THE SCOUTING REPORT: 1990

Produced by: STATS, Inc.
(Sports Team Analysis and Tracking Systems, Inc.)

John Dewan, Editor
Don Zminda, Associate Editor

Statistics by: STATS, Inc

1817

Harper & Row, Publishers, New York
Grand Rapids, Philadelphia, St. Louis, San Francisco
London, Singapore, Sydney, Tokyo, Toronto

The player photographs which appear in THE SCOUTING REPORT: 1990 were furnished individually by the 26 teams that comprise Major League Baseball. Their cooperation is gratefully acknowledged: Baltimore Orioles, Boston Red Sox, California Angels, Chicago White Sox, Cleveland Indians, Detroit Tigers, Kansas City Royals, Milwaukee Brewers, Minnesota Twins, New York Yankees, Oakland A's, Seattle Mariners, Texas Rangers, Toronto Blue Jays, Atlanta Braves, Chicago Cubs, Cincinnati Reds, Houston Astros, Los Angeles Dodgers, Montreal Expos, New York Mets, Philadelphia Phillies, Pittsburgh Pirates, St. Louis Cardinals, San Diego Padres and San Francisco Giants. Our appreciation is also extended to Coman Publishing, the Richmond Braves and the Columbus Clippers for their assistance in obtaining additional photographs.

FIRST EDITION

Designed by STATS, Inc.

ISSN 0743-1309

ISBN 0-06-096447-2

90 91 92 93 94 RRD 10 9 8 7 6 5 4 3 2 1

Acknowledgments

There are many people who are responsible for making this book a reality.

Don Zminda, my associate editor, has done a yeoman job in coordinating our scouts. He was also the first line of defense in editing, performing the primary editorial task for the scouting reports in this book. He added an extra dash of quality which is always inherent in his own work. Don, more than anyone else, is responsible for adding consistency to this book. Not a small task when the scouting reports are written by so many talented, but diverse, analysts.

Dr. Richard Cramer, the Founder and Chairman of the Board of STATS, Inc., is responsible, along with Steve Swope, for the hit location graphics which you can see on each player. Dick Cramer developed the Playball system which is used by STATS scorers in computerizing the direction and distance of every ball put in play. It was from that very detailed information stored within the STATS computer that these charts were digitized, through Dick Cramer's expertise and the computer's raw power. The Playball system he developed also keeps track of all information in every play of every game. This level of detail made it possible to supply all the other statistical breakdowns you'll find in this book.

Bob Mecca took on the role of statistical editor as well as copy editor. Using his in-depth knowledge of baseball, the STATS computer and his eagle eye, he was responsible for verifying the relevance and accuracy of the statistics quoted in the reports.

Matt Greenberger's job as copy editor also added yet another level of quality to the reports. Matt was also responsible for coordinating with the Major League Teams to provide the player photos.

Thanks to Irene and Clarence Waldock who helped turn many of the reports into electronic, computer readable form.

Daniel Bial, our editor at Harper and Row, was always there when we needed him. Besides lending his support and expertise, he added to the enjoyment of producing the book by being a super guy to work with.

Thanks to the rest of STATS, Inc. staff not mentioned above. They kept the ball rolling at STATS, while the rest of us worked on this book. This includes the STATS scorers throughout the country. Their accurate scoring of games during the season and using the Playball system helped make available all the wonderful statistics you'll find within this book.

And finally, my biggest thanks goes to Sue Dewan. Sue is much more than a loving and supportive wife. She is a charter member of the STATS Hall of Fame. Without her management and computer expertise, this book, and STATS as a whole, would not exist.

— John Dewan

The Scouting Staff

Writing a book of this magnitude requires writers who are well acquainted with the players on each major league team. To that end, we created a network composed of beat reporters and other writers who are known to STATS for their baseball expertise. These people are the unsung heroes of the book. They performed demanding, detailed work on short deadline, and we are deeply grateful for their efforts.

The scouting reports in this book were written by the following people, in conjunction with our board of editors:

Baltimore Orioles	Mike Lurie York Daily Record
	Kent Baker Baltimore Morning Sun
Boston Red Sox	Nick Cafardo Quincy Patriot-Ledger
California Angels	Rick Weinberg World Wide Sports Features
Chicago White Sox	Don Zminda and Don Gunning The Chicago Baseball Report & STATS, Inc.
Cleveland Indians	Paul Hoynes Cleveland Plain Dealer
Detroit Tigers	Steve Lysogorski
	Jon Heinlen
	John Benson Winning Rotisserie Baseball
Kansas City Royals	Marc Bowman STATS Inc.
Milwaukee Brewers	Tom Flaherty Milwaukee Journal
Minnesota Twins	Howard Sinker and Dennis Brackin Minneapolis Star-Tribune
New York Yankees	John Benson Winning Rotisserie Baseball
Oakland Athletics	Chuck Hildebrand Peninsula Times-Tribune
Seattle Mariners	Merrianna McCully Yakima Herald-Republic
Texas Rangers	Howard Sinker Minneapolis Star-Tribune
Toronto Blue Jays	Neil MacCarl Toronto Star
Atlanta Braves	Matt Greenberger STATS, Inc.

Chicago Cubs	Carmen Corica The Chicago Baseball Report & STATS, Inc.
Cincinnati Reds	Greg Gajus
	John Benson Winning Rotisserie Baseball
Houston Astros	Joe Heiling Beaumont Enterprise and Journal
Los Angeles Dodgers	Rick Weinberg World Wide Sports Features
Montreal Expos	Jack Romanelli Montreal Gazette
New York Mets	J. Randolph Burnham
	Jay Gregory
	Barry Rubinowitz
	John Benson Winning Rotisserie Baseball
Philadelphia Phillies	Pete DeCoursey Philadelphia Baseball File
Pittsburgh Pirates	John Perrotto Beaver County Times
San Diego Padres	Barry Bloom San Diego Tribune
San Francisco Giants	Rob Wood The Baseball Abstract
St. Louis Cardinals	Brock Hanke The Baseball Abstract

On a personal level, I would like to express my thanks to several people for their efforts in producing this book. The talented John Benson was able to step in time and again, as needed, and turn out splendid work on short notice. We appreciate your extraordinary effort, John. Matt Greenberger and Bob Mecca of the STATS office helped the writers get statistical information that was crucial to the reports. Matt and Carmen Corica not only did that, but wrote reports of their own. Thanks, fellows, for service above and beyond the call of duty.

Finally, I'd like to thank Dick Cramer and John and Sue Dewan, the driving forces behind STATS, for their work in bringing this project to fruition. The Scouting Report is only one of many projects STATS is involved in, but all of them made sure that this book would be as good as we could make it. Thank you all, both for that and the confidence you've shown in my work.

— Don Zminda

Table of Contents

Introduction

There are scouting reports on over 700 major league baseball players included in this book. They are the most complete and detailed reports the general public has ever had the opportunity to see. In fact, only the most progressive teams in Major League Baseball have this depth of information in their own scouting reports.

The Players

For each major league team, there are 25 to 30 players scouted here. Most of the players are covered in depth, with a full page of scouting information. They are listed alphabetically with the team they last played for in 1989. The lesser players, four to seven per team, follow the primary players on each team.

The Scouting Report Page

The Scouting Report page for primary players has two parts. The left side of the page provides an in-depth report by one of our expert scout/analysts who cover the teams on a daily basis. These reports are drawn from their day-to-day observation of the players.

The right-hand side of the page is chock full of information from the STATS computer. Starting at the top of the column it lists:

Position: The first position shown is the player's most common position in 1989. If a position player played at any other positions in 10 or more games, those positions are shown also. For pitchers, SP stands for starting pitcher and RP stands for relief pitcher. A second pitching position is shown if a starting pitcher relieved at least four times or a relief pitcher started at least twice.

Bats and Throws: L=lefthanded, R=righthanded, B=both (switch-hitter).

Opening Day Age: This is the player's age on April 5, 1990.

Born: Birth date and place.

ML Seasons: This number indicates the number of different major league seasons in which this player actually appeared. For example, if a player was called up to play in September in each

of the last three seasons, the number shown would be three (3). Note that this is different from the term Major League Service, which only counts the actual number of days a player appears on a major league roster.

Overall Statistics: These are traditional statistics for the player's 1989 season, and his career through 1989.

Hitting Diagrams

The hitting diagrams shown in these reports are the most advanced of their kind in baseball. Perhaps you've seen the diagrams in past editions of The Scouting Report. Those diagrams were based on subjective judgment and speculation. These new diagrams are based on cold, hard facts.

The hitting diagrams are based on our charting of every batted ball in the 1989 season. For every game and every ball hit into play last year (both hits and outs), our trained scorers entered data into the STATS computer. They kept track of the kind of batted ball -- flyball, groundball, popup, line drive or bunt. They also kept track of the direction and distance of each ball. Direction is kept by dividing the field into 26 "wedges" angling out from home plate. Distance is measured in 10-foot increments from home plate.

Shown below are Eddie Murray's hitting diagrams.

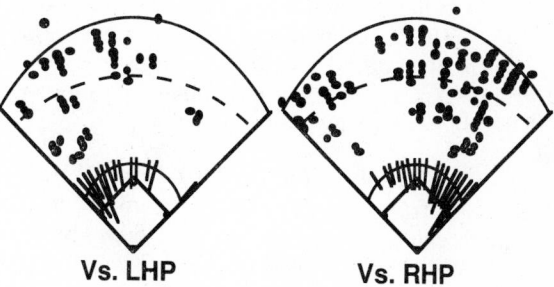

Vs. LHP   **Vs. RHP**

First of all, you'll notice that there are two charts. One chart shows where Murray hits the ball against lefthanded pitchers; the other shows him hitting against righties. For pitchers in these reports, opposition batters are broken down by lefties and righties.

In the diagrams, groundballs and short line drives are shown by the various length lines in the infield. The longer the line, the more groundballs and liners that were hit in that direction. When Murray is hitting against a RHP (batting lefty since he's a switch-hitter), you'll notice that he pulls a lot of balls on the first base side of the infield. There are a few balls in the shortstop area on over to second base, but most of his groundballs are pulled. There are no balls shown right at third base or down the third base line. For defensive purposes, the chart would indicate that a strong infield shift should be played when Murray is batting lefthanded.

In the outfield, batted balls are shown by dots. The dotted line in the outfield is 300 feet away from home plate. This line indicates about how deep an outfield would normally play. When Murray bats against a LHP (batting righthanded), he almost never hits to right field. The few times that he does, the ball is hit shallow. Murray tends to pull the ball on short liners; you'll notice quite a few dots in short left field between the line and straight-away left field. When he hits to center, he always hits deep. He also hits deep to left. Defensively, when Murray is batting righthanded, the right fielder should play shallow and the left fielder and centerfielder should play deep, with the left fielder shaded toward the line.

Against righties, Murray can hit the opposite way. In fact, he hits quite a few balls close to the line in left field. When Murray bats lefthanded, the left fielder should play deep and close to the line. The centerfielder and right fielder should both play deep, bunched towards right-centerfield. Give Murray left-center and the right field line when he's batting lefty.

Technical Information on the Diagrams

A lot of experimentation went into producing these charts. When we first started, we tried to show every single batted ball that was hit into play by each player. We found that the charts became very cluttered for everyday players. We began experimenting with trying to show only the most meaningful information. When all was said and done, here's what we ended up with:

a. Pop-ups and bunts are excluded. We excluded pop-ups because 95% of these are caught regardless of how fielders are positioned. We excluded bunts because defensing a bunt is a whole different strategy that is primarily used on a select number of players and situations.

b. Groundballs under 50 feet are excluded. These are swinging bunts and are somewhat rare. We exclude them because they don't provide a true indication of the direction of a batted ball reaching an infielder or going through the infield.

c. For everyday players, we excluded what we call isolated points in the outfield. If a player hit only one ball in a given area of the field with no other batted balls in the vicinity all season, we exclude it from the chart. We felt that one ball does not give a true indication of a tendency. This rule did not apply to balls hit farther than 380 feet; all batted balls over 380 feet are shown.

d. Similarly, for players who play infrequently, we expanded the data sample to create a larger pattern of dots in the outfield when he tended to hit in a given area more frequently.

e. For groundballs over 50 feet, we excluded only the rare isolated groundball. For most players, almost all of their groundballs are shown.

Other notes of interest:

The field itself is drawn to precise scale, with the outfield fence reaching 400 feet in centerfield and 330 feet down the lines. Keep in mind that parks are configured differently so that a dot that is shown inside of the diagram might actually have been a home run. Similarly, a dot outside the fence in the diagram might actually have been in play.

Liners under 170 feet are part of the infield. We give responsibility for short line drives to the infielders.

No distinction is made between hits and outs.

1989 Situational Stats

There are eight situational breakdowns for every primary player. **Home** and **Road** show performance between playing in his home park versus on the road. **Day** and **Night** show performance in day games versus night games. For hitters, **LHP** and **RHP** show the player's performance versus lefthanded pitchers and righthanded pitchers respectively. For pitchers, **LHB** and

RHB show how the opposition batters hit against that pitcher based on the side of the plate from which they hit. **Sc Pos** stands for Scoring Position. It shows batting performance when hitting with runners in scoring position. For pitchers, Sc Pos shows the opposition's batting statistics when there are men in scoring position against that pitcher.

The definition we use for **Clutch** here can be simply restated as the late innings of a close game. For those of you interested in the exact definition, clutch is when it is the seventh inning or later and the batting team is up by one run, tied, or has the tying run on base, at bat, or on deck. You'll notice a similarity to the save definition. This is intentional; it allows our definition of Clutch to be consistent with a very well-known statistic, the save.

1989 Rankings

This section shows how the player ranked against the league, against his teammates, and by position in significant categories. Thanks to the power of the STATS computer, we not only include traditional categories, but also the less traditional categories as shown in the Major League Leaders section of this book. The Definitions and Qualifications section below provides some details on these lesser known categories. Due to space considerations, when a player ranked high in numerous categories, we omitted the rankings by position. The abbreviations PA and IP stand for plate appearances and innings pitched, respectively.

Major League Leaders

The chapter immediately following this introduction is a complete listing of Major League Leaders. The top three players in each category are shown for each league separately. You'll notice a STATS flavor to these leaders. Not only do we show the leaders for the common categories like batting average, home runs and ERA, but you'll also find less traditional categories like steals of third, percentage of extra bases taken as a runner and pitches thrown.

Definitions and Qualifications

The following are definitions and qualifications for the Major League Leaders.

Definitions:

Times on Base - Hits plus walks plus hit by pitch.

Grounder/Flyball Ratio - The ratio of all groundballs

hit to flyballs and pop-ups hit. Bunts and line drives are excluded completely.

Percentage of extra bases taken as a runner - This figure measures how often a players takes an extra base on a single or double, advances on a groundout, or advances on a flyout.

Runs scored per time reached base - This is calculated by dividing Runs Scored by Times on Base.

Clutch - This category shows a player's batting average in the late innings of close games: the seventh inning or later with the batting team ahead by one, tied, or has the tying run on base, at bat, or on deck.

Bases Loaded - This category shows a player's batting average in bases loaded situations.

GDP per GDP situation - A GDP situation exists any time there is a man on first with less than two outs. This statistic measures how often a player grounds into a double play in that situation.

Percentage of Pitches Taken - This tells you how often a player lets a pitch go by without swinging.

Percentage of Swings Put into Play - This tells you how often a player hits the ball into fair territory when he swings.

Run Support per Nine Innings - This figure indicates how many runs are scored for a pitcher by his team while he was pitching translated into a per nine-inning figure.

Baserunners per Nine Innings - These are the hits, walks and hit batsmen allowed per nine innings.

Strikeout/Walk Ratio - This is simply a pitcher's strikeouts divided by his walks allowed.

Stolen Base Percentage Allowed - This figure indicates how successful opposing baseunners are when attempting a stolen base. It's stolen bases divided by stolen base attempts.

Save Percentage - This is saves divided by save opportunities. A save opportunity includes saves plus blown saves.

Blown Saves - A blown save is given any time a pitcher comes into a game where a save situation is in place and he loses the lead.

Holds - A hold is given to a pitcher when he comes into the game in a save situation, but is removed before the end of the game while maintaining his team's lead.

Percentage of Inherited Runners Scored - When a pitcher comes into a game with men already on base, these runners are called inherited runners. This statistic measures the percentage of these inherited runners that the relief pitcher allows to score.

First Batter Efficiency - This statistic tells you the batting average allowed by a relief pitcher to the first batter he faces.

Qualifications:

In order to be ranked, a player had to qualify with a minimum number of opportunities. The qualifications are as follows:

Batters

Batting average, slugging percentage, on-base average, home run frequency, grounder/flyball ratio, runs scored per time reached base, pitches seen per plate appearance, percentage of pitches taken, lowest percentage of swings that missed and percentage of swings put into play - 502 plate appearances

Percentage of extra bases taken as a runner - 40 opportunities to advance

Stolen base percentage - 20 stolen base attempts

Runners in scoring position - 100 plate appearances with runners in scoring position

Clutch - 50 plate appearances in the clutch

Bases loaded - 10 plate appearances with the bases loaded

GDP per GDP situation - 50 plate appearances with a man on first and less than two outs

Vs LHP - 125 plate appearances against lefthanded pitchers

Vs RHP - 377 plate appearances against righthanded pitchers

BA at home - 252 plate appearances at home

BA on the road - 252 plate appearances on the road

BA on 3-1 count - 20 plate appearances putting the ball into play or walking on a 3-1 count

BA with 2 strikes - 150 plate appearances with 2 strikes

BA on 0-2 count - 10 plate appearances putting the ball into play or striking out on a 0-2 count

BA on 3-2 count - 20 plate appearances with a 3-2 count

Pitchers

Earned run average, run support per nine innings, baserunners per nine innings, batting average allowed, on-base average allowed, slugging percentage allowed, home runs per nine innings, strikeouts per nine innings, strikeout/walk ratio, stolen base percentage allowed, GDPs per nine innings and grounder/flyball ratio off -162 innings pitched

GDPs induced per GDP situation - pitchers facing 30 batters in GDP situations

Save Percentage - 20 save opportunities

Percentage of inherited runners scoring - 30 inherited runners

First batter efficiency - 40 games in relief

BA allowed, runners in scoring position - pitchers facing 100 batters with men in scoring position

ERA at home - 81 innings pitched at home

ERA on the road - 81 innings pitched on the road

Vs LHB - 125 lefthanded batters faced

Vs RHB - 377 righthanded batters faced

Fielders

Percentage caught stealing by catchers - catchers with 75 stolen base attempts against them

Major League Leaders

1989 American League Leaders

Batters

Batting Average
Kirby PUCKETT .339
Carney LANSFORD .336
Wade BOGGS .330

Home Runs
Fred McGRIFF 36
Joe CARTER 35
Mark McGWIRE 33

RBIs
Ruben SIERRA 119
Don MATTINGLY 113
Nick ESASKY 108

Games
Joe CARTER 162
Cal RIPKEN 162
Ruben SIERRA 162

At Bats
Joe CARTER 651
Steve SAX 651
Cal RIPKEN 646

Runs
Wade BOGGS 113
Rickey HENDERSON 113
Ruben SIERRA 101
Robin YOUNT 101

Hits
Kirby PUCKETT 215
Wade BOGGS 205
Steve SAX 205

Singles
Steve SAX 171
Kirby PUCKETT 157
Carney LANSFORD 153

Doubles
Wade BOGGS 51
Kirby PUCKETT 45
Jody REED 42

Triples
Ruben SIERRA 14
Devon WHITE 13
Phil BRADLEY 10

Stolen Bases
Rickey HENDERSON 77
Cecil ESPY 45
Devon WHITE 44

Caught Stealing
Cecil ESPY 20
Harold REYNOLDS 18
Ozzie GUILLEN 17
Steve SAX 17

Walks
Rickey HENDERSON 126
Fred McGRIFF 119
Wade BOGGS 107

Intentional Walks
Wade BOGGS 19
Don MATTINGLY 18
Pete O'BRIEN 17

Hit by Pitch
Jim GANTNER 10
Carney LANSFORD 9
Gene LARKIN 9
Charlie O'BRIEN 9

Strikeouts
Bo JACKSON 172
Rob DEER 158
Jesse BARFIELD 150

Ground into Double Play
Julio FRANCO 27
Mark McGWIRE 23
Cal RIPKEN 22

Sacrifice Bunts
Felix FERMIN 32
Alvaro ESPINOZA 23
Billy RIPKEN 19

Sacrifice Flies
George BELL 14
Jeff LEONARD 12
Johnny RAY 12

Plate Appearances
Wade BOGGS 742
Steve SAX 717
Kevin SEITZER 715

Times on Base
Wade BOGGS 319
Rickey HENDERSON 277
Kevin SEITZER 275

Total Bases
Ruben SIERRA 344
Robin YOUNT 314
Joe CARTER 303

Slugging Percentage
Ruben SIERRA .543
Fred McGRIFF .525
Robin YOUNT .511

On-Base Average
Wade BOGGS .430
Alvin DAVIS .424
Rickey HENDERSON .411

HR frequency - ABs/HR
Mark McGWIRE 14.8
Fred McGRIFF 15.3
Bo JACKSON 16.1

Grounder/Flyball Ratio
Felix FERMIN 4.17
Steve SAX 3.99
Gary PETTIS 2.42

% Extra bases taken as runner
Mookie WILSON 64.2%
Willie WILSON 63.2
Lance JOHNSON 59.5

Runs scored/Time reached Base
Bo JACKSON 42.4%
Rob DEER 41.9
Glenn BRAGGS 38.7

SB Success %
Julio FRANCO 87.5%
Robin YOUNT 86.4
Steve FINLEY 85.0

Steals of third
Rickey HENDERSON 24
Steve SAX 11
Devon WHITE 11

Runners in Scoring Position
Julio FRANCO .407
Alvin DAVIS .362
Robin YOUNT .355

Clutch (late & close)
Danny TARTABULL .403
Al NEWMAN .386
Bob BOONE .379

BA with the Bases Loaded
Julio FRANCO	.667
B.J. SURHOFF	.625
Mark McGWIRE	.571

GDP per GDP situation
Dan PASQUA	0.0%
Cecil ESPY	2.7
Steve LYONS	3.0

BA vs LHP
Carney LANSFORD	.389
Alvaro ESPINOZA	.383
Steve SAX	.381

BA vs RHP
Kirby PUCKETT	.354
Wade BOGGS	.348
Harold BAINES	.330

BA at Home
Kirby PUCKETT	.390
Wade BOGGS	.377
Alvin DAVIS	.365

BA on the Road
Carney LANSFORD	.360
Robin YOUNT	.328
Harold BAINES	.322

BA on 3-1 Count
Gene LARKIN	.667
Paul MOLITOR	.667
Mickey TETTLETON	.600

BA with 2 Strikes
Wade BOGGS	.329
Brian HARPER	.309
Carney LANSFORD	.300

BA on 0-2 Count
Matt NOKES	.400
Carlton FISK	.370
Dan GLADDEN	.364

BA on 3-2 Count
Dave COCHRANE	.500
Don MATTINGLY	.435
Steve FINLEY	.429

Pitches Seen
Wade BOGGS	3,076
Kevin SEITZER	2,822
Rickey HENDERSON	2,765

Pitches Seen per PA
Jesse BARFIELD	4.2
Wade BOGGS	4.1
Gary PETTIS	4.1

% Pitches Taken
Rickey HENDERSON	71.0%
Alvin DAVIS	68.0
Scott FLETCHER	65.6

Lowest % Swings that Missed
Wade BOGGS	5.4%
Felix FERMIN	5.4
Carney LANSFORD	6.6

% Swings Put into Play
Harold REYNOLDS	59.9%
Carney LANSFORD	59.6
Don MATTINGLY	59.0

Bunts in Play
Felix FERMIN	42
Steve LYONS	42
Nelson LIRIANO	36

Pitchers

Earned Run Average
Bret SABERHAGEN	2.16
Chuck FINLEY	2.57
Mike MOORE	2.61

Wins
Bret SABERHAGEN	23
Dave STEWART	21
Storm DAVIS	19
Mike MOORE	19

Losses
Doyle ALEXANDER	18
Andy HAWKINS	15
Mike WITT	15

Win/Loss Pct
Bret SABERHAGEN	.793
Bert BLYLEVEN	.773
Mike HENNEMAN	.733

Games
Chuck CRIM	76
Rob MURPHY	74
Ken ROGERS	73

Games Started
Mark GUBICZA	36
Bob MILACKI	36
Dave STEWART	36

Complete Games
Bret SABERHAGEN	12
Jack MORRIS	10
Chuck FINLEY	9

Shutouts
Bert BLYLEVEN	5
Kirk McCASKILL	4
Bret SABERHAGEN	4

Saves
Jeff RUSSELL	38
Bobby THIGPEN	34
Dennis ECKERSLEY	33
Dan PLASAC	33
Mike SCHOOLER	33

Games Finished
Jeff RUSSELL	66
Jeff REARDON	61
Mike SCHOOLER	60

Innings
Bret SABERHAGEN	262.1
Dave STEWART	257.2
Mark GUBICZA	255.0

Hits Allowed
Dave STEWART	260
Mark GUBICZA	252
Mike WITT	252

Batters Faced
Dave STEWART	1,081
Mark GUBICZA	1,060
Roger CLEMENS	1,044

Runs Allowed
Andy HAWKINS	127
Bobby WITT	123
Mike WITT	119

Earned Runs Allowed
Andy HAWKINS	111
Bobby WITT	111
Mike WITT	111

Home Runs Allowed
Doyle ALEXANDER	28
Charlie HOUGH	28
Mike WITT	26

Walks Allowed
Bobby WITT	114
Nolan RYAN	98
Charlie HOUGH	95

Hit Batters
Dave STIEB	13
Mike BODDICKER	10
Mike SMITHSON	10

Strikeouts
Nolan RYAN	301
Roger CLEMENS	230
Bret SABERHAGEN	193

Wild Pitches

Nolan RYAN	19
Mike MOORE	17
Bud BLACK	13
Dave STEWART	13
Duane WARD	13

Balks

John DOPSON	15
Tom CANDIOTTI	8
4 tied with	5

Run Support per 9 IP

Allan ANDERSON	6.9
Storm DAVIS	6.5
Jeff BALLARD	6.1

Least Baserunners per 9 IP

Bret SABERHAGEN	8.7
Nolan RYAN	10.1
Bert BLYLEVEN	10.3

Batting Average Allowed

Nolan RYAN	.187
Tom GORDON	.210
Bret SABERHAGEN	.217

On-Base Average Allowed

Bret SABERHAGEN	.251
Nolan RYAN	.275
Mike MOORE	.286

Slugging Pct Allowed

Nolan RYAN	.283
Tom GORDON	.306
Mike MOORE	.307

HRs Allowed per 9 IP

Mark GUBICZA	.35
Tom CANDIOTTI	.44
Bret SABERHAGEN	.45

Strikeouts per 9 IP

Nolan RYAN	11.3
Tom GORDON	8.4
Roger CLEMENS	8.2

Strikeout/walk Ratio

Bret SABERHAGEN	4.5
Jimmy KEY	4.4
Chris BOSIO	3.6

Stolen Bases Allowed

Nolan RYAN	36
Bobby WITT	30
Jim ABBOTT	29

Caught Stealing

Roger CLEMENS	17
Jeff BALLARD	14
John CERUTTI	14

Lowest SB Pct Allowed

Bret SABERHAGEN	35.7%
Mike MOORE	41.2
Andy HAWKINS	42.1

GDPs Induced

Kirk McCASKILL	32
Bob MILACKI	29
Billy SWIFT	26

GDPs per 9 IP

Kirk McCASKILL	1.4
Storm DAVIS	1.3
Mike FLANAGAN	1.2

GDPs Induced / GDP situation

Tom FILER	.271
Tom McCARTHY	.258
Jeff RUSSELL	.236

Grd/Fly Ratio

Kevin BROWN	3.3
Mark GUBICZA	2.5
John DOPSON	2.1

Save Opportunities

Jeff RUSSELL	44
Bobby THIGPEN	43
Jeff REARDON	42

Save Percentage

Jeff RUSSELL	86.4%
Dennis ECKERSLEY	84.6
Lee SMITH	83.3

Blown Saves

Duane WARD	12
Jeff REARDON	11
Doug JONES	9
Dave RIGHETTI	9
Bobby THIGPEN	9

Holds

Rick HONEYCUTT	24
Chuck CRIM	17
Ken ROGERS	16

% Inherited Runners Scored

Bob McCLURE	14.0%
Tony FOSSAS	18.2
Dave RIGHETTI	19.4

First Batter Efficiency

Gene NELSON	.091
Jeff REARDON	.136
Gregg OLSON	.143

BA Allowed, Scoring Pos

Mike BODDICKER	.212
Bert BLYLEVEN	.213
Dave STEWART	.221

Pitches Thrown

Roger CLEMENS	4,243
Nolan RYAN	4,073
Bret SABERHAGEN	3,863

Pitches Thrown per Batter

Jeff BALLARD	3.3
Chris BOSIO	3.4
Bert BLYLEVEN	3.4

Pickoff Throws

Roger CLEMENS	295
Charlie HOUGH	277
John CERUTTI	249

ERA at Home

Bret SABERHAGEN	1.71
Mike MOORE	2.02
Chris BOSIO	2.06

ERA on the Road

Allan ANDERSON	2.24
Nolan RYAN	2.52
Bud BLACK	2.61

BA Allowed vs LHB

Gregg OLSON	.135
Bud BLACK	.158
Todd BURNS	.172

BA Allowed vs RHB

Dave STIEB	.187
Nolan RYAN	.197
Roger CLEMENS	.218

Fielders

Errors (all positions)

Felix FERMIN	26
Alvaro ESPINOZA	22
Kelly GRUBER	22
Ozzie GUILLEN	22
Jeff KUNKEL	22

% Caught Stealing by Catchers

Bob BOONE	42.3%
Dave VALLE	41.5
Don SLAUGHT	38.8

1989 National League Leaders

Batters

Batting Average
Tony GWYNN	.336
Will CLARK	.333
Lonnie SMITH	.315

Home Runs
Kevin MITCHELL	47
Howard JOHNSON	36
Eric DAVIS	34
Glenn DAVIS	34

RBIs
Kevin MITCHELL	125
Pedro GUERRERO	117
Will CLARK	111

Games
Bobby BONILLA	163
Jose OQUENDO	163
Pedro GUERRERO	162
Terry PENDLETON	162

At Bats
Todd BENZINGER	628
Roberto ALOMAR	623
Bobby BONILLA	616

Runs
Will CLARK	104
Howard JOHNSON	104
Ryne SANDBERG	104

Hits
Tony GWYNN	203
Will CLARK	196
Roberto ALOMAR	184

Singles
Tony GWYNN	165
Roberto ALOMAR	149
Brett BUTLER	138

Doubles
Pedro GUERRERO	42
Tim WALLACH	42
Howard JOHNSON	41

Triples
Robbie THOMPSON	11
Bobby BONILLA	10
Will CLARK	9
Vince COLEMAN	9
Andy VAN SLYKE	9

Stolen Bases
Vince COLEMAN	65
Roberto ALOMAR	42
Juan SAMUEL	42

Caught Stealing
Gerald YOUNG	25
Roberto ALOMAR	17
Brett BUTLER	16
Tony GWYNN	16

Walks
Jack CLARK	132
Von HAYES	101
Barry BONDS	93
Tim RAINES	93

Intentional Walks
Kevin MITCHELL	32
Spike OWEN	25
Eddie MURRAY	24

Hit by Pitch
Andres GALARRAGA	13
Robbie THOMPSON	13
Juan SAMUEL	11
Lonnie SMITH	11

Strikeouts
Andres GALARRAGA	158
Jack CLARK	145
Dale MURPHY	142

Ground into Double Play
Tim WALLACH	21
Chris JAMES	20
Ricky JORDAN	19
Tony PENA	19

Sacrifice Bunts
Roberto ALOMAR	17
Rick REUSCHEL	16
Tom BROWNING	14

Sacrifice Flies
Pedro GUERRERO	12
Eric DAVIS	11
9 tied with	8

Plate Appearances
Roberto ALOMAR	702
Bobby BONILLA	698
Eddie MURRAY	690

Times on Base
Will CLARK	275
Pedro GUERRERO	260
Tony GWYNN	260

Total Bases
Kevin MITCHELL	345
Will CLARK	321
Howard JOHNSON	319

Slugging Percentage
Kevin MITCHELL	.635
Howard JOHNSON	.559
Will CLARK	.546

On-Base Average
Lonnie SMITH	.415
Jack CLARK	.410
Will CLARK	.407

HR frequency - ABs/HR
Kevin MITCHELL	11.6
Eric DAVIS	13.6
Howard JOHNSON	15.9

Grounder/Flyball Ratio
Milt THOMPSON	2.43
Tony GWYNN	2.10
Jerome WALTON	2.05

% Extra bases taken as runner
Brett BUTLER	63.0%
Billy HATCHER	61.4
Jeff KING	61.4

Runs scored/Time reached Base
Vince COLEMAN	41.6%
Robbie THOMPSON	41.4
Howard JOHNSON	40.6

SB Success %
Billy DORAN	88.0%
Craig BIGGIO	87.5
Vince COLEMAN	86.7

Steals of third
Vince COLEMAN	17
Otis NIXON	9
Tim RAINES	9

Runners in Scoring Position
Lonnie SMITH	.418
Pedro GUERRERO	.400
Will CLARK	.389

Clutch (late & close)
Ozzie SMITH	.361
Luis SALAZAR	.359
Barry LARKIN	.358

BA with the Bases Loaded
Shawon DUNSTON	.563
Paul O'NEILL	.556
Mark GRACE	.556

GDP per GDP situation
Darrell EVANS	1.6%
Dave MARTINEZ	2.0
Tom FOLEY	2.8

BA vs LHP
Andres GALARRAGA	.385
Barry LARKIN	.372
Lloyd McCLENDON	.339

BA vs RHP
Tony GWYNN	.351
Will CLARK	.340
Mark GRACE	.336

BA at Home
Lonnie SMITH	.358
Mark GRACE	.337
Roberto ALOMAR	.329

BA on the Road
Tony GWYNN	.345
Will CLARK	.341
Pedro GUERRERO	.332

BA on 3-1 Count
Spike OWEN	.636
Gary REDUS	.615
Pedro GUERRERO	.571

BA with 2 Strikes
Tony GWYNN	.315
Barry LARKIN	.314
Bip ROBERTS	.302

BA on 0-2 Count
Barry LARKIN	.379
Spike OWEN	.364
Bip ROBERTS	.346

BA on 3-2 Count
Ken GRIFFEY	.450
Tommy HERR	.419
Mike LaVALLIERE	.409

Pitches Seen
Von HAYES	2,533
Barry BONDS	2,528
Roberto ALOMAR	2,520

Pitches Seen per PA
Jack CLARK	3.9
Von HAYES	3.9
Juan SAMUEL	3.8

% Pitches Taken
Willie RANDOLPH	64.3%
Jack CLARK	63.6
Spike OWEN	63.2

Lowest % Swings that Missed
Ozzie SMITH	6.2%
Tony GWYNN	7.2
Brett BUTLER	8.0

% Swings Put into Play
Tony GWYNN	61.0%
Willie RANDOLPH	59.6
Ozzie SMITH	56.2

Bunts in Play
Brett BUTLER	49
Vince COLEMAN	40
Roberto ALOMAR	37

Pitchers

Earned Run Average
Scott GARRELTS	2.28
Orel HERSHISER	2.31
Mark LANGSTON	2.39

Wins
Mike SCOTT	20
Greg MADDUX	19
Mike BIELECKI	18
Joe MAGRANE	18

Losses
Don CARMAN	15
Orel HERSHISER	15
Ken HILL	15

Win/Loss Pct
Sid FERNANDEZ	.737
Scott GARRELTS	.737
Danny DARWIN	.733

Games
Mitch WILLIAMS	76
Rob DIBBLE	74
Jeff PARRETT	72

Games Started
Tom BROWNING	37
Jose DeLEON	36
Greg MADDUX	35

Complete Games
Tim BELCHER	10
Bruce HURST	10
Tom BROWNING	9
Joe MAGRANE	9
Mike SCOTT	9

Shutouts
Tim BELCHER	8
Doug DRABEK	5
Tom GLAVINE	4
Orel HERSHISER	4
Mark LANGSTON	4

Saves
Mark DAVIS	44
Mitch WILLIAMS	36
John FRANCO	32

Games Finished
Mark DAVIS	65
Mitch WILLIAMS	61
Steve BEDROSIAN	60

Innings
Orel HERSHISER	256.2
Tom BROWNING	249.2
Jose DeLEON	244.2
Bruce HURST	244.2

Hits Allowed
Rick MAHLER	242
Tom BROWNING	241
Dennis MARTINEZ	227

Batters Faced
Orel HERSHISER	1,047
Tom BROWNING	1,031
Greg MADDUX	1,002

Runs Allowed
Rick MAHLER	113
Tom BROWNING	109
Bob WALK	106

Earned Runs Allowed
Kevin GROSS	98
Bob WALK	96
3 tied with	94

Home Runs Allowed
Tom BROWNING	31
Mike SCOTT	23
Don ROBINSON	22
John SMILEY	22
Ed WHITSON	22

Walks Allowed
Ken HILL	99
Fernando VALENZUELA	98
Mark LANGSTON	93

Hit Batters
Rick MAHLER	10
Mitch WILLIAMS	8
5 tied with	7

Strikeouts
Jose DeLEON	201
Tim BELCHER	200
Sid FERNANDEZ	198

Wild Pitches
Ken HOWELL	21
John WETTELAND	16
David CONE	14
Joe MAGRANE	14
Jeff ROBINSON	14

Balks
Pete SMITH	7
Rick SUTCLIFFE	6
6 tied with	5

Run Support per 9 IP
Bob WALK	5.4
Tom GLAVINE	5.2
David CONE	5.2

Least Baserunners per 9 IP
Scott GARRELTS	9.1
Jose DeLEON	9.5
Mike SCOTT	9.6

Batting Average Allowed
Jose DeLEON	.197
Sid FERNANDEZ	.198
John SMOLTZ	.212

On-Base Average Allowed
Scott GARRELTS	.258
Mike SCOTT	.267
Jose DeLEON	.268

Slugging Pct Allowed
Jose DeLEON	.309
Scott GARRELTS	.313
Ken HOWELL	.313

HRs Allowed per 9 IP
Joe MAGRANE	.19
Orel HERSHISER	.32
Ken HILL	.41

Strikeouts per 9 IP
Mark LANGSTON	8.9
Sid FERNANDEZ	8.1
Tim BELCHER	7.8

Strikeout/walk Ratio
Pascual PEREZ	3.4
Dennis MARTINEZ	2.9
Mike SCOTT	2.8

Stolen Bases Allowed
Mike SCOTT	39
Kevin GROSS	34
Dwight GOODEN	30

Caught Stealing
Rick MAHLER	17
Ken HOWELL	15
Fernando VALENZUELA	15

Lowest SB Pct Allowed
Mike BIELECKI	.417
Greg MADDUX	.478
Fernando VALENZUELA	.500

GDPs Induced
Orel HERSHISER	29
Joe MAGRANE	24
Dennis MARTINEZ	21

GDPs per 9 IP
Orel HERSHISER	1.017
Dennis RASMUSSEN	.931
Joe MAGRANE	.920

GDPs Induced / GDP Situation
Randy McCAMENT	.233
Atlee HAMMAKER	.200
Dan QUISENBERRY	.200

Grd/Fly Ratio
Orel HERSHISER	2.3
Greg MADDUX	2.2
Pascual PEREZ	2.2

Save Opportunities
Mark DAVIS	48
Mitch WILLIAMS	47
Tim BURKE	39
John FRANCO	39

Save Percentage
Mark DAVIS	91.7%
Bill LANDRUM	89.7
Jay HOWELL	87.5

Blown Saves
Tim BURKE	11
Mitch WILLIAMS	11
Joe BOEVER	9

Holds
Rob DIBBLE	23
Ken DAYLEY	22
Larry ANDERSEN	16
Calvin SCHIRALDI	16

% Inherited Runners Scored
Steve WILSON	15.7%
Ken DAYLEY	16.7
Randy MYERS	18.5

First Batter Efficiency
Greg W. HARRIS	.113
Bob KIPPER	.125
Calvin SCHIRALDI	.130

BA Allowed, Scoring Pos
Orel HERSHISER	.167
Mike SCOTT	.177
Tim BELCHER	.188

Pitches Thrown
Jose DeLEON	3,671
Tim BELCHER	3,636
Orel HERSHISER	3,615

Pitches Thrown per Batter
Tom BROWNING	3.2
Derek LILLIQUIST	3.3
Rick REUSCHEL	3.3

Pickoff Throws
Jim DESHAIES	355
Bruce HURST	253
Dennis MARTINEZ	251

ERA at Home
Scott GARRELTS	1.57
Doug DRABEK	1.85
Tim BELCHER	2.10

ERA on the Road
Orel HERSHISER	1.93
Mark LANGSTON	2.21
Ed WHITSON	2.27

BA Allowed vs LHB
Neal HEATON	.137
Zane SMITH	.143
Bill LANDRUM	.176

BA Allowed vs RHB
Jose DeLEON	.148
Mike SCOTT	.167
Sid FERNANDEZ	.198

Fielders

Errors (all positions)
Bobby BONILLA	35
Rafael RAMIREZ	30
Andres THOMAS	29

% Caught Stealing by Catchers
Benito SANTIAGO	41.0%
Mike SCIOSCIA	39.2
Terry KENNEDY	37.1

American League Players

HITTING:

The man the Red Sox hated to trade still has not hit as people expected.

It's hard to believe that two years ago, Anderson was the key man in a deal in which the Orioles parted with their most marketable starter, Mike Boddicker. They've given him plenty of opportunities, but he simply hasn't come through yet.

Injuries and a low average kept Anderson in the minors for much of the season. He was red-hot the opening week, but four early homers made Anderson think -- again -- that he can hit for power. With each home run, club coaches cringed. Anderson should be a contact hitter, but he seemed to make a lot of outs where he floated his wrists out in front and flailed at balls in an effort to lift them.

He keeps himself in great shape, and has fun by training for decathlon events. But all the muscles have not made him big or bulky. Some argued that the theories of former Red Sox hitting coach Walt Hriniak did not do Anderson any good. Others felt that Anderson, an extremely patient hitter, was simply letting too many good offerings go by. Whatever the case, he's been a big disappointment as a hitter.

BASERUNNING:

Anderson is fast, and aggressive. He could probably steal 35 bases or more if he played every day -- he was 16-for-20 in steals in '89, and that was in part-time action. Anderson runs the bases very well and scored a memorable run against the Twins early in the year by bashing his shoulder into a catcher and jarring the ball loose.

FIELDING:

This is Anderson's forte. Anderson and Steve Finley are clones in both body type and defensive ability. With his outstanding range and his ability to get a great jump on the ball, Anderson is a natural center fielder. His throwing arm is not exceptionally strong, but he gets rid of the ball quickly.

OVERALL:

It's hard to guess where Anderson will fit next year. His name keeps coming up in trade rumors. One figures the Orioles already have outfielders like him -- but better. But what would Anderson's value be with opposing clubs if the Orioles become the second team in two years to part ways with him?

BRADY ANDERSON

Position: CF
Bats: L **Throws:** L
Ht: 6' 1" **Wt:** 186

Opening Day Age: 26
Born: 1/18/64 in Silver Spring, MD
ML Seasons: 2

Overall Statistics

	G	AB	R	H	D	T	HR	RBI	SB	BB	SO	AVG
1989	94	266	44	55	12	2	4	16	16	43	45	.207
Career	188	591	75	124	25	6	5	37	26	66	120	.210

Where He Hits the Ball

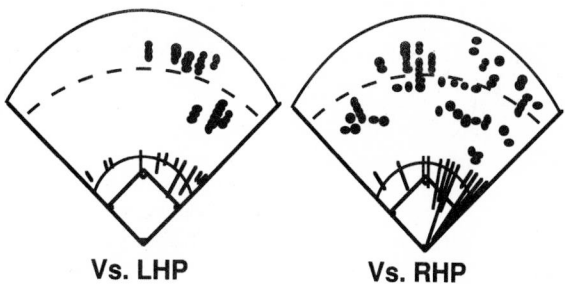

Vs. LHP   **Vs. RHP**

1989 Situational Stats

	AB	H	HR	RBI	AVG		AB	H	HR	RBI	AVG
Home	135	30	2	8	.222	LHP	70	9	1	2	.129
Road	131	25	2	8	.191	RHP	196	46	3	14	.235
Day	64	13	1	5	.203	Sc Pos	50	10	1	12	.200
Night	202	42	3	11	.208	Clutch	30	8	0	1	.267

1989 Rankings (American League)

➡ 8th in stolen base percentage (80% -16 for 20)

➡ 8th among all league players in percentage of pitches taken (66.1%)

➡ Led Orioles in extra bases taken per opportunity as a runner (54.2%)

STAFF ACE

JEFF BALLARD

Position: SP
Bats: L **Throws:** L
Ht: 6' 2" **Wt:** 198

Opening Day Age: 26
Born: 8/13/63 in Billings, MT
ML Seasons: 3

PITCHING:

Belief in himself and the development of a sinker carried Jeff Ballard to new heights in 1989. The lefty who had not previously had a winning season won 18 games and was a key figure in the Orioles' drive for a division title. Ballard acquired the confidence that was lacking in his previous two seasons and his team-mates didn't hurt his cause, averaging more than six runs per nine innings with Jeff on the mound.

Ballard is a low-ball, ground-ball pitcher who must depend on pinpoint control because he does not have overpowering stuff. The evidence is in the walks and strikeouts. The last pitcher to win 18 or more games with fewer strikeouts than Ballard's 62 was Dick Newsome with the 1941 Red Sox (58). Plus, Ballard walked only 57 batters in 215 innings, slightly less than 2.4 per nine innings. Last August 21 against Milwaukee, he became the first Oriole pitcher ever to throw a shutout without a walk or a strikeout.

Ballard now has four pitches, including an improved slider and curveball. He has average movement on the ball. Ballard has learned the poise to deal with tough situations and showed he has durability, going with three days' rest for the final month. Only once in his final 10 starts did he allow more than three earned runs, even though, because of his control, he allows a lot of hits. He now has a .500 record after starting his career 10-20 and has matured into a solid member of the rotation.

FIELDING:

Ballard is a good defensive player. He uses his quickness and intelligence to great advantage, is always aware of the game situation, and lands in a well balanced position. As a lefthander, he holds baserunners well and has a natural feel for their intentions. And, he will get better.

OVERALL:

Ballard knows now he can succeed at the major-league level. He had some hard luck in his final two starts, but, except for one fallow period in the middle of the season, was amazingly consistent. The future tests will come when he is not supported as well by the offense.

Overall Statistics

	W	L	ERA	G	GS	Sv	IP	H	R	BB	SO	HR
1989	18	8	3.43	35	35	0	215.1	240	95	57	62	16
Career	28	28	4.27	74	74	0	438.1	507	238	134	130	46

Where They Hit the Ball

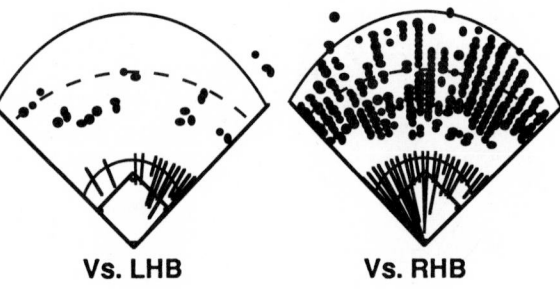

Vs. LHB   **Vs. RHB**

1989 Situational Stats

	W	L	ERA	Sv	IP		AB	H	HR	RBI	AVG
Home	9	4	3.19	0	110.0	LHB	139	39	4	15	.281
Road	9	4	3.67	0	105.1	RHB	697	201	12	62	.288
Day	4	5	3.95	0	57.0	Sc Pos	172	41	4	54	.238
Night	14	3	3.24	0	158.1	Clutch	67	15	0	2	.224

1989 Rankings (American League)

➡ 5th in wins (18)

➡ 3rd in run support received (6.1 runs per nine innings)

➡ 1st in least pitches thrown per batter (3.32)

➡ 7th in causing opponent GDPs (24)

➡ 3rd worst strikeout/walk ratio (1.09)

➡ Led Orioles in ERA (3.43), wins, CG (4), W/L Percentage (.692) and least HRs per 9 innings (.67) - *pitchers with 162 IP.*

HITTING:

Phil Bradley finished with a .277 average, 16 percentage points behind his major-league pace before '89. Normally a hot second-half hitter, he went through a couple of prolonged slumps after the All-Star Break. Of course, the Orioles needed all the offense they could get and they were counting on Bradley.

Despite the dropoff, though, he gave the club a lot to work with. Fine bat control is his chief strength. He was the perfect hit-and-run man, with a knack for pushing singles through the right side. Part of that tendency comes from a habit of swinging late at pitches. Bradley seems to wait on the ball and look, at times, as if he's fighting it off. When he makes solid contact, he can drive one out straight through centerfield. Every once in a while, he'll pull one. That's usually when he really connects. During the Orioles' final-series showdown of the year with Toronto, Bradley tattooed Todd Stottlemyre's first pitch several rows up in the SkyDome. It was not a typical homer, but Bradley was strong enough for 11 of them (his career high was 26 with Seattle in '85). Perhaps his biggest frustration was shifting between the No. 2 and leadoff spot. He does not like leading off, but Robinson liked to take advantage of Bradley's patient eye (70 walks in 144 games, third on the club).

BASERUNNING:

Bradley has good speed and smart instincts. He knows how to use all parts of the bag to beat a throw, and did so on a few occasions with some inventive slides. He's also a good base stealer and has stolen as many as 40 in a season, though last year's 20 is more his level.

FIELDING:

Oh, to have a solid outfield again. The Orioles had their best since Paul Blair's time with Bradley in left. He hits the cutoff man and his speed lets him cutoff numerous drives down the line. He also plays the corner in Memorial Stadium well.

OVERALL:

Essentially, Bradley was a big part of the Eddie Murray trade, albeit indirectly. The Orioles acquired Ken Howell from the Dodgers and sent him to the Phillies for Bradley. A protege of Al Bumbry's, Bradley loves being an Oriole and his superior work habits made hogwash out of the Phillies' charges that Bradley was a malcontent. Along with Cal Ripken, he's the most professional guy in the clubhouse.

PHIL BRADLEY

Position: LF
Bats: R **Throws:** R
Ht: 6' 0" **Wt:** 185

Opening Day Age: 31
Born: 3/11/59 in Bloomington, IN
ML Seasons: 7

Overall Statistics

	G	AB	R	H	D	T	HR	RBI	SB	BB	SO	AVG
1989	144	545	83	151	23	10	11	55	20	70	103	.277
Career	905	3273	506	950	165	41	74	345	138	382	657	.290

Where He Hits the Ball

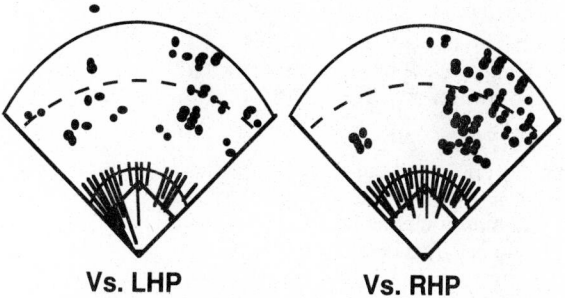

Vs. LHP   **Vs. RHP**

1989 Situational Stats

	AB	H	HR	RBI	AVG		AB	H	HR	RBI	AVG
Home	255	73	3	25	.286	LHP	192	57	8	22	.297
Road	290	78	8	30	.269	RHP	353	94	3	33	.266
Day	133	34	6	17	.256	Sc Pos	123	30	1	43	.244
Night	412	117	5	38	.284	Clutch	69	13	0	5	.188

1989 Rankings (American League)

➡ 3rd in triples (10)
➡ 7th in grounder/flyball ratio (1.97)
➡ 7th in HBP (7)
➡ Led Orioles in batting average (.277), slugging percent (.417), on-base average (.364), runs (83), triples and HBP - *players with 502 PA.*

HITTING:

Mike Devereaux was the guy Baltimore wanted all along when they made the Eddie Murray trade. The Dodgers didn't comply until months later, when they moved Devereaux during spring training for pitcher Mike Morgan. It was easy to see why the Orioles were interested. Devereaux became a good leadoff man, even though he had to be platooned. That's not easy for a rookie. Devereaux's ability to get on base a reasonable amount of time and make things happen showed that the Dodgers let a good one get away. Devereaux is an aggressive hitter. He'll go after the first pitch when he likes it, and as a result he had only 36 walks, which is pretty low for a leadoff man. He also struck out 60 times in 391 at bats, but that total balanced out against his eight homers. Three of his homers won games in sudden death. And one of those was easily the season's most infamous for Baltimore -- an extra-inning homer against the Angels in July that, to this day, still looks like a foul ball. He hits to all fields, and he probably has not yet tapped his full potential.

BASERUNNING:

Devereaux led the club with 22 steals -- he's capable of a 40-steal year if played every day -- and Frank Robinson claims he and Cal Ripken are the team's two best runners. It's been some time since the Orioles have had someone go from first to third as quickly.

FIELDING:

Devereaux made several fine plays in centerfield. Hard to believe, but with him and Steve Finley and part-timer Brady Anderson, the Orioles suddenly have too much quick outfield defense. Like Finley, Devereaux really needs to play every day. As a rookie, though, he still made platooning look easy. Certainly his defense never suffered. He has an adequate arm, and he normally throws to the right base. His speed is a big asset. He gets a good jump and can track most balls down once he kicks into gear.

OVERALL:

Some insiders with the Dodgers still scratch their heads about Devereaux's getting away. For some reason, his stock in the Los Angeles organization was never that high. But it is with Baltimore. He's a good man in the clubhouse, too. He's intelligent, polite and funny; his teammates like him.

MIKE DEVEREAUX

Position: CF/RF
Bats: R **Throws:** R
Ht: 6' 0" **Wt:** 195

Opening Day Age: 27
Born: 4/10/63 in Casper, WY
ML Seasons: 3

Overall Statistics

	G	AB	R	H	D	T	HR	RBI	SB	BB	SO	AVG
1989	122	391	55	104	14	3	8	46	22	36	60	.266
Career	171	488	66	121	18	3	8	52	25	41	80	.248

Where He Hits the Ball

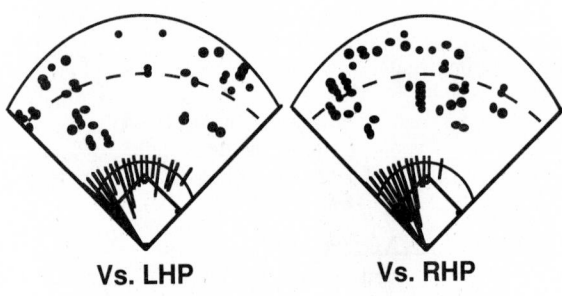

Vs. LHP **Vs. RHP**

1989 Situational Stats

	AB	H	HR	RBI	AVG		AB	H	HR	RBI	AVG
Home	191	47	4	19	.246	LHP	189	53	3	16	.280
Road	200	57	4	27	.285	RHP	202	51	5	30	.252
Day	102	33	2	4	.324	Sc Pos	108	26	4	39	.241
Night	289	71	6	42	.246	Clutch	60	14	3	9	.233

1989 Rankings (American League)

- 8th in steals of third (5)
- 4th worst in stolen base percentage (66.7%) among players with 20 attempts
- Led Orioles in stolen bases (22), caught stealing (11) and steals of third

HITTING:

It's easy to be deceived by Steve Finley's .249 average. Everyone in the Baltimore organization thinks this 14th-round pick could be a great one. He does everything naturally, and he makes good contact. He began '88 in Class A and by the end of the season was the best outfield prospect in Class AAA. For someone with two years' minor-league experience, hitting .250 while platooning against big-league pitching is nothing to be ashamed of.

Frank Robinson knows Finley has to play every day, and that's not easy to do in the Baltimore outfield. Finley led the International League in hitting two years ago (.314), the first Baltimore farmhand to do that since Rich Dauer led the IL in 1976. Finley undercut a few balls, and his lean build is representative of someone who should hit a lot of line drives. All he needs, most likely, is playing time. He's a decent bunter, although he popped up a crucial sacrifice attempt in game one of the Toronto series and was furious with himself for it.

BASERUNNING:

The Orioles think Finley has great instincts, and he usually showed them on the bases. He is very fast and stole 17 bases in 81 games while only being thrown out three times. But in that same Toronto game, he pinch ran and made a late break on a Randy Milligan double, which he should have scored on. That night Baltimore lost 2-1; Finley's run should have given Baltimore a 2-0 lead at the time. It was a mistake the youthful Finley probably won't make again.

FIELDING:

He's an outstanding fielder. He made the most famous catch of the season for Baltimore, robbing Mike Greenwell of a homer on Opening Day with a crashing catch against the outfield wall. It put Finley on the DL for three weeks. He throws well and plays centerfield like a young Fred Lynn.

OVERALL:

In the International League Finley was considered such an outstanding prospect that some observers rated him a better prospect than Gregg Jefferies. It just could be that people hear more of Finley this year. Coaches marveled at how he went about things. He looks like he's been around forever, though he's only 24. He really is a natural.

STEVE FINLEY

Position: RF/CF
Bats: L **Throws:** L
Ht: 6' 2" **Wt:** 175

Opening Day Age: 24
Born: 5/12/65 in Union City, TN
ML Seasons: 1

Overall Statistics

	G	AB	R	H	D	T	HR	RBI	SB	BB	SO	AVG
1989	81	217	35	54	5	2	2	25	17	15	30	.249
Career	81	217	35	54	5	2	2	25	17	15	30	.249

Where He Hits the Ball

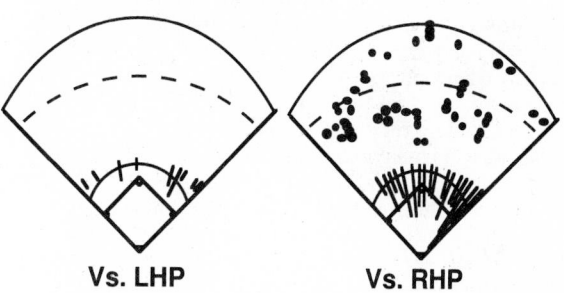

Vs. LHP   Vs. RHP

1989 Situational Stats

	AB	H	HR	RBI	AVG		AB	H	HR	RBI	AVG
Home	114	25	0	10	.219	LHP	38	6	1	6	.158
Road	103	29	2	15	.282	RHP	179	48	1	19	.268
Day	53	11	0	1	.208	Sc Pos	58	15	2	24	.259
Night	164	43	2	24	.262	Clutch	29	10	0	5	.345

1989 Rankings (American League)

- ➡ 3rd in stolen base percentage (85% - 17 for 20)
- ➡ Led Orioles with percent of swings where he put the ball into play (53.7%)
- ➡ Led AL Rightfielders in stolen base percentage and batting average on a 3-2 count (.429) - *players with 20 PA with a 3-2 count*

PITCHING:

The Orioles expected a lot of Pete Harnisch and his live arm when they recalled him at midseason last year. The results were somewhat mixed. Harnisch had some fine outings, but his 5-9 record and 4.62 ERA were well below expectations. Despite that, Robinson didn't give up on the youngster, even in the stretch. Harnisch lost a chance to pitch in the biggest game of his life at Toronto last September 29 when he stepped on a nail walking back to the team hotel.

A strong 23-year-old, Harnisch is a former number one draft choice who has had success wherever he's pitched. At every stop in the Oriole farm system, the righty had an ERA well below 3.00 and a high ratio of strikeouts to innings pitched. To continue that success in the majors, Harnisch must contain his nervous energy and channel it into pitching. He needs a lot of refinement, but the equipment is there. Harnisch throws a 90-plus fastball that has great movement, but must learn command of the strike zone with his slider and changeup. He performed reasonably well in the stretch last season, indicating he may be ready to handle the pressure. But his control is iffy and he throws too many pitches. If he can control his hyperactivity, control of the strike zone is likely to follow because Harnisch has loads of natural talent.

FIELDING:

Harnisch is not yet a good fielder because his pitching motion ends with him facing first base, out of position. And, he sometimes has a mental lapse covering the left side of the infield. Holding runners is another weakness. He has a slow release to the plate and a tendency to rush himself.

OVERALL:

No one gives up easily on this kind of talent. Harnisch finally won on the road after 10 straight losses last year and showed signs of settling down the last two months. Harnisch's stuff and minor league success indicate a pitcher who can win at the major league level. He will be given every shot to fill a place in the starting rotation.

PETE HARNISCH

Position: SP
Bats: R **Throws:** R
Ht: 6' 0" **Wt:** 195

Opening Day Age: 23
Born: 9/23/66 in Commack, NY
ML Seasons: 2

Overall Statistics

	W	L	ERA	G	GS	Sv	IP	H	R	BB	SO	HR
1989	5	9	4.62	18	17	0	103.1	97	55	64	70	10
Career	5	11	4.72	20	19	0	116.1	110	63	73	80	11

Where They Hit the Ball

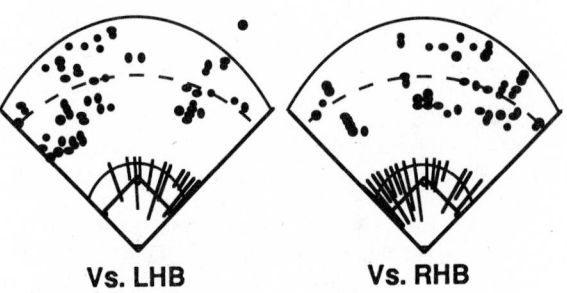

Vs. LHB   **Vs. RHB**

1989 Situational Stats

	W	L	ERA	Sv	IP		AB	H	HR	RBI	AVG
Home	3	1	3.41	0	34.1	LHB	181	47	3	17	.260
Road	2	8	5.22	0	69.0	RHB	209	50	7	19	.239
Day	1	3	3.79	0	38.0	Sc Pos	94	18	1	24	.191
Night	4	6	5.10	0	65.1	Clutch	25	6	1	2	.240

1989 Rankings (American League)

➡ Led Orioles in hit batsmen (5)

PITCHING:

Situational lefthander Kevin Hickey's story is an inspirational battle back from five years of minor-league obscurity. Thirty-three years old when 1989 began, Hickey had had some success with the White Sox in the early eighties, but hadn't pitched in the majors since 1983. Remembering Hickey's previous work from his years as the White Sox general manager, Oriole general manager Roland Hemond invited Kevin to spring training. The longest of long shots, Hickey made the ballclub and then had a solid year.

Hickey is basically a two-pitch pitcher (fastball, slider) who started 1989 with only a fastball. He must be used properly. He's best against tough opposing lefthanded hitters like Wade Boggs, George Brett and Don Mattingly. He held lefties to a .206 batting average (14-for-68), but also held righties to .229. However, his effectiveness faded somewhat during the final two months. Hickey allowed no hits or runs during his final six appearances, but he had to be spotted and was seldom seen for more than one or two hitters. He accepts his role graciously. Who wouldn't after what he's been through, including having to sleep in the clubhouse at Rochester in 1988. Continuing to handle righthanded hitters as well as he did in '89 would increase his value, but to do so he will need another effective pitch. Don't put it beyond him. Resurrected, Hickey will try anything to stay where he is. He is a good influence in the Orioles' young clubhouse.

FIELDING:

Hickey, who was originally discovered by the White Sox playing 16-inch softball in Chicago, is a decent athlete. He is strong, with quick feet, and has valuable experience in tough situations. Baserunners are careful about stealing with him on the mound and he knows most of their tendencies.

OVERALL:

Toward the end of 1989, Hickey showed signs of a tired arm. His control suffered, and he was not the Tug McGraw-type flash he had been the first half. But he is a gamer who did a good job overall and the Orioles like lefthanded relievers with savvy. He figures to return in the same role.

KEVIN HICKEY

Position: RP
Bats: L **Throws:** L
Ht: 6' 1" **Wt:** 195

Opening Day Age: 34
Born: 2/25/56 in Chicago, IL
ML Seasons: 4

Overall Statistics

	W	L	ERA	G	GS	Sv	IP	H	R	BB	SO	HR
1989	2	3	2.92	51	0	2	49.1	38	16	23	28	3
Career	7	11	3.38	175	0	16	192.0	172	84	82	91	15

Where They Hit the Ball

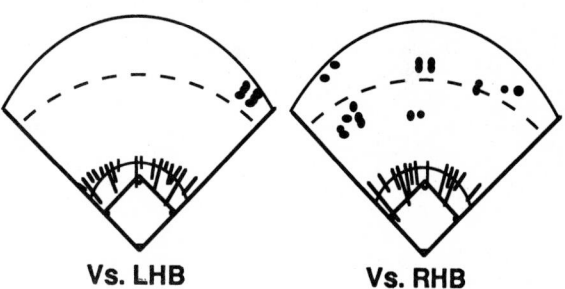

Vs. LHB   **Vs. RHB**

1989 Situational Stats

	W	L	ERA	Sv	IP		AB	H	HR	RBI	AVG
Home	1	3	3.28	1	24.2	LHB	68	14	2	10	.206
Road	1	0	2.55	1	24.2	RHB	105	24	1	7	.229
Day	0	1	5.79	0	9.1	Sc Pos	53	10	1	14	.189
Night	2	2	2.25	2	40.0	Clutch	57	12	1	6	.211

1989 Rankings (American League)

→ 8th in holds (12)

→ Led Orioles in holds and lowest batting average against righthanded batters (.229) - *all team pitchers*

PITCHING:

A key member of the world champion Dodger pitching staff in 1988 -- he had a 1.70 ERA and allowed only one run in six postseason innings -- Brian Holton came to the Orioles in the Eddie Murray deal and was expected to help shore up a very shaky pitching staff. As it turned out, the Oriole staff was much better than expected, but with little thanks to Holton. Working both as a starter and in relief, Holton turned in a mediocre 4.02 ERA and was pounded hard on many occasions. He was virtually buried in the Oriole bullpen the last three weeks, making only two nondescript appearances while the team strove for the pennant.

A former number one draft choice and a proficient pitcher for the Dodgers, Holton appeared to have lost some velocity off his fastball. Certainly he didn't seem to have confidence in it, and depended primarily on his two curveballs. He began the season as a starter and had some early success, beating Nolan Ryan and Kirk McCaskill, but he demonstrated little stamina beyond the fifth or sixth innings and finished the season in his familiar middle-man role. Holton's biggest problem is that the league became accustomed to all the curveballs and waited for them. Without a big-time fastball, he must use a slider and changeup efficiently and has to be reminded of that. He has to make perfect pitches and throw enough strikes to keep hitters honest.

FIELDING:

Holton does not have the pure athleticism to be a strong fielding pitcher, but he positions himself well and knows where to go with the ball. He hurts himself with all the slow curveballs he throws, giving baserunners time to pick up their feet and go.

OVERALL:

Holton needs to reacquire some speed on his fastball to take the heat off his other pitches, while maintaining near-flawless control. Holton is a good influence in the clubhouse, a quipster, but that may not be enough to keep him on the staff. Two years removed from that glorious '88 season, he may have to earn a job again.

BRIAN HOLTON

Position: RP/SP
Bats: R **Throws:** R
Ht: 6' 0" **Wt:** 195

Opening Day Age: 30
Born: 11/29/59 in McKeesport, PA
ML Seasons: 5

Overall Statistics

	W	L	ERA	G	GS	Sv	IP	H	R	BB	SO	HR
1989	5	7	4.02	39	12	0	116.1	140	63	39	51	11
Career	18	16	3.45	152	16	3	312.2	333	141	104	183	24

Where They Hit the Ball

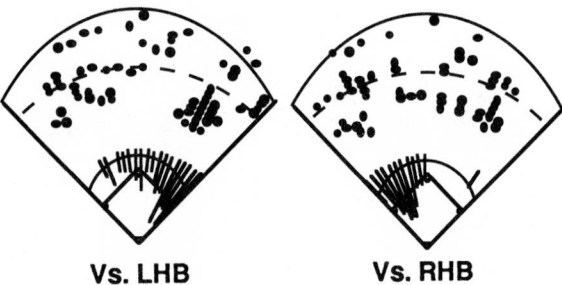

Vs. LHB   **Vs. RHB**

1989 Situational Stats

	W	L	ERA	Sv	IP		AB	H	HR	RBI	AVG
Home	3	4	3.53	0	66.1	LHB	230	71	7	29	.309
Road	2	3	4.68	0	50.0	RHB	237	69	4	31	.291
Day	1	3	4.44	0	26.1	Sc Pos	129	39	4	51	.302
Night	4	4	3.90	0	90.0	Clutch	53	20	2	5	.377

1989 Rankings (American League)

➡ Worst AL pitcher allowing inherited runners to score (53.3%) - *pitchers with 30 runners inherited*

HITTING:

Bob Melvin was a .220 hitter before the season began, so the Orioles did not get him for his offense. However, he hit .241 and drove in 32 runs in just 85 games. That was a real bonus for Baltimore. It wasn't until late August, at Yankee Stadium, that Melvin hit his one home run. He had 11 with the Giants in '87, but the wind must have been blowing out a lot that year at Candlestick. Melvin does not have a commanding presence in the batter's box. He also strikes out a bit -- 53 times in 278 at-bats. Still, he delivered in a number of clutch situations when he could look for the fastball. Key hits with the bases loaded helped the Orioles take control on about five different occasions. Melvin uses a small bat and, at times, looks as if he chokes up on it. It's surprising that he drives some balls as far as he does. It seemed as if his drives to the outfield landed just short of the outfield fence time after time.

BASERUNNING:

As catchers go, Melvin has adequate speed. At 205 pounds, his 6'4" frame looks lean. But the fact is, he's big. So while he doesn't confuse anyone with Gus Triandos, he doesn't threaten Al Bumbry's speed either. Like most catchers, he's not a base stealing threat and was thrown out four times in five steal attempts, most of them on broken hit-and-run plays.

FIELDING:

Roger Craig, who was the pitching coach at Detroit when Melvin played there, thought enough of the youngster's defense to part with both Eric King and Matt Nokes in the trade in which Melvin went to Craig's Giants. Defense is why the Orioles wanted Melvin also. They felt Terry Kennedy did not care about being a defensive catcher. Melvin does. He calls an excellent game. He also blocks a lot of balls in the dirt. Most pitchers say they are comfortable with him behind the plate. He has a strong throwing arm.

OVERALL:

A platoon of Bob Melvin and Mickey Tettleton is nothing to sneeze at. Melvin made the position stronger defensively, and he was invaluable the last two months after Tettleton's knee injury.

BOB MELVIN

Position: C
Bats: R **Throws:** R
Ht: 6' 4" **Wt:** 205

Opening Day Age: 28
Born: 10/28/61 in Palo Alto, CA
ML Seasons: 5

Overall Statistics

	G	AB	R	H	D	T	HR	RBI	SB	BB	SO	AVG
1989	85	278	22	67	10	1	1	32	1	15	53	.241
Career	391	1147	110	258	49	5	25	119	4	63	233	.225

Where He Hits the Ball

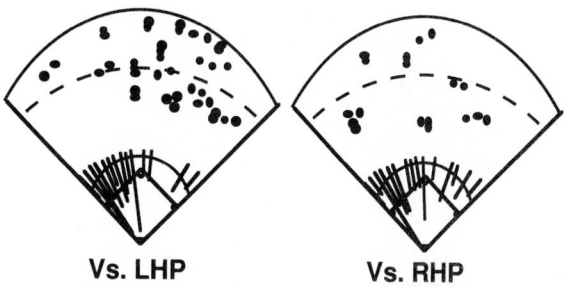

Vs. LHP   **Vs. RHP**

1989 Situational Stats

	AB	H	HR	RBI	AVG		AB	H	HR	RBI	AVG
Home	154	36	0	17	.234	LHP	151	46	1	20	.305
Road	124	31	1	15	.250	RHP	127	21	0	12	.165
Day	70	16	1	11	.229	Sc Pos	75	22	1	31	.293
Night	208	51	0	21	.245	Clutch	36	7	0	4	.194

1989 Rankings (American League)

➡ Led Orioles in batting against lefthanded pitchers (.305) - *all team players*

PITCHING:

Generally rated as the best pure pitcher on the Orioles, Bob Milacki finally put it all together last year after a long minor league apprenticeship. Drafted by the O's back in 1983--he'd originally been picked in the first round by the Padres, but didn't sign--Milacki spent five years at various stops in the Baltimore farm system. The righthander obviously learned his lessons, because he showed so much poise that it was hard to believe he was a rookie. He came to the majors knowing how to pitch. A workhorse, he tied for the American League lead with 36 starts. He went 243 innings, the most by an AL rookie since Roger Erickson of Minnesota threw 266 in 1978. Down the stretch, when the Orioles were expected to fold but never did, Milacki was one of the cornerstones of the Baltimore mound staff.

Milacki has power (90 mph fastball), finesse (a big curve), a slider and changeup and is not afraid to use any of them on any count. His size makes him an imposing figure to rival hitters. But he has had a tendency to throw too many different pitches to hitters he could retire with one or two. He pitched in tough luck all season or his 14 victories might have translated into 18 or 20. Stamina is no problem. Milacki goes into the seventh and eighth innings routinely and thrived on three days' rest (6-1 record). He went into the seventh 10 times in the last 11 starts that counted. He is receptive to teaching; the problem may be that he just doesn't know how good he is yet.

FIELDING:

Milacki moves deftly for a man his size and is improving rapidly in the field. Although he takes a while to unwind, he is very aware of baserunners and holds them well.

OVERALL:

A staff bulwark, Milacki has a very bright future. If he establishes his best pitches (fastball, changeup) early in games, there is no telling how good he can be. It would help immensely if the Orioles supported him with more runs. If he is this year's benefactor of offense, he can win 20 games.

BOB MILACKI

Position: SP
Bats: R **Throws:** R
Ht: 6' 4" **Wt:** 220

Opening Day Age: 25
Born: 7/28/64 in Trenton, NJ
ML Seasons: 2

Overall Statistics

	W	L	ERA	G	GS	Sv	IP	H	R	BB	SO	HR
1989	14	12	3.74	37	36	0	243.0	233	105	88	113	21
Career	16	12	3.46	40	39	0	268.0	242	107	97	131	22

Where They Hit the Ball

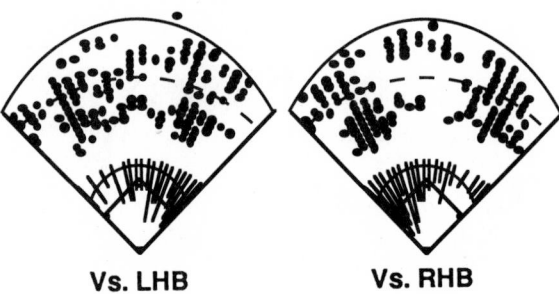

Vs. LHB   **Vs. RHB**

1989 Situational Stats

	W	L	ERA	Sv	IP		AB	H	HR	RBI	AVG
Home	7	7	3.53	0	130.0	LHB	463	118	10	39	.255
Road	7	5	3.98	0	113.0	RHB	456	115	11	53	.252
Day	2	1	2.72	0	39.2	Sc Pos	181	46	5	67	.254
Night	12	11	3.94	0	203.1	Clutch	101	19	1	4	.188

1989 Rankings (American League)

- ➡ 1st in games started (36)
- ➡ 2nd in causing opponent GDPs (29)
- ➡ 4th in batters faced (1,022)
- ➡ 5th in innings pitched (243.0)
- ➡ 10th worst in home runs allowed (21)
- ➡ Led Orioles in games started, shutouts (2), innings pitched, batters faced and strikeouts (113)

HITTING:

When the Mets gave up on Randy Milligan, he was a confused man. The 1987 Minor League Player of the Year, he nearly won the International League MVP. But the Mets, with Keith Hernandez at first, moved Milligan to Pittsburgh. Along the way he nearly took a huge offer to play in Japan. He stuck with the majors, but did not get untracked with the Bucs in '88 (.220, three homers in 40 games). The Orioles got him for minor league pitcher Pete Blohm and hoped they had a steal.

All things considered, they did. Milligan showed good power (12 homers) and a fine eye (74 walks) in 124 games. His .394 on-base percentage led the club in a year where he didn't take control of first base from the struggling Jim Traber until the second half. Milligan has a great sense of humor and coaches like how he approaches things. He was a contrast to Traber, whose style has been more talk than production. Of course, in fairness to Traber, Milligan took away some of Traber's opportunities. Randy was certainly more of a power threat, especially when he'd turn on a high fastball and really extend his arms. Milligan tends to use all portions of the field when he's going best, but hitting coach Tom McCraw helped him through a mid-season slump brought on when Milligan tried to pull pitches too often.

BASERUNNING:

Milligan probably gets a C+ on the bases. The plus is sufficient speed to go on the front end of a hit-and-run. Manager Frank Robinson likes to run. And with Milligan's high on-base percentage, it helped that he has decent speed for a big man, with a surprising nine stolen bases.

FIELDING:

By his own admission, Milligan is an average fielder. While he hustles, one almost gets the sense defense isn't a real priority for Milligan. In the Orioles' home finale, Milligan dropped a couple of balls, leading to an important Yankee run.

OVERALL:

It'll be interesting to see where Milligan fits into the club's plans. He was a big part of a harmonious clubhouse. His combination of high on-base percentage with occasional power might be enough to keep him his job. But the Orioles will look hard for a true home run threat during the winter, and that just might be another first baseman.

RANDY MILLIGAN

Position: 1B
Bats: R **Throws:** R
Ht: 6' 2" **Wt:** 225

Opening Day Age: 28
Born: 11/27/61 in San Diego, CA
ML Seasons: 3

Overall Statistics

	G	AB	R	H	D	T	HR	RBI	SB	BB	SO	AVG
1989	124	365	56	98	23	5	12	45	9	74	75	.268
Career	167	448	66	116	28	5	15	53	10	95	100	.259

Where He Hits the Ball

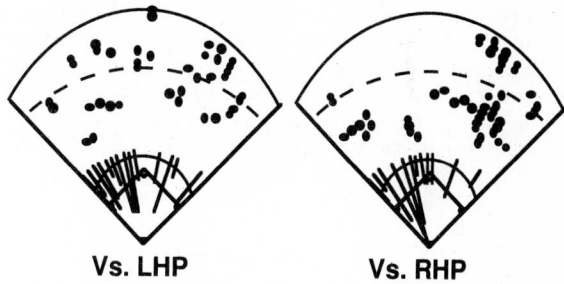

Vs. LHP   Vs. RHP

1989 Situational Stats

	AB	H	HR	RBI	AVG		AB	H	HR	RBI	AVG
Home	178	51	6	19	.287	LHP	169	38	6	22	.225
Road	187	47	6	26	.251	RHP	196	60	6	23	.306
Day	91	26	4	16	.286	Sc Pos	89	24	5	36	.270
Night	274	72	8	29	.263	Clutch	46	17	2	9	.370

1989 Rankings (American League)

➡ 4th in batting average in the clutch (.370) - *players with 50 PA*

➡ Led Orioles in walks (74)

➡ Led AL First Basemen in triples (5), steals of third (3), caught stealing (5) and batting average in the clutch

STOPPER

PITCHING:

Gregg Olson was the biggest surprise on THE surprising team of 1989. With just 10 games in the majors beforehand, he became one of the premier stoppers in the American League, thanks to a 93 miles-per-hour fastball and a nasty curve that has been compared favorably to Bert Blyleven's. Unhittable is sometimes the word used to describe the Orioles' rookie of the year. He thrives on the pressure with a perfect temperament for a late-inning closer. He wants the ball and, although he occasionally struggles with his control, Olson's great talent almost always gets him out of the jams he creates.

Olson had the longest road to travel last year of any Oriole pitcher. The fourth player selected in the '88 draft, he entered '89 with only 26 games of professional experience. Yet he saved 27 games--the second highest total in club history--did not allow a run in his last 21 appearances and became the toughest pitcher in the majors to homer against (one homer in 85 innings). The Orioles considered adding a change-up to his repertoire--Olson has worked on one--and making him a starter, but that seems a remote possibility after the season he had in the bullpen. The league batted under .200 against him and Olson relishes the role he has. A tremendous attitude is an asset and Olson just turned 23.

FIELDING:

The Achilles heel in Olson's game. He is not quite as agile as many pitchers and, although he isn't a liability, there is room for improvement. He is weak at holding baserunners because his release to home plate is slow. Opponents tend to take liberties from first and second base. But quickening his release may harm his effectiveness to hitters. It is a Catch-22 situation.

OVERALL:

This is a young man with a very bright future. His curveball sometimes breaks too sharply, leading to a team-high 9 wild pitches and he could improve defensively, but until conditions change, Olson is destined to be the team closer because of his talent and attitude. His erratic control but super overall talent can give managers gray hair, then broad smiles.

GREGG OLSON

Position: RP
Bats: R **Throws:** R
Ht: 6' 4" **Wt:** 211

Opening Day Age: 23
Born: 10/11/66 in Omaha, NE
ML Seasons: 2

Overall Statistics

	W	L	ERA	G	GS	Sv	IP	H	R	BB	SO	HR
1989	5	2	1.69	64	0	27	85.0	57	17	46	90	1
Career	6	3	1.88	74	0	27	96.0	67	21	56	99	2

Where They Hit the Ball

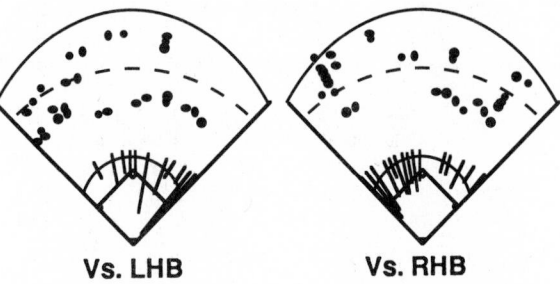

Vs. LHB   **Vs. RHB**

1989 Situational Stats

	W	L	ERA	Sv	IP		AB	H	HR	RBI	AVG
Home	3	0	0.77	12	46.2	LHB	141	19	0	6	.135
Road	2	2	2.82	15	38.1	RHB	163	38	1	13	.233
Day	0	1	4.85	3	13.0	Sc Pos	112	18	0	18	.161
Night	5	1	1.13	24	72.0	Clutch	195	33	0	10	.169

1989 Rankings (American League)

→ 1st in lowest batting average against left-handed batters (.135) - *pitchers facing 125 batters*

→ 3rd in first batter efficiency - (opposing batting average of .143)

→ 8th in Saves

→ Led Orioles in ERA (1.69), saves, games finished (52), wild pitches (9), lowest opponent batting average (.188), lowest opponent batting average with runners in scoring position (.161), lowest opponent slugging average (.247) - *all team pitchers*

HITTING:

For the second straight year, Joe Orsulak led the Orioles in hitting (.285, three points lower than '88). A man whom the Pirates didn't want, Orsulak proved he's a certifiable contact hitter. Occasionally he'll hit one out; he had two in the same game at Yankee Stadium in late August, on national TV no less. For the most part, though, he's a singles hitter who handles the fastball well.

Orsulak is a vintage Orioles no-name, whose 55 RBI in 123 games had a lot to do with the club's run production. His .351 on-base percentage was third best on the team. The Orioles used him in all nine spots of the order. It follows, then, that Orsulak (35 Ks) is a tough guy to strike out. Whatever power he has is usually to the right side, where he tends to jerk doubles (22) down the line. Orsulak also gets a lot of ground-ball hits. It's not so much that he swings down on the ball. Rather, he goes with the ball, even when it dips at the last second.

BASERUNNING:

Orsulak has OK speed. And consistent with his nature, he doesn't do anything stupid on the bases. He's stolen 24 bases twice with the Pirates, but with the Orioles that part of his game has been shut down. In two years with the O's he's stolen only 14 sacks while getting tossed out 11 times, a very poor percentage.

FIELDING:

Give Orsulak an 'A' for improvement. Despite a memorable throw to home plate in the '88 opener, he was a disaster in the outfield. He came a long way in '89. Steve Finley was a more reliable right fielder, but Orsulak did not represent too much of a drop. He still has a tendency to break late on balls, which is why he made so many sliding catches. His arm is average.

OVERALL:

Orsulak does not talk or show much emotion. But the Orioles like what he gets done and how hard he works. He figured to be the fifth outfielder in '89, but wormed his way into 123 games. He can pinch hit or start both ends of a doubleheader with equal effectiveness. Every time he seemed pushed to the background, he'd take over for someone in a slump and deliver some base hits. He's probably the kind of guy who could stick around the majors for a while. Down the road he might make a fine pinch hitter.

JOE ORSULAK

Position: RF/LF
Bats: L **Throws:** L
Ht: 6' 1" **Wt:** 186

Opening Day Age: 27
Born: 5/31/62 in Glen Ridge, NJ
ML Seasons: 6

Overall Statistics

	G	AB	R	H	D	T	HR	RBI	SB	BB	SO	AVG
1989	123	390	59	111	22	5	7	55	5	41	35	.285
Career	546	1645	233	458	77	22	17	126	65	119	139	.278

Where He Hits the Ball

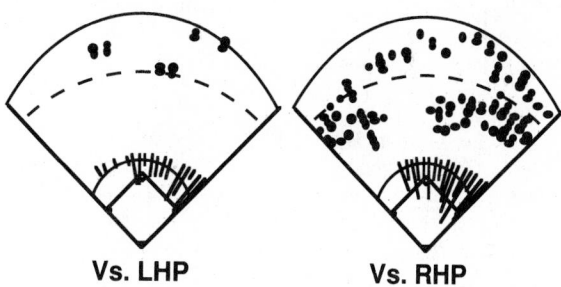

Vs. LHP   **Vs. RHP**

1989 Situational Stats

	AB	H	HR	RBI	AVG		AB	H	HR	RBI	AVG
Home	194	53	0	24	.273	LHP	84	17	0	5	.202
Road	196	58	7	31	.296	RHP	306	94	7	50	.307
Day	81	17	3	8	.210	Sc Pos	103	28	0	44	.272
Night	309	94	4	47	.304	Clutch	61	14	1	10	.230

1989 Rankings (American League)

- ➠ Led Orioles in batting average (.285), sacrifice flies (6), and hitting with the bases loaded (.444) - *all team players*
- ➠ Led AL Right Fielders in sacrifice bunts (7) and batting average with the bases loaded - *right fielders with 10 PA with the bases loaded*

HITTING:

Things improved for Bill Ripken offensively. He raised his average 32 percentage points from '88. In the end, though, the Orioles still hope he can become a more disciplined hitter. The problem, though Bill Ripken probably won't admit it, is trying to pull balls out like his brother Cal. Bill does not have the size, the strength, or the bat speed. He should be a contact, spray hitter. He was that when he came up in '87, and hit .308 in 58 games. Hitting coach Tom McCraw had Ripken go with the pitch more, but one also saw him trying too hard for power. Still, Ripken can put the ball in play on the hit-and-run. He's also a solid bunter.

Ripken will never be the hitter Cal is, but he can handle the low and medium fastball, particularly against lefty hurlers. He doesn't do nearly as well against breaking pitches, however, and still shows his old tendency to chase high fastballs that he really can't handle. He needs to work on his plate discipline so that he'll get more good pitches to hit.

BASERUNNING:

Like his brother, Bill Ripken comes from a sound school of fundamentals. He knows what to do on the bases and is not going to run a club out of an inning. He's also pretty fast. Ripken stole only one base in 1989, but was 8-for-10 in 1988.

FIELDING:

Ripken is an outstanding second baseman. He has fine range and quick hands. He's a master at charging the slow hit ball and throwing off-balance across his body. He preserved a few wins with his defense, and it is defense that makes Ripken still the man to beat at the position. A shoulder injury opened the way for Tim Hulett, who produced late in the season, but Hulett was no match defensively.

OVERALL:

Ripken is the clubhouse comedian. Privately, some crustier baseball people think he's a bit of a smart-aleck. Right now, though, he figures to mature in a few ways. If he becomes a more disciplined hitter, he should be one of the league's best second basemen.

BILLY RIPKEN

Position: 2B
Bats: R **Throws:** R
Ht: 6' 1" **Wt:** 183

Opening Day Age: 25
Born: 12/16/64 in Havre de Grace, MD
ML Seasons: 3

Overall Statistics

	G	AB	R	H	D	T	HR	RBI	SB	BB	SO	AVG
1989	115	318	31	76	11	2	2	26	1	22	53	.239
Career	323	1064	110	254	38	3	6	80	13	76	139	.239

Where He Hits the Ball

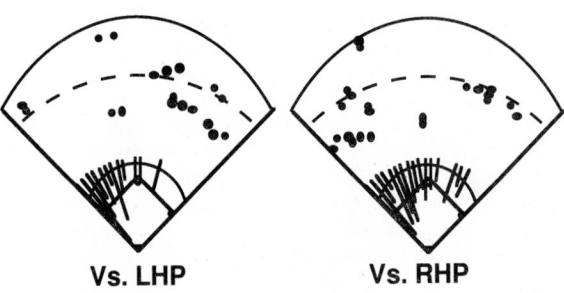

Vs. LHP   Vs. RHP

1989 Situational Stats

	AB	H	HR	RBI	AVG		AB	H	HR	RBI	AVG
Home	167	39	0	12	.234	LHP	103	28	0	9	.272
Road	151	37	2	14	.245	RHP	215	48	2	17	.223
Day	65	7	0	2	.108	Sc Pos	73	20	0	23	.274
Night	253	69	2	24	.273	Clutch	39	10	0	3	.256

1989 Rankings (American League)

→ 8th in bunts in play (24)
→ 3rd in sacrifice bunts (19)
→ Led Orioles in grounder/flyball ratio (2.62) and hitting with the bases loaded (.444) - *all team players*

HITTING:

If, if, if. If only Cal Ripken could have hit even .250 down the stretch ... well, who knows what would have happened to the '89 Orioles? He had some key hits in the final series with Toronto, but it was too late. Ripken hit .202 for September, a month where the Orioles lost to such clubs as Cleveland and Chicago. His final average: .257. Since batting .282 in '86, Ripken has hit .252, .264 and .257. He still hit 21 homers, which made him the first shortstop ever to have eight straight 20-homer seasons.

Ripken still relies on his father for a lot of advice. All one knows for sure is that Ripken changes his stance quite often. He just doesn't look as comfortable as he used to. He also looks at a lot of pitches. He's very patient. Sometimes too patient, waiting to do something with the perfect pitch. He did get some pitches to hit, walking 45 times less than he did in '88. But the Orioles have to wonder if he'll ever come close to .300 again. He went through some bad stretches and he was 1-for-14 with the bases loaded, hardly what the club wanted from its big gun.

BASERUNNING:

Ripken's not fast and has never stolen more than four bases in a season -- his lifetime totals are 19 steals, 22 caught stealings. But he's the best baserunner on the team. Ripken knows where to go, when to run, how to decoy, where to slide. They don't come much smarter.

FIELDING:

Ripken made just eight errors, an amazing total for someone who plays nearly every inning of the season. He still knows where to position himself. As team leader, he's easily the leader of the defense - as any shortstop should be. He may still stay at the position for a while, despite his size.

OVERALL:

With Eddie Murray gone, Ripken was the Orioles' role model. Murray was bitter by the time he'd left, while Ripken's spirit was a better example for a team of young players. But Ripken still does not like being the big dog. His leadership style is quiet. He works, and hopes others will follow. Ripken's lack of production in the clutch might have been a case of wanting to do too much. Still, Ripken is the quintessential Oriole, the Brooks Robinson of his generation. He's still a franchise player. Assuming the Orioles had won, what other .250 hitter could get serious consideration for MVP?

CAL RIPKEN

Position: SS
Bats: R **Throws:** R
Ht: 6' 4" **Wt:** 225

Opening Day Age: 29
Born: 8/24/60 in Havre de Grace, MD
ML Seasons: 9

Overall Statistics

	G	AB	R	H	D	T	HR	RBI	SB	BB	SO	AVG
1989	162	646	80	166	30	0	21	93	3	57	72	.257
Career	1315	5055	793	1402	266	24	204	744	19	553	635	.277

Where He Hits the Ball

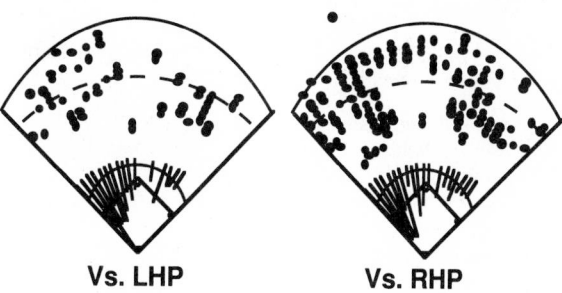

Vs. LHP   **Vs. RHP**

1989 Situational Stats

	AB	H	HR	RBI	AVG		AB	H	HR	RBI	AVG
Home	312	77	13	50	.247	LHP	196	46	5	22	.235
Road	334	89	8	43	.266	RHP	450	120	16	71	.267
Day	154	38	4	13	.247	Sc Pos	165	42	7	65	.255
Night	492	128	17	80	.260	Clutch	87	21	5	14	.241

1989 Rankings (American League)

- ➡ 1st in games played (162)
- ➡ 3rd in at bats (646)
- ➡ 3rd in GDPs (22)
- ➡ 5th worst hitting with bases loaded (.071)
- ➡ Led Orioles in games, at bats, hits (166), singles (115), doubles (30), total bases (259) and RBI (93)
- ➡ Led AL Shortstops in games, at bats, runs (80), hits, total bases, RBI, home runs (21) and slugging percentage (.401)

PITCHING:

Veteran righthander Dave Schmidt spent 1989 shifting between starting and relieving and was alternately effective and ineffective. After starting for most of the season--his 26 starts were the third most on the Baltimore staff --he ended the year working predominantly out of the bullpen, mostly as a middle man. For Schmidt the swing shift was a familiar role. He'd both started and relieved in all but one season since 1981, often with considerable success. He even went 8-5 for the woeful '88 Orioles; that was by far the best record on a club which lost 107 games.

In '89, the Orioles extracted considerable mileage from the veteran, particularly early in the season, but Schmidt's stuff does not seem conducive to regular starts. His greatest success has always come when used mostly out of the bullpen while making an occasional spot start. Schmidt was a willing workman and proved he could pitch into the sixth or seventh innings, but he stepped aside when younger starters arrived in droves.

Schmidt depends on a fastball and a palmball, with an occasional slider mixed in. If he gets behind he is often in trouble, and when his control is too good he is susceptible to the home run. A professional, he has learned how to adjust. It's now a question of whether a series of injuries to his arm have taken too much from him.

FIELDING:

Schmidt is a good athlete who reacts well and does the job. He has a high leg kick to the plate, so holding on runners is difficult for him. Still, Schmidt is better than average.

OVERALL:

Schmidt will be 33 in 1990, and though his '89 IP was the highest of his career, he appears to have some mileage left. Curiously--considering his past performance--he seems to want to continue working as a starter. As a free agent, Schmidt has a chance to continue his quest to be a starter elsewhere. If he stays with the Orioles, his future in that role is doubtful because he gives up too many hits (196 in 157 innings) and home runs.

DAVE SCHMIDT

Position: SP/RP
Bats: R **Throws:** R
Ht: 6' 1" **Wt:** 194

Opening Day Age: 32
Born: 4/22/57 in Niles, MI
ML Seasons: 9

Overall Statistics

	W	L	ERA	G	GS	Sv	IP	H	R	BB	SO	HR
1989	10	13	5.69	38	26	0	156.2	196	102	36	46	24
Career	51	51	3.76	335	63	37	846.2	888	396	219	453	79

Where They Hit the Ball

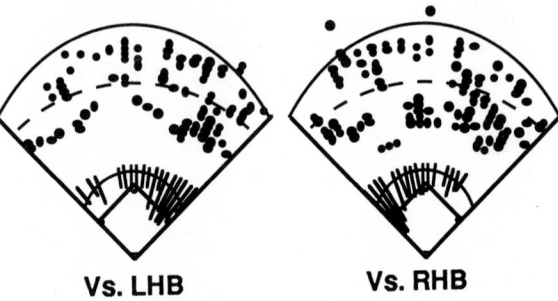

Vs. LHB   **Vs. RHB**

1989 Situational Stats

	W	L	ERA	Sv	IP		AB	H	HR	RBI	AVG
Home	3	3	6.67	0	56.2	LHB	310	94	12	44	.303
Road	7	10	5.13	0	100.0	RHB	322	102	12	48	.317
Day	2	2	6.31	0	25.2	Sc Pos	166	53	7	71	.319
Night	8	11	5.56	0	131.0	Clutch	25	5	1	3	.200

1989 Rankings (American League)

→ 4th worst in home runs allowed (24)

→ Worst on Orioles in losses (13) and home runs allowed.

HITTING:

This was the make-or-break year for Larry Sheets. It broke him. You've probably heard the story: 18 homers in 1986 and 31 the next season, then....

Perhaps expectations were simply too great after the 31-homer year; it came, after all, in 1987, the year of the homer and a season when a lot of players turned in power numbers they've never repeated. Except for that year, Sheets has never really been a complete hitter. He can handle the fastball, but can look pretty inept against a curve.

Sheets cares. He really does. He's a nice guy and he wants to do well. Players say when he doesn't perform, he takes it very hard. When the '89 season started poorly for him, his problems compounded. Sheets began swinging at the first pitch -- constantly, it seemed. Then he was more or less benched. Actually, a .359 slugging percentage and a .243 average paint a better picture for Sheets than the way it seemed. His season smacked of frustration. He hit a ton of line-drive outs. And it was Sheets who said how fitting it was for him to strike out against Tom Henke to clinch the Blue Jays' division championship celebration. In short, Sheets does not figure to be with Baltimore next season. He wants to play, but he feels neither loved nor needed with the Orioles.

BASERUNNING:

Sheets is very slow. Period. He's strictly a station-to-station runner and has never stolen more than two bases in a season.

FIELDING:

It's not an applicable question for Sheets. He proved in '88 that he's not an outfielder, and he was used exclusively at DH. His lack of defense certainly limits his future opportunities. With his weak glove, National League teams may not want him.

OVERALL:

Sheets is a sensitive man who wears his heart on his sleeve. If he can find the right situation, the right ballpark, get a few early hits... who knows? He has a lot to prove, and at 30 he still figures to have the talent. But he needs some coddling, someone to tell him he'll be OK. Chances are it won't be the Orioles.

LARRY SHEETS

Position: DH
Bats: L **Throws:** R
Ht: 6' 3" **Wt:** 236

Opening Day Age: 30
Born: 12/6/59 in Staunton, VA
ML Seasons: 6

Overall Statistics

	G	AB	R	H	D	T	HR	RBI	SB	BB	SO	AVG
1989	102	304	33	74	12	1	7	33	1	26	58	.243
Career	606	1907	233	511	80	3	84	286	5	149	308	.268

Where He Hits the Ball

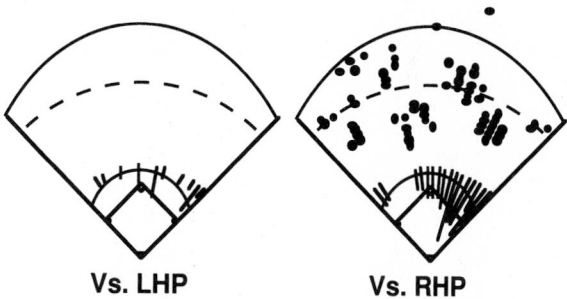

Vs. LHP   **Vs. RHP**

1989 Situational Stats

	AB	H	HR	RBI	AVG		AB	H	HR	RBI	AVG
Home	133	31	1	14	.233	LHP	39	6	0	1	.154
Road	171	43	6	19	.251	RHP	265	68	7	32	.257
Day	62	20	3	10	.323	Sc Pos	77	18	2	25	.234
Night	242	54	4	23	.223	Clutch	49	11	0	4	.224

1989 Rankings (American League)

➡ Hit only .056 (1 for 18) on hitter's counts (2-0 and 3-1)

➡ Led Orioles in intentional walks (10) and least frequent GDPs per GDP situation (7.5%)

HITTING:

A minor knee operation shortened Mickey Tettleton's season by four weeks. That's all that prevented him from hitting 30 homers. That he led the club with 26 surprised everyone. Now people will sit back and wonder whether Tettleton had a career year. The way Frank Robinson sees it, he's good for at least 15-20 homers per season. He had 11 homers in '88 (86 games), with the league's fourth-best home run frequency, so power isn't anything new for him. The Oakland A's knew that, but they were higher on Terry Steinbach two springs ago and let Tettleton go.

During the winter of '88-'89, Tettleton bulked up. His biceps were huge. But right before the season a cyst appeared on his knee. For all Tettleton knew, he had cancer. He survived that scare, but when the benign cyst was removed in early August, Tettleton went on the DL -- just as the Orioles emerged from their disastrous 2-12 road trip. Tettleton, a true competitor, hated being out. The injury limited him to DH duty. When he came back for September, he continued to hit home runs. Most of the shots went to the alleys. He always seemed to get great extension with his arms, emerging with a textbook power swing. Obviously, Tettleton has developed a good eye. He walked 73 times in 117 games and had a fine .369 on-base percentage. He also struck out 117 times, but Robinson said he's happy to sacrifice those outs for the power.

BASERUNNING:

Tettleton runs well for his size. He was even given the green light for stealing third on a couple of occasions. Tettleton has a lot of heart, which never hurts on the bases.

FIELDING:

He improved defensively, and pitchers liked how he called games. Tettleton is a gentle, soft-spoken man, and that can be pretty reassuring to young pitchers. And since the Orioles have plenty of those, Tettleton was a good guy to have around.

OVERALL:

Tettleton's folk-hero status lingers in Baltimore. Like the Orioles, he came out of nowhere in '89. Robinson is probably right -- 15-20 homers is a more reliable expectation. But if the club can get a proven power hitter, Tettleton and Cal Ripken would complete a solid middle of the order.

MICKEY TETTLETON

Position: C/DH
Bats: B **Throws:** R
Ht: 6' 2" **Wt:** 214

Opening Day Age: 29
Born: 9/16/60 in Oklahoma City, OK
ML Seasons: 6

Overall Statistics

	G	AB	R	H	D	T	HR	RBI	SB	BB	SO	AVG
1989	117	411	72	106	21	2	26	65	3	73	117	.258
Career	486	1403	181	337	58	4	59	183	13	209	383	.240

Where He Hits the Ball

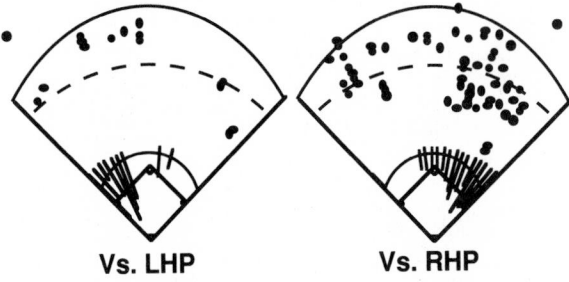

Vs. LHP   **Vs. RHP**

1989 Situational Stats

	AB	H	HR	RBI	AVG		AB	H	HR	RBI	AVG
Home	203	63	15	41	.310	LHP	139	34	10	20	.245
Road	208	43	11	24	.207	RHP	272	72	16	45	.265
Day	92	27	6	14	.293	Sc Pos	100	19	7	42	.190
Night	319	79	20	51	.248	Clutch	60	17	1	7	.283

1989 Rankings (American League)

- ➡ 8th in home runs (26)
- ➡ 4th worst hitting with runners in scoring position (.190)
- ➡ Led Orioles in home runs and strikeouts (117)
- ➡ Led AL Catchers in home runs, strikeouts, runs (72), total bases (209) and walks (73)

PITCHING:

A clearly defined role is no asset for Mark Thurmond, who frequently goes ten days without pitching. Thurmond really hasn't seen glory days since 1984, when he won fourteen games and started twice in the World Series. Since then it's been a struggle for him. After a horrible year at San Diego in 1986 (6.46 ERA), Thurmond has been shunted to the Tigers and then the Orioles, where he has assumed the thankless role of long man.

With Baltimore, Thurmond has made an occasional start, but is most utilized as the long-relief lefthander, the bridge between the starter and closer. Thurmond was so-so in that difficult role in 1989. He pitched well at times and displayed excellent control with 17 walks in 90 innings, but his ERA was on the high side (3.90) and he allowed 102 hits, a high number for the limited action he saw.

Thurmond has accepted his situation with equanimity and does his best by pitching in and out. He relies mostly on his guile, a cut fastball, slider and changeup and is fairly effective against righthanded hitters as well as lefties. Because he allows as many hits as he does, he needs his control to be effective. Fortunately for him, he seems to be able to pitch fairly well despite the long layoffs. More command of his pitches would help. Though not a dominating force, Thurmond had been good at keeping inherited runners from scoring until late in the season.

FIELDING:

His defense is okay, nothing spectacular, nothing exceptionally harmful. For a veteran lefthander, Thurmond does not have an especially dangerous pickoff move, but he is quick to the plate, removing some of the pressure.

OVERALL:

A basic major-league lefty, Thurmond is approaching seven years of service, so job security hasn't been a problem. But he is 33 now and will have to impress to maintain his spot on this staff. He was scored upon in three of his last four appearances, so a good spring training is a must for him.

MARK THURMOND

Position: RP
Bats: L **Throws:** L
Ht: 6' 0" **Wt:** 190

Opening Day Age: 33
Born: 9/12/56 in Houston, TX
ML Seasons: 7

Overall Statistics

	W	L	ERA	G	GS	Sv	IP	H	R	BB	SO	HR
1989	2	4	3.90	49	2	4	90.0	102	43	17	34	6
Career	38	43	3.71	271	97	17	781.0	837	369	244	296	63

Where They Hit the Ball

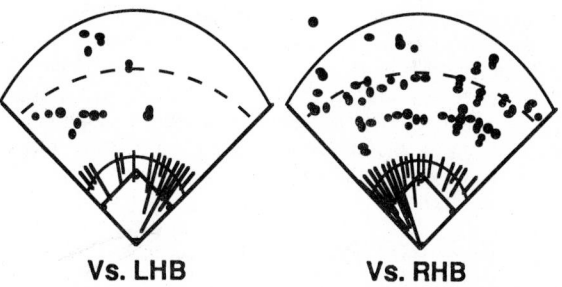

Vs. LHB   **Vs. RHB**

1989 Situational Stats

	W	L	ERA	Sv	IP		AB	H	HR	RBI	AVG
Home	2	3	3.83	1	44.2	LHB	106	30	1	17	.283
Road	0	1	3.97	3	45.1	RHB	248	72	5	36	.290
Day	0	2	2.25	1	20.0	Sc Pos	100	31	0	46	.310
Night	2	2	4.37	3	70.0	Clutch	31	9	1	5	.290

1989 Rankings (American League)

➡ 9th in most GDPs induced per GDP situation (19.3%)

PITCHING:

Mark Williamson came out of spring training as the best hope for the bullpen stopper's role, but, by last May, was the perfect setup man for Gregg Olson. It was a role he handled with aplomb. Williamson's ten relief wins, 65 appearances and 107.1 relief innings all ranked among the best in the majors. In addition, Williamson spelled Olson on occasion and recorded nine saves of his own.

Williamson's stuff is a little better than average. His best pitches are an 88-89 miles per hour fastball, a slider, and a palmball he uses as an off-speed delivery. What sets him apart are his bulldog determination and versatility. He is the glue of the staff, a pitcher who can go long, short, start or relieve. Williamson has a resilient arm which recovers well and he will pitch even when he doesn't feel well. He injured his hip throwing off the bullpen mound last year and it was feared he would go on the disabled list, but he returned to the mound two days later. The ten relief wins were the third most in Oriole history, and he converted nine of thirteen save chances. Those stats were a testament to both his character and his ability. On a staff which included outstanding performers like Gregg Olson and Jeff Ballard, he was among the most valuable.

FIELDING:

Williamson won't disgrace the team with bonehead plays on defense often. He rates above-average at coming off the mound and knows how to play his position. Baserunners occasionally can fool him, but he is not afraid to throw to first as often as he thinks is necessary to hold them.

OVERALL:

Between May 17 and September 28, Williamson lost only once. Then, he dropped two games in a row to Toronto that decided the American League East race. He may have been showing the effects of the long season at that point. Williamson will be back, refreshed and ready to perform in whatever role the Orioles ask. He is almost as indispensable as Olson, Ballard and Bob Milacki.

MARK WILLIAMSON

Position: RP
Bats: R **Throws:** R
Ht: 6' 0"   **Wt:** 171

Opening Day Age: 30
Born: 7/21/59 in Corpus Christi, TX
ML Seasons: 3

Overall Statistics

	W	L	ERA	G	GS	Sv	IP	H	R	BB	SO	HR
1989	10	5	2.93	65	0	9	107.1	105	35	30	55	4
Career	23	22	3.99	163	12	14	350.0	352	164	111	197	30

Where They Hit the Ball

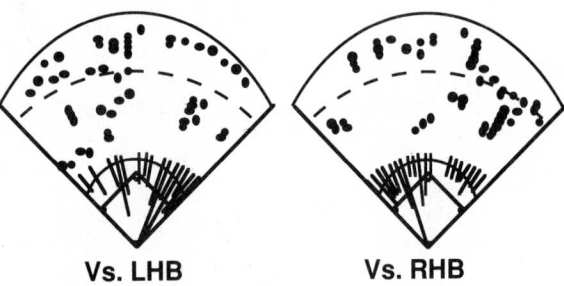

Vs. LHB   **Vs. RHB**

1989 Situational Stats

	W	L	ERA	Sv	IP		AB	H	HR	RBI	AVG
Home	7	2	2.61	4	58.2	LHB	177	46	0	19	.260
Road	3	3	3.33	5	48.2	RHB	226	59	4	38	.261
Day	1	2	6.53	2	20.2	Sc Pos	119	36	2	51	.303
Night	9	3	2.08	7	86.2	Clutch	196	59	4	38	.301

1989 Rankings (American League)

➡ 9th in games (65)

➡ 3rd worst in first batter efficiency (opposing batting average of .316)

➡ Led Orioles in blown saves (6)

HITTING:

Craig Worthington became everything the Orioles had hoped in 1989, and more. For several years he was a top prospect in a weak farm system. The Orioles saw a guy who could field with the best of them and occasionally pop one out. He did the latter 15 times, and a knack for delivering with the bases loaded gave Worthington 70 RBI. In fact, were it not for the presence of reliever Gregg Olson, Worthington likely would have received serious consideration for Rookie of the Year.

A number of Worthington's home runs were yanked down the short left-field line at Memorial Stadium. He has good bat speed and a compact swing. When pitchers jammed him, he had mixed results. Sometimes Worthington's strength allowed him to fist one out. Other times, he missed badly. Regardless, the Orioles don't think they have a fluke here. Worthington's numbers were just what they expected -- and good enough to stave off thoughts of moving Cal Ripken to third base and inserting minor-leaguer Juan Bell at shortstop. If Worthington gets a better handle on certain breaking pitches, he'll be a force for some time.

BASERUNNING:

Worthington is a slow runner. That didn't keep Frank Robinson from using him on the front end of a hit-and-run, if only because the club had decent contact guys behind him in the order. For what it's worth, Worthington doesn't make many glaring errors on the bases; he just can't get from one to the other fast enough. He's not a threat to steal.

FIELDING:

Worthington is the best third baseman the Orioles have seen since Doug DeCinces. He gets to everything and makes strong accurate throws when he has the chance to set himself. He went haywire for a bit in mid-season, making an error every third day over a 30-game span. Most of his problems were with making sidearm throws; Worthington said he was still learning not to rush them. Perhaps his only other fault was trying too hard -- cutting far over to his left for balls that Ripken had the easier bead on.

OVERALL:

More than anything, Worthington gives the Orioles options. He has solidified third base, at a time when Cal Ripken still seems to be the real thing at shortstop. The meaning: The Orioles could afford to deal Juan Bell, the centerpiece of the Eddie Murray trade and a promising young shortstop.

CRAIG WORTHINGTON

Position: 3B
Bats: R **Throws:** R
Ht: 6' 0" **Wt:** 190

Opening Day Age: 24
Born: 4/17/65 in Los Angeles, CA
ML Seasons: 2

Overall Statistics

	G	AB	R	H	D	T	HR	RBI	SB	BB	SO	AVG
1989	145	497	57	123	23	0	15	70	1	61	114	.247
Career	171	578	62	138	25	0	17	74	2	70	138	.239

Where He Hits the Ball

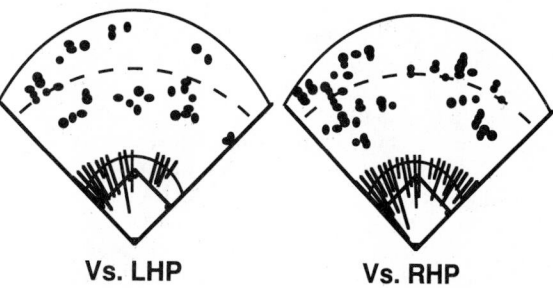

Vs. LHP   **Vs. RHP**

1989 Situational Stats

	AB	H	HR	RBI	AVG		AB	H	HR	RBI	AVG
Home	256	67	12	42	.262	LHP	155	40	4	19	.258
Road	241	56	3	28	.232	RHP	342	83	11	51	.243
Day	108	24	1	12	.222	Sc Pos	133	42	1	50	.316
Night	389	99	14	58	.254	Clutch	69	13	2	8	.188

1989 Rankings (American League)

- ➡ 6th in average pitches seen per plate appearance (4.0)
- ➡ Led Orioles in hitting with runners in scoring position (.316) and errors (20)

JOSE BAUTISTA

Position: SP/RP
Bats: R **Throws:** R
Ht: 6' 2" **Wt:** 203

Opening Day Age: 25
Born: 7/25/64 in Bani, Dominican Republic
ML Seasons: 2

Overall Statistics

	W	L	ERA	G	GS	Sv	IP	H	R	BB	SO	HR
1989	3	4	5.31	15	10	0	78.0	84	46	15	30	17
Career	9	19	4.61	48	35	0	249.2	255	132	60	106	38

PITCHING & FIELDING:

Two years ago, Jose Bautista was the team's most productive starter for several months. He finished that year with a 6-15 record, but Baltimore had high hopes for him in 1989. Unfortunately the righty never really got untracked. The Orioles demoted him twice last season after Bautista had tendencies to throw everything in the same hitting zone and lost command of his slider. He regained the slider, but pitched infrequently during the pennant race. Bautista needs some time to mature, control his emotions and regain his touch with the forkball, which often wound up in the bleachers. He had some problems with a blister on his pitching finger that cost him several home runs and caused Jose to pitch from behind to too many hitters. He is average on defense and holding runners.

OVERALL:

Bautista is still young at 25, but time is running out. He must demonstrate now that he is still a prospect and not a suspect after spending time in the minors every year but one since 1981.

RENE GONZALES

Position: 2B/3B
Bats: R **Throws:** R
Ht: 6' 2" **Wt:** 191

Opening Day Age: 28
Born: 9/3/61 in Austin, TX
ML Seasons: 5

Overall Statistics

	G	AB	R	H	D	T	HR	RBI	SB	BB	SO	AVG
1989	71	166	16	36	4	0	1	11	5	12	30	.217
Career	240	519	49	113	13	1	4	35	8	32	85	.218

HITTING, BASERUNNING, FIELDING:

Probably best known for his unusual uniform number -- 88 -- Rene Gonzales is what he is: a .220 hitter. He's the prototypical utility guy. He's a fine fielder, versatile, quick, with the ability to hit a couple homers per season. Baseball America once rated him a Top-10 prospect when he was Expos property, but he's never developed offensively. He's a decent bunter, but for someone his size you'd expect Gonzales to look tougher at the plate than he is. Gonzales makes the perfect pinch-runner, for he makes sense as a late-inning defensive replacement. He's a smart baserunner who moves well. On defense, Gonzales has a bullet arm and good hands. A natural shortstop, he's converted to stints at third base and second base with no problem. He had to begin the season at second for the injured Bill Ripken, and there was not a substantial dropoff.

OVERALL:

Gonzales can make a whole career out of being the utility guy, even though he'd like to be a regular.

TIM HULETT

Position: 2B
Bats: R **Throws:** R
Ht: 6' 0" **Wt:** 185

Opening Day Age: 30
Born: 1/12/60 in Springfield, IL
ML Seasons: 6

Overall Statistics

	G	AB	R	H	D	T	HR	RBI	SB	BB	SO	AVG
1989	33	97	12	27	5	0	3	18	0	10	17	.278
Career	406	1264	138	306	50	9	32	127	12	72	234	.242

HITTING, BASERUNNING, FIELDING:

Tim Hulett came up in late August when Bill Ripken hurt his shoulder. He hit so well -- .278, three homers 18 RBI in 33 games -- that Ripken had a hard time getting in even after he was healthy. The Orioles were sorely in need of punch, and they got it from Hulett, a man who's danced in and out of the majors since 1983. He's a patient hitter who has the nerve to jump on a first pitch when he likes it. He has power to left field and makes good contact when he does connect. He did, though, strike out 17 times. Hulett is not especially fast, nor is he a base stealing threat. He can play second or third adequately. He did cost the Orioles an important run in a loss to New York, making an ill-advised relay to home plate. The play let a runner advance to third and score an insurance run on a sacrifice fly.

OVERALL:

Hulett still may have a battle on his hands for a starting job, because Bill Ripken is stronger defensively. However, his pop with the bat might make him more versatile as a utility man than Rene Gonzales.

STAN JEFFERSON

Position: RF
Bats: B **Throws:** R
Ht: 5'11" **Wt:** 175

Opening Day Age: 27
Born: 12/4/62 in New York, NY
ML Seasons: 4

Overall Statistics

	G	AB	R	H	D	T	HR	RBI	SB	BB	SO	AVG
1989	45	139	20	34	7	0	4	21	10	4	26	.245
Career	224	696	101	152	17	9	14	57	49	54	148	.218

HITTING, BASERUNNING, FIELDING:

Once a hot prospect, Stan Jefferson came to Baltimore strictly to be a fill-in. He had his usual problems with strike zone judgment, but he hit four homers and figured more prominently in the Orioles' stretch drive than had been expected. The Orioles saw glimpses of why Jefferson was once a top Mets (and later Padres) farm product. His best asset is probably his great speed -- he's always a threat to steal. But he also has surprising power and can get hold of a fastball on occasion. Defense brought on Jefferson's demise with the Yankees and then-manager Dallas Green. The two got into a shouting match about his glovework, and there were times in Baltimore that Jefferson looked hopelessly lost in right field. Green thought he wasn't trying. He tried with the Orioles, but motivation has always been a problem for him.

OVERALL:

Jefferson is a scary guy to put in the outfield every day, and, as a hitter, he needs to make better contact. It's hard to figure where he'll fit in the Orioles' plans in 1990. The outfield is pretty crowded.

DAVE JOHNSON

Position: SP
Bats: R **Throws:** R
Ht: 5'11" **Wt:** 180

Opening Day Age: 30
Born: 10/24/59 in
Baltimore, MD
ML Seasons: 2

Overall Statistics

	W	L	ERA	G	GS	Sv	IP	H	R	BB	SO	HR
1989	4	7	4.23	14	14	0	89.1	90	44	28	26	11
Career	4	7	4.61	19	14	0	95.2	103	51	30	30	12

PITCHING & FIELDING:

If heart were the only criteria for success, Dave Johnson would have few peers. He pitched a masterful game as a substitute for Pete Harnisch when the Orioles were facing elimination and gave the team a big boost the last two months with his moxie. His stuff is average (fastball, curve, slider, change), but he moves the ball around well and has a knack for making big pitches. At 29, he was a rookie with a virtual lifetime in the minors; perhaps more than anything, he learned patience and is a positive thinker. Johnson pitches from many angles (over the top, three-quarters, even sidearm). He also has an unorthodox windup that can confuse hitters and is excellent at holding runners with a very quick move to first.

OVERALL:

It will not be new for Johnson to have to hustle to maintain his spot. Opponents could catch up to him after the first time around and his stuff may not compensate. But, with his heart, he always has a chance.

JAMIE QUIRK

Position: C
Bats: L **Throws:** R
Ht: 6' 4" **Wt:** 200

Opening Day Age: 35
Born: 10/22/54 in
Whittier, CA
ML Seasons: 15

Overall Statistics

	G	AB	R	H	D	T	HR	RBI	SB	BB	SO	AVG
1989	47	85	6	15	2	0	1	10	0	12	20	.176
Career	774	1765	152	418	84	5	37	193	5	131	345	.237

HITTING, BASERUNNING, FIELDING:

Jamie Quirk considered himself retired when the Orioles approached him after Mickey Tettleton injured his knee. He hit .176, which is about what the club expected, but the veteran is a good influence in the clubhouse and helped steady this young ballclub. He can still get a hold of a fastball on occasion, but not as often as he used to. Quirk has good speed as catchers go. He's been around and does not do many dumb things on the bases. On defense, he was just what the Orioles asked for: an experienced backstop in an emergency. He has pennant-race experience with Kansas City and an excellent disposition. In a fix, he was a fine answer for a young pitching staff.

OVERALL:

The 35-year-old Quirk is not getting any younger. One got a sense that the '89 Orioles experience recharged Quirk's battery, but with Tettleton and Bob Melvin healthy it's unknown if the Orioles will carry Quirk. Probably not, but lefty-hitting catchers seem to have nine lives.

JAY TIBBS

Position: SP
Bats: R **Throws:** R
Ht: 6' 1" **Wt:** 175

Opening Day Age: 28
Born: 1/4/62 in
Birmingham, AL
ML Seasons: 6

Overall Statistics

	W	L	ERA	G	GS	Sv	IP	H	R	BB	SO	HR
1989	5	0	2.82	10	8	0	54.1	62	17	20	30	2
Career	36	47	4.13	143	123	0	805.0	825	416	303	421	60

PITCHING & FIELDING:

Jay Tibbs was off and running with a 5-0 record before shoulder surgery ended his season prematurely. That was the sort of success that had long been expected of him. Though he's still only 28, Tibbs has been kicking around since 1980, pitching for four different systems. He's never had much success--his lifetime record is only 36-47--but Tibbs has the sort of stuff that intrigues managers and coaches. The difference in '89 was that he changed his repertoire. Working under coach Dick Bosman during a stint at Rochester, Tibbs junked his curve ball and improved his slider and changeup enormously. And he overcame his doubts about his ability, his confidence level rising appreciably with a simpler game plan. Tibbs can now throw the slider for strikes and changes speeds well. He is a better than average fielder and is a veteran who is conscious enough of baserunners. He has adopted a quicker move to first.

OVERALL:

Tibbs is one of the Orioles' biggest question marks entering 1990. He showed enough to justify staying in the rotation and could still be the No. 4 or 5 starter if healthy. He is no longer the pitcher who was 4-15 in 1988 and can provide a big lift if he bounces back.

JIM TRABER

Position: 1B
Bats: L **Throws:** L
Ht: 6' 0" **Wt:** 213

Opening Day Age: 28
Born: 12/26/61 in
Columbus, OH
ML Seasons: 4

Overall Statistics

	G	AB	R	H	D	T	HR	RBI	SB	BB	SO	AVG
1989	86	234	14	49	8	0	4	26	4	19	41	.209
Career	264	819	70	186	21	0	27	117	5	58	118	.227

HITTING, BASERUNNING, FIELDING:

In 1986, Jim Traber was the Local Hero from nearby Columbia, Md., who filled in so brilliantly for an injured Eddie Murray. A year later he had big power numbers at Class AAA. But in the majors, Traber continues to be what he is -- a .210-.240 hitter who hits an occasional big-impact homer and drives in a big run. He hardly saw playing time the last two months, and is almost self-deprecating about his chances with the club beyond '89. He's still prone to a lot of strikeouts; when he misses, he cocks his head to the right -- like he never saw the ball. Also, when will "The Whammer" lose some weight? It looks like his girth gets in the way. The poundage slows him down on the bases, but he's not a bad baserunner. At first base he excelled defensively, making only one error. No mammoth task, true, but nothing to be sneezed at.

OVERALL:

It seemed like Traber had a semi-weekly meeting with Frank Robinson about his status. The answer was simple: Traber was not producing, so he didn't play. It remains to be seen how much longer he'll be with the Orioles.

HITTING:

Marty Barrett is a thinking man's player. As a hitter Barrett has always been torn between spotting the ball where the fielders aren't or just going up and trying to hit the ball hard. In 1989, Barrett tried to place the ball and he had his worst season, hitting just .256. At the end of the year, Barrett vowed he was going to work on his wrists and try to hit everything hard, like his middle-infield partner, Jody Reed.

The prototypical No. 2 hitter, Barrett hits behind the runner well, is an excellent bunter and executes a hit-and-run as well as anyone. While Wade Boggs gets the credit for swinging and missing at few pitches, Barrett had perennially been No. 1 in that category. In an injury-filled 1989, which saw him undergo knee surgery, Barrett swung and missed 21 times in 596 swings. He did not strike out against a left-handed pitcher in 118 plate appearances. There's no easy way to pitch Barrett. Because he slaps the ball to all fields he is a good hitter against hard throwers. He is rarely overcome by the breaking pitch, but most pitchers will try to throw him high and inside, knowing he can't drive it over the fence.

BASERUNNING:

Barrett has average to below-average foot speed, but he is an intelligent base-runner who runs well between first and third. He is not a great candidate to steal a base, but Barrett picks the right spot to do so, which has kept his stealing percentage over 70 percent throughout his career.

FIELDING:

Many observers deride Barrett because he has very little range; others say he makes up for it with accurate positioning. One thing is for sure, if you want a ball hit in the Red Sox infield, you want it hit to Barrett. Barrett is excellent in turning the double-play; he has a tremendous sense of timing between himself and the incoming base-runner. He has a strong arm.

OVERALL:

A quiet leader and an astute observer of the game, Barrett is major league managerial timber. He's one of those players who isn't really noticed until he's gone. He's the type who detects little defects in an opposing pitcher's delivery and passes on the secrets to his teammates. Barrett accepted the three-way platoon at second and shortstop with he, Jody Reed and Luis Rivera, but would like his full-time role back next season. With a clean bill of health, it's quite probable he'll get it.

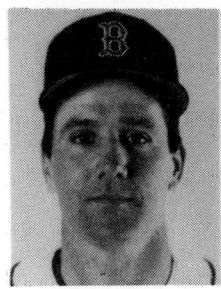

MARTY BARRETT

Position: 2B
Bats: R **Throws:** R
Ht: 5'10" **Wt:** 175

Opening Day Age: 31
Born: 6/23/58 in Arcadia, CA
ML Seasons: 8

Overall Statistics

	G	AB	R	H	D	T	HR	RBI	SB	BB	SO	AVG
1989	86	336	31	86	18	0	1	27	4	32	12	.256
Career	867	3203	402	899	158	9	17	298	53	289	193	.281

Where He Hits the Ball

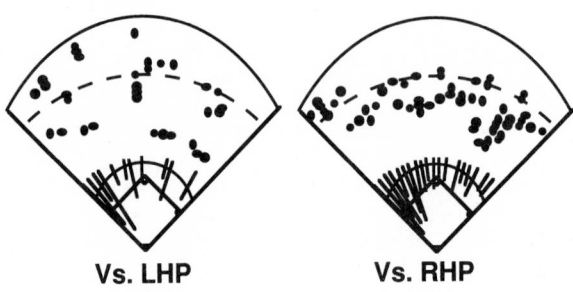

Vs. LHP   **Vs. RHP**

1989 Situational Stats

	AB	H	HR	RBI	AVG		AB	H	HR	RBI	AVG
Home	167	44	0	17	.263	LHP	104	27	0	5	.260
Road	169	42	1	10	.249	RHP	232	59	1	22	.254
Day	119	32	0	10	.269	Sc Pos	86	22	0	25	.256
Night	217	54	1	17	.249	Clutch	58	19	0	5	.328

1989 Rankings (American League)

→ 5th in sacrifice bunts (15)

→ 5th lowest percent of swings that missed (3.5%) - *all league players*

→ 7th in hitting with an 0-2 count (.308) - *players with 20 PA*

→ 3rd worst hitting with a 3-2 count (.043) - *players with 20 PA*

→ Led the Red Sox in sacrifice bunts, bunts in play (20), lowest percent of swings that missed, and hitting with the bases loaded (.444) - *all team players*

PITCHING:

Mike Boddicker's role as the team's number two starter fit him like a glove. He won 15 games. He did this despite the fact that he was a second half pitcher -- he struggles in cold weather with his curve ball, his bread and butter pitch. Boddicker's success came as a result of a change in his philosophy. In the past he was known as a finesse pitcher who threw several different speeds on a breaking pitch that ranked among the best in the game, in 1989 Boddicker featured his fastball more than ever. Though he throws it in the mid-80s, it's not a pitch that hitters sit on because they know he can make them look foolish with his other stuff. So many of Boddicker's fastballs are taken for strikes. He nibbles on both sides of the plate with his breaking stuff and usually drives hitters crazy.

When Boddicker has command of his breaking pitch there's no reason for the opposition to show up, because he can mix up his pitches and keep hitters off-balance. Boddicker suffers from what a lot of breaking pitchers have to deal with: umpires who give up on breaking pitches too soon. On the other hand, Boddicker's constant whining to umpires doesn't help his cause on close pitches. Boddicker was a far better pitcher on the road than at Fenway. He does give up long flyballs in big parks that get caught. He often gives up long balls to the right parts of Fenway, too, but it isn't the park best suited for Boddicker.

FIELDING:

Boddicker is an excellent athlete who can make the plays of an infielder. He's quick coming off the mound and his follow-through always puts him in perfect position to receive the ball. He can be stolen upon because his pitches take a while to make it to the plate.

OVERALL:

The Red Sox would like to see a better first half from Boddicker, who is relied on to be a top Sox starter after Roger Clemens. They would also like to see more leadership qualities from the veteran who has played in the post-season with the Orioles and Red Sox. He can be a big help to young pitchers because of his knowledge of the game, and is capable of carrying a pitching staff if need be.

MIKE BODDICKER

Position: SP
Bats: R **Throws:** R
Ht: 5'11" **Wt:** 186

Opening Day Age: 32
Born: 8/23/57 in Cedar Rapids, IA
ML Seasons: 10

Overall Statistics

	W	L	ERA	G	GS	Sv	IP	H	R	BB	SO	HR
1989	15	11	4.00	34	34	0	211.2	217	101	71	145	19
Career	101	87	3.70	239	228	0	1574.1	1500	726	541	1037	148

Where They Hit the Ball

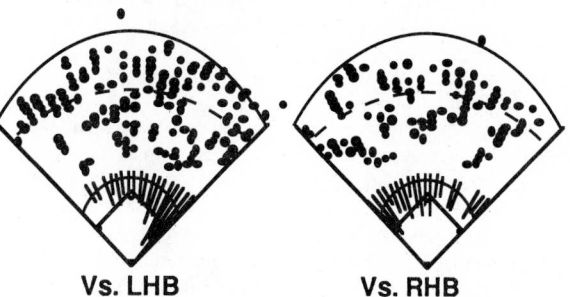

Vs. LHB   **Vs. RHB**

1989 Situational Stats

	W	L	ERA	Sv	IP		AB	H	HR	RBI	AVG
Home	7	8	4.89	0	103.0	LHB	444	124	12	54	.279
Road	8	3	3.15	0	108.2	RHB	369	93	7	29	.252
Day	2	5	5.70	0	53.2	Sc Pos	184	39	1	60	.212
Night	13	6	3.42	0	158.0	Clutch	59	9	1	2	.153

1989 Rankings (American League)

➡ 1st in lowest opponent batting average with runners in scoring position (.212) - *pitchers with 162 IP*

➡ Worst opponent on-base average when leading of an inning (.339)

➡ 2nd in hit batsmen (10)

➡ 8th in runs support per 9 innings (5.1)

➡ Led the Red Sox in hit batsmen, hits allowed (217), runs (101) and earned runs allowed (94), doubles allowed (43), triples allowed (4) and lowest opponent batting average with runners in scoring position.

HITTING:

Red Sox General Manager Lou Gorman said of Wade Boggs: "He can fall out of bed in December and get a hit." But it wasn't that easy in 1989. Boggs lacked patience during the first half of last season and wound up hitting .330, the second worst average of his career. Boggs, perhaps the greatest two-strike hitter of all time, was often seen swinging at first pitches. Though he denies it, it could be Boggs was trying to silence those who thought the Margo Adams affair was going to affect his hitting.

Boggs continued to be the made-for-Fenway Park hitter last year, hitting .377 there, while hitting 37 of his 51 doubles at Fenway, many of them high atop the left-field wall. The Red Sox wanted Boggs to pull the ball more, but he rarely got a pitch inside enough to turn on. More pitchers seemed to challenge Boggs in 1989. A good hard fastball high and away often had Boggs fishing, though he swung and missed only 59 times in 1,101 swings.

BASERUNNING:

Boggs was once timed down the first-base line by Gene Michael as the second fastest man in the American League. Injuries have slowed him a little, but when Boggs smells a hit there aren't too many faster. Yet Boggs has been known not to go from first to third on occasion, infuriating his manager. Boggs rarely attempts or steals a base despite being a leadoff hitter, which is another mystery since he runs so well.

FIELDING:

Those who watch him day in and day out wonder why Boggs has never won a Gold Glove. This natural hitter has made himself into an excellent third baseman with hard work. He is a master of the slow-roller and short-hop. If he lacks range, it's to his left. He has a strong and accurate arm. He always knows who's running and just how much he needs to put on his throw.

OVERALL:

The biggest rap on Boggs has been his lack of production and power, but Boggs never claimed to be that type of hitter, just one who gets 200 hits and 100 walks a year. He is a pitcher's nightmare because the hurler knows there's an excellent chance Boggs will get a hit or draw a walk. Even when Boggs makes an out, the pitcher has to work well into the count, and that helps the other Red Sox hitters.

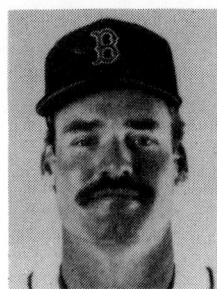

WADE BOGGS

Position: 3B
Bats: L **Throws:** R
Ht: 6' 2" **Wt:** 197

Opening Day Age: 31
Born: 6/15/58 in Omaha, NE
ML Seasons: 8

Overall Statistics

	G	AB	R	H	D	T	HR	RBI	SB	BB	SO	AVG
1989	156	621	113	205	51	7	3	54	2	107	51	.330
Career	1183	4534	823	1597	314	36	64	523	14	754	339	.352

Where He Hits the Ball

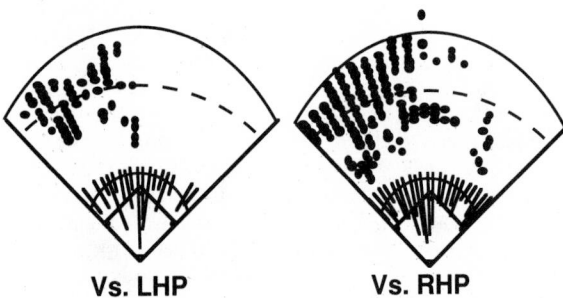

Vs. LHP   **Vs. RHP**

1989 Situational Stats

	AB	H	HR	RBI	AVG		AB	H	HR	RBI	AVG
Home	300	113	2	27	.377	LHP	210	62	0	17	.295
Road	321	92	1	27	.287	RHP	411	143	3	37	.348
Day	211	71	2	18	.336	Sc Pos	124	42	0	45	.339
Night	410	134	1	36	.327	Clutch	98	27	1	7	.276

1989 Rankings (American League)

➡ 1st in on-base average (.430), runs (113), doubles (51), intentional walks (19), plate appearances (742), pitches seen (3,076), times reached base (319), lowest percent of swings that missed (5.4%), and highest batting average with two strikes (.329) - *players with 502 PA*

➡ Led the Red Sox in batting average (.330), at bats (621), runs, hits, singles (144), doubles, triples, sacrifice flies (7), caught stealing (6), walks, intentional walks, hit by pitch (7), times reached base, games (156), plate appearances, pitches seen, on-base average, lowest percent of swings that missed, hitting with runners in scoring position (.339) and batting average with two strikes - *team players with 502 PA*

HITTING:

There have been shades of greatness in each of Ellis Burks's first three years in the major leagues, but something always holds him back. Last year injuries to each shoulder stopped him short. Despite that, Burks had a productive 97 games, hitting more than .300 with 12 home runs, 61 RBIs and 21 stolen bases.

Burks has pulled the ball more and more in the last two years as pitchers attempt to bust him inside with fastballs. If he has problems with any one pitch, it's the breaking pitch. Burks can be fooled by a slow, sharp break. Sometimes he will lunge at a pitch outside. He is an aggressive hitter whom the Red Sox would like to see become more patient.

The great debate in Boston has always been whether the Red Sox should take advantage of his speed by batting him lead-off, or to utilize his power and productivity by putting him in the three-hole. He seemed to answer that himself by hitting a whopping .325 in the No. 3 spot and .240 in other spots, including No. 1.

BASERUNNING:

Burks has speed galore and has had the green light in all three years as a major leaguer, but is afraid to get caught and thus only steals when he thinks the risk is low. It's almost as if he's torn between being a power hitter or a base-stealer. The Red Sox are trying to convince him he can be both.

FIELDING:

There isn't much Burks can't catch up to, and he makes many great catches. He errs at times in judgment, going back when he should come in and vice-versa. He has decent arm strength, but not the great arm that many rated Burks as having when he first came up. Burks often has a problem with accuracy. That could be due to his hand and shoulder injuries.

OVERALL:

The Red Sox want just one thing out of Burks: to play consistently at his full potential and intensity. Burks makes the Red Sox offense go because of his quick bat, his potential for power and his speed afoot. Burks also gets the most out of Mike Greenwell, the Sox' clean-up hitter, because Greenwell usually gets better pitches to hit and is usually in a men-on-base situation. He's also a potential club leader, but now the Sox are worried that he might be injury-prone.

ELLIS BURKS

Position: CF
Bats: R **Throws:** R
Ht: 6' 2" **Wt:** 188

Opening Day Age: 25
Born: 9/11/64 in Vicksburg, MS
ML Seasons: 3

Overall Statistics

	G	AB	R	H	D	T	HR	RBI	SB	BB	SO	AVG
1989	97	399	73	121	19	6	12	61	21	36	52	.303
Career	374	1497	260	432	86	13	50	212	73	139	239	.289

Where He Hits the Ball

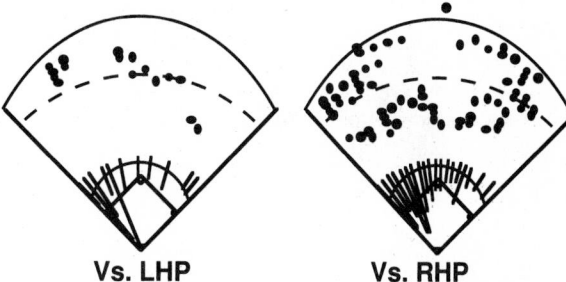

Vs. LHP   **Vs. RHP**

1989 Situational Stats

	AB	H	HR	RBI	AVG		AB	H	HR	RBI	AVG
Home	204	65	6	29	.319	LHP	104	29	2	12	.279
Road	195	56	6	32	.287	RHP	295	92	10	49	.312
Day	126	39	4	29	.310	Sc Pos	116	36	4	50	.310
Night	273	82	8	32	.300	Clutch	66	16	4	15	.242

1989 Rankings (American League)

➡ 6th in highest stolen base percentage (81% - 21 for 26)

➡ Led the Red Sox in stolen bases (21), stolen base percentage, and lowest percent of GDPs per GDP situation (7.5%)

HITTING:

Rick Cerone was acquired two years ago as a stop-gap when Rich Gedman got hurt. The plan was, as soon as Gedman returned, Cerone would make a nice back-up catcher. But Cerone, who had been released by the New York Yankees, became Boston's starting catcher and has kept the job for the past two years.

Cerone is a contact hitter. He goes with the pitch and usually doesn't try to over-swing at anything. He's benefitted by The Wall at Fenway Park where he has stroked a few soft doubles that would normally have been high fly ball outs. In this era of weak-hitting catchers, Cerone has hit .269 and .243 the past two years, which has been more than adequate.

Despite that success, Cerone is still prone to waving at tough breaking pitches out of the strike zone. For the most part, Cerone won't swing at much early in the count. He makes contact, which is why the Red Sox like to see him up with men on base. With a runner at third, Cerone can loft the ball for a sacrifice fly. Cerone's average has plummeted the second half of both seasons with the Sox, an indication he might be playing too much at his age.

BASERUNNING:

Cerone is pretty much a station-to-station runner, but he is considered a good base-runner who will not make any dumb mistakes. The Red Sox are at a disadvantage at Fenway as he usually has to be held up at third if a ball is hit to left field.

FIELDING:

Cerone's biggest problem is arm strength. He threw out only 28 percent of base stealers; some of that was the pitchers' fault, but when Cerone did have a chance, his throws either weren't on time or off the mark. He fields his position extremely well. Cerone handles nubbers well and welcomes home plate collisions. He calls an aggressive game and makes the pitcher feature his best pitch (example: Clemens' fastball).

OVERALL:

He has had the reputation of being a clubhouse lawyer and at times had to be spoken to by Red Sox management about it. But Cerone has a good knowledge of pitching and his experience is valuable at times. The Red Sox were hoping to bring him back to vie for the back-up catcher's spot, if they had acquired a frontliner over the winter.

RICK CERONE

Position: C
Bats: R **Throws:** R
Ht: 5'11" **Wt:** 195

Opening Day Age: 35
Born: 5/19/54 in Newark, NJ
ML Seasons: 15

Overall Statistics

	G	AB	R	H	D	T	HR	RBI	SB	BB	SO	AVG
1989	102	296	28	72	16	1	4	48	0	34	40	.243
Career	1157	3640	353	877	167	15	54	402	4	282	408	.241

Where He Hits the Ball

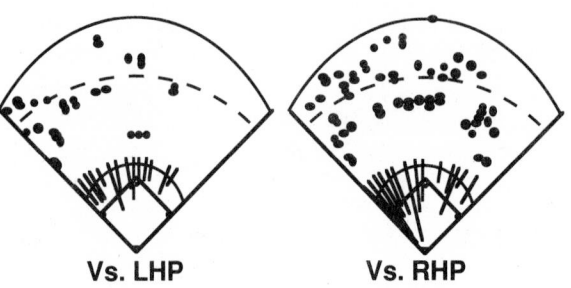

Vs. LHP   **Vs. RHP**

1989 Situational Stats

	AB	H	HR	RBI	AVG		AB	H	HR	RBI	AVG
Home	155	47	2	32	.303	LHP	119	34	2	23	.286
Road	141	25	2	16	.177	RHP	177	38	2	25	.215
Day	84	19	0	11	.226	Sc Pos	75	25	0	39	.333
Night	212	53	4	37	.250	Clutch	44	7	0	6	.159

1989 Rankings (American League)

➡ 4th worst in hitting in the clutch (.159)

➡ 5th worst throwing out opposing base stealers (28%)

ROGER CLEMENS

Position: SP
Bats: R **Throws:** R
Ht: 6' 4" **Wt:** 220

Opening Day Age: 27
Born: 8/4/62 in Dayton, OH
ML Seasons: 6

PITCHING:

Roger Clemens is still among the premiere pitchers in baseball, but his performance has steadily declined over the past four years as he makes the change from complete power pitcher to sometime power pitcher. Arm and shoulder injuries have caused Clemens to dabble in forkballs, sliders and sidearm pitches. He still throws his fastball most of the time, but not 80 percent of the time as he did in 1986. Still, when Clemens needs to be overpowering he can be.

Many pitchers would take time off when they have tendinitis, but Clemens elects to pitch through it. During those times when his arm is bothering him, he throws far too many forkballs, which can get him in trouble. Clemens has lost the slow, big-dropping curve he once had, but he still has an effective breaking pitch that can bite at the corners.

Clemens continued to be a extremely effective pitcher at Fenway Park, where he was 9-3 with a 2.90 ERA as opposed to an 8-8 mark and a 3.29 ERA on the road. Despite his arm problems, Clemens made all but one of his starts and again pitched more than 250 innings. Clemens is a battler who likes to challenge the opposing teams' best hitter. He isn't afraid to knock a big hitter off the plate to establish his territory. Clemens started throwing a sidearm fastball the second half of last season, which he threw once or twice a game with great effect. Clemens gets into trouble when he leaves a forkball over the plate or doesn't get his fastball either inside or outside enough.

FIELDING:

Clemens is as aggressive in fielding his position as he is on the mound. He's as quick as a big man can be, especially a pitcher whose follow-through is so pronounced. He doesn't have the best motion to first base, but he has become more mindful of runners on base than he was as a younger pitcher.

OVERALL:

He is the workhorse of the Boston staff and one of a few franchise players in baseball. Clemens needs more help in the Red Sox rotation so he doesn't feel the burden is squarely on his shoulders to produce a winner. It could be that Clemens needs to reduce his pitch-count and innings to be stronger throughout the year, but that's a hard thing to preach to a competitor like Clemens.

Overall Statistics

	W	L	ERA	G	GS	Sv	IP	H	R	BB	SO	HR
1989	17	11	3.13	35	35	0	253.1	215	101	93	230	20
Career	95	45	3.06	175	174	0	1284.2	1088	476	371	1215	95

Where They Hit the Ball

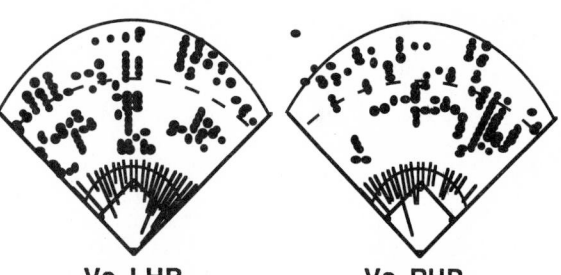

Vs. LHB   **Vs. RHB**

1989 Situational Stats

	W	L	ERA	Sv	IP		AB	H	HR	RBI	AVG
Home	9	3	2.90	0	105.2	LHB	503	122	7	43	.243
Road	8	8	3.29	0	147.2	RHB	426	93	13	42	.218
Day	4	3	2.71	0	86.1	Sc Pos	183	41	2	62	.224
Night	13	8	3.34	0	167.0	Clutch	114	28	3	8	.246

1989 Rankings (American League)

➡ 1st in pitches thrown (4,243), pickoff throws (295) and caught stealing (17)

➡ 2nd in strikeouts (230)

➡ 3rd in strikeouts per 9 innings (8.2) and batters faced (1,044)

➡ 9th in lowest opponent stolen base percentage (53%)

➡ Led the Red Sox in earned run average (3.13), wins, games started, complete games, shutouts, innings pitched, batters faced, walks, strikeouts, wild pitches (7), pitches thrown, pickoff throws, win/loss percentage (.607), caught stealing, lowest opponent stolen base percentage and lowest opponent batting average (.231) - *team pitchers with 162 IP*

PITCHING:

All the Red Sox wanted from John Dopson in 1989 was to show promise and maybe to pick up a few of the wins left by the departed Bruce Hurst. Dopson did that and more. The sinker/slider pitcher needed to have both pitches working in order to be effective earlier in the season, but toward the end Dopson learned to win without everything working at its best.

Dopson has a natural sinker that comes in at knee level or lower and which is absolutely unhittable. His bread and butter pitch might be the slider, which has tremendous movement and can be nasty on right-handed hitters. When Dopson gets into trouble, he gets his slider over the plate, or his sinker doesn't have the sharp drop it should. Dopson can throw in the high 80s and low 90s with great movement, but can lapse into spells where he loses control. Most of the time they are concentration problems which he seemed to get over as the season went on.

Dopson led the major leagues with 15 balks. That's after only one balk in 1988, the year of the balk. He sometimes needs a good swift kick to be motivated, but with improvement in that area along with more of a killer instinct, Dopson could be a force to be reckoned with. One of Dopson's biggest problems was stamina, but he began to solve that at the end of the 1989 season. Dopson is big at 6-4 and built similar to Roger Clemens, so the Red Sox would like him to be more of a workhorse in the future. One of Dopson's strengths is that he acts cool under pressure and doesn't usually change the way he pitches.

FIELDING:

As a sinker-ball pitcher, Dopson should be more aware that grounders could be shooting up the middle when he pitches. He could be in a lot better position on his follow-through to make the plays. The balks indicate his concern with runners, but they found his slow delivery easy to steal on.

OVERALL:

Dopson has a great will to be a top-notch starting pitcher. If he keeps his mistakes during a game to a minimum, Dopson has the potential to be a long-distance pitcher. He is a likeable player, the type a team can rally around. Being around Roger Clemens ought to help him in the future.

JOHN DOPSON

Position: SP
Bats: R **Throws:** R
Ht: 6' 4" **Wt:** 205

Opening Day Age: 26
Born: 7/14/63 in Baltimore, MD
ML Seasons: 3

Overall Statistics

	W	L	ERA	G	GS	Sv	IP	H	R	BB	SO	HR
1989	12	8	3.99	29	28	0	169.1	166	84	69	95	14
Career	15	21	3.79	59	57	0	351.0	341	170	131	200	33

Where They Hit the Ball

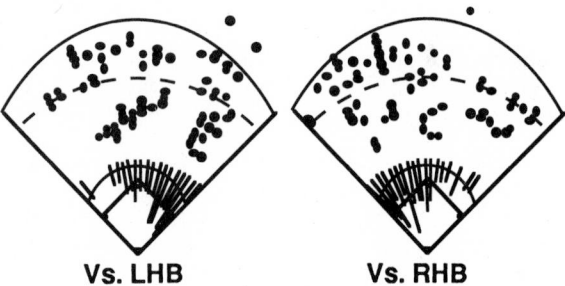

Vs. LHB   **Vs. RHB**

1989 Situational Stats

	W	L	ERA	Sv	IP		AB	H	HR	RBI	AVG
Home	6	5	4.07	0	104.0	LHB	316	78	5	27	.247
Road	6	3	3.86	0	65.1	RHB	331	88	9	41	.266
Day	6	1	2.83	0	60.1	Sc Pos	169	43	3	52	.254
Night	6	7	4.62	0	109.0	Clutch	45	11	0	2	.244

1989 Rankings (American League)

➡ 1st in balks (15)

➡ 3rd in grounder/flyball ratio (2.14)

➡ 4th in stolen bases allowed (28) and opponent stolen base percentage (85%)

➡ Led the Red Sox in balks, stolen bases allowed, grounder/flyball ratio, wild pitches (7), lowest strikeout/walk ratio (1.38), least pitches thrown per batter (3.6), most GDPs per 9 innings (1.01) - *team pitchers with 162 IP*

HITTING:

The prolonged slumps over the first five years of his career were a thing of the past for Nick Esasky once he hit Beantown. All of a sudden, Esasky, who produced career highs in home runs (30) and RBI (108), was able to rid himself of minor setbacks, usually by taking a day off now and then. Esasky benefitted by leaving the National League, whose pitchers often blew fastballs past the free-swinging first baseman. The more finesse-prone American League pitchers elected to vary their assortment to Esasky and many of his home runs came on off-speed pitches.

The key to Esasky's success is staying back in his stance and not getting too anxious. The 6-3, 210-pound right-handed hitter proved to be a tough man to pitch to. Pitch him inside and Esasky has the power to turn on the ball. Pitch him outside and Esasky can drill the ball over the fence in right-center and left-center, where the majority of his homers went.. Esasky, unlike most of his Red Sox colleagues, is a first-pitch hitter. He can be fooled by junk-ball left-handers, especially those who really change speeds constantly.

BASERUNNING:

Esasky has average speed, but he is a favorite pupil of Red Sox coaches because he gets the most out of his ability. Esasky will never steal more than 10 bases in a year, but he runs the bases with a great deal of intelligence and aggressiveness.

FIELDING:

He is a fine fielding first baseman whose forte is starting and finishing the 3-6-3 double-play. Esasky reacts very well to hard-hit balls, particularly those hit to the second base side. Esasky never makes a mental mistake in the field and is always looking to make the aggressive play.

OVERALL:

Esasky came to the Red Sox with the reputation of being too laid-back and too low-key, a label pinned on him mostly by ex-Reds Manager Pete Rose. What he showed with the Red Sox was a player who did his job and kept his mouth shut, one who was intense in his own way on the field and low-key off it. A fan favorite, Esasky was one of the few power hitters at Fenway in the past few years, and the Sox were fervently hoping to re-sign him.

NICK ESASKY

Position: 1B
Bats: R **Throws:** R
Ht: 6' 3" **Wt:** 215

Opening Day Age: 30
Born: 2/24/60 in Hialeah, FL
ML Seasons: 7

Overall Statistics

	G	AB	R	H	D	T	HR	RBI	SB	BB	SO	AVG
1989	154	564	79	156	26	5	30	108	1	66	117	.277
Career	801	2668	334	671	120	21	122	427	18	310	698	.251

Where He Hits the Ball

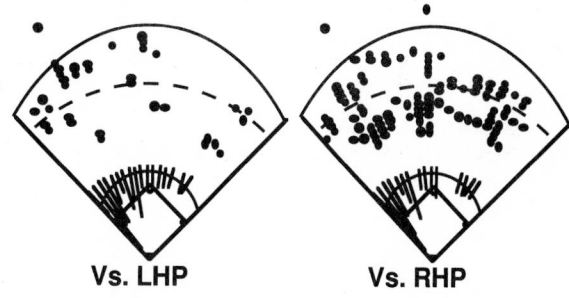

Vs. LHP   Vs. RHP

1989 Situational Stats

	AB	H	HR	RBI	AVG		AB	H	HR	RBI	AVG
Home	283	85	15	61	.300	LHP	172	43	11	31	.250
Road	281	71	15	47	.253	RHP	392	113	19	77	.288
Day	177	47	10	27	.266	Sc Pos	182	56	13	82	.308
Night	387	109	20	81	.282	Clutch	89	27	5	16	.303

1989 Rankings (American League)

➟ 3rd in RBIs (108)

➟ 4th in slugging percentage (.500)

➟ 5th in home runs (30)

➟ 7th in total bases (282) and least at bats per home run (18.8) - *players with 502 PA*

➟ Led the Red Sox in RBIs, slugging percentage, home runs, total bases, least at bats per home run and strikeouts (117) - team players with 502 PA

DWIGHT EVANS

Position: RF/DH
Bats: R **Throws:** R
Ht: 6' 3" **Wt:** 208

Opening Day Age: 38
Born: 11/3/51 in Santa Monica, CA
ML Seasons: 18

HITTING:

They say Dwight Evans is playing his career backwards. The first eight years were mediocre. The last nine have been good to great. At age 37, he is still one of the most feared hitters in the game. Evans can hit a home run at the most inopportune time for the opposition. He gears himself for the big situation and loves to come up when the game is on the line. A back injury prevented Evans from having the year he should have had in 1989. He probably could have hit 30 home runs if he had been able to swing more smoothly.

Most pitchers still can't throw hard enough to get it by Evans. Even though most pitchers know that Dewey rarely swings at the first pitch, they still don't come in with a strike as often as they should against him. In the past few years, Evans has pulled the ball more. The majority of his 20 homers were hit to left field and sometimes to left-center. Over the past nine years Evans, helped by former Red Sox hitting coach Walt Hriniak, has kept slumps to a minimum, though he usually goes through one big one every season.

BASERUNNING:

Evans is still a decent baserunner even though his injuries have diminished his speed. Up until last year, Evans was capable of stealing 10-15 bases, but running was painful last year and he became a station-to-station runner. When Evans is healthy, his experience allows him to steal a base now and then, usually when nobody is expecting it.

FIELDING:

Evans' arm isn't quite the rifle it used to be, but few runners bother finding out how much weaker it is. Injuries saw him used mostly as a DH last year and Evans could become a regular DH now, in the twilight of his career. In his hey-day (when he was winning his eight Gold Gloves), nobody played right field better and even now Evans can probably play it better than many.

OVERALL:

The Red Sox keep depending on Evans for incredible production year after year and he hasn't disappointed. But with age setting in, the Red Sox need to rely on him less. He started the season hitting sixth and ended it hitting third. He is one of the most intense players on the field and his youthful appearance and exuberance rub off on his teammates.

Overall Statistics

	G	AB	R	H	D	T	HR	RBI	SB	BB	SO	AVG
1989	146	520	82	148	27	3	20	100	3	99	84	.285
Career	2382	8281	1369	2262	456	69	366	1283	73	1270	1570	.273

Where He Hits the Ball

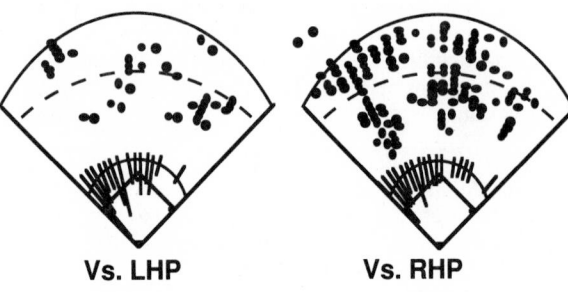

Vs. LHP   **Vs. RHP**

1989 Situational Stats

	AB	H	HR	RBI	AVG		AB	H	HR	RBI	AVG
Home	242	66	8	46	.273	LHP	155	47	4	22	.303
Road	278	82	12	54	.295	RHP	365	101	16	78	.277
Day	183	40	8	28	.219	Sc Pos	162	52	5	82	.321
Night	337	108	12	72	.320	Clutch	92	26	1	16	.283

1989 Rankings (American League)

→ 6th in walks (99), on-base average (.397) and percentage of pitches taken (64%)

→ 8th in RBIs (100)

→ 10th in times reached base (250)

→ Led the Red Sox in sacrifice flies (7)

→ Led AL Right Fielders in walks, times reached base and on-base average

PITCHING:

One of the great unsolved mysteries in Boston is: Why hasn't Wes Gardner ever realized his rightful talent? Nobody knows, least of all Gardner. The former Mets farmhand, once the International League's Fireman of the Year, has gone from starter to reliever and back again a few times. The Red Sox were relying on him to be a starter and a pitcher capable of winning 15 games, but that never got close to materializing.

Though the possessor of a 90-plus fastball and a nasty slider that can saw the bat off in a hitter's hands, Gardner always seems to make one or two mistakes that has him hitting the showers long before midgame. He has a tendency to hang his slider or to leave his fastball too far over the plate. There were times he didn't throw his fastball as hard as he's capable of throwing it. Injuries to his forearm and then a fractured cheekbone severely limited Gardner's opportunities in 1989.

When Gardner is on he's the type of pitcher who can overpower a hitter. He spots his fastball well and keeps it down in the strike zone. He'll tie up power hitters inside and the movement he has makes it tough for a hitter to drive the ball. Gardner showed signs of being that pitcher in 1987 when John McNamara converted him to a starter and he turned in several quality starts. But as a starter, Gardner lacked both stamina and a good off-speed pitch.

FIELDING:

As a fielder, Gardner is always aggressive. He is always prone to knocking down liners hit at him or stopping them with his body. Last August, Gardner got a ball that bounced and hit his cheekbone, fracturing three bones and ending his season. The question in 1990 will be whether that injury has left him a little apprehensive. Gardner does not hold runners well.

OVERALL:

A domestic problem and taking over duties as the team's player representative added a great deal of pressure on Gardner in 1989 and he'll have to overcome the affects of both in 1990 to be a solid contributor to the Red Sox. It is hard to give up on Gardner considering his skills, but the Red Sox need for him to emerge after three years of injuries and falling short of his potential.

WES GARDNER

Position: SP/RP
Bats: R **Throws:** R
Ht: 6' 4" **Wt:** 203

Opening Day Age: 28
Born: 4/29/61 in Benton, AR
ML Seasons: 6

Overall Statistics

	W	L	ERA	G	GS	Sv	IP	H	R	BB	SO	HR
1989	3	7	5.97	22	16	0	86.0	97	64	47	81	10
Career	15	22	4.83	138	35	13	363.0	367	214	169	288	45

Where They Hit the Ball

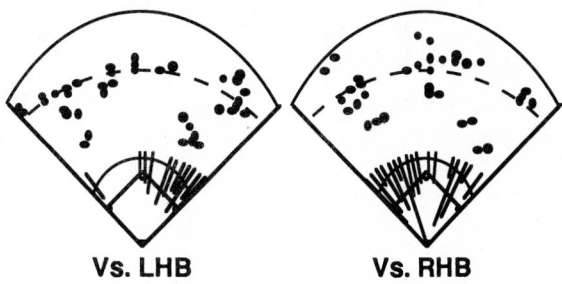

Vs. LHB　　　**Vs. RHB**

1989 Situational Stats

	W	L	ERA	Sv	IP		AB	H	HR	RBI	AVG
Home	2	2	4.33	0	35.1	LHB	147	46	2	25	.313
Road	1	5	7.11	0	50.2	RHB	191	51	8	32	.267
Day	0	2	6.45	0	22.1	Sc Pos	85	29	5	47	.341
Night	3	5	5.80	0	63.2	Clutch	27	6	0	3	.222

1989 Rankings (American League)

➡ Did not rank near the top or bottom of any categories

HITTING:

Nobody knows where the Rich Gedman of 1983-1986 went. He was then a power-hitting left-handed hitting catcher and a two-time All-Star. Over the past three years Gedman has struggled to hit in the low .200s and is now fighting to stay in baseball at age 30. A switch from his helicopter-like swing, where he took one hand off the bat with a distinctive follow-through to a two-handed swing, didn't seem to make much difference in Gedman's batting average. He often looked defeated at the plate before he even got up there.

Gedman saw a steady diet of breaking and off-speed pitches and would often look bad trying to make his bat meet with the ball. He was overanxious for a hit and often lunged at bad pitches. The fact that Gedman went from starting catcher to back-up catcher didn't help his chances to redeem his once potent swing. Even now when Gedman makes contact, he can hit line drives harder than any man in baseball. The problem is that it hasn't happened very often lately.

BASERUNNING:

Gedman is a slow runner, even for a catcher. It's not a matter of trying harder because Gedman runs out every ground ball and runs hard around the bases. He is tough to score from second and it takes a long fly ball to get him in from third.

FIELDING:

The Red Sox pitching staff was much better when Gedman caught then when Rick Cerone caught. The ERA was 3.67 with Gedman and 4.33 with Cerone. Most Red Sox pitchers will say they prefer Gedman catching. Gedman has a strong arm although you wouldn't know it from the numbers; he threw out only 25 percent of would-be base-stealers. He can block the plate well and has good instincts in the field.

OVERALL:

The Red Sox told Gedman he would be playing elsewhere in 1990. The team doesn't think Gedman can regain his old form with the Red Sox, but might be able to get it back some place else. Gedman still has good defensive skills and could make a decent back-up catcher. If Gedman could get his sense of timing back at the plate, he'd be a front-line catcher somewhere.

RICH GEDMAN

Position: C
Bats: L **Throws:** R
Ht: 6' 0" **Wt:** 215

Opening Day Age: 30
Born: 9/26/59 in Worcester, MA
ML Seasons: 10

Overall Statistics

	G	AB	R	H	D	T	HR	RBI	SB	BB	SO	AVG
1989	93	260	24	55	9	0	4	16	0	23	47	.212
Career	896	2841	312	738	164	12	83	356	3	201	442	.260

Where He Hits the Ball

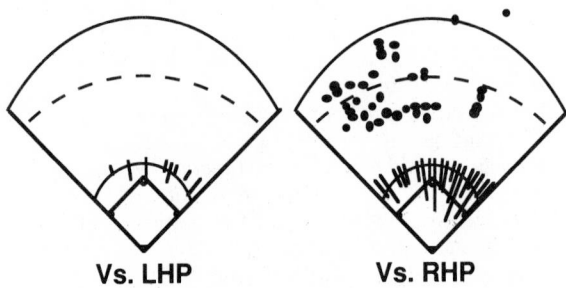

Vs. LHP   **Vs. RHP**

1989 Situational Stats

	AB	H	HR	RBI	AVG		AB	H	HR	RBI	AVG
Home	117	26	2	9	.222	LHP	37	10	1	4	.270
Road	143	29	2	7	.203	RHP	223	45	3	12	.202
Day	106	22	2	6	.208	Sc Pos	68	9	0	11	.132
Night	154	33	2	10	.214	Clutch	44	10	0	2	.227

1989 Rankings (American League)

➡ 3rd worst throwing out opposing base stealers (25%)

HITTING:

Mike Greenwell is a driven ballplayer who tries to smash the cover off the ball every time up. But in 1989, he found that pitchers weren't about to give him much to hit. Greenwell, who had hit over .320 in his two major league seasons, had to adjust to being a bona fide hitting star, meaning, don't expect much near the middle of the plate. His overall stats remained good, yet it was a quiet year.

Greenwell, who can turn on inside pitches and produce some extraordinary damage, got pitched away and out of reach of his wheelhouse. A good slider on the outside part of the plate usually gave him trouble. A mid-season ankle injury did not allow him to push off his back foot and thus diminished his power potential. Thus Greenwell tried to use his line drive hitting skills to spray the ball around the final two months of the season. Greenwell also had problems coming up with clutch hits, though he never really had a hot hitter in front of him the first half of the year.

BASERUNNING:

On a team of tortoises, Greenwell might be the best Red Sox base-runner. He doesn't have the speed of Ellis Burks, but Greenwell is just as intense on the basepaths as he is in the batter's box. His career percentage for steals is 67 percent with a season high of 16.

FIELDING:

Some baseball people think Greenwell will eventually be a DH. He has inherited the torch of great hitting left-fielders at Fenway, but he fields more like Ted Williams or Jim Rice than Carl Yastrzemski. Greenwell has learned to play the Green Monster and its caroms; he's an aggressive fielder, but sometimes he has troubles judging balls on the road. His arm is strong and usually accurate, but he's sometimes prone to throwing to the wrong base.

OVERALL:

Greenwell is one of the great hitters in the game. He's everyone's dream: an aggressive free-swinger who doesn't strike out much. Some think Greenwell should be more patient and draw more walks. He's odd in that he is prone to swinging at bad pitches, yet seldom fans. He's a hitter who loves one-on-one confrontations with pitchers, daring them to throw the ball by him. He is the heart and soul of the Red Sox team and the focal point of their offense.

MIKE GREENWELL

Position: LF
Bats: L **Throws:** R
Ht: 6' 0" **Wt:** 195

Opening Day Age: 26
Born: 7/18/63 in Louisville, KY
ML Seasons: 5

Overall Statistics

	G	AB	R	H	D	T	HR	RBI	SB	BB	SO	AVG
1989	145	578	87	178	36	0	14	95	13	56	44	.308
Career	476	1646	255	526	109	14	59	315	35	186	133	.320

Where He Hits the Ball

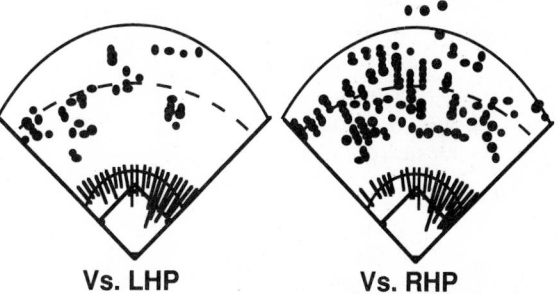

Vs. LHP   **Vs. RHP**

1989 Situational Stats

	AB	H	HR	RBI	AVG		AB	H	HR	RBI	AVG
Home	286	93	6	54	.325	LHP	202	55	2	28	.272
Road	292	85	8	41	.291	RHP	376	123	12	67	.327
Day	199	64	4	27	.322	Sc Pos	173	50	2	77	.289
Night	379	114	10	68	.301	Clutch	77	28	2	9	.364

1989 Rankings (American League)

➡ 4th in intentional walks (15) and grounded into double plays (21)

➡ 5th in hitting in the clutch (.364) - *batters with 50 PA*

➡ 7th in doubles (36)

➡ 8th in runs (87)

➡ 9th in batting average (.308)

➡ 10th in RBIs (95)

➡ Led the Red Sox in grounded into double plays, hitting in the clutch, and runs scored per times reaching base (33%) - *team players with 502 PA*

➡ Led AL Left Fielders in batting average, singles (128), intentional walks, grounded into double plays, and hitting in the clutch

HITTING:

The rap on Danny Heep was that he couldn't play a full season and still be an effective contributor. Due to injuries in the Red Sox lineup, Heep became more than a part-time player, and hit .300 for the first time in his career. Heep proved the Red Sox' top clutch hitter, hitting .337 with runners in scoring position. Heep is a spray hitter, but pulled the ball on occasion.

While he's a patient hitter, most of Heep's big hits came on the first pitch. Heep is a tough hitter to fool, but sharp sliders and forkballs on the outside half of the plate kept him off-stride from time to time. Heep is a low-ball hitter for the most part. Anything high and inside in the strike zone gave him problems. He was perhaps the most consistent Red Sox hitter. He suffered small slumps early in the season, but after a few days on the bench Heep was usually stroking the ball well again.

BASERUNNING:

Heep has good judgment on the basepaths, but is very slow. It wasn't often that Heep went successfully from first to third. He usually played it station-to-station, and didn't steal a base.

FIELDING:

Heep gets everything hit to him or near him, but his range is suspect as a right-fielder and his arm strength is average to below-average. Because he knows he can't get back on a hard-hit ball, he tries to position himself for the carom, which he does fairly well. He's also an adequate first baseman, again, one who makes the plays hit to him.

OVERALL:

Heep was the right man on the right team, particularly because injuries prevented right-fielder Dwight Evans from playing his normal position. Ideally, the Red Sox would like to use Heep less in 1990. While Heep was a .300 hitter, his production wasn't what they want out of their right- fielder. But if they can't acquire a power-hitter and Nick Esasky leaves them for the Atlanta Braves or another team, they won't hesitate to use Heep just as much.

DANNY HEEP

Position: RF/1B/LF
Bats: L **Throws:** L
Ht: 5'11" **Wt:** 177

Opening Day Age: 32
Born: 7/3/57 in San Antonio, TX
ML Seasons: 11

Overall Statistics

	G	AB	R	H	D	T	HR	RBI	SB	BB	SO	AVG
1989	113	320	36	96	17	0	5	49	0	29	26	.300
Career	828	1880	201	486	94	5	30	218	12	212	224	.259

Where He Hits the Ball

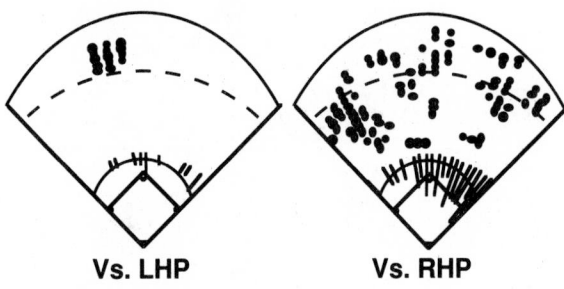

Vs. LHP   **Vs. RHP**

1989 Situational Stats

	AB	H	HR	RBI	AVG		AB	H	HR	RBI	AVG
Home	158	46	1	22	.291	LHP	21	4	0	1	.190
Road	162	50	4	27	.309	RHP	299	92	5	48	.308
Day	98	29	2	19	.296	Sc Pos	101	34	2	44	.337
Night	222	67	3	30	.302	Clutch	45	11	2	8	.244

1989 Rankings (American League)

➡ 8th in hitting with runners in scoring position (.337) - *players with 100 PA*

➡ Led AL Right Fielders in hitting with runners in scoring position and percent of swings put into play (58.6%)

PITCHING:

Like a fine wine, Dennis Lamp keeps getting better with age. The sinker-balling right-hander pitches with one motto: keep ahead in the count. You'll rarely see Lamp fall behind a hitter and his first pitch is usually right over the plate. The hitter often has trouble picking up the ball when Lamp delivers even though he knows exactly what's coming, a sinker or slider. Lamp led all relief pitchers in the major leagues with the longest outing per appearance, 2-2/3 innings. He was a main cog for the Red Sox in middle relief and as he continued to be more and more effective, Manager Joe Morgan wasn't afraid to see Lamp finish games. He did so for two saves.

Lamp's downfall comes when he does get behind on the count. Sometimes the sinker stays up and ends up getting cracked into the gaps or over the fence. His strikeout totals were way up as his slider seemed to have tremendous movement from the second half of the year on. Lamp's role changed as the season progressed. He fared well as a mop-up man in blowouts. From there, he was brought into games the Red Sox were trailing by one or two and then earned the right to be in games in which the Red Sox were ahead. At age 37, Lamp has a tremendous knowledge of pitching to the hitters' weaknesses. He gives power hitters fits by changing the speed and location of his pitches.

FIELDING:

For an older player, Lamp fields his position well and he's fundamentally sound in most phases of defense. He has a decent move to first base, but not great. His slow delivery makes him easy to run on.

OVERALL:

Lamp was a salvation to the Red Sox last year. He moved into a role normally fitted for Bob Stanley, who declined rapidly and eventually retired from baseball. Lamp will likely hold the same role with the Red Sox next season to support a pretty good bullpen which already has Rob Murphy and Lee Smith.

DENNIS LAMP

Position: RP
Bats: R **Throws:** R
Ht: 6' 3" **Wt:** 215

Opening Day Age: 37
Born: 9/23/52 in Los Angeles, CA
ML Seasons: 13

Overall Statistics

	W	L	ERA	G	GS	Sv	IP	H	R	BB	SO	HR
1989	4	2	2.32	42	0	2	112.1	96	37	27	61	4
Career	86	87	3.81	520	162	35	1605.1	1728	784	479	736	101

Where They Hit the Ball

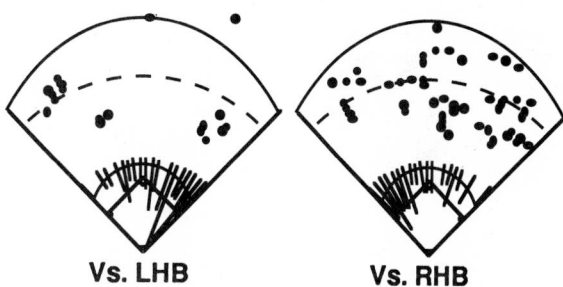

Vs. LHB   **Vs. RHB**

1989 Situational Stats

	W	L	ERA	Sv	IP		AB	H	HR	RBI	AVG
Home	3	1	2.93	2	73.2	LHB	180	52	2	19	.289
Road	1	1	1.16	0	38.2	RHB	228	44	2	19	.193
Day	2	2	2.65	2	51.0	Sc Pos	114	27	1	34	.237
Night	2	0	2.05	0	61.1	Clutch	51	16	1	6	.314

1989 Rankings (American League)

➡ 9th worst in stolen bases allowed (23)

➡ Led the Red Sox in earned run average (2.32), lowest on-base average allowed (.280), lowest baserunners allowed per nine innings (9.86), least hrs allowed per nine innings (.32), and most GDPs per GDP situation (16.4%) - *all team players*

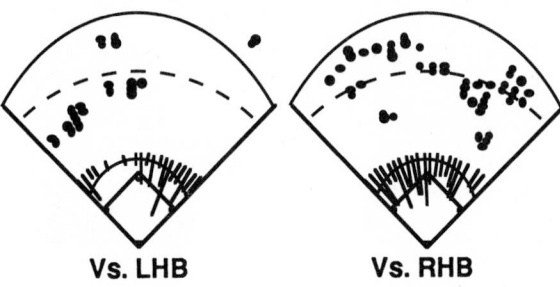

WORKHORSE

PITCHING:

The Red Sox had searched high and low to find a dominant left-handed reliever and they found one to trade for in Cincinnati named Rob Murphy. In his first full season with the Red Sox he did what no lefty reliever had done in the history of the franchise: he struck out more than 100 batters. It's not hard to tell what's coming when Murphy is pitching. It's going to be thrown hard and it's either a fastball or slider. Murphy is capable of throwing in the mid-90s but not consistently. There are times Murphy's fastball velocity drops off dramatically, but he always seems to have a nasty slider working on those days.

Murphy is an adrenaline pitcher. He gets up for the toughest of situations. He is capable of striking out the side with the bases loaded and nobody out if that's what he has to do. Murphy is tough against the best lefty hitters, folks like Don Mattingly, Alvin Davis, Pete O'Brien, lefties who can hit any other pitcher. Murphy is most effective when used in two or fewer innings. His slider is usually sharp, but when it's not up to snuff, it can hang long enough for a hitter to get a good whack and send it a long way. Murphy also dabbled with a knuckle ball as an off-speed pitch. He used the pitch less and less as the season progressed, but might resurrect it depending on his role.

FIELDING:

Murphy makes all the plays he can reach, but is not real quick or real fast afoot on balls hit up the middle at him. He controls the running game very well with a good move to first and a quick delivery.

OVERALL:

There are few days when Murphy doesn't want the ball. He can come back with minimum rest, has an exceptional attitude and keeps exhaustive records on every hitter he faces. When Murphy enters a game he's thoroughly prepared to pitch and he needs only about 10 pitches to warm up. Murphy could be a closer if the Red Sox decide to deal Lee Smith. If not, the Red Sox have a pretty tough righty-lefty combo closing games.

ROB MURPHY

Position: RP
Bats: L **Throws:** L
Ht: 6' 2" **Wt:** 205

Opening Day Age: 29
Born: 5/26/60 in Miami, FL
ML Seasons: 5

Overall Statistics

	W	L	ERA	G	GS	Sv	IP	H	R	BB	SO	HR
1989	5	7	2.74	74	0	9	105.0	97	38	41	107	7
Career	19	18	2.65	273	0	16	343.2	285	112	134	317	18

Where They Hit the Ball

Vs. LHB   **Vs. RHB**

1989 Situational Stats

	W	L	ERA	Sv	IP		AB	H	HR	RBI	AVG
Home	2	2	3.26	2	47.0	LHB	113	29	2	13	.257
Road	3	5	2.33	7	58.0	RHB	273	68	5	32	.249
Day	3	4	3.82	2	35.1	Sc Pos	129	35	3	40	.271
Night	2	3	2.20	7	69.2	Clutch	185	47	3	21	.254

1989 Rankings (American League)

➡ 2nd in games (74)
➡ 5th in holds (13)
➡ 6th in most blown saves (7)
➡ Led the Red Sox in games, holds and blown saves

HITTING:

Reed is one of the toughest hitters for a pitcher to face in the Red Sox lineup. Pitchers try to bust this short guy (5-9) high and inside, making it impossible for him to get his little body around on the ball -- but all Reed does then is slap doubles (42 last year) down the left-field line. Last year was an adjustment season for Reed, because word got out that he was a tough out. Thus, he started facing nastier pitching. Just when you thought the sophomore jinx was on, Reed hit .288. He can be fooled on breaking pitches away; because he's so used to pulling the inside pitch, sometimes an outside offering will leave him a little dumbfounded. He's not prone to striking out and he finished next to last on the team in strikeouts. Reed's problem this year was with runners in scoring position. He hit just .244 and it was that high only because of a surge the final two months of the season. Reed is one of those hitters who simply tries too hard at times and forgets his very simple mission of getting the ball in the air, deep enough to do some damage.

BASERUNNING:

Reed is an excellent baserunner. He goes from first to third well and he's also daring enough to go through a coach's sign now and then. Reed is not blessed with great speed and has not been a good base stealer.

FIELDING:

With injuries last year to Marty Barrett and the emergence of Luis Rivera, Reed split time between second and shortstop and did remarkably well at both. As a shortstop, he's a throwback to Rick Burleson, with a fine arm and good range. His range is even better at second, though shortstop is the position he prefers.

OVERALL:

Reed's the heart and soul of the Red Sox team. He has tremendous leadership/captain qualities, motivating others with his ability to get fired up and his always positive attitude. What the Red Sox need to decide is where Reed is best suited long-range, short or second.

JODY REED

Position: SS/2B
Bats: R **Throws:** R
Ht: 5' 9" **Wt:** 160

Opening Day Age: 27
Born: 7/26/62 in Tampa, FL
ML Seasons: 3

Overall Statistics

	G	AB	R	H	D	T	HR	RBI	SB	BB	SO	AVG
1989	146	524	76	151	42	2	3	40	4	73	44	.288
Career	264	892	140	259	66	4	4	76	6	122	65	.290

Where He Hits the Ball

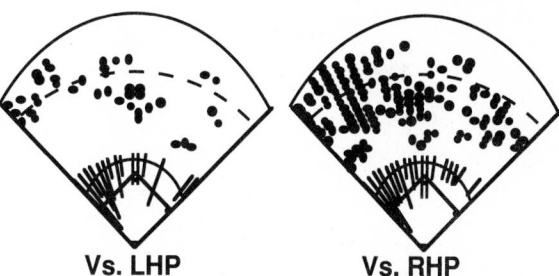

Vs. LHP   **Vs. RHP**

1989 Situational Stats

	AB	H	HR	RBI	AVG		AB	H	HR	RBI	AVG
Home	270	81	2	19	.300	LHP	140	45	1	17	.321
Road	254	70	1	21	.276	RHP	384	106	2	23	.276
Day	170	53	2	14	.312	Sc Pos	131	32	0	35	.244
Night	354	98	1	26	.277	Clutch	73	19	0	9	.260

1989 Rankings (American League)

- 3rd in doubles (42)
- 4th in hitting on an 0-2 count (.360) and percentage of pitches taken (65.5%) - *players with 502 PA*
- 5th in lowest percent of swings that missed (7.8%) - *players with 502 PA*
- 7th in sacrifice hits (13)
- Led the Red Sox in percent of swings put into play (58.8%), hitting vs. lefthanded pitchers (.321), and hitting on an 0-2 count - *team players with 502 PA*
- Led AL Shortstops in batting average (.288), doubles, walks (73), on-base average (.376) and hitting on an 0-2 count

HITTING:

Jim Rice's brilliant Boston career ended after 15 years, but he planned to continue with another team. By the end of last year, the once sweet, quick, powerful stroke had diminished into a slow swing with little power and often, little contact. He has been riddled with injuries the past few years - both knees have bothered him off and on and he underwent elbow surgery, twice, in 1988. The reasons for the sudden decline have been attributed to a decline in eyesight, his unwillingness to use a lighter bat and a naturally powerful body that softened due to a lack of care. Since 1986 Rice became more of a contact hitter, willing to hit the ball through the middle and often afraid to really cut loose with a patented Rice cut. Pitchers continued to pitch Rice like they had throughout his career, carefully. Hits that went for singles up the middle were the same pitches Rice used to crush to the centerfield fence. Rice feels he will rebound at age 36, if he stays healthy.

BASERUNNING:

Rice is slow, but he seldom make a baserunning blunder. He's aware of what's happening around him and has a good sense of whether or not he can score from second base.

FIELDING:

Rice always had an accurate arm with above-average strength, but that was mostly at Fenway Park; outside of Fenway he's a below-average outfielder. In recent years he's been strictly a DH. For years Rice has taken ground balls at first base and seems adept at being able to convert to the position if a National League team is interested in his services in 1990. Rice's worst problems in the outfield were always coming in on the ball since he wasn't that fast and his eye problems didn't allow him to read depth well.

OVERALL:

Rice still feels he can play every day, so he probably would not accept any part-time role. He'll need to lose some weight. Though he left the Red Sox with great ill-feeling, he is still viewed with a great deal of respect by opposing players. Rice showed no signs of being able to recapture his stroke of old, but with the incentive of trying to prove the Red Sox were wrong, Rice could have the greatest motivation of his career to get it back.

JIM
RICE

Position: DH
Bats: R **Throws:** R
Ht: 6' 2" **Wt:** 217

Opening Day Age: 37
Born: 3/8/53 in
Anderson, SC
ML Seasons: 16

Overall Statistics

	G	AB	R	H	D	T	HR	RBI	SB	BB	SO	AVG
1989	56	209	22	49	10	2	3	28	1	13	39	.234
Career	2089	8225	1249	2452	373	79	382	1451	58	670	1423	.298

Where He Hits the Ball

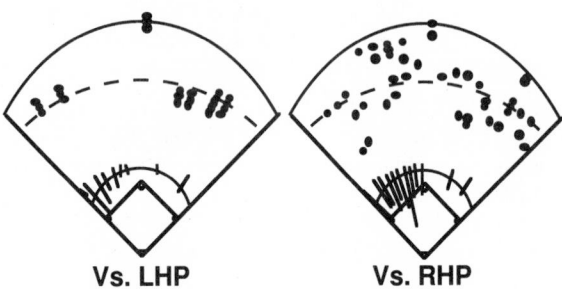

Vs. LHP   **Vs. RHP**

1989 Situational Stats

	AB	H	HR	RBI	AVG		AB	H	HR	RBI	AVG
Home	110	27	1	13	.245	LHP	63	16	1	8	.254
Road	99	22	2	15	.222	RHP	146	33	2	20	.226
Day	79	25	1	13	.316	Sc Pos	66	16	1	23	.242
Night	130	24	2	15	.185	Clutch	30	6	0	2	.200

1989 Rankings (American League)

- ➡ 3rd worst in percentage of extra bases taken as a runner (21.4%)
- ➡ Led AL Designated Hitters in triples (2)

HITTING:

Luis Rivera is a small man who is capable of hitting the ball hard. He is not a Punch-and-Judy shortstop; he hits line drives and occasionally tries to jerk the ball out of the park. Sometimes, his intensity at the plate doesn't get the desired result. He often tries to pull pitches he should go with. Still, Rivera showed the ability to get the big hit. Of his 29 RBI, 21 came with two outs. He seems to gain more confidence and intensity with men on base and was a dependable contributor.

Rivera is a fastball hitter who can be fooled by a steady diet of breaking pitches. He is a streak hitter who can go very good or very bad. When he goes bad he tends to strike out a lot, but Rivera will never cheat himself of a good swing. He does lack knowledge of the strike zone and he should be more patient, but what the Red Sox love about him is the way he attacks the ball, almost like Mike Greenwell, without the power. Rivera likes to swing for the fences, though he should probably try to hit the ball the other way more often.

BASERUNNING:

Rivera is considered one of the best baserunners on the Red Sox, he doesn't have blazing speed, but he is quick and reacts well on the basepaths. He is not a base stealer, however.

FIELDING:

Rivera is capable of making the sensational play. He has excellent range in the hole and often shows a cannon of an arm. For the most part, Rivera is steady in the infield, but he did prove to be nervous in tight situations. He can throw well off-balance and on the run and is not shy of contact while turning the double-play.

OVERALL:

While Rivera started in more than 90 games at short-stop, he did so because of an injury to Marty Barrett, forcing Jody Reed to second. When Barrett returned, Rivera worked nicely into a three-man platoon. The Red Sox will probably try to go back to a two-man middle-infield in 1990. They like Rivera's intensity on the field, though sometimes that intensity turns into a hot temper which has to be cooled down. His presence did make Reed and Barrett look over their shoulders. However, Rivera is the most likely candidate to be odd man out.

LUIS RIVERA

Position: SS
Bats: R **Throws:** R
Ht: 5' 9" **Wt:** 165

Opening Day Age: 26
Born: 1/3/64 in Cidra, Puerto Rico
ML Seasons: 4

Overall Statistics

	G	AB	R	H	D	T	HR	RBI	SB	BB	SO	AVG
1989	93	323	35	83	17	1	5	29	2	20	60	.257
Career	289	892	90	205	47	5	9	73	6	62	170	.230

Where He Hits the Ball

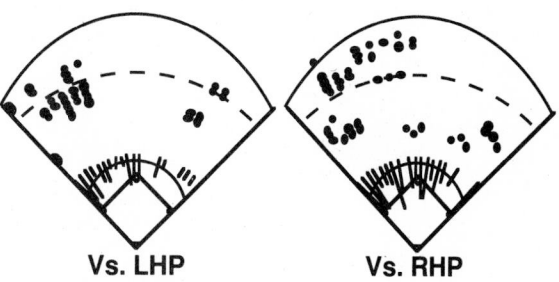

Vs. LHP   **Vs. RHP**

1989 Situational Stats

	AB	H	HR	RBI	AVG		AB	H	HR	RBI	AVG
Home	163	48	4	19	.294	LHP	102	28	2	12	.275
Road	160	35	1	10	.219	RHP	221	55	3	17	.249
Day	105	28	5	18	.267	Sc Pos	82	19	0	20	.232
Night	218	55	0	11	.252	Clutch	41	8	1	2	.195

1989 Rankings (American League)

➡ Did not rank near the top or bottom of any categories

HITTING:

Kevin Romine had a fire lit beneath him this season with the Red Sox. He started the season in Pawtucket, but once he was called up, he hit well over .400 during his first full month as a starting center-fielder while Ellis Burks recuperated from shoulder surgery. An inside-out hitter, he sprayed the ball consistently to right-center and right field throughout the year. He was an exceptional hitter against left-handed pitching, particularly away from Fenway Park where he hit .417 against lefties.

Romine's success was basically attributed to a more aggressive manner at the plate. In Romine's more patient days, he was often fooled on breaking stuff on the outside part of the plate. Romine has shown little power, but can hit the gaps for extra-base hits. He can be fooled with off-speed stuff, particularly a sharp dipping forkball. The best way to pitch Romine is high and tight, where he is not able to slap the bat-head out quick enough to send the ball spraying to the opposite field.

BASERUNNING:

Romine has above-average speed and the Red Sox would like to see him steal more bases. He also has problems judging whether to go from first to third, or to stop at second base on a sharp hit ball. Romine has the capability of stealing 25-30 bases if he plays full-time.

FIELDING:

Romine is a fine outfielder, playing all three positions with relative ease. He prefers to play center field and while he doesn't have blinding speed, he plays the position with enthusiasm and always seems to catch up to the ball. Romine has an average arm, though it has hampered him the past two years requiring off-season shoulder surgery.

OVERALL:

Despite starting 90 games for the Red Sox in the outfield, Romine is still best suited as an extra outfielder. Gifted with better than average overall talent, Romine hasn't always made the most of his abilities. At times he has had a defeatist attitude concerning his own plight, but motivated in the right way through playing time and back-patting, Romine can be an effective major league player.

KEVIN ROMINE

Position: CF/RF
Bats: R **Throws:** R
Ht: 5'11" **Wt:** 185

Opening Day Age: 28
Born: 5/23/61 in Exeter, NH
ML Seasons: 5

Overall Statistics

	G	AB	R	H	D	T	HR	RBI	SB	BB	SO	AVG
1989	92	274	30	75	13	0	1	23	1	21	53	.274
Career	217	439	61	112	21	1	2	34	6	34	87	.255

Where He Hits the Ball

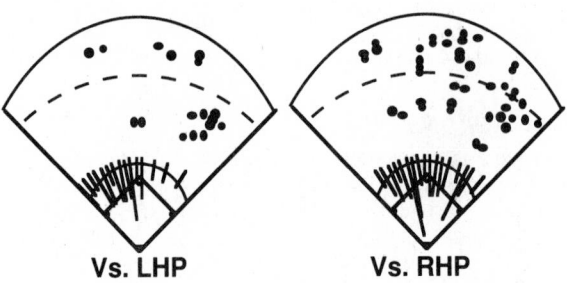

Vs. LHP **Vs. RHP**

1989 Situational Stats

	AB	H	HR	RBI	AVG		AB	H	HR	RBI	AVG
Home	131	34	1	18	.260	LHP	104	36	0	10	.346
Road	143	41	0	5	.287	RHP	170	39	1	13	.229
Day	103	30	0	5	.291	Sc Pos	72	20	0	22	.278
Night	171	45	1	18	.263	Clutch	39	12	0	2	.308

1989 Rankings (American League)

➡ Worst AL hitter with the bases loaded (.000) - *players with 10 or more PA*

➡ 8th in most GDPs per GDP situation (19.6%) - *players with 50 or more PA in GDP situations*

➡ Led the Red Sox in hitting on a 3-1 count (.571) - *all team players*

PITCHING:

Lee Smith has a fastball that still gets up into the high 90s and a slider that can break the bat of an opposing hitter. When Smith is in a save situation and he has his good fastball, you can just about call it a save for Boston and call it a loss for the other team. Smith converted on 25 saves in 30 chances, which is all a team can ask of its closer.

Smith has been a notoriously slow starter the past two seasons, but when the weather gets warmer Big Lee usually heats up too. After July 1 last year, hitters managed only a .162 average and he fanned 36 percent of the hitters he faced. That's power. Smith's fastball is explosive. Even when a hitter can make contact, he often pops the ball up or breaks his bat. If Smith has a fault, it is that he does not pitch inside. He tries to nip at the corners despite the fact that knocking a batter down now and then would make him even more effective.

Smith irritates his teammates and his manager by not getting as up for non-save situations as he does for save situations. When he blows saves it's because he can't spot his fastball and at times relies too much on his slider. But Smith's knee-high fastball is practically unhittable. Sometimes his performance is dictated by how stiff his back is. On the days he can't loosen up properly it's best not to bring him into a crucial situation. He also has other aches and pains and while he has never suffered a major injury to his arm, it often appears Smith's career is on its last legs, more by the way he moves around than by the way he performs.

FIELDING:

Smith is not a real agile player. He's not clumsy, but he's big and sometimes looks awkward fielding his position. Usually, fielding is a non-factor in his performances because he can be so overpowering to hitters. He has a slow move to first base and can be stolen on almost at will.

OVERALL:

Sometimes Smith's attitude gets in the way of what he is and should be: an effective and overpowering closer. He doesn't always feel up to pitching, but if there's a save on the line, Smith is usually at his dominating best. He and left-hander Rob Murphy comprise one of the best left-right closer combinations in baseball.

LEE SMITH

Position: RP
Bats: R **Throws:** R
Ht: 6' 6" **Wt:** 245

Opening Day Age: 32
Born: 12/4/57 in Jamestown, LA
ML Seasons: 10

Overall Statistics

	W	L	ERA	G	GS	Sv	IP	H	R	BB	SO	HR
1989	6	1	3.57	64	0	25	70.2	53	30	33	96	6
Career	50	57	2.96	586	6	234	836.1	716	304	334	836	51

Where They Hit the Ball

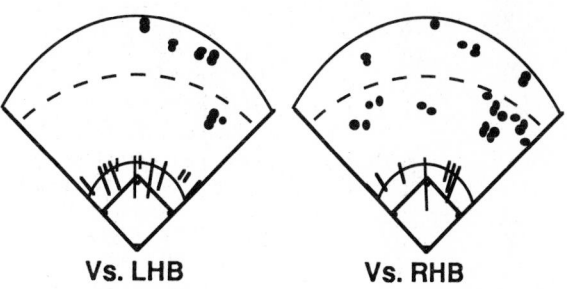

Vs. LHB   **Vs. RHB**

1989 Situational Stats

	W	L	ERA	Sv	IP		AB	H	HR	RBI	AVG
Home	6	0	4.06	12	37.2	LHB	121	27	5	21	.223
Road	0	1	3.00	13	33.0	RHB	132	26	1	13	.197
Day	2	0	4.44	11	26.1	Sc Pos	82	18	1	28	.220
Night	4	1	3.05	14	44.1	Clutch	156	35	5	28	.224

1989 Rankings (American League)

→ 3rd in save percentage (83.3%)

→ 5th in lowest percent of inherited runners scoring (21.4%) - *pitchers with 30 inherited runners*

→ 5th in strikeouts per nine innings (12.2) - *all league players*

→ 9th in saves (25)

→ 10th in games finished (50)

→ Led the Red Sox in saves, games finished, win/loss percentage (.857), save percentage, first batter efficiency (.196) and strikeouts per nine innings - *all team players*

PITCHING:

Here it is, hit it. That is how Mike Smithson has gone through his major league career which began in the Red Sox organization in 1976, continued in Texas and Minnesota, and now is back in Boston. Some years his philosophy has worked; other years it hasn't. Smithson is a sinker-ball pitcher with a side-arm motion that causes some problems to right-handed hitters. But conversely, left-handed hitters usually smack him around, to a tune of .311 in 1989, because they see the ball from a nice vantage point.

Smithson is capable of throwing hard at times, but he found through the years that the harder he threw, the straighter he threw and hitters were having feasts at his expense. So Smithson decided to take a few miles off his fastball, which allowed his ball to sink more. His forte is his heart. Smithson loves to pitch and will always ask to pitch. He has hurled some splendid games for Boston. But as good as he can be, he can be equally bad. When he goes bad he hangs pitches and gives up home runs.

Smithson has proved a versatile pitcher for the Red Sox the past two years. The Red Sox had him earmarked for long relief when they first signed him as a free-agent two years ago, but injuries to other pitchers had Smithson alternating between starting and relieving. His best outings have come as a starter, though so have his worst. Smithson is a gutsy pitcher, not afraid to brush back a hitter or to retaliate if a Red Sox hitter has been knocked down.

FIELDING:

Smithson works hard on his fielding because he has to. Because of his sidearm motion he's not often in the best position to field the ball, but Smithson hustles at his position and because of his height becomes a good target when covering the bag. He does an above average job of holding runners.

OVERALL:

Smithson is a popular player in the Red Sox clubhouse. He expounds often on the virtues of acting as a team and always fesses up to his mistakes. His versatility has bailed the Red Sox out of a tough time or two over the past two years. But whether that's enough for Smithson to keep his place on the roster is another matter.

MIKE SMITHSON

Position: RP/SP
Bats: L **Throws:** R
Ht: 6' 8" **Wt:** 215

Opening Day Age: 35
Born: 1/21/55 in Centerville, TN
ML Seasons: 8

Overall Statistics

	W	L	ERA	G	GS	Sv	IP	H	R	BB	SO	HR
1989	7	14	4.95	40	19	2	143.2	170	84	35	61	21
Career	76	86	4.58	240	204	2	1356.1	1473	745	383	731	168

Where They Hit the Ball

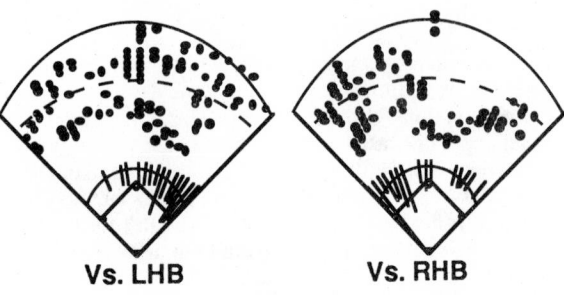

Vs. LHB   **Vs. RHB**

1989 Situational Stats

	W	L	ERA	Sv	IP		AB	H	HR	RBI	AVG
Home	5	6	4.88	1	79.1	LHB	289	90	13	39	.311
Road	2	8	5.04	1	64.1	RHB	284	80	8	38	.282
Day	3	4	4.63	2	56.1	Sc Pos	135	43	7	58	.319
Night	4	10	5.15	0	87.1	Clutch	39	12	3	7	.308

1989 Rankings (American League)

➡ 2nd in hit batsmen (10)

➡ 4th in most losses (14)

➡ 10th in most home runs allowed (21)

➡ Led the Red Sox in most losses, most hit batsmen, and most home runs allowed

GREG HARRIS

Position: RP
Bats: B **Throws:** R
Ht: 5'11" **Wt:** 165

Opening Day Age: 34
Born: 11/2/55 in
Lynwood, CA
ML Seasons: 9

Overall Statistics

	W	L	ERA	G	GS	Sv	IP	H	R	BB	SO	HR
1989	4	4	3.31	59	0	1	103.1	85	46	58	76	8
Career	35	45	3.52	383	45	38	791.0	700	360	344	626	75

PITCHING & FIELDING:

Greg Harris lives and dies with his breaking pitch. He throws it at different speeds, but it's the slow, big-breaking curve which has allowed Harris to stay in baseball for as long as he has. Harris can still throw his fastball in the mid-80s, but an effective breaking pitch is what makes his fastball effective. When his breaking pitch isn't up to par, Harris can have control problems and end up walking hitters. Then his fastball becomes a hitter's paradise. Harris, once a closer for the Texas Rangers, has not shown enough consistency in tough situations recently to believe he could ever perform that role effectively again. Harris is a good athlete who is quick off his feet and fields his position well. He has a good move to first and does a fine job of holding runners.

OVERALL:

Harris is intriguing to the Red Sox because he is ambidextrous and they would like to see how effective he could be as a left-handed pitcher. He has the ability to pitch frequently which gives the Red Sox another rubber-armed middle reliever in the bullpen.

ERIC HETZEL

Position: SP
Bats: R **Throws:** R
Ht: 6' 3" **Wt:** 175

Opening Day Age: 26
Born: 9/25/63 in
Crowley, LA
ML Seasons: 1

Overall Statistics

	W	L	ERA	G	GS	Sv	IP	H	R	BB	SO	HR
1989	2	3	6.26	12	11	0	50.1	61	39	28	33	7
Career	2	3	6.26	12	11	0	50.1	61	39	28	33	7

PITCHING & FIELDING:

Touted as a promising Red Sox prospect, Eric Hetzel came up to the Red Sox in August and proved to be a major disappointment. Despite the best run support of any major league pitcher with 10 or more starts, over eight runs per nine innings pitched, Hetzel squandered that by allowing 16.3 baserunners per nine innings, which was also the highest in baseball. Hetzel's forte is a sharp breaking forkball, but the lanky right-hander from Louisiana couldn't get it over for strikes. With a high 80s fastball and the forker, Hetzel was a strikeout pitcher in the minor leagues and the Red Sox still think he can do it in the majors. He has a strong arm and could be a bulldog, capable of pitching a lot of innings, if he gets past the fourth or fifth. Hetzel fields his position fairly well, though at times he'll go for an easier out when he could shoot for the lead runner. He has a good move to first.

OVERALL:

Hetzel is still in Boston's plans as a starting pitcher for 1990. He will get around-the-clock attention in spring training because if he can learn to throw his forkball for strikes, he could be a big winner.

SAM HORN

Position: DH
Bats: L **Throws:** L
Ht: 6' 5" **Wt:** 240

Opening Day Age: 26
Born: 11/2/63 in Dallas, TX
ML Seasons: 3

Overall Statistics

	G	AB	R	H	D	T	HR	RBI	SB	BB	SO	AVG
1989	33	54	1	8	2	0	0	4	0	8	16	.148
Career	103	273	36	61	9	0	16	46	0	36	91	.223

HITTING, FIELDING, BASERUNNING:

It has always been a case of unfulfilled potential where Sam Horn is concerned. The Red Sox have never since seen the player who hit 14 homers in 46 games at the end of the 1987 season. Horn's problems remain the same – he is fooled by the breaking pitch and now sees a steady diet of them. Horn is also pitched away quite often, and while he can hit some marathon shots to the opposite field, he much prefers to pull the ball. Horn is not that bad of a baserunner for a big, lumbering man. Defensively, Horn has worked hard at first base, but the Red Sox don't feel Horn will ever be an adequate first baseman.

OVERALL:

Horn needs a team that will take a chance with him and give him a long look. He could be a diamond in the rough for the right team, or he might just be a highly-touted No. 1 pick who never made it. Nobody questions his incredible power. His intensity has fluctuated over the years, but Horn's focus is in the right place.

RANDY KUTCHER

Position: RF/CF
Bats: R **Throws:** R
Ht: 5'11" **Wt:** 175

Opening Day Age: 29
Born: 4/20/60 in Anchorage, AK
ML Seasons: 4

Overall Statistics

	G	AB	R	H	D	T	HR	RBI	SB	BB	SO	AVG
1989	77	160	28	36	10	3	2	18	3	11	46	.225
Career	181	374	65	85	21	5	9	35	10	23	94	.227

HITTING, FIELDING, BASERUNNING:

Hitting is probably the least effective part of Randy Kutcher's game, but that's not to say the utilityman can't bleed the opposition once in a while. Kutcher can be fooled by off-speed pitches and will occasionally lunge for a pitch outside the strike zone. But put a fastball in the wrong place and Kutcher can drive it into the gaps, and, on occasion, out of the ballpark. He is by far the most aggressive Red Sox baserunner, much like a young Pete Rose with head-first slides. Kutcher has above-average speed and gets the optimum efficiency from his leg work. His best attribute is his versatility. Kutcher can play every position except pitcher. He made the Red Sox as a third catcher, but his best position is centerfield. He's also proven to be a good back-up third baseman.

OVERALL:

Kutcher is a breath of fresh air on a team and in a clubhouse. He loves to play baseball and it shows. He's a fundamentally sound player who gets the optimum out of his ability. He's a perfect utility player in that he likes the challenge of playing different positions.

JOE PRICE

Position: RP/SP
Bats: R **Throws:** L
Ht: 6' 4" **Wt:** 215

Opening Day Age: 33
Born: 11/29/56 in Inglewood, CA
ML Seasons: 10

Overall Statistics

	W	L	ERA	G	GS	Sv	IP	H	R	BB	SO	HR
1989	3	6	4.59	38	6	0	84.1	87	44	34	62	11
Career	42	45	3.65	322	84	13	840.2	777	379	313	603	87

PITCHING & FIELDING:

After coming over from San Francisco early in 1989, most of Joe Price's problems involved his inability to hold runners on base. Devon White stole second, third and home in a one inning sequence against the lefty. Price, a veteran, was distracted by personal problems with Manager Joe Morgan. Used as a spot starter and situation reliever, he has a good breaking pitch but didn't use it as often as the Red Sox had hoped. He spots the ball well and, like most pitchers who once had better fastballs, has learned how to pitch. Price can be tough against left-handed hitters using a sweeping breaking pitch that moves, but when he's not on the mark, he'll hang the curve or leave his mediocre fastball over the plate. Price had a lot of stiffness in his shoulder in 1989 and needed additional rest between appearances.

OVERALL:

Price can still be an effective situational pitcher or middle reliever if his shoulder is sound. He could be used as a spot starter. Despite his feud with Morgan, Price is considered an intelligent observer of the game and has a good effect on other pitchers.

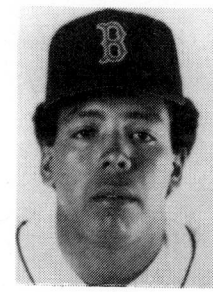

CARLOS QUINTANA

Position: RF
Bats: R **Throws:** R
Ht: 6' 2" **Wt:** 195

Opening Day Age: 24
Born: 8/26/65 in Miranda, Venezuela
ML Seasons: 2

Overall Statistics

	G	AB	R	H	D	T	HR	RBI	SB	BB	SO	AVG
1989	34	77	6	16	5	0	0	6	0	7	12	.208
Career	39	83	7	18	5	0	0	8	0	9	15	.217

HITTING, FIELDING, BASERUNNING:

Watching Carlos Quintana in the batting cage, Red Sox hitting coach Richie Hebner simply said, "I don't want to change a thing, yet." The Red Sox would like Quintana to eventually pull the ball more, but for now they are content to see him go with the pitch. Quintana is a low-ball hitter and feasts on fastballs, though he is still impatient and tends to lunge at breaking pitches. Quintana can go first-to-third, but is prone to base-running errors. He has average speed now but will probably slow down as he gets older because of his paunchy body shape. Defensively, Quintana is average to below average as an outfielder and first baseman. His future might be as a DH.

OVERALL:

There's little question Quintana can be an effective major league hitter if he becomes more selective. He probably will never be a big home run hitter, but the Red Sox are hoping he can eventually hit 20. Quintana is much more effective when used every day, but whether the Red Sox are willing to commit to him as an everyday player remains to be seen.

PITCHING:

One-handed sensation Jim Abbott authored one of the greatest and most heartwarming stories in the history of sports last season. Becoming only the fifteenth player (and ninth pitcher) since the 1965 amateur draft to skip the minor leagues, the lefthander won 12 games, posted a 3.92 ERA, pitched four complete games and threw two shutouts in his rookie season. His control gave him occasional problems, but Abbott proved without a doubt that, despite his inexperience, he's capable of dominating major league hitters.

Abbott, the Angels' No. 1 pick in the June 1989 draft and the eighth player selected overall, is equipped with a 90 mph fastball, a good curve and an assortment of sharp-breaking pitches. He's not afraid to pitch inside and uses the corners of the plate to his advantage. He has good control most of the time, good location, perfect pitching mechanics and a good head. He's as poised as a veteran. He handles himself extremely well on the mound, certainly not like your average 21-year-old rookie without any previous professional experience.

What made Abbott's performance even more sensational is that he had never experienced such a long, grinding season before. You cannot compare the major league schedule to a college schedule. But Abbott pushed through the tough times and had a sparkling season -- one for the record books.

FIELDING:

Abbott is an excellent athlete who fields his position beautifully. Fielding on the major league level is the one area where people figured Abbott might have problems. They were wrong. He's quick off the mound and is adept at removing his glove quickly enough to allow him to throw. Teams tried to bunt on him, but he was successful in foiling their ploy. That success, however, did not carry over to holding baserunners. Abbott committed two balks and allowed 29 stolen bases, the third highest total of any pitcher in the American League. He needs a lot of work in this area.

OVERALL:

Abbott was the talk of the baseball world last year. When he made his debut, it was a World Series atmosphere. Abbott handled the hoopla like a mature professional. In a way, that figured, because Abbott has been the center of attention from the time he walked onto a baseball diamond. He's poised beyond his years. Count on Abbott to be a consistent 15-to-20 game winner in the future.

JIM ABBOTT

Position: SP
Bats: L **Throws:** L
Ht: 6' 3" **Wt:** 200

Opening Day Age: 22
Born: 9/19/67 in Flint, MI
ML Seasons: 1

Overall Statistics

	W	L	ERA	G	GS	Sv	IP	H	R	BB	SO	HR
1989	12	12	3.92	29	29	0	181.1	190	95	74	115	13
Career	12	12	3.92	29	29	0	181.1	190	95	74	115	13

Where They Hit the Ball

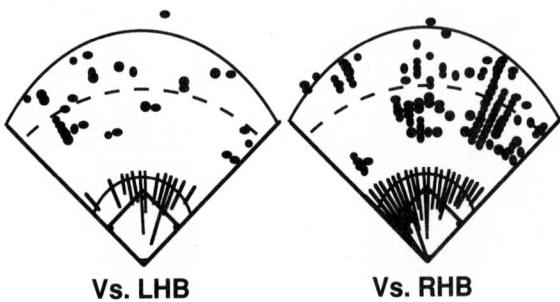

Vs. LHB   **Vs. RHB**

1989 Situational Stats

	W	L	ERA	Sv	IP		AB	H	HR	RBI	AVG
Home	5	5	4.84	0	87.1	LHB	123	40	2	19	.325
Road	7	7	3.06	0	94.0	RHB	571	150	11	54	.263
Day	3	4	3.00	0	42.0	Sc Pos	174	40	2	59	.230
Night	9	8	4.20	0	139.1	Clutch	40	16	0	4	.400

1989 Rankings (American League)

→ 2nd in most sacrifice hits allowed (11)

→ 3rd in most stolen bases allowed (29)

→ 4th in most GDPs per nine innings (1.14) and grounder/flyball ratio (1.98) - *pitchers with 162 IP*

→ 5th highest on-base average allowed (.345)

→ Led the Angels in stolen bases allowed, grounder/flyball ratio and wild pitches (8)

HITTING:

Kent Anderson is a righthanded contact hitter who often hits to the opposite field. He spent five years in the Angels' minor league system before receiving the call to the big leagues last season when Dick Schofield was sidelined with an injury. Anderson wound up playing in 86 games -- and playing well. He was a surprising factor in the Angels' run for the West Division title.

Anderson's .229 average doesn't reflect his overall effectiveness at the plate. He knows the strike zone well, but he needs to become a little more patient and work pitchers more. He walked only 17 times. Pitchers came right at him. The last thing pitchers wanted to do with a rookie like Anderson was walk him. He appeared to have trouble with inside fastballs and breaking stuff down and away. He looked particularly bad against the league's hard throwers. Anderson proved, though, to be a tough out. He doesn't have much power and went homerless, but he has the ability to hit a homer a two. His career high in homers in the minors was three. Anderson hits lefthanders pretty well, but has trouble with righthanders. His splits (.275 against lefthanders, .208 against righties) suggests a hitter who might be useful in a platoon role.

BASERUNNING:

Anderson had some baserunning difficulties last season, but that could be attributed to his inexperience. He is a smart runner with good instincts. He's aggressive. His speed is a little above average, and he'd be capable of around ten steals if he played every day.

FIELDING:

At first, Anderson was jittery and unsure of himself with the glove. Once he settled down, he was OK. Anderson isn't flashy. He doesn't make dazzling plays. He just gets the job done by making all the routine plays. His arm is above average. His range is good. With experience, he'll be very steady.

OVERALL:

Anderson received valuable experience last season. He got a lot of playing time when Dick Schofield was injured, and while he didn't overwhelm anyone, he didn't wilt in the pressure of the pennant race, either. He showed signs of having a future in the major leagues. Chances are he won't be able to hit enough to be a starting shortstop, but he definitely could be a solid, dependable backup.

KENT ANDERSON

Position: SS
Bats: R **Throws:** R
Ht: 6' 1" **Wt:** 180

Opening Day Age: 26
Born: 8/12/63 in Florence, SC
ML Seasons: 1

Overall Statistics

	G	AB	R	H	D	T	HR	RBI	SB	BB	SO	AVG
1989	86	223	27	51	6	1	0	17	1	17	42	.229
Career	86	223	27	51	6	1	0	17	1	17	42	.229

Where He Hits the Ball

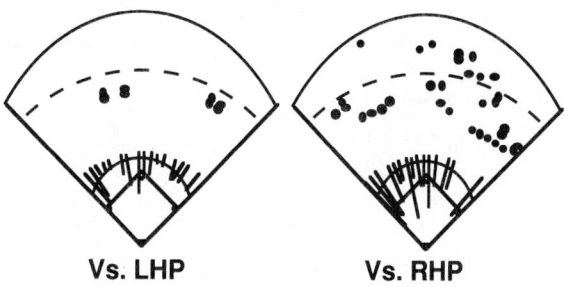

Vs. LHP   Vs. RHP

1989 Situational Stats

	AB	H	HR	RBI	AVG		AB	H	HR	RBI	AVG
Home	110	23	0	9	.209	LHP	69	19	0	3	.275
Road	113	28	0	8	.248	RHP	154	32	0	14	.208
Day	51	13	0	8	.255	Sc Pos	61	16	0	16	.262
Night	172	38	0	9	.221	Clutch	31	8	0	1	.258

1989 Rankings (American League)

➡ Did not rank near the top or bottom of any categories

TONY ARMAS

Position: RF
Bats: R **Throws:** R
Ht: 6' 1" **Wt:** 224

Opening Day Age: 36
Born: 7/2/53 in
Anzoatequi, Venezuela
ML Seasons: 14

HITTING:

The career of former American League home run and RBI king Tony Armas appeared to be over when the Red Sox released him after the 1986 season. He went to the Mexican League, hoping to be "rediscovered" and get back to the majors. Few thought it would happen, but Armas defied the odds and found his way back into the majors through the Angels' farm system. Needing outfield help, the Angels signed Armas in May of '87. Armas has turned out to be an extremely effective part-time player, even at the age of 36. He's hit 27 homers and driven in 88 runs in 651 at-bats over 2 1/2 seasons.

The righthanded power hitter has always been an excellent low-fastball hitter. Armas has never hit for average -- his career batting mark is .252 -- but he can hit a ball a long way and has had three seasons in which he's topped 35 homers and 100 RBIs. Though Armas' bat has slowed a little, his power hasn't declined much with age; last year he clubbed 11 homers in only 202 at bats. Despite that power, the free-swinging Armas is often an easy out. Get ahead of him by jamming him with fastballs, then throw some outside breaking pitches, and you usually see Armas heading back to the dugout. Armas has hurt his game by not being patient enough. He walked only seven times last year and has drawn only 260 bases on balls in his 14-year career. Armas has also always been a big strikeout man. He averaged about one strikeout for every four at bats last year, a fairly typical performance for him.

BASERUNNING:

Armas cannot run well any more, as age and leg injuries have caught up to him. He didn't attempt to steal a base last year and he has just three steals since 1983. He's always been an intelligent baserunner, however, utilizing the little speed he possesses.

FIELDING:

Armas was once one of the league's finest centerfielders with one of the best arms. Decent speed helped him defensively. Now that he has slowed down, his defense has suffered. His instincts and reactions are still very good.

OVERALL:

Considering his age, Armas' comeback has been remarkable. There's no reason to think he can't do it for another year -- as long as his legs are OK. Even with his slow bat and all the holes in his swing, he's still capable of producing in a bench role.

Overall Statistics

	G	AB	R	H	D	T	HR	RBI	SB	BB	SO	AVG
1989	60	202	22	52	7	1	11	30	0	7	48	.257
Career	1432	5164	614	1302	204	39	251	815	18	260	1201	.252

Where He Hits the Ball

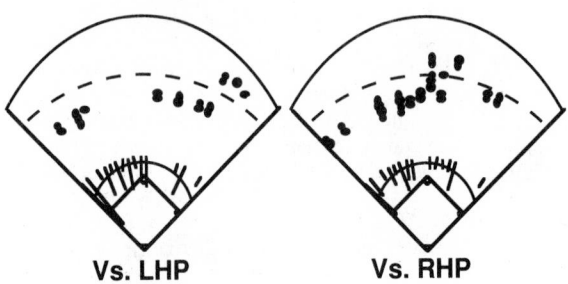

Vs. LHP **Vs. RHP**

1989 Situational Stats

	AB	H	HR	RBI	AVG		AB	H	HR	RBI	AVG
Home	104	23	5	11	.221	LHP	102	24	5	10	.235
Road	98	29	6	19	.296	RHP	100	28	6	20	.280
Day	46	6	2	5	.130	Sc Pos	49	15	3	21	.306
Night	156	46	9	25	.295	Clutch	41	8	2	7	.195

1989 Rankings (American League)

➡ Led the Angels with least at bats per home run (18.4) - *all team players*

PITCHING:

Bert Blyleven made one of the greatest comebacks in history, going from a 10-17 record with a 5.43 ERA for Minnesota in 1988 to 17-5 with a 2.73 ERA (fourth in the AL) for the Angels in 1989. He permitted just 14 homers last year -- after giving up 46 homers in 1987 (four shy of the major-league record of 50 he established in 1986). He had five shutouts last year -- equalling his total of the previous 3 1/2 seasons. He was super-tough in the clutch, holding opponents to a .213 average with runners in scoring position, second lowest in the American League.

Coming home (his hometown of Garden Grove is right next door to Anaheim) had a lot to do with Blyleven's comeback. So did his recovery from a sore thumb which had plagued him in '88. All in all, it was one of the most satisfying seasons in Blyleven's long and outstanding career, and one which greatly enhanced his chances for enshrinement at Cooperstown. Once thought to be a long shot for the Hall of Fame, Blyleven must now be considered a prime candidate.

Blyleven, a 39-year-old righthander and 20-year veteran, still possesses one of the best curveballs in the major leagues. His fastball is now only average; it's clocked these days in the 85-88 mph range. But his curve is so wicked, it keeps hitters off-balance and confused. He relies increasingly on pinpoint control, allowing only 1.64 walks per nine innings last year. Blyleven's 131 strikeouts in '89 were his lowest total since 1983, but he was able to pass the great Walter Johnson on the all-time strikeout list.

FIELDING:

Working hard has made Blyleven an effective fielder. He's a lot slower now than he used to be, so getting to first base is a chore. Runners are able to beat him to first base. Blyleven hardly hesitates in his stretch move, but he is nonetheless an easy man to steal on.

OVERALL:

After his magnificent 1989 season, Blyleven looks like he can be effective for several more years. He needs only 29 more wins to reach 300, and, judging by the way he pitched last season, you have to like his chances. Certainly the Angels are counting on him. One of sport's most comical players and pranksters, Blyleven keeps the Angels loose and laughing. He was credited with keeping his teammates from tightening up in a close pennant race.

BERT BLYLEVEN

Position: SP
Bats: R **Throws:** R
Ht: 6' 3" **Wt:** 205

Opening Day Age: 39
Born: 4/6/51 in Zeist, Netherlands
ML Seasons: 20

Overall Statistics

	W	L	ERA	G	GS	Sv	IP	H	R	BB	SO	HR
1989	17	5	2.73	33	33	0	241.0	225	76	44	131	14
Career	271	231	3.22	644	638	0	4702.1	4319	1868	1268	3562	398

Where They Hit the Ball

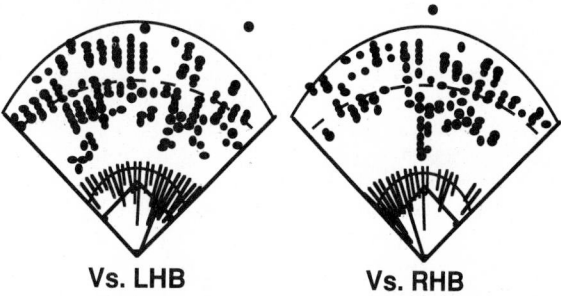

Vs. LHB   **Vs. RHB**

1989 Situational Stats

	W	L	ERA	Sv	IP		AB	H	HR	RBI	AVG
Home	8	1	2.64	0	119.1	LHB	485	122	4	31	.252
Road	9	4	2.81	0	121.2	RHB	422	103	10	38	.244
Day	4	3	3.17	0	65.1	Sc Pos	188	40	2	51	.213
Night	13	2	2.56	0	175.2	Clutch	96	23	1	8	.240

1989 Rankings (American League)

- ➡ 1st in shutouts (5)
- ➡ 2nd in win/loss percentage (.773) and lowest batting average with runners in scoring position (.213) - *pitchers facing 150 batters*
- ➡ 3rd in baserunners per nine innings (10.3) - *pitchers with 162 IP*
- ➡ 4th in earned run average (2.73) and complete games (8)
- ➡ Led the Angels in wins (17), games started (33), shutouts, innings (241), batters faced (973), hit batters (8), won/loss percentage, least pitches thrown per batter (3.4), baserunners per nine innings, lowest batting average with runners in scoring position and HRs per nine innings (.52) - *team players with 162 IP*

HITTING:

Chili Davis continues to be a solid 20-homer, 90-RBI player. In 1988, his first year with the Angels, he had 21 homers and 93 RBI. Last year he had 22 homers and 90 RBI. He became only the fourth player in Angels history to enjoy back-to-back 90-RBI seasons.

The switch-hitting Davis is not a high-average, contact hitter. His career average is .268, and he's hit over .300 only once in his career. He's much better batting lefthanded; most of Davis' home runs land in the right-field stands. Davis is a low-ball, fastball hitter from both sides of the plate. He has trouble with fastballs up and in. He swings hard, striking out 109 times last year and a career-high 118 times the year before. But Davis takes a lot of pitches and led the free swinging Angels with 61 walks. He's a superb clutch hitter. He hit .327 with nine homers and 75 RBI with runners in scoring position last year.

BASERUNNING:

Davis' ability to steal declines year after year. After back-to-back years with 16 steals in 1986-87, he stole nine bases while getting caught 10 times in 1988. He stole only three last season. He has good speed, but is a poor runner. He has poor instincts and concentration.

FIELDING:

Never considered a good fielder, Davis was a bust in right field his first year with California, committing a major-league high 19 errors. Davis turned even routine fly balls into an adventure. His .942 fielding percentage was brutal. Davis responded well when moved to left field after the arrival of Claudell Washington. He played much better all the way around. He reacted better and showed better range and concentration. He made just six errors.

OVERALL:

Signing Davis as a free agent before the '88 season turned out to be a sterling move by Angels General Manager Mike Port. Davis has been a big offensive boost to the club. Though he has his problems in the field and on the bases, he's only 30 and should be a fine offensive player for years to come. He's also been an influential figure in the clubhouse. He's turned into a club leader. With his sense of humor, quips and talkable nature, he's a media favorite. He also kept the loose Angels clubhouse a little looser with his jokes and pranks.

CHILI DAVIS

Position: LF
Bats: B **Throws:** R
Ht: 6' 3" **Wt:** 210

Opening Day Age: 30
Born: 1/17/60 in Kingston, Jamaica
ML Seasons: 9

Overall Statistics

	G	AB	R	H	D	T	HR	RBI	SB	BB	SO	AVG
1989	154	560	81	152	24	1	22	90	3	61	109	.271
Career	1186	4308	594	1153	197	24	144	601	107	478	805	.268

Where He Hits the Ball

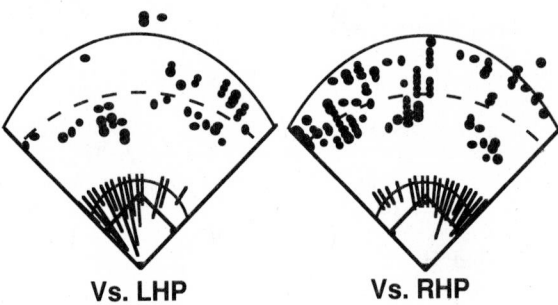

Vs. LHP   Vs. RHP

1989 Situational Stats

	AB	H	HR	RBI	AVG		AB	H	HR	RBI	AVG
Home	274	68	6	37	.248	LHP	200	49	8	28	.245
Road	286	84	16	53	.294	RHP	360	103	14	62	.286
Day	137	33	2	19	.241	Sc Pos	150	49	9	75	.327
Night	423	119	20	71	.281	Clutch	87	16	2	4	.184

1989 Rankings (American League)

➡ 4th in grounded into double play (21)

➡ 9th in intentional walks (12)

➡ Led the Angels in slugging percentage (.436), home runs (22), RBIs (90), walks (61), intentional walks, grounded into double play, and hitting with runners in scoring position (.327) - *team players with 100 PA*

HITTING:

Brian Downing is still going strong after seventeen years. Now 39, Downing hit .283 last season, his highest average since 1980, and his on base percentage was above .350 for the eleventh straight year. But Downing's power has decreased. He went from 25 homers in 1988 to 14 last year, ending a five-year streak of hitting at least 20 homers. And Downing's RBI total was his lowest since 1983, a season in which he played in only 113 games.

The righthanded hitting Downing hits from an unorthodox stance -- wide open and slanted to the left. He is a pull hitter who has always been very patient at the plate. He tries to work pitchers into deep counts, making them throw as much as possible. He waits for mistakes, then cashes in on them. Downing likes fastballs out over the plate. He is a guess hitter who has the ability to adjust and go to the opposite field to move a runner over or deliver an important run.

Downing can hit anywhere in the lineup. Former Manager Gene Mauch used to love leading Downing off because of his ability to get on base. Downing can hit anywhere from first to sixth. He has always been able to hit righthanders as well as lefthanders. Last year was only a slight exception: he hit .299 vs. lefties, .275 vs. righties.

BASERUNNING:

Downing doesn't have much speed any more, but he's very aggressive on the bases. He's every second baseman's nightmare since he goes into the base as hard as anyone this side of Kirk Gibson. Downing, who once stole 13 bases with Chicago in 1975, was thrown out on both of his stolen base attempts last year.

FIELDING:

Downing holds the American League record for consecutive games without an error (244). But he has slowed down considerably and will only play the outfield in an emergency. And certainly his catching days are long behind him. He's one of the few players who actually wants to be a DH.

OVERALL:

Downing is a tough, gritty and fiery player who has worked hard to become as good as he is. He was never expected to be this good or last for this long. He was never drafted. Yet he has been with the Angels since 1978 and has become a symbol of the franchise. After his success last year, there's no reason to think he won't play well again this year.

BRIAN DOWNING

Position: DH
Bats: R **Throws:** R
Ht: 5'10" **Wt:** 194

Opening Day Age: 39
Born: 10/9/50 in Los Angeles, CA
ML Seasons: 17

Overall Statistics

	G	AB	R	H	D	T	HR	RBI	SB	BB	SO	AVG
1989	142	544	59	154	25	2	14	59	0	56	87	.283
Career	2018	6796	1012	1807	307	24	234	934	48	1027	954	.266

Where He Hits the Ball

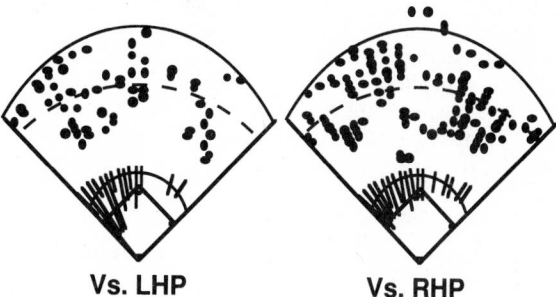

Vs. LHP   **Vs. RHP**

1989 Situational Stats

	AB	H	HR	RBI	AVG		AB	H	HR	RBI	AVG
Home	250	74	10	28	.296	LHP	187	56	8	18	.299
Road	294	80	4	31	.272	RHP	357	98	6	41	.275
Day	138	33	1	9	.239	Sc Pos	124	35	0	42	.282
Night	406	121	13	50	.298	Clutch	87	26	3	10	.299

1989 Rankings (American League)

→ 3rd in most runs scored per times reached base (24.8%) - *players with 502 PA*

→ 5th in most pitches per plate appearance (4.1) - *players with 502 PA*

→ 9th in hit by pitch (6)

→ Led the Angels in hit by pitch, on-base average (.354), pitches per plate appearance, lowest percent of GDPs per GDP Situation (6.3%), hitting in the clutch (.299) and hitting with the bases loaded (.417) - *team players with 502 PA*

→ Led AL Designated Hitters in singles (113), hit by pitch, lowest percent of GDPs per GDP situation, hitting in the clutch and hitting with the bases loaded

CY YOUNG STUFF

PITCHING:

In a season of amazing and unexpected performances by California Angel pitchers -- Bert Blyleven, Greg Minton and Bob McClure, to name three -- Chuck Finley's was far from the least. Maturing almost overnight, Finley became one of the American League's top lefthanded starters in only his third full season and only his second as a full-time starter.

Finley had only 28 games of professional experience -- all in Class A -- when the Angels brought him up in May of 1986. The Angels, who were in love with Finley's strong arm and makeup, were criticized for pushing Finley up the ladder without stopping at Double A or Triple A. After some initial success Finley struggled in 1987 and '88, and not a whole lot was expected of him in 1989. Finley surprised more than a few people by going 16-9 with a 2.57 ERA, second best in the league to Bret Saberhagen's 2.16. He also was the lone Angels pitcher to make the All-Star team. If Finley hadn't missed nearly a month because of a foot injury, he probably would have won 20 games -- and the Angels just might have upset the Oakland A's for the West Division title.

Finley, a tall and lean lefthander with a fluid motion, has an excellent fastball (90 mph), deceptively good changeup and a good curveball. He recently developed his forkball, which, combined with his fastball, enabled him to chalk up 156 strikeouts. The impressive part about that is that Finley is smart enough not to try and blow hitters away with heat all the time. He likes letting his fielders make some of the plays, realizing it conserves his energy for the late innings. Finley has overcome several problems that plagued him in previous seasons. He would often become flustered when he fell behind or when he was in jam. No more. He's as poised as a ten-year veteran.

FIELDING:

Finley's fielding is still improving. Finley gets off the mound well for someone who's 6'6". His concentration is good. He just needs to gain a little bit more agility and mobility. Finley's move to first is good, but should become even better with experience.

OVERALL:

Finley took his lumps his first few years because of his lack of experience. But he has adjusted and learned his craft well, and at 27 he should get even better. If he stays healthy, Finley might just become an annual 17-20 game winner.

CHUCK FINLEY

Position: SP
Bats: L **Throws:** L
Ht: 6' 6" **Wt:** 215

Opening Day Age: 27
Born: 11/26/62 in Monroe, LA
ML Seasons: 4

Overall Statistics

	W	L	ERA	G	GS	Sv	IP	H	R	BB	SO	HR
1989	16	9	2.57	29	29	0	199.2	171	64	82	156	13
Career	30	32	3.58	120	63	0	531.0	504	230	230	367	37

Where They Hit the Ball

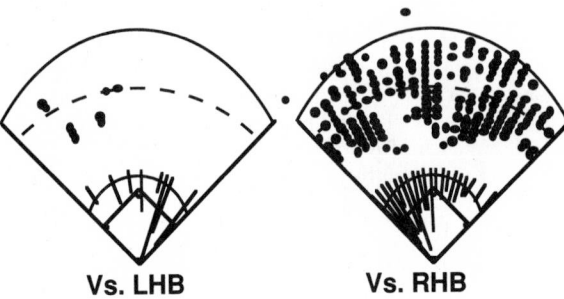

Vs. LHB　　　　　**Vs. RHB**

1989 Situational Stats

	W	L	ERA	Sv	IP		AB	H	HR	RBI	AVG
Home	8	7	2.23	0	113.0	LHB	99	17	0	3	.172
Road	8	2	3.01	0	86.2	RHB	634	154	13	55	.243
Day	1	1	2.79	0	19.1	Sc Pos	143	26	0	36	.182
Night	15	8	2.55	0	180.1	Clutch	91	23	3	9	.253

1989 Rankings (American League)

- ➡ 2nd in earned run average (2.57)
- ➡ 3rd in complete games (9)
- ➡ 5th in caught stealing (12)
- ➡ 6th in strikeouts per nine innings (7.0) - *pitchers with 162 IP*
- ➡ 7th in lowest opponent batting average (.233) - *pitchers with 162 IP*
- ➡ Led the Angels in caught stealing, lowest slugging percentage allowed (.334), earned run average, complete games, walks (82), strikeouts (156), lowest opponent batting average and strikeouts per nine innings - *team pitchers with 162 IP*

PITCHING:

With the acquisition of Bert Blyleven, the recovery of Kirk McCaskill and the addition of Jim Abbott, Willie Fraser worked out of the bullpen as a middle reliever last season after two years as a starter. He had a fine year and may have revived a career that was reeling after a disastrous 1988 campaign in which he gave up 33 home runs and was racked for a 5.41 ERA.

Rushed to the big leagues after only 38 games in the minors, Fraser had an impressive rookie season in 1987, but regressed completely in '88. He kept getting the ball up in the strike zone, mostly by hanging sliders. But after being shifted to the bullpen last year, Fraser was able to keep the ball down more and yielded just six four baggers. Armed with an 87-mph fastball, the slider and a changeup, Fraser is a tough, hard-nosed, gritty righthander. He battles and doesn't give in easily. That's an excellent attribute, especially for a youngster with only limited minor league experience. His fastball has good movement on it, and his change-up complements it well. Fraser hasn't developed enough confidence in his change-up to use it often. When he falls behind in the count, he is usually in trouble. He pitches inside effectively, but his control needs to improve. Lefthanders gave Fraser a lot of problems his first two years, but he improved against them last year.

FIELDING:

Fraser is a more than adequate fielder. He's a good athlete, and gets off the mound quickly. He doesn't make many mistakes afield. Once very easy to steal on, Fraser has improved his move to first and now is average or better at holding baserunners.

OVERALL:

Fraser will probably never be a staff ace or bullpen closer. His stuff, while good, just isn't that great. He has the potential, however, to be a decent third-to-fifth starter or an effective middle reliever, as he was in 1989. Fraser has a good arm and a good head. His inexperience has hurt him but he's learning and his control is improving. His future looks a whole lot brighter than it did a year ago.

WILLIE FRASER

Position: RP
Bats: R **Throws:** R
Ht: 6' 1" **Wt:** 208

Opening Day Age: 25
Born: 5/26/64 in New York, NY
ML Seasons: 4

Overall Statistics

	W	L	ERA	G	GS	Sv	IP	H	R	BB	SO	HR
1989	4	7	3.24	44	0	2	91.2	80	33	23	46	6
Career	26	30	4.45	115	56	3	467.1	449	251	167	240	65

Where They Hit the Ball

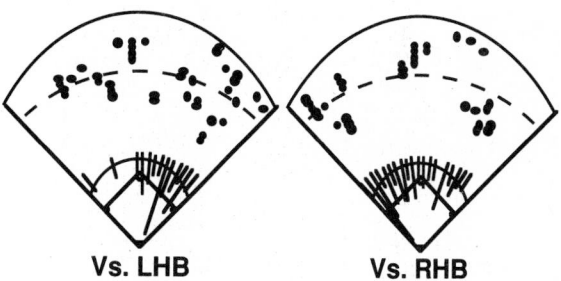

Vs. LHB   **Vs. RHB**

1989 Situational Stats

	W	L	ERA	Sv	IP		AB	H	HR	RBI	AVG
Home	3	2	1.98	1	50.0	LHB	135	34	4	21	.252
Road	1	5	4.75	1	41.2	RHB	205	46	2	22	.224
Day	0	2	3.72	0	9.2	Sc Pos	75	22	2	34	.293
Night	4	5	3.18	2	82.0	Clutch	125	32	3	18	.256

1989 Rankings (American League)

➡ Did not rank near the top or bottom of any categories

PITCHING:

With his 92-mph fastball and devastating forkball, Bryan Harvey has emerged as one of baseball's best closers. He still isn't talked about in the same breath as the Dennis Eckersleys, Jeff Reardons and Tom Henkes, but he should be. Harvey, a young fireballer, has 42 saves in two seasons, including 25 last season. He would have logged more saves last season if he hadn't missed a portion of the season due to a leg injury. The league hit only .183 against him. All this from a guy who was playing with his father on a nationally-known slo-pitch softball team, Howard's Furniture, when he was discovered by Angels scout Alex Cosmidis in 1985. Talk about your rags to riches stories!

Confident, even cocky, the hard-throwing Harvey has the ability to blow hitters away. He fanned 78 in only 55 innings in 1989. Harvey has a tendency to make his manager and teammates squirm a bit because of his propensity to go deep in a count and walk hitters. Harvey's control was excellent as a rookie, but last year he walked 41 men in only 55 innings as he concentrated on throwing as hard as possible. Despite his wildness, he is mentally tough and not afraid to pitch inside and challenge hitters with each and every pitch. His forkball is virtually impossible to hit when he has it working properly. It freezes hitters.

FIELDING:

Harvey has superb concentration and very good instincts. He's a solid, fundamentally sound defensive player. He has a strong, accurate arm and does not rush his throws. His move to first is also good and he holds baserunners better than most fireballers do.

OVERALL:

From the day Harvey arrived in the majors he has never been in awe of major league hitters. Nothing bothers him. He has a tremendous future; if he can cut down on his walks, he has the potential to become the best closer in baseball. He also needs to stay healthy. Harvey had bone chip surgery after the '88 season and last year the Angels used him carefully, never overworking him and seldom using him for more than one inning at a time. If Harvey's arm remains sound, Angel fans will be cheering this guy a lot in the years to come.

BRYAN HARVEY

Position: RP
Bats: R **Throws:** R
Ht: 6' 2" **Wt:** 212

Opening Day Age: 26
Born: 6/2/63 in Chattanooga, TN
ML Seasons: 3

Overall Statistics

	W	L	ERA	G	GS	Sv	IP	H	R	BB	SO	HR
1989	3	3	3.44	51	0	25	55.0	36	21	41	78	6
Career	10	8	2.58	104	0	42	136.0	101	43	63	148	10

Where They Hit the Ball

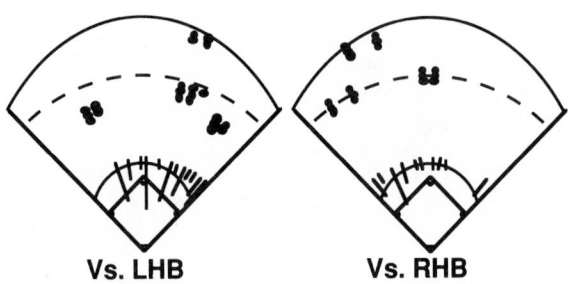

Vs. LHB   Vs. RHB

1989 Situational Stats

	W	L	ERA	Sv	IP		AB	H	HR	RBI	AVG
Home	2	0	2.56	16	31.2	LHB	100	16	3	16	.160
Road	1	3	4.63	9	23.1	RHB	97	20	3	11	.206
Day	0	0	1.50	6	12.0	Sc Pos	68	10	2	22	.147
Night	3	3	3.98	19	43.0	Clutch	134	26	4	21	.194

1989 Rankings (American League)

- → 3rd in strikeouts per nine innings (12.8) - *all league players*
- → 6th in most blown saves (7)
- → 9th in saves (25) and lowest opponent batting average - *all league players*
- → 9th in lowest percent of inherited runners scoring (22.5%)
- → Led the Angels in saves, games finished (42), and strikeouts per nine innings

HITTING:

Jack Howell has good power, but is extremely inconsistent and it doesn't appear as if he'll ever hit for a high average. The lefthanded hitting Howell has most of his problems with lefthanded pitchers -- and with breaking balls, regardless of who throws them. He hit .228 last year, the lowest average in his three years as a regular. He did hit 20 homers, but drove in only 52 runs -- a very poor homer/RBI ratio. He batted .140 against lefthanders with 45 strikeouts in 136 at-bats. Eighteen of his homers came against righthanders, only two against lefties.

Howell is a smooth swinger and a good fastball hitter. He is also a pull hitter. Lefthanders seldom throw him fastballs; they baffle him with breaking stuff. He is not patient nor a good contact hitter. His strikeout-to-walk ratio is well over 2-to-1. He struck out 125 times last year, 130 in 1988 and 118 times in 1987. What's surprising about Howell's offensive exploits is that he ripped apart minor league pitching. This is a guy who hit .373 with 13 homers in 79 games in Triple A at Edmonton in 1985 before being called up to the majors, where he proceeded to hit .197 in 43 games. He went back to Edmonton in 1986 and hit .359 in 44 games, was recalled again and hit a respectable .272. But he hasn't reached that level since.

BASERUNNING:

Howell has average speed and won't steal often. He attempted to steal three times last year and was caught all three times. He is aggressive, as he is in all facets of his game, and when he gets on, he runs the bases well. He has good judgement when running the bases, especially when taking the extra base.

FIELDING:

Howell may not have much range or quickness at third, but he has an excellent arm and is an accurate thrower. He throws hard and occasionally makes the spectacular play. He's versatile enough to play the outfield as well. He was the Angels' starting left fielder when the 1987 season began.

OVERALL:

Howell is a self-made player, an undrafted free agent who has worked hard to make the most of his ability. Some people may be questioning that ability after his regression last year. Howell, who could wind up being platooned, needs to cut down his swing and work the pitchers more. He has to wait for his pitch, rather than hit the pitcher's pitch.

JACK HOWELL

Position: 3B
Bats: L **Throws:** R
Ht: 6' 0" **Wt:** 201

Opening Day Age: 28
Born: 8/18/61 in Tucson, AZ
ML Seasons: 5

Overall Statistics

	G	AB	R	H	D	T	HR	RBI	SB	BB	SO	AVG
1989	144	474	56	108	19	4	20	52	0	52	125	.228
Career	542	1711	224	413	87	13	68	218	9	190	434	.241

Where He Hits the Ball

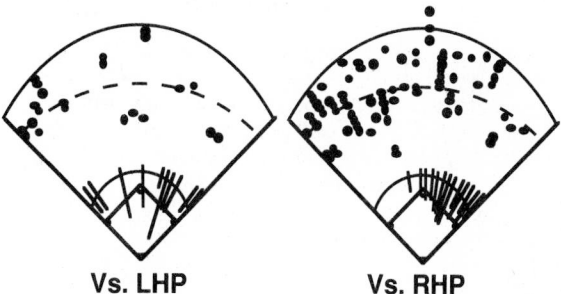

Vs. LHP   **Vs. RHP**

1989 Situational Stats

	AB	H	HR	RBI	AVG		AB	H	HR	RBI	AVG
Home	225	53	9	25	.236	LHP	136	19	2	9	.140
Road	249	55	11	27	.221	RHP	338	89	18	43	.263
Day	102	18	3	6	.176	Sc Pos	113	22	2	25	.195
Night	372	90	17	46	.242	Clutch	85	22	4	10	.259

1989 Rankings (American League)

- ➡ Lowest batting average against lefthanded pitchers (.140) - *players with 125 PA*
- ➡ 2nd worst batting average with two strikes (.104) - *players with 162 PA*
- ➡ 4th worst batting average overall (.228) - *players with 502 PA*
- ➡ 9th in strikeouts (125)
- ➡ Led Angels in least at bats per home run (23.7), highest batting average with a 3-1 count (.500) - *players with 10 PA*
- ➡ Led AL Third Basemen in least at bats per home run, strikeouts and home runs

WALLY JOYNER

Position: 1B
Bats: L **Throws:** L
Ht: 6' 2" **Wt:** 198

Opening Day Age: 27
Born: 6/16/62 in
Atlanta, GA
ML Seasons: 4

HITTING:

Wally Joyner is one of the baseball's top players in nearly every facet of the game. He has one of the most fluid and beautiful swings in the majors. He is a controlled hitter, a finesse hitter, but he can crash the ball out of the ballpark, too. A superb run producer, the left-handed hitting Joyner has been remarkably consistent in his first four seasons, hitting .290, .285, .295 and .282. His home run production remained low for the second straight year, but he's maintained all along that he's not a home run hitter. After whacking 22 homers as a rookie, then an astounding 34 in 1987, Joyner hit 13 in 1988 and 16 last year. Fourteen of his homers last year came after the All-Star break. Even in a down year, Joyner still drives in runs. The last two years have been considered mediocre for Joyner and he's driven in 85 and 79 runs, respectively. He broke in with California by driving in 100 runs, then followed it up with 117 RBI in his sophomore year.

Joyner has a good eye -- he doesn't fan often -- and can hit well to all fields. His home run production was down because pitchers kept the ball away from him, not allowing him to pull. But the patient and smart-hitting Joyner has the ability to adjust. Lefthanders work Joyner over with breaking balls away, but Joyner compensates by taking the ball to left field. Righthanders have trouble with Joyner. They can only hope to get ahead and hope he chases something in the dirt.

BASERUNNING:

Though Joyner doesn't have a lot of speed, he's a good baserunner. He's smart. He knows when he should run and when he shouldn't. He knows when he should take a chance. He can steal 5-10 bases a year for you.

FIELDING:

Joyner is a brilliant fielder. If not for Don Mattingly and his reputation, Joyner would have a Gold Glove or two. Coincidentally, Joyner is similar in style to Mattingly. He has excellent range, instincts and reactions. He also has soft hands. He has a good, accurate arm and is aggressive on defense.

OVERALL:

Joyner has emerged as one of the finest all-around first baseman in baseball. He can hit for average and power. He can field. He'll put up All-Star numbers for years to come. When someone hits .280-.290 with 80-90 RBI and people consider it a mediocre year, you know the guy is good.

Overall Statistics

	G	AB	R	H	D	T	HR	RBI	SB	BB	SO	AVG
1989	159	593	78	167	30	2	16	79	3	46	58	.282
Career	620	2347	341	676	121	8	85	381	24	230	231	.288

Where He Hits the Ball

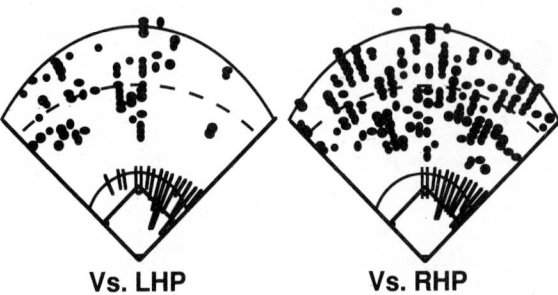

Vs. LHP   **Vs. RHP**

1989 Situational Stats

	AB	H	HR	RBI	AVG		AB	H	HR	RBI	AVG
Home	286	78	8	40	.273	LHP	206	54	6	32	.262
Road	307	89	8	39	.290	RHP	387	113	10	47	.292
Day	130	41	4	23	.315	Sc Pos	149	44	3	61	.295
Night	463	126	12	56	.272	Clutch	97	24	2	12	.247

1989 Rankings (American League)

- → 4th in lowest grounder/flyball ratio (.77) - *players with 502 PA*
- → 8th in games (159)
- → 9th in hit by pitch (6)
- → Led the Angels in hits (167), doubles (30), total bases (249), hit by pitch and games
- → Led AL First Basemen in percentage of extra bases taken as a runner (50.9%)

PITCHING:

As long as we're talking about the comebacks of Bert Blyleven and Chuck Finley, check out the one Kirk McCaskill made. After two years of arm problems, McCaskill compiled 15 victories and had a sparkling 2.93 ERA, fifth best in the league. An intelligent and gutsy righthander with a lot of heart, McCaskill has lost some of the velocity off his fastball because of his arm difficulties in 1987 and 1988. Once clocked in the 90's, his fastball now travels 86 mph at best. Luckily for McCaskill it sinks, thus increasing its effectiveness.

McCaskill has a crackling curve and good changeup, but his slider has become perhaps his most effective pitch. He's throwing it in mostly crucial situations -- times when he needs an out. Now, more than ever, McCaskill has to have good location to win. He is aggressive, but not as aggressive as before. After his arms problems he's had to make big adjustments. He's not pitching inside as much as he did before, and he's trying to hit the black of the plate more often. Because of his arm problems, McCaskill has had to change his style. He isn't able to blow hitters away anymore. He fanned only 107 batters in 212 innings after striking out 202 in 246 innings in '86. He now finesses hitters and has to rely on control and location.

FIELDING:

McCaskill is a superb athlete (he was an All-American hockey player at the University of Vermont and a fourth-round draft pick of the Winnipeg Jets in 1981). He fields as well as anyone. He's quick off the mound, fields bunts extremely well and is always under control to throw accurately. His move to first is also outstanding and he holds runners about as well as any righthander in baseball.

OVERALL:

If he's healthy, McCaskill is unquestionably one of the league's most effective pitchers. But that's a big if. Bone chips in his right elbow ended his 1987 season prematurely. Nerve irritation in his right arm ended his 1988 season. He recovered in '89, making the difficult transition from power pitcher to finesse pitcher. Unquestionably, McCaskill is a survivor. But his history of arm trouble makes it difficult for the Angels to count on him without hesitation.

KIRK MCCASKILL

Position: SP
Bats: R **Throws:** R
Ht: 6' 1" **Wt:** 195

Opening Day Age: 29
Born: 4/9/61 in Kapuskasing, Ontario
ML Seasons: 5

Overall Statistics

	W	L	ERA	G	GS	Sv	IP	H	R	BB	SO	HR
1989	15	10	2.93	32	32	0	212.0	202	73	59	107	16
Career	56	44	3.90	133	130	0	869.0	837	406	310	565	81

Where They Hit the Ball

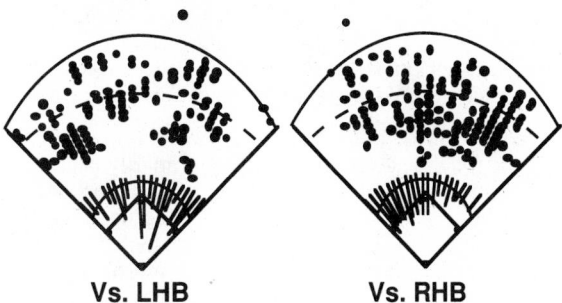

Vs. LHB   **Vs. RHB**

1989 Situational Stats

	W	L	ERA	Sv	IP		AB	H	HR	RBI	AVG
Home	10	4	3.12	0	112.1	LHB	399	100	10	31	.251
Road	5	6	2.71	0	99.2	RHB	396	102	6	36	.258
Day	3	1	2.76	0	45.2	Sc Pos	171	38	3	52	.222
Night	12	9	2.98	0	166.1	Clutch	77	14	2	4	.182

1989 Rankings (American League)

→ 1st in GDPs (32) and most GDPs per nine innings (1.36) - *pitchers with 162 PA*

→ 2nd in shutouts (4)

→ 4th in lowest batting average with runners in scoring position (.222) - *pitchers with 150 batters faced*

→ 5th in earned run average (2.93)

→ 7th in lowest stolen base percentage (50.0%) - *pitchers with 162 PA*

→ Led the Angels in GDPs, most GDPs per nine innings, lowest stolen base percentage and pickoff throws (186)

PITCHING:

Bob McClure enjoyed his finest major league season last year at the age of 36. Signed as a free agent before the '89 season, McClure turned out to be another one of General Manager Mike Port's coups. In his fifteenth season McClure compiled a career-best 1.55 ERA, and his 6-1 record matched his best winning percentage. McClure held the opposition to a meager .212 average, easily the best performance of his career. All this from a pitcher who'd been released by both the Expos and Mets in a period of less than four months in 1988.

Given a new lease on life by California, McClure proved to be exactly what the Angels needed. A seasoned veteran who pitched for Milwaukee in the 1982 World Series and played a bit role in helping the Mets to a division title in 1988, McClure's not the kind of guy who's going to beat himself very often. He's never been overpowering; he's always had to rely on guile to get hitters out, and his intelligence makes him an excellent role model for younger hurlers.

McClure, who has a tight, unorthodox windup and delivery, has stayed in the majors primarily because of his effectiveness against lefthanders. His best pitch is a sharp-breaking curveball, but he has a good fastball and an ability to change speeds. He depends on the curve to handle lefties, relying mostly on his changeup versus righthanders. McClure has superb location and control. He's a thorough professional, throwing strikes and not wasting time on the mound. He has a knack for getting ahead of hitters and then getting them to chase pitches out of the strike zone.

FIELDING:

McClure gets off the mound well and fields his position well. That comes from experience and McClure has learned his lessons well. He's also outstanding at holding baserunners. McClure's pickoff move is so good that few runners even venture very far from first with him on the mound.

OVERALL:

McClure seems to be in good hands pitching for manager Doug Rader, who's shown a definite ability to get the most out of a mound staff. A year ago McClure looked washed up, but coming to California seems to have revived his career. He caught Angel-itis last year: nearly every Angel pitcher pitched well, turning the club into one of the surprise teams in baseball. He should be pitching for another year or two, though probably not quite up to his 1989 level.

BOB MCCLURE

Position: RP
Bats: R **Throws:** L
Ht: 5'11" **Wt:** 170

Opening Day Age: 36
Born: 4/29/53 in Oakland, CA
ML Seasons: 15

Overall Statistics

	W	L	ERA	G	GS	Sv	IP	H	R	BB	SO	HR
1989	6	1	1.55	48	0	3	52.1	39	14	15	36	2
Career	62	53	3.77	557	73	52	1058.2	1016	500	451	645	92

Where They Hit the Ball

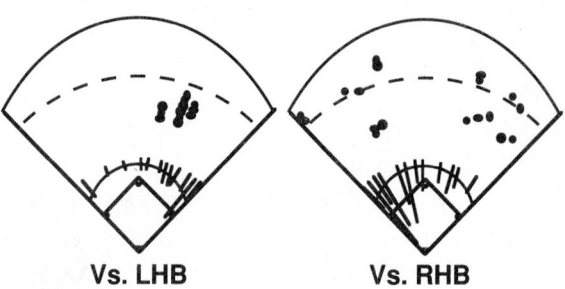

Vs. LHB   **Vs. RHB**

1989 Situational Stats

	W	L	ERA	Sv	IP		AB	H	HR	RBI	AVG
Home	4	0	1.88	1	24.0	LHB	65	10	1	9	.154
Road	2	1	1.27	2	28.1	RHB	119	29	1	10	.244
Day	4	0	0.90	1	20.0	Sc Pos	46	10	1	15	.217
Night	2	1	1.95	2	32.1	Clutch	83	13	1	4	.157

1989 Rankings (American League)

- ➡ 1st in lowest percent of inherited runners scored (14.0%) - *pitchers with 30 inherited runners*
- ➡ 5th in earned run average (1.55) - *all league players*
- ➡ Led the Angels in lowest percent of inherited runners scored and won/loss percentage (.857) - *all team pitchers*

PITCHING:

Greg Minton's career appeared to be over in 1987. He was overweight. He was pitching ineffectively for the Giants. He was being booed -- even while warming up in the bullpen. He was released in May of that year. The Angels, in desperate need of relief help at the time, signed him up immediately. Chalk one up for California; acquiring Minton was a coup. He went on a strict diet and exercise program, lost weight, and has turned out to be an effective setup man for Bryan Harvey. He can also close a game himself every once in a while. Minton has exceeded the Angels' expectations. He had a 2.20 ERA last season to go along with eight saves and four victories. Since California got him off the scrap heap, Minton has 25 saves and a 2.68 ERA.

The key pitch for Minton, a 12-year righthanded veteran, is a sinker. It's been his most effective pitch for years. It leaves hitters beating the ball into the ground time and again. Minton, who pitched for the Giants from 1975 to 1987, used his 87-mph fastball to set up his sinker. He also mixes in a changeup and an occasional slider. He has excellent pitching mechanics, pitches inside, and is fearless. He seldom gives up home runs. He permitted only two homers in a span of 64 appearances and 116 innings from July 1987 to the end of the '88 season. He allowed just five homers in his first 156 innings as an Angel. He has allowed just 42 homers in 1115 2/3 innings in his career. That's one homer every 26.5 innings.

FIELDING:

Ever since he got back in shape, Minton has been a solid fielder. His concentration is good and he's aggressive coming off the mound. His move to first is average.

OVERALL:

Minton gives the Angels flexibility: he can close games if need be or can serve as a setup man. His presence in the clubhouse has also been a boost to California, as an experienced veteran who's been through some pennant races. He also has a tremendous sense of humor, which keeps others around him loose.

GREG MINTON

Position: RP
Bats: B **Throws:** R
Ht: 6' 2" **Wt:** 207

Opening Day Age: 38
Born: 7/29/51 in Lubbock, TX
ML Seasons: 15

Overall Statistics

	W	L	ERA	G	GS	Sv	IP	H	R	BB	SO	HR
1989	4	3	2.20	62	0	8	90.0	76	22	37	42	4
Career	58	64	3.11	699	7	150	1115.2	1071	448	476	475	42

Where They Hit the Ball

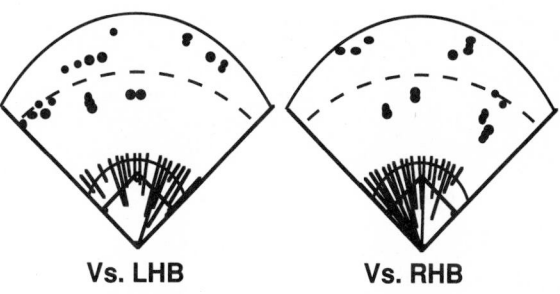

Vs. LHB   **Vs. RHB**

1989 Situational Stats

	W	L	ERA	Sv	IP		AB	H	HR	RBI	AVG
Home	4	2	1.97	3	50.1	LHB	146	31	0	17	.212
Road	0	1	2.50	5	39.2	RHB	185	45	4	22	.243
Day	1	0	2.45	1	14.2	Sc Pos	103	24	0	34	.233
Night	3	3	2.15	7	75.1	Clutch	161	30	3	22	.186

1989 Rankings (American League)

➡ 4th in holds (15)

➡ 7th in first batter efficiency (.172) - *40 first batters faced*

➡ Led the Angels in games (62), holds and first batter efficiency

PITCHING:

If you've been released by the Seattle Mariners, you know you're in trouble. Rich Monteleone was released by Seattle in May 1988. The Angels didn't care. The 6'2" righthanded middle relief specialist was picked up by California, shipped to AAA Edmonton (where his brother-in-law Chuck Hernandez is pitching coach) and Monteleone had one of his typical seasons: losing record, high ERA. No matter. When the Angels got in trouble and needed pitching help last year, they looked, somewhat in desperation, toward Monteleone, who once went 6-12, 8-12 and 6-13 during a three-year span in the minor leagues (1985-87) and had only 11.1 innings at the major league level before last season.

The results were better than anyone could have reasonably expected. With the Angels, Monteleone compiled the best ERA (3.18) of his less-than-impressive eight-year professional career. Equipped with an 90-mph fastball, good forkball and curve, Monteleone is not overpowering, but he has a sound arm. He has a tendency to work on hitters more than a man with his sort of stuff should have to. By going deep into the count so often, Monteleone gets into trouble and then has to come in with a fastball that's less than his best. That's exactly what hitters hope to see from him.

FIELDING:

Monteleone is an adequate fielder. He doesn't get off the mound as well as others, but he has a good, accurate arm. For a righthander who's primarily a power pitcher, he has a pretty good move to first and does a decent job of holding baserunners.

OVERALL:

Monteleone has some talent. He's a former number one draft choice and was considered a good enough prospect to be traded even up for another tarnished but talented prospect, Darnell Coles. Until last year, Monteleone had shown little ability to be an effective pitcher, even at the minor league level. With the Angels he got one last chance and made the most of it. It's possible he's a late bloomer. Working in middle relief, where there wasn't much pressure on him, he did a more than decent job. If Monteleone can duplicate what he did last year, he'll have earned a major league job at last.

RICH MONTELEONE

Position: RP
Bats: R **Throws:** R
Ht: 6' 2" **Wt:** 217

Opening Day Age: 27
Born: 3/22/63 in Tampa, FL
ML Seasons: 3

Overall Statistics

	W	L	ERA	G	GS	Sv	IP	H	R	BB	SO	HR
1989	2	2	3.18	24	0	0	39.2	39	15	13	27	3
Career	2	2	3.35	30	0	0	51.0	53	20	18	32	5

Where They Hit the Ball

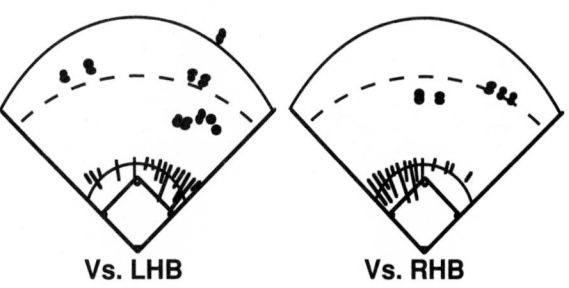

Vs. LHB   **Vs. RHB**

1989 Situational Stats

	W	L	ERA	Sv	IP		AB	H	HR	RBI	AVG
Home	0	0	1.10	0	16.1	LHB	75	20	1	6	.267
Road	2	2	4.63	0	23.1	RHB	78	19	2	13	.244
Day	0	1	9.53	0	5.2	Sc Pos	33	11	1	14	.333
Night	2	1	2.12	0	34.0	Clutch	29	9	0	5	.310

1989 Rankings (American League)

➡ 1st in least stolen base attempts (0) - *all league pitchers*

HITTING:

Lance Parrish rebounded well after two atrocious years in Philadelphia and was instrumental in helping the Angels to an improbable 91-victory season with his leadership, his handling of the pitching staff and his occasional power. He hit only .238, but that was an improvement on the .215 average he'd posted the previous season with the Phillies. It should have been a lot better. Parrish had 15 homers by the first week of August, but hit just two the rest of the way, mainly because his chronic back problem acted up, spoiling his season.

Parrish, a 12-year veteran, is a dead pull hitter who enjoys fastballs at the waist. When he gets in the hole, pitchers can usually get him out on outside breaking pitches. He is impatient, as his 104 strikeouts in 433 at bats illustrate. He is especially impatient against righthanders, who attempt to get ahead of him with fastballs, then try to get him out with breaking pitches. Lefthanders change speeds on him and keep the ball down and away, out of his power zone.

BASERUNNING:

Pitchers needn't bother to hold Parrish close to first. He won't run. He has no speed whatsoever, but in 1989 he finally got his first stolen base since 1985.

FIELDING:

Parrish has one of the strongest arms in baseball. He's also accurate. But his back problems have prevented him from excelling the way he's capable. He is fundamentally sound, but he is not all that quick behind the plate -- mainly because of his physical limitations.

OVERALL:

If he didn't have those back problems, Parrish would still be one of the game's top and most consistent catchers. At this point, it's clear that those problems may prevent Parrish from playing more than another year or two. He was cruising along last year until the back problems became severe. He was on track for a 25-homer, 75-RBI year when his back went out.

Returning to the American League, where he enjoyed tremendous success with Detroit, and to his hometown of Anaheim, Parrish was happy, especially since his two-year stay in Philadelphia was an absolute nightmare. Playing for a loser was a big part of Parrish's problems in Philly. He thrives in a pennant chase, as he proved for most of last year. Problem is, it may have been his last pennant race.

LANCE PARRISH

Position: C
Bats: R **Throws:** R
Ht: 6' 3" **Wt:** 220

Opening Day Age: 33
Born: 6/15/56 in McKeesport, PA
ML Seasons: 13

Overall Statistics

	G	AB	R	H	D	T	HR	RBI	SB	BB	SO	AVG
1989	124	433	48	103	12	1	17	50	1	42	104	.238
Career	1523	5596	711	1431	251	26	261	877	23	470	1148	.256

Where He Hits the Ball

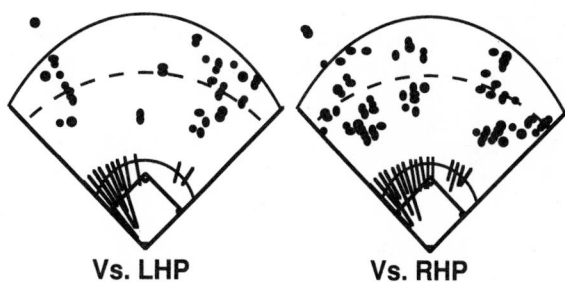

Vs. LHP   **Vs. RHP**

1989 Situational Stats

	AB	H	HR	RBI	AVG		AB	H	HR	RBI	AVG
Home	215	54	8	25	.251	LHP	144	34	7	20	.236
Road	218	49	9	25	.225	RHP	289	69	10	30	.239
Day	85	22	4	10	.259	Sc Pos	100	21	4	34	.210
Night	348	81	13	40	.233	Clutch	78	17	2	5	.218

1989 Rankings (American League)

➡ 8th worst throwing out opposing base stealers (28.7%) - *catchers with 75 attempts*

HITTING:

Johnny Ray is one of the game's steadiest hitters, perennially in the .290-.300 range. The switch-hitting Ray, who spent six years in Pittsburgh and will enter his third full season with the Angels, is a superb contact hitter. Ray has a smooth, compact swing, great knowledge of the strike zone, is very patient and doesn't strike out much. Ray fanned only 30 times in 530 at-bats last year and only 38 times in 602 at-bats in 1988. He's never fanned more than 47 times in any of his eight years in the big leagues. Though a good hitter from both sides, Ray is better lefthanded; last year he hit .304 lefthanded, .262 righthanded, typical splits for him.

Ray waits on breaking pitches as well as anyone in baseball. Pitchers try to jam him; that's where they have the greatest success. Ray's a good clutch hitter, but he has limited power and has never hit more than seven homers in a season. Most of those four baggers come from the left side of the plate. For a long time Ray has been known as one of the finest doubles hitters in the game. He averaged 36 doubles per 600 at bats entering last year, with NL-leading figures of 38 in 1983-84 and an Angels-high 42 in 1988. But he fell to 16 doubles last year. At 33 it's possible he may be starting to slow down a little.

BASERUNNING:

Ray's speed is below average at this point of his career. He stole 18 bases in 1983, but hasn't approached that level since. Last year he swiped six bases and was caught three times. Ray doesn't commit many blunders on the bases, but that's because he doesn't run much.

FIELDING:

Ray is a reasonably sure-handed fielder who doesn't have much range. He has difficulty pivoting on the double play and is far better on grass than on turf. His difficulties on defense were a major factor when Pittsburgh dealt him. The Angels tried to convert Ray into a leftfielder in 1988, but the experiment was a flop when Ray committed five errors in 40 games.

OVERALL:

The Angels think so much of Ray that they gave him a three-year extension during the season. The Angels have one of the toughest organizations to negotiate with and seldom perform such an act. Though Ray is somewhat of a liability in the field, and doesn't possess speed, his bat is valuable. He may wind up being a designated hitter when age finally catches up with Brian Downing.

JOHNNY RAY

Position: 2B
Bats: B **Throws:** R
Ht: 5'11" **Wt:** 189

Opening Day Age: 33
Born: 3/1/57 in Chouteau, OK
ML Seasons: 9

Overall Statistics

	G	AB	R	H	D	T	HR	RBI	SB	BB	SO	AVG
1989	134	530	52	153	16	3	5	62	6	36	30	.289
Career	1248	4784	557	1390	271	36	48	551	78	334	285	.291

Where He Hits the Ball

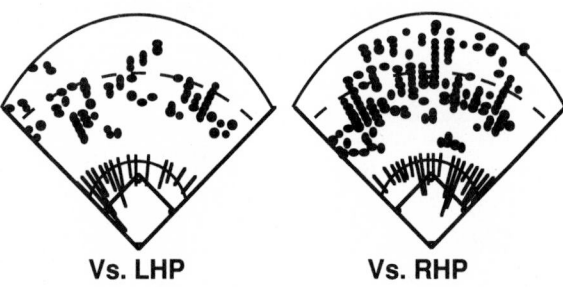

Vs. LHP   **Vs. RHP**

1989 Situational Stats

	AB	H	HR	RBI	AVG		AB	H	HR	RBI	AVG
Home	268	71	3	30	.265	LHP	195	51	1	21	.262
Road	262	82	2	32	.313	RHP	335	102	4	41	.304
Day	128	44	0	17	.344	Sc Pos	108	32	1	54	.296
Night	402	109	5	45	.271	Clutch	75	15	0	10	.200

1989 Rankings (American League)

- ➡ 2nd in sacrifice flies (12)
- ➡ 5th in most runs scored per times reached base (25.0%) - *players with 502 PA*
- ➡ 6th in least percent of swings that missed (8.0%) - *players with 502 PA*
- ➡ Led the Angels in batting average (.289), singles (129), sacrifice flies, percent of swings that missed, percent of swings put into play (53.2%)
- ➡ Led AL Second Basemen in hitting on the road (.313) and sacrifice flies

HITTING:

Everyone in the Angels' organization has been waiting for Dick Schofield to bust loose at the plate. That day has yet to come. He opened his career hitting .193 and .219; his job was in jeopardy. Schofield kept it by hitting .249 with 13 homers in 1986, then improved to .251 in 1988, which is what the Angels want him to hit, though they feel he's capable of .270. But Schofield dipped to .239 in 1988, then to .228 last year with only four homers and 26 RBI in 91 games.

The right-handed hitting Schofield is a pull hitter who has always had problems going to the opposite field. He has never learned how to go with the pitch. Consequently, pitchers throw him breaking stuff down and away, and the undisciplined Schofield usually chases it. Righthanders give Schofield a lot of problems. He hit .206 against righties last year and .260 against southpaws. He's a career .252 hitter vs. righties, .215 against lefties.

For a little guy, Schofield has decent power. He hit a career-high 13 homers in 1986, by far his best season to date, but dropped to nine homers in 1987, six homers in 1988 and only four last year (in 302 at-bats).

BASERUNNING:

Most people don't realize how much speed Schofield has and what an intelligent baserunner he is. He stole 23 bases out of 28 attempts in 1986, 19 out of 22 in 1987 and 20 out of 25 in 1988. He dipped to nine out of 12 last season. He is aggressive on the bases, takes the extra base whenever he can and seldom makes a mistake.

FIELDING:

Ozzie Smith, Tony Fernandez and Ozzie Guillen may cover a little more ground than Schofield, but no one is steadier. Schofield is not dazzling or flashy. He gets the job done and done well. He is quick, has excellent range, soft hands and a strong, accurate arm. He led the league in fielding percentage in 1987 and 1988 and committed just seven errors all last season.

OVERALL:

If only Schofield hit a little more, he'd be mentioned in the same breath as Cal Ripken Jr. and Alan Trammell. On a winning team, Schofield is the perfect shortstop. He's a standout defensive player and runner, but he must learn how to hit major league pitching on a consistent basis. Former Manager Gene Mauch contends that some day Schofield will hit .300 with 22 homers, 85 RBI and 25 stolen bases. However, now at age 27, these kind of numbers are highly unlikely.

DICK SCHOFIELD

Position: SS
Bats: R **Throws:** R
Ht: 5'10" **Wt:** 175

Opening Day Age: 27
Born: 11/21/62 in Springfield, IL
ML Seasons: 7

Overall Statistics

	G	AB	R	H	D	T	HR	RBI	SB	BB	SO	AVG
1989	91	302	42	69	11	2	4	26	9	28	47	.228
Career	827	2658	315	613	87	23	47	229	87	227	379	.231

Where He Hits the Ball

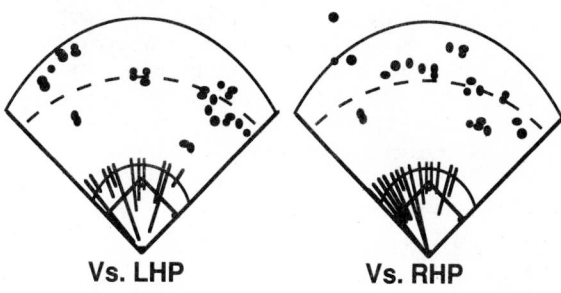

Vs. LHP   **Vs. RHP**

1989 Situational Stats

	AB	H	HR	RBI	AVG		AB	H	HR	RBI	AVG
Home	143	29	1	11	.203	LHP	127	33	1	7	.260
Road	159	40	3	15	.252	RHP	175	36	3	19	.206
Day	73	22	0	8	.301	Sc Pos	65	15	1	22	.231
Night	229	47	4	18	.205	Clutch	39	11	0	3	.282

1989 Rankings (American League)

➡ Led the Angels in sacrifice hits (11)

HITTING:

Bill Schroeder's seven years of experience makes him one of the finest backup catchers in baseball. He's had some good seasons with the bat, hitting 14 homers twice and batting .332 in one of those years, 1987, while batting only 250 times. Though he's now 31 and has never played more than 75 games in a season, Schroeder could probably start for a few clubs. How the Angels seized him from Milwaukee for only Gus Polidor before the '89 season is a mystery.

Schroeder can obviously hit for power. He batted only .203 last year, but showed his usual pop by hitting six homers in 138 at-bats. He's a pull hitter who likes low fastballs. He also has the ability to adjust and can occasionally punch the ball to the opposite field. If there's a reason Schroeder has never been given a chance to play regularly, it's because of his tendency to take a wild cut. He fanned 44 times in 41 games last year and over his career has averaged nearly a strikeout a game. Schroeder never has been a very patient hitter, but last year he was more undisciplined than ever, walking only three times. His strikeout-to-walk ratio (44 to 3) had to be one of the more amazing figures in baseball. Maybe it was playing for a new club, but last year Schroeder seemed to come up the plate strictly with the idea of trying to hit a homer.

BASERUNNING:

Schroeder can run pretty well for a big guy (6'2", 200). He stole five bases in 1987. Though he hasn't stolen a base since, he is a smart runner with good instincts.

FIELDING:

Schroeder is underrated as a gloveman. He has a good, accurate arm and is adept at calling a game. He works well with pitchers and is known for calling a good game. He'll give a veteran hurler some rope, but he's not afraid to take charge with a young pitcher who needs some guidance.

OVERALL:

Schroeder's value is high as a backup because of his ability to fill in and produce. One gets the feeling that he might thrive if he played in the right platoon catcher arrangement, especially for a manager like Earl Weaver who knew how to get the most of players with sharply defined, but limited skills. Playing for California, a team whose other catchers also hit right-handed, Schroeder won't get that chance. But the Angels are very glad to have him.

BILL SCHROEDER

Position: C
Bats: R **Throws:** R
Ht: 6' 2" **Wt:** 200

Opening Day Age: 31
Born: 9/7/58 in
Baltimore, MD
ML Seasons: 7

Overall Statistics

	G	AB	R	H	D	T	HR	RBI	SB	BB	SO	AVG
1989	41	138	16	28	2	0	6	15	0	3	44	.203
Career	358	1204	146	290	46	1	57	143	6	57	333	.241

Where He Hits the Ball

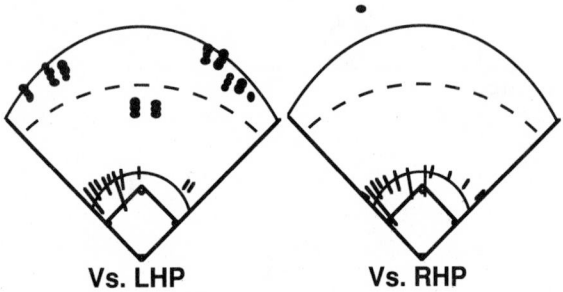

Vs. LHP   Vs. RHP

1989 Situational Stats

	AB	H	HR	RBI	AVG		AB	H	HR	RBI	AVG
Home	55	14	2	6	.255	LHP	66	12	4	6	.182
Road	83	14	4	9	.169	RHP	72	16	2	9	.222
Day	54	13	3	7	.241	Sc Pos	36	6	2	11	.167
Night	84	15	3	8	.179	Clutch	15	1	0	0	.067

1989 Rankings (American League)

➡ Did not rank near the top or bottom in any categories

HITTING:

Everyone always expected Claudell Washington to hit .300, bash 30 homers and drive in 100 runs. The Oakland Athletics did. The Texas Rangers did. So did the Chicago White Sox, New York Mets, Atlanta Braves and New York Yankees -- all the clubs Washington previously played for. By the time he reached California, the Angels realized what Washington was actually capable of: .280, 15 homers, 75 RBI. He didn't exactly reach those figures in his first year with the Angels in '89, as injuries and a family crisis cut down his playing time. But Washington was instrumental in helping California to its improbable run at the division crown with his leadership and clutch hitting.

The lefthanded hitting Washington is a streaky hitter who loves pitches low in the strike zone. Over the years, he's adjusted and hit high pitches more consistently. He's also learned to go to the opposite field. At 35, his bat may be beginning to slow down a little. Washington struck out 84 times in 418 at-bats, his highest strikeout total since he fanned 103 times in 1983. He also walked just 27 times. Never a very patient hitter, Washington has only walked as many as 35 times three times in his 16 major league seasons.

BASERUNNING:

Washington, who keeps himself in superb physical condition, has good speed and excellent instincts. He stole 13 bases in 18 attempts last season; not bad for a 35-year-old. He stole 15 bases the previous year -- the most in four years. Washington isn't aggressive on the bases, but he doesn't make mistakes. The last few years, he's excelled on the bases because he's played regularly.

FIELDING:

Once known as an adequate outfielder with occasional concentration lapses, Washington has turned himself into an excellent defensive player. Basically, the more he's played, the better he's become. He used to make blunders on routine plays. No more. He gets an outstanding jump on the ball, moves extremely well to his left and right and has sharp instincts. His arm isn't as strong as it once was, however, and runners challenge him more often than they used to.

OVERALL:

Washington's talents were never really appreciated -- until last year. The Angels simply knew what to expect out of Washington, received it, and were happy. Formerly considered a malingerer and a clubhouse problem, Washington has turned into a role model for some of the younger Angels, and was especially influential with centerfielder Devon White, a potential superstar.

CLAUDELL WASHINGTON

Position: RF
Bats: L **Throws:** L
Ht: 6' 2" **Wt:** 195

Opening Day Age: 35
Born: 8/31/54 in Los Angeles, CA
ML Seasons: 16

Overall Statistics

	G	AB	R	H	D	T	HR	RBI	SB	BB	SO	AVG
1989	110	418	53	114	18	4	13	42	13	27	84	.273
Career	1867	6673	919	1865	332	68	163	815	308	464	1241	.279

Where He Hits the Ball

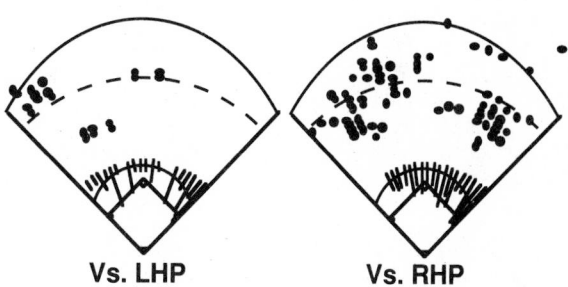

Vs. LHP   Vs. RHP

1989 Situational Stats

	AB	H	HR	RBI	AVG		AB	H	HR	RBI	AVG
Home	210	62	9	25	.295	LHP	102	30	0	5	.294
Road	208	52	4	17	.250	RHP	316	84	13	37	.266
Day	98	28	4	15	.286	Sc Pos	87	23	1	24	.264
Night	320	86	9	27	.269	Clutch	60	15	0	4	.250

1989 Rankings (American League)

➡ 8th in steals of third (5)

GREAT SPEED

DEVON WHITE

Position: CF
Bats: B **Throws:** R
Ht: 6' 2" **Wt:** 178

Opening Day Age: 27
Born: 12/29/62 in Kingston, Jamaica
ML Seasons: 5

HITTING:

At 27 and after three full seasons, Devon White still has the potential to become one of baseball's brightest stars. White just has to become more disciplined at the plate. He has to stop swinging at nearly ever pitch that comes his way. The switch-hitting White has the devastating combination of speed and power, but he has never hit for a high average in his three major-league seasons. It doesn't appear, at this point, that he has the mental makeup to do so.

White is an excellent fastball hitter, so pitchers throw him mostly breaking balls and off-speed pitches. He won't see a lot of fastballs until he's able to hit breaking pitches with consistency. Low pitches give him trouble -- especially low breaking pitches. White has not shown a great ability to improve annually. He hit .245 last year -- 14 points lower than the previous season and 18 points lower than in '87. He hit 12 homers last year, one more than '88 -- but 12 less than in 1987. He drove in 56 runs last year, five more than in '88 -- but 31 less than in 1987. He's a better hitter from the left side of the plate, especially in the power department. Ten of his 12 homers and 39 of his 56 RBI came against righties. He hit only .228 with runners in scoring position -- a poor showing for a player of White's caliber.

BASERUNNING:

When White gets going, watch out. He's a blur. His problem is taking off. He's slow getting out of the batter's box. Regardless, he is blessed with amazing speed -- as his career-high 44 stolen bases last year illustrates. The drawback was Devon's 16 times caught stealing last year.

FIELDING:

White has great range, mobility, instincts and reactions and a Gold Glove to prove it. His speed enables him to chase down nearly everything. His great leaping ability enables to rob opponents of home runs, and his arm is strong and accurate to boot. If White has one problem defensively, it's getting the ball out of his glove and getting rid of it fast enough. Runners have caught on and have taken advantage of the deficiency.

OVERALL:

White has all the tools to be a superstar. With speed, power and great defensive skills, he's been compared to Willie Davis, the former Dodgers great. If White can become disciplined, he could hit .300-.330 with 30 homers, 40-50 steals and 100 RBI. But to reach that level, he has to make pitchers work harder. Much harder.

Overall Statistics

	G	AB	R	H	D	T	HR	RBI	SB	BB	SO	AVG
1989	156	636	86	156	18	13	12	56	44	31	129	.245
Career	487	1788	280	455	74	21	48	197	102	100	359	.254

Where He Hits the Ball

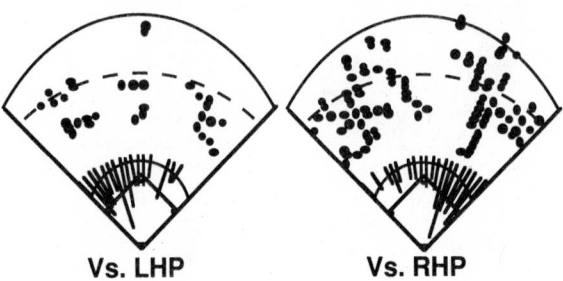

Vs. LHP   **Vs. RHP**

1989 Situational Stats

	AB	H	HR	RBI	AVG		AB	H	HR	RBI	AVG
Home	317	77	9	26	.243	LHP	214	53	2	17	.248
Road	319	79	3	30	.248	RHP	422	103	10	39	.244
Day	149	37	2	10	.248	Sc Pos	136	31	1	39	.228
Night	487	119	10	46	.244	Clutch	85	18	0	4	.212

1989 Rankings (American League)

- ➡ 2nd in triples (13) and steals of third (11)
- ➡ 3rd in stolen bases and lowest on-base average (.282) - *players with 502 PA*
- ➡ 4th in at bats (636)
- ➡ 5th in caught stealing (16)
- ➡ 8th in strikeouts (129)
- ➡ 10th in runs (86)
- ➡ Led the Angels in stikeouts, at bats, runs, triples, stolen bases, caught stealing, plate appearances (678), stolen base percentage (73.3%), bunts in play (20) and steals of third
- ➡ Led AL Centerfielders in triples and steals of third

PITCHING:

What's happened to Mike Witt, once one of the league's most dominant hurlers? Once the ace of the staff, Witt has fallen to the Angels' No. 4 pitcher -- maybe even No. 5. A 6-foot-7 righthander with one of the best curveballs in baseball, Witt won 15 games in both 1984 and '85 and was brilliant in the Angels' title season of 1986, winning 18 games, completing 14 and posting a 2.84 ERA. He's gone downhill ever since. His ensuing ERAs are 4.01 in 1987, 4.15 in 1988 and 4.54 last year. His strikeouts have decreased from 208 (in 1986) to 192 (1987) to 133 (1988) to 123 (last season). Last season, he compiled his worst record -- 9-15 -- since going 7-14 in 1983.

The theory is that all the innings Witt has logged over the years have taken a toll on his arm, causing a decrease in velocity. He did, after all, pitch 246 innings or more for five straight years (1984-88). His fastball once got up to about 93-94 mph, but it tops out now at 90. He's had to rely on his curveball more, and when he doesn't get it over, hitters sit on his fastball and crank it. His curveball, though, can drive hitters batty and make them look like minor leaguers. Witt, who throws with a straight overhand motion, also has a changeup, but doesn't use it much. He doesn't have the confidence in it that he does in his fastball and curve. Hitters teed off against Witt last year, belting 26 homers -- 12 more than they hit off him in 1988. Witt permitted 252 hits in 220 innings, easily the worst hits-to-innings ratio of his career.

FIELDING:

Witt is a below-average fielder. He often freezes and waves at balls as they whiz by. Former Angels Manager Gene Mauch often ripped Witt for his inability to field comebackers. Witt also has problems fielding bunts and slow grounders. Witt has an excellent move to first, however, and is very tough to steal on.

OVERALL:

Witt's rapid decline is a mystery. He hasn't complained of arm or shoulder soreness, so it doesn't appear as if he needs surgery. Maybe it's psychological. Witt was seeing a psychologist at one time to help him become more positive and optimistic, but said last year that he had no interest in resuming the sessions. Something has to be done, though. Witt simply shouldn't be washed up at 29. But three consecutive poor years is reason for the Angels to be concerned.

MIKE WITT

Position: SP
Bats: R **Throws:** R
Ht: 6' 7" **Wt:** 198

Opening Day Age: 29
Born: 7/20/60 in Fullerton, CA
ML Seasons: 9

Overall Statistics

	W	L	ERA	G	GS	Sv	IP	H	R	BB	SO	HR
1989	9	15	4.54	33	33	0	220.0	252	119	48	123	26
Career	109	104	3.78	304	272	5	1945.0	1913	917	643	1269	166

Where They Hit the Ball

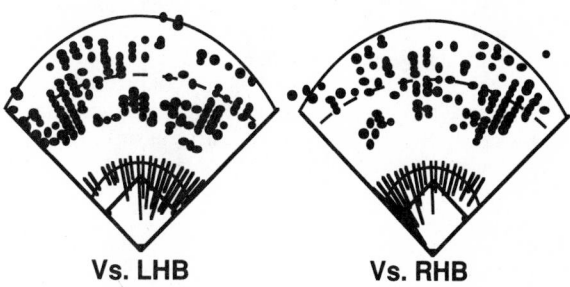

Vs. LHB   Vs. RHB

1989 Situational Stats

	W	L	ERA	Sv	IP		AB	H	HR	RBI	AVG
Home	5	7	4.85	0	107.2	LHB	432	128	12	44	.296
Road	4	8	4.25	0	112.1	RHB	432	124	14	59	.287
Day	6	4	3.06	0	100.0	Sc Pos	174	54	5	76	.310
Night	3	11	5.78	0	120.0	Clutch	75	27	1	7	.360

1989 Rankings (American League)

➡ Worst opponent batting average (.292) - *pitchers with 162 IP*

➡ 2nd in most losses (15) and most hits allowed (252)

➡ 3rd most home runs allowed (26)

➡ 5th in worst earned run average (4.54) - *pitchers with 162 IP*

➡ Led the Angels in games started (33), most losses, most hits allowed, most home runs allowed and most pitches thrown (3,471)

DANTE BICHETTE

Position: RF/LF
Bats: R **Throws:** R
Ht: 6' 3" **Wt:** 215

Opening Day Age: 26
Born: 11/18/63 in West Palm Beach, FL
ML Seasons: 2

GLENN HOFFMAN

Position: 3B/SS
Bats: R **Throws:** R
Ht: 6' 2" **Wt:** 190

Opening Day Age: 31
Born: 7/7/58 in Orange, CA
ML Seasons: 9

Overall Statistics

	G	AB	R	H	D	T	HR	RBI	SB	BB	SO	AVG
1989	48	138	13	29	7	0	3	15	3	6	24	.210
Career	69	184	14	41	9	0	3	23	3	6	31	.223

Overall Statistics

	G	AB	R	H	D	T	HR	RBI	SB	BB	SO	AVG
1989	48	104	9	22	3	0	1	3	0	3	13	.212
Career	766	2163	247	524	106	9	23	210	5	136	309	.242

HITTING, FIELDING, BASERUNNING:

Someday, Dante Bichette will be a mighty fine player. That's what the Angels are thinking -- and hoping for. Bichette, a free-swinging righthander still in the learning stages, gave the Angels a taste of what they can expect when he launched a 450-foot home run in Cleveland last year. But though he has great potential and talent, Bichette has a lot to learn. He strikes out a bit too much and walks too little. He has also had trouble with inside fastballs and breaking balls down and away. He especially has trouble against righthanders (he hit only .192 against righties) and hasn't learned to hit the opposite way consistently. At 6'3", 215 pounds, Bichette runs surprisingly well. He stole 25 bases at AA Quad City in 1985 and was 3 for 3 in steals for the Angels last year. He appears capable of stealing 12-15 bases during a full season. Defense may be Bichette's best attribute at this point. He has good instincts and reaction. He moves well in the outfield and has a good arm.

OVERALL:

Bichette has many skills and appears to be capable of hitting .290 with 20 homers and 75-80 RBI. He'll need to work to reach that level.

HITTING, FIELDING, BASERUNNING:

Glenn Hoffman was the starting shortstop for the Red Sox in 1982 and 1983, but he lost his job due to injuries and ineffectiveness; his career hasn't been the same since. Signed by the Angels as a free agent before last year, Hoffman is a good contact hitter who has a little power. He has a short, compact stroke and a good knowledge of the strike zone. He knows his capabilities. He can hit well to the opposite field, doesn't strike out much, and can hit an occasional homer. Hoffman is an intelligent baserunner who doesn't have a lot of speed, but also doesn't make mistakes on the bases. In the field he doesn't possess much range -- which was why he lost his job as a regular with Boston -- but he can play several positions and makes all the routine plays. His arm is only average.

OVERALL:

Hoffman had a few decent years with the bat in Boston. Now he is only an adequate backup infielder. He is no longer considered a potential starter. At 31, he can still help, offensively and defensively, but only as a fil-in.

MARK MCLEMORE

Position: 2B
Bats: B **Throws:** R
Ht: 5'11" **Wt:** 195

Opening Day Age: 25
Born: 10/4/64 in San Diego, CA
ML Seasons: 4

Overall Statistics

	G	AB	R	H	D	T	HR	RBI	SB	BB	SO	AVG
1989	32	103	12	25	3	1	0	14	6	7	19	.243
Career	252	773	111	183	27	6	5	71	44	81	121	.237

HITTING, FIELDING, BASERUNNING:

Poor Mark McLemore. When Bobby Grich retired in 1987, McLemore, a talented switch-hitter, was handed the starting job. He was doing very well when suddenly, out of the blue, the Angels acquired Johnny Ray from Pittsburgh; McLemore was out of a job for the rest of the pennant race. He got it back in '88 when the Halos moved a protesting Ray to left field. But when nerve irritation in McLemore's right arm took him out of the lineup, Ray returned to second. And McLemore hasn't been back since.

Still only 25, McLemore has the ability to hit for a decent average. He also has a little pop in his bat. He has a nice level swing, is patient, not overanxious, and knows the strike zone. He has good speed and stole 25 bases in 1987 and six in seven attempts last year. On defense McLemore has occasional lapses, but he has the potential and makeup to become one of the best in the league. McLemore has good range and mobility and a good arm.

OVERALL:

One of these days, second base will belong to McLemore. When it does, watch him blossom. He can hit, field and run. That combination equals success.

JOHN ORTON

Position: C
Bats: R **Throws:** R
Ht: 6' 1" **Wt:** 195

Opening Day Age: 24
Born: 12/8/65 in Santa Cruz, CA
ML Seasons: 1

Overall Statistics

	G	AB	R	H	D	T	HR	RBI	SB	BB	SO	AVG
1989	16	39	4	7	1	0	0	4	0	2	17	.179
Career	16	39	4	7	1	0	0	4	0	2	17	.179

HITTING, FIELDING, BASERUNNING:

John Orton is being billed as the Angels' catcher of the future. If so, the Angels received a glimpse of that future last year. They called Orton up when Lance Parrish was out with an injury. Playing in 16 games, Orton opened some eyes, especially with his defensive skills. He got off to a good start offensively, then struggled. One of his hits, though, was bases-loaded double that won a game. Orton, a righthanded hitter, has a smooth swing with a little pop in his bat. He has a short stroke but has to become more disciplined. Orton has good speed, but more importantly, he is a smart baserunner. He takes the extra base and doesn't make mistakes. Where Orton really shines is behind the plate. He has a good, strong arm. He's mobile and quick. He received many plaudits for his game-calling ability.

OVERALL:

Orton will travel up the Angels' minor league ladder fast. He will probably play at AAA Edmonton in 1990 and be in Anaheim by 1991. The Angels figure that will be his permanent address.

DAN
PETRY

Position: RP/SP
Bats: R **Throws:** R
Ht: 6' 4" **Wt:** 215

Opening Day Age: 31
Born: 11/13/58 in Palo Alto, CA
ML Seasons: 11

Overall Statistics

	W	L	ERA	G	GS	Sv	IP	H	R	BB	SO	HR
1989	3	2	5.47	19	4	0	51.0	53	32	23	21	8
Career	113	92	3.85	298	271	0	1829.2	1720	878	730	951	190

PITCHING & FIELDING:

Once one of the American League's elite pitchers, Dan Petry has been the victim of injury. The righthander with the herky-jerky motion won at least 15 games for four straight seasons (1982-85) before developing bone chips in his elbow, possibly caused by the stress from throwing his hard slider. Petry, who had a career record of 93-64 after the '85 season, is only 20-28 with an ERA over 4.50 since then.

Last season Petry was beaten out of the Angels' fifth starting spot by rookie Jim Abbott and worked middle relief with little success. He uses four pitches -- a fastball, changeup, curve and slider -- but has only regained a little of the velocity on his fastball. It still isn't adequate. The tenacious and intense Petry isn't afraid to pitch inside or challenge hitters. He's a super competitor. Despite being 6-foot-4, Petry gets off the mound quickly and is fundamentally sound on defense. He has a poor move to first.

OVERALL:

Petry hasn't had much success getting by on finesse. To win with an 86-mph fastball, he must have his breaking stuff working well and must be able to spot the ball well. You hate to write off a guy who's only 31, but so far the mix hasn't worked.

MAX
VENABLE

Position: RF
Bats: L **Throws:** R
Ht: 5'10" **Wt:** 185

Opening Day Age: 32
Born: 6/6/57 in Phoenix, AZ
ML Seasons: 10

Overall Statistics

	G	AB	R	H	D	T	HR	RBI	SB	BB	SO	AVG
1989	20	53	7	19	4	0	0	4	0	1	16	.358
Career	552	1021	126	242	40	12	11	86	57	85	157	.237

HITTING, FIELDING, BASERUNNING:

Max Venable, the epitome of a journeyman, enjoyed tremendous success with the Angels last season after his recall from AAA Edmonton. Formerly the property of the Dodgers, Giants, Expos, Reds and Orioles, Venable, a 32-year-old lefthanded hitter, did not even play in organized ball in 1988. Yet he amazed the Angels and everyone else by hitting .358 in 20 games. For Venable, it was the highest he's batted since entering professional ball in 1976. Previously, Venable's best major league season was in 1985 with the Reds, when he batted .289 in 77 games.

Venable is a good contact hitter who has a little power. He is able to hit to all fields. He has good bat control. He could display a little more patience; he walked once in 53 at-bats with California. He has good speed and once stole 46 bases in the minors. He's an average fielder, but can cover some ground.

OVERALL:

Venable may have extended his career a little longer with last year's performance. He doesn't have much of a chance to be a starter, especially at this point of his career. But he could fit in as a spare outfielder and pinch hitter.

IVAN CALDERON

Position: RF/DH/1B/LF
Bats: R **Throws:** R
Ht: 6' 1" **Wt:** 221

Opening Day Age: 28
Born: 3/19/62 in
Fajardo, Puerto Rico
ML Seasons: 6

HITTING:

A shoulder injury wrecked his 1988 campaign, but in 1989 Ivan Calderon was a one-man gang, leading the White Sox in at bats, runs, hits, doubles, triples, homers and RBIs. Though few noticed because he was playing for a last place club, Calderon dominated the club's leader board like no Sox hitter since Minnie Minoso in 1954.

Calderon is an aggressive hitter and loves to jump on the first pitch and drive it into the gaps. Because of that he'll never draw many walks, but he'll be successful as long as he lays off bad pitches. Pitchers who nibble, especially righthanders, can make him look foolish at times. Though he's capable of belting 450-foot homers, Calderon's a line drive hitter who hits the ball a long way to left and right center, rather than being a classic pull hitter. With his long, full swing he takes a long time to get out of the batter's box, and thus tends to hit into a lot of double plays.

BASERUNNING:

Calderon possesses good running speed but has never stolen many bases. His stolen base percentage in '89 was excellent (7 for 8), but the Sox were reluctant to send him, perhaps out of fear that he might reinjure his shoulder. Such conservatism is unlike Calderon. When he hits a gapper he's always trying to stretch a single into a double or a double into a triple, and gets many of his extra base hits that way. That aggressiveness costs him at times; he has gotten thrown out quite easily on the bases on a few occasions.

FIELDING:

While he makes some spectacular catches in right field, Calderon seems to lack good defensive instincts. He often dives recklessly, missing a catch or letting a ball get by him. He possesses a strong but not always accurate throwing arm. The White Sox experimented with Calderon at first base, though they limited his action there to protect his shoulder. He looked awkward there, but appears capable of learning the position. In truth, Calderon's best position is DH, but he has had trouble hitting when used in that slot.

OVERALL:

Often described as moody and temperamental, Calderon quieted his critics with his performance at bat in '89. Defense will always be a problem with him, but when healthy, Calderon is a potent offensive force.

Overall Statistics

	G	AB	R	H	D	T	HR	RBI	SB	BB	SO	AVG
1989	157	622	83	178	34	9	14	87	7	43	94	.286
Career	502	1826	271	499	110	16	67	249	29	167	358	.273

Where He Hits the Ball

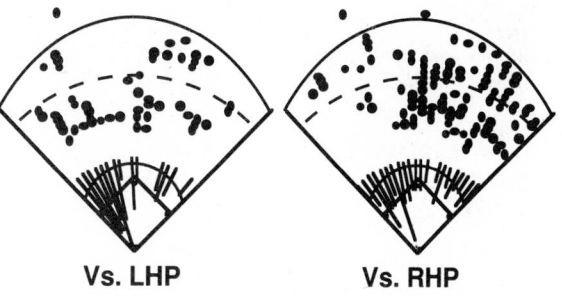

Vs. LHP **Vs. RHP**

1989 Situational Stats

	AB	H	HR	RBI	AVG		AB	H	HR	RBI	AVG
Home	286	71	2	34	.248	LHP	184	61	4	29	.332
Road	336	107	12	53	.318	RHP	438	117	10	58	.267
Day	174	49	5	31	.282	Sc Pos	163	44	5	69	.270
Night	448	129	9	56	.288	Clutch	100	30	1	14	.300

1989 Rankings (American League)

➡ 4th in triples (9) and road batting average (.318) - *players with 252 road PA*

➡ 8th in at bats (622)

➡ Led the White Sox in batting average (.286), home runs (14), at bats (622), runs (83), hits (178), doubles (34), triples, RBI (87), total bases (272), slugging percentage (.437), on-base average (.332), strikeouts (94), sacrifice flies (6), times on base (224), grounded in to double plays (20) and plate appearances (676) - *players with 502 PA*

➡ Led AL Right Fielders in singles (121), intentional walks (7), grounded into double plays and road batting average

PITCHING:

Richard Dotson was once a fastballer who won as many as 22 games. But he has seen his career jeopardized by chronic arm and shoulder problems. That career seemed about over when the Yankees released him in midseason '89, but the White Sox took a chance that he had something left. Though his 5-12 record doesn't show it, Dotson pitched well enough for Chicago to give him some hope for the future.

In his prime, Dotson had a fastball which reached the low nineties; he mixed that with an effective change, slider and curve. When injuries began to rob him of the fastball, Dotson relied more and more on his other pitches, especially the changeup. With the Yankees, even the change was getting raked around, but the Sox saw some flaws in Dotson's delivery and worked hard to reconstruct it. It took a while, but eventually the efforts paid off. Dotson's ERA after September 1 was 2.87. More heartening, the change and all his other pitches looked sharper. He even struck out 27 batters in 37.2 innings, a hopeful sign as the strikeout had almost disappeared from Dotson's arsenal.

Since his shoulder began to ache early in the '85 season, Dotson's major problem has been lack of consistency. He'd look good for a few outings, but then would go through periods where he simply couldn't get anyone out. To his credit, Dotson never complained about his injuries and has always been ready to take his turn whether he has his good stuff or not. But given his past problems, there has to be doubt about whether Dotson is able to sustain his September efforts over a full season. If he pitches like he did for the Yankees in '89, Dotson will have trouble holding a major league job.

FIELDING:

A thorough professional, Dotson has always helped himself by being an excellent glove man. He handles everything hit his way and holds baserunners extremely well.

OVERALL:

Dotson was a free agent after the '89 season and figured to get a few offers from clubs which need pitching. Certainly the White Sox were interested in bringing him back. With his excellent work habits and bulldog tenacity, Dotson is an excellent role model for the young Sox pitching staff. However, he'll have to prove he can continue his September work; if he can't, his future is very much in doubt.

RICH DOTSON

Position: SP
Bats: R **Throws:** R
Ht: 6' 0" **Wt:** 203

Opening Day Age: 31
Born: 1/10/59 in Cincinnati, OH
ML Seasons: 11

Overall Statistics

	W	L	ERA	G	GS	Sv	IP	H	R	BB	SO	HR
1989	5	12	4.46	28	26	0	151.1	181	84	58	69	16
Career	111	109	4.16	297	288	0	1828.1	1841	935	726	964	191

Where They Hit the Ball

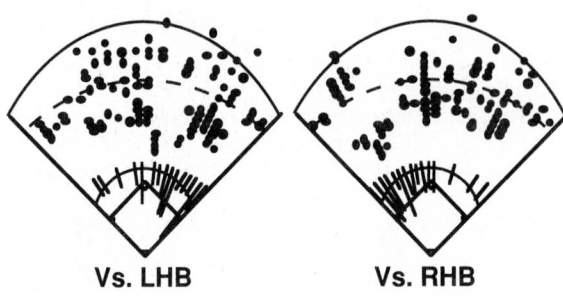

Vs. LHB   **Vs. RHB**

1989 Situational Stats

	W	L	ERA	Sv	IP		AB	H	HR	RBI	AVG
Home	3	7	4.54	0	73.1	LHB	313	91	9	44	.291
Road	2	5	4.38	0	78.0	RHB	302	90	7	30	.298
Day	2	2	4.76	0	39.2	Sc Pos	153	40	1	51	.261
Night	3	10	4.35	0	111.2	Clutch	34	6	0	1	.176

1989 Rankings (American League)

➡ 3rd in lowest winning percentage (.294) - *pitchers with 15 or more decisions*

HITTING:

Although injuries caused Carlton Fisk to miss a substantial portion of the season for the second year in a row, he continued to be among the top catchers in the American League in 1989. It's hard to believe this man is 42 and that the White Sox tried to end his catching career four years ago. The Fisk-to-left-field move was quickly aborted and, thereafter, Fisk has amassed some of his best numbers since the early 1980's.

There is no real way to get Pudge out consistently. He's best against the high fastball and has hit lefties better than righties in recent years, but he's strong against all types of pitching. The big change in '89 was that, under the tutelage of new Sox hitting coach Walt Hriniak, Fisk cut down on his swing a little and went with the pitch more to center and right field. The result was his highest average since 1977 . . . but also his lowest homer total since '81.

BASERUNNING:

As a catcher, Fisk is no longer the base-stealing threat who once swiped 17. In '89 he was successful in his only attempt of the season. As a baserunner, though, he moves surprisingly well for a player of his age and position. He's a smart aggressive runner who's unafraid of barreling into a base.

FIELDING:

Long one of the top fielding catchers in the AL, Fisk's skills have lessened somewhat as the years have passed. But his handling of the Sox young pitching staff and his knowledge of opposing hitters still make him an extremely valuable backstop. The Sox staff ERA was approximately one run lower with Fisk in the game than with other catchers. Carlton threw out 30% of opposing baserunners trying to steal against him, a fair average.

OVERALL:

As a team leader and role model for younger players, not to mention first-rate hitter and catcher, Fisk's value to the White Sox remains very high. But he's now 42 and may not last much beyond 1990. Sometime during the '90 season (barring injury) he figures to hit his 328th home run as a catcher, breaking Johnny Bench's all-time record. There's little else he hasn't accomplished during a Hall of Fame career.

CARLTON FISK

Position: C/DH
Bats: R **Throws:** R
Ht: 6' 2" **Wt:** 225

Opening Day Age: 42
Born: 12/26/47 in Bellows Falls, VT
ML Seasons: 20

Overall Statistics

	G	AB	R	H	D	T	HR	RBI	SB	BB	SO	AVG
1989	103	375	47	110	25	2	13	68	1	36	60	.293
Career	2141	7603	1155	2063	371	46	336	1166	117	731	1178	.271

Where He Hits the Ball

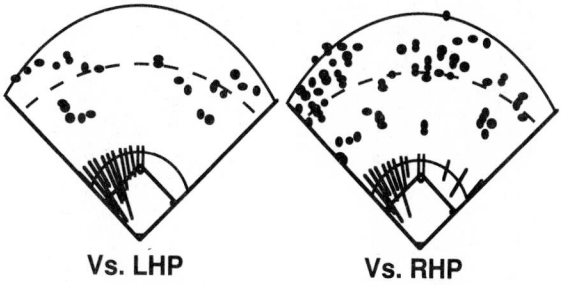

Vs. LHP	Vs. RHP

1989 Situational Stats

	AB	H	HR	RBI	AVG		AB	H	HR	RBI	AVG
Home	172	59	4	32	.343	LHP	120	39	4	22	.325
Road	203	51	9	36	.251	RHP	255	71	9	46	.278
Day	55	14	3	12	.255	Sc Pos	105	37	4	49	.352
Night	320	96	10	56	.300	Clutch	70	21	2	15	.300

1989 Rankings (American League)

- → 2nd in hitting on an 0-2 count (.370) - *players with 20 PA*
- → 4th in hitting with runners in scoring position (.352) - *players with 100 PA*
- → Led the White Sox in hitting on an 0-2 count and hitting with runners in scoring position
- → Led AL Catchers in doubles (25), RBI (68), intentional walks (8), hitting with runners in scoring position and hitting against left-handed pitchers (.325) - *catchers with 125 PA against LHP*

HITTING:

Scott Fletcher was acquired from Texas along with Sammy Sosa and Wilson Alvarez in the controversial Harold Baines trade. It was hoped that he would bring some stability to the second base position, where many hopefuls have enjoyed mixed (at best) success over the past few seasons. By the end of the year, Scotty had done exactly that, and has made his part of the trade hold up quite well.

Fletcher is basically a singles hitter. He uses the whole field and seldom tries to pull the ball. He has better success against left-handed pitchers and sometimes struggles against those with slow, breaking stuff. Scotty seldom hits home runs -- his lone homer this year was his first in over two years -- but he can find the outfield gaps with enough regularity to put up some pretty good doubles numbers. He's a patient hitter, willing to wait for a good pitch to hit. Over his career he's walked more times than he has struck out. With only 42 RBIs for the season, he's not a big run producer; his value comes from his ability to get on base and move runners along.

BASERUNNING:

Scotty is now 31 years old and has never been a big base-stealer (56 over his career). He has probably lost a step and he attempted only 3 steals this year. But he runs the bases well and seldom makes a costly error.

FIELDING:

Though he played little at second base during his years with Texas, Fletcher looked right at home there with the White Sox. He played errorless ball at second with the Sox and showed better than average range. He also worked well with Ozzie Guillen on the double play, making a good pivot and getting off a good throw back to first. His overall play rates him as a solid second baseman, and along with Guillen gives the Sox two dependable performers up the middle.

OVERALL:

Although his salary is on the high side for the thrifty White Sox, Fletcher looks like he'll be the regular Sox second baseman for awhile. The Sox will be perfectly happy if he can continue his good performance of last August and September into next year, but with more work with Sox hitting coach Walt Hriniak, Scotty may even be able to improve on it a bit. Unless he's traded, the Sox search for a second baseman seems to be over.

SCOTT FLETCHER

Position: SS/2B
Bats: R **Throws:** R
Ht: 5'11" **Wt:** 173

Opening Day Age: 31
Born: 7/30/58 in Fort Walton Beach, FL
ML Seasons: 9

Overall Statistics

	G	AB	R	H	D	T	HR	RBI	SB	BB	SO	AVG
1989	142	546	77	138	25	2	1	43	2	64	60	.253
Career	997	3268	436	875	147	24	17	302	56	350	343	.268

Where He Hits the Ball

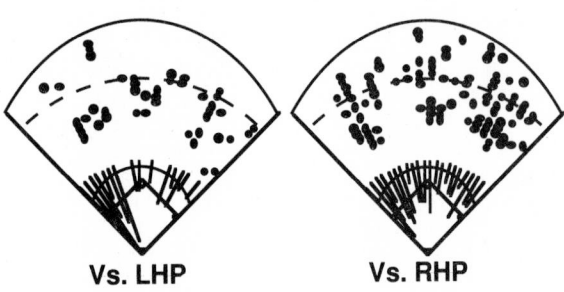

Vs. LHP   Vs. RHP

1989 Situational Stats

	AB	H	HR	RBI	AVG		AB	H	HR	RBI	AVG
Home	270	69	0	21	.256	LHP	164	46	0	10	.280
Road	276	69	1	22	.250	RHP	382	92	1	33	.241
Day	128	31	0	8	.242	Sc Pos	138	33	0	41	.239
Night	418	107	1	35	.256	Clutch	84	17	0	6	.202

1989 Rankings (American League)

→ 3rd in worst home run frequency (546 ABs per HR) and percentage of pitches taken (65.6%) - *players with 502 PA*

→ 4th lowest slugging percentage (.311)

→ 7th in percentage of swings put into play (56.0%)

→ 8th in bunts in play (24)

→ 9th in grounder/flyball ratio (1.92)

→ Led AL Shortstops in runs scored per time reached base (33.8%)

HITTING:

Will the real Dave Gallagher please stand up? After nine minor league seasons, Gallagher made the most of his first extended chance when he batted .303 in 1988. Some called it a fluke, but in midseason last year Gallagher was hitting .300 again, drawing some walks and looking like the best White Sox leadoff man in years. But from then on Gallagher hit only .221, an especially unacceptable average for someone who's strictly a singles hitter. At first it seemed like just a temporary slump, but as the bad times continued, Gallagher began to press. He consistently chased pitches out of the strike zone -- he drew only eleven walks after the All Star break -- and soon lost his leadoff slot to Lance Johnson. Gallagher continued to appear in every game, but by September he was being used more and more as a late-inning sub.

Gallagher is an intelligent player who markets his own batting aid called the "Stride Tutor." At his best, he is a stinging, line-drive hitter who belts the ball up the middle. He handles the bat well and is an excellent hit-and-run man. He's also an excellent bunter who can lay one down for a hit on occasion. He's shown a weakness against high inside fastballs, and will need to do better against those offerings if he wants to hold a regular job.

BASERUNNING:

Gallagher, who possesses only above average speed, is not a good base stealer. In two Chicago seasons he's stolen a total of only ten bases while being thrown out the same number of times. He is, however, very aggressive running the bases and gets the absolute maximum out of what speed he has. He is easily the best baserunner on the White Sox team.

FIELDING:

Gallagher has spent most of his White Sox years playing center field, in part because the Sox had no viable alternative. He lacks the blazing speed a good center fielder needs, though he plays hitters very well and tracks down everything he can reach. He has a good, accurate throwing arm.

OVERALL:

Since he lacks both speed and power, Gallagher really needs to hit at least .280, and maybe more, to justify an everyday spot. His second-half performance in '89 casts doubt on his ability to do that. But with his other skills and great intelligence, Gallagher figures to stick in the majors, if only as a reserve.

DAVE GALLAGHER

Position: CF/RF
Bats: R **Throws:** R
Ht: 6' 0" **Wt:** 180

Opening Day Age: 29
Born: 9/20/60 in Trenton, NJ
ML Seasons: 3

Overall Statistics

	G	AB	R	H	D	T	HR	RBI	SB	BB	SO	AVG
1989	161	601	74	160	22	2	1	46	5	46	79	.266
Career	277	984	135	269	38	6	6	78	12	77	124	.273

Where He Hits the Ball

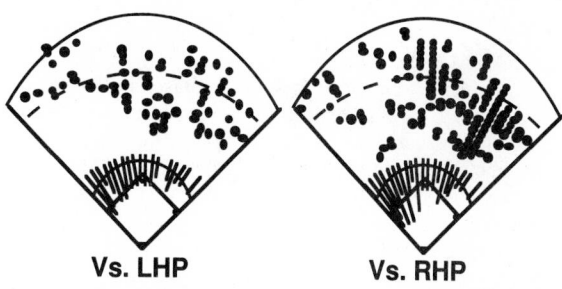

Vs. LHP   **Vs. RHP**

1989 Situational Stats

	AB	H	HR	RBI	AVG		AB	H	HR	RBI	AVG
Home	289	78	1	21	.270	LHP	200	56	0	20	.280
Road	312	82	0	25	.263	RHP	401	104	1	26	.259
Day	168	42	1	10	.250	Sc Pos	153	39	1	45	.255
Night	433	118	0	36	.273	Clutch	98	19	0	5	.194

1989 Rankings (American League)

- ➥ 1st in worst home run frequency (601 ABs per HR)
- ➥ 4th in sacrifice bunts (16) and games (161)
- ➥ 5th in lowest slugging percentage (.314) and bunts in play (32) - *players with 502 PA*
- ➥ 9th in singles (135)
- ➥ Led the White Sox in singles, sacrifice bunts, pitches seen (2,536), games, pitches seen per plate appearance (3.8), and batting average with 2 strikes (.256)
- ➥ Led AL Center Fielders in sacrifice bunts, pitches seen, bunts in play, and lowest percentage of swings that missed (11.6%) - *players with 502 PA*

GREAT RANGE

OZZIE GUILLEN

Position: SS
Bats: L **Throws:** R
Ht: 5'11" **Wt:** 153

Opening Day Age: 26
Born: 1/20/64 in Miranda, Venezuela
ML Seasons: 5

HITTING:

After five full seasons as the White Sox regular short-stop, Ozzie Guillen is still only 26 and should be approaching the prime of his baseball career. So it is somewhat bothersome to notice the lack of progress Ozzie has displayed at the plate.

Ozzie's average has declined from his high of .279 in 1987 to just .253 in '89. And even that .253 mark would have been considerably lower if Ozzie had not had a .311 hot streak in July. Never one to accept a base on balls if the pitch is in the same zip code, Ozzie also walked only 15 times in '89, adding up to a poor .270 on base percentage. Not a power hitter, Ozzie likes to go to the opposite field and has his best success dumping liners into short left field. He's a good fastball hitter, especially in situations where he can expect a hard one on the first pitch. Guillen hit well with men in scoring position last year and had a new career high in RBIs with 54.

BASERUNNING:

Ozzie had his career high in stolen bases in '89 with 36, but was caught stealing 17 times, not an outstanding success rate. He is aggressive on the bases and often challenges the opposition by going for the extra base. His 8 triples were good enough for second on the White Sox, trailing only Ivan Calderon.

FIELDING:

It is in the field that Guillen really shines. Over the past few years he has been among the top defensive shortstops in the game. He covers an incredible amount of ground, has a strong arm capable of making the throw from deep in the hole, and possesses sure, soft hands that seldom miss those scalded grounders and tricky short hops. He is also outstanding on the double play, a big reason why the Sox were second in the Majors in this department. About his only weakness is that he makes an occasional careless error.

OVERALL:

Ozzie is a big part of the White Sox plans for the future, and figures to be their starting shortstop for a long time to come. But he needs to turn his offensive game around and be more patient at the plate to be a truly outstanding all-around shortstop. If he can do that, he can be one of the best shortstops in the game in the early nineties.

Overall Statistics

	G	AB	R	H	D	T	HR	RBI	SB	BB	SO	AVG
1989	155	597	63	151	20	8	1	54	36	15	48	.253
Career	769	2761	314	726	98	35	6	224	101	86	228	.263

Where He Hits the Ball

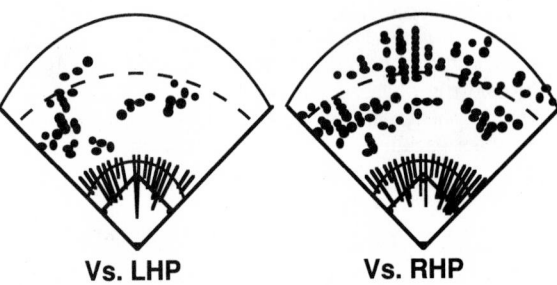

Vs. LHP   **Vs. RHP**

1989 Situational Stats

	AB	H	HR	RBI	AVG		AB	H	HR	RBI	AVG
Home	292	70	0	23	.240	LHP	209	53	0	17	.254
Road	305	81	1	31	.266	RHP	388	98	1	37	.253
Day	163	44	0	12	.270	Sc Pos	155	42	0	50	.271
Night	434	107	1	42	.247	Clutch	110	33	0	12	.300

1989 Rankings (American League)

→ 2nd in worst home run frequency (597 ABs per HR), lowest percentage of pitches taken (41.2%), on-base average (.270), and errors (22) - *players with 502 PA*

→ 3rd in caught stealing (17) and least pitches seen per plate appearance (2.9)

→ 7th in stolen bases (36)

→ 8th in triples (8) and hitting on an 0-2 count (.300) - *players with 20 PA on an 0-2 count*

→ Led the White Sox in stolen bases, caught stealing, grounder/flyball ratio (1.69), and lowest percentage of swings that missed (11.4%)

→ Led AL Shortstops in singles (122), stolen bases, and caught stealing

PITCHING:

One of the few bright spots in a lackluster 1989 White Sox season was the emergence of Greg Hibbard as a dependable major league pitcher. Hibbard was brought up at the end of May when most of the other Sox starters were ineffective. For the rest of the year he was the most consistent starter on the staff. And, as we shall see below, the unluckiest.

Hibbard has a fair fastball, but he relies mainly on his breaking stuff to keep the hitters off balance. Because he doesn't throw really hard and keeps the ball down, he allowed only 5 home runs in his 137 innings, an excellent ratio. Greg doesn't strike out a lot of batters, but he helps himself by not walking many either. These two factors combined to help him post a team leading 3.21 ERA (among starters) even though opposing hitters batted a fairly lusty .268 against him.

Hibbard was a model of consistency; his monthly ERAs ranged from 3.00 to 3.42 and only once in 23 starts did he give up as many as five runs. He often tires around the fifth or sixth inning and reached the seventh in only nine of his starts. With a bit more support from his teammates, Greg's record might have been much more respectable. He lost seven times, and in those games the Sox offense scored a grand total of seven runs on his behalf, getting shut out in three of them. In his 10 no-decision starts, he gave up two runs or less four times, but came away with nothing to show for it. With a little better luck he might well have finished up closer to 12-5 for the season. Whoever said it's better to be lucky than good just might be onto something.

FIELDING:

Hibbard has a good move to first and holds opposing baserunners close enough to give his catcher a chance to throw them out. Defensively, he seldom hurts himself on the field and plays his position well.

OVERALL:

Based on his strong '89 performance, the Sox are relying on Hibbard to be part of the starting rotation in 1990. With the consistency he showed last year, it would be a surprise indeed if his game fell off drastically. With a few more runs to work with from his teammates, and a turn for the better in his fortunes, he figures to turn in a solid 1990 season.

GREG HIBBARD

Position: SP
Bats: L **Throws:** L
Ht: 6' 0" **Wt:** 180

Opening Day Age: 25
Born: 9/13/64 in New Orleans, LA
ML Seasons: 1

Overall Statistics

	W	L	ERA	G	GS	Sv	IP	H	R	BB	SO	HR
1989	6	7	3.21	23	23	0	137.1	142	58	41	55	5
Career	6	7	3.21	23	23	0	137.1	142	58	41	55	5

Where They Hit the Ball

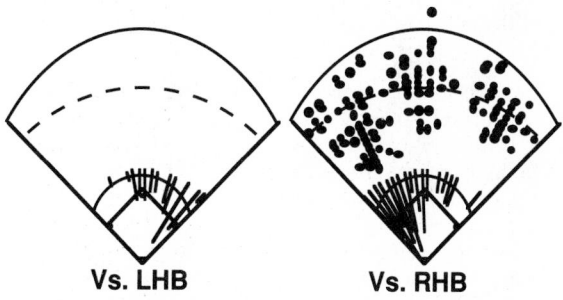

Vs. LHB   **Vs. RHB**

1989 Situational Stats

	W	L	ERA	Sv	IP		AB	H	HR	RBI	AVG
Home	4	3	2.86	0	69.1	LHB	68	21	0	8	.309
Road	2	4	3.57	0	68.0	RHB	461	121	5	40	.262
Day	3	1	3.57	0	35.1	Sc Pos	126	31	0	38	.246
Night	3	6	3.09	0	102.0	Clutch	31	10	0	0	.323

1989 Rankings (American League)

➡ Led the White Sox in complete games (2) and least HRs per 9 innings (.33) - *all team pitchers*

PITCHING:

Shawn Hillegas was once considered one of the gems of the Dodger farm system, but he has yet to achieve major league success. It's hard to see why he hasn't, because he certainly appears to have the stuff. A big, hard-throwing righthander, Hillegas possesses a fastball that can reach the 90 mile mark along with a decent curve and changeup.

Hillegas began 1989 as a member of the White Sox starting rotation, but had pitched his way out of it before the end of May. Relegated to a middleman/set-up role, Hillegas immediately began to pitch much better. The difference may have been that, in relief, Hillegas could simply rear back and throw without worrying about getting cute. At any rate, he worked effectively out of the pen for three months. But when the Sox returned him to the rotation in September, he floundered once more. For the year Hillegas had a hideous 6.00 ERA as a starter; in relief his ERA was 3.19.

If Hillegas is ever going to be a successful major league hurler, he will need to sharpen his control. His '89 walk ratio was on the high side (3.8 per nine innings); more significantly, he had considerable difficulty when he got behind in the count. In plate appearances in which Hillegas got the first pitch over for a strike, he held opponents to a .234 average. But when the first pitch was a ball, opponents lit him up for a .302 mark.

Hillegas also needs to improve his work against left-handed hitters, who batted over .300 against him in '89. The problem may be that he doesn't pitch inside enough to keep lefty swingers from digging in.

FIELDING:

Hillegas is only an average glove man but makes up for that with his ability to hold baserunners. In '89 opponents stole only six bases off him while being thrown out eight times. That record is surprisingly good for a righthanded fastballer.

OVERALL:

Hillegas is only 25 and still has time to become a winning major league hurler. He certainly has the ability. What he needs to do is believe in himself more, stop nibbling and get a little more aggressive. His bullpen work in '89 suggests that he's heading in the right direction, but he will have to prove himself as a starter to join the starting rotation again.

SHAWN HILLEGAS

Position: RP/SP
Bats: R **Throws:** R
Ht: 6' 2" **Wt:** 208

Opening Day Age: 25
Born: 8/21/64 in Dos Palos, CA
ML Seasons: 3

Overall Statistics

	W	L	ERA	G	GS	Sv	IP	H	R	BB	SO	HR
1989	7	11	4.74	50	13	3	119.2	132	67	51	76	12
Career	17	20	4.13	79	39	3	274.1	268	136	117	183	26

Where They Hit the Ball

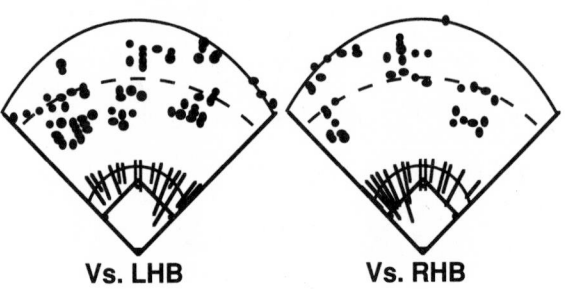

Vs. LHB   **Vs. RHB**

1989 Situational Stats

	W	L	ERA	Sv	IP		AB	H	HR	RBI	AVG
Home	6	5	4.62	1	60.1	LHB	226	70	4	32	.310
Road	1	6	4.85	2	59.1	RHB	247	62	8	31	.251
Day	1	4	7.97	0	20.1	Sc Pos	133	37	4	50	.278
Night	6	7	4.08	3	99.1	Clutch	109	32	2	12	.294

1989 Rankings (American League)

→ Led the White Sox in lowest stolen base percentage (42.9%) and holds (9) - *all team pitchers*

HITTING:

Lance Johnson was obtained from the Cardinals in a big '88 deal that featured Rick Horton and Jose Deleon. But he batted only .185 that year and was considered a bitter disappointment. Given only a cursory look last year in spring training, he spent the first half of the season in the minors. When the Sox recalled him in late July, expectations were so low that Lance's role figured to consist mostly of pinch-running and late-inning defensive work.

Thank goodness for second chances. Johnson got a start, performed well, and after that the Sox simply couldn't get him out of the lineup. A bit overawed in his '88 trial, Johnson relaxed and resembled the prospect who had hit over .300 four times in his minor league career. Johnson is a Matty Alou-type hitter; he possesses little power but has excellent bat control and can slap the ball to all fields. He gets a good number of leg hits and usually tries drag bunting at least once a game. A natural lefthanded hitter, he did exhibit some weakness against southpaws; toward the end of the season, the Sox began sitting him down when a lefthander took the hill. Johnson also looked overmatched at times versus good fastballers. He is not an especially patient hitter and needs to draw more walks in order to be a top leadoff man.

BASERUNNING:

Once he gets to first base, Johnson is capable of wreaking havoc on enemy pitchers. A brilliant base stealer, he swiped 16 bases in 19 attempts and injected some badly needed excitement into the White Sox attack. He reads pitchers' moves intently and almost always seems to get a good jump. Johnson does get overly aggressive when running the bases and occasionally gets caught trying to take the extra base.

FIELDING:

Johnson is an outstanding flychaser who has great range and instincts for the ball. In his two-month stint last year he made a number of brilliant catches, robbing opponents of home runs on a couple of occasions. Johnson is a small man; he does not have a strong arm and is thus better suited for left field than either center or right.

OVERALL:

Johnson's play in the last two months of '89 quite literally resurrected his career. The White Sox desperately need speed on both offense and defense, so he figures to get lots of playing time in 1990. With any consistency, Johnson will easily steal 50 bases.

LANCE JOHNSON

Position: LF
Bats: L **Throws:** L
Ht: 5'11" **Wt:** 155

Opening Day Age: 26
Born: 7/7/63 in Lincoln Hts, OH
ML Seasons: 3

Overall Statistics

	G	AB	R	H	D	T	HR	RBI	SB	BB	SO	AVG
1989	50	180	28	54	8	2	0	16	16	17	24	.300
Career	116	363	43	90	14	4	0	29	28	27	41	.248

Where He Hits the Ball

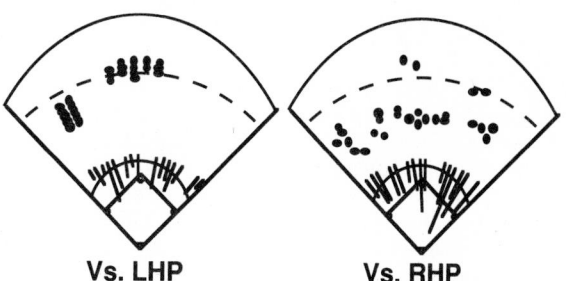

Vs. LHP   **Vs. RHP**

1989 Situational Stats

	AB	H	HR	RBI	AVG		AB	H	HR	RBI	AVG
Home	84	23	0	7	.274	LHP	58	15	0	4	.259
Road	96	31	0	9	.323	RHP	122	39	0	12	.320
Day	50	12	0	3	.240	Sc Pos	45	14	0	15	.311
Night	130	42	0	13	.323	Clutch	34	8	0	0	.235

1989 Rankings (American League)

➡ 3rd in percentage of extra bases taken per opportunity (59.5%) - *players with 40 opportunities*

➡ 8th in times thrown out trying to advance an extra base (5)

➡ Led the White Sox in steals of third (3) and percentage of extra bases taken per opportunity

➡ Led AL Left Fielders in percentage of extra bases taken per opportunity

RON KARKOVICE

Position: C
Bats: R **Throws:** R
Ht: 6' 1" **Wt:** 215

Opening Day Age: 26
Born: 8/8/63 in Union, NJ
ML Seasons: 4

HITTING:

After hitting just .168 in portions of three previous seasons with the White Sox, it looked like Ron Karkovice would never be more than a good-field, no-hit catcher. But thanks to a special effort by new Sox hitting coach Walt Hriniak, Ron hit a solid .264 in '89, a remarkable turnaround. Once a total sucker for a curveball in the dirt, he particularly improved against breaking balls. He also showed surprising bunting ability, working several successful squeezes and beating out a few bunt hits.

Ron began the season as Fisk's backup, but saw a lot of playing time when Carlton went on the DL. Through the first half of the season, Karko was hitting around .220, no major improvement. But he ignited in July and August, hitting over .350 those two months.

In spite of the improved batting average, Ron still has a lot of room for improvement. He seldom walks and he strikes out too much for a hitter without good power. A good fastballer can still blow him away. He hit only .225 in late-inning clutch situations, striking out almost half the time. But Karkovice is a hard worker, and given the tremendous progress he's made this year, further improvement is likely. Last year's performance helped Karko believe in himself as a major league hitter, and that confidence should serve him well in the future.

BASERUNNING:

For a catcher, Karkovice has pretty good speed. He can steal an occasional base and leg out a few extra base hits. He was used as a pinch runner on occasion by the Sox in '89 and gets around the bases fairly well.

FIELDING:

Karkovice probably has the strongest arm of any catcher in baseball, and makes it even more effective by his ability to get rid of the ball so quickly on throws to the bases. Karko has thrown out about 50% of the runners that have attempted to steal a base against him in the last two years, a simply phenomenal rate. His work in handling pitchers could still use some improvement. With Fisk catching, the team's ERA was almost a full run lower (3.80) in 1989 than with Karko behind the plate (4.75).

OVERALL:

Karkovice figures to begin next season as Fisk's backup, but with Carlton's retirement looming in the foreseeable future, the '90 season will be a most important one for Ron. If he can show that his hitting in '89 was not a fluke, and continue to improve his offensive game, he'll get his chance as a starting major league catcher.

Overall Statistics

	G	AB	R	H	D	T	HR	RBI	SB	BB	SO	AVG
1989	71	182	21	48	9	2	3	24	0	10	56	.264
Career	193	479	51	98	20	2	12	53	8	33	163	.205

Where He Hits the Ball

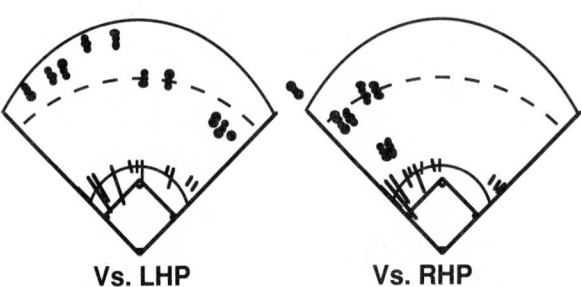

Vs. LHP   **Vs. RHP**

1989 Situational Stats

	AB	H	HR	RBI	AVG		AB	H	HR	RBI	AVG
Home	87	21	0	8	.241	LHP	88	25	1	13	.284
Road	95	27	3	16	.284	RHP	94	23	2	11	.245
Day	104	28	3	18	.269	Sc Pos	50	14	2	21	.280
Night	78	20	0	6	.256	Clutch	40	9	0	2	.225

1989 Rankings (American League)

→ 5th in throwing out base stealers (49.0%) - *all league catchers*

→ Led the White Sox in least GDPs per GDP situation (0%)

→ Led AL Catchers in bunts in play (20) and least GDPs per GDP situation

PITCHING:

The 1989 season was Eric King's first real opportunity as a regular starting pitcher. Despite an injury that forced him to spend a month on the disabled list, he put together a pretty impressive season.

King went through a few different stages last season. After losing his first three starts he entered a phase where he was almost untouchable, allowing only four earned runs in four starts, but then began having control problems, walking five to seven men in some games. After five straight losses, he went on the DL with a sore shoulder. Maybe he was trying to throw too hard. When he returned from the DL, he was much more effective. His control returned, but his strikeouts also declined. He finished up the season with a snappy ERA of 1.98 in September.

King is a hard thrower and throws several different pitches, including a couple of different fastballs -- one that rides into a righthanded hitter and one that moves away -- as well as a good hard curve. In past years he was capable of blowing hitters away, but his strikeout total was way down last year, perhaps because of his arm trouble. Whatever the case, he was much more of a finesse hurler with the Sox than he'd been with Detroit. He was most effective when he kept the ball down in the strike zone, and threw more double play balls than any pitcher on the Sox staff.

Sox Manager Jeff Torborg let King throw a lot of pitches in the beginning of the season -- more than 100 in 8 of 10 consecutive starts, with a high of 140. This, no doubt, contributed to his arm problems soon afterward. After his return, Torborg watched King more closely and let him go over 100 pitches in only 3 of his last 12 starts. The results show that King is much more effective when used this way.

FIELDING:

King did well holding runners close to first base; only 13 of 21 baserunners stole successfully against him. Defensively, Eric needs some work fielding his position. He needs to improve his play covering first; several times during the year opposition runners were safe because King didn't get over to cover the bag in time.

OVERALL:

King figures to be one of the regular Sox starters during the '90 season. At his young age, he has a chance to contribute to the Sox staff for many years to come.

ERIC KING

Position: SP
Bats: R **Throws:** R
Ht: 6' 2" **Wt:** 180

Opening Day Age: 26
Born: 4/10/64 in Oxnard, CA
ML Seasons: 4

Overall Statistics

	W	L	ERA	G	GS	Sv	IP	H	R	BB	SO	HR
1989	9	10	3.39	25	25	0	159.1	144	69	64	72	13
Career	30	24	3.79	136	50	15	482.1	423	218	221	285	44

Where They Hit the Ball

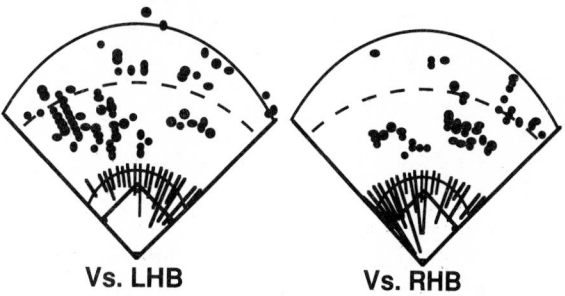

Vs. LHB   Vs. RHB

1989 Situational Stats

	W	L	ERA	Sv	IP		AB	H	HR	RBI	AVG
Home	6	7	3.20	0	98.1	LHB	308	71	11	30	.231
Road	3	3	3.69	0	61.0	RHB	283	73	2	25	.258
Day	1	4	4.45	0	30.1	Sc Pos	123	30	2	41	.244
Night	8	6	3.14	0	129.0	Clutch	52	11	0	2	.212

1989 Rankings (American League)

- ➡ 4th in GDPs induced (25)
- ➡ 8th in GDPs induced per GDP situation (19.4%) - *pitchers with 30 GDP situations*
- ➡ Led the White Sox in GDPs induced and won/loss percentage (.474) - *pitchers with 15 or more decisions*

HITTING:

Ron Kittle was a favorite of White Sox fans during his previous tour of duty with the team. He was reacquired as a free agent by the Sox before the beginning of the '89 season. Fondly remembered for his prodigious home run clouts (including six onto the Comiskey park roof), Kittle got off to a fine start that earned him AL player of the month honors in May. Always a powerful home run hitter, Ron had never hit for much of an average -- his lifetime batting average was .237 after the 1988 season. But under the tutelage of Walt Hriniak, Kittle flourished, posting a .371 May batting average and winding up with a .302 mark, by far his best batting average ever. Ron hit well with men in scoring position and was a dependable clutch hitter. Unfortunately, the season ended early in June for Kittle, when a nagging back problem required surgery.

Kittle is not at all the slugging Dave Kingman type he's sometimes dismissed as. He's had a bad habit of chasing breaking balls in the dirt, but he seems to be learning some discipline. He's primarily a pull hitter, but he's capable of going the other way enough to keep the defense honest. And he hits righthanders as well or better than he does lefties.

BASERUNNING:

Like many power hitters, Kittle has little foot speed and must be a cautious baserunner. Stealing bases is usually out of the question for him unless the opposition is napping. He must be classified with the slow runners in the league, and after his back surgery will likely be even slower.

FIELDING:

Employed in the past as an outfielder and more recently at designated hitter, Kittle spent some time at first base for the Sox last season and didn't embarrass himself at the position. With his physical problems, his days as an outfielder are probably over, and he will probably play mostly as a DH in the future, with occasional first base play.

OVERALL:

We'll probably have to wait until spring training to see if Kittle can make a full recovery from last year's injury; if he does, he can provide the Sox with some much needed power. Ronny made great strides in his offensive game last year; if he can pick up where he left off, he can be among the league leaders in homers.

RON KITTLE

Position: 1B/DH
Bats: R **Throws:** R
Ht: 6' 4" **Wt:** 220

Opening Day Age: 32
Born: 1/5/58 in Gary, IN
ML Seasons: 8

Overall Statistics

	G	AB	R	H	D	T	HR	RBI	SB	BB	SO	AVG
1989	51	169	26	51	10	0	11	37	0	22	42	.302
Career	721	2323	316	561	84	3	156	407	16	205	644	.241

Where He Hits the Ball

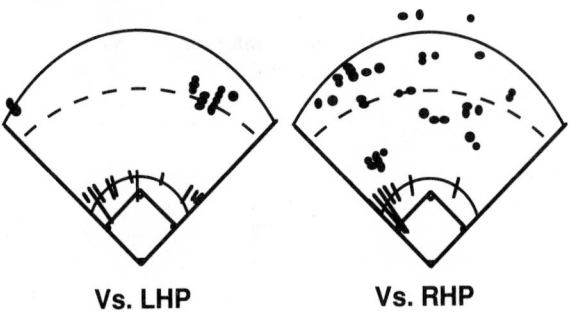

Vs. LHP   **Vs. RHP**

1989 Situational Stats

	AB	H	HR	RBI	AVG		AB	H	HR	RBI	AVG
Home	70	19	6	20	.271	LHP	55	16	4	10	.291
Road	99	32	5	17	.323	RHP	114	35	7	27	.307
Day	45	13	2	8	.289	Sc Pos	38	13	2	23	.342
Night	124	38	9	29	.306	Clutch	26	12	1	4	.462

1989 Rankings (American League)

➡ 5th in slugging percentage (.556) - *all league players*

➡ 6th in ABs per HR (15.4) - *all league players*

➡ Led the White Sox in ABs per HR and slugging percentage - *all team players*

➡ Led AL First Basemen in slugging percentage

HITTING:

Steve Lyons is a former number one draft choice. He was once considered an outstanding prospect; indeed, the White Sox thought enough of him to trade Tom Seaver for him in 1986. Chicago has given him a chance to play, but by now it's apparent that Lyons will never be more than a good fill-in and supersub.

As a minor leaguer, Lyons displayed some power, belting as many as seventeen homers, but in the majors his bat has shown little pop. Basically, he's a hacker, a guy who likes to jump on the first pitch and spray line drives around the diamond. He likes the fastball, but has his problems against lefthanded breaking ball pitchers. He handles the bat well and is a good hit-and-run man. He's also an excellent bunter who gets numerous bunt singles. He performed well as a pinch-hitter in '89, leading the White Sox in that department.

BASERUNNING:

Lyons is known as "Psycho," and if you've ever watched him run the bases you can easily understand why. He's one of those guys who runs with a lot of enthusiasm but not much brains. Though he has good speed, his lifetime stolen base percentage is only a little over .500, and he often runs into foolish outs. He also slides into first base a lot while trying to beat out singles -- not exactly the sign of an astute ballplayer.

FIELDING:

Lyons' best asset by far is his versatility. He's played every position but pitcher during his major league career and has handled most of them well. He's a fine outfielder at all three positions but doesn't hit with enough power to play regularly there. He was surprisingly good at second in his first real shot there in '89, fielding .982 and displaying decent range. He makes some fine plays at third, the position he's played most frequently, but commits way too many errors.

OVERALL:

Lyons yearns to be a regular, but his skills are best suited to a bench role. If he can accept this, he should be around for a number of years; in the age of the 24-man roster, versatility like his is a prized commodity.

STEVE LYONS

Position: 2B/1B/3B
Bats: L **Throws:** R
Ht: 6' 3" **Wt:** 195

Opening Day Age: 29
Born: 6/3/60 in Tacoma, WA
ML Seasons: 5

Overall Statistics

	G	AB	R	H	D	T	HR	RBI	SB	BB	SO	AVG
1989	140	443	51	117	21	3	2	50	9	35	68	.264
Career	596	1726	218	452	83	13	14	164	29	130	275	.262

Where He Hits the Ball

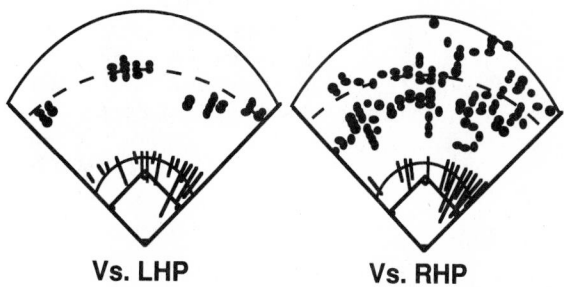

Vs. LHP   **Vs. RHP**

1989 Situational Stats

	AB	H	HR	RBI	AVG		AB	H	HR	RBI	AVG
Home	207	45	0	15	.217	LHP	94	20	0	9	.213
Road	236	72	2	35	.305	RHP	349	97	2	41	.278
Day	133	38	1	14	.286	Sc Pos	125	35	2	47	.280
Night	310	79	1	36	.255	Clutch	83	25	1	12	.301

1989 Rankings (American League)

- ➡ 1st in bunts in play (42)
- ➡ 3rd in least GDPs per GDP situation (3.0%) - *players with 50 PA in GDP situations*
- ➡ Led the White Sox in bunts in play, hitting in the clutch (.301) and hitting vs. righthanded pitchers (.278) - *team players with 50 PA in the clutch and 377 PA against RHP*
- ➡ Led AL Second Basemen in bunts in play and least GDPs per GDP situation

HITTING:

In his first extended major league tryout, Carlos Martinez acquitted himself very nicely in 1989. Brought up from Triple A soon after the beginning of the season, he was played sparingly. But after the All-Star break, White Sox manager Jeff Torborg decided to take a long look at what this highly regarded prospect could do. The results were generally quite positive.

After hitting .248 in the first half of the season, Martinez caught fire in the second, hitting a robust .321 to finish at .300 for the season. Though he hit only 5 home runs, he also connected for 22 doubles, showing good power to the left and right field gaps. A tall, lanky ballplayer (6'5"; 175 pounds), Carlos could probably benefit by adding some pounds and increasing his strength; his power stats would likely benefit.

Though his natural talent is unquestioned, Martinez has sometimes been his own worst enemy. He's moody and not always alert -- the Sox sat him down for a couple of days after he'd missed a couple of bunt signs. As a hitter he goes through spells where he'll overstride or swing at pitches over his head. To succeed he'll need to continue the growth he began showing in '89.

BASERUNNING:

Although he once stole 23 bases in the minors, Carlos has shown little inclination to steal in the big leagues. In 1989 he attempted just six stolen bases and was successful on four of those. With his big body it just takes a bit longer to get everything in motion.

FIELDING:

Martinez played at third base, at first base, and a few games in left field last season. Finding the right position for him may be difficult. While making a lot of errors he showed promise at third, but with Robin Ventura waiting in the wings it's unlikely there's a future for him there. He seemed uncomfortable in his limited tryout at first and will concentrate more on that position before the '90 season begins.

OVERALL:

Martinez established himself as a good young hitter with his 1989 performance, but it's hard to predict how he will be used next season. The Sox have a couple of veteran first basemen coming off injuries, and rookie Ventura may be ready to take over at third. Barring a trade, it will likely take until spring training to see what Martinez' role will be.

CARLOS MARTINEZ

Position: 3B/1B
Bats: R **Throws:** R
Ht: 6' 5" **Wt:** 175

Opening Day Age: 24
Born: 8/11/65 in La Guaira, Venezuela
ML Seasons: 2

Overall Statistics

	G	AB	R	H	D	T	HR	RBI	SB	BB	SO	AVG
1989	109	350	44	105	22	0	5	32	4	21	57	.300
Career	126	405	49	114	23	0	5	32	5	21	69	.281

Where He Hits the Ball

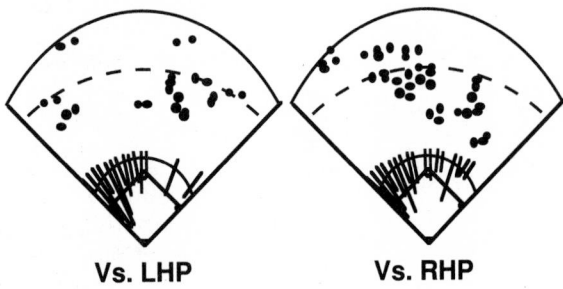

Vs. LHP   **Vs. RHP**

1989 Situational Stats

	AB	H	HR	RBI	AVG		AB	H	HR	RBI	AVG
Home	171	48	2	15	.281	LHP	132	39	2	16	.295
Road	179	57	3	17	.318	RHP	218	66	3	16	.303
Day	103	22	2	10	.214	Sc Pos	96	22	0	26	.229
Night	247	83	3	22	.336	Clutch	53	15	1	9	.283

1989 Rankings (American League)

→ 8th in errors (20)
→ Led AL Third Basemen in sacrifice bunts (6)

PITCHING:

After beginning the season in the minor leagues, Tom McCarthy was called up to the White Sox in May. A ten-year minor league veteran, McCarthy had appeared in only nine late-season major league games prior to 1989. But with the White Sox '89 pitching problems, McCarthy's chance finally came and he spent the majority of the season on the Sox staff.

Early in his minor league career, McCarthy was a hard-throwing wild man who averaged nearly one strikeout and one walk per inning. But as he's matured, McCarthy has become a finesse hurler, relying on a sinker and pinpoint control. When he's on his game, he gets lots of groundouts and double play balls; when he's not, he has games like the harrowing night in Milwaukee when he toiled six innings in a blowout, yielding 11 runs (nine earned) and 14 hits. Although he finished the season with a respectable 3.51 ERA, McCarthy was inconsistent over the course of the season. He had a promising beginning with a 3.10 ERA for May, but then began to flounder in June, winding up the month with a 5.28 ERA. A little after the Milwaukee nightmare, McCarthy was sent to Vancouver.

When he returned in early August, McCarthy seemed like a new pitcher. He allowed no earned runs in August in 14.1 innings pitched, but then faded a bit in September, having some health problems and making only four brief appearances. Opposing batters hit a solid .280 off him for the season, but he generally had good control. McCarthy was susceptible to the long ball, giving up 8 homers in his limited appearances.

FIELDING:

McCarthy has a pretty good move to first base for a right-handed pitcher. Defensively, he has no obvious flaws; he is a good athlete who plays his position well.

OVERALL:

McCarthy will turn 29 during the 1990 season; with the White Sox committed to trying to develop their younger pitching prospects, McCarthy probably doesn't fit into their long range plans. But if the young arms aren't quite ready for the big leagues yet, McCarthy is capable of providing some help.

TOM McCARTHY

Position: RP
Bats: R **Throws:** R
Ht: 6' 0" **Wt:** 180

Opening Day Age: 28
Born: 6/18/61 in Lundstahl, West Germany
ML Seasons: 3

Overall Statistics

	W	L	ERA	G	GS	Sv	IP	H	R	BB	SO	HR
1989	1	2	3.51	31	0	0	66.2	72	32	20	27	8
Career	3	2	3.61	40	0	1	84.2	88	40	26	34	9

Where They Hit the Ball

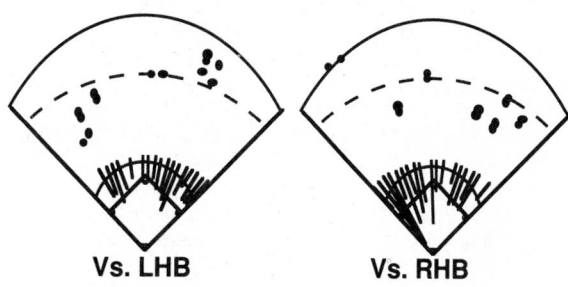

Vs. LHB   **Vs. RHB**

1989 Situational Stats

	W	L	ERA	Sv	IP		AB	H	HR	RBI	AVG
Home	1	1	2.75	0	39.1	LHB	104	31	1	13	.298
Road	0	1	4.61	0	27.1	RHB	153	41	7	24	.268
Day	0	0	2.65	0	17.0	Sc Pos	72	16	1	30	.222
Night	1	2	3.81	0	49.2	Clutch	36	10	2	4	.278

1989 Rankings (American League)

➡ 2nd in GDPs induced per GDP situation (25.8%) - *pitchers with 30 GDP situations*

➡ 4th in worst percentage of inherited runners scoring (48.4%) - *pitchers with 30 inherited runners*

➡ Led the White Sox in GDPs induced per GDP situation and grounder/flyball ratio (2.53) - *all team players*

PITCHING:

Donn Pall was a so-so starter through most of his minor league career, but he saw his career revived when the White Sox shifted him to the bullpen at Vancouver in '88. The Sox recalled him later that year, and he has been relatively effective since then as a middle reliever and setup man.

It's easy to see why Pall would be more effective in a relief role. He has a decent fastball that can reach the high eighties, but his best pitch by far is his split-fingered fastball; without it, Pall wouldn't have much of a career. When it's working, the splitter produces both strikeouts and groundouts in good number. For the most part he has good control of the splitter. But when he gets behind on the count and has to rely on his fastball, Pall is likely to be hit hard. A good competitor, Pall is fearless about pitching inside. His eight hit batters were by far the most on the Sox staff.

After a strong spring, Pall was the closer on opening day and picked up a save in relief of Jerry Reuss. The closer's role was only temporary while Bobby Thigpen battled a streak of ineffectiveness. Once Thigpen returned to form, Pall became the set-up man, working as the closer himself when Thigpen needed a rest. The results were mixed. At times he was very effective, reeling off a string of 17.2 consecutive scoreless innings at one point. And Pall's first batter efficiency was excellent -- he held opponents to a .188 average. But he converted only six of ten save opportunities, and he allowed nearly half of his inherited runners to score. Pall will have to pitch better than that if he wants to keep the set-up role.

FIELDING:

Pall is a good fielder who helps himself with his glove work. He also holds baserunners well, allowing only three stolen bases in 1989.

OVERALL:

Pall enters 1990 competing for the Sox set-up role with Barry Jones and possibly Shawn Hillegas. His so-so '89 stats indicate that it might be a losing battle. But if Pall doesn't get the set-up job, he has enough stuff to pitch effectively in long relief.

DONN PALL

Position: RP
Bats: R **Throws:** R
Ht: 6' 1" **Wt:** 180

Opening Day Age: 28
Born: 1/11/62 in Chicago, IL
ML Seasons: 2

Overall Statistics

	W	L	ERA	G	GS	Sv	IP	H	R	BB	SO	HR
1989	4	5	3.31	53	0	6	87.0	90	35	19	58	9
Career	4	7	3.35	70	0	6	115.2	129	46	27	74	10

Where They Hit the Ball

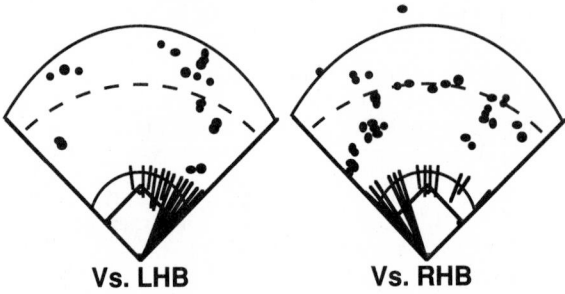

Vs. LHB   **Vs. RHB**

1989 Situational Stats

	W	L	ERA	Sv	IP		AB	H	HR	RBI	AVG
Home	1	2	3.38	3	37.1	LHB	157	40	4	17	.255
Road	3	3	3.26	3	49.2	RHB	176	50	5	30	.284
Day	1	0	1.61	3	28.0	Sc Pos	108	27	1	34	.250
Night	3	5	4.12	3	59.0	Clutch	148	38	6	19	.257

1989 Rankings (American League)

➡ 2nd in worst percentage of inherited runners scoring (48.9%) - *pitchers with 30 inherited runners*

➡ 5th in hit batsmen (8)

➡ 10th in first batter efficiency (.188) - *pitchers with 40 games in relief*

➡ Led the White Sox in hit batsmen

HITTING:

Dan Pasqua has been plagued by injuries since he was acquired from the Yankees after the 1987 season. Twice this season, when he seemed to be hitting the ball well, injuries forced him to the bench. First a broken hand sidelined him for a month just after the beginning of the season, and then a knee problem ended his season in August.

Pasqua is a left-handed hitter with good power. His 1989 average of .248 is right on his career mark of .243. He has a pretty good eye and can coax a walk out of a pitcher, but like many power hitters he strikes out frequently. Danny has always hit much better during day games than night games -- his '89 marks of .318 day, .222 night are not atypical -- and experimented with glasses in an attempt to pick up the ball better at night.

Pasqua has always had sharply defined strengths and weaknesses. A definite pull hitter, he likes the ball inside and is especially strong against righthanded breaking ball pitchers. But outside pitches give him trouble and almost any kind of lefty pitching has stopped him completely. He did show some definite improvement against southpaws last year, belting four homers, including a mighty roof shot off Frank Tanana.

BASERUNNING:

Pasqua was never a fast runner, but in the past he showed himself to be an intelligent runner on the bases, seldom getting himself into trouble. But with his recent injury problems, he may find it necessary to be very conservative on the bases.

FIELDING:

Pasqua is a surprisingly good defensive outfielder, and can also fill in at first base adequately. He has a strong arm and good range. He plays the hitters well and seldom makes defensive mistakes. But due to his knee problems he was forced to play with a knee brace late last season, and this may hamper his mobility next year if the brace is still a necessity.

OVERALL:

There will be a lot of competition for starting jobs in the White Sox outfield next season; as of this writing no one has any of the outfield positions locked up. A good spring showing will be needed for Dan to win one of them. But if he does, and is able to stay healthy all year, he could be a big producer for the Sox and be a 25-30 homer man.

DAN PASQUA

Position: LF/RF
Bats: L **Throws:** L
Ht: 6' 0" **Wt:** 205

Opening Day Age: 28
Born: 10/17/61 in Yonkers, NY
ML Seasons: 5

Overall Statistics

	G	AB	R	H	D	T	HR	RBI	SB	BB	SO	AVG
1989	73	246	26	61	9	1	11	47	1	25	58	.248
Career	477	1414	177	344	52	5	73	209	4	174	373	.243

Where He Hits the Ball

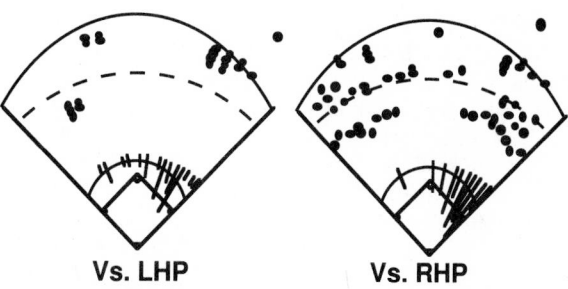

Vs. LHP   Vs. RHP

1989 Situational Stats

	AB	H	HR	RBI	AVG		AB	H	HR	RBI	AVG
Home	113	29	5	18	.257	LHP	76	17	3	11	.224
Road	133	32	6	29	.241	RHP	170	44	8	36	.259
Day	66	21	2	18	.318	Sc Pos	65	21	1	34	.323
Night	180	40	9	29	.222	Clutch	41	7	1	9	.171

1989 Rankings (American League)

➡ 1st in least GDPs per GDP situation (0%) - *players with 50 PA in GDP situations*

➡ Worst batting average with 2 strikes (.103) - *players with 162 PA*

➡ 8th in hitting with the bases loaded (.455) - *players with 10 PA with the bases loaded*

➡ Led the White Sox in least GDPs per GDP situation and hitting with the bases loaded

➡ Led AL Left Fielders in least GDPs per GDP situation and hitting with the bases loaded

CHICAGO WHITE SOX

PITCHING:

After an outstanding rookie season in which he won a dozen games, Melido Perez was expected to be the young ace of the White Sox staff in 1989. It never happened; the 23-year-old righty struggled until late in the year. Perez did have a good September, going 4-1 with a 3.53 ERA, but all in all the season was a big disappointment for the young righthander.

Perez possesses a fastball that can reach the high eighties, but his money pitch is his split-fingered fastball. In '88 the pitch had been Melido's bread and butter; in '89 it was his undoing. Perez had control problems for most of the year, often bouncing the splitter in the dirt. He'd get behind on the count and either walk the batter or get creamed for an extra base hit. Perez was particularly inept at the start of games, with a first inning ERA of around 7.00. The result was a long and depressing season in which he led the White Sox in both walks and home runs allowed.

Though the White Sox weren't saying, it's possible that Perez was suffering from a tired arm for most of the year. After working 197 innings for the Sox in '88, Perez went back home to the Dominican Republic and threw 79 more innings in his country's winter league. Melido's winter work was outstanding -- 8-1 with a 1.48 ERA -- and the Sox had every reason to expect a big year from him in '89. The result, instead, was disaster. It's quite possible that the frail Perez was paying the price for his heavy 1988 workload.

FIELDING:

Defensively, Perez is an average workman. He gets off the mound fairly well but often reacts slowly to balls hit up the middle. He has a good move to first and holds baserunners well. Only 60% of the runners who attempted to steal on Perez in '89 were successful--a very good record.

OVERALL:

After one very good year and one bad one, the White Sox don't know quite what to expect from Melido Perez in 1990. His talent is undeniable; he has the stuff to be a winning pitcher for many years. Were his problems in 1989 mechanical, physical or mental? The Sox can only work with Perez and try to get him on track again.

MELIDO PEREZ

Position: SP
Bats: R **Throws:** R
Ht: 6' 4" **Wt:** 180

Opening Day Age: 24
Born: 2/15/66 in San Cristobal, Dominican Republic
ML Seasons: 3

Overall Statistics

	W	L	ERA	G	GS	Sv	IP	H	R	BB	SO	HR
1989	11	14	5.01	31	31	0	183.1	187	106	90	141	23
Career	24	25	4.47	66	66	0	390.2	391	223	167	284	51

Where They Hit the Ball

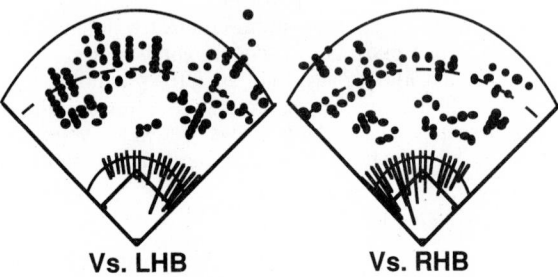

Vs. LHB   **Vs. RHB**

1989 Situational Stats

	W	L	ERA	Sv	IP		AB	H	HR	RBI	AVG
Home	4	6	5.06	0	78.1	LHB	369	97	12	41	.263
Road	7	8	4.97	0	105.0	RHB	339	90	11	46	.265
Day	5	5	5.13	0	66.2	Sc Pos	181	45	7	64	.249
Night	6	9	4.94	0	116.2	Clutch	41	11	1	2	.268

1989 Rankings (American League)

- 2nd worst ERA (5.01) - *pitchers with 162 IP*
- 3rd in most baserunners per 9 innings (13.7) and highest on-base average allowed (.348)
- 4th in losses (14) and lowest grounder/fly-ball ratio (.95)
- 5th in most home runs allowed (23), walks allowed (90), caught stealing (12), HRs per 9 innings (1.13) and batting average with runners in scoring position (.249)
- Led the White Sox in wins (11), losses, games started (31), complete games (2), innings (183), hits allowed (187), home runs allowed (23) walks allowed (90), strikeouts (141) and wild pitches (12)

PITCHING:

After some modest success as a reliever in 1988, Steve Rosenberg was thrust into the White Sox starting rotation last year. Though the move was made partly out of desperation -- Sox starters were getting hammered regularly at the time -- there was reason to think it might work. Rosenberg's fastball won't break any speed records, but he has good variety of pitches, and all of them move; he sets up the fastball with both a screwball and a good slow curve. He keeps the ball down in the strike zone and gets a good share of groundball outs and double play balls. Adding all that up, the top brass felt that Rosenberg had enough stuff to succeed in a starting role. Unfortunately, it proved to be yet another White Sox theory gone awry. Rosenberg wound up with a 4-13 record and averaged only a shade more than five innings per start. As a starter his ERA was 5.45; in 17 relief appearances it was 3.38.

Rosenberg's situational stats suggest a hurler better suited to bullpen duty, especially against lefthanded hitters. Though his opponents' batting averages against lefties and righties were roughly even, Rosenberg allowed 13 homers to righty swingers but only one to a lefty. For the first 15 pitches of his appearances, he held opponents to a .217 average; from pitch 16 on, his opponents' average was .289. A move back to the pen seemed totally logical, but Rosenberg complained bitterly when the Sox finally took him out of the rotation. Doesn't this fellow know where he's well off?

FIELDING:

A decent glove man, Rosenberg commits an occasional error but handles himself smartly on the mound. He is especially good at starting the 1-6-3 double play. But though he looks as though he has a good move to first, Rosenberg was second on the White Sox staff in stolen bases allowed last year. Perhaps he was distracted by his difficulties as a starter; in '88 Rosenberg was quite effective in holding runners.

OVERALL:

Originally a product of the Yankee farm system, Rosenberg was a successful reliever throughout his minor league career. His work in 1989 clearly indicates that this, rather than starting, is the proper role for him. Rosenberg will likely end up competing with Ken Patterson for the role of lefty specialist and set-up man.

STEVE ROSENBERG

Position: SP/RP
Bats: L **Throws:** L
Ht: 6' 0" **Wt:** 185

Opening Day Age: 25
Born: 10/31/64 in Brooklyn, NY
ML Seasons: 2

Overall Statistics

	W	L	ERA	G	GS	Sv	IP	H	R	BB	SO	HR
1989	4	13	4.94	38	21	0	142.0	148	92	58	77	14
Career	4	14	4.79	71	21	1	188.0	201	114	77	105	19

Where They Hit the Ball

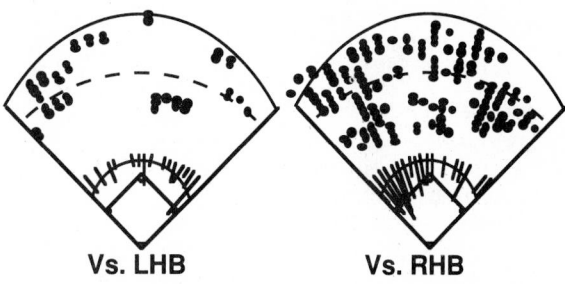

Vs. LHB   Vs. RHB

1989 Situational Stats

	W	L	ERA	Sv	IP		AB	H	HR	RBI	AVG
Home	2	7	4.73	0	70.1	LHB	97	26	1	11	.268
Road	2	6	5.15	0	71.2	RHB	444	122	13	62	.275
Day	1	6	5.69	0	49.0	Sc Pos	139	41	3	55	.295
Night	3	7	4.55	0	93.0	Clutch	43	11	1	2	.256

1989 Rankings (American League)

➡ Worst won/loss percentage (.235) - *pitchers with 15 or more decisions*
➡ Led the White Sox in complete games (2) and pickoff throws (154)

HITTING:

Only 21, Sammy Sosa was a key to the big deal in which the White Sox sent Harold Baines to Texas. He has, as they say, all the tools: he can hit with power, field, run and throw. Though his August-September trial was far from a complete success, Sosa showed enough ability to definitely mark himself a potential star.

Like most young players, Sosa loves the fastball. But breaking balls have given him all kinds of trouble. American League pitchers soon discovered this and began feeding him a steady diet of curves and sliders. At first the youngster was completely confused. After being helped by White Sox hitting coach Walt Hriniak, Sosa showed enough discipline to stop chasing so many pitches in the dirt; he even drew a few walks for the first time in his career. Still, good righthanders were able to tie him up completely. Sosa's enormous platoon differential (156 points) shows how much he needs to learn about handling major league pitching.

BASERUNNING:

Sosa possesses great speed; discipline is another matter. He loves to steal bases but has yet to master the art of reading pitchers' moves. As a result he gets thrown out way too much for someone so fast. He is extremely aggressive when running the bases, which helps make him an exciting player. It also helps make him look pretty foolish at times.

FIELDING:

With his speed and great range, Sosa is a natural choice to roam the acreage of Comiskey Park's vast center field. Here again, his inexperience shows; he still needs to learn a lot about playing hitters. He appears to be a good student, so it should be just a matter of absorbing lessons from his coaches. Sosa has an outstanding throwing arm and can uncork the long throw from right field as well as center.

OVERALL:

Sosa has such great potential that it's difficult to remember that he's young and very raw. At this stage of his career, he's no Harold Baines, and at first his performance won't justify trading one of the great players in White Sox history. Sosa is going to make a lot of mistakes, and that will require patience on the part of the White Sox and their fans. Platooning him for a while until he learns the ropes might be in his best interests.

SAMMY SOSA

Position: CF/LF
Bats: R **Throws:** R
Ht: 6' 0" **Wt:** 165

Opening Day Age: 21
Born: 11/10/68 in San Pedro de Macoris, Dominican Republic
ML Seasons: 1

Overall Statistics

	G	AB	R	H	D	T	HR	RBI	SB	BB	SO	AVG
1989	58	183	27	47	8	0	4	13	7	11	47	.257
Career	58	183	27	47	8	0	4	13	7	11	47	.257

Where He Hits the Ball

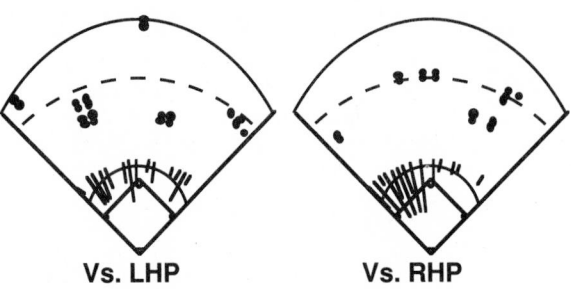

Vs. LHP   **Vs. RHP**

1989 Situational Stats

	AB	H	HR	RBI	AVG		AB	H	HR	RBI	AVG
Home	67	19	1	5	.284	LHP	78	27	2	9	.346
Road	116	28	3	8	.241	RHP	105	20	2	4	.190
Day	37	10	1	2	.270	Sc Pos	38	8	0	8	.211
Night	146	37	3	11	.253	Clutch	26	5	0	0	.192

1989 Rankings (American League)

➡ Led the White Sox in hitting vs. lefthanded pitchers (.382) - *all team players*

PITCHING:

After only two full seasons as a closer, Bobby Thigpen has established himself as one of the best relief pitchers in baseball. His 68 saves in 1988-89 were quite a feat; the struggling White Sox gave him few leads to protect, and didn't help his efforts much with their sloppy defense. A thorough professional, Thigpen seldom let such lapses bother him.

Thigpen throws an occasional slider, but his best weapon is a good hard fastball that is consistently in the low nineties. Despite such velocity, he seldom blows hitters away; a typical Thigpen outing will feature numerous pop-ups and weak grounders rather than an overpowering amount of strikeouts. In years past, Bobby had trouble with lefthanded hitters. But by busting the ball inside more consistently in '89, he was largely able to eliminate that problem.

Despite his success, Thigpen does have a couple of weaknesses. One of them, in 1989 anyway, was his control. Last year he issued more than one walk for every two innings pitched, an unacceptably high ratio. His tendency is to be wild high, and that was doubly dangerous to him in '89. In addition to all the walks, Thigpen yielded 10 homers in only 77 innings of work, a very high gopher ball rate.

Another problem for Thigpen is that he tends to be much less effective in non-save situations than he is when the game is on the line. Lack of concentration could be the culprit.

FIELDING:

Thigpen is an outstanding athlete who was a designated hitter on the Mississippi State team which featured Will Clark and Rafael Palmeiro. Bobby doesn't get a chance to hit in the American League -- the Sox have, at times, considered using him as a pinch hitter -- but his athletic ability really shows in his defensive work. Thigpen is probably the best fielding pitcher on the White Sox staff. He does a decent job of holding runners, but his high leg kick makes him vulnerable to the good base stealers.

OVERALL:

Still relatively unheralded, Bobby Thigpen has become one of the rarest of stars: relief ace for a perennial loser. There's always a debate of whether such a pitcher is being "wasted," since his club won't win many games anyhow. Because of that, Thigpen's name always comes up when the White Sox are talking trade. Little wonder -- almost every club in baseball would love to have him.

BOBBY THIGPEN

Position: RP
Bats: R **Throws:** R
Ht: 6' 3" **Wt:** 195

Opening Day Age: 26
Born: 7/17/63 in Tallahassee, FL
ML Seasons: 4

Overall Statistics

	W	L	ERA	G	GS	Sv	IP	H	R	BB	SO	HR
1989	2	6	3.76	61	0	34	79.0	62	34	40	47	10
Career	16	19	3.06	200	0	91	293.2	270	109	109	181	27

Where They Hit the Ball

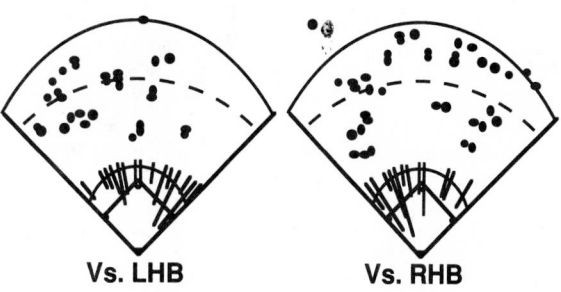

Vs. LHB   **Vs. RHB**

1989 Situational Stats

	W	L	ERA	Sv	IP		AB	H	HR	RBI	AVG
Home	1	2	3.60	18	40.0	LHB	136	26	5	26	.191
Road	1	4	3.92	16	39.0	RHB	149	36	5	20	.242
Day	0	2	2.45	13	22.0	Sc Pos	82	21	5	37	.256
Night	2	4	4.26	21	57.0	Clutch	206	44	7	36	.214

1989 Rankings (American League)

- ➡ 2nd in saves (34)
- ➡ 3rd in blown saves (9)
- ➡ 4th in games finished (56)
- ➡ 5th in batting average vs. lefthanded batters (.191) - *pitchers with 125 PA vs. LHB*
- ➡ 9th in save percentage (79.1%) and first batters efficiency (.182) - *pitchers with 40 games in relief*
- ➡ Led the White Sox in games (61), saves, blown saves, games finished, batting average vs. lefthanded batters, save percentage and first batter efficiency

HITTING:

After two totally unproductive campaigns, Greg Walker enters 1990 with his major league career in jeopardy. A return to full health would be a big first step. In 1988, Walker was experiencing his worst major league season when he was felled by a frightening seizure during pregame drills. His recovery was slow and painful, but Walker worked diligently and looked like his old self last year during spring training. However, he fell into a deep slump as soon as the season began. The snap in his swing was gone, and he displayed none of the power which had produced three 20-homer seasons. Doctors and Walker both insisted that he had completely recovered from the seizures. Late in the season they discovered that an old shoulder injury was acting up again. Walker underwent surgery and finished the year on the disabled list.

When completely healthy, Walker possesses a long, rhythmic swing that even Ted Williams has admired. He likes the low fastball and can pull it with considerable power. Good lefties have always given him trouble, and he's never hit much for average, but he has become a more disciplined hitter as he's matured. At the top of his game he's a dependable run producer good for 25 homers and 90 RBIs a year.

BASERUNNING:

Walker stole an occasional base early in his career, when Tony LaRussa liked to send him as a surprise move. But he has slowed down in recent years and has not had a successful steal since 1987. He is a conservative baserunner who prefers to advance one base at a time. He seldom makes a mental mistake on the bases.

FIELDING:

Once a terrible fielder, Walker has worked hard on his defense and now rates as an above-average gloveman. Sure-handedness is his best attribute. He has never had great range, and has always had difficulty turning the 3-6-3 double play. He once had difficulty with pop flies, but overcame that weakness through hard work.

OVERALL:

Walker is a blue-collar type who is one of the most popular players on the White Sox. He will be given more opportunities than most players to show whether he has recovered from his injuries. The Sox renewed his contract for 1990 and are obviously hoping for the best. But first base is a power position, and unless he can return to his 1987 form, Walker may soon find himself out of a job.

GREG WALKER

Position: 1B/DH
Bats: L **Throws:** R
Ht: 6' 3" **Wt:** 210

Opening Day Age: 30
Born: 10/6/59 in Douglas, GA
ML Seasons: 8

Overall Statistics

	G	AB	R	H	D	T	HR	RBI	SB	BB	SO	AVG
1989	77	233	25	49	14	0	5	26	0	23	50	.210
Career	839	2825	366	740	164	19	113	442	18	265	509	.262

Where He Hits the Ball

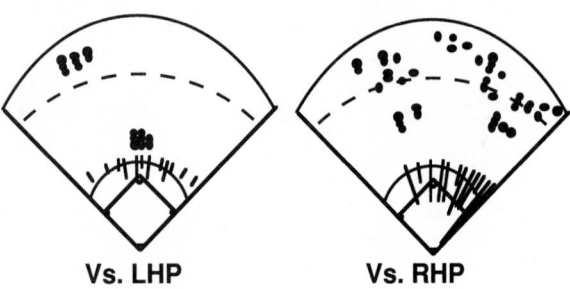

Vs. LHP   **Vs. RHP**

1989 Situational Stats

	AB	H	HR	RBI	AVG		AB	H	HR	RBI	AVG
Home	91	15	4	11	.165	LHP	48	9	0	3	.188
Road	142	34	1	15	.239	RHP	185	40	5	23	.216
Day	70	19	0	6	.271	Sc Pos	61	14	0	20	.230
Night	163	30	5	20	.184	Clutch	36	5	0	3	.139

1989 Rankings (American League)

➡ Did not rank near the top or bottom in any category

DARYL BOSTON

Position: LF/RF
Bats: L **Throws:** L
Ht: 6' 3" **Wt:** 203

Opening Day Age: 27
Born: 1/4/63 in Cincinnati, OH
ML Seasons: 6

Overall Statistics

	G	AB	R	H	D	T	HR	RBI	SB	BB	SO	AVG
1989	101	218	34	55	3	4	5	23	7	24	31	.252
Career	495	1350	179	323	63	13	38	123	51	109	240	.239

HITTING, FIELDING, BASERUNNING:

Once considered the top prospect in the White Sox farm system, Boston has seen his stock shrink year by year. In '89 he never came close to winning a regular position; his role was strictly that of a part-time platoon outfielder and pinch-hitter. Lefty hurlers have always given Boston trouble, and almost all his plate appearances were against righthanders. Boston did attempt to learn the theories of new Sox hitting coach Walt Hriniak, and was able to raise his batting average by 35 points over 1988. But that improvement was at the expense of power; Boston's home run output declined from 15 to 5. Boston was fairly effective as a pinch-hitter and was often used as a defensive replacement. He is a fleet outfielder with good range and a decent throwing arm. He can also steal a base, though he has never really tapped his speed.

OVERALL:

Still only 27, Boston has been given several chances but has never really asserted himself. He does have major league ability and can help a club coming off the bench, as he did for the White Sox in '89. But at this point stardom seems extremely unlikely.

BARRY JONES

Position: RP
Bats: R **Throws:** R
Ht: 6' 4" **Wt:** 225

Opening Day Age: 27
Born: 2/15/63 in Centerville, IN
ML Seasons: 4

Overall Statistics

	W	L	ERA	G	GS	Sv	IP	H	R	BB	SO	HR
1989	3	2	2.37	22	0	1	30.1	22	12	8	17	2
Career	11	13	3.40	139	0	8	193.1	178	90	90	122	17

PITCHING & FIELDING:

Barry Jones' '89 season was mostly spent on the DL -- after a May elbow injury required surgery, he wasn't able to return to the bullpen until the end of August. But in the last month, he was able to demonstrate that he could still pitch effectively, and that made prospects for next year seem brighter.

Jones was primarily used as a set-up man for closer Bobby Thigpen and he filled that role well. Opposing batters hit only .208 against him and he held the first batter faced in relief to a .190 average. He has a good fastball and improved his control this year, walking only eight batters in over 30 innings. And he was effective in shutting down rallies when he did enter the game; only 22% of the runners on base when he came into a game eventually scored. He's a good fielder, but the opposition had good success running against Jones, converting all six stolen base attempts.

OVERALL:

Jones figures to be the principal set-up man for the White Sox next year. Still only 27, he should just be entering his prime. If he can pick up where he left off in '89, he should fill that role very capably.

BILL LONG

Position: RP/SP
Bats: R **Throws:** R
Ht: 6' 0" **Wt:** 185

Opening Day Age: 30
Born: 2/29/60 in Cincinnati, OH
ML Seasons: 4

Overall Statistics

	W	L	ERA	G	GS	Sv	IP	H	R	BB	SO	HR
1989	5	5	3.92	30	8	1	98.2	101	49	37	51	8
Career	21	25	4.33	110	52	4	455.2	492	240	113	213	53

PITCHING & FIELDING:

Bill Long is a nibbler, the kind of pitcher whose fastball is never going to impress major league scouts. Long was 27 before he got his first real major league shot, and though he continues to be a marginal performer, there is no question he makes the most of his abilities. Strictly a finesse pitcher, Long relies mostly on control and a big-breaking curve to survive as a major league hurler. He's never allowed less than a hit per inning and has always given up a generous number of homers. His strengths are his competitive nature -- he's fearless about pitching inside -- and his ability to work effectively as both as starter and reliever. His peripheral skills, in fielding and holding baserunners, are good.

OVERALL:

Long will never be more than the seventh or eighth pitcher on a staff, but in that role he's very dependable. He's bulldog-tough; it took him a long time to reach the majors, and even though he spent some time at Vancouver in '89, one suspects that Long will figure out a way to land a job on a club that needs pitching.

KEN PATTERSON

Position: RP
Bats: L **Throws:** L
Ht: 6' 4" **Wt:** 210

Opening Day Age: 25
Born: 7/8/64 in Costa Mesa, CA
ML Seasons: 2

Overall Statistics

	W	L	ERA	G	GS	Sv	IP	H	R	BB	SO	HR
1989	6	1	4.52	50	1	0	65.2	64	37	28	43	11
Career	6	3	4.59	59	3	1	86.1	89	48	35	51	13

PITCHING & FIELDING:

Ken Patterson is a big lefthander with a fastball that can reach the low nineties and a good hard curveball. He had some success working out of the White Sox bullpen in 1989. When his control is on and his pitches are popping, Patterson can breeze through a lineup. He runs into trouble when he has to take something off his pitches to get them over the plate; too often in '89, the result was a long ball over the fence. Patterson also had a surprising amount of trouble against lefthanded hitters last year. He is an average fielder, and with his high leg kick, is relatively easy to steal against.

OVERALL:

Despite his mediocre numbers in 1989, the White Sox liked Patterson's arm and carefully nursed him through a late-season shoulder injury. Lefty relievers of even modest talent always seem to get numerous chances. Since he has a live arm, Patterson figures to be pitching somewhere in the majors during the next few years.

TOP PROSPECT

ROBIN VENTURA

Position: 3B
Bats: L **Throws:** R
Ht: 6' 1" **Wt:** 185

Opening Day Age: 22
Born: 7/14/67 in Santa Maria, CA
ML Seasons: 1

Overall Statistics

	G	AB	R	H	D	T	HR	RBI	SB	BB	SO	AVG
1989	16	45	5	8	3	0	0	7	0	8	6	.178
Career	16	45	5	8	3	0	0	7	0	8	6	.178

HITTING, FIELDING, BASERUNNING:

Robin Ventura -- his future's so bright, he's got to wear shades. Projected as the White Sox third baseman for years to come, Ventura is out of the Wade Boggs mold. He will probably never be a big home run man, but his short quick stroke is capable of producing line drives to all fields. In time, a .310 average with 40 doubles doesn't seem beyond his reach. Like Boggs, Ventura has a great batting eye and figures to draw 100 walks per year. He possesses only average speed but did steal nine bases at Birmingham and runs the bases with intelligence. Ventura is not yet regarded as an outstanding fielder, but his September defensive work with the Sox was surprisingly good. With practice his glove work figures to improve.

OVERALL:

There seems little doubt that Ventura will soon be a major league regular, and quite possibly a star. But Opening Day 1990 may be a little too soon. Ventura batted only .278 in Double A ball and 100 points less than that in his September trial with the Sox. He might still need a half year or so in Triple A before he's ready to stick.

EDDIE WILLIAMS

Position: 3B
Bats: R **Throws:** R
Ht: 6' 0" **Wt:** 175

Opening Day Age: 25
Born: 11/1/64 in Shreveport, LA
ML Seasons: 4

Overall Statistics

	G	AB	R	H	D	T	HR	RBI	SB	BB	SO	AVG
1989	66	201	25	55	8	0	3	10	1	18	31	.274
Career	103	293	39	71	12	0	4	16	1	27	56	.242

HITTING, FIELDING, BASERUNNING:

Eddie Williams is a former number one draft choice with a good minor league record. He began 1989 with his first real chance to play regularly in the major leagues. For a time it seemed like he'd made it at last -- Williams batted .338 in April and showed some fancy glove work at third base. Unfortunately, the success was short-lived. Though his bat mark never dipped below .270, Williams showed little of the power he'd displayed in the minor leagues. His work with runners in scoring position (a .122 average) was especially anemic. To top it all off, that fancy glove turned out to have holes in it; Williams fielded only .908 (16 errors) and became a member of the embarrassing "more errors than RBIs" club. All in all, he seemed overmatched. The White Sox returned Williams to Triple A in early July and pretty much forgot about him.

OVERALL:

Though he flubbed a major chance in 1989, Williams is still young enough at 25 to get another opportunity. With the White Sox committed to Robin Ventura as their third sacker of the future, Williams' best hope is that another club needing a third baseman will want to give him a look.

ANDY ALLANSON

Position: C
Bats: R **Throws:** R
Ht: 6' 5" **Wt:** 225

Opening Day Age: 28
Born: 12/22/61 in
Richmond, VA
ML Seasons: 4

HITTING:

There is a price for success. Andy Allanson made that painful discovery last season. In 1988, Allanson appeared to be one of the rising young catchers in the big leagues. He hit .263, drove in 50 runs, called a sweet game behind the plate and led Indians' hitters with a .306 average with runners in scoring position. The future looked bright.

Last year, somebody turned the lights out. Pitchers had always treated Allanson as an automatic out. However, he drew much closer attention last year. He got pitchers' A game -- breaking balls, sliders and split-fingered fastballs -- from opening day, and didn't pass the test. Allanson didn't adjust to the adjustment the pitchers made against him. Instead of the short, compact swing he used in 1988, he kept using a long, slow power swing. Based on his power production -- three homers and 17 RBI -- it was the wrong approach. Despite his size, 6'5", 225 pounds, Allanson is more suited to be an action-type offensive player instead of a power hitter. He can hit behind the runner, go to right field and move a runner along with a sacrifice bunt. Yet all those elements that made him successful in 1988 were missing from his game in 1989.

BASERUNNING:

Allanson once stole 22 bases in the minors, but those days are gone. Still, he can steal a base in the right situation if called upon. He doesn't run the bases well, looks unsure of himself going from first to third and often loafs to first base.

FIELDING:

Allanson has a good head for the game. He's analytical behind the plate and the pitching staff loves to throw to him. Last year, though, he let his lack of offense affect his catching. At times, he lost his concentration during games. He has a decent arm, but had a terrible year throwing out base stealers. His kill ratio was 28 percent (30 of 106). He does not block the plate well.

OVERALL:

Allanson's stock plunged last year. He had personal problems off the field, and they hurt his game. He didn't work hard in the off-season and it showed. He finally came around at the end of the year under interim manager John Hart, hitting .320 in his last 28 games. Overall, the Indians were disenchanted with his lack of hustle and he appeared headed for a change of address.

Overall Statistics

	G	AB	R	H	D	T	HR	RBI	SB	BB	SO	AVG
1989	111	323	30	75	9	1	3	17	4	23	47	.232
Career	395	1204	121	296	33	4	12	112	20	71	176	.246

Where He Hits the Ball

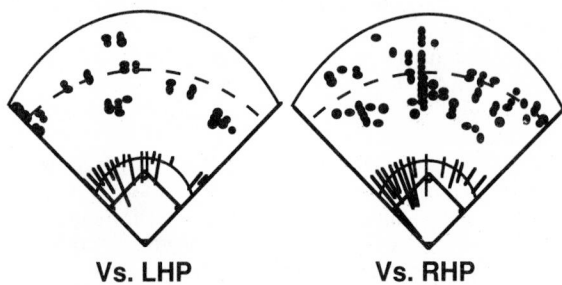

Vs. LHP   **Vs. RHP**

1989 Situational Stats

	AB	H	HR	RBI	AVG		AB	H	HR	RBI	AVG
Home	149	31	1	8	.208	LHP	94	27	0	3	.287
Road	174	44	2	9	.253	RHP	229	48	3	14	.210
Day	106	19	1	3	.179	Sc Pos	80	13	0	12	.162
Night	217	56	2	14	.258	Clutch	47	14	2	4	.298

1989 Rankings (American League)

➡ Led AL catchers in percentage of extra bases per opportunity as a runner (44.4%) - *catchers with 40 opportunities to advance*

PITCHING:

Everyone keeps saying Scott Bailes should be better than he is, but so far he's content to let people feed on their own words. Last year he opened in the bullpen, making 16 appearances. Then he replaced Rich Yett in the rotation and made 11 straight starts before wearing down and injuring his left shoulder. His last six appearances of the season were as a set-up man and/or long reliever. In 1988, Bailes and the Indians tried a different approach. He made 21 straight starts to open the season, before pitching his way back into the bullpen. His inconsistency drove former manager Doc Edwards into temper tantrums. In 1987, it was the same story. Bailes made 17 starts and 21 relief appearances. Is a pattern developing here, or what?

Bailes' best spot is probably in a middle or set-up relief role. He has a good slider, decent sinking fastball -- if he doesn't overthrow it -- and he works quickly, which keeps the defense alert. However, hitters catch up to him after he goes through the lineup once.

When Bailes came off the DL on Sept. 6, he worked on a new delivery. He had always favored an elaborate wind up featuring a high leg kick. It looked pretty, but gave would-be basestealers a huge jump on their way to second base, not a good practice when you're a left-handed pitcher. His new delivery offers a quicker, no-frills approach, getting the ball to the plate faster.

FIELDING:

Bailes cost himself at least two victories due to bad fielding last year. He has a problem with comebackers. He falls off the mound toward first base after his delivery and doesn't give himself a chance to get in front of balls hit back to the mound. With his new delivery, he is more effective at cutting down the running game.

OVERALL:

Bailes visited a sports psychologist on a regular basis following the 1988 season. The Indians wanted Bailes, a constant worrywart, to improve his concentration and confidence during game situations. He has natural movement on all his pitches, but at times tries to be too fine instead of throwing the ball and letting his talent take its course. His visits with the psychologist didn't improve his won-loss record, but Bailes was more focused and confident last year. Always a subject of trade rumors, Bailes is the ideal utility pitcher.

SCOTT BAILES

Position: RP/SP
Bats: L **Throws:** L
Ht: 6' 2" **Wt:** 175

Opening Day Age: 27
Born: 12/18/62 in Chillicothe, OH
ML Seasons: 4

Overall Statistics

	W	L	ERA	G	GS	Sv	IP	H	R	BB	SO	HR
1989	5	9	4.28	34	11	0	113.2	116	57	29	47	7
Career	31	41	4.70	172	59	13	491.2	533	291	165	225	62

Where They Hit the Ball

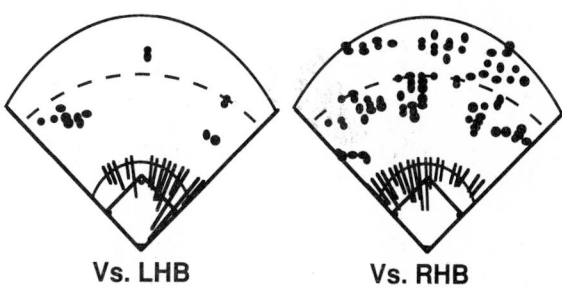

Vs. LHB   **Vs. RHB**

1989 Situational Stats

	W	L	ERA	Sv	IP		AB	H	HR	RBI	AVG
Home	5	2	4.09	0	61.2	LHB	122	29	1	13	.238
Road	0	7	4.50	0	52.0	RHB	309	87	6	44	.282
Day	2	2	2.92	0	40.0	Sc Pos	116	32	2	49	.276
Night	3	7	5.01	0	73.2	Clutch	59	16	2	6	.271

1989 Rankings (American League)

➡ Led the Indians in most GDPs induced per GDP situation (17.7%) - *team pitchers with 30 GDP situations*

HITTING:

Joey Belle made the jump from Class AA to the big leagues last July. Based on what he showed the Indians in 63 games, he won't be jumping back too soon. Belle brought two reputations with him -- one as a power hitter, the other as a hot-headed troublemaker. Both were deserved. The Indians suspended Belle twice during the 1988 minor league season. He even got kicked out of the Mexican League, a rare accomplishment, during the 1988 winter ball season. In Cleveland, though, Belle was a model citizen. The only person he got upset with was himself when he failed to perform on the field.

Belle hits out of a slightly closed right-handed stance. Most of his power is to left field, but he can drive the ball the opposite way as well. He has a disturbing habit of "stepping into the bucket" with his front foot just before starting his swing. When he's going good, it doesn't upset his timing. When he's slumping, however, it makes him pull off the ball and fail to make contact. Belle has a good working knowledge of the strike zone, a rarity for a young hitter. His final stats (55 strikeout, 12 walks) don't bear that out, but that's due more to rookie impatience than anything else. The thing that really impressed the Indians was Belle's ability to produce runs.

BASERUNNING:

Belle has average speed, and might develop into the kind of player who steals between 10-15 bases a year if he works at it. He'll go hard into second to break up a double play and isn't afraid to take an extra base.

FIELDING:

Belle looks awkward in the outfield, but showed he could close on soft hit bloopers and go back on well-hit line drives. He needs to tame a strong and wild arm. It will help when he learns where he's supposed to throw the ball in game situations.

OVERALL:

Belle has convinced the Indians he deserves serious consideration for a fulltime outfield job. He even caused Cory Snyder to take a seat on the bench for extended periods of time last year. He still needs polishing. His swing has large holes in it, and he must learn to lay off sliders and breaking balls just off the plate. But the talent -- power, a developing sense of the strike zone and a strong arm -- is there.

JOEY BELLE

Position: RF/DH/LF
Bats: R **Throws:** R
Ht: 6' 2" **Wt:** 200

Opening Day Age: 23
Born: 8/25/66 in Shreveport, LA
ML Seasons: 1

Overall Statistics

	G	AB	R	H	D	T	HR	RBI	SB	BB	SO	AVG
1989	62	218	22	49	8	4	7	37	2	12	55	.225
Career	62	218	22	49	8	4	7	37	2	12	55	.225

Where He Hits the Ball

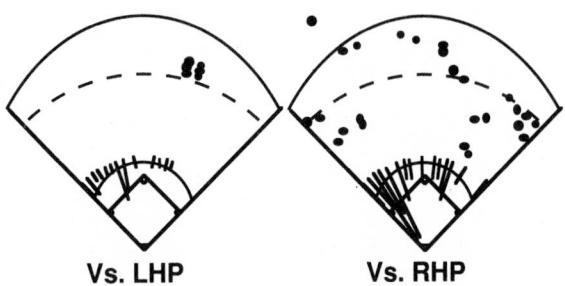

Vs. LHP　　　　**Vs. RHP**

1989 Situational Stats

	AB	H	HR	RBI	AVG		AB	H	HR	RBI	AVG
Home	115	28	3	25	.243	LHP	58	15	3	11	.259
Road	103	21	4	12	.204	RHP	160	34	4	26	.213
Day	56	15	1	13	.268	Sc Pos	59	20	2	30	.339
Night	162	34	6	24	.210	Clutch	39	10	1	11	.256

1989 Rankings (American League)

➡ Led the Indians in hitting with runners in scoring position (.339) - *all team players*

PITCHING:

Bud Black is back. The classy left-hander fell into baseball's bottomless hole -- middle relief -- after the 1985 season and didn't resurface until last year. It was a long climb back, but worth the wait. Black could have won 16 to 18 games if he had received the slightest bit of help from the Indians' offense. Talk about non-support. Black led the staff with 10 no decisions. In three of his 11 losses, the Indians were shut out. In nine of his losses, they scored three runs or less.

The key to 1989 for Black was a strong left elbow and the opportunity to be a starter. After the Indians acquired Black from Kansas City in 1988 for Pat Tabler, he was bothered by a sore left elbow and bounced from the disabled list to the bullpen to the rotation. Last year, Black's elbow was healthy and the Indians put him in the rotation from the first day of spring training and left him there. He responded by leading the staff in starts, innings pitched and shutouts and was second in complete games. It was the first time he'd won 12 or more games since 1984 and he was the only Tribe starter who didn't miss a start.

Black came up with a cut fastball last year that broke in on righthanded hitters and jammed them. It made him a five-pitch pitcher and he was able to throw them all for strikes -- fastball, slider, curveball, cutter and change up. The opposition hit .253 against him, but he dominated left-handed hitters (.158). Oddly enough, Black was third in the league with 13 wild pitches. He had a tendency to overthrow his pitches when a runner reached second base and they often ended up in the dirt.

FIELDING:

Black is a good fielder. He always covers first base on grounders to the right side of the infield. Black has a decent move to first base, but baserunners rattle him, especially when they reach second, so often he simply ignores them.

OVERALL:

Black's ability to throw five different pitches for strikes was the reason for his success in 1989. He's a finesse pitcher who has to pitch to locations to get people out. He's always prepared, knows how to work a hitter, and is intense during a game. He has a professional attitude, and never let the Indians' lack of offense hurt his performance on the field. It helped him retain his sanity and stay consistent on the mound.

BUD BLACK

Position: SP
Bats: L **Throws:** L
Ht: 6' 2" **Wt:** 180

Opening Day Age: 32
Born: 6/30/57 in San Mateo, CA
ML Seasons: 9

Overall Statistics

	W	L	ERA	G	GS	Sv	IP	H	R	BB	SO	HR
1989	12	11	3.36	33	32	0	222.1	213	95	52	88	14
Career	70	71	3.72	267	167	11	1260.0	1216	587	367	640	120

Where They Hit the Ball

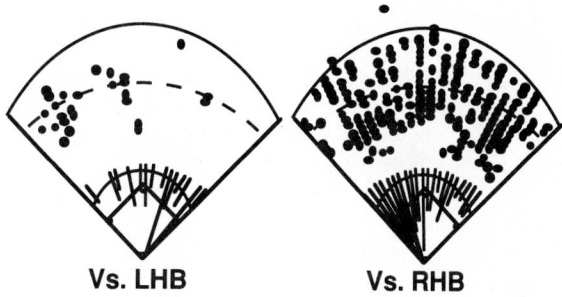

Vs. LHB   **Vs. RHB**

1989 Situational Stats

	W	L	ERA	Sv	IP		AB	H	HR	RBI	AVG
Home	5	9	4.06	0	115.1	LHB	120	19	2	6	.158
Road	7	2	2.61	0	107.0	RHB	724	194	12	69	.268
Day	3	6	3.63	0	67.0	Sc Pos	176	40	4	59	.227
Night	9	5	3.24	0	155.1	Clutch	104	30	2	11	.288

1989 Rankings (American League)

- ➡ 2nd in batting average vs. lefthanded batters (.158) - *pitchers facing 125 lefthanded batters*
- ➡ 3rd in wild pitches (13)
- ➡ 4th in shutouts (3)
- ➡ 5th in lowest strikeouts per 9 innings (3.6) - *pitchers with 162 IP*
- ➡ Led the Indians in games started (32), shutouts, innings (222.1), batters faced (912), wild pitches (13), GDPs induced (19), least baserunners per 9 innings (10.8), and lowest batting average with runners in scoring position (.226) - *team pitchers with 162 IP*

JERRY BROWNE

Position: 2B
Bats: B **Throws:** R
Ht: 5'10" **Wt:** 170

Opening Day Age: 24
Born: 2/13/66 in St. Croix, Virgin Islands
ML Seasons: 4

HITTING:

Jerry Browne is the man who saved Hank Peters' hide. At the winter meetings following the 1988 season, Peters, the Indians' president, sent proven .300 hitter Julio Franco to the Texas Rangers for Pete O'Brien, Oddibe McDowell and Browne. Browne was supposed to be a an extra body in the trade. He turned out to be its salvation when O'Brien had a mediocre year and McDowell didn't last the season, while Franco had a career year. The switch-hitting second baseman moved into the lead-off spot on May 29 when McDowell bombed and never looked back. Browne hit .303 in 114 games as a lead-off hitter, scoring 67 runs with a .385 on-base percentage. He hit .350 (36 for 103) leading off the first inning and needed one hit in his last at-bat of the season to hit .300 for the year. Instead, he sacrificed the winning run to third base as the Indians beat the Chicago White Sox, 1-0.

Browne is a line-drive, contact hitter with occasional power. The key to his season was the ability to make adjustments from one at-bat to the next. His longest slump of the season was only 0 for 16. Browne has a good idea of the strike zone. He walked more times than he struck out (68 to 64), while scoring 83 runs.

BASERUNNING:

Not overly fast, Browne led the Indians in stolen bases with 14; they'd like to see him steal more in the future. He runs the bases well and will break up a double play. He has enough speed to score from first on an extra base hit.

FIELDING:

Browne is a decent fielder with above average range and an adequate arm. He's especially effective going to his left at second base and charging slow hit balls to the right side of the mound. His pivot on the double play needs work. He made 15 errors, the majority of them coming on routine grounders.

OVERALL:

Browne ran out of gas at the end of the season, but still produced 20 percent of the Indians' runs. That's amazing for a lead-off hitter. The question is, can he do it again? He has never come close to that kind of production over a full season, so 1990 will be a telling year. Ideally, the Indians would like to move him to the No. 2 spot in the lineup if they could obtain a lead-off hitter with speed.

Overall Statistics

	G	AB	R	H	D	T	HR	RBI	SB	BB	SO	AVG
1989	153	598	83	179	31	4	5	45	14	68	64	.299
Career	370	1290	178	361	58	12	7	103	48	155	151	.280

Where He Hits the Ball

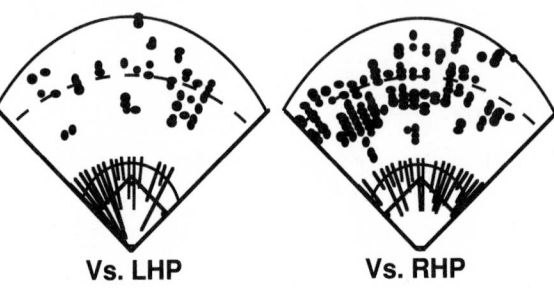

Vs. LHP   **Vs. RHP**

1989 Situational Stats

	AB	H	HR	RBI	AVG		AB	H	HR	RBI	AVG
Home	316	105	1	24	.332	LHP	175	54	2	17	.309
Road	282	74	4	21	.262	RHP	423	125	3	28	.296
Day	199	58	2	14	.291	Sc Pos	115	32	1	39	.278
Night	399	121	3	31	.303	Clutch	97	29	1	4	.299

1989 Rankings (American League)

- 3rd highest leadoff on-base average (.385) - *players with 150 PA batting leadoff*
- 6th in sacrifice bunts (14)
- 8th in singles (139)
- 9th in batting average with 2 strikes (.271) - *players with 162 PA*
- 10th in plate appearances (685)
- Led the Indians in batting average (.299), hits (179), singles, stolen bases (14), caught stealing (6), times on base (248), pitches seen (2,440), on-base average (.370), batting average with 2 strikes, hitting with runners in scoring position (.278), hitting in the clutch (.299) - *team players with 502 PA*

PITCHING:

Tom Candiotti finally did it. He put solid numbers on the board for two straight seasons. It might not sound like much, but for a guy who throws a knuckleball anywhere from 50 to 90 percent of the time, that's an accomplishment. The knuckleball is a unpredictable pitch and Candiotti's statistics in his four seasons in Cleveland have matched its erratic flight. In 1986, The Candy Man went 16-12. The next year he fell to 7-18 before going 14-8 in 1988. Last year Candiotti went 13-10 with a 3.10 earned run average, his lowest ever. He did it by becoming a mix master. He has the knuckleball, featured at two speeds, a variety of curveballs and an 82 mph fastball that's used for shock treatment.

Most of the time, Candiotti throws softer than a good batting practice pitcher. He has a slow and fast knuckler and a slow curveball that has been clocked at less than 60 mph. When Candiotti needs to throw a strike, he goes to the curveball. He'll vary speeds on it, but it's the one pitch he feels he can throw over the plate at any time in any situation. A thinking man's pitcher, he frustrates the opposing lineup with knuckleballs and slow curves. Then he'll slip in his 82 mph fastball; at that point, the fastball looks like Roger Clemens threw it.

In a jam, Candiotti will drop down to a sidearm motion against righthanded hitters. Whether he throws a knuckler or a curve, he's almost unhittable in that situation. He dominates free-swinging, power-hitting teams. However, patient contact hitters give him the most trouble.

FIELDING:

One of the better athletes on the Tribe pitching staff, Candiotti gets off the mound quickly and always backs up the right base on extra base hits. He has an excellent pickoff move to first, so would-be base-stealers can't take too many liberties against his slow-moving knuckleball.

OVERALL:

Candiotti is obviously a fine pitcher, but his health is a concern. He's spent time on the disabled list the last two seasons for shoulder and rotator cuff problems. It's a paradox since he doesn't throw that hard, but changing speeds and arm angles has taken a toll. He's a workhorse, pitching over 200 innings in each of four straight seasons, but he must be watched carefully so he isn't overworked. The last two years, he's learned to tell the manager when his tank is empty.

TOM CANDIOTTI

Position: SP
Bats: R **Throws:** R
Ht: 6' 2" **Wt:** 200

Opening Day Age: 32
Born: 8/31/57 in Walnut Creek, CA
ML Seasons: 6

Overall Statistics

	W	L	ERA	G	GS	Sv	IP	H	R	BB	SO	HR
1989	13	10	3.10	31	31	0	206.0	188	80	55	124	10
Career	56	54	3.69	148	142	0	964.2	940	452	333	583	80

Where They Hit the Ball

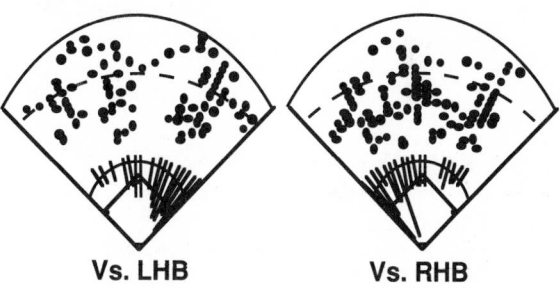

Vs. LHB   Vs. RHB

1989 Situational Stats

	W	L	ERA	Sv	IP		AB	H	HR	RBI	AVG
Home	7	3	2.95	0	100.2	LHB	395	97	5	38	.246
Road	6	7	3.25	0	105.1	RHB	383	91	5	29	.238
Day	5	3	3.41	0	71.1	Sc Pos	162	40	2	57	.247
Night	8	7	2.94	0	134.2	Clutch	77	18	0	5	.234

1989 Rankings (American League)

- ➡ 2nd in balks (8), lowest run support per 9 innings (3.5), on-base average leading off innings (.242) and HRs per 9 innings (.44) - *pitchers with 162 IP*

- ➡ 4th in least GDPs per 9 innings (.48) and pickoff throws (247)

- ➡ Led the Indians in ERA (3.10), wins (13), balks, pickoff throws, stolen bases allowed (24), lowest opponent batting average (.242), lowest on-base average allowed (.294), lowest slugging percentage allowed (.319) and least HRs per 9 innings - *team pitchers with 162 IP*

HITTING:

What a maddening season Joe Carter had in 1989. So maddening that it's hard to get a true reading on it. While playing for the lowest scoring team in the American League, Carter finished second in the league in home runs and tied for fourth in RBI with 105. He produced 25 percent of the Indians' 604 runs, a worthy achievement. Yet Carter batted only .243, his all-time low, and struck out 112 times, his all-time high. The most disturbing thing about Carter's performance was his refusal to adjust his hitting style. He struck out on the same pitches that he struck out on as a rookie in 1984.

Carter is a sucker for any kind of breaking ball down and away when he's behind on the count. Throw a slider or curveball on the outside part of the plate and he'll swing and miss until his head falls off. Another problem is that he's turned into a dead pull hitter to left field. He's closed his stance and tries to yank everything out of the ballpark. He's a different player from 1986, when he hit .302 with 29 homers, 121 RBI and went to right field all the time. Now Carter refuses to go with the pitch.

BASERUNNING:

This is another area of Carter's game that has deteriorated. Between 1985 and 1988, Carter averaged over 27 stolen bases per season. But last year, he stole just 13 bases. Carter said his legs ached from playing centerfield. Then he said he was trying to leave the hole open between first and second for the left-handed hitting Pete O'Brien. But the fact was, he just stopped running. When he feels like it, he can still run the bases aggressively.

FIELDING:

After a stellar year in centerfield in 1988, Carter looked like he'd never played the position before in 1989. He misjudged several balls early in the season and played scared the rest of the way. His play did improve when he moved to left field. He has an above average arm and runners take the extra base on him less than they do on most other center fielders.

OVERALL:

Carter played the 1989 season like a man trying to get out of Cleveland. He battled with the media, the fans, and the front office. Carter can be a free agent after 1990 and the Indians went into the 1989 offseason seriously considering trading him. When he's happy, Carter is an amazing talent. But he wasn't happy in 1989.

JOE CARTER

Position: CF/1B/LF
Bats: R **Throws:** R
Ht: 6' 3" **Wt:** 215

Opening Day Age: 30
Born: 3/7/60 in Oklahoma City, OK
ML Seasons: 7

Overall Statistics

	G	AB	R	H	D	T	HR	RBI	SB	BB	SO	AVG
1989	162	651	84	158	32	4	35	105	13	39	112	.243
Career	862	3307	462	885	165	23	151	531	127	169	537	.268

Where He Hits the Ball

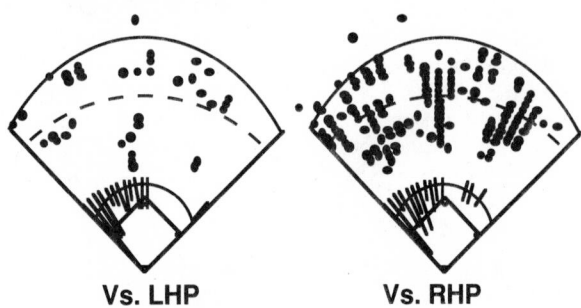

Vs. LHP   Vs. RHP

1989 Situational Stats

	AB	H	HR	RBI	AVG		AB	H	HR	RBI	AVG
Home	329	80	16	55	.243	LHP	187	40	8	26	.214
Road	322	78	19	50	.242	RHP	464	118	27	79	.254
Day	213	48	5	22	.225	Sc Pos	179	49	6	66	.274
Night	438	110	30	83	.251	Clutch	108	20	5	15	.185

1989 Rankings (American League)

- ➡ 1st in games (162) and at bats (651)
- ➡ 2nd in home runs (35)
- ➡ 3rd in total bases (303)
- ➡ 4th in RBI (105)
- ➡ 5th in hit by pitch (8) and plate appearances (705)
- ➡ Led the Indians in at bats, home runs, runs (84), doubles (32), total bases (303), RBI, hit by pitch, plate appearances, games, slugging percentage (.465) and least ABs per HR (18.6) - *team players with 502 PA*
- ➡ Led AL Center Fielders in home runs, at bats, RBI, hit by pitch, plate appearances, games and least ABs per HR

HITTING:

Dave Clark is caught in the age-old baseball vise. He's a player who needs to play every day in order to hit, but hasn't been able to get himself off the bench to get the opportunity. Clark did open last season as the Indians' left-handed designated hitter, but was never able to get hot enough to take over the job fulltime despite receiving a career high 253 at-bats. He started only five of the Indians' last 34 games.

Clark is a line-drive hitter, but he developed a severe contact problem last year. He fanned 63 times, showing little patience at the plate. At the beginning of the year, he hit for a decent average (.295 on May 10), by hitting singles and doubles to left field. But he wasn't producing many runs and the Indians suggested he try and pull the ball more to right field. Clark hit his major-league high eight home runs in 1989, but he was constantly pulling off the pitch too soon in an effort to jerk it over the fence. It was a problem he never corrected. High fastballs and breaking balls gave him the most problems. As to whether he's more than a platoon-type hitter, it's hard to say. The Indians really never gave him a chance to find out if he could hit left- handers. Last year he had just nine at bats against lefties.

BASERUNNING:

Clark once stole 27 bases in the minors, but he's grown fat and slowed down since then. Scouts remarked over how much weight Clark had put on last year. He'll go into second base hard to break up a double play, and will go from first to third when the opportunity presents itself. But his days as a base stealer are behind him.

FIELDING:

Clark is an average to below average outfielder. He can play left and right field, with right being his best position. He has a strong arm, but he doesn't get to use it very often.

OVERALL:

If Clark is still with the Indians in 1990 -- and that's questionable -- he seems destined to play the role of a spare part. Unfortunately, in years past he's been unable to produce offensively when coming off the bench. However, last year he hit .241 as a pinch-hitter with two home runs. So maybe he's learned something. If not, his days in the big leagues are numbered.

DAVE CLARK

Position: DH/LF
Bats: L **Throws:** R
Ht: 6' 2" **Wt:** 200

Opening Day Age: 27
Born: 9/3/62 in Tupelo, MS
ML Seasons: 4

Overall Statistics

	G	AB	R	H	D	T	HR	RBI	SB	BB	SO	AVG
1989	102	253	21	60	12	0	8	29	0	30	63	.237
Career	212	554	53	135	22	1	17	68	2	56	126	.244

Where He Hits the Ball

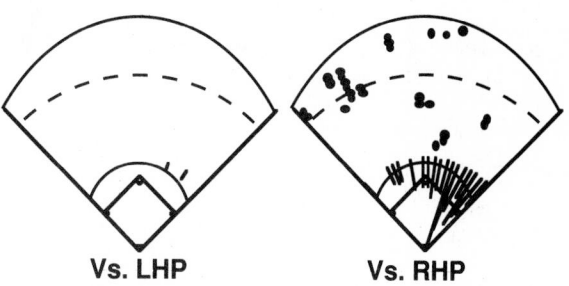

Vs. LHP   Vs. RHP

1989 Situational Stats

	AB	H	HR	RBI	AVG		AB	H	HR	RBI	AVG
Home	123	29	4	15	.236	LHP	9	1	0	0	.111
Road	130	31	4	14	.238	RHP	244	59	8	29	.242
Day	105	21	5	14	.200	Sc Pos	63	12	1	20	.190
Night	148	39	3	15	.264	Clutch	58	14	2	7	.241

1989 Rankings (American League)

➡ Did not rank near the top or bottom in any category

PITCHING:

Baseball is a series of games within a game. Adjustments are a key to winning those games. John Farrell has shown he can make those adjustments. Now he just has to prove he can win on a consistent basis. Farrell's first adjustment got him to the big leagues late in the 1987 season. He'd floundered in the Indians' minor league system for most of four seasons before he reduced his delivery, allowing him to get the ball to the plate faster. But the new windup also presented problems. In 1988 Farrell went 14-10, but his right elbow suffered from too much strain. He went on the disabled list with an inflamed elbow in both '88 and spring training '89. But with the help of pitching coach Mark Wiley, Farrell changed his new motion again, coming over the top more to relieve pressure on the elbow.

While Farrell's elbow stayed pain free, it took him more than half a season to feel comfortable with the new delivery. It proved to be worth the wait. Farrell's fastball climbed from the 87-88 mph range to a consistent 92-94 mph, and he became one of the hardest throwing, albeit unknown, starters in the American League. A three-pitch pitcher, he features the fastball, a much-improved slider and a change-up. The change-up is brutal on righthanders, but at times he forgets about his change up and gets hit. Like all Indian starters, Farrell would have fared better in the won-loss column with any kind of offensive support.

FIELDING:

Farrell is quick off the mound on bunts and check-swing nubbers in front of the plate. He always covers first base and can start the 1-6-3 double play without throwing the ball into center field. He helps himself as a fielder. He has worked hard on his pickoff move, but runners were successful on 20 of 23 steal attempts against Farrell last year.

OVERALL:

Farrell could become the ace of the Indians' staff. With lefty Greg Swindell prone to injury, Farrell has the size, strength and endurance to be the Tribe's No.1 starter. Yet he himself must stay injury free and must also cut down on his pitches. He gets excellent movement on the ball, and at times is simply overpowering, but he throws too many balls out of the strike zone. A good competitor, he looks like a Marine getting ready to charge an enemy bunker on days he pitches.

JOHN FARRELL

Position: SP
Bats: R **Throws:** R
Ht: 6' 4"   **Wt:** 210

Opening Day Age: 27
Born: 8/4/62 in Monmouth PK, NJ
ML Seasons: 3

Overall Statistics

	W	L	ERA	G	GS	Sv	IP	H	R	BB	SO	HR
1989	9	14	3.63	31	31	0	208.0	196	97	71	132	14
Career	28	25	3.86	72	70	0	487.1	480	232	160	252	36

Where They Hit the Ball

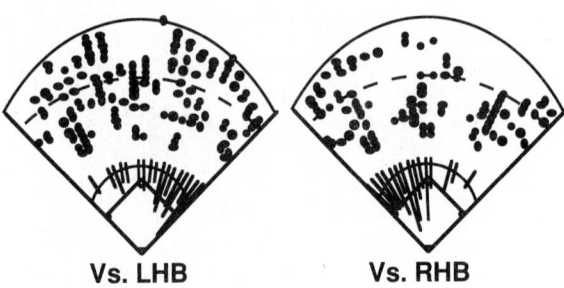

Vs. LHB   Vs. RHB

1989 Situational Stats

	W	L	ERA	Sv	IP		AB	H	HR	RBI	AVG
Home	5	6	3.21	0	109.1	LHB	420	98	6	43	.233
Road	4	8	4.10	0	98.2	RHB	383	98	8	36	.256
Day	2	8	4.88	0	75.2	Sc Pos	195	49	2	63	.251
Night	7	6	2.92	0	132.1	Clutch	78	18	3	8	.231

1989 Rankings (American League)

➡ 2nd in worst stolen base percentage allowed (87.0%) and least GDPs per 9 innings (.216) - *pitchers with 162 IP*

➡ 4th in losses (14)

➡ Led the Indians in losses, complete games (7), walks allowed (71), hit batsmen (7), strikeouts (132) and pitches thrown (3,246)

CLEVELAND INDIANS

HITTING:

Felix (The Cat) Fermin played his first full season in the big leagues last year. When it was over, the right-handed hitting shortstop had compiled a peculiar array of statistics. He led the American League in sacrifice bunts with 32. It was the most sacrifice bunts by a major league player since 1979, and the most by an Indians' player since Joe Sewell had 41 in 1929. The Cat was the third hardest player to strike out in the league, fanning just 27 times in 484 at bats. Fermin also had 21 RBIs in 156 games. That's the fewest RBIs by a player who appeared in 150 or more games in one season in AL history.

The Cat makes contact, can hit and run and will move a runner a long with a sac-bunt. Just don't ask him to produce runs. He has three triples, nine doubles and no home runs in 739 major league at bats. Fermin chokes up on the bat and uses a compact swing. He makes contact with almost every kind of pitch, but loves fastballs. He hits almost exclusively to right field, and that presented a problem. Due to Fermin's lack of power, opposing right fielders played so shallow that at times they could have held hands with the second and first basemen. The Indians asked Fermin to go on a weight-training program to have enough muscle to be able to neutralize that kind of defense.

BASERUNNING:

Fermin isn't especially fast, but he'll go from first to third on almost any hit that leaves the infield. He can steal a base in certain situations.

FIELDING:

This is where The Cat earns his kitty chow. He made plays at shortstop that Cleveland fans haven't seen in years. He has great range to his left and right, but his favorite play is grabbing a ground ball on the outfield grass behind second, doing a 360 and throwing to first for the out. He did commit 26 errors and wore down physically in the second half. He has a strong arm that he uses wisely.

OVERALL:

A good offensive team could easily carry a defensive specialist like Fermin. But with the Indians Fermin becomes a liability. He must improve his upper body strength or the Indians might go searching for a more offensive-minded shortstop despite Fermin's magic paws.

FELIX FERMIN

Position: SS
Bats: R **Throws:** R
Ht: 5'11" **Wt:** 170

Opening Day Age: 26
Born: 10/9/63 in Mao, Dominican Republic
ML Seasons: 3

Overall Statistics

	G	AB	R	H	D	T	HR	RBI	SB	BB	SO	AVG
1989	156	484	50	115	9	1	0	21	6	41	27	.238
Career	222	639	65	156	9	3	0	27	9	53	46	.244

Where He Hits the Ball

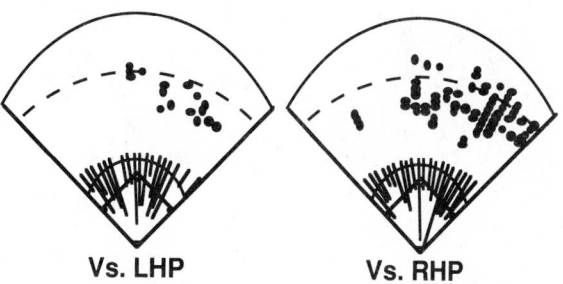

Vs. LHP   Vs. RHP

1989 Situational Stats

	AB	H	HR	RBI	AVG		AB	H	HR	RBI	AVG
Home	235	53	0	10	.226	LHP	130	32	0	8	.246
Road	249	62	0	11	.249	RHP	354	83	0	13	.234
Day	162	41	0	4	.253	Sc Pos	109	20	0	21	.183
Night	322	74	0	17	.230	Clutch	66	18	0	4	.273

1989 Rankings (American League)

→ 1st in lowest slugging percentage (.260), bunts in play (42), grounder/flyball ratio (4.17), sacrifice bunts (32), and errors (26) - *players with 502 PA*

→ 2nd in lowest percent of swings that missed (5.4%) and lowest batting average with runners in scoring position (.183)

→ Led the Indians in sacrifice bunts, GDPs (15), grounder/flyball ratio, bunts in play, lowest percentage of swings that missed and errors

→ Led AL Shortstops in sacrifice bunts, grounder/flyball ratio, bunts in play, lowest percentage of swings that missed and errors

HITTING:

What kind of year did Brook Jacoby have last season? He had a grind-it-out, get-it-done season that marked his return from the ashes of 1988. On the last day of the year, with absolutely nothing to prove, Jacoby went 3 for 4 to finish the season with a respectable .272 batting average. It was a 31 point improvement over the .241 he hit in 1988.

That wasn't the only number that rose from the dead. His home runs increased from nine to 14 and his RBI climbed from 49 to 64. Not flashy numbers, to be sure. But Jacoby isn't a flashy kind of player. He improved last year because he regained the feel for his strike zone. In 1988, pitchers worked him inside with high fastballs and he couldn't get around on them. Last year, he laid off that pitch and waited for them to come down in the strike zone. He got better pitches to hit and also increased his walks from 48 to 62.

As a result, Jacoby became a better breaking-ball hitter. Instead of trying to pull those pitches, he went the opposite way. He also changed his stance. In 1988, he used a closed stance and would jam himself when he tried to turn on a fastball. Last season, he used a straight-up stance that gave him more control of the strike zone.

BASERUNNING:

Jacoby is a poor baserunner. He hustles down to first and will try to break up a double play at second, but the instincts just aren't there. He's very cautious when it comes to going from first to third and has difficulty reading the ball off the bat. He'll steal one or two bases a year, usually involving a double steal.

FIELDING:

Jacoby is a maligned and underrated defensive third baseman. He doesn't have much range, but over the years has learned to position himself correctly. He's also become more aggressive. He never used to dive for balls down the line or to his left. Now he does. He also charges bunts well.

OVERALL:

Last year was a comeback season for Jacoby. But he hasn't come back all the way. He might never hit 32 home runs or drive in 87 runs again, but the Indians need him to be a consistent offense force on the club. That means he has to start hitting in the clutch, a weak point over the last two years.

BROOK JACOBY

Position: 3B
Bats: R **Throws:** R
Ht: 5'11" **Wt:** 195

Opening Day Age: 30
Born: 11/23/59 in Philadelphia, PA
ML Seasons: 8

Overall Statistics

	G	AB	R	H	D	T	HR	RBI	SB	BB	SO	AVG
1989	147	519	49	141	26	5	13	64	2	62	90	.272
Career	914	3257	400	888	152	19	98	390	13	321	598	.273

Where He Hits the Ball

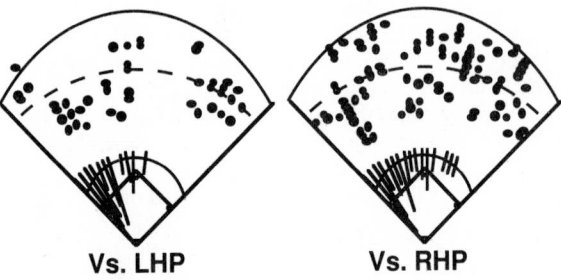

Vs. LHP   Vs. RHP

1989 Situational Stats

	AB	H	HR	RBI	AVG		AB	H	HR	RBI	AVG
Home	248	66	7	32	.266	LHP	152	45	6	19	.296
Road	271	75	6	32	.277	RHP	367	96	7	45	.262
Day	174	41	2	20	.236	Sc Pos	108	24	2	43	.222
Night	345	100	11	44	.290	Clutch	91	24	3	14	.264

1989 Rankings (American League)

- ➡ 1st in lowest percentage of runs scored per time on base (21.5%) - players with 502 PA
- ➡ Led the Indians in triples (5), sacrifice flies (8), and GDPs (15)

HITTING:

Dion James did something most of his teammates had a hard time doing last year. He hit the baseball consistently. The Indians acquired James from Atlanta for Oddibe McDowell on July 2. He was the only Indian with 70+ games to hit over .300. James is a good line drive hitter with some power. The Indians even gave him a chance to face lefties on occasion.

The Indians used James mostly as their No.2 hitter. Although he's a below average runner at best, he handled the bat well enough to take advantage of lead-off hitter Jerry Browne's .370 on-base percentage. He can hit behind the runner, and works the hit and run well. James, though, is the kind of hitter who could bat almost anywhere in the lineup. He's versatile at the plate, and doesn't mind doing the little things necessary to win ballgames. He has a good knowledge of the strike zone. Breaking balls give him the most problems, but he fears no pitcher. He likes to hit, and believes he can hit, which wasn't the case with some of his teammates last year. James performed much better as an everyday player. He had trouble coming off the bench, batting just .167 (2 for 12) as a pinch-hitter.

BASERUNNING:

James hustles, but he's a below average runner. He isn't afraid to dive into first base head first on an infield single, but most of the times he doesn't get close enough to do it. He's a fair baserunner going from first to third, but should never be called on to steal a base.

FIELDING:

Under Doc Edwards, James saw most of his playing time in left field or at DH. Edwards felt James was a defensive liability. When interim manager John Hart replaced Edwards on Sept. 12, James started seeing more playing time in center field, and he did an adequate job. He has trouble coming in on balls and his range is limited. His arm is only fair. The Indians asked him to lose weight and get in better shape to increase his range in preparation for 1990.

OVERALL:

The Indians like James, but mostly as a bench player. They see him as a fourth or fifth outfielder, who can DH and pinch-hit late in a game. If he plays the outfield for them regularly, it means he's either hitting a ton or the Indians are in trouble.

DION JAMES

Position: LF/DH/RF
Bats: L **Throws:** L
Ht: 6' 1" **Wt:** 170

Opening Day Age: 27
Born: 11/9/62 in Philadelphia, PA
ML Seasons: 6

Overall Statistics

	G	AB	R	H	D	T	HR	RBI	SB	BB	SO	AVG
1989	134	415	41	119	18	0	5	40	2	49	49	.287
Career	557	1751	225	499	92	16	19	165	32	217	220	.285

Where He Hits the Ball

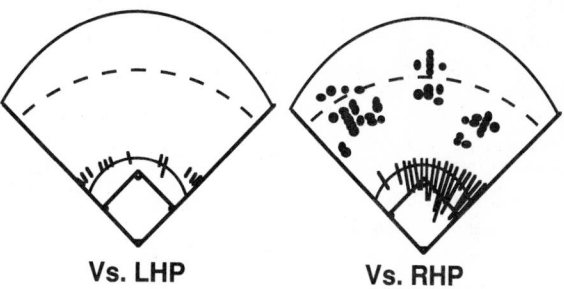

Vs. LHP   **Vs. RHP**

1989 Situational Stats

	AB	H	HR	RBI	AVG		AB	H	HR	RBI	AVG
Home	200	44	1	16	.220	LHP	52	11	0	2	.212
Road	215	75	4	24	.349	RHP	363	108	5	38	.298
Day	137	50	2	14	.365	Sc Pos	95	22	0	28	.232
Night	278	69	3	26	.248	Clutch	76	18	0	7	.237

1989 Rankings (American League)

➡ Led the Indians in batting average (.306) - *all team players*

DOUG JONES

Position: RP
Bats: R **Throws:** R
Ht: 6' 2" **Wt:** 195

Opening Day Age: 32
Born: 6/24/57 in Covina, CA
ML Seasons: 4

PITCHING:

Doug Jones is a stopper who out-guesses hitters even though he throws only a change-up and a fastball. Those two pitches are more like six, because Jones varies the speed on his pitches, making them do different things at different times. The key for him is the gap between his fastball and change-up. The bigger the gap, the more effective he is. Jones can sometimes hit 88 mph with his fastball. That makes his slow-motion change even more effective.

Jones figured in 53 percent of the Tribe's wins last season. In 1988, he had a hand in 51 percent of the Wahoos' wins. In just three seasons he has become the Tribe's all-time save leader. He did it the hard way, too. Jones spent almost ten years in the minors before the Indians gave him a shot. No one thought he threw hard enough to be a closer; he proved them wrong.

Jones is all business on the mound. He doesn't make eye contact with hitters. Instead, he pulls his cap down low and appears to be staring straight at the ground. What he's really doing is checking the positioning of the batter's feet so he'll know where to throw the next pitch. He throws every pitch with the same action, same mechanics and same release point. That way hitters don't know if Jones is throwing them a fastball or change of pace.

FIELDING:

Jones is not a pretty fielder, although he has improved from 1987 when he committed five errors. He has some trouble getting off the mound for hits in front of the plate. He does cover first base on grounders and is fearless when it comes to starting the 1-6-3 double play. He does an outstanding job of holding baserunners; only one runner tried to steal off Jones last year, and he was thrown out.

OVERALL:

Though he's had two straight good years, it's possible Jones may need a new pitch. In 1988, the opposition hit .218 against him. Last year, they hit .251. He also blew nine save opportunities. The key for him is throwing strikes; over the last two years, Jones has 137 strikeouts and only 29 walks (seven of them intentional) in 164 innings.

Overall Statistics

	W	L	ERA	G	GS	Sv	IP	H	R	BB	SO	HR
1989	7	10	2.34	59	0	32	80.2	76	25	13	65	4
Career	17	19	2.60	170	0	78	273.1	264	101	59	236	9

Where They Hit the Ball

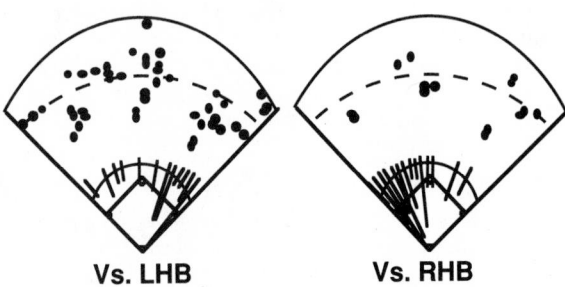

Vs. LHB   **Vs. RHB**

1989 Situational Stats

	W	L	ERA	Sv	IP		AB	H	HR	RBI	AVG
Home	6	4	2.15	15	46.0	LHB	160	39	4	17	.244
Road	1	6	2.60	17	34.2	RHB	143	37	0	15	.259
Day	1	3	1.47	10	18.1	Sc Pos	93	22	3	31	.237
Night	6	7	2.60	22	62.1	Clutch	264	67	4	32	.254

1989 Rankings (American League)

→ 2nd in worst first batter efficiency (.327) - pitchers with 40 games in relief

→ 3rd in blown saves (9)

→ 4th in strikeout/walk ratio (5.00) - *all league pitchers*

→ 5th in save percentage (78.0%) - *pitchers with 20 save opportunities*

→ 6th in saves (32) and games finished (53)

→ Led the Indians in saves, games finished, saves percentage, least stolen bases allowed (0), and percent of inherited runners scoring (22.5%) - *pitchers with 30 inherited runners*

HITTING:

Brad Komminsk was a pleasant surprise in an otherwise ugly season for the Indians. They signed him after the 1988 season as a minor league free agent. Komminsk made the Tribe's 24-man roster when they discovered he could play center field. Little did they know that Komminsk's defensive ability would eventually force Joe Carter to left field. An asthma attack sent Komminsk back to Class AAA, but he was recalled on June 29 and stayed the rest of the season. The former No.1 pick from Atlanta, the can't-miss prospect who kept missing, had his best overall season in the big leagues.

Komminsk is a one zone hitter. Put the ball in that zone, and he'll hit it. However, if pitchers move the ball around in the strike zone, he's going to struggle. He tried to reduce his long swing, but still fanned 55 times in 198 at bats. Still, he can look bad for three at bats, and then hit a game-winning home run in the late innings. The Indians were 8-0 when he homered, and in one stretch he hit three straight game-winning homers -- one of them coming in the ninth inning and another in the tenth.

BASERUNNING:

Komminsk is one of the fastest players on the Indians. He could have stolen a few more bases, but his playing time was so erratic he never got into a groove. He gets a good jump on the pitcher, can score from first on extra base hits and goes from first to third with ease.

FIELDING:

Komminsk hadn't played center field since the low minors, but when he moved to that position in spring training, it looked like he'd been playing it his whole life. He has all the tools a centerfielder needs -- speed into the left and right field gaps, the ability to get a quick jump on the ball, and no fear of the fence. His arm, average at best, is his only defensive liability.

OVERALL:

Komminsk is another player the Indians would like to use to improve their bench. So far his offense has been too inconsistent to deserve regular playing time, but he can pinch-run or pinch-hit late in the game because of his power and speed. He can also play late-inning defense. He also showed the Indians he could play well for a week or two if a regular went down with an injury.

BRAD KOMMINSK

Position: CF
Bats: R **Throws:** R
Ht: 6' 2" **Wt:** 205

Opening Day Age: 29
Born: 4/4/61 in Lima, OH
ML Seasons: 6

Overall Statistics

	G	AB	R	H	D	T	HR	RBI	SB	BB	SO	AVG
1989	71	198	27	47	8	2	8	33	8	24	55	.237
Career	298	855	119	187	32	5	20	95	37	97	218	.219

Where He Hits the Ball

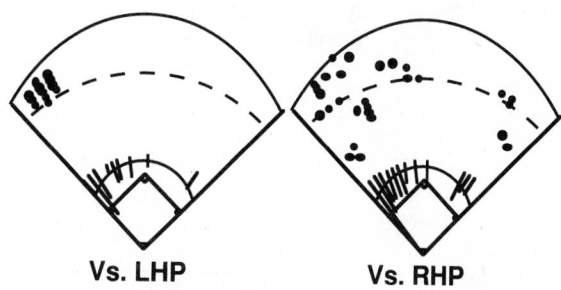

Vs. LHP   **Vs. RHP**

1989 Situational Stats

	AB	H	HR	RBI	AVG		AB	H	HR	RBI	AVG
Home	115	31	6	23	.270	LHP	65	11	1	9	.169
Road	83	16	2	10	.193	RHP	133	36	7	24	.271
Day	50	13	2	10	.260	Sc Pos	61	16	3	25	.262
Night	148	34	6	23	.230	Clutch	32	6	2	6	.188

1989 Rankings (American League)

➡ Led the Indians in stolen base percentage (80%) - *all team players*

PITCHING:

At times last year, Rod Nichols looked more than ready to be the Indians' fifth starter in 1990. At other times, he looked lost. That's typical of a young pitcher trying to break into the big leagues. Nichols started the year in Class AAA and went 8-1 overall between two promotions to Cleveland. He won his first three starts with the Tribe, but then lost five of his last six decisions. Such is life for a struggling young pitcher.

Nichols is deceptive on the mound. During his wind up, he turns his back entirely to the batter, a la Luis Tiant. He has a good fastball and slider, but it's his off-speed pitch that makes him distinctive. He throws a big-breaking curveball for his change of pace pitch. He'll throw it at any time in the count and can usually throw it for strikes. It's enough to wobble a right-handed hitter's knees and break his heart at the same time. But he had a lot of problems with left-handed hitters. They could see his off-speed stuff coming from a long way off and were ready for it.

Nichols used to have trouble controlling his temper on the mound. In 1985 at Class A Batavia, he became so upset at one of his performances that he tried to flush his glove down a toilet after the game. He's in much better control of his emotions now, but he's still extremely competitive. He's not afraid to work the inside part of the plate on a hitter, and he'll retaliate if the opposing pitcher brushes back one of his team-mates.

FIELDING:

Nichols won't embarrass himself defensively. He gets off the mound quickly and always covers first base. His move to first is below average.

OVERALL:

The next step in Nichols' career is up to him. If he proves he can be consistent, he could move into the starting rotation on a fulltime basis. Last year, he had stretches where he was unhittable. At other times, he had trouble getting out of the first inning because he couldn't throw a strike. The Indians must find out if he can pitch late into a ballgame. If not, they'll have to go get him after six or seven innings.

ROD NICHOLS

Position: SP
Bats: R **Throws:** R
Ht: 6' 2" **Wt:** 190

Opening Day Age: 25
Born: 12/29/64 in Burlington, IA
ML Seasons: 2

Overall Statistics

	W	L	ERA	G	GS	Sv	IP	H	R	BB	SO	HR
1989	4	6	4.40	15	11	0	71.2	81	42	24	42	9
Career	5	13	4.72	26	21	0	141.0	154	83	47	73	14

Where They Hit the Ball

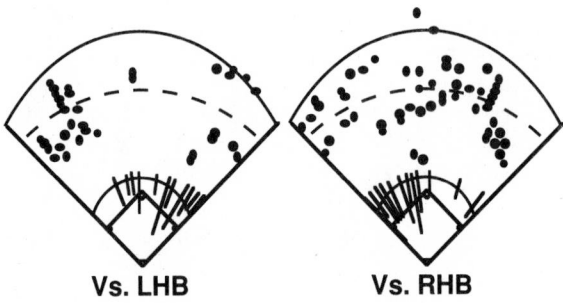

Vs. LHB   **Vs. RHB**

1989 Situational Stats

	W	L	ERA	Sv	IP		AB	H	HR	RBI	AVG
Home	2	2	3.22	0	44.2	LHB	127	41	5	15	.323
Road	2	4	6.33	0	27.0	RHB	157	40	4	23	.255
Day	0	1	4.15	0	8.2	Sc Pos	53	18	2	26	.340
Night	4	5	4.43	0	63.0	Clutch	33	10	3	8	.303

1989 Rankings (American League)

→ Did not rank near the top or bottom in any category

HITTING:

The Indians expected better things from Pete O'Brien in 1989. So did Pete O'Brien. For the third straight season, O'Brien's production in home runs and runs batted in slipped. In fact, O'Brien's .260 batting average was his lowest since 1983 and his 12 home runs were the fewest he's hit in a full big-league season. Certainly he lacked consistency. On April 30, he was hitting .400. By the All-Star break, he had slumped to .278. He built his average back to .289, but overall he hit just .238 after the break. What's more, O'Brien stopped driving the ball. He hit just two homers after June 24, a span of 81 games covering 300 at bats. He turned into a singles hitter.

Part of O'Brien's problem was frustration. He spent most of the season hitting behind Joe Carter, an all or nothing-type player who either cleared the bases or struck out. That meant O'Brien didn't have many RBI opportunities. And when there were runners on base, the opposition usually didn't pitch to him. He walked 83 times, including 17 intentional walks. O'Brien grew impatient because he was being pitched around, but his ability to draw walks helped him prevent a real disaster. He reached base by a hit or walk in 121 of his 153 games (79%).

BASERUNNING:

O'Brien is not fast, but he has excellent baserunning instincts. He reads the ball off the bat very well, and can gamble in certain situations. He'll go hard into second base to break up a double play and will go from first to third when the opportunity presents itself. O'Brien is not a base stealer, however.

DEFENSE:

O'Brien gave the Indians their best defensive performance at first base since the days of Mike Hargrove. He's excellent at scooping low throws out of the dirt. He also has soft hands and starts the 3-6-3 double play very well. O'Brien has good range at first and any foul pops he can track down, he'll catch.

OVERALL:

The Indians wanted to re-sign O'Brien, a free agent, because they have no one else in their system who can play first. But at press time they still hadn't reached an agreement. O'Brien went on record as saying he would only return to the Indians if they improved their offense. He said he needed people who could get on base hitting in front and behind him to be successful.

PETE O'BRIEN

Position: 1B
Bats: L **Throws:** L
Ht: 6' 2" **Wt:** 205

Opening Day Age: 32
Born: 2/9/58 in Santa Monica, CA
ML Seasons: 8

Overall Statistics

	G	AB	R	H	D	T	HR	RBI	SB	BB	SO	AVG
1989	155	554	75	144	24	1	12	55	3	83	48	.260
Career	1101	3905	494	1058	185	17	126	542	22	487	421	.271

Where He Hits the Ball

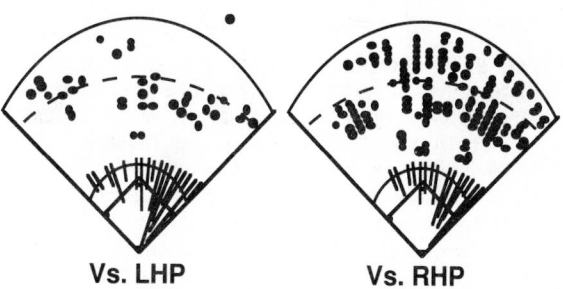

Vs. LHP   **Vs. RHP**

1989 Situational Stats

	AB	H	HR	RBI	AVG		AB	H	HR	RBI	AVG
Home	261	75	5	33	.287	LHP	167	49	4	19	.293
Road	293	69	7	22	.235	RHP	387	95	8	36	.245
Day	184	49	6	17	.266	Sc Pos	135	31	3	44	.230
Night	370	95	6	38	.257	Clutch	86	16	0	7	.186

1989 Rankings (American League)

- ➡ 3rd in intentional walks (17)
- ➡ 5th in percentage of swings put into play (57.6%) - *players with 502 PA*
- ➡ 10th in walks (83)
- ➡ Led the Indians in walks, intentional walks, percentage of swings put into play and hitting with the bases loaded (.333) - *team players with 10 PA with the bases loaded*

PITCHING:

In 36 innings and 25 games, the rookie with the submarine throwing motion made a solid impression. The Indians, hurting for middle relief pitching for more than two seasons, think Olin can solve part of the problem. There's a bonus, too. While pitching in a middle relief or set-up role, he can be groomed as a stopper. Olin went 4-1 and saved 24 games for Colorado Springs in the Pacific Coast League before the Indians called him to Cleveland.

Like most right-handed submariners, Olin is especially effective against right-handed batters. He keeps the ball down in the strike zone and produces a lot of ground ball outs. Left-handed batters and patient right-handers gave him the most trouble. The lefties picked up his ball early and had time to adjust to it. The righties, who were willing to wait until he made a mistake with a fastball, would go the opposite way to right field.

Olin throws a fastball and a slider. He needs a pitch that will let him jam left-handers. If he can't develop one, he's going to become strictly a situational pitcher. He was used as a closer in Triple A, and showed a resilient arm when in Cleveland. He also did a nice job of picking up his fellow pitchers, allowing just four of 22 inherited runners to score. Toward the end of the year, he seemed to wear down. His control suffered and he started to issue more walks. Olin had 46 strikeouts and 15 walks at Triple A, but his strikeout to walk ratio in Cleveland dropped to 24-14.

FIELDING:

He's an average fielder. He has problems with bunts and slow rollers hit down the first base line. His pickoff move is below average.

OVERALL:

Olin is a definite prospect who should help the Indians' bullpen in seasons to come. He has moved through the Tribe's minor-league system quickly. He spent the 1988 season in two Class A leagues before jumping to Class AAA and then the big leagues. His submarine delivery gives hitters a different look, but it will be interesting to see what adjustments the hitters make to him and he makes to the hitters in the future. A trick delivery is nice, but it wears thin if it doesn't produce quality pitches.

STEVE OLIN

Position: RP
Bats: R **Throws:** R
Ht: 6' 2" **Wt:** 185

Opening Day Age: 24
Born: 10/10/65 in Portland, OR
ML Seasons: 1

Overall Statistics

	W	L	ERA	G	GS	Sv	IP	H	R	BB	SO	HR
1989	1	4	3.75	25	0	1	36.0	35	16	14	24	1
Career	1	4	3.75	25	0	1	36.0	35	16	14	24	1

Where They Hit the Ball

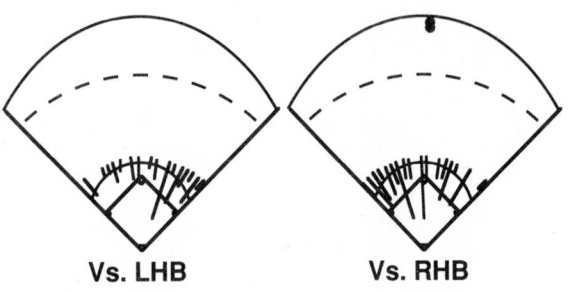

Vs. LHB   Vs. RHB

1989 Situational Stats

	W	L	ERA	Sv	IP		AB	H	HR	RBI	AVG
Home	0	2	3.32	0	19.0	LHB	51	17	1	10	.333
Road	1	2	4.24	1	17.0	RHB	86	18	0	5	.209
Day	0	1	3.86	0	9.1	Sc Pos	43	12	1	14	.279
Night	1	3	3.71	1	26.2	Clutch	44	14	0	5	.318

1989 Rankings (American League)

➡ 4th in lowest percentage of inherited runners scoring (18.2%) - *all league pitchers*

➡ 6th in highest grounder/flyball ratio (4.17) - *all league pitchers*

➡ Led the Indians in lowestage percent of runners scoring and highest grounder/flyball ratio

PITCHING:

The Indians thought Jesse Orosco might bring a World Series with him when he signed as a free agent before the start of the 1989 season. After all, Orosco helped the New York Mets win the series in 1986 and Los Angeles do the same in 1988. Well, the World Series never made it to the shores of Lake Erie, but Orosco did. His critics said he was washed up. They said his slider had lost its zip and his fastball had faded. Yet Orosco, making his American League debut, opened scouts' eyes from coast-to-coast with his velocity. He set a career high with 69 appearances, struck out 79 in 78 innings and had the lowest earned run average (2.08) for a Cleveland reliever since Vincente Romo had a 1.62 ERA in 1968.

Orosco was used almost strictly as a set-up man for closer Doug Jones. When he did get an opportunity to save a game, he looked shaky and unsure of himself. That seemed unusual for a man who had saved 21 games for the world champion Mets in 1986, but perhaps it explains why he's only saved 12 games in the last two years. The Indians view him as a two-inning pitcher. When he went beyond that limit last year, his effectiveness dropped dramatically, and he developed a nasty habit of giving up big home runs in the late innings. The blame was almost always mechanical. When Orosco gets his hand under the ball while throwing his slider, the pitch rises in the strike zone and is easy to hit. But when he stays on top of the ball, his slider stays down and is nearly unhittable.

FIELDING:

Orosco has made just two errors in 10 big-league seasons. Over the last four years, he's fielded his position flawlessly. He could use some work on comebackers, but he always helps himself with his defense. He has a fine move to first and does a good job of controlling the running game.

OVERALL:

The Indians signed Orosco to ease the burden on Doug Jones. They didn't want Jones pitching two or three innings for a save like he did in 1988. In that regard, Orosco did his job and then some. He's an aggressive pitcher and proved that his arm is healthy. It would be nice to see him show a little more assertiveness in save situations, but if used correctly he can be a valuable part of any bullpen.

JESSE OROSCO

Position: RP
Bats: R **Throws:** L
Ht: 6' 2" **Wt:** 185

Opening Day Age: 32
Born: 4/21/57 in Santa Barbara, CA
ML Seasons: 10

Overall Statistics

	W	L	ERA	G	GS	Sv	IP	H	R	BB	SO	HR
1989	3	4	2.08	69	0	3	78.0	54	20	26	79	7
Career	53	53	2.66	496	4	119	726.1	575	245	296	628	51

Where They Hit the Ball

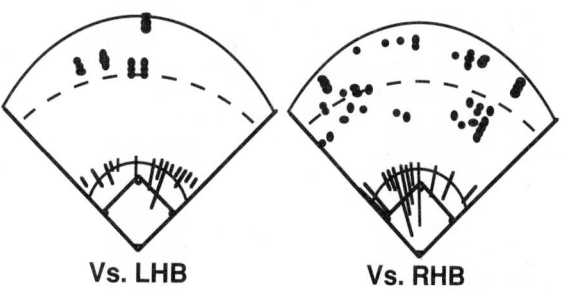

Vs. LHB   **Vs. RHB**

1989 Situational Stats

	W	L	ERA	Sv	IP		AB	H	HR	RBI	AVG
Home	2	2	1.69	1	42.2	LHB	87	12	0	8	.138
Road	1	2	2.55	2	35.1	RHB	186	42	7	22	.226
Day	2	1	2.30	1	15.2	Sc Pos	68	10	0	21	.147
Night	1	3	2.02	2	62.1	Clutch	163	34	4	19	.209

1989 Rankings (American League)

- 6th in games (69)
- 8th in holds (12)
- 9th in lowest batting average with runners in scoring position (.147) - *all league pitchers*
- Led the Indians in ERA (2.08), games, holds and first batter efficiency (.213) - *all team pitchers (ERA) and team pitchers with 40 relief games (first batter efficiency)*

HITTING:

Is Joel Skinner a starting catcher or a backup? The Indians acquired him from the New York Yankees in an attempt to find out, but they didn't do a very good job of it. Under former manager Doc Edwards, Skinner saw limited playing time. Edwards thought Andy Allanson worked the pitching staff better and stuck with him no matter how much Allanson struggled offensively.

Even in limited playing time, Skinner hit the ball well. He was hitting .276 at the All-Star break in just 87 at-bats. But then he virtually disappeared, playing in only 30 games after the break. When Edwards was fired on September 12, Skinner's playing time increased. He started 11 of the final 19 games, hitting .259, but the damage was already done. It raised his second half average to just .198.

Skinner is a line-drive, spray hitter who has major problems with breaking balls. He's been the kind of player who does his best hitting during batting practice. He just can't carry it over into the game when someone younger and stronger than a 50-year-old first base coach is pitching. When Skinner makes contact, he hits the ball hard, and he hits it to all fields. His raw ability keeps tantalizing teams. If he could ever develop, the Tribe projects him as the kind of player who could hit .250-.270 with 15 to 20 home runs. But right now, that projection is a long way off.

BASERUNNING:

Skinner is one of the slowest players in the game. He just can't run, period.

FIELDING:

Skinner is ranked as one of the best defensive catchers in the league, but he struggled last year. He threw out only 28 percent of the would-be base stealers he faced and committed nine errors. In spite of that, he has a strong throwing arm and makes a low accurate throw to second base. He's excellent at blocking the plate on bang-bang plays, and never shies away from contact.

OVERALL:

Skinner came to the Indians with the reputation of a defensive catcher with the ability to develop offensively. He never got that chance, which is one of the reasons Doc Edwards was fired as manager. Yet a look at Skinner's career shows he's never been a starter anywhere in the big leagues, so maybe Edwards saw something that the front office didn't. His ability to call a quality game behind the plate is still unproven.

JOEL SKINNER

Position: C
Bats: R **Throws:** R
Ht: 6' 4" **Wt:** 205

Opening Day Age: 29
Born: 2/21/61 in La Jolla, CA
ML Seasons: 7

Overall Statistics

	G	AB	R	H	D	T	HR	RBI	SB	BB	SO	AVG
1989	79	178	10	41	10	0	1	13	1	9	42	.230
Career	416	1018	80	225	44	2	14	96	3	59	276	.221

Where He Hits the Ball

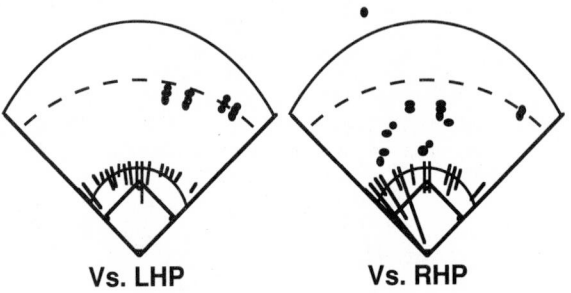

Vs. LHP   Vs. RHP

1989 Situational Stats

	AB	H	HR	RBI	AVG		AB	H	HR	RBI	AVG
Home	94	21	0	7	.223	LHP	55	13	0	4	.236
Road	84	20	1	6	.238	RHP	123	28	1	9	.228
Day	59	14	0	4	.237	Sc Pos	43	7	0	11	.163
Night	119	27	1	9	.227	Clutch	26	6	0	2	.231

1989 Rankings (American League)

➡ 9th in grounder/flyball ratio (3.50) - *all league players*

HITTING:

Cory Snyder had a pitiful season in 1989. Once thought to be one of the most promising young players in the game, Snyder struggled like a raw rookie in 1989. He literally swung -- and missed -- almost every pitch thrown to him. It's mystifying, because from 1987 to 1988, Snyder had improved his batting average from .236 to .272, while cutting his strikeouts from a club-record 166 to 101. He carried that momentum into spring training with him last year. After a great spring, he was hitting .339 on April 22. But shortly after that, Snyder injured his back while hitting the outfield wall in Baltimore.

Snyder kept playing with a sore back until the All-Star break. The Indians finally put him on the disabled list and sent him to class AA to get his swing back. Snyder never found it. Pitchers would pound him inside with fastball after fastball and then strike him out by throwing curveballs and sliders low and away. Hurlers have been getting Snyder out with the same pattern of pitches for more than three seasons. Yet, Snyder has refused to adjust. He still swings for the fences in every at bat, and hardly ever goes to right field or works the pitcher for a walk. He struck out 134 times in 132 games and hit just .190 (33 for 174) after coming off the disabled list on July 30.

BASERUNNING:

Snyder gets the most out of his speed. He runs out every ground ball as if it were his last. He'll go from first to third and last year stole a career-high six bases in 11 attempts.

FIELDING:

Snyder remains one of the best right fielders in the league. He finished second in the league to Jesse Barfield with 17 assists. A former infielder, he gets to the ball quickly and almost dares runners to take the extra base. Once reckless, he played more cautiously after his back injury. He still has a problem judging balls hit into the power alley, often trying to cut the ball off only to watch it sail over his head.

OVERALL:

If Cory Snyder doesn't adjust his offensive game, he's not going to be in the big leagues very long despite all his ability. He has power to spare, but he has to learn that he's not going to hit a home run in every at-bat. Last year, he lost his confidence and then went into a shell. Big League players don't do that.

CORY SNYDER

Position: RF
Bats: R **Throws:** R
Ht: 6' 3" **Wt:** 185

Opening Day Age: 27
Born: 11/11/62 in Englewood, CA
ML Seasons: 4

Overall Statistics

	G	AB	R	H	D	T	HR	RBI	SB	BB	SO	AVG
1989	132	489	49	105	17	0	18	59	6	23	134	.215
Career	534	1993	252	493	86	6	101	285	18	112	524	.247

Where He Hits the Ball

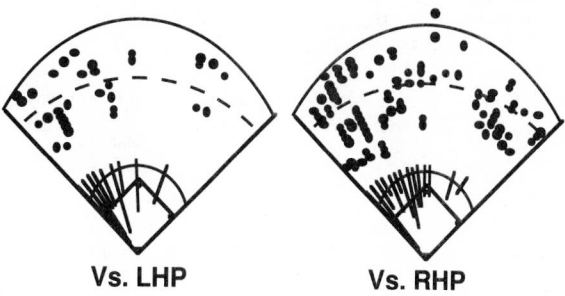

Vs. LHP   Vs. RHP

1989 Situational Stats

	AB	H	HR	RBI	AVG		AB	H	HR	RBI	AVG
Home	246	51	6	25	.207	LHP	165	41	10	27	.248
Road	243	54	12	34	.222	RHP	324	64	8	32	.198
Day	159	28	3	15	.176	Sc Pos	119	27	3	38	.227
Night	330	77	15	44	.233	Clutch	99	14	0	3	.141

1989 Rankings (American League)

➡ Lowest on-base average (.251) - *players with 502 PA*

➡ 2nd lowest batting average (.215)

➡ 3rd in highest percentage of swings that missed (31.8%) and lowest batting average in the clutch (.141)

➡ 5th in strikeouts (134) and lowest batting average with 2 strikes (.113)

➡ Led the Indians in strikeouts (134)

PITCHING:

Greg Swindell is a pitcher who keeps sidestepping greatness. On July 20 of last year, Swindell was 13-2 with a 2.51 earned run average and was a legitimate threat to win the Cy Young award. But his left elbow was hurting and after one more start he went on the disabled list with a strained ligament in the elbow. He didn't return until Aug. 30. Overpitched in his three-year career at the University of Texas, Swindell has never had one pain-free year with the Indians. In 1987, he strained the same elbow ligament and missed the last three games of the season. In 1988, he was 10-1 with a 2.11 ERA on May 30. Then he went into a prolonged slump due to a tired left shoulder before righting himself for a final record of 18-14.

When Swindell is healthy, he's one of the dominant pitchers in the league. He has a great feel for pitching, and can throw four pitches for strikes -- fastball, slider, change-up and curveball. He's primarily a fastball-slider pitcher. The slider is his out pitch, but it's brutal on his elbow. It has been blamed for his two elbow injuries and he was under orders not to throw it in his first few starts after coming off the DL last year.

Swindell does not have an overpowering fastball, but he knows when and where to use it. Control is a vital part of his game. Before going on the DL last year, he'd walked only 38 batters in 154 innings. When he returned, his control was shot, and he didn't recover it until his final two starts of the season.

FIELDING:

Swindell is an average fielder, but his physical conditioning is questionable. He's listed at 6-3 and 225 pounds, but he was near 240 last year. He doesn't get off the mound quickly and teams can bunt on him. But he does an excellent job of holding baserunners, especially for a power pitcher.

OVERALL:

In normal circumstances, Swindell would be the logical choice around whom to build the Indian staff. But in the last two years, the Indians have nosedived dramatically when Swindell has been on the DL or pitching at less than 100 percent. What they need is a strong wire-to-wire season from him.

GREG SWINDELL

Position: SP
Bats: R **Throws:** L
Ht: 6' 3" **Wt:** 225

Opening Day Age: 25
Born: 1/2/65 in Fort Worth, TX
ML Seasons: 4

Overall Statistics

	W	L	ERA	G	GS	Sv	IP	H	R	BB	SO	HR
1989	13	6	3.37	28	28	0	184.1	170	71	51	129	16
Career	39	30	3.69	86	85	0	590.1	573	265	148	452	61

Where They Hit the Ball

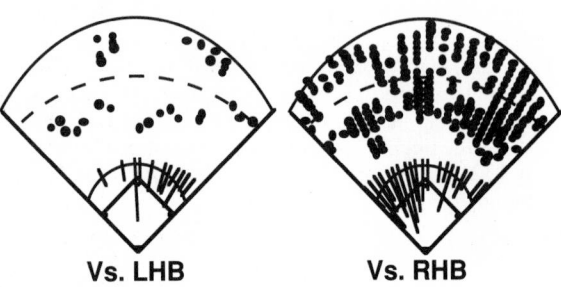

Vs. LHB **Vs. RHB**

1989 Situational Stats

	W	L	ERA	Sv	IP			AB	H	HR	RBI	AVG
Home	6	4	3.34	0	94.1	LHB		107	23	1	8	.215
Road	7	2	3.40	0	90.0	RHB		583	147	15	49	.252
Day	4	0	0.96	0	56.1	Sc Pos		127	27	1	36	.213
Night	9	6	4.43	0	128.0	Clutch		69	16	0	2	.232

1989 Rankings (American League)

→ 3rd in lowest grounder/flyball ratio (.94) - *pitchers with 162 IP*

→ 4th in caught stealing (13)

→ 5th in least GDPs per 9 innings (.49)

→ 8th in least baserunners allowed per 9 innings (10.8) and won/loss percentage (.684)

→ Led the Indians in wins (13), home runs allowed (16), won/loss percentage, strikeouts per 9 innings (6.3), caught stealing, and lowest stolen base percentage allowed (58.1%) - *team pitchers with 162 IP*

PITCHING:

For a while it looked like Rich Yett had actually learned how to pitch. Guess again. In 1988, Yett looked like he could be a solid fourth or fifth starter. After yo-yoing between the bullpen and the rotation for parts of two seasons, he had his first winning year in the big leagues, doing it almost exclusively as a starter. In one stretch, he went 3-1 with a 2.43 earned run average in six starts. Not Hall of Fame stuff, certainly, but it was enough to show promise. But last year Yett pitched himself out of the rotation in just 12 starts, averaging less than five innings per outing. He spent the rest of the year manning the mop and bucket brigade.

Yett's problems were mostly mechanical. In 1988, he appeared to have finally gotten the upper hand on his forkball. He would get ahead of batters with his fastball and then throw the forkball out of the strike zone or in the dirt, and the batters had little choice but to swing. He also grew more and more confident with his curveball. Last year that strategy evaporated because he couldn't keep any of his pitches out of the dirt. Yett threw seven wild pitches as he bounced every pitch he had in the dirt around home plate. That pushed him even farther to the back of the bullpen bus because the coaching staff was hesitant to bring a guy into a game with the tying run on third base when his best pitch was a down and dirty forkball past the catcher.

FIELDING:

Yett is a solid fielder. He doesn't leap off the mound like a gazelle on bunts and check-swings in front of the plate, but he gets the job done. He once did an outstanding job of holding runners, but regressed in '89, possibly because of his pitching problems.

OVERALL:

Yett's career has reached a fork in the road. He can keep pitching like he did last year and end up back home in Mesa, Ariz. Or he can try to develop some consistency, as a starter or reliever. It's going to be difficult because Yett has always been wildly inconsistent in his big league career. He has a good arm and likes to pitch, but he hasn't put the numbers on the board.

RICHARD YETT

Position: RP/SP
Bats: R **Throws:** R
Ht: 6' 2" **Wt:** 187

Opening Day Age: 27
Born: 10/6/62 in Pomona, CA
ML Seasons: 5

Overall Statistics

	W	L	ERA	G	GS	Sv	IP	H	R	BB	SO	HR
1989	5	6	5.00	32	12	0	99.0	111	56	47	47	10
Career	22	24	4.98	132	49	2	410.0	438	240	190	227	52

Where They Hit the Ball

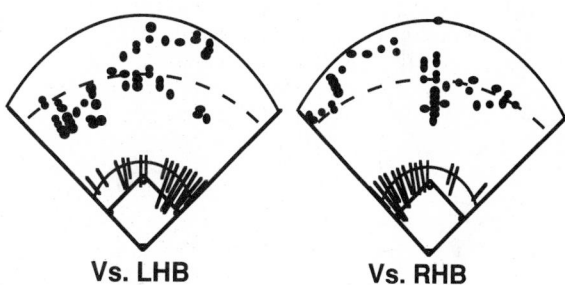

Vs. LHB   **Vs. RHB**

1989 Situational Stats

	W	L	ERA	Sv	IP		AB	H	HR	RBI	AVG
Home	2	3	5.10	0	47.2	LHB	197	59	7	23	.299
Road	3	3	4.91	0	51.1	RHB	195	52	3	26	.267
Day	4	2	3.65	0	44.1	Sc Pos	106	30	2	39	.283
Night	1	4	6.09	0	54.2	Clutch	16	4	0	0	.250

1989 Rankings (American League)

➡ Did not rank near the top or bottom in any category

LUIS AGUAYO

Position: 3B
Bats: R **Throws:** R
Ht: 5' 9" **Wt:** 195

Opening Day Age: 31
Born: 3/13/59 in Vega Baja, Puerto Rico
ML Seasons: 10

Overall Statistics

	G	AB	R	H	D	T	HR	RBI	SB	BB	SO	AVG
1989	47	97	7	17	4	1	1	8	0	7	19	.175
Career	568	1104	142	260	43	10	37	109	7	94	220	.236

HITTING, FIELDING, BASERUNNING:

The Indians let Luis Aguayo rot on the bench last year and then expressed dismay when he couldn't hit and suffered defensive lapses. A utility player's job is to sit and wait, but Aguayo only received 97 at-bats all year. That's ridiculous. Aguayo is a fastball hitter who can hit a home run now and then. One year in Philadelphia, he hit 12 homers in 209 at bats. Yet his value to a ballclub is his versatility on defense. He can play second and his best position is third base, but it was his inability to play short that caused the Indians to release him at the end of last season. Aguayo has a decent glove, but does not have the range to play shortstop for an extended period of time. Aguayo has below average speed and has never been a base stealing threat.

OVERALL:

Aguayo's work habits are good and his bat still has some juice left; he'll play somewhere in the majors this year. He may be better suited for the National League, where managers make much more use of their bench than in the American League.

KEITH ATHERTON

Position: RP
Bats: R **Throws:** R
Ht: 6' 4" **Wt:** 200

Opening Day Age: 31
Born: 2/19/59 in Mathews, VA
ML Seasons: 7

Overall Statistics

	W	L	ERA	G	GS	Sv	IP	H	R	BB	SO	HR
1989	0	3	4.15	32	0	2	39.0	48	22	13	13	7
Career	33	41	3.99	342	0	26	566.1	546	268	215	349	75

PITCHING & FIELDING:

Keith Atherton was a bust in Cleveland. Pure and simple. The Indians obtained him from Minnesota, expecting him to be a right-handed reliever who could set up closer Doug Jones. Atherton's credentials said he could do that job. He'd done it for the Twins in both 1987 and 1988. Yet he didn't do it in Cleveland.

Atherton's main problem was keeping the ball in the ballpark. In one explosive stretch in late June, he gave up five home runs in a 10-inning span covering 10 appearances. A trip to the minors didn't straighten him out, and Cleveland suggested he go back to AAA. Atherton refused and was given his release. Atherton is a decent fielder who usually doesn't hurt himself with his defense. He does an average-to-below average job of holding runners.

OVERALL:

Atherton is mostly a power pitcher. Unfortunately, everything he threw last year was straight and high in the hitting zone. He said he suffered from lack of work. That may have been the case since the Indians lost confidence in him early and used him only in blowout situations. His track record says he can still pitch in the big leagues.

STEVE DAVIS

Position: RP
Bats: L **Throws:** L
Ht: 5'11" **Wt:** 185

Opening Day Age: 29
Born: 8/4/60 in San Antonio, TX
ML Seasons: 3

Overall Statistics

	W	L	ERA	G	GS	Sv	IP	H	R	BB	SO	HR
1989	1	1	8.06	12	2	0	25.2	34	24	14	12	2
Career	3	2	6.44	25	7	0	57.1	65	45	32	39	9

PITCHING & FIELDING:

Steve Davis had a much more enjoyable season at Class AAA than he did in the big leagues last year. It might not have been an accident. At Colorado Springs, the left-hander went 12-2 with a 2.45 earned run average but his two trips to Cleveland didn't bring him much more than frustration and an 8.06 ERA. Davis is a slider/fastball pitcher. Once a top prospect in the Toronto system, he made it to the big leagues with the Blue Jays in 1985 before seriously injuring his pitching shoulder. He impressed the Indians in spring training by jamming right-handed hitters with his fastball. The strategy continued to work in Class AAA, but not in Cleveland. Davis is a good fielder who holds runners close at first with a decent move.

OVERALL:

Davis is probably in the wrong organization. He showed he can't pitch out of the bullpen and his stuff isn't good enough to break into a Cleveland rotation that had the second lowest ERA in the American League East. He's basically a good Class AAA pitcher, who could offer borderline help to a big league club in the right situation.

LUIS MEDINA

Position: DH
Bats: R **Throws:** L
Ht: 6'3" **Wt:** 195

Opening Day Age: 27
Born: 3/26/63 in Santa Monica, CA
ML Seasons: 2

Overall Statistics

	G	AB	R	H	D	T	HR	RBI	SB	BB	SO	AVG
1989	30	83	8	17	1	0	4	8	0	6	35	.205
Career	46	134	18	30	1	0	10	16	0	8	53	.224

HITTING, FIELDING, BASERUNNING:

Luis Medina blew the opportunity of a lifetime last season. The Indians traded Mel Hall and Carmen Castillo and planned to platoon Medina with Dave Clark at DH. But Medina batted just .205 in 83 at-bats with 35 strikeouts. The Indians farmed him out on June 18 and he never made it back. Medina is strictly a power hitter, with a compact stroke. If he gets a fastball in his zone, he'll hit it a long way. If he doesn't, he'll strike out. Medina, who led all of Class AAA baseball with 27 homers in 1988, could not adjust to being platooned. His swing suffered from lack of work and he pressed. He is a liability in the outfield or at first base. He started one game in left field and one game in right field, making errors both times. His speed is below average.

OVERALL:

Medina is the kind of player who will go as far as his bat will take him. Last year it didn't take him very far. By the end of the season, Medina had other problems. He suffered a 50 to 80 percent tear of his left rotator cuff, and the injury might be career threatening.

MARK SALAS

Position: DH
Bats: L **Throws:** R
Ht: 6' 0" **Wt:** 205

Opening Day Age: 29
Born: 3/8/61 in Montebello, CA
ML Seasons: 6

Overall Statistics

	G	AB	R	H	D	T	HR	RBI	SB	BB	SO	AVG
1989	30	77	4	17	4	1	2	7	0	5	13	.221
Career	402	1071	122	276	45	10	28	112	3	68	125	.258

HITTING, FIELDING, BASERUNNING:

The Indians shuttled players between Cleveland and their Class AAA team so much last year that Colorado Springs became known as "Stiff Central." That's because almost every hitter the Indians promoted flopped with a loud thud. Mark Salas was one of the few exceptions. Salas' numbers weren't great in his 30-game stay with the Tribe, but at least he made opposing pitchers sweat. The left-handed hitter has plenty of big-league experience and he knows how to hit. Plus he has some pop in his bat if he gets the right kind of pitch. He makes contact, but struggled as a pinch-hitter. As a catcher, Salas is a good receiver, but he's not going to throw anybody out. He runs like you'd expect a catcher to -- slowly, very slowly.

OVERALL:

Salas underwent surgery to have bone chips removed from his elbow at the end of last season. He might have a chance to make it as a bench player with the Indians, but it's highly unlikely. His best chance might be trying to hook on with another team.

MIKE YOUNG

Position: DH
Bats: B **Throws:** R
Ht: 6' 2" **Wt:** 206

Opening Day Age: 30
Born: 3/20/60 in Oakland, CA
ML Seasons: 8

Overall Statistics

	G	AB	R	H	D	T	HR	RBI	SB	BB	SO	AVG
1989	32	59	2	11	0	0	1	5	1	6	13	.186
Career	635	1840	244	454	80	6	72	235	22	237	465	.247

HITTING, FIELDING, BASERUNNING:

The Indians gave Mike Young what was essentially a free ride in 1989. A man who once hit 28 homers for Baltimore, he barely got the ball out of the infield. In fact, it's thought Young stayed around only because Hank Peters and Tom Giordano, who called the shots for Baltimore during Young's glory days, were running the Indians' front office. Cleveland was his third big-league club since the Orioles traded him to Milwaukee on Aug. 24, 1988. In all that time, he's hit two home runs. Mechanically, his swing is so messed up that when he hits the ball in the air, it's reason for celebration. As his offensive skills have deteriorated, so have his defensive skills. He could once play the outfield and had a good arm. The Indians rarely let him play the outfield last year, using him mostly as a DH and pinch-hitter.

OVERALL:

Young said all you wanted to know when asked if he was happy to be called up to Cleveland for a second time last season. Young's response was "I really don't know." It was obvious he would have preferred to stay in Class AAA. In 1990, he may get his wish.

PAUL ZUVELLA

Position: SS
Bats: R **Throws:** R
Ht: 6' 0" **Wt:** 178

Opening Day Age: 31
Born: 10/31/58 in San Mateo, CA
ML Seasons: 8

Overall Statistics

	G	AB	R	H	D	T	HR	RBI	SB	BB	SO	AVG
1989	24	58	10	16	2	0	2	6	0	1	11	.276
Career	207	491	41	109	17	2	2	20	2	34	50	.222

HITTING, FIELDING, BASERUNNING:

Just call Paul Zuvella "The Stretchmaster." Zuvella goes through an elaborate pre-game stretching routine, sometimes starting an hour or two before game-time. Zuvella has played second, short and third in the big leagues. For the last three seasons, he's had super seasons at Class AAA, but has never been able to adjust to big-league pitching. Last year, though, the hyper Zuvella hit .276 for the Tribe in 34 games, his best showing ever with three different big-league clubs. Some believe Zuvella has finally grown comfortable with the fact that he's good enough to play in the big leagues. Zuvella could hit at the top or bottom of the order. He has good bat control and isn't afraid to give himself up with a sacrifice bunt. His range is a little better than average and his arm is accurate, but not overpowering. He is not a base stealing threat.

OVERALL:

Zuvella may be in line to win the Tribe's utility job this year. Mentally, he's finally ready to accept the role, rather than dreaming and striving to be a starter. His forte is defense, especially shortstop. That's a key skill where a utility man is concerned.

PITCHING:

Doyle Alexander gives you everything you could expect from a 39 year-old pitcher. He has exceptional poise and mound smarts. He has a huge repertoire of pitches and motions that will often leave opposition hitters mumbling to themselves. He has a proven ability to be a winner long after others have given up on him. And most important, he has a well-earned reputation for winning big games and responding well in pressure situations.

Doyle has been working on a knuckleball for years, and he began using it more extensively in 1989. Among his other pitches, he has a fastball that he can throw at various speeds and from numerous release points, a big, looping curve, and a slider that looks very much like his low, downward-dipping fastball.

All of Alexander's pitches, especially the smorgasbord of fastballs, require pinpoint control, because they lack velocity. Doyle's adoption of the knuckleball is an obvious response to his wish for something that does not require him to work like a dart thrower who needs a Triple Twenty. Although nobody has to throw a knuckleball to spots, every pitcher must be able to throw it in the strike zone. Doyle had some trouble with this requirement in 1989, and it cost him. He frequently pitched from behind in the count, meaning he threw a lot of weak cheese to hitters eagerly expecting it, and he issued a lot of free passes, too.

After the All Star break, he walked 3.5 batters per 9 innings pitched, 3.1 for the full year. Not once since 1981 had he given up more than 2.3 walks per 9 innings in any season; the 1.8 he yielded in 1988 is about right if he wants to be successful. No pitcher can absorb a 70% increase in his walk frequency without a serious impact, and Doyle's 18 losses in 1989 are an accurate measure of the impact on him.

FIELDING:

Alexander is a good athlete, and carries himself well around the mound. He is always attentive, knows where to go instinctively, and exercises fine judgement. He holds runners well.

OVERALL:

Only Doyle knows to what extent he was just experimenting in a meaningless season. If he cannot do any better than what we saw in the second half of 1989, someone may as well stick a fork in him -- he's done. It is, however, certainly conceivable that Alexander could learn to throw his knuckler for strikes, and beat old Father Time again. He has done it before.

DOYLE ALEXANDER

Position: SP
Bats: R **Throws:** R
Ht: 6' 3" **Wt:** 200

Opening Day Age: 39
Born: 9/4/50 in Cordova, AL
ML Seasons: 19

Overall Statistics

	W	L	ERA	G	GS	Sv	IP	H	R	BB	SO	HR
1989	6	18	4.44	33	33	0	223.0	245	118	76	95	28
Career	194	174	3.76	561	464	3	3366.1	3376	1541	978	1528	324

Where They Hit the Ball

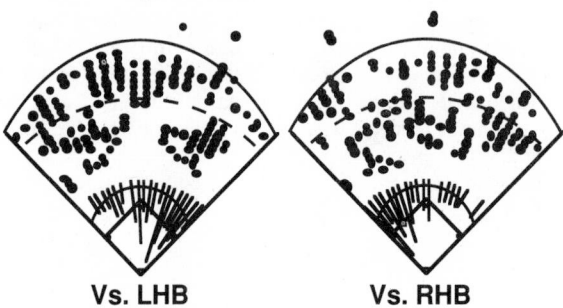

Vs. LHB   **Vs. RHB**

1989 Situational Stats

	W	L	ERA	Sv	IP		AB	H	HR	RBI	AVG
Home	3	9	4.44	0	119.2	LHB	486	138	13	58	.284
Road	3	9	4.44	0	103.1	RHB	390	107	15	50	.274
Day	3	5	4.08	0	68.1	Sc Pos	196	46	4	73	.235
Night	3	13	4.60	0	154.2	Clutch	83	25	3	8	.301

1989 Rankings (American League)

- 1st in losses (18), home runs allowed (28) and least run support per 9 innings (3.0) - *pitchers with 162 IP*
- 2nd worst won/loss percentage (.250) - *pitchers with 15 or more decisions*
- 4th in worst slugging percentage allowed (.434), highest HRs allowed per 9 innings (1.13), hits allowed (245) and strikeout/walk ratio (1.25) - *pitchers with 162 IP*
- 10th in lowest batting average with runners in scoring position (.235)
- Led the Tigers in losses, games started (33), hits allowed, batters faced (977), home runs allowed, walks (76) and lowest batting average with runners in scoring position

HITTING:

Dave Bergman was informed by Sparky Anderson at the beginning of 1989 that he would see only limited duty, but by season's end he had established personal highs for most hits and most games played in a single season. Bergman personifies the term "bench strength." He's a superior situational hitter who can be deadly in a critical at bat. At his best when platooned against right-handers, Bergman is that rare part-time player who can assume a starting role without weakening his team's offensive or defensive capabilities.

As a hitter, Bergman seldom wastes an at bat. He's a good lowball hitter, particularly against the fastball. He is extremely aware of the pitches he can best handle and does his best to lay off the ones he can't. He has a good eye and is patient enough to draw his share of walks. Although not considered a pure power hitter, he has a solid stroke with some pop, as his 13 doubles and 7 home runs indicate. Additionally, he's an effective bunter. Traditionally, Bergman has been extremely dangerous in clutch situations.

BASERUNNING:

Bergman possesses slightly below average speed, and he's basically a station-to-station type of baserunner. Bergman knows his speed limitations and avoids taking unnecessary chances. Any stolen bases are likely to be the result of failed hit-and-run attempts. He managed one steal in four attempts last year.

FIELDING:

Bergman fields his position quietly and steadily. He has spent much of his career in Detroit as a late-inning defensive replacement. His mobility at first is not exceptional and his range somewhat limited, but he makes most of the routine plays and occasionally pulls off a fielding gem. The arm is solid and his throws are on target. His experience gives him a big defensive edge. So does the fact that he happens to be the only legitimate first baseman on Detroit's roster. Although it happened several years ago, he's the last Tiger to execute the hidden ball trick.

OVERALL:

With the departures of Lance Parrish, Kirk Gibson and Darrell Evans in consecutive seasons, the Tigers spent much of 1989 searching for a team leader. By season's end, Bergman had assumed that role. Given his past contributions, failure to re-sign him for 1990 would be second-rate and downright foolish.

DAVE BERGMAN

Position: 1B
Bats: L **Throws:** L
Ht: 6' 2" **Wt:** 190

Opening Day Age: 36
Born: 6/6/53 in
Evanston, IL
ML Seasons: 14

Overall Statistics

	G	AB	R	H	D	T	HR	RBI	SB	BB	SO	AVG
1989	137	385	38	103	13	1	7	37	1	44	44	.268
Career	1076	2099	251	545	77	14	44	224	14	292	271	.260

Where He Hits the Ball

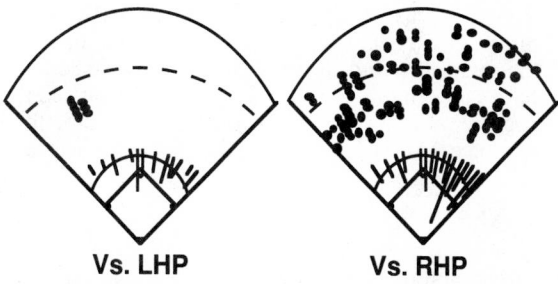

Vs. LHP   **Vs. RHP**

1989 Situational Stats

	AB	H	HR	RBI	AVG		AB	H	HR	RBI	AVG
Home	173	43	6	15	.249	LHP	61	13	0	9	.213
Road	212	60	1	22	.283	RHP	324	90	7	28	.278
Day	137	38	3	13	.277	Sc Pos	89	27	0	29	.303
Night	248	65	4	24	.262	Clutch	59	12	0	4	.203

1989 Rankings (American League)

➡ Led AL First Basemen in bunts in play (7)

HITTING:

At the beginning of 1989, Mike Brumley was considered at least a marginal major league prospect. The son of the former big league catcher of the same name, Brumley had previously been a throw-in in deals involving such big names as Bill Buckner, Dennis Eckersley, Goose Gossage and Keith Moreland. Teams seemed to find him worth a gamble, and Brumley's stock went up considerably after he hit .315 for Las Vegas in '88. The Tigers obtained him early in 1989, primarily as an emergency replacement for Alan Trammell. The woeful Bengals gave Brumley some chances to play, but he didn't show much. Brumley is a decent fastball hitter, and he did well in situations where he was almost certain a hard one was coming. In particular, he likes to swing at the first pitch and did pretty well when he made contact with first offerings. But Brumley was helpless when he got behind in the count. Breaking balls tied him up completely and he chased numerous pitches in the dirt. It didn't help that he was seldom in the lineup long enough to find his stroke. Batting righthanded -- he's a switch-hitter -- Brumley's numbers at least approached respectability. But his work did little to reinforce the notion that he could help a major league club with his bat.

BASERUNNING:

Brumley possesses above average speed and succeeded in 8 of 12 steal attempts. When running the bases, there were occasions when he would stay put when advancement was guaranteed or would attempt the extra base when failure was clearly evident. But overall his base-running was quite good in 1989.

FIELDING:

Brumley made appearances at short, second and a few games at third in 1989. He displayed decent range and a strong arm at all positions. The somewhat unpredictable accuracy of his throws, however, made for an inordinate amount of suspense as plays unfolded. The inexperience of youth is a trite but sound baseball truism. Brumley's 12 errors were primarily the result of throws that would best have been unattempted. Brumley's effort and willingness to play where needed were admirable. The fielding ability is there.

OVERALL:

Ideally Brumley is a contact, singles-hitter. His value would increase were he to shorten his swing and work to actually make contact more often. His good speed is negated by lack of batting punch. Based on his 1989 performance, to assign him a role exceeding second-line utility man status is begging for disappointment.

MIKE BRUMLEY

Position: SS/2B
Bats: B **Throws:** R
Ht: 5'10" **Wt:** 165

Opening Day Age: 27
Born: 4/9/63 in Oklahoma City, OK
ML Seasons: 2

Overall Statistics

	G	AB	R	H	D	T	HR	RBI	SB	BB	SO	AVG
1989	92	212	33	42	5	2	1	11	8	14	45	.198
Career	131	316	41	63	7	4	2	20	15	24	75	.199

Where He Hits the Ball

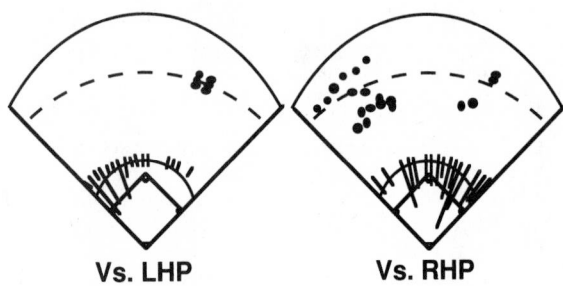

Vs. LHP   **Vs. RHP**

1989 Situational Stats

	AB	H	HR	RBI	AVG		AB	H	HR	RBI	AVG
Home	101	21	1	9	.208	LHP	69	17	1	6	.246
Road	111	21	0	2	.189	RHP	143	25	0	5	.175
Day	71	15	0	3	.211	Sc Pos	60	8	0	9	.133
Night	141	27	1	8	.191	Clutch	32	5	0	0	.156

1989 Rankings (American League)

- ➥ 10th in percent of extra bases taken as a runner (55.3%) - *players with 40 opportunities to advance*
- ➥ Led the Tigers in percent of runs scored per time on base (49.3%) - *all team players*

PITCHING:

Classify Paul Gibson as a late-bloomer. After toiling anonymously in the Tigers' farm system for a number of years, he finally earned a place on Detroit's roster in 1988. At age 28, not much was expected of him and he was relegated to long relief. Gibson was a surprise that year, posting an overall 4-2 record with a 2.93 ERA while winning his only start. Given that success, more was expected of Gibson in '89, especially after injuries to Mike Henneman and Willie Hernandez decimated the Detroit pitching staff. But Gibson struggled all year while working as both a starter and a reliever. In general, his primary shortcoming last year was a tendency to surrender damaging home runs.

Gibson has a decent fastball, but he's not the overpowering type. He depends primarily on location, but last year his control was clearly off. He walked too many hitters and often got into trouble after he fell behind on the count. He has the stuff to be an effective major league hurler, but he needs better control of his offerings. In his two major league seasons Gibson has been much more effective pitching in Tiger Stadium than he has been on the road. That's a little surprising because he's not a groundball pitcher and tends to work up in the strike zone. But Gibson's stuff is tough to pull and he's able to keep the ball in the spacious middle of the Detroit outfield.

FIELDING:

Gibson has displayed a propensity for irksome defensive lapses. Intent on the pitching game, he occasionally is a bit slow covering first or cleanly handling the routine bunt. Holding base runners has also been a weakness for him.

OVERALL:

Gibson has value as a versatile, if unspectacular, performer. He has had success in a long-relief role and has also shown himself to be a workmanlike starter. He has also demonstrated a willingness to accept the role of staff swing-man and make the best of it. From his '89 performance, he'd have a lot of difficulty making a quality major league staff. But on a club hurting for pitching like the Tigers, Gibson will probably be given a good opportunity to straighten himself out.

PAUL GIBSON

Position: RP/SP
Bats: R **Throws:** L
Ht: 6' 0" **Wt:** 165

Opening Day Age: 30
Born: 1/4/60 in Southampton, NY
ML Seasons: 2

Overall Statistics

	W	L	ERA	G	GS	Sv	IP	H	R	BB	SO	HR
1989	4	8	4.64	45	13	0	132.0	129	71	57	77	11
Career	8	10	3.94	85	14	0	224.0	212	104	91	127	17

Where They Hit the Ball

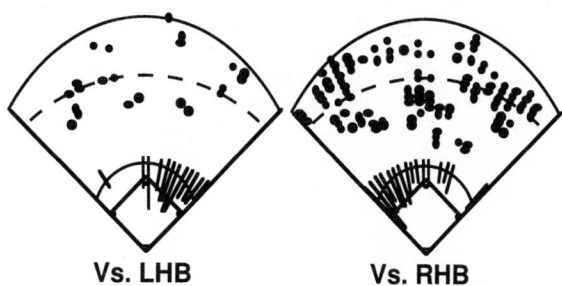

Vs. LHB   **Vs. RHB**

1989 Situational Stats

	W	L	ERA	Sv	IP		AB	H	HR	RBI	AVG
Home	2	3	3.49	0	69.2	LHB	117	31	4	19	.265
Road	2	5	5.92	0	62.1	RHB	381	98	7	42	.257
Day	2	2	4.19	0	43.0	Sc Pos	132	37	4	52	.280
Night	2	6	4.85	0	89.0	Clutch	56	13	1	4	.232

1989 Rankings (American League)

➡ Led the Tigers in lowest batting average against righthanded batters - *team pitchers facing 377 righthanded batters*

HITTING:

Mike Heath got a chance to play full time from June until the end of the season because of a serious knee injury to Matt Nokes. Heath became a mainstay behind the plate, and proved that he is more than just a part-time catcher.

Heath loves to face southpaws. Last year he hit almost 100 points higher against them than righties. He is also the consummate first-ball, fastball hitter. Pitchers like Bert Blyleven and Tom Candiotti, who try to confuse hitters with an assortment of slow breaking-balls, will eat Heath up.

Heath should try to develop more patience. Heath is an excellent 3-0, 3-1 hitter because he can sit back and wait on the fastball. Unfortunately, he swings at way too many first pitches.

Heath is a spray hitter who doesn't try to pull the ball. He will take the outside pitch to rightfield most of the time. This prevents him from having any extended slumps and kept his batting average between .260 and .275 for most of the season. However, with the game on the line, Heath would not be one of your choices to come to the plate.

BASERUNNING:

Heath is not a significant threat on the bases. But he picks his time to run very carefully and therefore has a high success rate. For a catcher, Heath is not that slow. However, he plays on a team that scratches and claws for runs and can't afford to have any runner thrown out.

FIELDING:

Heath is best known for his defensive abilities. He possesses a strong and accurate throwing arm and is not afraid to block pitches in the dirt. For the year, Heath threw out 35% of prospective basestealers. He is also an excellent handler of pitchers. Dealing with Jack Morris' temper and Kevin Ritz's wildness is not the easiest job in the world. Heath is also adept at coming from behind the plate fielding bunts. He makes the pivot and turn on that play as well as anyone other than Lance Parrish.

OVERALL:

Heath is a solid veteran. He has been around long enough to know what it takes to win. Heath is very important to Detroit. With Matt Nokes' knee injury a constant source of concern, Heath's role is that much bigger. He figures to be platooned next year if Nokes recovers fully. This would be the ideal setup for Heath.

MIKE HEATH

Position: C
Bats: R **Throws:** R
Ht: 5'11" **Wt:** 180

Opening Day Age: 35
Born: 2/5/55 in Tampa, FL
ML Seasons: 12

Overall Statistics

	G	AB	R	H	D	T	HR	RBI	SB	BB	SO	AVG
1989	122	396	38	104	16	2	10	43	7	24	71	.263
Career	1154	3703	412	932	152	24	78	419	47	252	519	.252

Where He Hits the Ball

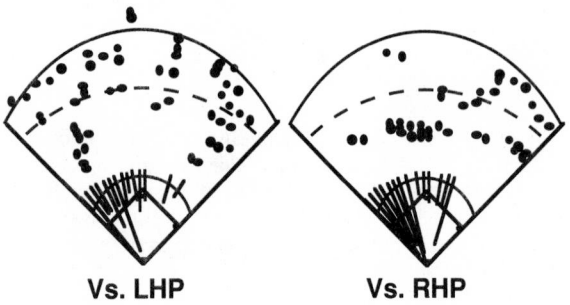

Vs. LHP   **Vs. RHP**

1989 Situational Stats

	AB	H	HR	RBI	AVG		AB	H	HR	RBI	AVG
Home	189	45	5	20	.238	LHP	162	52	5	18	.321
Road	207	59	5	23	.285	RHP	234	52	5	25	.222
Day	105	28	1	11	.267	Sc Pos	88	20	3	32	.227
Night	291	76	9	32	.261	Clutch	85	25	5	12	.294

1989 Rankings (American League)

➡ 4th in throwing out opposing base stealers (35.0%) - *catchers with 75 attempts*

➡ 5th in highest percent GDPs per GDP situation (22.0%) - *players with 50 PA in GDP situations*

PITCHING:

On the bright side of the Tigers 1989 season, Mike Henneman led the team in victories, albeit with the lowest win total to lead a Tigers staff since 1953. Without that 11th win, snatched during the final week of the season, Henneman was in line to lead the staff with the most modest win total in club history. More significantly, closers are supposed to amass saves rather than wins, and Henneman's save total of eight was only second best on the team (Hernandez posted 15). In 1989, it seemed Henneman turned opportunities to save games for others into potential win/loss opportunities for himself. He wasn't being selfish, just uncharacteristically ineffective. Most of those lapses were translated into wins, as his 11-4 record indicates.

At the top of his game, Henneman can overpower any batter. He has a good high-80s fastball that sinks, a split fingered pitch and a slider, and all the pitches are effective. In 1989, however, injuries limited his stretches in top form.

Over the season, Henneman experienced three absolutely dreadful outings that added 13 earned runs to his stats in just 2.2 innings of work. Toss out those three appearances and you get a 2.47 ERA, which compares favorably to his previous lifetime ERA of 2.44.

FIELDING:

While no gazelle, Henneman fields his position in a solid, no-nonsense manner. He knows how to get the sure out and has enough sense to take it. He doesn't create potential outs while pitching, only to give them back with slipshod defensive work. Henneman improved somewhat in '89 at holding baserunners, once the weakest part of his game.

OVERALL:

Henneman's style displays confidence bordering on cockiness, and seems to say, "I know how well I can throw; let's see how well you can hit." Call it brashness or call it guts. Although his saves total was down substantially from 1988 and his ERA the highest of his career, these should be attributed to a nagging groin pull which sidelined him several times during the season. The resulting lay-offs probably prevented him from honing his timing and mechanics to their usual degree of sharpness. With Hernandez questionable for 1990, Mike Henneman remains the cream of the Tigers bullpen crop.

MIKE HENNEMAN

Position: RP
Bats: R **Throws:** R
Ht: 6' 4" **Wt:** 195

Opening Day Age: 28
Born: 12/11/61 in St. Charles, MO
ML Seasons: 3

Overall Statistics

	W	L	ERA	G	GS	Sv	IP	H	R	BB	SO	HR
1989	11	4	3.70	60	0	8	90.0	84	46	51	69	4
Career	31	13	2.85	180	0	37	278.0	242	105	105	202	19

Where They Hit the Ball

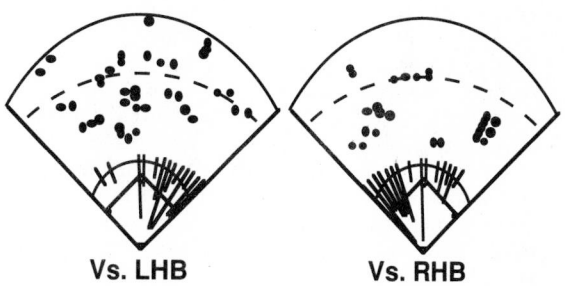

Vs. LHB   **Vs. RHB**

1989 Situational Stats

	W	L	ERA	Sv	IP		AB	H	HR	RBI	AVG
Home	8	0	3.65	5	49.1	LHB	155	41	1	16	.265
Road	3	4	3.76	3	40.2	RHB	180	43	3	22	.239
Day	1	2	5.13	4	26.1	Sc Pos	89	23	0	32	.258
Night	10	2	3.11	4	63.2	Clutch	191	51	3	18	.267

1989 Rankings (American League)

- ➡ 3rd in win/loss percentage (.733) - *pitchers with 15 or more decisions*
- ➡ Led the Tigers in wins (11), games (60), games finished (35), holds (6), win/loss percentage and lowest percent of inherited runners scoring (26.3%) - *team pitchers with 30 runners inherited*

TOUGH ON LEFTIES

WILLIE HERNANDEZ

Position: RP
Bats: L **Throws:** L
Ht: 6' 2" **Wt:** 185

Opening Day Age: 35
Born: 11/14/54 in Aguada, P. R.
ML Seasons: 13

PITCHING:

In theory, 1989 saw Willie Hernandez relinquish the role of closing relief ace to Mike Henneman. Even so, he led the Tigers in saves with 15, despite several stints on the DL, including a season-ending departure in August to undergo major elbow surgery deemed career-threatening by Tigers brass. Last year was the final year of a bonanza contract signed following his MVP/Cy Young season in 1984. In retrospect, that 1984 season was not only his shining moment, but also his greatest bane. With it, he created a vociferous monster--the monster of unrealistic fan expectations. The resulting boos have dogged him ever since. Hernandez is tenacious and sensitive; the fan abuse he has endured is a crime. The succeeding seasons have been disappointments only as measured against the 1984 yardstick.

Hernandez has complained of arm soreness over several seasons but some questioned his fortitude, so on he pitched. Last season, the arm blew. The injury aborted what might have been his best year since the hallowed '84. His screwball, which had been erratic over the past few years, was back and just as devastating as ever. The velocity on his fast ball had also returned. In just 31.1 innings of work, he fanned 30 while walking 16. He dominated left-hand hitters, holding them to a .205 average. His ERA was high, mostly due to stretches of injury-related inactivity. Hernandez needs frequent work to maintain his sharpness. He appeared in only 32 games for the Tigers; about half his yearly average. His 15 saves emerged from just 17 save opportunities. He not only topped the staff, but also accumulated more saves than the rest of the relief corps combined. Had the elbow been sound, the man could have fashioned a remarkable season.

FIELDING:

Hernandez is quick and always in the game. He will frequently play for a lead runner, at either second or third, on a routine bunt. He instinctively differentiates between dumb plays and percentage plays. His pitching motion is tough to gage. He always appears as if he might throw to first, which freezes runners.

OVERALL:

Guillermo's future with Detroit is cloudy, perhaps returning this spring as a non-roster invitee. The tough, proud competitor must prove in Lakeland (or elsewhere) that his gifted arm still has some major league innings left in it. In management's view, a return to form would be an unexpected plus.

Overall Statistics

	W	L	ERA	G	GS	Sv	IP	H	R	BB	SO	HR
1989	2	2	5.74	32	0	15	31.1	36	21	16	30	4
Career	70	63	3.38	744	11	147	1045.0	952	431	349	788	97

Where They Hit the Ball

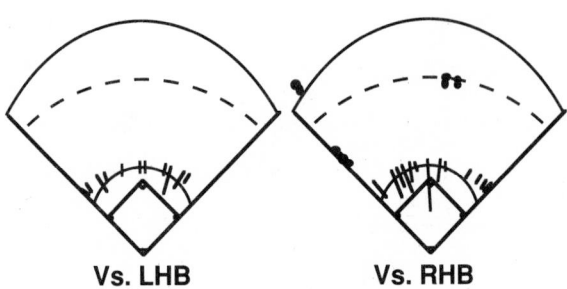

Vs. LHB **Vs. RHB**

1989 Situational Stats

	W	L	ERA	Sv	IP		AB	H	HR	RBI	AVG
Home	2	2	8.00	8	18.0	LHB	39	8	1	5	.205
Road	0	0	2.70	7	13.1	RHB	84	28	3	25	.333
Day	0	0	4.61	8	13.2	Sc Pos	42	16	3	28	.381
Night	2	2	6.62	7	17.2	Clutch	76	20	1	18	.263

1989 Rankings (American League)

➡ Led the Tigers in saves (15) and strikeouts per 9 innings (8.6) - *all team pitchers*

HITTING:

Tracy Jones was once considered an outstanding hitting prospect, but he has gone from the Reds to the Expos to the Giants to the Tigers in less than two years. He came to the Tigers with brief but impressive career numbers, entering 1989 with a .299 average and 15 homers in 669 lifetime at bats. You then wondered: If he's so good, why is he so expendable? One answer may be that he's prone to injury. Jones has never batted more than 359 times in a season and has spent five separate stints on the disabled list in only four years. More to the point, Jones has gotten the reputation for having an attitude problem. He's considered moody, stubborn, and difficult to manage. That reputation won't win him any points with Sparky Anderson, who loves those "we" ballplayers. Anderson likes to start with an open mind about people, as he did with Chris Brown, but Jones will clearly be on trial in 1990.

Certainly Jones has talent. Never a big home run man, he has good line drive power to the gaps. He's a slashing-type hitter, with a quick, short stroke, and can attack the high fastball. Jones is not nearly as good a breaking ball hitter, which won't help him at all in the American League, and he's always been much more effective against lefties than righties. But unquestionably, he can hit when healthy.

BASERUNNING:

Jones is swift but lacks blazing speed. In the past he was an outstanding base stealer, swiping 31 in only 117 games in 1987. But injuries have really taken away this part of his game. He stole two for the Giants last year and then went one of two in Detroit. When healthy and when more familiar with American League pitchers, this total should rise. He is a useful man to have aboard when the hit and run is in order.

FIELDING:

Jones is valued as much for his fielding as his hitting. The same speed he shows on the bases serves him well in the outfield. He has good range, and a strong, accurate arm which makes him a suitable choice at any outfield position. Jones made only one error with the Tigers.

OVERALL:

With his talent, Jones is one of the few members of Detroit's outfield corps who could yet mature into a consistently effective offensive force. If he can stay healthy and get his head straightened out a little, Jones can be a very useful player in 1990. Certainly he deserves a long look in a platoon role.

TRACY JONES

Position: LF/RF
Bats: R **Throws:** R
Ht: 6' 3" **Wt:** 220

Opening Day Age: 29
Born: 3/31/61 in Inglewood, CA
ML Seasons: 4

Overall Statistics

	G	AB	R	H	D	T	HR	RBI	SB	BB	SO	AVG
1989	86	255	22	59	14	0	3	38	3	21	30	.231
Career	339	924	120	259	40	4	18	116	59	73	93	.280

Where He Hits the Ball

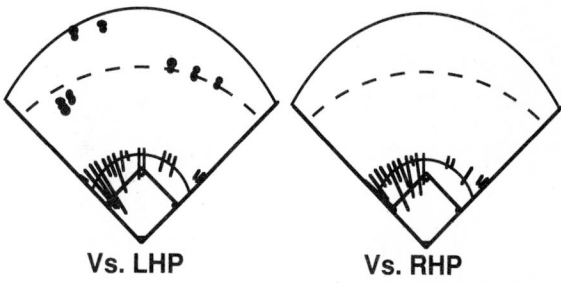

Vs. LHP   Vs. RHP

1989 Situational Stats

	AB	H	HR	RBI	AVG		AB	H	HR	RBI	AVG
Home	135	32	3	23	.237	LHP	102	30	1	22	.294
Road	120	27	0	15	.225	RHP	153	29	2	16	.190
Day	89	20	2	14	.225	Sc Pos	76	22	1	35	.289
Night	166	39	1	24	.235	Clutch	53	14	1	9	.264

1989 Rankings (American League)

➥ Led the Tigers in hitting with runners in scoring position (.319) - *all team players*

➥ Led AL Left Fielders in grounder/flyball ratio (3.86) - *all left fielders*

HITTING:

When a 34 year-old .276 lifetime hitter produces a .237 season, there is reason to be concerned. Chet Lemon's great hitting days appear to be in his past.

Lemon has shown the ability to hit for average and to hit with power. On different occasions, he has produced back-to-back .300 seasons, and consecutive 20 HR seasons. In 1989, however, Lemon was a weak producer of both singles and homers. Lemon's bat speed appeared to deteriorate, as his strikeouts/walks ratio jumped from 1.10 in 1988 to 1.54 last year, a bad sign for a veteran player.

Chet is a good mistake hitter. He likes fastballs up and out over the plate. The book of most pitchers is to give him many breaking balls and sinkers, and to let him crowd the plate if he wants. He has been a good pull hitter for years, but can be jammed when his stance is closed. Lemon has a history of hitting lefties better than righties.

BASERUNNING:

Although blessed with good speed, Lemon has not been a threat to steal since 1976 when he swiped 13 sacks. He shows good hustle on the bases, but he does not get a good jump, and his instincts and judgment are below average. The raw speed that used to help him overcome these deficiencies is now on the wane.

FIELDING:

Lemon's ability is a matter of record, literally. He holds the A.L. marks for most putouts by an outfielder in a season (512) and most seasons with 400 or more putouts (5). But all those numbers came in 1984 or earlier. Lemon has lost a step, moved from center field to right, and is now just adequate there. Lemon might also be well-advised to follow the old softball axiom, "always throw to second base." When he has to make a decision, all too often he chooses the wrong place to throw. His arm is strong but not very accurate.

OVERALL:

Since signing an eight-year contract that pays him through 1992, Lemon has produced enough good baseball to prove that he is not loafing. Indeed, he is an all-out, hustling player. The problem is simply that time is catching up with him. But even if a younger player takes away his role as a regular, Chet should have enough productive years left to finish his contract gracefully.

CHET LEMON

Position: RF/DH
Bats: R **Throws:** R
Ht: 6' 0" **Wt:** 190

Opening Day Age: 35
Born: 2/12/55 in Jackson, MS
ML Seasons: 15

Overall Statistics

	G	AB	R	H	D	T	HR	RBI	SB	BB	SO	AVG
1989	127	414	45	98	19	2	7	47	1	46	71	.237
Career	1884	6546	934	1792	380	57	210	852	55	701	963	.274

Where He Hits the Ball

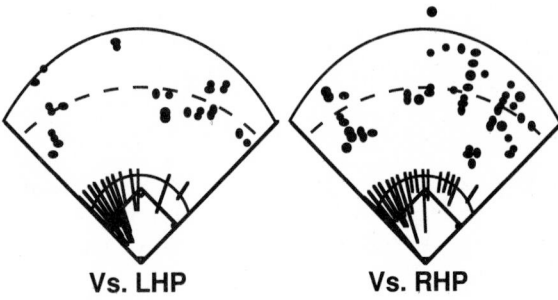

Vs. LHP **Vs. RHP**

1989 Situational Stats

	AB	H	HR	RBI	AVG		AB	H	HR	RBI	AVG
Home	189	43	4	23	.228	LHP	154	43	5	27	.279
Road	225	55	3	24	.244	RHP	260	55	2	20	.212
Day	121	26	0	14	.215	Sc Pos	104	30	1	36	.288
Night	293	72	7	33	.246	Clutch	79	16	0	7	.203

1989 Rankings (American League)

➡ 5th in hit by pitch (8)

➡ Led the Tigers in hit by pitch and hitting with the bases loaded (.333) - *team players with 10 PA with the bases loaded*

➡ Led AL Right Fielders in hit by pitch

HITTING:

What a difference the environment makes. In spring training, Fred Lynn was the best hitter on the team. However, when the team went north, Lynn's batting average went south. From Opening Day until the end of the season, Lynn found himself mired in a slump he could not get out of. After hitting between 21 and 25 homers for seven straight seasons, Lynn could manage only 11 round-trippers.

For most of his career, Lynn has been a patient hitter. But in 1989, he was extremely aggressive. He was anxious at the plate and jumped at the ball instead of striding into it. The most basic cause for Lynn's decline was simple. Age finally caught up to him. Lynn was overmatched all year on the fastball. Also, a good, hard breaking-ball on the fists would eat him up.

Lynn also turned into a dead pull hitter in '89. Instead of taking the outside pitch to leftfield, he would play pepper with the first and second basemen. Despite all his problems at the plate, Lynn still produced some game-winning hits. At least he didn't forget how to produce in the clutch.

BASERUNNING:

Lynn is a smart baserunner with no speed. He is daring, though, and will not hesitate to gamble for the extra base. His days of being a base-stealing threat are over. Five steals would be a banner year for him.

FIELDING:

At least Lynn didn't let his poor hitting affect his play in the field. His range isn't what it used to be, but he still gets an excellent jump on the ball. His arm is still above average and he also plays the corner as well as anyone. Lynn is a fearless leftfielder who is not afraid to dive or crash into fences to make a play.

OVERALL:

Fred Lynn's days in Detroit are numbered. The Tigers are going with the youth movement and Lynn is anything but a youngster. Maybe Lynn's disappointing season was just a fluke. Then again it could be the beginning of a steady decline. More than likely it is the latter. Lynn may latch on to another team, but his influence would probably be minimal.

FRED LYNN

Position: LF/DH
Bats: L **Throws:** L
Ht: 6' 1" **Wt:** 190

Opening Day Age: 38
Born: 2/3/52 in Chicago, IL
ML Seasons: 16

Overall Statistics

	G	AB	R	H	D	T	HR	RBI	SB	BB	SO	AVG
1989	117	353	44	85	11	1	11	46	1	47	71	.241
Career	1879	6729	1045	1913	385	42	300	1088	70	835	1072	.284

Where He Hits the Ball

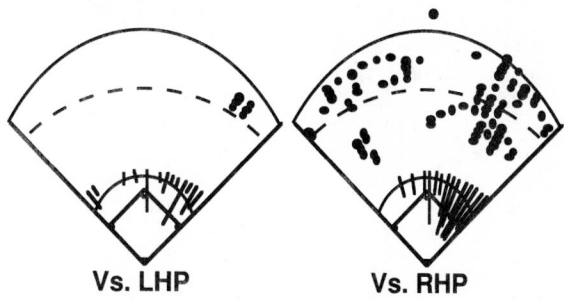

Vs. LHP   Vs. RHP

1989 Situational Stats

	AB	H	HR	RBI	AVG		AB	H	HR	RBI	AVG
Home	173	37	9	29	.214	LHP	64	12	0	1	.188
Road	180	48	2	17	.267	RHP	289	73	11	45	.253
Day	127	33	5	20	.260	Sc Pos	90	24	2	33	.267
Night	226	52	6	26	.230	Clutch	57	10	1	2	.175

1989 Rankings (American League)

➡ Led the Tigers in lowest GDPs per GDP situation (5.5%) - *team players with 50 PA in GDP situations*

JACK MORRIS

Position: SP
Bats: R **Throws:** R
Ht: 6' 3" **Wt:** 200

Opening Day Age: 34
Born: 5/16/55 in St. Paul, MN
ML Seasons: 13

PITCHING:

All good things must come to an end. For Jack Morris, the winningest pitcher of the 1980's, the 1989 season was a living nightmare. He missed two months of the season with a fractured bone in his pitching elbow. After his return, Morris struggled to regain his old form.

Even after the injury, Morris is still a pitcher who relies on power. His fastball, slider and split finger fastball are his best pitches in a tight situation. However, Morris must pitch from ahead in the count to be effective. His split finger is nearly unhittable, but can't be thrown when the count is 2-0 and 3-1. Most of the homeruns that Morris allows are off the change-up that he has never quite mastered.

Morris' competitive drive makes him a strong and durable pitcher. He is a firm believer in finishing what he starts. However, this drive can also be his undoing. Morris often fights himself on the mound and loses his temper and composure whenever a teammate makes an error or the umpire misses a pitch. Over the last few years Morris has learned to control his emotions better. What separates Morris from the rest of the pack is his desire to pitch the big game. He was 3-0 in post season play in 1984. When the chips are down, Morris wants the ball.

FIELDING:

Morris is without question the best fielding pitcher on the Tigers. Even though his follow-through leaves him in awful fielding position, he is athletic enough to recover in time to make the difficult play look routine. But one of Morris' major problems is holding runners on first. His delivery is much too slow and deliberate, making it nearly impossible for the catcher to throw anyone out.

OVERALL:

Morris is still the ace of the Tiger staff. His poor showing in 1989 is partly due to the elbow injury but mostly due to the sinfully bad team he was a part of. Put Morris on a team that can field and score some runs and he will prove why he is still one of the top ten pitchers in the game today.

Overall Statistics

	W	L	ERA	G	GS	Sv	IP	H	R	BB	SO	HR
1989	6	14	4.86	24	24	0	170.1	189	102	59	115	23
Career	183	132	3.66	394	372	0	2793.2	2536	1238	989	1818	295

Where They Hit the Ball

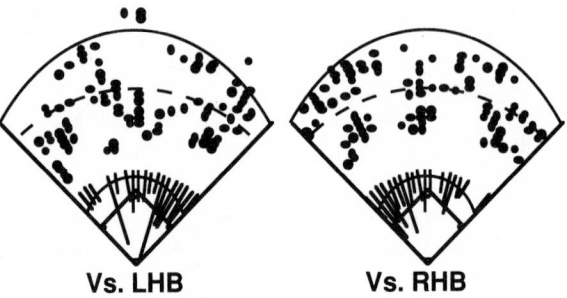

Vs. LHB　　　　　**Vs. RHB**

1989 Situational Stats

	W	L	ERA	Sv	IP		AB	H	HR	RBI	AVG
Home	4	6	4.75	0	85.1	LHB	307	91	11	45	.296
Road	2	8	4.98	0	85.0	RHB	362	98	12	46	.271
Day	2	4	4.35	0	39.1	Sc Pos	166	52	1	62	.313
Night	4	10	5.02	0	131.0	Clutch	94	24	2	12	.255

1989 Rankings (American League)

➡ 2nd in worst slugging percentage allowed (.450), most HRs allowed per 9 innings (1.22) and complete games (10) - *pitchers with 502 PA*

➡ 3rd in worst ERA (4.86) and worst run support per 9 innings (3.54)

➡ 4th in losses (14)

➡ 5th in home runs allowed (23) and lowest won/loss percentage (.300) - *pitchers with 15 or more decisions*

➡ Led the Tigers in complete games, wild pitches (12), stolen bases allowed (24), grounder/flyball ratio (1.34), least pitches thrown per batter (3.5) and strikeouts per 9 innings (6.1) - *team pitchers with 162 IP*

HITTING:

Matt Nokes is a fine hitter, but not as good as his fabulous rookie season would indicate. He is a typical example of first-year success raising unreasonable expectations, and a perfect case of a rookie's second half numbers giving a true indication of future performance. In 1987, Nokes hit .289 with great power, but most of his success came in the first half, when he hit .313 while every pitcher challenged him. After the All Star break, he hit just .251. Nokes pleased some forecasters by hitting exactly .251 in 1988 and .250 in an injury-riddled 1989.

The story of 1987 tells a lot about how to pitch to Nokes. Come after him with a nice fat fastball, and he will park it for you. It is safer to keep the ball down and away, and to start him off with something unhittable. If the first pitch is in the strike zone, he will swing at it. Matt is a pull hitter who loves fastballs, and he loves them up. The pitches that get him out are breaking balls (nothing too easy to jerk), fastballs that he cannot reach, and change-ups. Nokes does not hit lefties well, and does not get to face them very often. Southpaws are able to jam him effectively, so they can choose whatever pitch is their strongest, and take the direct approach.

BASERUNNING:

The stolen base is not a part of Nokes' offensive arsenal; he is simply not a track star. He's a conservative baserunner.

FIELDING:

Nokes has just reached age 26, and it is fair to say that he is still learning subjects like opposing hitters' weaknesses. But he is not a subnormal fielder, as has often been reported. His arm is a particular strength, powerful enough to offset a somewhat delayed release. Matt cuts down his share of opposing baserunners.

OVERALL:

Sparky Anderson's once admitted that if Lance Parrish had stayed in Detroit, Matt Nokes would have stayed in Toledo. Qualified catchers often reach age 26 without reaching the majors, and Nokes might still be an unknown if he had not been given his chance.

MATT NOKES

Position: C/DH
Bats: L **Throws:** R
Ht: 6' 1" **Wt:** 185

Opening Day Age: 26
Born: 10/31/63 in San Diego, CA
ML Seasons: 5

Overall Statistics

	G	AB	R	H	D	T	HR	RBI	SB	BB	SO	AVG
1989	87	268	15	67	10	0	9	39	1	17	37	.250
Career	370	1188	142	315	45	2	60	186	3	88	175	.265

Where He Hits the Ball

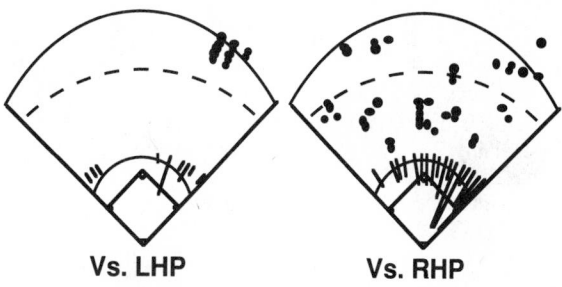

Vs. LHP   **Vs. RHP**

1989 Situational Stats

	AB	H	HR	RBI	AVG		AB	H	HR	RBI	AVG
Home	127	34	7	20	.268	LHP	43	11	2	9	.256
Road	141	33	2	19	.234	RHP	225	56	7	30	.249
Day	93	27	6	21	.290	Sc Pos	75	18	2	27	.240
Night	175	40	3	18	.229	Clutch	40	10	1	8	.250

1989 Rankings (American League)

➡ 1st in batting average on an 0-2 count (.400) - *players with 20 PA with an 0-2 count*

➡ 2nd in lowest percent of extra bases taken per opportunity (19.2%) - *players with 40 opportunities*

HITTING:

Gary Pettis learned that in order to be successful he had to hit the ball on the ground. In 1989 he sported the 3rd highest groundball/flyball ratio in the American League. Combined with a career high 84 walks, Gary posted a sparkling .375 on-base average, placing him firmly among the league leaders.

Pettis is a sucker for the letter high fastball. Considering the fact that he has no power and terrible bat speed, this should be the last pitch he swings at. When Pettis is in a good groove at the plate, he lays off the high fastball and goes to the opposite field on any pitch from the middle of the plate on out.

Pettis is a fine leadoff man because of his speed and on-base average, but is a strikeout candidate against any pitcher with just a mediocre fastball. The Tigers, like the Angels before them, have been preaching to Pettis about swinging down on the ball to induce more grounders, but the downside has been a dramatic leap in his GDPs, from 4 to 14 over the last two years.

BASERUNNING:

Pettis is an excellent baserunner who is a threat to steal anytime. He is the only player on the Tigers that has the greenlight to steal whenever he wants. If Pettis can maintain his high on-base average, he will continue to steal 40-50 bases per year. 1989's drop in his SB success rate is some cause for alarm, but not panic.

FIELDING:

Pettis is probably the best centerfielder in the game today. His range is outstanding which helps cover up for what is only an average arm. Pettis plays one of the shallowest centerfields in the league, but is very adept at going back on the ball. He will rarely get a bad jump on a ball and plays all caroms to perfection. If the ball has enough hang time on it, Pettis will make the play.

OVERALL:

Pettis is still an all-star defensively, and at age 31 he finally came into his own as an offensive player. Pettis should be the Tigers' everyday centerfielder for a long time, although prospect Milt Cuyler is waiting in the wings. Pettis is an important element on what is right now a rather non-descript Detroit team.

GARY PETTIS

Position: CF
Bats: B **Throws:** R
Ht: 6' 1" **Wt:** 160

Opening Day Age: 32
Born: 4/3/58 in Oakland, CA
ML Seasons: 8

Overall Statistics

	G	AB	R	H	D	T	HR	RBI	SB	BB	SO	AVG
1989	119	444	77	114	8	6	1	18	43	84	106	.257
Career	832	2765	438	661	81	33	17	197	273	381	704	.239

Where He Hits the Ball

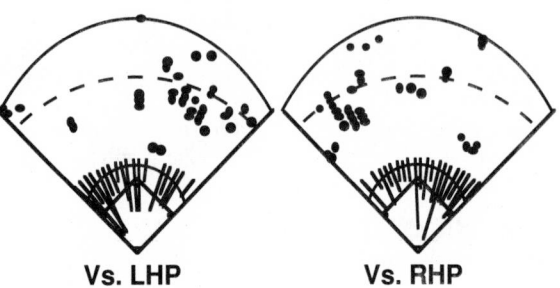

Vs. LHP   **Vs. RHP**

1989 Situational Stats

	AB	H	HR	RBI	AVG		AB	H	HR	RBI	AVG
Home	234	62	1	12	.265	LHP	152	40	0	7	.263
Road	210	52	0	6	.248	RHP	292	74	1	11	.253
Day	119	31	0	5	.261	Sc Pos	84	16	0	15	.190
Night	325	83	1	13	.255	Clutch	68	18	0	9	.265

1989 Rankings (American League)

➡ 3rd in lowest slugging percentage (.309), highest grounder/flyball ratio (2.42) and pitches seen per plate appearance (4.1) - *players with 502 PA*

➡ 4th in stolen bases (43) and lowest home run frequency (444 ABs per HR)

➡ Led the Tigers in batting average (.257), runs (77), singles (99), triples (6), sacrifice bunts(8), stolen bases, caught stealing, on-base average (.375), grounder/flyball ratio, bunts in play (23), steals of third, batting average with 2 strikes (.233), strikeouts and percentage of extra bases taken as a runner (55.6%) - *team players with 502 PA*

PITCHING:

Jeff Robinson is going to be a good one, if he can ever stay healthy for an entire season. In 1988 it was a circulatory problem in his fingers that caused him to miss the last month and a half. In 1989, Robinson had various shoulder, elbow, and stomach injuries that shelved him for most of the season.

When not on the DL, Robinson can be a very dominant power pitcher. On his best nights, Robinson's fastball will reach 91-94 mph. He also mixes in a good slider and an excellent split finger pitch that was taught to him by San Francisco manager Roger Craig.

One of Robinson's biggest problems last season was control. Part of this is attributable to his arm problems. Robinson fell behind too many hitters with 2-0 and 3-1 counts and was unable then to throw his split finger pitch.

Robbie has been much more successful at Tiger Stadium than in enemy ballparks. The main cause for this is that he is a groundball pitcher and is helped immensely by the tall infield grass in Detroit. Robinson often struggles in any park with artificial turf. He is also a consistent pitcher. Robinson will very rarely get knocked out of the box early. He is usually good for at least 6 or 7 innings per start, which over the course of a season will save a lot of wear and tear on the bullpen.

FIELDING:

Robinson is very agile and is quick off the mound on bunt plays. He has even waved off other infielders in order to catch pop-ups. In short, Robinson will not beat himself with physical errors. But he is a very easy pitcher to steal on. His long leg kick and love for throwing the split finger pitch make it simple to get a good jump on him. Pitching coach Billy Muffett is working with Robinson on quickening his delivery to the plate, but so far the results have not been noticeable.

OVERALL:

Robinson's attitude is outstanding. He has maintained a positive outlook despite all of the setbacks he has incurred. Each time Robinson has been injured, he has worked hard and diligently to come back. If he stays healthy it is only a matter of time before he becomes a solid 18-20 game winner.

JEFF M. ROBINSON

Position: SP
Bats: R **Throws:** R
Ht: 6' 6" **Wt:** 210

Opening Day Age: 28
Born: 12/14/61 in Ventura, CA
ML Seasons: 3

Overall Statistics

	W	L	ERA	G	GS	Sv	IP	H	R	BB	SO	HR
1989	4	5	4.73	16	16	0	78.0	76	47	46	40	10
Career	26	17	4.15	69	60	0	377.1	329	194	172	252	45

Where They Hit the Ball

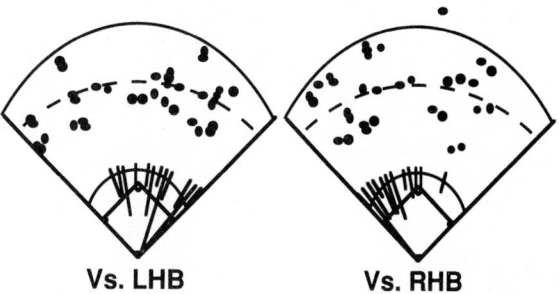

Vs. LHB   **Vs. RHB**

1989 Situational Stats

	W	L	ERA	Sv	IP		AB	H	HR	RBI	AVG
Home	4	2	2.76	0	45.2	LHB	145	39	6	20	.269
Road	0	3	7.52	0	32.1	RHB	149	37	4	17	.248
Day	2	1	3.16	0	25.2	Sc Pos	73	20	3	27	.274
Night	2	4	5.50	0	52.1	Clutch	7	0	0	0	.000

1989 Rankings (American League)

➡ Led the Tigers in shutouts (1)

HITTING:

Rick Schu was scrounged from the Baltimore organization and employed as Detroit's third hot corner solution of 1989, after dismal showings by Chris Brown and Al Pedrique. Given plenty of playing time, Schu didn't seize the opportunity. He showed a little pop with seven homers, but his .214 average was a career low. The righthanded hitter showed little of the ability that had produced an average which ranged from .252 to .276 in all but one of his previous five seasons.

Schu is primarily a high fastball hitter. Although he's never hit more than eight home runs, he still prefers to pull the ball and try to drive it. He's never been a very good breaking-ball hitter, and pitches low and away have always bothered him. Schu has the habit of trying to do more with pitches than he really can, and in '89 those tendencies were worse than ever. He was especially anemic against righthanded breaking-ball pitchers. Perhaps playing a power position in a home run park made him think (again) that he was a slugger. Whatever the case, he was totally messed up.

BASERUNNING:

Schu has decent overall speed and has always been a smart baserunner. He's no threat to steal, however. He stole only base in '89, and in his career has swiped only 17 bases while getting tossed out 16 times -- a terrible ratio.

FIELDING:

The trade of the aging Tom Brookens threw into turmoil what, for years, had been a solid if unspectacular position. Schu, of all last season's hot corner itinerants, came closest to providing the dependable defense Brookens always provided. He's not a Gold Glover, merely the type who can make the routine play. He has average range and a decent arm. Schu committed 12 errors last year. The other Tiger third sackers committed 28.

OVERALL:

The steady Brookens always seemed to win the Tiger third base job after all the other candidates played themselves out of contention. The 28-year old Schu may find himself in the same position in 1990, especially if he shows he can return his average to its previous .250-plus level. The Tigers will probably try to find a replacement, but Schu could well win the job by default.

RICK SCHU

Position: 3B
Bats: R **Throws:** R
Ht: 6' 0" **Wt:** 194

Opening Day Age: 28
Born: 1/26/62 in Philadelphia, PA
ML Seasons: 6

Overall Statistics

	G	AB	R	H	D	T	HR	RBI	SB	BB	SO	AVG
1989	99	266	25	57	11	0	7	21	1	24	37	.214
Career	501	1385	169	342	59	13	35	118	17	127	250	.247

Where He Hits the Ball

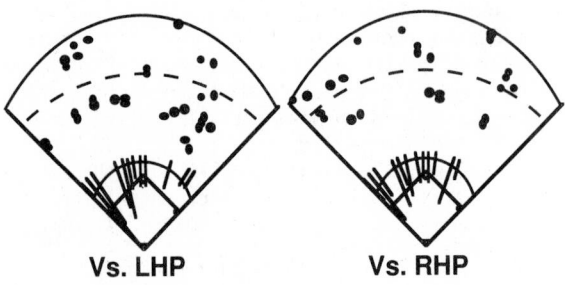

Vs. LHP   **Vs. RHP**

1989 Situational Stats

	AB	H	HR	RBI	AVG		AB	H	HR	RBI	AVG
Home	130	25	3	11	.192	LHP	143	38	5	14	.266
Road	136	32	4	10	.235	RHP	123	19	2	7	.154
Day	81	16	1	6	.198	Sc Pos	60	10	0	11	.167
Night	185	41	6	15	.222	Clutch	51	9	0	0	.176

1989 Rankings (American League)

➡ Did not rank near the top or bottom in any category

HITTING:

Unless Doug Strange starts to hit the ball with more consistency, his career in the bigs will be short-lived. Strange is a switch hitter who hits the ball much better from the left side. In his '89 trial Strange didn't do much hitting of any kind, batting only .214 with a single home run.

Strange's biggest problem is that he hits too many balls in the air. He may have fancied himself a power hitter after belting 13 homers at Glens Falls in 1987 and 8 more in 304 at bats for Toledo early in '89. In truth, Strange is a singles hitter who should be trying to slap the ball on the ground and utilize his decent speed. He probably wouldn't have been in the big leagues at all last year if the Tigers hadn't been so desperate for thirdbase help. He didn't make the Tigers' list of top ten prospects the last two years and his minor league record, though it showed flashes of promise, was terribly uneven.

Strange does have some offensive skills. He batted over .300 twice in the minors and legged out a lot of doubles. But he struggled even at the Triple A level, so major league success is not going to come easily for him.

BASERUNNING:

Strange has above average speed and could conceivably steal 15-20 bases a year. Unfortunately, he can't steal first base. He is also a smart baserunner who takes the extra base when the opportunity is there.

FIELDING:

Strange's defensive play was horrendous. He led the Tigers in errors despite being up for only half the season. Strange will make the tough plays but loses his concentration on the easy ones. His range is good but he doesn't charge balls as well as he should.

OVERALL:

Strange is going to get every opportunity to play in Detroit. The Tigers have him pegged as their third baseman of the future. Strange figures to get lots of playing time in spring training and a chance to become the everyday third sacker next season. He'll need some major improvement, however, to avoid a return to Triple A.

DOUG STRANGE

Position: 3B
Bats: B **Throws:** R
Ht: 6' 2" **Wt:** 170

Opening Day Age: 25
Born: 4/13/64 in Greenville, SC
ML Seasons: 1

Overall Statistics

	G	AB	R	H	D	T	HR	RBI	SB	BB	SO	AVG
1989	64	196	16	42	4	1	1	14	3	17	36	.214
Career	64	196	16	42	4	1	1	14	3	17	36	.214

Where He Hits the Ball

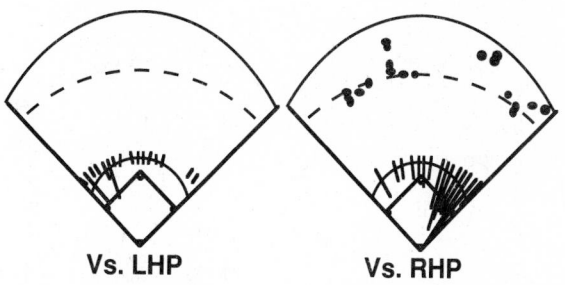

Vs. LHP   Vs. RHP

1989 Situational Stats

	AB	H	HR	RBI	AVG		AB	H	HR	RBI	AVG
Home	96	20	1	8	.208	LHP	42	8	0	0	.190
Road	100	22	0	6	.220	RHP	154	34	1	14	.221
Day	45	10	1	5	.222	Sc Pos	45	12	0	13	.267
Night	151	32	0	9	.212	Clutch	39	7	0	3	.179

1989 Rankings (American League)

➡ Led the Tigers in errors (19)

PITCHING:

Frank Tanana will never again be accused of over-powering the batters. On occasion, his fastball probably doesn't even break the speed limit. What Tanana does instead is outsmart the hitters and destroy their timing. By throwing an assortment of curveballs, change-ups, and even a screwball, Tanana has become the ultimate finesse pitcher.

Tanana's most effective pitch is undoubtedly his curveball. He throws this pitch at various speeds and also drops down from the side against lefthanded batters. Tanana's fastball, while anything but fast, looks quicker than it really is because of the way he sets it up. Tanana's control is excellent. Of course, for him to be successful it has to be. Tanana is a model of consistency. He rarely finishes a game but also rarely gets knocked out before the sixth. When Tanana starts, you can usually count on 6-8 strong innings.

Tanana would be a good candidate to pitch a deciding game. The game he is most remembered for since joining Detroit was his 1-0 division clinching gem against Jimmy Key and Toronto on the final day of the 1987 season. He is a veteran with experience, which is important when it's put up or shut up time.

The fact that Tanana has made the successful conversion from a power pitcher to a finesse pitcher is a story in itself. When Tanana was with the California Angels in the early '70's he threw in the mid 90's and just blew everyone away. However, after his surgery he was able to change his way of pitching and become a successful junkballer.

FIELDING:

Another reason for Tanana's success is his ability to hold runners on and field his position. Tanana's persistence in throwing to first is something. He will not hesitate to throw over five or six times each batter. Tanana also fields anything and everything he can get his hands on. In short, Tanana does not beat himself with silly mistakes.

OVERALL:

Tanana was the best pitcher on the Tigers in 1989. With any support at all he would have won 15-18 games. He and Brian DuBois are the only lefties on the staff. Assuming he's still with them, Tanana will be used as the third starter behind Morris and Robinson in 1990.

FRANK TANANA

Position: SP
Bats: L **Throws:** L
Ht: 6' 3" **Wt:** 195

Opening Day Age: 36
Born: 7/3/53 in Detroit, MI
ML Seasons: 17

Overall Statistics

	W	L	ERA	G	GS	Sv	IP	H	R	BB	SO	HR
1989	10	14	3.58	33	33	0	223.2	227	105	74	147	21
Career	198	188	3.49	507	491	0	3403.2	3252	1496	966	2345	347

Where They Hit the Ball

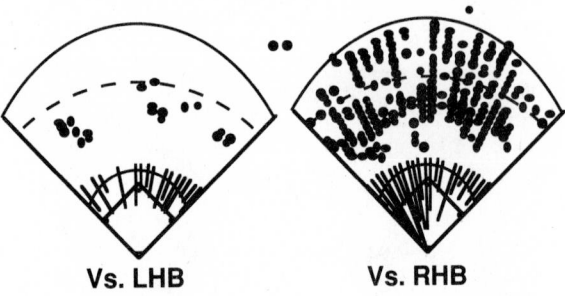

Vs. LHB   Vs. RHB

1989 Situational Stats

	W	L	ERA	Sv	IP		AB	H	HR	RBI	AVG
Home	4	6	3.48	0	119.0	LHB	118	36	2	15	.305
Road	6	8	3.70	0	104.2	RHB	738	191	19	82	.259
Day	5	8	3.63	0	91.2	Sc Pos	172	49	3	71	.285
Night	5	6	3.55	0	132.0	Clutch	76	21	3	5	.276

1989 Rankings (American League)

➡ 4th in losses (14) and lowest run support per 9 innings (3.66) - *pitchers with 162 IP*

➡ 5th in hit batters (8) and caught stealing (12)

➡ 10th in games started (33), home runs allowed (21), innngs (223), stolen bases allowed (22)

➡ Led the Tigers in ERA (3.58), games started, shutouts (1), innings, hit batters, strikeouts (147), pitches thrown (3,651), pickoff throws (196), GDPs induced (20), lowest opponent batting average (.265) and lowest HRs per 9 innings (.85) - *team pitchers with 162 PA*

HITTING:

Alan Trammell got off to a slow start at the plate in 1989, built his average back to within shouting distance of his lifetime numbers by early June, then nose-dived through a horrendous slump in July and August before displaying hints of his old batting form for much of September. A bad back, which plagued Trammell for most of the season, is probably the primary culprit for a paltry .243 batting average, his lowest since becoming a Tigers regular in 1978. Trammell's fence-clearing stroke also departed in 1989, leaving him with just 5 round-trippers at season's end. Again, blame the bad back. When he's healthy, Trammell is one of the best offensive shortstops in baseball. He has a beautiful short stroke and can turn with great power on anything inside. He's weakest against righthanded breaking-ball pitchers who can keep the ball low and away. But when he's healthy and on his game, no kind of pitching is consistently effective against him.

Trammell is one of the few major league hitters versatile enough to handle both the number two and number four spots in the batting order. He has great bat control and can make contact and hit behind the runner when batting second. Yet used as a cleanup man with the '87 division champions, Trammell responded with 28 homers and 105 RBIs.

BASERUNNING:

Trammell is an intelligent runner who seldom commits a blunder. Trammell being thrown out taking an ill-advised extra base or getting nailed at the plate would be major news. He still goes easily from first to third on singles. He remains the team's most judicious stealer, succeeding 10 of 12 times last year.

FIELDING:

Although age and injuries may be slowing them a bit, the Trammell/Whitaker tandem remains the defensive heart and soul of the Tigers. Trammell's range has decreased to some degree, but he compensates with knowledge and experience. He positions himself against hitters as well as any shortstop in the game. Trammell's arm isn't the most powerful, but it's adequate and as accurate as an atomic clock. He makes all the routine plays with stellar consistency.

OVERALL:

Bad back, bad wrist, and bad leg all added up to a bad season for Trammell in 1989. Attribute the decline in Trammell's statistics to physical ailments, not declining skills. A move to first base might extend a solid career in danger of being curtailed by the wear and tear on an unselfish player.

ALAN TRAMMELL

Position: SS
Bats: R **Throws:** R
Ht: 6' 0"   **Wt:** 175

Opening Day Age: 32
Born: 2/21/58 in
Garden Grove, CA
ML Seasons: 13

Overall Statistics

	G	AB	R	H	D	T	HR	RBI	SB	BB	SO	AVG
1989	121	449	54	109	20	3	5	43	10	45	45	.243
Career	1689	6143	938	1759	292	49	138	721	187	639	657	.286

Where He Hits the Ball

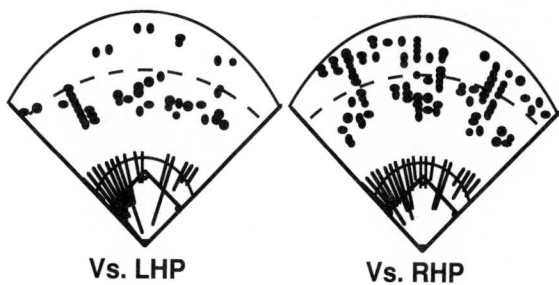

Vs. LHP   **Vs. RHP**

1989 Situational Stats

	AB	H	HR	RBI	AVG		AB	H	HR	RBI	AVG
Home	236	59	2	25	.250	LHP	163	47	1	18	.288
Road	213	50	3	18	.235	RHP	286	62	4	25	.217
Day	145	41	1	12	.283	Sc Pos	100	26	0	35	.260
Night	304	68	4	31	.224	Clutch	73	22	1	9	.301

1989 Rankings (American League)

- ➥ 2nd worst slugging for a cleanup hitter (.324) - *players with 150 PA batting cleanup*
- ➥ Led the Tigers in lowest percent of swings that missed (11.4%) and hitting in the clutch (.301) - *players with 50 PA in the clutch*
- ➥ Led AL Shortstops hitting in the clutch

HITTING:

With the release of Larry Herndon, Detroit needed an experienced righthanded hitter capable of generating some power. In Gary Ward, they landed a proven hitter, a seasoned outfielder, and an attractive DH option. He was more a success than a disappointment with his assignment, but unanticipated shortcomings at numerous other positions made Ward's contributions largely meaningless. While Ward batted only .253, he was obtained primarily to hit lefties, and he did the job in that department, batting .278. His overall .397 slugging average was third best on the team, and most of that power was against lefties. His work with runners in scoring position was terrible, but for the most part Ward performed about as expected.

Ward likes the ball over the plate. He hits the fastball pretty well and is still capable of driving the ball a long way. Righthanders have found Ward very vulnerable to low and away sliders, especially as he's gotten older.

BASERUNNING:

A former base-stealing threat whose speed merchant days are gone, Ward nabbed one of four in 1989. Losing a step or two to age was a factor in 10 double play ground outs. Overall, however, experience and aggressiveness make for an intelligent and prudent runner.

FIELDING:

Defensively, Ward will give you a good effort with serviceable results. His range is not the most expansive in baseball, but what he gets to he hangs on to. Although not in the acrobatic Fred Lynn mold, he hustles and stays within his limitations. He may not amaze you often, but neither will frequent defensive gaffes leave you slapping your forehead in despair. Ward's arm is average, with reliable accuracy. He plays a conservative rather than renegade left field. Unlike many left fielders, he is not a defensive disaster waiting to happen. His glove work is both dependable and consistent.

OVERALL:

Fred Lynn's value is questionable, Gary Pettis may elect free agency, Ken Williams was a disappointment, Scott Lusader and Tracy Jones are unproven. Detroit's outfield prospects are muddled, with an aging Chet Lemon still the cornerstone. Until the professed youth movement yields results, good old Gary Ward is worth retaining.

GARY WARD

Position: LF/DH/1B/RF
Bats: R **Throws:** R
Ht: 6' 2" **Wt:** 202

Opening Day Age: 36
Born: 12/6/53 in Los Angeles, CA
ML Seasons: 11

Overall Statistics

	G	AB	R	H	D	T	HR	RBI	SB	BB	SO	AVG
1989	113	292	27	74	11	2	9	30	1	24	59	.253
Career	1181	4170	562	1157	185	39	121	551	81	321	725	.277

Where He Hits the Ball

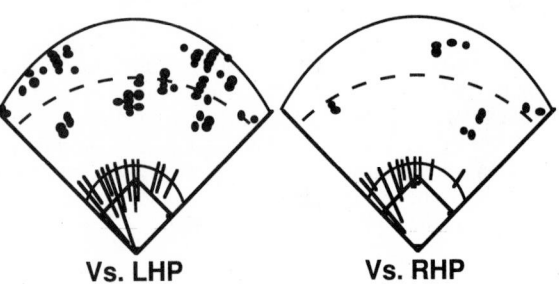

Vs. LHP   **Vs. RHP**

1989 Situational Stats

	AB	H	HR	RBI	AVG		AB	H	HR	RBI	AVG
Home	139	36	6	18	.259	LHP	187	52	9	24	.278
Road	153	38	3	12	.248	RHP	105	22	0	6	.210
Day	83	16	2	4	.193	Sc Pos	75	14	1	21	.187
Night	209	58	7	26	.278	Clutch	62	13	1	4	.210

1989 Rankings (American League)

- ➡ 1st in lowest batting average with the bases loaded (.000) - *players with 10 PA with the bases loaded*
- ➡ 3rd lowest batting average with 2 strikes (.107) - *players with 162 PA with 2 strikes*

OVERLOOKED

LOU WHITAKER

Position: 2B
Bats: L **Throws:** R
Ht: 5'11" **Wt:** 160

Opening Day Age: 32
Born: 5/12/57 in Brooklyn, NY
ML Seasons: 13

HITTING:

If age is catching up with Lou Whitaker after 13 years with the Tigers, nobody has broken the news to him. In 1989, Whitaker was the daily bright spot in a dark and dreary season. Steady to stellar, both in the field and at the plate, Whitaker set personal season highs in home runs, walks and RBIs. He led the team in at bats, hits, home runs, doubles, RBIs, and walks.

After slumping to only 12 homers in 1988, Whitaker worked hard last year to restore his pull-hitting stroke. He did that, and then some. He was able to get around on the fastballs which gave him trouble in '88; many of those offerings ended up in the seats. Lefthanders continued to work him away in 1989, both with fastballs and breaking stuff, and Whitaker continued to struggle against those offerings. Whitaker has not hit over .230 against lefties since 1983. As he ages, Whitaker may need to be platooned a little.

BASERUNNING:

Whitaker is a dangerous, effective man on the bases. Occasionally, aggressiveness wins out over judgment and an unexpected out results. For the most part, if there's a way to score, Whitaker will find it. Despite fair speed, stealing is one aspect of the game that he hasn't chosen to develop.

FIELDING:

As one-half of the longest running double-play duo in baseball history, it's easy to view Whitaker and Trammell as a single defensive entity. This is true of the way they instinctively mesh to execute the double play. On the right side of the infield, however, Whitaker is totally individual and special. He goes to his right or his left with equal facility (though now with diminished range) and is almost unerring going back to snag short pops to the outfield. He did drop such a bases-loaded fly in 1989--the only time in recent memory that a Whitaker error cost Detroit a game.

OVERALL:

Forget the tag "Sweet Lou." Instead, try "Consistent Lou." Over the past decade, you would be hard pressed to find a second baseman not named Sandberg who has performed at such a steadfast level of offensive and defensive excellence. Those "Lous" in Tiger Stadium have never turned to boos, and probably never will. Whitaker should have at least a couple of years left as regular second sacker. After that, he'll play as long as he can hit, and that should be for a while.

Overall Statistics

	G	AB	R	H	D	T	HR	RBI	SB	BB	SO	AVG
1989	148	509	77	128	21	1	28	85	6	89	59	.251
Career	1695	6221	965	1719	279	58	149	721	116	802	803	.276

Where He Hits the Ball

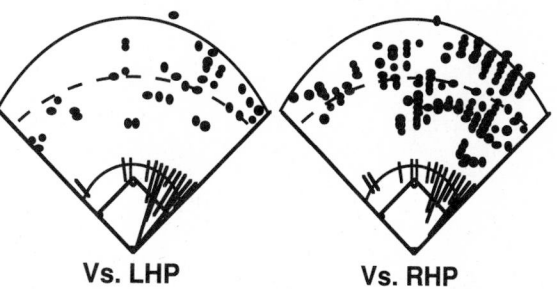

Vs. LHP   **Vs. RHP**

1989 Situational Stats

	AB	H	HR	RBI	AVG		AB	H	HR	RBI	AVG
Home	235	62	17	45	.264	LHP	149	28	5	14	.188
Road	274	66	11	40	.241	RHP	360	100	23	71	.278
Day	155	44	11	30	.284	Sc Pos	125	37	6	56	.296
Night	354	84	17	55	.237	Clutch	82	18	7	21	.220

1989 Rankings (American League)

➡ 2nd lowest batting average against left-handed pitchers (.188) - *players with 125 PA against LHP*

➡ 5th in highest home run frequency (18.2 ABs per HR) and lowest grounder/flyball ratio (.81) - *players with 502 PA*

➡ 7th in home runs (28) and walks (89)

➡ Led the Tigers in home runs, at bats (509), runs (77), hits (128), doubles (21), total bases (235), RBI (85), sacrifice flies (9), walks, intentional walks (6), pitches seen (2,245), plate appearances (611), games (148), home run frequency and slugging percentage (.462) - *team players with 502 PA*

PITCHING:

Frank Williams is another in the exceedingly long line of players who came to Detroit via the National League. The Tigers have a penchant for such deals. In many cases, the results have been extremely gratifying. Williams was not a personal favorite of Pete Rose (as it now appears few players were) and the Reds rather surprisingly released him after a good season in 1988. Detroit signed Williams to bolster their right-handed, middle relief strength. Until falling victim to the curse of the lame and infirm which stalked the Tigers' roster all year, he was quite effective. Williams began the year in his expected long-relief role, but was utilized at times as a closer when early-season injuries disabled Hernandez and Henneman. More effective as a middleman -- he has only eight career saves -- Williams quickly returned to that role and was fairly effective. He sat out much of July and August and made only two more appearances after September 1st.

Not a particularly hard thrower, Williams is a sidearmer who keeps the ball low in the strike zone. With his sweeping delivery, he can be very tough on right-handed hitters. His strengths are his durability -- he's pitched in as many as 85 games in a season -- and an ability to get a lot of groundball outs. That makes him ideally suited for Tiger Stadium, where the long grass is perfect for groundball pitchers. But Williams' pitches have a tendency to drop out of the strike zone, and he needs control to be effective. In 1989 he didn't have it, allowing 46 walks in 71.2 innings. The result was a season somewhat below Williams' previous efforts, though his injuries probably had something to do with that.

FIELDING:

Williams's delivery leaves him in good defensive position to make whatever play may be necessary. He doesn't rate as panther-quick, but he gets the job done. Holding baserunners was a bit of a problem for him in 1989. In 10 steal attempts, 7 runners found safe haven.

OVERALL:

Compared to his career stats, Williams' 1989 ERA was a bit swollen; but, at times, so was his arm. Blame injury and inactivity for the rise, not that he needs excuses for the season he posted. A healthy Williams could be a key performer in a bullpen short on depth.

FRANK WILLIAMS

Position: RP
Bats: R **Throws:** R
Ht: 6' 1" **Wt:** 205

Opening Day Age: 32
Born: 2/13/58 in Seattle, WA
ML Seasons: 6

Overall Statistics

	W	L	ERA	G	GS	Sv	IP	H	R	BB	SO	HR
1989	3	3	3.64	42	0	1	71.2	70	37	46	33	5
Career	24	14	3.00	333	1	8	471.2	418	194	227	314	23

Where They Hit the Ball

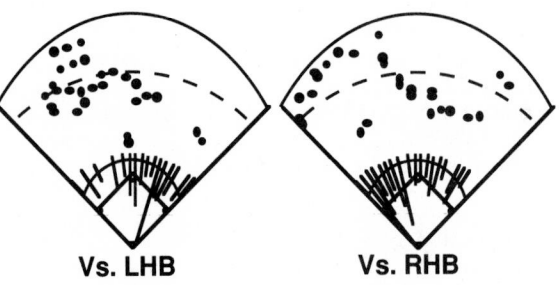

Vs. LHB   **Vs. RHB**

1989 Situational Stats

	W	L	ERA	Sv	IP		AB	H	HR	RBI	AVG
Home	1	1	4.25	0	36.0	LHB	124	32	3	20	.258
Road	2	2	3.03	1	35.2	RHB	152	38	2	18	.250
Day	2	0	4.97	0	25.1	Sc Pos	94	19	2	33	.202
Night	1	3	2.91	1	46.1	Clutch	52	15	1	9	.288

1989 Rankings (American League)

➡ Led the Tigers in holds (6)

HITTING:

Ken Williams arrived in Detroit last spring to replace the injured Gary Pettis. Williams maintained that injuries had caused his disastrous offensive showing in 1988. He vowed that people would see a new Kenny Williams in '89. "Honchos" enthusiastically allowed that, with a modicum of production, he might easily turn out to be the Tigers new full-time center fielder. Then, the season started and the fairy tale ended. Unhappily. Through April, Williams's average was bogged down near .200 and remained mired there through May. A rib cage injury, after a .125 average for early June, swamped him. Pettis returned to action as the once and future center fielder. Williams finished the year subbing for injured outfielders, when he wasn't injured himself.

A great athlete who was a wide receiver and sprinter at Stanford University, Williams is still struggling to prove himself as a major league hitter. He possesses both power and great bat speed and is capable of turning a fastball around and hitting it a long way. But he has little strike zone judgment and is an easy mark for any pitcher who works on him intelligently. Williams has backslid tremendously since 1987, when he hit .281 with 11 homers in part-time work for the White Sox. A disastrous experiment as a third baseman the next spring seemed to destroy his confidence. Despite his big talk last spring, he still may not have recovered.

BASERUNNING:

Williams possesses outstanding speed, and while no Gary Pettis, has the ability of stealing 20 to 30 bases a year. Of course, more walks and more hits would help Williams develop his base-stealing potential into a more forceful and reliable offensive weapon. He's a good, aggressive baserunner.

FIELDING:

Williams' great speed gives him a big boost afield. He gets a good jump on the ball and is good at determining quickly the point where his glove and the ball are likely to intersect. He covered center field while Pettis was out of action and spent the rest of his playing time last year primarily in left. He puts good steam into throws and his arm is reasonably accurate.

OVERALL:

Over four seasons, Williams has been unable to establish the batting skills required of a full-time starter. He's still only 26 and could fulfill his great potential, but he needs to get to work. The evidence to date suggests a career as a defensive replacement.

KEN WILLIAMS

Position: CF/LF/RF
Bats: R **Throws:** R
Ht: 6' 1" **Wt:** 187

Opening Day Age: 26
Born: 4/6/64 in Berkeley, CA
ML Seasons: 4

Overall Statistics

	G	AB	R	H	D	T	HR	RBI	SB	BB	SO	AVG
1989	94	258	29	53	5	1	6	23	9	18	63	.205
Career	298	900	97	202	27	5	26	102	37	39	221	.224

Where He Hits the Ball

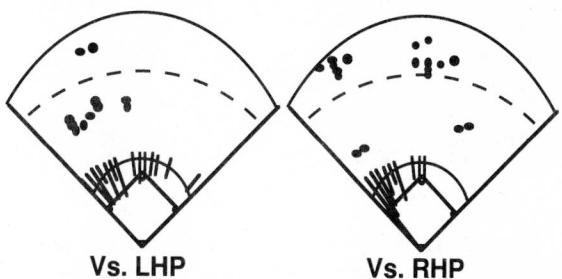

Vs. LHP   **Vs. RHP**

1989 Situational Stats

	AB	H	HR	RBI	AVG		AB	H	HR	RBI	AVG
Home	119	24	3	14	.202	LHP	129	29	3	10	.225
Road	139	29	3	9	.209	RHP	129	24	3	13	.186
Day	92	16	1	10	.174	Sc Pos	63	15	1	16	.238
Night	166	37	5	13	.223	Clutch	48	6	0	3	.125

1989 Rankings (American League)

➡ Lowest AL batting average in the clutch (.125) - *players with 50 PA in the clutch*

➡ 3rd lowest batting average on an 0-2 count - *players with 20 PA with an 0-2 count*

SCOTT LUSADER

Position: RF
Bats: L **Throws:** L
Ht: 5'10" **Wt:** 165

Opening Day Age: 25
Born: 9/30/64 in Chicago, IL
ML Seasons: 3

Overall Statistics

	G	AB	R	H	D	T	HR	RBI	SB	BB	SO	AVG
1989	40	103	15	26	4	0	1	8	3	9	21	.252
Career	79	166	26	42	7	1	3	19	4	15	32	.253

HITTING, FIELDING, BASERUNNING:

Lusader saw his most action ever in 1989, which is not surprising, since Detroit was peering under every rock in their farm system, hoping to uncover an overlooked gem. Considered one of the better prospects in a very weak organization, Lusader turned in a disappointing performance. He's a good defensive outfielder with fine speed and a strong throwing arm, so he definitely can make it as a reserve. But to play regularly, he'll have to improve his stickwork. In '89 Lusader showed little of the power that produced as many as 17 homers in the minors. He preferred to concentrate on base hits. But Lusader batted only .252 and proved easy to strike out, often chasing high pitches. His speed and defensive skills, at least, remained intact.

OVERALL:

Lusader has appeared in parts of three seasons with Detroit. At 25, he remains unproven, but he hasn't really been given much of a chance yet, and he's very young compared to most of the fading elders on this team. Perhaps not the rightfielder of Detroit's future, his potential still earns him some consideration for 1990.

ED NUNEZ

Position: RP
Bats: R **Throws:** R
Ht: 6'5" **Wt:** 240

Opening Day Age: 26
Born: 5/27/63 in Humacao, Puerto Rico
ML Seasons: 8

Overall Statistics

	W	L	ERA	G	GS	Sv	IP	H	R	BB	SO	HR
1989	3	4	4.17	27	0	1	54.0	49	33	36	41	6
Career	19	25	4.15	242	14	36	396.2	395	209	169	296	54

PITCHING & FIELDING:

Edwin Nunez was acquired in June, when injuries to Hernandez and Henneman made a shambles of the bullpen. He was Detroit's patron saint of lost causes -- eating up innings and mopping up other people's messes. From June through August he proved extremely effective at keeping his team in ball games. Usually, the wake-up call didn't arrive for his offense, but that wasn't Ed's department. From September on, however, Nunez seemed to loose steam. Like most players on Detroit's roster, he couldn't stay healthy and a sore arm led to an ever-swelling ERA as the season wound down. Primarily a power pitcher, Nunez still relies mostly on his outstanding fastball. But he often sacrifices control for speed and last year averaged a hideous six walks per nine innings pitched. No better than average defensively, he wasn't likely to aid his cause with brilliant work afield. He was effective at holding runners and discouraging larceny on the bases.

OVERALL:

September slump aside, for much of the year Nunez stood above the crowd of Tigers pitchers. After eight seasons in the majors, he's still only 26, and if healthy, could win a job once more on the shaky Tiger staff.

AL PEDRIQUE

Position: SS
Bats: R **Throws:** R
Ht: 6' 0" **Wt:** 155

Opening Day Age: 29
Born: 8/11/60 in Aragua, Venezuela
ML Seasons: 3

Overall Statistics

	G	AB	R	H	D	T	HR	RBI	SB	BB	SO	AVG
1989	31	69	1	14	3	0	0	5	0	2	15	.203
Career	174	449	32	111	18	1	1	36	5	29	61	.247

HITTING, FIELDING, BASERUNNING:

Acquired as a reserve infielder, Pedrique briefly became the Tigers' starting third baseman when Chris Brown, another off-season prize, proved to be as unmotivated in Detroit as he had been in San Diego. Weak stickwork quickly returned Pedrique to the bench. He's had some major league success with the bat, hitting .294 for the Mets and Pirates in '87, but he has no power and no strike zone judgment and will often chase pitches over his head. Good breaking stuff still gets him out pretty easily. Pedrique can play second, short and third adequately. His range is decent but he still makes too many errors to make up for his weak bat. He's an aggressive, but not especially smart, baserunner.

OVERALL:

Envisioned as the "new" Luis Salazar, who was a proven winner foolishly traded, Pedrique quickly became a proven washout. He has a chance to make a major league team as a reserve infielder, but not as a regular. And he'll have to hit a lot better.

KEVIN RITZ

Position: SP
Bats: R **Throws:** R
Ht: 6' 4" **Wt:** 195

Opening Day Age: 24
Born: 6/8/65 in Eatonstown, NJ
ML Seasons: 1

Overall Statistics

	W	L	ERA	G	GS	Sv	IP	H	R	BB	SO	HR
1989	4	6	4.38	12	12	0	74.0	75	41	44	56	2
Career	4	6	4.38	12	12	0	74.0	75	41	44	56	2

PITCHING & FIELDING:

When Kevin Ritz beat Milwaukee on August 7, he became the first Tiger pitcher of 1989 to win three consecutive games. A welcome addition to a beleaguered staff, Ritz has a fastball in the high 80's and likes to pitch inside. He also has a big curve, a change-up, and he throws an occasional slider. He mixes speeds and locations, and he can throw eight or ten flawless pitches in a row. But Ritz is prone to make mistakes, and they are often costly.

Ritz loves to pitch ahead in the count. On the other hand, he gives in too easily when he falls behind, leading to weak offerings on 2-0 and 2-1 counts. He needs to show more confidence in his breaking pitches, and not worry about location on the fastball even when he trails in the count. Kevin is a fine fielder with excellent range and poise. His ability to hold runners is already good, and he is still improving.

OVERALL:

Ritz has not yet produced a winning season with any professional team, but he seems to have all the necessary tools. Kevin just needs to avoid mistakes and show the increased confidence that comes with experience.

MIKE SCHWABE

Position: RP/SP
Bats: R **Throws:** R
Ht: 6' 4" **Wt:** 200

Opening Day Age: 25
Born: 7/12/64 in
Fort Dodge, IA
ML Seasons: 1

Overall Statistics

	W	L	ERA	G	GS	Sv	IP	H	R	BB	SO	HR
1989	2	4	6.04	13	4	0	44.2	58	33	16	13	6
Career	2	4	6.04	13	4	0	44.2	58	33	16	13	6

PITCHING & FIELDING:

Mike Schwabe's brief stay in the majors was rather unsuccessful. Pitching in 13 games after his call up from Double A London (Ontario), Schwabe struggled with his control.

Schwabe is a finesse pitcher who relies on his curve, change-up and split finger pitch to get hitters out. His most effective pitch is a sharp breaking curve that is tough on right-handers. Schwabe was not a mystery for lefties who lit him up for a .362 average.

One aspect of Schwabe's game that is positive is his fielding. He moves extremely well to his left and right on bunt plays. His follow-through leaves him in good position to field anything up the middle. Schwabe's move to first is adequate at best. He needs to shorten his stride home in order to give his catchers a chance to throw out base-stealers.

OVERALL:

Schwabe is still young, so there is plenty of time for him to overcome his control problems. He has the tools to become a very successful pitcher. Schwabe may or may not pitch in Detroit next year. The Tigers' might decide to let him pitch in Toledo (Triple A) for one season. Regardless, Schwabe should be a regular on the staff by 1991.

PITCHING:

When Floyd Bannister was lost to a season ending injury, Luis Aquino got his chance to become a regular starter for the Royals. In the past, Aquino served as a long relief specialist, getting an occasional start. He did well as a starter at first, but later got hit hard and was replaced in the rotation by Tom Gordon. Aquino lost four of twelve decisions with a 4.26 ERA as a starter.

Serving as both long reliever and stopper in the minors, Aquino was the Carolina League's top reliever in 1984 when he recorded 20 saves. Aquino hasn't fully adjusted to the starting role; he rarely lasts more than six innings. Aquino is best suited to a long relief job until he can develop better command of his breaking pitches.

Aquino relies mainly on his fastball, but also throws curves and sliders, using them as set up pitches. He doesn't have good command of all his pitches and will usually resort to the fastball when behind in the count. Aquino gets into trouble the second or third time through a batting order; hitters know what to expect and can better time his fastball. He has more success when he uses fewer pitches in the early innings.

A power pitcher in the minors, Aquino averaged 6.4 strikeouts per nine innings in parts of three years at Triple A. In the majors he has collected only 4.2 strikeouts per nine innings. As his strikeout totals have diminished, Aquino's control has gotten better. He allowed nearly four walks per nine innings at Triple A; in 1989 he gave up just 2.2 per nine innings.

FIELDING:

Aquino has a good pickoff move, but is deliberate in his delivery. Baserunners have limited success when running against Aquino; six of 10 base stealers were caught. He is an average fielder. He's relatively fast in getting to the ball but doesn't always use the best judgement when throwing to the bases. Aquino does a good job of fielding bunts and his throws are accurate.

OVERALL:

1990 will mean a return to the bullpen for Aquino; he may even begin the season in Omaha. The Royals figure to have five or six healthy starters ready in spring training, so if Aquino makes the team, he will pitch in long relief. But, when the injuries strike, Aquino may once again be thrust into a starting role.

LUIS AQUINO

Position: RP/SP
Bats: R **Throws:** R
Ht: 6' 1" **Wt:** 175

Opening Day Age: 24
Born: 5/19/65 in Rio Piedras, Puerto Rico
ML Seasons: 3

Overall Statistics

	W	L	ERA	G	GS	Sv	IP	H	R	BB	SO	HR
1989	6	8	3.50	34	16	0	141.1	148	62	35	68	6
Career	8	9	3.57	48	21	0	181.2	195	85	55	84	9

Where They Hit the Ball

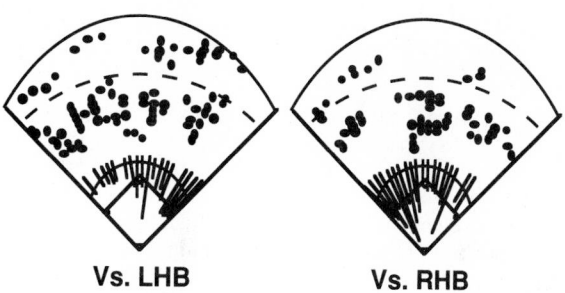

Vs. LHB	Vs. RHB

1989 Situational Stats

	W	L	ERA	Sv	IP		AB	H	HR	RBI	AVG
Home	4	3	3.03	0	65.1	LHB	252	73	3	27	.290
Road	2	5	3.91	0	76.0	RHB	294	75	3	32	.255
Day	3	0	1.16	0	31.0	Sc Pos	133	37	2	51	.278
Night	3	8	4.16	0	110.1	Clutch	40	11	0	3	.275

1989 Rankings (American League)

➡ Did not rank near the top or bottom in any category

PITCHING:

A rotator cuff tear ended Floyd Bannister's season in mid-June, leaving the Royals pitching staff short on starters. His absence opened the way for Luis Aquino and, later, rookie Tom Gordon to step into starting roles. Bannister was missed the most late in the year when the Royals opted to use a four man rotation, but had trouble finding an effective fourth starter.

Bannister has been among the league leaders in strike-outs in past seasons; he led the league with 209 Ks for the Mariners in 1982. Despite having good control of a hard fastball, Bannister has never been able to win consistently. He has little else to go with the fastball except a straight change and has trouble throwing breaking pitches for strikes. He has had just three winning seasons since beginning his career with Houston in 1977 (not including injury-shortened 1989). Bannister's 1989 ERA was his highest since 1985, but his career ERA is 4.03 and last year marked the eighth time in his career his ERA has been over 4.00.

Constant reliance upon the fastball has diminished Bannister's stamina. Once able to throw more than 200 innings per year, he has only reached that plateau once since 1985. Whereas he used to regularly pitch into the eighth or ninth inning, Bannister is now lifted before completing the seventh inning. He has averaged under six innings per start in 1988 and 1989. Likewise, his strikeouts per game have reduced from over seven per nine innings prior to 1986 to under five per nine innings during the last four years. After eleven complete games in 1986, Bannister has completed just two of his last 45 starts.

FIELDING:

Lefthandedness, a quick delivery, and a good fastball all contribute to Bannister's success at holding baserunners close, even though he does not possess a great pickoff move. Bannister is an average fielder who makes the easy plays and doesn't hurt himself with mistakes. He is content to take the easy out at first base on sacrifice bunts. Bannister fields better on artificial turf.

OVERALL:

The Royals need Bannister to be their fourth starter in 1990. His surgery was deemed successful and he will be ready to pitch in spring training. However, some questions remain about his durability and his ability to continue throwing a 90-plus MPH fastball. If Bannister loses too much off his fastball, he will have difficulty with big league hitters.

FLOYD BANNISTER

Position: SP
Bats: L **Throws:** L
Ht: 6' 1" **Wt:** 190

Opening Day Age: 34
Born: 6/10/55 in Pierre, SD
ML Seasons: 13

Overall Statistics

	W	L	ERA	G	GS	Sv	IP	H	R	BB	SO	HR
1989	4	1	4.66	14	14	0	75.1	87	40	18	35	8
Career	133	142	4.03	379	363	0	2325.2	2256	1150	815	1677	283

Where They Hit the Ball

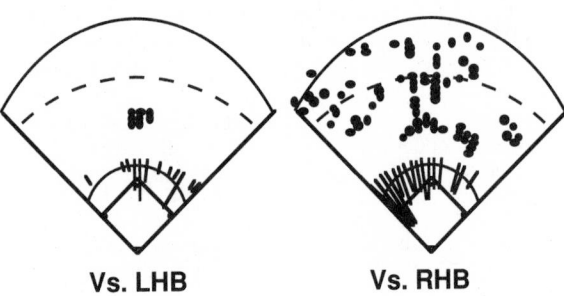

Vs. LHB   **Vs. RHB**

1989 Situational Stats

	W	L	ERA	Sv	IP		AB	H	HR	RBI	AVG
Home	2	1	4.60	0	45.0	LHB	48	17	1	7	.354
Road	2	0	4.75	0	30.1	RHB	252	70	7	24	.278
Day	1	0	6.23	0	13.0	Sc Pos	63	18	1	21	.286
Night	3	1	4.33	0	62.1	Clutch	16	6	0	2	.375

1989 Rankings (American League)

➡ Did not rank near the top or bottom in any category

CLUTCH HITTER

BOB BOONE

Position: C
Bats: R **Throws:** R
Ht: 6' 2" **Wt:** 207

Opening Day Age: 42
Born: 11/19/47 in San Diego, CA
ML Seasons: 18

HITTING:

At the age of 41, Bob Boone again had a productive offensive year. He hit .274 with 43 RBI while hitting in the eighth spot in the order for much of the season. Early in the year, he drove in several key runs with bloop singles to the opposite field.

Boone stands deep in the batter's box and uses a wide-open stance as he tries to slap the ball into the outfield. He fights off the fastballs, waiting for a high breaking ball that he can drive into a gap. With two strikes on him, Boone throws his bat at the ball in order to stay alive at the plate (he had a few run-scoring singles in that manner, including a two-run bloop hit to beat the Orioles early in the year). This tendency makes Boone one of the most difficult Royals players to strike out and a good hit-and-run candidate.

Lacking any real power (.323 slugging, one homer), Boone can be overmatched by fastballs on the outside part of the plate. The Royals sometimes try to avoid the double play by having Boone bunt, a task at which he is particularly adept. Boone's slashing batting style is particularly effective in spacious Royals Stadium, where he batted .317.

BASERUNNING:

Boone is arguably the slowest baserunner in the majors. On several occasions, he grounded softly into a double play where the pivot man had time to leap over the sliding runner, right himself, then make the throw to first in time. Boone rarely makes a baserunning mistake by trying to take the extra base, but it is difficult to score him from second base with a single.

FIELDING:

The recipient of six Gold Gloves, Boone is the premier fielding catcher in the league. He helped keep opposition baserunners under control while calling a superb game from behind the plate. Boone is the all-time leader in career games caught. His experience behind the plate has helped make the Royals pitching staff one of the best in baseball.

OVERALL:

Boone's value to the Royals is in his defensive ability. He is the on-field manager who tries to keep the young Royals pitchers under control. The Royals hope Boone can mold Mike Macfarlane into a successful big league catcher. Boone's role in 1990 will probably be reduced from previous years; as his offensive ability deteriorates, he will gradually be replaced by Macfarlane.

Overall Statistics

	G	AB	R	H	D	T	HR	RBI	SB	BB	SO	AVG
1989	131	405	33	111	13	2	1	43	3	49	37	.274
Career	2224	7128	668	1810	300	26	105	817	37	646	596	.254

Where He Hits the Ball

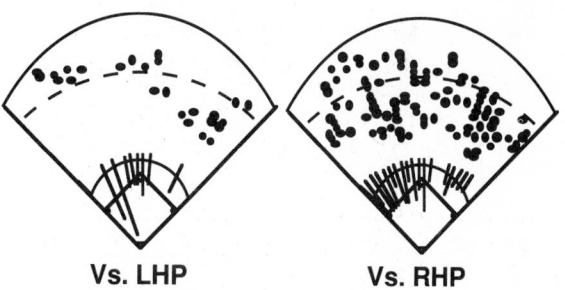

Vs. LHP   **Vs. RHP**

1989 Situational Stats

	AB	H	HR	RBI	AVG		AB	H	HR	RBI	AVG
Home	199	63	1	24	.317	LHP	97	28	0	9	.289
Road	206	48	0	19	.233	RHP	308	83	1	34	.269
Day	80	22	1	15	.275	Sc Pos	100	35	1	41	.350
Night	325	89	0	28	.274	Clutch	66	25	0	8	.379

1989 Rankings (American League)

- ➡ 1st in throwing out opposing base stealers (42.3%) - *catchers with 75 attempts*
- ➡ 3rd in hitting in the clutch (.379) - *players with 50 PA in the clutch*
- ➡ 5th in hitting with runners in scoring position (.350) - *players with 100 PA with runners in scoring position*
- ➡ Led the Royals in hitting with runners in scoring position, hitting with the bases loaded (.444) and sacrifice bunts (8)
- ➡ Led AL Catchers in sacrifice bunts, games (131), and hitting in the clutch

HALL OF FAMER

GEORGE BRETT

HITTING:

Despite more than a month on the DL due to a knee injury and a very slow start, George Brett had another successful summer with the bat. With 80 RBI, 67 runs scored, and a .282 average, he was one of the Royals' leading hitters. As usual, Brett helped carry the Royals during the pennant race.

Brett is well known as a Charlie Lau disciple and as an extremely patient hitter. He swings only at strikes and has remarkable judgement. Brett was one of three Royals to walk more often than strike out; his .362 on-base average was third on the team. In recent years, Brett's hitting style has started to change. Once a high average spray hitter, Brett has begun to pull the ball more and hit for power. Likewise, he is now a more aggressive hitter, especially late in the game; Brett usually swings at the first offering from relief pitchers.

Brett is the man the Royals want to see at the plate with the game on the line. He thrives on game breaking situations and has always performed well in the heat of the pennant chase. Brett is a lifetime .337 hitter (with 10 home runs) in post-season play.

BASERUNNING:

Brett has a good deal of baserunning savvy and displays occasional base stealing ability. In fact, his stolen base totals have been rising since 1983 and 1984 when he had no steals. Brett almost never makes a baserunning blunder and does a good job of taking an extra base on outfield hits.

FIELDING:

After making the transition from third base in 1987, Brett has gradually grown into the first base role. He still shows a third baseman's range and has developed an ability to scoop low throws from other infielders. Brett won his only Gold Glove in 1985. Brett's throwing arm has always been accurate, but it is not his strong point. While playing first base, his arm is less important and he can concentrate more upon his hitting. Brett committed just two errors in 1989.

OVERALL:

Destined for the Hall of Fame, Brett is nearing the twilight of his remarkable career. He still has several productive years left and has a reasonable chance to get 3000 career hits. His value as a leader is obvious in his positive affect on the young Royal hitters. Brett will probably play 1990 at first base before eventually becoming a regular designated hitter.

Position: 1B/DH
Bats: L **Throws:** R
Ht: 6' 0" **Wt:** 200

Opening Day Age: 36
Born: 5/15/53 in Glen Dale, WV
ML Seasons: 17

Overall Statistics

	G	AB	R	H	D	T	HR	RBI	SB	BB	SO	AVG
1989	124	457	67	129	26	3	12	80	14	59	47	.282
Career	2137	8148	1300	2528	514	120	267	1311	175	908	634	.310

Where He Hits the Ball

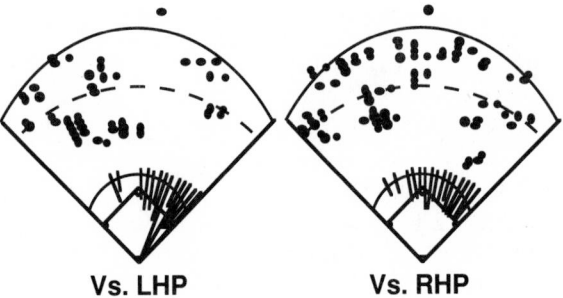

Vs. LHP   **Vs. RHP**

1989 Situational Stats

	AB	H	HR	RBI	AVG		AB	H	HR	RBI	AVG
Home	229	63	3	37	.275	LHP	167	37	2	24	.222
Road	228	66	9	43	.289	RHP	290	92	10	56	.317
Day	101	26	2	20	.257	Sc Pos	133	39	2	63	.293
Night	356	103	10	60	.289	Clutch	65	21	1	13	.323

1989 Rankings (American League)

→ 6th in intentional walks (14)

→ 9th in sacrifice flies (9)

→ Led the Royals in sacrifice flies, intentional walks, and GDPs (18)

→ Led AL First Basemen in stolen bases (14) and batting average vs. righthanded pitchers (.317)

HITTING:

Forty-year-old Bill Buckner is near the end of a long and successful career. The two-time batting champion had the lowest batting average (.216) and fewest at bats (176) of his career in 1989. Buckner was unsuccessful in his primary role as a left-handed pinch hitter; he hit .200 coming off the bench and drove in just five runs as a pinch hitter. It now appears Buckner will not reach the 3000 hit mark.

Though he has never drawn many walks, Buckner does not swing at many bad pitches and usually watches until he has seen at least one strike. He is a hard batter to fan and struck out just eleven times in 1989. Buckner will use the whole field, but tries to pull inside pitches into the corner for extra bases.

Buckner is a singles hitter with occasional power. He was once capable of 15 to 18 homers each year, but has not had more than five in any year since 1986, when he peaked at eighteen homers and also drove in 102 runs. Buckner has usually been a good clutch hitter in the past and is often called on as a pinch hitter late in close games.

BASERUNNING:

With his legendary bad ankles, Buckner is a poor baserunner. He was once replaced at second base with pinch runner Jamie Quirk, a 36-year-old catcher. Yet Buckner was successful in his only steal attempt of 1989 and has managed at least one stolen base in all 19 of his full big league seasons.

FIELDING:

Buckner has never been a good glove man. He played sparingly at first base when George Brett was injured in 1989, but still managed three errors, one more than Brett made playing in 100 more games. He is very slow at this point in his career and has a weak throwing arm. Buckner does not scoop low throws well and makes pitchers work hard when they cover first base. As a fielder, Buckner makes a good designated hitter.

OVERALL:

After many successful summers as a major league hitter, Buckner will likely hang up his spikes after a short stint in 1990. He wants to play next year so he can have participated in the majors in four different decades (1960's through 1990's). Buckner is currently unsigned and may opt for a final fling at free agency.

BILL BUCKNER

Position: 1B/DH
Bats: L **Throws:** L
Ht: 6' 1" **Wt:** 195

Opening Day Age: 40
Born: 12/14/49 in Vallejo, CA
ML Seasons: 21

Overall Statistics

	G	AB	R	H	D	T	HR	RBI	SB	BB	SO	AVG
1989	79	176	7	38	4	1	1	16	1	6	11	.216
Career	2495	9354	1073	2707	498	49	173	1205	183	447	451	.289

Where He Hits the Ball

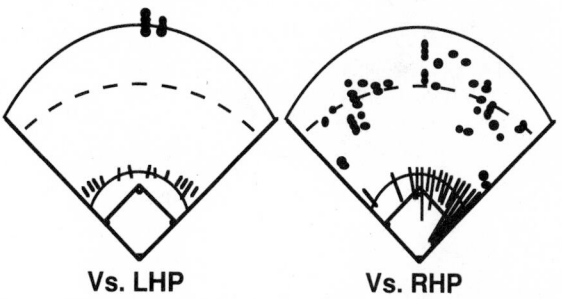

Vs. LHP   **Vs. RHP**

1989 Situational Stats

	AB	H	HR	RBI	AVG		AB	H	HR	RBI	AVG
Home	84	16	0	7	.190	LHP	23	8	0	4	.348
Road	92	22	1	9	.239	RHP	153	30	1	12	.196
Day	61	14	0	5	.230	Sc Pos	42	9	0	13	.214
Night	115	24	1	11	.209	Clutch	38	10	0	5	.263

1989 Rankings (American League)

➡ Led the Royals in lowest percentage of swings that missed (9.5%) - *all team players*

PITCHING:

Steve Crawford was resurrected with the Royals in 1989 after parts of seven seasons with the Red Sox. His 2.83 ERA and three victories provided a late-season boost to the sagging Royals relief corps. Crawford was at his best in late August and September when the Royals were in a pennant chase.

Relying primarily on a fastball and a straight change, Crawford usually throws the breaking ball only as a set-up pitch; his "out pitch" is the fastball. Crawford allows a lot of fly balls, especially on fastballs, and spacious Royals Stadium helps keeps them in play. Crawford has good control with the fastball, but has difficulty throwing breaking balls for strikes. He allowed over three walks per nine innings in 1989 and nearly four per nine innings with Boston in 1987. His career strikeout to walk ratio is just 1.6 to 1. Crawford works slowly and he becomes even more deliberate when he doesn't have his best stuff.

Although he usually only throws for an inning or two at a time, Crawford occasionally went four or more innings in relief of a failed or injured starter. He began his career as a starter, but was converted to a relief role while with Boston; he earned 12 of his career 17 saves for the Red Sox in 1985. The Royals used Crawford in pressure situations mainly during long, extra-inning games.

FIELDING:

Baserunners have had limited success against Crawford. He doesn't possess a good move to first and is slow in his delivery to the plate. However, he throws to first frequently to cut down on the runner's lead and his reliance on fastballs gives the catcher a chance to throw out potential base stealers. Crawford makes the difficult plays but has trouble with routine plays. In particular, he may make a poor throw to first if he has time to wait. But, if he has to hurry, the throw is usually good. Crawford is slow to cover bunts and sometimes throws erratically to the bases.

OVERALL:

The Royals needed a reliable long reliever in 1989, and Crawford filled that role; his success should give him an opportunity for a similar position in 1990. However, the Royals have several youngsters in the minors who are ready for the majors, so Crawford may find himself pressed next season.

STEVE CRAWFORD

Position: RP
Bats: R **Throws:** R
Ht: 6' 5" **Wt:** 225

Opening Day Age: 31
Born: 4/29/58 in Pryor, OK
ML Seasons: 8

Overall Statistics

	W	L	ERA	G	GS	Sv	IP	H	R	BB	SO	HR
1989	3	1	2.83	25	0	0	54.0	48	19	19	33	2
Career	22	17	3.98	198	16	17	436.0	504	229	145	228	44

Where They Hit the Ball

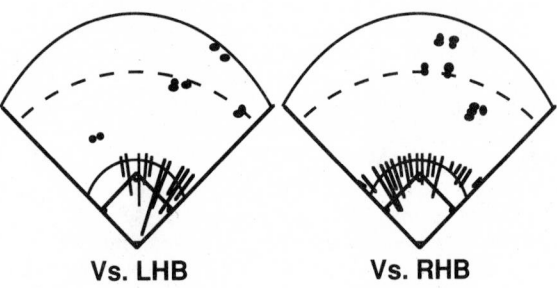

Vs. LHB   **Vs. RHB**

1989 Situational Stats

	W	L	ERA	Sv	IP		AB	H	HR	RBI	AVG
Home	1	0	4.07	0	24.1	LHB	104	27	2	14	.260
Road	2	1	1.82	0	29.2	RHB	94	21	0	11	.223
Day	1	0	2.53	0	10.2	Sc Pos	68	17	1	24	.250
Night	2	1	2.91	0	43.1	Clutch	48	7	0	1	.146

1989 Rankings (American League)

➡ Did not rank near the top or bottom in any category

HITTING:

Jim Eisenreich began the season as the Royals' fourth outfielder and occasional designated hitter. But injuries to regulars gave Eisenreich a starting role and he responded phenomenally, leading the team in batting average, doubles, triples and steals, while placing high in many other offensive categories. Eisenreich's surprising emergence as a star is a big reason the Royals were contenders in 1989.

Eisenreich tries to hit the ball up the middle. His line drives are conducive to Royals Stadium's artificial turf and wide open spaces. Primarily a first pitch, fastball hitter, Eisenreich is very aggressive and rarely walks. He doesn't strike out much either, suffering only 44 Ks in 516 plate appearances. Eisenreich gets into trouble by looking only for fastballs; he can be fooled by change-ups and has difficulty with low, inside curves.

The 1989 Royals were a great comeback team, especially at home, and Eisenreich always played a large role. He frequently started the late-inning, game-winning rallies, or drove in the winner. He hit one of the Royals' two pinch-hit homers in 1989, providing another come-from-behind victory. Eisenreich batted .319 with runners in scoring position.

BASERUNNING:

Eisenreich led the Royals with 27 stolen bases and had a fine 77% success rate. He is a smart baserunner who rarely over extends himself. Eisenreich is an excellent front end to a hit-and-run play.

FIELDING:

Eisenreich has good speed and uses it well in the outfield where he filled in admirably at all three outfield positions. He had the best fielding average among the Royals outfielders and he usually gets a good jump on fly balls. Eisenreich has just an average arm, but throws accurately and always hits the cut-off man. He appears to be more at home in rightfield, but is more than adequate in center or in left. With Eisenreich's good speed he is exactly the kind of player the Royals need to patrol the large Royals Stadium outfield.

OVERALL:

It is hard to say what the future holds for Eisenreich. He is just coming into his own, but will be 31 years old in 1990. His value as a left-handed hitter is enormous for the Royals and he's a fine outfielder. Eisenreich figures to continue his substitute outfield role in 1990, but the team needs to get him in the lineup every day.

JIM EISENREICH

Position: CF/LF/RF
Bats: L **Throws:** L
Ht: 5'11" **Wt:** 195

Opening Day Age: 30
Born: 4/18/59 in St. Cloud, MN
ML Seasons: 6

Overall Statistics

	G	AB	R	H	D	T	HR	RBI	SB	BB	SO	AVG
1989	134	475	64	139	33	7	9	59	27	37	44	.293
Career	308	920	112	247	57	10	16	111	39	64	106	.268

Where He Hits the Ball

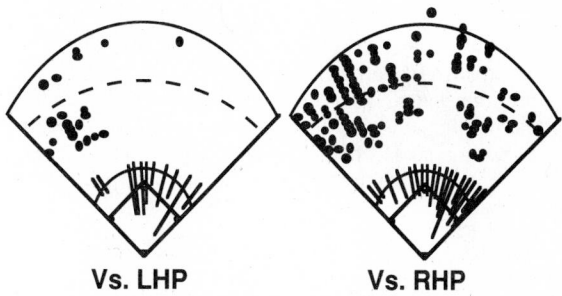

Vs. LHP   **Vs. RHP**

1989 Situational Stats

	AB	H	HR	RBI	AVG		AB	H	HR	RBI	AVG
Home	228	70	4	29	.307	LHP	107	36	2	17	.336
Road	247	69	5	30	.279	RHP	368	103	7	42	.280
Day	129	44	1	19	.341	Sc Pos	116	37	3	50	.319
Night	346	95	8	40	.275	Clutch	66	19	1	7	.288

1989 Rankings (American League)

➡ 4th in steals of third (7) and least pitches seen per plate appearance (3.0) - *players with 502 PA*

➡ 5th in batting average with 2 strikes (.286) - *players with 162 PA with 2 strikes*

➡ 9th in stolen bases (27)

➡ Led the Royals in batting average (.293), doubles (33), triples (7), stolen bases, steals of third, and batting average with 2 strikes

➡ Led AL Center Fielders in intentional walks (9) and batting average with 2 strikes

PITCHING:

Steve Farr began the year as the Royals' closer. He was somewhat effective in the role, collecting 18 saves in 22 opportunities before a knee injury and surgery in August nearly finished his season. When Farr returned in late-September, he was mainly used as the set-up man for Jeff Montgomery and also got two starting assignments to spare the injury-riddled starting staff.

A 90-mph fastball is Farr's primary pitch. He also throws a slider and a curve, but rarely for strikes. Farr's fastball tends to ride up and in to right handed batters. He has become more of a power pitcher since taking on relief duties. Since moving permanently to the bullpen in 1986, Farr has struck out 7.8 batters per nine innings pitched. As a closer, he has struck out over eight per nine innings pitched.

Farr was successful as a minor league starter, twice leading the league in ERA and posting fine win-loss records. However, in the majors he has rarely lasted into the seventh inning. Farr succeeds best when he can throw hard for an inning or two of relief, instead of pacing himself for six or seven innings as a starter. Also, as a reliever, Farr can use his best pitch, the fastball, more often.

Although he did a competent job as a closer, Farr lacks the stopper's mentality to bear down and blow away the hitters with a hard fastball. He allowed his failures to multiply by not using his fastball in the most crucial situations. Farr prefers the role of set-up man to that of closer or starter.

FIELDING:

Baserunners can steal against Farr; he lacks an impressive move to first base and he doesn't have a quick delivery. He is a fine fielder and also has displayed good judgement about which base to throw to on sacrifice bunts and grounders. He is quick to field the ball and throws accurately to all bases. Farr rarely hurts himself with the glove.

OVERALL:

Farr will be the set-up man in the Royals bullpen in 1990. Should the closer heir-apparent, Montgomery, falter or become injured, the Royals can rely on Farr as a proven closer. He may also see some duty as a spot starter if injuries and ineffectiveness continue to damage the Royals' starting staff.

STEVE FARR

Position: RP
Bats: R **Throws:** R
Ht: 5'11" **Wt:** 200

Opening Day Age: 33
Born: 12/12/56 in Cheverly, MD
ML Seasons: 6

Overall Statistics

	W	L	ERA	G	GS	Sv	IP	H	R	BB	SO	HR
1989	2	5	4.12	51	2	18	63.1	75	35	22	56	5
Career	24	28	3.67	263	22	49	500.0	476	222	201	418	45

Where They Hit the Ball

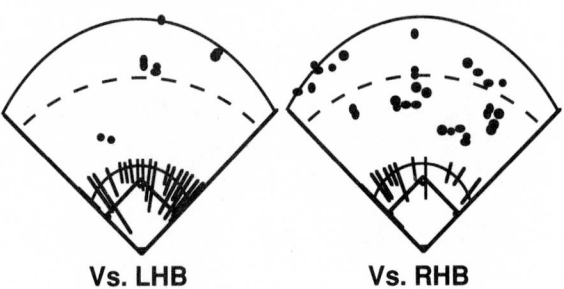

Vs. LHB   **Vs. RHB**

1989 Situational Stats

	W	L	ERA	Sv	IP		AB	H	HR	RBI	AVG
Home	2	1	3.00	14	36.0	LHB	125	35	0	12	.280
Road	0	4	5.60	4	27.1	RHB	128	40	5	22	.313
Day	2	1	4.24	2	17.0	Sc Pos	69	18	2	29	.261
Night	0	4	4.08	16	46.1	Clutch	107	31	4	16	.290

1989 Rankings (American League)

- 8th in save percentage (81.8%) - *pitchers with 20 save opportunities*
- Led the Royals in saves (18), games finished (40) and save percentage

CY YOUNG STUFF

TOM GORDON

Position: RP/SP
Bats: R **Throws:** R
Ht: 5' 9" **Wt:** 160

Opening Day Age: 22
Born: 11/18/67 in Sebring, FL
ML Seasons: 2

PITCHING:

Rookie of the Year candidate Tom "Flash" Gordon burst onto the major league scene with 17 victories and a 3.64 earned run average. Gordon began the year in the bullpen, where he collected his first 10 wins and one save, and then moved into the starting rotation in July when Luis Aquino became ineffective. He went on to post victories in six of his first eight starts before running into control trouble in September. Gordon lost five of his last six decisions.

Gordon's primary weapon is a sharp-breaking curve that he will throw on any count. He also has a fastball that runs away from right-handers and a slider; both are used as set-up pitches for the nasty, knee-buckling curve. In 163 innings pitched, Gordon struck out 153, one of the highest strikeout rates in the majors. He was one of only two American League pitchers to record a save and also throw a shutout last year. Batters hit just .210 versus Gordon in 1989, the second lowest average in the American League.

To be successful, Gordon needs good control. When first placed into the rotation, he had pin-point control and confidence to throw the curve, frequently for strikes, even when behind in the count. Later, when his control began to elude him, Gordon lost confidence in his ability to throw the curve for strikes, instead relying on a less effective fastball. He allowed 4.7 walks per nine innings in 1989 after experiencing control problems in the minors.

FIELDING:

At this point in his career, Gordon is easy to run against. He doesn't hold runners well and his reliance on curveballs gives basestealers an edge. Gordon will need to develop a better move to first base to hold future runners. Gordon is still unsure of himself with the glove. He is sometimes hesitant after fielding grounders. Early in the year, he occasionally failed to cover first base on grounders to the right side, costing the Royals some outs. These mental mistakes have lessened as Gordon has gained experience.

OVERALL:

Gordon is one of the best young pitchers in the game, and figures to play a prominent role in the Royals plans for 1990 and beyond, whether pitching out of the bullpen or as a member of the starting rotation. The future is bright for Gordon; he is likely to get even better with experience.

Overall Statistics

	W	L	ERA	G	GS	Sv	IP	H	R	BB	SO	HR
1989	17	9	3.64	49	16	1	163.0	122	67	86	153	10
Career	17	11	3.78	54	18	1	178.2	138	76	93	171	11

Where They Hit the Ball

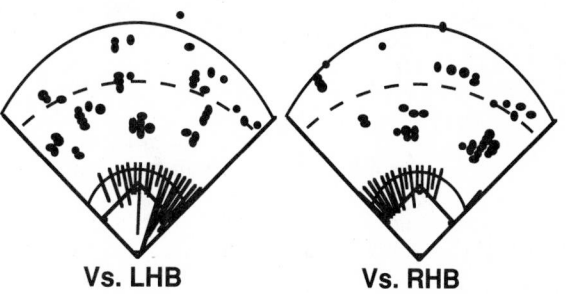

Vs. LHB   **Vs. RHB**

1989 Situational Stats

	W	L	ERA	Sv	IP		AB	H	HR	RBI	AVG
Home	11	5	3.38	0	98.2	LHB	305	67	4	38	.220
Road	6	4	4.06	1	64.1	RHB	277	55	6	36	.199
Day	3	3	5.24	0	34.1	Sc Pos	147	42	3	64	.286
Night	14	6	3.22	1	128.2	Clutch	179	33	3	23	.184

1989 Rankings (American League)

➡ 2nd in lowest opponent batting average (.210), lowest opponent slugging average (.306), highest strikeouts per 9 innings (8.4) - *pitchers with 162 IP*

➡ 3rd in highest percentage of inherited runners scoring (48.5%) - *pitchers with 30 runners inherited*

➡ 5th in GDPs per 9 innings (1.1)

➡ 6th in wins (17) and wild pitches (12)

➡ Led the Royals in lowest opponent batting average, lowest opponent slugging average, highest strikeouts per 9 innings, GDPs per 9 innings, wild pitches, GDPs induced (20) and blown saves - *team pitchers with 162 IP*

PITCHING:

After emerging as one of baseball's top pitchers in 1988, Mark Gubicza continued his pre-eminence in 1989. He placed among the league leaders in several categories, including innings pitched, ERA, strikeouts and games started. Gubicza has won 35 games over the last two years, ranking behind only Dave Stewart and teammate Bret Saberhagen in the American League.

Gubicza has always possessed the raw talent to succeed at the major league level. While his best pitch is still an overpowering fastball, his hard slider has kept the hitters honest. Breaking ball control has also contributed to Gubicza's success. He has reduced his walks allowed from over four per game prior to 1988 to 2.5 per game in 1988 and 1989. Six shutouts and 16 complete games in the last two years attest to Gubicza's stamina. He averaged over seven innings pitched per start since 1987 and pitched at least seven innings in 28 of his 35 starts in 1989.

Gubicza was a workhorse for the Royals in 1989 and performed well in several important games late last season, carrying an ERA of 1.76 from mid-August through September 18th. Also, he threw seven shutout innings just hours after signing a multi-million dollar deal for 1990 through 1992. If he has a weakness, it's that trying too hard for the strikeout can get him into trouble. He tends to overthrow the ball and get behind in the count. Also, he has been known to get upset at poor defensive play behind him or at himself if he walks a batter. Gubicza led the Royals' staff with 14 unearned runs allowed.

FIELDING:

Gubicza doesn't have a great pickoff move and his height makes it difficult for him to have a quick release. He tries to compensate with frequent throws to first to cut down on the runner's lead. Gubicza occasionally makes critical fielding mistakes when under pressure. He tries for the more difficult play instead of taking the easy out at first on sacrifice bunts. Gubicza's height helps him snare high bouncers over the mound that might otherwise get through the infield.

OVERALL:

Gubicza was eligible for free agency in 1990, but re-signed with the Royals late in 1989. His three year, $7.4 million deal places him among the highest paid in major league baseball. At age 27, Gubicza is one of the top starting pitchers in the game and a key to the Royals success in the 1990s.

MARK GUBICZA

Position: SP
Bats: R **Throws:** R
Ht: 6' 5" **Wt:** 210

Opening Day Age: 27
Born: 8/14/62 in Philadelphia, PA
ML Seasons: 6

Overall Statistics

	W	L	ERA	G	GS	Sv	IP	H	R	BB	SO	HR
1989	15	11	3.04	36	36	0	255.0	252	100	63	173	10
Career	84	67	3.51	199	187	0	1313.1	1207	563	502	850	74

Where They Hit the Ball

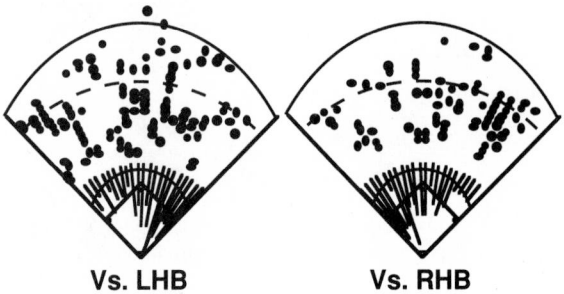

Vs. LHB   **Vs. RHB**

1989 Situational Stats

	W	L	ERA	Sv	IP		AB	H	HR	RBI	AVG
Home	8	6	3.17	0	142.0	LHB	510	126	4	36	.247
Road	7	5	2.87	0	113.0	RHB	463	126	6	47	.272
Day	4	3	3.15	0	65.2	Sc Pos	229	51	2	69	.223
Night	11	8	2.99	0	189.1	Clutch	125	30	0	5	.240

1989 Rankings (American League)

- ➡ 1st in least HRs per 9 innings (.35) and games started (36)
- ➡ 2nd in hits allowed (252) and batters faced (1,060)
- ➡ 3rd in innings (255)
- ➡ 4th in strikeouts (173) and complete games (8)
- ➡ 5th in lowest batting average with runners in scoring position (.223)
- ➡ Led the Royals in games started, hits allowed, batters faced, lowest batting average with runners in scoring position, least HRs per 9 innings, losses (11), GDPs induced (20) and grounder/flyball ratio (2.48)

FUTURE MVP?

BO JACKSON

Position: LF/DH
Bats: R **Throws:** R
Ht: 6' 1" **Wt:** 222

Opening Day Age: 27
Born: 11/30/62 in Bessemer, AL
ML Seasons: 4

HITTING:

Does Bo know baseball? Absolutely! At one point he had a lot to learn about the game, and still does. But his 1989 performance, and dramatic All-Star game home run have shut up all his detractors.

The sight of Bo Jackson swinging a bat is truly a thrill. Whether he hits a monstrous home run or strikes out, every Jackson at bat is an event. Last year was Jackson's most productive yet. He set career highs in virtually every department and had one of the Royals' all-time best seasons with the bat. Jackson led Kansas City in home runs, RBIs, and slugging average.

Jackson usually looks for the fastball, but doesn't always hit it. He is especially prone to "climbing the ladder" – swinging at progressively higher fastballs until he strikes out. Jackson will also chase a curve in the dirt. But don't throw him fastballs out and over the plate; he thrives on outer-half fastballs. Many of Jackson's 32 homers were hit to rightfield off such mistakes.

By striking out 172 times, Jackson led the American League and set an all-time Royals single season mark for futility. Jackson's first pitch aggression often left him deep in a hole and an easy target for low curves, or high unhittable fastballs.

BASERUNNING:

Jackson provides an excellent blend of power and raw speed. He has stolen 53 bases in the last two years despite missing 65 games over that span. His lifetime 78% success rate is good; he is certain to run even more in the future.

FIELDING:

Perhaps Jackson's most unpredictable feature is his fielding. He will make an incredible running or diving catch, only to misplay routine flies in the same game. He has difficulty with soft line drives, usually starting back before correcting himself. His great speed allows him to make up for mistakes and he should become better as his judgement improves. Jackson has one of the greatest throwing arms in the game. A throw in Seattle that nailed Harold Reynolds at the plate, saving a ninth-inning, game-winning run, still has people amazed; Jackson's homer won the game. He is rapidly winning respect around the league for his throwing ability.

OVERALL:

Injuries -- and maybe football -- are the only things standing between Jackson and diamond greatness. He has the ability to learn and improve in his weakest areas. Jackson will eventually cut down his strikeouts and reduce his errors in the field. If he stays healthy all year, he may have MVP numbers. Bo can do it all.

Overall Statistics

	G	AB	R	H	D	T	HR	RBI	SB	BB	SO	AVG
1989	135	515	86	132	15	6	32	105	26	39	172	.256
Career	409	1432	204	350	50	13	81	235	66	101	510	.244

Where He Hits the Ball

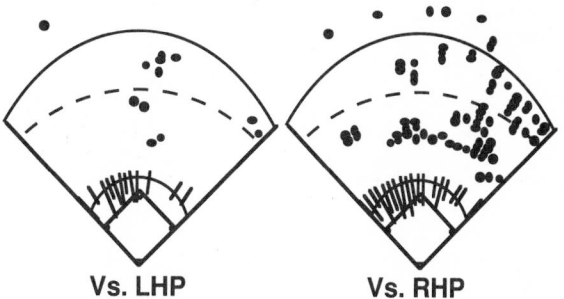

Vs. LHP   **Vs. RHP**

1989 Situational Stats

	AB	H	HR	RBI	AVG		AB	H	HR	RBI	AVG
Home	248	58	11	46	.234	LHP	128	34	7	20	.266
Road	267	74	21	59	.277	RHP	387	98	25	85	.253
Day	118	33	8	26	.280	Sc Pos	156	41	13	82	.263
Night	397	99	24	79	.249	Clutch	83	20	5	11	.241

1989 Rankings (American League)

- ➡ 1st in strikeouts (172), percent of swings that missed (38.6%) and runs scored per time reached base (42.4%) - *players with 502 PA*
- ➡ 3rd highest home run frequency (16.1 ABs per HR)
- ➡ 4th in home runs (32) and RBI (105)
- ➡ 6th in slugging percentage (.495)
- ➡ Led the Royals in strikeouts, slugging percentage, runs scored per time reached base, home run frequency, home runs, runs, total bases (255), RBI and caught stealing (9)
- ➡ Led AL Left Fielders in strikeouts, slugging percentage, runs scored per time reached base, home run frequency, home runs and RBI

PITCHING:

Terry Leach's fine career won/loss record of 29 wins and 15 losses is mainly due to an 11 and 1 mark with the Mets in 1987. But sparkling winning percentages are nothing new for Leach; he won seven versus just two losses for the Mets in 1988 and had a 10-2 record for Tidewater in 1984. The Royals hoped that success would follow Leach to Kansas City, but were disappointed. He pitched a few times in relief before getting some starting assignments. Leach had little success as a starter, getting pounded in two of his three starts. He had more success pitching in long relief, when he only went through the line-up once.

To Kansas City fans, Leach's sidearm delivery is reminiscent of Dan Quisenberry. He throws sinkers and curves low and away from the hitters trying to get them to chase balls in the dirt. His breaking pitches move away from right-handed batters, and he has always been very tough on them. But lefties have always been able to handle Leach rather easily.

Leach prefers to get the hitters to beat the ball into the ground. He has collected just 4.5 strikeouts per nine innings pitched in his career; he struck out only 4.2 per game in 1989. Leach runs into control trouble when trying to be too fine with his breaking pitches. His career 140 walks (2.7 per nine innings) is good, but his 36 walks with the Royals (4.2 per nine innings) is a cause for concern. In 1989 gave he recorded only 0.9 strikeouts per walk. Leach once walked three consecutive batters on 12 pitches.

FIELDING:

Baserunners don't need a big lead to steal against Leach. His slow sidearm delivery allows the runners a quick jump and his reliance on low breaking balls gives the catchers a difficult pitch to handle. Leach's sidearm delivery leaves him off to the third base side of the mound; he is sometimes out of position to field grounders through the middle. Otherwise, Leach does a creditable job with the glove by throwing well to the bases and handling bunts quickly.

OVERALL:

Despite his outstanding success in the past, Leach didn't fare well in Kansas City. He will be challenged by other long relief specialists for a spot on the Royals roster, especially at the age of 36. Unless Leach can be more consistent, and regain his pre-1989 control, he may end up in Triple-A or released.

TERRY LEACH

Position: RP/SP
Bats: R **Throws:** R
Ht: 6' 0" **Wt:** 191

Opening Day Age: 36
Born: 3/13/54 in Selma, AL
ML Seasons: 8

Overall Statistics

	W	L	ERA	G	GS	Sv	IP	H	R	BB	SO	HR
1989	5	6	4.17	40	3	0	95.0	97	57	40	36	5
Career	29	15	3.33	207	21	7	462.0	452	201	142	228	32

Where They Hit the Ball

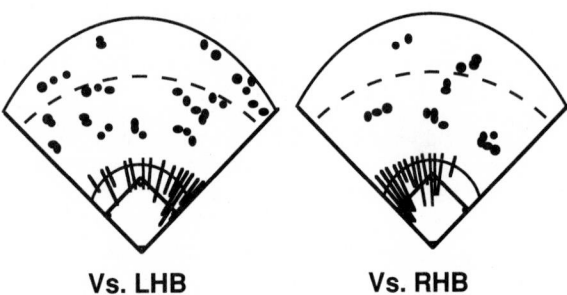

Vs. LHB   **Vs. RHB**

1989 Situational Stats

	W	L	ERA	Sv	IP		AB	H	HR	RBI	AVG
Home	3	0	2.61	0	48.1	LHB	173	53	3	30	.306
Road	2	6	5.79	0	46.2	RHB	186	44	2	26	.237
Day	1	2	3.95	0	27.1	Sc Pos	106	34	2	51	.321
Night	4	4	4.26	0	67.2	Clutch	38	5	0	1	.132

1989 Rankings (American League)

➡ Did not rank near the top or bottom in any category

PITCHING:

Charlie Leibrandt would like to forget 1989. The veteran lefthander was coming off five straight winning seasons, with at least 11 victories in each year since 1984, and was expected to be a solid part of a good starting rotation. But Leibrandt never got started last year. His usually splendid control deserted him and opposition batters racked him for a .304 average. Eventually, Leibrandt was relegated to a middle relief role and suffered his first losing season as a member of the Royals.

Leibrandt is the ultimate in finesse pitchers. He will never overpower batters with a fastball or dazzle them with a sharp breaking curve. Instead, he uses a variety of well-placed sliders, curves, fastballs and changeups to befuddle opposing hitters. Leibrandt spots his fastball well and changes speeds, but primarily uses the slider to get outs. But Leibrandt became very hittable when he lost his pin-point control. He tended to nibble at corners; he'd fall behind and end up having to groove one. The hitters responded by slugging 13 homers (tied with Bret Saberhagen for the team high) in only 161 innings pitched. His 5.14 ERA was more than a point higher than his previous Royals high of 4.09 in 1986.

Historically, Leibrandt has been a model of consistency. He nearly always lasted into the eighth inning, completing 23 percent of his starts since 1985. In 1989, Leibrandt finished only three of his 27 starts, with one shutout. He had been used heavily in important starts for the Royals since 1984, succeeding in most. In contrast, Leibrandt was removed from the rotation in 1989 just when the pennant race began in earnest and the Royals became desperate for starting pitching.

FIELDING:

Leibrandt has a deceptive move to first base and is usually successful in keeping baserunners close, but his slow delivery and less than powerful fastball give the base stealers a slight edge. Leibrandt is an average fielder who will not hurt himself with the glove. He does a fine job of covering bunts and also provides easy throws to handle when starting a double play.

OVERALL:

Leibrandt's failure in 1989 may be indicative of a pitcher without overpowering stuff finally losing his touch. If he can find his control again, Leibrandt will be the Royals primary left-handed starter in 1990. If not, the end is near for Leibrandt; the Royals have several youngsters ready to take his place.

CHARLIE LEIBRANDT

Position: SP/RP
Bats: R **Throws:** L
Ht: 6' 3" **Wt:** 200

Opening Day Age: 33
Born: 10/4/56 in Chicago, IL
ML Seasons: 10

Overall Statistics

	W	L	ERA	G	GS	Sv	IP	H	R	BB	SO	HR
1989	5	11	5.14	33	27	0	161.0	196	98	54	73	13
Career	92	78	3.77	276	229	2	1572.2	1654	729	478	724	121

Where They Hit the Ball

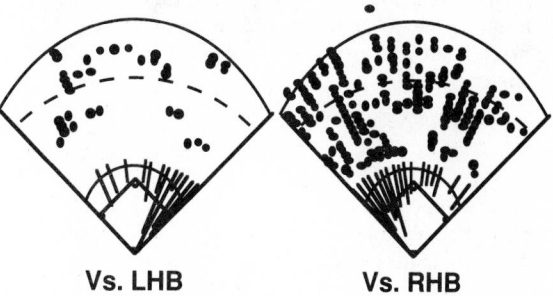

Vs. LHB   **Vs. RHB**

1989 Situational Stats

	W	L	ERA	Sv	IP		AB	H	HR	RBI	AVG
Home	3	3	3.71	0	68.0	LHB	124	43	0	14	.347
Road	2	8	6.19	0	93.0	RHB	520	153	13	65	.294
Day	1	3	5.64	0	44.2	Sc Pos	166	44	1	59	.265
Night	4	8	4.95	0	116.1	Clutch	49	13	0	4	.265

1989 Rankings (American League)

➡ 3rd highest opponent batting average vs. lefthanded batters (.347) - *pitchers facing 125 LHB*

➡ 4th highest opponent batting average vs. righthanded batters (.294) - *pitchers facing 377 RHB*

➡ Led the Royals in losses (11), home runs allowed (13), pickoff throws (147), stolen bases allowed (14) and caught stealing (9)

MIKE MACFARLANE

Position: C
Bats: R **Throws:** R
Ht: 6' 1" **Wt:** 200

Opening Day Age: 25
Born: 4/12/64 in Stockton, CA
ML Seasons: 3

HITTING:

After a promising rookie season in 1988, Macfarlane served as backup to Bob Boone for the 1989 campaign. The year was disappointing as Macfarlane failed to hit as well as expected. After posting a .265 rookie batting average, he fell to .223 with only two homers, slugging just .299. Yet, there were bright spots for Macfarlane. He continued to demonstrate good clutch hitting and the ability to produce runs; Macfarlane batted .314 with runners in scoring position and drove in 19 runs in only 157 at bats.

Macfarlane is a fastball hitter who pulls the ball to left and left-center. His power stroke is to the left-centerfield alley. He has the most trouble with breaking pitches, especially low in the strike zone. Macfarlane takes advantage of the wide open spaces of Royals Stadium; he batted .290 at home, but only .179 on the road. Impatient at the plate, Macfarlane strikes out frequently and has whiffed 66 times in 387 career at bats. He drew a fair amount of walks in 1988, but just seven in 1989.

BASERUNNING:

Macfarlane is very slow and rarely takes an extra base as a runner. It is difficult to score from second base with a single and he has no base-stealing ability. He attempted no stolen bases in 1989 and has no successful steals in his career. In short, he runs like a catcher.

FIELDING:

A fine fielding catcher, Macfarlane blocks low pitches well and moves quickly to prevent wild pitches. He has an accurate throwing arm and committed just one error in 1989. Macfarlane had a partial tear of his rotator cuff in his throwing arm in 1986 and is still rebuilding his strength in that arm. Macfarlane erased only 11 of 54 base-stealers as a rookie in 1988, yet his throws were strong and accurate enough to twice catch Rickey Henderson that year. Defense is Macfarlane's forte.

OVERALL:

The Royals hope Boone's experience will help Macfarlane to become a successful big-league catcher. As age gradually erodes Boone's offensive abilities, Macfarlane will begin to take on more of the catching duties. After one more year as an understudy, Macfarlane should be ready to become the Royals' regular catcher by 1991.

Overall Statistics

	G	AB	R	H	D	T	HR	RBI	SB	BB	SO	AVG
1989	69	157	13	35	6	0	2	19	0	7	27	.223
Career	147	387	38	95	22	0	6	48	0	30	66	.245

Where He Hits the Ball

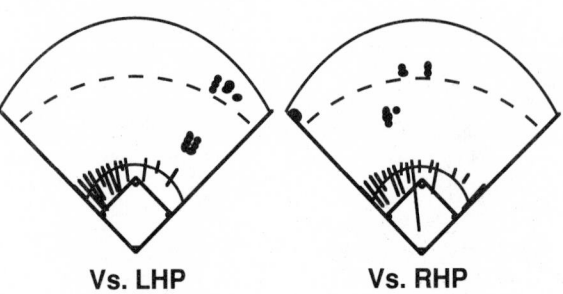

Vs. LHP   **Vs. RHP**

1989 Situational Stats

	AB	H	HR	RBI	AVG		AB	H	HR	RBI	AVG
Home	62	18	0	7	.290	LHP	64	11	0	6	.172
Road	95	17	2	12	.179	RHP	93	24	2	13	.258
Day	58	14	1	8	.241	Sc Pos	35	11	1	18	.314
Night	99	21	1	11	.212	Clutch	31	7	1	4	.226

1989 Rankings (American League)

➡ Did not rank near the top or bottom in any category

PITCHING:

The Royals turned to Jeff Montgomery as the team's closer in August, when a knee injury began to limit Steve Farr's efficiency. He responded well, recording 18 saves in 24 chances during the pennant drive. This role is familiar to Montgomery; he was a successful stopper at two minor league levels. Montgomery has a stopper's tenacity.

Montgomery is the classic fireballing reliever; he uses a high velocity fastball almost exclusively. He enjoys challenging the hitters with high, hard heat. Montgomery's curve and slider are merely for show, he does not usually throw them where they can be hit, his out pitch is the fastball. He will occasionally lose control of his fastball; Montgomery unleashed six wild pitches and hit two batters in 1989 and has thrown nine wild pitches in only 154.2 innings pitched since 1988.

Despite recording more than a strikeout per inning pitched in 1989, Montgomery allowed only 2.4 walks per nine innings. His strikeout to walk ratio of 3.8 to one is remarkable for a pitcher who throws so hard. Montgomery allowed 66 hits in 92 innings pitched; opponents batted just .198 and had an on-base percentage of only .257 versus Montgomery. His sparkling ERA of 1.37 led the Royals staff and lowered his career ERA with the Royals to 2.21. Montgomery has been blessed with good offensive support by the Royals. This run support has helped him earn 14 wins to go with his 19 saves in just a year and a half.

FIELDING:

Montgomery has a good move to first, but throws erratically when attempting to pickoff a baserunner. All of his four errors in 1989 were throwing, three of them on pickoff attempts. Montgomery does a good job of handling bunts and is quick to cover first base on grounders to the right side. Occasionally, he will get into trouble by trying to get the lead runner on sacrifice attempts, throwing late or wildly and setting up a big inning for the opposition.

OVERALL:

The role of closer will be won by Montgomery in spring training in 1990, with Farr returning to set-up status. Montgomery needs to learn another pitch to become a stopper of Dennis Eckersley or Mark Davis proportions. In the meantime, Montgomery may become the best closer the Royals have had since Dan Quisenberry was in top form.

JEFF MONTGOMERY

Position: RP
Bats: R **Throws:** R
Ht: 5'11" **Wt:** 180

Opening Day Age: 28
Born: 1/7/62 in Wellston, OH
ML Seasons: 3

Overall Statistics

	W	L	ERA	G	GS	Sv	IP	H	R	BB	SO	HR
1989	7	3	1.37	63	0	18	92.0	66	16	25	94	3
Career	16	7	2.69	122	1	19	174.0	145	56	64	154	11

Where They Hit the Ball

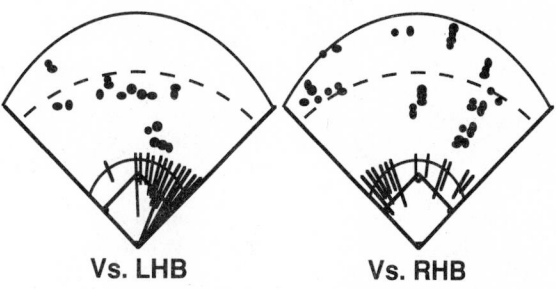

Vs. LHB   **Vs. RHB**

1989 Situational Stats

	W	L	ERA	Sv	IP		AB	H	HR	RBI	AVG
Home	6	3	1.32	9	47.2	LHB	152	32	2	8	.211
Road	1	0	1.42	9	44.1	RHB	182	34	1	16	.187
Day	1	1	1.96	5	23.0	Sc Pos	80	13	1	21	.162
Night	6	2	1.17	13	69.0	Clutch	183	39	1	19	.213

1989 Rankings (American League)

→ 4th in ERA (1.37) - *all league pitchers*

→ 4th in lowest save percentage (75.0%) - *pitchers with 20 save opportunities*

→ 6th in lowest slugging percentage allowed (.251) - *all league pitchers*

→ 9th in lowest on-base percentage allowed (.257) - *all league pitchers*

→ Led the Royals in ERA, games (63), saves (18), save opportunities (24), holds (11), opponent batting average (.198), lowest slugging percentage allowed, strikeouts per 9 innings (9.2) and blown saves (6) - *all team pitchers*

PINPOINT CONTROL

PITCHING:

Not only did Bret Saberhagen win his second Cy Young Award last year, he also became the second pitcher in Royals history to win 20 games in two different seasons, and he set a Royals season high in victories with 23. He placed among the league leaders in several categories, including finishing first in earned run average, victories and complete games. Saberhagen's four shutouts were second to Bert Blyleven in the American League.

By combining remarkable control with excellent command of several pitches, Saberhagen has become perhaps the most dominant pitcher in the American League. He uses low curveballs and sliders to set up his fastball, which can be thrown at several different speeds and with good movement. Saberhagen throws hard enough to get away with throwing high in the strike zone. He also uses his high overhand delivery to dish out a very deceptive change-up. Primarily a power pitcher, Saberhagen has a knack getting a strikeout when he needs it most. Unlike a traditional power pitcher, however, he issues few walks. Saberhagen allowed just 37 unintentional walks in 262.1 innings (1.3 per nine innings pitched) while his strikeout to walk ratio was 4.5 to 1.

When the pennant race heated up, Saberhagen really got rolling. He won 13 of his last 14 starts (three were shutouts) with a 1.57 ERA to give the Royals a much needed lift in the last half of the season. Saberhagen was nearly unbeatable at home; he won 11 of 12 decisions with a 1.71 ERA. As injuries took their toll, Saberhagen eventually became the Royals' only effective starter.

FIELDING:

Saberhagen owns one of the best pickoff moves among major league right-handers. He erased 12 runners in 1989 while committing just one balk. His good pickoff move combined with a hard fastball makes Saberhagen difficult to run against. Opposing baserunners succeeded in only five of 14 steal attempts, a success rate of 36 percent. Generally regarded as one of the best fielding pitchers in the game, Saberhagen frequently pounces on bunts and throws out the lead runner to thwart sacrifice attempts. Occasionally, Saberhagen fields infield pop ups himself and twice in 1989 raced into foul ground to snare popped up bunts.

OVERALL:

Still only 26, Saberhagen has once again become the most dominant pitcher in the league. As he enters his prime, the Royals can only dream about what he might accomplish. Saberhagen has all the tools to be successful for a decade.

BRET SABERHAGEN

Position: SP
Bats: R **Throws:** R
Ht: 6' 1" **Wt:** 185

Opening Day Age: 26
Born: 4/11/64 in Chicago Heights, IL
ML Seasons: 6

Overall Statistics

	W	L	ERA	G	GS	Sv	IP	H	R	BB	SO	HR
1989	23	6	2.16	36	35	0	262.1	209	74	43	193	13
Career	92	61	3.23	204	178	1	1329.0	1240	522	258	870	105

Where They Hit the Ball

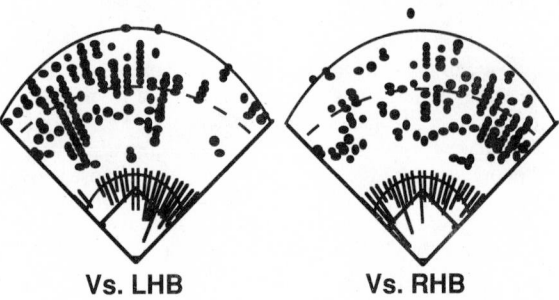

Vs. LHB   **Vs. RHB**

1989 Situational Stats

	W	L	ERA	Sv	IP		AB	H	HR	RBI	AVG
Home	11	1	1.71	0	131.1	LHB	524	102	8	29	.195
Road	12	5	2.61	0	131.0	RHB	437	107	5	36	.245
Day	4	3	3.38	0	61.1	Sc Pos	184	41	2	48	.223
Night	19	3	1.79	0	201.0	Clutch	128	29	3	12	.227

1989 Rankings (American League)

→ 1st in wins (23), ERA (2.16), complete games (12), baserunners per 9 innings (8.7), on-base average allowed (.251), innings (262.1), won/loss percentage (.793), strikeout/walk ratio (4.5) and lowest opponent stolen base percentage (35.7%) - *pitchers with 162 IP*

→ Led the Royals in wins, ERA, complete games, baserunners per 9 innings, on-base average allowed, innings, won/loss percentage, strikeout/walk ratio, lowest opponent stolen base percentage, caught stealing (9), shutouts (4), strikeouts (193), pitches thrown and home runs allowed (13)

HITTING:

The Royals moved Kevin Seitzer to the lead-off spot in 1989 to take advantage of his ability to get on base. Seitzer's .387 on-base average and 102 walks in 1989 led Kansas City and he was one of three Royals to walk more often than strike out. Seitzer's high batting average makes him ideal for a spot at or near the top of the order. His .281 average in 1989 was his lowest at any professional level; Seitzer is a career .304 hitter.

Seitzer makes good use of spacious Royals Stadium by hitting to all fields. He is a line drive hitter who is willing to wait for his pitch. Seitzer takes what is offered by the pitcher and by the defense; he will hit to right field on pitches away from him and pull pitches on the inside part of the plate. Mostly, Seitzer tries to hit the ball back up the middle.

By being selective, Seitzer can usually coax the pitcher into throwing a fastball, his favorite pitch to hit. But, he is equally capable of hitting breaking balls. On the other hand, Seitzer has trouble with hard fastballs thrown up and in or big-breaking curves thrown low and away.

BASERUNNING:

While stealing bases is not Seitzer's forte, he does have limited ability in this area. His 17 successful thefts, versus eight times being caught, made him one of six Royals to steal at least 10 bases. Seitzer's exuberance leads to baserunning mistakes, especially when going from first to third; he has been out easily at third on occasion.

FIELDING:

Seitzer throws well enough from the hot corner but is erratic. With 20 miscues, he made more errors than any other Royal. Seitzer's biggest problem is going for balls hit hard to his right. Seitzer sometimes waves at them instead of gloving them. He allows his mistakes to multiply, at times compounding one error with another. Seitzer has a dramatic flair to his fielding. He has a knack for making a sparkling play at a critical point in a game. He has decent range, but might be better suited to the outfield or first base.

OVERALL:

The Royals have long been lacking a consistent lead-off hitter and they have found one in Seitzer. Even with his fielding difficulties, Seitzer will be a valuable player for many years to come.

KEVIN SEITZER

Position: 3B
Bats: R **Throws:** R
Ht: 5'11" **Wt:** 180

Opening Day Age: 28
Born: 3/26/62 in Springfield, IL
ML Seasons: 4

Overall Statistics

	G	AB	R	H	D	T	HR	RBI	SB	BB	SO	AVG
1989	160	597	78	168	17	2	4	48	17	102	76	.281
Career	498	1893	289	576	86	16	26	202	39	273	239	.304

Where He Hits the Ball

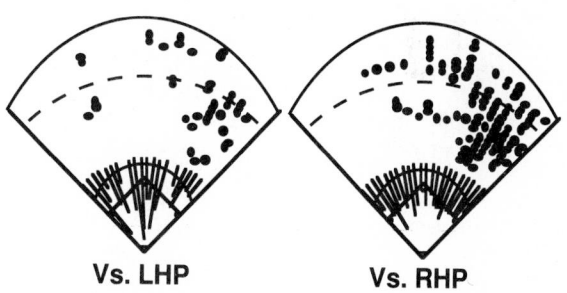

Vs. LHP   Vs. RHP

1989 Situational Stats

	AB	H	HR	RBI	AVG		AB	H	HR	RBI	AVG
Home	299	93	2	22	.311	LHP	175	45	3	12	.257
Road	298	75	2	26	.252	RHP	422	123	1	36	.291
Day	136	43	0	17	.316	Sc Pos	132	38	0	42	.288
Night	461	125	4	31	.271	Clutch	85	27	1	11	.318

1989 Rankings (American League)

- ➡ 2nd in pitches seen (2,822)
- ➡ 3rd in plate appearances (715) and times on base (275)
- ➡ 4th in walks (102)
- ➡ 5th in singles (145)
- ➡ Led the Royals in at bats (597), hits (168), singles, walks, hit by pitch (5), times on base, pitches seen, plate appearances, games, on-base average (.387), grounder/flyball ratio (1.75), bunts in play (19) and errors (20) - *team players with 502 PA*
- ➡ Led AL Third Basemen in games and bunts in play

HITTING:

Once again, Kurt Stillwell quietly had a fine offensive season to go with solid play at shortstop. He slugged .380 while scoring 52 runs in just 130 games. He produces from everywhere in the batting order; since joining the Royals in 1988, Stillwell has batted in every position except third, fourth and fifth.

Stillwell's patience at the plate may let him settle into the second spot in the order. However, he doesn't thrive on fastballs as expected of second place hitters; he's sometimes overmatched by high heat. Stillwell has a good batting eye and usually waits for his pitch, but, in potential RBI situations, he expands his strike zone in order to drive in runs. He adjusts well to the situation; he had 54 RBIs with only three double play grounders. Stillwell batted .292 with runners in scoring position.

Steadiness and offensive versatility are Stillwell's most valuable traits. He has occasional power (17 homers since 1988), can steal bases (15 steals in two years), drive in runs (166 RBI in 493 games), or score them (200 career runs scored). Stillwell produces from either side of the plate; he batted .264 right-handed and .260 as a lefty. While he doesn't have fence- busting power or blazing speed, Stillwell has few weaknesses; he contributes in many ways.

BASERUNNING:

Stillwell can steal bases when necessary. He is still learning the American League pitchers and doesn't always get a good jump off first. Stillwell makes occasional mistakes when trying for an extra base on outfield hits.

FIELDING:

Although he lacks flashiness or a rifle throwing arm, Stillwell is a solid performer at shortstop. He and second baseman Frank White helped make the Royals one of the American League's best fielding teams in 1989. Stillwell committed just 16 errors in 600 chances, but he doesn't have the best range among shortstops. He is still learning to position himself for the hitters. He appears to play too close at times, especially on artificial turf; this may have contributed to the low number of double plays turned by the Royals. His range should get better as he learns to position himself better.

OVERALL:

The Royals should be set at shortstop for the next decade. After years of a revolving door at the position, Stillwell's steadiness is refreshing. He continues to learn and should get even better. At age 24, Stillwell is just now entering his most productive years.

KURT STILLWELL

Position: SS
Bats: B **Throws:** R
Ht: 5'11" **Wt:** 175

Opening Day Age: 24
Born: 6/4/65 in Glendale, CA
ML Seasons: 4

Overall Statistics

	G	AB	R	H	D	T	HR	RBI	SB	BB	SO	AVG
1989	130	463	52	121	20	7	7	54	9	42	64	.261
Career	493	1596	200	402	74	20	21	166	25	151	237	.252

Where He Hits the Ball

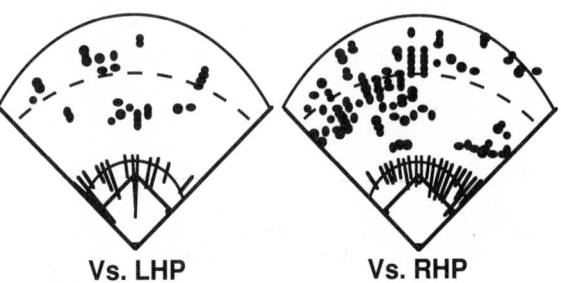

Vs. LHP   Vs. RHP

1989 Situational Stats

	AB	H	HR	RBI	AVG		AB	H	HR	RBI	AVG
Home	217	49	2	30	.226	LHP	121	32	1	12	.264
Road	246	72	5	24	.293	RHP	342	89	6	42	.260
Day	105	25	0	8	.238	Sc Pos	120	35	2	46	.292
Night	358	96	7	46	.268	Clutch	61	12	0	2	.197

1989 Rankings (American League)

➡ 4th in lowest GDPs per GDP situation (3.2%) - *players with 50 PA in GDP situations*

➡ 10th in triples (7)

➡ Led the Royals in lowest GDPs per GDP situation and triples

➡ Led AL Shortstops in lowest GDPs per GDP situation and road batting average (.293)

HITTING:

Historically, Pat Tabler does two things well, driving in runs and hitting for a high average. Yet, in 1989, he could do neither consistently. His .259 average, 42 RBIs and 101 hits were full season lows for Tabler and he hit only .231 with runners in scoring position.

Tabler uses a short batting stroke to punch the ball through the infield and he prefers hitting fastballs. As a starter, Tabler is selective only in his first plate appearance as he gauges the pitcher's stuff. Later, he becomes more aggressive, usually swinging at the first offering. When pinch hitting, Tabler comes out looking for fastballs and swinging away. He's a solid contact man, seldom either striking out or walking. His 42 Ks in 1989 were the fewest by Tabler in a full major league season; he was one of the more difficult Royals to strike out. Tabler only walked 37 times in 435 plate appearances in 1989.

Tabler's hitting is paradoxical. He has a high average, yet fails to get on base with regularity; Tabler's 1989 on-base average of .325 is in line with of his career .349 on-base average. He lacks power, yet drives in runs; Tabler has a high RBI per at bats ratio over his career despite hitting only 44 homers.

BASERUNNING:

Lacking any real speed, Tabler is a below average baserunner. He takes few chances, however, and is rarely put out on the bases. Tabler made no stolen base attempts in 1989 and was occasionally replaced by late-inning pinch runners.

FIELDING:

Tabler's versatility in the field hides his lack of fielding ability. He is a poor fielder who is usually replaced in the field whenever his bat becomes expendable. Tabler does not really have a regular fielding position; instead, he is used in the outfield, at first base, and on occasion at third base. The four errors committed by Tabler in 1989 in limited duty don't show his frequent misplays and weak throwing arm. The designated hitter role is a perfect fit for Tabler.

OVERALL:

Tabler has value to the Royals as a part-time designated hitter and right-handed pinch hitter. However, he is a defensive liability and his lack of any true fielding position limits his contribution to the team. The Royals need a consistent run producer, and as long as Tabler can drive in runs he will have at least a part-time role.

PAT TABLER

Position: DH/1B/LF/RF
Bats: R **Throws:** R
Ht: 6' 2" **Wt:** 200

Opening Day Age: 32
Born: 2/2/58 in Hamilton, OH
ML Seasons: 9

Overall Statistics

	G	AB	R	H	D	T	HR	RBI	SB	BB	SO	AVG
1989	123	390	36	101	11	1	2	42	0	37	42	.259
Career	979	3353	405	962	165	23	44	446	16	312	495	.287

Where He Hits the Ball

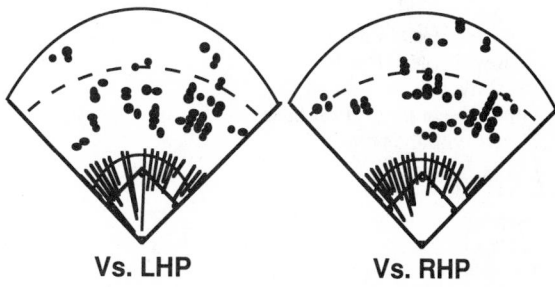

Vs. LHP   **Vs. RHP**

1989 Situational Stats

	AB	H	HR	RBI	AVG		AB	H	HR	RBI	AVG
Home	181	49	2	21	.271	LHP	160	56	2	21	.350
Road	209	52	0	21	.249	RHP	230	45	0	21	.196
Day	99	31	1	13	.313	Sc Pos	121	28	2	39	.231
Night	291	70	1	29	.241	Clutch	66	19	1	9	.288

1989 Rankings (American League)

➡ 6th in batting average vs. lefthanded pitchers (.350) - *players with 125 PA vs. LHP*

➡ 10th in most GDPs per GDP situation (19.2%) - *players with 50 PA in GDP situations*

➡ Led the Royals in batting average vs. lefthanded pitchers

➡ Led AL Designated Hitters in bunts in play (6) and batting average vs. lefthanded pitchers

HITTING:

Injuries limited Danny Tartabull's effectiveness for much of the 1989 campaign. Career lows in virtually every offensive category resulted in Tartabull moving out of the clean-up spot. Tartabull batted just .207 with runners in scoring position. However, he still contributed in many ways. Tartabull's 18 homers and .369 on-base average were second best for the Royals. He also hit 22 doubles and drove in 62 runs and was one of the team's leading hitters.

Tartabull combines a good average with even better power. His .283 career average complements his 26 homers and 90 RBI per year since 1986. He has 239 extra bases hits in 2122 career at bats. Tartabull usually hits left and righthanded pitching equally, but batted .317 against lefties and .248 versus righthanders in 1989, perhaps because of his injuries. He's a pull hitter who prefers to wait for his pitch, a fastball out and over the plate. His power is mostly to the alleys. Tartabull is prone to striking out, especially on low curves. But he also draws a lot of walks; Tartabull was second on the team with 69 bases on balls. His career .371 on-base average is excellent for a hitter with his power.

BASERUNNING:

Despite having good speed, Tartabull is a poor base runner. He rarely gets a good jump when stealing and has a below average success rate as a base stealer. Tartabull's four steals in 1989 were a career low, but were at least partially due to suffering from injuries all year.

FIELDING:

Tartabull started as a second baseman, but he is now more at home in the outfield. He is fast enough to be effective in wide open Royals Stadium, but appears to be slow to respond on balls hit deep to rightfield. Tartabull doesn't go back on flies as well as he comes in for them and he tries to compensate for this tendency by playing too deep at times. While Tartabull's arm is not overly strong, it is accurate; he committed just two errors in 1989 and has always had a good fielding average.

OVERALL:

Tartabull is one of the most important hitters in the Royals line-up. He has been remarkably consistent in his four full seasons and provides protection for George Brett and Bo Jackson. Tartabull's high batting average and on-base avearge give him an added dimension; he is not just a power hitter. Sometimes unappreciated by Royals fans, Tartabull remains a very valuable performer.

DANNY TARTABULL

Position: RF/DH
Bats: R **Throws:** R
Ht: 6' 1" **Wt:** 205

Opening Day Age: 27
Born: 10/30/62 in Miami, FL
ML Seasons: 6

Overall Statistics

	G	AB	R	H	D	T	HR	RBI	SB	BB	SO	AVG
1989	133	441	54	118	22	0	18	62	4	69	123	.268
Career	603	2122	316	601	120	13	106	375	26	295	552	.283

Where He Hits the Ball

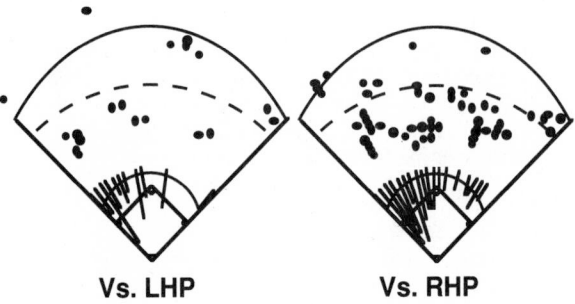

Vs. LHP   **Vs. RHP**

1989 Situational Stats

	AB	H	HR	RBI	AVG		AB	H	HR	RBI	AVG
Home	214	60	9	31	.280	LHP	125	39	8	22	.312
Road	227	58	9	31	.256	RHP	316	79	10	40	.250
Day	110	32	4	18	.291	Sc Pos	116	24	2	40	.207
Night	331	86	14	44	.260	Clutch	67	27	5	21	.403

1989 Rankings (American League)

- ➡ 1st in hitting in the clutch (.403) - *players with 50 PA in the clutch*
- ➡ 2nd in percent of swings that missed (33.3%) - *players with 502 PA*
- ➡ 3rd in slugging percentage vs. lefthanded pitchers (.577) - *players with 125 PA vs LHP*
- ➡ 7th in hitting on a 3-1 count (.533) - *players with 10 PA with a 3-1 count*
- ➡ Led the Royals in clutch hitting, hitting on a 3-1 count and hitting on a 0-2 count (.261)
- ➡ Led AL Right Fielders in hitting in the clutch and hitting on a 3-1 count

HITTING:

Brad Wellman saw increased middle infield duty in 1989 when Royals regulars Frank White and Kurt Stillwell were injured or being rested; Wellman played more at second base, but usually as a late inning substitute. He set career highs in appearances (103) and runs scored (30) and had his most at bats in any season since 1984. Wellman was an important player for the Royals in 1989.

Wellman is sometimes overmatched by big league pitching; he has trouble with big breaking curves and high, tight fastballs. Wellman prefers to hit sliders or low fastballs; he is primarily a mistake hitter. Wellman uses the whole field, attempting to slap the ball through the infield, especially on artificial turf. Frequently a strikeout victim, Wellman had a strikeout to walk ratio of over five to one in 1989. His career ratio is just under three to one, but Wellman has struck out 95 times in the last 476 at bats since 1985, about once every five at bats. He doesn't match this high strikeout rate with a lot of walks, though. In the same 476 at bats, Wellman walked just 18 times.

BASERUNNING:

Wellman has average speed. He has been used as a pinch runner in late innings by the Royals, although he is not often asked to steal a base. Wellman's five stolen bases in 1989 are the best since he swiped 10 for the Giants in 1984. He runs the bases well and makes few baserunning errors.

FIELDING:

Wellman was adequate as a fill-in for White and Stillwell. He has the range of a middle infielder, but makes a lot of errors. Wellman committed just two errors in 1989 but has a career fielding average under .970. Wellman is more comfortable at second base, where he plays more often, but can also play shortstop or even third base. He has an accurate throwing arm that is strong enough to allow him to play anywhere on the infield.

OVERALL:

Wellman is a marginal major league player who has been able to survive through versatility and by maximizing his best talents. He is a glove man who doesn't hit enough to play a regular role for the Royals. Wellman will be pushed by Bill Pecota for a similar job with the 1990 Royals.

BRAD WELLMAN

Position: 2B/SS
Bats: R **Throws:** R
Ht: 6' 0" **Wt:** 170

Opening Day Age: 30
Born: 8/17/59 in Lodi, CA
ML Seasons: 8

Overall Statistics

	G	AB	R	H	D	T	HR	RBI	SB	BB	SO	AVG
1989	103	178	30	41	4	0	2	12	5	7	36	.230
Career	441	927	97	214	30	2	6	77	26	59	176	.231

Where He Hits the Ball

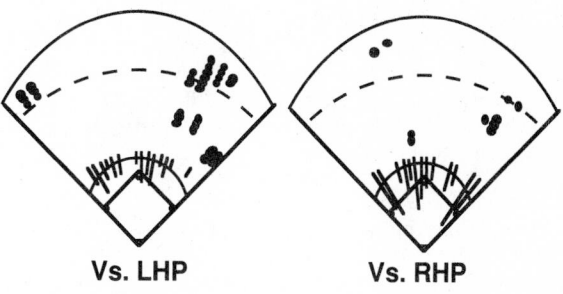

Vs. LHP   **Vs. RHP**

1989 Situational Stats

	AB	H	HR	RBI	AVG		AB	H	HR	RBI	AVG
Home	86	14	0	4	.163	LHP	64	18	1	7	.281
Road	92	27	2	8	.293	RHP	114	23	1	5	.202
Day	75	19	0	5	.253	Sc Pos	43	8	0	10	.186
Night	103	22	2	7	.214	Clutch	21	9	0	1	.429

1989 Rankings (American League)

➤ Led the Royals in grounder/flyball ratio (2.1) and hitting in the clutch - *all team players*

➤ Led AL second basemen in percent of extra bases taken as a runner (54.5%) - *second basemen with 40 opportunities to advance*

HITTING:

As Frank White's power numbers continued to decline last year, he was relegated to a role at the bottom of the batting order. White was once a clean-up hitter, but spent most of 1989 in the seventh and eighth spots. Last season's two homers and 36 RBI were White's worst since the mid-1970's; his .328 slugging average was his second worst for a full season. Nevertheless, White did contribute offensively by improving his batting average and on-base average. He hit .289 with runners in scoring position and, after hitting in the low .200s for much of the first half of the year, White rebounded to .256; his second best average since 1984.

For the third consecutive year, White reduced his strikeout total. His batting style is gradually changing from that of an aggressive, fastball hitter to more of a contact hitter. White still pulls the ball frequently, but has begun to use more of the field in recent years. White is a good clutch hitter, as evidenced by his homers in playoff, World Series, and All-Star play. He has usually been at his best during the stretch drives at the end of the year. White handles the bat well and is a good bunter.

BASERUNNING:

At age 39, White is a conservative runner, unlikely to take chances on extra bases. But he still has some speed; he stole three bases in 1989 (after seven in 1988) and was used occasionally in hit and run plays.

FIELDING:

White is tied with Bill Mazeroski for the most Gold Gloves ever by a second baseman, with eight. White is a superb fielder who never fails to glove a ball within reach and has made just 14 errors in the last two years, a span of 280 games. White's .984 fielding percentage in over 2000 games at second base is the all-time best. Knee injuries and age have cut down his range, but White uses excellent positioning to make the plays. He still has one of the best range factors in the league based upon plays made per nine innings.

OVERALL:

White is currently unsigned and wishes to test the free agent market. Either way, he probably has no more than a couple of years left and will be rested frequently. Age and bad knees will continue to take a toll on his offensive abilities, but White can still contribute in many ways.

FRANK WHITE

Position: 2B
Bats: R **Throws:** R
Ht: 5'11" **Wt:** 190

Opening Day Age: 39
Born: 9/4/50 in Greenville, MS
ML Seasons: 17

Overall Statistics

	G	AB	R	H	D	T	HR	RBI	SB	BB	SO	AVG
1989	135	418	34	107	22	1	2	36	3	30	52	.256
Career	2242	7618	892	1954	393	57	158	865	177	402	1003	.256

Where He Hits the Ball

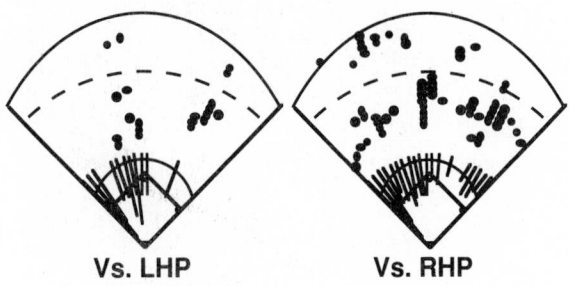

Vs. LHP   **Vs. RHP**

1989 Situational Stats

	AB	H	HR	RBI	AVG		AB	H	HR	RBI	AVG
Home	210	50	1	20	.238	LHP	125	30	0	10	.240
Road	208	57	1	16	.274	RHP	293	77	2	26	.263
Day	75	16	0	8	.213	Sc Pos	97	28	0	34	.289
Night	343	91	2	28	.265	Clutch	64	18	1	6	.281

1989 Rankings (American League)

➡ 10th in hitting with the bases loaded (.444) - *players with 10 PA with the bases loaded*

➡ Led the Royals in hitting with the bases loaded

HITTING:

The 1989 season was arguably Willie Wilson's worst. His .253 batting average represented a career low and he was replaced in the leadoff spot by Kevin Seitzer. His lost leadoff role was primarily due to an abysmal .300 on-base average in 1989 after a similarly low OBP in 1988. After his league leading .332 average in 1982, Wilson's hitting has declined every year since; his last year over the .300 mark was 1984 (.301). He has hit just .267 for the last four years and 1989 was the first full season in which Wilson didn't collect at least 100 hits.

Notorious for swinging at almost anything, Wilson is especially overmatched by low fastballs and curves. He doesn't make use of his speed; he hits fly balls instead of grounders he might beat out. Wilson tries to pull the ball, resulting in pop ups or strike outs. Wilson strikes out a lot, but rarely walks. His 39 walks in 1984 were a career high and the only year in which his strikeout to walk ratio was less than two to one. Only once has Wilson collected more walks than RBIs (1987), a bad sign for a leadoff hitter.

BASERUNNING:

Wilson is known mainly for his baserunning and stealing. Yet, he has led the league in steals just once although he has topped 47 steals twice since 1980. Wilson is a smart thief; his success rate is usually more than 80%. Few runners go first to third faster than Wilson and he scores from second on any kind of outfield hit.

FIELDING:

Once an excellent fielder with outstanding range, Wilson is just average now. Nagging injuries and age have slowed him gradually; he no longer cuts off the ball in the gap like he once did. Wilson has never had any throwing ability. His arm has been weak throughout his career, but recently baserunners are starting to take advantage of him. Not only do they move up one base on flies to medium deep center, but runners on first go to second, and nearly every runner takes an extra base on hits to center.

OVERALL:

Wilson can best be classified as a fading star. His future value to the Royals is limited. At times it appears he plays only because of his lifetime contract. The team is best served by platooning Wilson and batting him ninth where his speed will help and his low on-base average won't hurt.

WILLIE WILSON

Position: CF
Bats: B **Throws:** R
Ht: 6' 3" **Wt:** 195

Opening Day Age: 34
Born: 7/9/55 in Montgomery, AL
ML Seasons: 14

Overall Statistics

	G	AB	R	H	D	T	HR	RBI	SB	BB	SO	AVG
1989	112	383	58	97	17	7	3	43	24	27	78	.253
Career	1672	6492	1011	1879	228	130	38	467	588	330	933	.289

Where He Hits the Ball

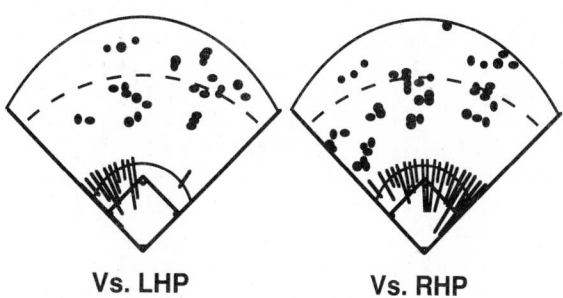

Vs. LHP   **Vs. RHP**

1989 Situational Stats

	AB	H	HR	RBI	AVG		AB	H	HR	RBI	AVG
Home	197	53	1	19	.269	LHP	123	34	1	18	.276
Road	186	44	2	24	.237	RHP	260	63	2	25	.242
Day	77	24	1	8	.312	Sc Pos	91	24	0	36	.264
Night	306	73	2	35	.239	Clutch	50	10	1	9	.200

1989 Rankings (American League)

➟ 2nd in percent of extra bases taken as a runner (63.2%) - *players with 40 opportunities to advance*

➟ 10th in triples (7)

➟ Led the Royals in percent of extra bases taken as a runner, triples and stolen base percentage (80.0%) - *team players with 20 stolen base attempts*

➟ Led AL Center Fielders in sacrifice flies (6)

KEVIN APPIER

Position: SP
Bats: R **Throws:** R
Ht: 6' 2" **Wt:** 180

Opening Day Age: 22
Born: 12/6/67 in Lancaster, CA
ML Seasons: 1

Overall Statistics

	W	L	ERA	G	GS	Sv	IP	H	R	BB	SO	HR
1989	1	4	9.14	6	5	0	21.2	34	22	12	10	3
Career	1	4	9.14	6	5	0	21.2	34	22	12	10	3

PITCHING & FIELDING:

Kevin Appier came close to making the Royals team out of spring training; he was one of the last players cut. His surprising progress (he was not on the 40-man roster over the previous winter) brought him to the majors June 2nd, but Appier was overmatched by big league batters who hit .374 with three homers against him. Appier won just one of his five starting assignments (losing four) and lasted into the sixth inning in only two starts before returning to Omaha July 4th.

Appier has a slider and a curve, but mostly relies on a hard fastball. He occasionally has trouble controlling the fastball, as his high walk ratio indicates. Appier has a good move to first but his wildness sometimes allows baserunners to advance. He is quick getting to bunts and covering first base, and displays a good temperament considering his lack of experience.

OVERALL:

Thought to be one of the bright young prospects in the Royals organization, Appier may be ready to assume a starting role in 1990. Although he may not make the majors straight out of spring training, look for Appier to join the Royals early in the year.

LUIS DELOS SANTOS

Position: 1B
Bats: R **Throws:** R
Ht: 6' 5" **Wt:** 190

Opening Day Age: 23
Born: 12/29/66 in San Cristobal, Dominican Republic
ML Seasons: 2

Overall Statistics

	G	AB	R	H	D	T	HR	RBI	SB	BB	SO	AVG
1989	28	87	6	22	3	1	0	6	0	5	14	.253
Career	39	109	7	24	4	2	0	7	0	9	18	.220

HITTING, FIELDING, BASERUNNING:

Luis delos Santos got his shot in the majors when an April knee injury forced George Brett out of the line-up for more than a month. Delos Santos hit for average well enough, but he had no power and had difficulty driving in runs. Eventually he was relegated to a platoon role before returning to Omaha when Brett got well. At times, delos Santos appeared over-matched by big league curveballs. Usually a patient hitter, he began pressing and swinging wildly. Delos Santos succeeds when he waits for his pitch and hits to all fields.

A below average baserunner, delos Santos was often replaced by a pinch-runner in the late innings; he has little base-stealing ability. Although not considered a "glove man," he filled in well at first base in Brett's absence. He made a few rookie mistakes, but displayed good range and an above average throwing arm. He had some trouble digging out low throws.

OVERALL:

No significant role will be forthcoming for delos Santos with the Royals in 1990 unless Brett is again injured. Brett still has several productive years left; meanwhile, delos Santos will have to wait.

RICK LUECKEN

Position: RP
Bats: R **Throws:** R
Ht: 6' 6" **Wt:** 210

Opening Day Age: 29
Born: 11/15/60 in
McAllen, TX
ML Seasons: 1

Overall Statistics

	W	L	ERA	G	GS	Sv	IP	H	R	BB	SO	HR
1989	2	1	3.42	19	0	1	23.2	23	9	13	16	3
Career	2	1	3.42	19	0	1	23.2	23	9	13	16	3

PITCHING & FIELDING:

After rapid progress in the minors since 1987, Rick Luecken made it to the majors for the first time in 1989. He acquitted himself well with the Royals, posting a 3.42 ERA and collecting a save while serving as a set-up man. Relying mainly upon a fastball, Luecken had some control difficulties; he allowed nearly as many walks as strikeouts. Luecken had some good strikeout totals in the minors; he recorded 57 Ks in 64.2 innings at Double A and Triple A in 1988.

Luecken usually pitched the seventh or eighth inning to get to the stopper, or in a mop up role with the game already out of reach. He normally pitched to no more than six batters at a stretch. Luecken has been groomed in the minors as a short relief specialist; he could take over the stopper role in a pinch. An average fielder, Luecken's inexperience showed when he occasionally had trouble with throws to the bases.

OVERALL:

Although Luecken is likely to begin next season in Triple A, he can provide the Royals with a reliable set-up man. Luecken will probably practice his closer role at Omaha before being recalled early in 1990.

LARRY McWILLIAMS

Position: RP/SP
Bats: L **Throws:** L
Ht: 6' 5" **Wt:** 181

Opening Day Age: 36
Born: 2/10/54 in
Wichita, KS
ML Seasons: 12

Overall Statistics

	W	L	ERA	G	GS	Sv	IP	H	R	BB	SO	HR
1989	4	13	4.11	48	21	0	153.1	154	82	57	78	5
Career	78	90	3.95	357	224	3	1550.0	1538	759	533	933	135

PITCHING & FIELDING:

Obtained as a swingman for the pennant drive, Larry McWilliams became a reliable fourth starter; his two victories came after Royals losses and his only defeats were suffered against shutouts. He pitched well for the Royals under pennant-drive pressure.

McWilliams uses a compact delivery that hides his point of release. He relies primarily upon the curve, using fastballs and sliders as set-up pitches. Baserunners have difficulty reading McWilliams' unusual delivery; he works rapidly and his quick release helps keep them close to base. Once a consistent starter, McWilliams suffered arm injuries that have relegated him to a long-relief role in recent years. Last season's 153.1 innings are the most he has pitched since 1984. His unusual delivery sometimes leaves him out of position to field grounders through the box. He is not particularly fast in fielding bunts and has difficulty throwing to second base.

OVERALL:

As a late-season fill in, McWilliams did an excellent job. However, he will have to overcome his inconsistency to have a regular role with the Royals in the future. McWilliams figures to be a left-handed long reliever in 1990.

REY PALACIOS

Position: 3B
Bats: R **Throws:** R
Ht: 5'10" **Wt:** 190

Opening Day Age: 27
Born: 11/8/62 in Brooklyn, NY
ML Seasons: 2

Overall Statistics

	G	AB	R	H	D	T	HR	RBI	SB	BB	SO	AVG
1989	55	47	12	8	2	0	1	8	0	2	14	.170
Career	60	58	14	9	2	0	1	8	0	2	18	.155

HITTING, FIELDING, BASERUNNING:

Rey Palacios was a disappointment in 1989. He was expected to be an occasional pinch hitter or pinch runner and late-inning defensive substitute, but hit just .170 with no power. Palacios spent the better part of the season at Omaha, where he also had trouble with the bat.

At this point in his career, Palacios is overmatched by big league pitching. He struck out 14 times in only 47 at bats, and collected just two walks. Palacios is primarily a fastball hitter. Despite his occasional use as pinch runner, Palacios isn't a great baserunner, nor does he have exceptional speed. He was caught in his only steal attempt in 1989 and has no major league steals. In extremely limited duty, Palacios did demonstrate fine versatility. He played at third, first, in the outfield, and served as the Royals' third catcher. Palacios has shown good throwing ability as a minor league catcher, but he lacks the range to play regularly anywhere else. His value as a utility player is questionable.

OVERALL:

At age 27, Palacios is no prospect. His minor league numbers are unimpressive and he has been disappointing in limited major league duty. Palacios is destined for Omaha in 1990.

BILL PECOTA

Position: SS
Bats: R **Throws:** R
Ht: 6' 2" **Wt:** 190

Opening Day Age: 30
Born: 2/16/60 in Redwood City, CA
ML Seasons: 4

Overall Statistics

	G	AB	R	H	D	T	HR	RBI	SB	BB	SO	AVG
1989	65	83	21	17	4	2	3	5	5	7	9	.205
Career	233	446	71	103	14	6	7	36	17	43	71	.231

HITTING, FIELDING, BASERUNNING:

Bill Pecota's weak bat once again had him shuttling between Kansas City and Omaha. His Triple A numbers were unimpressive and he hit just .205 in the majors; Pecota has hit above .208 just once in four part-time big league seasons. He did have a few bright spots in 1989. He slugged .410 with nine extra base hits in 83 at bats and had a spectacular double header performance against the Yankees in which he homered three times (tying a Royals record). His hitting in the majors should improve; Pecota has succeeded at several minor league levels. A good baserunner, Pecota was successful in all five steal attempts in 1989 and has 17 career steals while only being caught three times. He is a versatile fielder. He has enough range and accuracy in throwing to succeed as an infielder and he is fast enough to play the outfield. Pecota has a strong arm and played at two outfield positions and all four infield spots.

OVERALL:

Despite his lack of batting prowess, Pecota has become a valuable utility player. His ability to fill in anywhere on the diamond is especially important with the 24-man rosters.

GARY THURMAN

Position: CF
Bats: R **Throws:** R
Ht: 5'10" **Wt:** 175

Opening Day Age: 25
Born: 11/12/64 in
Indianapolis, IN
ML Seasons: 3

Overall Statistics

	G	AB	R	H	D	T	HR	RBI	SB	BB	SO	AVG
1989	71	87	24	17	2	1	0	5	16	15	26	.195
Career	133	234	42	52	5	1	0	12	28	27	66	.222

HITTING, FIELDING, BASERUNNING:

Last year was another wasted season for Gary Thurman. He rode the bench for much of 1989 and wound up getting injured when his opportunity to play arrived. After a meteoric rise throughout the minors, Thurman has now had two consecutive sub-par seasons.

Thurman still has trouble hitting major league pitching consistently. Big breaking curves and high heat give him trouble. Thurman has learned to beat the ball into the artificial turf, trying to use his speed to get on base. He uses a short swing to try to slap the ball through the infield. He's a great baserunner and tied a league record by stealing 16 bases without getting caught. Thurman has led three different minor leagues in stolen bases. He's also a fine outfielder. He has exceptional speed, ideal for spacious Royals Stadium. Thurman owns an outstanding throwing arm; he had 16 assists in Omaha in 1988.

OVERALL:

Thurman has reached a cross-roads in 1990; he has nothing more to prove in the minors and must prove he can perform in the big leagues. But his time is running out. Thurman will likely open the year in Omaha, but should be recalled early.

MATT WINTERS

Position: RF
Bats: L **Throws:** R
Ht: 6'3" **Wt:** 215

Opening Day Age: 30
Born: 3/18/60 in
Buffalo, NY
ML Seasons: 1

Overall Statistics

	G	AB	R	H	D	T	HR	RBI	SB	BB	SO	AVG
1989	42	107	14	25	6	0	2	9	0	14	23	.234
Career	42	107	14	25	6	0	2	9	0	14	23	.234

HITTING, FIELDING, BASERUNNING:

A career minor leaguer, Matt Winters got his chance in the majors when Danny Tartabull was injured. Winters made the most of his opportunity by slugging .346 and serving well as an extra left-handed bat. Winters has a fine batting eye; he drew 14 walks in only 122 plate appearances, while striking out 23 times. He has always had a good strikeout to walk ratio; Winters walked 147 times versus 88 strikeouts at two minor league levels in 1982. Although Winters is well past his base stealing days, he ran the bases with abandon when first recalled from AAA Omaha. He is willing to gamble for an extra base. In the field, Winters' lack of experience as a major league outfielder was apparent in his short stint with the Royals. He frequently misplayed routine flies and had trouble going back on flies over his head. Winters has a below average arm and committed three errors in limited outfield playing time.

OVERALL:

Winters performed as expected after his recall from Omaha. He hit well as a substitute rightfielder and pinch hitter. With Bill Buckner's status still uncertain, the Royals may look for Winters to be their left-handed pinch hitter.

PITCHING:

After posting a 13-7 record and 3.09 ERA in his rookie season, Don August was the Brewers' opening day pitcher in 1989. He lost to the Cleveland Indians, 1-0, and that was almost the highlight of his season.

August is a breaking ball pitcher, one who lives and dies with his sharp breaking curve. If he can't get the breaking ball over the plate, he is not going to get many hitters out with his below-average fastball. He wasn't getting it over the plate for most of the first half of the season and was shipped out to Denver in August when his ERA ballooned to 5.49 with a 9-11 record. Hitters were batting .309 against him. He returned in September and had a little more success, going 3-1 and lowering his ERA, slightly, to 5.31.

Although August pitched a little better in September, he was not consistent. He had a few outings when his breaking ball was working well and he could mix it up with an effective change-up. Just when he would seem to be getting his act together again, he would revert to the problems he had early in the season.

August has never been a strikeout pitcher, but he had good walk-strikeout ratios in the minor leagues and in his rookie season. The 1989 season was just the opposite. He walked 58 batters in 142.1 innings while striking out only 51. With hitters sitting on his fastball or taking their hacks at hanging breaking balls, he led the team by giving up 17 home runs.

FIELDING:

August doesn't look like an athlete but is surprisingly agile. He doesn't hurt himself on defense, fielding his position well and doing a good job of covering first base. His pick-off move is average, but runners can take advantage of his breaking ball to steal against him.

OVERALL:

August's problems in 1989 can't be blamed on the sophomore jinx. He simply did not pitch as well as he did in his rookie season. To be successful, he will need his good breaking ball because he won't be able to blow any hitters away. He will have to have an outstanding spring to win his spot in the rotation. If he isn't in the rotation, he will be back at Denver at the start of the 1990 season.

DON AUGUST

Position: SP/RP
Bats: R **Throws:** R
Ht: 6' 3" **Wt:** 190

Opening Day Age: 26
Born: 7/3/63 in Inglewood, CA
ML Seasons: 2

Overall Statistics

	W	L	ERA	G	GS	Sv	IP	H	R	BB	SO	HR
1989	12	12	5.31	31	25	0	142.1	175	93	58	51	17
Career	25	19	4.18	55	47	0	290.2	312	148	106	117	29

Where They Hit the Ball

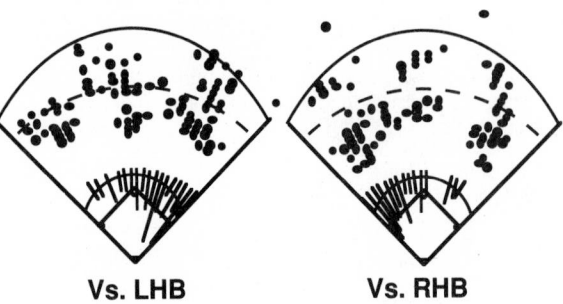

Vs. LHB   **Vs. RHB**

1989 Situational Stats

	W	L	ERA	Sv	IP		AB	H	HR	RBI	AVG
Home	5	5	5.54	0	50.1	LHB	292	89	6	31	.305
Road	7	7	5.18	0	92.0	RHB	287	86	11	47	.300
Day	5	2	2.31	0	50.2	Sc Pos	127	33	8	65	.260
Night	7	10	6.97	0	91.2	Clutch	36	16	3	5	.444

1989 Rankings (American League)

→ 3rd worst road ERA (5.18) - *pitchers with 81 road IP*

→ Led the Brewers in losses (12), home runs allowed (17), walks allowed (58), runs allowed (93), earned runs allowed (84) and caught stealing (7)

PITCHING:

Two years ago in 1988, Chris Bosio had a season that anyone would like to forget. He set a team record with 11 straight losses, earning a brief demotion to the minor leagues in the process. The losing streak was totally unexpected. When it started, he was among the league leaders in earned run average, complete games and shutouts. But Bosio erased those bad memories in 1989. With Teddy Higuera troubled with an assortment of ailments, the Brewers needed someone to step into the role as their No. 1 starter. Bosio, who wasn't even guaranteed a spot in the rotation going into spring training, quickly claimed that job.

His success is no real surprise to Bosio watchers. The husky righthander has always had a lively arm, a competitive nature and a knack for being able to pick up a new pitch almost immediately. His biggest problem was Chris Bosio. Too often his emotions would overflow, and he would lose his cool and self destruct.

Bosio can throw hard but has learned that a lot of strikeouts don't necessarily make a winning pitcher. He still gets his share of strikeouts, but is willing to settle for a ground ball to short on his second or third pitch instead of a strikeout on a 3-2 count. His repertoire is big and constantly growing. At the end of the season, he was using five pitches -- two different fastballs, a nasty slider, a change-up and a split-finger fastball. He can throw any of them for strikes at any time in the count. Hitters can't wait him out. He walked only 48 last season.

FIELDING:

Bosio is improving, but he still has trouble holding runners on first base. Base stealers have a high success rate when he is on the mound. He can field his position but occasional lapses will sometimes keep him from covering first base in time on balls hit to the first baseman.

OVERALL:

Bosio has the ability to be a big winner in the major leagues. He also has the versatility and arm to be used either as a starting pitcher or a closer. With Dan Plesac around, the Brewers don't need a closer, though Bosio has had success as a short reliever.

CHRIS BOSIO

Position: SP
Bats: R **Throws:** R
Ht: 6' 3" **Wt:** 210

Opening Day Age: 27
Born: 4/3/63 in Carmichael, CA
ML Seasons: 4

Overall Statistics

	W	L	ERA	G	GS	Sv	IP	H	R	BB	SO	HR
1989	15	10	2.95	33	33	0	234.2	225	90	48	173	16
Career	33	37	3.93	127	78	8	621.1	643	299	149	436	56

Where They Hit the Ball

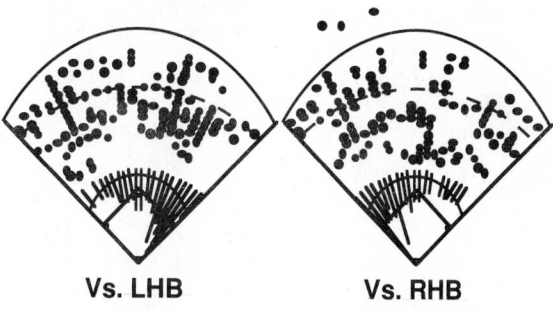

Vs. LHB   **Vs. RHB**

1989 Situational Stats

	W	L	ERA	Sv	IP		AB	H	HR	RBI	AVG
Home	9	3	2.06	0	127.0	LHB	458	113	8	39	.247
Road	6	7	4.01	0	107.2	RHB	447	112	8	37	.251
Day	5	5	2.24	0	96.1	Sc Pos	185	44	4	57	.238
Night	10	5	3.45	0	138.1	Clutch	77	19	1	3	.247

1989 Rankings (American League)

➡ 2nd in least pitches thrown per batter (3.4) - *pitchers with 162 IP*

➡ 3rd in highest strikeout/walk ratio (3.6)

➡ 4th in run support per 9 innings (5.4), strikeouts (173) and complete games (8)

➡ Led the Brewers in wins (15), ERA (2.95), games started (33), complete games, shutouts (2), innings (234), hits allowed (225), batters faced (969), strikeouts, pitches thrown (3,268), lowest opponent batting average (.249), lowest opponent slugging percentage (.336), lowest opponent on-base percentage (.289), highest strikeout/walk ratio (3.6), least baserunners per 9 innings (10.7) and run support per 9 innings

HITTING:

Glenn Braggs is one of the Brewers' biggest puzzles. This guy seems to have everything. He's big, strong and has good speed. He seems to have the tools to be an impact player. Although he has shown flashes of the production the Brewers had hoped for, his overall numbers have been mediocre. Braggs started out the 1988 season as one of the league leaders in RBIs after two months, and the Brewers thought he had finally arrived. An impinged nerve in his right shoulder silenced his bat in June, however, and he underwent surgery in July. He returned to the lineup in '89, but had another disappointing year, hitting .247 with 15 home runs and only 66 RBI.

One of his problems has been a tendency to overswing. He's strong enough to hit the ball out of the park with a short, smooth stroke and has had his best success when he remembers to cut down on his swing. Unfortunately, he doesn't remember often enough.

Because of his strength, Braggs shouldn't have any problems hitting 20-30 home runs a season, but he has never hit more than 15 in the major leagues. His run production also has been a big disappointment. He batted just .238 with runners in scoring position last season and .243 in late-inning clutch situations. He handles lefthanders well, hitting over .300 against them in '89, but righthanders give him big trouble.

BASERUNNING:

Although he has good speed and stole 17 bases in 1989, Braggs is not a good baserunner. He makes a lot of mistakes while running the bases. He runs and slides hard and will break up an attempted double play.

FIELDING:

Braggs has his problems in the outfield, too. A centerfielder in the minor leagues, Braggs was used in left field in his rookie season and had all kinds of problems judging fly balls. He had better success when he was moved to right field the next season, but shoulder surgery in the middle of the 1988 season forced him to return to left field last year. He has worked hard on his defense but still has a long way to go.

OVERALL:

Braggs is only 27 years old and is still loaded with potential. The big question in Milwaukee at the end of the season was whether the Brewers had run out of patience. Braggs might benefit from a change of scenery. And that could happen. His name was often mentioned in trade rumors at the end of the season.

GLENN BRAGGS

Position: LF/DH
Bats: R **Throws:** R
Ht: 6' 3" **Wt:** 210

Opening Day Age: 27
Born: 10/17/62 in San Bernadino, CA
ML Seasons: 4

Overall Statistics

	G	AB	R	H	D	T	HR	RBI	SB	BB	SO	AVG
1989	144	514	77	127	12	3	15	66	17	42	111	.247
Career	406	1506	193	385	62	12	42	203	36	114	314	.256

Where He Hits the Ball

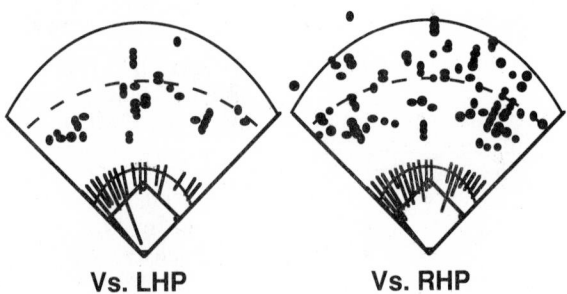

Vs. LHP   Vs. RHP

1989 Situational Stats

	AB	H	HR	RBI	AVG		AB	H	HR	RBI	AVG
Home	275	58	8	36	.211	LHP	142	43	6	25	.303
Road	239	69	7	30	.289	RHP	372	84	9	41	.226
Day	184	37	6	25	.201	Sc Pos	130	31	1	45	.238
Night	330	90	9	41	.273	Clutch	74	18	1	6	.243

1989 Rankings (American League)

➡ 2nd in lowest batting average vs. right-handed pitchers (.226) - *players with 377 PA vs RHP*

➡ 3rd in runs scored per time reached base (38.7%)

➡ Led the Brewers in GDPs (13)

HITTING:

Greg Brock is a line-drive hitter who was once expected to hit 20 or more home runs a season. Primarily a pull hitter, Brock did hit 12 home runs in 107 games for the Brewers last season, but that was still far below the production the Brewers hoped for when they traded Tim Leary for the veteran first baseman. However, Brock's .265 average was more than 20 points above his career average going into the season. The primary reason for the improvement was that he hit lefthanders better than ever before in his career.

Unlike most lefthanded hitters, Brock prefers pitches up in the strike zone. He likes the ball over the plate but has problems with breaking stuff and pitches that jam him. He made some adjustments against inside pitches in 1989, and that helped him a lot against lefties. He has also shown some improvement in key situations in recent years. In 1988, he batted a career-high .314 in late-inning pressure situations. In '89, he held his own with a .262 average with runners in scoring position.

BASERUNNING:

Because of his lack of speed, Brock would seldom be a threat to steal a base for most teams. With the Brewers' running game, however, he will have a half dozen thefts a season, often as part of a double steal. He is a smart baserunner, who will go for the extra base if available, but the ball has to be hit in the right place to move him from first to third.

FIELDING:

Although he has never won a Gold Glove, Brock is an excellent first baseman and may be as good as anyone in the league. He has good hands and will dig balls out of the dirt and take extra-base hits away with diving stops on balls hit down the line. Despite his lack of speed, he has above-average range at first base.

OVERALL:

Brock was slowed by injuries the last two seasons, which probably affected his overall performance. His improvement in clutch situations has made him a more dangerous hitter, but the decline in power has been a puzzle. At age 32, he has never reached the level scouts predicted for him when he was a young player. He is a good player but not a star.

GREG BROCK

Position: 1B
Bats: L **Throws:** R
Ht: 6' 3" **Wt:** 205

Opening Day Age: 32
Born: 6/14/57 in McMinnville, OR
ML Seasons: 8

Overall Statistics

	G	AB	R	H	D	T	HR	RBI	SB	BB	SO	AVG
1989	107	373	40	99	16	0	12	52	6	43	49	.265
Career	859	2775	369	686	114	6	102	406	36	377	415	.247

Where He Hits the Ball

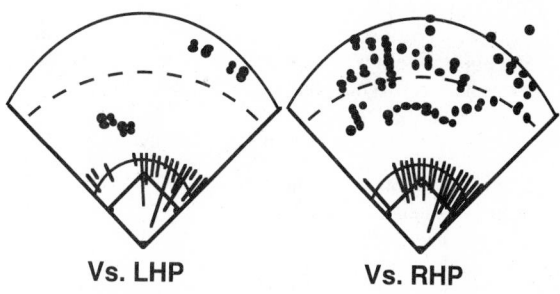

Vs. LHP   Vs. RHP

1989 Situational Stats

	AB	H	HR	RBI	AVG		AB	H	HR	RBI	AVG
Home	176	46	7	28	.261	LHP	90	30	2	20	.333
Road	197	53	5	24	.269	RHP	283	69	10	32	.244
Day	102	23	5	14	.225	Sc Pos	107	28	3	39	.262
Night	271	76	7	38	.280	Clutch	51	11	1	10	.216

1989 Rankings (American League)

➡ 4th lowest batting average with an 0-2 count (.167) - *players with 20 PA with an 0-2 count*

WORKHORSE

CHUCK CRIM

Position: RP
Bats: R **Throws:** R
Ht: 6' 0" **Wt:** 185

Opening Day Age: 28
Born: 7/23/61 in Van Nuys, CA
ML Seasons: 3

PITCHING:

Chuck Crim loves to pitch, and the Brewers have given him a lot of opportunities. He has led the American League in appearances the last two seasons. A pitcher who can pitch three innings one day and come back and pitch another the next is a valuable man to have around. Crim has been doing that for three seasons with no apparent arm problems.

He is a sinker/slider pitcher who has been very successful as Dan Plesac's set-up man and what Manager Tom Trebelhorn likes to refer to as a middle inning "stopper." His fastball is above the major league average, but hardly a match for Nolan Ryan's readings on the radar gun. Crim has been rather successful because of his competitive nature more than the quality of his pitches . He doesn't mess around and goes right after the hitter. If he has a bad day, he is anxious to go out again the next day and face the same hitters.

Crim was a little less successful last year than in 1988. His big problem was lack of success against the first hitter he faced. They batted a whopping .377 against him. But he got tougher after that, finishing with a 2.83 ERA. Overall, hitters batted .259 against Crim.

Crim isn't a big strikeout pitcher. He looks for the ground ball that will produce an inning-ending double play. He has good control and walked only 36 batters in 117.2 innings.

FIELDING:

Crim is only average defensively and will hurt himself occasionally with a bad play. His delivery is compact and he finishes in a good position to field a ball. Most of his errors are from throwing the ball away, usually to second base. He gets off the mound quickly and aggressively fields bunts and topped ground balls. He pays attention to baserunners and has a quick move to first. He throws over there a lot.

OVERALL:

Crim's 1989 season wasn't as good as the previous one, but he still performed very well. His rubber arm is his biggest asset, and he also is very versatile. Although he has been used mainly in middle relief, he has had some success as a closer and even made five starts when he was a rookie in 1987. Despite all the work he has had in his first three seasons, Crim shows no signs of wearing out.

Overall Statistics

	W	L	ERA	G	GS	Sv	IP	H	R	BB	SO	HR
1989	9	7	2.83	76	0	7	117.2	114	42	36	59	7
Career	22	21	3.16	199	5	28	352.2	342	140	103	173	33

Where They Hit the Ball

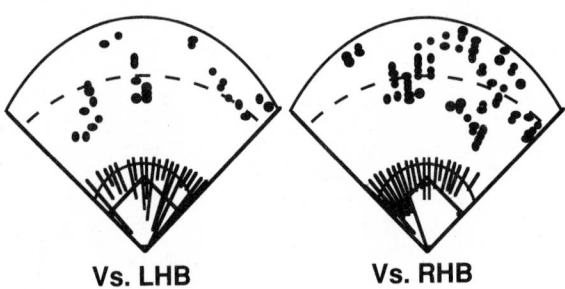

Vs. LHB   **Vs. RHB**

1989 Situational Stats

	W	L	ERA	Sv	IP		AB	H	HR	RBI	AVG
Home	4	3	2.60	5	65.2	LHB	166	45	3	16	.271
Road	5	4	3.12	2	52.0	RHB	274	69	4	41	.252
Day	6	4	3.96	4	38.2	Sc Pos	133	32	1	48	.241
Night	3	3	2.28	3	79.0	Clutch	208	52	4	26	.250

1989 Rankings (American League)

→ 1st in games (76) and worst first batter efficiency (.377) - *pitchers with 40 games in relief*

→ 2nd in holds (17)

→ 6th in blown saves (7)

→ Led the Brewers in games, holds, blowns saves, least pitches thrown per batter (3.3) and GDPs induced (20)

HITTING:

Rob Deer has led the power-hungry Brewers in home runs ever since he joined the team in 1986. When he connects, the ball goes a long, long distance. Unfortunately for the Brewers, Deer doesn't connect often enough.

Although he is usually one of the team leaders in walks, Deer is a big swinger who will chase almost anything. A high fastball hitter, he is especially susceptible to breaking balls down and away. In 1987 he set an American League record with 186 strikeouts. Deer undoubtedly would have broken Bobby Bonds' major league record of 189 strikeouts in a season if he hadn't been injured and missed the last week of the '87 season. In 1989, Deer became the first player to strike out 150 or more times four seasons in a row.

Despite his many strikeouts, Deer can be a dangerous hitter because of his power. He hits in streaks, however, and has ended every season except 1988 in a long slump. After coming off the disabled list in late July, Deer never did get untracked. He went 7 for 68 with just one home run and three RBIs after returning to the lineup. A flat-out pull hitter, Deer is not much of a threat in clutch situations.

BASERUNNING:

Deer has decent speed for a big man and will steal an occasional base, especially with Brewer Manager Tom Trebelhorn's running game. He is an aggressive runner and will take the extra base.

FIELDING:

Despite his shortcomings in several areas of the game, Deer plays hard and makes up for his inadequacies with hustle. His play in the outfield is a case in point. Although he may misjudge a ball, he will often bust his tail and still make the play. He has good range and a strong and accurate arm. His fielding has steadily improved since his rookie season with the San Francisco Giants in 1985, but sometimes his aggressive play will cost him.

OVERALL:

Deer's playing time dwindled late in the 1989 season, and his future with the Brewers is questionable. Despite his power, he has too many weaknesses as a hitter, and the Brewers need a more reliable cleanup hitter. The Brewers like him because he works hard and is an aggressive player, but his high strikeout totals make him one of the weakest links in a weak lineup.

ROB DEER

Position: RF
Bats: R **Throws:** R
Ht: 6' 3" **Wt:** 210

Opening Day Age: 29
Born: 9/29/60 in Orange, CA
ML Seasons: 6

Overall Statistics

	G	AB	R	H	D	T	HR	RBI	SB	BB	SO	AVG
1989	130	466	72	98	18	2	26	65	4	60	158	.210
Career	624	2084	316	477	79	8	121	339	31	299	757	.229

Where He Hits the Ball

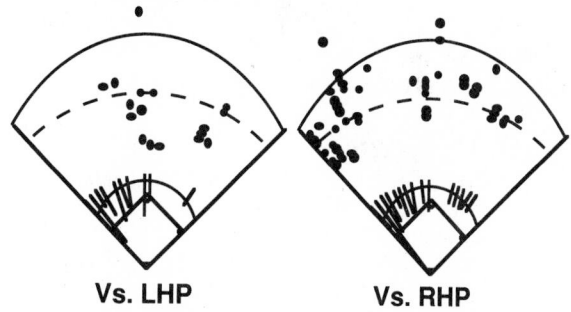

Vs. LHP   Vs. RHP

1989 Situational Stats

	AB	H	HR	RBI	AVG		AB	H	HR	RBI	AVG
Home	234	47	15	35	.201	LHP	134	34	8	18	.254
Road	232	51	11	30	.220	RHP	332	64	18	47	.193
Day	172	38	10	26	.221	Sc Pos	127	30	7	41	.236
Night	294	60	16	39	.204	Clutch	63	14	4	10	.222

1989 Rankings (American League)

➡ Worst batting average (.210) - *players with 502 PA*

➡ Worst batting average against righthanded pitchers (.193) - *players with 377 PA vs. RHP*

➡ 2nd in runs scored per time reached base (41.9%)

➡ 3rd in lowest grounder/flyball ratio (.70)

➡ 4th in home run frequency (17.9 ABs per HR) and percent of swings that missed (31.4%)

➡ Led the Brewers in strikeouts (158), home run frequency, home runs, pitches seen per plate appearance (4.0) and runs scored per time reached base

HITTING:

Every now and then, the 5-foot, 8-inch Mike Felder tries to drive a ball. When he does, he's usually in trouble. Felder's asset is his speed, and he does best when he tries to take advantage of it. That means punching, poking and bunting the ball and legging out his hits.

Felder is a switch hitter who has more success batting righthanded. He hit .277 righthanded in 1989 and only .224 lefthanded, even though he faced more than twice as many righthanders. He doesn't drive in many runs, which isn't hard to figure out when you look at his averages in clutch situations. He batted just .217 with runners in scoring position and a feeble .182 in late-inning clutch situations.

He makes good contact and is good at advancing a baserunner, especially with his bunting ability, He was one of the Brewers' leaders in sacrifice bunts despite playing in a back-up role. He isn't a real selective hitter and doesn't walk much for a player his size.

BASERUNNING:

Felder is one of the fastest runners in the league and will steal a lot of bases. He stole 26 bases and was caught stealing only five times in 1989. Most of those were when he was picked off first base, not the result of a catcher throwing him out. He is often used as a pinch runner, especially in situations where a stolen base is needed or when a fast runner is needed to score from second base.

FIELDING:

Felder is a good defensive player who can play all three outfield positions. Because of his great speed, he can run down balls a lot of outfielders would never get to. His arm is a little above average, but his throws aren't always on target and runners will take chances against him. He was originally signed as an infielder and was used some at second base last season. He fielded the position without any problems but had trouble turning the double play.

OVERALL:

Felder's speed keeps him in the major leagues. He isn't likely to become an everyday player, but he is a valuable player to have around to steal a base or go in as a late-inning defensive replacement. He fits in well with the running game used by Brewers Manager Tom Trebelhorn.

MIKE FELDER

Position: RF/LF/CF
Bats: B **Throws:** R
Ht: 5' 8" **Wt:** 160

Opening Day Age: 27
Born: 11/18/62 in Richmond, CA
ML Seasons: 5

Overall Statistics

	G	AB	R	H	D	T	HR	RBI	SB	BB	SO	AVG
1989	117	315	50	76	11	3	3	23	26	23	38	.241
Career	334	896	144	215	20	14	6	72	88	69	94	.240

Where He Hits the Ball

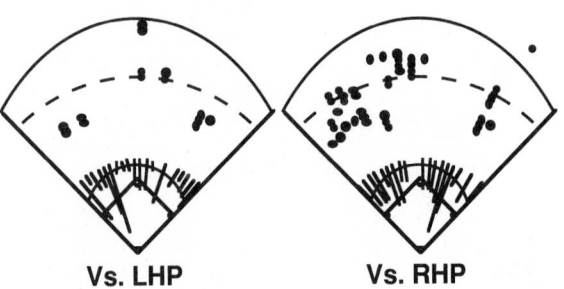

Vs. LHP   **Vs. RHP**

1989 Situational Stats

	AB	H	HR	RBI	AVG		AB	H	HR	RBI	AVG
Home	139	25	1	8	.180	LHP	101	28	0	6	.277
Road	176	51	2	15	.290	RHP	214	48	3	17	.224
Day	104	18	1	4	.173	Sc Pos	69	15	1	19	.217
Night	211	58	2	19	.275	Clutch	55	10	2	5	.182

1989 Rankings (American League)

➡ 5th in stolen base percentage (83.9%) - *players with 20 stolen base attempts*

➡ 7th in bunts in play (25)

➡ 8th in steals of third (5)

➡ Led the Brewers in bunts in play, steals of third and percent of extra bases taken as a runner (47.5%) - *team players with 40 opportunities to advance*

➡ Led AL Right Fielders in stolen bases (26), bunts in play, steals of third and sacrifice bunts (7)

PITCHING:

Patience paid off for Tony Fossas. At age 30, he finally made it to the major leagues. The native of Havana, Cuba, had been pitching in professional baseball since 1979 in the Texas Rangers' system. He spent all of his time in the minor leagues until 1988, when he pitched in five games for the Rangers. When the Rangers didn't protect him on their 40-man roster, the Brewers signed him as a minor-league free agent.

The Brewers liked his sinking fastball and assigned him to Denver to open the season. He was called up early and used mainly to come in and face a left-handed hitter or two. He's the guy they called on when they needed someone to strike out a hitter. He did that job superbly, holding lefties to a .185 average. Fossas had some problems with righties, but overall he did a fine job, striking out 42 in 61.0 innings and turning in a 3.54 ERA.

Besides his fastball, Fossas also mixes in frequent sliders and an occasional change-up. In his role, he doesn't really need the third pitch and can rely on his sinker and slider. He challenges the hitters and does a good job of keeping the ball in the ballpark. He pitched very well at County Stadium but was hit hard on the road.

FIELDING:

Like most lefthanders, Fossas keeps runners close to first base. His follow-through carries him to the third base side of the mound and doesn't leave him in the best position to field ground balls, especially to the first-base side.

OVERALL:

Fossas did a good job filling in as a stop-gap replacement, but he is another pitcher who will have to battle to win a job if everyone is healthy next spring. He's best suited for his current role as a set-up man and isn't likely to develop into the kind of reliever who could be used as a stopper. After all those years in the minor leagues, however, he isn't likely to give up his spot on the roster without a battle. He showed during the season that he was a good competitor, and that should help him.

TONY FOSSAS

Position: RP
Bats: L **Throws:** L
Ht: 6' 0" **Wt:** 180

Opening Day Age: 31
Born: 9/23/58 in Havana, Cuba
ML Seasons: 2

Overall Statistics

	W	L	ERA	G	GS	Sv	IP	H	R	BB	SO	HR
1989	2	2	3.54	51	0	1	61.0	57	27	22	42	3
Career	2	2	3.65	56	0	1	66.2	68	30	24	42	3

Where They Hit the Ball

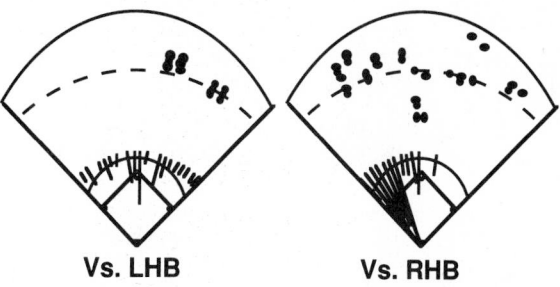

Vs. LHB   Vs. RHB

1989 Situational Stats

	W	L	ERA	Sv	IP		AB	H	HR	RBI	AVG
Home	2	0	2.79	1	38.2	LHB	81	15	1	10	.185
Road	0	2	4.84	0	22.1	RHB	142	42	2	17	.296
Day	1	0	3.20	1	25.1	Sc Pos	76	18	1	24	.237
Night	1	2	3.79	0	35.2	Clutch	37	10	0	6	.270

1989 Rankings (American League)

➡ 2nd in lowest percent of inherited runners scoring (18.2%) - *pitchers with 30 inherited runners*

➡ 5th in holds (13)

➡ Led the Brewers in balks (3), lowest percent of inherited runners scoring and 1st batter efficiency (.209) - *team pitchers with 40 games in relief*

HITTING:

Terry Francona's .232 average almost looks like a typographical error in his year-by-year breakdown. This is a guy who always has been able to hit the ball. The big drop in batting average could be from lack of use. He batted only 233 times and only had 38 at-bats in the last two months of the season.

Francona is a contact hitter who has a knack for finding holes in the defense. He is not much of a power threat, but can deliver a base hit in a key situation. He batted .310 with runners in scoring position. Early in his career he hit well against both left-handers and right-handers, but knee problems have turned him into a part-time player, and he has been used mostly against right-handers.

He is a spray hitter who is more likely to go to the opposite field than to pull the ball. He likes the ball up in the strike zone and will have problems with breaking balls down and away. Francona hardly ever draws a walk; his lifetime batting average is .274, but his career on base percentage is only .301.

BASERUNNING:

Knee and leg problems throughout his career have slowed Francona down, and he is no threat on the basepaths. He is an intelligent baserunner and won't make a lot of mistakes, but he doesn't have the speed to go for too many extra bases.

FIELDING:

The Brewers used Francona at first base a lot early in the season when Greg Brock was injured, and he was barely adequate at that position. He gets a good jump on a ball in the outfield, but his range is not great because of a lack of speed due to his leg problems. His arm is below average for an outfielder.

OVERALL:

Francona can be a handy player to have around on a team looking for a veteran who can handle a bat. The best way to use him probably would be as a left-handed designated hitter. It's unfortunate that he had the knee problems early in his career because he could have developed into one of the better hitters in the game. He was bidding for a batting title at Montreal in 1984 when he tore up the knee.

TERRY FRANCONA

Position: 1B/DH/RF
Bats: L **Throws:** L
Ht: 6' 1" **Wt:** 175

Opening Day Age: 30
Born: 4/22/59 in New Brighton, PA
ML Seasons: 9

Overall Statistics

	G	AB	R	H	D	T	HR	RBI	SB	BB	SO	AVG
1989	90	233	26	54	10	1	3	23	2	8	20	.232
Career	705	1727	162	474	74	6	16	143	12	65	119	.274

Where He Hits the Ball

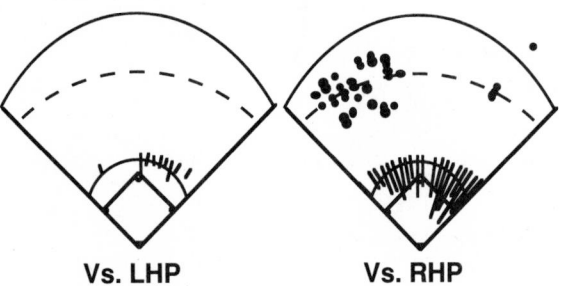

Vs. LHP   Vs. RHP

1989 Situational Stats

	AB	H	HR	RBI	AVG		AB	H	HR	RBI	AVG
Home	128	29	1	9	.227	LHP	21	5	0	5	.238
Road	105	25	2	14	.238	RHP	212	49	3	18	.231
Day	92	19	0	8	.207	Sc Pos	58	18	1	21	.310
Night	141	35	3	15	.248	Clutch	40	8	0	2	.200

1989 Rankings (American League)

➡ Did not rank near the top or bottom in any category

HITTING:

Jim Gantner is a scrappy little guy who will do anything to beat you -- except, perhaps, hit a home run. He has not hit a home run in the last two seasons. Although he isn't a power hitter, he likes to pull the ball and hits many ground balls to the second baseman. Still, he is a pesky hitter who will deliver in clutch situations, averaging .307 with runners in scoring position in 1989.

Not a big RBI man, Gantner makes good contact, can hit behind the runner and is a good bunter, all assets for a No. 2 man in the lineup. Pitchers with a good breaking ball can give him fits, especially lefthanders. He likes pitches up in the strike zone and will sometimes chase a high fastball.

Gantner apparently has no preference whether he faces a lefthander or a righthander, batting an identical .274 against both last season. That was no fluke. In 1988, he batted .274 against lefthanders and .277 against righthanders. His rare bursts of power have been against righthanded pitching, however; only two of his 44 career home runs have come off lefties.

BASERUNNING:

Although he has good speed and is always a threat to steal, Gantner had never done a lot of running until 1988 when he stole 20 bases. In 1989 he swiped 20 again despite missing the last month of the season. Just as he does everything else, Gantner runs hard and isn't afraid to make a solid contact to knock the ball away from an infielder or catcher.

FIELDING:

Gantner's specialty is turning the double play. He doesn't scare easily and hangs in better than anyone in the league. Ironically, that asset of his game now has made his future questionable. A rolling block by Marcus Lawton of the New York Yankees resulted in a serious knee injury, and the Brewers aren't sure Gantner will be able to play next season. He doesn't have the greatest range, but he knows the hitters well and is never out of position. He has a strong arm and can also play third base.

OVERALL:

The Brewers have a good reason for hoping Gantner recovers from his knee injury. He isn't their best player, but his competitive nature makes him a valuable member of the team. Observers don't think it was coincidental that the Brewers fell out of the pennant race after they lost their fiery second baseman.

JIM GANTNER

Position: 2B
Bats: L **Throws:** R
Ht: 5'11" **Wt:** 175

Opening Day Age: 36
Born: 1/5/54 in Eden, WI
ML Seasons: 14

Overall Statistics

	G	AB	R	H	D	T	HR	RBI	SB	BB	SO	AVG
1989	116	409	51	112	18	3	0	34	20	21	33	.274
Career	1472	5084	605	1399	215	28	44	478	109	315	431	.275

Where He Hits the Ball

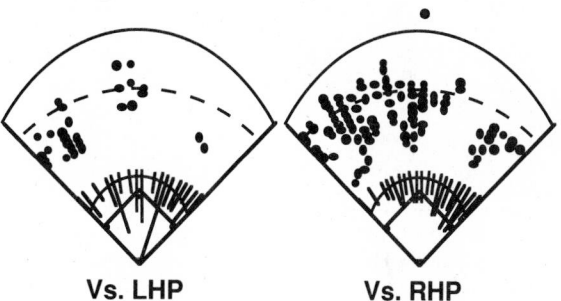

Vs. LHP   Vs. RHP

1989 Situational Stats

	AB	H	HR	RBI	AVG		AB	H	HR	RBI	AVG
Home	189	48	0	14	.254	LHP	113	31	0	10	.274
Road	220	64	0	20	.291	RHP	296	81	0	24	.274
Day	135	38	0	11	.281	Sc Pos	91	28	0	33	.308
Night	274	74	0	23	.270	Clutch	58	19	0	6	.328

1989 Rankings (American League)

- ➡ 1st in hit by pitch (10)
- ➡ Led the Brewers in hit by pitch and sacrifice bunts (8)
- ➡ Led AL Second Basemen in hit by pitch

PITCHING:

Last year was a lost season for Teddy Higuera. He missed the first month of the season after undergoing surgery to remove a herniated disc from his back in January. When he finally returned to the mound, he was bothered by a bad left ankle for most of the remainder of the season. The ankle forced him to miss a few starts, and when he did pitch, he had trouble driving off the foot at the end of his delivery. After winning at least 15 games in each of his first four seasons and earning a reputation as one of the top pitchers in the major leagues, Higuera had to settle for a 9-6 record to go with a 3.46 ERA. Like most of the Brewers' pitchers, Higuera suffered from a lack of support and could have had a much better record.

Higuera relies on three pitches, a fastball in the high 80s, a sharp breaking ball that he curls over the corner of the plate, and a change-up that makes big swingers look silly. He is a very intelligent pitcher and keeps the hitters guessing because he will throw any of his pitches at any time in the count. He is very aggressive and competitive and loves pitching in important games. He especially enjoys pitching against the New York Yankees, against whom he has a 12-2 lifetime record and 2.45 ERA.

Although he isn't a flamethrower, Higuera strikes out a lot of hitters. He struck out 240 in 1987 to set a team record. He has almost pinpoint control and can throw any of his pitches wherever he wants.

FIELDING:

Higuera fields his position as well as any pitcher in the big leagues. He's quick and has good reflexes, but just as important, he works at his defense as hard as he does at everything else. When working on fundamental drills in spring training, Higuera goes after the ball with the same determination as he would in a game. His pickoff move is good, but opposing baserunners did manage to steal 18 bases against him in 1989.

OVERALL:

Because of his physical problems, Higuera wasn't the same pitcher that American League hitters had seen in previous years. If he is healthy, and there is no reason to believe he won't be, Higuera can be expected to be the ace of the Brewers' staff again next season. Higuera is a very hard worker, and probably will show up at spring training already in midseason form.

TED HIGUERA

Position: SP
Bats: B **Throws:** L
Ht: 5'10" **Wt:** 180

Opening Day Age: 31
Born: 11/9/58 in Las Mochis, Mexico
ML Seasons: 5

Overall Statistics

	W	L	ERA	G	GS	Sv	IP	H	R	BB	SO	HR
1989	9	6	3.46	22	22	0	135.1	125	56	48	91	9
Career	78	44	3.28	154	152	0	1085.0	941	431	331	857	96

Where They Hit the Ball

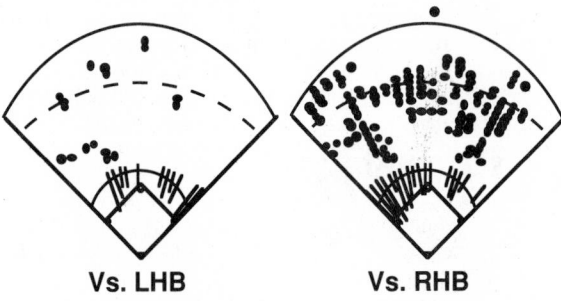

Vs. LHB   **Vs. RHB**

1989 Situational Stats

	W	L	ERA	Sv	IP		AB	H	HR	RBI	AVG
Home	7	3	2.94	0	82.2	LHB	89	20	2	10	.225
Road	2	3	4.27	0	52.2	RHB	415	105	7	38	.253
Day	0	3	4.69	0	40.1	Sc Pos	113	26	0	34	.230
Night	9	3	2.94	0	95.0	Clutch	24	6	0	1	.250

1989 Rankings (American League)

→ Led the Brewers in won/loss percentage (.600) and stolen bases allowed - *team pitchers with 15 or more decisions*

PITCHING:

In the middle of the 1988 season, the Milwaukee Brewers gave a Japanese team permission to talk to Mark Knudson, who was pitching for their Denver farm club at the time. Even though the Brewers didn't seem to have any plans for him in their future, Knudson turned down a chance to make more money in Japan. He figured he could still be a successful pitcher in the major leagues. It turns out that he was right.

In a season in which the Brewers' pitching staff was decimated by injuries, Knudson turned out to be a handy guy to have around. He was used as both a starter and long reliever and finished with an 8-5 record and 3.35 ERA. He was more successful as a starter and earned a shot at a spot in the rotation next season. In seven starts, Knudson had a 6-1 record and 2.23 ERA. Six of his last seven appearances were as a starter, and he won five of those starts, including a complete game.

Knudson has always insisted that he feels more comfortable starting a game than coming in relief. He had been primarily a starter in the minor leagues and wasn't used as a reliever until his first trial with the Brewers in 1986. His performance in 1989 indicates that he was right again.

Knudson throws a fastball, slider and forkball. The fastball is his No. 1 pitch, but his velocity tends to take a big drop in late innings. He has to keep the ball down to be successful. If he gets a pitch up in the strike zone, it can be inviting, resulting in 15 home runs in 123.2 innings.

FIELDING:

Knudson is an average fielder with a quick move to hold runners on first base. He is fundamentally sound and does a good job of getting over to cover first base on ground balls to the right side of the infield.

OVERALL:

Now 29, Knudson appears to finally have earned a solid position on the Brewers' pitching staff. His next goal will be to win a spot in the starting rotation during spring training. His performance in 1989 will help his chances.

MARK KNUDSON

Position: RP/SP
Bats: R **Throws:** R
Ht: 6' 5" **Wt:** 215

Opening Day Age: 29
Born: 10/28/60 in Denver, CO
ML Seasons: 5

Overall Statistics

	W	L	ERA	G	GS	Sv	IP	H	R	BB	SO	HR
1989	8	5	3.35	40	7	0	123.2	110	50	29	47	15
Career	13	17	4.32	75	25	0	273.0	306	148	68	113	35

Where They Hit the Ball

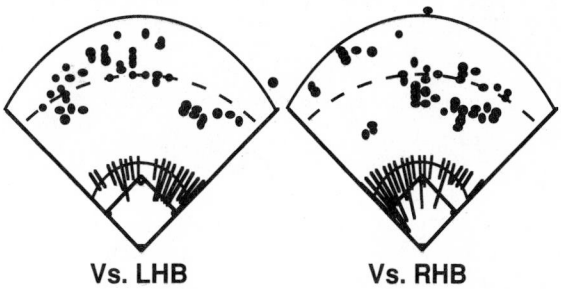

Vs. LHB   Vs. RHB

1989 Situational Stats

	W	L	ERA	Sv	IP		AB	H	HR	RBI	AVG
Home	3	3	2.41	0	56.0	LHB	198	47	5	17	.237
Road	5	2	4.12	0	67.2	RHB	266	63	10	32	.237
Day	5	2	2.53	0	57.0	Sc Pos	86	24	6	36	.279
Night	3	3	4.05	0	66.2	Clutch	65	26	2	11	.400

1989 Rankings (American League)

➡ Did not rank near the top or bottom in any category

PITCHING:

Bill Krueger is a veteran lefty who will be 32 shortly after the 1990 season begins. He had pitched in six scattered major league seasons, with little success, until last year. A 15-5 year at Albuquerque in 1988 revived some major league interest in him, but Krueger looked like he'd be stuck in Triple A when the Brewers signed him to a minor league contract on April 1, after he was released by the Pittsburgh Pirates. Krueger got a little lucky. Before April was over, he was called up to replace Paul Mirabella, who went on the disabled list with a shoulder injury. Krueger ended up pitching very well as a lefthanded long reliever.

He made five starts, but was most effective when he was called on in the early innings to hold an opponent and keep a game from getting out of hand. He ended up pitching in 34 games and turned in some very good numbers, including a 3-2 record and 3.84 ERA. He gave up a respectable 96 hits in 93 2/3 innings while recording 72 strikeouts and walking only 33. Opponents batted .264 against him.

Krueger throws an average fastball, a big breaking curveball and a slider. The curve is especially effective against lefthanded hitters and it makes his fastball seem to have better velocity. Krueger has bounced around a little bit, but he has good knowledge of pitching and knows how to set up hitters.

FIELDING:

Krueger has a good move to first base, but his big breaking ball will give runners an edge if they guess right. He's an average fielder, and his follow through leaves him in good position to handle balls back to the mound. His fundamentals are good.

OVERALL:

Signing Krueger turned out to be a very good move for the Brewers, whose pitching staff was decimated by injuries. If everybody is healthy next season, however, he will have to battle to make the team in spring training. He won't be the ace of anyone's staff, but he will eat up a lot of innings for you in long relief and do a good job of holding the score down.

BILL KRUEGER

Position: RP/SP
Bats: L **Throws:** L
Ht: 6' 5" **Wt:** 210

Opening Day Age: 31
Born: 4/24/58 in Waukegan, IL
ML Seasons: 7

Overall Statistics

	W	L	ERA	G	GS	Sv	IP	H	R	BB	SO	HR
1989	3	2	3.84	34	5	3	93.2	96	43	33	72	9
Career	30	33	4.44	132	72	4	541.1	577	324	264	262	42

Where They Hit the Ball

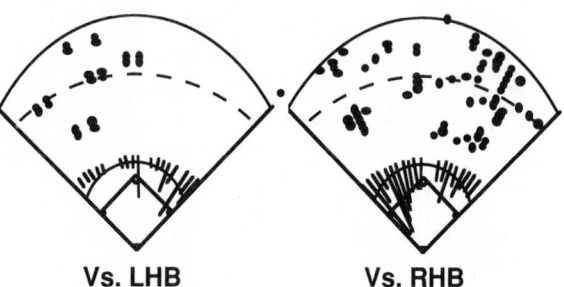

Vs. LHB   **Vs. RHB**

1989 Situational Stats

	W	L	ERA	Sv	IP		AB	H	HR	RBI	AVG
Home	2	2	3.61	1	47.1	LHB	94	21	0	6	.223
Road	1	0	4.08	2	46.1	RHB	270	75	9	39	.278
Day	1	0	3.97	0	11.1	Sc Pos	106	26	2	34	.245
Night	2	2	3.83	3	82.1	Clutch	33	7	0	0	.212

1989 Rankings (American League)

➡ 9th in wild pitches (10)
➡ Led the Brewers in wild pitches

HITTING:

Paul Molitor was dubbed "The Ignitor" early in his career, and the description is a good one. When Molitor gets on base, the Brewers have a good chance of scoring a run.

He has been a lead-off hitter for most of his career and has been more successful in the number one spot. Unlike the textbook leadoff hitters, he is an aggressive hitter and does not look for a walk. He is a notorious first-pitch fastball hitter, which can make him susceptible to a good slider.

Molitor always scores a lot of runs but doesn't get the opportunity to drive many in. He usually doesn't hit well with runners in scoring position, though he did hit .328 in 1989. He has struggled at times when used in the number three spot in the batting order, but went on a 19-game hitting streak when used there at the end of last year. Molitor has some power but is mostly a line drive hitter who sprays the ball around. He is extremely quick and will wait on a pitch until the last moment. Because of his speed, Molitor is always a threat to bunt for a hit.

BASERUNNING:

In some polls of American League managers, Molitor was named the best baserunner in the league. He doesn't steal as many bases as Rickey Henderson, but always has a high success ratio when he does run. He is quick, has good instincts, and excels at turning singles into doubles and taking the extra base.

FIELDING:

Molitor is a good athlete and can play almost any position, although he has been used primarily as a third baseman since 1982. He has good hands and range, but has had problems throwing since undergoing reconstructive surgery of his right elbow in 1984. Most of his errors have been throwing errors, and he occasionally has to be used as designated hitter to give his arm a rest. Molitor might move back to second base in 1990 if Jim Gantner is unable to come back from a knee injury.

OVERALL:

Frequent injuries throughout his career have probably kept Molitor from becoming one of the dominating players in the game, but he is still a very good one. Although he was able to avoid any major injuries in 1989, he still had his share of nagging aches and pains and he stole only 27 bases, down from 41 in 1988. Eventually, his fragile body may force him to become a full-time designated hitter.

PAUL MOLITOR

Position: 3B/DH/2B
Bats: R **Throws:** R
Ht: 6' 0" **Wt:** 175

Opening Day Age: 33
Born: 8/22/56 in St. Paul, MN
ML Seasons: 12

Overall Statistics

	G	AB	R	H	D	T	HR	RBI	SB	BB	SO	AVG
1989	155	615	84	194	35	4	11	56	27	64	67	.315
Career	1437	5828	989	1751	310	60	119	581	344	568	703	.300

Where He Hits the Ball

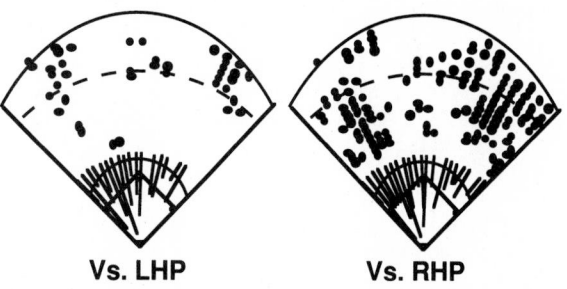

Vs. LHP   **Vs. RHP**

1989 Situational Stats

	AB	H	HR	RBI	AVG		AB	H	HR	RBI	AVG
Home	296	97	6	28	.328	LHP	157	51	4	13	.325
Road	319	97	5	28	.304	RHP	458	143	7	43	.312
Day	206	70	1	17	.340	Sc Pos	119	39	2	46	.328
Night	409	124	10	39	.303	Clutch	69	22	1	4	.319

1989 Rankings (American League)

- ➡ 5th in hits (194)
- ➡ 6th in batting average (.315), singles (144), times on base (262) and plate appearances (696)
- ➡ 8th in doubles (35)
- ➡ 9th in stolen bases (27)
- ➡ Led the Brewers in at bats (615), singles, stolen bases, walks (64), grounder/flyball ratio (1.48), lowest percent of swings that missed (13.2%) and steals of third (5)
- ➡ Led AL Third Basemen in sacrifice flies (9) and hitting in the clutch (.319) - *third basemen with 50 PA in the clutch*

PITCHING:

Going into the 1989 season, the Brewers saw Jaime Navarro as a talented young pitcher who would play a big role in their future. For Navarro, the future turned out to be now. In just his third professional season, Navarro started out with El Paso of the Texas League and quickly earned a promotion to Denver of the American Association. By the middle of June, he was in the Brewers' starting rotation. The Brewers hadn't planned to rush him that fast, but with Juan Nieves, Bill Wegman, Mike Birkbeck and Bryan Clutterbuck on the disabled list, they needed starting pitching. Navarro had one of the best arms available. When he arrived, his performance showed that he wasn't out of his element. Navarro finished the season with a 7-8 record and a very impressive 3.12 ERA. His won-lost record was misleading. In his first six losses, the Brewers didn't score a run for him while he was in the ball game. With any kind of support, he could have been a big winner.

Navarro has an outstanding fastball, which is his main pitch. He also throws a breaking ball and a changeup. The breaking ball was only marginal when he was first called up, but it was much improved by the end of the season after working with pitching coach Chuck Hartenstein. Late in the season, he had enough confidence in the breaking ball to throw it when he was behind in the count.

Navarro's composure was also impressive. He wasn't overawed by any of the hitters and wasn't afraid to challenge them. Although his fastball is in the 90-mph range, Navarro didn't strike out a lot of hitters, letting them put the ball in play and giving his defense a chance to take care of things. His control was good. He walked only 32.

FIELDING:

Navarro is a good athlete and handles himself well on defense. He gets off the mound quickly to field bunts or ground balls around the mound. His pickoff move is only average, and he will have to work on holding runners on first base.

OVERALL:

Navarro is way ahead of schedule and should have a bright future. The improvement in his breaking ball after he joined the Brewers shows that he is willing to learn. He has the arm and the ability to become a big winner in the near future.

JAIME NAVARRO

Position: SP
Bats: R **Throws:** R
Ht: 6' 4" **Wt:** 210

Opening Day Age: 23
Born: 3/27/67 in Bayamon, Puerto Rico
ML Seasons: 1

Overall Statistics

	W	L	ERA	G	GS	Sv	IP	H	R	BB	SO	HR
1989	7	8	3.12	19	17	0	109.2	119	47	32	56	6
Career	7	8	3.12	19	17	0	109.2	119	47	32	56	6

Where They Hit the Ball

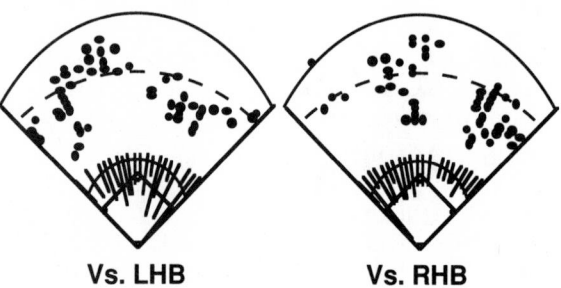

Vs. LHB   **Vs. RHB**

1989 Situational Stats

	W	L	ERA	Sv	IP		AB	H	HR	RBI	AVG
Home	6	4	2.82	0	67.0	LHB	194	53	2	12	.273
Road	1	4	3.59	0	42.2	RHB	236	66	4	26	.280
Day	3	5	2.93	0	46.0	Sc Pos	96	27	0	28	.281
Night	4	3	3.25	0	63.2	Clutch	26	10	1	3	.385

1989 Rankings (American League)

➡ Did not rank near the top or bottom in any category

HITTING:

Charlie O'Brien's forte is his defense, and any hitting the Brewers get out of him is a bonus. It turned out that they got a big bonus from him in 1989. His overall average of .234 was hardly spectacular, but O'Brien was one of the team's top hitters in key situations. He batted .380 with runners in scoring position.

O'Brien is a spray hitter with only occasional power. He did hit six home runs in 188 at-bats, however, and three of them came with runners on base. Early in the season, he was used almost exclusively against left-handed pitchers but ended up starting most of the time late in the season because of his defensive ability and skill at handling pitchers. He had his problems hitting against righthanders, however.

O'Brien makes good contact and doesn't strike out a lot, making him an effective hitter in hit-and-run situations. He also is a good bunter and shared the team lead with Jim Gantner with eight sacrifice bunts.

BASERUNNING:

O'Brien runs like a catcher, which means he's not going to be running wild on the basepaths. He did not attempt to steal a base in 1989, the only player on the team who was not called on to run. He also won't stretch many singles into doubles and won't be called on to go from first to third on a routine single.

FIELDING:

For the last few years, everybody has been talking about B. J. Surhoff as one of the game's next star catchers. By the end of the 1989 season, however, O'Brien was doing most of the catching for the Brewers. That says a lot about O'Brien's defense. He has strong and accurate arm for cutting down would-be base stealers and handles himself extremely well behind the plate. He has good hands and does an excellent job of blocking balls in the dirt. Just as important, he knows the hitters and his pitchers; he calls an excellent game behind the plate.

OVERALL:

O'Brien will be a valuable guy to have around for several years because of his defensive ability. He will never be a big hitter, but his defense is strong enough for him to start on many teams that have line-ups full of heavy hitters. With Surhoff around and expected to improve offensively and defensively, however, O'Brien probably will be the back-up catcher again with the Brewers.

CHARLIE O'BRIEN

Position: C
Bats: R **Throws:** R
Ht: 6' 2" **Wt:** 190

Opening Day Age: 29
Born: 5/1/60 in Tulsa, OK
ML Seasons: 4

Overall Statistics

	G	AB	R	H	D	T	HR	RBI	SB	BB	SO	AVG
1989	62	188	22	44	10	0	6	35	0	21	11	.234
Career	128	352	39	80	20	1	8	45	0	33	34	.227

Where He Hits the Ball

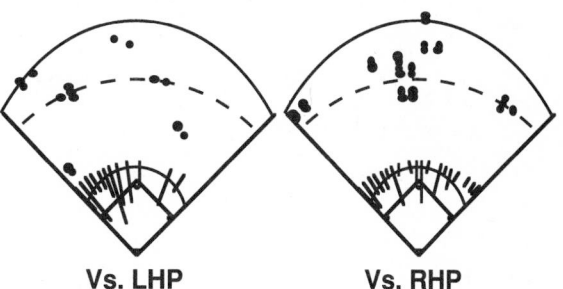

Vs. LHP   **Vs. RHP**

1989 Situational Stats

	AB	H	HR	RBI	AVG		AB	H	HR	RBI	AVG
Home	90	22	4	14	.244	LHP	89	22	3	9	.247
Road	98	22	2	21	.224	RHP	99	22	3	26	.222
Day	68	15	3	14	.221	Sc Pos	50	19	3	30	.380
Night	120	29	3	21	.242	Clutch	12	3	0	1	.250

1989 Rankings (American League)

- ➡ 2nd in hit by pitch (9)
- ➡ 7th in most GDPs per GDP situation (21.2%) - *batters with 50 PA in GDP situations*
- ➡ Led the Brewers in sacrifice flies (8)
- ➡ Led AL Catchers in sacrifice bunts (8) and hit by pitch

STOPPER

PITCHING:

Dan Plesac has only been the Milwaukee Brewers' closer for three seasons, but he's already the most successful short reliever in the team's history. OK, so the Brewers had some pretty lean years in the bullpen for much of their history. Rollie Fingers, the most successful reliever in the history of the game, finished his career in Milwaukee, winning an MVP award in the process. Ken Sanders was the American League's fireman of the year in the Brewers' second season in Milwaukee. Plesac wiped both names out of the team's record book in 1989. He saved 33 games, to break Sanders' record of 31, set in 1971. And he increased his four- year total to 100, topping Fingers' team record of 97. He also pitched in his third straight All-Star Game.

The tall lefthander doesn't try to fool anybody when he walks to the mound. Hitters know what they're going to get -- hard stuff. Plesac is going to throw them either a 95-mph fastball or a wicked slider. "Here it is, gentlemen, try to hit it!" More often than not, they don't. Plesac's fastball is not just fast, but moves a lot also. He mixes it up with his hard slider, which takes a wicked break as it reaches the plate. As hard as he throws, Plesac doesn't need pinpoint control, but he throws strikes and rarely gets himself in trouble by walking someone.

FIELDING:

Plesac's follow-through doesn't leave him in the best position to field a ball, and he will have trouble getting to a ball hit to the first-base side of the mound. That isn't really important. He's a strikeout pitcher and isn't looking for a ground ball when he walks onto the mound. He has a good pickoff move but normally pays more attention to the hitter than to the baserunners.

OVERALL:

Plesac already had established himself as an outstanding closer, but there were questions about his durability going into the 1989 season. He had missed most of the final month of the season in both 1987 and '88 because of injuries, and there were rumors that his arm couldn't hold up in the role of a closer. He squelched those rumors with an injury-free season. If the Brewers' offense can give him a few more leads to protect, look for him to add another 10 saves to his club record for a single season.

DAN PLESAC

Position: RP
Bats: L **Throws:** L
Ht: 6' 5" **Wt:** 210

Opening Day Age: 28
Born: 2/4/62 in Gary, IN
ML Seasons: 4

Overall Statistics

	W	L	ERA	G	GS	Sv	IP	H	R	BB	SO	HR
1989	3	4	2.35	52	0	33	61.1	47	16	17	52	6
Career	19	19	2.63	210	0	100	284.0	237	94	81	268	21

Where They Hit the Ball

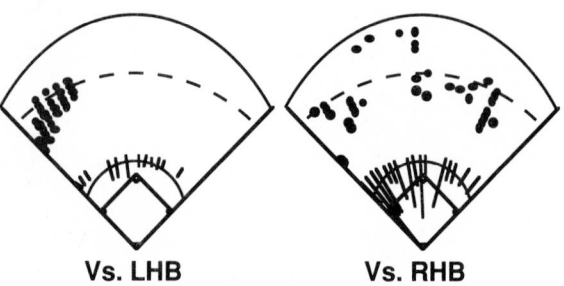

Vs. LHB   **Vs. RHB**

1989 Situational Stats

	W	L	ERA	Sv	IP		AB	H	HR	RBI	AVG
Home	2	1	1.89	15	33.1	LHB	47	11	1	10	.234
Road	1	3	2.89	18	28.0	RHB	174	36	5	18	.207
Day	1	0	0.37	12	24.1	Sc Pos	68	16	2	23	.235
Night	2	4	3.65	21	37.0	Clutch	165	37	6	28	.224

1989 Rankings (American League)

➡ 3rd in saves (33)

➡ 5th in save opportunities (40)

➡ 6th in save percentage (82.5%) and blown saves (7) - *pitchers with 20 save opportunites*

➡ 9th in games finished (51)

➡ Led the Brewers in saves, games finished, save percentage and blown saves

HITTING:

Gus Polidor is one of those players whose glove keeps him in the major leagues. As a hitter, he's not much of a threat. Polidor is a slap hitter with no power, but he will make contact and doesn't strike out very much. He bunts well and can be counted on to sacrifice to move a runner up. Righthanded pitchers will have success by jamming him with pitches on his fists. He is an impatient hitter who is up there swinging and does not draw a lot of walks.

Polidor's role as a utility infielder probably has had an adverse affect on his hitting. He has hit well in the minor leagues, batting .285 at Edmonton in 1985 and .300 for the same club a year later. He even belted 5 homers and drove in 61 runs in '86. Unfortunately, Polidor rarely has had a chance to play regularly in the major leagues. He had his most success in 1987, when he was with the California Angels. He played every day for almost two months when shortstop Dick Schofield was injured and ended up batting .263 in 63 games that season.

BASERUNNING:

In nine years in professional baseball, Polidor's highest total of stolen bases was seven for Edmonton of the Pacific Coast League in 1986. It's obvious that he doesn't run much, but he was successful in all three of his attempts last season with the Brewers. Overall, he runs the bases well and will not make a lot of mistakes.

FIELDING:

Polidor was used all over the infield last season, but his best position is shortstop. He has a strong arm and does a good job of chasing down balls hit into the hole. He also handles himself well at second and third and is a reliable backup at either of those positions. If he could hit a little better, he could be a steady starting shortstop for some team.

OVERALL:

Because of his weak bat, Polidor isn't likely to make anybody's starting line-up, but he is a good man to have on the bench. His ability to play more than one position increases his value as a utility infielder.

GUS POLIDOR

Position: 2B/3B/SS
Bats: R **Throws:** R
Ht: 6' 0" **Wt:** 184

Opening Day Age: 28
Born: 10/26/61 in Caracas, Venezuela
ML Seasons: 5

Overall Statistics

	G	AB	R	H	D	T	HR	RBI	SB	BB	SO	AVG
1989	79	175	15	34	7	0	0	14	3	6	18	.194
Career	204	413	33	88	14	0	2	34	3	12	44	.213

Where He Hits the Ball

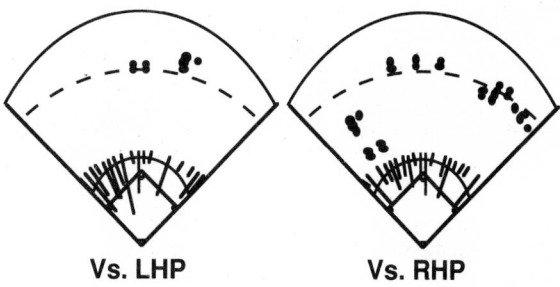

Vs. LHP   **Vs. RHP**

1989 Situational Stats

	AB	H	HR	RBI	AVG		AB	H	HR	RBI	AVG
Home	81	21	0	10	.259	LHP	85	15	0	10	.176
Road	94	13	0	4	.138	RHP	90	19	0	4	.211
Day	63	13	0	5	.206	Sc Pos	42	12	0	14	.286
Night	112	21	0	9	.188	Clutch	21	6	0	1	.286

1989 Rankings (American League)

➡ Did not rank near the top or bottom in any category

HITTING:

Gary Sheffield was almost everybody's pre-season choice for American League rookie of the year. It didn't work out that way. The young shortstop had problems at the plate and in the field and was farmed out to Denver shortly after the All-Star Game. While he was at Denver, it was discovered that he had been playing with a broken bone in his foot, and he was placed on the Brewers' disabled list. Sheffield returned to action in September and finished with a .247 batting average, five home runs and 32 RBIs. He batted only .219 with runners in scoring position.

Despite the disappointing season, Sheffield is still an extremely promising hitter. He was only 20 years old during the 1989 season, and a lot was expected of him. Sheffield himself expected a lot more. Although his numbers were not impressive, Sheffield gave a lot of indications that he knows what he is doing when he has a bat in his hands. He wasn't intimidated by any pitcher he faced and could get his bat on a good fastball or breaking ball. Sheffield is a line drive hitter who pulls the ball and has good power. You can expect him to hit 20 or more home runs in a season.

BASERUNNING:

Sheffield's speed is above average, and he can be a threat to steal. So far, he's an average baserunner, but he is young and still learning. He has good instincts, is a smart player, and should learn fast.

FIELDING:

Defense is Sheffield's biggest problem. He prefers to play shortstop, but his range is limited and he has trouble starting a double play. Sheffield probably will wind up at third base – especially because it looks like Bill Spiers has earned the starting shortstop job – but he isn't likely to win a Gold Glove there, either. Sheffield's defense needs a lot of work, but it must be remembered that he signed out of high school and was in the major leagues after less than three years in the minor leagues. His biggest asset is his arm, one of the strongest on the Brewers' team.

OVERALL:

Most scouts still predict stardom for Sheffield, who is a nephew of Dwight Gooden of the New York Mets. His immaturity caused a lot of his problems in his rookie season. Early in the season he accused the Brewers' pitchers of not protecting him and expressed unhappiness with the Brewers' organization. Obviously he has a lot of growing up to do.

GARY SHEFFIELD

Position: SS/3B
Bats: R **Throws:** R
Ht: 5'11" **Wt:** 190

Opening Day Age: 21
Born: 11/18/68 in Tampa, FL
ML Seasons: 2

Overall Statistics

	G	AB	R	H	D	T	HR	RBI	SB	BB	SO	AVG
1989	95	368	34	91	18	0	5	32	10	27	33	.247
Career	119	448	46	110	19	0	9	44	13	34	40	.246

Where He Hits the Ball

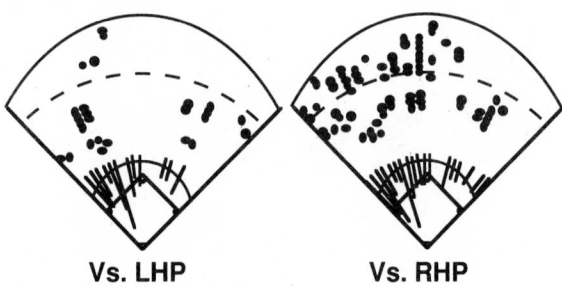

Vs. LHP   **Vs. RHP**

1989 Situational Stats

	AB	H	HR	RBI	AVG		AB	H	HR	RBI	AVG
Home	198	51	2	12	.258	LHP	113	33	3	14	.292
Road	170	40	3	20	.235	RHP	255	58	2	18	.227
Day	146	33	1	9	.226	Sc Pos	96	21	0	26	.219
Night	222	58	4	23	.261	Clutch	56	14	1	5	.250

1989 Rankings (American League)

➡ 10th in least GDPs per GDP situation (4.7%)
 - *batters with 50 PA in GDP situations*

HITTING:

Bill Spiers got a surprise a few days after the Brewers sent him to their minor-league camp during spring training. He was called back to the major-league camp and ended up winning a spot on the opening day roster. By midseason, he had won the starting shortstop job. Don't expect anyone to take it away for a long time.

Spiers is a line-drive hitter who uses the whole playing field. Although he has not been a big home run threat so far, scouts expect him to contribute more than an occasional long ball as he develops. Although Spiers's .255 batting average is respectable for a rookie shortstop, it is misleading. He was batting just .229 in June when he wasn't playing much and the Brewers sent him on a brief trip to Denver to get more playing time. His average climbed considerably when he started playing on a regular basis.

The Brewers used Spiers as a leadoff hitter late in the season, and he seemed to thrive in that spot. His average jumped from .233 to his final .255 after he moved to the top spot. Spiers had problems in clutch situations, but that should improve with maturity.

BASERUNNING:

Spiers stole 10 bases and was only caught twice, so he obviously has good speed and the ability to get a good jump on a pitcher. He undoubtedly will do more running when he gets more experience and gets to know the pitchers better. He gets out of the batter's box quickly and will take the extra base.

FIELDING:

Spiers made his biggest impression with his defense. He has excellent range and a rifle arm. He goes into the hole well, but his most impressive play is cutting off balls hit up the middle. He makes the play behind second base better than any Milwaukee shortstop since Robin Yount's shoulder problems forced his move to the outfield. Also impressive is his ability to make a strong, accurate throw while running or off balance.

OVERALL:

A lot of people couldn't understand why the Brewers used their No. 1 pick to select a shortstop in the first round of the 1987 draft, just a year after selecting Gary Sheffield, also a shortstop. Spiers answered that question less than three years later. Although he was rushed to the major leagues, Spiers impressed everyone with his defensive play. In the coming years, he probably will impress them with his hitting as well.

BILL SPIERS

Position: SS
Bats: L **Throws:** R
Ht: 6' 2" **Wt:** 190

Opening Day Age: 23
Born: 6/5/66 in Orangeburg, SC
ML Seasons: 1

Overall Statistics

	G	AB	R	H	D	T	HR	RBI	SB	BB	SO	AVG
1989	114	345	44	88	9	3	4	33	10	21	63	.255
Career	114	345	44	88	9	3	4	33	10	21	63	.255

Where He Hits the Ball

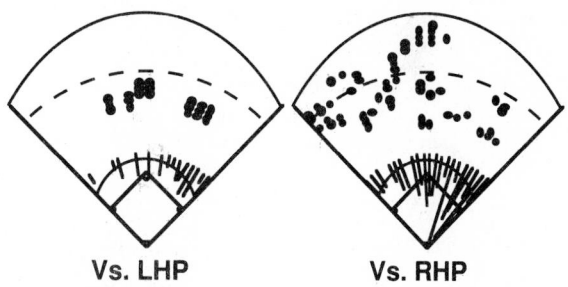

Vs. LHP   Vs. RHP

1989 Situational Stats

	AB	H	HR	RBI	AVG		AB	H	HR	RBI	AVG
Home	172	47	1	17	.273	LHP	70	19	1	9	.271
Road	173	41	3	16	.237	RHP	275	69	3	24	.251
Day	126	33	2	12	.262	Sc Pos	83	23	1	29	.277
Night	219	55	2	21	.251	Clutch	50	12	0	2	.240

1989 Rankings (American League)

➡ 5th in least GDPs per GDP situation (3.6%) - *players with 50 PA in GDP situations*

➡ 6th in errors (21)

➡ Led the Brewers in least GDPs per GDP situation and errors

HITTING:

The Brewers selected catcher B. J. Surhoff as the first pick in the 1985 draft, and most scouts agreed that they had made the right choice. That pick looked even better two years later, when Surhoff batted .299 as a rookie in 1987. Since then, Surhoff's career has been in a steady decline and Brewers fans are asking why they didn't pick Will Clark, the No. 2 pick who has become one of the game's biggest stars for the San Francisco Giants.

Surhoff is a line-drive spray hitter with occasional power. He hits pitches up in the strike zone, and pitchers have been getting him out by keeping the ball low the last two seasons. He doesn't strike out a lot, but he has had difficulty making consistent solid contact for the last two seasons. This has led to extensive slumps. A lefthanded hitter, he actually had a higher average against lefties last season although he was used mostly against righthanders in the last half of the season.

Surhoff is an excellent bunter and will bunt for a base hit. In his rookie year, he won a game in the ninth inning by driving in a run with a two-out bunt against the Yankees' Dave Righetti.

BASERUNNING:

Surhoff has exceptional speed for a catcher and is always a threat to run. His total of 14 steals in '89 was down quite a bit from his high of 21 in 1988, however. He is a heady runner who will take the extra base and has enough speed to challenge an outfielder's arm.

FIELDING:

Surhoff has tremendous agility and quickness to go with good hands and a strong arm. Some scouts have said that his play behind the plate is similar to the way a shortstop plays his position, which would figure since Surhoff played a lot of shortstop in college. But despite his athletic ability and talent, Surhoff's throwing has been erratic, and he's also had some problems handling pitchers.

OVERALL:

Surhoff has so much ability that his last two seasons shouldn't be an accurate gauge of what he can do. He is only 25 years old and should get better both offensively and defensively. Some observers believe that Surhoff tends to get down on himself, which affects his play. Scouts still predict that he will soon be the best catcher in the American League.

B.J. SURHOFF

Position: C/DH
Bats: L **Throws:** R
Ht: 6' 1" **Wt:** 190

Opening Day Age: 25
Born: 8/4/64 in Bronx, NY
ML Seasons: 3

Overall Statistics

	G	AB	R	H	D	T	HR	RBI	SB	BB	SO	AVG
1989	126	436	42	108	17	4	5	55	14	25	29	.248
Career	380	1324	139	347	60	7	17	161	46	92	108	.262

Where He Hits the Ball

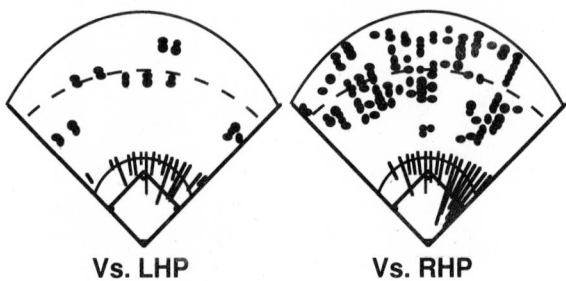

Vs. LHP   **Vs. RHP**

1989 Situational Stats

	AB	H	HR	RBI	AVG		AB	H	HR	RBI	AVG
Home	213	51	3	29	.239	LHP	84	26	2	17	.310
Road	223	57	2	26	.256	RHP	352	82	3	38	.233
Day	142	38	2	14	.268	Sc Pos	97	26	2	48	.268
Night	294	70	3	41	.238	Clutch	70	19	1	10	.271

1989 Rankings (American League)

- → Worst stolen base percentage (53.8%) - *players with 20 stolen base attempts*
- → 2nd in hitting with the bases loaded (.625) - *players with 10 PA with the bases loaded*
- → 3rd lowest on-base average vs. righthanded pitchers (.281) - *batters with 377 PA vs. RHP*
- → 4th lowest slugging percentage vs. righthanded pitchers (.313) - *batters with 377 PA vs. RHP*
- → Led the Brewers in sacrifice flies (10), caught stealing (12) and hitting with the bases loaded
- → Led AL Catchers in triples (4), sacrifice flies, stolen bases (14), caught stealing, steals of third (3) and hitting with the bases loaded

HITTING:

Robin Yount may be one of baseball's most under-rated players as far as the fans are concerned. As far as opposing players are concerned, the Brewers' centerfielder is one of the most respected players in baseball. There is good reason.

Yount is a patient hitter who waits for his pitch and is capable of driving it to any part of the ball park. He likes the ball inside and low; he'll chase an occasional breaking ball, but he has no real weakness. Although he is basically a line-drive hitter, he has enough power to hit 15-20 home runs a year. He hits for a high average against lefthanders or righthanders and is an excellent run-producer. He batted over .300 in 1989 for the fourth straight season and seventh in his career. He drove in more than 100 runs for the third time.

Yount is an excellent bunter and has the speed to bunt for a base hit, but will usually be swinging away because he is the best hitter in a weak line-up.

BASERUNNING:

Yount has good speed and has a high success rate as a base stealer, although he doesn't run that often. He is a very aggressive baserunner, and is always looking to take the extra base. He is as good as anyone at going from first to third on a routine single.

FIELDING:

Earlier in his career Yount was a Gold Glove-winning shortstop, but had to move to the outfield because of a shoulder injury. He adapted to his new position immediately, running down almost everything with his long, smooth strides. Baserunners took advantage of his weakened shoulder for the first few seasons, but his arm is strong again, and opponents can no longer run at will when the ball is hit to Yount in center field. Just as with his hitting and baserunning, Yount's speed and instincts on defense have made him one of the best outfielders in the league.

OVERALL:

Yount has been an everyday player since he was 18 years old and could finish with some very impressive statistics. He isn't impressed with numbers, however, and has often said he will play the game only as long as it's still fun. At age 34, he was still having fun and played the game as hard as he did as a rookie.

ROBIN YOUNT

Position: CF/DH
Bats: R **Throws:** R
Ht: 6' 0" **Wt:** 180

Opening Day Age: 34
Born: 9/16/55 in Danville, IL
ML Seasons: 16

Overall Statistics

	G	AB	R	H	D	T	HR	RBI	SB	BB	SO	AVG
1989	160	614	101	195	38	9	21	103	19	63	71	.318
Career	2291	8907	1335	2602	481	111	208	1124	226	737	1008	.292

Where He Hits the Ball

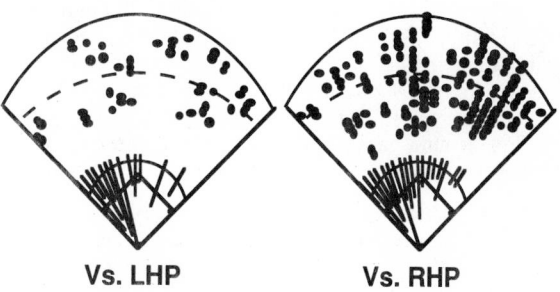

Vs. LHP   **Vs. RHP**

1989 Situational Stats

	AB	H	HR	RBI	AVG		AB	H	HR	RBI	AVG
Home	300	92	14	59	.307	LHP	167	57	6	25	.341
Road	314	103	7	44	.328	RHP	447	138	15	78	.309
Day	208	74	7	35	.356	Sc Pos	152	54	5	78	.355
Night	406	121	14	68	.298	Clutch	83	28	0	17	.337

1989 Rankings (American League)

➡ 2nd in stolen base percentage (86.4%) and total bases (314)

➡ 3rd in runs (101), slugging percentage (.511) and hitting with runners in scoring position (.355)

➡ 4th in batting average (.318), hits (195) and triples (4) - *players with 502 PA*

➡ 5th in doubles (38) and times on base (264)

➡ Led the Brewers in batting average, runs, hits, doubles, triples, total bases , RBI (103), intentional walks (9), times on base, games (160), on-base average (.384), stolen base percentage, hitting with runners in scoring position, slugging percentage and hitting in the clutch (.337)

MIKE BIRKBECK

Position: SP
Bats: R **Throws:** R
Ht: 6' 2" **Wt:** 185

Opening Day Age: 29
Born: 3/10/61 in Orrville, OH
ML Seasons: 4

Overall Statistics

	W	L	ERA	G	GS	Sv	IP	H	R	BB	SO	HR
1989	0	4	5.44	9	9	0	44.2	57	32	22	31	4
Career	12	17	5.12	49	46	0	235.2	285	146	90	133	22

PITCHING & FIELDING:

Mike Birkbeck insists that he is not a breaking-ball pitcher. If he's not, he is in trouble. Although his fastball is a little above average, Birkbeck needs his big breaking ball to be working for any kind of success. In 1989, he didn't have much success at all and was demoted to Denver after going 0-4 with a 5.44 ERA in nine games. Birkbeck spent the rest of the season on the disabled list with a shoulder problem.

When his big breaking ball is working, Birkbeck can be very impressive. The problem is consistency. The only time he pitched well over an extended period was in 1988, when he returned from a brief demotion to Denver and won seven of his first eight decisions. Except for that stretch, he's struggled.

OVERALL:

Birkbeck was supposed to be one of several "promising young arms" the Brewers brought to camp in 1986. The others included Juan Nieves, Dan Plesac and Bill Wegman. Plesac has had a lot of success and Nieves pitched a no-hitter in his second season. Wegman has been steady. Birkbeck is still trying to establish himself. He is running out of time.

BRYAN CLUTTERBUCK

Position: SP
Bats: R **Throws:** R
Ht: 6' 4" **Wt:** 223

Opening Day Age: 30
Born: 12/17/59 in Detroit, MI
ML Seasons: 2

Overall Statistics

	W	L	ERA	G	GS	Sv	IP	H	R	BB	SO	HR
1989	2	5	4.14	14	11	0	67.1	73	39	16	29	11
Career	2	6	4.21	34	11	0	124.0	141	71	32	67	19

PITCHING & FIELDING:

Bryan Clutterbuck appeared to have triumphed in his comeback attempt from one career-threatening injury when he was felled by another. After undergoing surgery to reconstruct his elbow in 1987, Clutterbuck won a spot on the pitching staff last year and turned out to be one of the Brewers' most consistent starters early in the season. Before he had time to celebrate, he injured his shoulder and was sidelined for the rest of the season. A sinker/slider pitcher who battles the hitters, Clutterbuck is aggressive and thrives on competition. Best of all, he throws strikes. He is an average fielder with a good move towards first base. Although Clutterbuck is a big man, he will get off the mound in a hurry on a bunt and to cover first base.

OVERALL:

Clutterbuck doesn't have the greatest ability, but he is a battler. After watching him battle back from the elbow surgery, the Brewers aren't likely to give up on him now. He can be a valuable pitcher because he can be used as a starter or out of the bullpen. Clutterbuck doesn't care which way they use him. He just likes to pitch.

TOM
FILER

Position: SP
Bats: R **Throws:** R
Ht: 6' 1" **Wt:** 198

Opening Day Age: 33
Born: 12/1/56 in
Philadelphia, PA
ML Seasons: 4

Overall Statistics

	W	L	ERA	G	GS	Sv	IP	H	R	BB	SO	HR
1989	7	3	3.61	13	13	0	72.1	74	30	23	20	6
Career	20	13	4.27	51	46	0	263.1	270	130	92	98	25

PITCHING & FIELDING:

Tom Filer opened the 1989 season at Denver. That was in part because of a shoulder injury that bothered him at the end of '88, but Filer came back up to post a 7-3 record in 13 starts for the Brewers. Filer is a sinker/slider pitcher with good control. He keeps the ball down and gets a lot of outs on ground balls. Many of those ground balls go through the infield for singles, but many are also turned into double plays. Opponents batted .271 against him in '89. He's a smart pitcher who won't beat himself. He's also a good athlete who fields his position well and has a decent move to first.

OVERALL:

Although his injuries have limited him to less than three full seasons in the major leagues, Filer is a versatile, smart veteran who can be used as a starter or in middle relief; that makes him a good guy to have around. His injuries have taken away what could have been his most productive seasons, but he can be a steady contributor for a few more years.

JERRY
REUSS

Position: SP
Bats: L **Throws:** L
Ht: 6' 5" **Wt:** 227

Opening Day Age: 40
Born: 6/19/49 in St. Louis, MO
ML Seasons: 21

Overall Statistics

	W	L	ERA	G	GS	Sv	IP	H	R	BB	SO	HR
1989	9	9	5.13	30	26	0	140.1	171	88	34	40	19
Career	220	191	3.64	624	546	11	3661.0	3726	1697	1124	1906	244

PITCHING & FIELDING:

The Brewers picked up Jerry Reuss in late July from the White Sox to aid the pennant drive, but Reuss was slowed by a nagging hamstring injury and won only one game for his new club. Since Reuss will be 41 in 1990 and had an ERA of over 5.00 last year, it might seem that the end is near for him. But Reuss has been in the same position several times before and has always bounced back. When healthy, he keeps his good cut fastball in on the hands of righthanded hitters; that sets up his slow curve and change-up. The mixture requires pinpoint control, and when he has it, Reuss can breeze through a game in 90 pitches. But there's little middle ground; when Reuss isn't on his game, he's usually gone early. Reuss helps his cause by being a good fielder, and his move to first is outstanding.

OVERALL:

While no Nolan Ryan, Reuss still has enough stuff to be a winning major league pitcher if healthy. He keeps himself in excellent shape, and his playful manner is an asset in any clubhouse.

ED
ROMERO

Position: 2B/3B
Bats: R **Throws:** R
Ht: 5'11" **Wt:** 180

Opening Day Age: 32
Born: 12/9/57 in
Santurce, Puerto Rico
ML Seasons: 11

Overall Statistics

	G	AB	R	H	D	T	HR	RBI	SB	BB	SO	AVG
1989	68	182	18	39	8	0	1	10	0	7	17	.214
Career	698	1842	210	457	76	1	8	151	9	134	155	.248

HITTING, FIELDING, BASERUNNING:

Ed Romero has had a successful major league career because of his ability to play several defensive positions in a backup role. Romero thinks of himself as a hitter. Occasionally, a television camera would pan the dugout and catch Romero with an imaginary bat in his hands, poised and ready to swing. He's not a bad hitter, averaging over .250 for most of his career. He's a good contact hitter who makes sure he gets in his hacks. His real value is his defense. He's a good backup shortstop with good hands and a very strong arm, and more than adequate at second or third. He can even fill in as an outfielder. He does not have great speed and has never been a big threat to steal.

OVERALL:

Romero, who is 32, is still an adequate infielder, and his arm is still strong. He ended up wearing a Brewers uniform again because of injuries to Jim Gantner and Billy Bates, but isn't likely to be around in 1990. It's not that he can't still do the job defensively, but he has been around long enough to command a fairly high salary. Most teams will be looking for someone younger -- and cheaper.

TOP PROSPECT

GREG
VAUGHN

Position: LF/DH
Bats: R **Throws:** R
Ht: 6'1" **Wt:** 175

Opening Day Age: 24
Born: 7/3/65 in
Oklahoma City, OK
ML Seasons: 1

Overall Statistics

	G	AB	R	H	D	T	HR	RBI	SB	BB	SO	AVG
1989	38	113	18	30	3	0	5	23	4	13	23	.265
Career	38	113	18	30	3	0	5	23	4	13	23	.265

HITTING, FIELDING, BASERUNNING:

Greg Vaughn had some excellent numbers in the minor leagues, and a lot was expected of him when the Brewers called him up in August. In 38 games, Vaughn was impressive, hitting for power and excelling in pressure situations. Pitchers learned in a hurry that they couldn't blow him away with a fastball. A good breaking ball will give him some problems, but he will hammer a mistake. He is strong enough to fight off an inside pitch when pitchers try to jam him. Vaughn runs the bases well and is a threat to steal. He stole four bases in five attempts after joining the Brewers, and stole 36 bases for Beloit of the Class A Midwest League in 1987. He is a good defensive outfielder who gets a good jump on the ball and has the speed to run a ball down.

OVERALL:

Vaughn isn't the first Brewer rookie to bring along a can't-miss label. Glenn Braggs and B. J. Surhoff haven't made it yet. But Vaughn appears to be the real thing, and his performance at the end of the season probably was good enough to win a starting job in the outfield next season.

BILL
WEGMAN

Position: SP
Bats: R **Throws:** R
Ht: 6' 5" **Wt:** 200

Opening Day Age: 27
Born: 12/19/62 in
Cincinnati, OH
ML Seasons: 5

Overall Statistics

	W	L	ERA	G	GS	Sv	IP	H	R	BB	SO	HR
1989	2	6	6.71	11	8	0	51.0	69	44	21	27	6
Career	34	42	4.62	115	107	0	691.0	739	389	170	301	96

PITCHING & FIELDING:

For his first couple of years, Bill Wegman was known as the Brewers' hard-luck pitcher. Hard luck would have been good luck for him in 1989. He pitched in 11 games before going on the disabled list with a shoulder injury that eventually needed surgery.

Wegman isn't an overpowering pitcher. He has a fastball that is slightly above average, but has to depend upon a good breaking ball and keeping the ball down. He also throws a change-up. Although he isn't a power pitcher, he will attempt to blow the ball past hitters at times, and that gets him into trouble. He is extremely competitive and won't back down from anyone, even when it might be a good idea. Wegman is an exceptional athlete and fields his position as well as anyone. He also has a good move to first.

OVERALL:

Wegman is expected to be fully recovered from his shoulder problems in time for spring training and will be back in the starting rotation next season. He doesn't have the ability to be the ace of a good staff, but he is a solid pitcher who will perform well as a No. 3 or No. 4 starter.

PITCHING:

Rick Aguilera is the most experienced pitcher Minnesota got when Frank Viola was traded to the Mets, and at times he can be overpowering. He throws a 90-mile-per-hour fastball that has a tendency to rise, and also mixes in a split-fingered fastball that's better than average, as well as a curve and slider. He has good stuff, but one thing that might have to change is Aguilera's pitch selection. In the National League, with its bigger stadiums, Aguilera could throw his rising fastball and challenge the hitters to do with it what they could. That won't work in the smaller parks of the American League. The Metrodome turns lazy fly balls to right into home runs and doubles.

With the Mets in 1989, Aguilera was used as a late-inning reliever, either setting up Randy Myers or finishing games when Myers wasn't available. However, Aguilera yearned to return to the starting rotation, and the Twins appear willing to give him that chance. The split-fingered pitch should help Aguilera make the move to a starting role. He's a smart pitcher who doesn't get easily rattled, and those attributes should help him adjust to the American League. Aguilera has always had good control, which allows opponents to dig in and take their cuts unless he makes an effort to back them off the plate. As a starter, he'll do that more often.

Aguilera will also have to build up his arm strength. The Twins were willing to bring him along slowly last year, but now he'll be expected to last into the eighth and ninth innings. He showed earlier in his career that he was capable, and shows no ill effects from the shoulder problems that shortened his 1987 and 1988 seasons.

FIELDING:

Unlike some hard throwers whose follow-through take them off the mound, Aguilera throws easily enough that he's in good position to field -- squared around and facing home plate. He reacts well and has a quick delivery that keeps runners from getting too quick of a jump. His move to first is OK.

OVERALL:

If he can combine skill with good health, Aguilera has the potential to be an important member of the Twins starting staff for years to come. The other option is that he returns to the bullpen as a set-up man or a closer, work the Mets found he was suited for, even if Aguilera didn't care for it.

RICK AGUILERA

Position: RP/SP
Bats: R **Throws:** R
Ht: 6' 5" **Wt:** 200

Opening Day Age: 28
Born: 12/31/61 in San Gabriel, CA
ML Seasons: 5

Overall Statistics

	W	L	ERA	G	GS	Sv	IP	H	R	BB	SO	HR
1989	9	11	2.79	47	11	7	145.0	130	51	38	137	8
Career	40	32	3.53	125	70	7	548.2	546	243	154	408	45

Where They Hit the Ball

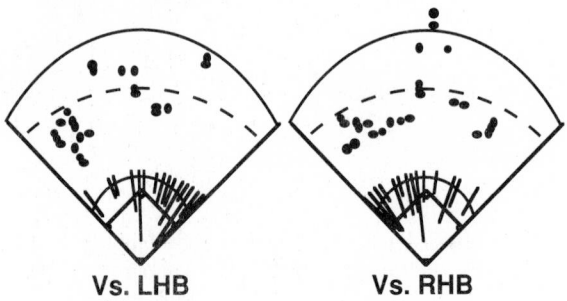

Vs. LHB   **Vs. RHB**

1989 Situational Stats

	W	L	ERA	Sv	IP		AB	H	HR	RBI	AVG
Home	6	5	2.61	3	72.1	LHB	276	71	3	28	.257
Road	3	6	2.97	4	72.2	RHB	269	59	5	27	.219
Day	3	2	2.58	1	59.1	Sc Pos	132	31	2	44	.235
Night	6	9	2.94	6	85.2	Clutch	127	32	3	16	.252

1989 Rankings (American League)

→ Led the Twins in most GDPs per GDP situation (14.3%) - *team players with 30 GDP situations*

STAFF ACE

PITCHING:

With the departure of Frank Viola, Allan Anderson is the acknowledged ace of the Twins staff. Anderson's rise has been meteoric for a pitcher left unprotected on the Twins' major league roster after the 1987 season. Anderson, purchased from Portland in late April, 1988, went 16-9 with a league-leading 2.45 ERA with the Twins. He followed that with a solid 1989, posting a 17-10 record with a 3.80 ERA.

Anderson's personal story should serve as an inspiration to aspiring young pitchers. He was a hard-throwing phenom in high school, drafted in the second round of the 1982 free agent draft. But he suffered an elbow injury in his first professional season, forcing him to make the difficult transformation from power to finesse. Anderson had the good fortune to join the Twins during Viola's Cy Young Award season of 1988. He became a Viola disciple, earning the moniker "Little Frankie" in the Twins clubhouse and, more important, learning the change-up that is the key to Viola's success. When Anderson is on his game, his change-up is in Viola's class. Anderson's fastball is average, but he mixes pitches so effectively that it often appears better than it is. Control is the key. Last year Anderson walked just 53 batters in 196.2 innings. He's not a strikeout pitcher, as evidenced by his 69 whiffs.

Anderson's 1989 season was not without its distressing aspect. Twins officials are befuddled over Anderson's home-road disparity, and what it might mean to the lefthander's future success in the Dome. Anderson struggled at home all season in '89. But there's good reason to believe that the numbers were a one-season aberration. In 1988, Anderson was 9-2 with a 2.29 ERA at home, 7-7, 2.60 ERA on the road.

FIELDING:

Anderson is one of the league's quickest pitchers off the mound. He's a self-made pitcher, a master of technique and that includes defense as well as his move to first.

OVERALL:

Anderson, who turned 26 in January, is a quality pitcher, but he needs to be at the top of his game to keep winning consistently. He is not overpowering enough to get by when his control is even slightly off. He has shown in the past two years that he understands his limitations, and knows what it takes to win. There's no reason he shouldn't be a consistent 15-game winner for years to come.

ALLAN ANDERSON

Position: SP
Bats: L **Throws:** L
Ht: 6' 0" **Wt:** 194

Opening Day Age: 26
Born: 1/7/64 in Lancaster, OH
ML Seasons: 4

Overall Statistics

	W	L	ERA	G	GS	Sv	IP	H	R	BB	SO	HR
1989	17	10	3.80	33	33	0	196.2	214	97	53	69	15
Career	37	25	3.72	88	75	0	495.2	539	236	130	206	43

Where They Hit the Ball

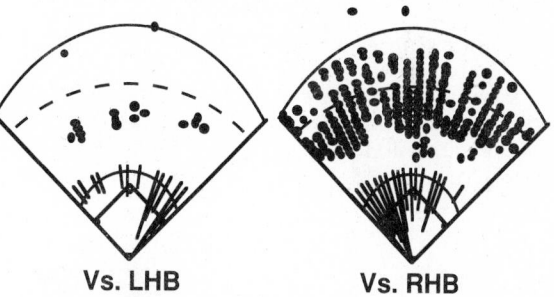

Vs. LHB   **Vs. RHB**

1989 Situational Stats

	W	L	ERA	Sv	IP		AB	H	HR	RBI	AVG
Home	6	5	6.47	0	72.1	LHB	113	31	2	15	.274
Road	11	5	2.24	0	124.1	RHB	664	183	13	71	.276
Day	7	3	2.76	0	75.0	Sc Pos	183	50	1	63	.273
Night	10	7	4.44	0	121.2	Clutch	19	4	1	1	.211

1989 Rankings (American League)

➡ 1st in run support per 9 innings (6.9) and road ERA (2.24) - *pitchers with 81 road IP*

➡ 4th in lowest strikeout rate per 9 innings (3.2) - *pitchers with 162 IP*

➡ 6th in wins (17)

➡ Led the Twins in wins, games started (33), innings (196.2), hits allowed (214), batters faced (846), hit batters (7), pitches thrown (2,948), GDPs induced (22), won/loss percentage (.630), run support per 9 innings, least HRs per 9 innings (.69), GDPs per 9 innings (1.0) and lowest slugging percentage allowed (.395) - *team pitchers with 162 IP*

HITTING:

The Twins obtained Wally Backman, a switch-hitter, with the intention of making him their everyday second baseman. A 1989 season marred by shoulder miseries leaves the jury still out on whether Backman can hit well enough righthanded to fill that role. Backman endured two separate stints on the disabled list last year because of an injury to his right shoulder. When he came off the disabled list for the first time in May, the nagging shoulder woes limited him to batting left-handed.

Backman came to the Twins before the 1989 season with career averages of .306 against right-handed pitchers, .150 against lefthanders. When he did play, Backman showed some signs of being able to hit American League lefthanders. He hit .281 from the right side, although batting just 57 times. But Backman spoiled that by struggling against righties.

Backman is primarily a ground-ball hitter, spraying singles and an occasional double. He likes high pitches when batting from the right side, but prefers low pitches batting lefty. He has a good eye and can draw some walks. He's also an excellent bunter.

BASERUNNING:

Backman combined to steal 62 bases with the Mets in 1984 and 1985. But his running speed has decreased, perhaps due to nagging hamstring problems he experienced in his final years with the Mets. Backman stole just one base with the Twins last year, an accurate portrayal of the threat he posed on the bases.

FIELDING:

Early in the season, Backman's range appeared terribly limited. He was hesitant, but he did exhibit better range after making a late-season return. He made six errors in only 87 games, not a great mark for a second baseman. But his shoulder was largely to blame, because his hands remain steady.

OVERALL:

Backman will have to answer several serious questions in 1990. At age 30, does he have the range to be a quality major league second baseman? And if he proves himself capable in the field, can he hit well enough righthanded to play everyday? Backman remains confident, almost cocky in his ability, and his pesky attitude is a clubhouse plus. But time appears to be running out.

WALLY BACKMAN

Position: 2B
Bats: B **Throws:** R
Ht: 5' 9" **Wt:** 168

Opening Day Age: 30
Born: 9/22/59 in Hillsboro, CA
ML Seasons: 10

Overall Statistics

	G	AB	R	H	D	T	HR	RBI	SB	BB	SO	AVG
1989	87	299	33	69	9	2	1	26	1	32	45	.231
Career	852	2668	392	739	104	16	8	191	107	292	380	.277

Where He Hits the Ball

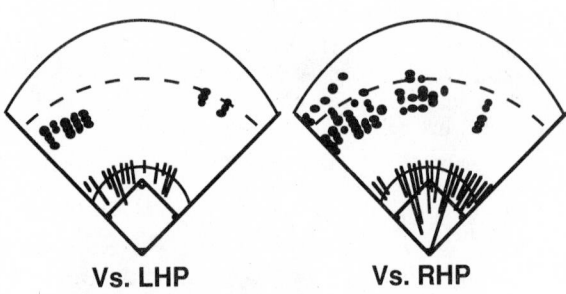

Vs. LHP   **Vs. RHP**

1989 Situational Stats

	AB	H	HR	RBI	AVG		AB	H	HR	RBI	AVG
Home	150	37	0	14	.247	LHP	57	16	0	9	.281
Road	149	32	1	12	.215	RHP	242	53	1	17	.219
Day	89	19	1	6	.213	Sc Pos	71	18	0	24	.254
Night	210	50	0	20	.238	Clutch	33	9	0	2	.273

1989 Rankings (American League)

➡ 5th lowest batting average on a 3-1 count (.167) - *players with 10 PA with a 3-1 count*

PITCHING:

Juan Berenguer still throws his fastball at 90-miles plus, making him a valuable middle-inning set-up man for closer Jeff Reardon. Berenguer, as always, averaged close to a strikeout an inning last year and posted an excellent 9-3 record with three saves.

But the hard-throwing righthander turned 35 in November, and there were signs his days as an overpowering thrower are past. The most distressing stat was that lefthanded batters hit .329 with seven home runs against Berenguer. He walked almost as many lefthanders as he struck out (23 walks, 33 strikeouts). Berenguer was still torture against righthanded batters, who managed a paltry .185 batting average and just four homers. His best pitch remains his fastball. When he's able to control his off-speed pitch -- a nasty split-fingered fastball -- Berenguer is difficult to hit. When lefthanded batters are able to sit on his fastball, however, the numbers speak for themselves.

With the Twins, Berenguer has done a good job of controlling a temper that once wreaked havoc with his concentration on the mound. Berenguer has for the most part stayed in control of himself, decreasing the streaks of wildness for which he was once known. However, Berenguer still draws the ire of opposing hitters for his arm gestures that frequently follows strikeouts. Berenguer is an emotional player, and the Twins have decided they'd rather the emotion come out via an arm salute than a pitch sailing over the backstop.

FIELDING:

At 5-11, 225 pounds, Berenguer looks out of shape. But he fields his position surprisingly well for a hard-thrower. He's grabbed numerous balls that appeared headed up the middle, and although he's no gazelle, he gets to first base fast enough to keep teams from dragging bunts with any degree of success. With his high leg kick, Berenguer has always been easy to steal on.

OVERALL:

Berenguer's disparity between righthanded and lefthanded batters suggest his days as an overpowering pitcher may be behind him. But it may be too early to write him off. As long as his fastball stays in the 90-mile range, and he stays in control of himself, Berenguer is a solid middle reliever.

JUAN BERENGUER

Position: RP
Bats: R **Throws:** R
Ht: 5'11" **Wt:** 223

Opening Day Age: 35
Born: 11/30/54 in Aguadulce, Panama
ML Seasons: 12

Overall Statistics

	W	L	ERA	G	GS	Sv	IP	H	R	BB	SO	HR
1989	9	3	3.48	56	0	3	106.0	96	44	47	93	11
Career	55	49	3.93	343	93	14	963.0	829	463	490	800	92

Where They Hit the Ball

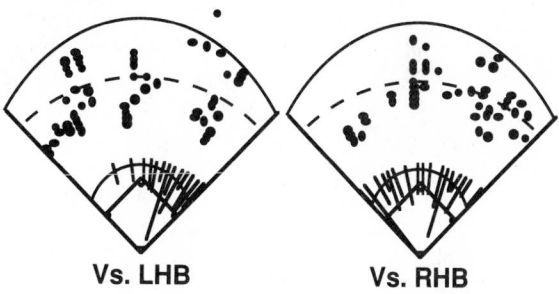

Vs. LHB   **Vs. RHB**

1989 Situational Stats

	W	L	ERA	Sv	IP		AB	H	HR	RBI	AVG
Home	8	2	3.36	2	69.2	LHB	164	54	7	30	.329
Road	1	1	3.72	1	36.1	RHB	227	42	4	23	.185
Day	2	0	5.86	2	27.2	Sc Pos	108	26	2	40	.241
Night	7	3	2.64	1	78.1	Clutch	134	29	4	21	.216

1989 Rankings (American League)

➡ Led the Twins in balks (3), stolen bases allowed (16) and strikeouts per 9 innings (7.9) - *all team players*

HITTING:

Much to his chagrin, Randy Bush has been a platoon player through his entire major-league career. The only time he'll bat against lefthanded pitching is when the manager is reluctant to lift him in mid-game for fear of having to send his replacement against a tough righty reliever in the late innings. Bush has made the most of his platoon opportunities, however, and has gained a reputation as a solid and reliable hitter who can adjust to the situation at hand. Since his rookie season, 1982, he has been in double figures for home runs in every season but one, while never getting more than 400 at-bats. Bush is primarily a fastball hitter, although power pitchers can tie him up with inside heat. He might sometimes look a bit awkward battling off-speed pitches, but he can't be fooled by a steady diet of junk the way some others can.

One change over the years: There was a time when Bush was such a fly ball hitter that he rarely grounded into double plays. In 1989, he was among the team leaders in that category despite his part-time status. Bush has always drawn more than his share of walks.

BASERUNNING:

Bush knows what he's doing on the bases, but doesn't have the speed to do everything that he'd like. He'll steal if given the opportunity, but a pitcher who watches him or a catcher with an accurate arm will keep him from causing much trouble. Bush goes from first to third well, and is more likely to beat a tag with finesse than by trying to overpower the fielder.

FIELDING:

Once exclusively a designated hitter, Bush did well enough as a part-time left fielder to shake the hitting-only label. His range and arm are both OK. He now plays in right field most of the time because there's less ground to cover there at the Metrodome. He also has put in some time at first base and, once again, he's OK.

OVERALL:

Bush has carved himself a solid niche with the Twins as a third or fourth outfielder, back-up first baseman, designated hitter, and pretty good pinch hitter. His talents have developed over the years, although it's unlikely he'll ever improve much over his recent statistics. Other teams have shown interest in Bush, but the Twins have never come close to trading him.

RANDY BUSH

Position: RF/1B/LF
Bats: L **Throws:** L
Ht: 6' 1" **Wt:** 184

Opening Day Age: 31
Born: 10/5/58 in Dover, DE
ML Seasons: 8

Overall Statistics

	G	AB	R	H	D	T	HR	RBI	SB	BB	SO	AVG
1989	141	391	60	103	17	4	14	54	5	48	73	.263
Career	918	2472	335	623	126	24	82	343	32	285	403	.252

Where He Hits the Ball

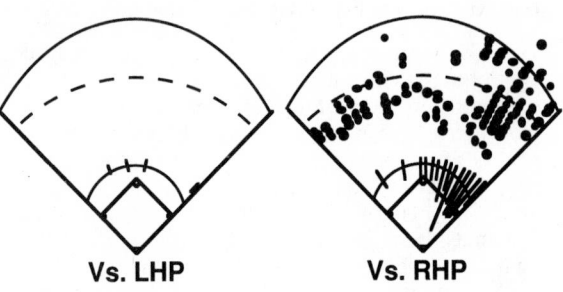

Vs. LHP   **Vs. RHP**

1989 Situational Stats

	AB	H	HR	RBI	AVG		AB	H	HR	RBI	AVG
Home	181	48	6	23	.265	LHP	20	5	0	3	.250
Road	210	55	8	31	.262	RHP	371	98	14	51	.264
Day	111	32	6	15	.288	Sc Pos	95	28	4	40	.295
Night	280	71	8	39	.254	Clutch	57	13	1	5	.228

1989 Rankings (American League)

➥ Led AL Right Fielders in caught stealing (8)

HITTING:

When Carmen Castillo got off to a quick start in his first season with Minnesota, Twin officials were intrigued by the possibility of his shedding his platoon label. No way. This guy can hit lefthanded pitching, and some hard-throwing righthanders, but he has no chance against a righthander with a decent breaking ball. Castillo's former employer, the Cleveland Indians, used him with some success against hard-throwing righthanders like Boston's Roger Clemens. Castillo generally has enough power to make the gamble that he'll connect worthwhile. But after a short trial the Twins decided they could not afford that gamble, and he was quickly shuttled back into a platoon role.

In fairness to Castillo, he was victimized by a variety of injuries that limited his power. He dislocated a finger early in the season, then injured his right shoulder crashing into a fence in mid-season.

BASERUNNING:

Castillo has adequate speed on the bases, but is not considered a threat to run. Castillo stole just one base in three attempts last year. He seldom embarrasses himself with baserunning blunders, which fits into the Twins conservative running game.

FIELDING:

One reason the Twins wanted to look at Castillo as an everyday player is that he's the closest thing to Tom Brunansky in right field that the organization has had since dispatching Brunansky to St. Louis. Castillo has an accurate arm and gets a good jump on the ball. He mastered the Dome's sometimes tricky lighting system, and made a number of eye-opening catches in his first season as a Twin. Castillo played the field with reckless abandon, dislocating a finger trying to make a diving catch and injuring his shoulder crashing into the fence going for another ball.

OVERALL:

If Castillo could only hit righthanded pitching better, he'd have a chance to be an everyday player. He has power and showed last season that he can be an asset in the field. The injuries of last season could prompt Twins officials to take a closer look at Castillo against righthanders next season. But at 31, he's getting a little old to shed labels that are a decade old.

CARMEN CASTILLO

Position: RF
Bats: R **Throws:** R
Ht: 6' 1" **Wt:** 190

Opening Day Age: 31
Born: 6/8/58 in San Francisco de Macoris, Dominican Republic
ML Seasons: 8

Overall Statistics

	G	AB	R	H	D	T	HR	RBI	SB	BB	SO	AVG
1989	94	218	23	56	13	3	8	33	1	15	40	.257
Career	558	1370	179	351	67	7	55	185	15	87	266	.256

Where He Hits the Ball

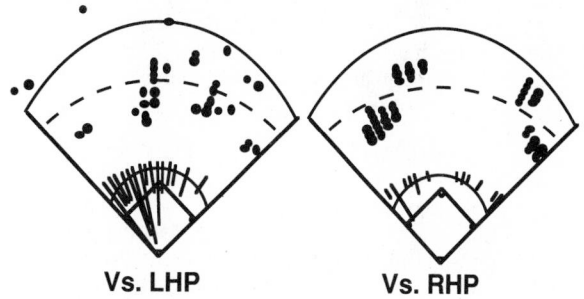

Vs. LHP   **Vs. RHP**

1989 Situational Stats

	AB	H	HR	RBI	AVG		AB	H	HR	RBI	AVG
Home	111	27	2	14	.243	LHP	155	49	8	30	.316
Road	107	29	6	19	.271	RHP	63	7	0	3	.111
Day	71	25	2	14	.352	Sc Pos	72	17	2	26	.236
Night	147	31	6	19	.211	Clutch	39	16	2	7	.410

1989 Rankings (American League)

➡ 4th in slugging percentage vs. lefthanded pitchers (.572) - *batters with 125 PA vs. LHP*

HITTING:

Gary Gaetti was hampered by injuries last season and lost the groove that has led people to expect 30 home runs and 100 RBIs per season from him. He's a high-power, high-strike sort of hitter, but has switched from being a dead-pull hitter to also having some power to right-center when opponents try to work him outside. He's overcome the tendency to swing wildly and go into prolonged slumps, although some have suggested that he needs to think more about making contact when he falls behind in the count.

Gaetti likes the ball up, and most of his homers have been to left-center, the deepest corner of the Metrodome. Pitchers have success working him down and away. He'll lay off sliders that are destined to break in the dirt, but outside fastballs are a pretty effective way of keeping him honest. Gaetti has traditionally grounded into a lot of double plays -- mostly of the 6-4-3 and 5-4-3 variety. Artificial turf allows some of his hard one-hoppers to scoot through for base hits, although his turf and grass averages weren't that far apart last year.

BASERUNNING:

Gaetti was a standout quarterback and defensive back in school, and opposing fielders have felt his punishing collisions throughout his career. His recent injuries may slow him down a bit, and make him think twice about running through somebody when sliding around them might prolong his health. Gaetti will take advantage of a pitcher who doesn't watch him at first base.

FIELDING:

Gaetti won two straight Gold Gloves, but his range was a bit limited early last year, and he sometimes seemed wooden in the field. However, Gaetti has a good arm and, when healthy, can handle the hot corner with the best of them. He moves well in either direction, and also handles bunts without much trouble. Sometimes his throws sail high, a quirk that hinders him for a couple of stretches every season.

OVERALL:

Since Gaetti's conversion to fundamentalist Christianity, there have been questions about whether he has the same enthusiasm for the game that was the trademark of his younger years. His numbers last year indicate a less productive player, but he was also nagged by assorted injuries. Gaetti still has to place on any list of the top third baseman, and the Twins can expect more years of high production if he's healthy.

GARY GAETTI

Position: 3B
Bats: R **Throws:** R
Ht: 6' 0" **Wt:** 200

Opening Day Age: 31
Born: 8/19/58 in Centralia, IL
ML Seasons: 9

Overall Statistics

	G	AB	R	H	D	T	HR	RBI	SB	BB	SO	AVG
1989	130	498	63	125	11	4	19	75	6	25	87	.251
Career	1207	4412	585	1144	225	20	185	673	68	322	776	.259

Where He Hits the Ball

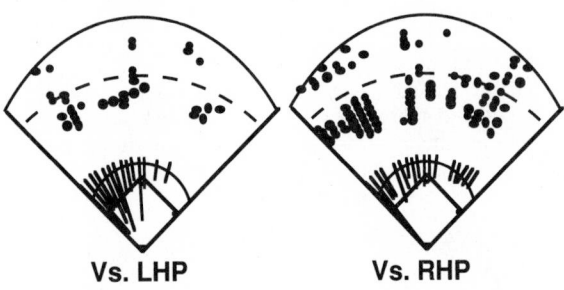

Vs. LHP   Vs. RHP

1989 Situational Stats

	AB	H	HR	RBI	AVG		AB	H	HR	RBI	AVG
Home	249	62	10	40	.249	LHP	152	35	5	24	.230
Road	249	63	9	35	.253	RHP	346	90	14	51	.260
Day	172	46	10	33	.267	Sc Pos	132	29	7	56	.220
Night	326	79	9	42	.242	Clutch	82	19	6	15	.232

1989 Rankings (American League)

- → 1st in lowest percent of pitches taken (40.9%) - *players with 502 PA*
- → 4th in lowest on-base average (.286)
- → 9th in sacrifice flies (9)
- → Led the Twins in strikeouts (87), home run frequency (26.2 ABs per HR) and sacifice flies
- → Led AL Third Basemen in RBIs (75) and sacrifice flies

HITTING:

Greg Gagne had his best year in 1989, hitting over .270 for the first time in his career. But he continued to be an impatient hitter, walking only 17 times. Last year the Twins, who have tried various approaches with Gagne, brought in Don Baylor for a week specifically to work with Gagne and help him become less anxious and find more consistency. Gagne had taken a liking to Baylor when he came to Minnesota for the final weeks of the 1987 season. Still, Gagne's pattern didn't change much.

Gagne has pretty good power for a middle infielder -- owing to his strong build -- but he doesn't have a particularly quick swing. Balls that a quicker bat would pull over the leftfield wall become routine flies to center. Gagne doesn't chase as many bad pitches as he used to, but the Twins would still like to see him cut down on his strikeout total while increasing his walks. He has always handled righthanded pitchers reasonably well, and in fact, has suffered at times against lefties. He's improved in that area, and one only needs to recall 1985, when Gagne batted .255 as an overmatched rookie, to appreciate some of the progress he's made. The real question may be whether expectations are too high.

BASERUNNING:

Gagne is not a great base stealer, but his skills have improved in that area. He has learned to read pitchers better than he used to, and more work could turn him into a feared thief because Gagne is as fast as anyone on the team. Gagne also has the sort of sliding technique that aspiring ballplayers should emulate.

FIELDING:

You don't hear his name mentioned in the same sentence as Ozzie Smith or Tony Fernandez, but Gagne can make spectacular plays at shortstop -- and has become much steadier on the routine ones. The Twins haven't been afraid to give him some bench time now and then, in favor of Newman, and that may help keep him from getting mentally weary.

OVERALL:

There might be a year when Gagne puts everything together and gains a reputation beyond the Minnesota border. In the meantime, the Twins don't have to worry about looking for a shortstop as long as Gagne is around. Perhaps he would look better if his offense was compared to other shortstops, instead of to Puckett, Hrbek and Gaetti.

GREG GAGNE

Position: SS
Bats: R **Throws:** R
Ht: 5'11" **Wt:** 177

Opening Day Age: 28
Born: 11/12/61 in Fall River, MA
ML Seasons: 7

Overall Statistics

	G	AB	R	H	D	T	HR	RBI	SB	BB	SO	AVG
1989	149	460	69	125	29	7	9	48	11	17	80	.272
Career	717	2151	309	537	115	29	47	216	54	119	445	.250

Where He Hits the Ball

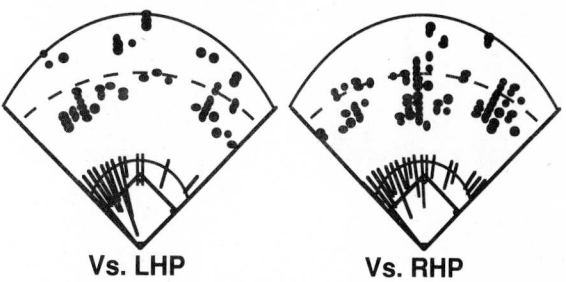

Vs. LHP   **Vs. RHP**

1989 Situational Stats

	AB	H	HR	RBI	AVG		AB	H	HR	RBI	AVG
Home	218	65	5	25	.298	LHP	171	50	5	16	.292
Road	242	60	4	23	.248	RHP	289	75	4	32	.260
Day	142	40	3	18	.282	Sc Pos	110	23	1	37	.209
Night	318	85	6	30	.267	Clutch	60	12	0	5	.200

1989 Rankings (American League)

➡ 10th in triples (7)
➡ Led the Twins in triples and errors (18)
➡ Led AL Shortstops in strikeouts (80)

HITTING:

When the Twins were known as a collection of sluggers a few years back, they needed Dan Gladden to provide some balance. Even though he wasn't going to hit .300 or draw 100 walks, Minnesota needed Gladden in the leadoff position to get on base and steal second. He's filled that role well enough, but other challengers have emerged for the top spot and as a result, Gladden has filled other spots in the line-up. Gladden has responded by keeping his average up and establishing himself as a guy who'll take a pitcher deep just when you start to forget about his power.

Gladden thrives on pressure situations and seems to come up with more than his share of important hits. He doesn't back down from tough pitchers and sprays the ball to all fields, although most of his power is down the leftfield line. Gladden isn't a great bunter, but he's always a threat to beat out those that he does lay down.

Gladden can be frustrated by off-speed pitchers, and Kelly benched Gladden when such hurlers took the mound against the Twins. Gladden chafes at not being able to play, however, and it's hard to keep him out of the line-up unless he's physically unfit.

BASERUNNING:

Speaking of unfit, a hamstring injury forced Gladden to the sidelines for much of last summer -- and hampered him on the bases, too. When healthy, Gladden reads pitchers well and combines that skill with above-average speed. His injuries haven't seemed to slow him down too much, though Gladden would be the last to let on if something was bothering him.

FIELDING:

Gladden broke into the majors as a center fielder, but wasn't going to move into that spot because of a guy named Puckett. He's established himself as a reckless left fielder whose errors usually come from being overly aggressive. His throwing arm isn't as strong as the Twins would like, but he has good range..

OVERALL:

One vision of the 1987 Series is Cardinals starter Joe Magrane throwing to first, time after time, to keep Gladden close. Gladden is that sort of pesky player, good enough at all phases of the game to be a real pain to opponents. While you wouldn't label him a standout at this point in his career, he can be expected to have several more valuable years ahead.

DAN GLADDEN

Position: LF
Bats: R **Throws:** R
Ht: 5'11" **Wt:** 175

Opening Day Age: 32
Born: 7/7/57 in San Jose, CA
ML Seasons: 7

Overall Statistics

	G	AB	R	H	D	T	HR	RBI	SB	BB	SO	AVG
1989	121	461	69	136	23	3	8	46	23	23	53	.295
Career	731	2733	425	753	126	22	43	256	170	224	384	.276

Where He Hits the Ball

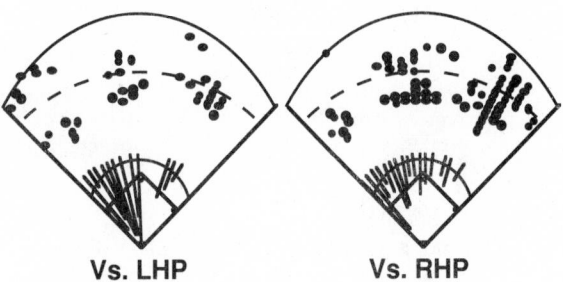

Vs. LHP   Vs. RHP

1989 Situational Stats

	AB	H	HR	RBI	AVG		AB	H	HR	RBI	AVG
Home	222	63	1	21	.284	LHP	157	48	3	11	.306
Road	239	73	7	25	.305	RHP	304	88	5	35	.289
Day	144	37	4	14	.257	Sc Pos	105	25	1	35	.238
Night	317	99	4	32	.312	Clutch	66	23	1	9	.348

1989 Rankings (American League)

➡ 3rd in hitting on an 0-2 count (.364) - *players with 20 PA on an 0-2 count*

➡ 8th in hitting in the clutch (.348) - *players with 50 PA in the clutch*

➡ Led the Twins in hitting on an 0-2 count, stolen base percentage (76.7%) and hitting on the road (.305)

➡ Led AL Left Fielders in sacrifice bunts (5), hitting vs. lefthanded pitchers (.306) and hitting on an 0-2 count

PITCHING:

German Gonzalez has spent parts of the last two seasons as a set-up man for Jeff Reardon, although arm problems sidelined him for a significant portion of last season. He has a unique sidearm style that can be more difficult for lefthanded batters to hit than righties. Common wisdom would be that lefty batters would get a better look at the ball from a sidearm righthander. The secret is probably in the pitches on which Gonzalez relies.

He tends to use a fastball that tails away from lefties and a slider that breaks down and in. The fastball doesn't have much of a downward break, meaning that he's throwing it much of the time right into the hitting zones of righthanders. His style is different enough that, despite not being overpowering, Gonzalez averaged more than a strikeout per inning in the minors, and has gotten 7.9 Ks per nine innings in his major league career.

The Twins worry about overexposing Gonzalez, and it remains to be seen if batters facing him for the third or fourth time will figure out his game plan. Gonzalez doesn't appear to be in a position to come up with another pitch. Despite the trend toward overpowering late-inning relievers, Gonzalez shouldn't be written off merely because he doesn't blow people away. Doug Jones of Cleveland faced that sort of bias before he became one of the best.

FIELDING:

With his sweeping motion, Gonzalez falls off the mound when he follows through, which keeps him from being in good fielding position. He has a fairly quick release with runners on base, which helps make him fairly tough to steal on. He does not hold runners well.

OVERALL:

Gonzalez will have to continue convincing the Twins of his value if he is to be an important part of their bullpen. He made a good impression in his '88 debut, but didn't look nearly as good in a longer look last year. At this point, management appears to be more interested in other candidates. Gonzalez is only 24 and has time to improve and fool the experts.

GERMAN GONZALEZ

Position: RP
Bats: R **Throws:** R
Ht: 6' 0" **Wt:** 170

Opening Day Age: 24
Born: 10/3/65 in Rio Caribe, Venezuela
ML Seasons: 2

Overall Statistics

	W	L	ERA	G	GS	Sv	IP	H	R	BB	SO	HR
1989	3	2	4.66	22	0	0	29.0	32	17	11	25	2
Career	3	2	4.11	38	0	1	50.1	52	25	19	44	6

Where They Hit the Ball

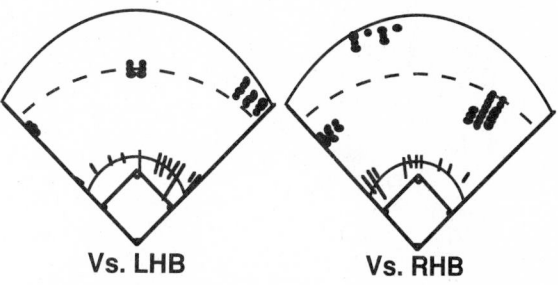

Vs. LHB **Vs. RHB**

1989 Situational Stats

	W	L	ERA	Sv	IP		AB	H	HR	RBI	AVG
Home	2	1	3.45	0	15.2	LHB	58	17	0	8	.293
Road	1	1	6.08	0	13.1	RHB	59	15	2	6	.254
Day	1	1	6.35	0	11.1	Sc Pos	37	10	0	12	.270
Night	2	1	3.57	0	17.2	Clutch	20	6	0	2	.300

1989 Rankings (American League)

➡ Led the Twins in balks (3)

HITTING:

Brian Harper is a consummate contact hitter who somehow wandered through almost a decade of journeyman status before finding a regular job with the Twins last season. He batted .325, his best mark as a major leaguer, after previous stints with California, Pittsburgh, St. Louis, Detroit and Oakland.

Harper struck out only 16 times in 385 at bats, an amazingly low ratio of strikeouts to at bats. He led the Twins in strikeout ratio in 1988 as well, fanning once every 15.2 plate appearances that year. He's a solid line drive hitter to all fields who is seldom fooled and almost always gets a solid piece of the ball. Harper will hit a long one occasionally -- his eight homers were a career high -- but mostly he likes to hit the ball hard into the gaps. If he has a glaring weakness, American League pitchers have yet to find it.

Surprisingly, Harper walked just 13 times, a low total for a contact hitter who seldom strikes out. But Harper, like most of his Twins teammates, is a free swinger. The difference is, Harper is more apt to make contact when he does swing.

BASERUNNING:

Harper is certainly no blazer on the bases, having been thrown out on four of six basestealing attempts. Even that was an improvement, as he entered the 1989 season with one major league stolen base in 265 games. Harper's redeeming grace is his heady baserunning, plus finally getting to play a position that does not require speed as a prerequisite.

FIELDING:

Until coming to the Twins in 1988, Harper had never been given a chance to win a catching job at the major league level. His few previous opportunities came primarily at third base and in the outfield. Twins officials were originally skeptical of Harper's defensive skills, but by season's end he had erased most doubts. He threw out a respectable percentage of would-be basestealers and did a good job blocking errant pitches. Harper was clearly entrenched as the Twins No. 1 catching job by mid-season.

OVERALL:

Harper, at age 30, proved last year that he is capable of being a regular major league catcher. Twins manager Tom Kelly continues to express the belief that Harper must be spotted, playing about four times a week. But Harper's consistent bat, plus improving defensive play, could force a change in that strategy.

BRIAN HARPER

Position: C/DH
Bats: R **Throws:** R
Ht: 6' 2" **Wt:** 195

Opening Day Age: 30
Born: 10/16/59 in Los Angeles, CA
ML Seasons: 10

Overall Statistics

	G	AB	R	H	D	T	HR	RBI	SB	BB	SO	AVG
1989	126	385	43	125	24	0	8	57	2	13	16	.325
Career	391	941	91	265	50	2	22	127	3	36	69	.282

Where He Hits the Ball

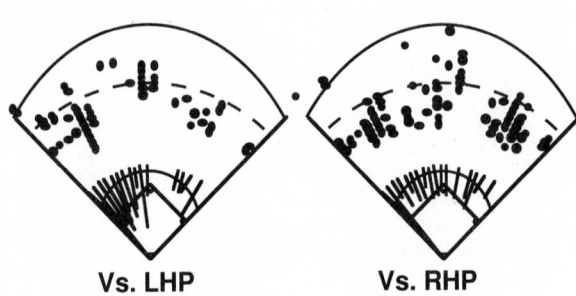

Vs. LHP   **Vs. RHP**

1989 Situational Stats

	AB	H	HR	RBI	AVG		AB	H	HR	RBI	AVG
Home	181	55	4	27	.304	LHP	155	48	3	21	.310
Road	204	70	4	30	.343	RHP	230	77	5	36	.335
Day	114	43	2	20	.377	Sc Pos	109	36	2	49	.330
Night	271	82	6	37	.303	Clutch	57	18	2	10	.316

1989 Rankings (American League)

➡ 2nd in hitting with 2 strikes (.309) - *players with 162 PA with 2 strikes*

➡ 5th in throwing out base stealers (32.9%) - *catchers with 75 attempts*

➡ 9th in hit by pitch (6)

➡ Led the Twins in hitting with 2 strikes and hitting with runners in scoring position (.330) - *team players with 100 PA with runners in scoring position*

➡ Led AL Catchers in hits (125), batting average with 2 strikes and errors (11)

KENT HRBEK

Position: 1B/DH
Bats: L **Throws:** R
Ht: 6' 4" **Wt:** 250

Opening Day Age: 29
Born: 5/21/60 in
Minneapolis, MN
ML Seasons: 9

HITTING:

The thing that sets Kent Hrbek apart from so many others is that his talent has come so naturally. Hrbek toys with different stances at the plate, switching from one to another when it's necessary to break out of a slump. He never goes too long without hitting, and he goes on a tear now and then when he's just about impossible to retire.

The short rightfield wall at the Metrodome provides Hrbek with an advantage for his home-run stroke, but he's always prided himself on being able to hit to all fields. Hrbek has sent several long homers over the wall in straight-away center and left-center. He doesn't fall into the trap of trying to pull lefties. In fact, lefthanders have enjoyed more success against Hrbek in the past couple of years by working him inside with fastballs.

Hrbek's health has been a big question recently. He suffered a separated shoulder in 1989 that was slow to heal, and was nagged by other problems. He's been encouraged to take better care of himself, but Hrbek seems happy as a 250-pounder and the Twins haven't made a huge deal out of his conditioning.

BASERUNNING:

What do you expect from a 250-pounder? Hrbek has slowed markedly over the years, and now takes the bases one at a time.

FIELDING:

What do you expect from a 250-pounder? Not as much as you get from Hrbek, who has remained one of the game's best fielders. Only Don Mattingly has stood between Hrbek and several Gold Gloves. He fields grounders well, starts the double play as well as anyone and has saved infielders many errors with his ability to handle poor throws. Hrbek played hockey as a youngster, and has the moves of a good goalie at first base.

OVERALL:

Can Hrbek remain healthy? If so, the Twins have a hitting machine who can help them for years to come, and a solid defensive player. If the body doesn't cooperate, Hrbek might find himself moving closer to being a full-time designated hitter. It will be interesting to see if Hrbek starts to pay more attention to his body when the alternative is missing 50 or 60 games per season. Remember that as a rookie in 1982, Hrbek weighed only 218 pounds. At this point, he'd look skinny at 230.

Overall Statistics

	G	AB	R	H	D	T	HR	RBI	SB	BB	SO	AVG
1989	109	375	59	102	17	0	25	84	3	53	35	.272
Career	1156	4178	624	1212	224	16	201	724	19	523	564	.290

Where He Hits the Ball

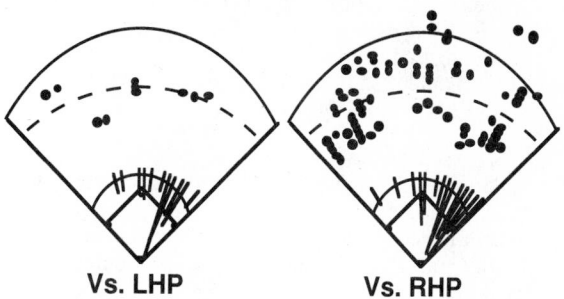

Vs. LHP   **Vs. RHP**

1989 Situational Stats

	AB	H	HR	RBI	AVG		AB	H	HR	RBI	AVG
Home	191	54	17	56	.283	LHP	109	29	6	25	.266
Road	184	48	8	28	.261	RHP	266	73	19	59	.274
Day	100	23	6	15	.230	Sc Pos	109	32	8	64	.294
Night	275	79	19	69	.287	Clutch	53	16	6	13	.302

1989 Rankings (American League)

→ 4th in home run frequency (15.0 ABs per HR) - *all league players*

→ 6th in batting average with 2 strikes (.274) - *players with 162 PA with 2 strikes*

→ 10th in home runs (25)

→ Led the Twins in home run frequency and home runs

→ Led AL First Basemen in batting average with 2 strikes and least GDPs per GDP situation (6.2%)

HITTING:

Gene Larkin came to the majors without a position. He wasn't going to move Kent Hrbek off first base and hadn't played third base, Gary Gaetti's position, since his college years at Columbia. As a result, he was a rarity -- a youngster who was a switch-hitting DH. He was given the title, "Gene, the Hitting Machine," for his ability to smoke line drives from either side of the plate. Yet the Twins always hoped there would be more, that Larkin would either develop into a .300 hitter, who would be a solid RBI man, or add more power to his repertoire. The Twins are still waiting, and wondering if he'll develop on either front.

Although he can hold his own from either side, Larkin has had much more success against lefties for the last couple of years. Part of Larkin's problem may be that he tries to pull the ball too much from the left. From the right, he uses the entire field and can be very frustrating to defend against. Though a plate-crowder who gets plunked by a lot of pitches, Larkin has yet to homer in double figures.

BASERUNNING:

Larkin doesn't have a lot of speed, but he runs the bases intelligently, rarely getting into trouble. If he can get to second base in time to make a difference, he isn't afraid to go in hard to break up a double play. He'll steal a base on occasion.

FIELDING:

With little chance of playing the infield, except as a backup to Kent Hrbek, Larkin volunteered to learn the outfield -- and made his debut in right field last season. He turned some routine plays into adventures, but earned a passing grade. His arm isn't strong, and opponents could take advantage of his inexperience. He's an average first baseman who got a chunk of time at that position when Hrbek was injured.

OVERALL:

The Twins would still like to see Larkin bloom into a feared hitter. He hit over .300 at every minor-league stop and this will only be his fourth season in the majors. Being able to play the field makes him more valuable, and being a switch-hitter also helps his cause. He must hit better from the left side, though, in order to be considered a true switch-hitter, and to increase his chances of remaining on the roster.

GENE LARKIN

Position: 1B/DH/RF
Bats: B **Throws:** R
Ht: 6' 3" **Wt:** 212

Opening Day Age: 27
Born: 10/24/62 in Flushing, NY
ML Seasons: 3

Overall Statistics

	G	AB	R	H	D	T	HR	RBI	SB	BB	SO	AVG
1989	136	446	61	119	25	1	6	46	5	54	57	.267
Career	370	1184	140	316	66	5	18	144	9	147	143	.267

Where He Hits the Ball

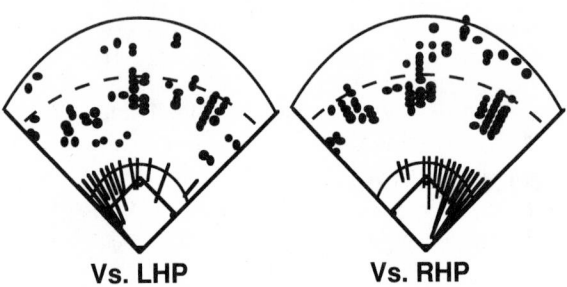

Vs. LHP   Vs. RHP

1989 Situational Stats

	AB	H	HR	RBI	AVG		AB	H	HR	RBI	AVG
Home	239	62	3	25	.259	LHP	156	57	1	20	.365
Road	207	57	3	21	.275	RHP	290	62	5	26	.214
Day	147	45	0	10	.306	Sc Pos	122	29	2	41	.238
Night	299	74	6	36	.247	Clutch	70	18	1	4	.257

1989 Rankings (American League)

➡ 1st in batting average on a 3-1 count (.667) - *players with 10 PA with a 3-1 count*

➡ 2nd in hit by pitch (9) and on-base average vs. lefthanded pitchers (.438) - *players with 125 PA vs. LHP*

➡ 5th in batting average vs. lefthanded pitchers (.365)

➡ Led the Twins in hit by pitch, batting average vs. lefthanded pitchers and hitting on a 3-1 count

➡ Led AL First Basemen in sacrifice bunts (5), hit by pitch, bunts in play (7), batting average vs. lefthanded pitchers and batting average on a 3-1 count

HITTING:

Tim Laudner took another step backward at the plate in 1989, but it may have had more to do with physical ailments than physical limitations. Laudner underwent knee surgery in early September, and a summer of pain made him an offensive asset only when he wasn't crouching behind the plate. Laudner batted .194 when he was catching, but had a .339 average at designated hitter, pinch hitter, or on first base.

Not that Laudner is any threat to bat .300, even on a part-time basis. He finished with a .222 average last season, only slightly less than his major league average entering the season (.225). Laudner has twice batted under .200 in his seven full seasons in the majors.

This much is now certain: A hard-throwing righthander ties Laudner in knots with inside fastballs. He is often off-balance at the plate, striking out almost three times as often as he walks throughout his major league career. His redeeming grace offensively is that when he connects, he has power. Laudner, who once hit 42 home runs as a minor leaguer, had six home runs in 239 at bats last year. He had reached double figures in roundtrippers in each of the three previous seasons.

BASERUNNING:

Laudner's speed is befitting that of a 214-pound catcher with sore knees. Laudner is simply slow. He did steal one base last year, giving him a major league career total of three. He does possess decent baserunning instincts, and is seldom embarrassed because of mental blunders.

FIELDING:

The knee pain created obvious problems for Laudner behind the plate. He appeared to be making strides in 1988, throwing out 30 percent of potential basestealers while doing a decent job of blocking the plate on low outside breaking balls. But he struggled last year against opposing basestealers. He also drew the wrath of manager Tom Kelly for a variety of defensive shortcomings, ranging from questionable pitch selections to failing to catch a foul pop in an early-season loss at Baltimore.

OVERALL:

Laudner lost the No. 1 catching job last year to Brian Harper. Even so, his power makes him enticing to Twins management. But if his knees affect his ability to catch, Laudner's career could be in jeopardy because his penchant for striking out coupled with his lack of speed makes him a less-than-desirable designated-hitter.

TIM LAUDNER

Position: C/DH
Bats: R **Throws:** R
Ht: 6'3" **Wt:** 214

Opening Day Age: 31
Born: 6/7/58 in Mason City, IA
ML Seasons: 9

Overall Statistics

	G	AB	R	H	D	T	HR	RBI	SB	BB	SO	AVG
1989	100	239	24	53	11	1	6	27	1	25	65	.222
Career	734	2038	221	458	97	5	77	263	3	190	553	.225

Where He Hits the Ball

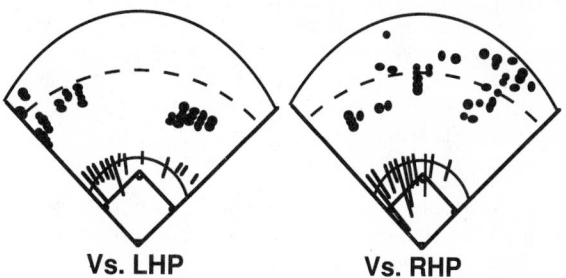

Vs. LHP   Vs. RHP

1989 Situational Stats

	AB	H	HR	RBI	AVG		AB	H	HR	RBI	AVG
Home	132	29	2	12	.220	LHP	91	23	2	12	.253
Road	107	24	4	15	.224	RHP	148	30	4	15	.203
Day	79	14	2	10	.177	Sc Pos	53	11	1	20	.208
Night	160	39	4	17	.244	Clutch	37	6	1	6	.162

1989 Rankings (American League)

➡ 4th in batting average on a 3-1 count (.600) - *players with 10 PA with a 3-1 count*

➡ Led AL Catchers in batting average on a 3-1 count

HITTING:

John Moses is a switch-hitter, but he spent the off-season prior to 1989 trying to improve as a righthanded batter, in hopes that it would result in increased playing opportunities. Moses did improve, though he remained primarily a left-handed batting platoon player for the Twins.

The significant stats: Moses batted .209 against lefthanders for Seattle in 1987, and .222 (in just nine at bats) for the Twins in 1988. Against righthanded pitchers, he batted .264 in 1987, .320 in 1988. So Moses worked on his righthanded hitting, and the improvement was noticeable. Moses batted .286 against lefthanded pitchers last season, increasing his overall value.

Moses is a good contact hitter who can hit to all fields. He struck out just 23 times in 267 plate appearances. He's an excellent fastball hitter, but like most of the free-swinging Twins, he has some problems timing off-speed offerings. Moses doesn't have much power, however. He's never hit more than three homers in a season, and despite his good speed, his career high in doubles is 16.

BASERUNNING:

A smart baserunner, rather than a blazer, Moses affords the Twins the opportunity to hit-and-run or steal bases when he's in the line-up. He stole a combined 48 bases in two seasons for Seattle in 1986-87, but at age 32 he's probably lost a step. Moses was successful on 14 of 21 stolen base attempts last year.

FIELDING:

Moses is decent with the glove, but a weak arm has prevented him from being an everyday player. After primarily playing centerfield for the Mariners, Moses has provided insurance at all three outfield positions for the Twins. With Kirby Puckett in center, Moses has logged most of his time in left field, subbing for oft-injured Dan Gladden, or platooning in right field.

OVERALL:

Moses ia a solid role player who can be an asset to a contending team. He makes contact at the plate, does a good job on the bases, and is adequate defensively. He does his job without complaints, whatever the task. He'll never be a superstar, but there will always be a spot at the major league level for players with his ability.

JOHN MOSES

Position: RF/LF/CF
Bats: B **Throws:** L
Ht: 5'10" **Wt:** 170

Opening Day Age: 32
Born: 8/9/57 in Los Angeles, CA
ML Seasons: 8

Overall Statistics

	G	AB	R	H	D	T	HR	RBI	SB	BB	SO	AVG
1989	129	242	33	68	12	3	1	31	14	19	23	.281
Career	620	1508	213	396	64	16	10	129	95	117	196	.263

Where He Hits the Ball

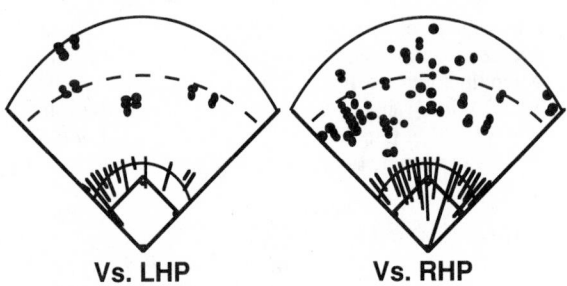

Vs. LHP   **Vs. RHP**

1989 Situational Stats

	AB	H	HR	RBI	AVG		AB	H	HR	RBI	AVG
Home	97	30	0	19	.309	LHP	63	18	0	9	.286
Road	145	38	1	12	.262	RHP	179	50	1	22	.279
Day	96	26	0	14	.271	Sc Pos	59	20	0	29	.339
Night	146	42	1	17	.288	Clutch	56	14	0	8	.250

1989 Rankings (American League)

➡ 5th in lowest stolen base percentage (66.7%)
- *players with 20 stolen base attempts*

HITTING:

Al Newman is devoid of power, but that doesn't mean he's devoid of skill. He'll poke the ball over and around infielders, getting doubles and triples when those hits bounce up the power alleys and into the corner. Listed at 5'9", Newman also can be a pain to deal with for a pitcher. He spent a lot of time in the leadoff spot last season, and had a respectable on-base percentage. He also led the Twins in stolen bases with 25.

As you might imagine, Newman gets into trouble when he tries to hit the ball in the air. He did pick up a few extra-base hits last year by lofting the ball over the outfield and may surprise everyone some day by clearing the short, high wall in right at the Metrodome.

Newman shows that you can't judge a switch-hitter by one season's statistics. His statistics from the left and right have varied markedly in his three seasons with Minnesota. In 1988, he batted only .174 against lefties, while last season his stats were fairly even. A disproportionate number of Newman's extra-base hits comes against lefties, while he seems to take a closer look at pitches against righties. Newman is also a good bunter.

BASERUNNING:

Newman has improved over the last couple of years from merely being fast to having both speed and talent on the bases. The key is his acceleration; Newman no longer needs three or four short, choppy strides to get going. He seems to have benefited from working with Jerry White, the Twins' base running coach.

FIELDING:

Newman can play second, short and third -- and handles all three positions reasonably well. Injuries to other players allowed Newman to get more playing time in 1989 than in any previous season, and the Twins could do worse than give Newman a chance to be their regular second baseman. He looks more comfortable in the field than he did as a younger player, when he sometimes appeared to be fighting the ball.

OVERALL:

The Twins have penciled in Newman as a role player, but he'd like to do much more. Under the right circumstances, he could establish himself as a regular. He is a very intelligent player who makes the most of his talents and works within his limitations.

AL NEWMAN

Position: 2B/3B/SS
Bats: B **Throws:** R
Ht: 5' 9" **Wt:** 183

Opening Day Age: 29
Born: 6/30/60 in
Kansas City, MO
ML Seasons: 5

Overall Statistics

	G	AB	R	H	D	T	HR	RBI	SB	BB	SO	AVG
1989	141	446	62	113	18	2	0	38	25	59	46	.253
Career	476	1227	171	281	44	7	1	95	65	146	131	.229

Where He Hits the Ball

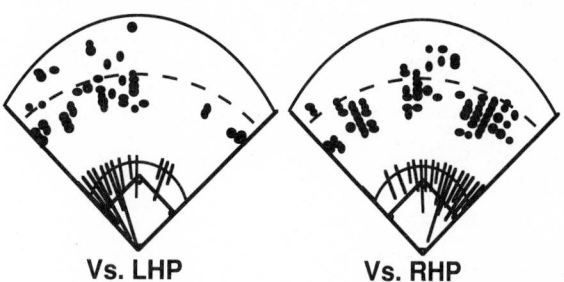

Vs. LHP   **Vs. RHP**

1989 Situational Stats

	AB	H	HR	RBI	AVG		AB	H	HR	RBI	AVG
Home	224	58	0	14	.259	LHP	163	41	0	17	.252
Road	222	55	0	24	.248	RHP	283	72	0	21	.254
Day	142	41	0	18	.289	Sc Pos	104	26	0	35	.250
Night	304	72	0	20	.237	Clutch	70	27	0	8	.386

1989 Rankings (American League)

- ➡ 2nd in lowest slugging percentage (.303) - *players with 502 PA*
- ➡ 2nd in hitting in the clutch (.386) - *players with 50 PA in the clutch*
- ➡ 6th in grounder/flyball ratio (2.02)
- ➡ Led the Twins in sacrifice bunts (10), stolen bases (25), caught stealing (12), walks (59), bunts in play (23), lowest percent of swings that missed (13.0%), percent of swings put into play (55.8%), stals of third (4), least GDPs per GDP situation (5.9%) and hitting in the clutch (.386)
- ➡ Led AL Second Basemen in hitting in the clutch

IN HIS PRIME

KIRBY PUCKETT

Position: CF
Bats: R **Throws:** R
Ht: 5' 8" **Wt:** 210

Opening Day Age: 29
Born: 3/14/61 in Chicago, IL
ML Seasons: 6

HITTING:

The only thing textbook about Kirby Puckett's approach at the plate is the bottom line. He has emerged as the game's premier righthanded hitter despite a style that borders on reckless abandon. Puckett is an impatient, bad-ball hitter, but would you change him?

Puckett's .339 average in 1989 marked the fourth straight year he has hit .328 or better and collected more than 200 base hits. The stocky outfielder has more than 1,200 hits in his six major league seasons, putting him on a Hall of Fame course for the magic 3,000. He does it his way, hacking at pitches above his head, flailing at offerings down and away. As often as not, he gets a good piece of the pitch and sends it on a line into the outfield.

Puckett entered 1989 wanting to increase his base on balls total, which was a paltry 23 in 657 official at bats in 1988. Puckett did walk 41 times last year, but he seemed to grow less patient at the plate as the year went on. He also managed to decrease his strikeouts from 83 in 1988 to 59 last year. The biggest mystery with Puckett is his steady power decline. He hit 31 home runs in 1986, but has decreased each year since, from 28 to 24 to a stunningly low nine last year. Oftentimes last year he seemed to be reverting to his rookie form, when he hit most balls to right field.

BASERUNNING:

At 5-8, 210 pounds, Puckett looks muscle-bound. But he actually has better than average speed, evidenced by his 11 steals in 15 attempts in 1989. Puckett has twice stolen more than 20 bases as major leaguer, but batting No. 3 in a power-hitting lineup has reduced his opportunities to run.

FIELDING:

A perennial Gold Glove winner, Puckett's strengths are a strong throwing arm and a vertical jump that has often allowed him to leap over the Dome's fence to take away would-be home runs from opposing batters. Puckett does have defensive weaknesses. He plays a relatively deep centerfield, allowing singles to fall in that some outfielders might get to. Puckett has worked at playing shallower, and he made strides in that direction last year.

OVERALL:

A strong argument can be built that Puckett is the game's best overall player. Puckett's case would be stronger if his home run stroke returned, but his 45 doubles are evidence that he's far from just another singles hitter. Best of all, Puckett has retained an Ernie Banks-like demeanor that makes him one of baseball's best ambassadors.

Overall Statistics

	G	AB	R	H	D	T	HR	RBI	SB	BB	SO	AVG
1989	159	635	75	215	45	4	9	85	11	41	59	.339
Career	924	3844	542	1243	197	38	96	506	84	187	488	.323

Where He Hits the Ball

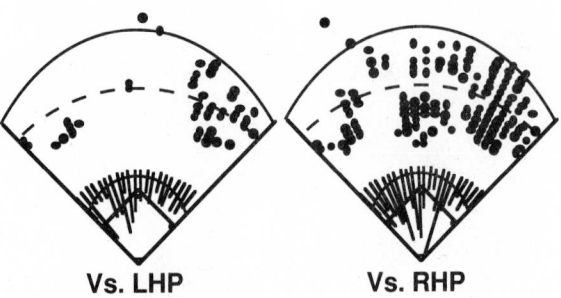

Vs. LHP   **Vs. RHP**

1989 Situational Stats

	AB	H	HR	RBI	AVG		AB	H	HR	RBI	AVG
Home	328	128	7	52	.390	LHP	191	58	1	19	.304
Road	307	87	2	33	.283	RHP	444	157	8	66	.354
Day	198	71	2	24	.359	Sc Pos	176	58	2	70	.330
Night	437	144	7	61	.330	Clutch	91	32	3	16	.352

1989 Rankings (American League)

➡ 1st in batting average (.339), hits (215), batting average vs. righthanded pitchers (.354) and hitting at home (.390) - *players with 502 PA*

➡ 2nd in singles (157), doubles (45) and least pitches seen per plate appearance (2.8)

➡ 4th in GDPs (21)

➡ Led the Twins in batting average, at bats (635), runs (75), hits, singles, doubles, totals bases (295), RBIs (85), intentional walks (9), times on base (259), GDPs, pitches seen (1,900), plate appearance (684), games (159), on-base average (.379), slugging percentage (.465), grounder/flyball ratio (2.26) and hitting vs. righthanded pitchers

PITCHING:

The Twins got Shane Rawley after the '88 campaign, giving up Tommy Herr, the man for whom they'd surrendered Tom Brunansky. They didn't expect miracles, but thought Rawley would flash the steady form that produced 78 wins from 1982 through 1987, with every season in double figures. They figured Rawley to be the third starter in their rotation last year, but what they got was a pitcher who knew more struggles than success. An ERA above five doesn't allow for many excuses. Rawley's fastball, which was never great, appeared to lose some velocity, and his other pitches didn't pick up the slack. He walked almost as many batters as he struck out and was frequently hurt by home runs, further proof that his pitches weren't fooling anyone. Rawley's fastball never had much movement in his harder throwing years, and his curve and change-up have never been great.

Rawley's success, when he had it, was frequently the result of a slider that has been one part of his game that's improved over the years. At age 34, it will be interesting to see if Rawley is able to make some further adjustments that could prolong his career. Several teams weren't willing to take that risk last season when the Twins were shopping Rawley to pennant contenders without asking much in return. His future in Minnesota may be limited because of the younger (and lower-paid) pitchers in the organization.

Rawley has a tendency to fall behind in the count, which especially bothered the Twins when he was pitching with a lead.

FIELDING:

Rawley fields his position well, both in his follow-through and covering first base on ground balls. He has a pretty good move to first base. There are times when he seems to pay too much attention to baserunners, and other times when the attention he gives them is cursory.

OVERALL:

Rawley has reached the point in his career where he's going to have to make some changes to survive. Since he was never an overpowering pitcher, it's hard to imagine what he might come up with. Rawley is a cerebral sort, and may come up with something. One suggestion: let him pitch only against the Dodgers, against whom he's 9-0. Seriously, it might not be too late for him to work on his change-up.

SHANE RAWLEY

Position: SP
Bats: L **Throws:** L
Ht: 6' 0" **Wt:** 185

Opening Day Age: 34
Born: 7/27/55 in Racine, WI
ML Seasons: 12

Overall Statistics

	W	L	ERA	G	GS	Sv	IP	H	R	BB	SO	HR
1989	5	12	5.21	27	25	0	145.0	167	89	60	68	19
Career	111	118	4.02	469	230	40	1870.2	1934	917	734	991	153

Where They Hit the Ball

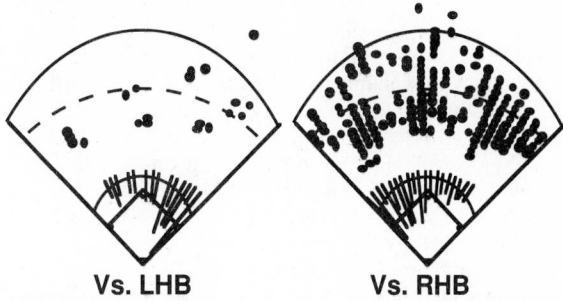

Vs. LHB   **Vs. RHB**

1989 Situational Stats

	W	L	ERA	Sv	IP		AB	H	HR	RBI	AVG
Home	2	7	6.18	0	78.2	LHB	113	41	4	16	.363
Road	3	5	4.07	0	66.1	RHB	456	126	15	60	.276
Day	3	4	3.88	0	65.0	Sc Pos	143	44	4	55	.308
Night	2	8	6.30	0	80.0	Clutch	45	17	0	6	.378

1989 Rankings (American League)

➡ 4th lowest won/loss percentage (.294) - *pitchers with 15 or more decisions*

➡ Led the Twins in losses (12), walks allowed (60) and pickoff throws (91)

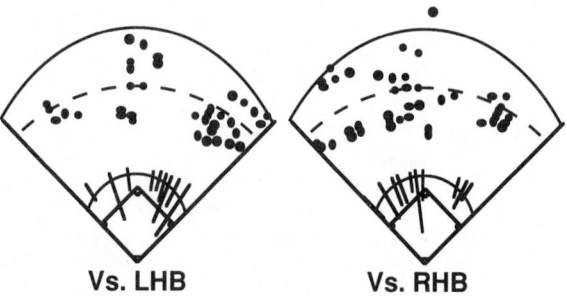

PITCHING:

By his own imposing standards -- he's the only pitcher who has saved over 40 games in each league -- Jeff Reardon's performance dropped off last season. The big question is whether the righthander has lost something off his fastball that will be impossible to get back. There were times last year when Reardon just didn't look as sharp as in previous years. His fastball didn't seem to have the same zip that marked previous successes. At the same time, however, the Twins were struggling enough that Reardon didn't get the regular work on which he thrives -- and inactivity bothers Reardon more than overwork. Closers are hard to find and the Twins will probably be willing to gamble that the 34-year-old Reardon didn't lose anything that can't be regained.

Reardon brings two pitches in from the bullpen -- a fastball and a curve that can fool batters even when they know it's coming. The fastball seems to rise when Reardon is on top of his game and flattens out when he gets pounded. Critics urged him to use the curve more last season, but Reardon is a power pitcher, and even the best of curves can be timed if used too often. His outs usually come on fly balls and strikeouts, and one can see how pitching in the Metrodome can be a challenge for him. Reardon has dabbled with a change-up, but prefers to stay with the hard stuff. The back problems that Reardon experienced with Montreal no longer bother him, and there was some thought that using him too often -- especially warming him up when he didn't enter the game -- contributed to that soreness. With the Twins, Reardon rarely warms up without coming into a game.

FIELDING:

Reardon gets paid handsomely for his pitching arm, not his fielding glove. That's a good thing, because Reardon's motion leaves him out of position for fielding balls back through the middle. He's easy to steal against, too.

OVERALL:

The coming year will be an interesting one for Reardon. He should get the chance to prove that he has another good year or two left. Whether he does it with continued power or adds some more wrinkles to his pitch assortment remains to be seen. It should be remembered that Reardon was booed just as heavily at times in 1987, when he helped lead the Twins to the World Series title, as he was last year.

JEFF REARDON

Position: RP
Bats: R **Throws:** R
Ht: 6' 0" **Wt:** 200

Opening Day Age: 34
Born: 10/1/55 in Pittsfield, MA
ML Seasons: 11

Overall Statistics

	W	L	ERA	G	GS	Sv	IP	H	R	BB	SO	HR
1989	5	4	4.07	65	0	31	73.0	68	33	12	46	8
Career	57	62	3.03	647	0	266	892.1	757	321	301	722	82

Where They Hit the Ball

Vs. LHB   **Vs. RHB**

1989 Situational Stats

	W	L	ERA	Sv	IP		AB	H	HR	RBI	AVG
Home	4	2	4.12	19	39.1	LHB	129	32	5	22	.248
Road	1	2	4.01	12	33.2	RHB	147	36	3	24	.245
Day	1	2	4.01	9	24.2	Sc Pos	82	21	3	36	.256
Night	4	2	4.10	22	48.1	Clutch	179	44	6	38	.246

1989 Rankings (American League)

- → 2nd in blown saves (11), games finished (61) and first batter efficiency (.136) - *pitchers with 40 games in relief*
- → 3rd in lowest save percentage (73.8%) and save opportunites (42)
- → 7th in saves (31)
- → 9th in games (65)
- → Led the Twins in games, saves, games finished, first batter efficiency, blown saves, lowest batting average vs. lefthanded batters (.248) and on-base average allowed (.280)

PITCHING:

It took Roy Smith a long time to win the respect of the Twins' coaching staff. There was a time when other pitchers were getting called up from the minors, even though Smith was putting together more impressive statistics. They felt he couldn't throw hard enough and that he could only be effective one time through the order. When the Twins ran out of options last season, Smith finally got his chance to pitch regularly, and made the most of it.

His assortment of slow curves and good enough fastballs can tie hitters in knots. Smith was a hard thrower in his younger days in the Phillies and Indians organizations, but now his fastball is in the low or mid-80s. Smith needs to be in command of his breaking pitches; otherwise hitters can wait for the fastballs. That happened a couple of times last season, leading to very early exits. He also has trouble with the home-run ball. Hanging curves that stay up and over the plate always have the potential to be launched into the cheap seats.

Fielders like playing behind Smith because he doesn't walk a lot of batters and works at a brisk pace. He strikes out more batters than you might expect and understands that he has to use the brushback pitch to keep opponents from getting too comfortable, the lot of control pitchers.

FIELDING:

Smith twists into an awkward position after releasing the ball, and isn't in a good position to handle grounders up the middle. What Smith can get to, however, he handles well, and he isn't a slowpoke about covering first. The combination of not having a strong move to first base and his reliance on off-speed pitches make him a mark for base-stealers, but Twins catchers did manage to throw out 47% of opposing basestealers in 1989 while Smith was on the mound. Smith's defensive limitations appear to be a natural result of his pitching style.

OVERALL:

Whether 1989 was Smith's one good season or if he'll continue to improve remains to be seen. If the Twins develop a staff of hard-throwing youngsters, Smith could fit in well as a spot starter and long reliever. He could also end up as the fourth starter this year, and with continued improvement, make himself more valuable. Smith is only 28, which is young for a finesse pitcher.

ROY SMITH

Position: SP/RP
Bats: R **Throws:** R
Ht: 6' 3" **Wt:** 217

Opening Day Age: 28
Born: 9/6/61 in Mt. Vernon, NY
ML Seasons: 6

Overall Statistics

	W	L	ERA	G	GS	Sv	IP	H	R	BB	SO	HR
1989	10	6	3.92	32	26	1	172.1	180	82	51	92	22
Career	20	17	4.31	87	56	1	384.2	417	201	131	208	51

Where They Hit the Ball

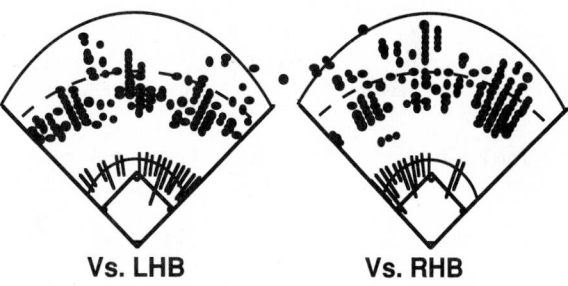

Vs. LHB   **Vs. RHB**

1989 Situational Stats

	W	L	ERA	Sv	IP		AB	H	HR	RBI	AVG
Home	5	1	4.22	1	85.1	LHB	314	85	5	33	.271
Road	5	5	3.62	0	87.0	RHB	354	95	17	40	.268
Day	2	3	3.57	0	63.0	Sc Pos	156	42	2	44	.269
Night	8	3	4.12	1	109.1	Clutch	49	10	0	2	.204

1989 Rankings (American League)

- ➡ 1st in lowest grounder/flyball ratio (.77) - *pitchers with 162 IP*
- ➡ 3rd in most HRs allowed per 9 innings (1.15)
- ➡ 8th in lowest stolen base percentage allowed (52.6%)
- ➡ 9th in home runs allowed (22)
- ➡ Led the Twins in home runs allowed, lowest stolen base percentage allowed and caught stealing (9)

PITCHING:

The Twins were forced to keep Gary Wayne at the major league level last year after selecting him from Montreal's unprotected list in the major league draft. Wayne appeared overmatched the first month, posting a 5.90 ERA in his first 12 big league appearances. He walked 13 in 18.1 innings during that span. But the Twins stuck with him rather than risk losing him to the Expos for one-half the $25,000 they had paid for him. The gamble paid off. Manager Tom Kelly spotted Wayne, saving the tightest spots for veterans Juan Berenguer and Jeff Reardon. But Wayne showed a veteran's poise on several occasions, earning his first major league victory in a 4-3, 11 inning game against Seattle. The lefthanded reliever settled into a groove and finished with a very respectable 3.30 ERA.

In retrospect, Wayne's early-season problems should have been no surprise. He suffered a stress fracture to his right foot three times within a seven-month period beginning in October 1987 in the Expos instructional league. He underwent surgery the following April and pitched in just eight games in 1988, seven of them in August.

The key to Wayne's success is his herky-jerky delivery. He appears to be throwing with an incredibly rigid motion, but Twins pitching coach Dick Such said that, contrary to appearances, the rookie's mechanics are actually excellent. Wayne's fastball is in the mid-80s, average by major league standards. His effectiveness depends largely on getting the split-fingered fastball he uses as a change-up over the plate. Wayne did that with consistency after his rocky start and became the Twins' best lefty reliever in recent memory.

FIELDING:

Wayne has overcome his foot problems, showing no limitations in his movement. Despite his pitching motion, Wayne's follow-through is excellent, affording him good defensive position. He's quick off the mound and an excellent athlete. He has a fair move to first.

OVERALL:

The Twins like Wayne's attitude as much as his physical attributes. He's a happy-go-lucky sort who doesn't dwell on past failures. He has a lefthander's flakiness; among the options Wayne said he'd consider if he wasn't pitching in the big leagues is the professional bowlers tour. That endeared him to veteran team leader Kent Hrbek, who signed Wayne on as a member of his annual winter bowling league team.

GARY WAYNE

Position: RP
Bats: L **Throws:** L
Ht: 6' 3" **Wt:** 185

Opening Day Age: 27
Born: 11/30/62 in Dearborn, MI
ML Seasons: 1

Overall Statistics

	W	L	ERA	G	GS	Sv	IP	H	R	BB	SO	HR
1989	3	4	3.30	60	0	1	71.0	55	28	36	41	4
Career	3	4	3.30	60	0	1	71.0	55	28	36	41	4

Where They Hit the Ball

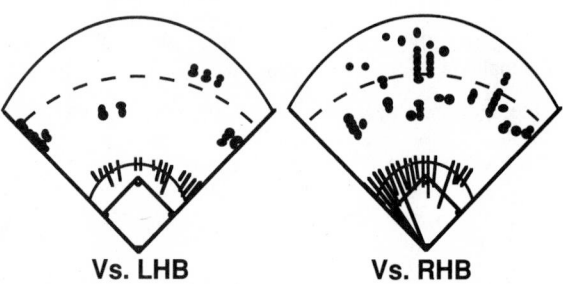

Vs. LHB   **Vs. RHB**

1989 Situational Stats

	W	L	ERA	Sv	IP		AB	H	HR	RBI	AVG
Home	2	0	2.16	1	41.2	LHB	81	15	2	15	.185
Road	1	4	4.91	0	29.1	RHB	178	40	2	19	.225
Day	0	2	5.89	0	18.1	Sc Pos	86	20	2	31	.233
Night	3	2	2.39	1	52.2	Clutch	73	13	0	9	.178

1989 Rankings (American League)

➡ Led the Twins in wild pitches (7), holds (10), ERA at home (2.16) and lowest percent of inherited runners scoring (27.8%) - *team players with 30 inherited runners*

PITCHING:

David West was considered the brightest pitching prospect in the Mets organization when the Twins obtained him among five players in exchange for 1988 Cy Young winner Frank Viola. West, who had been ineffective in brief stints with the Mets, looked overrated when he posted a 16.62 ERA in his first five relief appearances with Minnesota.

The exasperated Twins coaching staff moved West into the starting rotation, hoping it would change his fortunes. Presto. West teamed with Jeff Reardon for a 1-0 shutout in his American League debut as a starter, then beat Texas five nights later. The lefthander finished the season as a regular starter. Team officials theorize that West, 6-6, 220, benefits by the extra warm-up time afforded starting pitchers compared to their bullpen counterparts. There is also an obvious psychological plus to starting for West, since he considers himself best suited for that role.

Twins coaches blame West's early major league struggles on mechanical, rather than talent, deficiencies. Pitching coach Dick Such said West arrived from the Mets with a tendency to throw from the side, rather than over the top. That led to control problems, most significantly a number of high pitches within the strike zone that resulted in line-drive base hits. West does appear to have a quality major league arm. His fastball is above average in the high 80s. He also has showed glimpses of an outstanding breaking ball. West appeared to have problems changing speeds working out of the bullpen, but as a starter he seemed to have a better change-up.

FIELDING:

West still needs work on his mechanics defensively. He isn't exceptionally quick, which is no surprise considering his size. He's a good natural athlete, though, and there's every reason to believe he will be at least adequate defensively when Twins coaches finally get his rhythm straightened out. His move to first is already good and should improve.

OVERALL:

West was largely perceived as the key for the Twins when Minnesota sent Viola to the Mets for five players July 31. That put obvious pressure on West's shoulders, but to his credit his confidence remained steadfast throughout his early struggles out of the bullpen. Although the Mets have been guilty of overrating farm products in the past, West appears as if he will be a solid member of the Twins starting staff for years to come.

DAVID WEST

Position: RP/SP
Bats: L **Throws:** L
Ht: 6' 6" **Wt:** 220

Opening Day Age: 25
Born: 9/1/64 in Memphis, TN
ML Seasons: 2

Overall Statistics

	W	L	ERA	G	GS	Sv	IP	H	R	BB	SO	HR
1989	3	4	6.79	21	7	0	63.2	73	49	33	50	9
Career	4	4	6.46	23	8	0	69.2	79	51	36	53	9

Where They Hit the Ball

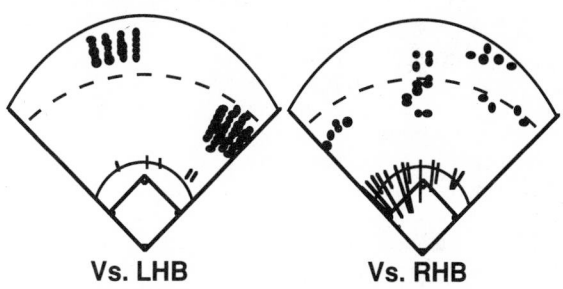

Vs. LHB   **Vs. RHB**

1989 Situational Stats

	W	L	ERA	Sv	IP		AB	H	HR	RBI	AVG
Home	3	3	7.68	0	41.0	LHB	48	7	0	3	.146
Road	0	1	5.16	0	22.2	RHB	205	66	9	43	.322
Day	0	0	5.11	0	12.1	Sc Pos	69	24	2	34	.348
Night	3	4	7.19	0	51.1	Clutch	29	8	1	4	.276

1989 Rankings (American League)

➡ Did not rank near the top or bottom in any category

DOUG BAKER

Position: 2B/SS
Bats: B **Throws:** R
Ht: 5' 9" **Wt:** 165

Opening Day Age: 29
Born: 4/3/61 in Fullerton, CA
ML Seasons: 6

Overall Statistics

	G	AB	R	H	D	T	HR	RBI	SB	BB	SO	AVG
1989	43	78	17	23	5	1	0	9	0	9	18	.295
Career	133	245	38	51	11	2	0	22	3	18	62	.208

HITTING, FIELDING, BASERUNNING:

Doug Baker has spent portions of the last six seasons in the majors, being called up from Triple A when a regular is sidelined by injury. He has done well, but not well enough to threaten the established starters. Baker is a contact hitter who strikes out too much. In other words, he's often overmatched by the good fastballs and breaking stuff that he doesn't often see in Triple A. Baker has pretty good speed, but isn't considered a threat to steal. Shortstop is his main position, and he can also handle second base. Baker has a reputation as a solid fielder with pretty good range and very good hands. He won't make the spectacular play, but he's not going to make many mistakes, either.

OVERALL:

Baker will probably always be a role player in the majors. It would be a victory for him, at this point, just to stay on a major league roster for an entire season. Despite coming and going since 1984, his official major league service time is right around the two-year mark. He's the sort of player who would be helped by major league expansion.

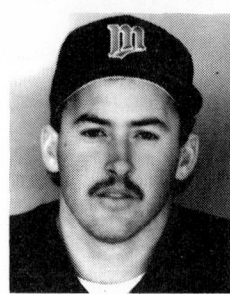

MIKE DYER

Position: SP
Bats: R **Throws:** R
Ht: 6' 3" **Wt:** 195

Opening Day Age: 23
Born: 9/8/66 in Upland, CA
ML Seasons: 1

Overall Statistics

	W	L	ERA	G	GS	Sv	IP	H	R	BB	SO	HR
1989	4	7	4.82	16	12	0	71.0	74	43	37	37	2
Career	4	7	4.82	16	12	0	71.0	74	43	37	37	2

PITCHING & FIELDING:

After being a fourth round draft choice in 1986, Mike Dyer advanced quickly the Twins minor-league system, moved ahead of others who were getting more publicity, and joined the Twins during the middle of the 1989 season. The Twins had more confidence in Dyer, however, than he had in himself -- and his first few appearances made it look like all the hoopla surrounding his arrival was totally misguided. Dyer couldn't find the plate and, when he did, enough was taken off the pitch that hitters quickly figured him out. Then, Dyer found that his assortment of pitches -- fastball, curve and slider -- was good enough for the majors. Dyer doesn't do anything fancy on the mound, but his pitches all have good movement. When he overthrows his fastball it has a tendency to flatten out and stay hittable. Dyer is a good fielder, although he was rarely put into situations last year where base-stealers tested him.

OVERALL:

The Twins rate Dyer right at the top of the young pitchers who figure in their future plans, and have him rated as one of their 1990 starters. They feel his potential is limitless, providing that he stays healthy and keep a mature frame of mind.

MARK GUTHRIE

Position: SP/RP
Bats: B **Throws:** L
Ht: 6' 4" **Wt:** 202

Opening Day Age: 24
Born: 9/22/65 in Buffalo, NY
ML Seasons: 1

Overall Statistics

	W	L	ERA	G	GS	Sv	IP	H	R	BB	SO	HR
1989	2	4	4.55	13	8	0	57.1	66	32	21	38	7
Career	2	4	4.55	13	8	0	57.1	66	32	21	38	7

PITCHING & FIELDING:

Mark Guthrie was rushed to the majors after less than one minor league season above the Class A level. The 24-year old lefthander showed Twins officials that he deserves consideration for 1990 with a strong final two months. Guthrie's strengths are composure and a split-fingered fastball. He has superb control of the pitch for one so young. His fastball, average by big-league standards, is used primarily to set-up his split-finger pitch. After one rough late-season outing, catcher Tim Laudner was criticized by Twins manager Tom Kelly for calling too many straight fastballs and not enough split-fingered pitches.

Guthrie was a seventh-round pick in 1987 who has yet to find a league where he can't succeed. He was 8-3 with a 1.97 ERA in 14 starts at AA Orlando last year before going 3-4, with a 3.65 ERA at AAA Portland. He walked just 54 in 140 1/3 innings at those two stops, striking out 138. He holds baserunners well.

OVERALL:

Guthrie, at an early age, is a pitcher rather than a thrower. He needs some further refinements -- an improved breaking ball for one -- but he has the temperament and pitch control to be a solid major league pitcher.

CHIP HALE

Position: 2B
Bats: L **Throws:** R
Ht: 5'11" **Wt:** 180

Opening Day Age: 25
Born: 12/2/64 in Santa Clara, CA
ML Seasons: 1

Overall Statistics

	G	AB	R	H	D	T	HR	RBI	SB	BB	SO	AVG
1989	28	67	6	14	3	0	0	4	0	1	6	.209
Career	28	67	6	14	3	0	0	4	0	1	6	.209

HITTING, FIELDING, BASERUNNING:

For a player selected in the 17th round of the 1987 amateur draft, Chip Hale has had a rapid ascent to the majors. There's one reason for that: his solid left-handed batting stroke. Hale is a line drive, contact hitter who struck out infrequently as a minor leaguer and showed he might be able to hold his own against major leaguers. He has only average speed on the bases, but he's a smart, intense player. His major weakness is in the field. Hale's hands are a question mark, but thus far he's made up for his shortcomings with a blue-collar work ethic. Hale's "gamer" attitude is the kind manager Tom Kelly prefers, which should help his chances.

OVERALL:

After Wally Backman's disappointing 1989 season, the Twins might take a long look at Hale at second base in spring training. Hale is similar in many ways to a young Backman: a pesky line-drive hitter with a bulldog intensity approach to his job. Hale's price tag is right, and if he shows he can do an adequate job defensively, he could contend for at least semi-regular duty in 1990.

HITTING:

Pushed aside by more talented first basemen and repeatedly released, Steve Balboni enjoyed something of a revival when Yankees found themselves devoid of right-handed power and turned to "Bye Bye" for help. Steve did about as well as anyone could expect.

Balboni is a dead pull hitter, and a mistake-punisher. He is not much interested in singles; almost half his hits in 1989 were for extra bases. His stance is deceptively closed, with his left foot almost on the plate. But his first motion is always the front foot toward third base, setting him in a pull position.

The consensus among A.L. scouts is that Balboni is least dangerous when given a steady diet of breaking balls, but a couple of organizations prefer to feed him fastballs away. Everyone agrees that a predictable, lukewarm heater over the plate is likely to be smashed over the left field fence, while an effectively set up curve in the dirt will usually strike him out.

Steve likes to guess at pitches and locations. His personal preference is to face pitchers with pinpoint control and a known repertoire. Hurlers with uncertain control or good movement on their fastball are the hardest for him to hit. Lefties have given him just as much trouble as righties over the past three years, although he did somewhat better against the southpaws in 1989 (.247 with 13 HR).

BASERUNNING:

Balboni is not built for speed, but he gives a good effort. Shortstops are well advised to avoid daydreaming while Steve is hustling to first on a deep grounder. He legged out two triples in 1989. Stolen bases are simply not part of his game, and he made only 3 extra base advances on hits and outs in 1989, but he is alert and avoids obvious mistakes.

FIELDING:

Steve can give a journeyman's performance at first base when called upon to give the regular a rest. He is not especially error-prone, but that is due to not reaching too many balls. He has little range and cannot be regarded as a defensive presence.

OVERALL:

At Columbus in 1982 it looked as if Steve Balboni, not Don Mattingly, would be the Yankees' first baseman of the future. The future was not as it appeared, however, and Steve is now at or near the end of his career. But Balboni is serious about physical conditioning, and may have another season or two left in him.

STEVE BALBONI

Position: DH/1B
Bats: R **Throws:** R
Ht: 6' 3" **Wt:** 225

Opening Day Age: 33
Born: 1/16/57 in Brockton, MA
ML Seasons: 9

Overall Statistics

	G	AB	R	H	D	T	HR	RBI	SB	BB	SO	AVG
1989	110	300	33	71	12	2	17	59	0	25	67	.237
Career	842	2849	327	660	121	11	164	461	1	238	763	.232

Where He Hits the Ball

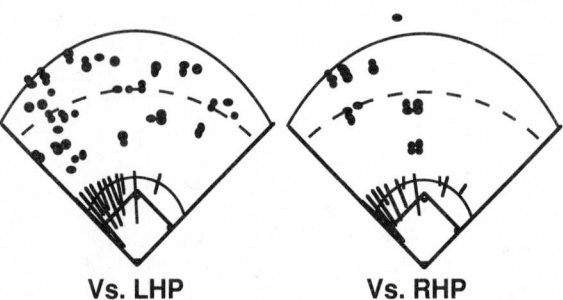

Vs. LHP   **Vs. RHP**

1989 Situational Stats

	AB	H	HR	RBI	AVG		AB	H	HR	RBI	AVG
Home	127	30	7	25	.236	LHP	194	48	13	46	.247
Road	173	41	10	34	.237	RHP	106	23	4	13	.217
Day	88	18	4	13	.205	Sc Pos	100	23	3	36	.230
Night	212	53	13	46	.250	Clutch	44	12	2	7	.273

1989 Rankings (American League)

- ➡ 1st in lowest percentage of extra bases taken as a runner (13.3%) - *players with 40 opportunities to advance*
- ➡ 10th in home run frequency (17.6 ABs per HR) - *all league players*
- ➡ Led the Yankees in home run frequency - *all team players*
- ➡ Led AL Designated Hitters in batting average with 2 strikes (.250) - *designated hitters with 162 PA with 2 strikes*

STRONG ARM

HITTING:

Barfield is still recuperating from wrist surgery he underwent in 1988. Of the 18 home runs that he in hit in 1988, 16 came after his operation. The comeback continued in 1989, in a stadium notoriously unfriendly to righthanded sluggers. Jesse's RBI production was low. Of course he did not bat third behind Sax, Henderson, etc., but the major cause of Barfield's low output was his tendency to fan. His 150 whiffs trailed only Bo Jackson and Rob Deer in the American League. The old book of mixing pitches, speeds, and locations is still the right approach to Barfield; keep him off balance and uncertain. Throw some weak cheese on a 2-0 count, however, and you will soon be asking the ump for a new ball.

The jury is still pondering what to expect from Barfield in 1990. His batting average slipped further in 1989, and he continued his tendency to chase unhittable pitches. However, Jesse drew 87 walks in 1989, for an on-base average of .345 -- better than Wally Joyner, George Bell or Jose Canseco, and his run scoring was surpassed only by Steve Sax among the Yankees.

A key number to watch is Barfield's K/BB ratio. From 1984 through 1987 (his "prime" years) this number tracked 2.3, 2.2, 2.1, and 2.4 respectively, then rose to 2.6 in his troubled year of 1988. In 1989, however, the K/BB ratio not only rebounded but reached a career best of 1.7. There is strong evidence that Barfield is still improving, certainly in his knowledge of the strike zone.

BASERUNNING

Not since copping 22 stolen bases in 1985 has Jesse been a special concern for pitchers and catchers. But he still has good speed and an excellent sense for knowing when to steal (5 for 5 in 1989) or take an extra base. He rarely makes an unnecessary out or misses a possible advance.

FIELDING:

Even in his off years, Jesse has always been a star in right field. In 1989 he joined the select company of DiMaggio, Mantle and Murcer as the only Yankee outfielders with 20 assists in a season since 1935. Barfield is alert, gets to the ball quickly, and throws with one of the best arms in the game today.

OVERALL:

Jesse Barfield needed a good year to rejuvenate his career in 1989, and he got it. He was a success on the field, and with fans, media, and the front office in New York. Jesse believes that his wrist is still regaining strength after his 1988 disability, and the evidence supports his contention.

JESSE BARFIELD

Position: RF/CF
Bats: R **Throws:** R
Ht: 6' 1" **Wt:** 200

Opening Day Age: 30
Born: 10/29/59 in Joliet, IL
ML Seasons: 9

Overall Statistics

	G	AB	R	H	D	T	HR	RBI	SB	BB	SO	AVG
1989	150	521	79	122	23	1	23	67	5	87	150	.234
Career	1160	3904	601	1025	181	28	197	583	60	424	977	.263

Where He Hits the Ball

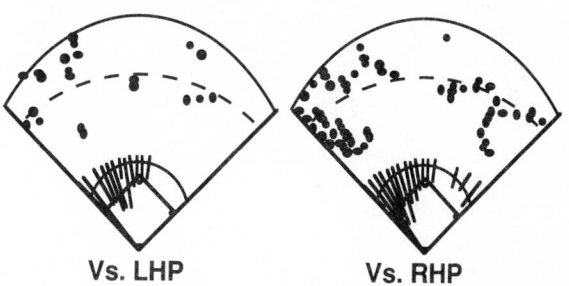

Vs. LHP   **Vs. RHP**

1989 Situational Stats

	AB	H	HR	RBI	AVG		AB	H	HR	RBI	AVG
Home	261	63	7	30	.241	LHP	160	38	8	16	.237
Road	260	59	16	37	.227	RHP	361	84	15	51	.233
Day	169	33	9	25	.195	Sc Pos	137	26	7	46	.190
Night	352	89	14	42	.253	Clutch	75	10	3	11	.133

1989 Rankings (American League)

- ➡ 1st in pitches seen per plate appearance (4.2) - *players with 502 PA*

- ➡ 2nd in lowest batting average in the clutch (.133) - *players with 50 PA in the clutch*

- ➡ 3rd in strikeouts (150) and lowest batting average with runners in scoring position (.190) - *players with 100 PA with runners in scoring position*

- ➡ 5th in percentage of swings that missed (30.0%)

- ➡ Led the Yankees in strikeout (122), home run frequency (24.5 ABs per HR), walks (82), pitches seen per plate appearance (4.2) and runs scored per time reached base (34.0%) - *team players with 502 PA*

PITCHING:

With Oakland, Greg Cadaret made a successful change from minor league starter to major league reliever. In 1989 he had some trouble changing back from reliever to starter in mid-season.

Cadaret is basically a fastball pitcher. A student of Dave Duncan, he likes to pitch inside. In 1988, in short relief with numerous lefty vs. lefty confrontations, Greg used his curve and forkball sparingly. Holding the lefthanded hitters to a .198 average, Greg posted an impressive 2.89 ERA. The success continued into 1989. In 29 relief appearances through July 1, he had a 2.70 ERA. After that, things fell apart.

The Yankees found themselves with four good southpaws in the bullpen and a shortage of starters. The solution: simply instruct Cadaret to revitalize his seldom-used windup, start throwing his curve and forkball more frequently (for strikes of course) and finally, be prepared to throw 100 pitches or more every outing, not 15 or 20.

These changes caused some problems. The rusty breaking pitches did not always find the strike zone. Opposing hitters watched them go by, waiting for the fastball. With more righthanded hitters to face (73% of opponents' at bats in 1989), more innings to labor, and more batters knowing what was coming, the fastball became eminently hittable. Cadaret's ERA ballooned to 4.57 in the second half. The longer outings were especially damaging, as Greg allowed opposing hitters a .349 batting average after the sixth inning. In summary, the mid-season conversion to starter was a bad idea that did not work.

FIELDING:

Cadaret is a good athlete with above-average fielding ability. As a lefty reliever accustomed to pitching from the stretch with runners on base, he has a good pickoff move and holds runners effectively. As a starter, however, the mechanics of his windup need polishing, and he is still re-learning some of the fine points related to fielding.

OVERALL:

Although they never told him so, Oakland's management always felt that Cadaret could succeed as a major league starter. But giving him this role in the middle of 1989 was an act of desperation by the Yankees, not a carefully executed plan. Given Greg's professional approach and past record of success in a clearly defined role, there is no reason to judge his future performance on the basis of problems encountered in 1989. If given time to make the adjustment, he should be able to fulfill the role of starter effectively.

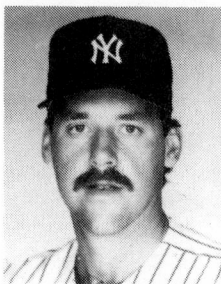

GREG CADARET

Position: RP/SP
Bats: L **Throws:** L
Ht: 6' 3" **Wt:** 205

Opening Day Age: 28
Born: 2/27/62 in Detroit, MI
ML Seasons: 3

Overall Statistics

	W	L	ERA	G	GS	Sv	IP	H	R	BB	SO	HR
1989	5	5	4.05	46	13	0	120.0	130	62	57	80	7
Career	16	9	3.77	133	13	3	231.1	227	110	117	174	15

Where They Hit the Ball

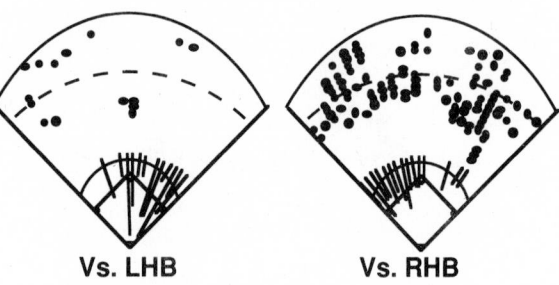

Vs. LHB   **Vs. RHB**

1989 Situational Stats

	W	L	ERA	Sv	IP		AB	H	HR	RBI	AVG
Home	4	2	4.41	0	63.1	LHB	123	31	1	16	.252
Road	1	3	3.65	0	56.2	RHB	341	99	6	44	.290
Day	2	3	5.02	0	28.2	Sc Pos	134	44	3	52	.328
Night	3	2	3.74	0	91.1	Clutch	41	15	0	8	.366

1989 Rankings (American League)

- ➡ 5th worst batting average vs. righthanded batters (.290) - *pitches facing 377 RHB*
- ➡ Led the Yankees in wild pitches (6)

PITCHING:

Chuck Cary was one of the few pleasant surprises on a beleaguered pitching staff. He learned the screwball from Luis Arroyo in winter ball, and put it to good use. Cary has a fine repertoire: a lively fastball, a nice biting slider, and the screwball, which he can throw at different speeds. He uses the scroogie mainly against lefthanders, inside.

After eight relief appearances through June 1, in which Cary had earned a 1.50 ERA with only 10 baserunners in 12 innings, the Yankees gave him two extended outings (75 to 80 pitches) and then his first start on June 14. It took a while to get used to the longer workouts, but Cary adjusted well, reaching his peak as a starter with two consecutive complete game victories, allowing just three runs in total, on July 29 and August 3.

The impacts of year-round baseball and changing workload finally took their toll, and Cary became tired. Three of four outings in late August were rather shaky. Chuck worked little in September/October, as the Yankees looked at their late-season callups.

Many pitchers would have complained bitterly with all the changes that Cary endured in 1989, but Chuck took it all in stride. He finished with a .500 record and the best ERA among 17 pitchers who made a start for the Yankees last year.

In the end, Cary proved effective against every classification of opposing batters, but he was especially tough on lefties (.197 BA, only 4 walks), first man faced (.143 BA with only one walk and one extra base hit), and hitters after the sixth inning (.165 average, .069 isolated power).

FIELDING:

Cary once pitched 108 innings without making a single error. Unfortunately, this feat indicated slowness and inability to stop ground balls. Cary is really not a good fielder. In 1989, he made only eight plays and committed 2 errors. Opposing runners stole six bases in seven attempts (86%) against Cary in 1989, for a rate of .58 SB's per nine innings, among the worst of all Yankees.

OVERALL:

After failing to stick with the Tigers and Braves, Cary had good reason to be pleased with his 1989 performance. Few pitchers show big improvement at age 29; when they do, it is almost always a sign of increased knowledge -- and a new pitch. Cary showed the world that he has not stopped learning, and that his physical abilities remain strong. Chuck must be regarded as one of the front-runners for a spot in the 1990 Yankees rotation.

CHUCK CARY

Position: SP/RP
Bats: L **Throws:** L
Ht: 6' 4" **Wt:** 210

Opening Day Age: 30
Born: 3/3/60 in Whittier, CA
ML Seasons: 5

Overall Statistics

	W	L	ERA	G	GS	Sv	IP	H	R	BB	SO	HR
1989	4	4	3.26	22	11	0	99.1	78	42	29	79	13
Career	6	8	3.51	80	11	3	179.2	152	82	60	144	22

Where They Hit the Ball

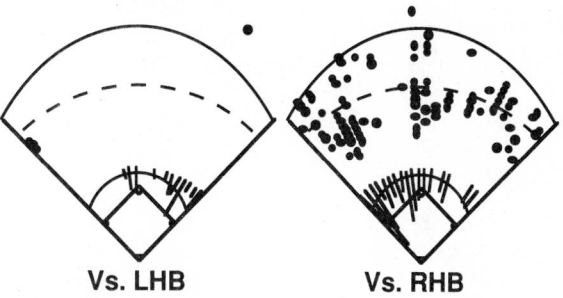

Vs. LHB   **Vs. RHB**

1989 Situational Stats

	W	L	ERA	Sv	IP		AB	H	HR	RBI	AVG
Home	3	2	3.26	0	60.2	LHB	66	13	2	13	.197
Road	1	2	3.26	0	38.2	RHB	307	65	11	29	.212
Day	2	0	2.68	0	37.0	Sc Pos	81	20	6	34	.247
Night	2	4	3.61	0	62.1	Clutch	26	6	0	1	.231

1989 Rankings (American League)

➡ Led the Yankees in lowest opponent batting average (.209), lowest opponent on-base percentage (.266), lowest baserunners per 9 innings (9.7) and wild pitches (6) - *all team players*

HITTING:

When Rafael Santana became unavailable, the Yankees began a frantic search for a regular shortstop. But Pat Corrales advised the front office to look no further than Columbus, and his advice proved sound indeed. Alvaro Espinoza exceeded expectations as much as anyone in pinstripes in 1989.

Espinoza is the ultimate contact hitter, one of the best in baseball. He absorbed a good deal of knowledge from his first major league roommate, Kirby Puckett. Well suited to bat number two, Alvaro is an excellent bunter, and was second in the majors in sacrifice hits. With a slow and compact swing, Alvaro maximizes opportunities for the bat to touch the ball. The result is a multitude of singles, and not much else. With runners at second or third, Espinoza is even more determined to put the ball in play. One fourth of his hits came with runners in scoring position, but only two of his 18 doubles.

Espinoza likes to see the ball up in the strike zone. The pitchers who give him the most trouble are those who throw heavy, sinking fastballs and sliders that break down as well as fade. Kevin Brown and Bert Blyleven are two who especially impressed him.

BASERUNNING:

Shortstops are often a source of speed, but not in the case of Espinoza. His main strength as a runner is that he is always able to size up the situation. Espinoza took 46 extra base advances on hits and outs in 1989, third best of all Yankees. So there are abilities at work to compensate for the lack of raw speed.

FIELDING:

The same qualities that make Espinoza a good baserunner make him a good fielder: he studies the pitchers and hitters, knows where to position himself and what to expect. Alvaro moves well to both sides, and gets to many balls that could elude other major league shortstops. In 1989, he ranked second in double plays turned -- not bad for an unexpected newcomer.

OVERALL:

Espinoza was one of the pleasant surprises for the Yankees in 1989. Although he slumped noticeably in September, Espinoza improved his batting average from .266 at the All Star break, to .282 at year's end. The old logic of looking at the second half to know what a rookie will do in coming years is a good method. We should expect to see plenty of Alvaro Espinoza at the major league level.

ALVARO ESPINOZA

Position: SS
Bats: R **Throws:** R
Ht: 6' 0" **Wt:** 170

Opening Day Age: 28
Born: 2/19/62 in Valencia, Venezuela
ML Seasons: 4

Overall Statistics

	G	AB	R	H	D	T	HR	RBI	SB	BB	SO	AVG
1989	146	503	51	142	23	1	0	41	3	14	60	.282
Career	218	605	60	166	26	1	0	51	3	16	79	.274

Where He Hits the Ball

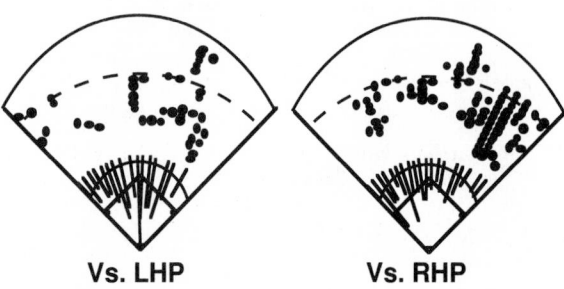

Vs. LHP   Vs. RHP

1989 Situational Stats

	AB	H	HR	RBI	AVG		AB	H	HR	RBI	AVG
Home	241	72	0	22	.299	LHP	162	62	0	12	.383
Road	262	70	0	19	.267	RHP	341	80	0	29	.235
Day	151	39	0	11	.258	Sc Pos	111	35	0	38	.315
Night	352	103	0	30	.293	Clutch	70	21	0	6	.300

1989 Rankings (American League)

➡ 1st in least pitches seen per plate appearance (2.8)

➡ 2nd in sacifice bunts (23), errors (22) and hitting vs. lefthanded pitchers (.383) - *players with 125 PA vs. LHP*

➡ 3rd in lowest percentage of pitches taken (41.8%) - *players with 502 PA*

➡ 4th in bunts in play (34)

➡ Led the Yankees in sacrifice bunts, bunts in play, hitting vs. lefthanded pitchers and errors

➡ Led AL Shortstops in hitting vs. lefthanded pitchers, batting average with 2 strikes (.245) and hitting with runners in scoring position (.315)

HITTING:

As San Diego's first-round pick in 1979, Bob Geren hung around the Padres' clubhouse, to see what it felt like to be a major leaguer. It took him over nine years to find out for sure.

Bob has proven power, but his .288 average (over .300 almost all year) must have surprised everyone except hitting instructor Champ Summers, who saw him improve from a .221 hitter at Double A Albany to a .271 hitter at Triple A Columbus.

After 10 years of minor league experience, Geren had a reputation. For a rookie, he got respect. Knowledgeable pitchers approached him carefully, with offspeed and breaking balls. Bob has finally learned to lay off the change of pace. Early in the year, he looked bad falling into a change-up; by September he had learned not to swing, unless he was expecting it.

Bob is a good bat handler, useful in any situation. His strikeout frequency (21%) is about average for a power hitter, but he can protect the plate well, he can bunt, and he can go with a pitch.

BASERUNNING:

Geren will rarely attempt to steal, and he is unlikely to try for extra bases on hits and outs (only nine advances in 1989). But he is attentive on the basepaths, and will not make blunders.

FIELDING:

Bob has always had excellent defensive stats, leading four leagues in fielding percentage or assists. Bob is an ace at throwing out runners. His release is not especially quick, but he throws with great velocity and accuracy. In 1989, he cut down 41% of steal attempts, an outstanding percentage. Geren made big advancements as a game-caller and pitcher-handler in 1989. He learned that pitchers' strengths are just as important as hitters' weaknesses, and he learned that some major league pitchers need to be pampered. It takes big league experience to become a big league catcher, but Bob made the adjustment quickly.

OVERALL:

Without announcement or fanfare, Bob Geren has become the Yankees' number one catcher. After only half a season, he can do it all: hit for average, hit for power, call a game, handle pitchers, throw out runners, and field his position. His success in 1989 was a happy ending after 10 years in the minors. Bob has never been on the D.L., never been thrown out of a game, and never had a heated argument with a teammate, coach or manager. In short, he has earned it.

BOB GEREN

Position: C
Bats: R **Throws:** R
Ht: 6' 3"   **Wt:** 205

Opening Day Age: 28
Born: 9/22/61 in San Diego, CA
ML Seasons: 2

Overall Statistics

	G	AB	R	H	D	T	HR	RBI	SB	BB	SO	AVG
1989	65	205	26	59	5	1	9	27	0	12	44	.288
Career	75	215	26	60	5	1	9	27	0	14	47	.279

Where He Hits the Ball

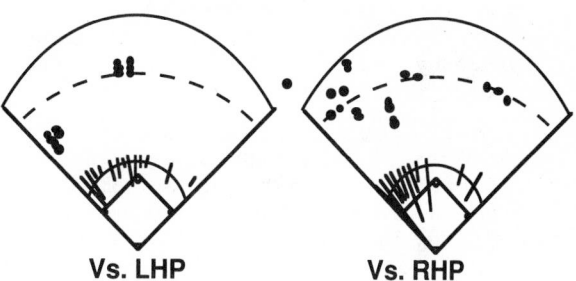

Vs. LHP   **Vs. RHP**

1989 Situational Stats

	AB	H	HR	RBI	AVG		AB	H	HR	RBI	AVG
Home	106	33	4	12	.311	LHP	67	19	2	10	.284
Road	99	26	5	15	.263	RHP	138	40	7	17	.290
Day	81	25	5	14	.309	Sc Pos	47	13	1	15	.277
Night	124	34	4	13	.274	Clutch	37	10	2	6	.270

1989 Rankings (American League)

➡ Did not rank near the top or bottom in any category

PITCHING:

Lee Guetterman has an excellent assortment of pitches for a reliever. Unlike many converted starters, Lee has not reduced his repertoire. He has a good fastball in the 88-90 MPH range, a curve, a slider, and a straight change. The fastball is doubly effective, because he can also throw a sinker. These pitches do not all work well in every game. If they did, Lee would be unhittable. Guetterman likes the fastball best, because he is most confident about controlling it. He selects from the slider, sinker, curve and change (in approximately that order of preference) depending on what is working best, each time out.

In his role of short reliever, Guetterman exerts himself fully and tires quickly. He gave up no runs until May 24, when Chili Davis homered and Johnny Ray uncorked a bases loaded, two-out double. It was only the second time in 20 appearances that Guetterman had thrown as many as 40 pitches. On July 9, Lee really extended himself with a season-high 57 pitches. In his next seven outings, he incurred four losses, and his July ERA ballooned to 6.48.

Guetterman is best suited for situation pitching, with short workouts. He is especially effective against the first hitter (.159 average, no homers, only 2 extra base hits in 63 at bats). And he is definitely more effective against lefty hitters (.236 average, .283 slugging, compared to .266 and .358 for righties). He seems to have bad luck with switch hitters.

FIELDING:

Guetterman made the most errors of any Yankee pitcher (3), but he also made the most assists, 24, and 6 putouts. For a large man, he comes off the mound well, and is especially effective covering first base, a position he played at Liberty Baptist College and left to Sid Bream when he graduated. Lee is about average at holding runners, though the opposition attempted only seven steals all season. And despite the errors in 1989, he is a superior fielder.

OVERALL:

Guetterman has been underappreciated in New York, partly because of Dave Righetti's presence in the bullpen. But based solely on the numbers, it looks like Guetterman, not Rags, should have been the Yankees' lefthanded closer in 1989. He was 100% (13 for 13) in save opportunities and he was the **only** Yankee pitcher to post an ERA under 3.00 (and Lee was way under). With Righetti moving to the starting rotation, Guetterman will either take his place as a closer, or find a new "big name" to overshadow him.

LEE GUETTERMAN

Position: RP
Bats: L **Throws:** L
Ht: 6' 8" **Wt:** 225

Opening Day Age: 31
Born: 11/22/58 in Chattanooga, TN
ML Seasons: 5

Overall Statistics

	W	L	ERA	G	GS	Sv	IP	H	R	BB	SO	HR
1989	5	5	2.45	70	0	13	103.0	98	31	26	51	6
Career	17	15	4.30	159	23	13	337.1	381	181	107	148	28

Where They Hit the Ball

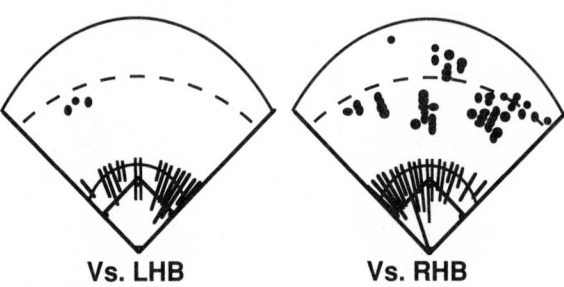

Vs. LHB   **Vs. RHB**

1989 Situational Stats

	W	L	ERA	Sv	IP		AB	H	HR	RBI	AVG
Home	3	1	2.30	8	58.2	LHB	106	25	1	10	.236
Road	2	4	2.64	5	44.1	RHB	274	73	5	31	.266
Day	2	2	2.43	4	37.0	Sc Pos	111	27	2	34	.243
Night	3	3	2.45	9	66.0	Clutch	171	48	3	16	.281

1989 Rankings (American League)

➡ 1st in save percentage (100%) - *all league pitchers*

➡ 5th in games (70) and first batter efficiency (.159) - *pitchers with 40 relief games*

➡ 6th in GDPs per GDP situation (20.0%) - *pitchers with 30 GDP situations*

➡ 8th in holds (12)

➡ Led the Yankees in ERA (2.45), games, holds, save percentage, first batter efficiency and GDPs per GDP situation

HITTING:

Mel Hall is a marvelous bundle of talent, separated from stardom by an incomplete awareness of events around him. If he could stay alert and show better judgment, he could be a first-class platoon outfielder or designated hitter. Unfortunately, Mel often looks out of touch with the game situation.

Hall is a pull hitter, effective against righthanded pitching (lifetime .283 average), but has never hit lefties well (career .154 and dropping). He is a natural to be platooned. Mel likes fastballs, but he likes them all over the place. During 1989, he was prone to chase high heat, even on 3-0 and 3-1 counts. He does not strike out excessively (only 10.2% in 1989), but he does not walk much, either. Mel would rather swing the bat than think about the strike zone. Hurlers with a superior fastball can handle Mel rather easily. He hit .250 against all power pitchers, but only .153 against flyball pitchers (generally, those who throw a high or rising fastball).

Hall has other exploitable weaknesses. He can be backed off the plate with an inside fastball, and then caught looking at an outside curve or lunging at a fat pitch way off the plate. Finally, Mel's hitting has a recent tendency to get untracked late in the season. He hit just .184 in September/October in each of the last two years.

BASERUNNING:

Mel has fair speed and excellent hustle, but shows little understanding of situations. He is the kind of runner who gets thrown out stretching a single when his team is far behind. He is not a threat to steal, presumably because the coaches will not let him try.

FIELDING:

Hall's reputation as a butcher is only partly deserved. He can make splendid catches and great throws. The problem is that Mel is prone to inappropriate moves, like throwing to the wrong man, or diving for a catch when it is vital to contain the ball. He looks unprepared on some fly balls, as if he did not expect anything to be hit at him.

OVERALL:

While some of his skills have leveled off and others have begun to decline (his batting average has dropped for five consecutive years), Mel has not shown any offsetting increase in smarts, as one would expect from a veteran. Hall has become a cult anti-hero in New York, frequently mentioned as a symbol of the Yankee's slide into mediocrity.

MEL HALL

Position: LF/DH/RF
Bats: L **Throws:** L
Ht: 6' 1"   **Wt:** 205

Opening Day Age: 29
Born: 9/16/60 in Lyons, NY
ML Seasons: 9

Overall Statistics

	G	AB	R	H	D	T	HR	RBI	SB	BB	SO	AVG
1989	113	361	54	94	9	0	17	58	0	21	37	.260
Career	845	2777	390	772	147	18	88	408	27	205	432	.278

Where He Hits the Ball

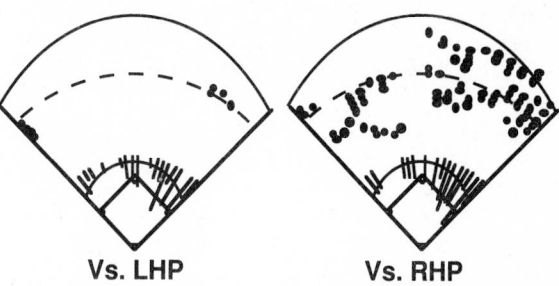

Vs. LHP   **Vs. RHP**

1989 Situational Stats

	AB	H	HR	RBI	AVG		AB	H	HR	RBI	AVG
Home	202	57	11	29	.282	LHP	69	11	1	11	.159
Road	159	37	6	29	.233	RHP	292	83	16	47	.284
Day	130	34	5	22	.262	Sc Pos	88	24	2	39	.273
Night	231	60	12	36	.260	Clutch	50	14	2	8	.280

1989 Rankings (American League)

→ Led the Yankees in percentage extra bases taken as a runner (54.5%) - *team players with 40 opportunities to advance*

PITCHING:

Andy Hawkins won more games in 1989 than any other two Yankees combined. This achievement was not so much a success for Hawkins as it was a failure for the Bombers. Hawkins is a good enough pitcher, but he is misplaced in the role of ace. Even in his 18-8 year with the Padres, Andy gave up more than a hit per inning. In the next two years, he was a losing pitcher, with ERA's of 4.30 and 5.05. Andy's successful 1988 season (14-11, 3.35 ERA) was well-timed for free agency.

Hawkins has a sharp fastball, a cut fastball, and a hard slider. He does not throw any big, slow breaking pitch, just an occasional straight change. The key to his game is good control and good movement on the fastball. With 19 complete games at San Diego, and five more with the Yankees, Hawkins obviously likes to finish what he starts. However, his durability should not be overestimated. Andy's ability to go the distance depends on good control. He threw more than 126 pitches only twice in 1989, and he was pulled 14 times before reaching 100.

Andy gave definition to the phrase "mid-season form" in 1989. He was at the top of his game in mid-June to mid-July, winning six of seven, and four straight. He reached his pinnacle by sandwiching the All Star break with two consecutive shutouts (just eight hits and one walk in 18 innings pitched). His June-July composite ERA was only 2.68.

FIELDING:

Hawkins has good range. He picks up his share of grounders, covers first effectively, and grabs an occasional pop fly. He made a couple of errors in 1989, but was second in putouts among Yankee pitchers. Andy has an excellent move to first, and American League runners really had trouble stealing against him. They got away with eight bases but were cut down 11 times. Hawkins' 0.35 ratio of steals per nine innings was among the lowest of all regulars on the Bronx staff.

OVERALL:

Hawkins has a leader's attitude, focused on the big "W" as his one and only goal when he takes the mound. He is clearly established as the dominant force among returning Yankee starters going into 1990. Success in pitching can be short-lived, and so can success in the Bronx. The last Yankee pitcher who had twice as many wins as the #2 starter was Dennis Rasmussen, and he proved dispensable. Hawkins can expect more deference during his stay in New York.

ANDY HAWKINS

Position: SP
Bats: R **Throws:** R
Ht: 6' 3" **Wt:** 217

Opening Day Age: 30
Born: 1/21/60 in Waco, TX
ML Seasons: 8

Overall Statistics

	W	L	ERA	G	GS	Sv	IP	H	R	BB	SO	HR
1989	15	15	4.80	34	34	0	208.1	238	127	76	98	23
Career	75	73	4.00	233	206	0	1311.0	1327	658	488	587	122

Where They Hit the Ball

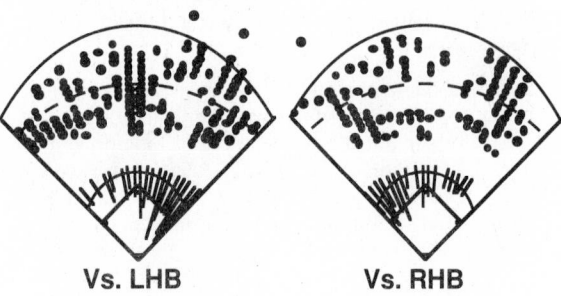

Vs. LHB   **Vs. RHB**

1989 Situational Stats

	W	L	ERA	Sv	IP		AB	H	HR	RBI	AVG
Home	9	10	4.54	0	125.0	LHB	436	141	14	61	.323
Road	6	5	5.18	0	83.1	RHB	384	97	9	43	.253
Day	6	1	2.64	0	47.2	Sc Pos	192	67	4	77	.349
Night	9	14	5.43	0	160.2	Clutch	48	23	3	9	.479

1989 Rankings (American League)

→ 1st in worst slugging percentage allowed (.460), most baserunners allowed per 9 innings (13.8) and doubles allowed (56) - *pitchers with 162 IP*

→ 2nd in losses (15), worst opponent batting average (.290) and worst opponent on-base average allowed (.354)

→ 3rd in lowest stolen base percentage (42.1%)

→ 4th in worst ERA (4.80)

→ Led the Yankees in wins (15), losses, games started (34), complete games (5), shutouts (2), innings (208), hits allowed (238), home runs allowed (23), walks (76), hit batters (6) and strikeouts (98)

GREAT SPEED

HITTING:

One of the Yankee's best trades NOT made in 1989 was Roberto Kelly to Atlanta for Jeff Blauser. Kelly blossomed into a prize rookie centerfielder, while the Yankees found their shortstop in their own back yard.

Roberto surprised almost everyone by hitting .302 with a .369 on-base average. His minor league history was mediocre until 1988, when he hit .333 in a short stay with AAA Columbus. But at age 24, improvement can happen, and it happened for Kelly in 1989.

Despite his glittering average, Bobby has visible weaknesses. He swings too hard with two strikes, and he chases unhittable, low and outside breaking pitches much too often. The book on pitching Kelly is to throw lots of low breaking balls and an occasional fastball up and out. Roberto's free swinging gave him more K's than any Yankee except slugger Jesse Barfield. But his problems are due to inexperience, and he is learning.

BASERUNNING:

Kelly has great speed, and seems able to extend himself in crucial situations. His 35 stolen bases led all American League rookies by a wide margin. He showed improved selectivity and SB efficiency as the season progressed; he was caught only four times after the All Star break. As he learns the pitchers better, Kelly could become a real burner, having already exceeded 50 SB's in a minor league season. He will sharpen his baserunning skills with more experience.

FIELDING:

Speed is a great asset to a centerfielder in Yankee Stadium, as Kelly proved by running down many fly balls at the wall. He looked like a rookie at times, but learned on the job during 1989. Only one of his six errors came after the All Star break. Roberto has great range and is improving his jump on the ball. His arm has always been more like a pop gun than a cannon, but he exceeded expectations when it came to hitting the cutoff man and exercising judgment.

OVERALL:

Roberto has graduated from prospect to potential star, and fans will follow his career with increased interest as his stats accumulate. The man who once wrapped his sprained wrist with garlic has not yet shown his full potential. Rookies who can hit .300 and steal 35 bases are rare. Kelly attracted little attention as the Yankees were out of contention all summer, but in retrospect, his emergence was one of the more interesting stories of 1989.

ROBERTO KELLY

Position: CF
Bats: R **Throws:** R
Ht: 6' 4" **Wt:** 185

Opening Day Age: 25
Born: 10/1/64 in Panama City, Panama
ML Seasons: 3

Overall Statistics

	G	AB	R	H	D	T	HR	RBI	SB	BB	SO	AVG
1989	137	441	65	133	18	3	9	48	35	41	89	.302
Career	198	570	86	166	25	4	11	62	49	49	119	.291

Where He Hits the Ball

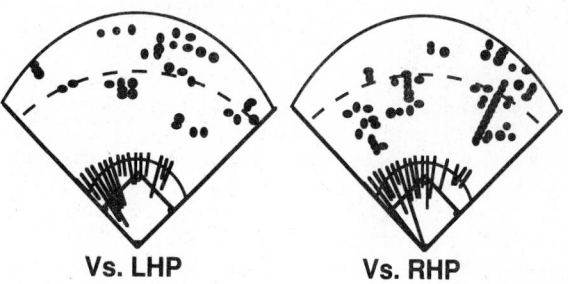

Vs. LHP   Vs. RHP

1989 Situational Stats

	AB	H	HR	RBI	AVG		AB	H	HR	RBI	AVG
Home	205	65	2	26	.317	LHP	145	54	3	16	.372
Road	236	68	7	22	.288	RHP	296	79	6	32	.267
Day	133	38	1	8	.286	Sc Pos	105	30	1	38	.286
Night	308	95	8	40	.308	Clutch	79	26	2	10	.329

1989 Rankings (American League)

- ➡ 2nd in times picked off (4)
- ➡ 3rd in on-base average vs. lefthanded pitchers (.429) - *players with 125 PA vs. left-handed pitchers*
- ➡ 4th in batting average vs. lefthanded pitchers (.372)
- ➡ 8th in stolen bases (35)
- ➡ 9th in caught stealing (12) and hit by pitch (6)
- ➡ Led the Yankees in triples (6), hit by pitch, times picked off, hitting in the clutch (.329) and hitting with the bases loaded (.308)
- ➡ Led AL Center Fielders in times picked off and batting average vs. lefthanded pitchers

PITCHING:

The Yankees do not seem to understand that pitching is fragile. Tiny shifts in ability can make a big difference in numbers. For Dave LaPoint, small factors produced big stats in 1988: career bests in wins, innings pitched, ERA, games, and longest winning streak. New York doled out big bucks with apparent confidence that LaPoint had reached some new plateau. The plateau turned out to be a spike. Junkballers do not usually achieve new levels of dominance at age 30. The key to LaPoint's success in 1988 was excellent control: 41 more K's than walks. In 1989 the difference dropped to six, and LaPoint's game dropped with it.

LaPoint didn't just return to his old form in 1989; he had his worst year ever. He allowed 1.28 hits per inning, walked about as many as he struck out, had a losing record, and produced the highest ERA of his career. He lacked stamina, allowing opposing hitters a .410 average after the 6th inning.

Dave throws all kinds of stuff, including a change-up so deceptive that it has been called a "change of space." He also has a decent slider and a lukewarm fastball. But all of these pitches require pinpoint placement, or they become batting practice material. One of the more hittable pitches that LaPoint threw in 1989 struck him on the left hand August 2, off the bat of Kirby Puckett. Dave was done for the season.

LaPoint's performance in 1989 was consistent. He did not discriminate between lefties and righties, and he gave up runs generously at home and away, day and night, on grass and turf, and every month (4.60 ERA or higher in every breakdown).

FIELDING:

Like most pitchers who worked for St. Louis in the 1980's, LaPoint is very good at holding runners. He helps himself in the field by avoiding bonehead plays, but he is nothing special when it comes to glovework.

OVERALL:

Ever since George Steinbrenner rebuilt the Yankees around Catfish Hunter, he has been trying to buy pennants with high priced pitching. Unfortunately, starters who can be predicted to win 40 games in two years (as Catfish did after coming to New York) are rare indeed. In Dave LaPoint, the Yankees acquired a lifetime 67-66, 3.81 ERA pitcher whose performance in 1989, the year he turned 30, should not have been a shock. The Yankees would have been well advised to spend their money on a third baseman.

DAVE LAPOINT

Position: SP
Bats: L **Throws:** L
Ht: 6' 3" **Wt:** 215

Opening Day Age: 30
Born: 7/29/59 in Glens Falls, NY
ML Seasons: 10

Overall Statistics

	W	L	ERA	G	GS	Sv	IP	H	R	BB	SO	HR
1989	6	9	5.62	20	20	0	113.2	146	73	45	51	12
Career	73	75	3.96	264	198	1	1324.1	1408	654	496	732	106

Where They Hit the Ball

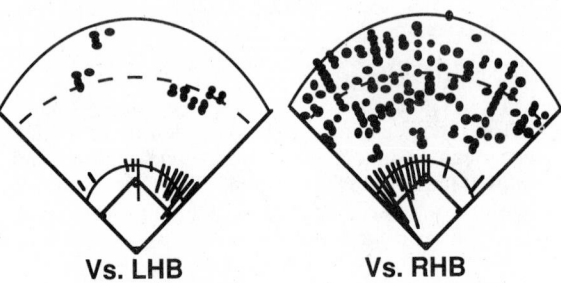

Vs. LHB   **Vs. RHB**

1989 Situational Stats

	W	L	ERA	Sv	IP		AB	H	HR	RBI	AVG
Home	3	3	4.60	0	47.0	LHB	83	26	4	17	.313
Road	3	6	6.35	0	66.2	RHB	387	120	8	44	.310
Day	0	3	5.64	0	22.1	Sc Pos	108	35	1	45	.324
Night	6	6	5.62	0	91.1	Clutch	22	11	0	2	.500

1989 Rankings (American League)

➥ Worst batting average allowed vs. right-handed batters (.310) - *pitchers facing 377 RHB*

IN HIS PRIME

HITTING:

Don Mattingly is the first Yankee since Joe DiMaggio who hits homers almost as often as he strikes out. Is he the best hitter in the American League? Well, Wade Boggs fans should consider that Boggs and Mattingly both hit about .400 in Fenway Park, where Boggs plays half his games. Don is a rare hitter who can produce a .300 BA, 20 home runs and 100 RBI, and be accused of having a bad year. There have been reports of back trouble. But if there was a problem in 1989, it was the epidemic of malaise that spread through the Bronx. Don hit .342 with seven dingers and 29 RBI in his final 31 games. In September, he enjoyed teasing reporters, "Oh, my back is really killing me today!"

Mattingly has a trademark hitting style. He likes to look at the first pitch, real close. Once satisfied, Don is prepared to smash it in any direction. Opposing pitchers say that Don can go through streaks of 20 or more at bats without failing to drive the ball every time; they wish he would walk more.

Most pitchers have learned to get the first pitch in for a strike, but this is a minimal advantage, because Don is at ease no matter what the count. And Mattingly will occasionally punish those who start him off with cheese down the middle, especially with runners in scoring position. Mattingly hit lefties better than righties in 1989 (.338 vs. .282). His explanation is that southpaws are too optimistic about giving him inside heat, while righties know better.

BASERUNNING:

Don has little speed and not much instinct on the bases. He steals a base or two per year just to stay in shape.

FIELDING:

Mattingly knows the pitchers and hitters, and concentrates. He is always in great position, and gets a prescient jump on the ball. Don thus has an appearance of speed and quickness far above his natural ability. His soft glove takes away E's from his teammates and H's from his opponents.

OVERALL:

Don Mattingly is a presence, one of the few great impact players in the game today. He functions as an extra coach whenever he is on the field, on offense or defense. He is a consummate professional, quiet but mentally aggressive. Even among fans who adore him, there is little appreciation for the intelligence and intensity that Don brings onto the field.

DON MATTINGLY

Position: 1B/DH
Bats: L **Throws:** L
Ht: 6' 0" **Wt:** 175

Opening Day Age: 28
Born: 4/20/61 in Evansville, IN
ML Seasons: 8

Overall Statistics

	G	AB	R	H	D	T	HR	RBI	SB	BB	SO	AVG
1989	158	631	79	191	37	2	23	113	3	51	30	.303
Career	1015	4022	615	1300	272	15	164	717	8	314	238	.323

Where He Hits the Ball

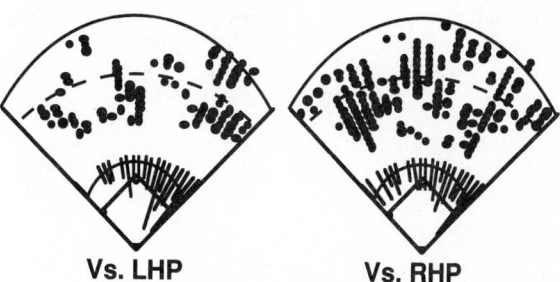

Vs. LHP   **Vs. RHP**

1989 Situational Stats

	AB	H	HR	RBI	AVG		AB	H	HR	RBI	AVG
Home	317	106	19	72	.334	LHP	237	80	8	52	.338
Road	314	85	4	41	.271	RHP	394	111	15	61	.282
Day	201	67	9	42	.333	Sc Pos	172	57	5	86	.331
Night	430	124	14	71	.288	Clutch	89	27	4	21	.303

1989 Rankings (American League)

→ 2nd in RBIs (113) and intentional walks (18)

→ 4th in total bases (301)

→ 6th in doubles (37)

→ 7th in slugging percentage (.477), hits (191), at bats (631) and plate appearances (693) - *players with 502 PA*

→ Led the Yankees in home runs (23), doubles, total bases, RBIs, sacrifice flies (10), intentional walks, games (158), slugging percentage and hitting with runners in scoring position (.331)

→ Led AL First Basemen in at bats, hits, singles (129), doubles, total bases, RBI, intentional walks and plate appearances

LANCE McCULLERS

Position: RP
Bats: B **Throws:** R
Ht: 6' 1" **Wt:** 218

Opening Day Age: 26
Born: 3/8/64 in Tampa, FL
ML Seasons: 5

PITCHING:

For three years, Lance McCullers was a dominating pitcher. When the Yankees acquired him, he had a lifetime ERA under 3.00 and had accumulated 36 saves as the setup man for Rich Gossage and Mark Davis, with almost one strikeout per inning. But everything seemed to come unglued for Lance in New York. He had an ERA of 6.27 in June and 9.00 in July. During this time, he kept using his fastball, and kept accumulating strikeouts (.84 per inning). But the more Lance threw his heater, the more hitters looked for it. Finally, Dave Righetti convinced him to try something different.

McCullers had the tools to make the adjustments. He possesses a slider that breaks down sharply, and his fastball is complemented with an excellent change-up. Using these off-speed pitches, Lance began his mid-year comeback. In August, McCullers posted an ERA of 2.49 with more than one K per IP. His fastball became effective again, as hitters were unable to predict its arrival. In September, he worked little, while the Yankees looked at youngsters.

FIELDING:

McCullers is an average fielder whose occasional errors are due to carelessness, not lack of ability. Although he throws to first frequently and has a reputation for holding runners close, McCullers was the easiest Yankee hurler to steal from in 1989. He gave up the most stolen bases (11), the most steals per nine innings (1.2), and he only caught one runner stealing. American League runners do not give Lance the respect that he enjoyed in the senior circuit.

OVERALL:

McCullers is arguably the most talented pitcher owned by the Yankees. As the only established major leaguer obtained in exchange for Jack Clark, he has been highly scrutinized, but praised by only a few among the New York media. It appears that Lance did not enjoy the pressure of pitching in the Big Apple. His home numbers are worse than road in almost every category, and his four worst appearances all occurred in the Bronx. Lance explains his adjustment to the American League as a matter of learning the hitters. He was impressed by the number of free-swinging sluggers, and came to appreciate the need for a good breaking ball. True, the two leagues are different, but not quite as much as New York is different from San Diego.

Overall Statistics

	W	L	ERA	G	GS	Sv	IP	H	R	BB	SO	HR
1989	4	3	4.57	52	1	3	84.2	83	46	37	82	9
Career	25	31	3.25	281	8	39	476.2	394	196	225	408	43

Where They Hit the Ball

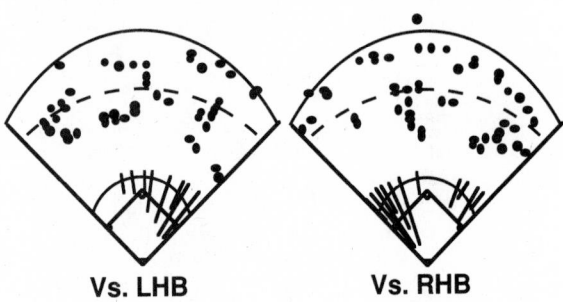

Vs. LHB   Vs. RHB

1989 Situational Stats

	W	L	ERA	Sv	IP		AB	H	HR	RBI	AVG
Home	2	1	5.13	3	52.2	LHB	143	36	3	19	.252
Road	2	2	3.66	0	32.0	RHB	182	47	6	37	.258
Day	1	1	6.27	2	37.1	Sc Pos	106	31	5	48	.292
Night	3	2	3.23	1	47.1	Clutch	94	23	2	17	.245

1989 Rankings (American League)

→ 1st in lowest GDPs per GDP situation (0.0%) - *pitchers with 30 GDP situations*

→ 6th in first batter efficiency (.159) - *pitchers with 40 games in relief*

→ Led the Yankees in stolen bases allowed (11) and strikeouts per 9 innings (8.7) - *all team players*

PITCHING:

Dale Mohorcic continued his downward slide with New York in 1989. Four months into the season, he had just 2 saves, and a 4.59 ERA. On July 19, he gave up four runs including a three-run dinger to Carlton Fisk, and did not appear in the major leagues again until September. In 16 appearances at Columbus, he produced a 1.69 ERA and allowed only 1.05 runners per inning. Shortly after Bucky Dent got the call to New York, he summoned Mohorcic to join him. Unfortunately, Mohorcic did no better in September than he did in July. Overall, his numbers after the All Star break amounted to 12 earned runs in 12 innings, an atrocious 9.00 ERA. He was worse than the numbers indicate, and frequently appeared in the role of arsonist in some of the hottest pyrotechnics displayed by the Yankee bullpen. Too often, he left a game in ashes, with Dallas Green or Bucky Dent smoldering on the mound.

Like most sinkerball pitchers, Mohorcic likes regular work to stay loose. Aside from the sinker, he has a rather standard repertoire. He can mix speeds effectively, and has an off-speed slider. Control is critical no matter what he throws, and his control depends on confidence and frequent appearances. It was a vicious circle that worked unfavorably in 1989.

FIELDING:

Mohorcic is just a fair fielder. He is not especially quick off the mound, but he avoids foolish mistakes, and made no errors in 1989. He is usually competent, but rarely graceful. Dale is not very effective at holding runners, although he watches them closely and throws to first frequently. His ratio of .64 stolen bases allowed per nine innings was among the worst of Yankee pitchers.

OVERALL:

Dale does not like to talk about 1989. But he has had to deal with frustration before, and has handled it well. Nobody spends nine years in the minors with a give-up attitude. This year will be a make or break year for Mohorcic. The most recent evidence says that he is great at Triple A, but not so good against major league hitters. At age 34, he will be fortunate to keep getting regular work. His future is uncertain, at best.

DALE MOHORCIC

Position: RP
Bats: R **Throws:** R
Ht: 6' 3" **Wt:** 220

Opening Day Age: 34
Born: 1/25/56 in Cleveland, OH
ML Seasons: 4

Overall Statistics

	W	L	ERA	G	GS	Sv	IP	H	R	BB	SO	HR
1989	2	1	4.99	32	0	2	57.2	65	41	18	24	8
Career	15	19	3.53	220	0	31	310.2	322	142	81	145	31

Where They Hit the Ball

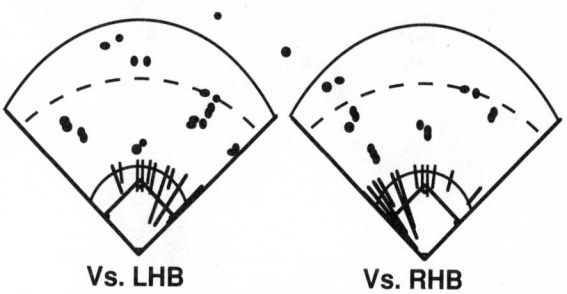

Vs. LHB   **Vs. RHB**

1989 Situational Stats

	W	L	ERA	Sv	IP		AB	H	HR	RBI	AVG
Home	1	0	6.37	1	29.2	LHB	100	32	4	23	.320
Road	1	1	3.54	1	28.0	RHB	127	33	4	23	.260
Day	0	0	11.32	0	10.1	Sc Pos	85	25	3	38	.294
Night	2	1	3.61	2	47.1	Clutch	36	11	1	7	.306

1989 Rankings (American League)

➡ Led the Yankees in hit batsmen (6)

PITCHING:

After four years of excellent progress through the minor leagues, Clay Parker took his place in the Yankee starting rotation on May 16. As a starter he wasn't overwhelming, but Parker's excellent control was evident all year. In 120 innings, Clay walked only 31 batters, a ratio of 2.2 per game. He never gave up more than four walks in any outing. Among all Yankees, only John Candelaria had clearly better command of the strike zone.

Parker has a good, lively fastball and is capable of accumulating K's. At Columbus in 1988, he was the only regular starter to exceed one whiff per inning. Clay's repertoire also includes a curve, a slider and his big out pitch, a palm ball. The palm-change, as he calls it, usually breaks straight down, inducing ground balls, if it can be hit at all.

Although he has been a starter throughout his pro career, and although the New York bullpen was over-crowded late in the season, the Yankees experimented with Parker as a reliever in August and September. Local media made a big deal about George Steinbrenner's wish to see Eric Plunk as a starter; regardless of who said what, it is a matter of record that Parker was the one displaced, sometimes unceremoniously. On September 16, Plunk was inserted in Parker's place after Parker had been published as the starter.

FIELDING:

Parker is an excellent athlete, and it shows in his fielding play. The former LSU punter (veteran of Orange Bowl and Sugar Bowl games) has great range, quickness in all directions, and sure hands. He also possesses great poise and the ability to make the right decision instantly. Clay has a good move to first, and he pays close attention. Runners stole only four bases from him in 1989.

OVERALL:

Clay is eager to pitch, whatever his role. For the record, he did very well in relief (1.56 ERA, 14 hits and four walks in 17+ innings), and certainly better than Eric Plunk did as a starter. If "Manager George" had instigated the switch because he wanted Parker as a fireman, he would have looked like a genius. At age 27, Parker appears ready, willing and able to do whatever job the Yankees want. He finished just one game under .500 on a team that was 13 games under, and had the lowest ERA of any Yankee with 12 or more starts. As a reliever, he appeared truly dominant.

CLAY PARKER

Position: SP/RP
Bats: R **Throws:** R
Ht: 6' 1" **Wt:** 185

Opening Day Age: 27
Born: 12/19/62 in Columbia, LA
ML Seasons: 2

Overall Statistics

	W	L	ERA	G	GS	Sv	IP	H	R	BB	SO	HR
1989	4	5	3.67	22	17	0	120.0	123	53	31	53	12
Career	4	5	4.09	25	18	0	127.2	138	63	35	61	14

Where They Hit the Ball

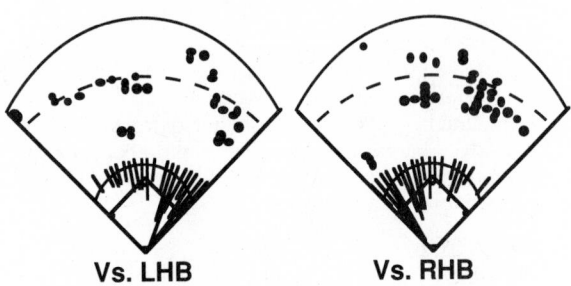

Vs. LHB   **Vs. RHB**

1989 Situational Stats

	W	L	ERA	Sv	IP		AB	H	HR	RBI	AVG
Home	2	2	3.83	0	56.1	LHB	217	61	4	27	.281
Road	2	3	3.53	0	63.2	RHB	249	62	8	19	.249
Day	2	2	4.86	0	53.2	Sc Pos	109	29	1	33	.266
Night	2	3	2.71	0	66.1	Clutch	21	5	1	1	.238

1989 Rankings (American League)

→ Did not rank near the top or bottom in any category

PITCHING:

Eric Plunk, twice involved in trades for Rickey Henderson, became a topic in the rift between Dallas Green and George Steinbrenner. Dallas liked Plunk as a short reliever, the role he had with Oakland. George wanted Eric to become a starter again. Guess who won . . .

Plunk got seven starts late in the season, and showed that he is capable of making the adjustment back to a starting role. It will take a little time, however. Eric is a modified fastball pitcher: that is, he wishes he could throw fastballs all the time, but has modified his thinking to include a curveball. His curve is good, and breaks almost straight down. Eric has always had a change-up, and he has tinkered with a slider, but he never liked to use these pitches much. In his recent return to the rotation, Plunk has shown a soft curve/change that really works. In 1989 it certainly had the element of surprise. Whatever he adds to his repertoire, however, he will always like the heater best.

Much publicity has been given to Eric's improved mechanics over the past three years, but Eric feels that the pressure-packed short relief role was the key to getting his 90 MPH heater over the plate consistently. Now that he is a starter again, Plunk wants to use the same philosophy, and go after every hitter directly. Eric does not mix his pitches extensively. He has a tendency to throw almost all fastballs the first time through a batting order, and then favor the curve more in later innings.

FIELDING:

Defense is an area where Plunk is still learning. He has shown much-improved presence of mind, and he is now able to get to ground balls more effectively, and make the right play promptly. He still needs to work on things like always looking to the catcher for directions.

OVERALL:

The key factor in Eric Plunk's success has always been good control. When he was a short reliever, the question was one of getting his fastball into the strike zone. Now in a starter's role, Plunk has got to be able to throw his curve for strikes, to set up the fastball and change. He is definitely not sharp enough to throw his fastball to locations, so he must keep the hitters guessing as much as possible.

ERIC PLUNK

Position: RP/SP
Bats: R **Throws:** R
Ht: 6' 5" **Wt:** 210

Opening Day Age: 26
Born: 9/3/63 in Wilmington, CA
ML Seasons: 4

Overall Statistics

	W	L	ERA	G	GS	Sv	IP	H	R	BB	SO	HR
1989	8	6	3.28	50	7	1	104.1	82	43	64	85	10
Career	23	21	4.19	157	33	8	397.2	326	198	267	352	38

Where They Hit the Ball

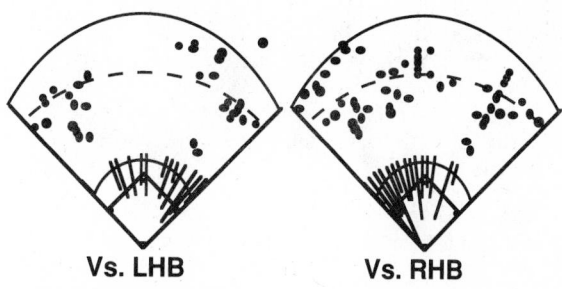

Vs. LHB   **Vs. RHB**

1989 Situational Stats

	W	L	ERA	Sv	IP		AB	H	HR	RBI	AVG
Home	4	2	2.32	0	50.1	LHB	166	37	6	18	.223
Road	4	4	4.17	1	54.0	RHB	207	45	4	32	.217
Day	2	2	3.00	0	27.0	Sc Pos	90	21	3	40	.233
Night	6	4	3.38	1	77.1	Clutch	68	16	3	10	.235

1989 Rankings (American League)

➡ 5th in highest percentage of inherited runners scoring (47.2%) - *pitchers with 30 inherited runners*

➡ 9th in wild pitches (10)

➡ Led the Yankees in wild pitches, balks (3) and lowest batting average allowed vs. left-handed batters (.236) - *team pitchers facing 125 lefthanded batters*

HITTING:

Luis Polonia is a typical speedster, hitting for high average, stealing bases, and getting more triples than homers. He can hit most fastballs, he can chop down effectively on tough sinkers and forkers, and he is a good bunter. Luis expects to be pitched away, and likes to go with outside fastballs. Most teams play the switch-hitting Polonia like a righthanded hitter. The book is to pitch him way outside, mix in plenty of low breaking balls, and try to surprise him with occasional inside heat. He likes to look at the first pitch.

The Yankees late-season experiment with Polonia as a DH, batting second, was a success. Polonia batted .357 over his last 22 games.

BASERUNNING:

Polonia really hustles. He is exciting to watch, running on his toes with many rapid, digging steps, not especially long strides. If legs are wheels, Luis has the highest RPM's on the team. The 20-plus bases that Luis steals every year are taken with pure speed. He gets only an average jump. Once he gets moving, Polonia is an excellent runner. He had one of the best ratios of extra bases taken per opportunity in the league.

FIELDING:

Polonia is usually competent in left field, and sometimes spectacular. He gets only a fair jump on the ball, but his speed gives him range. His throwing arm is just adequate. He can be erratic, a symptom of failing to get set promptly. The main problem with Luis is that he shows poor judgement at times, making dramatic attempts at impossible plays. His awareness of situations is questionable. Too often, he helps the opposition by refusing to make simple, safe plays, and getting himself tied up in knots, with the ball rolling around behind him. Yankee Stadium is not a good place for such antics.

OVERALL:

Polonia aimed to make New Yorkers forget Rickey Henderson. At times, he succeeded. Little Luis is a gritty, aggressive player, who charged the mound with a flying drop kick at 6'5" 215 lb. Mark Knudson. He is always trying to do the impossible and the impractical. Polonia seems destined to fall short of stardom. But at age 25, he is still learning, and his problems with the law in Milwaukee show he needs to mature. But he is a valuable platoon player already, and has upward potential, if he could only learn his limits and play within them.

LUIS POLONIA

Position: LF
Bats: B **Throws:** L
Ht: 5' 8" **Wt:** 155

Opening Day Age: 25
Born: 10/12/64 in Santiago City, Dominican Republic
ML Seasons: 3

Overall Statistics

	G	AB	R	H	D	T	HR	RBI	SB	BB	SO	AVG
1989	125	433	70	130	17	6	3	46	22	25	44	.300
Career	334	1156	199	339	44	20	9	122	75	78	148	.293

Where He Hits the Ball

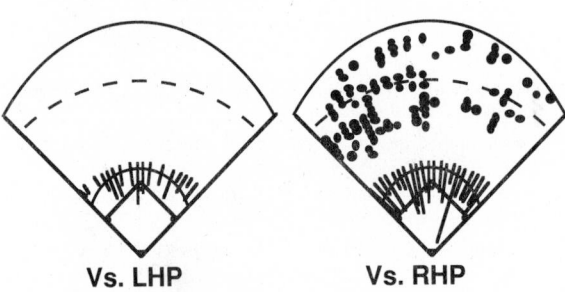

Vs. LHP   **Vs. RHP**

1989 Situational Stats

	AB	H	HR	RBI	AVG		AB	H	HR	RBI	AVG
Home	199	74	1	26	.372	LHP	71	22	0	6	.310
Road	234	56	2	20	.239	RHP	362	108	3	40	.298
Day	159	57	1	15	.358	Sc Pos	119	34	1	41	.286
Night	274	73	2	31	.266	Clutch	71	20	1	6	.282

1989 Rankings (American League)

➡ 4th in batting average with 2 strikes (.297) - *players with 162 PA with 2 strikes*

➡ 7th in percentage of extra bases taken as a runner (56.3%) - *players with 40 opportunities to advance*

➡ Led AL Left Fielders in bunts in play (17) and batting average with 2 strikes

PITCHING:

Dave Righetti ceased being a premier reliever three years ago; it has just taken the Yankees a while to catch on. In his prime, Righetti was as good as anybody; over the past three years, he has been below average among major league closers. Since 1984, his stats in important categories like ERA and baserunners per nine innings have gradually but definitely worsened.

The critical factor for Righetti is movement on the slider. His fastball does not have the velocity or the movement that it once did. He needs the second pitch, and he needs it working well, to be effective. In recent years, Dave has only experimented with the curve and change that used to help him as a starter. He has relied on the fastball and slider almost exclusively in game situations.

After the 1989 season, Dave went to instruction camp to work on his third and fourth pitches, in preparation for a return to the starting rotation. If he is given a role as starter, he will be in the rotation as long as he wants. The Yankees were obviously not inclined to change his role in mid-season.

FIELDING:

Rags made no errors in 1989, but he was also the only regular Yankee pitcher who did not cover first successfully or catch a pop fly even once during the season. With his athletic ability, he should be flashing a lot more leather. Dave has two problems with his fielding: (1) His whole approach to the game is devoted to throwing good pitches; he simply prefers to focus on pitching, not fielding; (2) His delivery motion leaves him leaning toward third base; since his range is not well-developed anyway, he has particular trouble reaching anything hit to his left. Concentrating as much on the hitter as he does, Righetti has always been fairly easy to steal on.

OVERALL:

Righetti is a thoughtful and introspective student of his craft. At age 31 he is already filling the role of coach for some of the young and struggling pitchers around him. He is open-minded, willing to experiment, and naturally curious; these qualities should help him through changes and difficulty. 1990 will begin with a short honeymoon period for Rags, as he makes the readjustment to starting. But in the pressure-cooker Yankee atmosphere, he will be expected to produce and produce quickly.

DAVE RIGHETTI

Position: RP
Bats: L **Throws:** L
Ht: 6' 4" **Wt:** 210

Opening Day Age: 31
Born: 11/28/58 in San Jose, CA
ML Seasons: 10

Overall Statistics

	W	L	ERA	G	GS	Sv	IP	H	R	BB	SO	HR
1989	2	6	3.00	55	0	25	69.0	73	32	26	51	3
Career	73	60	3.09	469	76	188	1083.0	951	424	447	897	57

Where They Hit the Ball

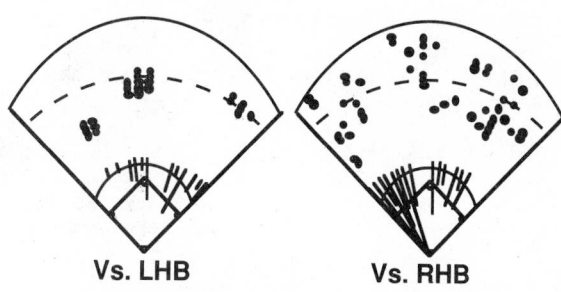

Vs. LHB   Vs. RHB

1989 Situational Stats

	W	L	ERA	Sv	IP		AB	H	HR	RBI	AVG
Home	0	1	3.16	10	31.1	LHB	62	17	1	8	.274
Road	2	5	2.87	15	37.2	RHB	202	56	2	28	.277
Day	0	0	1.57	9	23.0	Sc Pos	83	23	0	31	.277
Night	2	6	3.72	16	46.0	Clutch	180	47	3	24	.261

1989 Rankings (American League)

➡ 2nd lowest save percentage (73.5%) - *pitchers with 20 save opportunites*

➡ 3rd in blown saves (9) and lowest percentage of inherited runners scoring (19.4%) - *pitchers with 30 inherited runners*

➡ 6th in games finished (53)

➡ 9th in saves (25)

➡ Led the Yankees in saves, games finished, lowest percentage of inherited runners scoring and blown saves

HITTING:

Willie Who? Steve Sax has taken New York by storm, elected by fans as the Most Popular Yankee in his first year.

Sax is a marvelous, professional hitter. He takes the whole plate from any pitcher who will not back him off. If you throw him a high fastball, it better be well above the strike zone, or he can hit it hard. Down and in, he is also very strong, dropping his shoulder to go with the pitch. He is a disciplined, up-the-middle hitter; most teams give him the lines.

As a contact hitter, base-stealer and catalyst, Sax stepped in admirably to replace Rickey Henderson as leadoff batter. Few players could even attempt to fill that role. Steve's walks/strikeouts ratio of 1.18 was better than any other Yankee but Don Mattingly, and one of the best in the American League.

With Henderson or Roberto Kelly in front of him most of the season, Sax produced a career high 63 RBI. He is excellent at reading defenses and taking advantage of open spots.

BASERUNNING:

Not since Snuffy Stirnweiss stole 55 bases (against World War II replacements) has any Yankee second baseman been able to steal as many as Sax did. Steve excels at all aspects of the running game: he gets a good jump, runs with superior speed, has sharp instincts, studies the opposition well, and always knows the situation. Sax has now compiled five seasons of 40 or more steals, and has stolen over 30 bases seven times in eight years. His credentials as a burner are clearly established.

FIELDING:

Steve is a superb fielder, and has been superb for years. He has sure hands, good range, excellent positioning, and a strong and accurate throwing arm. He ranked first in fielding percentage among American League second basemen. Seven years ago, he started the 1983 season with a bizarre period of errant throwing. The problem stopped as suddenly as it had started, and it never recurred. But unfounded prejudices still remain.

OVERALL:

Steve Sax replaced two popular Yankees: Willie Randolph at second base, and Rickey Henderson in the leadoff spot. He stepped into both roles with complete confidence, and performed both jobs with excellence, not bad for one year's work!

STEVE SAX

Position: 2B
Bats: R **Throws:** R
Ht: 5'11" **Wt:** 185

Opening Day Age: 30
Born: 1/29/60 in Sacramento, CA
ML Seasons: 9

Overall Statistics

	G	AB	R	H	D	T	HR	RBI	SB	BB	SO	AVG
1989	158	651	88	205	26	3	5	63	43	52	44	.315
Career	1249	4963	662	1423	185	38	35	396	333	415	450	.287

Where He Hits the Ball

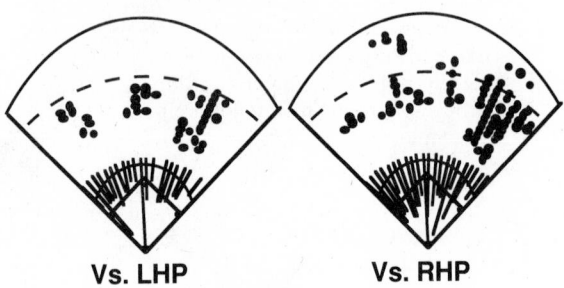

Vs. LHP   **Vs. RHP**

1989 Situational Stats

	AB	H	HR	RBI	AVG		AB	H	HR	RBI	AVG
Home	324	105	2	37	.324	LHP	202	77	2	17	.381
Road	327	100	3	26	.306	RHP	449	128	3	46	.285
Day	203	54	0	16	.266	Sc Pos	171	50	2	59	.292
Night	448	151	5	47	.337	Clutch	92	29	1	12	.315

1989 Rankings (American League)

➡ 1st in at bats (651) and singles (171)

➡ 2nd in hits (205), grounder/flyball ratio (3.99), steals of third (11) and plate appearances (717)

➡ 3rd in hitting vs. lefthanded pitchers (.381) and caught stealing (17)

➡ 4th in stolen bases (43)

➡ 6th in runs (88)

➡ Led the Yankees in batting average (.315), at bats, runs, hits, singles, triples (3), stolen bases, caught stealing, times on base (258), GDPs (19), pitches seen (2,490), plate appearances (717), games (158), on-base average (.364), steals of third and batting average with 2 strikes (.264) - *players with 502 PA*

HITTING:

Slaught was having a career year in 1986 when a Dennis Boyd pitch struck him in the face. He has not been quite the same since. Slaught revived somewhat after the Rangers gave him to the Yankees, but in 1989 his career took another downward turn, as bothersome injuries and the emergence of Bob Geren pushed Sluggo aside. After hitting .285 in the first half, Don slumped to .168 with limited use following the All Star break.

Don can hit for average, and he can hit for power when he tries to pull the ball. He is not a natural pull hitter, however. The book on Slaught is to give him a mixture of breaking balls away, with an occasional fastball in. Although he can be blown away with a sizzling heater (.226 against power pitchers, .211 against flyball pitchers), he will give a long ride to hanging curves or fat fastballs. Slaught is a professional hitter, with one of the highest lifetime averages among American League catchers.

BASERUNNING:

Slaught has average speed for a catcher, meaning he is not a threat to steal. In the total population of baserunners, Sluggo is slower than most, gets a shorter lead and a smaller jump, and is below average at taking extra bases. But for a catcher, he is OK.

FIELDING:

Since leaving Texas, Slaught has become good at throwing out baserunners. He nailed 38.8% of all attempts in 1989. The large number of lefties and veterans on the Yankee pitching staff is a factor that helps, but Don has definitely improved. A number of Yankee pitchers did better in the second half, after Bob Geren became the regular catcher. If Slaught is not the most popular backstop any longer, that could be one more factor in his losing playing time. Although Don tied for the American League lead in catcher's errors in 1988, he is solid in every aspect of his position, and brings an alert and knowledgeable approach onto the field.

OVERALL:

Slaught has had numerous long hot streaks during his career, and he has frequently risen to be among the top catchers in the league. But at age 31, he is past his prime. His personal bests for hits, homers, RBIs and stolen bases all came in the years 1984-86. Don has a long history of disabilities due to injury, and now seems to wear out as the season wears on.

DON SLAUGHT

Position: C
Bats: R **Throws:** R
Ht: 6' 1" **Wt:** 190

Opening Day Age: 31
Born: 9/11/58 in Long Beach, CA
ML Seasons: 8

Overall Statistics

	G	AB	R	H	D	T	HR	RBI	SB	BB	SO	AVG
1989	117	350	34	88	21	3	5	38	1	30	57	.251
Career	756	2366	248	637	141	19	50	256	13	154	356	.269

Where He Hits the Ball

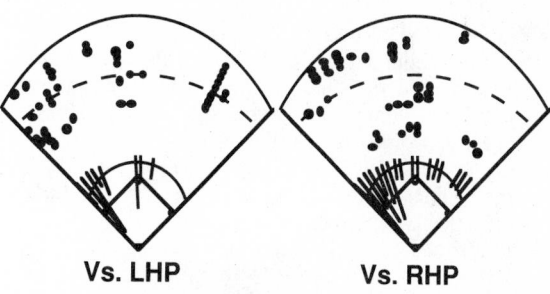

Vs. LHP	Vs. RHP

1989 Situational Stats

	AB	H	HR	RBI	AVG		AB	H	HR	RBI	AVG
Home	169	47	3	24	.278	LHP	131	31	2	13	.237
Road	181	41	2	14	.227	RHP	219	57	3	25	.260
Day	95	19	2	14	.200	Sc Pos	88	25	0	33	.284
Night	255	69	3	24	.271	Clutch	66	20	0	9	.303

1989 Rankings (American League)

- ➡ 3rd in throwing out base stealers (38.8%) - *catchers with 75 attempts*
- ➡ 4th in lowest batting average with 2 strikes (.112) - *players with 162 PA with 2 strikes*
- ➡ Led the Yankees in triples (3)

PITCHING:

It seems like every pitching staff has at least one "crafty lefty," but Walt Terrell is one of the few crafty righties in the game. He throws a hard sinker, a slider, and a revitalized palm ball that may appear any time. Terrell wisely uses location appropriate to every hitter and situation. Not everything works well all the time, however.

Walt was a major disappointment for San Diego. He had good control, as usual (1.9 walks per 9 innings) but got smacked around pretty well by National League hitters. The Padres shipped Terrell and his 5-13 record to New York in late July. Walt's return to the American League was an unceremonious shelling by Cleveland. Terrell eventually regrouped, however, and finished the season with two strong outings and a winning record for New York; he seemed to sense that his future could be on the line.

Without dominating stuff, Walt is in no position to be sensitive about setbacks. He battles in every game, giving up more than a hit per inning, but always keeping his composure. Terrell is sharpest when he can get opposing hitters to swing at difficult offerings early in the count. When Walt starts serving up hittable cookies on the first pitch, he usually gets hammered. He will throw a lot of pitches, pitch a lot of innings, and rarely miss a turn in the rotation. The Yankees gave him regular work but normally pulled him after six or seven innings.

FIELDING:

Terrell is a good fielder, always sure of what to do and usually doing it right. He made no errors with the Yankees, and picked up his share of ground balls, although he is not exactly a cat on the mound. In 1989, Walt had some trouble holding runners on -- previously one of his strong points. Opposing runners stole 8 bases in 11 attempts.

OVERALL:

Terrell battled his 1989 season the same way he often battles in games: get in trouble, fall behind, achieve a little success here and there, and leave the opposition with some tough memories even if they beat you. The Yankees have stockpiled a large number of undistinguished pitchers, hoping that somewhere in the bunch, there will be one or two gems. This method of using quantity to get quality works best with young talent. Unfortunately for Terrell, the youngsters have a better chance to improve and earn work in 1990.

WALT TERRELL

Position: SP
Bats: L **Throws:** R
Ht: 6' 2" **Wt:** 205

Opening Day Age: 31
Born: 5/11/58 in Jeffersonville, IN
ML Seasons: 8

Overall Statistics

	W	L	ERA	G	GS	Sv	IP	H	R	BB	SO	HR
1989	11	18	4.49	32	32	0	206.1	236	117	50	93	23
Career	84	89	4.01	221	219	0	1473.1	1486	732	564	724	137

Where They Hit the Ball

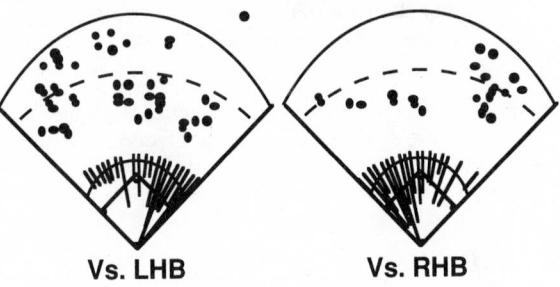

Vs. LHB   Vs. RHB

1989 Situational Stats

	W	L	ERA	Sv	IP		AB	H	HR	RBI	AVG
Home	4	9	4.73	0	83.2	LHB	415	128	13	60	.308
Road	7	9	4.33	0	122.2	RHB	401	108	10	44	.269
Day	0	11	4.98	0	68.2	Sc Pos	171	57	5	79	.333
Night	11	7	4.25	0	137.2	Clutch	76	24	6	14	.316

1989 Rankings (American League)

➡ 5th worst batting average allowed vs. left-handed batters (.333) - *pitchers facing 125 LHB*

MIKE BLOWERS

Position: 3B
Bats: R **Throws:** R
Ht: 6' 2" **Wt:** 190

Opening Day Age: 24
Born: 4/24/65 in
Wurzburg, West
Germany
ML Seasons: 1

Overall Statistics

	G	AB	R	H	D	T	HR	RBI	SB	BB	SO	AVG
1989	13	38	2	10	0	0	0	3	0	3	13	.263
Career	13	38	2	10	0	0	0	3	0	3	13	.263

HITTING, FIELDING, BASERUNNING:

Unless the Yankees make a big acquisition, Mike Blowers will have a genuine chance to prove himself at third base in 1989. Blowers looked like a "good hit, bad field" prospect during his September call-up. The "good hit" part is true. Mike has averaged 15 home runs and 62 RBI in minor league play from 1987 through 1989. He is still improving his knowledge of the strike zone (13 strikeouts in 38 at bats), and could gain power with improved mechanics.

Mike looked shaky in the field, making four errors in 13 games. Most likely, the bumbling was just an anomaly. Mike's reputation and minor league performance both indicate a sure-handed fielder with average range. Blowers is no more than a competent baserunner, without much speed. Over the course of a season, he can steal five or six bases by seizing opportunities, not by outrunning catchers' arms.

OVERALL:

Blowers will turn 25 during the 1990 season. With just one year at the Triple A level, he can be viewed as still developing. With increased patience, a better knowledge of the strike zone, and a chance to learn American League pitchers, Mike could turn into a good, old-fashioned, power-hitting third baseman, something the Yankees could well use.

TOM BROOKENS

Position: 3B
Bats: R **Throws:** R
Ht: 5'10" **Wt:** 170

Opening Day Age: 36
Born: 8/10/53 in
Chambersburg, PA
ML Seasons: 11

Overall Statistics

	G	AB	R	H	D	T	HR	RBI	SB	BB	SO	AVG
1989	66	168	14	38	6	0	4	14	1	11	27	.226
Career	1272	3711	459	909	168	38	70	411	86	267	580	.245

HITTING, FIELDING, BASERUNNING:

In 1989 Tom Brookens was limited to the role of platooner vs. left-handed pitching, and then was sidelined by a pulled muscle from late July until September. He finished with only 169 at bats, a weak .226 average, and was unspectacular in the field. At age 36, he must be thinking about the end of his playing career.

Brookens can be mastered by almost any pitcher who has good control and an assortment of pitches. Tom likes to work the count and then look for a fastball, but is at a loss facing pitchers who throw strikes consistently, especially breaking balls when behind in the count. Brookens is, however, good at reading changes of speeds, and can punish a hurler who has only one pitch under control on a given day.

On the basepaths, Brookens is alert and shows excellent judgment. He is no longer a threat to steal (only one in four attempts in 1989), but he is not going to waste any opportunities with inattention or make outs being overly optimistic.

OVERALL:

Brookens may still have value as a substitute infielder. Considering his knowledge, attitude and personality, his future may lie in the coaching or managing ranks.

GOOSE GOSSAGE

Position: RP
Bats: R **Throws:** R
Ht: 6' 3" **Wt:** 226

Opening Day Age: 38
Born: 7/5/51 in
Colorado Springs, CO
ML Seasons: 18

Overall Statistics

	W	L	ERA	G	GS	Sv	IP	H	R	BB	SO	HR
1989	3	1	2.95	42	0	5	58.0	46	22	30	30	2
Career	113	98	2.92	853	37	307	1636.0	1339	594	656	1379	98

PITCHING & FIELDING:

The Goose had an ERA of 2.68 last year when the Giants cut him loose. They knew that he was not as good as his numbers. At age 38, Gossage needs more than a fastball. Unfortunately, Rich does not have good command of his breaking pitches, not even his once-great slider. With no reliable breaking ball, Gossage often tries to spot his fastball, keeping it away from right-handed hitters. But he is not accustomed to throwing at spots, so he walks a lot of people, even with fastballs. In 1989, Rich had just as many walks as strikeouts. In his prime, he produced two to three times as many K's.

Gossage has never had great fielding ability. Whatever he has learned from experience has been offset by increased age. His move to first is mediocre at best.

OVERALL:

If Gossage could unveil a new pitch, like a forkball or even a working curve, he is strong enough to return to dominance. But after four years of looking for that big adjustment, it is doubtful that he is ever going to find it.

JIMMY JONES

Position: SP/RP
Bats: R **Throws:** R
Ht: 6' 2" **Wt:** 190

Opening Day Age: 25
Born: 4/20/64 in Dallas, TX
ML Seasons: 4

Overall Statistics

	W	L	ERA	G	GS	Sv	IP	H	R	BB	SO	HR
1989	2	1	5.25	11	6	0	48.0	56	29	16	25	7
Career	22	22	4.19	73	60	0	390.2	412	218	117	173	36

PITCHING & FIELDING:

Jimmy Jones has a classic fastball, curveball, and change-up. He spent the winter working on a slider to unveil in 1990. Although he likes to show the curve to every hitter, his main pitch is the 88 to 90 MPH heater.

Jimmy puts slight variations on his fastball to get different kinds of movement. His basic #1 moves down and slightly away from a righthanded hitter. He can also throw a sinking fastball, which moves into a righthander. Jones mixes pitches well and he is a durable hurler.

Jones is good at holding runners on. In 48 innings, the opposition stole just one base from him, while two runners were thrown out trying. He is a competent fielder as well, with good range coming off the mound.

OVERALL:

Jimmy feels that he had the best stuff of his career in 1989. He was somewhat bewildered to be shuttled between New York and Columbus. Jones is going to have to get accustomed to inexplicable treatment if he hopes to succeed in New York. Just 25 on opening day 1990, Jimmy is still improving, and should be among the leading candidates for a regular spot in the rotation.

HENSLEY MEULENS

Position: 3B
Bats: R **Throws:** R
Ht: 6' 3" **Wt:** 190

Opening Day Age: 22
Born: 6/23/67 in
Curacao, Netherlands
Antilles
ML Seasons: 1

Overall Statistics

	G	AB	R	H	D	T	HR	RBI	SB	BB	SO	AVG
1989	8	28	2	5	0	0	0	1	0	2	8	.179
Career	8	28	2	5	0	0	0	1	0	2	8	.179

HITTING, FIELDING, BASERUNNING:

Since leading the Carolina League with 28 homers in 1987, Hensley "Bam Bam" Meulens has been hyped as the Yankees main hope for a home-grown slugger. Rushed to the majors in '89, he looked overmatched. Hensley can be punched out by most pitchers, especially those with excellent control. With his open, off-the-plate stance, Meulens can't cover the whole strike zone; he will probably have to move in some. He is an anxious, free swinger, and strikes out often. In the field, Hensley is good at grabbing line drives and picking low smashes out of the dirt, but he is error prone on any play requiring steps toward the ball, especially when moving to his left. Meulens is an alert runner with surprising ability to steal a base from a sleepy defense (he stole 14 in 1987). In New York he will not be given the green light too often, however.

OVERALL:

At age 22, Meulens is too young to be written off as a non-prospect, although the Big Apple media have tried. His most visible faults can be corrected with experience. An intelligent man (he speaks four languages), Hensley should continue to improve, especially if he is not rushed.

DEION SANDERS

Position: CF
Bats: L **Throws:** L
Ht: 6' 1" **Wt:** 195

Opening Day Age: 22
Born: 8/9/67 in Ft.
Myers, FL
ML Seasons: 1

Overall Statistics

	G	AB	R	H	D	T	HR	RBI	SB	BB	SO	AVG
1989	14	47	7	11	2	0	2	7	1	3	8	.234
Career	14	47	7	11	2	0	2	7	1	3	8	.234

HITTING, FIELDING, BASERUNNING:

With tons of talent and an ounce of experience, "Neon Deion" flashed on and off the New York scene twice in 1989. Both call-ups were intended to entice Sanders away from pro football. But he is not really ready to play major league baseball.

Deion showed discipline at bat, usually looking at the first pitch. For someone who looks like he is swinging an axe, Sanders is very effective putting the bat on the ball. He can fight off tough pitches and produce long at bats as well as hits. Only the low breaking ball gives him serious trouble, especially a hard slider down and in. On the basepaths, Deion takes a large lead and runs with great speed. In the field, he depends on speed to keep him in some plays, chasing down long flies. He holds onto the ball a little too long, while thinking about where to throw it.

OVERALL:

It would be great fun to watch Sanders develop as a baseball player. But anyone who saw him leave his team in the middle of a game, to sign with the Atlanta Falcons, must believe that his interests lie elsewhere.

RANDY VELARDE

Position: 3B
Bats: R **Throws:** R
Ht: 6' 0" **Wt:** 185

Opening Day Age: 27
Born: 11/24/62 in
Midland, TX
ML Seasons: 3

Overall Statistics

	G	AB	R	H	D	T	HR	RBI	SB	BB	SO	AVG
1989	33	100	12	34	4	2	2	11	0	7	14	.340
Career	89	237	31	58	10	2	7	24	1	15	44	.245

HITTING, FIELDING, BASERUNNING:

Randy Velarde is ready to become the Yankees' number one infield backup. He is a good hitter, as evidenced by his .300-plus seasons at Albany and Columbus. Velarde waits well on the breaking ball, especially when it is up in the strike zone. With his hands extended, he can really drive a ball. He can pull a ball or use all fields. If he has a visible weakness, it is low breaking balls. Dave Stewart's forkball and Dave Stieb's bottomless slider are the two pitches Randy likes to see least. The book on Velarde is to come right at him with fastballs, and mix in something that sinks if you have it.

Velarde has good range, and versatility to play second base, third base or short, but he is error-prone. His throwing and footwork are somewhat erratic. On the bases, Velarde has fair speed. He needs to work on his lead and his knowledge of opposing pitchers.

OVERALL:

The Yankees have been disappointed by a series of veteran utility infielders over the past few years. Velarde is no kid (age 27), but he is a fresh face, and in 1990 he should get his chance to stay in the majors.

OVERLOOKED

PITCHING:

Todd Burns burst upon the scene rather suddenly in 1988, when he went 8-2 as the A's fifth starter. His role changed in 1989, and he showed his adaptability as well as his potential. Burns pitched more innings in relief than any other A's pitcher in 1989. In addition to starting two games, he was used as a long man, a set-up man and even as a closer during the time that Dennis Eckersley was injured. His versatility was the main reason the A's were able to trade relief pitchers Eric Plunk and Greg Cadaret to the Yankees for Rickey Henderson.

Burns doesn't have great arm speed, but he has a well-developed lower body and enhances his velocity by driving well off the mound. He keeps most of his pitches down, and isn't afraid to move a batter off the plate to lay claim to the inside corner. Burns was strictly a fastball pitcher during four run of the mill minor league seasons. Now, however, he has a fastball, curveball, forkball and change-up that he is willing to throw virtually at any time. As a starter, Burns will use all of his pitches. As a reliever, Burns usually will concentrate on ascertaining his two most effective pitches as he is loosening up. He usually will stick with those two pitches when he is called into the game, and the fact he doesn't experiment helps him get better mastery of whatever pitches he decides are working for him.

FIELDING:

Burns isn't the most mobile of athletes, but his fielding was much improved in 1989. His move is adequate, and he usually keeps runners close.

OVERALL:

The A's haven't established a long-term role for Burns; it could be that he winds up back in the starting rotation in 1990. But it's virtually certain that he'll be a part of their plans. He is much like Gene Nelson, except for the fact he is more durable, and he gives the A's a wild card in the event of problems either in the starting rotation or in the bullpen. He handles the difficult starter/reliever swingman role as well as any pitcher in the major leagues.

TODD BURNS

Position: RP
Bats: R **Throws:** R
Ht: 6' 2" **Wt:** 186

Opening Day Age: 26
Born: 7/6/63 in Maywood, CA
ML Seasons: 2

Overall Statistics

	W	L	ERA	G	GS	Sv	IP	H	R	BB	SO	HR
1989	6	5	2.24	50	2	8	96.1	66	27	28	49	3
Career	14	7	2.71	67	16	9	199.0	159	65	62	106	11

Where They Hit the Ball

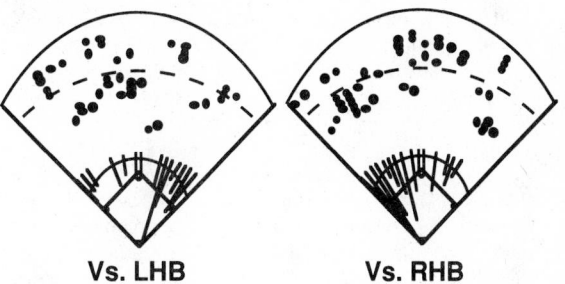

Vs. LHB   Vs. RHB

1989 Situational Stats

	W	L	ERA	Sv	IP		AB	H	HR	RBI	AVG
Home	4	2	2.59	5	48.2	LHB	134	23	0	6	.172
Road	2	3	1.89	3	47.2	RHB	203	43	3	20	.212
Day	2	1	1.70	6	37.0	Sc Pos	76	14	0	19	.184
Night	4	4	2.58	2	59.1	Clutch	108	26	2	14	.241

1989 Rankings (American League)

➡ 3rd in lowest batting average vs. lefthanded batters (.172) - *pitchers facing 125 LHB*

➡ 4th in lowest percent of inherited runners scoring (20.0%) - *pitchers with 30 runners inherited*

➡ 7th in lowest baserunners per 9 innings (8.9) - *all league pitchers*

➡ Led the A's in lowest batting average vs. lefthanded batters and lowest percent of inherited runners scoring

HITTING:

It wasn't until late August that Jose Canseco again became a celebrity for doing what he does best. It was at that point that Canseco made people forget all his other troubles by going on a week-long tear that produced five home runs, 14 RBIs and a sense that baseball's first 40-homer, 40-steal man had returned to 1988 form. Well, not quite. Canseco never fully recovered from the wrist injury, and it showed when he tried to hit to the opposite field. He lunged at outside pitches instead of wristing them, and he tended to overswing, especially when he got ahead on the count and began guessing fastball instead of reacting to whatever pitch that was thrown.

Canseco also began tinkering with his stance -- a problem to which he was vulnerable earlier in his career. During his August streak, he finally settled on a back-of-the-box, hands-low stance that helped him wait on the outside pitch. Once the pain in his wrist began to subside, his patience began to improve. Canseco saw more breaking balls than in 1989 because of all the lunging he did, but after his August binge, pitchers returned to the up-and-in, low-and-away pattern that he saw most often in 1988.

BASERUNNING:

Canseco's baserunning aggression seemed like an outlet for him immediately after he came off the disabled list; it was as if he thought the first step toward recapturing his combativeness at the plate was to do so on the bases. Consequently, he was very aggressive on the bases, although he didn't try to steal as much as he did in 1988.

FIELDING:

Canseco's wrist problems didn't affect his defense. He has a no-trespassing sign on his arm and moves up on a ball as well as any right fielder in the league. His first move usually is forward, which hurts him occasionally on balls hit behind him. But he is an excellent defensive outfielder overall.

OVERALL:

Canseco survived everything that was thrust upon him last season, both on and off the field. The A's organization became more than mildly irritated with his difficulties early in the season. But later the thinking was that the experiences of 1989 could be of long-range benefit to him in terms of maturity. Nobody ever has questioned that when Jose Canseco is 100 percent, nobody in the game can do as many things as well.

JOSE CANSECO

Position: RF
Bats: R **Throws:** R
Ht: 6' 3" **Wt:** 230

Opening Day Age: 25
Born: 7/2/64 in Havana, Cuba
ML Seasons: 5

Overall Statistics

	G	AB	R	H	D	T	HR	RBI	SB	BB	SO	AVG
1989	65	227	40	61	9	1	17	57	6	23	69	.269
Career	568	2163	342	583	110	5	128	424	77	220	560	.270

Where He Hits the Ball

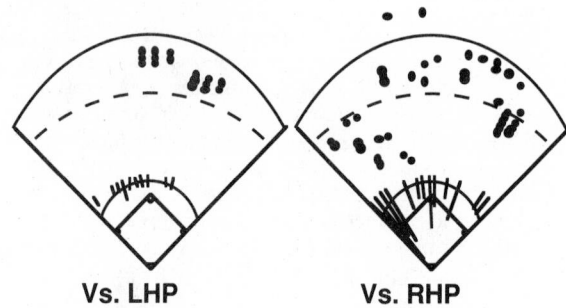

Vs. LHP   **Vs. RHP**

1989 Situational Stats

	AB	H	HR	RBI	AVG		AB	H	HR	RBI	AVG
Home	104	28	8	23	.269	LHP	50	13	7	18	.260
Road	123	33	9	34	.268	RHP	177	48	10	39	.271
Day	74	20	4	16	.270	Sc Pos	65	23	6	41	.354
Night	153	41	13	41	.268	Clutch	31	9	2	8	.290

1989 Rankings (American League)

- ➡ 2nd in home run frequency (13.4 ABs per HR) - *all league players*
- ➡ Led the A's in slugging percentage and least GDPs per GDP situation (5.8%) - *team players with 50 PA in GDP situations*
- ➡ Led AL Right Fielders in home run frequency

PITCHING:

Jim Corsi is one of the more intriguing unknown quantities in the A's organization. Corsi, 28, was released by the Yankees and Red Sox before reaching Class AAA in either organization, and it doesn't seem likely that the A's will find a long-term role for him, either. He was with the big club most of the season, yet got into only 22 games and pitched only seven innings after Aug. 16.

Nevertheless, the A's like him, and it's easy to see why opposing hitters don't. Corsi is a muscular man with an offensive lineman's lower body, and he explodes at the hitter with arms, legs and torso all seemingly going in different directions. He is a high-strikeout, high-risk pitcher who showed promise as a closer at Class AAA Tacoma, but the A's have used him primarily in mop-up roles, so it has been difficult for him to show what he can do in high-stress, major league situations. Corsi is strictly a fastball/slider pitcher who doesn't bother much with finesse. Pitching coach Dave Duncan has been teaching him a forkball, as he does with all of the A's pitchers; that could be the off-speed pitch that Corsi needs.

FIELDING:

Corsi generates so much force coming off the mound that his follow-through leaves him out of position to field. He isn't a bad athlete, though, and seems to react well when the ball is hit back at him. His fielding against bunts must improve; so must his ability to hold runners on. But he is extremely competitive, and sources in the A's organization say most of his fielding defects can be corrected.

OVERALL:

If looks alone could get batters out, Corsi wouldn't be a fringe reliever. His build, delivery, velocity and growling mound demeanor give him the look of the ideal closer. The problem is that the A's simply don't need any more relief pitchers, and Corsi is too unpolished to help them now. But he could turn out to be like Cleveland's Doug Jones, who bounced around for several years before finding himself with the Indians. Keep an eye on this guy; he could emerge as somebody's star closer at some point.

JIM CORSI

Position: RP
Bats: R **Throws:** R
Ht: 6' 1" **Wt:** 210

Opening Day Age: 28
Born: 9/9/61 in Newton, MA
ML Seasons: 2

Overall Statistics

	W	L	ERA	G	GS	Sv	IP	H	R	BB	SO	HR
1989	1	2	1.88	22	0	0	38.1	26	8	10	21	2
Career	1	3	2.56	33	1	0	59.2	46	18	16	31	3

Where They Hit the Ball

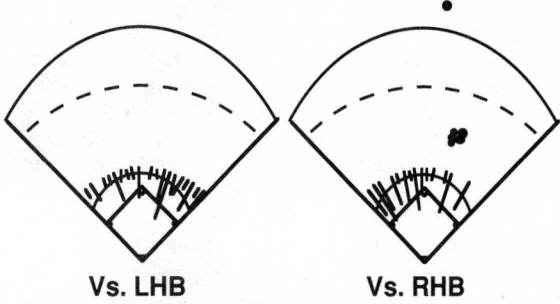

Vs. LHB   **Vs. RHB**

1989 Situational Stats

	W	L	ERA	Sv	IP		AB	H	HR	RBI	AVG
Home	1	1	2.84	0	19.0	LHB	60	9	0	2	.150
Road	0	1	0.93	0	19.1	RHB	74	17	2	13	.230
Day	1	0	0.82	0	11.0	Sc Pos	32	8	0	12	.250
Night	0	2	2.30	0	27.1	Clutch	27	6	0	3	.222

1989 Rankings (American League)

➡ 5th in lowest baserunners per 9 ininngs (8.7) - *all league pitchers*

➡ 7th in lowest slugging percentage allowed (.254) - *all league pitchers*

➡ 8th in lowest on-base percentage allowed (.252) - *all league pitchers*

➡ Led the A's in grounder/flyball ratio (2.29) - *all team pitchers*

PITCHING:

Early in the 1989 season, Storm Davis established himself as perhaps the best No. 4 starter in baseball. Late in the season, he was as good as anybody the A's had. Davis finished with a fluffy earned run average, but he lost only two games after August 1 on his way to a 19-7 season. That surge came at a time when Bob Welch and Mike Moore were struggling, and it reinforced Davis' long-standing reputation as a second-half pitcher. Davis is a sensitive individual who doesn't pitch well in a hard-nosed regime, such as Larry Bowa's operation when Davis was pitching for the Padres. A's pitching coach Dave Duncan has done wonders with Davis in terms of giving him the confidence he needs.

Davis is a straight-over-the-top pitcher who throws a heavy ball that he tries to keep down. His release point is particularly important; he usually gets hit if he isn't driving his arm through before he releases the ball. But he is usually around the plate; his strikeout-to-walk ratio was respectable in 1989, mainly because he doesn't often try to be too fine. Davis' No. 2 pitch is an overhand curve, which, like the fastball, he occasionally hangs because his release point is too high. With both pitches, he usually tries to work in and out rather than up and down. He overthrows occasionally, but has learned to slow himself down when he slips into that habit. He doesn't change speeds a great deal, although he does throw the forkball that Duncan teaches to all the A's pitchers.

FIELDING:

Davis has a quick motion in the stretch, which makes him difficult to run on even though his move isn't that good. He takes a long stride after he releases the ball, and that sometimes leaves him out of fielding position, but he is quick on his feet and doesn't embarrass himself as a fielder. It's a good thing for Davis that he pitches in the American League; he is a terrible hitter.

OVERALL:

The acquisition of Davis from San Diego has proven to be the best something-for-nothing deal of Sandy Alderson's general managership. Freed from a manager who wasn't attuned to the fact Davis doesn't respond well to harsh treatment, Davis at 28 figures to be part of the A's rotation for many years to come.

STORM DAVIS

Position: SP
Bats: R **Throws:** R
Ht: 6' 4" **Wt:** 200

Opening Day Age: 28
Born: 12/26/61 in Dallas, TX
ML Seasons: 8

Overall Statistics

	W	L	ERA	G	GS	Sv	IP	H	R	BB	SO	HR
1989	19	7	4.36	31	31	0	169.1	187	91	68	91	19
Career	92	62	3.86	244	200	1	1319.0	1315	616	488	769	102

Where They Hit the Ball

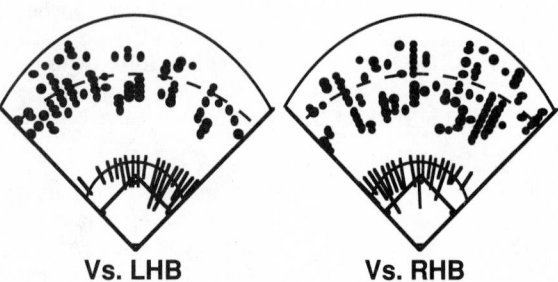

Vs. LHB   **Vs. RHB**

1989 Situational Stats

	W	L	ERA	Sv	IP		AB	H	HR	RBI	AVG
Home	9	3	4.70	0	82.1	LHB	314	83	10	35	.264
Road	10	4	4.03	0	87.0	RHB	335	104	9	44	.310
Day	9	4	4.85	0	78.0	Sc Pos	160	43	3	59	.269
Night	10	3	3.94	0	91.1	Clutch	33	9	2	4	.273

1989 Rankings (American League)

➡ 1st in worst on-base average allowed (.354) - *pitchers with 162 IP*

➡ 2nd in run support per 9 innings (6.48) and most GDPs per 9 innings (1.28)

➡ 3rd in wins (19), worst slugging percent allowed (.434), highest opponent batting average (.288)

➡ 4th in highest baserunners allowed per 9 innings (13.7) and best won/loss percentage (.731)

➡ Led the A's in caught stealing (10), GDPs induced (24), won/loss percentage, run support per 9 innings and GDPs per 9 innings

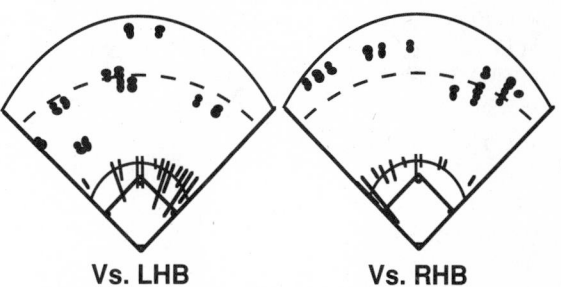

PITCHING:

Dennis Eckersley is a novelty among major league relief pitchers -- partly because he is so good, and partly because he is motivated by the fear of being bad. Eckersley at one time was one of the sport's more renowned roisterers, and his in-your-face competitive zeal made him something less than popular among opponents. But he has undergone treatment for alcoholism, and now the introspective side of Eckersley is dominant. He admits to thinking in terms of not failing, rather than succeeding, when he is sent to close a game, and unlike most relief pitchers, he has made that fear of failure work for him. His 45-save performance in 1988 was overshadowed by the World Series home run he gave up to Kirk Gibson, but Eckersley had another outstanding season for the A's in 1989 despite missing 40 games with a strained right shoulder.

Eckersley at age 35 can still be overpowering, although his velocity is no longer his calling card. He has a sidearm motion that enables his fastball to ride in on right-handed hitter. Against lefties, especially pull hitters, Eckersley can turn the ball over and sink it. Regardless of the hitter, Eckersley almost never gets behind on the count. He doesn't try to paint the corners, and as a result is one of the best control pitchers in baseball.

Eckersley gets into trouble with off-speed stuff, like the Gibson home run pitch. Like most closers, he generally stays with his best pitch and relies more on location and aggression than on deception. Eckersley, who has a history of arm trouble, is spotted carefully by A's manager Tony La Russa. La Russa seldom uses Eckersley on successive days, and is reluctant to pitch him for more than one inning at a time.

FIELDING:

Eckersley's pickoff move is average at best; he doesn't concern himself much with baserunners. He's occasionally slow to react to bunts, but his sidearm motion gives him a follow-through that enables him to make most plays on balls hit back to him.

OVERALL:

Eckersley never can be an every-day-and-twice-on-Sunday closer, and his arm is too delicate to say with certainty that he can put together many more seasons of the quality that he produced in 1988 and 1989. But for the A's, who have one of the deepest bullpens in baseball, Eckersley is the ideal closer.

DENNIS ECKERSLEY

Position: RP
Bats: R **Throws:** R
Ht: 6' 2" **Wt:** 195

Opening Day Age: 35
Born: 10/3/54 in Oakland, CA
ML Seasons: 14

Overall Statistics

	W	L	ERA	G	GS	Sv	IP	H	R	BB	SO	HR
1989	4	0	1.56	51	0	33	57.2	32	10	3	55	5
Career	152	131	3.64	507	337	95	2555.0	2437	1111	565	1713	273

Where They Hit the Ball

Vs. LHB   **Vs. RHB**

1989 Situational Stats

	W	L	ERA	Sv	IP		AB	H	HR	RBI	AVG
Home	2	0	2.01	19	31.1	LHB	97	20	1	6	.206
Road	2	0	1.03	14	26.1	RHB	101	12	4	13	.119
Day	2	0	1.65	17	27.1	Sc Pos	32	5	1	13	.156
Night	2	0	1.48	16	30.1	Clutch	146	20	5	19	.137

1989 Rankings (American League)

➡ 1st in strikeout/walk ratio (18.3) - *all league players*

➡ 2nd in least baserunners per 9 innings (5.6), save percentage (84.6% - *players with 20 opportunites*), and lowest on-base average allowed (.175) - *all league players*

➡ 3rd in saves (33)

➡ Led the A's in saves, games finished (46), lowest opponent batting average (.162), least baserunners per 9 innings, blown saves (6), ERA (1.56), on-base average allowed and lowest batting average vs. righthanded batters (.119) - *all team players*

HITTING:

Mike Gallego, whose glove and versatility first earned him a major league job, showed in 1989 that his bat can help keep him in the show. A 5'8", 160-pounder whose size belies surprising strength, Gallego flirted with the .400 mark for the first few weeks of the season. He tailed off after that, but kept his average around the .250 mark most of the season. He drew almost as many walks (35) as he had strike-outs (43). That gave the A's a useful "second leadoff man" at the bottom of the order, especially after the A's obtained Rickey Henderson.

Gallego's an excellent bunter, and the A's will hit and run with him because he makes consistent contact. He's a very good reaction hitter who will wrist the ball over or around the infielders. Gallego is a top-hand hitter who usually hits low pitches better than high ones. He usually is smart enough to avoid trying to hit under the ball. Most pitchers try to go hard and in on him, then curve him away. Teams usually play him around to right and shallow, but left fielders usually respect his power to the left-center gap.

BASERUNNING:

Gallego is a very smart, make-things-happen baserunner with above-average speed. He doesn't steal much, but will take the extra base and doesn't make many mental mistakes.

FIELDING:

Gallego, a second baseman by inclination, played every day at shortstop after Walt Weiss was injured and surprised everybody, himself included. His exceptional range is as useful at shortstop as it is at second, and he compensates for an average arm with a release that almost is as quick as Weiss'. Even after Weiss returned, Gallego got almost as much time at shortstop as Walt. He also filled in at second and third.

OVERALL:

Mike Gallego has gone from a marginal major league in 1987, to a valuable utilityman in 1988, to one of the A's most valuable players in 1989. Gallego is an overachiever who in 1989 began to gain the confidence he needs to become a consistent contributor with the bat. He gives the A's an insurance policy at three positions, and an "I'll do anything!" attitude in the clubhouse and on the bench.

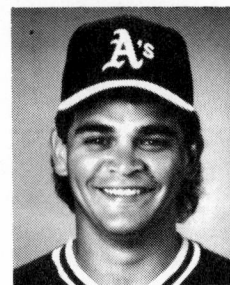

MIKE GALLEGO

Position: SS/2B
Bats: R **Throws:** R
Ht: 5' 8" **Wt:** 160

Opening Day Age: 29
Born: 10/31/60 in Whittier, CA
ML Seasons: 5

Overall Statistics

	G	AB	R	H	D	T	HR	RBI	SB	BB	SO	AVG
1989	133	357	45	90	14	2	3	30	7	35	43	.252
Career	430	872	116	205	35	3	8	77	10	94	137	.235

Where He Hits the Ball

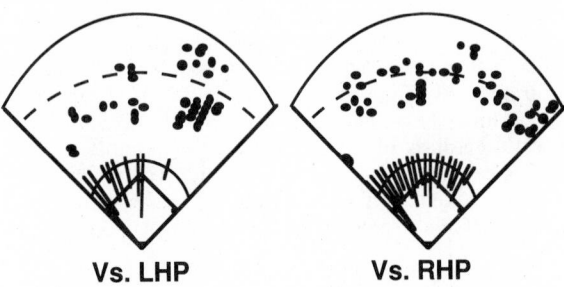

Vs. LHP   **Vs. RHP**

1989 Situational Stats

	AB	H	HR	RBI	AVG		AB	H	HR	RBI	AVG
Home	178	49	2	17	.275	LHP	125	33	0	9	.264
Road	179	41	1	13	.229	RHP	232	57	3	21	.246
Day	129	32	1	15	.248	Sc Pos	83	18	0	25	.217
Night	228	58	2	15	.254	Clutch	49	9	0	2	.184

1989 Rankings (American League)

- ➡ 4th in percent extra bases taken as a runner (58.0%) - *players with 40 opportunities to advance*
- ➡ 9th in hit by pitch (6)
- ➡ Led the A's in sacrifice bunts (8), bunts in play (15) and errors (19)
- ➡ Led AL Shortstops in hit by pitch and percent extra bases taken as a runner

HITTING:

Ron Hassey remains valuable to the A's, but not as an everyday catcher, and his play in 1989 indicated that he may be near the end at age 36. Hassey, a valuable scrap-heap addition for the A's in 1988, contributed the knowledge that the A's expected, and offense they had no reason to expect that season. By the end of 1989, though, he had largely lost his platoon-player status, and his main contribution was his expertise. He batted only .228 in 97 games, and slumped badly toward the end of the season as his workload decreased.

Hassey, a lefthanded hitter who never was overly inclined to pull the ball, has become almost exclusively an opposite-field hitter with the A's. Hassey stands close to the plate and tries to take the inside pitch away from the pitcher. He also bats with an open stance, which gives him an additional split second to adjust to inside pitches and doesn't prevent him from making a late adjustment to outside pitches. Hassey usually won't try to turn on an inside fastball, and will take a lot more pitches than he used to if teams try to pitch him that way. He prefers the ball up, but will put the bat head on top of the low outside pitch and drive it to left.

BASERUNNING:

Hassey actually stole a base in his only attempt; nobody is sure how. He never has run well, even for a catcher, and he has slowed almost to a walk now. He doesn't take many chances.

FIELDING:

Hassey, once one of the better defensive catchers in the American League, now has to get by on guile. He had a lot of problems with pitches low and to his right, and he threw out only 22 of 73 would-be base stealers (30 percent). Because of his knee trouble, he gets out of his crouch slowly. Hassey still calls a fine game, though, and the A's veteran pitchers like working with him.

OVERALL:

Hassey has had a solid career, but it hasn't much longer to run. He doesn't move well behind the plate anymore, and his throwing is weak. Even so, it wouldn't be a surprise if the A's re-sign Hassey for 1990. He's a good influence on the younger pitchers, and he is a font of knowledge. But his role in 1990 probably will be strictly as a backup.

RON HASSEY

Position: C
Bats: L **Throws:** R
Ht: 6' 2" **Wt:** 195

Opening Day Age: 37
Born: 2/27/53 in Tucson, AZ
ML Seasons: 12

Overall Statistics

	G	AB	R	H	D	T	HR	RBI	SB	BB	SO	AVG
1989	97	268	29	61	12	0	5	23	1	24	45	.228
Career	1046	3067	325	833	157	7	65	402	13	345	333	.272

Where He Hits the Ball

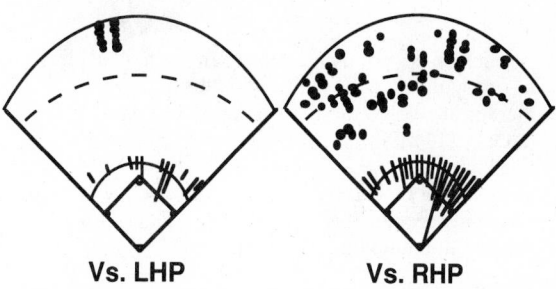

Vs. LHP   **Vs. RHP**

1989 Situational Stats

	AB	H	HR	RBI	AVG		AB	H	HR	RBI	AVG
Home	121	27	3	12	.223	LHP	34	8	1	3	.235
Road	147	34	2	11	.231	RHP	234	53	4	20	.226
Day	109	21	3	12	.193	Sc Pos	58	13	0	16	.224
Night	159	40	2	11	.252	Clutch	43	10	2	5	.233

1989 Rankings (American League)

➡ Did not rank near the top or bottom in any category

HITTING:

After his breakthrough 1988 season, Dave Henderson's 1989 numbers reverted to the level that marked him as an underachiever during his six seasons with the Seattle Mariners. But unlike Henderson's Seattle bosses, A's manager Tony La Russa considers the 31-year-old indispensable. La Russa talks constantly about the little things Henderson does to help win games, and how he plays hurt and tired without complaint. This is somewhat different than the hot-dog image Henderson once had.

Henderson, who had a career-high 24 home runs in 1988, seemed intent on matching or exceeding that total in 1989. His RBI production (80) remained solid, but his home-run total (15) and his average (.250) both fell off. He hit under the ball more than in 1988, and spent too much time trying to pull outside pitches. He was far and away the easiest Oakland player to strike out.

Henderson is most dangerous when pitched inside; he has very quick wrists and holds the bat low so that there is no wasted motion when he turns on the inside pitch. He'll bunt, both to get on base and to pull the third baseman in a few steps. He'll occasionally overswing and look bad on breaking balls, but he'll make adjustments and isn't often made to look bad a second time on the same pitch.

BASERUNNING:

Henderson runs well, but isn't noted for his base-stealing. The A's will hit and run with him on the bases, though, where he is very aggressive and physical. He batted second until Carney Lansford seized that role, and that says something about his wheels.

FIELDING:

Henderson still infuriates some opponents with his habit of leaning sideways and feigning indifference when he handles an easy chance. But he has excellent range to either side, and under manager Tony La Russa has become much better at hitting cutoff men. He throws accurately and well, and few baserunners test him anymore.

OVERALL:

Henderson, the Mariners' first-round draft choice in 1977, never lived up to expectations in Seattle. He has resurrected his career with the A's, who expect him to be solid but don't expect him to be spectacular. Henderson at 31 has matured into a dependable, sturdy player who figures to stick with Oakland for a while.

DAVE HENDERSON

Position: CF
Bats: R **Throws:** R
Ht: 6' 2" **Wt:** 210

Opening Day Age: 31
Born: 7/21/58 in Dos Palos, CA
ML Seasons: 9

Overall Statistics

	G	AB	R	H	D	T	HR	RBI	SB	BB	SO	AVG
1989	152	579	77	145	24	3	15	80	8	54	131	.250
Career	1078	3465	494	902	191	16	127	474	39	317	730	.260

Where He Hits the Ball

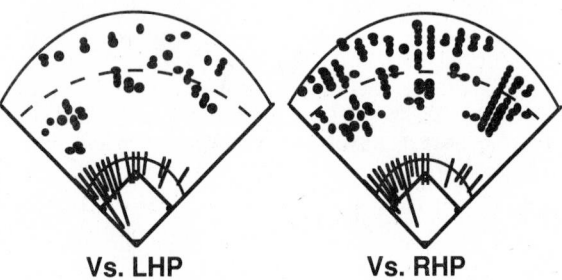

Vs. LHP   Vs. RHP

1989 Situational Stats

	AB	H	HR	RBI	AVG		AB	H	HR	RBI	AVG
Home	289	81	10	45	.280	LHP	171	49	5	27	.287
Road	290	64	5	35	.221	RHP	408	96	10	53	.235
Day	220	60	8	32	.273	Sc Pos	154	44	2	58	.286
Night	359	85	7	48	.237	Clutch	79	20	4	16	.253

1989 Rankings (American League)

➡ 2nd lowest batting average on the road (.221) - *players with 252 PA on the road*

➡ 7th in strikeouts (131)

➡ Led the A's in at bats (579), pitches seen (2,420), plate appearances (643), games (152) and strikeouts

➡ Led AL Center Fielders in strikeouts and sacrifice flies (6)

HALL OF FAMER

RICKEY HENDERSON

Position: LF
Bats: R **Throws:** L
Ht: 5'10" **Wt:** 195

Opening Day Age: 31
Born: 12/25/58 in Chicago, IL
ML Seasons: 11

HITTING:

Rickey Henderson's return to his hometown on June 20 seemed to bring him a new sense of inner tranquility. Henderson, who was batting only .254 for the Yankees, immediately began to move closer to the .300 range while scoring at least one run 61 of his first 67 games with Oakland and stealing 40 bases during that span.

Henderson had lapsed into impatient hitting with the Yankees, never drawing as many as 100 walks while with them. He moved farther back in the box after rejoining the A's, and waited better on pitches, thus giving him more reaction time against breaking balls; the result was 126 walks. Henderson's on base ability not only resulted in better pitches to hit for number two man Carney Lansford, but for the whole A's lineup.

Henderson is the all-time career leader in home runs leading off games. His power numbers also went up dramatically after he came to Oakland. He's a pure line-drive hitter who will take outside pitches he can't handle. He's also a good breaking-ball hitter who doesn't overswing. Teams usually try to pitch him away to negate his power, and he is usually played to pull to left and to spray to right-center. Henderson doesn't bunt often, but will do so if the third baseman is playing him deep.

BASERUNNING:

No embellishment of Henderson's magnificent statistics is required. But one difference from his previous stay in Oakland is that he has no qualms about accepting a red light from A's manager Tony La Russa if he's thinking about stealing third. He resented red lights earlier in his career.

FIELDING:

Henderson goes back on balls as well as any left fielder in the league, and never hesitates when approaching walls or essaying diving catches. He's content now to hit his cutoff man instead of trying to make the spectacular throw; he has only slightly better than average arm strength, but he throws accurately.

OVERALL:

This is a new Rickey Henderson -- affable with the media, ready to kid his teammates or be kidded by them, and relaxed to a degree that surprised everyone who remembers the sulking, moody Rickey Henderson who was with the A's before. And he has given the A's the leadoff man they had lacked. Look for Henderson's second stay in Oakland to be longer, happier, and more productive than his first.

Overall Statistics

	G	AB	R	H	D	T	HR	RBI	SB	BB	SO	AVG
1989	150	541	113	148	26	3	12	57	77	126	68	.274
Career	1472	5524	1171	1603	261	47	138	561	871	996	736	.290

Where He Hits the Ball

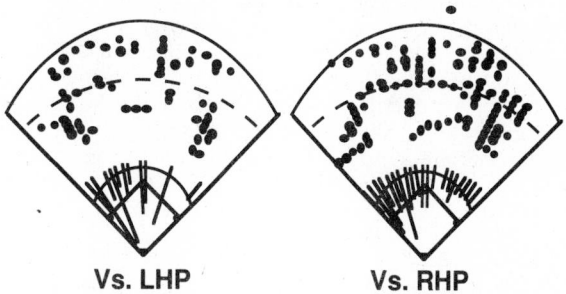

Vs. LHP   **Vs. RHP**

1989 Situational Stats

	AB	H	HR	RBI	AVG		AB	H	HR	RBI	AVG
Home	253	73	7	31	.289	LHP	173	48	1	13	.277
Road	288	75	5	26	.260	RHP	368	100	11	44	.272
Day	165	49	8	25	.297	Sc Pos	124	29	2	41	.234
Night	376	99	4	32	.263	Clutch	78	20	2	11	.256

1989 Rankings (American League)

➡ 1st in runs (113), stolen bases (77), walks (126), percent of pitches taken (71.0%), times picked off (8) and steals of third (24) - *players with 502 PA*

➡ 2nd in times on base (277)

➡ 3rd in on-base average (.411) and pitches seen (2,765)

➡ 4th in stolen base percentage (84.6%) and pitches seen per plate appearance (4.1)

➡ Led the A's in stolen bases (52), stolen base percentage (89.7%), times picked off (4) and steals of third (18)

PITCHING:

Rick Honeycutt in 1989 completed his transformation from starter to reliever, and it was a good thing for the A's that he did. Honeycutt teamed with Todd Burns to give the A's an effective lefty-righty closing combination while Dennis Eckersley was out with a shoulder injury. Honeycutt appeared in 64 games, most on the team and a career high, and he recorded 12 saves after registering only eight during his previous 11 major league seasons.

Honeycutt is a location pitcher who usually tries to sink the ball on the black of the plate. He no longer throws hard enough to challenge hitters, and he gets into trouble when he does. Honeycutt gave up only two earned runs in his final 13 innings of regular season work, and both of those runs came on solo home runs. Honeycutt has a good slider, which he runs down and in to righthanded hitters, and he uses a forkball as an off-speed pitch. Generally, though, he depends more on location than on fooling hitters with off-speed stuff. Honeycutt usually was used as the setup man for Eckersley when the latter was healthy. But he hasn't lost all of the stamina from his starting days; he also was used for up to three innings on a few occasions. He is intelligent and seldom tries to overthrow.

FIELDING:

Honeycutt is an average fielder who can handle balls through the middle, but he isn't a fifth-infielder type when he has to move off the mound, and he can be bunted on. He has a good move to first, and generally does a good job of keeping runners close.

OVERALL:

The acquisition of Honeycutt in 1987 cost the A's Tim Belcher, who has become a fine starter for the Dodgers. But Honeycutt has been well worth the expenditure, and was particularly valuable in 1989 as a substitute closer when Dennis Eckersley was injured. Honeycutt benefits from the fact that he is a control pitcher on a staff with other relievers who are fastball pitchers. Consequently, the hitters usually have to adjust to him instead of the other way around. At 35, Honeycutt seems to have settled into a new career as a reliever. It would be a surprise if he were not a prominent factor in the A's bullpen plans for 1990.

RICK HONEYCUTT

Position: RP
Bats: L **Throws:** L
Ht: 6' 1" **Wt:** 190

Opening Day Age: 35
Born: 6/29/54 in Chattanooga, TN
ML Seasons: 13

Overall Statistics

	W	L	ERA	G	GS	Sv	IP	H	R	BB	SO	HR
1989	2	2	2.35	64	0	12	76.2	56	26	26	52	5
Career	95	125	3.76	428	268	20	1858.0	1906	903	558	850	163

Where They Hit the Ball

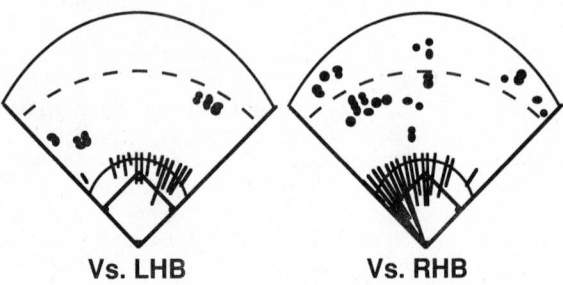

Vs. LHB   **Vs. RHB**

1989 Situational Stats

	W	L	ERA	Sv	IP		AB	H	HR	RBI	AVG
Home	0	2	2.85	6	41.0	LHB	90	14	1	5	.156
Road	2	0	1.77	6	35.2	RHB	181	42	4	21	.232
Day	0	0	2.89	4	28.0	Sc Pos	57	15	1	21	.263
Night	2	2	2.03	8	48.2	Clutch	178	36	1	16	.202

1989 Rankings (American League)

➡ 1st in holds (24)

➡ 4th in first batter efficiency (.158) - *pitchers with 40 relief games*

➡ Led the A's in games (64), holds and most GDPs per GDP situation (17.9%)

HITTING:

Stan Javier went from key contributor to expendable outfielder during the 1989 season, even though that transformation wasn't his fault. Javier was one of the A's top hitters in April, but he slumped into the .250 range and missed considerable time with a wrist injury. By the time he returned, Jose Canseco was healthy and the A's had obtained Rickey Henderson. So Javier's time melted to almost zero, even though his batting average held steady through the latter stages of the season.

Javier is a switch hitter who is far more effective from the left side than from the right. He has almost no power from the left side and slaps the ball over the infield, usually to the left side. He'll hit the ball where it is pitched as a lefthander, and will get an occasional hit off a drag bunt. He can be jammed, though. As a righthanded hitter, Javier has more power but far fewer weapons; he is less patient and more willing to chase pitches out of the strike zone. Most pitchers threw him breaking balls away, and he is too willing to chase them. The A's feel Javier could be a competent righthanded hitter if he saw more lefthanded pitching, but unfortunately for Stan, they have a lot of good righthanded hitters.

BASERUNNING:

Javier is one of the A's best baserunners, and he sometimes is used as a designated rabbit late in games. He stole 20 bases in 21 attempts in 1988 and was 12 for 14 in 1989, and has been used as a leadoff hitter on occasion. Like all the A's, he goes in hard on takeouts.

FIELDING:

Javier's main forte is his versatility; the A's have used him at all three outfield positions. He can also play first base in a pinch. His arm is decent -- short on strength, long on accuracy, although he has been known to miss a cutoff man now and then. He plays the outfield intelligently and doesn't often throw to the wrong base. His range is such that the A's have used him as their regular centerfielder for brief periods.

OVERALL:

Javier at age 24 seems to have a long-term future in baseball, but probably not as a member of the A's. The thinking is that the A's eventually will send him to a club that will use him on an everyday basis.

STAN JAVIER

Position: RF/LF/CF
Bats: B **Throws:** R
Ht: 6' 0" **Wt:** 185

Opening Day Age: 25
Born: 1/9/65 in San Francisco de Macoris, Dominican Republic
ML Seasons: 5

Overall Statistics

	G	AB	R	H	D	T	HR	RBI	SB	BB	SO	AVG
1989	112	310	42	77	12	3	1	28	12	31	45	.248
Career	384	979	127	231	36	7	5	80	43	98	169	.236

Where He Hits the Ball

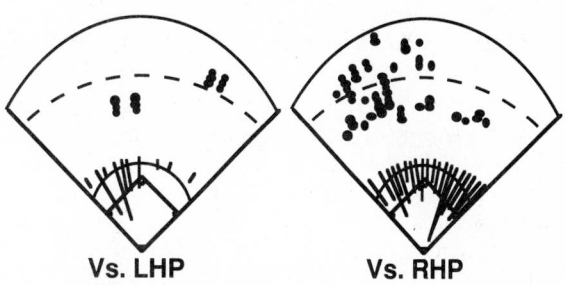

Vs. LHP   Vs. RHP

1989 Situational Stats

	AB	H	HR	RBI	AVG		AB	H	HR	RBI	AVG
Home	138	31	1	9	.225	LHP	74	17	1	7	.230
Road	172	46	0	19	.267	RHP	236	60	0	21	.254
Day	138	27	1	8	.196	Sc Pos	76	19	0	25	.250
Night	172	50	0	20	.291	Clutch	61	18	0	8	.295

1989 Rankings (American League)

➡ Led the A's in hitting in the clutch - *team players with 50 PA in the clutch*

➡ Led AL Right Fielders in grounder/flyball ratio (2.64) - *all league right fielders*

HITTING:

Rickey Henderson helped Carney Lansford, already a solid hitter, come close to his second batting title in the 1980s. Lansford has been such a discerning hitter that he seldom swung at pitches outside the strike zone. He usually hit the ball where it was pitched -- up the middle and to the gaps, which is where teams usually played him. Hence, he had more than his share of hard-luck outs.

After the A's re-acquired Henderson, Lansford was placed in the No.2 position. To protect Rickey, Lansford had to swing at pitches he would have taken in the past. The result is that Lansford was more aggressive. He started hitting to right field and hitting the ball down the left-field line more. Instead of bunching him toward the middle, teams now shade him around to right field -- and that opens up the gaps that Lansford previously had not been able to exploit. His walk-strikeout ratio improved markedly. Entering this season, he averaged roughly two walks for every three strikeouts. In 1989, he walked 51 times and had only 25 strikeouts.

Lansford handles breaking balls and off-speed pitches well because he is a "late" hitter who can make adjustments even when he is fooled. He does particularly well with the high-outside pitch. The best way to pitch him is down and in.

BASERUNNING:

With Canseco and McGwire missing early-season time because of injuries, the A's needed Lansford's baserunning acumen more than usual. As result, he had a career-high 37 steals in 1989. He has better-than-average speed and almost never unnecessarily runs the A's out of an inning.

FIELDING:

Lansford's instincts at third remain excellent, and his range is above average. He is best at charging balls and can get the ball off quickly. His only problem is that he usually throws sidearm, and the ball sometimes tails on the first baseman. Most of Lansford's errors this past season were throwing errors. He is a stabilizing influence on young infielders like shortstop Walt Weiss.

OVERALL:

Lansford is a consummate professional who will play hurt, and he has played through personal tragedy (the death of a son) in the past. He is one of the fiercest competitors on a fiercely competitive team. He should be a fixture in Oakland for many more years to come.

CARNEY LANSFORD

Position: 3B/1B
Bats: R **Throws:** R
Ht: 6' 2" **Wt:** 195

Opening Day Age: 33
Born: 2/7/57 in San Jose, CA
ML Seasons: 12

Overall Statistics

	G	AB	R	H	D	T	HR	RBI	SB	BB	SO	AVG
1989	148	551	81	185	28	2	2	52	37	51	25	.336
Career	1588	6139	884	1807	287	38	141	748	201	465	628	.294

Where He Hits the Ball

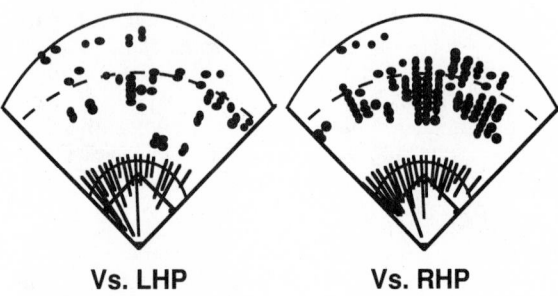

Vs. LHP   **Vs. RHP**

1989 Situational Stats

	AB	H	HR	RBI	AVG		AB	H	HR	RBI	AVG
Home	259	80	1	33	.309	LHP	149	58	1	14	.389
Road	292	105	1	19	.360	RHP	402	127	1	38	.316
Day	198	72	1	24	.364	Sc Pos	133	38	0	47	.286
Night	353	113	1	28	.320	Clutch	82	23	0	5	.280

1989 Rankings (American League)

- 1st in batting average vs. lefthanded pitchers (.389) - *players with 125 PA vs. LHP*
- 2nd in batting average (.336), percent swings put into play (59.6%) and hit by pitch (9) - *players with 502 PA*
- 3rd in lowest percent of swings that missed (6.6%) and singles (153)
- 4th in GDPs (21)
- Led the A's in batting average, runs (81), hits (185), singles, doubles (28), caught stealing (15), hit by pitch, times on base (245), on-base average (.398), grounder/flyball ratio (1.93), percent swings put into play, lowest percent of swings that missed and batting average with 2 strikes (.300)

HITTING:

Mark McGwire's third major league season marked him as a candidate to become the Dave Kingman of the 1990s, although the A's had Kingman before they had McGwire and certainly wouldn't want to make an exchange. In 1989, McGwire saw innumerable well-hit balls become warning-track outs. He didn't alter his characteristic uppercut, though, and the result was a significant drop in his batting average and a slight drop in his power numbers. A's manager Tony La Russa, who batted McGwire fourth throughout most of the 1988 season, dropped him to sixth and even to seventh on occasion last year.

McGwire lofts almost everything thrown to him above waist level, and most pitchers will go up and in to him, especially since he has shown a tendency to overreact when he thinks somebody is throwing at him. McGwire is a better hitter when the pitch is down and he has to concentrate on dropping the bat head on top of the ball. He also has excellent power to right field, and likes to extend his arms, so most outside pitches he sees are off-speed. His walk total went up substantially in 1989, mainly because he is laying off more breaking balls. He'll still chase balls outside the strike zone, but batting farther down in the order seemed to help him in terms of discipline.

BASERUNNING:

McGwire appears awkward when running, and he is neither fast nor particularly daring on the basepaths. But he is a good athlete with equivalent athletic instincts, and he knows his limitations and usually won't try to exceed them.

FIELDING:

McGwire has surprising range around the bag for a man his size and build, and is adept at chasing down foul popups -- an invaluable skill at the spacious Coliseum. McGwire is better than adequate on low throws, and his height obviously is an asset on high throws. The A's aren't wild about the idea of him throwing the ball, but he usually shows restraint and discretion in such situations.

OVERALL:

McGwire undoubtedly will be one of the top home-run producers of the 1990s, assuming he stays healthy. The A's would like to see improvement in his batting average, and they'd like to see him hit more line drives and fewer towering fly balls. But he has so many other assets that the A's will take the bad with the good.

MARK McGWIRE

Position: 1B
Bats: R **Throws:** R
Ht: 6' 5" **Wt:** 225

Opening Day Age: 26
Born: 10/1/63 in Pomona, CA
ML Seasons: 4

Overall Statistics

	G	AB	R	H	D	T	HR	RBI	SB	BB	SO	AVG
1989	143	490	74	113	17	0	33	95	1	83	94	.231
Career	467	1650	268	427	68	5	117	321	2	234	360	.259

Where He Hits the Ball

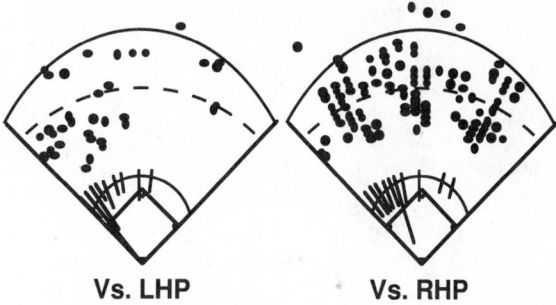

Vs. LHP   Vs. RHP

1989 Situational Stats

	AB	H	HR	RBI	AVG		AB	H	HR	RBI	AVG
Home	246	57	12	45	.232	LHP	132	31	6	25	.235
Road	244	56	21	50	.230	RHP	358	82	27	70	.229
Day	183	49	17	42	.268	Sc Pos	118	32	9	63	.271
Night	307	64	16	53	.208	Clutch	67	16	3	15	.239

1989 Rankings (American League)

- ➡ 1st in home run frequency (14.8 ABs per HR) - *players with 502 PA*
- ➡ 2nd in GDPs (23), lowest grounder/flyball ratio (.66)
- ➡ 3rd in home runs (33), hitting with the bases loaded (.571) and lowest batting average vs. righthanded pitchers (.229)
- ➡ 4th in sacrifice flies (11)
- ➡ 5th in lowest batting average (.231)
- ➡ Led the A's in home runs, home run frequency, slugging percentage (.467), sacrifice flies, walks (83), GDPs and hitting with the bases loaded

PITCHING:

Mike Moore turned out to be well worth the $1.7 million contract the A's tendered him as a free agent before the 1989 season. Moore demonstrated that his 66-96 major league record entering 1989 was less Moore and more Mariners. Given the support that he never had in Seattle, he went 19-11 and helped give the A's the top four-man rotation in the majors since the Baltimore Orioles had four 20-game winners in 1971.

Moore earned the late-inning confidence that manager Tony La Russa previously had reserved for staff ace Dave Stewart. He has an overpowering sinking fastball that he runs in and out without giving the hitter a discernible pattern to follow. He uses a forkball for his off-speed pitch, and paces himself well so that he is strong in the late innings. He has a whiplike forearm motion, which follows his weight shift, that gives him the extension that he needs to keep the ball down. At his best he is throwing nothing but ground balls, although his ball sinks so rapidly that many hitters swing over the pitch and he winds up with a strikeout total that makes him look more like a power-obsessed pitcher than he really is.

When Moore has control problems, it's usually because he isn't getting that extension. He also has had problems with opening his body too fast; therefore, his energy is expended before he releases the ball. When that happens, he gets wild high, and although he still has good enough stuff to overpower some hitters, opponents can draw a lot of walks by laying off high pitches. The Coliseum's generous dimensions and huge expanse of foul territory also helped Moore.

FIELDING:

Moore is a good fielder who moves off the mound well for a big man. His move is good, but sometimes he is so focused on the batter, he'll forget the runner and thus is run on more than he probably should be.

OVERALL:

At age 30, Moore is coming off his first All-Star season, and it probably won't be his last. Freed from the obscurity and uncertainty of the Seattle organization, Moore has the arm and stamina to become a consistent 20-game winner; he only needs to become constant with his mechanics to overcome the periodic wildness that hurt him in 1989.

MIKE MOORE

Position: SP
Bats: R **Throws:** R
Ht: 6' 4" **Wt:** 205

Opening Day Age: 30
Born: 11/26/59 in Eakly, OK
ML Seasons: 8

Overall Statistics

	W	L	ERA	G	GS	Sv	IP	H	R	BB	SO	HR
1989	19	11	2.61	35	35	0	241.2	193	82	83	172	14
Career	85	107	4.13	262	252	2	1698.2	1691	865	618	1109	160

Where They Hit the Ball

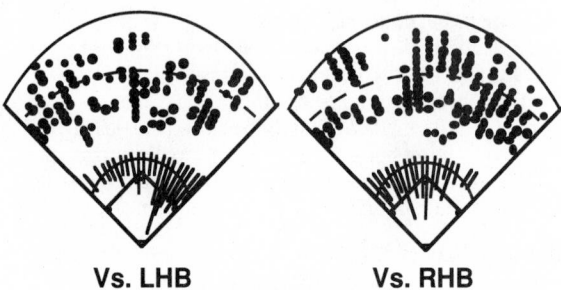

Vs. LHB   **Vs. RHB**

1989 Situational Stats

	W	L	ERA	Sv	IP		AB	H	HR	RBI	AVG
Home	10	4	2.02	0	124.2	LHB	426	93	3	30	.218
Road	9	7	3.23	0	117.0	RHB	454	100	11	41	.220
Day	7	2	1.36	0	72.2	Sc Pos	164	38	5	58	.232
Night	12	9	3.14	0	169.0	Clutch	79	17	1	7	.215

1989 Rankings (American League)

→ 1st in lowest on-base average allowed to leadoff batters (.241) - *pitchers facing 150 leadoff batters*

→ 2nd in home ERA (2.02), lowest stolen base percentage allowed (41.2%) and wild pitches (17)

→ 3rd in lowest on-base average allowed (.286), lowest slugging percentage allowed (.307), ERA (2.61), and wins (19)

→ Led the A's in ERA, losses (11), shutouts (3), walks (83), strikeouts (183), wild pitches, lowest opponent batting average (.219), lowest on-base average allowed, lowest slugging percentage allowed and least HRs per 9 innings (.52)

PITCHING:

Gene Nelson's cubicle in the Oakland A's Coliseum clubhouse is immediately adjacent to that of Dennis Eckersley. It's no coincidence; they are close friends, they are very much alike in terms of their quiet-yet-intense personalities, and their methods of retiring batters are similar. Like Eckersley, whom Nelson usually precedes as the A's righthanded set-up man, Nelson is a no-nonsense, confrontational pitcher. And while his results aren't as spectacular as Eckersley, Nelson more than gets the job done. After working a lot as a starter early in his career, Nelson has worked between 50 and 54 games each of the last four years, turning in consistently good efforts.

Nelson has a good slider and will throw an occasional forkball, but his forte is a low, hard fastball that will sometimes sail when Nelson, whose arm angle is low, drops down further. He doesn't try to paint the corners, and he doesn't get behind on many counts. Nelson, like many of the A's relief pitchers, is versatile and can work on a regular basis. He didn't start any games for the A's in 1989, but has done so in the past. He can go three or four innings in relief if need be.

FIELDING:

Nelson isn't the most athletic of the A's pitchers, but he is heady and usually makes the correct fielding play. His move to first is acceptable, but he doesn't hold runners on particularly well, mainly because he focuses so much concentration on the hitter. His delivery from the stretch is relatively slow, but not to the extent that it causes him serious problems.

OVERALL:

Gene Nelson's situation with the A's is that of the right place with the right manager at the right time. Nelson did fine work for Tony La Russa when the latter was managing the Chicago White Sox, and Nelson has been even better with Oakland. La Russa has stuck with Nelson through some trying circumstances, and Nelson pitches like a man intent on rewarding La Russa for his faith. He's a hard-nosed, versatile pitcher who doesn't often beat himself, and his future in Oakland should be secure as long as La Russa is managing and Nelson's arm is sound.

GENE NELSON

Position: RP
Bats: R **Throws:** R
Ht: 6' 0" **Wt:** 172

Opening Day Age: 29
Born: 12/3/60 in Tampa, FL
ML Seasons: 9

Overall Statistics

	W	L	ERA	G	GS	Sv	IP	H	R	BB	SO	HR
1989	3	5	3.26	50	0	3	80.0	60	33	30	70	5
Career	46	50	4.14	318	66	18	844.0	818	420	332	536	92

Where They Hit the Ball

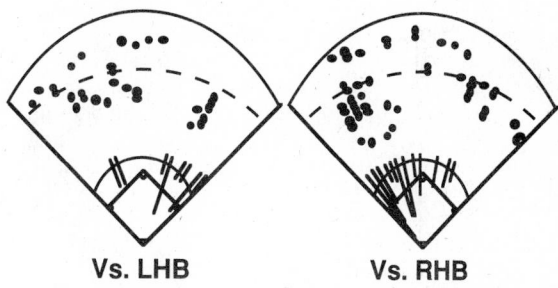

Vs. LHB   **Vs. RHB**

1989 Situational Stats

	W	L	ERA	Sv	IP		AB	H	HR	RBI	AVG
Home	3	2	3.18	0	39.2	LHB	112	28	3	11	.250
Road	0	3	3.35	3	40.1	RHB	184	32	2	19	.174
Day	1	0	2.97	1	30.1	Sc Pos	73	13	0	24	.178
Night	2	5	3.44	2	49.2	Clutch	97	22	2	7	.227

1989 Rankings (American League)

- ➡ 1st in first batter efficiency (.091) - *pitchers with 40 relief games*
- ➡ 5th in holds (13)
- ➡ Led the A's in first batter efficiency

HITTING:

Dave Parker is 38 and no longer the "Cobra" who was the National League's most feared hitter in the late 1970s, but his bat still has fangs. Parker competed with Mark McGwire for the team RBI lead all season and finished two ahead of McGwire with 97, just missing his sixth triple-figure RBI season. He started 67 games in the No. 3 position occupied throughout 1988 by Jose Canseco, and he was one of the main reasons the A's survived the pre All-Star break period without Canseco.

Parker has chronic knee problems and cannot generate the raw power that he once had. He compensates by swinging harder, making him more vulnerable to off-speed pitches, and often knocks himself off-balance when he doesn't connect. But when he does, he can still hit the ball farther than most hitters in the American League.

Most teams play Parker straightaway and deep. His power is to the gaps, and he only occasionally hits the ball up the middle. He'll chase the letter-high fastball, and it is on that pitch that he overswings and pops up or strikes out most often. He'll adjust on the breaking ball, especially if it is outside, and take it to left field.

BASERUNNING:

Parker, once the sport's fastest big man, has lost most of his straight-ahead speed. But he has lost none of the tenacity and still is respected on the basepaths. He'll go hard into a middle infielder without hesitation to break up a double play.

FIELDING:

Parker seldom is seen in the field any more; his age is most noticeable when he plays in the outfield. He still has a strong throwing arm, but he can't get to balls that he once handled with ease. It's likely that he'll be exclusively a DH for the remainder of his career.

OVERALL:

Parker has been everything the A's expected when they got him from Cincinnati two years ago. His lefthanded bat balances a lineup that is top-heavy with righthanded hitters, and his hard-nosed approach to the game despite the fact he plays in pain has made him much admired among his younger teammates. He also helps keep the clubhouse loose with his heavy-handed sense of humor.

DAVE PARKER

Position: DH
Bats: L **Throws:** R
Ht: 6' 5" **Wt:** 245

Opening Day Age: 38
Born: 6/9/51 in Jackson, MS
ML Seasons: 17

Overall Statistics

	G	AB	R	H	D	T	HR	RBI	SB	BB	SO	AVG
1989	144	553	56	146	27	0	22	97	0	38	91	.264
Career	2177	8246	1154	2416	470	70	307	1342	147	609	1337	.293

Where He Hits the Ball

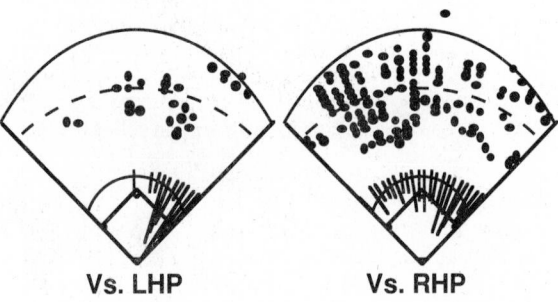

Vs. LHP **Vs. RHP**

1989 Situational Stats

	AB	H	HR	RBI	AVG		AB	H	HR	RBI	AVG
Home	272	76	10	50	.279	LHP	127	29	6	26	.228
Road	281	70	12	47	.249	RHP	426	117	16	71	.275
Day	212	57	12	49	.269	Sc Pos	152	45	6	72	.296
Night	341	89	10	48	.261	Clutch	77	14	3	7	.182

1989 Rankings (American League)

- 2nd in lowest on-base average vs. lefthanded pitchers (.233) - *players with 125 PA vs. LHP*
- 4th in GDPs (21)
- 7th in intentional walks (13)
- 9th in RBI (97)
- Led the A's in total bases (239), RBI, intentional walks and hitting with runners in scoring position (.296) - *team players with 100 PA with runners in scoring position*
- Led AL Designated Hitters in total bases, RBI, intentional walks, GDPs and hitting with runners in scoring position

HITTING:

Ken Phelps' tenure in New York City marked the confluence of two major oddities of the 1980's: Phelps is one of the great all-time power hitters against righthanded pitching, but he reached the age of 32 before anyone noticed. And the Yankees love to use big, strong righthanded DH's who are totally misplaced in Yankee stadium. So in 1989, the man second only to Babe Ruth in home run percentage sat on the bench, watching Steve Balboni and others take their cuts for the power-starved mini-Bombers. He finally ended up in Oakland, where he was a useful sub for a championship team.

Phelps is basically a pull hitter, but he has learned to hit outside pitches to left field with tremendous power as well. Ken has an excellent knowledge of the strike zone, always getting a mile of walks and compiling impressive on-base averages. The best way to get him is with low, sinking stuff when he must protect the plate.

At age 35, he has lost some of his ability to get around on a crackling fastball. But given the role of pinch hitter, Ken gave a stellar performance. He led A.L. pinch hitters in hits (11), homers (3), and RBIs (13). He is a valuable weapon on any bench, even if his skills are on the wane.

BASERUNNING :

The best thing about Ken Phelps as a baserunner is that he hits a lot of fly balls, avoiding DP's. He used to steal about a base a year, but he has always been a slow runner.

FIELDING:

When Ken appears at first base on rare occasions, it is a contingency move, not a defensive replacement. He has little range, but still makes his share of errors. In the future, we will likely see even less of him roaming the field.

OVERALL:

Phelps' glittering percentages dropped in 1989, while he sat underutilized. It is unclear which caused the other. Ken may have a little drama left in his bat, but the big question will necessarily go unanswered: what could Phelps have produced, if he had been given 10 or 11 seasons with 350 to 400 at bats per year against right-handed pitching? He might have had about 300 homers, and nearly 1000 walks. But we will never know.

KEN PHELPS

Position: DH
Bats: L **Throws:** L
Ht: 6' 1" **Wt:** 204

Opening Day Age: 35
Born: 8/6/54 in Seattle, WA
ML Seasons: 10

Overall Statistics

	G	AB	R	H	D	T	HR	RBI	SB	BB	SO	AVG
1989	97	194	26	47	4	0	7	29	0	31	47	.242
Career	705	1734	298	425	62	7	122	307	9	368	428	.245

Where He Hits the Ball

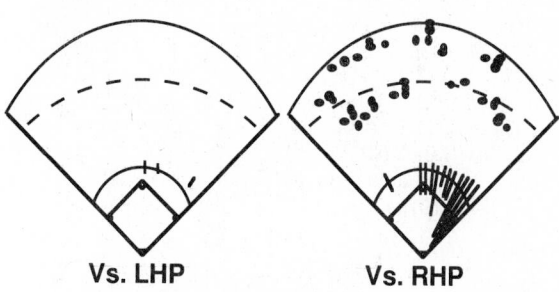

Vs. LHP   **Vs. RHP**

1989 Situational Stats

	AB	H	HR	RBI	AVG		AB	H	HR	RBI	AVG
Home	104	27	4	16	.260	LHP	11	2	0	2	.182
Road	90	20	3	13	.222	RHP	183	45	7	27	.246
Day	77	18	4	12	.234	Sc Pos	49	11	3	23	.224
Night	117	29	3	17	.248	Clutch	37	10	2	8	.270

1989 Rankings (American League)

➡ 2nd worst batting average on a 3-2 count (.029) - *players with 20 PA with a 3-2 count*

HITTING:

Tony Phillips in 1989 completed a cycle that began in 1984 and for most of that time included more pain than gain. Phillips was the A's regular second baseman throughout most of the season -- the same position he occupied in 1984, before his problems began with injuries and what was at one time considered an indifferent attitude.

Phillips, perhaps the A's most versatile player offensively as well as defensively, did his best work when used in the first or second positions in the order. He proved particularly resourceful at the top of the order, and tended to concentrate more on manipulating the bat. As a lefthanded batter, Phillips has surprising power to the gaps and is a good low-ball hitter who doesn't often chase the high fastball anymore. He snaps the bat instead of looping it as he often had done earlier in his career, and as a result he fared better against breaking pitches. He'll occasionally slice the outside pitch down the left-field line; teams tend to shade him that way, and to pitch him inside when possible. He doesn't have as much power from the right side, but he tended to be more patient and willing to draw walks. He doesn't go to the opposite field as often righthanded as he does lefthanded. Phillips is a much-improved bunter and will drag periodically.

BASERUNNING:

Phillips, never a high-percentage base stealer, didn't change that characteristic in 1989. He does have above-average speed, though, and has become less reckless as he has matured.

FIELDING:

Phillips isn't outstanding at any particular position, but is good enough overall to have played all four infield positions and two outfield posts in 1989. He often plays more than one position in a game, and seldom is removed for defensive purposes. Phillips moves very well to his left, probably because his most extensive defensive experience is at second base. He turns the double play acceptably, and his arm is adequate for second base, though a trifle weak for shortstop.

OVERALL:

Phillips, whose future with the A's was bleak in 1987 and still uncertain in 1988, probably will go into 1990 as the A's regular second baseman after his first injury-free season since 1984. He has learned to channel the frustration that he once vented in negative ways, and now seems to enjoy being at the ballpark even if he isn't playing.

TONY PHILLIPS

Position: 2B/3B/SS
Bats: B **Throws:** R
Ht: 5'10" **Wt:** 175

Opening Day Age: 30
Born: 4/15/59 in Atlanta, GA
ML Seasons: 8

Overall Statistics

	G	AB	R	H	D	T	HR	RBI	SB	BB	SO	AVG
1989	143	451	48	118	15	6	4	47	3	58	66	.262
Career	835	2588	354	649	107	25	33	259	56	342	490	.251

Where He Hits the Ball

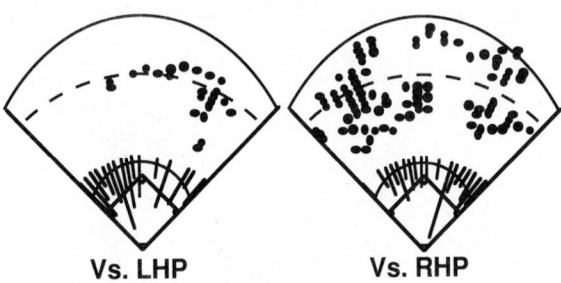

Vs. LHP   Vs. RHP

1989 Situational Stats

	AB	H	HR	RBI	AVG		AB	H	HR	RBI	AVG
Home	214	58	2	23	.271	LHP	139	36	0	10	.259
Road	237	60	2	24	.253	RHP	312	82	4	37	.263
Day	181	49	0	12	.271	Sc Pos	112	26	0	37	.232
Night	270	69	4	35	.256	Clutch	73	17	1	9	.233

1989 Rankings (American League)

- → 2nd in lowest percent of runs scored per time reached base (24.1%) - *players with 502 PA*
- → Led the A's in triples (6)
- → Led AL Second Basemen in pitches seen per plate appearance (3.8)

HITTING:

Terry Steinbach became an American League All-Star before he became the A's fulltime catcher. He demonstrated that he deserved both designations in 1989 as the A's went 59-33 in games he started behind the plate. His next step is to demonstrate that he can put together two solid halves in the same season. In 1988 Steinbach had a poor first half, but a strong finish. His 1989 season was exactly the opposite. He batted .322 before the All-Star Game, but only .216 from then on. Some A's people felt he had a slow bat in August and September – perhaps because of the fatigue factor, and perhaps because he was seeing more righthanded pitchers against whom Ron Hassey usually played in the past.

Steinbach has more power than his home run total of seven suggests, but he tends to drop under the ball and take too big a swing. That results in a lot of deep fly outs at the spacious Coliseum. Teams usually play him deep and around slightly to left field, but he has good power to the right-center field alley and will hit the hanging breaking ball there. Steinbach's walk-to-strikeout ratio went down in 1989, but he is an intelligent hitter who knows the strike zone fairly well. He likes to extend his arms, and when he doesn't overswing, he does his best hitting up the middle, a la Carney Lansford. Teams usually try to jam Steinbach; he must refrain from trying to pull that pitch.

BASERUNNING:

Steinbach stole only one base in 1989, but his speed isn't far below average. The A's have started him in hit-and-run situations, and he seldom runs into a foolish out.

FIELDING:

Steinbach threw out 26 of 64 would-be base stealers last year for a solid 41%. He is very quick behind the plate and has rid himself of the habit of reaching instead of shifting his feet. Steinbach called some of his own games in 1989, taking over that chore from pitching coach Dave Duncan -- another sign of his maturity. Steinbach can also play third, first and right field.

OVERALL:

Steinbach, entering his third full major league season, is solid in every respect. If he puts together two solid halves in 1990, he has a chance to be recognized as one of the sport's catching elite. He also has become a tension-reliever in the clubhouse because of his good nature and wry sense of humor.

TERRY STEINBACH

Position: C
Bats: R **Throws:** R
Ht: 6' 1" **Wt:** 195

Opening Day Age: 28
Born: 3/2/62 in New Ulm, MN
ML Seasons: 4

Overall Statistics

	G	AB	R	H	D	T	HR	RBI	SB	BB	SO	AVG
1989	130	454	37	124	13	1	7	42	1	30	66	.273
Career	362	1211	148	333	48	5	34	153	5	96	179	.275

Where He Hits the Ball

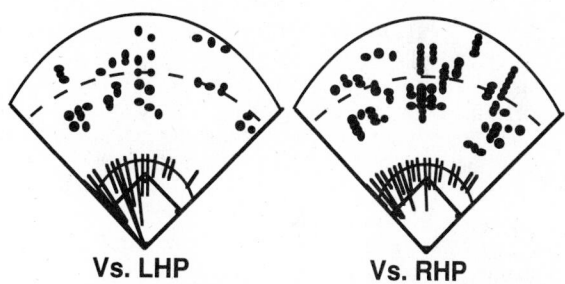

Vs. LHP   Vs. RHP

1989 Situational Stats

	AB	H	HR	RBI	AVG		AB	H	HR	RBI	AVG
Home	216	63	5	23	.292	LHP	159	41	3	18	.258
Road	238	61	2	19	.256	RHP	295	83	4	24	.281
Day	167	48	3	21	.287	Sc Pos	107	28	2	36	.262
Night	287	76	4	21	.265	Clutch	59	14	2	8	.237

1989 Rankings (American League)

→ Led the A's in hitting on a 3-1 count (.400) - *team players with 10 PA with a 3-1 count*

→ Led AL Catchers in at bats (454), singles (103), plate appearances (491) and errors (11)

STAFF ACE

DAVE STEWART

Position: SP
Bats: R **Throws:** R
Ht: 6' 2" **Wt:** 200

Opening Day Age: 33
Born: 2/19/57 in Oakland, CA
ML Seasons: 10

PITCHING:

Dave Stewart has a style that some of the greats of the distant past would have appreciated. Christy Mathewson and Grover Cleveland Alexander, to name two, became immortals not just because they had immortal stuff. Both pitched to spots only when they were in a jam. Both were smart enough to pace themselves and keep an ace in the hole against each hitter. Both were hit liberally on occasion, but neither made a habit of throwing the single bad pitch that could cost him a ballgame.

Stewart, a fringe major leaguer when he overthrew and tried to be too fine, now pitches to areas rather than to spots. He challenges hitters to hit the pitches that are working for him, which is why he gives up a lot of solo home runs. But he uses every at-bat to his advantage, and almost never gives up home runs in a situation where one can beat him.

Stewart always has had a good riding fastball, which he varies with the use of finger pressure. His best fastball rides up and in; hitters tend to hit it into the air at the Coliseum, where home runs are difficult to come by. Stewart also has a tight slider that has little movement but lots of rotation. He gets most of his ground-ball outs with that. The missing pitch in Stewart's portfolio before he came to Oakland, though, was the forkball he has developed. His outstanding forker makes it impossible for hitters to sit on his power pitches as they once did.

FIELDING:

Stewart is one of the best fielding pitchers in the league, and he would be a good hitting pitcher in the National League. He runs well, and even though his pickoff move isn't outstanding, he does a good job of keeping runners close.

OVERALL:

Jose Canseco, Mark McGwire and Dennis Eckersley probably are better known on the national scene than Stewart, but this Oakland native's story parallels that of this once-dying franchise. No pitcher in baseball is better at keeping a team in a game, and none has meant more to a franchise in terms of his work in the community. Stewart is one of the classiest acts in baseball, and he has never tried to run away from his well-documented troubles in Texas. This 20-game winner of the last three seasons finally received his due with the 1989 World Series MVP award.

Overall Statistics

	W	L	ERA	G	GS	Sv	IP	H	R	BB	SO	HR
1989	21	9	3.32	36	36	0	257.2	260	105	69	155	23
Career	101	74	3.68	357	182	19	1560.2	1455	704	594	1036	139

Where They Hit the Ball

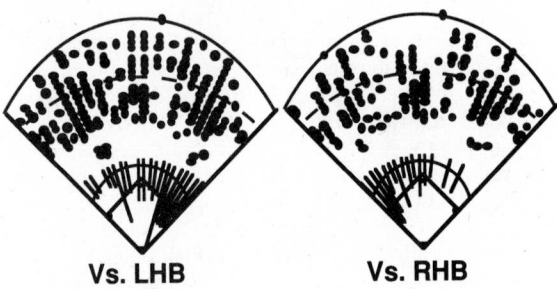

Vs. LHB **Vs. RHB**

1989 Situational Stats

	W	L	ERA	Sv	IP		AB	H	HR	RBI	AVG
Home	11	4	2.77	0	133.1	LHB	522	138	12	55	.264
Road	10	5	3.91	0	124.1	RHB	464	122	11	41	.263
Day	10	3	3.09	0	110.2	Sc Pos	235	52	2	67	.221
Night	11	6	3.49	0	147.0	Clutch	91	26	0	5	.286

1989 Rankings (American League)

→ 1st in games started (36), hits allowed (260) and batters faced (1,081)

→ 2nd in wins (21) and innings (257.2)

→ 3rd in wild pitches (13) and lowest opponent batting average with runners in scoring position (.221) - *pitchers facing 150 batters with runners in scoring position*

→ 4th in complete games (8)

→ 5th in home runs allowed (23), pitches thrown (3,820) and won/loss percentage (.700)

→ Led the A's in wins, games started, complete games, innings, hits allowed, batters faced, home runs allowed (23), hit batsmen (6) and least pitches thrown per batter (3.5)

HITTING:

The knee injury that interrupted Walt Weiss' second major league season didn't affect his hitting as much as it did his fielding. Nevertheless, his numbers went down slightly from his Rookie of the Year totals of 1988. Weiss is a low-ball hitter who, when healthy, doesn't try to pull inside pitches and doesn't strike out that much. But in 1989 his knee wasn't healthy even upon his return from the disabled list. His balance and timing at the plate were not up to his 1988 standards, and he lunged at breaking balls more than he did during his rookie season.

Most teams jammed Weiss when he batted lefthanded in 1988, but he generally was played slightly around to left field because that's where most of his left-handed power is. Weiss can, however, turn on the ball if he chooses to; he has reached the upper deck in right field at Tiger Stadium in Detroit. He is a good bunter who will drag for a hit occasionally. Weiss is not a particularly good righthanded hitter, and usually sat against lefties late in 1989. He tends to try to pull the ball too much, so he generally was pitched and played away. He needs to improve as a righty swinger in order to play every day.

BASERUNNING:

Weiss is a good baserunner. His speed obviously was affected by his knee injury in 1989, but his decisions usually were sound. He is relatively conservative as a baserunner but stole six bases in seven attempts in 1989.

FIELDING:

It was in this category that the effects of Weiss' injury were most obvious. Weiss' mobility and ability to keep his balance while throwing were severely affected by his bad knee. His range to his right was limited most; the injury was to his right knee, and he had trouble driving off that knee to get into the hole. Weiss still displayed an excellent, accurate arm, and didn't back down on the double play turn even when he was playing hurt.

OVERALL:

Weiss virtually played on one leg for most of the 1989 season, and his play reflected that. He wound up sharing the shortstop job with Mike Gallego, but it's likely that he will win it back; Weiss is only 26, and it wasn't believed that the knee problem will be long-term in nature.

WALT WEISS

Position: SS
Bats: B **Throws:** R
Ht: 6' 0"   **Wt:** 175

Opening Day Age: 26
Born: 11/28/63 in Tuxedo, NY
ML Seasons: 3

Overall Statistics

	G	AB	R	H	D	T	HR	RBI	SB	BB	SO	AVG
1989	84	236	30	55	11	0	3	21	6	21	39	.233
Career	247	714	77	180	32	3	6	61	11	58	97	.252

Where He Hits the Ball

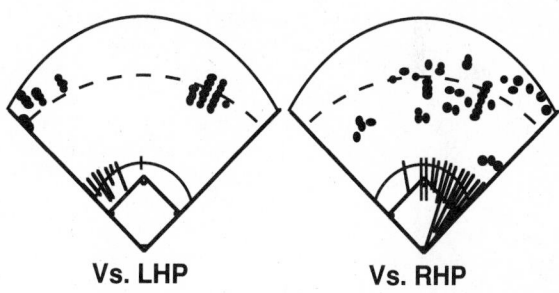

Vs. LHP   **Vs. RHP**

1989 Situational Stats

	AB	H	HR	RBI	AVG		AB	H	HR	RBI	AVG
Home	120	24	2	10	.200	LHP	57	13	0	4	.228
Road	116	31	1	11	.267	RHP	179	42	3	17	.235
Day	93	18	0	7	.194	Sc Pos	65	15	1	17	.231
Night	143	37	3	14	.259	Clutch	33	5	0	2	.152

1989 Rankings (American League)

➡ Did not rank near the top or bottom in any category

PITCHING:

Perhaps the most notable characteristic that Bob Welch has added since joining the A's is a relative sense of serenity on the mound. While with Los Angeles, Welch was known to teammates and opponents as a fidgety, edgy pitcher who was aggravating to face, but difficult to play behind. Now his demeanor on the mound is more calm and controlled, although the fierce competitive nature that he had as a young pitcher still is very much in evidence.

Welch is a let-it-all-hang-out pitcher who doesn't have to worry about completing games – he had only one CG in 1989 – because of the A's deep bullpen. He always has challenged hitters and doesn't get cute. He wants the inside fringe of the plate and will move hitters off that area if they crowd him. Welch still has an above-average fastball, which he can ride in on righthanded hitters. He'll cut the ball to lefthanded hitters and try to get them to swing at high pitches. His breaking pitches are good but not great, and he generally uses them to set up the fastball, not as "out" pitches. He has a straight change, and while he doesn't use the forkball as much as most of the A's other pitchers, it works for him because of the element of surprise. Welch uses the spacious Coliseum to his advantage; he is 23-6 there since joining the A's. He throws a lot of fly balls, and fly balls usually wind up as outs in the spacious Coliseum.

FIELDING:

Welch is athletic and instinctive enough to make spectacular plays on the mound, but he also has been known to mess up easy chances. His move to first is only fair, and he could do a better job of holding runners on base. But he uncoils quickly and isn't easy for a baserunner to read.

OVERALL:

Welch probably never will reach the superstardom that once was predicted for him, but on this staff he doesn't have to be a superstar. Like the other A's starting pitchers, he isn't required to carry a disproportionate share of the load or assume a win-or-else mandate in any game. That has helped Welch become more relaxed on the mound; that, in turn, has made him a more reliable pitcher.

BOB WELCH

Position: SP
Bats: R **Throws:** R
Ht: 6' 3" **Wt:** 195

Opening Day Age: 33
Born: 11/3/56 in Detroit, MI
ML Seasons: 12

Overall Statistics

	W	L	ERA	G	GS	Sv	IP	H	R	BB	SO	HR
1989	17	8	3.00	33	33	0	209.2	191	82	78	137	13
Career	149	103	3.18	361	336	8	2274.1	2059	891	724	1587	168

Where They Hit the Ball

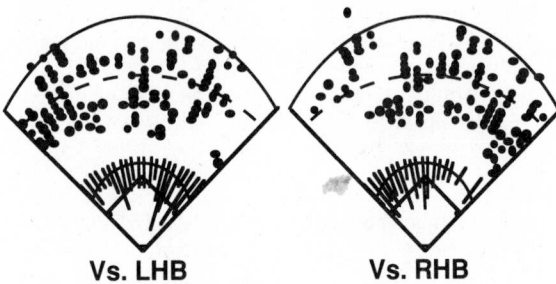

Vs. LHB   **Vs. RHB**

1989 Situational Stats

	W	L	ERA	Sv	IP		AB	H	HR	RBI	AVG
Home	10	2	2.77	0	107.1	LHB	417	87	3	28	.209
Road	7	6	3.25	0	102.1	RHB	375	104	10	40	.277
Day	11	3	2.37	0	95.0	Sc Pos	190	43	4	53	.226
Night	6	5	3.53	0	114.2	Clutch	51	13	1	3	.255

1989 Rankings (American League)

- ➡ 6th in wins (17)
- ➡ 7th in ERA (3.01), run support per 9 innings (5.2) and lowest opponent on-base average leading off an inning (.267) - *pitchers facing 150 leadoff batters*
- ➡ 9th in won/loss percentage (.680), lowest opponent batting average with runners in scoring position (.226) and lowest batting average vs. lefthanded batters (.208)
- ➡ Led the A's in hit batsmen (6), stolen bases allowed (22) and grounder/flyball ratio (1.36)

PITCHING:

Curt Young in 1989 was the odd man out on the A's staff. Yet his potential is such that the A's, who don't have another lefthanded starter, believe he still can be part of their future. Young was the A's fifth starter in 1989, and pitched only 111 innings (he worked 156 the previous year). The A's during the offseason added Mike Moore to their rotation, and that left only 20 starts for Young.

Partly because his workload was sporadic, Young had trouble both with control and with the long ball; his home runs-to-innings pitched ratio was the second-worst on the staff behind Storm Davis. Nevertheless, he pitched several good games in which he received little support, and finished strongly. His problem in the past has been putting six good months together in a single season.

Young has a downward-darting fastball that he throws with a laconic-looking motion when he is at his best. His curve, slider and forkball all are good at times and bad at others; he has become better at hiding the ball and at taking speed off the pitches other than his fastball. He isn't a strikeout pitcher, and his periodic inability to get his secondary pitches over for strikes early in the count have made him susceptible to bombardment when he has to come in with a fastball.

FIELDING:

Young is a decent overall fielder who gets off the mound well, but he has been known to make erratic throws after fielding comebackers. He doesn't have a great move to first, but he is persistent. He is working on getting rid of the ball more quickly when going to the plate from the stretch.

OVERALL:

Many baseball people believe Curt Young would thrive with regular work and an established role. The problem is that he hasn't been in that situation with the pitching-rich A's, who are at the point where they should decide either to commit to him or move him. Young at his best can match stuff with any of the A's front four starters; the problem is that he hasn't yet learned to survive when he doesn't have good stuff. As a left-hander, he has value to the A's, either with them or in trade, and it will be interesting during spring training to see what they decide to do with him.

CURT YOUNG

Position: SP/RP
Bats: R **Throws:** L
Ht: 6' 1" **Wt:** 175

Opening Day Age: 29
Born: 4/16/60 in Saginaw, MI
ML Seasons: 7

Overall Statistics

	W	L	ERA	G	GS	Sv	IP	H	R	BB	SO	HR
1989	5	9	3.73	25	20	0	111.0	117	56	47	55	10
Career	51	42	4.20	158	130	0	832.0	841	431	256	429	115

Where They Hit the Ball

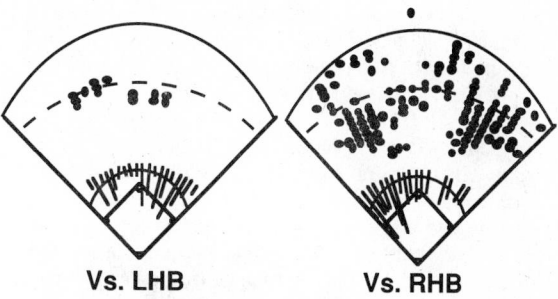

Vs. LHB   **Vs. RHB**

1989 Situational Stats

	W	L	ERA	Sv	IP		AB	H	HR	RBI	AVG
Home	3	4	4.05	0	60.0	LHB	80	17	0	6	.213
Road	2	5	3.35	0	51.0	RHB	364	100	10	43	.275
Day	3	1	3.60	0	30.0	Sc Pos	109	29	1	37	.266
Night	2	8	3.78	0	81.0	Clutch	21	6	1	3	.286

1989 Rankings (American League)

➡ 7th in balks (4)
➡ Led the A's in balks

BILLY BEANE

Position: RF
Bats: R **Throws:** R
Ht: 6' 4" **Wt:** 208

Opening Day Age: 28
Born: 3/29/62 in
Orlando, FL
ML Seasons: 6

Overall Statistics

	G	AB	R	H	D	T	HR	RBI	SB	BB	SO	AVG
1989	37	79	8	19	5	0	0	11	3	0	13	.241
Career	148	301	30	66	14	0	3	29	5	11	80	.219

HITTING, FIELDING, BASERUNNING:

At 6'4" and 210 pounds, Billy Beane looks like a power hitter, but he doesn't always hit like one. Beane's tendency to loop the bat and hit up at the ball results in a lot of flyball outs. Beane isn't disciplined at the plate and didn't draw a single walk in 79 at-bats with the A's. But he can hit the ball a long way when he is pitched at the letters, and he has power to the gaps when he is able to extend his arms. Beane runs well, although at 28 he has lost some of the acceleration he had while in the Mets organization. An outfielder his entire career, Beane has kept himself a marketable commodity in the age of the 24-man roster by taking up catching. He is a functional outfielder with a strong arm and good speed.

OVERALL:

Beane should be able to stay in the majors, mainly because he can function as a third catcher in addition to playing the outfield. He is a good-natured individual who won't complain about any role assigned to him, and he does have power. Those attributes make him the ideal 24th player on a 24-man roster.

LANCE BLANKENSHIP

Position: 2B/RF
Bats: R **Throws:** R
Ht: 6' 0" **Wt:** 185

Opening Day Age: 26
Born: 12/6/63 in
Portland, OR
ML Seasons: 2

Overall Statistics

	G	AB	R	H	D	T	HR	RBI	SB	BB	SO	AVG
1989	58	125	22	29	5	1	1	4	5	8	31	.232
Career	68	128	23	29	5	1	1	4	5	8	32	.227

HITTING, FIELDING, BASERUNNING:

Blankenship, considered the A's second baseman of the future, eventually could give the A's the hitting they have lacked at that position. A powerfully-built right-handed batter, he has power to the gaps and is a very aggressive hitter. He is a first-ball hitter who needs to learn to stay back on breaking balls outside the strike zone. Blankenship stole five bases in 58 games for Oakland in 1989, and has stolen as many as 40 in the minors. He has fine acceleration and likes to take chances; he may have to curb his aggression on the bases somewhat. In the field, Blankenship has quick feet and a choppy stride, and gets a good break to either side. He doesn't have a great arm, but gets rid of the ball quickly. He has played several positions besides second base in the minors, and played some outfield for the A's in 1989.

OVERALL:

Blankenship is one of the top prospects in the A's organization, and could make a serious run for the starting second base job in 1990 if Tony Phillips falters. His style is somewhat reminiscent of a young Ryne Sandberg, which is high praise indeed.

FELIX JOSE

Position: RF
Bats: B **Throws:** R
Ht: 6' 1"   **Wt:** 190

Opening Day Age: 24
Born: 5/8/65 in Santo Domingo, Dominican Republic
ML Seasons: 2

Overall Statistics

	G	AB	R	H	D	T	HR	RBI	SB	BB	SO	AVG
1989	20	57	3	11	2	0	0	5	0	4	13	.193
Career	28	63	5	13	3	0	0	6	1	4	14	.206

HITTING, FIELDING, BASERUNNING:

Felix Jose won the A's rightfield job, vacated by the injured Jose Canseco, by tearing up the Cactus League during spring training. But Jose, considered the best prospect in the A's system, soon demonstrated that he wasn't ready to face big-league pitching on a day-to-day basis. Jose, a switch-hitter, swung with power from the right side. But he made almost no contact from the left side, and demonstrated poor strike-zone awareness. He can hit for power and for average, although he needs to wait for his pitch instead of lunging at breaking balls. Jose is extremely fast on the bases, although he is undisciplined and hasn't yet learned to fully harness that speed. He has good outfield instincts, and his arm strength has given him a modest reputation. But he misses too many cutoff men, and still is adjusting to the hitters and the ballparks.

OVERALL:

The A's put Jose in a difficult position at the start of 1989, and his troubles were somewhat predictable. But he has all the tools to be an outstanding major league player, and they will probably have to make room for him within a year or two.

MATT YOUNG

Position: RP/SP
Bats: L **Throws:** L
Ht: 6' 3"   **Wt:** 205

Opening Day Age: 31
Born: 8/9/58 in Pasadena, CA
ML Seasons: 6

Overall Statistics

	W	L	ERA	G	GS	Sv	IP	H	R	BB	SO	HR
1989	1	4	6.75	26	4	0	37.1	42	31	31	27	2
Career	43	60	4.48	230	98	25	730.2	773	413	306	490	65

PITCHING & FIELDING:

Matt Young was considered one of the principals in the trade that also brought the A's Bob Welch before the start of the 1988 season. But Young has not become the lefthanded closer the A's envisioned. After missing the entire 1988 season and undergoing Tommy John-type reconstructive surgery on his elbow in September, Young wasn't able to come off the disabled list until after the 1989 season had started. After a rehabilitation period, Young joined the starting rotation for a brief time. But Young's control was horrendous, largely because he was trying to work on too many pitches.

Young at his best is a down-and-dirty fastball pitcher. As a starter he fell behind while trying to use other pitches, forcing him to come in with fat fastballs. La Russa finally moved Young back to the bullpen at midseason, and his control improved markedly. In the bullpen he regained some of his aggression and confidence. When his mechanics are right, Young's fastball can both ride and tail against lefties. He throws a slider, but doesn't change speeds much.

Young's fielding instincts, once good, were diminished somewhat by his long layoff and his lack of work. He has a decent move to first, although he takes a long time to uncoil.

OVERALL:

With lefthanded relief pitchers being as much in demand as they are, Young probably can hook on somewhere if he doesn't make the A's in the spring. After missing the entire 1988 season and getting comparatively little work in 1989, he has to prove himself again as a major league pitcher. His arm apparently is OK, but whether he is with the A's in 1990 could depend not as much on his performance as on the development of some of the younger pitchers in the organization.

SCOTT BANKHEAD

Position: SP
Bats: R **Throws:** R
Ht: 5'10" **Wt:** 185

Opening Day Age: 26
Born: 7/31/63 in Raleigh, NC
ML Seasons: 4

PITCHING:

A year ago, Scott Bankhead was facing a clouded future. No one had ever questioned the ability of this former number one draft choice. But after he'd gone through two seasons of shoulder problems in 1987 and '88, people were saying that Bankhead might never be anything more than a No. 4 or 5 starter. With what seemed to be a chronically weak shoulder, a 200 inning season was unlikely. Indeed, Bankhead had never worked even 150 innings in any of his three previous campaigns, and had yet to win in double figures.

But Bankhead's determination to overcome his injuries has brought his career to a higher level. He's worked relentlessly with Mariner trainer Rick Griffin, and the rehabilitation work has paid off. Last year Bankhead worked 210.1 innings and turned in a 14-6 record, an outstanding mark for a hurler on a sixth place team. Bankhead reeled off nine straight wins in midseason, and by year's end was the ace of the Mariner staff.

Bankhead has a high eighties fastball he uses about 75% of the time. He also possesses a curve, slider and change-up. He can strike hitters out, but location is the key to his success. Bankhead owns the half inch on both sides of the plate and uses his pinpoint control to keep hitters off balance. There is no pattern to his pitch sequence and he won't pitch any batter the same way twice. He's not afraid to come inside. Because of his shoulder problems the Mariners limited Bankhead to 100-115 per game pitches last year, but with his control, he was still able get into the seventh or eighth inning on a consistent basis. Bankhead is a top competitor, and though youthful himself at 26, has set an example for the inexperienced pitchers on the Seattle staff. Brian Holman in particular learned a lot from Bankhead's excellent work habits.

FIELDING:

Bankhead is an exceptional fielder. He's quick and handles all grounders flawlessly. His delivery to the plate is on the slow side, so he has to work on holding baserunners. His pickoff move is very good.

OVERALL:

They say it takes a few years to really evaluate a trade, and in Bankhead's case, it's taken three. If 1989 is an indication of what's to come, then the Danny Tartabull deal looks a lot more even. Bankhead is now the Mariners' ace. If he stays healthy, he's capable of being a 15 to 20 game winner for years to come.

Overall Statistics

	W	L	ERA	G	GS	Sv	IP	H	R	BB	SO	HR
1989	14	6	3.34	33	33	0	210.1	187	84	63	140	19
Career	38	32	4.03	105	96	0	615.2	591	299	175	431	76

Where They Hit the Ball

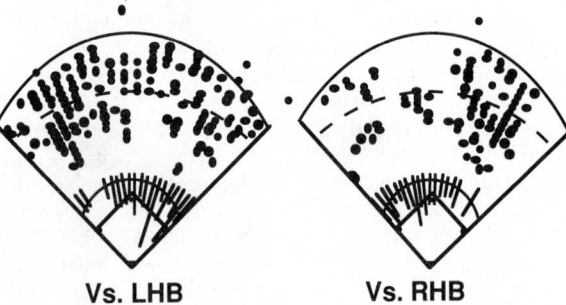

Vs. LHB   **Vs. RHB**

1989 Situational Stats

	W	L	ERA	Sv	IP		AB	H	HR	RBI	AVG
Home	7	3	3.40	0	106.0	LHB	413	95	12	37	.230
Road	7	3	3.28	0	104.1	RHB	371	92	7	37	.248
Day	2	3	3.43	0	39.1	Sc Pos	156	37	4	48	.237
Night	12	3	3.32	0	171.0	Clutch	41	9	1	2	.220

1989 Rankings (American League)

→ 2nd in lowest grounder/flyball ratio (.82) - *pitchers with 162 IP*

→ 5th in pickoff throws (240)

→ 6th in won/loss percentage (.700) - *pitchers with 15 or more decision*

→ Led the Mariners in ERA (3.34), wins (14), games started (33), shutouts (2), innings (210.1), hits allowed (187), batters faced (862), home runs allowed (19), strikeouts (140), pitches thrown (3,296), pickoff throws, won/loss percentage, lowest opponent batting average (.239), lowest opponent on-base average (.295) and lowest opponent slugging percentage (.376)

HITTING:

Though not a great hitter, Scott Bradley is one of the best contact hitters in the AL. He's very aggressive and it's a rarity when he doesn't swing at the first pitch. Bradley's theory is that the first pitch might be the best one that he will see in an at bat, so he comes up swinging. That philosophy has helped Bradley compile a .271 career average and kept his strikeout total low, but it's also prevented him from getting on base as often as he might. Bradley drew only 21 walks in 1989, and that was a career high for him.

Although he's a spray hitter who mostly hits line drives, Bradley can belt the ball on occasion. He likes the low fastball and any home runs that he hits are pulled. He does not hit lefthanded pitching well and will usually only start against southpaws in an emergency. Bradley's role as a Mariner has always been that of back-up catcher and pinch hitter off the bench. He's a fine pinch hitter and can fill in at other positions. Bradley has often been sought by other clubs, but the Mariners would be reluctant to let him go. Because of yearly injuries to starting catcher Dave Valle, Bradley has been the everyday catcher on numerous occasions. In fact, over the last three years, Bradley has logged both more plate appearances and games behind the plate than Valle has.

BASERUNNING:

Bradley is on the slow side, but not as slow as most catchers. He's a pretty heady baserunner and won't make many mistakes.

FIELDING:

Once considered such a weak receiver that he spent a lot of time playing other positions, Bradley has worked hard and improved. He still doesn't have the fielding skills to make him an everyday catcher, but he's the kind where you don't panic if the main man goes down. Bradley blocks the ball decently but falls short in throwing out baserunners. He handles the pitchers well and at one time was Mark Langston's personal catcher. In a pinch he can play third, first, or the outfield without embarrassing himself.

OVERALL:

A solid veteran, Bradley is valuable in his backup role and a steadying influence in the Mariner clubhouse. He can fill in and do a good job when Valle's hurt . . . which is often. It would take a good offer for the Mariners to part with him.

SCOTT BRADLEY

Position: C
Bats: L **Throws:** R
Ht: 5'11" **Wt:** 185

Opening Day Age: 30
Born: 3/22/60 in
Montclair, NJ
ML Seasons: 6

Overall Statistics

	G	AB	R	H	D	T	HR	RBI	SB	BB	SO	AVG
1989	103	270	21	74	16	0	3	37	1	21	23	.274
Career	413	1237	127	335	59	6	17	144	3	68	70	.271

Where He Hits the Ball

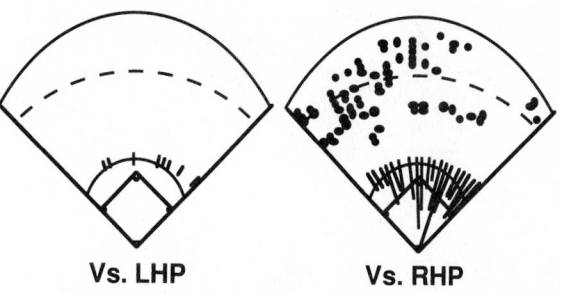

Vs. LHP   **Vs. RHP**

1989 Situational Stats

	AB	H	HR	RBI	AVG		AB	H	HR	RBI	AVG
Home	131	36	1	12	.275	LHP	14	2	0	2	.143
Road	139	38	2	25	.273	RHP	256	72	3	35	.281
Day	84	23	1	18	.274	Sc Pos	70	20	2	35	.286
Night	186	51	2	19	.274	Clutch	59	16	1	5	.271

1989 Rankings (American League)

➡ 2nd worst in throwing out base-stealers (19.7%) - *catchers with 75 attempts*

OVERLOOKED

GREG BRILEY

Position: LF
Bats: L **Throws:** R
Ht: 5' 8" **Wt:** 165

Opening Day Age: 24
Born: 5/24/65 in Bethel, NC
ML Seasons: 2

HITTING:

Some people say that if rookie Greg Briley would flap his left elbow, it would put the finishing touch to his likeness to Joe Morgan. Others compare him to Kirby Puckett because of his intensity at the plate. So intense is Briley in fact, that most of the Mariners' fans have yet to see him smile. Briley might not be convinced that he has nailed down the job in left field, but most others are. His rookie year was excellent. Although overshadowed by teammate Ken Griffey, Briley ended the year with a .266 average, 13 HRs, 52 RBIs and 11 stolen bases in 394 at bats. In 455 at bats, Griffey had a .264 average, 16 HRs, 61 RBIs and 16 stolen bases in 455 at bats -- not much difference.

For his size, Briley has a surprising amount of pop in his bat. The media guide lists him at 5'9", but he has admitted to being only 5'7½", which creates a small strike zone and makes him a little tough to pitch to. He's a line-drive pull hitter, but can go the other way. He likes the ball low and inside and turns on the pitch quickly. He hits lefties well and that will keep him an everyday player. He has patience, makes good contact, has good speed and is a natural number two hitter, though one with power.

BASERUNNING:

Briley's ability as a baserunner has yet to be explored, but he has the potential to be an above average base stealer. In three minor league seasons, Briley accumulated a total of 87 stolen bases. As Briley gathers major league experience, one has to speculate that he will eventually steal 25 or more bases.

FIELDING:

It's difficult to give an accurate evaluation of Briley's abilities as an outfielder, as the position is new to him. Briley's natural position is second base, but the Mariners have a Gold Glover there. After a shift to third at Calgary, he was recalled and put in left field when Jeff Leonard developed foot problems. As an outfielder Briley has good speed and range and an average arm. He'll get better.

OVERALL:

Already a solid number two hitter, Briley has star potential, but will probably become best known as one of the three young Mariner outfielders. Teamed with Ken Griffey Jr. and Jay Buhner, it appears that Seattle has a solid defensive and offensive outfield for years to come.

Overall Statistics

	G	AB	R	H	D	T	HR	RBI	SB	BB	SO	AVG
1989	115	394	52	105	22	4	13	52	11	39	82	.266
Career	128	430	58	114	24	4	14	56	11	44	88	.265

Where He Hits the Ball

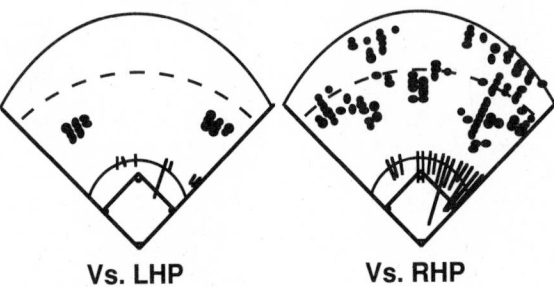

Vs. LHP   Vs. RHP

1989 Situational Stats

	AB	H	HR	RBI	AVG		AB	H	HR	RBI	AVG
Home	164	34	5	23	.207	LHP	53	17	1	7	.321
Road	230	71	8	29	.309	RHP	341	88	12	45	.258
Day	105	34	6	16	.324	Sc Pos	90	20	2	35	.222
Night	289	71	7	36	.246	Clutch	68	15	0	5	.221

1989 Rankings (American League)

- ➡ 5th in percentage of extra bases taken as a runner (57.1%) - *players with 40 opportunities to advance*
- ➡ 6th in batting on the road (.309) - *players with 252 road PA*
- ➡ 8th in batting on a 3-1 count (.529) - *players with 10 PA with a 3-1 count*
- ➡ Led the Mariners in percentage of extra bases taken as a runner and batting on a 3-1 count
- ➡ Led AL Left Fielders in batting on the road and batting on a 3-1 count

HITTING:

Jay Buhner had a problem getting started from nearly the first day of spring training last year. He began the year as the subject of trade rumors that included him in the proposed Langston trade with the Mets. Buhner sulked, knowing his chances of playing every day with the Mariners were far better than they would have been with the Mets. The deal fell through, but by then Buhner had developed a sullen, lifeless attitude. Buhner was so unimpressive in spring training that he started the year in Triple A Calgary.

Buhner loves the game of baseball, however, and it didn't take long for him to get his head on straight and make it back to the majors. The Yankees traded him because he had a hitch in his swing, and Buhner had returned to his old bad habits. He was swinging from an upright position and not making contact. He continually chased high fast balls out of the strike zone and was striking out at an alarming rate. While he was in Calgary, he changed his stance to a more crouched position. The change helped tremendously and the hitch is now gone. The high fast balls are now over his head, eliminating the temptation to chase them.

Buhner is a power hitter with gobs of raw talent waiting to be harnessed. He ended last year with a .275 average and .490 slugging percentage which reflects the kind of numbers he's capable of. He can pull the ball but also hits with power to center and right-centerfield. He likes ball low in the strike zone. A full year with a healthy body and attitude could produce 30 plus homers in the cozy Kingdome.

BASERUNNING:

Buhner is a good baserunner with skills that could still be developed. Right now, he not a base stealing threat, but the feeling is that with time and experience, 15 stolen bases are possible.

FIELDING:

Buhner has not had a great deal of major league experience but has already developed a reputation for his defensive range and instincts, and his cannon arm is demanding a great deal of respect. There is little doubt that he will soon rank among the best outfielders in the American League.

OVERALL:

Buhner certainly has star potential. All he needs is a healthy year and no trade rumors. It appears that the Mariners feel the same way and right field will be Buhner's for years to come.

JAY BUHNER

Position: RF
Bats: R **Throws:** R
Ht: 6' 3" **Wt:** 205

Opening Day Age: 25
Born: 8/13/64 in Louisville, KY
ML Seasons: 3

Overall Statistics

	G	AB	R	H	D	T	HR	RBI	SB	BB	SO	AVG
1989	58	204	27	56	15	1	9	33	1	19	55	.275
Career	150	487	63	117	30	2	22	72	2	48	154	.240

Where He Hits the Ball

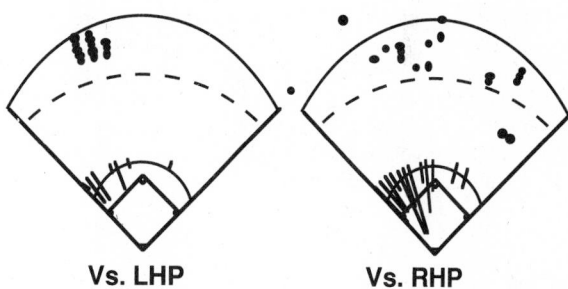

Vs. LHP   **Vs. RHP**

1989 Situational Stats

	AB	H	HR	RBI	AVG		AB	H	HR	RBI	AVG
Home	104	29	7	16	.279	LHP	60	14	2	6	.233
Road	100	27	2	17	.270	RHP	144	42	7	27	.292
Day	60	22	3	9	.367	Sc Pos	50	15	1	21	.300
Night	144	34	6	24	.236	Clutch	36	10	2	5	.278

1989 Rankings (American League)

- ➡ 5th in lowest percentage of extra bases taken as a runner - *players with 40 opportunities to advance*

- ➡ 8th in batting average with 2 strikes (.272) - *players with 162 PA with 2 strikes*

- ➡ Led the Mariners in home run frequency (22.7 ABs per HR) and batting average with 2 strikes - *all team players*

- ➡ Led AL Right Fielders in batting average with 2 strikes

HITTING:

Darnell Coles is a contact hitter with power to right field. He chokes up on the bat about an inch and uses all fields, quite often hitting the gaps for extra bases. Coles likes the fastball inside, so hurlers tend to work him down and away with breaking stuff; once a strong pull hitter, Coles goes with the pitch more these days. He's not selfish and is very good at moving baserunners along. Coles loves the Kingdome and his performance inside the dome last year far exceeded his output on the road. One of Darnell's goals for 1990 should be to equal his Kingdome accomplishments away from home. If he could, he'd be a big boost to the team's offense.

Mariner manager Jim Lefebvre likes Coles, but finding a spot for him to play was difficult. Lefebvre wanted Coles to have 600 at bats, but ended up doing a juggling act to keep him in the line-up. Coles ended the year with 535 at bats, third most on the team, but he had to play several different positions (left field, right field, first, third and DH) to do it. Considering the constant defensive changes, Coles was productive with the bat, driving in 59 runs, but the feeling is that he is capable of much more consistent and better numbers. He hit 20 home runs in Detroit in 1986 and there's no reason to believe that he can't accomplish that same feat in the Kingdome under the right circumstances.

BASERUNNING:

Coles does not have great speed and has stolen only 18 bases in seven seasons while being thrown out the same number of times. He's a fairly conservative baserunner.

FIELDING:

Which position? Third base is Coles' natural position and the one that he prefers to play. He has good range to his right and has made some spectacular plays going that way. He has trouble to his left. He has an excellent arm and did well throwing to first, a bugaboo for him in the past in Detroit. The arm helps him in the outfield, where he's still learning.

OVERALL:

Coles is important to the team and that was made clear when Lefebvre got him 535 at bats without a permanent position. To have 'hot Coles' all season long, it's imperative that the Mariners find a him a permanent home and tack his name over the door. In all probability, that is third base.

DARNELL COLES

Position: RF/DH/1B/3B
Bats: R **Throws:** R
Ht: 6' 1" **Wt:** 185

Opening Day Age: 27
Born: 6/2/62 in San Bernardino, CA
ML Seasons: 7

Overall Statistics

	G	AB	R	H	D	T	HR	RBI	SB	BB	SO	AVG
1989	146	535	54	135	21	3	10	59	5	27	61	.252
Career	606	2024	239	500	101	9	57	271	18	176	310	.247

Where He Hits the Ball

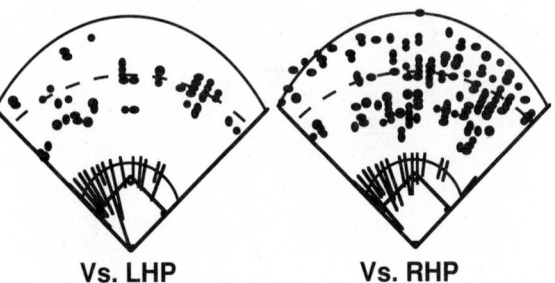

Vs. LHP   **Vs. RHP**

1989 Situational Stats

	AB	H	HR	RBI	AVG		AB	H	HR	RBI	AVG
Home	241	69	4	29	.286	LHP	157	38	2	16	.242
Road	294	66	6	30	.224	RHP	378	97	8	43	.257
Day	129	34	0	12	.264	Sc Pos	128	31	2	46	.242
Night	406	101	10	47	.249	Clutch	83	24	3	10	.289

1989 Rankings (American League)

➡ 9th in hit by pitch (6)
➡ Led AL Right Fielders in errors (12)

PITCHING:

Lefthanded relief pitchers don't die, they just find another team to play for. Thirty-four year old Keith Comstock has done just that time after time after time. In 14 years of professional baseball, he's pitched for seven different organizations, and in several different countries as well. What other pitcher can you name who was released by the Yomiuri Giants of the Japanese league ... only to be signed by the *San Francisco Giants?*

Yet up until the time that he joined the Mariners, Comstock's service in the majors totaled just 71 innings. Comstock began 1989 pitching for the Padres' AAA farm team at Las Vegas. He did well, but when San Diego refused to recall him, Comstock guttily demanded his release and signed with Seattle's Calgary farm team. The rest, as they say, is history. Mariner manager Jim Lefebvre was looking for lefthanded relief and he liked Comstock's screwball. Comstock was the ultimate specialist for Seattle, working only 25.2 innings in his 31 appearances. He did well, but in an odd sort of way. Most of the time he came in to face one or two lefthanded batters, but with his screwball Comstock was markedly more effective against righties. He faced enough of them, including pinch hitters, to earn his keep. Comstock failed to record an out in only three appearances and allowed his own baserunners to score in just four appearances. In his last 16 outings, he allowed only one run for an ERA of 1.04.

FIELDING:

Comstock is an average fielder and handles most anything hit within his range. He has a good move to first and allowed only one stolen base in his 31 appearances.

OVERALL:

They are rare, lefthanded relief pitchers. So if you find one that is effective, you keep him. Comstock has been very effective for the Mariners and has earned the right to return next year. He'll need to improve his work against lefthanded hitters, but as long as he pitches as well as he did last year, the Mariners won't complain. After years of wandering and stubborn determination, it appears that perhaps Comstock has found a permanent home and a place to finish out his adventuresome career. But then again, there's always Australia ... or maybe the Italian league.

KEITH COMSTOCK

Position: RP
Bats: L **Throws:** L
Ht: 6' 0" **Wt:** 174

Opening Day Age: 34
Born: 12/23/55 in San Francisco, CA
ML Seasons: 4

Overall Statistics

	W	L	ERA	G	GS	Sv	IP	H	R	BB	SO	HR
1989	1	2	2.81	31	0	0	25.2	26	8	10	22	2
Career	3	3	4.56	83	0	1	96.2	92	50	48	92	10

Where They Hit the Ball

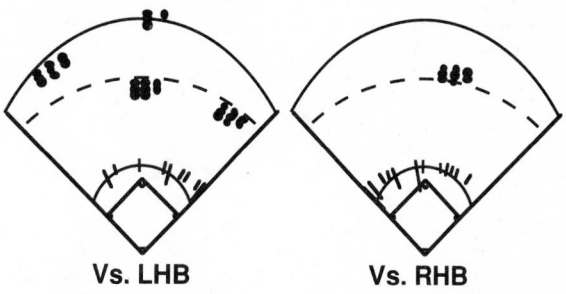

Vs. LHB   **Vs. RHB**

1989 Situational Stats

	W	L	ERA	Sv	IP		AB	H	HR	RBI	AVG
Home	1	1	3.95	0	13.2	LHB	45	15	1	8	.333
Road	0	1	1.50	0	12.0	RHB	52	11	1	5	.212
Day	0	1	3.38	0	5.1	Sc Pos	22	7	1	11	.318
Night	1	1	2.66	0	20.1	Clutch	31	12	0	5	.387

1989 Rankings (American League)

➡ Did not rank near the top or bottom in any category

HENRY COTTO

Position: LF/CF/RF
Bats: R **Throws:** R
Ht: 6' 2" **Wt:** 180

Opening Day Age: 29
Born: 1/5/61 in New York, NY
ML Seasons: 6

HITTING:

Henry Cotto is a line drive hitter to all fields with a surprising amount of power to left. He has a very quick, compact swing and can turn on the ball. He makes good contact and normally bats second unless Greg Briley and Harold Reynolds are both playing. In just 295 at bats last year, Cotto had nine homers, two triples and 11 doubles and scored 44 runs. Cotto still has a tendency to chase bad pitches and has never walked enough to be a complete offensive player. But overall, 1989 was Cotto's best season, and he was very productive in the role that he filled.

Many consider Cotto the best fourth outfielder on any American League team. For that reason, his name surfaces frequently in trade talks. Several teams have spots where he could play every day. Cracking the Mariner outfield next year will be virtually impossible with Greg Briley in left, Ken Griffey, Jr. in center and Jay Buhner in right. So Cotto will have to be content as a role player again. He doesn't seem to mind the assignment and keeps himself ready to play at all times.

BASERUNNING:

Cotto is the smartest of the Mariner baserunners and has a high percentage of successful steals -- his career success rate of 81% is one of the best in the majors. Cotto is very fast, but doesn't seem to be as aggressive as he could be. It's very possible that he's not running on his own, and he's not in the lineup often enough to keep his skills as sharp as he should.

FIELDING:

Cotto can play all three outfield positions and is an above average fielder. He has the speed to run down most anything in centerfield but just doesn't cover the ground Griffey can. His range is good and he can go back on the ball well. His arm is adequate, but he's not going to overwhelm anyone with his throwing abilities.

OVERALL:

Cotto is as important to the Mariners as any fourth outfielder in baseball. One would guess that that will be his role again in 1990. However, the possibility of including him in a trade package looms heavily since so much interest has been expressed in his possible availability.

Overall Statistics

	G	AB	R	H	D	T	HR	RBI	SB	BB	SO	AVG
1989	100	295	44	78	11	2	9	33	10	12	44	.264
Career	475	1112	154	287	48	3	24	106	54	56	184	.258

Where He Hits the Ball

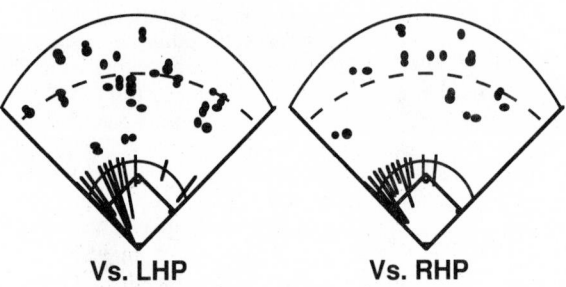

Vs. LHP   Vs. RHP

1989 Situational Stats

	AB	H	HR	RBI	AVG		AB	H	HR	RBI	AVG
Home	149	37	5	16	.248	LHP	160	42	5	19	.262
Road	146	41	4	17	.281	RHP	135	36	4	14	.267
Day	66	17	1	5	.258	Sc Pos	55	17	1	18	.309
Night	229	61	8	28	.266	Clutch	53	13	2	4	.245

1989 Rankings (American League)

➡ Did not rank near the top or bottom in any category

HITTING:

The word's getting around. After years of being hidden in obscurity in Seattle, Alvin Davis is finally getting his just due. The whole world might not be informed of his consistent success, but those with some baseball knowledge know that there is more than just one good first baseman by the name of Davis. A very selective hitter, Alvin has an excellent knowledge of the strike zone and has one of the most mechanically perfect swings in baseball. Davis has been a consistent power hitter since breaking in with the Mariners in 1984. He's averaged 22 homers, 88 RBIs and 88 walks while hitting under .284 only once.

In an effort to get more good pitches, Alvin has moved very close to the plate. He likes the ball low and inside so he can drive it to left field. He's successful at hitting the inside pitch because he's so quick with the bat. He has a short stride and a swift swing loaded with power. He's very adept at taking the outside pitch to right. Part of the problem with Alvin in the line-up is finding the right kind of hitter to protect him. Jeff Leonard was to provide that protection, but pitchers still pitched around Davis. With the emergence of Ken Griffey, Jr., Davis might yet find the protection that he needs.

BASERUNNING:

Davis is probably faster than Steve Balboni, but that's up for debate. It was noted last year that Jeffrey Leonard's RBI total probably would have surpassed 100 if Davis had possessed the speed to score from first base on a double. Alvin knows his limitations and so does the third base coach.

FIELDING:

Davis is an average fielder with little range. Along with not being fast, he's not quick. He's been fortunate to have Harold Reynolds plugging the holes he can't. He scoops the ball well. Many feel that Davis would be best utilized as the DH, opening a position for another offensive and defensive infielder.

OVERALL:

Alvin Davis is the mainstay of the Mariner team. He's been rewarded with a hefty three-year contract and there's no reason to believe that he will be traded. However, the search is on for a first baseman and if found, Alvin will move to the permanent DH spot and Jeff Leonard will play outfield, or more likely be traded.

ALVIN DAVIS

Position: 1B/DH
Bats: L **Throws:** R
Ht: 6' 1" **Wt:** 190

Opening Day Age: 29
Born: 9/9/60 in Riverside, CA
ML Seasons: 6

Overall Statistics

	G	AB	R	H	D	T	HR	RBI	SB	BB	SO	AVG
1989	142	498	84	152	30	1	21	95	0	101	49	.305
Career	881	3180	461	921	176	9	131	530	7	531	403	.290

Where He Hits the Ball

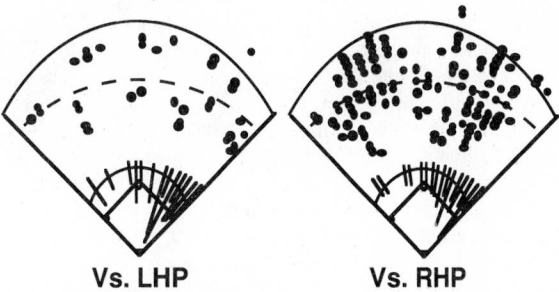

Vs. LHP   **Vs. RHP**

1989 Situational Stats

	AB	H	HR	RBI	AVG		AB	H	HR	RBI	AVG
Home	249	91	13	56	.365	LHP	154	49	6	41	.318
Road	249	61	8	39	.245	RHP	344	103	15	54	.299
Day	132	49	9	34	.371	Sc Pos	127	46	6	72	.362
Night	366	103	12	61	.281	Clutch	77	16	3	16	.208

1989 Rankings (American League)

➡ 2nd in on-base average (.424), hitting with runners in scoring position (.362) and percentage of pitches taken (68.0%) - *players with 502 PA*

➡ 3rd in batting at home (.365) - *players with 252 PA at home*

➡ 4th in intentional walks (15)

➡ 5th in slugging percentage (.496) and walks (101)

➡ Led the Mariners in batting average (.305), doubles (30), total bases (247), RBI (95), walks, intentional walks, hit by pitch (6), times on base (259), GDPs (15), on-base average, slugging percentage and hitting with runners in scoring position

PITCHING:

Mike Dunne came to the Mariners in an April trade with Pittsburgh involving shortstop Rey Quinones. Seattle was desperate for pitching help and worked Dunne into the starting rotation immediately. They were hoping that he would regain the success that he experienced when he was the 1987 Sporting News National League Rookie Pitcher of the Year. Unfortunately, the change in scenery didn't help. Dunne finished his first year with Seattle with some of the same problems that haunted him the year before in Pittsburgh. Dunne won only twice in 15 starts for Seattle, and his 5.27 Mariner ERA was a far cry from the 3.03 mark he'd recorded only two years previously.

Dunne's pitches include a fastball, slider, changeup and forkball. His fastball can reach the 90's but he relies mostly on the sharp-breaking slider. If the breaking ball is not effective, he tends to get behind in the count and then into trouble. Dunne has the stamina to go the distance but usually pitches himself into a hole before he gets very deep into a game. As a starter in Seattle, he averaged only 5.69 innings pitched per start. He appears to have lost the confidence that he needs to be aggressive. He has talent -- the usually astute Cardinals made him the seventh player selected in the 1984 draft -- and on occasion has put together a superior performance, which tends to encourage management. Surprisingly, Dunne has been more successful in the Kingdome than he's been on the road. His ERA in the hitters' park was a respectable 3.76.

FIELDING:

Mike Dunne will not win any Gold Gloves in the near future. He's an average or below-average fielder, which is not particularly an asset for a ground ball pitcher. However, considering his size, 6'4", he gets around the mound well enough. His lack of concentration tends to get him in trouble when holding baserunners.

OVERALL:

Dunne's future as a starting pitcher for the Mariners in on the bubble. One has to believe that Seattle will be seeking a solid veteran starter during the off season and if they're successful, Dunne would need a very impressive spring training to make the team. He still has the tools and perhaps a new year could make the difference. The other consideration is that he might be included in some sort of trade package.

MIKE DUNNE

Position: SP
Bats: R **Throws:** R
Ht: 6' 4" **Wt:** 200

Opening Day Age: 27
Born: 10/27/62 in South Bend, IN
ML Seasons: 3

Overall Statistics

	W	L	ERA	G	GS	Sv	IP	H	R	BB	SO	HR
1989	3	10	5.60	18	18	0	99.2	125	73	46	42	8
Career	23	27	3.97	71	69	0	433.0	431	227	202	184	33

Where They Hit the Ball

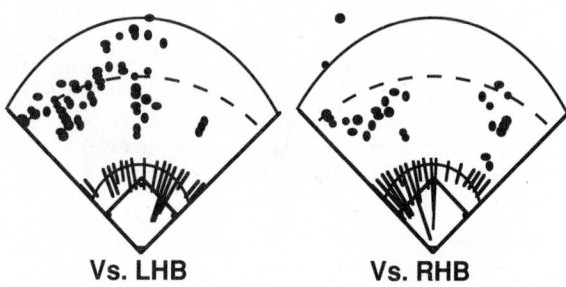

Vs. LHB   Vs. RHB

1989 Situational Stats

	W	L	ERA	Sv	IP		AB	H	HR	RBI	AVG
Home	3	5	4.29	0	63.0	LHB	204	70	4	34	.343
Road	0	5	7.85	0	36.2	RHB	199	55	4	20	.276
Day	1	1	8.49	0	11.2	Sc Pos	112	32	2	45	.286
Night	2	9	5.22	0	88.0	Clutch	10	3	0	1	.300

1989 Rankings (American League)

➥ 4th worst batting average allowed vs. left-handed batters (.333) - *pitchers facing 125 LHB*

➥ Led the Mariners in wild pitches (7)

FUTURE ALL-STAR

HITTING:

It's hard to become a household name while playing for the Seattle Mariners, but Ken Griffey, Jr. is one player who can buck the odds. Only 20, Griffey has the tools to be one of the top players in the game. He can hit for power and average, run the bases and field. He hasn't begun to tap his abilities yet.

Griffey has a very quick swing with little leg kick or wasted motion. He has the ability to make adjustments not only between at bats, but during at bats. He's already a patient hitter and will have a lot of quality plate appearances. He likes the ball low in the center of the strike zone and his big sweeping swing can drive it deep. He has the knack for the dramatic in clutch situations, the earmark of a superstar.

Griffey got off to an excellent start last year, but a broken hand suffered in a hotel shower may have cost him the AL Rookie of the Year title. When Griffey returned, his performance declined. That really didn't worry the Mariners; hand injuries often take a while to heal, and it was a very long year for a 19-year old rookie who was constantly in the media spotlight. Nonetheless, Griffey's rookie season was all anyone could have expected. He wasn't overawed by being in the major leagues and showed more than enough to indicate a very big future.

BASERUNNING:

Griffey is a smart baserunner for a youngster. He stole 16 bases in his first year, but twice that amount is certainly a possibility. An aggressive baserunner, he has excellent speed and will make the mistakes of a youngster, but he can only improve with experience. His slide is ragged and he spent the winter at the Instructional League to sharpen his skills.

FIELDING:

Griffey plays very shallow and stops hearts with his ability to chase balls down. He appears lackadaisical on routine plays but displays all out abandon on the tougher chances. His catch in Fenway last season will be on highlight films for years to come. Griffey has a strong and accurate arm, but again will make youthful mistakes.

OVERALL:

Griffey is a future superstar. He can do it all on the field and has the charisma a great player needs. The Mariners have put together what some call the most potentially dangerous outfield of the '90s, both offensively and defensively. Ken Griffey, Jr. is its nucleus.

KEN GRIFFEY JR

Position: CF
Bats: L **Throws:** L
Ht: 6' 3" **Wt:** 195

Opening Day Age: 20
Born: 11/21/69 in Donora, PA
ML Seasons: 1

Overall Statistics

	G	AB	R	H	D	T	HR	RBI	SB	BB	SO	AVG
1989	127	455	61	120	23	0	16	61	16	44	83	.264
Career	127	455	61	120	23	0	16	61	16	44	83	.264

Where He Hits the Ball

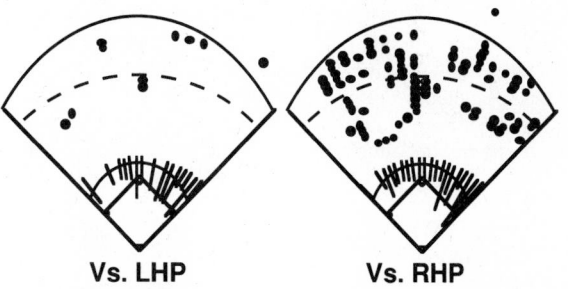

Vs. LHP   **Vs. RHP**

1989 Situational Stats

	AB	H	HR	RBI	AVG		AB	H	HR	RBI	AVG
Home	218	57	10	32	.261	LHP	118	25	3	12	.212
Road	237	63	6	29	.266	RHP	337	95	13	49	.282
Day	120	29	3	15	.242	Sc Pos	111	32	1	42	.288
Night	335	91	13	46	.272	Clutch	72	16	4	11	.222

1989 Rankings (American League)

- 8th in least GDPs per GDP situation (4.3%) - *players with 50 PA in GDP situations*
- Led the Mariners in runs scored per time reached base (32.6%) and steals of third (4)
- Led AL Center Fielders in errors (10)

PITCHING:

Every team in baseball could probably play the "what if" game, but the Eric Hanson "what if" is legitimate. If Hanson had exercised properly in the 1988-1989 off-season, it's possible he would have been the American League Rookie of the Year last year. Instead he spent half the season rebuilding his muscles on the disabled list instead of muscling American League hitters with his nasty curve ball. Even so, Hanson had a 9-5 record while making only 17 starts.

Hanson has a fastball in the low 90's with excellent movement. He has a good change-up that can eventually make him even more effective if he uses it more. His bread and butter pitch, however, is the curve. Not many big leaguers throw curve balls with the movement that Hanson's has, possibly because he holds the ball farther back in the palm of the hand than most pitchers do. Hanson's ERA of 3.18 has to be admired for a rookie who pitched half his games in the Kingdome. Even more impressive was his consistency: 70% of his outings were quality starts. He also displayed outstanding control, walking only 2.54 batters per nine innings. Hanson wasn't the recipient of an overabundance of runs, but he made the most of what he had. In the 9 games where he was supported with 3 or fewer runs, Hanson won five and lost three with an ERA of 2.24. A winning record in that situation is highly unlikely and a true measure of a premier pitcher.

FIELDING:

Hanson is very tall at 6'6", but handles his lanky frame well. He's an excellent fielder and smart player. Like teammate Randy Johnson, Hanson can get to first base in short order. Hanson has one of the better slide steps in baseball and his quick delivery makes base stealing extremely difficult. Opposing runners stole only two bases with Hanson on the mound, while getting thrown out nine times.

OVERALL:

Hanson has all the earmarks of a consistent big winner. Obviously his ability is very important to the Mariner's future in the aftermath of losing Mike Moore and Mark Langston. Hanson is the number two starter after Scott Bankhead, but appears to have the stuff to eventually become the ace of any staff.

ERIK HANSON

Position: SP
Bats: R **Throws:** R
Ht: 6' 6" **Wt:** 205

Opening Day Age: 24
Born: 5/18/65 in Kinnelon, NJ
ML Seasons: 2

Overall Statistics

	W	L	ERA	G	GS	Sv	IP	H	R	BB	SO	HR
1989	9	5	3.18	17	17	0	113.1	103	44	32	75	7
Career	11	8	3.19	23	23	0	155.0	138	61	44	111	11

Where They Hit the Ball

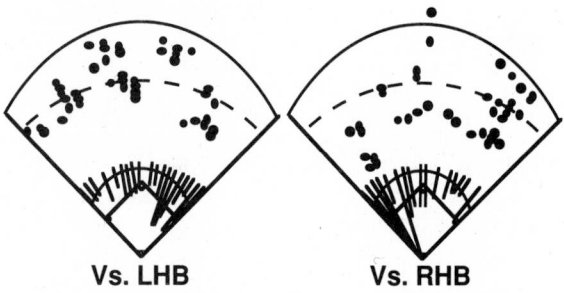

Vs. LHB   Vs. RHB

1989 Situational Stats

	W	L	ERA	Sv	IP		AB	H	HR	RBI	AVG
Home	5	2	3.57	0	58.0	LHB	225	48	2	16	.213
Road	4	3	2.77	0	55.1	RHB	198	55	5	18	.278
Day	3	0	2.11	0	21.1	Sc Pos	83	19	1	22	.229
Night	6	5	3.42	0	92.0	Clutch	39	9	0	1	.231

1989 Rankings (American League)

➡ Led the Mariners in caught stealing (9)

PITCHING:

Brian Holman is one of three pitchers Seattle acquired from Montreal in the Mark Langston trade. Although it appeared that Randy Johnson was the key acquisition, Holman has turned out to be a pleasant surprise. The righthander has a high 80's fastball with tremendous movement that is often compared to Mike Moore's fastball. He also has a slider, curve and change-up. The curve is crisp with a big break. Both the slider and curve can be devastating when Holman's ahead in the count. Holman is not afraid to pitch inside and has enough confidence in his breaking pitches to use them when he's behind in the count.

Holman seems to be blossoming in the American League and had some excellent outings last year, including two shutouts and six complete games. He has the makeup to go the distance and be a workhorse; he averaged 7.17 innings pitched per start. He had 22 starts in a Mariner uniform and sported an ERA of 3.44 which is encouraging considering he's pitching in the Kingdome. Even though his first year in Seattle showed a lot of promise, Holman lacks the consistency of a veteran pitcher. That probably is most noticeable in his low percentage of quality starts (50%). However, it appears that he has the good stuff and mental toughness to become more consistent and reliable.

Holman's role model has become Scott Bankhead and he attributes some of his success to his observance of the Mariner's ace. He's impressed with Bankhead's ability to throw strikes and get ahead of the hitters. Apparently Bankhead's approach to the game has rubbed off somewhat. In Holman's first 13 appearances, he average 4.08 walks per nine innings pitched. But in his last nine outings, he cut that average drastically to 2.49.

FIELDING:

Holman has above average fielding abilities. He's agile for his height and will handle most anything hit his way. He falls off the mound to the left, but it doesn't seem to hinder him any. He holds baserunners reasonably well, though 73% of the runners who tried to steal off him were successful.

OVERALL:

Barring a bad spring training, Holman has to be considered the third or fourth starter behind Scott Bankhead and Eric Hanson. It seems that he has a solid hold on his position in the rotation and should be an important part of the Mariner starting staff for years to come.

BRIAN HOLMAN

Position: SP/RP
Bats: R **Throws:** R
Ht: 6' 4" **Wt:** 185

Opening Day Age: 25
Born: 1/25/65 in Denver, CO
ML Seasons: 2

Overall Statistics

	W	L	ERA	G	GS	Sv	IP	H	R	BB	SO	HR
1989	9	12	3.67	33	25	0	191.1	194	86	77	105	11
Career	13	20	3.52	51	41	0	291.2	295	125	111	163	14

Where They Hit the Ball

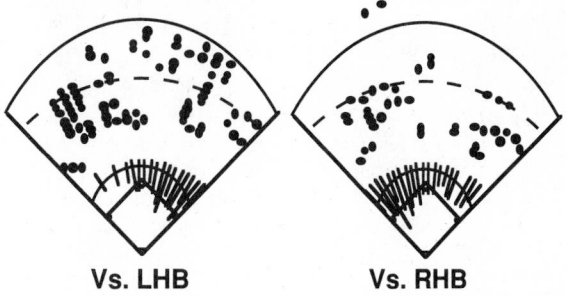

Vs. LHB   **Vs. RHB**

1989 Situational Stats

	W	L	ERA	Sv	IP		AB	H	HR	RBI	AVG
Home	4	5	4.16	0	80.0	LHB	351	93	5	34	.265
Road	5	7	3.31	0	111.1	RHB	388	101	6	40	.260
Day	4	4	3.58	0	55.1	Sc Pos	190	40	1	59	.211
Night	5	8	3.71	0	136.0	Clutch	62	19	2	8	.306

1989 Rankings (American League)

➡ Led the Mariners in losses (10), complete games (6), shutouts (2) and hit batsmen (6)

PITCHING:

Last spring, the Mariners had the luxury of choosing their stopper from among three applicants. The door to the job was left open for Mike Schooler, Tom Niedenfuer and Mike Jackson. As many guessed, Jackson ended up being the set-up man for Schooler. The difference between the two is Schooler throws strikes. Schooler ended the year with more hits per innings pitched, but his ratio of strikeouts to walks (69 to 19) was much better than Jackson's (94 to 54).

Jackson is a power pitcher with a fastball in the low 90's that has lots of good movement. He also throws a hard slider, a curve, and an offspeed pitch. He has fallen in love with the offspeed pitch and should be using the fastball more. When he has his good stuff, his darting fastball is nearly unhittable. Being the set-up man is not an assignment that Jackson likes, but he appeared to have accepted it with less fuss than in 1988. Like many middle relievers, he'd rather have the more profitable role of closer.

Jackson started the year slowly and through June had an ERA of 4.18 and a 2-2 record. His ERA after June was 2.08 and he ended the year very strongly at 3.17. Jackson is very durable and finished with 65 appearances, second on the club only to Schooler's 67. He allowed just 81 hits in 99.1 innings pitched. Jackson is rapidly becoming known for his abilities and is considered one of the best middle relief pitchers in the American League. He is often compared to Lee Smith, who has a similar delivery and even lumbers to the mound in the same fashion.

FIELDING:

Before he was converted to a pitcher, Jackson was an infielder when he joined the Phillies. That explains why he had such good fielding instincts. He's quick for a big man and can handle most anything within his range. He has a quick move to first for a righthanded pitcher and usually pays close attention to baserunners.

OVERALL:

Jackson is a very talented and dependable relief pitcher. If Schooler went down for some reason, Jackson could step into the closer's role with ease. He is very valuable to the team in his present role of set-up man and should continue to fill that capacity in 1990. That is, if the Mariners don't give in to tempting trade offers. With two good years back to back, the demand for his services should be high.

MICHAEL JACKSON

Position: RP
Bats: R **Throws:** R
Ht: 6' 0" **Wt:** 185

Opening Day Age: 25
Born: 12/22/64 in Houston, TX
ML Seasons: 4

Overall Statistics

	W	L	ERA	G	GS	Sv	IP	H	R	BB	SO	HR
1989	4	6	3.17	65	0	7	99.1	81	43	54	94	8
Career	13	21	3.36	191	7	12	321.1	255	140	157	266	36

Where They Hit the Ball

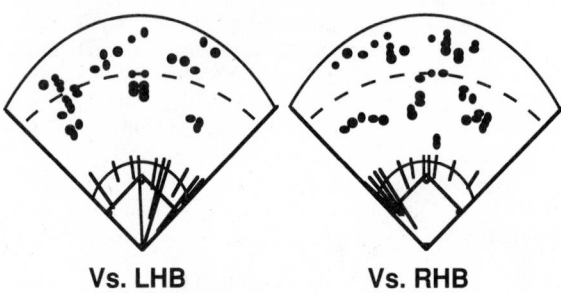

Vs. LHB   **Vs. RHB**

1989 Situational Stats

	W	L	ERA	Sv	IP		AB	H	HR	RBI	AVG
Home	2	2	3.50	4	54.0	LHB	158	35	5	26	.222
Road	2	4	2.78	3	45.1	RHB	205	46	3	25	.224
Day	0	1	4.91	2	18.1	Sc Pos	128	33	1	41	.258
Night	4	5	2.78	5	81.0	Clutch	165	37	2	23	.224

1989 Rankings (American League)

→ 9th in games (65)

→ Led the Mariners in hit batsmen (6), first batter efficiency (.250) and strikeouts per 9 innings (8.5)

PITCHING:

Some call him "Big Bird," his teammates call him "Big Unit" and by now, we all know that Randy Johnson is the tallest pitcher in major league history at 6'10". Johnson came to the Mariners along with Brian Holman and Gene Harris in the now famous "Langston Deal." Of the three pitchers Seattle obtained, Johnson was considered the best prospect. He was even rated a National League Rookie of the Year candidate, though he struggled with the Expos in his early '89 outings and had to be returned to the minors.

Johnson is a lefthanded power pitcher with a fastball in the mid 90's. Although his motion is fairly fluid for someone his size, he throws from a three quarters delivery and tends to sling the ball. That makes him tough on lefthanded hitters, but some feel that there would be better movement on his fastball if he came over the top more. Johnson throws a curve and a change, but the fastball and a hard slider are his best pitches and the reason he racks up impressive strikeout totals. His ratio of hits to innings pitched with Seattle was good (118/131), but his control was erratic, with more than one walk for every two innings pitched. Johnson has a reputation for blowing his cool -- as a Montreal farmhand he once punched a dugout wall, breaking his right hand -- and some feel that he loses his concentration too easily. He did bear down in close games -- in the 12 contests where he was supported with three or less runs, Johnson's ERA was 3.60. But when his teammates scored four runs or more, Johnson's ERA inflated to 5.46.

FIELDING:

Johnson fields fairly well for a big guy and can get to first base in about three giant steps. He has several moves to first including a Mark Langston flip toss which he will hurl into the stands on occasion. As one would guess, Johnson is extremely easy to steal on due to the time it takes for him to uncoil.

OVERALL:

It's a toss-up between Holman and Johnson for the third and fourth spot in the Mariner rotation. Johnson is an important part of the Mariner future, but it's imperative that he improve his control and get his head together a little more.

RANDY JOHNSON

Position: SP
Bats: R **Throws:** L
Ht: 6'10" **Wt:** 225

Opening Day Age: 26
Born: 9/10/63 in Walnut Creek, CA
ML Seasons: 2

Overall Statistics

	W	L	ERA	G	GS	Sv	IP	H	R	BB	SO	HR
1989	7	13	4.82	29	28	0	160.2	147	100	96	130	13
Career	10	13	4.48	33	32	0	186.2	170	108	103	155	16

Where They Hit the Ball

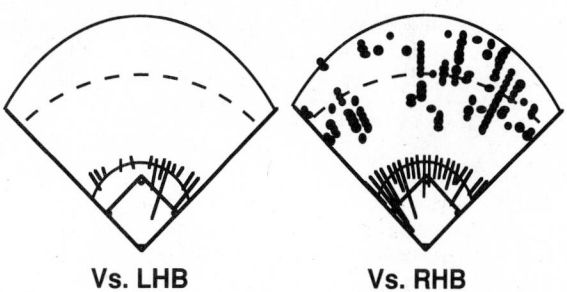

Vs. LHB   **Vs. RHB**

1989 Situational Stats

	W	L	ERA	Sv	IP		AB	H	HR	RBI	AVG
Home	2	6	4.76	0	70.0	LHB	87	17	2	14	.195
Road	5	7	4.86	0	90.2	RHB	506	130	11	71	.257
Day	3	3	6.16	0	38.0	Sc Pos	171	49	5	72	.287
Night	4	10	4.40	0	122.2	Clutch	42	10	0	1	.238

1989 Rankings (American League)

➡ 3rd in balks (5)

➡ 6th in stolen bases allowed (24)

➡ Led the Mariners in balks, stolen bases allowed and walks allowed (70)

HITTING:

With a handle like Hac-Man, you have to be an aggressive hitter. Jeffrey Leonard is. He's a power pull hitter but will go the other way on occasion. Leonard stands well off the plate and the normal pattern is to pitch him high and tight and then breaking stuff low and outside. He can also be worked up the ladder. Leonard is a good low ball hitter and likes to turn on low offerings and drive them with power.

Much credit has to be given to manager Jim Lefebvre for his insight in obtaining Leonard as a free agent after Milwaukee chose not to renew his contract. The Mariners took a big chance and subjected themselves to criticism when they signed Leonard to a two year, 1.6 million dollar contract, especially when Leonard was coming off the worst year of his career. When he heard of the signing, Atlanta Braves Manager, Russ Nixon commented: "We're desperate for help, but not that desperate." Leonard proved that such comments were way off base. He reached career highs in homers (24) and RBIs (93), and his presence in the lineup behind Alvin Davis gave Alvin some much-needed protection.

BASERUNNING:

Leonard is the oldest Mariner at 34, but not the slowest by any means. He's sneaky fast and a very smart base runner. He has good instincts and is aggressive, especially when trying to break up double plays.

FIELDING:

When last season started, Leonard had a lock on left field, but he lost his grip on the job with a nagging foot injury and the emergence of rookie Greg Briley. For most of the season, Leonard filled the role of DH. With the speed of Griffey, Buhner and Briley, it appears that it will be a rare occasion when Leonard gets an outfield assignment. He has lost a lot of his fielding skills, but will do a sufficient job if called upon.

OVERALL:

Leonard is a solid veteran who has been everything that the Mariners hoped for. With a intimidating nickname like Penitentiary Face, many find his true presence in the clubhouse hard to believe. Leonard's had a definite positive influence on the young Mariners, especially Griffey. Filling the DH role again in 1990 seems likely, but there is talk about Seattle seeking a first baseman and moving Alvin Davis to DH. If that happens, Leonard might become trade bait.

JEFF LEONARD

Position: DH/LF
Bats: R **Throws:** R
Ht: 6' 4" **Wt:** 200

Opening Day Age: 34
Born: 9/22/55 in Philadelphia, PA
ML Seasons: 13

Overall Statistics

	G	AB	R	H	D	T	HR	RBI	SB	BB	SO	AVG
1989	150	566	69	144	20	1	24	93	6	38	125	.254
Career	1281	4567	575	1222	203	37	134	648	159	305	903	.268

Where He Hits the Ball

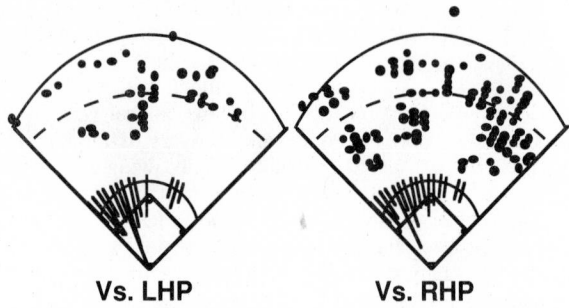

Vs. LHP   Vs. RHP

1989 Situational Stats

	AB	H	HR	RBI	AVG		AB	H	HR	RBI	AVG
Home	258	67	9	44	.260	LHP	157	44	8	27	.280
Road	308	77	15	49	.250	RHP	409	100	16	66	.244
Day	142	30	3	12	.211	Sc Pos	151	36	7	71	.238
Night	424	114	21	81	.269	Clutch	90	21	3	11	.233

1989 Rankings (American League)

- ➡ 2nd in sacrifice flies (12)
- ➡ 9th in strikeouts (125)
- ➡ 10th in home run frequency (23.5 ABs per HR) - *players with 502 PA*
- ➡ Led the Mariners in strikeouts, home run frequency, home runs (24) and sacrifice flies
- ➡ Led Designated Hitters in strikeouts, home run frequency, home runs, at bats (566), sacrifice flies, stolen bases (6), plate appearances (621), games (150) and runs scored per time reached base (32.5%)

HITTING:

Jim Presley has tremendous power to left and left centerfield when he makes contact. Making contact has always been Presley's trouble. After a 27 homer, 107 RBI season in 1986 -- a season in which he struck out 172 times -- Presley's numbers have declined year by year. The strikeouts have come down a little on a per-at-bat basis, but the power figures have come down even more. Last season's 12 homers and 41 RBIs were Presley's worst figures since his 70 game debut in 1984.

Presley is a pull hitter who has the ability to go the other way, but he seldom does. He iikes the fastball out over the plate where he can get his arms extended. Unfortunately, he can't get his arms extended far enough to hit the low-and-away breaking pitches he continually chases. He also has problems with the off-speed pitch and his power can be stifled by pitching him up and in. Obviously, with his strike out ratio and low walk total, Presley is not a patient hitter.

Presley was a promising young star only a few years ago, but all that talent has fizzled. One has to wonder if artificial turf and back problems, combined with Seattle's continual management turnover, have hindered Presley's career. It's hard to call Presley a fading veteran. A change to a new home, especially one covered with grass, could well rekindle Presley's career.

BASERUNNING:

Presley is not a base stealing threat. If he steals any, it's probably the result of a mistake or missed sign. He is not fleet of foot but is a fairly smart baserunner. He will make aggressive slides into second to break up attempted double plays.

FIELDING:

Presley has average range with a good but often erratic arm. He can made the spectacular play, especially to his right. He has the ability to recover quickly and made a strong throw. His defense seems to suffer when his offense is sour.

OVERALL:

You can almost bet the farm that Presley won't be a Mariner in 1990. He's just not in the plans. Darnell Coles should inherit his third base job. The problem is unloading Presley with his hefty contract. Woody Woodward has to work some magic to pull off a profitable trade.

JIM PRESLEY

Position: 3B/1B
Bats: R **Throws:** R
Ht: 6' 1" **Wt:** 190

Opening Day Age: 28
Born: 10/23/61 in Pensacola, FL
ML Seasons: 6

Overall Statistics

	G	AB	R	H	D	T	HR	RBI	SB	BB	SO	AVG
1989	117	390	42	92	20	1	12	41	0	21	107	.236
Career	799	2946	351	736	147	13	115	418	8	177	713	.250

Where He Hits the Ball

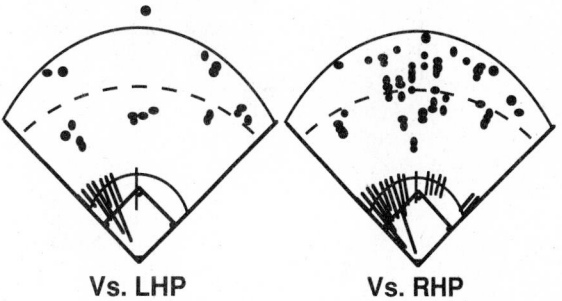

Vs. LHP   **Vs. RHP**

1989 Situational Stats

	AB	H	HR	RBI	AVG		AB	H	HR	RBI	AVG
Home	213	55	7	22	.258	LHP	116	38	4	11	.328
Road	177	37	5	19	.209	RHP	274	54	8	30	.197
Day	103	14	2	8	.136	Sc Pos	98	22	2	24	.224
Night	287	78	10	33	.272	Clutch	65	11	4	6	.169

1989 Rankings (American League)

➡ Worst batting average with an 0-2 count (.029) - *players with 20 PA with an 0-2 coun*t

➡ Led the Mariners in errors (18)

PITCHING:

Jerry Reed has quietly done a very respectable job for the Mariners in his very glamorless role as a long reliever. There's few stats for his kind of work, and those that exist are new and still awaiting popular acceptance. Long relief is a pretty thankless job, but one which Reed has handled very well in his four seasons with Seattle. Reed's seven wins and 52 appearances last year were a career high, and his 3.19 ERA was the second lowest of his career.

Reed has the basic stuff, throwing a fastball, curve and slider. His fastball is ordinary, reaching the high eighties on a good day, and given his age (34), it's not going to get any faster. Reed's pitches move, however; his breaking stuff tends to move down and sharply away from righthanded hitters, and for that reason he has always been markedly more effective against righty swingers than against lefties. Reed pays a price for that movement. He threw a lot of wild pitches last year, and he has a tendency to get a little wild, particularly against the lefty swingers who bother him. When Reed gets behind in the count and has to take something off his offerings, he's in trouble -- the result is often a ball over the fence. He needs to stay ahead of the hitters to be successful, and that's not always possible with the kind of stuff he possesses. He's a smart hurler, one who's made the most out of what talent he possesses.

FIELDING:

Reed is an above average fielder and an excellent athlete. He works hard to keep himself in top condition. He's quick off the mound and fields anything hit his way. Reed was once very easy to steal on, but he's worked hard at keeping baserunners close, and is now one of the better Seattle pitchers at holding baserunners.

OVERALL:

Reed has been very important to the Mariners over the last few years. He accepts the job he's been handed and can be used as a spot starter. If no trades or major changes occur and the Mariners pick up the veteran starter they are looking for, it seems logical that the five bullpen occupants would be Mike Schooler, Mike Jackson, Keith Comstock, Bill Swift and Jerry Reed.

JERRY REED

Position: RP
Bats: R **Throws:** R
Ht: 6' 1" **Wt:** 190

Opening Day Age: 34
Born: 10/8/55 in Bryson City, NC
ML Seasons: 8

Overall Statistics

	W	L	ERA	G	GS	Sv	IP	H	R	BB	SO	HR
1989	7	7	3.19	52	1	0	101.2	89	44	43	50	10
Career	18	17	3.83	205	12	16	427.1	414	207	153	229	45

Where They Hit the Ball

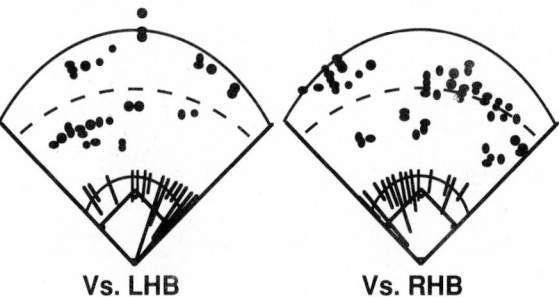

Vs. LHB   **Vs. RHB**

1989 Situational Stats

	W	L	ERA	Sv	IP		AB	H	HR	RBI	AVG
Home	6	4	2.75	0	52.1	LHB	148	38	4	20	.257
Road	1	3	3.65	0	49.1	RHB	231	51	6	26	.221
Day	1	0	3.62	0	27.1	Sc Pos	117	22	3	33	.188
Night	6	7	3.03	0	74.1	Clutch	80	29	1	11	.363

1989 Rankings (American League)

➡ Led the Mariners in percentage of inherited runners scoring (25.5%) - *team players with 30 inherited runners*

HITTING:

Switch-hitting Harold Reynolds is a line drive spray hitter. His best weapon is his speed on ground balls, giving him the ability to leg out a lot of infield hits. His slashing, chopping swing is not picture perfect, but it's effective as he makes solid contact. Reynolds goes to the opposite field at will and pulls the ball well from the left side.

Reynolds is least successful when pitched in on the hands. He'll jump all over mistakes, but he also hits a lot of bad pitches. Some feel that Reynolds should be more selective and improve his on-base percentage via the walk. He is improving in that area, however, and his 55 walks last year were a career high. Reynolds bunts well and likes to drag the ball, but could probably do so even more than he does now.

Reynolds' offensive stats have improved each year since he was a rookie. He can thank Dick Williams for that. Williams had the foresight to recognize Reynolds' talents and the patience to stick with him through two seasons of meager numbers. It was Reynolds' work ethic and dedication that kept him in Williams' favor, not an easy assignment for anyone. Reynolds has done an excellent job since being put in the leadoff spot by Manager Jim Lefebvre. Harold is a team player and does all the little things that are important.

BASERUNNING:

Reynolds has the speed to be among the top base stealers in the AL. His 60 stolen bases led the league in '87, but both his totals and success rate have gone down since coach Bobby Tolan was let go. He's not reading the pitchers well and has been caught stealing 47 times in the last two seasons.

FIELDING:

No one plays second base better than Reynolds. Watching him on a daily basis will make even the worst skeptics into believers. He plays all out 100% of the time. His range is exceptional and his instincts outstanding, and he seems to average at least one circus catch a game on a pop fly. Reynolds is also fearless at turning the double play.

OVERALL:

Reynolds is the foundation of a potentially outstanding up-the-middle defense. Coupled with Valle, Vizquel and Griffey, one couldn't ask for a stronger foursome defensively. Reynolds' future is brighter than ever and he's already proven himself as a star second sacker.

HAROLD REYNOLDS

Position: 2B
Bats: B **Throws:** R
Ht: 5'11" **Wt:** 165

Opening Day Age: 29
Born: 11/26/60 in Eugene, OR
ML Seasons: 7

Overall Statistics

	G	AB	R	H	D	T	HR	RBI	SB	BB	SO	AVG
1989	153	613	87	184	24	9	0	43	25	55	45	.300
Career	694	2359	293	628	107	34	6	150	154	193	196	.266

Where He Hits the Ball

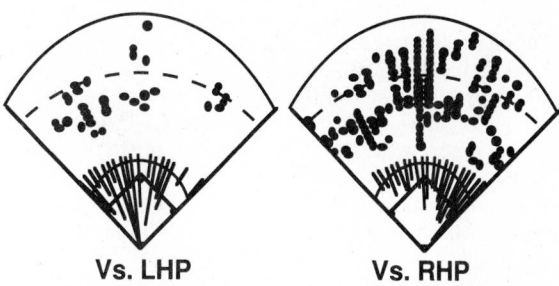

Vs. LHP   Vs. RHP

1989 Situational Stats

	AB	H	HR	RBI	AVG		AB	H	HR	RBI	AVG
Home	307	92	0	27	.300	LHP	170	55	0	14	.324
Road	306	92	0	16	.301	RHP	443	129	0	29	.291
Day	141	40	0	7	.284	Sc Pos	113	32	0	42	.283
Night	472	144	0	36	.305	Clutch	77	27	0	6	.351

1989 Rankings (American League)

➡ 1st in percentage of swings put into play (59.9%) - *players with 502 PA*

➡ 2nd in worst stolen base percentage (58.1%) and caught stealing (18)

➡ 4th in triples (9), lowest percentage of swings that missed (6.7%) and singles (151)

➡ Led the Mariners in at bats (613), runs (87), hits (184), singles, triples, stolen bases (25), caught stealing, plate appearances (677), games (153), percentage of swings put into play, percentage of swings that missed, steals of third (4), least GDPs per GDP situation (4.2%) and hitting in the clutch (.351) - *team players with 502 PA*

STOPPER

MIKE SCHOOLER

Position: RP
Bats: R **Throws:** R
Ht: 6' 3" **Wt:** 220

Opening Day Age: 27
Born: 8/10/62 in Anaheim, CA
ML Seasons: 2

PITCHING:

A year ago, Mike Schooler had to earn the job as the Mariners' closer in competition with Tom Niedenfuer and Mike Jackson. In 1990, there'll be no competition; after a 33 save season in 1989, Schooler already rates as the best finisher in Seattle history. Schooler's debut as a late-inning man has been one of the strongest in major league history. If he can earn saves in his first two 1990 appearances, he'll tie Todd Worrell's record for reaching 50 saves faster than any other reliever (109 games).

Schooler has the equipment that a dominating closer needs. He throws a fastball in the low 90's with good movement, an excellent slider, and he'll mix in a curve on occasion. He can get ahead in the count with his fastball, then freeze hitters with the slider that dips low and away from righthanded hitters. And he's getting even better. Schooler improved his ERA from 3.54 in 1988 to 2.81 in 1989, and he allowed only two home runs last year despite the fact that he pitches in one of the smallest ballparks in the major leagues. Perhaps his most significant improvement was his reduction in walks. In 1988 he yielded 4.47 walks per nine innings, which was the main reason why he had to vie for the closer role last year in spring training. In 1989 Schooler cut that figure by more than half, walking only 2.22 men per nine innings. Surprisingly, he yielded more than one hit per inning. Schooler seemed to be taking a little off his pitches to get them over, and indeed his strikeout rate dropped from 10.05 per nine innings to a still-respectable 8.06. It's hard to knock the results.

FIELDING:

Schooler has a quick delivery and holds baserunners well. There's little movement in his landing and he finishes his delivery in an excellent position to field most anything. He's big at 6'3", but very agile and capable of fielding the more difficult plays.

OVERALL:

Schooler has proven that he can handle the late-inning job with the best of closers. His record last year was only 1-7, but that doesn't bother the Mariners. They're more interested in his .825 save percentage, which was fifth best in the American league and ranked ahead of such stellar relief men as Gregg Olson and Bobby Thigpen. Schooler is only 27; with a strong arm and a fierce competitive nature that helps him rebound from subpar outings, he should be a fixture in the Mariner bullpen for years.

Overall Statistics

	W	L	ERA	G	GS	Sv	IP	H	R	BB	SO	HR
1989	1	7	2.81	67	0	33	77.0	81	27	19	69	2
Career	6	15	3.09	107	0	48	125.1	126	48	43	123	6

Where They Hit the Ball

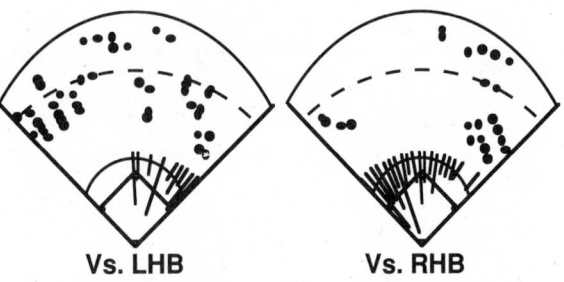

Vs. LHB   **Vs. RHB**

1989 Situational Stats

	W	L	ERA	Sv	IP		AB	H	HR	RBI	AVG
Home	1	4	3.32	20	43.1	LHB	140	40	1	20	.286
Road	0	3	2.14	13	33.2	RHB	164	41	1	15	.250
Day	0	0	0.98	6	18.1	Sc Pos	108	30	0	32	.278
Night	1	7	3.38	27	58.2	Clutch	227	63	2	28	.278

1989 Rankings (American League)

- ➡ 3rd in saves (33) and games finished (60)
- ➡ 5th in save percentage (82.5%) and worst first batter efficiency (.302) - *pitchers in 40 games in relief*
- ➡ 6th in blown saves (7)
- ➡ 7th in games (67)
- ➡ Led the Mariners in games, saves, games finished, save percentage, blown saves and least home runs per 9 innings (.23) - *all team players*

PITCHING:

Billy Swift is a sinker/slider pitcher with a fair fastball. When Swift's breaking pitches are working, it's almost impossible for hitters to get the ball off the ground and into the air. That's certainly an asset if you pitch in the cozy Kingdome. So effective is his bread and butter pitch that the Mariner infield holds the major league record (22) for infield assists in a 9 inning game. The record was set in 1988 behind nine strong innings by Billy Swift. However, when the sinker doesn't sink and the slider doesn't slide, Swift gets lit up like a Christmas tree.

Manager Jim Lefebvre used Swift both in the pen and as a starter in 1989. It appears that his niche is in long relief. In 44.2 innings as a reliever, Swift gave up 41 hits with an ERA of 3.02, allowing only 10.48 baserunners per nine innings. He was highly successful coming into situations where a ground ball was needed to get out of a jam. His record as a starter was 5-3, but that was because his teammates saved his bacon by scoring an average of 5.56 runs per game. As a starter, Swift allowed 99 hits in 85.1 innings, 13.50 baserunners per nine innings and had a 5.17 ERA. For that reason, Swift was excused to the bullpen. However, he did start twice at the end of the year and was very effective.

FIELDING:

Swift fields well and would be in big trouble if he didn't. A ground ball pitcher has to be able to handle comebackers. He's very quick off the mound and handles most grounders flawlessly. Swift holds baserunners extremely well and was one of the toughest Mariner pitchers to steal on.

OVERALL:

It's unlikely that Swift would be considered for the starting rotation in 1990 if the Mariners are successful in obtaining the veteran starter that they are seeking. It would seem that Swift's true value would be in the pen in long relief. Swift has the stuff and the stamina to start, however, and would be highly successful if he can make his pitches work on a more consistent basis. In either role, Swift can be very valuable to the Mariners.

BILLY SWIFT

Position: RP/SP
Bats: R **Throws:** R
Ht: 6' 0" **Wt:** 180

Opening Day Age: 28
Born: 12/27/61 in Portland, ME
ML Seasons: 4

Overall Statistics

	W	L	ERA	G	GS	Sv	IP	H	R	BB	SO	HR
1989	7	3	4.43	37	16	1	130.0	140	72	38	45	7
Career	23	34	4.78	127	78	1	540.2	618	327	206	202	30

Where They Hit the Ball

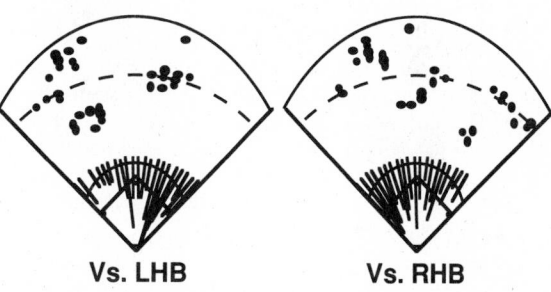

Vs. LHB　　　　**Vs. RHB**

1989 Situational Stats

	W	L	ERA	Sv	IP		AB	H	HR	RBI	AVG
Home	3	2	4.93	0	73.0	LHB	231	73	3	31	.316
Road	4	1	3.79	1	57.0	RHB	273	67	4	32	.245
Day	2	2	3.79	1	40.1	Sc Pos	129	35	2	52	.271
Night	5	1	4.72	0	89.2	Clutch	37	6	1	3	.162

1989 Rankings (American League)

➡ 3rd in GDPs induced (26)

➡ 5th in most GDPs per GDP situation (20.6%) - *pitchers with 30 GDP situations*

➡ Led the Mariners in GDPs induced and most GDPs per GDP situation

HITTING:

Though a low average hitter, Dave Valle has some pop in his bat. He can pull the fastball and has averaged 18 homers per 550 at bats in his career, with nearly half his four baggers coming away from Seattle. Valle's problem is that he is not a patient hitter and swings at too many bad pitches. He makes contact and doesn't strike out that often, but surely would be more effective is he were patient enough to wait for his pitch. Valle is a very intense player and tries too hard to hit the five run homer when a single to the opposite field would do. He likes the ball low and out over the plate where he can get his arms extended. A 20 homer season is certainly within reach if Valle could just get in a full year.

Valle is considered Seattle's regular catcher, but regular is not an aptly applied adjective. In three full years with the Mariners, he has yet to play in 100 games in a season. In fact, the so-called back-up catcher, Scott Bradley, has 17 more at bats and 27 more games under his belt during that same span of time. Valle's missed games have all been due to injury. The most devastating injury came last year when Milwaukee's Bill Spiers hooked Valle's leg on a play at the plate, just at a time when Valle had everything going. The injury to Valle's knee was serious and put an end to a possible All Star season.

BASERUNNING:

Valle is a catcher with a bum knee so he's not a base stealing threat. He's a smart baserunner and is dangerous when plowing into second on double play balls.

FIELDING:

Valle is an excellent backstop and has become a pitcher's catcher. He's gaining a reputation for one of the best arms in the American League. He has a quick release and throws out an unusually high percentage of base stealers. He's also very adept at blocking pitches.

OVERALL:

As long as he's healthy, Valle is the Mariner catcher now and for several years to come. If he could manage to get in a full year, his value to the team would become even more apparent and his abilities as a catcher more prominent.

DAVE VALLE

Position: C
Bats: R **Throws:** R
Ht: 6' 2" **Wt:** 200

Opening Day Age: 29
Born: 10/30/60 in Bayside, NY
ML Seasons: 6

Overall Statistics

	G	AB	R	H	D	T	HR	RBI	SB	BB	SO	AVG
1989	94	316	32	75	10	3	7	34	0	29	32	.237
Career	347	1080	117	262	46	8	35	160	2	71	145	.243

Where He Hits the Ball

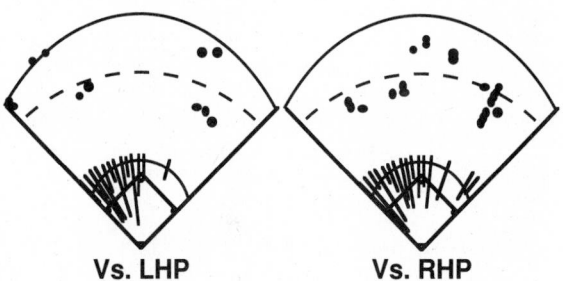

Vs. LHP   **Vs. RHP**

1989 Situational Stats

	AB	H	HR	RBI	AVG		AB	H	HR	RBI	AVG
Home	163	41	1	17	.252	LHP	106	25	4	10	.236
Road	153	34	6	17	.222	RHP	210	50	3	24	.238
Day	66	17	2	5	.258	Sc Pos	78	17	0	25	.218
Night	250	58	5	29	.232	Clutch	55	9	1	5	.164

1989 Rankings (American League)

- ➡ 1st in worst batting average on a 3-1 count (.083) - *players with 10 PA on a 3-1 count*
- ➡ 2nd in throwing out base-stealers (41.5%) - *catchers with 75 attempts*
- ➡ 5th in worst batting average in the clutch (.164) - *players with 50 PA in the clutch*
- ➡ 6th in most GDPs per GDP situation (21.7%) - *players with 50 PA in GDP situations*
- ➡ 9th in hit by pitch (6)
- ➡ Led the Mariners in hit by pitch

HITTING:

Rey Quinones forced the Mariners to make a move that they probably would not have made for another year or two. When Seattle got tired of Quinones' sullen attitude early in 1989, they quickly traded the shortstop to Pittsburgh and handed the job to 22-year old Omar Vizquel. Talk about a raw rookie: Vizquel had only played 33 games at the Triple A level and hadn't batted higher than .263 since he left the rookie league. But he had a good glove, and the Mariners were desperate. Take it away, Omar!

All in all, the rookie performed about as expected. His defense was fine, but with the bat Vizquel quickly made people recall Omar Moreno's old nickname of "Omar the Out Maker." Vizquel hit only .220, drove in just 20 runs, didn't draw many walks and had only 11 extra base hits in 387 at bats. He did make good contact (only 40 strikeouts), but usually hit the ball on the ground right at someone. A switch-hitter, he was slightly better from the left side. Vizquel has no power and has to rely on hitting to all fields. He bunts well, which is an asset he needs to take advantage of more often.

BASERUNNING:

Vizquel can run, and collected 32 stolen bases with Vermont and Calgary in 1988. However, in his first year in the bigs, he swiped only one base while getting thrown out four times. Obviously he's capable of doing a lot better. Vizquel runs the bases pretty well; with contact hitter Harold Reynolds hitting behind him, he's often the lead man on hit-and-run plays.

FIELDING:

Vizquel's glove is the reason he landed a major league job. He has good range, with the ability to go far to his right and make a strong throw without taking the time to set up. Vizquel doesn't quite cover the ground that Quinones did, but he'll make the routine plays, a feat which often baffled Quinones. It didn't take long for Vizquel to mesh with Reynolds and form a strong double play combination. He also has a very strong and accurate arm.

OVERALL:

Vizquel is still very young, but the Mariners already have to ask how far they can go with him. He's a fine glove man, but with his weak bat he'd have to field like Ozzie Smith to keep his job. Vizquel isn't in that category, so he'll have to improve his hitting. The Mariners will give him the chance in 1990.

OMAR VIZQUEL

Position: SS
Bats: B **Throws:** R
Ht: 5' 9" **Wt:** 155

Opening Day Age: 22
Born: 5/15/67 in Caracas, Venezuela
ML Seasons: 1

Overall Statistics

	G	AB	R	H	D	T	HR	RBI	SB	BB	SO	AVG
1989	143	387	45	85	7	3	1	20	1	28	40	.220
Career	143	387	45	85	7	3	1	20	1	28	40	.220

Where He Hits the Ball

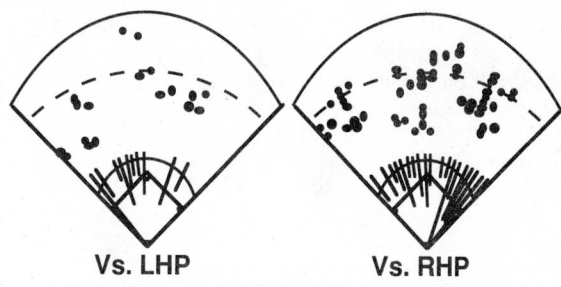

Vs. LHP   **Vs. RHP**

1989 Situational Stats

	AB	H	HR	RBI	AVG		AB	H	HR	RBI	AVG
Home	189	43	1	12	.228	LHP	102	20	1	6	.196
Road	198	42	0	8	.212	RHP	285	65	0	14	.228
Day	105	23	1	7	.219	Sc Pos	90	16	0	19	.178
Night	282	62	0	13	.220	Clutch	52	13	0	0	.250

1989 Rankings (American League)

- ➡ 1st in worst batting average with runners in scoring position (.178) - *players with 100 PA with runners in scoring position*
- ➡ 6th in worst home run frequency (387 ABs per HR) - *all league players*
- ➡ 7th in sacrifice bunts (13)
- ➡ Led the Mariners in sacrifice bunts, bunts in play (23) and errors (18)

MICKEY BRANTLEY

Position: LF/RF
Bats: R **Throws:** R
Ht: 5'10" **Wt:** 180

Opening Day Age: 28
Born: 6/17/61 in Catskill, NY
ML Seasons: 4

Overall Statistics

	G	AB	R	H	D	T	HR	RBI	SB	BB	SO	AVG
1989	34	108	14	17	5	0	0	8	2	7	7	.157
Career	302	1138	154	295	56	8	32	125	34	67	136	.259

HITTING, FIELDING, BASERUNNING:

Just last year, Mickey Brantley appeared to have a lock on one of the Mariner outfield positions. But with the emergence of the Briley-Griffey-Buhner trio and the acquisition of Jeff Leonard, Brantley found himself on the bench. He didn't handle the situation well and hit only .157 with no homers in a reserve role. He eventually was sent to AAA. Brantley has an open stance and holds the bat high over his head. He likes to pull the ball and has a hard time with pitches away. Brantley has power to right but can hit the ball to all fields. He has good baserunning instincts and is an above-average base stealing threat. He's also a solid fielder and can play all three outfield positions, although he calls left field home. He has an average but accurate arm. He's an aggressive fielder with the speed to cover the ground.

OVERALL:

The best guess is that the consistent Henry Cotto will be the fourth outfielder for the Mariners.and Brantley will be trade material. A trade involving Jeffrey Leonard could also open a spot and have an effect on Brantley's future with the Mariners.

DAVE COCHRANE

Position: SS
Bats: B **Throws:** R
Ht: 6' 2" **Wt:** 180

Opening Day Age: 27
Born: 1/31/63 in Riverside, CA
ML Seasons: 2

Overall Statistics

	G	AB	R	H	D	T	HR	RBI	SB	BB	SO	AVG
1989	54	102	13	24	4	1	3	7	0	14	27	.235
Career	73	164	17	36	6	1	4	9	0	19	49	.220

HITTING, FIELDING, BASERUNNING:

At 6'2" and 180-185 pounds, Dave Cochrane is not your stereotype utility player, but his main strength is that he adds depth and muscle to the bench. He's a switch hitter with some power; at AAA Calgary in 1988, Cochrane hit 15 homers and drove in 61 runs. He hits to all fields, but had trouble making contact against major league pitching in '89. Cochrane has average speed and is not a base stealing threat. It's Cochrane's versatility as a fielder that makes him so important to the Mariners. He's one of those rare players who can play every position, and has. He has a great arm and had a trial as a pitcher while in the White Sox minor league system. Probably the most important position that Cochrane can play is back-up catcher. He gives the Mariners that rare privilege of having three receivers. Cochrane plays all positions well and with confidence. Changing from one position to another doesn't appear to bother him.

OVERALL:

Due to his ability to play virtually anywhere, Cochrane should have a good chance again next year to be the Mariners' main utility player.

MARIO DIAZ

Position: SS
Bats: R **Throws:** R
Ht: 5'10" **Wt:** 160

Opening Day Age: 28
Born: 1/10/62 in Humacao, Puerto Rico
ML Seasons: 3

Overall Statistics

	G	AB	R	H	D	T	HR	RBI	SB	BB	SO	AVG
1989	52	74	9	10	0	0	1	7	0	7	7	.135
Career	91	169	19	39	5	1	1	19	0	10	16	.231

HITTING, FIELDING, BASERUNNING:

Mario Diaz in a utility infielder with just 169 at bats in the majors over the course of three seasons. He maintained an average over .300 in '87 and '88, but slipped miserably to .135 in 74 at bats in 1989. He had some elbow problems that could explain his slump. Diaz is a singles hitter with no power. He can hit to all fields and makes good contact. He is strictly a back-up player and had a chance to help the Mariners as a utility man, but flubbed the opportunity with his weak hitting. Diaz is not fast nor a basestealing threat, and has average baserunning instincts. Though primarily a shortstop, Diaz can play all four infield positions. He's a consistent fielder and will make the routine plays. He does not have great range. His arm is average, but accurate.

OVERALL:

Dave Cochrane is more versatile, so it's doubtful that Diaz can contend for the infield utility job. He is a marginal fill-in and might not even be protected on the 40 man roster. At least he's used to playing in Calgary.

GENE HARRIS

Position: RP/SP
Bats: R **Throws:** R
Ht: 5'11" **Wt:** 190

Opening Day Age: 25
Born: 12/5/64 in Sebring, FL
ML Seasons: 1

Overall Statistics

	W	L	ERA	G	GS	Sv	IP	H	R	BB	SO	HR
1989	2	5	5.91	21	6	1	53.1	63	38	25	25	4
Career	2	5	5.91	21	6	1	53.1	63	38	25	25	4

PITCHING & FIELDING:

Gene Harris was the third pitcher in the Mark Langston trade with Montreal, ranking behind Randy Johnson and Brian Holman. Some sources say that Harris was the sleeper in the deal and should have a bright future. Harris is a power pitcher with a fastball, curve and change. He doesn't have much of a leg kick and really doesn't appear to be throwing hard, but he is. Despite his good stuff, Harris didn't have the success that was hoped for in his first year as a Mariner. He won only one game and had a monumental 6.48 ERA. Part of the problem could be attributed to injury, the rest to inexperience. Defensively, Harris appears to be an excellent athlete. His fielding abilities should get better with age and experience. With his short leg kick, he is tough to steal on.

OVERALL:

Harris is valuable to the Mariners down the road, but probably not in 1990. He surely will get a chance to gain a position with the team in spring training, but will have to turn in a dazzling performance to do so. If he were lefthanded, his chances would certainly be a lot better.

MIKE KINGERY

Position: CF
Bats: L **Throws:** L
Ht: 6' 0" **Wt:** 180

Opening Day Age: 29
Born: 3/29/61 in St. James, MN
ML Seasons: 4

Overall Statistics

	G	AB	R	H	D	T	HR	RBI	SB	BB	SO	AVG
1989	31	76	14	17	3	0	2	6	1	7	14	.224
Career	270	762	98	195	42	9	15	81	18	65	110	.256

HITTING, FIELDING, BASERUNNING:

Mike Kingery is a singles hitter who can hit to all fields. He normally makes good contact and had a fairly good year when he first came to the Mariners in 1987. At that time, his biggest asset was his ability to get a hit with runners in scoring position. He also showed a little power, belting nine homers in 354 at bats. It first appeared that Kingery might become the Mariners' everyday right fielder, but his power declined and he just didn't have the pop to fill the position. He's now 29 and can only hope that his lefthanded bat can get him a utility job. Kingery has above average speed and is quite often used as a pinch runner. He's aggressive on the basepaths and seems to have good instincts. He's also a solid fielder and filled in nicely when Griffey was injured. He has an average arm.

OVERALL:

Kingery, at best, is a fifth outfielder, but being left-handed could keep him with the Mariners for another year. He has good peripheral skills; all he needs to do is hit a little better than he did last year.

EDGAR MARTINEZ

Position: 3B
Bats: R **Throws:** R
Ht: 5'11" **Wt:** 175

Opening Day Age: 27
Born: 1/2/63 in New York, NY
ML Seasons: 3

Overall Statistics

	G	AB	R	H	D	T	HR	RBI	SB	BB	SO	AVG
1989	65	171	20	41	5	0	2	20	2	17	26	.240
Career	92	246	26	66	14	2	2	30	2	23	38	.268

HITTING, FIELDING, BASERUNNING:

Edgar Martinez has been groomed to take over third base for Seattle, but it hasn't worked. While he continues to walk all over minor league pitching, Martinez has yet to prove that he can hit the guys who throw in the bigs. Perhaps the problem is not enough time to prove himself. However, the Mariners have too much youthful inexperience and cannot afford much time to groom Martinez in the majors. Martinez is a line drive contact hitter and hits to all fields. He's very patient and has a good eye. If he could get it together, he would hit for a high average and have a high on base percentage. Martinez is not a base stealing threat, but has good base running instincts. He has the glove to play third, handling routine plays flawlessly with decent range and a strong, accurate arm.

OVERALL:

It certainly appears that Darnell Coles will be playing third in 1990, but if Martinez is still with the Mariners, he will try to challenge for the job in spring training. If he doesn't get the assignment, it's hard to say where he would fit into the team's plans.

TOM NIEDENFUER

Position: RP
Bats: R **Throws:** R
Ht: 6' 5" **Wt:** 224

Opening Day Age: 30
Born: 8/13/59 in St. Louis Park, MN
ML Seasons: 9

Overall Statistics

	W	L	ERA	G	GS	Sv	IP	H	R	BB	SO	HR
1989	0	3	6.69	25	0	0	36.1	46	29	15	15	7
Career	36	40	3.28	432	0	95	588.0	535	225	201	442	57

PITCHING & FIELDING:

In Seattle, Tom Niedenfuer's 1989 season brought back memories of Steve Trout, another big-name hurler who was a total flop with the Mariners. In Niedenfuer's defense, he was injured in spring training. But he appeared to have lost a great deal off his fastball and found it nearly impossible to get batters out. Signed as a free agent for big money, Niedenfuer was expected to challenge Mike Schooler and Mike Jackson for the closer's role. Instead he became an expensive mop-up man. He was horrid from the start, allowing 31 hits and 19 earned runs in his first 18 innings. Niedenfuer improved after that, but not nearly enough to redeem himself. He was especially prone to the home run ball, yielding nearly one for every five innings pitched. Niedenfuer is a good fielder for his size and does a decent job of holding baserunners.

OVERALL:

No fool, Niedenfuer has already sold his house in Redmond and has conceded the fact that his future in Seattle is bleak. Unless Niedenfuer has a sudden turnaround, the Mariners will probably have to swallow some or all of his big contract, even if someone else wants him.

DENNIS POWELL

Position: RP
Bats: R **Throws:** L
Ht: 6' 3" **Wt:** 200

Opening Day Age: 26
Born: 8/13/63 in Moultrie, GA
ML Seasons: 5

Overall Statistics

	W	L	ERA	G	GS	Sv	IP	H	R	BB	SO	HR
1989	2	2	5.00	43	1	2	45.0	49	25	21	27	6
Career	7	16	4.81	114	14	3	192.2	205	109	85	109	23

PITCHING & FIELDING:

Dennis Powell is a power pitcher with a fastball, slider and curve. His biggest problem is his lack of control. He tries to be too fine and is often behind in the count. Powell started off last season with lots of confidence and a fastball with good movement. In his first 13 appearances in relief, Powell went 20 innings giving up 7 hits and 4 runs for an ERA of 1.80. It appeared early on that the Mariners finally found the Dennis Powell they had been looking for since trading Matt Young to the Dodgers to acquire him. But from there it went downhill fast. Between June 19 and July 22, Powell failed to record an out in six of 11 outings. He was sent to Calgary and not recalled until September, when he continued to struggle. Powell is an average fielder and moves around the mound with ease for his size. He does a fine job of holding baserunners.

OVERALL:

Powell wasn't protected on the Mariners' 40 man roster and one would guess that he might be picked up by another team. If he's still around, he'll surely be invited to spring training again.

CLINT ZAVARAS

Position: SP
Bats: R **Throws:** R
Ht: 6' 1" **Wt:** 175

Opening Day Age: 23
Born: 1/4/67 in Denver, CO
ML Seasons: 1

Overall Statistics

	W	L	ERA	G	GS	Sv	IP	H	R	BB	SO	HR
1989	1	6	5.19	10	10	0	52.0	49	33	30	31	4
Career	1	6	5.19	10	10	0	52.0	49	33	30	31	4

PITCHING & FIELDING:

Injuries forced the Mariners to look at one of their top prospects last year, and they liked what they saw in the raw talent of 22 year old Clint Zavaras, despite a poor overall record. Zavaras has a fastball, curve, slider and change. The curve has good velocity and rotation and is his out pitch; some say that only Eric Hanson on the Mariners has a better curve. Zavaras' fastball trails away from lefties and he often uses the curve to set up the fastball. He mixes his pitches well and seems to have an idea on how to pitch and how to set up batters. At this point Zavaras has proven he has the stuff to pitch in the majors; now he needs to improve his control and consistency. Zavaras appears to be an above average fielder, but he needs a lot of work on holding baserunners.

OVERALL:

Any pitcher with an arm like Zavaras' has to be important to his club. However, the Mariners need a veteran pitcher to balance the fine young arms on their staff and it's doubtful that Zavaras will make the squad within the next year or two.

HITTING:

After a somewhat subpar 1988 campaign, Harold Baines had a strong first half for the White Sox, then was traded to Texas in a deal that the Rangers hoped would net them a division title. Baines couldn't be blamed when that didn't happen, but the Rangers had to be a little disappointed in his performance. After hitting .321 with 13 homers for the Sox, Baines batted only .284 with but three dingers for Texas. His overall .309 batting average matched his career high, and Baines' .395 on base average was a personal best and ranked him among the league leaders. But Baines is expected to drive in runs, and his 72 RBIs were his lowest total since 1981.

A classic Walt Hriniak/Charley Lau disciple, Baines stands off the plate and attacks the ball where it's pitched, showing his best power to left and right center. Baines learned these theories from Lau himself in the early '80s. Hriniak, who became the Sox hitting coach reinforced them, and added a new wrinkle: he got Baines, sometimes a wild swinger in the past, to lay off bad pitches more than at any time in his career. The results were higher batting and on base averages, but where was the power?

BASERUNNING:

Never particularly fast, Baines has had his speed seriously curtailed by chronic knee problems. He hasn't stolen a base since 1986 and sometimes gets cut down trying to take an extra base. With his knees healthier in 1989, Baines did show more speed than he had in several years. Nonetheless, he has to be rated in the slow category, though he seldom gets caught napping.

FIELDING:

Baines was an excellent defensive player in his younger days, but he has been regulated to spot duty by his injuries; he played a bit in right field for the White Sox, but the Rangers used him exclusively as a DH. When he does play in the field, his range is much more limited than it once was. He plays hitters well, however, and hardly ever makes either a mental or physical mistake. His throwing arm remains accurate, though not exceptionally strong.

OVERALL:

The Rangers, hungry for a productive DH, parted with two top prospects and their regular shortstop, Scott Fletcher, in order to obtain Baines. Though his power figures were disappointing, he nonetheless was a productive performer. If healthy in 1990, Baines, who will be 31, figures to return to the 80-plus RBI level he reached every year from 1982 through 1988.

HAROLD
BAINES

Position: DH/RF
Bats: L **Throws:** L
Ht: 6' 2" **Wt:** 195

Opening Day Age: 31
Born: 3/15/59 in Easton, MD
ML Seasons: 10

Overall Statistics

	G	AB	R	H	D	T	HR	RBI	SB	BB	SO	AVG
1989	146	505	73	156	29	1	16	72	0	73	79	.309
Career	1428	5363	679	1547	276	44	189	835	29	449	809	.288

Where He Hits the Ball

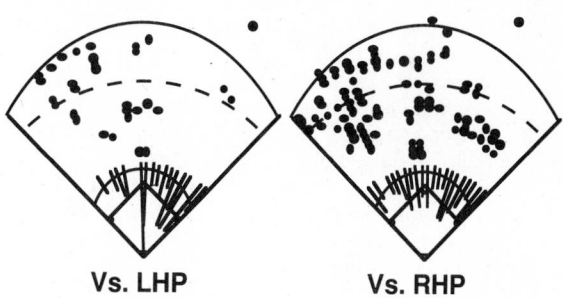

Vs. LHP   **Vs. RHP**

1989 Situational Stats

	AB	H	HR	RBI	AVG		AB	H	HR	RBI	AVG
Home	247	73	5	34	.296	LHP	156	41	4	26	.263
Road	258	83	11	38	.322	RHP	349	115	12	46	.330
Day	126	51	4	21	.405	Sc Pos	121	33	5	55	.273
Night	379	105	12	51	.277	Clutch	76	17	3	9	.224

1989 Rankings (American League)

- ➡ 3rd in hitting vs. righthanded pitchers (.330) - *players with 377 PA vs. RHP*
- ➡ 4th in on-base average vs. righthanded pitchers (.415)
- ➡ 5th in slugging percentage vs. righthanded pitchers
- ➡ 7th in intentional walks (13) and on-base average (.395) - *players with 502 PA*
- ➡ 8th in batting average (.309)
- ➡ Led AL Designated Hitters in batting average, runs (73), hits (156), doubles (29), walks (73), intentional walks, on-base average, slugging percentage, grounder/flyball ratio (1.81) and hitting vs. righthanded pitchers

PITCHING:

Some guys get all the breaks. In Kevin Brown's case, that means he has been blessed with the ability to throw a sinking fastball that's effective even when hitters know it's coming. It seemed like every opposing manager ended up raving about that pitch, which produced many more double play grounders than any other Texas pitcher could net. His fastball moves down and away to righthanded batters and, in his hottest performances, Brown would typically get 15 groundouts and an easy win. He did struggle from time to time, but Brown's 12 wins tied for second on the Rangers, and his overall work had a stabilizing effect on an up-and-down staff.

Looking at Brown pitch in '89, it was easy to see the pitcher who was the fourth player picked in the 1986 draft. But the truth was that Brown had struggled through a lot of his minor league career and turned in a 1-11 record in 1987 while making stops at three different minor league teams. What happened? Brown used to throw a fastball that was clocked at 97 miles per hour. It was fast and straight. No movement at all. Groove enough fastballs and one -- more than one, really -- will get belted. With some coaching and coaxing, Brown found out that he could throw the ball in the low 90s and get a lot more movement on the pitch. Now he throws the sinking fastball and can still fire the ball past hitters when he needs to.

FIELDING:

Brown has an average move to first base and pays attention to runners without going overboard. Compared to other Texas pitchers, he's a wizard at those things. He fields his position well, although he has a habit of throwing underhand to first base on balls hit back at him.

OVERALL:

Texas wasn't counting on Brown during spring training last year. His work convinced the Rangers to put him in the rotation, which allowed them to move Jeff Russell to the bullpen -- a double bonus, as it turned out. Now that he finally seems to have it all together, Brown could be a consistent major league winner.

KEVIN BROWN

Position: SP
Bats: R **Throws:** R
Ht: 6' 4" **Wt:** 198

Opening Day Age: 25
Born: 3/14/65 in McIntyre, GA
ML Seasons: 3

Overall Statistics

	W	L	ERA	G	GS	Sv	IP	H	R	BB	SO	HR
1989	12	9	3.35	28	28	0	191.0	167	81	70	104	10
Career	14	10	3.45	33	33	0	219.1	206	98	78	120	12

Where They Hit the Ball

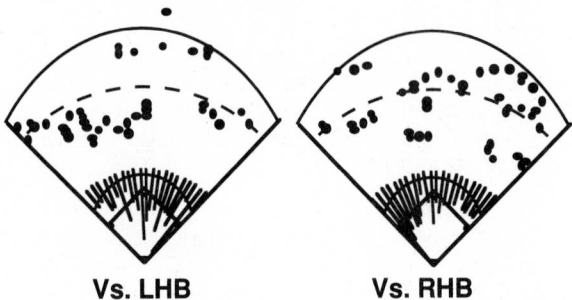

Vs. LHB   **Vs. RHB**

1989 Situational Stats

	W	L	ERA	Sv	IP		AB	H	HR	RBI	AVG
Home	6	3	3.25	0	80.1	LHB	351	79	5	26	.225
Road	6	6	3.42	0	110.2	RHB	364	88	5	41	.242
Day	1	2	3.18	0	51.0	Sc Pos	147	37	2	53	.252
Night	11	7	3.41	0	140.0	Clutch	82	15	2	10	.183

1989 Rankings (American League)

➥ 1st in grounder/flyball ratio (3.31) - *pitchers with 162 IP*

➥ 4th in lowest HRs per 9 innings (.47) and allowed slugging percentage allowed (.312)

➥ 6th in lowest batting average allowed vs. righthanded batters (.242) - *pitchers facing 377 RHB*

➥ 8th in GDPs per 9 innings (1.04) and lowest opponent batting average (.234)

➥ Led the Rangers in complete games (7), GDPs induced (22), grounder/flyball ratio, least pitches thrown per batter (3.7), HRs per 9 innings, GDPs per 9 innings and lowest stolen base percentage allowed (54.5%)

HITTING:

Depending on what you're looking for and what position he's playing, Steve Buechele either makes the most of his abilities or is overmatched. Buechele has pretty good power, reaching double figures in home runs during all four of his seasons as a regular, but isn't especially dangerous when compared to other third baseman. He'd be a more valuable performer at second, where the Rangers played him late last year. His offensive stats would be pretty good for a middle infielder.

Buechele is a dangerous low-ball hitter who appears to have better success against off-speed pitches. He's vulnerable to fastballs, both being jammed and pitches that are high and outside. He'll often chase the latter and has a tendency to fall behind in the count. Buechele doesn't adjust well.

You keep waiting for Buechele to learn from his mistakes, but he hasn't given signs of being anything but a .230 to .240 hitter. His performance doesn't drop off against righthanders, and his statistics are pretty even in all situations.

BASERUNNING:

Buechele is in that select group of players who've been caught stealing more often than they've been successful. What does that tell you? While his speed is below average, Buechele gets a good jump on the bases, and will go from first to third in some situations where others would hold. Opponents tend to discount him on the bases, and he'll make them pay once in a while.

FIELDING:

Buechele won't make the spectacular play very often, but he has earned a reputation for consistency in the field. His hands are excellent, his range above average. Buechele does have streaks during which he makes the first baseman work too hard. Maybe he should have a session on accuracy with his old college roommate, an NFL quarterback named Elway. You can rank Buechele with the top four or five players at third and not get much of an argument.

OVERALL:

If Buechele is considered a third baseman, the Rangers will probably be looking for someone who can combine his glove with more consistent offense. He'd be better at second, but the Rangers would have to shuffle a number of players to put him there. If he's not going to contribute more to the offense, look for Buechele to become a role player, albeit one who could make important contributions like a Mickey Hatcher or a Lloyd McClendon.

STEVE BUECHELE

Position: 3B/2B
Bats: R **Throws:** R
Ht: 6' 2" **Wt:** 190

Opening Day Age: 28
Born: 9/26/61 in Lancaster, CA
ML Seasons: 5

Overall Statistics

	G	AB	R	H	D	T	HR	RBI	SB	BB	SO	AVG
1989	155	486	60	114	22	2	16	59	1	36	107	.235
Career	668	2032	249	486	88	11	69	242	13	178	388	.239

Where He Hits the Ball

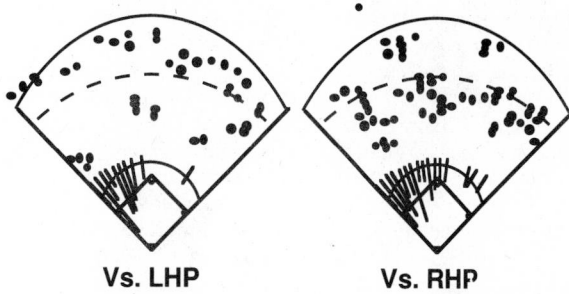

Vs. LHP   **Vs. RHP**

1989 Situational Stats

	AB	H	HR	RBI	AVG		AB	H	HR	RBI	AVG
Home	227	51	7	17	.225	LHP	148	38	6	17	.257
Road	259	63	9	42	.243	RHP	338	76	10	42	.225
Day	93	19	5	11	.204	Sc Pos	125	28	2	39	.224
Night	393	95	11	48	.242	Clutch	71	17	2	6	.239

1989 Rankings (American League)

➡ 3rd in most GDPs per GDP situation (22.6%) - *players with 50 PA in GDP situations*

➡ 4th in GDPs (21)

➡ Led the Rangers in most pitches seen per plate appearance (3.8) - *team players with 502 PA*

CECIL ESPY

Position: CF
Bats: B **Throws:** R
Ht: 6' 3" **Wt:** 195

Opening Day Age: 27
Born: 1/20/63 in San Diego, CA
ML Seasons: 4

HITTING:

Put this guy at the top of the order and watch him fly. If Cecil Espy gets on base, he can be a dangerous asset for the Rangers. But the Texas front office would feel better about Espy if it was his batting average hovering around .300 instead of his on-base percentage. The Rangers are hoping that he'll show some improvement, or else he could end up as a role player.

Espy needs to be more selective in the pitches he chases and give himself more chances to use his speed. That means striking out less and slapping more balls on the ground, especially when the Rangers are playing on artificial turf. He's an adept bunter and should continue to develop that skill. He rarely grounds into double plays -- mostly because of his speed but also, in part, because he strikes out so much.

BASERUNNING:

After Rickey Henderson and Vince Coleman, no major leaguer stole as many bases as Espy. However, he also led the league in being caught stealing and his thievery rate slowed markedly as the season progressed. If Espy can become more efficient, the other question is how many bases he could steal if he got on base more often. Few players have the potential to drive pitchers to such distraction -- and it would help both Espy and those batting behind him if he reached base, say, 50 more times in a season.

FIELDING:

Espy has a fairly strong arm but doesn't take charge as one would expect from a centerfielder. That was more of a problem with balls hit to right-center. As happens with many young outfielders, teams have wanted to test Espy's arm, and he's often risen to the occasion. If he ends up sitting on the Texas bench, it won't be because of his defense.

OVERALL:

Espy shows promise, but the Rangers need more than they've seen. He can be their leadoff batter and centerfielder for years to come, and Rangers fans have reason to be excited about an outfield of Espy (the speedster), Incaviglia (the slugger) and Sierra (the superstar). One need only to cite the questions surrounding Coleman, the National League stolen base leader in '89, to know that speed alone doesn't kill in the majors. Whether he can improve on some of his natural talent may be the difference between becoming an important player or another Mike Felder.

Overall Statistics

	G	AB	R	H	D	T	HR	RBI	SB	BB	SO	AVG
1989	142	475	65	122	12	7	3	31	45	38	99	.257
Career	299	841	116	211	30	13	5	71	80	60	187	.251

Where He Hits the Ball

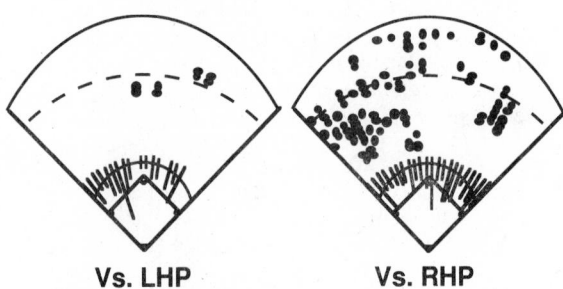

Vs. LHP   **Vs. RHP**

1989 Situational Stats

	AB	H	HR	RBI	AVG		AB	H	HR	RBI	AVG
Home	239	65	2	14	.272	LHP	95	23	3	9	.242
Road	236	57	1	17	.242	RHP	380	99	0	22	.261
Day	88	23	0	2	.261	Sc Pos	106	22	0	28	.208
Night	387	99	3	29	.256	Clutch	65	22	0	7	.338

1989 Rankings (American League)

➡ 1st in caught stealing (20)

➡ 2nd in stolen bases (45) and least GDPs per GDP situation (2.7%) - *players with 50 PA in GDP situations*

➡ 4th in steals of third (7)

➡ Led the Rangers in stolen bases, caught stealing, sacrifice bunts (10), grounder/flyball ratio (1.80), bunts in play (29), steals of third (7), least GDPs per GDP situation and hitting in the clutch (.338)

➡ Led AL Center Fielders in stolen bases, caught stealing and least GDPs per GDP situation

CLUTCH HITTER

JULIO FRANCO

Position: 2B
Bats: R **Throws:** R
Ht: 6' 0" **Wt:** 165

Opening Day Age: 28
Born: 8/23/61 in San Pedro de Macoris, Dominican Republic
ML Seasons: 8

HITTING:

Julio Franco came over from Cleveland before last season and tore up American League pitching for the first half of the season. He tailed off in the second half, but Franco was a force for the Rangers for most of the season, spraying line drives to all fields, hitting more homers than ever before and maintaining his reputation for causing havoc on the bases.

Franco had always been considered a terror against lefties, but righthanders felt most of the heat in 1989. He's an aggressive hitter who'll murder high fastballs and low breaking pitches. A pitcher needs to change speeds to be effective. What gets Franco out in the first and third innings might be the pitch that loses the game in the sixth or eighth. He can drag bunt, though he's weak on the sacrifice. He traditionally has grounded into a lot of double plays, the downside of his slap-hitting prowess.

BASERUNNING:

Franco does well enough at other aspects of the game that his stealing skills often go unnoticed. He was second on the team to Cecil Espy last year, even though his total lagged from previous seasons. Franco is a gambler on the bases, and sometimes his team will pay for those chances. He's not afraid of contact.

FIELDING:

At shortstop, which he played for the Indians until moving to second a couple of seasons back, Franco made errors in bunches. He moved to second base, and quickly established himself as one of the best in the American League. He's especially tough going to his left and has done a pretty good job of learning the double-play pivot. He will make the flashy play, but doesn't have great hands. There has been talk of moving him to first base, although such a switch is by no means a certainty.

OVERALL:

Franco provided the Rangers with a spark and seemed comfortable with the idea that he was one of the leaders on his new team. He should be an important member of the Rangers for years to come. All you have to do is look at his average with men in scoring position last year (.407), to know the Rangers had picked up a gamer from Cleveland.

Overall Statistics

	G	AB	R	H	D	T	HR	RBI	SB	BB	SO	AVG
1989	150	548	80	173	31	5	13	92	21	66	69	.316
Career	1064	4138	584	1232	188	36	58	524	152	337	459	.298

Where He Hits the Ball

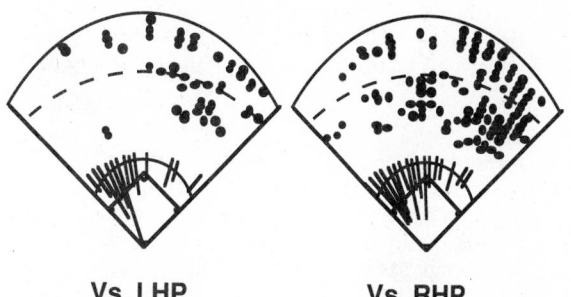

Vs. LHP   **Vs. RHP**

1989 Situational Stats

	AB	H	HR	RBI	AVG		AB	H	HR	RBI	AVG
Home	267	95	9	52	.356	LHP	161	46	5	28	.286
Road	281	78	4	40	.278	RHP	387	127	8	64	.328
Day	108	30	0	13	.278	Sc Pos	140	57	3	76	.407
Night	440	143	13	79	.325	Clutch	77	25	2	15	.325

1989 Rankings (American League)

➡ 1st in hitting with runners in scoring position (.407), stolen base percentage (87.5%), hitting with the bases loaded (.667), GDPs (27) and most GDPs per GDP situation (24.5%)

➡ 4th in hitting vs. righthanded pitchers (.328) - *players with 377 PA vs RHP*

➡ 5th in batting average (.316)

➡ Led the Rangers in batting average, singles (124), walks (66), intentional walks (11), times on base (240), GDPs, on-base average (.386), stolen base percentage, hitting with runners in scoring position, hitting with the bases loaded and hitting vs. righthanded pitchers

PITCHING:

On a staff loaded with hard throwers, Cecilio Guante provides a contrast because he comes at batters, especially righthanders, from a variety of angles. He throws an especially nasty breaking pitch. His slider is the main reason that he averaged a strikeout per inning during his 50 relief appearances, fanning about 30 percent of the righties that he faced. His stuff provided a marked contrast to most of the Texas starters and closer Jeff Russell, making him a valuable guy for the manager to call upon.

The nagging question is whether Guante could ever be a legitimate closer on his own. He's spent his career setting up some of the best -- Dave Righetti with the Yankees; Robinson, Candelaria and Tekulve in younger days with the Pirates -- and has earned some saves in the process. Given a chance to finish some games a couple of seasons back with the Yankees, the reviews were mixed: He earned 11 saves but also surrendered four game-ending homers, which explains his ticket to Texas late in the 1988 season.

What he might need is another pitch to use on lefthanders, who sometimes seem to time his slider. Guante faced far more righties in 1989, but allowed five of his seven homers to lefties and also walked more of them than he struck out. Guante doesn't have pinpoint control, which probably gets him into as much trouble as the hits he gives up. If Guante were used in more late-game situations he'd probably face more pinch hitters from the left. Middle relievers are the last guys on a pitching staff to get recognition, and Guante certainly has kept a low profile over the years.

FIELDING:

Guante doesn't hold runners close and doesn't finish in good position to field grounders back through the middle, which shouldn't be a surprise given his pitching motion. He sometimes gets a late start when he should be covering first.

OVERALL:

We've probably seen the best that Guante has to offer. His success against righthanders is such that he's best used in situations where the other team isn't likely to send up a pinch hitter. Get him in there for a batter or two, and get him out before he gets overexposed. You would rather see Guante face a tough righty batter than a journeyman lefty. Used properly, Guante can be a bullpen asset.

CECILIO GUANTE

Position: RP
Bats: R **Throws:** R
Ht: 6' 3" **Wt:** 205

Opening Day Age: 30
Born: 2/2/60 in Jacagua, Dominican Republic
ML Seasons: 8

Overall Statistics

	W	L	ERA	G	GS	Sv	IP	H	R	BB	SO	HR
1989	6	6	3.91	50	0	2	69.0	66	35	36	69	7
Career	27	31	3.35	337	0	35	548.1	474	230	218	473	51

Where They Hit the Ball

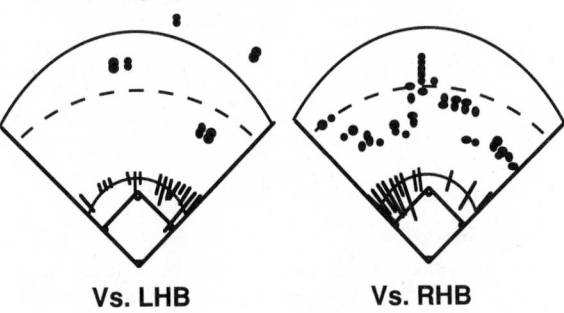

Vs. LHB   **Vs. RHB**

1989 Situational Stats

	W	L	ERA	Sv	IP		AB	H	HR	RBI	AVG
Home	5	3	2.95	1	39.2	LHB	86	22	5	12	.256
Road	1	3	5.22	1	29.1	RHB	179	44	2	22	.246
Day	1	1	4.97	0	12.2	Sc Pos	95	19	1	26	.200
Night	5	5	3.67	2	56.1	Clutch	105	26	2	10	.248

1989 Rankings (American League)

➡ 7th in lowest percentage of inherited runners scoring (22.2%) - *pitchers with 30 inherited runners*

PITCHING:

The Rangers thought they were getting more when they picked up Drew Hall from the Cubs along with Rafael Palmiero and Jamie Moyer. In fact, they thought he might be able to take over the bullpen role vacated by Mitch Williams. It didn't work out. Hall has a reputation in the minors for being a hard-thrower, but he didn't establish a top-level fastball last season. The Rangers thought about giving him a shot at starting, but it didn't happen. He'd been a starter in the minors, throwing six shutouts in 48 starts over two years, until the Cubs moved him to the bullpen after the 1986 season.

Hall didn't win any points in 1989 for being one of the slowest-working pitchers in baseball. There were several problems in this regard. Hall went to deep counts with many batters, going 3-and-1 and 3-and-2 time after time after time; he took too much time between pitches and he would spend a disproportionate amount of time looking runners back, especially to second base. Those are signs of a pitcher who lacks confidence in his stuff.

Toward the end of the season, Hall had some success pitching long relief. That's not much consolation when a team is expecting more. Hall also had problems with his control, which kept him from being a guy who could be brought in to face one batter in a tough situation. The control problem was a constant during his minor league years, too. He's fairly tough on lefthanded batters, with a fastball that runs away from them when sharp, and doesn't give up many home runs.

FIELDING:

Hall spends a lot of time checking runners and throwing to first base. Otherwise, his fielding skills are above average. He fields most balls hit up the middle and doesn't have problems covering first base and handling bunts.

OVERALL:

The Rangers learned last year why Hall split the previous three seasons between the Cubs and their minor league teams. That the Rangers aren't swimming in lefty relievers is to his advantage, but that doesn't mean he'll get an infinite number of chances. The 1990 season could be a make or break campaign for Hall because, at age 27, he can no longer be considered a youngster.

DREW HALL

Position: RP
Bats: L **Throws:** L
Ht: 6' 4" **Wt:** 220

Opening Day Age: 27
Born: 3/27/63 in Louisville, KY
ML Seasons: 4

Overall Statistics

	W	L	ERA	G	GS	Sv	IP	H	R	BB	SO	HR
1989	2	1	3.70	38	0	0	58.1	42	24	33	45	3
Career	5	5	5.26	83	4	2	137.0	132	87	66	108	14

Where They Hit the Ball

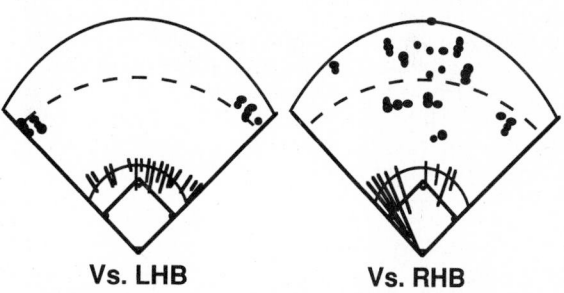

Vs. LHB   Vs. RHB

1989 Situational Stats

	W	L	ERA	Sv	IP		AB	H	HR	RBI	AVG
Home	0	1	2.83	0	35.0	LHB	63	10	1	9	.159
Road	2	0	5.01	0	23.1	RHB	140	32	2	11	.229
Day	0	0	5.68	0	6.1	Sc Pos	52	11	0	16	.212
Night	2	1	3.46	0	52.0	Clutch	23	5	0	0	.217

1989 Rankings (American League)

➡ 6th in lowest percentage of inherited runners scoring (.220) - *pitchers with 30 inherited runners*

➡ Led the Rangers in lowest percentage of inherited runners scoring

PITCHING:

Charlie Hough, the senior statesman of the Texas staff until Nolan Ryan came along, found himself struggling to get past batters whom he fooled in previous seasons. The knuckler didn't seem to move as much and batters were able to get better swings at it. Remember that if Hough can't fool you with the knuckler, he can't fool you. He throws a fastball that doesn't crack 80 on the radar gun, and a slider. Hough has been able to throw the knuckler at different speeds, adding another dimension to its unpredictability.

It could be that Hough's heavy workload is finally catching up with him. He pitched at least 228 innings in every year from 1982 through 1988, and made 40 starts as recently as 1987. Whatever the case, he certainly wasn't as effective. There were seasons when Hough's won-loss record didn't indicate how well he pitched, but 1989 wasn't one of them.

Whether Hough can recapture his magic for another season or two is a big question. Hough was on the disabled list with tendinitis, his first arm injury since coming to the Rangers in 1980. The Dodgers gave up on him 10 years ago, selling his contract to Texas and setting up his most productive years. But that was a long time ago.

FIELDING:

A knuckleball pitcher should be easy to steal against. But Hough has a barely-stopping motion when pitching from the stretch that keeps runners close. The motion, with hands held well in front of his body, was among those that umpires picked on during the balk craze of 1988. Even when Hough modified it, he was tougher to run against than you would expect. Hough works faster with runners on base, which his fielders appreciate. He is also a slick glove man who has always been among the top fielding pitchers.

OVERALL:

While not a standout athlete, Hough has worked hard on conditioning and changed his spring training routine a few years to avoid the slow Aprils that plagued him previously. If the knuckler flutters more faithfully, Hough is an interesting addition to a staff of hard throwers. He had a 5-2 record after coming off the disabled list last season.

CHARLIE HOUGH

Position: SP
Bats: R **Throws:** R
Ht: 6' 2" **Wt:** 190

Opening Day Age: 42
Born: 1/5/48 in Honolulu, HI
ML Seasons: 20

Overall Statistics

	W	L	ERA	G	GS	Sv	IP	H	R	BB	SO	HR
1989	10	13	4.35	30	30	0	182.0	168	97	95	94	28
Career	174	157	3.60	713	297	61	2888.0	2446	1330	1263	1874	282

Where They Hit the Ball

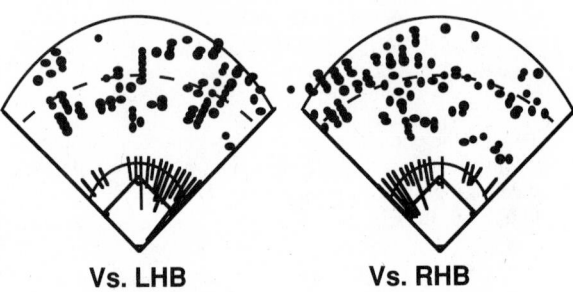

Vs. LHB   **Vs. RHB**

1989 Situational Stats

	W	L	ERA	Sv	IP		AB	H	HR	RBI	AVG
Home	5	6	4.88	0	79.1	LHB	336	80	9	32	.238
Road	5	7	3.94	0	102.2	RHB	349	88	19	50	.252
Day	3	3	4.11	0	50.1	Sc Pos	157	30	1	45	.191
Night	7	10	4.44	0	131.2	Clutch	41	14	5	8	.341

1989 Rankings (American League)

- ➡ 1st in home runs allowed (28), most home runs allowed per 9 innings (1.39) and lowest strikeout/walk ratio (.99) - *pitchers with 162 IP*
- ➡ 2nd in pickoff throws (277)
- ➡ 3rd in walks allowed (95) and balks (5)
- ➡ 5th in stolen bases allowed (26)
- ➡ Led the Rangers in losses (13), home runs allowed, balks, pickoff throws, lowest strikeout/walk ratio, caught stealing (9) and lowest batting average allowed with runners in scoring position

HITTING:

When Pete Incaviglia--without a day in the minors-- hit 30 home runs as a rookie in 1986, the message was that he would be a force to be reckoned with for the next couple of decades. Well, it wasn't that simple. The rest of the league caught up with Incaviglia and his home run total has dropped every year, sinking to 21 last season with a career low batting average. Even so, Incaviglia remains a productive player, especially in a lineup which possesses so many other offensive threats.

Like most sluggers, Incaviglia can pull pitches, but he prefers the ball away from the plate because he has unusual power to right field and right-center. It's an all-or-nothing game for pitchers who challenge him in that zone, either home run or strikeout. Breaking balls away have always been a problem as have pitches on the inside corner. Incaviglia has yet to learn how to swing for anything but the fences. He's tried to make adjustments and it only seems to confuse him more. Incaviglia is an analytical sort, but hasn't been able to find the answers that work for him. With each season, he's drawn fewer walks, another pattern that needs to be reversed.

BASERUNNING:

As you might expect from a guy with Incaviglia's muscular build, he can make life tough on second basemen and catchers with his aggressive running style. Incaviglia has to pick his spots to take an extra base because his speed is below average.

FIELDING:

In his rookie season, Incaviglia made playing left field look about as simple as playing Rachmaninoff. But Incaviglia has dedicated himself to his defense, and has made marked improvement. He used to miss fly balls and cut-off men. Now, at least he doesn't look like an impostor in the outfield. He was even used in centerfield last year. One Ranger observer went so far as to say that those who laughed at Incaviglia's defense, at this point in his career, are really showing their own ignorance.

OVERALL:

Incaviglia plays the game with such enthusiasm and dedication that you want him to overcome his weaknesses. Realistically, what we've seen is probably what we're going to get. There will be long home runs and lots of strikeouts. If Incaviglia stops working on his defense, he'll probably end up as a full-time designated hitter.

PETE INCAVIGLIA

Position: LF
Bats: R **Throws:** R
Ht: 6' 1" **Wt:** 220

Opening Day Age: 26
Born: 4/2/64 in Pebble Beach, CA
ML Seasons: 4

Overall Statistics

	G	AB	R	H	D	T	HR	RBI	SB	BB	SO	AVG
1989	133	453	48	107	27	4	21	81	5	32	136	.236
Career	541	1920	274	484	93	13	100	303	23	174	642	.252

Where He Hits the Ball

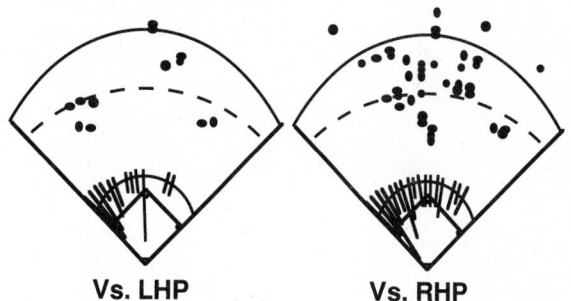

Vs. LHP   **Vs. RHP**

1989 Situational Stats

	AB	H	HR	RBI	AVG		AB	H	HR	RBI	AVG
Home	223	56	13	46	.251	LHP	148	31	6	19	.209
Road	230	51	8	35	.222	RHP	305	76	15	62	.249
Day	81	18	5	15	.222	Sc Pos	129	37	7	61	.287
Night	372	89	16	66	.239	Clutch	79	17	4	13	.215

1989 Rankings (American League)

- ➡ 3rd lowest on-base average vs. lefthanded pitchers (.264) - *players with 125 PA vs. LHP*
- ➡ 4th in strikeouts (136)
- ➡ 5th lowest batting average vs. lefthanded pitchers (.209)
- ➡ Led the Rangers in strikeouts, home run frequency (21.6 ABs per HR) and hit by pitch (6)

PITCHING:

Entering 1989, Mike Jeffcoat was best known as a journeyman lefthander who had once been involved in a deal for the immortal Johnnie LeMaster. Realizing it was make-or-break time, Mike Jeffcoat worked hard last year to erase the doubts that had accumulated during a 10-year professional career. It was said that Jeffcoat gained enough confidence in his ability to be successful. The Rangers had to gain some confidence in him as well, considering that they returned him to the minors last spring after only one exhibition appearance. He'd made the team the previous year, but was sent down to Triple-A after two losing starts and allowing a grand slam in his only relief outing.

Whatever Jeffcoat did to revive his career last year, it worked. The southpaw who had won a total of six games in five previous major league seasons found himself going 9-6, with a fine 3.58 ERA. Observers said that Jeffcoat threw harder last season, at age 30, than he had during previous stints in the majors. He also had a curve, and a split-fingered fastball that he used an off-speed pitch. He varies the speed on all of his pitches and usually worked from ahead of the batters. Jeffcoat was especially tough on lefthanders, who didn't get many good swings against him.

FIELDING:

Jeffcoat fields his position well, using a motion that leaves him in good position to handle comebackers aimed right at him. He also has a fine pickoff move and allowed only two steals in six attempts last year.

OVERALL:

With his fine work last year Jeffcoat has a revived career and an excellent chance to be a part of the Ranger rotation again in 1990. After his past lack of success it's a little early to guarantee his future, but he went a long way in 1989 toward convincing people that he should have a permanent major league address. He's the sort of pitcher who teammates enjoy playing behind because he keeps the pace of the game quick.

MIKE JEFFCOAT

Position: SP
Bats: L **Throws:** L
Ht: 6' 2" **Wt:** 189

Opening Day Age: 30
Born: 8/3/59 in Pine Bluff, AR
ML Seasons: 6

Overall Statistics

	W	L	ERA	G	GS	Sv	IP	H	R	BB	SO	HR
1989	9	6	3.58	22	22	0	130.2	139	65	33	64	7
Career	15	16	4.01	131	30	1	287.1	318	147	91	134	25

Where They Hit the Ball

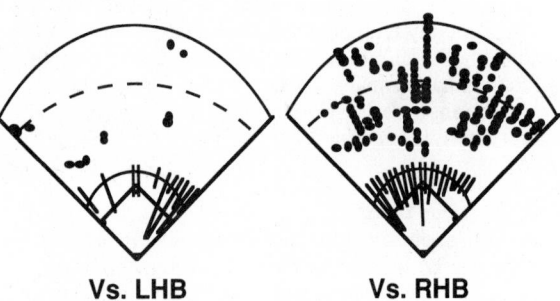

Vs. LHB   **Vs. RHB**

1989 Situational Stats

	W	L	ERA	Sv	IP		AB	H	HR	RBI	AVG
Home	5	1	3.60	0	60.0	LHB	96	25	1	10	.260
Road	4	5	3.57	0	70.2	RHB	418	114	6	41	.273
Day	0	1	1.65	0	16.1	Sc Pos	111	32	2	40	.288
Night	9	5	3.86	0	114.1	Clutch	31	13	0	1	.419

1989 Rankings (American League)

➡ Led the Rangers in shutouts (2)

HITTING:

The Rangers had Chad Kreuter start with them last season after playing at the Double A level in 1988. It looked like skipping one level in the minors was a mistake, as Kreuter struggled at the plate all season, not living up to his billing on either side of a midseason trip to Class AAA Oklahoma City. He finished the season hitting .152 and frequently looked more like a pitcher at the plate than a catcher. Kreuter did show a pretty good eye at the plate with 27 walks.

In his defense, part of the problem could have been the way he was used. Kreuter started switch-hitting several years ago. Originally, he was a righthanded swinger and has always been stronger from that side. When the season started, however, Kreuter got most of his at bats from the left because he was sharing time behind the plate with righthanded Jim Sundberg. That helped neither his confidence nor batting average and, later in the season, there were times when he batted righthanded against righty pitching. His average wasn't much better from the right, but he showed some power. Kreuter is expected to improve with time and experience, although the Rangers have two other catchers -- Geno Petralli and Mike Stanley -- who rate considerably ahead of him from an offensive standpoint. Ironically, Petralli used to be a switch-hitter and gave it up. It will be interesting to see if Kreuter makes a similar decision.

BASERUNNING:

You wouldn't be able to judge because Kreuter hardly got on base enough to draw any conclusions. Throughout his minor league career, he was caught stealing almost as often as he stole successfully. He apparently has average speed for a catcher.

DEFENSE:

In the minors, Kreuter earned kudos for his strong arm, quick release and pitch blocking skills. He didn't do any of those things very well with the Rangers. He led the league in passed balls. Some of that was from catching the knuckleballs of Charlie Hough, some of that was simply missing pitches that an ordinary catcher would have handled. Whether those were rookie jitters or a premature decline in skills is a valid question to ask.

OVERALL:

If Kreuter had proven himself as a standout in the minors, it might be possible to defend the decision to rush him. But it appears now that the Rangers' expectations of him were simply unrealistic. Kreuter will have to work hard to regain his confidence. Otherwise he simply may be a footnote in history as the man who caught Nolan Ryan's 5000th strikeout.

CHAD KREUTER

Position: C
Bats: R **Throws:** R
Ht: 6' 2" **Wt:** 190

Opening Day Age: 25
Born: 8/26/64 in Marin County, CA
ML Seasons: 2

Overall Statistics

	G	AB	R	H	D	T	HR	RBI	SB	BB	SO	AVG
1989	87	158	16	24	3	0	5	9	0	27	40	.152
Career	103	209	19	38	5	1	6	14	0	34	53	.182

Where He Hits the Ball

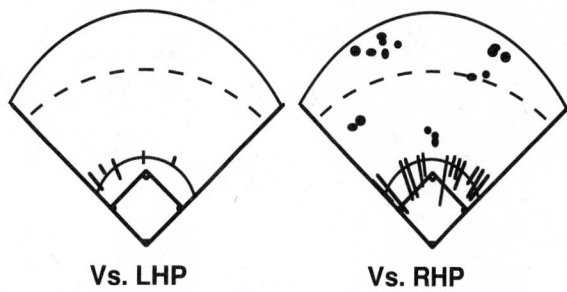

Vs. LHP   Vs. RHP

1989 Situational Stats

	AB	H	HR	RBI	AVG		AB	H	HR	RBI	AVG
Home	74	13	2	5	.176	LHP	35	8	3	4	.229
Road	84	11	3	4	.131	RHP	123	16	2	5	.130
Day	24	3	1	1	.125	Sc Pos	27	2	0	4	.074
Night	134	21	4	8	.157	Clutch	11	2	0	0	.182

1989 Rankings (American League)

➡ Worst percentage throwing out base stealers (17.9%) - *catchers with 75 attempts*

JEFF KUNKEL

Position: SS/CF
Bats: R **Throws:** R
Ht: 6' 2" **Wt:** 190

Opening Day Age: 28
Born: 3/25/62 in West Palm Beach, FL
ML Seasons: 6

HITTING:

After several seasons of shuttling between Triple-A and the big time, Jeff Kunkel got a chance to show the Rangers what he could do in 1989. Kunkel showed that he could turn in a respectable performance against major-league pitching, even though he still has some improvements to make.

Kunkel long had a reputation for swinging at most everything, and he appeared to recognize that late last year. He had only 10 walks through the first five months of last year, but almost doubled that total in September. Still, he needs to battle his way on base whenever possible because, even in the minors, Kunkel never hit for average with any consistency.

It makes sense for opposing pitchers to change speeds on Kunkel and try to get him to chase balls outside of the strike zone. If Kunkel breaks that habit, he might see more fastballs, and be able to show off the power he started to exhibit last season. He needs to continue making progress, because he has yet to play well enough to merit being a full-time starter.

BASERUNNING:

Kunkel doesn't do many things wrong on the bases, but doesn't have the speed to be a base stealer. He will take an extra base when an outfielder gets lazy, but doesn't go from first to third as well as some teammates. Like the rest of his game, his baserunning skills could stand to be a bit better.

FIELDING:

Nobody has ever questioned Kunkel's arm strength. Accuracy is another subject, however, and the Rangers had Kunkel play some centerfield last season to see if that would aid his throwing. Some people feel he's a better outfielder than a shortstop, if only because his long throws tended to be more accurate. But the Baines-for-Fletcher deal opened up the shortstop position, and the Rangers returned him to the infield during the final two months. If he can improve his accuracy, look for Kunkel to have the inside track at being Fletcher's replacement in 1990.

OVERALL:

The Rangers made Kunkel the third player selected in the 1983 amateur draft and had him in the majors midway through the next season. Surely they expected he would be a major contributor to their lineup by now. It's too soon to give up hope, because Kunkel has shown signs of overcoming some of his weaknesses. The jury may be skeptical, but it's still out.

Overall Statistics

	G	AB	R	H	D	T	HR	RBI	SB	BB	SO	AVG
1989	108	293	39	79	21	2	8	29	3	20	75	.270
Career	238	638	71	154	32	8	15	55	7	26	160	.241

Where He Hits the Ball

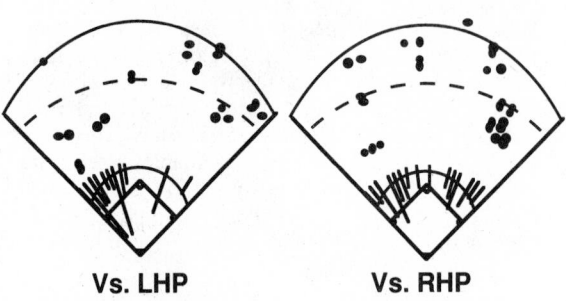

Vs. LHP   **Vs. RHP**

1989 Situational Stats

	AB	H	HR	RBI	AVG		AB	H	HR	RBI	AVG
Home	145	37	8	17	.255	LHP	140	43	3	16	.307
Road	148	42	0	12	.284	RHP	153	36	5	13	.235
Day	67	19	2	4	.284	Sc Pos	62	18	1	20	.290
Night	226	60	6	25	.265	Clutch	41	9	0	1	.220

1989 Rankings (American League)

➡ Led the Rangers in sacrifice bunts (10) and errors (22)

HITTING:

Rick Leach signed with the Rangers as a free agent, and seemed to get into a position similar to the one he was in with Toronto, where he was the fourth outfielder behind the Bell-Moseby-Barfield combination. Still, he has proven to be an adequate fill-in against righthanded pitchers. He won't hit for power, but he'll drive the ball to all fields.

One of Leach's strengths is that he can sit on the bench for days, come to the plate and look like he hasn't missed a beat. There aren't many pitchers who can throw the ball by him, but pitchers who work the ball around in the strike zone do tend to give him problems. You want a testimonial? Ask the Minnesota Twins, against whom Leach could pass for Wade Boggs.

When he's in a groove, Leach seems to be hitting from ahead in the count more often than not. He doesn't bunt much, probably because he doesn't have enough speed to take advantage of doing so. He has never hit for much power, save for one season in Triple-A ball, and has done a good job of improving his average. Still, there were higher hopes for Leach, who shared the Detroit outfield years back with another former football player named Kirk Gibson. Leach was a quarterback from Michigan, Gibson a wide receiver from Michigan State. The Spartans have to get the upper hand sometimes.

BASERUNNING:

Leach isn't particularly fast. In fact, in 4 1/2 years with Toronto, he was 0- for-2 in stolen bases. He got a couple with the Rangers. Leach won't get into trouble on the bases and, befitting a former football player, will go hard into second base to break up a double play.

FIELDING:

Leach can handle what he gets to. He's been used mostly in left and right field, and doesn't have particularly good range. Opposing runners tend to take an extra base on him.

OVERALL:

The biggest question mark may be Leach's off-the-field reputation. He disappeared from the team during a trip to New York last season and pulled a similar disappearing act with the Blue Jays. That sort of thing doesn't sit well with management. Still, if Leach can be judged as a player, he should have a role as a fourth outfielder who can come off the bench and help his team.

RICK LEACH

Position: DH/LF
Bats: L **Throws:** L
Ht: 6' 0" **Wt:** 195

Opening Day Age: 32
Born: 5/4/57 in Ann Arbor, MI
ML Seasons: 9

Overall Statistics

	G	AB	R	H	D	T	HR	RBI	SB	BB	SO	AVG
1989	110	239	32	65	14	1	1	23	2	32	33	.272
Career	721	1545	181	409	87	10	16	167	8	155	197	.265

Where He Hits the Ball

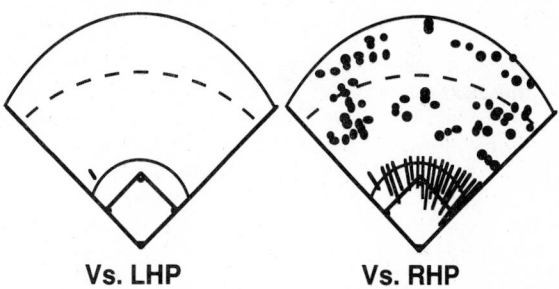

Vs. LHP   Vs. RHP

1989 Situational Stats

	AB	H	HR	RBI	AVG		AB	H	HR	RBI	AVG
Home	117	25	0	8	.214	LHP	7	1	0	0	.143
Road	122	40	1	15	.328	RHP	232	64	1	23	.276
Day	43	11	0	3	.256	Sc Pos	68	13	0	21	.191
Night	196	54	1	20	.276	Clutch	39	10	0	6	.256

1989 Rankings (American League)

➡ Did not rank near the top or bottom in any category

HITTING:

Throughout his major league career, Fred Manrique was seen as the guy who got in the lineup because of his glove -- and was buried at the bottom of the order. Well, Manrique showed in 1989, as he'd done in spurts during earlier years, that he has the potential to make some noise with his bat. Manrique was in the lineup more than half the time in 1989 and flirted with the .300 mark for much of the season.

Manrique doesn't draw many walks, but you can call him a "contact hitter" without mumbling the second word of the phrase. His career-high batting average was 52 points better than the .242 career mark with which he entered the season. What happened? For one thing, Manrique seemed to become more patient at the plate, no longer the kind of guy you could fool with a breaking pitch and burn with a fastball. Getting the chance to hit against more righthanders also may have gotten him into a groove.

While he doesn't hit for power, Manrique can flex his muscles and show off some extra-base prowess on occasion. He sprays the ball and does a lot of damage hitting to right-center and right fields. He's a pretty good bunter, too. Whether he can continue improving his skills or merely maintain the prowess he showed last season, Manrique can now make a contribution to the offense.

BASERUNNING:

While hardly a slowpoke, Manrique has never been able to master the skills necessary to be a base-stealing threat. He gets out of the batter's box pretty quickly and is an intelligent baserunner, albeit a cautious one.

FIELDING:

The Rangers are unsettled at two infield positions -- maybe three if Julio Franco moves over to first base -- and Manrique has proven that he can play second, short or third. He's strongest at second base, where he has pretty good range and turns the double play. But he shouldn't be ruled out as a starting shortstop. It has to be reassuring for manager Bobby Valentine to know that Manrique can be worked around his other personnel decisions.

OVERALL:

Former White Sox broadcaster (and veteran major leaguer) Del Crandall always thought highly of Manrique, and another year like 1989 could get that chorus to grow. Manrique can definitely help Texas with his glove, and may actually turn out to be a more complete player than anyone had reckoned.

FRED MANRIQUE

Position: 2B/SS
Bats: R **Throws:** R
Ht: 6' 1" **Wt:** 175

Opening Day Age: 28
Born: 11/5/61 in Bolivar, Venezuela
ML Seasons: 7

Overall Statistics

	G	AB	R	H	D	T	HR	RBI	SB	BB	SO	AVG
1989	119	378	46	111	25	1	4	52	4	17	63	.294
Career	420	1088	127	283	49	11	15	122	16	59	203	.260

Where He Hits the Ball

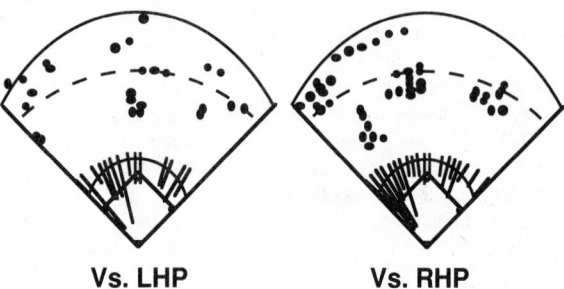

Vs. LHP   **Vs. RHP**

1989 Situational Stats

	AB	H	HR	RBI	AVG		AB	H	HR	RBI	AVG
Home	174	55	1	23	.316	LHP	141	43	1	21	.305
Road	204	56	3	29	.275	RHP	237	68	3	31	.287
Day	94	30	2	18	.319	Sc Pos	85	33	1	42	.388
Night	284	81	2	34	.285	Clutch	60	18	1	11	.300

1989 Rankings (American League)

➡ 6th in errors (21)
➡ 7th in sacrifice hits (13)

PITCHING:

He doesn't have a world of talent, but Gary Mielke earned himself a place on the Texas staff with his attitude as much as his right arm. Mielke is a competitor who didn't back down from his opponents during his rookie season, coming inside with a fastball when it looked like opponents were getting too comfortable in the batter's box. Mielke never looked like a nervous rookie on the mound, showing instead the poise of a veteran. His overall stats -- one win, a save and a 3.26 ERA -- were modest, but Mielke formed an important bridge between the Ranger starters and closer Jeff Russell.

Mielke relies on two pitches, a hard sinking fastball and a big-breaking slider. Both pitches can be tough on righthanded batters, but there are some doubts about his effectiveness against lefties. He isn't expected to develop into a closer, but that doesn't mean he can't fill a valuable role. The Rangers usually used him in mid-game situations where he was expected to pitch for an inning or two, and he had the ability to pitch for several consecutive days. The defense liked working behind him because he keeps the ball in play. He showed no after effects of the shoulder surgery that sidelined him for the final six weeks of the Triple A season in 1988.

FIELDING:

Mielke did a decent job of holding baserunners during his first full year in the majors. He also fields his position reasonably well.

OVERALL:

A hurler like Mielke never has a certain future in the majors, but his competitive nature can't help but be a plus if the front office has to make a close call. The Rangers think he has the makeup and skills to do the things that have made Gene Nelson such a valuable reliever for the White Sox and Athletics. Mielke hasn't reached that level yet, and needs to find a way to be more effective against lefties if he wants to make a bigger contribution to his team.

GARY MIELKE

Position: RP
Bats: R **Throws:** R
Ht: 6' 3"   **Wt:** 180

Opening Day Age: 27
Born: 1/28/63 in St. James, MN
ML Seasons: 2

Overall Statistics

	W	L	ERA	G	GS	Sv	IP	H	R	BB	SO	HR
1989	1	0	3.26	43	0	1	49.2	52	18	25	26	4
Career	1	0	3.42	46	0	1	52.2	55	20	26	29	6

Where They Hit the Ball

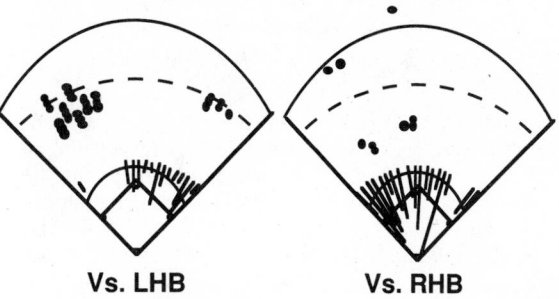

Vs. LHB   **Vs. RHB**

1989 Situational Stats

	W	L	ERA	Sv	IP		AB	H	HR	RBI	AVG
Home	0	0	2.37	1	30.1	LHB	50	12	1	6	.240
Road	1	0	4.66	0	19.1	RHB	136	40	3	29	.294
Day	0	0	1.69	0	5.1	Sc Pos	72	25	2	31	.347
Night	1	0	3.45	1	44.1	Clutch	37	13	1	5	.351

1989 Rankings (American League)

➡ Did not rank near the top or bottom in any category

PITCHING:

Jamie Moyer didn't get a true chance to show what he could contribute to the Rangers last season because a severely strained shoulder muscle kept him sidelined from the end of May until August. In limited service his record was spotty. But he showed flashes of brilliance, particularly in one game against Toronto in which he struck out 13 batters.

After walking only 55 batters in 202 innings for the Cubs in 1988, Moyer came to Texas billed as a control pitcher. But last year he walked 33 in only 76 innings. He didn't have good control of the changeup -- being injured could be a valid explanation -- and was forced to pitch from behind more often than a finesse pitcher should. As a result, batters could wait on his fastball and drill it. When he has to rely on it, his fastball is merely average. But when Moyer can control the change, the fastball becomes a better pitch. That's crucial to him because he can give up home runs in bunches even though he usually gets more outs on grounders than fly balls.

It didn't help Moyer that until last year he was pitching in Wrigley Field, which definitely favors hitters. Texas Stadium should be more forgiving, but the tradeoff comes when Moyer hits the road and pitches in American League bandboxes such as the Kingdome and Tiger Stadium. The jury is still out about how he'll fare in those venues. Fifteen appearances isn't a fair sample on which to judge.

FIELDING:

Moyer is a good fielder who reacts well on balls hit up the middle. He does a decent job of holding runners, but does not have the slick pickoff move you'd expect of a lefty finesse pitcher. He allows more steals than the average hurler, mostly because he allows so many runners to reach first.

OVERALL:

Several pitchers passed Moyer on the Texas depth chart last season and he needs to reestablish that he can help the team. He'll be among those battling to fill a spot at the end of the rotation. If the Rangers give up, there should be a place somewhere else for Moyer because lefthanded pitchers with good control are always in demand somewhere. Moyer has earned a reputation over the years as a smart pitcher who's always looking for way to better himself. That's another point in his favor.

JAMIE MOYER

Position: SP
Bats: L **Throws:** L
Ht: 6' 0" **Wt:** 170

Opening Day Age: 27
Born: 11/18/62 in Sellersville, PA
ML Seasons: 4

Overall Statistics

	W	L	ERA	G	GS	Sv	IP	H	R	BB	SO	HR
1989	4	9	4.86	15	15	0	76.0	84	51	33	44	10
Career	32	43	4.48	100	94	0	566.1	613	314	227	357	68

Where They Hit the Ball

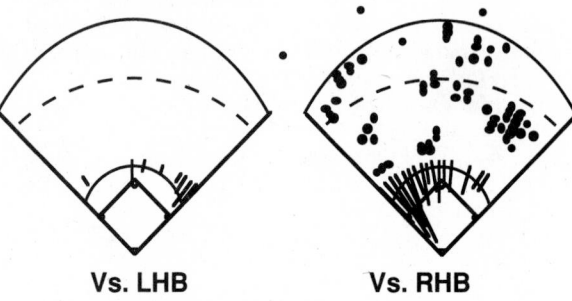

Vs. LHB   **Vs. RHB**

1989 Situational Stats

	W	L	ERA	Sv	IP		AB	H	HR	RBI	AVG
Home	3	4	4.34	0	47.2	LHB	42	9	1	4	.214
Road	1	5	5.72	0	28.1	RHB	255	75	9	35	.294
Day	1	1	2.00	0	18.0	Sc Pos	62	18	2	26	.290
Night	3	8	5.74	0	58.0	Clutch	13	4	1	2	.308

1989 Rankings (American League)

➡ Did not rank near the top or bottom in any category

HITTING:

The Rangers acquired Rafael Palmeiro from the Cubs in one of the big offseason trades. They expected him to hit for average and show some power. Palmiero didn't do either, and there was talk that the struggle between average and power sent him into a half-season of limited production. At age 25, however, it would seem too early to write off Palmiero based on one season in which he failed to live up to offensive expectations.

Palmiero doesn't strike out much and is a line drive hitter who favors driving the ball into the left-center field gap. When he's on a streak, Palmiero can be among the toughest outs in baseball. He has a quick stroke and a good eye at the plate. You can't get him out consistently with the same strategy. He carried the rap with the Cubs of not being able to hit with runners in scoring position, but those figures evened out last season in Texas. The trouble was that the Rangers expected more hitting in all situations. In particular, his doubles production was down, and he didn't hit southpaws as well as he had with the Cubs.

BASERUNNING:

Palmiero doesn't have great speed, but he'll go from first to third on a single where some runners would hold at second. The Rangers didn't ask him to steal bases the way the Cubs did in 1988, when he was 12 for 14.

FIELDING:

Moved from the outfield to first base, his natural position, Palmiero did an acceptable job, but would fall short in comparison with Pete O'Brien, his predecessor. Maybe it was rustiness, but Palmiero had some trouble fielding bunts. His weak arm shouldn't bother him at first, but might prevent the Rangers from moving him back to the outfield.

OVERALL:

The Rangers are still banking that Palmiero will return more than he did last season. He can be one of the top pure hitters in the game. It will be interesting to see if he can become more of a power hitter as his career progresses, and whether he can do it while maintaining his average.

RAFAEL PALMEIRO

Position: 1B
Bats: L **Throws:** L
Ht: 6' 0" **Wt:** 180

Opening Day Age: 25
Born: 9/24/64 in Havana, Cuba
ML Seasons: 4

Overall Statistics

	G	AB	R	H	D	T	HR	RBI	SB	BB	SO	AVG
1989	156	559	76	154	23	4	8	64	4	63	48	.275
Career	414	1433	192	411	83	10	33	159	19	125	114	.287

Where He Hits the Ball

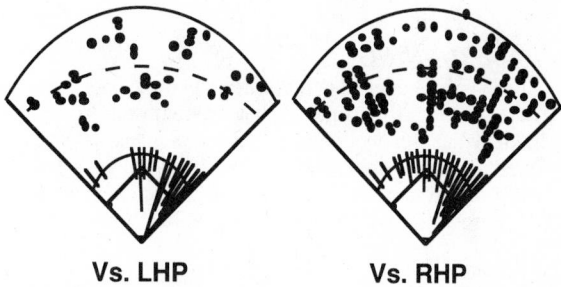

Vs. LHP   Vs. RHP

1989 Situational Stats

	AB	H	HR	RBI	AVG		AB	H	HR	RBI	AVG
Home	263	68	4	29	.259	LHP	165	41	2	20	.248
Road	296	86	4	35	.291	RHP	394	113	6	44	.287
Day	102	30	4	16	.294	Sc Pos	133	37	1	50	.278
Night	457	124	4	48	.271	Clutch	72	20	2	7	.278

1989 Rankings (American League)

➥ 10th in lowest percentage of swings that missed (10.2%)

➥ Led the Rangers in lowest percentage of swings that missed, highest percentage of swings put into play (53.6%), hit by pitch (6) and batting average with 2 strikes (.262)

➥ Led AL First Basemen in grounder/flyball ratio (1.39)

HITTING:

Geno Petralli has gotten a lot of attention for chasing the errant balls thrown by the youngsters and knuckleballers of the Texas staff. What's been overlooked is that he has established himself as a solid major league hitter who will cause trouble for anyone taking him lightly.

Petralli's 1989 season was limited by a knee injury that kept him under 300 at-bats for the first time in three seasons. Still, Petralli finished with a .304 average, playing almost exclusively against righthanded pitchers. With a nice stroke, Petralli hits mostly to right and right-center, but can take an outside pitch to the opposite field. He doesn't strike out much and has a fairly good eye at the plate. In addition, he has always hit better against pitchers who try to keep the ball on the ground. He can be overpowered by hard throwers, especially those who can tie him up with a nasty slider.

BASERUNNING:

Speed? You better look elsewhere. Petralli once stole four bases in a season, but that was with the Rookie League team in Medicine Hat, Alberta, back in 1978. He's strictly a one-base-at-a-time guy. Always had been, always will be. Petralli won't take chances on the bases. He understands his limitations.

FIELDING:

Petralli has been Charlie Hough's designated catcher more often than not, and the results have not been pretty. Petralli holds the record for most passed balls in a season and has tied marks for most PBs in a game (6) and an inning (4). Petralli feels he gets a bad rap on some of those calls. His position: Just because he touches a knuckler doesn't mean he should catch it. No word yet on whether Petralli plans a seminar for official scorers. He has an average arm and, of course, has been hindered by trying to throw out stealers who get an extra step on the Hough knuckler.

OVERALL:

The Rangers have been looking at young catchers to share time with Petralli. Health permitting, he provides them with the stability to bring others along slowly, and will probably do as much catching as anyone in 1990. His bat alone will probably keep him in a job for several more years because the major league catching pool is pretty limited. There are no areas of the game, save for foot speed, in which Petralli doesn't make a contribution.

GENO PETRALLI

Position: C/DH
Bats: L **Throws:** R
Ht: 6' 1" **Wt:** 180

Opening Day Age: 30
Born: 9/25/59 in Sacramento, CA
ML Seasons: 8

Overall Statistics

	G	AB	R	H	D	T	HR	RBI	SB	BB	SO	AVG
1989	70	184	18	56	7	0	4	23	0	17	24	.304
Career	436	1025	108	294	45	7	20	120	4	103	138	.287

Where He Hits the Ball

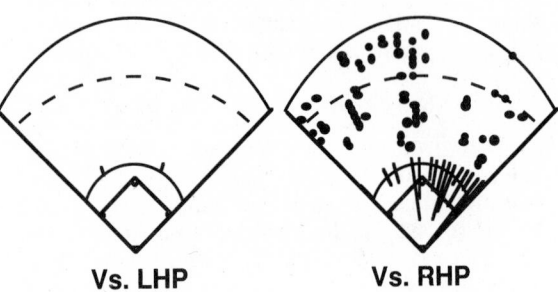

Vs. LHP   **Vs. RHP**

1989 Situational Stats

	AB	H	HR	RBI	AVG		AB	H	HR	RBI	AVG
Home	88	17	1	6	.193	LHP	9	1	0	0	.111
Road	96	39	3	17	.406	RHP	175	55	4	23	.314
Day	35	14	1	3	.400	Sc Pos	54	13	1	19	.241
Night	149	42	3	20	.282	Clutch	26	8	0	2	.308

1989 Rankings (American League)

➡ Led the Rangers in hitting on a 3-2 count (.333) - *team players with 20 PA on a 3-2 count*

PITCHING:

Had you been making a list of Texas prospects going into last season, and used minor-league statistics as primary criteria, Kenny Rogers would have been nowhere to be found. He'd compiled a 19-38 record and 4.25 ERA in seven seasons of banging from rotation to bullpen throughout the Rangers system. That he was a 39th round draft choice back in 1982 didn't help his chances. Neither did the surgery performed on his left elbow in 1987.

Yet when 1989 was in the record books, Rogers had established himself as the key lefthander in the Texas bullpen. He pitched in 73 games, kept his ERA under three and allowed only two home runs in 73.2 innings. He didn't earn much recognition for his work outside of the Lone Star State, but the Rangers knew they had a guy who could combine a 90-plus fastball with a better-than-average slider. That he skipped pitching in Triple A didn't seem to affect his poise, which makes him something of a novelty among the young Ranger pitchers.

The Rangers used Rogers frequently, but picked their spots with him. He usually pitched to only a couple of batters, and rarely stayed around to finish a game. That didn't hurt the Rangers, though, because Jeff Russell had such an extraordinary year. Without Rogers, there wouldn't have been a consistent reliever to force opposing managers to get some of their left-handed bats out of the lineup. Rogers is primarily a two-pitch guy, but would sometimes show off a change-up, which he'd usually keep out of the strike zone.

FIELDING:

Rogers has earned a reputation as the Rangers' best fielding pitcher, traits he probably acquired as a left-handed high school shortstop. He follows through in good fashion and is in good position to field grounders. He gets off the mound well on bunts and moves quickly to first base. Baserunners couldn't take advantage of Rogers the way they could against other Texas pitchers.

OVERALL:

Texas hopes that Rogers can finish off more games, and would like him to be the one they turn to if Russell falters or needs a rest. They would like it if Rogers could rack up about 10 saves this season and improve his control a bit. Rogers has found a niche with the Rangers.

KEN ROGERS

Position: RP
Bats: L **Throws:** L
Ht: 6' 1" **Wt:** 200

Opening Day Age: 25
Born: 11/10/64 in Savannah, GA
ML Seasons: 1

Overall Statistics

	W	L	ERA	G	GS	Sv	IP	H	R	BB	SO	HR
1989	3	4	2.93	73	0	2	73.2	60	28	42	63	2
Career	3	4	2.93	73	0	2	73.2	60	28	42	63	2

Where They Hit the Ball

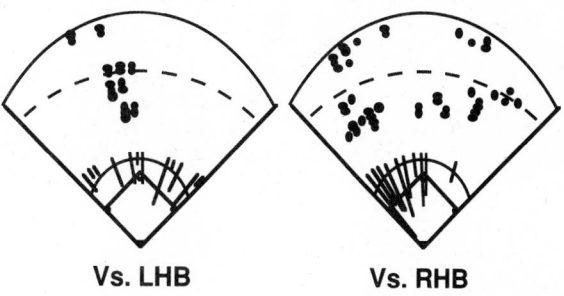

Vs. LHB   **Vs. RHB**

1989 Situational Stats

	W	L	ERA	Sv	IP		AB	H	HR	RBI	AVG
Home	3	3	3.33	1	46.0	LHB	81	14	0	11	.173
Road	0	1	2.28	1	27.2	RHB	178	46	2	26	.258
Day	1	0	0.00	1	9.2	Sc Pos	94	24	1	36	.255
Night	2	4	3.38	1	64.0	Clutch	109	24	1	17	.220

1989 Rankings (American League)

➡ 3rd in games (73) and holds (16)

➡ Led the Rangers in games and holds

JEFF RUSSELL

Position: RP
Bats: R **Throws:** R
Ht: 6' 3" **Wt:** 210

Opening Day Age: 28
Born: 9/2/61 in
Cincinnati, OH
ML Seasons: 7

STOPPER

PITCHING:

The Rangers spent several seasons figuring out how Jeff Russell could best help them, and discovered in 1989 that they had one of the premier closers in baseball. He led the American League with 38 saves and was consistent enough to finish the season with an ERA below 2.00. He hardly looked like the same guy who entered 1989 with a 33-44 career record and a 4.24 lifetime ERA. The difference was that as a stopper Russell could put away batters with his 90-plus fastball without having to worry about improving the rest of his arsenal. Russell has always struggled with his off-speed and breaking pitches. Last year, they were merely diversions as he allowed less than one runner per inning in 71 appearances.

Want more evidence about how much better Russell could be once he could just rear back and throw? As a starter/middle reliever in 1988, Russell averaged less than one strikeout every two innings ... but as a closer he more than doubled that rate. He allowed only four homers in 73.2 innings last year. The rest of his repertoire includes a hard slider and a change-up, but as a late man the fastball and slider are really all he needs. The Rangers were fortunate to find enough starting pitchers during spring training to allow them to make the move with Russell.

FIELDING:

Russell used to make life tough on his catchers because he didn't have a good move to first. That's another benefit of short relief. Baserunners often can't take a chance on stealing when getting caught can take their team out of a game. Russell fields his position well, showing good reactions and movements.

OVERALL:

It's Easy to Forget, Part I: The Rangers obtained Russell in a deal in which they gave up longtime favorite Buddy Bell. That trade, very controversial at the time, looks pretty good right now. At age 28, Russell should be able to handle Texas bullpen duties for years to come. It's Easy to Forget, Part II: Russell and Mitch Williams, who had 36 saves for the Cubs last year, were on the same pitching staff for a couple of seasons.

Overall Statistics

	W	L	ERA	G	GS	Sv	IP	H	R	BB	SO	HR
1989	6	4	1.98	71	0	38	72.2	45	21	24	77	4
Career	39	48	4.02	250	79	43	752.2	740	385	287	460	71

Where They Hit the Ball

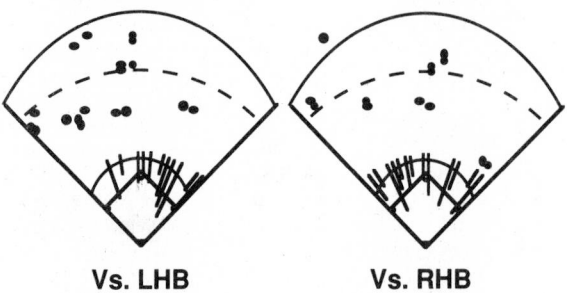

Vs. LHB   **Vs. RHB**

1989 Situational Stats

	W	L	ERA	Sv	IP		AB	H	HR	RBI	AVG
Home	2	1	1.64	24	38.1	LHB	112	23	0	15	.205
Road	4	3	2.36	14	34.1	RHB	135	22	4	23	.163
Day	5	2	2.25	5	20.0	Sc Pos	85	20	0	31	.235
Night	1	2	1.88	33	52.2	Clutch	176	36	3	34	.205

1989 Rankings (American League)

- ➡ 1st in save percentage (86.4%), games finished (66), saves (38) and save opportunities (44)
- ➡ 3rd in most GDPs per GDP situation (23.6%) - *pitchers with 30 GDP situations*
- ➡ 4th in games (71)
- ➡ Led the Rangers in ERA (1.98), saves, games finished, save opportunities, save percentage, first batter efficiency (.180), least baserunners per 9 innings (8.9), most GDPs per 9 innings (1.61), blown saves (6), lowest on-base average allowed (.260) and lowest slugging percentage allowed (.279) - *all team pitchers*

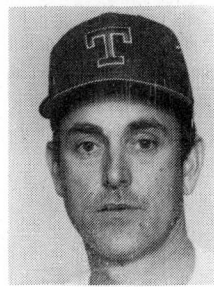

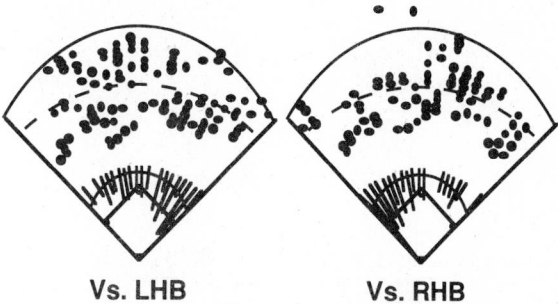

HALL OF FAMER

NOLAN RYAN

Position: SP
Bats: R **Throws:** R
Ht: 6' 2" **Wt:** 220

Opening Day Age: 43
Born: 1/31/47 in
Refugio, TX
ML Seasons: 23

PITCHING:

Reading about Nolan Ryan doesn't do him justice. You have to watch the 43-year-old pitcher in order to experience the thrill of his fastball simply overpowering players young enough to be his children. After his awesome 1989 season, it's easy to forget that there were doubts about whether he could still help a team when he came to the Rangers as a free agent. All Ryan did was strike out 301 batters while compiling a 16-10 record. It was the sixth time in his career that Ryan had struck out more than 300 in a season, but the first since 1977. How impressive was the strikeout total? The American League runner-up, Roger Clemens, had 230. The National League leader, Jose DeLeon, had 201 -- not to be confused with 301.

Although Ryan hasn't won 20 games since 1974, you could argue that he was a better pitcher last year than ever before. Certainly his control has improved with time. He used to walk 100 batters in a season pretty regularly, but hasn't done that since 1983. He threatened that streak last year, bringing 98 into his final start -- and didn't walk anyone while striking out 13 in a three-hit shutout. Ryan reached the 5,000-strikeout mark last season while only one other pitcher, Steve Carlton, has even reached 4,000.

Seeing 1989 as a personal challenge, Ryan wanted to reestablish that he could go the distance. His previous team, Houston, had taken to limiting the number of pitches he would throw before being removed. Ryan had been bothered by an assortment of small injuries with the Astros, but the superior physical condition that preserved his fastball also allowed him to battle the aches and pains. As a Ranger, he tossed six complete games, his most since 1982, and his 239.1 innings were his highest total since 1977.

FIELDING:

It's no secret that Ryan has neither a good move to first base nor a delivery that keeps runners close. He prefers to concentrate on the hitter, and it's hard to knock the results. Ryan has never been a good fielder and sometimes hurts himself with his poor defense.

OVERALL:

Without question Ryan proved in 1989 that he can be a valuable asset to a pitching staff, and that reports of his demise were premature. Another season like 1989 would be unprecedented for a 43-year old ... but then Nolan Ryan is used to going places no man has gone before.

Overall Statistics

	W	L	ERA	G	GS	Sv	IP	H	R	BB	SO	HR
1989	16	10	3.20	32	32	0	239.1	162	96	98	301	17
Career	289	263	3.15	710	676	3	4786.1	3492	1912	2540	5076	277

Where They Hit the Ball

Vs. LHB **Vs. RHB**

1989 Situational Stats

	W	L	ERA	Sv	IP		AB	H	HR	RBI	AVG
Home	9	6	3.68	0	139.1	LHB	446	79	8	39	.177
Road	7	4	2.52	0	100.0	RHB	421	83	9	38	.197
Day	3	0	1.96	0	41.1	Sc Pos	203	48	4	61	.236
Night	13	10	3.45	0	198.0	Clutch	108	23	2	7	.213

1989 Rankings (American League)

➡ 1st in strikeouts (301), lowest opponent batting average (.187), lowest opponent slugging average (.283), most stolen bases allowed (36), most strikeouts per 9 innings (11.3), most pitches thrown per batter (4.1), least GDPs per 9 innings (.15) and wild pitches (19) - *pitchers with 162 IP*

➡ 2nd in lowest on-base average allowed (.275), walks allowed (98) and pitches thrown (4,073)

➡ Led the Rangers in ERA (3.20), wins (16), games started (32), shutouts (2), innings (239.1), batters faced (988), hit batsmen (9), won/loss percentage (.677) - *team pitchers with 502 PA*

FUTURE MVP?

RUBEN SIERRA

Position: RF
Bats: B **Throws:** R
Ht: 6' 1" **Wt:** 175

Opening Day Age: 24
Born: 10/6/65 in Rio Piedras, Puerto Rico
ML Seasons: 4

HITTING:

What didn't Ruben Sierra do for the Rangers in 1989? At age 23 he hit for both average and power while leading the league in RBIs. He was a terror with runners in scoring position and didn't care whether opposing teams made him bat lefthanded or right. Kirby Puckett of the Twins gets more attention, but Sierra may be close to being considered an equal as an all-around player. More consistency will be required before that comparison is fully justified.

Through his first couple of seasons, Sierra was considered a stronger hitter from the left side. But for the past two years, he has been tougher from the right, though he shows about equal power from either direction. You wouldn't bring in a reliever to turn Sierra around, the way you would do with many other switch-hitters.

Earlier in his career, Sierra was thought to be vulnerable to outside pitches from righthanders. He seems to have conquered that problem. He also became more patient. He can hit with power to all fields.

BASERUNNING:

After going 18 for 22 in stolen bases in 1988, Sierra didn't have stealing as a high priority in 1989. That's because the Rangers need Sierra to drive home runs much more than to score them. He'll take an extra base when an outfielder stops hustling and rarely makes a bad move on the paths. There are times when it looks like he doesn't get a good jump on a pitcher, but he has enough sheer speed to make up for it.

FIELDING:

Good range, excellent arm -- Sierra has been a constant force in an outfield of changing characters. He's made more errors that you would expect during his career and there have been questions about his concentration in the field. Count on Sierra becoming a better defensive player as he gets older, especially if the Rangers become contenders.

OVERALL:

Only time will tell how much better Sierra will become. He can only benefit from some of the experienced players with whom the Rangers have surrounded him. There will probably be a time when Sierra is in the same mentor's role, and the Rangers are expecting more leadership qualities from him than he's exhibited to this point in his career. You'll probably see him on a Hall of Fame ballot some time in the 21st century.

Overall Statistics

	G	AB	R	H	D	T	HR	RBI	SB	BB	SO	AVG
1989	162	634	101	194	35	14	29	119	8	43	82	.306
Career	589	2274	325	620	115	30	98	374	49	148	352	.273

Where He Hits the Ball

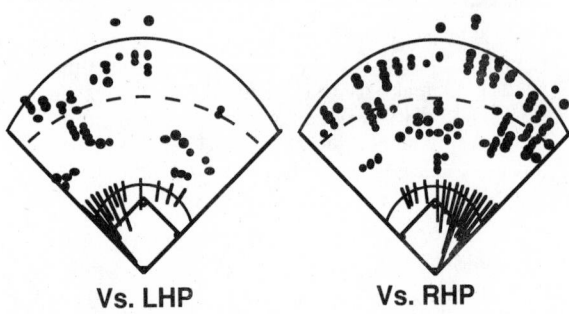

Vs. LHP   **Vs. RHP**

1989 Situational Stats

	AB	H	HR	RBI	AVG		AB	H	HR	RBI	AVG
Home	309	98	21	73	.317	LHP	205	70	10	44	.341
Road	325	96	8	46	.295	RHP	429	124	19	75	.289
Day	123	33	5	21	.268	Sc Pos	167	56	8	85	.335
Night	511	161	24	98	.315	Clutch	84	26	4	16	.310

1989 Rankings (American League)

→ 1st in slugging percentage (.543), triples (14), RBI (119), games (162) and total bases (344)

→ 3rd in runs (101)

→ 5th in hits (194) and sacrifice flies (10)

→ Led the Rangers in home runs (29), at bats (634), runs, hits, doubles (35), triples, total bases, RBIs, sacrifice flies, games, slugging percentage, and runs scored per time reached base (36.6%)

→ Led AL Right Fielders in batting average (.306), home runs, at bats, runs, hits, doubles, triples, total bases, RBIs, sacrifice flies, games and slugging percentage

PITCHING:

There doesn't seem to be much middle ground with Bobby Witt. He can be very, very tough or very, very disappointing. After showing signs in 1988 that he was going to conquer the control woes that had always plagued him, Witt struggled again. He's going to have to make control a priority if he wants to live up to the billing that made him a No. 1 draft pick five years ago. If he can't do it, the Rangers might finally run out of patience with him.

On the good days, Witt throws a 95-plus fastball, a hard slider similar to the one thrown by Dave Stieb of the Blue Jays, and a curve. However, the starts in which he can get all three of those pitches over are in the minority. His fastball has an exploding effect, rising and handcuffing righthanded hitters especially. When Witt is wild he should throw his fastball without worrying about nipping the corners and using his other pitches less frequently.

There was a stretch in '88 when he threw nine straight complete games and appeared on the way to becoming a total pitcher. The streak was especially significant because Witt had only two career complete games before it started. The streak also was the longest since Bert Blyleven had 10 straight for Cleveland in 1985. But Witt completed only five games in 1989.

If Witt could do nothing more than throw hard, he could be dismissed as a novelty. But the fact that he can throw a good slider and a decent curve makes his lack of success that much more frustrating. There's still time for him to put it all together, as long as his arm doesn't fall apart.

FIELDING:

It used to be that a walk from Witt was as good as a double because he barely bothered to look over to first base. He's worked on his move to the point of keeping runners honest. Call it average. For a hard thrower, Witt gets off the mound and fields his position fairly well.

OVERALL:

Witt finished strongly in 1988, only to backslide last season, which means that he'll have to show something over a sustained period in order to satisfy the skeptics. Nobody expects Witt to become the staff ace, but some consistency would help the Rangers round out a rotation in which the search for five solid starters has been an ongoing battle.

BOBBY WITT

Position: SP
Bats: R **Throws:** R
Ht: 6' 2" **Wt:** 205

Opening Day Age: 25
Born: 5/11/64 in Canton, MA
ML Seasons: 4

Overall Statistics

	W	L	ERA	G	GS	Sv	IP	H	R	BB	SO	HR
1989	12	13	5.14	31	31	0	194.1	182	123	114	166	14
Career	39	42	4.85	110	109	0	669.1	560	392	498	648	55

Where They Hit the Ball

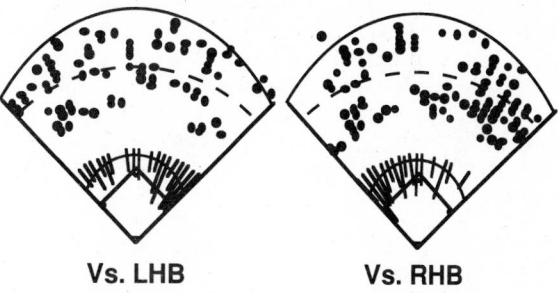

Vs. LHB **Vs. RHB**

1989 Situational Stats

	W	L	ERA	Sv	IP		AB	H	HR	RBI	AVG
Home	5	7	4.74	0	89.1	LHB	349	87	10	54	.249
Road	7	6	5.49	0	105.0	RHB	384	95	4	48	.247
Day	1	2	6.53	0	20.2	Sc Pos	205	59	4	87	.288
Night	11	11	4.98	0	173.2	Clutch	47	9	0	1	.191

1989 Rankings (American League)

- ➡ 1st in worst ERA (5.14), walks allowed (114) and highest stolen base percentage allowed (88.2%) - *pitchers with 162 IP*
- ➡ 2nd in stolen bases allowed (30), most baserunners per 9 innings (13.8) and worst batting average allowed with runners in scoring position (.288)
- ➡ 4th in highest on-base average allowed (.347) and strikeouts per 9 innings (7.7)
- ➡ 7th in strikeouts (166)
- ➡ Led the Rangers in losses (13), hits allowed (182) and walks allowed

BRAD ARNSBERG

Position: RP
Bats: R **Throws:** R
Ht: 6' 4" **Wt:** 205

Opening Day Age: 26
Born: 8/20/63 in
Seattle, WA
ML Seasons: 3

THAD BOSLEY

Position: LF
Bats: L **Throws:** L
Ht: 6' 3" **Wt:** 175

Opening Day Age: 33
Born: 9/17/56 in
Oceanside, CA
ML Seasons: 13

Overall Statistics

	W	L	ERA	G	GS	Sv	IP	H	R	BB	SO	HR
1989	2	1	4.13	16	1	1	48.0	45	27	22	26	6
Career	3	4	4.42	24	4	1	75.1	80	42	36	43	12

Overall Statistics

	G	AB	R	H	D	T	HR	RBI	SB	BB	SO	AVG
1989	37	40	5	9	2	0	1	9	2	3	11	.225
Career	754	1552	180	426	50	12	19	155	46	139	268	.274

PITCHING & FIELDING:

Give Brad Arnsberg credit for an extraordinary come-back. He missed the entire 1988 season because of Tommy John-like surgery. His right elbow was reconstructed with the aid of a tendon from his left wrist. He spent that year on the disabled list and hopes weren't high for his future. He pitched mostly in long relief last year, and his arm appeared healthy. But questions remain about the quality of his stuff. He throws a fastball clocked in the high 80s, a curveball and a forkball for an off-speed pitch. Arnsberg was effective against right-handers, but had a lot of trouble retiring lefties, often being forced to come in with 2-and-0 or 3-and-1 fastballs. He either needs to come up with another pitch to use against lefties or show through all-around improvement that he wasn't working at 100 percent last year.

OVERALL:

Arnsberg either will show talent he hasn't yet displayed on the major league level or become a journeyman who'll always have to fight for his spot on a pitching staff. The latter represents quite a tumble considering that he was once one of the Yankees' top prospects.

HITTING, FIELDING, BASERUNNING:

At this stage of his career, Thad Bosley is the sort of journeyman pinch hitter who will attract the attention of teams needing some extra offensive punch. Bosley has been used over the years almost exclusively against righthanded pitchers, and while he'll usually hit the ball to right or right-center, he can take an outside pitch to the opposite field. He's always lacked power. He defies being typecast as either a first-ball or a patient hitter, instead doing what the situation warrants. He can hit fastballs and breaking pitches, and likes the ball on the inside half of the plate. Bosley doesn't run the bases as well as he did when younger, but still has average speed. More than anything else, Bosley's defense has kept him from being a regular. He lacks range and has an arm that allows runners to take an extra base.

OVERALL:

At this point, Bosley should be considered lucky to find a roster spot given the 24-man roster and his defensive limitations. While it would be interesting for Bosley to get to hit 400 times in a season, don't hold your breath waiting for it to happen.

JACK DAUGHERTY

Position: 1B
Bats: B **Throws:** L
Ht: 6' 0" **Wt:** 185

Opening Day Age: 29
Born: 6/3/60 in Hialeah, FL
ML Seasons: 2

Overall Statistics

	G	AB	R	H	D	T	HR	RBI	SB	BB	SO	AVG
1989	52	106	15	32	4	2	1	10	2	11	21	.302
Career	63	116	16	33	5	2	1	11	2	11	24	.284

HITTING, FIELDING, BASERUNNING:

Nothing has come easy in baseball for Jack Daugherty. Though he had a fine minor league record including a cool .402 season at Helena in 1984, he didn't get his big league chance until this year. He certainly made the most of it.

Daugherty showed the Rangers a lively bat from either side of the plate and an ability to handle off-speed pitches as well as fastball. He is a patient hitter who can hit line drives to all fields. The Rangers had some success with him a pinch hitter, a job to which most rookies have difficulty adapting. He runs the bases well and doesn't take long to reach full speed, and that quickness also helps on defense.

Daugherty showed off some nice glovework around first base and also played the outfield. He has stronger fielding skills than the other Texas first basemen. His arm is just average, which works against his being an outfielder on a regular basis. Given the Rangers' regular lineup, that versatility should pay off for him.

OVERALL:

With the uncertainty about who's going to play where for Texas this season, Daugherty provides the Rangers with some flexibility. He doesn't really hit with enough power to guarantee a regular role, but he should see considerable action.

CRAIG MCMURTRY

Position: RP
Bats: R **Throws:** R
Ht: 6' 5" **Wt:** 195

Opening Day Age: 30
Born: 11/5/59 in Temple, TX
ML Seasons: 6

Overall Statistics

	W	L	ERA	G	GS	Sv	IP	H	R	BB	SO	HR
1989	0	0	7.43	19	0	0	23.0	29	21	13	14	3
Career	28	38	4.01	178	76	4	615.2	592	305	297	331	50

PITCHING & FIELDING:

In 1988, the Rangers thought that Craig McMurtry was on the verge of recapturing the effectiveness that won him recognition five years earlier as the National League's top rookie pitcher. He was used as a reliever and gave batters fits by having control of a fastball, slider and change-up, and being able to throw any of those pitches in any situation. He maintained none of that prowess in 1989, getting hit hard and having control troubles, too. Last year McMurtry's pitches were often up in the strike zone and lacked both speed and movement. His health adds another variable to the equation. McMurtry was on the disabled list with a strained rotator cuff, limiting him to only 19 appearances.

McMurtry brought a good move to first base over from the National League, where it was considered one of the best for a righthanded pitcher. Otherwise, his defensive skills are inconsistent. He'll make some nice plays and then throw some balls away.

OVERALL:

The Rangers have identified middle relief as an area that needs improvement. McMurtry will be one of the contestants, but the Rangers will want to see the consistency that eluded him in 1989.

MIKE
STANLEY

Position: DH/C
Bats: R **Throws:** R
Ht: 6' 0" **Wt:** 185

Opening Day Age: 26
Born: 6/25/63 in Ft.
Lauderdale, FL
ML Seasons: 4

Overall Statistics

	G	AB	R	H	D	T	HR	RBI	SB	BB	SO	AVG
1989	67	122	9	30	3	1	1	11	1	12	29	.246
Career	254	617	68	156	22	2	11	76	5	83	146	.253

HITTING, FIELDING, BASERUNNING:

After slumping at the plate for most of the 1989 season, Mike Stanley got a chance to play with some regularity in the final weeks and showed off a major league bat. He was 21 for 65 in the last 34 games, and the feeling was that Stanley finally got enough at-bats to iron out some of his flaws. Stanley has always been a high fastball hitter. He can be tied up by pitches that are in at the knees, and isn't much of a low-ball hitter under any circumstances.

Behind the plate, Stanley calls a good game and has a take-charge attitude. Pitchers like working with him for those talents. At the same time, it's accepted that he's not going to throw out many baserunners.

OVERALL:

Stanley doesn't hit well enough to be a DH and doesn't play a position well enough to hold it down regularly. Chances are he'll stay in the majors as the 23rd or 24th man on a roster because he can play several positions, including catcher, and hit with some authority. That versatility is his strong suit as much as any of his skills.

PITCHING:

Is Jim Acker a Toronto Brave or an Atlanta Blue Jay? Even Acker must have to gaze down at his uniform shirt from time to time in order to make sure he knows which of the two teams he's pitching for. A former number one draft choice of the Braves, Acker was drafted by Toronto and pitched effectively for the Jays from 1983 to 1986. Then he was traded back to Atlanta, where his work was strictly mediocre. Finally, last August, Blue Jay GM Pat Gillick decided the Jays needed to upgrade their middle relief corps. Who else would he deal for but Jim Acker?

Though seen by some as a minor move, the re-acquisition of Acker paid big dividends. In 14 games Acker recorded a 1.59 ERA, serving as a bridge between the Blue Jay starters and closer Tom Henke. While Acker wasn't the biggest factor in Toronto's drive to a division title, he was an important element. Without him they might have fallen short. And in the championship series against Oakland, Acker was one of the few Blue Jays who held his own. The veteran righty appeared in all five games, allowing only one earned run in 6.1 innings.

There isn't anything complicated in the way Acker works. At 31 he may not throw quite as hard as he used to, but he keeps the ball consistently down in the strike zone, getting lots of groundouts and double play balls. In addition to his excellent sinker, Acker has developed an effective change-up. He also throws a slider and has good control of all his pitches. Acker's pitches move, and he can get some strikeouts. He can be very tough on righthanded hitters. But basically Acker relies on his infielders to do the work.

FIELDING:

Maybe it's more experience, but Acker seems cooler now in fielding ground balls and bunts. Acker also has a good pickoff move and does an outstanding job of holding baserunners. Opposing base stealers were successful only 6 times in 15 attempts with Acker on the mound last year.

OVERALL:

Acker seems completely recovered from the elbow problems that had threatened his career in Atlanta. He knows his role and performs it well. Acker is eligible for free agency, but the Blue Jays want to keep him. No doubt the Braves want him back, as well.

JIM
ACKER

Position: RP
Bats: R **Throws:** R
Ht: 6' 2" **Wt:** 212

Opening Day Age: 31
Born: 9/24/58 in Freer, TX
ML Seasons: 7

Overall Statistics

	W	L	ERA	G	GS	Sv	IP	H	R	BB	SO	HR
1989	2	7	2.43	73	0	2	126.0	108	36	32	92	6
Career	26	40	3.78	337	28	28	693.2	693	326	251	373	53

Where They Hit the Ball

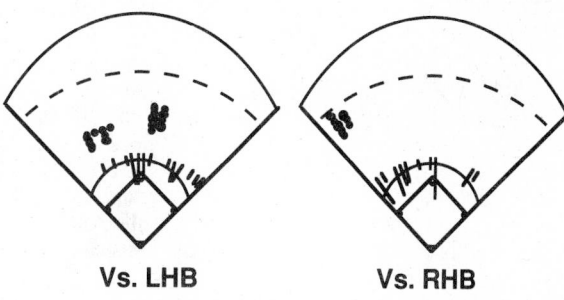

Vs. LHB   **Vs. RHB**

1989 Situational Stats

	W	L	ERA	Sv	IP		AB	H	HR	RBI	AVG
Home	1	3	1.97	0	64.0	LHB	224	64	3	17	.286
Road	1	4	2.90	2	62.0	RHB	232	44	3	22	.190
Day	2	2	3.21	0	33.2	Sc Pos	126	26	1	33	.206
Night	0	5	2.14	2	92.1	Clutch	167	42	0	14	.251

1989 Rankings (American League)

➡ Did not rank near the top or bottom in any category

HITTING:

Often criticized, George Bell has been the Jays' best run producer, averaging over 100 RBIs for the past six seasons. He's had problems with his right shoulder and his left knee for several years and that may have contributed to a reduction in power. In 1989, Bell's home run output (18) was his lowest since he became a regular in 1984. He went 38 games without a home run during June and July and did not hit one from Sept. 15 until his final at bat in the ALCS.

Though his homers were down, Bell survived by making adjustments. He hit more to right field and hit 41 doubles, a career high. Bell was tough in the clutch, batting a team-leading .337 with runners in scoring position. He was consistent down the stretch and had a 22 game hitting streak in the second half. Always known as a power hitter who doesn't strike out much -- his career high is 90, and that was back in 1985 -- Bell was more of a contact man than ever. He whiffed only 60 times, his lowest full-season total, and fanned only six times in his last 34 games.

A free swinger who seldom walks, Bell has always been known as a great fastball hitter. He doesn't like off speed stuff away from him, preferring somebody who challenges him. He's a low-ball hitter, and sometimes will hit a pitch almost in the dirt. In the ALCS, Oakland pitchers were successful by consistently working him inside.

BASERUNNING:

Because of his gimpy knee, Bell is no longer a threat to steal bases. He still runs aggressively and will go for the extra base at times. He slides hard, and will try to break up a double play.

FIELDING:

Bell is no threat to win a Gold Glove, but he's an adequate left fielder. He had a poor season afield in 1988, but played with considerably more enthusiasm last year after Cito Gaston replaced Williams. Bell's arm is strong and accurate when he's healthy, but a sore elbow bothered him last year and he had only four assists.

OVERALL:

George Bell wants to win. After ripping the Blue Jay fans, Bell was upset at the barrage of boos. But his bat won the fans over. He's a gamer and will play hurt. When he couldn't throw at the end of the season because of his sore elbow, he willingly DH'd. Even with a reduced home run output, Bell is a very valuable player.

GEORGE BELL

Position: LF/DH
Bats: R **Throws:** R
Ht: 6' 1" **Wt:** 202

Opening Day Age: 30
Born: 10/21/59 in San Pedro de Macoris, Dominican Republic
ML Seasons: 8

Overall Statistics

	G	AB	R	H	D	T	HR	RBI	SB	BB	SO	AVG
1989	153	613	88	182	41	2	18	104	4	33	60	.297
Career	1039	3966	574	1145	212	32	181	654	56	223	484	.289

Where He Hits the Ball

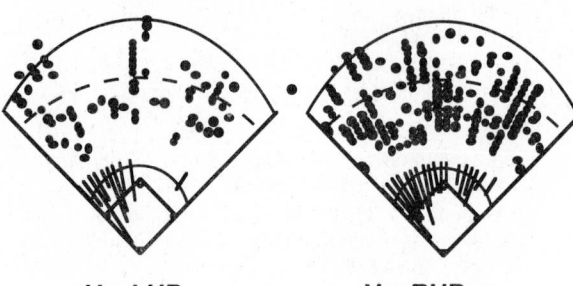

Vs. LHP   **Vs. RHP**

1989 Situational Stats

	AB	H	HR	RBI	AVG		AB	H	HR	RBI	AVG
Home	281	86	8	47	.306	LHP	178	51	9	39	.287
Road	332	96	10	57	.289	RHP	435	131	9	65	.301
Day	192	47	3	29	.245	Sc Pos	172	58	4	85	.337
Night	421	135	15	75	.321	Clutch	97	32	3	20	.330

1989 Rankings (American League)

→ 1st in sacrifice flies (14)

→ 4th in doubles (41)

→ 6th in hitting on an 0-2 count (.318) - *players with 10 PA on an 0-2 count*

→ 7th in hitting with runners in scoring position (.337) - *players with 100 PA with runners in scoring position*

→ Led the Blue Jays in batting average (.297), at bats (613), hits (182), singles (121), doubles (41), RBI (104), sacrifice flies (14), GDPs (18), highest percentage of swings put into play (51.8%), hitting with runners in scoring position, hitting in the clutch (.330) and hitting on an 0-2 count

HITTING:

Pat Borders is a fine hitting prospect who has batted over .300 at numerous minor league stops. He has assumed the role that was shouldered for years by Buck Martinez. Borders has the hitting talent to play every day, but the lefty-swinging Ernie Whitt hasn't shown many signs of losing his hitting stroke. So Borders has been restricted to playing against left-handers, and in that role he's done well. Borders' overall figures declined last year from his '88 numbers, but he hit .281 against lefties, which is what the Blue Jays were most interested in.

As a hitter Borders is aggressive with a capital A. In his rookie debut in '88, Borders demonstrated his love for the first pitch fastball, but word soon got around. Last year he saw a steady diet of breaking pitches, and he didn't always respond well to it. In almost every category, his batting figures declined. His average dropped from .273 to .257; his slugging percentage fell from .448 to .349; his home runs declined from five to three. Borders has not shown the inclination to take a walk, and pitchers often won't bother to throw him strikes. After drawing only three walks in 160 plate appearances as a rookie, Borders drew 11 in 256 a year ago -- an improvement, but not by much. At the same time, he almost doubled his strikeouts, going from 24 to 45. Borders will have to stop chasing bad pitches if he's going to improve as a hitter.

BASERUNNING:

Borders is a big man who weighs over 200 pounds and runs like most catchers. He got his first two career stolen bases last year, but he's no threat on the bases. As a baserunner he's strictly the station-to-station type.

FIELDING:

A converted infielder, Borders is still learning the catching position. For the most part he throws well, but he's very aggressive and has a tendency to rush. He did gun down 17 of 48 runners attempting to steal, a decent percentage, and got three pickoffs. When Borders was in a hitting slump early in the season it bothered him defensively, and Gaston let him DH in order to let him concentrate on his hitting.

OVERALL:

Borders is an ideal platoon catcher who should continue to improve with experience. He needs to work on his plate discipline and improve against breaking stuff, but he has the talent. With Whitt getting older, Gaston may need to give him some starts against righthanded pitching.

PAT BORDERS

Position: C/DH
Bats: R **Throws:** R
Ht: 6' 2" **Wt:** 205

Opening Day Age: 26
Born: 5/14/63 in Columbus, OH
ML Seasons: 2

Overall Statistics

	G	AB	R	H	D	T	HR	RBI	SB	BB	SO	AVG
1989	94	241	22	62	11	1	3	29	2	11	45	.257
Career	150	395	37	104	17	4	8	50	2	14	69	.263

Where He Hits the Ball

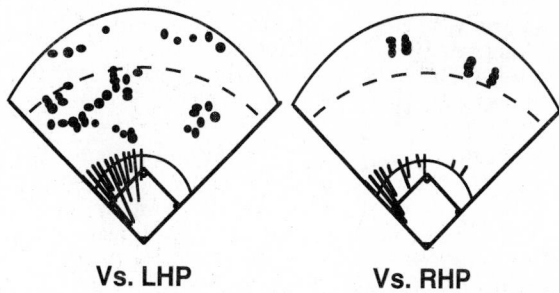

Vs. LHP   **Vs. RHP**

1989 Situational Stats

	AB	H	HR	RBI	AVG		AB	H	HR	RBI	AVG
Home	105	26	1	13	.248	LHP	171	48	2	25	.281
Road	136	36	2	16	.265	RHP	70	14	1	4	.200
Day	76	14	1	9	.184	Sc Pos	59	17	1	25	.288
Night	165	48	2	20	.291	Clutch	46	12	1	6	.261

1989 Rankings (American League)

➡ Did not rank near the top or bottom in any category

PITCHING:

John Cerutti, a veteran lefty, handled the difficult starter/reliever swingman role with great effectiveness for three seasons. Cerutti always wanted to be a regular starter, however, and he finally got his chance last year. Though not the biggest winner on the Toronto staff -- his record was only 11 and 11 -- Cerutti was the Jays' most consistent pitcher. In his first 22 starts, Cerutti never allowed over four earned runs, and he allowed as many as four on only three occasions. Cerutti's 3.07 ERA was the lowest of any Toronto starter and among the best in the league. Unfortunately, he did not get the offensive support necessary to get a lot of wins. Cerutti failed to last five innings only three times, and two of those were in August when he had a brief slump, going winless in four successive starts.

Prior to '89 Cerutti had relied mostly on a decent fastball that can reach the high eighties, and a good change-up. He'd always kept the ball up in the strike zone, giving up a lot of flyballs and a lot of home runs as well -- as many as 30 in a season (1987). But last spring Cerutti worked hard to develop a sinker. As a result he was more effective than ever before, and especially got more groundball outs. He even threw the sinker too much on occasion, which was the cause of his brief slump. Cerutti has not really turned into a groundball pitcher however. Despite his new pitch, he led the Jays in home runs allowed with 19.

FIELDING:

Cerutti is a good glove man and gets a lot of practice on balls hit right back at him. He's not as quick getting off the mound to cover first as Stieb or Key, but he's not a liability. Cerutti has always been good at holding runners, with a deceptive pickoff move that caught Rickey Henderson in last year's playoffs. Only 12 of the 26 runners who tried to steal off Cerutti were successful.

OVERALL:

Big and strong, Cerutti finally logged over 200 innings for the first time in his career last season. His versatility cost him at the end of last year, when the Jays put him in the bullpen for the playoffs in order to have a second lefty there. He got no significant work in the playoffs and will probably return to the regular rotation in 1990.

JOHN CERUTTI

Position: SP
Bats: L **Throws:** L
Ht: 6' 2" **Wt:** 200

Opening Day Age: 29
Born: 4/28/60 in Albany, NY
ML Seasons: 5

Overall Statistics

	W	L	ERA	G	GS	Sv	IP	H	R	BB	SO	HR
1989	11	11	3.07	33	31	0	205.1	214	90	53	69	19
Career	37	28	3.67	161	85	2	632.1	638	301	205	320	87

Where They Hit the Ball

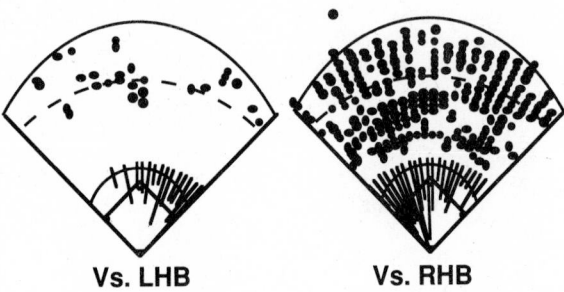

Vs. LHB   Vs. RHB

1989 Situational Stats

	W	L	ERA	Sv	IP		AB	H	HR	RBI	AVG
Home	5	5	2.63	0	102.2	LHB	124	27	3	7	.218
Road	6	6	3.51	0	102.2	RHB	661	187	16	68	.283
Day	3	4	3.08	0	79.0	Sc Pos	144	38	4	53	.264
Night	8	7	3.06	0	126.1	Clutch	81	25	2	5	.309

1989 Rankings (American League)

- ➡ 2nd in caught stealing (14)
- ➡ 3rd in pickoff throws (249) and lowest strikeouts per 9 innings (3.0) - *pitchers with 162 IP*
- ➡ 5th in ERA at home (2.63) and lowest stolen base percentage allowed (46.2%)
- ➡ 7th in lowest strikeout/walk ratio (1.30)
- ➡ 9th in ERA (3.07)
- ➡ Led the Blue Jays in ERA, caught stealing, home runs allowed (19), pickoff throws, lowest stolen base percentage allowed and ERA at home

JUNIOR FELIX

Position: RF/CF
Bats: B **Throws:** R
Ht: 5'11" **Wt:** 165

Opening Day Age: 22
Born: 10/3/67 in Laguna Sabada, Dominican Republic
ML Seasons: 1

HITTING:

Not many rookies have broken in like Junior Felix did a year ago. He homered in his first at bat in the AL, just as he had done in Triple A. For a while he hit up a storm, with six triples, seven homers and 41 RBIs in his first 58 games. But then Felix cooled off completely, with only four ribbies in the second half. He spent a lot of time on the bench as the Blue Jays were driving to a division title.

Despite the hot-and-cold performance, Felix remains a tremendous prospect. He has both speed and power, an ideal combination. A switch-hitter, he was much stronger from the left side. Either way, he loved the fastball but had a lot of trouble with breaking stuff. Felix did not show a lot of discipline. He seldom walked and struck out almost once in every four at bats. He has a strong tendency to overswing.

With his speed, all Felix really needs to do is put the ball in play. He can beat out a lot of grounders for hits, and is an excellent bunter. Typical of his Jekyll and Hyde season, Felix had 13 bunt singles by July 17, but none thereafter. Part of his second half slump may have been due to injuries. He hurt one shoulder in a headfirst slide at the plate, and later jammed the other one in a collision with an outfield fence. By the time Felix was healthy, the Jays had added Mookie Wilson.

BASERUNNING:

Felix has tremendous speed on the bases. He stole 18 bases, but with 12 caught stealings, he needs to improve in that area. He has problems getting the proper lead off first, and he must eliminate his tendency to be foolishly over-aggressive.

FIELDING:

Felix has good arm strength, but needs to improve his mechanics getting rid of the ball. He was used more in right than center, but his speed makes him a natural for the spacious center field of the SkyDome. Felix almost caused a number of collisions by trying to catch everything, and needs to become more of a team player.

OVERALL:

Only 22, Felix has fantastic potential. He has surprising power for his size. He should be a star if he doesn't try to do everything himself, and learns to adjust to the ups-and-downs of major league play.

Overall Statistics

	G	AB	R	H	D	T	HR	RBI	SB	BB	SO	AVG
1989	110	415	62	107	14	8	9	46	18	33	101	.258
Career	110	415	62	107	14	8	9	46	18	33	101	.258

Where He Hits the Ball

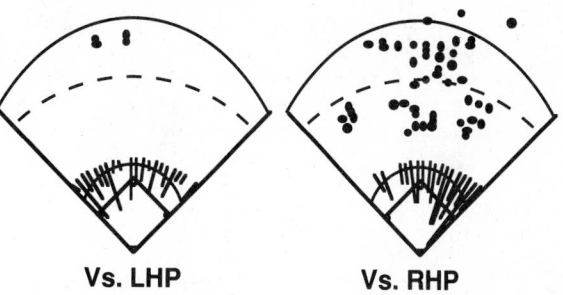

Vs. LHP   Vs. RHP

1989 Situational Stats

	AB	H	HR	RBI	AVG		AB	H	HR	RBI	AVG
Home	199	50	4	16	.251	LHP	129	26	2	15	.202
Road	216	57	5	30	.264	RHP	286	81	7	31	.283
Day	136	38	3	16	.279	Sc Pos	111	27	3	38	.243
Night	279	69	6	30	.247	Clutch	67	15	4	11	.224

1989 Rankings (American League)

- ➡ 3rd in worst stolen base percentage (60.0%) - *players with 20 stolen base attempts*
- ➡ 4th in lowest batting average vs. lefthanded pitchers (.202) - *players with 125 PA vs. LHP*
- ➡ 8th in triples (8) and bunts in play (24)
- ➡ 9th in caught stealing (12)
- ➡ Led the Blue Jays in caught stealing, least GDPs per GDP situation (7.0%) and batting on a 3-1 count (.455)

GREAT RANGE

TONY FERNANDEZ

Position: SS
Bats: B **Throws:** R
Ht: 6' 2" **Wt:** 170

Opening Day Age: 27
Born: 6/30/62 in San
Pedro de Macoris,
Dominican Republic
ML Seasons: 7

HITTING:

Tony Fernandez is an outstanding shortstop who batted .322 in 1987, but he saw his average tumble all the way to .257 last year. Tony's season started disastrously when he was hit in the face by a Cecilio Guante pitch during the first week. Fernandez missed a month with a fractured jaw, and when he returned he was never completely able to regain his batting stroke. The season did have its pluses. Fernandez belted 11 homers, a career high, and probably would have set a career high in RBIs if he hadn't missed so much time with the broken jaw.

A good contact hitter, Fernandez jumps at pitches early in the count and seldom either walks or strikes out. He's primarily a lowball hitter from the left side, a highball hitter from the right side, and he's a fine bunter. Fernandez has been a line drive hitter throughout his career, but he hit the ball in the air much more during 1989. That's reflected in Tony's career-high 10 sacrifice flies (he'd never had more than four in any previous season) and in the 11 homers. The homer total which would have been greater if he hadn't been playing in the spacious SkyDome -- nine of Fernandez' 11 homers came on the road.

BASERUNNING:

Fernandez had a career-high 32 steals in 1987 before tearing up his left knee. It took him a long time to recover, but in '89 he finally appeared to be running without a problem. Tony's 22 steals in 28 attempts was his best percentage ever, and his nine triples matched his second best total.

FIELDING:

Gold Glover Fernandez was at his best during 1989, committing only six errors to set a league record. Tony still tracks down balls in the hole, but he no longer tries to make a throw on everything, and thus commits fewer throwing errors. Fernandez still has amazing agility and the ability to throw from any position.

OVERALL:

Cito Gaston has always insisted that Fernandez will eventually hit 15 or more homers. Though the SkyDome won't help Tony any, Gaston may well be right. Tony's reduced average last year was probably due to both swinging for more for power and the after-effects of getting hit in the face. It remains to be seen whether he'll hit .322 again, but Fernandez is an outstanding shortstop even if he only hits as well as he did in 1989.

Overall Statistics

	G	AB	R	H	D	T	HR	RBI	SB	BB	SO	AVG
1989	140	573	64	147	25	9	11	64	22	29	51	.257
Career	867	3317	426	967	165	44	36	338	112	214	274	.292

Where He Hits the Ball

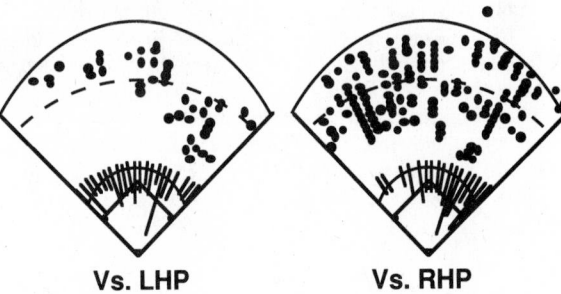

Vs. LHP   **Vs. RHP**

1989 Situational Stats

	AB	H	HR	RBI	AVG		AB	H	HR	RBI	AVG
Home	276	66	2	24	.239	LHP	185	50	2	21	.270
Road	297	81	9	40	.273	RHP	388	97	9	43	.250
Day	170	46	2	12	.271	Sc Pos	127	32	2	50	.252
Night	403	101	9	52	.251	Clutch	82	21	1	7	.256

1989 Rankings (American League)

➡ 4th in triples (9)

➡ 5th in sacrifice flies (10) and lowest on-base average (.291) - *players with 502 PA*

➡ 9th in stolen base percentage (78.6%)

➡ Led the Blue Jays in triples, grounder/flyball ratio (1.17), stolen base percentage and lowest percentage of swings that missed (11.4%)

➡ Led AL Shortstops in triples, sacrifice flies and stolen base success percentage

PITCHING:

Mike Flanagan, now 38, has seen glorious days. He was the Cy Young Award winner in 1979, when he won 23 games and started twice in the World Series. The Blue Jays trusted Flanagan enough to start him in the crucial fourth game of the playoffs last year, but his current plight is best reflected in the mammoth home run Jose Canseco hit off him in that game. Flanagan took the tape measure job in stride, as always, but the truth is that he may be nearing the end of a fine career which has produced 163 victories.

Flanagan still has his good outings, but he doesn't have consistently good games the way he used to. He averaged less than six innings per start last year, and was kayoed eight times in five or less innings. Never an overpowering pitcher, Flanagan needs a good fastball to set up his great breaking ball. But his fastball these days barely reaches the low eighties and he's no longer able to finish off a hitter: his strikeout ratio of 2.46 strikeouts per nine innings last year was one of the lowest in the majors. More than most pitchers, Flanagan needs pinpoint control in order to be effective. He moves the ball around and changes speeds and deliveries, coming in sidearm at times against lefthanded hitters. Flanagan continued to be very effective against lefty swingers last year, holding them to a .206 average with no homers. But he was lit up by righties, especially on days when his control was off even a little.

FIELDING:

Still a stylish fielder, Flanagan handles both bunts and ground balls well, and is good at covering first base. He's always been known for his good pickoff move, but Flanagan has a slow delivery to home plate. He also needs to concentrate on the hitter more these days, and the result is that he's become pretty easy to steal on.

OVERALL:

With a flock of good young arms coming along from the Jays farm system, Flanagan will have difficulty sticking in the rotation for the final year of his contact. It would not be a great shock if he's traded or released. One factor greatly in his favor is that all the younger Toronto pitchers look up to him. He has a great sense of humor and is a good man to have in the clubhouse. That may not be enough to save his job, however.

MIKE FLANAGAN

Position: SP
Bats: L **Throws:** L
Ht: 6' 0" **Wt:** 195

Opening Day Age: 38
Born: 12/16/51 in Manchester, NH
ML Seasons: 15

Overall Statistics

	W	L	ERA	G	GS	Sv	IP	H	R	BB	SO	HR
1989	8	10	3.93	30	30	0	171.2	186	82	47	47	10
Career	163	134	3.89	415	398	1	2616.2	2644	1226	834	1414	239

Where They Hit the Ball

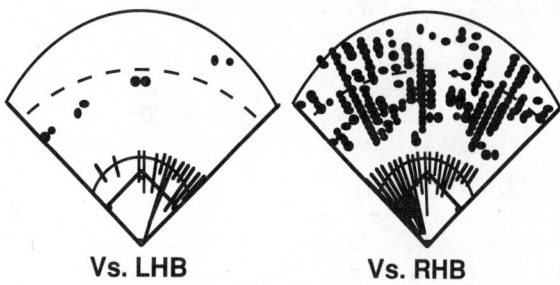

Vs. LHB   **Vs. RHB**

1989 Situational Stats

	W	L	ERA	Sv	IP		AB	H	HR	RBI	AVG
Home	5	4	3.51	0	84.2	LHB	97	20	0	7	.206
Road	3	6	4.34	0	87.0	RHB	561	166	10	65	.296
Day	1	4	3.92	0	43.2	Sc Pos	138	47	2	60	.341
Night	7	6	3.94	0	128.0	Clutch	41	8	0	2	.195

1989 Rankings (American League)

- ➡ 1st in lowest strikeouts per 9 innings (2.5) - *pitchers with 162 IP*
- ➡ 2nd in lowest strikeout/walk ratio (1.0)
- ➡ 3rd in GDPs per 9 innings (1.21)
- ➡ 4th in fewest pitches thrown per batter (3.4)
- ➡ 5th in highest opponent batting average (.283)
- ➡ Led the Blue Jays in GDPs induced (23), grounder/flyball ratio (1.62), fewest pitches thrown per batter and GDPs per nine innings

HITTING:

In his third full season with Toronto, Kelly Gruber continued to improve as a hitter. Gruber's .290 average, 18 home runs, 83 runs scored and .448 slugging average were all career highs. He did this while becoming more of a contact man than ever. In three seasons Gruber has cut his strikeout rate almost in half, going from one per 4.9 at bats in 1987 to one per 9.1 at bats a year ago. In 1989 Gruber fanned only 60 times, a remarkably low total for a power hitter. On the debit side, he drew only 30 walks, an unacceptably low total.

Gruber has always been a good high fastball hitter, but as he's matured he's begun using the entire field. His RBI total last year was a little disappointing, dropping to 73 after he'd driven in 81 in 1988. But that was due in good part to the fact that the Jays had no reliable on-base men at the top of their lineup. An injury also hampered him. Gruber was hitting .308 at the All-Star break, and seemed on his way to a banner season. Then he injured his right hand in a collision with umpire Don Denkinger on August 9. It was the second year in a row he was slowed by a hand injury in August, and he had a difficult time recovering from it.

BASERUNNING:

Gruber runs aggressively, taking the extra base whenever possible. But he pays a price for that aggressiveness. His nagging hand injuries have sometimes resulted from his headfirst slides on the bases. Gruber may need to return to a conventional feet first slide. His stolen base total slipped from 23 in 1988 to 10 a year ago, but that was due in large part to his injuries.

FIELDING:

A fine athlete, Gruber has great range and an outstanding arm, but he made too many errors (22). Part of this resulted from his versatility. When the Jays had some injuries, Gruber played the outfield, and in his first game back in the infield he had three errors. He'll improve.

OVERALL:

At age 27, and in only his second season as a regular, Gruber was picked as an extra man on the All-Star squad because of his versatility. Kelly can only get better. He's capable of hitting .300 with 25 homers and 100 RBIs, but he'll have to keep his hands out of trouble.

KELLY GRUBER

Position: 3B/RF
Bats: R **Throws:** R
Ht: 6' 0" **Wt:** 185

Opening Day Age: 28
Born: 2/26/62 in Bellaire, TX
ML Seasons: 6

Overall Statistics

	G	AB	R	H	D	T	HR	RBI	SB	BB	SO	AVG
1989	135	545	83	158	24	4	18	73	10	30	60	.290
Career	538	1627	229	428	75	13	52	208	47	90	256	.263

Where He Hits the Ball

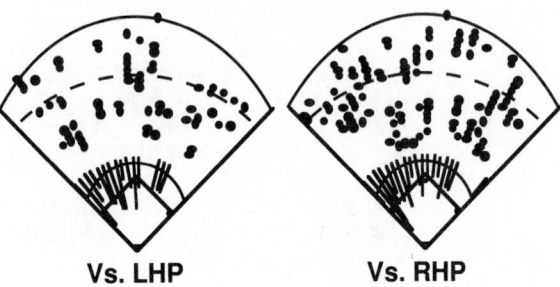

Vs. LHP   **Vs. RHP**

1989 Situational Stats

	AB	H	HR	RBI	AVG		AB	H	HR	RBI	AVG
Home	278	82	8	34	.295	LHP	166	54	7	23	.325
Road	267	76	10	39	.285	RHP	379	104	11	50	.274
Day	174	45	2	23	.259	Sc Pos	141	39	4	55	.277
Night	371	113	16	50	.305	Clutch	81	23	2	12	.284

1989 Rankings (American League)

- ➡ 2nd in errors (22)
- ➡ 5th in most runs scored per time on base (38.2%) - *players with 502 PA*
- ➡ 10th in slugging percentage vs. lefthanded pitchers (.509) - *players with 125 PA vs. LHP*
- ➡ Led the Blue Jays in errors, runs scored per time on base and hitting vs. lefthanded pitchers (.325)
- ➡ Led AL Third Basemen in errors and runs scored per time on base

STOPPER

TOM HENKE

Position: RP
Bats: R **Throws:** R
Ht: 6' 5" **Wt:** 225

Opening Day Age: 32
Born: 12/21/57 in
Kansas City, MO
ML Seasons: 8

PITCHING:

Though he finished the year with very strong numbers, Tom Henke had an unusual season in 1989. To his credit Henke fought his way back from a disastrous first half, then in the second half pitched as good as he ever has.

Henke's early-season problems started when Ruben Sierra of the Rangers tagged him for a game winning home run during the first week of the season. Then Mark McGwire nailed him for a grand slam on May 2. Henke's confidence was shattered, and soon manager Jimy Williams lost confidence in his ace reliever. Henke didn't pitch effectively enough to get the work he needed to be sharp. Soon, he wasn't even being used in save situations.

Henke didn't get a save from April 7 until June 23, but began righting himself after the Jays fired Williams and made Cito Gaston their new manager. Gaston restored Henke to the closer's role and the righthander finished with 17 saves in 20 chances. He was remarkably consistent and didn't blow a save from May 2 to September 19. Not only did Henke regain full velocity on his 90s plus fastball, but he also had an effective forkball to go with it. Opposing batters averaged only .205 against him, one of the best marks in the league, and he struck out 116 men in 89 innings.

The Henke of late-season '89 was as overpowering as he's ever been in his career. He made five appearances in the crucial last week of the season, garnering three saves and only faltering once when he blew a save in Detroit. Fittingly, he was on the mound to strike out Larry Sheets for the final out in the Sept. 30 pennant clincher.

FIELDING:

Like many hard throwers, Henke is not the most agile of fielders. He's only average in covering first base. Henke has a decent move to first and does a better job of holding runners than most power pitchers.

OVERALL:

Now 32, Henke is as much of a flamethrower as ever. From July 2 until September 2, he had at least one strikeout in every outing. He should benefit from having fought his way through adversity. He's got the forkball mastered to go with his fastball, and should be a dominant reliever for several more years.

Overall Statistics

	W	L	ERA	G	GS	Sv	IP	H	R	BB	SO	HR
1989	8	3	1.92	64	0	20	89.0	66	20	25	116	5
Career	27	22	2.81	320	0	122	442.1	346	150	146	521	32

Where They Hit the Ball

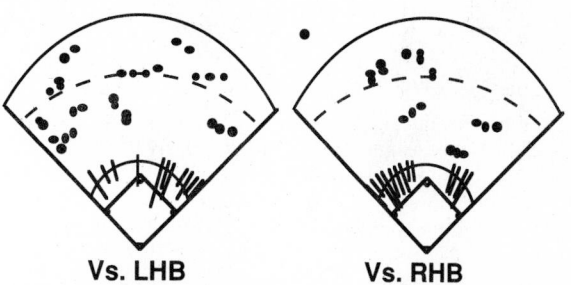

Vs. LHB   **Vs. RHB**

1989 Situational Stats

	W	L	ERA	Sv	IP		AB	H	HR	RBI	AVG
Home	6	0	2.48	7	36.1	LHB	149	29	3	18	.195
Road	2	3	1.54	13	52.2	RHB	173	37	2	18	.214
Day	1	2	4.42	4	18.1	Sc Pos	85	20	4	34	.235
Night	7	1	1.27	16	70.2	Clutch	198	38	5	31	.192

1989 Rankings (American League)

- ➡ 4th in save percentage (83.3%), worst first batter efficiency (.311) and games finished (56)

- ➡ 6th in lowest batting average vs. lefthanded batters - *pitchers facing 125 LHB*

- ➡ 7th in strikeouts per 9 innings (11.7) - *all league pitchers*

- ➡ Led the Blue Jays in saves (20), games finished, hits per inning (.74), lowest batting average vs. lefthanded batters and save percentage

PINPOINT CONTROL

JIMMY KEY

Position: SP
Bats: R **Throws:** L
Ht: 6' 1" **Wt:** 190

Opening Day Age: 28
Born: 4/22/61 in Huntsville, AL
ML Seasons: 6

PITCHING:

Jimmy Key was the American League ERA leader in 1987, but he has been slowed by arm injuries the last two seasons. In 1988 Key missed 10 weeks after undergoing elbow surgery, but came back to pitch effectively, with a 12-5 record and a 3.29 ERA in 21 starts. He seemed fully recovered, and in 1989 it looked for awhile like he might become the Jays' first 20-game winner. Key got off to a 6-2 start last year, but then suddenly ran into a prolonged slump, losing 11 of his next 12 decisions. His arm clearly wasn't right, and in August he had to be put on the disabled list again with a strained elbow. Key rested the arm for 15 days, and when he returned he was once again the Key of old. He was brilliant in the Jays' pennant drive, winning six of his last seven decisions with a 3.39 ERA. In the playoffs Key recorded the Blue Jays' only victory against Oakland. Once more Key seemed fully recovered. But then he revealed that he'd experienced some shoulder fatigue in the late innings after his return. A post-season examination revealed a slight tear in the rotator cuff of his left shoulder.

When healthy, Key rates as one of the top lefties in the American League. He doesn't get nearly the publicity that Teddy Higuera does, but in fact his stats rate only a little below the Milwaukee lefty's. Over the past five years Higuera is 78-44 with a 3.28 ERA. Key, working 32 fewer innings, is 70-44 with the same 3.28 ERA. Key is not overpowering, but he has a great curve ball, a good fastball and change-up, and uncanny control. He did not walk a batter in 15 of his 33 starts. He moves the ball around, inside and out, and changes speeds. He's extremely tough against left-handed hitters, holding them to a .200 average (45 for 225) over the last two years while allowing only three homers.

FIELDING:

Key is one of the best fielding pitchers in the league. He's quick as a cat at pouncing on bunts, and also good on balls hit back at him. His pickoff move is excellent, and few runners (Rickey Henderson excepted) even try to run on him.

OVERALL:

Key is an outstanding pitcher when healthy, but he has had elbow and shoulder problems the last two seasons. He's missed time and suffered reduced effectiveness. Blue Jay followers can only hope their ace lefty will be able to make a complete recovery in 1990.

Overall Statistics

	W	L	ERA	G	GS	Sv	IP	H	R	BB	SO	HR
1989	13	14	3.88	33	33	0	216.0	226	99	27	118	18
Career	74	49	3.36	224	157	10	1115.0	1043	459	279	614	109

Where They Hit the Ball

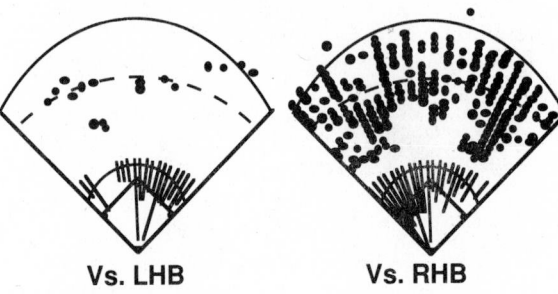

Vs. LHB   **Vs. RHB**

1989 Situational Stats

	W	L	ERA	Sv	IP		AB	H	HR	RBI	AVG
Home	7	8	3.81	0	120.1	LHB	150	34	2	19	.227
Road	6	6	3.95	0	95.2	RHB	688	192	16	72	.279
Day	3	5	4.58	0	55.0	Sc Pos	173	49	4	69	.283
Night	10	9	3.63	0	161.0	Clutch	67	17	1	6	.254

1989 Rankings (American League)

- ➝ 2nd in strikeout/walk ratio (4.37) - *pitchers with 162 IP*
- ➝ 4th in losses (14)
- ➝ 5th in least baserunners per 9 innings (10.7)
- ➝ 6th in lowest on-base average allowed (.292)
- ➝ 9th in hits allowed (226) and least pitches thrown per batter (3.5)
- ➝ Led the Blue Jays in losses, games started (33), complete games (5), innings (216), hits allowed, batters faced (886), pitches thrown (3,121), least baserunners per 9 innings, lowest on-base average allowed and strikeouts per 9 innings (4.9) - *team players with 162 IP*

HITTING:

Manny Lee is only 24 years old, but he's already a five year veteran. Lee has never really been a regular -- he's yet to bat 400 times in a season -- and has mostly played on and off at second base or filled in for Tony Fernandez at shortstop when Tony's been injured. In that role Lee has been a valuable performer, but he'd like the opportunity to do more.

In 1989 Lee finally worked mainly as a platoon second baseman, alternating with Nelson Liriano. It's a role in which he can have considerable value. Though a switch-hitter, Lee is much stronger as a righthanded batter. Over the last three seasons, he has hit .313, .336 and .295 batting righty. As a lefty swinger he's batted .219, .268 and .230. Either way he doesn't have much power. Lee also has little plate discipline. He seldom draws a walk and last year struck out once for every five times at bat, a very high strikeout ratio for a singles hitter.

Lee is a little man at 5'9" and 161 pounds; he may need to cut down on his swing in order to be more effective. He's often simply overpowered by a good fastball, and like most anxious hitters, he's prone to chasing breaking pitches out of the strike zone. He has some hitting talent, as his figures batting righty would indicate. He should improve with experience and hard work.

BASERUNNING:

Lee stole 24 bases in class A ball back in 1984, but his overall speed is only a little above average, if that. As a major leaguer he's stolen only 10 bases in five years while getting thrown out the same number of times. Lee's four steals in 1989 were a career high.

FIELDING:

Lee's original position was shortstop and that's where he would prefer to play. He did a fine job last year when Tony Fernandez was injured, showing good range. But with the Jays Lee has played mostly at second base. He has shown steady improvement in turning the double play and mastering the position.

OVERALL:

Despite his weakness as a lefthanded hitter, Lee has a .265 lifetime average. That's acceptable for a good gloveman, and many people still think he'd be a fine everyday shortstop. Considering his youth and the shortage of quality major league shortstops, Lee would appear to be a good bet to be traded.

MANNY LEE

Position: 2B/3B/SS
Bats: B **Throws:** R
Ht: 5' 9" **Wt:** 161

Opening Day Age: 24
Born: 6/17/65 in San Pedro de Macoris, Dominican Republic
ML Seasons: 5

Overall Statistics

	G	AB	R	H	D	T	HR	RBI	SB	BB	SO	AVG
1989	99	300	27	78	9	2	3	34	4	20	60	.260
Career	370	920	96	244	27	9	7	90	10	58	156	.265

Where He Hits the Ball

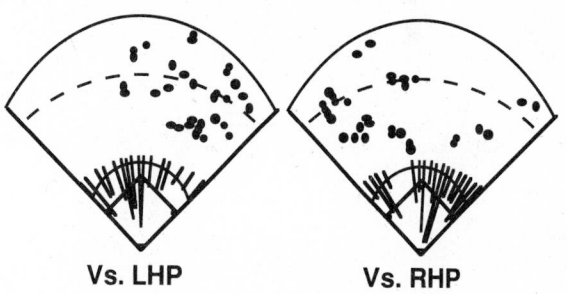

Vs. LHP   **Vs. RHP**

1989 Situational Stats

	AB	H	HR	RBI	AVG		AB	H	HR	RBI	AVG
Home	126	30	1	13	.238	LHP	139	41	1	20	.295
Road	174	48	2	21	.276	RHP	161	37	2	14	.230
Day	80	18	1	11	.225	Sc Pos	75	21	1	29	.280
Night	220	60	2	23	.273	Clutch	56	13	1	9	.232

1989 Rankings (American League)

➡ Did not rank near the top or bottom in any category

HITTING:

On the surface, Nelson Liriano had a fairly nondescript 1989 season. He followed a .264 average in 1988 with a .263 year in '89. For the most part he worked in a second base platoon with Manny Lee, but that was mainly for Lee's benefit. Both Lee and Liriano are switch-hitters, but Lee has always hit better from the right side, while Liriano's figures are virtually identical either way. He does have slightly more power from the left side.

But Liriano caused some excitement with his bat during 1989. Within a span of five days in April, he spoiled two no-hitters in the ninth inning. On April 23, Liriano broke up Nolan Ryan's bid for a sixth no-hitter with a one-out triple in the ninth inning. Five days later, Liriano ruined Kirk McCaskill's no-hitter with a ninth inning double. Liriano stayed hot with his bat in the early season, hitting .341 in May and winning an American League Player of the Week Award during that month. His stickwork helped keep the Blue Jays afloat when they were floundering in the early weeks.

Liriano's biggest hit of the year was a bases-loaded shot off the right field fence to win a crucial Sept. 19 game against the Red Sox. That helped cement his reputation as a good clutch hitter. Liriano hit well with runners in scoring position in both '88 and '89. He had 53 RBIs in only 418 at bats in 1989, when he also came through with four pinch hits in seven at bats, including two doubles and a home run. Liriano is also the best bunter on the Blue Jay team. He's a good breaking ball hitter and has some patience at the plate.

BASERUNNING:

Liriano runs well, with a career-high 16 steals a year ago. He has the potential to increase his stolen base total to 20 or more. He's a fairly smart baserunner.

FIELDING:

Though not as good a glove man as Manny Lee, Liriano has good range at second. He also turns the double play very well. He needs to improve on pop-ups.

OVERALL:

Liriano looked like the Jays' second baseman of the future when he first came up late in 1987. He lost the job when he failed to hit early in '88, but redeemed himself a lot last year. He's a tough out and might get the job fulltime if Lee is traded.

NELSON LIRIANO

Position: 2B
Bats: B **Throws:** R
Ht: 5'10" **Wt:** 165

Opening Day Age: 25
Born: 6/3/64 in Puerto Plata, Dominican Republic
ML Seasons: 3

Overall Statistics

	G	AB	R	H	D	T	HR	RBI	SB	BB	SO	AVG
1989	132	418	51	110	26	3	5	53	16	43	51	.263
Career	268	852	116	221	38	7	10	86	41	70	113	.259

Where He Hits the Ball

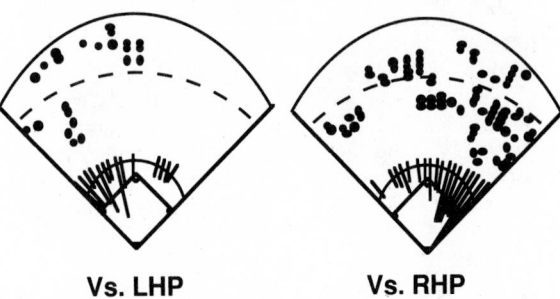

| Vs. LHP | Vs. RHP |

1989 Situational Stats

	AB	H	HR	RBI	AVG		AB	H	HR	RBI	AVG
Home	208	52	3	28	.250	LHP	109	29	0	16	.266
Road	210	58	2	25	.276	RHP	309	81	5	37	.262
Day	138	38	0	22	.275	Sc Pos	120	37	1	47	.308
Night	280	72	5	31	.257	Clutch	85	20	0	13	.235

1989 Rankings (American League)

→ 3rd in bunts in play (36)

→ 4th in hitting with the bases loaded (.500) - *players with 10 PA with the bases loaded*

→ Led the Blue Jays in sacrifice bunts (10), bunts in play, percentage of swings put into play (55.1%), steals of third (2), batting average with 2 strikes (.252) and hitting with the bases loaded

HITTING:

Fred McGriff had an outstanding season in 1989, but his year was soured somewhat by a late-season slump. McGriff hit only one home run in his last 24 games, and none in the championship series against Oakland. Worse still, he did not have an extra base hit after September 13. Down the stretch and in the playoffs, McGriff did not respond well to the pennant pressure. One problem was that pitchers stopped throwing him strikes. McGriff, who was second in the league with 119 walks, drew 30 in his final 28 games. Finally the Jays shifted him to the third slot in the batting order, ahead of George Bell. But even that change didn't help McGriff snap out of his slump.

Even with the muted finish, McGriff had great numbers for the second straight year. He led the league with 36 homers and was fifth in runs scored, second in slugging percentage, fourth in on-base percentage and second in home run frequency. Over the last two years McGriff has averaged 35 homers, 87 RBIs, 99 runs scored and 99 walks. The Blue Jays will take those figures any day, and clearly McGriff has established himself as one of the top sluggers in baseball.

McGriff is a man for all fields -- almost half of his 36 homers were hit to left and left center. It's when he tries to pull everything that he gets into trouble. Cito Gaston, as his hitting guru, constantly preaches patience and laying off bad pitches; McGriff has absorbed those lessons thoroughly. McGriff has learned to lay off the high fastball away, and with two strikes, to shun the pitch he can't drive. Lefthanders still bother him; only five of McGriff's 36 homers came off southpaws.

BASERUNNING:

A big man, McGriff does not have great speed but can steal a base occasionally. He sometimes makes running mistakes by not going all out until the ball reaches the outfield.

FIELDING:

After leading the league in fielding percentage with only five errors in 1988, McGriff committed 17 in '89. Coach Mike Squires worked with him, and he improved his range, but many of McGriff's errors were a result of simply not catching the ball, possibly due to lack of concentration.

OVERALL:

Despite his poor finish, McGriff's potential is unlimited. When the Jays first moved into the SkyDome, it was feared McGriff's home run production would suffer, but he soon showed otherwise. Concentration or whatever, he needs to cut down his errors and improve his hitting against lefthanders.

FRED McGRIFF

Position: 1B
Bats: L **Throws:** L
Ht: 6' 3" **Wt:** 208

Opening Day Age: 26
Born: 10/31/63 in Tampa, FL
ML Seasons: 4

Overall Statistics

	G	AB	R	H	D	T	HR	RBI	SB	BB	SO	AVG
1989	161	551	98	148	27	3	36	92	7	119	132	.269
Career	425	1387	257	373	78	7	90	217	16	258	387	.269

Where He Hits the Ball

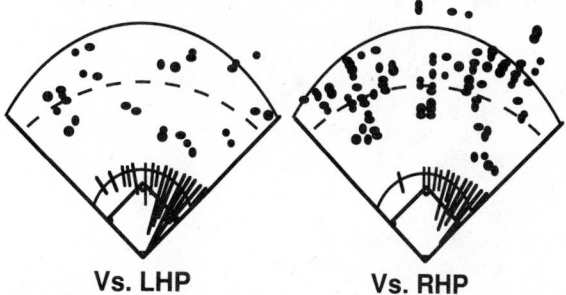

Vs. LHP   **Vs. RHP**

1989 Situational Stats

	AB	H	HR	RBI	AVG		AB	H	HR	RBI	AVG
Home	273	77	18	48	.282	LHP	189	48	5	23	.254
Road	278	71	18	44	.255	RHP	362	100	31	69	.276
Day	178	43	5	20	.242	Sc Pos	135	34	8	54	.252
Night	373	105	31	72	.282	Clutch	89	26	4	15	.292

1989 Rankings (American League)

- ➡ 1st in home runs (36) and slugging percentage vs. righthanded pitchers (.597) - *players with 377 PA vs. RHP*
- ➡ 2nd in home run frequency (15.3 ABs per HR), slugging percentage (.525) and walks (119) - *players with 502 PA*
- ➡ 3rd in on-base average vs. righthanded pitchers (.417)
- ➡ Led the Blue Jays in home run frequency, home runs, runs (98), total bases (289), walks, intentional walks (12), times on base (271), pitches seen (2,647), plate appearances (680), games (161), on-base percentage (.399), slugging percentage and strikeouts (132)

HITTING:

Lloyd Moseby is only 30, but he's slipped a long way offensively since '87 when he hit 26 homers and drove in 96 runs. After a disastrous '88 season, he showed up in spring training last year in his best shape ever. Then his mother died, and he never seemed to recover. Jays' manager Cito Gaston showed great patience and kept giving Moseby every opportunity, and Moseby did hit better in September. Moseby played a key role in the crucial season-ending series against Baltimore, and was one of the Blue Jays' better performers in the disastrous playoff series against Oakland. But overall, the numbers were not what was expected for $2.3 million.

Moseby has always been primarily a high fastball hitter, which is somewhat unusual for a lefthanded hitter. He likes the ball over the plate, so pitchers tend to work him low and away, then high and tight. Once a power hitter who averaged 20 homers a year in the period from 1983 to 1987, Moseby has been more of a spray hitter the last two years. He still belts an occasional longball but his power numbers (a total of 21 homers in 1988-89) are not nearly what they used to be. Moseby takes a lot of pitches and consequently draws an above average number of walks. For that reason Gaston used him a lot as a leadoff hitter. But Moseby also strikes out 100 or more times a season, and his .306 on-base percentage is woefully low for a leadoff man.

BASERUNNING:

A very fast runner, Moseby had another good year on the bases last year, stealing 24 bases in 31 attempts. That marked a decline, however, as he had stolen at least 31 for five straight years. The main problem in 1989 was that he had difficulty getting on base, limiting his running game. He remains a sharp and aggressive baserunner.

FIELDING:

Once considered an outstanding centerfielder, Moseby is now one of the weaker men playing the position. He has good range laterally, but a lot of balls fall in front of him in shallow center. His throwing arm was never great and runners are taking more chances on him all the time.

OVERALL:

Moseby's future with Toronto is tenuous. He's had problems with his lower back and legs, and he blames the aches on artificial turf. He is still young enough to have several productive years; he might be rejuvenated if he went to a team which plays on grass.

LLOYD MOSEBY

Position: CF/DH
Bats: L **Throws:** R
Ht: 6' 3" **Wt:** 200

Opening Day Age: 30
Born: 11/5/59 in Portland, OR
ML Seasons: 10

Overall Statistics

	G	AB	R	H	D	T	HR	RBI	SB	BB	SO	AVG
1989	135	502	72	111	25	3	11	43	24	56	101	.221
Career	1392	5124	768	1319	242	60	149	651	255	547	1015	.257

Where He Hits the Ball

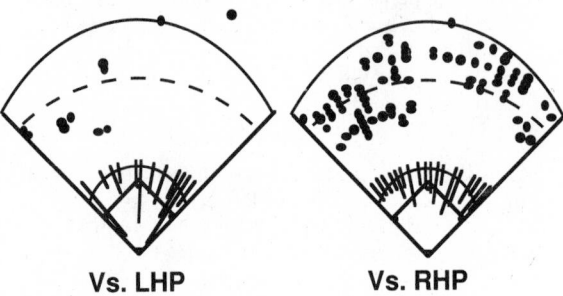

Vs. LHP   **Vs. RHP**

1989 Situational Stats

	AB	H	HR	RBI	AVG		AB	H	HR	RBI	AVG
Home	222	40	4	13	.180	LHP	138	27	2	10	.196
Road	280	71	7	30	.254	RHP	364	84	9	33	.231
Day	148	33	3	13	.223	Sc Pos	114	27	2	29	.237
Night	354	78	8	30	.220	Clutch	88	21	1	8	.239

1989 Rankings (American League)

- ➡ 1st in lowest batting average at home (.180) - *players with 252 home PA*
- ➡ 2nd in lowest slugging percentage vs. left-handed pitchers (.273) - *players with 125 PA vs. LHP*
- ➡ 3rd in lowest batting average (.221) - *players with 502 PA*
- ➡ 10th in stolen base percentage (77.4%)
- ➡ Led the Blue Jays in stolen bases (24), hit by pitch (6) and batting average on a 3-2 count (.340) - *team players with 20 PA on a 3-2 count*

HITTING:

Rance Mulliniks's 1989 season was quite a comedown from what the Blue Jays had come to expect from the veteran third baseman-DH. Mulliniks had been a jewel of consistency in 1987 and '88, batting .310 and .300, hitting 28 and then 21 doubles, and belting 11 and 12 homers. That was typical of the numbers the lefty swinger had been recording since coming to Toronto in 1982. But in 1989 Mulliniks never got untracked. He batted only .238, his worst average since 1981, and managed only 11 doubles and three homers. That really hurt the Blue Jays, who went from the best DH numbers in the league to the worst.

When he's on his game Mulliniks is a patient and productive hitter platooning against righthanders. He likes the low fastball but can handle breaking pitches as well, going to the opposite field against offspeed offerings. He's so disciplined that pitchers have to work hard even when they get him out. That's when he's on his game, however. In 1989 Mulliniks looked like his bat had slowed considerably. He had trouble getting around on good fastballs and looked anxious a lot of the time. He started swinging at bad pitches for the first time in years. Mulliniks' total of unintentional walks was his lowest since coming to Toronto.

BASERUNNING:

Mulliniks has never been a base stealer. His career high in stolen bases is three, and that was back in 1982. He had no stolen base attempts at all in 1989. But he's a smart baserunner who knows his own limitations.

FIELDING:

Mulliniks, a former shortstop, has always been an underrated third baseman with good range to both sides. He also has a strong arm. With Kelly Gruber entrenched at third base, Mulliniks has had little playing time at third in recent years. But he filled in for an injured Gruber for a little while last year and did a fine job, even though his range has decreased a little.

OVERALL:

Though a fan favorite and a fine performer for years, Mulliniks' future in Toronto is doubtful. He once had a comfortable platoon with Garth Iorg at third base, but Gruber is now entrenched there. He could still see action as a DH, but the Blue Jays showed what they thought of him by using the since-released Lee Mazzilli during the playoffs. If Mulliniks is to prove he can still hit, it may well be for another team.

RANCE MULLINIKS

Position: DH/3B
Bats: L **Throws:** R
Ht: 6' 0" **Wt:** 175

Opening Day Age: 34
Born: 1/15/56 in Tulare, CA
ML Seasons: 13

Overall Statistics

	G	AB	R	H	D	T	HR	RBI	SB	BB	SO	AVG
1989	103	273	25	65	11	2	3	29	0	34	40	.238
Career	1168	3230	406	883	210	16	69	395	13	393	492	.273

Where He Hits the Ball

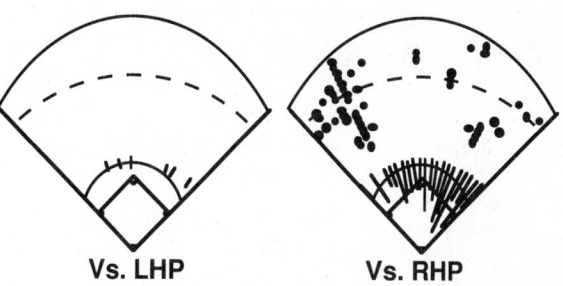

Vs. LHP   **Vs. RHP**

1989 Situational Stats

	AB	H	HR	RBI	AVG		AB	H	HR	RBI	AVG
Home	117	27	1	14	.231	LHP	16	3	0	2	.188
Road	156	38	2	15	.244	RHP	257	62	3	27	.241
Day	78	19	0	4	.244	Sc Pos	82	16	2	26	.195
Night	195	46	3	25	.236	Clutch	46	11	0	1	.239

1989 Rankings (American League)

➡ 4th in most GDPs per GDP situation (22.2%)
  - *players with 50 PA in GDP situations*

PITCHING:

Now 32 and an 11-year veteran, Dave Stieb has been a consistent winner, though never a big winner. In 1989 Stieb won 17 games for the third time, matching his career high. Though no longer the overpowering pitcher he once was, Stieb had a very impressive year in '89. Stieb held righthanded hitters to a .187 average, the best figure in the American League. He was also among the leaders in overall opponents' batting average (.219) and fewest home runs per nine innings (.523). Stieb has now won 148 games for Toronto, making him the club's all time team leader.

For most of his career Stieb has been a power pitcher, relying on a high 80's fastball, a very effective hard slider, a curve and a change-up. He loves to pitch inside and plunked 13 batters in 1989, leading the league in that category for the fifth time. But age and elbow injuries have caught up with him, and Stieb has begun to rely more on finesse. In 1989 he struck out only 101 batters, his lowest total yet in a full season. Despite that, Stieb is capable of overpowering hitters on good nights. He lost three no-hitters with two outs in the ninth in 1988 and '89 -- the one he lost in '89 had been a perfect game against the Yankees. On that night, his big pitch was a sharp breaking curve that many thought was a slider. Stieb switched to throwing it three-quarters because the batters had been hitting it when he came over the top.

FIELDING:

Stieb, a former outfielder, has always been an excellent fielder. He's very good at handling balls hit back to him, fielding bunts and covering first. He did not commit an error last year in 47 chances. Stieb is also very good at holding baserunners. His move to first is among the best of all righthanded pitchers.

OVERALL:

Once regarded as the best pitcher in the American League, Stieb has slipped from that perch, but only a little. He's still a mainstay of the Blue Jay staff and looks like he'll still be effective even when he can no longer overpower hitters. His arm is no longer as strong as it once was, but he's capable of 200 innings and 16 to 17 wins with a little help from his bullpen.

DAVE STIEB

Position: SP
Bats: R **Throws:** R
Ht: 6' 0" **Wt:** 195

Opening Day Age: 32
Born: 7/22/57 in Santa Ana, CA
ML Seasons: 11

Overall Statistics

	W	L	ERA	G	GS	Sv	IP	H	R	BB	SO	HR
1989	17	8	3.35	33	33	0	206.2	164	83	76	101	12
Career	148	117	3.37	357	349	1	2458.1	2158	1024	873	1432	194

Where They Hit the Ball

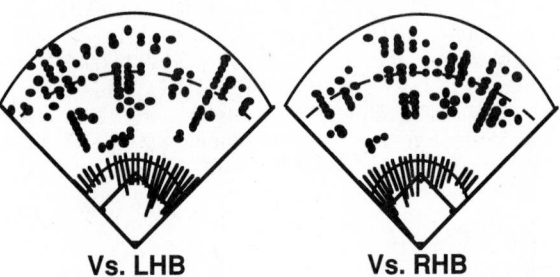

Vs. LHB   Vs. RHB

1989 Situational Stats

	W	L	ERA	Sv	IP		AB	H	HR	RBI	AVG
Home	7	4	3.34	0	94.1	LHB	385	96	7	41	.249
Road	10	4	3.36	0	112.1	RHB	363	68	5	29	.187
Day	4	4	4.77	0	77.1	Sc Pos	165	44	3	58	.267
Night	13	4	2.51	0	129.1	Clutch	38	8	0	3	.211

1989 Rankings (American League)

➡ 1st in hit batters (13) and lowest batting average vs. righthanded batters (.187) - *pitchers facing 377 RHB*

➡ 4th in lowest opponent batting average (.219) - *pitchers with 162 IP*

➡ 5th in lowest opponent slugging percentage (.316)

➡ Led the Blue Jays in wins (17), games started (33), shutouts (2), walks allowed (76), hit batters, won/loss percentage (.680), lowest opponent batting average, lowest opponent slugging percentage and lowest batting average vs. righthanded batters - *team pitchers with 162 IP*

PITCHING:

The son of Mel Stottlemyre, the former Yankee star who is now pitching coach for the Mets, Todd Stottlemyre has finally established himself in the Blue Jay starting rotation. Stottlemyre returned from the minors at the end of last June and didn't make an impact for a while. But down the stretch he was a key member of the starting staff. Like a lot of players from baseball families -- Todd's brother Mel, Jr., is a pitcher in the Royals organization -- Stottlemyre has poise beyond his 24 years. The Jays had enough confidence in the youngster to start him in the crucial first game of the season-ending series against Baltimore. Stottlemyre responded well, allowing only four hits and one run in five innings. He also started, and lost, the second game of the playoffs against Oakland. Stottlemyre's work in that game wasn't great, but the experience had to be good for him.

A power pitcher, Stottlemyre has a good fastball, a slider, curve and change-up. The fastball is Stottlemyre's best pitch and the reason he reached the majors. Both in 1988 and early last season he had a tendency to overthrow when he got into difficulty. Stottlemyre's not afraid to pitch inside, and he can be very tough on righthanded hitters. But lefties have bothered him a lot, and he's been prone to the home run ball, yielding 26 in 225.2 big league innings.

The Jays tried Stottlemyre in long relief last year, but he's always been groomed to start. His progress was rapid. Stottlemyre seemed to make the transition from thrower to pitcher, winning seven of ten decisions after an 0-4 start.

FIELDING:

Stottlemyre needs to work on his defense. His five errors last year were more than any pitcher on the Blue Jay staff. The miscues usually came on errant pickoff throws, or when he rushed a throw after fielding a bunt or a squibber. Stottlemyre also needs a lot of work on holding baserunners. He allowed 21 stolen bases last year, by far the most on the Blue Jay staff.

OVERALL:

Stottlemyre may be about ready to blossom as a workhorse of the Blue Jay staff. Maybe because of his name, people expected too much from him too soon. This will be only his fifth season of pro ball, and his development is right on schedule.

TODD STOTTLEMYRE

Position: SP/RP
Bats: L **Throws:** R
Ht: 6' 0" **Wt:** 190

Opening Day Age: 24
Born: 5/20/65 in Prosser, WA
ML Seasons: 2

Overall Statistics

	W	L	ERA	G	GS	Sv	IP	H	R	BB	SO	HR
1989	7	7	3.88	27	18	0	127.2	137	56	44	63	11
Career	11	15	4.67	55	34	0	225.2	246	126	90	130	26

Where They Hit the Ball

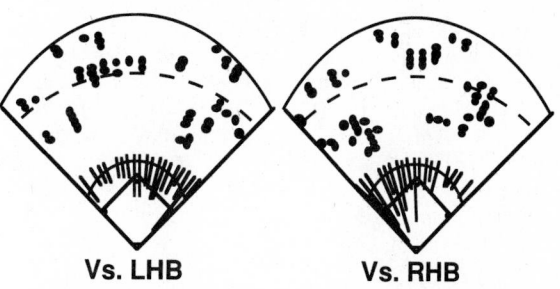

Vs. LHB   **Vs. RHB**

1989 Situational Stats

	W	L	ERA	Sv	IP		AB	H	HR	RBI	AVG
Home	4	3	3.53	0	79.0	LHB	219	70	7	24	.320
Road	3	4	4.44	0	48.2	RHB	267	67	4	24	.251
Day	2	3	5.53	0	40.2	Sc Pos	119	22	0	32	.185
Night	5	4	3.10	0	87.0	Clutch	43	16	0	7	.372

1989 Rankings (American League)

➡ Led the Blue Jays in stolen bases allowed (21)

PITCHING:

As he approaches his 26th birthday, Duane Ward finds himself in a frustrating position. He's earned his spurs as a reliever, working as a set-up man for Tom Henke and taking the closer's role himself when Henke is overworked or going through periods of ineffectiveness. Ward has done the job in that role, for the most part. Over the last two seasons Henke has earned 45 saves. Ward has earned 30, 15 in each season.

But last season, while he did capture 15 saves, he led the league with 12 blown saves. He assumed the closer role for awhile early in the year, when Henke was being hit hard, but Ward couldn't hold it. This was partly due to his own difficulties, but also because Henke soon righted himself. Though he has overpowering stuff, Ward needs to overcome his habit of walking the first batter he faces. That led to many of his 10 losses.

With his stuff, Ward only needs a little improvement. He not only throws hard -- over 90 mph -- but he also throws a heavy sinker. His slider has a tight spin, and it's sometimes uncatchable as well as unhittable. When Ward gets the slider into the dirt, as he often does, it's apt to elude the catcher. Ward had 13 wild pitches, the third highest total in the league after Nolan Ryan and Mike Moore, but easily the highest on a per-inning basis.

FIELDING:

Ward is a hard thrower whose follow-through creates some problems on ground balls. He's not always as quick in covering first as he should be. Ward's move to first is average, but he has a high leg kick and is pretty easy to steal on.

OVERALL:

Working behind the sometimes-erratic Tom Henke, Ward will get a chance to post some saves, even if he doesn't hold the top job himself. He'd improve his chances of being the closer himself if he were a little more consistent. Like the little girl with the curl, when he's good he's very, very good. Other times, he struggles with his control.

DUANE WARD

Position: RP
Bats: R **Throws:** R
Ht: 6' 4" **Wt:** 205

Opening Day Age: 25
Born: 5/28/64 in Parkview, NM
ML Seasons: 4

Overall Statistics

	W	L	ERA	G	GS	Sv	IP	H	R	BB	SO	HR
1989	4	10	3.77	66	0	15	114.2	94	55	58	122	4
Career	14	15	4.01	154	2	30	256.0	234	127	142	232	11

Where They Hit the Ball

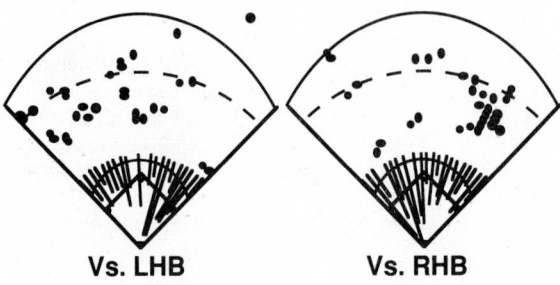

Vs. LHB   **Vs. RHB**

1989 Situational Stats

	W	L	ERA	Sv	IP		AB	H	HR	RBI	AVG
Home	2	6	3.81	8	54.1	LHB	172	45	2	23	.262
Road	2	4	3.73	7	60.1	RHB	236	49	2	34	.208
Day	3	4	5.67	3	39.2	Sc Pos	140	33	2	54	.236
Night	1	6	2.76	12	75.0	Clutch	245	58	3	38	.237

1989 Rankings (American League)

- ➡ 1st in blown saves (12) and worst save percentage (55.6%) - *pitchers with 20 save opportunities*
- ➡ 3rd in wild pitches (13)
- ➡ 8th in games (66)
- ➡ Led the Blue Jays in games, strikeouts (122), wild pitches, save opportunities (27), blown saves and grounder/flyball ratio (2.66) - *all team pitchers*

PITCHING:

In a crowded Blue Jay bullpen, David Wells hasn't really had a chance to show his true potential. Certainly Wells has the tools to be a premier reliever. He's a lefthander with a 90-plus fastball, a tough slider and a great overhand curve. Wells had his best major league season in 1989, with a 7-4 record, 2.40 ERA, and nearly a strikeout per inning (78 in 86.1 innings). Working in 54 games, Wells struck out almost three times as many men as he walked and held the opposition to a .207 batting average. About the only problem he had was that no one noticed. Working out of a bullpen in which Tom Henke, Duane Ward and even Jim Acker excelled, Wells's performance was largely forgotten.

Wells was mostly a long reliever in the past, but he was used both short and long in '89; he even recorded a couple of saves (though he also had seven blown saves). He showed no recurrence of the elbow problem that limited his effectiveness in 1988. His return to health was a big factor in his '89 success, but the other was improved control. It wasn't only that Wells walked fewer batters. He was also ahead in the count much more of the time, and as a result he was in far fewer situations where he simply had to throw a strike. The end result was a drastic reduction in home runs allowed. After yielding 12 homers in 64.1 innings in 1988, Wells permitted only five a year ago. And Wells was even better last year against righties than lefties, meaning that he could be used without hesitation in any situation.

FIELDING:

Wells is an oversized lefthander, and thus a little slow off the mound fielding grounders. His move to first base is okay, but he could learn from Key and Flanagan. Of course, as a power pitcher with a high leg kick, he'll probably always have trouble controlling the running game.

OVERALL:

Wells pitched all last season with the effectiveness he had demonstrated in the final month of 1987. He established his credentials as an up-and-coming reliever, and he's only 26. As long as Wells keeps his weight in check -- always a problem for him -- he should be around a long time.

DAVID WELLS

Position: RP
Bats: L **Throws:** L
Ht: 6' 4" **Wt:** 225

Opening Day Age: 26
Born: 5/20/63 in Torrance, CA
ML Seasons: 3

Overall Statistics

	W	L	ERA	G	GS	Sv	IP	H	R	BB	SO	HR
1989	7	4	2.40	54	0	2	86.1	66	25	28	78	5
Career	14	12	3.45	113	2	7	180.0	168	75	71	166	17

Where They Hit the Ball

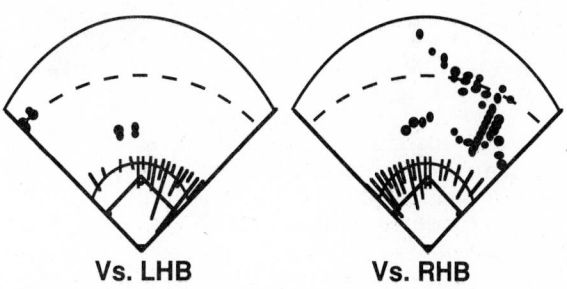

Vs. LHB   **Vs. RHB**

1989 Situational Stats

	W	L	ERA	Sv	IP		AB	H	HR	RBI	AVG
Home	5	2	2.40	1	48.2	LHB	77	18	1	7	.234
Road	2	2	2.39	1	37.2	RHB	242	48	4	20	.198
Day	2	1	2.19	0	24.2	Sc Pos	85	17	0	19	.200
Night	5	3	2.48	2	61.2	Clutch	155	39	4	16	.252

1989 Rankings (American League)

- ➡ 6th in blown saves (7)
- ➡ Led the Blue Jays in holds (8), lowest percentage of inherited runners scoring (30.0%) and first batter efficiency (.204)

HITTING:

Ernie Whitt, approaching his 38th birthday, remains a productive hitter and one of the better batsmen among American League catchers. Whitt's performance in 1989 has to give the Blue Jays a little cause for alarm, however. A notoriously slow starter over the years, Whitt had his best ever first half, hitting .300 at the break. In the second half, he dropped off, hitting only .229. He had some trouble adjusting to the SkyDome and went 37 games without a home run before connecting off Oakland's Todd Burns on July 13. Possibly because of the SkyDome, he had more doubles and less homers. Whitt didn't hit well at home last year and seemed to miss cozy Exhibition Stadium.

Whitt is a pull hitter and likes the ball up and out over the plate, but has some trouble handling the fastball in on him. He plays pretty much exclusively against righthanders, who work on him with breaking stuff and changeups. Whitt is a very patient hitter who makes hurlers work on him and then feeds off their mistakes. He's also one of the better bunters on a team that seldom sacrifices.

BASERUNNING:

As an aging catcher, Whitt lacks speed on the bases. He doesn't get out of the batter's box very well, but he's an intelligent baserunner. Whitt will surprise the opposition by stealing a base occasionally if ignored. His five stolen bases in 1989 matched his career high.

FIELDING:

This is the part of Whitt's game which has deteriorated the most. He doesn't block low pitches as well as he once did and he drops a lot of pitches, committing 12 passed balls last year. Nor does Whitt block the plate well. He had a bad year throwing out runners in '88 and this continued in '89, as he gunned down only 28 of 89. In the ALCS Whitt was even worse; Rickey Henderson stole eight times without being thrown out, and Whitt tossed out only one of 14.

OVERALL:

Whitt is a father figure in the Blue Jay clubhouse, a quiet leader who is not afraid to say what he feels, as he did in his book when he ripped Joe Brinkman's umpiring crew. He still calls a good game, and despite his dropoff in 1989, he can still hit. With Greg Myers waiting in the wings, Whitt may see some duty as the DH.

ERNIE WHITT

Position: C
Bats: L **Throws:** R
Ht: 6' 2" **Wt:** 200

Opening Day Age: 37
Born: 6/13/52 in Detroit, MI
ML Seasons: 13

Overall Statistics

	G	AB	R	H	D	T	HR	RBI	SB	BB	SO	AVG
1989	129	385	42	101	24	1	11	53	5	52	53	.262
Career	1226	3532	428	892	166	15	132	521	22	405	452	.253

Where He Hits the Ball

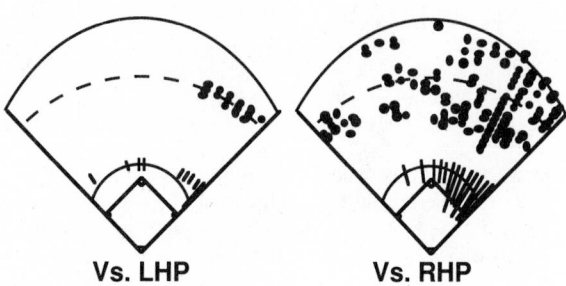

Vs. LHP　　　　**Vs. RHP**

1989 Situational Stats

	AB	H	HR	RBI	AVG		AB	H	HR	RBI	AVG
Home	184	43	8	27	.234	LHP	44	7	1	7	.159
Road	201	58	3	26	.289	RHP	341	94	10	46	.276
Day	118	30	5	15	.254	Sc Pos	96	24	5	40	.250
Night	267	71	6	38	.266	Clutch	65	16	2	9	.246

1989 Rankings (American League)

➥ Led AL catchers in hitting vs. righthanded pitchers (.276) - *catchers with 377 PA vs. RHP*

HITTING:

Mookie Wilson, dumped by the Mets after getting off to a .205 start, revived his career overnight with Toronto. Once he shook off the rust that he had accumulated riding the Met bench, Wilson became a real offensive sparkplug for a club which badly needed one. He helped in other ways as well. Always known as a clubhouse leader, Wilson was an excellent role model for the younger Blue Jays, and his spirit seemed to lift the veterans also. To top it off, he became an instant fan favorite, the first new hero in the new SkyDome.

A switch-hitter, Wilson was frequently platooned with the lefty-swinging Lenny Dykstra during his later Met years. That suggests he's better hitting right-handed, but in fact Wilson's left-right splits have been pretty even in recent years, and he was actually better hitting lefthanded during each of the last three years. He likes the ball up as a righty hitter, down as a lefty. From either side Wilson is a cutting, slashing fastball hitter who sprays the ball around without much power. He's never been the patient type and his free-swinging was more pronounced than ever after the Blue Jays acquired him. Wilson drew only three walks in 247 plate appearances for the Jays. Despite a good batting average his on-base percentage for Toronto was only .311, a low figure for a man who bats at the top of the lineup.

BASERUNNING:

At 34, Wilson still has outstanding speed. His career stolen base success rate is 76 percent, and he was successful 12 times in 13 tries with Toronto. He runs the bases aggressively, even scoring from first base on a single late in the season.

FIELDING:

Cito Gaston used him in all three outfield spots, and Wilson made good use of his speed in tracking down balls in the spacious SkyDome. His arm is very weak, however, and opposing baserunners take advantage of it.

OVERALL:

Wilson has made a place for himself with the Blue Jays, but the problem is trying to find the best spot for him. His arm is too weak to be in rightfield every day. If George Bell would accept the DH role, Wilson could play left, or the two could share both slots. Some National League observers caution that Wilson might not be able to produce over a full season as he did in his two months with Toronto.

MOOKIE WILSON

Position: CF/LF/RF
Bats: B **Throws:** R
Ht: 5'10" **Wt:** 170

Opening Day Age: 34
Born: 2/9/56 in Bamberg, SC
ML Seasons: 10

Overall Statistics

	G	AB	R	H	D	T	HR	RBI	SB	BB	SO	AVG
1989	134	487	54	122	19	2	5	35	19	13	84	.251
Career	1170	4265	624	1183	179	63	62	359	293	243	729	.277

Where He Hits the Ball

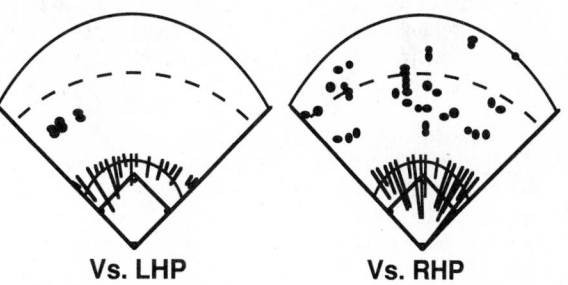

Vs. LHP   **Vs. RHP**

1989 Situational Stats

	AB	H	HR	RBI	AVG		AB	H	HR	RBI	AVG
Home	247	55	2	15	.223	LHP	200	47	1	14	.235
Road	240	67	3	20	.279	RHP	287	75	4	21	.261
Day	168	37	0	7	.220	Sc Pos	121	24	0	29	.198
Night	319	85	5	28	.266	Clutch	87	18	0	6	.207

1989 Rankings (American League)

➡ 1st in highest percentage of extra bases taken as a runner (64.2%) - *players with 40 opportunities to advance*

ROB DUCEY

Position: RF
Bats: L **Throws:** R
Ht: 6' 2" **Wt:** 175

Opening Day Age: 24
Born: 5/24/65 in Toronto, Canada
ML Seasons: 3

Overall Statistics

	G	AB	R	H	D	T	HR	RBI	SB	BB	SO	AVG
1989	41	76	5	16	4	0	0	7	2	9	25	.211
Career	102	178	32	42	9	1	1	19	5	22	42	.236

HITTING, FIELDING, BASERUNNING:

The Blue Jays would love to see Rob Ducey make it big, and not just because he's a native of Toronto on a club looking for a Canadian hero. Ducey's an excellent outfielder with a good throwing arm. He would probably do a better job of covering centerfield in the spacious SkyDome than anyone on the Jays except for Junior Felix. A year ago Ducey made the Blue Jays' opening day roster after an outstanding spring in which he led the team with a .462 Grapefruit League average. But Jimy Williams didn't use him. Then, when a shortage of outfielders developed, Ducey hurt his right knee in a freak accident in the SkyDome. On rehab assignment at Syracuse, he aggravated the injury and wasn't activated until September. All in all, he had a wasted and depressing season. He has good speed, some power and a fine minor league hitting record.

OVERALL:

Despite his '89 problems, at 24 Ducey is still young enough to make an impact. Whether he makes the Jays or not depends on what happens with other outfielders, including George Bell, Lloyd Moseby, Mookie Wilson and Glenallen Hill, but after three years at Syracuse, Ducey is about as ready as he'll ever be.

MAURO GOZZO

Position: RP/SP
Bats: R **Throws:** R
Ht: 6' 3" **Wt:** 212

Opening Day Age: 24
Born: 3/7/66 in New Britain, CT
ML Seasons: 1

Overall Statistics

	W	L	ERA	G	GS	Sv	IP	H	R	BB	SO	HR
1989	4	1	4.83	9	3	0	31.2	35	19	9	10	1
Career	4	1	4.83	9	3	0	31.2	35	19	9	10	1

PITCHING & FIELDING:

Originally signed by the Mets, Mauro Gozzo was traded to Kansas City in the deal for pitcher David Cone. The Royals left Gozzo unprotected in the minor league player draft last December and Pat Gillick, who has excelled in his selections in this draft, took him. Thus far it looks like another shrewd move from the man who picked up George Bell, Kelly Gruber and Manny Lee in exactly the same manner. Gozzo was 7-0 in Double A and 5-1 in Triple A, finally losing for the first time at the end of July. When Jimmy Key went on the DL in early August, Gozzo was summoned and pitched eight shutout innings in his Major League debut. He won two more starts against Boston and Baltimore, and picked up a win in relief. Gozzo has an excellent sinker and a competitive attitude that reminds some people of Pete Vuckovich. He fields his position decently and does a good job of holding baserunners.

OVERALL:

Gozzo's not a hard thrower -- he had only 10 strikeouts in 31.2 innings -- but he's smart and knows how to pitch. Undoubtedly he'll get a long look next spring, unless he is used in a trade package.

GLENALLEN HILL

Position: RF
Bats: R **Throws:** R
Ht: 6' 2" **Wt:** 210

Opening Day Age: 25
Born: 3/22/65 in Santa Cruz, CA
ML Seasons: 1

Overall Statistics

	G	AB	R	H	D	T	HR	RBI	SB	BB	SO	AVG
1989	19	52	4	15	0	0	1	7	2	3	12	.288
Career	19	52	4	15	0	0	1	7	2	3	12	.288

HITTING, FIELDING, BASERUNNING:

Glenallen Hill is known as "Thrill," but thus far not in the same sense that Will Clark is. In Hill's case, the thrill has often been the way Hill screwed himself into the ground after uncorking one of the hardest swings in baseball. The Hill legend was firmly created back in 1985, when he struck out a staggering 210 times at Kingston in the Carolina League. Hill belted 20 homers that year, however, and the Jays slowly moved him up their system. But Hill seemed stymied in 1988, when he played poorly and was demoted from Triple A back to Knoxville in Double A because of his attitude. He was then left unprotected in the Rule 5 draft, and although the Jays lost five players, nobody would gamble $50,000 on Hill. Given a reprieve, he caught fire in 1989, hitting .321 with 21 homers and 21 steals for Syracuse. He did well in a September call-up, with a grand slam homer his first game, and good defense in the outfield. Hill runs and throws well.

OVERALL:

The Blue Jay outfield picture is crowded, but Hill has a definite chance after his '89 performance. If Lloyd Moseby doesn't return and George Bell accepts a DH role, his chances will improve. Now 25, Hill is definitely a prospect again.

TOM LAWLESS

Position: 3B
Bats: R **Throws:** R
Ht: 5'11" **Wt:** 165

Opening Day Age: 33
Born: 12/19/56 in Erie, PA
ML Seasons: 7

Overall Statistics

	G	AB	R	H	D	T	HR	RBI	SB	BB	SO	AVG
1989	59	70	20	16	1	0	0	3	12	7	12	.229
Career	328	519	77	109	17	2	2	23	53	41	84	.210

HITTING, FIELDING, BASERUNNING:

Though he'll probably be remembered in history as the man who was traded even up for Pete Rose, Tom Lawless is still a useful player. Lawless is a career .210 hitter who has 23 RBIs in 519 career at bats, so obviously the Jays don't prize him for his bat. He's a handy guy who can play second, third and the outfield. He even caught for the first time in the major leagues last year, and threw out Billy Ripken trying to steal. His best position is probably second base, but Lawless has a strong arm and is versatile enough to do a good job at any position. Lawless's best moments last year came as Cito Gaston's designated runner, however. He stole 12 bases in 13 attempts, including a crucial steal against Baltimore on the last weekend that led to a big run. Lawless's running was all the more impressive because the steals usually came in obvious running situations.

OVERALL:

Lawless is now 33, and will probably have a major league job as long as he can field and run. He has 53 steals in 64 career attempts, and his '89 performance indicates that he isn't slowing down yet.

AL LEITER

Position: SP
Bats: L **Throws:** L
Ht: 6' 3" **Wt:** 210

Opening Day Age: 24
Born: 10/23/65 in Toms River, NJ
ML Seasons: 3

Overall Statistics

	W	L	ERA	G	GS	Sv	IP	H	R	BB	SO	HR
1989	1	2	5.67	5	5	0	33.1	32	23	23	26	2
Career	7	8	4.92	23	23	0	113.1	105	66	71	114	11

PITCHING & FIELDING:

On the last Sunday of April, the Blue Jays traded Jesse Barfield to the Yankees to acquire Al Leiter, a hard-throwing lefty whom GM Pat Gillick had long coveted. The move was more than a little curious. Though considered a top prospect, Leiter has never won more than six games in any of his seasons in organized baseball. And the trade came with the move to the spacious SkyDome only a month away -- a curious time to get rid of your best defensive outfielder, not to mention a former major league home run king. All the Jays got was one start from Leiter before he was put on the DL with a sore shoulder. Eventually he was sent to Dunedin in Class A on rehab assignment. After three starts there, he again experienced stiffness in his shoulder and his season was over.

OVERALL:

The Jays expect Leiter to make a comeback next year, and still consider him a top prospect to be a big winner. Although they already have three lefty starters, Leiter is different because he throws heat.

LEE MAZZILLI

Position: DH
Bats: B **Throws:** R
Ht: 6' 1" **Wt:** 195

Opening Day Age: 35
Born: 3/25/55 in Brooklyn, NY
ML Seasons: 14

Overall Statistics

	G	AB	R	H	D	T	HR	RBI	SB	BB	SO	AVG
1989	76	126	22	26	5	0	6	18	5	34	35	.206
Career	1475	4124	571	1068	191	24	93	460	197	642	627	.259

HITTING, FIELDING, BASERUNNING:

Now 35, Lee Mazzilli has entered the "have bat, will travel" phase of his career. A useful fill-in outfielder/first baseman/pinch-hitter when the Mets picked him up in 1986, Mazzilli has hit only .147 and .206 the last two years. And he's been released by two teams, the Mets and Blue Jays, who are among the few clubs he could figure to help. Though a switch-hitter, Mazzilli does almost all of his damage from the left side. He has occasional power (six homers in 126 at bats last year), but his best attribute is his patience. He seldom swings at bad pitches, draws a lot of walks and can spray line drives to all fields. He's slowed down, but he's a smart baserunner and was five-for-five in stealing attempts last year. He's below average in both the outfield and at first base, with a notoriously weak throwing arm.

OVERALL:

Mazzilli's skills have narrowed in recent years and he simply has to hit in order to help a club. Neither the Mets nor the Blue Jays thought he could do it any more. Mazzilli may get another chance, but he'll have to prove himself pretty quickly.

FRANK WILLS

Position: RP/SP
Bats: R **Throws:** R
Ht: 6' 2" **Wt:** 200

Opening Day Age: 31
Born: 10/26/58 in New Orleans, LA
ML Seasons: 7

Overall Statistics

	W	L	ERA	G	GS	Sv	IP	H	R	BB	SO	HR
1989	3	1	3.66	24	4	0	71.1	65	31	30	41	4
Career	16	21	5.01	106	31	6	332.1	329	192	155	207	35

PITCHING & FIELDING:

Frank Wills is a 31-year old veteran who's pitched for the Royals, Mariners, Indians and Blue Jays. He finally got his big moment of fame last September 30. Relieving starter Jimmy Key, Wills allowed only one hit in four innings and was the winning pitcher as Toronto clinched its second division title. That was quite a triumph for a pitcher who's been released three times in a rather lackluster career. A former first-round draft choice, Wills once had a 94 mph fastball that he threw almost exclusively. Age and arm injuries have reduced his velocity, but Wills still relies mostly on the fastball, mixing in an occasional change-up and curve. Control has always been a problem for him. Wills needs to stay ahead in the count to be effective; when he gets behind, he's liable to give up home runs.

OVERALL:

Wills pitched well for Toronto last year, working in middle relief and making an occasional spot start. But the Jays' addition of Jim Acker makes his Toronto future doubtful. Wills has a live arm, however, and even though his career ERA is 5.01, someone always seems to be willing to give him a chance.

National League Players

HITTING:

Jeff Blauser took a giant step forward this year, becoming an offensive force on the Braves second only to Lonnie Smith. He raised his average nearly 30 points, hit 12 homers, and shook off any doubts about his ability to play every day. He hit for average and slugged lefties and righties equally. Early in the season Jeff was briefly among the league leaders in doubles, ended up with 38 extra base hits, and sported a fine .410 slugging percentage.

The most disturbing aspect of Blauser's hitting is his high strikeout total, but there were encouraging signs; except for a slight drop-off in September, his on-base percentage rose each month. He was still striking out, but he learned to take a walk and that bodes well for the future. His low RBI total can be placed squarely at Russ Nixon's feet; although Jeff had the third highest slugging average on the team behind Smith and McDowell, he had only nine at bats in the 3-4-5 spots. He showed some real talent hitting second in the lineup, and did not let his revolving-door defensive assignments affect his hitting. Jeff takes a full cut, and can tag a fastball.

BASERUNNING:

Blauser is a good baserunner and has above average speed -- he was a centerfielder in high school. He attempted only seven steals this year and was successful five times, but it seems that he could attempt more. Jeff stole 36 bases in 1985 at Sumpter and seems to have the ability to swipe 15 plus for the Braves.

FIELDING:

Blauser made a lot of errors this year (21) at a lot of positions. In spite of that, and in spite of displaying uneven range, Jeff has the tools to master second, third, or short. He dives with abandon to the left or the right and shows good balance. Blauser has a good arm and played only shortstop in the minors. When he settles into a regular position he should perform better.

OVERALL:

Although Blauser's talents might seem good to ordinary on another team, he is very valuable to the Braves, who badly need to solidify several positions. Writing in his name at second, third, or short would help Jeff and the Braves, and at this point he must be considered one of their two or three best everyday players. He will be only 24 during the 1990 season, and if the trade rumors that swirled around his head in 1989 subside, he could be around for the Braves' next pennant.

JEFF BLAUSER

Position: 3B/2B/SS
Bats: R **Throws:** R
Ht: 6' 0" **Wt:** 170

Opening Day Age: 24
Born: 11/8/65 in Los Gatos, CA
ML Seasons: 3

Overall Statistics

	G	AB	R	H	D	T	HR	RBI	SB	BB	SO	AVG
1989	142	456	63	123	24	2	12	46	5	38	101	.270
Career	211	688	81	179	33	6	16	68	12	58	146	.260

Where He Hits the Ball

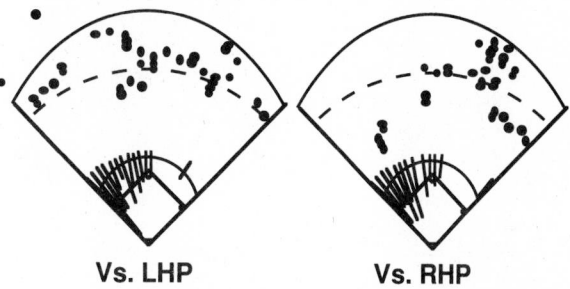

Vs. LHP   **Vs. RHP**

1989 Situational Stats

	AB	H	HR	RBI	AVG		AB	H	HR	RBI	AVG
Home	229	57	5	19	.249	LHP	197	55	4	16	.279
Road	227	66	7	27	.291	RHP	259	68	8	30	.263
Day	95	29	3	12	.305	Sc Pos	78	25	0	33	.321
Night	361	94	9	34	.260	Clutch	100	26	2	11	.260

1989 Rankings (National League)

- ➡ 8th in errors (21)
- ➡ 10th in most pitches seen per plate appearance (3.7) - *players with 502 PA*
- ➡ Led the Braves in sacrifice hits (8)
- ➡ Led NL Third Basemen in sacrifice hits, pitches seen per plate appearance and hitting with runners in scoring position (.321)

PITCHING:

After racking up 110 minor league saves, mostly in the relief-rich St. Louis Cardinals system, Joe Boever was only penciled in for the '89 season because Atlanta still hoped for a return on their Bruce Sutter investment. But Boever wasted no time assuming the stopper role by not giving up an earned run in his first seven appearances. His big weapon is a sharp-dropping palmball, which he sets up with a fastball that is only average. If Boever starts a batter with the palmball he will throw the fastball out of the strike zone, where it tempts hitters looking for the palmball.

From April through July, Boever appeared in 45 games and only gave up earned runs eight times. He was absolutely devastating in July, with an ERA of 0.48, with five saves and two wins. He had only two really bad outings, and in both of them he was allowed to pitch an absurd amount, throwing over 60 pitches. But in early August Boever gave up his first homerun, a game winner off the mighty bat of Mariano Duncan, and his season went south. He lost eight games in August and September and saved only three, all of the saves coming in August.

Boever started throwing the palmball too low, it was dropping out of the strike zone, and he was falling behind in the count. He had to come in with that fastball and hitters knew it. Naturally, he started giving up hits like crazy, including six home runs. Mike Stanton began to get the save opportunities, and it was a good thing, since Boever was completely ineffective.

FIELDING,HITTING,BASERUNNING:

Boever is a good fielder with excellent range and reflexes, and he makes the smart play. He did not commit an error in 1989. Unlike most Braves pitchers, he doesn't hold runners particularly well, and since he throws a slow pitch that often ends up in the dirt, he is an easy pitcher to run on. Because he was a stopper he had only one at bat, and did nothing.

OVERALL:

Stanton's presence and those eight losses down the stretch tend to distort what has to be considered a triumphant vindication for Boever. He has probably earned the right to be considered a rival for the closer position. In 1990 he will have to prove that his late season swoon is correctable, and not the reason he was allowed to earn those 110 saves in the minors instead of the majors.

JOE BOEVER

Position: RP
Bats: R **Throws:** R
Ht: 6' 1" **Wt:** 200

Opening Day Age: 29
Born: 10/4/60 in St. Louis, MO
ML Seasons: 5

Overall Statistics

	W	L	ERA	G	GS	Sv	IP	H	R	BB	SO	HR
1989	4	11	3.94	66	0	21	82.1	78	37	34	68	6
Career	5	14	3.79	120	0	22	159.0	155	69	62	121	16

Where They Hit the Ball

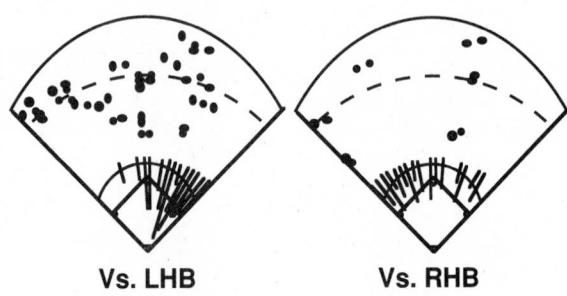

Vs. LHB   **Vs. RHB**

1989 Situational Stats

	W	L	ERA	Sv	IP		AB	H	HR	RBI	AVG
Home	4	6	3.53	9	51.0	LHB	183	46	2	17	.251
Road	0	5	4.60	12	31.1	RHB	126	32	4	21	.254
Day	0	2	3.68	7	22.0	Sc Pos	83	21	1	32	.253
Night	4	9	4.03	14	60.1	Clutch	202	50	5	25	.248

1989 Rankings (National League)

- ➡ 1st in lowest save percentage (70.0%) - *pitchers with 20 save opportunities*
- ➡ 3rd in blown saves (9) and lowest won/loss percentage (.267) - *pitchers with 15 decisions*
- ➡ 5th in games finished (53)
- ➡ 6th in lowest percentage of inherited runners scoring (17.4%) - *all league pitchers*
- ➡ 7th in save opportunities (30)
- ➡ Led the Braves in games (66), games finished, save opportunities, saves (21), lowest percentage of inherited runners scoring, first batter efficiency (.258) and blown saves

PITCHING:

Marty Clary threw only 86 pitches for his first major league victory, a complete game four-hitter. That is the type of game Clary will pitch when he is on. Clary is a control pitcher who relies more on stuff than guile. He goes right at hitters, throwing his fastball on the black, a nice change-up, and a low curveball. Marty is extremely tough when ahead on the count, and for a pitcher who throws in the strike zone he doesn't give up many hits.

Clary doesn't get many strikeouts, so he is dependent on his defense. When the curve is working well, his strikeouts go up and that is when he has his best games. Marty allowed lefties a meager .236 BA and a .290 on-base percentage, which was handy since he faced far more lefties than righties. When he isn't going well, he tends to miss low with his breaking ball, and good low-ball hitters will give him a hard time. Clary pitched in some bad luck at times, but he showed that he is a Major League pitcher.

Clary often had trouble at the beginning of games, and some of that seemed to be a problem figuring out a particular umpire's strike zone. Because he likes to paint the corners, slight differences in ball/strike calls can hurt him and his walks would rise. He learned fast, though, and would be very tough on hitters the second time through the order.

FIELDING, HITTING, BASERUNNING:

When Clary pitches there are a lot of balls put into play, and he helps his cause with his defense. He has good range and is very cool snaring line-drives. He made no errors in 1989. He holds runners close and had only five bases stolen against him and 10 caught stealing, which is excellent, but was vulnerable to late-inning stolen bases when pitching in trouble. He can sacrifice if you need it, and has a good eye at the plate, but only had 31 at bats so his hitting is still a question. He is not a threat on the bases.

OVERALL:

Once considered a top prospect, Clary made steady if unspectacular progress through the minors and pitched in a few games for the Braves in 1987. He was not effective and spent all of '88 in the minors. He will be 29 in 1990 and the Braves' corp of young pitchers may push him out, but his '89 performance should allow him a good shot in 1990.

MARTIN CLARY

Position: SP
Bats: R **Throws:** R
Ht: 6' 4" **Wt:** 190

Opening Day Age: 29
Born: 8/9/60 in Detroit, MI
ML Seasons: 2

Overall Statistics

	W	L	ERA	G	GS	Sv	IP	H	R	BB	SO	HR
1989	4	3	3.15	18	17	0	108.2	103	47	31	30	6
Career	4	4	3.50	25	18	0	123.1	123	60	35	37	8

Where They Hit the Ball

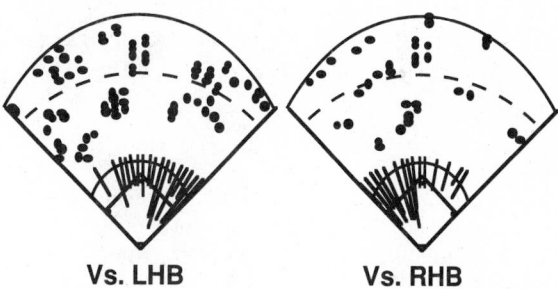

Vs. LHB   **Vs. RHB**

1989 Situational Stats

	W	L	ERA	Sv	IP		AB	H	HR	RBI	AVG
Home	3	1	3.27	0	55.0	LHB	257	61	3	17	.237
Road	1	2	3.02	0	53.2	RHB	155	42	3	19	.271
Day	1	0	2.33	0	27.0	Sc Pos	100	17	2	28	.170
Night	3	3	3.42	0	81.2	Clutch	39	12	0	4	.308

1989 Rankings (National League)

➡ Did not rank near the top or bottom in any category

HITTING:

Jody Davis raised his average 25 points in 1989 against the lefthanded pitching that bothered him in 1988. To .204. His average against righties fell 125 points to .145, below Mendoza's Grandmother's Line. His overall average of .169 is a dramatic dropoff from 1988, which in turn was a troubling drop from his established career levels. In view of his age (33), however, Davis's 1989 totals seem to be a true reflection of his ability at this stage of his career. Davis caught more innings than any Braves catcher, but was used sparingly in the last two months. The rest must have done him some good because he hit pretty well in September.

Davis has gained weight and lost bat speed. He used to play in Wrigley Field where his hitting stats always looked good, but even cozy Fulton County Stadium can't help him now. He hit one of his four homers there. Davis was part of the worst-hitting catching corps in all of baseball. Braves catchers hit .185; the next worse staff, Philadelphia's, hit .211. The Braves may be the one team that could benefit from hitting the pitchers ahead of the catchers.

BASERUNNING:

Davis has stolen one base since 1985 while being caught six times. He grounds into a lot of double plays and goes station to station with some effort. It takes quite a deep fly ball to get him home from third. Jody scored only 12 runs although he had 219 at bats, and four of those were on homers.

FIELDING:

Davis has a good arm, and combining his skills with a staff that holds runners well, he had a 41% caught stealing percentage last year. He has limited mobility behind the plate, as his six passed balls and six errors attest. His work behind the plate often exasperated manager (and former catcher) Russ Nixon, and the Braves seem worried about placing their precious young pitchers in Davis' hands. He seemed particularly damaging to Tom Glavine.

OVERALL:

The Braves have no promising catchers in the high minors, and it will be a while before first round draft pick Tyler Houston gets some seasoning. Jody's hitting in partial September duty indicated that he might be of some value as a backup catcher. But seriously, although the Brave's minor league catchers have shown very little ability, how much worse can they be? It will be interesting to see how long the Braves stay with Davis in 1990.

JODY DAVIS

Position: C
Bats: R **Throws:** R
Ht: 6' 3" **Wt:** 210

Opening Day Age: 33
Born: 11/12/56 in Gainesville, GA
ML Seasons: 9

Overall Statistics

	G	AB	R	H	D	T	HR	RBI	SB	BB	SO	AVG
1989	78	231	12	39	5	0	4	19	0	23	61	.169
Career	1070	3557	364	875	164	11	127	489	7	330	709	.246

Where He Hits the Ball

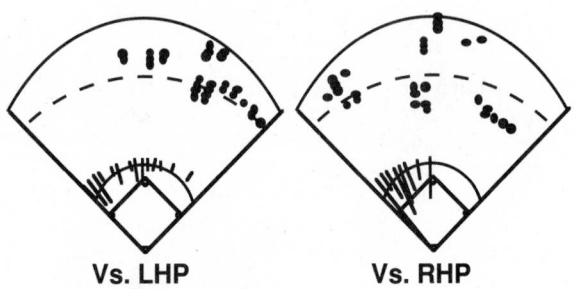

Vs. LHP   Vs. RHP

1989 Situational Stats

	AB	H	HR	RBI	AVG		AB	H	HR	RBI	AVG
Home	105	15	1	10	.143	LHP	93	19	1	10	.204
Road	126	24	3	9	.190	RHP	138	20	3	9	.145
Day	58	11	1	5	.190	Sc Pos	48	9	0	12	.188
Night	173	28	3	14	.162	Clutch	52	7	0	3	.135

1989 Rankings (National League)

➡ 1st in lowest batting average with 2 strikes (.044) - *players with 162 PA with 2 strikes*

➡ 4th in lowest batting average in the clutch (.135) - *players with 50 PA in the clutch*

PITCHING:

Mark Eichhorn pitched in 45 games for the Braves last year in spite of wild swings of effectiveness. The problems that developed for Eichhorn in Toronto continued in Atlanta. When hitters learn to let his change-up go by, he falls behind in the count, a position where he is extremely vulnerable. His submarine pitch is puzzling, but he doesn't throw it hard and when he leaves it in the strike zone hitters just tattoo it. Eichhorn was effective against righthanded hitters, holding them to a .213 average and walking only six with 31 strikeouts, but in nearly identical appearances against lefties, he was battered for a .336 average and a .484 slugging percentage. He allowed 90 baserunners in 68.1 innings.

Eichhorn's change-up and fastball both tail away from righthanders. That, combined with his delivery, which starts far to the left of the hitter, makes the ball appear to be passing in front of the batter rather than at him. Lefties can see the ball leave Eichhorn's hand and watch it come at them. The ball appears to rise into the strike zone and if he doesn't have much on it, it's almost as if it were thrown underhanded. He is most effective when used for just an inning or less, against tough righties, but his role with the Braves as a middle reliever forced Eichhorn to pitch several innings in each outing, and he got worked over pretty well.

FIELDING:

Eichhorn is a good fielder, although he hasn't much range to his left. He saved himself many times by snaring line drives, and did not commit an error in 1989. In spite of his mediocre move to first, Eichhorn was not victimized much by the stolen base; his side-arm delivery allows him to keep a better eye on first than pitchers with conventional wind-up or stretch deliveries.

OVERALL:

Eichhorn must get some zip back in his fastball; hitters are wise to his change-up. His past success with Toronto should allow him another opportunity to earn a role with the Braves, but he needs a better showing than his last two seasons, or any work that he gets will be in a very limited role.

MARK EICHHORN

Position: RP
Bats: R **Throws:** R
Ht: 6' 3" **Wt:** 200

Opening Day Age: 29
Born: 11/21/60 in San Jose, CA
ML Seasons: 5

Overall Statistics

	W	L	ERA	G	GS	Sv	IP	H	R	BB	SO	HR
1989	5	5	4.35	45	0	0	68.1	70	36	19	49	6
Career	29	23	3.19	247	7	15	457.2	404	175	157	355	35

Where They Hit the Ball

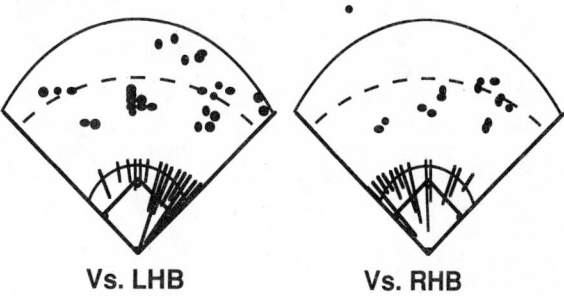

Vs. LHB   **Vs. RHB**

1989 Situational Stats

	W	L	ERA	Sv	IP		AB	H	HR	RBI	AVG
Home	1	3	5.40	0	31.2	LHB	128	43	2	21	.336
Road	4	2	3.44	0	36.2	RHB	127	27	4	25	.213
Day	0	3	2.45	0	14.2	Sc Pos	84	24	5	43	.286
Night	5	2	4.86	0	53.2	Clutch	97	25	4	23	.258

1989 Rankings (National League)

➡ 2nd in worst batting average allowed vs. lefthanded batters (.336) - *pitchers facing 125 LHB*

➡ Led the Braves in holds (8)

DARRELL EVANS

Position: 1B/3B
Bats: L **Throws:** R
Ht: 6' 2" **Wt:** 205

Opening Day Age: 42
Born: 5/26/47 in Pasadena, CA
ML Seasons: 21

HITTING:

Darrell Evans is like the little old lady who hikes in the mountains; "I can still go every where I used to go," she says, "it just takes me longer." If Darrell had gotten a full season of at bats in '89 he would have had the 20-homer, 80-RBI, and 80-walks type of season he had in '88. Darrell has lost some pop and he is just holding his strikeout/walk ratio at about even, though he used to be a prodigious walker. But if he is losing his eye, it's only about a decade later than most players do. While few have noticed, the quiet Evans is the active leader in career home runs, with 414.

Evans still stands stock still in the box, with his bat straight up and down, but he has lost some bat speed. His great virtue now is patience; if he can get ahead in the count he is deadly. He can no longer adjust to the curve and if a pitcher can throw it for strikes, Darrell is done for. It is when a pitcher has to come in with some heat that Evans does his damage, and the longer he can work the count, the more success he has.

BASERUNNING:

Remember that little old lady? Darrell was caught stealing in his one stolen base attempt, but he did hit a triple in '89. He does not run well, and never has, but he hit into only one double play so he isn't costing his team much on the basepaths. Darrell hits some mighty long singles now, but is wise to stop at first.

FIELDING:

Injuries – and the failure of Ron Gant to cut it at third – forced Evans to the hot corner during 28 games, far more than Darrell or the Braves expected. He has lost the mobility that made him the premier fielding third baseman in the National League in the mid-70's, and does not throw with authority any more. He doesn't pinch hit well, so his value must be as a part-time first baseman.

OVERALL:

Evans has been a fine ballplayer, almost a great one, although his time may be up as a major leaguer. The Braves announced that they will not re-sign him, but he may latch on with someone, and his power and experience could help a team for one more year. If not, he's had a heckuva career.

Overall Statistics

	G	AB	R	H	D	T	HR	RBI	SB	BB	SO	AVG
1989	107	276	31	57	6	1	11	39	0	41	46	.207
Career	2687	8973	1344	2223	329	36	414	1354	98	1605	1410	.248

Where He Hits the Ball

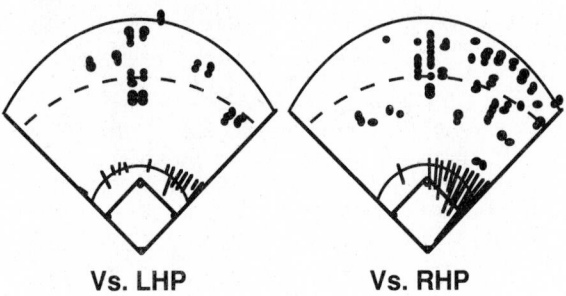

Vs. LHP   **Vs. RHP**

1989 Situational Stats

	AB	H	HR	RBI	AVG		AB	H	HR	RBI	AVG
Home	144	33	5	22	.229	LHP	73	18	2	17	.247
Road	132	24	6	17	.182	RHP	203	39	9	22	.192
Day	71	15	6	15	.211	Sc Pos	64	16	1	26	.250
Night	205	42	5	24	.205	Clutch	63	9	0	3	.143

1989 Rankings (National League)

→ 1st in fewest GDPs per GDP situation (1.6%) - *players with 50 PA in GDP situations*

HITTING:

The problem was supposed to be finding Ron Gant a position to play. It turned out, they had to find it in the minor leagues. Gant started slowly last year, hitting for some power and walking a little. But his average was right around his weight and he began to press. His walks all but disappeared as his strikeouts rose and his batting average fell. He wasn't cutting it at third base so sending him down was the right thing to do.

Gant worked extensively with Hank Aaron in the minors. When Ron came back up in September his average remained low but he raised his slugging to his '88 level. His quick wrists and big swing make it imperative that he hit for power because he is going to strike out a lot. He also has trouble adjusting to relief pitchers, which could be an area that will improve with experience. Gant's ability to draw walks and his high strikeout totals are about what you would expect from a young power hitter, and you would hope that he could improve a little there. His power seems to be intact, and he managed 20 extra-base hits, including nine homers, in his up-and-down half season.

BASERUNNING:

Gant is fast, runs and slides smoothly, and should improve his baserunning if he can get on base. Ron's 23 steals in 1988 are probably about as good as he'll get since he will not be on base that much, but he will cut his caught-stealings; after his September call-up he was three for three as a base stealer but only six for 12 during his early season stint.

FIELDING:

Gant is just awful in the infield, lacking the experience to make the right play instinctively. He made 16 errors in only 53 games during the third base experiment, eclipsing his own 26 errors in 122 games fiasco at second in 1988. He was schooled in centerfield during his demotion, but that was before Oddibe McDowell came over and put his name on the position. First base or another outfield position are possibilities, but it does not look as if he will go back to second or third.

OVERALL:

Everything depends on Gant's bat. The Braves are desperate for his kind of power and will accept many failings if he can slug in the .400s and keep his average above .250. If he can't hit, no degree of fielding improvement will keep him with Atlanta.

RON GANT

Position: 3B/CF
Bats: R **Throws:** R
Ht: 6' 0" **Wt:** 172

Opening Day Age: 25
Born: 3/2/65 in Victoria, TX
ML Seasons: 3

Overall Statistics

	G	AB	R	H	D	T	HR	RBI	SB	BB	SO	AVG
1989	75	260	26	46	8	3	9	25	9	20	63	.177
Career	242	906	120	214	40	11	30	94	32	67	192	.236

Where He Hits the Ball

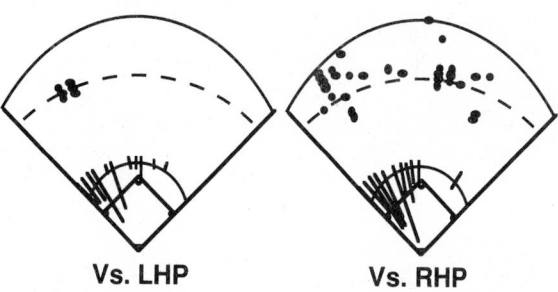

Vs. LHP   **Vs. RHP**

1989 Situational Stats

	AB	H	HR	RBI	AVG		AB	H	HR	RBI	AVG
Home	135	24	5	13	.178	LHP	79	9	1	6	.114
Road	125	22	4	12	.176	RHP	181	37	8	19	.204
Day	63	7	0	3	.111	Sc Pos	56	8	0	13	.143
Night	197	39	9	22	.198	Clutch	44	4	1	2	.091

1989 Rankings (National League)

➡ 5th in worst batting average with 2 strikes (.112) - *players with 162 PA with 2 strikes*

FUTURE ALL-STAR

TOM GLAVINE

Position: SP
Bats: L **Throws:** L
Ht: 6' 0" **Wt:** 175

Opening Day Age: 24
Born: 3/25/66 in
Concord, MA
ML Seasons: 3

PITCHING:

Tom Glavine led the Braves last year with 14 victories, but you can't really credit his great run-support (over five runs per game). He tossed four complete-game shut-outs and another complete game with a single unearned run. In fact, Tom allowed only 16 earned runs in his 14 victories, while surrendering 60 in his 15 other starts. Consistency was obviously a problem. It wasn't that he endured long slumps -- he had only one losing month, July at 1-2 -- but he would pitch a great game and then go out and get pounded the next time. His fastball was often the culprit.

Tom improved by getting a little more on his fastball and going inside with it more. His slider and curve both move downward and batters pound them into the ground. As the Braves solidify their infield defense, Glavine should become even more effective. Because his fastball won't overpower a hitter he gets in trouble with it. After showing some improvement towards the end of '88 he relapsed and gave up 20 home runs in 1989, especially in Fulton County Stadium where righties took him deep 13 times. All his home runs were to righthanded hitters; he handles lefties with ease. Glavine has always been a tough competitor and he showed fortitude in '89, bouncing back from every losing streak with good pitching.

FIELDING & HITTING:

Tom is a good fielder with pretty good range. Sometimes his big motion carries him off to the right and out of position to field easily, but he recovers well. He did commit four errors, but also started four double plays. He will throw to first base all day -- 185 throws in '89 -- and allowed only 12 stolen bases with 11 caught stealing, a sign that the throws to first are working. Glavine finagled a few walks and hits, but is not a big contributor with the bat, but he gets his cuts, and strikes out a lot.

OVERALL:

Glavine and John Smoltz should anchor the young Braves staff. If Tom can cut down on the home run ball he will be able to stay in more games. Glavine doesn't have a stamina problem and he throws easily, so he could compile some impressive inning totals, and his already fine record of complete games (6) could be even better. Since he is still only 24, and he works with weights, Glavine could add the little extra to his fastball that would make him a dominating pitcher. The Braves' future depends a great deal on Glavine.

Overall Statistics

	W	L	ERA	G	GS	Sv	IP	H	R	BB	SO	HR
1989	14	8	3.68	29	29	0	186.0	172	88	40	90	20
Career	23	29	4.29	72	72	0	431.2	428	233	136	194	37

Where They Hit the Ball

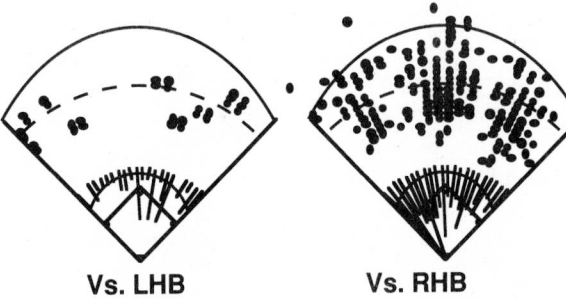

Vs. LHB   **Vs. RHB**

1989 Situational Stats

	W	L	ERA	Sv	IP		AB	H	HR	RBI	AVG
Home	6	4	3.72	0	94.1	LHB	106	23	0	7	.217
Road	8	4	3.63	0	91.2	RHB	603	149	20	62	.247
Day	3	2	5.10	0	30.0	Sc Pos	117	30	4	47	.256
Night	11	6	3.40	0	156.0	Clutch	60	11	3	7	.183

1989 Rankings (National League)

→ 2nd in most run support per 9 innings (5.2) - *pitchers with 162 IP*

→ 3rd in shutouts (4) and most home runs allowed per nine innings (.97)

→ 7th in lowest stolen base percentage allowed (52.2%) and pickoff throws (185)

→ Led the Braves in complete games (6), shut-outs, wins (14), home runs allowed (20), won/loss percentage (.636), strikeout/walk ratio (2.25), grounder/flyball ratio allowed (1.39), run support per nine innings and caught stealing (11)

HITTING:

Tommy Gregg was supposed to be a fill-in, a spare outfielder and a bat off the bench against righthanders. But he was off to a hot start last year --.389 with good power, in 13 games -- when he suffered a foot injury that disrupted his season. Gregg missed six weeks with the injury -- it came a day after he went five for five -- and he was not a factor after he returned. Tommy hit only .221 with 41 strikeouts and only 14 walks the rest of the way. Despite that, Gregg has shown some good ability to hit for average, is a fine hit-and-run man, and could be a solid doubles hitter who will hit the ball to all fields. What he hasn't shown is an ability to hit lefties, or hit outside of Fulton County Stadium.

Much has been said about Tommy's career as a college football player, and he does appear to have a football mentality. He hit much better when he was involved in the hitting attack – with runners on base, and at the top of the batting order. He has a deliberate, serious approach at the plate, and appears to be trying to have the perfect at bat, the perfect swing. He is a gung-ho player, and during April his approach worked well. But as the season went on and his deliberate approach so often resulted in failure, he seemed to get a little discouraged at the plate. In September he struck out 10 times in 32 at bats.

BASERUNNING:

Gregg has pretty good straight ahead speed, but is not too good on the bases for an old kick returner. He stole only three bases and was caught four times, and has a choppy running style that doesn't give him great acceleration. Gregg has stolen as many as 35 bases in the minors, but his broken foot may have affected his speed.

FIELDING:

Gregg played mostly at first and in right field. He made a couple of errors in the outfield, and his arm was below average. He was pretty good at first base, making no errors and showing some good moves on groundballs, particularly to his right.

OVERALL:

Tommy Gregg has very little major league experience, and it is possible that he could hit for good average in Atlanta, provided he has a position to play. His average against righties is traditionally good enough that he could find a good deal of playing time at first base or in right field.

TOMMY GREGG

Position: RF/1B
Bats: L **Throws:** L
Ht: 6' 1" **Wt:** 190

Opening Day Age: 26
Born: 7/29/63 in Boone, NC
ML Seasons: 3

Overall Statistics

	G	AB	R	H	D	T	HR	RBI	SB	BB	SO	AVG
1989	102	276	24	67	8	0	6	23	3	18	45	.243
Career	137	328	32	82	13	0	7	30	3	21	53	.250

Where He Hits the Ball

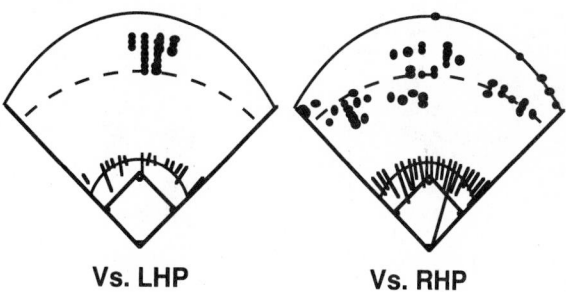

Vs. LHP   Vs. RHP

1989 Situational Stats

	AB	H	HR	RBI	AVG		AB	H	HR	RBI	AVG
Home	116	34	2	10	.293	LHP	57	13	0	2	.228
Road	160	33	4	13	.206	RHP	219	54	6	21	.247
Day	54	17	1	8	.315	Sc Pos	56	13	1	15	.232
Night	222	50	5	15	.225	Clutch	67	14	1	5	.209

1989 Rankings (National League)

➡ Did not rank near the top or bottom in any category

PITCHING:

Derek Lilliquist was one of the first pieces acquired by the Braves as they started the long rebuilding process in 1987. The former first-round draft pick got an education in 1989. The fastball that moved away from righthanded batters proved too predictable, and often ended up moving away from batters and into the seats. Derek has fine control -- only 34 walks in 30 starts -- but he gave up hits when he left his curve ball in the strike zone or left his fastball up. He was at his best when ahead in the count, but again was too predictable; batters knew he was coming over the plate, and hit his first pitch at a .380 clip. His troubles were compounded by his teammates; in 20 of his starts they supported him with only 19 runs. Nevertheless, he was giving up a ton of extra base hits, and almost 13 baserunners per nine innings. This was not the future ace everyone had expected.

After struggling all season and only getting into the seventh three times, Lilliquist made some much needed adjustments in September. He added a cut fastball that bore in on righties. Hitters had to look inside after spending the year hitting the ball on the outside of the plate. His ERA dropped a couple of runs from his July and August outings, and he began to last longer in games. Hitters began to swing and miss more, and over his last five starts he struck out 21 while walking only two in 33 innings.

FIELDING, HITTING, BASERUNNING:

Lilliquist has a compact motion that leaves him in a good position to field the ball. He is an adequate fielder for a big man, with little range but few mistakes. Derek holds runners well and had only six bases swiped against him. Lilliquist, who batted a respectable .190 in 1989, was a very good hitter in college, and has some potential with the bat. He is not a daring baserunner.

OVERALL:

Lilliquist has always had terrific control, but he needs to use it to his advantage, rather than letting hitters use it to theirs. Because he is young and took the frustrations of his maiden voyage well, the improvements of his last month are especially encouraging. If his new philosophy of pitching in and out works as well as it seemed to, it could signal the beginning of a fine career. He will get every chance with the Braves.

DEREK LILLIQUIST

Position: SP
Bats: L **Throws:** L
Ht: 6' 0" **Wt:** 200

Opening Day Age: 24
Born: 2/20/66 in Winter Park, FL
ML Seasons: 1

Overall Statistics

	W	L	ERA	G	GS	Sv	IP	H	R	BB	SO	HR
1989	8	10	3.97	32	30	0	165.2	202	87	34	79	16
Career	8	10	3.97	32	30	0	165.2	202	87	34	79	16

Where They Hit the Ball

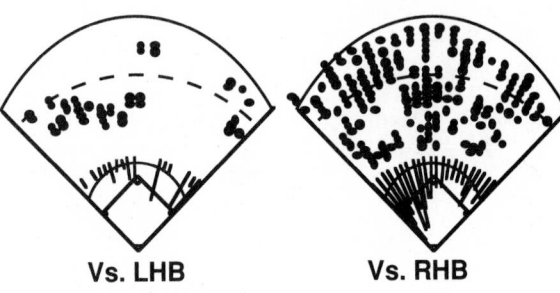

Vs. LHB   Vs. RHB

1989 Situational Stats

	W	L	ERA	Sv	IP		AB	H	HR	RBI	AVG
Home	5	5	3.32	0	97.2	LHB	102	27	3	15	.265
Road	3	5	4.90	0	68.0	RHB	569	175	13	58	.308
Day	4	3	5.04	0	44.2	Sc Pos	145	47	3	54	.324
Night	4	7	3.57	0	121.0	Clutch	33	14	1	4	.424

1989 Rankings (National League)

- ➡ 1st in worst slugging percentage allowed (.435) and highest batting average allowed (.301) - *pitchers with 162 IP*
- ➡ 2nd in least pitches thrown per batter (3.3)
- ➡ 3rd in lowest run support per 9 innings (3.4)
- ➡ 4th in lowest stolen base percentage allowed (50.0%)
- ➡ 5th in highest on-base average allowed (.335) and highest ERA (3.97)
- ➡ Led the Braves in games started (30), hit batsmen (2), least pitches thrown per batter, most GDPs per 9 innings (.71), lowest stolen base percentage allowed and hits allowed (202)

HITTING:

If the Braves made one move last season that had to be considered a step in the right direction, it was the acquisition of Oddibe McDowell. Injuries, including a freak run-in with a butter knife, have made some inroads on Oddibe's progress. He spent time in the minors as recently as 1988, although why is still a bit of a mystery. But he is a fine player, 27 years old, and his combination of speed, power, and ability to hit righties add up to a nice package for Atlanta.

McDowell is a slashing hitter with a flat swing, and should hit a lot of doubles in Fulton County Stadium. He's an excellent bunter. Whether he can raise his on-base percentage the 20-30 points he needs to justify the leadoff spot is a question. Although Oddibe is not a big man, he should show more power in The Launching Pad, and could hit 10-15 home runs. If he continues to lower his strikeouts (down every year since 1986), then the Braves have a player they can write on the line-up card every day.

BASERUNNING:

McDowell is a first-class basestealer, never swiping fewer than 24 bases even when his seasons have been as short as 111 games. His percentages before '89 have ranged from good (33 for 48, 69%) to spectacular (24 for 26, 92%), and his 15 for 25 for the Braves must be assumed to be the adjustment to a new league. He is fast and smart, and runs the bases well. McDowell didn't ground into a single double play with the Braves.

FIELDING:

Oddibe has never been a great fielder, mostly because his arm is not first class, and runners will take the extra base on him. He is an acrobat, and his speed and polish have allowed him to play left or centerfield; he could play either for the Braves.

OVERALL:

McDowell has not become the dominating player he was expected to become. He is a bit like Juan Samuel in his breadth of skills, and like Samuel was penciled in for stardom but then labeled a disappointment. McDowell is certainly not too old to improve, and he's changed the thinking in Atlanta about the future of centerfield. It is quite possible that there is a standout player sleeping in McDowell, and being traded twice in one season might be just the wake-up call he needed.

ODDIBE MCDOWELL

Position: CF/LF
Bats: L **Throws:** L
Ht: 5' 9" **Wt:** 160

Opening Day Age: 27
Born: 8/25/62 in Hollywood, FL
ML Seasons: 5

Overall Statistics

	G	AB	R	H	D	T	HR	RBI	SB	BB	SO	AVG
1989	145	519	89	138	23	6	10	46	27	52	73	.266
Career	658	2341	377	593	106	27	66	226	142	245	458	.253

Where He Hits the Ball

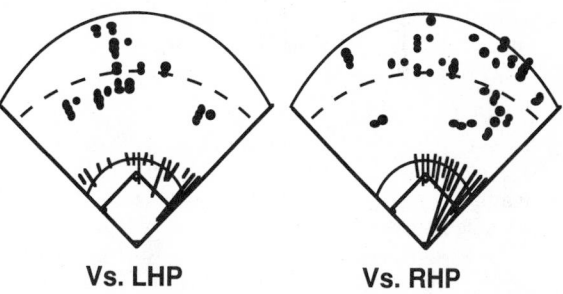

Vs. LHP   **Vs. RHP**

1989 Situational Stats

	AB	H	HR	RBI	AVG		AB	H	HR	RBI	AVG
Home	232	67	3	23	.289	LHP	170	38	0	10	.224
Road	287	71	7	23	.247	RHP	349	100	10	36	.287
Day	154	38	1	9	.247	Sc Pos	102	24	2	33	.235
Night	365	100	9	37	.274	Clutch	76	18	2	7	.237

1989 Rankings (National League)

- ⇒ 2nd in worst stolen base percentage (60.0%) - *players with 20 stolen base attempts*
- ⇒ 6th in batting average on a 3-2 count (.389) - *players with 20 PA on a 3-2 count*
- ⇒ 8th in percentage of extra bases taken as a runner (59.6%) - *players with 40 opportunities to advance*
- ⇒ 9th in bunts in play (21) -- finished 8th in the AL with 24 bunts in play before being traded
- ⇒ Led the Braves in triples (4), bunts in play, hitting in the clutch (.277), percentage of extra bases taken as a runner, hitting on a 3-1 count (.462) and hitting on a 3-2 count (3.89)
- ⇒ Led NL Center Fielders in hitting on a 3-2 count

HALL OF FAMER

DALE MURPHY

Position: CF/RF
Bats: R **Throws:** R
Ht: 6' 4" **Wt:** 215

Opening Day Age: 34
Born: 3/12/56 in Portland, OR
ML Seasons: 14

HITTING:

Although Dale Murphy's home runs, RBI totals, and batting average last year were not terribly different from his poor 1988 totals, there were many signs of further erosion of his talents. His road batting average was .201. His trickle of triples dried up, and he suffered a devastating drop in doubles from an excellent 35 to a meager 16. He had the fewest total bases of any of his 400 at bat seasons. His strikeouts were up and his walks were down.

In many ways 1989 resembles Murphy's pre-star, 1978 campaign; the difference is that he had his best days ahead of him then, not behind him. Dale struck out on four pitches or less 92 times, and his bat helicoptering over the infield after he threw it at a pitch out of the strike zone became a common sight. During the season Murphy seemed to think that he would snap out of his slump at any moment, but he never did. Dale's days in the four spot are best behind him, and his future is probably as a number five or six hitter, protecting the next Dale Murphy.

BASERUNNING:

Murphy's career 70% success rate is good, but he's lost a lot of speed, as reflected by his drop in doubles and the move from center to right. Dale is six for 13 over the last two years, and it is unlikely that he will again be a serious base stealing threat. He still runs the bases intelligently, though, and is dangerous to any fielder blocking his path to a base.

FIELDING:

Dale made a good adjustment to right, and goes to the wall well. His arm, excellent through 1988, was a distinct liability in '89, when runners consistently took the extra base. An outfield of Smith, McDowell, and Murphy would not be a great defensive unit.

OVERALL:

Murphy should be able to reach 400 home runs and 2000 hits with the Braves. He still has value because of his ability to draw walks and hit the long ball, and will play for the Braves if he maintains a level of production somewhere between his '88 and '89 performances. Only three years removed from being one of the best three or four players in the league, it is possible for Dale to rebound somewhat. Because of his stature and class, you can bet that all the people who don't believe he can make a comeback would be glad to be proven wrong.

Overall Statistics

	G	AB	R	H	D	T	HR	RBI	SB	BB	SO	AVG
1989	154	574	60	131	16	0	20	84	3	65	142	.228
Career	1829	6749	1065	1820	292	37	354	1088	151	871	1497	.270

Where He Hits the Ball

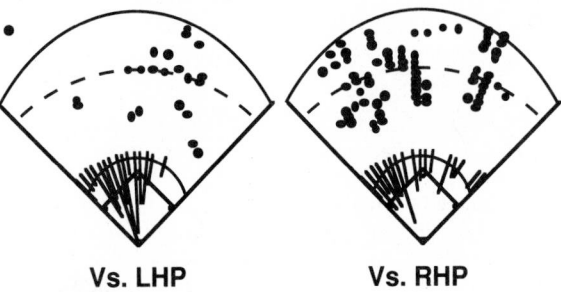

Vs. LHP   **Vs. RHP**

1989 Situational Stats

	AB	H	HR	RBI	AVG		AB	H	HR	RBI	AVG
Home	276	71	9	47	.257	LHP	172	42	5	19	.244
Road	298	60	11	37	.201	RHP	402	89	15	65	.221
Day	141	37	2	21	.262	Sc Pos	151	43	9	67	.285
Night	433	94	18	63	.217	Clutch	95	24	3	18	.253

1989 Rankings (National League)

- ➡ 2nd in highest percentage of swings that missed (29.3%) - *players with 502 PA*
- ➡ 3rd in strikeouts (142)
- ➡ 4th in lowest batting average (.228)
- ➡ 5th in lowest percentage of swings put into play (37.1%)
- ➡ Led the Braves in strikeouts, at bats (574), intentional walks (10), plate appearances (647), games (154), RBIs (84), and pitches seen (2,280)
- ➡ Led NL Center Fielders in strikeouts and GDPs (15)

HITTING:

Nice month. In April Gerald Perry drew 19 walks; his previous season high was 48. He hit .314 with power, and looked like he had taken another step beyond his 1988 campaign when he made a run at the batting title for most of the season. Unfortunately Perry's shoulder problems became the determining factor of his '89 season. He began to miss games in May, and was out for the season by the end of July. Gerald suffered through a pitiful streak of futility while trying to stay in the line-up. In 43 games, over 164 at bats, from April 24th to June 29th, Gerald did not drive in a run. He had opportunities, too. The Braves were really counting on Perry for RBIs in 1989 and his failure was devastating to the team.

Gerald feasts on fastballs, but can really hit any pitcher when he is on. His dismal showing against righties (.198) in '89 has to be blamed on the shoulder, but how do you account for the way he pounded the lefties that have given him a problem in the past? He hit .337 with power against them. If that is a real improvement, and Gerald can recover from his health problems, then he may again be a factor in a future batting race.

BASERUNNING:

Perry is fast but gets thrown out trying to steal with bad jumps, thinking he can outrun the ball. His numbers before last year were good but erratic, with a high of 42 steals in 1987. When healthy, Gerald is good for 25-30 steals. Although Perry did much better last season, he generally hits into far too many double plays for a lefty with his speed.

FIELDING:

Perry was on a pace to make more than 1988's 17 errors at first base, with nine in only 72 games. In an early season game Gerald turned to argue a call with the umpire at first and the run scored from third. Although he is mobile, and often wonderful on line drives, particularly to his left, he is not a good first baseman.

OVERALL:

Because his shoulder went out three times last year and he doesn't have the power people expect from a first baseman, Perry's future is unclear. At 29, Perry would have to do all the things he has done in the past, plus show the eye he had in April, to be considered for the regular job. His bat will insure a major role somewhere, provided he stays healthy.

GERALD PERRY

Position: 1B
Bats: L **Throws:** R
Ht: 6' 0" **Wt:** 190

Opening Day Age: 29
Born: 10/30/60 in Savannah, GA
ML Seasons: 7

Overall Statistics

	G	AB	R	H	D	T	HR	RBI	SB	BB	SO	AVG
1989	72	266	24	67	11	0	4	21	10	32	28	.252
Career	643	2040	247	551	96	5	37	246	105	213	214	.270

Where He Hits the Ball

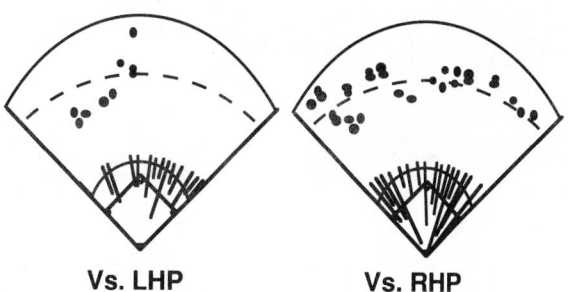

Vs. LHP   **Vs. RHP**

1989 Situational Stats

	AB	H	HR	RBI	AVG		AB	H	HR	RBI	AVG
Home	142	41	2	12	.289	LHP	104	35	3	10	.337
Road	124	26	2	9	.210	RHP	162	32	1	11	.198
Day	65	20	4	10	.308	Sc Pos	69	14	1	15	.203
Night	201	47	0	11	.234	Clutch	39	6	1	2	.154

1989 Rankings (National League)

➡ Led NL First Basemen in bunts in play (7)

HITTING:

John Russell had the dubious distinction of being the least-used member of the worst-hitting catching corps in the Major Leagues. The Braves trio of Benedict, Davis, and Russell were remarkable for their similarities; they all had the same weaknesses and the same strength. Each hit between .169 and .195, each hit between one and four home runs, and each slugged below .242. Russell is quite a free swinger, and he was constantly behind in the count. He struck out far more often than he reached base. He can hit righthanders a little, and for that reason he should have played more, since Davis and Benedict both managed to hit over .200 against lefties but not righties.

Russell had a couple of decent years with Philadelphia, particularly in 1986 when Darren Daulton went down and Russell was asked to step into the breach. He showed good power that year (13 homers and 60 RBIs in only 315 at bats) but changes in the catching situation in Philly reduced him to just a bit player. With the Braves, Russell actually hit a little better as a catcher than he did at other positions.

BASERUNNING:

Is there a new way to say that a catcher is slow? Russell runs like he's paired with Jody Davis in a three-legged race. Actually, he is much faster than Davis, and scored 14 runs to Davis' 12, and in far fewer at bats and half the home runs. He is a threat on the bases only if he's on your team.

FIELDING:

Russell is a catcher because he could never hit enough to play in the outfield. He handled pitchers to a 4.05 ERA, but had the best winning percentage on the team at .414 (12-17). He has a fine arm, like the rest of the Braves catchers, and with the help of the pitching staff tossed out 21 of 38 basestealers. Russell played a little bit in right, left, at first, and at third. He was pretty bad in right in limited duty. John's versatility is a matter of question. You wouldn't want to use him for extended duty at any position other than catcher.

OVERALL:

The Braves are looking for a young catcher, but don't really have anyone who can step in right away. None of their immediate possibilities are better than Russell, so, since he has the added bonus of versatility, it is likely that John will return in 1990.

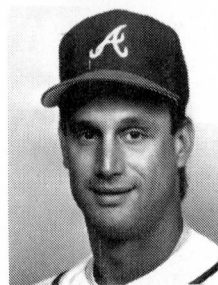

JOHN RUSSELL

Position: C
Bats: R **Throws:** R
Ht: 6' 0" **Wt:** 195

Opening Day Age: 29
Born: 1/5/61 in Oklahoma City, OK
ML Seasons: 6

Overall Statistics

	G	AB	R	H	D	T	HR	RBI	SB	BB	SO	AVG
1989	74	159	14	29	2	0	2	9	0	8	53	.182
Career	333	900	92	201	45	3	31	115	2	69	293	.223

Where He Hits the Ball

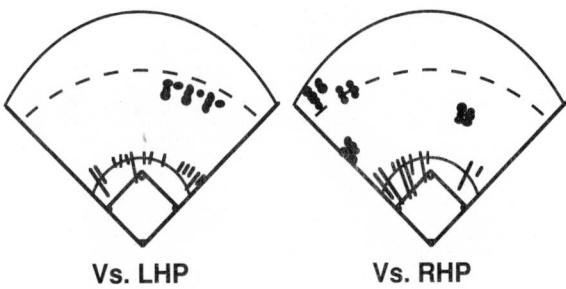

Vs. LHP   **Vs. RHP**

1989 Situational Stats

	AB	H	HR	RBI	AVG		AB	H	HR	RBI	AVG
Home	72	12	1	4	.167	LHP	68	8	1	1	.118
Road	87	17	1	5	.195	RHP	91	21	1	8	.231
Day	43	4	0	0	.093	Sc Pos	28	6	0	6	.214
Night	116	25	2	9	.216	Clutch	39	6	0	3	.154

1989 Rankings (National League)

➡ Did not rank near the top or bottom in any category

HITTING:

The stories started last winter about the great things Lonnie Smith was doing in the Caribbean League. Smith came to camp hungry for a job, won it and continued the magic all season. Lonnie has returned from his drug problems a far more dangerous hitter than he has ever been in the past. He established career highs in walks and homers, slugging and on-base percentage, killed lefties and righties, and was consistent. Smith had his worst month in September when he hit only .269 (but still scored 16 runs and drove in 15) and, if he wore down at the end it's no surprise considering he'd played all year round.

Smith lifted his game another notch with runners on base or in scoring position; he hit over .400 and slugged over .630. He looks bigger in the upper body now, but still has that high-held, "dangerous me!" wave to his bat. His wrists are so quick that he hits the ball hard everywhere. In 1989 he was by far the best hitter on the team, and one of the best in baseball.

BASERUNNING:

If Smith's speed has never been tamed, it has not deserted him, either. He swiped 25 bases in '89, and was nine for 11 in April, which is amazing when you consider that he was nursing a bad ankle for the first two months. Lonnie is prone to lapses on the bases, and was picked off three times in 1989.

FIELDING:

"Skates" Smith has a history of defensive problems, as any fan knows. A mid-season Sporting News issue gave straight-faced kudos to Lonnie for being the top left fielder in baseball, and while his numbers look OK, they fib. Lonnie kicks balls, he will fall asleep in the field, he won't hustle after misplayed balls, and if he does make a mistake, he will play cautiously, surrounding balls hit his way. His throws are an adventure, though his arm is only a little below average. He is fast and can run under some drives, but it can't be said that he uses his speed much on defense.

OVERALL:

The Braves are incredibly lucky to have Smith, especially now that Dale Murphy seems unable to put punch in the lineup. Even if Lonnie loses some of last year's magic, he will still be productive. Smith has played on three world championship teams, and that can't hurt the young Braves players. Comeback Player of the Year.

LONNIE SMITH

Position: LF
Bats: R **Throws:** R
Ht: 5'9" **Wt:** 170

Opening Day Age: 34
Born: 12/22/55 in Chicago, IL
ML Seasons: 12

Overall Statistics

	G	AB	R	H	D	T	HR	RBI	SB	BB	SO	AVG
1989	134	482	89	152	34	4	21	79	25	76	95	.315
Career	1134	3911	700	1136	210	42	68	385	337	436	609	.290

Where He Hits the Ball

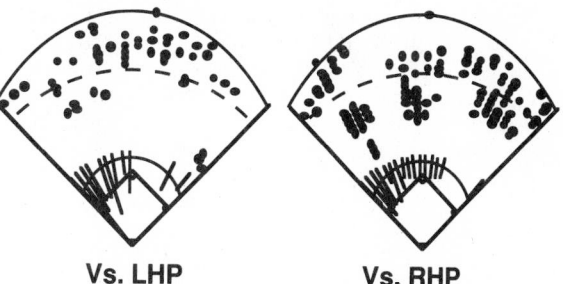

Vs. LHP   **Vs. RHP**

1989 Situational Stats

	AB	H	HR	RBI	AVG		AB	H	HR	RBI	AVG
Home	226	81	10	46	.358	LHP	165	53	7	28	.321
Road	256	71	11	33	.277	RHP	317	99	14	51	.312
Day	107	35	8	16	.327	Sc Pos	98	41	4	54	.418
Night	375	117	13	63	.312	Clutch	67	18	3	11	.269

1989 Rankings (National League)

- ➡ 1st in on-base average (.415), hitting with runners in scoring position (.418) and batting at home (.358) - *players with 502 PA*

- ➡ 3rd in batting average (.315), lowest percent of swings put into play (35.6%) and hit by pitch (11)

- ➡ 4th in pitches seen per plate appearance (3.8)

- ➡ Led the Braves in batting average, home runs (21), runs (89), doubles (34), triples (4), stolen bases (25), walks (76), total bases (257), sacrifice flies (7), caught stealing (12), hit by pitch, on-base average, slugging percentage (.533), runs scored per time reached base (34.4%) and hitting with runners in scoring position

PITCHING:

Pete Smith was allowed to go 7-15 in 1988 and 5-14 in 1989 for two reasons; the Braves have time, and he can throw the baseball. Smith has a 90+ mph fastball, a hard slider, a curveball, and in '89 he developed a circle change. Pete can really spot the fastball, as his 115 strikeouts in 142 innings indicate. He will throw it inside against righthanded hitters and simply freeze them. Against righties he struck out 65 and walked only 12. With two full seasons as a major league starter, he is still only 24. So much for the good news.

Smith was rushed to the Braves based on his heater and not much else. His minor league history is similar to his major league performance; about a hit per inning, fair to lousy ERA, and poor win/loss record. In 1988 Smith was going about six innings per start because he was being nursed along, though he did pitch five complete games and three shutouts. But in '89 he just couldn't go longer, lasting as far as seven innings in only four starts. Smith had some bad luck, too. He gave up a total of only two earned runs in those four starts, but was only 1-1. Pete doesn't seem to be able to master all of his pitches. The change was supposed to be the missing piece of the puzzle, but it was just another problem for him.

FIELDING:

Smith will just throw and throw over to first, but runners were 17 of 26 stealing on him. He balked seven times with all those throws. Pete is good on ground balls and liners past the mound, and only made one error in 1989. His range is only fair. Pete isn't much of a factor at the plate, although he does put the ball into play.

OVERALL:

Sometimes you have to wonder if the Braves just don't know what to do with Smith. He seemed to be less effective as the game went on; his fastball seemed to lose a yard, and his strikeouts would drop. That is also when he gave up most of his home runs. Perhaps, with that good fastball, he would be more effective as a reliever? Because of his youth, stuff, and proven ability to keep going out there, it is certain that the Braves will give him more opportunities to develop as a starter, but he might be a guy who can bring it for an inning or two and save 30 games.

PETE SMITH

Position: SP
Bats: R **Throws:** R
Ht: 6' 2" **Wt:** 185

Opening Day Age: 24
Born: 2/27/66 in Abington, MA
ML Seasons: 3

Overall Statistics

	W	L	ERA	G	GS	Sv	IP	H	R	BB	SO	HR
1989	5	14	4.75	28	27	0	142.0	144	83	57	115	13
Career	13	31	4.20	66	65	0	369.0	366	193	159	250	31

Where They Hit the Ball

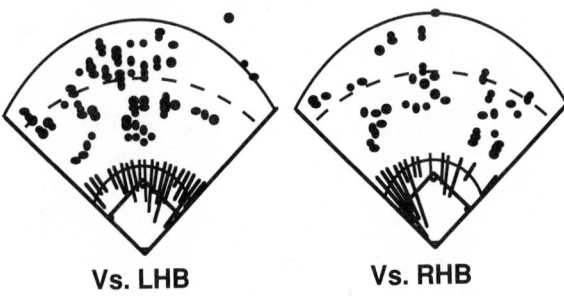

Vs. LHB   **Vs. RHB**

1989 Situational Stats

	W	L	ERA	Sv	IP		AB	H	HR	RBI	AVG
Home	2	7	4.48	0	72.1	LHB	328	84	7	35	.256
Road	3	7	5.04	0	69.2	RHB	219	60	6	30	.274
Day	2	2	2.60	0	27.2	Sc Pos	123	37	2	49	.301
Night	3	12	5.27	0	114.1	Clutch	23	5	0	2	.217

1989 Rankings (National League)

- 1st in balks (7)
- 2nd in lowest won/loss percentage (.263) - *pitchers with 15 decisions*
- 4th in losses (14)
- 5th in pickoff throws (217)
- Led the Braves in balks, losses, pickoff throws and stolen bases allowed (17)

JOHN SMOLTZ

Position: SP
Bats: R **Throws:** R
Ht: 6' 3" **Wt:** 185

Opening Day Age: 22
Born: 5/15/67 in
Detroit, MI
ML Seasons: 2

CY YOUNG STUFF

PITCHING:

John Smoltz has been touted for years as a future staff ace, a pitcher with the kind of overpowering stuff that 20 game winners are made of. Smoltz's fastball has always been his money pitch, and he throws it in the 90s, but the question was if he would be able to harness his big curve. In '88 the answer was no. He walked 33 batters in 64 innings, and had to come in with the fastball. As good as the heater is, it's hittable when batters know it's coming, and Smoltz gave up 74 hits, including 10 homers.

The Braves weren't worried because Smoltz occasionally threw pitches that simply blew hitters away. He started strong in '89 with the curve working and an effective change-up to go with the heater. In May he was 4-1 with 12 walks and 36 strikeouts, and allowed only 30 hits in 49 innings with a 1.84 ERA. Although his arm tired in August, Smoltz still finished with an impressive record. Lefties and righties hit him at an equally futile .212 pace, and only Sid Fernandez and Jose DeLeon held opponents to a lower average. His heater and big curve racked up the strikeouts, but also led to eight wild pitches. John had an ERA in Fulton County Stadium a half run better than on the road, despite surrendering 12 Fulton homers. Smoltz gives up extra base hits -- 30 doubles, 3 triples, 15 homers -- and that is some cause for concern.

FIELDING, HITTING, BASERUNNING:

Smoltz made seven errors in 1989 and generally had problems in the field. He does have pretty good range, and his error total was bloated by miscues on balls he was really stretching for. Smoltz does not hold runners very well, and often seems to ignore the runner. He has a good move though, and picked off three runners. Although his average was poor, John is a hitter up there, and hit for the cycle during the course of the season -- he had one of each. The homer went 430 feet.

OVERALL:

For a team as maligned as a collector of talent as Atlanta, the acquisition of Smoltz for Doyle Alexander in '87 has to be heartening. John's 1989 season can only be seen as a final step towards stardom. His elbow troubles of late 1989 are not expected to affect him. He has great stuff and a fine arm. It would be surprise if he did not soon take his place among the best pitchers in the league.

Overall Statistics

	W	L	ERA	G	GS	Sv	IP	H	R	BB	SO	HR
1989	12	11	2.94	29	29	0	208.0	160	79	72	168	15
Career	14	18	3.54	41	41	0	272.0	234	119	105	205	25

Where They Hit the Ball

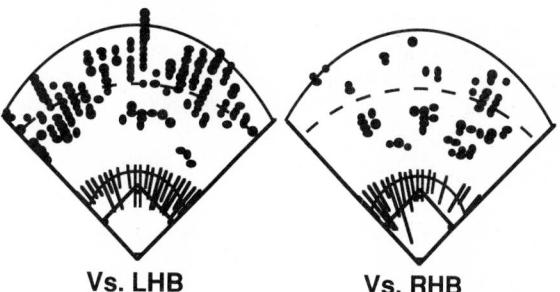

Vs. LHB　　　　**Vs. RHB**

1989 Situational Stats

	W	L	ERA	Sv	IP		AB	H	HR	RBI	AVG
Home	6	4	2.63	0	99.1	LHB	458	97	6	45	.212
Road	6	7	3.23	0	108.2	RHB	298	63	9	27	.211
Day	5	0	1.49	0	54.1	Sc Pos	163	32	2	51	.196
Night	7	11	3.46	0	153.2	Clutch	105	19	1	7	.181

1989 Rankings (National League)

- ➡ 3rd in lowest batting average allowed (.212) - *pitchers with 162 IP*
- ➡ 4th in lowest run support per 9 innings (3.5)
- ➡ 5th in lowest slugging percentage allowed (.319)
- ➡ 6th in strikeouts per 9 innings (7.3)
- ➡ 8th in lowest on-base average allowed (.280)
- ➡ Led the Braves in ERA (2.94), innings (208), walks allowed (72), strikeouts (168), pitches thrown (3,193), lowest batting average allowed, lowest HRs per 9 innings (.649), highest strikeouts per 9 innings (7.3), lowest on-base average allowed, lowest slugging percentage allowed

PITCHING:

Mike Stanton is just the kind of wild, hard throwing young reliever that is all the rage these days. He's not wild with his pitches, however, as he walked only eight and struck out 27 in his 24 innings with the Braves. He is a wild and restless presence in the bullpen. He's fidgety and as the game goes on, he gets more wound up and nervous. On the mound he talks to himself between pitches, smiling to himself, giving himself pep talks and pumping himself up.

Stanton got the call when Jim Acker got traded and Joe Boever was fading. He set a record in Double A Greenville with 19 saves and was doing the job in Richmond -- eight saves -- when the Braves sent for him. He was only going to get a look, but gave every indication that he's ready for the majors. He throws a fastball in the 90s that he keeps low, and a curveball that keeps batters honest. After heat, heat, and more heat, the curveball will simply paralyze hitters. He gets a few more groundouts than flyouts, and quite a few strikeouts. What he doesn't do is give up hits, only 17 in his 24 innings. His seven saves were earned in only eight save opportunities.

FIELDING, HITTING, BASERUNNING:

Stanton has a big motion, but appears to be watching the pitch rather than positioning himself to field the ball. He was an outfielder when he was drafted and has only been pitching for three years, so he does not have an infielder's instincts. He keeps runners close and they don't often try to run on him; there was one base stolen on him, in one attempt. The former outfielder may never get to strut his stuff at the plate; stoppers don't hit.

OVERALL:

Last season was the first year that Stanton pitched in relief; he was a starter for two years before that. It looks as if he's found his role. The presence of Joe Boever might suggest that Stanton will work in a platoon role in 1990, but he handles lefties and righties so well, and is such a force on the mound that it is unlikely that he will have to share duties if he proves up to the task. Boever is a good insurance policy, but the Braves will try to groom Stanton for the ace stopper role.

MIKE STANTON

Position: RP
Bats: L **Throws:** L
Ht: 6' 1" **Wt:** 190

Opening Day Age: 22
Born: 6/2/67 in Houston, TX
ML Seasons: 1

Overall Statistics

	W	L	ERA	G	GS	Sv	IP	H	R	BB	SO	HR
1989	0	1	1.50	20	0	7	24.0	17	4	8	27	0
Career	0	1	1.50	20	0	7	24.0	17	4	8	27	0

Where They Hit the Ball

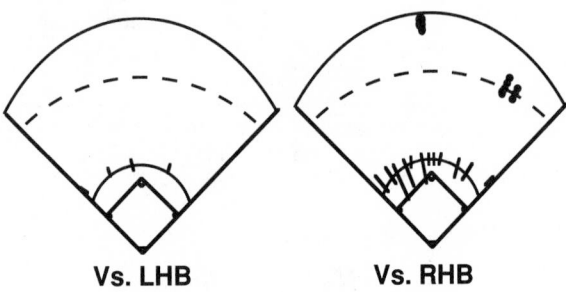

Vs. LHB   **Vs. RHB**

1989 Situational Stats

	W	L	ERA	Sv	IP		AB	H	HR	RBI	AVG
Home	0	1	2.63	3	13.2	LHB	14	3	0	5	.214
Road	0	0	0.00	4	10.1	RHB	68	14	0	4	.206
Day	0	0	0.00	1	6.2	Sc Pos	32	6	0	9	.188
Night	0	1	2.08	6	17.1	Clutch	61	14	0	7	.230

1989 Rankings (National League)

➡ 7th in ERA (1.50) - *all league pitchers*

➡ Led the Braves in save percentage (87.5%)

HITTING:

Andres Thomas' power may be his undoing. He started the season hot, Dale Murphy didn't, and on April 13th Thomas found himself hitting fourth. The Braves won and Andres got three hits and drove in a run, starting a flirtation with the cleanup slot that eventually ran to 97 at bats. He was really good hitting cleanup and even better in the three spot. By the end of June he had 10 homers and 41 RBIs. He hurt his ankle early in July, but came back quickly and continued to hit cleanup. It may have been the ankle or maybe it was just the swinging for the fences, but from July 1st on Thomas hit .180 with 16 RBIs. He slowly sank back to the seven spot.

Thomas holds the bat high and cocked and loops into his flat, level swing, making it very difficult to adjust to the breaking ball. Andres is extremely impatient at the plate and nearly half the time puts the ball in play on the first or second pitch. His 1988 .268 on base percentage now seems Ruthian next to last year's absurd .228 OBP. Thomas almost has to hit for average, because, though he has a little power, he doesn't do anything else well enough to justify his starting position.

BASERUNNING:

Andres was three for six as a basestealer, which is consistent with his career. Combined with few doubles, no triples, and 17 GDPs, it seems clear that Andres does not use his speed well on offense.

FIELDING:

Thomas' natural quickness and ability often allow him to make spectacular plays. His arm is good, but he will throw from the hole when he should eat the ball. Because he prefers to approach the ball from the side, rather than get in front of it in the classic manner, Thomas continues to be among the worst regular shortstops in fielding percentage (29 errors in 1989). He committed more errors than he had RBIs in the second half.

OVERALL:

Thomas has not made the improvements that would cement his hold on an everyday shortstop job, and in fact suffered a serious decline in 1989. His successful love affair with the 3-4 spots must be considered the luck of a hot streak. Although his power is good for a shortstop, you pay a high price in negatives for a few homers. Thomas does not take his failures lightly, and will try to find some answers, but the Braves would probably be better served starting Blauser or one of the rookies at short.

ANDRES THOMAS

Position: SS
Bats: R **Throws:** R
Ht: 6' 1" **Wt:** 185

Opening Day Age: 26
Born: 11/10/63 in Santo Domingo, Dominican Republic
ML Seasons: 5

Overall Statistics

	G	AB	R	H	D	T	HR	RBI	SB	BB	SO	AVG
1989	141	554	41	118	18	0	13	57	3	12	62	.213
Career	493	1825	156	432	68	4	37	198	20	48	258	.237

Where He Hits the Ball

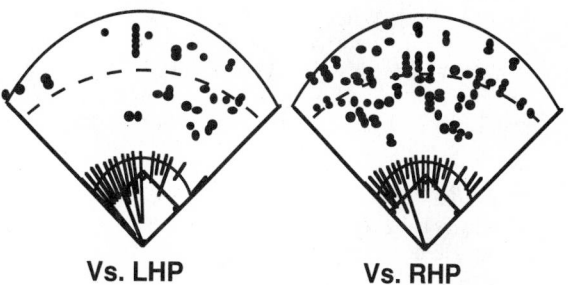

Vs. LHP　　　**Vs. RHP**

1989 Situational Stats

	AB	H	HR	RBI	AVG		AB	H	HR	RBI	AVG
Home	251	49	5	26	.195	LHP	173	36	4	18	.208
Road	303	69	8	31	.228	RHP	381	82	9	39	.215
Day	131	28	4	13	.214	Sc Pos	133	31	1	40	.233
Night	423	90	9	44	.213	Clutch	107	29	4	11	.271

1989 Rankings (National League)

➡ 1st in worst batting average (.213), worst on-base average (.228), and worst batting average at home (.195) - *players with 502 PA*

➡ 3rd in errors (29)

➡ 4th in lowest percentage of pitches taken (45.3%)

➡ 5th in GDPs (17) and worst slugging percentage (.316)

➡ Led the Braves in GDPs, grounder/flyball ratio (1.22), hitting with the bases loaded (.273) and errors

➡ Led NL Shortstops in home run frequency (42.6 ABs per HR) and GDPs (17)

HITTING:

First, Jeff Treadway had injury problems in Cincinnati. Then he fought a long slump that, combined with the reemergence of Ron Oester, made him expendable. As they did with Oddibe McDowell later, the Braves showed a willingness to go with a younger player whose value was down, and they hit pay dirt with Treadway. While there is a large question about his ability to hit lefthanded pitching (he was allowed 106 at bats and hit only .198), it is clear that he can help the club if used correctly.

Treadway is a contact hitter and hit at least .300 every year of his organized baseball career until 1988. He's a good fastball hitter and likes the ball inside. But at Cincinnati, Treadway's lack of power and below-average speed forced him into low-RBI and runs scored spots near the bottom of the order. He had over half his at bats with the Braves in the one-two spots, however, and performed well in those spots against righthanders. When Oddibe McDowell arrived, Treadway's RBI totals from the two spot increased dramatically. He is a good bunter and struck out only 38 times, but you would like to see more than his 30 walks. For such a good contact hitter, he was only two for eight on the hit-and-run.

BASERUNNING:

Treadway has average speed, but is not a basestealing threat. He does not often take the extra base, but he won't cost his team foolish outs on the bases. He grounded into nine double plays, which is a lot for a lefthanded batter, but some of those came on the busted hit-and-run.

FIELDING:

Treadway's style at second would have to be called hard-nosed rather than graceful. He will knock down a ball on a diving stop, where another second baseman would glove the same ball and make the play. That type of play may be why he was charged with only 12 errors. Treadway worked well with Andres Thomas and was involved in 79 double plays, which place him squarely among the top National League second sackers. He showed improvement during the year, and could easily become a steady, competent fielder.

OVERALL:

If Mark Lemke is finally ready for The Show, he and Treadway could be a fine second base platoon. At 27, it is time for Treadway to consolidate his obvious skills and see if he can make the few small adjustments -- a few more walks and a few less miscues in the field -- that would establish him in the majors.

JEFF TREADWAY

Position: 2B
Bats: L **Throws:** R
Ht: 5'11" **Wt:** 170

Opening Day Age: 27
Born: 1/22/63 in Columbus, GA
ML Seasons: 3

Overall Statistics

	G	AB	R	H	D	T	HR	RBI	SB	BB	SO	AVG
1989	134	473	58	131	18	3	8	40	3	30	38	.277
Career	260	858	97	235	41	7	12	67	6	59	74	.274

Where He Hits the Ball

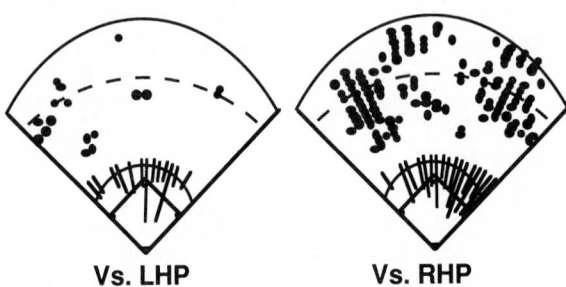

Vs. LHP   **Vs. RHP**

1989 Situational Stats

	AB	H	HR	RBI	AVG		AB	H	HR	RBI	AVG
Home	234	61	2	22	.261	LHP	106	21	0	10	.198
Road	239	70	6	18	.293	RHP	367	110	8	30	.300
Day	126	34	1	7	.270	Sc Pos	90	23	1	31	.256
Night	347	97	7	33	.280	Clutch	94	24	2	9	.255

1989 Rankings (National League)

- ➡ 3rd in least pitches seen per plate appearance (3.0) - *players with 502 PA*
- ➡ 6th in percentage of swings put into play (54.2%)
- ➡ 7th in hitting on the road (.293)
- ➡ 8th in hitting vs. righthanded pitchers (.300) and lowest percentage of swings that missed (9.2%)
- ➡ Led the Braves in singles (102), percentage of swings that missed, percentage of swings put into play, batting average with 2 strikes (.261), hitting vs. righthanded pitchers and hitting on the road
- ➡ Led NL Second Basemen in hitting on the road

JAY ALDRICH

Position: RP
Bats: R **Throws:** R
Ht: 6' 3" **Wt:** 210

Opening Day Age: 28
Born: 4/14/61 in
Alexandria, LA
ML Seasons: 2

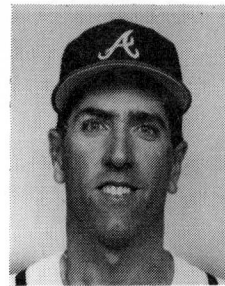

JOSE ALVAREZ

Position: RP
Bats: R **Throws:** R
Ht: 5'11" **Wt:** 175

Opening Day Age: 34
Born: 4/12/56 in
Tampa, FL
ML Seasons: 4

Overall Statistics

	W	L	ERA	G	GS	Sv	IP	H	R	BB	SO	HR
1989	2	2	3.29	24	0	1	38.1	31	16	19	19	3
Career	5	3	4.28	55	0	1	96.2	102	49	32	41	11

Overall Statistics

	W	L	ERA	G	GS	Sv	IP	H	R	BB	SO	HR
1989	3	3	2.86	30	0	2	50.1	44	18	24	45	4
Career	8	9	2.99	98	0	5	162.1	140	56	79	134	12

PITCHING, FIELDING, HITTING:

Righthander Jay Aldrich came to the Braves just in time to have young Mike Stanton emerge ahead of him. Aldrich had previously pitched in the Brewer system, and had been groomed as a closer since '84. Not overpowering, he had good numbers with the Braves, but the results were better than the pitching would seem to warrant. He started out behind in the count a lot; his nearly one-to-one strikeout to walk ratio was a sign of that, and learning a new league. He was death to lefties and there is where his real value lies, although he would be okay against righties if he could stop giving up the long hit. His 2.19 ERA with the Braves was excellent, but the limited duty makes it difficult to know how much to rely on it. He is not a good fielder, and does not hold baserunners particularly well.

OVERALL:

Aldrich has been at his best in closer situations, but there are only so many spots in the Braves bullpen. However, if Jay can produce the good results for the team that he did in his short 1989 stint, he will find work with them next season.

PITCHING, FIELDING, HITTING:

At 32, Jose Alvarez was the fourth oldest rookie in history when he came up to the Braves in 1988. He compiled an impressive 2.99 ERA in 60 games that year, and filled the middle relief role admirably. Jose throws a variety of breaking pitches, but his down-breaking curve is his money pitch. He moves the ball around the strike zone and doesn't throw hard. Because breaking pitches sometimes hang, he gives up a few homers and doubles, and because he is reluctant to come into a batter when behind on the count, he gives up walks. He is a good fielder, especially on bunts, but he doesn't hold runners and with all of his slow junk, runners go. Alvarez was breezing in 1989 when a knee problem began to bother him. Jose's pitching was affected and he was getting beat up in June when he went on the disabled list with tendinitis. He finally was forced to have knee surgery and was out for the season.

OVERALL:

Alvarez fills an important role and does it well. But he is 34 years old and is coming off of surgery. If healthy, Alvarez should fill the long relief role again in 1990. If he doesn't bounce back well, it could be year 11 in the minor leagues.

GERONIMO BERROA

Position: RF
Bats: R **Throws:** R
Ht: 6' 0" **Wt:** 165

Opening Day Age: 25
Born: 3/18/65 in Santo
Domingo, Dominican
Republic
ML Seasons: 1

Overall Statistics

	G	AB	R	H	D	T	HR	RBI	SB	BB	SO	AVG
1989	81	136	7	36	4	0	2	9	0	7	32	.265
Career	81	136	7	36	4	0	2	9	0	7	32	.265

HITTING, FIELDING, BASERUNNING:

Geronimo Berroa did a creditable job last year as a righty bat off the bench, and although he had a couple of slumps during the season, he gained some much needed experience. His effectiveness as a pinch-hitter was limited -- .234 with no power -- but he hit reasonably well when filling in right field, although everyone and their grandmother ran on him. He has to work on his arm, but his range is okay. Berroa's minor league record is that of a slugger, with a ton of power and a ton of strikeouts. He struck out with the Braves about a quarter of the time, with low, but not terrible power. Berroa suffered through two slumps that really hurt his final numbers, but there were moments when he showed some real promise. After striking out three times against Fernando Valenzuela he swore revenge, and then smacked his first big league homer. He isn't a base-stealing threat.

OVERALL:

Last season was Berroa's first year in the Braves organization, after being drafted out of the Blue Jays system. Berroa gave the impression of a young man studying a new situation. His power is intriguing, and while it is difficult to figure where he could play, it is also difficult to ignore the promise he showed in 1989.

TONY CASTILLO

Position: RP
Bats: L **Throws:** L
Ht: 5'10" **Wt:** 177

Opening Day Age: 27
Born: 3/1/63 in Lara,
Venezuela
ML Seasons: 2

Overall Statistics

	W	L	ERA	G	GS	Sv	IP	H	R	BB	SO	HR
1989	1	2	5.67	29	0	1	27.0	31	19	14	15	0
Career	2	2	4.71	43	0	1	42.0	41	24	16	29	2

PITCHING, FIELDING, HITTING:

Tony Castillo, acquired from Toronto in the Jim Acker trade, has made a fine recovery from a 1986 rotator cuff injury. Castillo, 27, throws a good fastball and his curveball, which tends to sail, serves as an offspeed pitch. He is working on a slider. Lefthanders have given him a problem and they really worked him over in 1989. Castillo's minor league record shows how effective he can be as a set-up man. He gets a lot of strikeouts and has steadily reduced his walk totals throughout his career. Tony is not afraid to pitch inside. With the fastball as his bread and butter, he needs to keep hitters off of the plate, and that will be especially important in Atlanta. His high leg kick reduces his fielding range but he handles everything he can get to. His kick also hurts his ability to watch runners; even with the heater, he is an easy mark for basestealers.

OVERALL:

Castillo has had to pitch in two new leagues in two years, so it's hard to say how much weight you can put on his mediocre 1989 season. Another lefty in the pen would be a plus, but it's going to be crowded out there. Castillo will have to pitch well in the spring.

CHARLIE PULEO

Position: RP
Bats: R **Throws:** R
Ht: 6' 3" **Wt:** 200

Opening Day Age: 35
Born: 2/7/55 in Glen Ridge, NJ
ML Seasons: 8

Overall Statistics

	W	L	ERA	G	GS	Sv	IP	H	R	BB	SO	HR
1989	1	1	4.66	15	1	0	29.0	26	15	16	17	2
Career	29	39	4.25	180	76	2	632.2	621	335	319	387	59

PITCHING, FIELDING, HITTING:

Charlie Puleo shaved off his mustache, and he did look younger, but he didn't fool Atlanta. Their commitment to their young pitchers led to Charlie's innings dropping to only 29 from 106.1 in '88, and he pitched in only 15 games. In April he started the second game of a double-header, but failed to get out of the third inning, and got his brains beat in, ending speculation that he would spot-start. Puleo is a classic fastball, curve, changeup pitcher with a big, easy motion. Charlie's big problem last year was that when he gave up hits, they went a long way -- nine of his 26 hits surrendered went for extra bases. Puleo had achieved decent levels of strikeouts to walks during the 1987-88 seasons; last year's 17 walks to only 16 strikeouts could be a sign that age has caught up with him, or simply a function of pitching so little. He does not hold runners well and surrendered five stolen bases.

OVERALL:

If Puleo has a role with Atlanta, and that's doubtful, it will be in middle relief, since the young Atlanta pitchers will be starters somewhere, either in Fulton County Stadium or in the minors. However, the Braves will fill his roster spot more profitably with anyone who can give them more than 29 innings..

SERGIO VALDEZ

Position: RP
Bats: R **Throws:** R
Ht: 6' 1" **Wt:** 190

Opening Day Age: 24
Born: 9/7/65 in Elias Pina, Dominican Republic
ML Seasons: 2

Overall Statistics

	W	L	ERA	G	GS	Sv	IP	H	R	BB	SO	HR
1989	1	2	6.06	19	1	0	32.2	31	24	17	26	5
Career	1	6	6.40	24	6	0	57.2	70	44	28	46	7

PITCHING, FIELDING, HITTING:

Sergio Valdez got his chance when Jose Alvarez needed knee surgery, and he showed some promise, despite his 6.06 ERA. Valdez has an assortment of dropping pitches; a forkball, a slider, and a split-fingered fastball. He also throws a straight fastball that he spots. He has a very measured, almost jerky motion, that is at the same time very easy. One, touch my belt, two, raise my knee, three, throw to the plate. You can almost see him count it out to himself, and it seems as if he could throw about as well with no wind-up, his stops between the motions are so pronounced. On the few occasions that he pitched well, he breezed through the lineup, and made hitters look silly. For the most part he was pummeled, however. In spite of all the ugly numbers, Valdez does not allow many hits. It's the distance of them and the walks that killed him in 1989. Valdez had a hit in his only at bat, and looks like a good athlete.

OVERALL:

Valdez's easy motion and his fine minor league numbers make him an intriguing prospect, although the Braves are particularly rich in pitching prospects. It is likely that he will begin the 1990 season in the minors.

JEFF WETHERBY

Position: LF
Bats: L **Throws:** L
Ht: 6' 2" **Wt:** 195

Opening Day Age: 26
Born: 10/18/63 in Granada Hills, CA
ML Seasons: 1

Overall Statistics

	G	AB	R	H	D	T	HR	RBI	SB	BB	SO	AVG
1989	52	48	5	10	2	1	1	7	1	4	6	.208
Career	52	48	5	10	2	1	1	7	1	4	6	.208

HITTING, FIELDING, BASERUNNING:

After four years in the minor leagues, Jeff Wetherby got the call in June of 1989. The lefty swinger had a nice month, with four hits and a walk in 10 plate appearances, but spent the rest of the year watching, and occasionally pinch hitting. Wetherby was primarily a DH in the minors. In his few forays into the Braves outfield he handled his chances cleanly, but at no time was he allowed significant playing time. He is not very fast, but is valuable because he has shown some real power, even in his limited duty with the Braves. Of his 10 hits for the season, four of them were for extra bases. He didn't hit for much average (.208). Wetherby thought he might get a real shot in 1989, and when he was caught in a roster squeeze in July when Gerald Perry decided against going on the disabled list, he took it badly.

OVERALL:

The Braves gave a lot of their 24-26 year old players a look this year, because as the youth movement gains steam, decisions have to be made about the players already in the pipeline. Wetherby probably needs more playing time in the minors before being asked to take a seat on the Major League bench for another season.

ED WHITED

Position: 3B
Bats: R **Throws:** R
Ht: 6' 3" **Wt:** 195

Opening Day Age: 26
Born: 2/9/64 in Bristol, PA
ML Seasons: 1

Overall Statistics

	G	AB	R	H	D	T	HR	RBI	SB	BB	SO	AVG
1989	36	74	5	12	3	0	1	4	1	6	15	.162
Career	36	74	5	12	3	0	1	4	1	6	15	.162

HITTING, FIELDING, BASERUNNING:

Ed Whited was slated for another season in the minors last year, but Ron Gant's problems ended that. The slugging third baseman came to the Braves in the Rafael Ramirez trade. He had demolished Class A pitching, but had less success in Double A and was struggling at Richmond when the Braves called him up. He seemed lost when behind in the count and was usually fooled badly when hitting with two strikes on him. In the minors he displayed a fine eye, and drew 97 walks in Greenville in 1988, so it's highly possible that he will improve. Whited showed good speed in the minors and was successful in his one Atlanta stolen base attempt; he was picked off once, as well. Ed made five errors in 29 games, but showed some tools at third base.

OVERALL:

The Braves sacrificed Whited's 1989 development in favor of Ron Gant's, so you have to wonder how committed the team is to his future. He has now had four seasons as a professional and is 26, so he must make a move soon. The Braves are rich in infield prospects, which won't help him.

PITCHING:

Paul Assenmacher puts up power pitcher numbers but relies on off-speed pitches and control to be effective. His fastball is only average and when he is forced to come in with it he becomes very hittable. Assenmacher struck out 9.3 batters per nine innings pitched last season, relying mainly on his overhand curveball. He has enough confidence to throw the curve on any count. When he can spot his curveball he becomes especially tough because then he can throw the fastball by the hitter.

With his sidearm motion, Assenmacher can be very tough against lefthanded batters. The opposition's batting average was about .250 from both sides of the plate last year, but he didn't yield a home run to a lefthander last season. Against lefties he only surrendered two extra-base hits, whereas the righthanders had 13 doubles and 3 home runs. Lefthanded batters draw fewer walks and strikeout more often, but righthanders hit into more doubleplays.

Assenmacher is seldom given the ball in a save situation. With his stuff, he's used best in middle relief for about 30 pitches. After that, his control rapidly decreases. When he can't get the curve over, it's time for the showers because his fastball simply isn't good enough.

HITTING, FIELDING, BASERUNNING:

Since Assenmacher is rarely called on to hit, his opportunities to run the bases are rare and he is a threat neither at the plate nor on the basepaths. His fielding is above average. He has a good follow-through and is ready for balls hit back to the mound. Assenmacher is quick off the mound when he is needed to cover first base and always backs up third and home. He also has a deceptive move to first which freezes most runners even when he is going to the plate.

OVERALL:

Used effectively, Assenmacher can be an effective middle reliever, but two innings is usually as far as he can go. His control will determine how much gas he has left. He keeps the ball in the park against lefthanded batters and when he is right he will get the righthanders. He has done his best work as a set-up man.

PAUL ASSENMACHER

Position: RP
Bats: L **Throws:** L
Ht: 6' 3" **Wt:** 200

Opening Day Age: 29
Born: 12/10/60 in Detroit, MI
ML Seasons: 4

Overall Statistics

	W	L	ERA	G	GS	Sv	IP	H	R	BB	SO	HR
1989	3	4	3.99	63	0	0	76.2	74	37	28	79	3
Career	19	15	3.58	240	0	14	279.0	265	129	110	245	20

Where They Hit the Ball

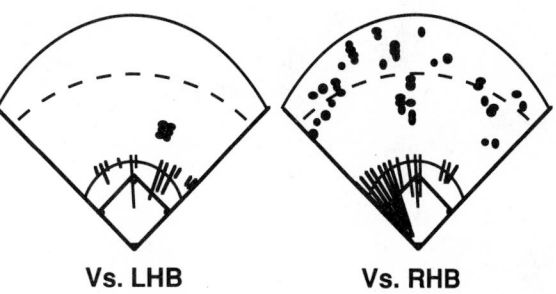

Vs. LHB   Vs. RHB

1989 Situational Stats

	W	L	ERA	Sv	IP		AB	H	HR	RBI	AVG
Home	3	3	3.86	0	42.0	LHB	85	21	0	9	.247
Road	0	1	4.15	0	34.2	RHB	205	53	3	28	.259
Day	2	0	4.94	0	27.1	Sc Pos	91	23	1	33	.253
Night	1	4	3.47	0	49.1	Clutch	129	41	1	17	.318

1989 Rankings (National League)

➡ 7th in holds (13)

HITTING:

With catchers in so much demand, Damon Berryhill's many abilities make him a nearly priceless commodity. Berryhill combines fine defense with decent offense, a rare combination these days.

A switch-hitter, Berryhill needs only to keep the stroke he has from the right side. He hits for good power and average, but has the same affliction that seems to bother all Cubs -- the inability to take a walk. Damon pulls the ball more from the right side of the plate, but his power is to the alleys. With any kind of breeze in Wrigley and a lefthander on the mound, he becomes a power threat. From the left side he is more of a defensive hitter, just protecting the plate and trying to spray the ball around. His power as a left-hander is down the line and mostly due to the wind.

Like most young hitters, Berryhill sits on the fastball and protects against the curve and the change-up. From the left side he'll chase the pitch down and away. Like most hitters he is more susceptible when he gets behind on the count, but getting two strikes doesn't make Damon an easy strikeout. That makes him an excellent batter for the hit-and-run during any count and from either side of the plate.

BASERUNNING:

Berryhill has one gear -- slow. Scoring from second can be an adventure for this stocky catcher, but he has a ballplayer's instincts and never runs through stop signs, for obvious reasons. His only stolen base last season came in the shadows of a night game on a swinging strike with the hit-and-run on.

FIELDING:

Berryhill is one of the best catchers in the majors at throwing out would-be basestealers. He failed to pick any runners off base last season, but he did get 45% of the runners attempting to steal, an excellent percentage. He blocks pitches out of the strike zone very well. He needs a little more experience on calling the game, a skill that will be fine-tuned with experience.

OVERALL:

At a time when great catchers are only a memory, Berryhill can be one of the exceptions. He has the tools to be outstanding defensively. With time he can learn the hitters and be one of the premier receivers in the majors. Until then, school is in session and Damon will have to work to get to the head of the class.

DAMON BERRYHILL

Position: C
Bats: B **Throws:** R
Ht: 6' 0" **Wt:** 205

Opening Day Age: 26
Born: 12/3/63 in South Laguna, CA
ML Seasons: 3

Overall Statistics

	G	AB	R	H	D	T	HR	RBI	SB	BB	SO	AVG
1989	91	334	37	86	13	0	5	41	1	16	54	.257
Career	198	671	58	171	33	1	12	80	2	36	115	.255

Where He Hits the Ball

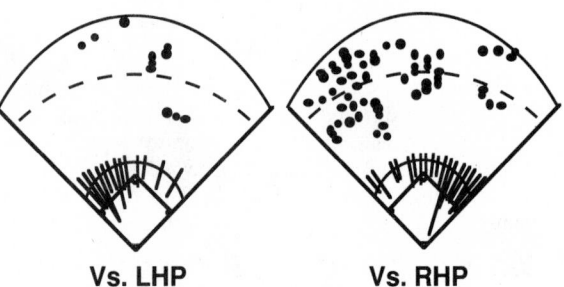

Vs. LHP   **Vs. RHP**

1989 Situational Stats

	AB	H	HR	RBI	AVG		AB	H	HR	RBI	AVG
Home	148	46	2	22	.311	LHP	97	33	3	13	.340
Road	186	40	3	19	.215	RHP	237	53	2	28	.224
Day	163	46	2	23	.282	Sc Pos	92	30	0	34	.326
Night	171	40	3	18	.234	Clutch	54	14	1	4	.259

1989 Rankings (National League)

→ 7th in hitting with runners in scoring position (.326) - *players with 100 PA with runners in scoring position*

→ 7th in most GDPs per GDP situation (17.6%) - *players with 50 PA in GDP situations*

→ 9th in hitting with the bases loaded (.444) - *players with 10 PA with the bases loaded*

→ Led the NL Catchers in sacrifice flies (5), hitting with runners in scoring position and hitting with the bases loaded

PITCHING:

Last season was a year of firsts for Mike Bielecki. It was the first year he pitched without injuries. It was the first year that he was a member of the starting rotation out of spring training. And it was the first year he lived up to the potential baseball folks thought he had.

Not much was expected from Bielecki when the Cubs picked him up in a minor deal last season. What they got was the most consistent starter on the staff. Mike has four pitches he can throw for strikes: fastball, forkball, curveball and change-up. He shows no preference and will use any of them during any count. It's a mistake to sit on the fastball if ahead in the count because Bielecki may still come in with his forkball and the pitch will be pounded into the ground. He is especially tough on righthanded hitters.

Bielecki gets stronger as the game progresses. In a typical start he will get into a bit of trouble in the first inning, settle down until the fifth inning and then get stronger from the sixth on. After the sixth inning the league only batted .192 against Bielecki. Finally, at about the 120 pitch mark, he's ready for the showers.

FIELDING, HITTING, BASERUNNING:

Bielecki may be called the "Style Master" by teammates because of his fancy clothes, but up at the plate he has no style at all. He had only three basehits all season and is usually given congratulations for foul balls. That he hit a two-run single in the playoff game against Rick Reuschel was truly extraordinary.

Mike's move to firstbase is one of the best in the league. He keeps runners very close. There were only 12 stolen base attempts while Mike was on the mound and seven of those failed. Mike is tough to beat on the bases. His fielding is average. He has a good follow-through, is ready to cover first, and handle bunts adequately, but there is no gold glove in his future.

OVERALL:

Mike has shown that he can be a winner in the Major Leagues. But at age 30, there are a lot of "ifs." Mike has to stay healthy, and keep his new-found command of his repertoire of pitches. If he can do this, there is no reason to think he won't continue to be a 15-20 game winner.

MIKE BIELECKI

Position: SP
Bats: R **Throws:** R
Ht: 6' 3" **Wt:** 195

Opening Day Age: 30
Born: 7/31/59 in
Baltimore, MD
ML Seasons: 6

Overall Statistics

	W	L	ERA	G	GS	Sv	IP	H	R	BB	SO	HR
1989	18	7	3.14	33	33	0	212.1	187	82	81	147	16
Career	30	26	3.85	107	80	0	505.0	483	242	223	311	41

Where They Hit the Ball

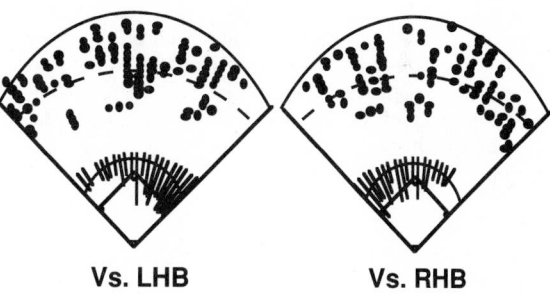

Vs. LHB　　　　**Vs. RHB**

1989 Situational Stats

	W	L	ERA	Sv	IP		AB	H	HR	RBI	AVG
Home	9	3	2.83	0	114.1	LHB	421	106	10	22	.252
Road	9	4	3.49	0	98.0	RHB	368	81	6	38	.220
Day	10	5	4.08	0	123.2	Sc Pos	161	38	2	42	.236
Night	8	2	1.83	0	88.2	Clutch	49	13	2	6	.265

1989 Rankings (National League)

➡ 1st in lowest stolen base percentage allowed (41.7%) - *pitchers with 162 IP*

➡ 3rd in wins (18)

➡ 4th in won/loss percentage (.720) - pitchers with 15 decisions

➡ 6th in shutouts (3)

➡ 7th in GDPs induced (18) and games started (7)

➡ Led the Cubs in lowest stolen base percentage allowed, shutouts, GDPs induced, won/loss percentage, lowest opponent batting average (.237), ERA at home (2.83), GDPs per 9 innings (.76) and strikeouts per 9 innings (6.2)

HITTING:

Andre Dawson is a possible Hall of Famer. At the height of his career he batted for a good average, had power, speed and outstanding defensive abilities. He is past that prime, however. Now 35, Dawson hit only .252 last year, a 51 point drop from 1988, and had his worst season since 1984.

Dawson is not a patient hitter. He loves fastballs and looks for them on nearly every pitch. Unless a ball is not even close to the strike zone, Andre will probably take a swing at it. He looks for the fastball more often now than he did earlier in his career because he doesn't want it thrown by him. This leaves him very vulnerable to a good change-up or curveball. With less than two strikes or three balls, Andre should be fed slow stuff low and away. This will lead to strike-outs and groundballs to short.

For the most part Dawson is still a line drive hitter. He hits the ball hard to the alleys in left and right center and can still take the ball out of the park to any field. He rarely hits the ball to right field on the ground and the right side of the infield should be slightly shifted to defense this.

BASERUNNING:

While he may have lost a step since his younger days, Dawson is a veteran and rarely makes a mistake on the basepaths. He goes from first to third very well and still has enough speed to steal bases though his attempts are diminishing with age. Dawson cannot be take for granted but neither is he the threat he once was.

FIELDING:

Dawson is still one of the best right fielders in the game. He gets a good jump on balls hit to him, knows the game situation when the ball is hit to him and rarely throws to a wrong base or past the cutoff man. His arm is still strong and running on Andre in a game situation is not recommended.

OVERALL:

While his skills have narrowed, Dawson still has many of the tools that made him a great ballplayer. But there are more weaknesses to work on now and if pitched to carefully, Andre can be handled. Nonetheless he always plays well fundamentally and is an asset to a contending team.

ANDRE DAWSON

Position: RF
Bats: R **Throws:** R
Ht: 6' 3" **Wt:** 195

Opening Day Age: 35
Born: 7/10/54 in Miami, FL
ML Seasons: 14

Overall Statistics

	G	AB	R	H	D	T	HR	RBI	SB	BB	SO	AVG
1989	118	416	62	105	18	6	21	77	8	35	62	.252
Career	1871	7256	1058	2037	368	83	319	1131	284	458	1134	.281

Where He Hits the Ball

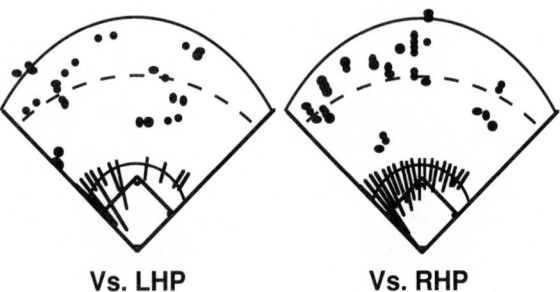

Vs. LHP   Vs. RHP

1989 Situational Stats

	AB	H	HR	RBI	AVG		AB	H	HR	RBI	AVG
Home	218	52	6	35	.239	LHP	114	34	8	28	.298
Road	198	53	15	42	.268	RHP	302	71	13	49	.235
Day	229	64	12	45	.279	Sc Pos	115	33	6	57	.287
Night	187	41	9	32	.219	Clutch	61	10	3	9	.164

1989 Rankings (National League)

➡ 3rd in most GDPs per GDP situation (18.8%) - *players with 50 PA in GDP situations*

➡ 4th in slugging percentage of lefthanded pitchers (.579) - *players with 125 PA vs. LHP*

➡ 7th in GDPs (16)

➡ 9th in hitting on a 3-1 count (.500) - *players with 10 PA on a 3-1 count*

➡ Led the Cubs in sacrifice flies (7), triples (6) and GDPs

➡ Led NL Right Fielders in triples, GDPs and hitting on an 0-2 count (.235)

STRONG ARM

SHAWON DUNSTON

Position: SS
Bats: R **Throws:** R
Ht: 6' 1" **Wt:** 175

Opening Day Age: 27
Born: 3/21/63 in
Brooklyn, NY
ML Seasons: 5

HITTING:

Shawon Dunston had his best season in 1989, even though he may be the most impatient hitter on the planet. After an exceptionally slow start with Dunston hitting under .200 for April and May, the Shawon-o-Meter finally stopped at a career-high .278, and the key was better contact Dunston cut his strikeouts from 108 in 1988 to 86 a year ago.

Dunston's 30 walks were also a career high, but that's deceiving since half of them were intentional. Other than his walks, Shawon only got to a three ball count 39 times. The way he goes after bad pitches is a used car salesman's dream. Dunston loves to swing at the first pitch, and batted .300 when he put the first offering in play last year. But when he swings at the first pitch and doesn't put it into play, he's in big trouble.

Dunston is a line drive hitter who can spray the ball to all fields. He isn't a big power threat but when he gets hot and is thrown strikes, he can be dangerous. Shawon is both more patient and more successful against lefthanders, especially ones who specialize in throwing fastballs. He's quick with the bat and it's difficult to throw fastballs past him. Muscle against muscle isn't the way to go after Dunston, though. He's too easily fooled with breaking pitches.

BASERUNNING:

Dunston is an excellent baserunner who isn't given the green light to steal often enough. He runs out everything so hard that even the slightest bobble is enough for him to reach safely. Dunston may be the best in all of baseball at going from first to third or scoring from second on a base hit.

FIELDING:

Once so erratic that the Cubs considered shifting him to another position, Dunston is now one of the best defensive shortstops in baseball. His range is outstanding and he continues to improve on the double play with Ryne Sandberg. Dunston has the finest infield arm in baseball, and he's learning not to throw the ball when he doesn't have a play.

OVERALL:

Even if he only batted .250, Dunston would be an asset to his team. He stands out defensively, is one of the best on the bases, is always hustling, and isn't afraid to work on a part of his game that needs fine tuning. If he learns to draw walks and stays healthy he can be one of the best of his era.

Overall Statistics

	G	AB	R	H	D	T	HR	RBI	SB	BB	SO	AVG
1989	138	471	52	131	20	6	9	60	19	30	86	.278
Career	612	2223	267	569	110	22	44	224	85	96	418	.256

Where He Hits the Ball

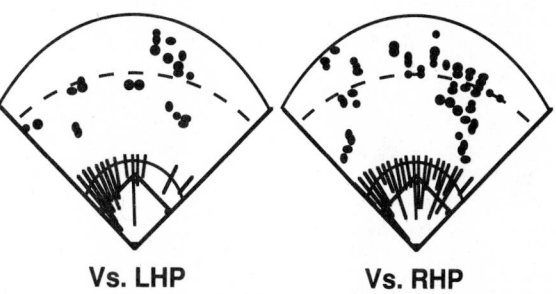

Vs. LHP   **Vs. RHP**

1989 Situational Stats

	AB	H	HR	RBI	AVG		AB	H	HR	RBI	AVG
Home	225	69	3	32	.307	LHP	139	47	2	26	.338
Road	246	62	6	28	.252	RHP	332	84	7	34	.253
Day	249	73	5	36	.293	Sc Pos	120	35	3	52	.292
Night	222	58	4	24	.261	Clutch	75	20	0	5	.267

1989 Rankings (National League)

➡ 1st in hitting with the bases loaded (.563) - *players with 10 PA with the bases loaded*

➡ 3rd in lowest percentage of pitches taken (44.6%) - *players with 502 PA*

➡ 4th in batting average vs. lefthanded pitchers (.338) - *players with 125 PA vs LHP*

➡ Led the Cubs in strikeouts (86), caught stealing (11), intentional walks (15), triples (6), hitting with bases loaded and errors (17)

➡ Led NL Shortstops in strikeouts (86), slugging percentage (.403), batting average (.278), caught stealing, RBI (60), steals of third (4), hitting with the bases loaded and percentage of extra bases taken as a runner (57.8%)

HITTING:

Joe Girardi is still learning to hit major league pitching, but based on his 1989 season, he is a willing and capable student. He showed steady improvement and may have too much talent to be a backup catcher for more than a couple of years. Girardi didn't display much power in his rookie season, but his stocky build suggests that the power may not be a long way off. Early in the season he was overmatched by National League hurlers. A good fastball could be thrown by him and he was nearly defenseless on change-ups and curveballs.

But when Girardi got the chance to play regularly late in the season, due to Damon Berryhill's shoulder injury, he showed definite improvement. Fastballs were no longer being thrown past him. He was hitting line drives to left and right center and finished the year strongly. Curveballs that were thrown for strikes still gave him trouble, but if they were off the plate, Girardi was able to lay off them.

Girardi came through with runners on base in September and his confidence seemed to grow with each plate appearance. It seemed that the later it got in the game, the better he was able to hit. If Girardi continues to improve as a hitter, it's going to be hard to keep him out of the lineup.

BASERUNNING:

Girardi is slow and will never be a base stealer. He's an aggressive runner, however, and will go into second hard to break up the doubleplay, and he will bowl the catcher over on a play to the plate. Girardi will not try to take the extra base on an outfielder.

FIELDING:

Girardi's greatest strength is his defense. He threw out 37% of the baserunners attempting to steal on him last season. He needs to work on calling games but he is learning. He blocks the plate well on plays at the plate and keeps pitches in the dirt in front of him. His head is always in the game.

OVERALL:

Backup catchers of Girardi's quality are difficult to find. In another couple of years he may be among the better catchers overall. His hitting is steadily improving and his defense is already very good. His big problem will be playing time. If Damon Berryhill, another fine young catcher, is healthy in 1990, Girardi may not get the experience he needs to polish his game.

JOE GIRARDI

Position: C
Bats: R **Throws:** R
Ht: 5'11" **Wt:** 195

Opening Day Age: 25
Born: 10/14/64 in Peoria, IL
ML Seasons: 1

Overall Statistics

	G	AB	R	H	D	T	HR	RBI	SB	BB	SO	AVG
1989	59	157	15	39	10	0	1	14	2	11	26	.248
Career	59	157	15	39	10	0	1	14	2	11	26	.248

Where He Hits the Ball

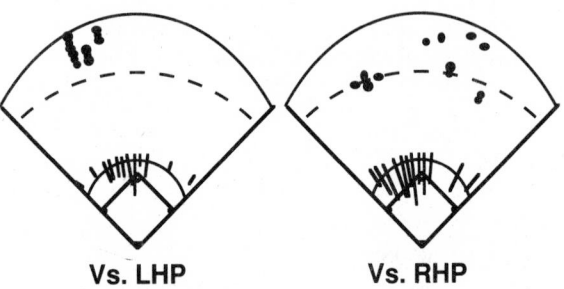

Vs. LHP   Vs. RHP

1989 Situational Stats

	AB	H	HR	RBI	AVG		AB	H	HR	RBI	AVG
Home	78	21	0	8	.269	LHP	50	11	0	6	.220
Road	79	18	1	6	.228	RHP	107	28	1	8	.262
Day	91	21	0	9	.231	Sc Pos	36	10	0	12	.278
Night	66	18	1	5	.273	Clutch	23	7	0	0	.304

1989 Rankings (National League)

➡ Did not rank near the top or bottom in any category

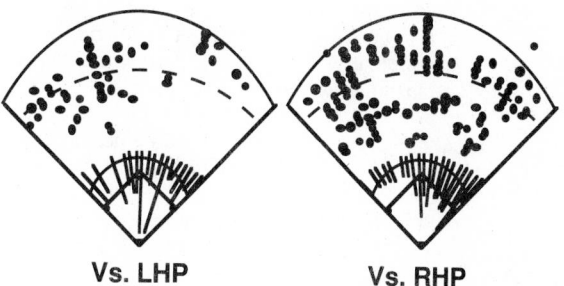

HITTING:

Mark Grace has the potential to win more than one batting title. He shows patience at the plate, doesn't chase bad pitches and hits the ball with authority. Teams have been pitching Mark away and playing the outfield shifted toward left, but since he is a line drive hitter, his hits still fall in. Despite the way he is defensed, Mark hits the ball to all fields. Many of his multi-hit games include a hit to left field when the pitcher tries to keep the ball away, then a hit to right field on a pitch inside.

Grace will wait on the curve and is quick enough to get around on the fastball. He will stay in against the lefties, as Randy Myers learned when Grace hit a ninth inning, game-winning homer against him. Grace has not shown much power in his two years with the Cubs, but with good size and Wrigley Field going for him, he has the potential to hit 20 homers or more.

Grace makes the pitcher throw strikes and then can hit any ball that is in the strike zone. He is not fooled often and does not chase a pitcher's pitch. The defense can coordinate with the pitching in an attempt to defense Grace, but he can hit the ball anywhere on the diamond with authority. When the game is on the line, it's best to pitch around him.

FIELDING:

Grace is quietly becoming one of the best fielding first basemen in the National League. His range is limited, but if he can put his glove on the ball he can catch it. He protects the line very well and his reflexes are quick enough to stop hard hit balls hit there. He is able to scoop most low throws and has saved fellow infielders countless errors on throws in the dirt.

BASERUNNING:

Grace has little natural speed but can steal bases, with 14 steals last year. Most of them are on broken hit-and-run plays. His instincts are good and he is rarely thrown out on the bases, though he doesn't take many chances.

OVERALL:

Mark Grace's potential seems almost limitless. He already has one of the top batting averages in the league, he doesn't chase bad pitches, and his defense is good and improving. Mark comes as close to an untouchable ballplayer as there is in the majors.

MARK GRACE

Position: 1B
Bats: L **Throws:** L
Ht: 6' 2" **Wt:** 190

Opening Day Age: 25
Born: 6/28/64 in Winston-Salem, NC
ML Seasons: 2

Overall Statistics

	G	AB	R	H	D	T	HR	RBI	SB	BB	SO	AVG
1989	142	510	74	160	28	3	13	79	14	80	42	.314
Career	276	996	139	304	51	7	20	136	17	140	85	.305

Where He Hits the Ball

Vs. LHP   **Vs. RHP**

1989 Situational Stats

	AB	H	HR	RBI	AVG		AB	H	HR	RBI	AVG
Home	258	87	8	44	.337	LHP	159	42	4	24	.264
Road	252	73	5	35	.290	RHP	351	118	9	55	.336
Day	278	87	4	40	.313	Sc Pos	135	42	2	59	.311
Night	232	73	9	39	.315	Clutch	69	24	3	9	.348

1989 Rankings (National League)

→ 1st in on-base average vs. righthanded pitchers (.433) - *players with 377 PA vs. RHP*

→ 2nd in batting average at home (.337) - *players with 252 PA at home*

→ 3rd in batting average vs. righthanded pitchers (.336)

→ 4th in batting average (.314), on-base average (.405) and highest percentage of swings put into play (55.8%) - *players with 502 PA*

→ Led the Cubs in batting average, singles (116), doubles (28), RBIs (79), walks (80), on-base average, times on base (240), lowest percentage of swings that missed (8.6%), highest percentage of swings put into play and hitting in the clutch (.348)

PITCHING:

Paul Kilgus began last season as the Cubs' number four starter. After the All-Star break he lost his starting job and was moved into the bullpen. He got three more starts in September but he helped the team most when he pitched middle and long relief.

Kilgus is a lefthanded breaking ball pitcher with good control but no strikeout pitch. He struck out only 12 more batters than he walked in 145 innings last season. Most times his control works against him. Since he doesn't challenge hitters, they dig in and take good swings even when he is ahead in the count. One of Paul's problems last season may have been that he was new to the league. Adding to his lack of experience was the fact that his catchers had less than two years Major League experience. Both he and his catchers were learning the National League hitters on the job.

As a starter, Kilgus seems to start out slow and then peter out completely. His average start lasted only five and a third innings and his ERA during starts in 1989 was 4.72. He did much better in his 12 relief appearances. He saved two games because he had the stamina to pitch three or four innings in relief when the starter couldn't get past the fifth inning. The Cubs will use Kilgus as the number five starter again unless they pick up a starter in the off-season. If they do get a starter, Paul will be more valuable to the team as their third lefthander in the bullpen with Major League experience.

FIELDING, HITTING, BASERUNNING:

In his first major league opportunity to hit and run the bases, Kilgus looked like he was still feeling his way around, as could be expected. He fields the ball well but often takes foolish chances trying to get a lead runner. He has a fine move to first.

OVERALL:

Kilgus is still young and looking for his role on the team. Without a great fastball he is going to need to improve his control in order to hold onto a starter's spot. He will also have trouble being a closer since he can't enter the game and be overpowering. His best role may be that of a middle reliever.

PAUL KILGUS

Position: SP/RP
Bats: L **Throws:** L
Ht: 6' 1" **Wt:** 175

Opening Day Age: 28
Born: 2/2/62 in Bowling Green, KY
ML Seasons: 3

Overall Statistics

	W	L	ERA	G	GS	Sv	IP	H	R	BB	SO	HR
1989	6	10	4.39	35	23	2	145.2	164	90	49	61	9
Career	20	32	4.23	92	67	2	438.1	449	240	151	191	41

Where They Hit the Ball

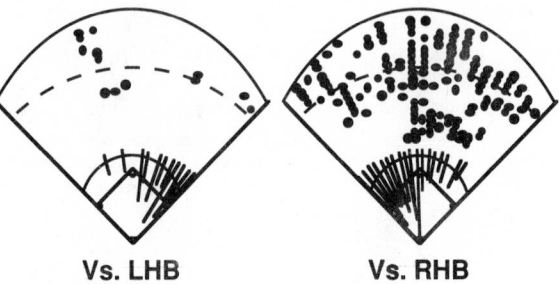

Vs. LHB   **Vs. RHB**

1989 Situational Stats

	W	L	ERA	Sv	IP		AB	H	HR	RBI	AVG
Home	3	4	3.68	1	85.2	LHB	107	27	3	17	.252
Road	3	6	5.40	1	60.0	RHB	472	137	6	53	.290
Day	2	4	3.76	0	76.2	Sc Pos	135	41	3	56	.304
Night	4	6	5.09	2	69.0	Clutch	54	15	1	4	.278

1989 Rankings (National League)

- ⟶ 5th worst in batting average allowed vs. righthanded batters (.290) - *pitchers facing 377 RBH*

- ⟶ Led the Cubs in least pitches thrown per batter (3.2) and most GDPs per GDP situation (13.1%) - *all team pitchers*

PITCHING:

Les Lancaster's career took a sharp upward turn in 1989. He didn't make the roster after spring training and wasn't called up by the Cubs until mid-June. From that point on he was the best pitcher in the Cubs bullpen. Lancaster's biggest single improvement was his ability to get ahead of the batters. This allowed him to nibble more at the corners without the fear of walking batters. He also cut down on his walks, allowing only 15 in 72.2 innings. Only nine times all season did he get as far behind as three balls and no strikes.

Lancaster is basically a fastball/slider pitcher with an occational change-up. He'll move his pitches in and out and up and down. When he is called in from the bullpen it's best to swing at the first pitch since it will probably be a fastball and a strike.

As a short reliever, Lancaster seems to hold up very well. His second inning is usually as strong as his first. If he hasn't thrown many pitches, he can give a quality third inning. Once he has reached the 40 pitch mark he becomes suspect.

The conventional wisdom of sending a lefthander up against the righthanded Lancaster may be a mistake. Lancaster held lefthanders 40 points lower than righthanders in batting and 80 points lower in slugging. The only two homers he surrendered were to righthanders.

FIELDING, HITTING, BASERUNNING:

Lancaster's not a great hitter, but he had the game winning hit in an extra inning ball game last season. He's a slow runner.

Lancaster has a smooth delivery and leaves himself in position to field his position well. He moves well to first on grounders to the right side but sometimes fails to take charge on pop-ups in the infield. He does a fine job of holding baserunners.

OVERALL:

As long as Lancaster continues to get in front of the hitters, he can be an excellent reliever. There is plenty of movement on his fastball, and his change-up is also an out pitch when his fastball is moving. He will have problems if he relapses and has control problems with his off-speed pitches. He cannot afford to rely on his fastball alone.

LES LANCASTER

Position: RP
Bats: R **Throws:** R
Ht: 6' 2" **Wt:** 200

Opening Day Age: 27
Born: 4/21/62 in Dallas, TX
ML Seasons: 3

Overall Statistics

	W	L	ERA	G	GS	Sv	IP	H	R	BB	SO	HR
1989	4	2	1.36	42	0	8	72.2	60	12	15	56	2
Career	16	11	3.68	113	21	13	290.2	287	130	100	170	20

Where They Hit the Ball

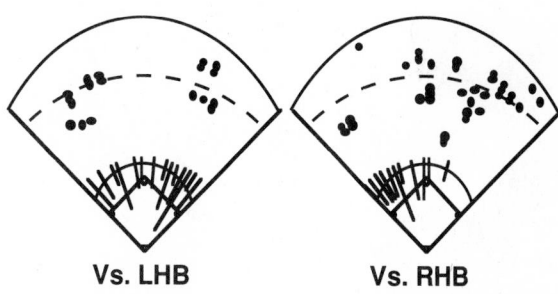

Vs. LHB   Vs. RHB

1989 Situational Stats

	W	L	ERA	Sv	IP		AB	H	HR	RBI	AVG
Home	3	1	1.75	3	36.0	LHB	133	27	0	5	.203
Road	1	1	0.98	5	36.2	RHB	132	33	2	16	.250
Day	2	2	1.38	5	39.0	Sc Pos	74	12	0	19	.162
Night	2	0	1.34	3	33.2	Clutch	148	35	1	12	.236

1989 Rankings (National League)

➡ 6th in ERA (1.36) - *all league pitchers*

➡ Led the Cubs in ERA, batting average allowed vs. lefthanded batters (.201), least baserunners per 9 innings (9.3) and lowest batting average with runners in scoring position (.162) - *all team pitchers*

HITTING:

Vance Law had a career year in 1988 and raised the expectations of Cub fans. But those expectations were dashed in 1989. Law is a career .257 hitter and will probably not have another .290 year in the big leagues.

Law is a fastball hitter who hits in streaks. When he is hot he will go the other way with the outside pitch and hit an inside pitch with authority. When Vance is struggling, breaking pitches give him trouble. If he is behind in the count, he will chase a pitch in the dirt.

Law has a little power and has belted as many as 17 homers in a season. Hang a curve inside and he can pull it with power. He cannot reach the fences when he goes to right field. The outfield is best played shifted toward left and shallow. When he hits long fly balls, there is usually time to get under them.

Because he hits the ball on the ground more often than not, Law's average has been better on turf than on natural grass. Righthanders gave him a lot of trouble last year, clouding his future as an everyday third baseman. Last year he failed in all of his 10 attempts to pinch hit. This is probably due to the fact that Law still considers himself a starter and needs to readjust his thinking about his role on the team.

BASERUNNING:

Law is not quick on the bases but is a smart baserunner. His stolen bases mostly come on busted hit-and-run plays. He takes a conservative lead off of first base and takes very few chances on the basepaths. One throw to first is usually enough to freeze him for the next couple of pitches. Because of his conservative approach he gets a late jump on the hit and run.

FIELDING:

The biggest contribution Vance can make to a ballclub is his defense. He can play both second adequately and has proven himself to be a fine third baseman. Law can contribute coming off the bench by being a late inning defensive replacement or by giving the regulars a day off.

OVERALL:

Law is at the point in his career where he can help a contending team as a part-time player. He can come off the bench defensively, and if he works on it he can be a valuable pinch hitter. He can probably no longer start for a team that is in contention.

VANCE LAW

Position: 3B
Bats: R **Throws:** R
Ht: 6' 1" **Wt:** 190

Opening Day Age: 33
Born: 10/1/56 in Boise, ID
ML Seasons: 10

Overall Statistics

	G	AB	R	H	D	T	HR	RBI	SB	BB	SO	AVG
1989	130	408	38	96	22	3	7	42	2	38	73	.235
Career	1138	3668	442	944	186	25	71	433	34	390	575	.257

Where He Hits the Ball

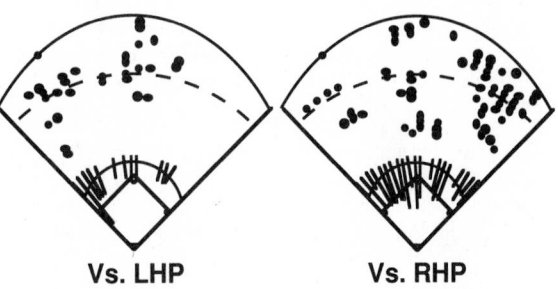

Vs. LHP   Vs. RHP

1989 Situational Stats

	AB	H	HR	RBI	AVG		AB	H	HR	RBI	AVG
Home	187	44	4	22	.235	LHP	111	33	3	14	.297
Road	221	52	3	20	.235	RHP	297	63	4	28	.212
Day	208	50	6	24	.240	Sc Pos	117	23	0	35	.197
Night	200	46	1	18	.230	Clutch	61	8	0	5	.131

1989 Rankings (National League)

- ➡ 2nd in worst hitting in the clutch (.131) - *players with 50 PA in the clutch*
- ➡ 3rd in worst hitting with runners in scoring position (.197) - *players with 100 PA with runners in scoring position*
- ➡ Led the Cubs in sacrifice flies (7)
- ➡ Led NL Third Basemen in sacrifice flies

GREG MADDUX

STAFF ACE

Position: SP
Bats: R **Throws:** R
Ht: 6' 0" **Wt:** 170

Opening Day Age: 23
Born: 4/14/66 in San Angelo, TX
ML Seasons: 4

PITCHING:

Finding a weakness in Greg Maddux is difficult. Whether he is at home or on the road, on turf or natural grass, during the day or at night, his numbers are all excellent. Though Maddux is not yet 24, he pitches like a 10-year veteran.

Maddux has four pitches he can throw for strikes. His fastball is in the high eighties and it explodes as it get to the plate. Greg moves the fastball in and out, mixes it with his slider and has very good control. He works so hard on hitting the corners that at times he gets into trouble by trying to be too fine. His curve ball is only average and he'll only go to it when he is ahead in the count.

The best way to take advantage of Maddux is to load the lineup with lefthanded batters. Lefthanders hit 60 points higher, had more extra base hits and drew more walks. Greg will jam righthanded batters by keeping the fastball down and in. He shoots for the same corner against lefties but when he misses they are able to extend their arms and hit the ball hard.

It's important to get to Maddux early in the game. As the game gets into the later innings, he gets stronger. He only surrendered one home run last season after the sixth inning. The league's slugging percentage against Greg from the seventh inning on was only .267.

FIELDING, HITTING, BASERUNNING:

A fine hitter, though one with little power, Maddux was second among pitchers in base hits in the National League last season. Once on base Greg knows what he wants to do. He has good speed and is used occasionally as a pinch runner. He even stole a base last year.

Maddux has excellent mechanics on the mound. His follow-through brings him to a good fielding position and he handles his position well. He seldom takes chances on bunts and usually elects to take the sure out at first. For a righthander, he does an outstanding job of holding baserunners. Only 11 of 23 runners who tried to steal on Maddux last year were successful.

OVERALL:

Maddux can beat a team on the bases, with the bat and especially on the mound. They don't come much better than that.

Overall Statistics

	W	L	ERA	G	GS	Sv	IP	H	R	BB	SO	HR
1989	19	12	2.95	35	35	0	238.1	222	90	82	135	13
Career	45	38	3.77	105	101	0	674.0	677	318	248	396	46

Where They Hit the Ball

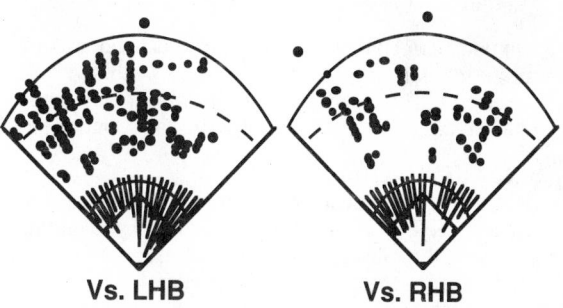

Vs. LHB   **Vs. RHB**

1989 Situational Stats

	W	L	ERA	Sv	IP		AB	H	HR	RBI	AVG
Home	10	5	3.03	0	113.0	LHB	498	138	4	36	.277
Road	9	7	2.87	0	125.1	RHB	392	84	9	42	.214
Day	10	5	2.80	0	115.2	Sc Pos	201	45	0	56	.224
Night	9	7	3.08	0	122.2	Clutch	81	16	0	2	.198

1989 Rankings (National League)

➡ 2nd in wins (19) and lowest stolen base percentage allowed (47.8%) - *pitchers with 162 IP*

➡ 3rd in games started (35) and batters faced (1,002)

➡ Led the Cubs in ERA (2.95), wins, losses (12), games started, innings (238), walks allowed (82), pitches thrown (3,395), strikeout/walk ratio (1.65), grounder/flyball ratio (2.24), least pitches thrown per batter (3.4), least HRs per 9 innings (.49), caught stealing (12), lowest slugging percentage allowed (.343) and most run support per 9 innings (4.9) - *team pitchers with 162 IP*

HITTING:

At age 30, Lloyd McClendon exploded onto the scene in 1989 by hitting a three-run homer in his first at bat. He spent the remainder of the season coming off the bench and helping the Cubs with his timely hitting. McClendon hit for both power and average in 1989. Righthanders cut down on his average because he is more likely to chase a ball out of the strike zone. But when a righthander makes a mistake against this stocky utility man, the ball could end up out of the park.

McClendon's main value is as a platoon player against lefties. Against southpaws McClendon is patient, powerful and hits for good average. He will not chase a pitch out of the strike zone against lefties and hits the curve as well as he does the fastball. His power is to left and left center but when he hits it to the opposite field, it is usually a line drive.

The most effective way to pitch to McClendon is to move the ball around, alternating between the off-speed and the fastball. If a pitcher falls into a pattern against him, McClendon will control the situation.

BASERUNNING:

McClendon has deceptive speed on the bases. He is not a threat to steal on a regular basis but if you ignore him he will steal second. The same is true when he is on the basepaths. If the outfielders relax for a second, he will take the extra base. His stocky build makes him appear slow but he can get around.

FIELDING:

McClendon will not win a Gold Glove at any position but he can practically play them all. He is used mostly in left field and does an adequate job when he is out there. He can also play first and thirdbase but has limited range. Finally, he is used as a late inning replacement for the catcher when his team is trying to improve the offense. He can and should be run on as a catcher since his arm is strong but not accurate.

OVERALL:

McClendon is about the most valuable player a team can have coming off the bench. He can play numerous positions and can pinch hit with great effectiveness. He's a team player who understands his role and is willing to play it to the best of his ability.

LLOYD MCCLENDON

Position: LF/1B
Bats: R **Throws:** R
Ht: 5'11" **Wt:** 195

Opening Day Age: 31
Born: 1/11/59 in Gary, IN
ML Seasons: 3

Overall Statistics

	G	AB	R	H	D	T	HR	RBI	SB	BB	SO	AVG
1989	92	259	47	74	12	1	12	40	6	37	31	.286
Career	209	468	64	119	21	1	17	67	11	56	68	.254

Where He Hits the Ball

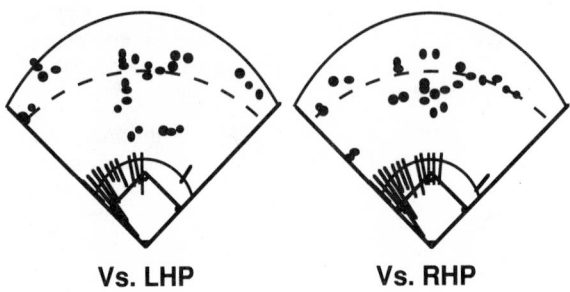

Vs. LHP   Vs. RHP

1989 Situational Stats

	AB	H	HR	RBI	AVG		AB	H	HR	RBI	AVG
Home	133	40	9	25	.301	LHP	121	41	6	22	.339
Road	126	34	3	15	.270	RHP	138	33	6	18	.239
Day	140	45	9	26	.321	Sc Pos	61	17	1	27	.279
Night	119	29	3	14	.244	Clutch	42	11	0	3	.262

1989 Rankings (National League)

→ 3rd in batting average vs. lefthanded pitchers (.339) and on-base average vs. lefthanded pitchers (.432) - *players with 125 PA vs. LHP*

→ 5th in hitting on a 3-1 count (.545) - *players with 10 PA on a 3-1 count*

→ 7th in slugging percentage vs. lefthanded pitchers (.554)

→ Led the Cubs in sacrifice flies (7), hitting vs. lefthanded pitchers and hitting on a 3-1 count

→ Led NL Left Fielders in sacrifice flies, hitting vs. lefthanded pitchers and hitting on a 3-1 count

HITTING:

Luis Salazar is a line drive hitter. He never goes to the plate looking for a base on balls. If Salazar is walked, it is probably intentional. He looks for any fastball and adjusts to the curve. He will drive the outside fastball to rightfield and pull the inside fastball to leftfield.

Salazar hits lefthanded pitchers with more authority than righthanders; however, righties don't give him a lot of trouble. He cuts down on his swing against the righties, happy to put the ball in play to any field. Against lefthanders he is both more patient and more powerful. He is less likely to chase a bad pitch against the lefthander which makes him more of a power threat when he gets ahead in the count.

If his showing with the Cubs late last season is any indication, Salazar is a good player to have coming to the plate with the game on the line. He stays within himself and atop the game situation. He is usually batting sixth or seventh in the batting order and it may be wiser to pitch around him late in the game to face a less experienced number eight hitter.

BASERUNNING:

Salazar has stolen as many as 32 bases in a season and was six for six as recently as 1988. But he looked slower in 1989 and ran only when a hit-and-run was called. He gets a good jump off of the bases on a ball put into play and will take out the middle infielder to break up the double play.

FIELDING:

Salazar is a jack of all trades and the master of none. Last season he played all defensive positions except catcher and secondbase. He is best at third base and has a solid arm for that position. His reflexes aren't the fastest, but if he gets a glove on it, he can usually make the play. Because of his strong arm he also fills in well in the outfield, though his lack of speed is a liability.

OVERALL:

Salazar can be an excellent bench player on a good team. He can fill in for almost any injured player for short periods, but the full baseball schedule is too long for him to keep up the intensity. He is a capable pinch hitter and can be counted on in the clutch.

LUIS SALAZAR

Position: 3B
Bats: R **Throws:** R
Ht: 5' 9" **Wt:** 180

Opening Day Age: 33
Born: 5/19/56 in Barcelona, Venezuela
ML Seasons: 10

Overall Statistics

	G	AB	R	H	D	T	HR	RBI	SB	BB	SO	AVG
1989	121	326	34	92	12	2	9	34	1	15	57	.282
Career	986	3103	340	827	110	27	63	345	113	134	515	.267

Where He Hits the Ball

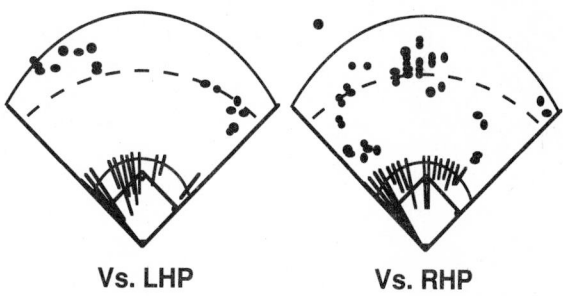

Vs. LHP   **Vs. RHP**

1989 Situational Stats

	AB	H	HR	RBI	AVG		AB	H	HR	RBI	AVG
Home	174	45	6	18	.259	LHP	125	37	5	22	.296
Road	152	47	3	16	.309	RHP	201	55	4	12	.274
Day	114	29	2	12	.254	Sc Pos	76	21	1	21	.276
Night	212	63	7	22	.297	Clutch	64	23	2	9	.359

1989 Rankings (National League)

- ➡ 2nd in hitting in the clutch (.359) - *players with 50 PA in the clutch*
- ➡ Led the Cubs in hitting in the clutch and hitting with 2 strikes (.311) - *all team players*
- ➡ Led NL Third Basemen in hitting in the clutch

GREAT RANGE

RYNE SANDBERG

Position: 2B
Bats: R **Throws:** R
Ht: 6' 2" **Wt:** 180

Opening Day Age: 30
Born: 9/18/59 in Spokane, WA
ML Seasons: 9

HITTING:

Ryne Sandberg is in the prime of his career and at the peak of his hitting game. He has exceptional power for a middle infielder. He hits for average. He's a defensive standout. Championship teams look for eight guys like him.

Last year Sandberg tied Hack Wilson's 1930 Cub record by homering in five consecutive games. His power is to left and left center, but in Wrigley, where the power alleys are short and the wind can make them seem even shorter, he'll take the ball out in any direction. He loves to hit the first pitch fastball; don't throw it if any other pitch is working. Getting ahead of Sandberg isn't easy, though. He doesn't chase many bad pitches until he gets behind in the count. He doesn't like to draw walks and will swing at a pitch close to the strike zone even when ahead in the count.

When Sandberg isn't hitting for power he's spraying line drives. The best way to defense him is to play straight away and hope the ball is hit at someone. He'll go with the outside pitch and pull the inside pitch. Worse yet, he'll hit them both with authority. With runners in scoring position Ryne cuts down on his swing and just tries to put the ball into play.

BASERUNNING:

Sandberg is an excellent baserunner. He'll go first to third on most singles to rightfield and has excellent judgement on line drives. As a base stealer he is cautious and will not run if he feels he doesn't have a good jump. With Zimmer as his manager there is almost no threat Sandberg will run when the Cubs are behind.

FIELDING:

Unquestionably, Sandberg is one of the best defensive second basemen of all time. He has no weakness, great range, sure hands, and the ability to make the double play. Sandberg has now gone 90 games without an error, a National League record which he'll try to extend on Opening Day.

OVERALL:

Sandberg is the second baseman you want if you are putting together a team of the best at their positions. Offensively, he's outstanding when he's hot, and good when he's cold. In the field no one is better. In the clubhouse he leads by example. He loves to play team ball which makes this superstar a most valuable player.

Overall Statistics

	G	AB	R	H	D	T	HR	RBI	SB	BB	SO	AVG
1989	157	606	104	176	25	5	30	76	15	59	85	.290
Career	1234	4893	756	1395	226	54	139	549	250	414	702	.285

Where He Hits the Ball

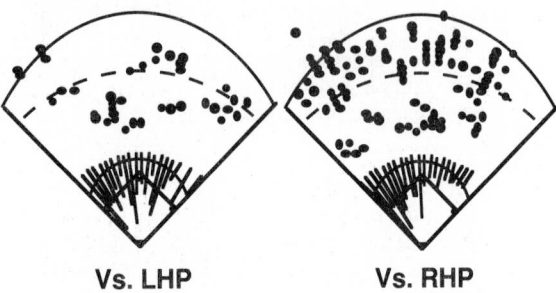

Vs. LHP   **Vs. RHP**

1989 Situational Stats

	AB	H	HR	RBI	AVG		AB	H	HR	RBI	AVG
Home	303	90	16	50	.297	LHP	172	54	7	20	.314
Road	303	86	14	26	.284	RHP	434	122	23	56	.281
Day	326	104	16	47	.319	Sc Pos	130	30	0	36	.231
Night	280	72	14	29	.257	Clutch	94	26	4	10	.277

1989 Rankings (National League)

➡ 1st in runs (104)

➡ 5th in at bats (606), total bases (301) and runs scored per time reached base (38.1%) - *players with 502 PA*

➡ Led the Cubs in at bats, singles (116), total bases, plate appearances (672), games (157), home runs (30), runs, hits (176), pitches seen (2,275), runs scored per time reached base, hitting on an 0-2 count (.256), hitting on a 3-2 count (.377), home run frequency (20.2 ABs per HR) and slugging percentage (.497)

➡ Led NL Second Basemen in slugging percentage, total bases, home runs, runs, RBIs (76) and intentional walks (8)

PITCHING:

Scott Sanderson returned to the big leagues after major back surgery, demonstrating his attitude, desire and devotion to baseball. Sanderson didn't need the grueling routine he was forced to endure to return to the bigs and is financially independent. This is a man who always gives you his best.

But Father Time is wandering slowly into the career of Sanderson. At 33 his fastball has lost more than a few inches and he is no longer able to rely on throwing heat to get out of an inning. He now relies on changing speeds and movement. Often that's not enough. Late last year, Don Zimmer clearly felt that Sanderson had lost something. During the crucial last two months, he started Sanderson only four times, using him mostly as a long reliever.

Despite his loss in velocity, Sanderson's fastball is still his best pitch. His curveball is second rate but he keeps it off the plate. Sanderson will try to retire a hitter without throwing many strikes, and patient hitters can get the best of him by refusing to nibble at his bad offerings. They'll get good wood off him and frequently take him out of the ballpark. Scott averaged just under a homer per nine innings pitched last season.

Sanderson seldom hurts himself with the base on balls. His strongest suit is his control. If he walks a batter early in the game, it's probably not his day. If he walks one later in the game, it's probably time to get someone up in the bullpen. Anytime he walks two batters in the same inning, the hook had better be ready.

FIELDING, HITTING, BASERUNNING:

Sanderson has excellent mechanics and fields his position well. He gets to first on balls hit to the right side very well and is above average at handling the bunt defensively. He is average at holding runners on and, because he throws so many off speed pitches, base stealers are generally successful against him. Sanderson is a poor hitter, a decent bunter, and very slow on the bases.

OVERALL:

While his better days may be behind him, a man like Sanderson can be a good spot starter and an intangible asset as a member of the team. Like Ryne Sandberg, Sanderson leads by example. But it remains to be seen whether Don Zimmer has enough confidence in Sanderson to return him to the rotation.

SCOTT SANDERSON

Position: SP/RP
Bats: R **Throws:** R
Ht: 6' 5" **Wt:** 198

Opening Day Age: 33
Born: 7/22/56 in Dearborn, MI
ML Seasons: 12

Overall Statistics

	W	L	ERA	G	GS	Sv	IP	H	R	BB	SO	HR
1989	11	9	3.94	37	23	0	146.1	155	69	31	86	16
Career	98	89	3.55	309	252	5	1620.0	1567	701	412	1081	162

Where They Hit the Ball

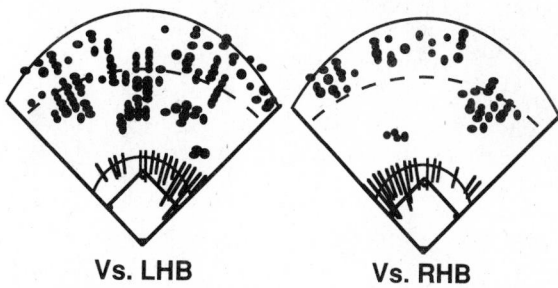

Vs. LHB   **Vs. RHB**

1989 Situational Stats

	W	L	ERA	Sv	IP		AB	H	HR	RBI	AVG
Home	6	3	3.75	0	69.2	LHB	343	100	8	39	.292
Road	5	6	4.11	0	76.2	RHB	223	55	8	24	.247
Day	6	4	3.30	0	84.2	Sc Pos	124	34	4	46	.274
Night	5	5	4.82	0	61.2	Clutch	51	14	1	3	.275

1989 Rankings (National League)

➡ Led the Cubs in run support per 9 innings (5.8)

HITTING:

Dwight Smith was the best hitting rookie in the major leagues last season. He didn't win the Rookie of the Year award because he wasn't up all season and didn't play against lefthanders. But that wasn't his fault.

Smith, a lefthanded hitter, didn't display any glaring weaknesses at the plate. His at bats against lefthanders were limited to a couple of dozen but he was not overmatched at those times. Against righthanders Dwight got the upper hand. Because he isn't a big threat to strike out, he is a good number two batter. He can be used to hit-and-run and he will take a pitch to allow the runner to steal a base.

Smith has better than average power and uses his speed to turn balls in the gap into doubles and triples. He protects the plate well when he is behind in the count and is an outstanding hitter when ahead in the count. He likes the ball out over the plate and low, and drives that pitch to left and left center. Dwight will pull the inside pitch and it is difficult to throw fastballs past him.

Any weaknesses Smith possesses have yet to be discovered. As National League pitchers made adjustments from inside to outside and fastball to change-up, Dwight adjusted with them. If he can continue to makes those adjustments he may have a batting title in his future.

BASERUNNING:

Smith made the typical rookie mistakes on the basepaths. He has excellent speed, but wasn't asked to steal much last season; he did well in his limited attempts, however. In the future, Smith should be able to swipe a lot more. But he will have to improve his ability to read a pitcher's move since he generally gets a poor jump.

FIELDING:

It was Smith's bat that got him to the majors, not his glove. While he is quick and can get to balls other outfielders can't get to, his glove is unsteady. His arm is also not among the best and he can be run on.

OVERALL:

Offensively, Dwight Smith only needs to stay as good as he already is to assure himself a spot on the Cubs roster. The rest of his game can improve, and will, as he gains experience. If he works on his baserunning and defense, Smith will almost assure himself a starting role, even against lefthanders.

DWIGHT SMITH

Position: LF/RF
Bats: L **Throws:** R
Ht: 5'11" **Wt:** 175

Opening Day Age: 26
Born: 11/8/63 in Tallahassee, FL
ML Seasons: 1

Overall Statistics

	G	AB	R	H	D	T	HR	RBI	SB	BB	SO	AVG
1989	109	343	52	111	19	6	9	52	9	31	51	.324
Career	109	343	52	111	19	6	9	52	9	31	51	.324

Where He Hits the Ball

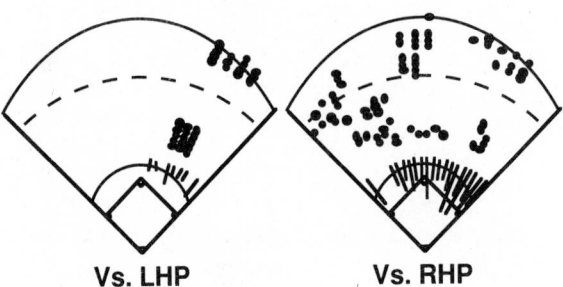

Vs. LHP   **Vs. RHP**

1989 Situational Stats

	AB	H	HR	RBI	AVG		AB	H	HR	RBI	AVG
Home	157	57	5	28	.363	LHP	29	7	1	5	.241
Road	186	54	4	24	.290	RHP	314	104	8	47	.331
Day	183	62	4	28	.339	Sc Pos	91	27	2	39	.297
Night	160	49	5	24	.306	Clutch	49	12	1	6	.245

1989 Rankings (National League)

- ➡ 8th in least GDPs per GDP situation (3.8%) - *players with 50 PA in GDP situations*

- ➡ 9th in percentage of extra bases taken as a runner (59.4%) - *players with 40 opportunities to advance*

- ➡ Led the Cubs in triples (6), least GDPs per GDP opportunity, percentage of extra bases taken as a runner and batting at home (.363) - *all team players*

PITCHING:

Rick Sutcliffe is not as consistently good as he once was, but he still reaches his old heights on occasion. He won't be winning any more Cy Young Awards. But on any given day, or during the course of any game, Sutcliffe still has the talent to stop any team cold.

Rick still relies heavily on his fastball and slider. He is most effective when he keeps the ball down in the strike zone. Because the fastball isn't the same one he was throwing five years ago, when he gets it high in the strike zone the opposition often hits it high in the bleachers. For that reason Wrigley Field gives Sutcliffe more trouble as the years go by. His ERA at home (4.80) was more than two runs higher than his road ERA last season.

Further evidence that age is catching up to Sutcliffe is his inability to complete games. He finished only five games last season and a couple of those were because the Cubs had a big lead and the manager was on auto-pilot. Rick is at his best during his first 75 pitches, which occurs generally about the sixth inning. After the seventh inning he loses another foot off the fastball; the league batting average off him from the seventh inning on jumped to .292.

FIELDING, HITTING, BASERUNNING:

Sutcliffe is a fine hitter. The Cubs have successfully hit-and-run with Rick and, once in a while, he can take one out of the park. Once he does reach base however, he's a very slow baserunner.

In the field he charges bunts well, knocks down balls hit back to the box, and covers first base well on balls hit to the right side. If Sutcliffe has a glaring weakness, it's his inability to hold runners on. Even though Rick had some of the best catchers in baseball making the throws, National League runners were successful in 25 of 32 attempts.

OVERALL:

Sutcliffe is a former Rookie of the Year and a former Cy Young award winner. He is aging, but at times he can still pitch as well as he did in those seasons. Rick helps the staff as a veteran pitcher because he can work with the younger pitchers and he can set a work ethic. There are still a couple of years left in his arm and there are few number three pitchers who are better.

RICK SUTCLIFFE

Position: SP
Bats: L **Throws:** R
Ht: 6' 7" **Wt:** 215

Opening Day Age: 33
Born: 6/21/56 in Independence, MO
ML Seasons: 13

Overall Statistics

	W	L	ERA	G	GS	Sv	IP	H	R	BB	SO	HR
1989	16	11	3.66	35	34	0	229.0	202	98	69	153	18
Career	133	103	3.81	352	291	6	2109.0	1985	970	844	1405	176

Where They Hit the Ball

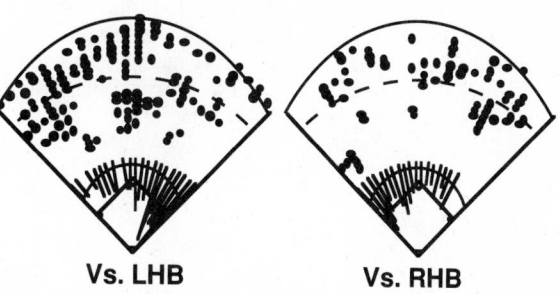

Vs. LHB   **Vs. RHB**

1989 Situational Stats

	W	L	ERA	Sv	IP		AB	H	HR	RBI	AVG
Home	5	7	4.80	0	99.1	LHB	507	123	11	48	.243
Road	11	4	2.78	0	129.2	RHB	335	79	7	30	.236
Day	7	8	4.08	0	123.2	Sc Pos	167	37	3	57	.222
Night	9	3	3.16	0	105.1	Clutch	53	18	2	8	.340

1989 Rankings (National League)

➡ 1st in worst ERA at home (4.80) - *pitchers with 81 IP at home*

➡ 2nd in balks (6)

➡ 4th in games started (34), pickoff throws (222) and worst stolen base percentage allowed (78.1%) - *pitchers with 162 IP*

➡ 6th in wins (16)

➡ Led the Cubs in wild pitches (12), balks, home runs allowed (18), strikeouts (153), pickoff throws, stolen bases allowed (25), ERA on the road, lowest on-base average allowed (.296) and lowest batting average with runners in scoring position (.222) - *team pitchers with 162 IP*

GREAT SPEED

JEROME WALTON

Position: CF
Bats: R **Throws:** R
Ht: 6' 1" **Wt:** 175

Opening Day Age: 24
Born: 7/8/65 in Newnan, GA
ML Seasons: 1

HITTING:

Jerome Walton won the Rookie of the Year Award last year, as he deserved to; he hit consistently in all situations. In every situation -- runners in scoring position, grass/turf, home/road, whatever -- Walton produced. He's a hitter.

Jerome has a wide open stance and his first move is to close up as he strides into the pitch. He is vulnerable to a fastball on or just off the inside corner. His quick reflexes allow him to inside-out an off-speed pitch. Most pitchers seem to want to go after the outside corner, feeling that Jerome can't reach it. That is a mistake.

There is very little power in Jerome's bat. He may never hit 10 home runs in a season but with his speed he should hit over 30 doubles consistently. Injuries to his hamstrings hampered him during his entire rookie season. When healthy he will get even more infield and bunt singles. His ability to bunt keeps the corners short and allows him to swing away against a drawn-in infield. Walton's career is off to a terrific start, but his future will depend on him making the needed adjustments at the plate as the pitchers in the league try to find his weaknesses.

BASERUNNING:

When Walton wasn't hampered by hamstring injuries, he was one of the quickest players in the league on the bases. If he learns how to get a better jump off of first, he may be able to steal 75 bases in a season. Walton scores from second on nearly any hit that reaches the outfield, but he could make better use of his coaches. This is probably a result of skipping over Triple A ball, but the problem should be corrected in time.

FIELDING:

Walton muffed the first ball hit to him last season but only made one more error for the rest of the season, a throwing error. Jerome uses his speed to great advantage in centerfield, but if he has a weakness it's his hesitancy to take charge. His arm is weak but accurate. The faster runners in the league will challenge Walton.

OVERALL:

Walton is one of the best defensively, and is a capable leadoff hitter. He only had three minor league seasons and there's no reason to think he can't continue to improve. It's best that opposing teams challenge him both offensively and defensively, since he is still prone to the mistakes made by younger ballplayers.

Overall Statistics

	G	AB	R	H	D	T	HR	RBI	SB	BB	SO	AVG
1989	116	475	64	139	23	3	5	46	24	27	77	.293
Career	116	475	64	139	23	3	5	46	24	27	77	.293

Where He Hits the Ball

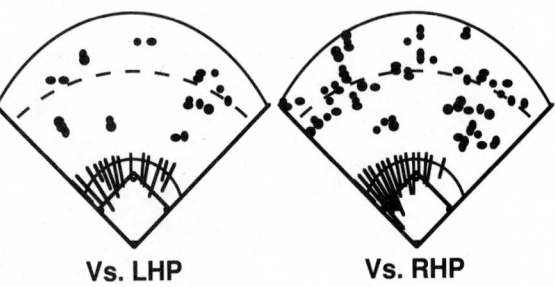

Vs. LHP   **Vs. RHP**

1989 Situational Stats

	AB	H	HR	RBI	AVG		AB	H	HR	RBI	AVG
Home	231	70	3	24	.303	LHP	128	41	2	19	.320
Road	244	69	2	22	.283	RHP	347	98	3	27	.282
Day	255	82	3	30	.322	Sc Pos	92	32	0	41	.348
Night	220	57	2	16	.259	Clutch	66	15	0	9	.227

1989 Rankings (National League)

➡ 3rd in grounder/flyball ratio (2.05) - *players with 502 PA*

➡ 4th in bunts in play (34)

➡ 5th in hitting with runners in scoring position (.248) - *players with 100 PA with runners in scoring position*

➡ 6th in hit by pitch (6)

➡ 7th in batting average (.293)

➡ 10th in steals of third (5)

➡ Led the Cubs in hit by pitch, stolen bases (24), grounder/flyball ratio, stolen base percentage (77.4%), bunts in play and hitting with runners in scoring position

HITTING:

Mitch Webster began the 1989 season as the starting left fielder for the Chicago Cubs. He hit well until the end of April when he went into a 1 for 30 slump. Webster then lost the job to Dwight Smith and was on the bench for the rest of the season. Once a fine hitter for Montreal, where he had two seasons with more than 50 extra-base hits each, Webster has failed to reach that level of production with the Cubs.

Webster twice homered in double figures for Montreal, but he had only three last year, just one of those in Wrigley Field. These days Webster is a groundball and line drive hitter. When things are going right for him he hits the ball up the middle, but his extra base hits tend to be down the line. It's best to pitch Webster away as a righthanded batter and jam him as a lefty. Keep the outfield shifted the same way.

Webster was used a lot as a pinch hitter last year, but did not do well. His batting average dropped as the inning numbers went up. Pinch hitting is a skill Webster will have to refine if he hopes to remain a useful major leaguer.

BASERUNNING:

This is the best part of Webster's game. As a base stealer he takes a big enough lead so that he has to dive back to reach first safely. When he runs he gets a good break from first and is tough to catch. He goes from first to third on nearly everything hit to center and right field and will challenge the arms in the outfield if he has a chance to score.

FIELDING:

Another advantage Mitch gives the ballclub is his versatility in the outfield. He can play all three positions but is most comfortable in center. His speed allows him to get to a lot of balls in the alleys, but he is often guilty of not taking charge of the outfield when he is in center. His arm is average. Runners will challenge him when he is in right but only the best will run on him while he is in left and center.

OVERALL:

Webster gives a team a fine defensive outfielder with good speed and the ability to play all three positions. Offensively he hasn't helped the Cubs much except on the bases. He is best suited to bench duty and can fill that role well as long as it isn't expanded beyond his capabilities.

MITCH WEBSTER

Position: LF/CF/RF
Bats: B **Throws:** L
Ht: 6' 1" **Wt:** 185

Opening Day Age: 30
Born: 5/16/59 in Larned, KS
ML Seasons: 7

Overall Statistics

	G	AB	R	H	D	T	HR	RBI	SB	BB	SO	AVG
1989	98	272	40	70	12	4	3	19	14	30	55	.257
Career	671	2205	342	603	99	36	43	204	120	234	356	.273

Where He Hits the Ball

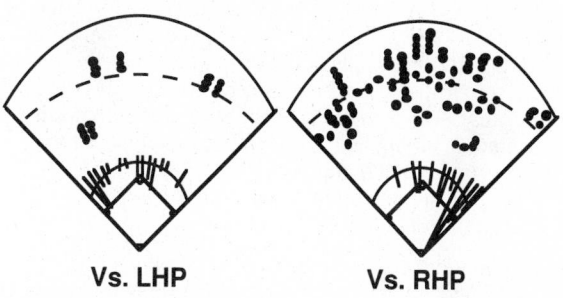

Vs. LHP **Vs. RHP**

1989 Situational Stats

	AB	H	HR	RBI	AVG		AB	H	HR	RBI	AVG
Home	132	33	1	9	.250	LHP	61	19	1	2	.311
Road	140	37	2	10	.264	RHP	211	51	2	17	.242
Day	149	37	2	10	.248	Sc Pos	62	13	1	16	.210
Night	123	33	1	9	.268	Clutch	50	8	1	3	.160

1989 Rankings (National League)

➡ 9th in steals of third (6)
➡ Led the Cubs in steals of third

PITCHING:

Mitch "Wild Thing" Williams says, "I pitch like my hair is on fire." Truer words were never spoken. To understand that statement you only need to see his pitching motion once; there's nothing like it in all of baseball. But it wasn't just his hair that was sizzling in 1989. His 36 saves led the Cubs out of the cellar and into the penthouse of the National League's East division.

Williams is a power pitcher who relies strictly on his fastball. There is no trickery when he is on the mound. He goes right after every hitter. It is not necessary to try to hit his first pitch fastball. Whether the first pitch is a ball or a strike he will come back with another fastball. He doesn't use his off-speed pitch unless he has two strikes on the batter and even then it is not guaranteed.

Williams's nickname, "Wild Thing," is more than accurate. While he struck out 7.4 batters per nine innings he also walked 5.7 batters per nine. His control problems make him vulnerable in many ways. Because of it he is most effective when he comes in to start an inning and has open bases, allowing room for error. If his control is not with him, Williams is likely to take something off his fastball in order to find the plate. At that point he's in trouble.

Williams has good stamina and can usually go as long as 45 pitches before he starts to tire. But like most hard throwers, he wears down with the season. He was consistently effective last year until August, but then was gradually hit harder. His control is about the same when he tires but the speed of the fastball drops dramatically.

FIELDING, HITTING, BASERUNNING:

Hitting and baserunning are not among the things that Mitch Williams gets paid to do. He'll get less than a half a dozen at bats per season and when he does, the game is out of reach. Williams falls off to the third base side on every pitch, and with that follow-through can barely defend himself, much less field his position. He took a frightening shot off his head down the stretch, but was not seriously hurt. But he's outstanding at holding baserunners, and picked off six runners last year with his slick move.

OVERALL:

Mitch Williams is a closer. When he brings his control to the park he will shut down the opposition. Patience is the way to beat Williams. Unfortunately when he is brought into the game, time is usually of the essence and patience is not an affordable commodity.

MITCH WILLIAMS

Position: RP
Bats: L **Throws:** L
Ht: 6' 4" **Wt:** 200

Opening Day Age: 25
Born: 11/17/64 in Santa Ana, CA
ML Seasons: 4

Overall Statistics

	W	L	ERA	G	GS	Sv	IP	H	R	BB	SO	HR
1989	4	4	2.64	76	0	36	81.2	71	27	52	67	6
Career	22	23	3.46	308	1	68	356.1	251	151	272	347	27

Where They Hit the Ball

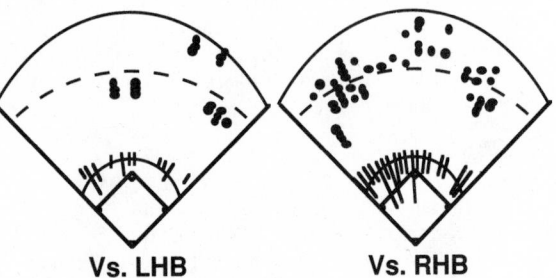

Vs. LHB   **Vs. RHB**

1989 Situational Stats

	W	L	ERA	Sv	IP		AB	H	HR	RBI	AVG
Home	3	2	3.65	15	37.0	LHB	71	18	0	12	.254
Road	1	2	1.81	21	44.2	RHB	227	53	6	28	.233
Day	2	1	3.21	18	42.0	Sc Pos	109	23	2	34	.211
Night	2	3	2.04	18	39.2	Clutch	225	49	5	33	.218

1989 Rankings (National League)

- 1st in games (76) and blown saves (11)
- 2nd in saves (36), games finished (61), hit batsmen (8) and save opportunities (47)
- 4th in lowest save percentage (76.6%) - *pitchers with 20 or more save opportunities*
- 5th in worst GDPs induced per GDP situation (3.3%) - *pitchers with 30 GDP situations*
- Led the Cubs in games, games finished, hit batsmen, saves and blown saves

HITTING:

Marvell Wynne has long been a streaky lefthanded hitter, one capable of going on significant tears before he begins to bottom out. When he's hot, the idea is to play him until he no longer sizzles. But when he stops hitting, get him out of the lineup before he becomes a detriment. Wynne simply wears down after several weeks of continuous play.

Wynne is a good man to have coming off the bench because he is capable of hitting with occasional power. He's a good contact hitter and will usually put the ball in play. But he's never been a patient hitter and it looks like he never will be -- last year's total of 13 walks was a career low for him. The lefty-swinging Wynne has almost always been platooned, but he's batted .340 (34 for 100) against lefthanded pitching over the last two years.

Though he has some talent, Wynne is one of those hitters who is just not good enough to hit a high quality fastball -- it took him seven years to get a hit off the Mets' Dwight Gooden -- or good quality breaking pitches. If you're pegging Wynne for your starting lineup, it is a yardstick of the weakness of your team.

BASERUNNING:

A speedy base runner, Wynne often negates that asset by making bonehead plays and silly decisions. Last August, representing the tying run with two outs in the ninth inning against Atlanta, he fell for the hidden ball trick, ending the rally and the game. It wasn't an isolated incident. During his Padre years, Wynne was known for blowing so many base-running signs that coaches considered using cue cards.

FIELDING:

Wynne can play all three outfield positions, but with his speed, is probably best suited for centerfield. He's a very competent late-inning defensive replacement, but again, is not suited for a starting role in any of these positions. He has decent range and a mediocre arm. You can count on Wynne to miss several cutoff men during the course of a season.

OVERALL:

Though Wynne falls just a shade short in almost every facet as a player, he is a useful spot player and a good guy to have around the clubhouse. Many Padres players were quite disturbed when the upbeat and well-liked Wynne was traded because he was such an important ingredient of the club's chemistry.

MARVELL WYNNE

Position: CF/LF/RF
Bats: L **Throws:** L
Ht: 5'11" **Wt:** 185

Opening Day Age: 30
Born: 12/17/59 in Chicago, IL
ML Seasons: 7

Overall Statistics

	G	AB	R	H	D	T	HR	RBI	SB	BB	SO	AVG
1989	125	342	27	83	13	2	7	39	6	13	48	.243
Career	848	2507	279	626	99	26	36	225	77	177	373	.250

Where He Hits the Ball

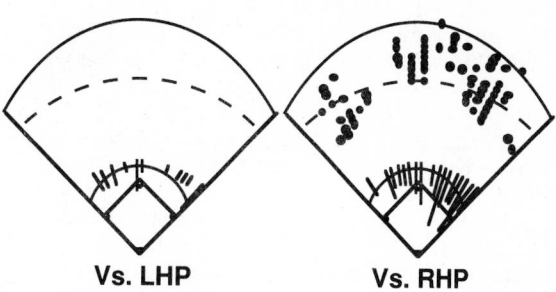

Vs. LHP   Vs. RHP

1989 Situational Stats

	AB	H	HR	RBI	AVG		AB	H	HR	RBI	AVG
Home	150	38	3	12	.253	LHP	45	16	1	7	.356
Road	192	45	4	27	.234	RHP	297	67	6	32	.226
Day	125	34	2	15	.272	Sc Pos	84	23	3	31	.274
Night	217	49	5	24	.226	Clutch	57	16	0	5	.281

1989 Rankings (National League)

➡ Led NL Center Fielders in hitting vs. left-handed pitchers (.356) - *all NL center fielders*

DOUG DASCENZO

Position: CF
Bats: B **Throws:** L
Ht: 5'8" **Wt:** 160

Opening Day Age: 25
Born: 6/30/64 in
Cleveland, OH
ML Seasons: 2

Overall Statistics

	G	AB	R	H	D	T	HR	RBI	SB	BB	SO	AVG
1989	47	139	20	23	1	0	1	12	6	13	13	.165
Career	73	214	29	39	4	0	1	16	12	22	17	.182

HITTING, FIELDING, BASERUNNING:

The Cubs continue to try to force Doug Dascenzo into the leadoff role, though he didn't hit for a high average or draw many walks even at the minor league level. Doug's on-base percentage could be improved if he would work on his patience; with his 5'8" stature, he should be capable of drawing plenty of walks. Dascenzo has no power, but he can get a lot of leg hits. His offensive strength is his ability to steal bases. With a little more experience he can be an excellent baserunner. Defensively, Dascenzo is at the front of the class. His speed allows him to run down fly balls in the gaps and cut off line drives that might normally fall in for singles. He has good hands and will hold onto any balls he gets his glove on. He can also play left and right field but his arm is only average and should be considered before putting him in right.

OVERALL:

Without a drastic improvement in his batting average and on-base percentage, Dascenzo will have trouble sticking with the Cubs. His defense and baserunning ability are fine but there are few jobs available for defensive replacements in the outfield.

JEFF PICO

Position: RP/SP
Bats: R **Throws:** R
Ht: 6'2" **Wt:** 170

Opening Day Age: 24
Born: 2/12/66 in
Antioch, CA
ML Seasons: 2

Overall Statistics

	W	L	ERA	G	GS	Sv	IP	H	R	BB	SO	HR
1989	3	1	3.77	53	5	2	90.2	99	43	31	38	8
Career	9	8	3.98	82	18	3	203.1	207	100	68	95	14

PITCHING, FIELDING, HITTING:

Jeff Pico threw a complete game shutout in his first major league appearance in 1988. Since then nearly everything Pico has done indicates he needs more minor league experience if he is to become an effective major league pitcher.

Pico is strictly a finesse pitcher. To his credit, he doesn't make mistakes with pitches on bad counts. If he falls behind a hitter, he'll still shoot for the corners. If he gets in front of the batter, he'll stay off the plate rather than give him anything to hit. When Jeff is effective it is because he's getting in front of hitters. Unfortunately this also becomes his problem. Knowing that the first pitch would be around the plate, the league batted .400 on a 0-0 count and only dropped to .345 on 0-1 pitches.

Pico doesn't have great stuff. His fastball is barely average. He has a decent curveball but can't rely on getting it over the plate if he falls behind the hitter. He is effective at keeping the ball in the park against righthanded batters but lefties fall over each other getting to the plate.

Pico has struggled as a hitter, and has had few opportunities on the bases. He is a capable fielder on bunts and balls hit back to the box, but he is a little slow getting over to first base on groundballs. Pico's move to first is outstanding; he allowed only one stolen base last year, while five were caught stealing.

OVERALL:

Pico will come to camp looking for a job. If he spent the off-season working on his pitching and shows some improvement, he may catch on as the tenth man. Otherwise it may be back to the minors for more schooling.

DOMINGO RAMOS

Position: SS/3B
Bats: R **Throws:** R
Ht: 5'10" **Wt:** 154

Opening Day Age: 32
Born: 3/29/58 in
Santiago, Dominican
Republic
ML Seasons: 10

GARY VARSHO

Position: LF
Bats: L **Throws:** R
Ht: 5'11" **Wt:** 190

Opening Day Age: 28
Born: 6/20/61 in
Marshfield, WI
ML Seasons: 2

Overall Statistics

	G	AB	R	H	D	T	HR	RBI	SB	BB	SO	AVG
1989	85	179	18	47	6	2	1	19	1	17	23	.263
Career	409	860	87	201	29	2	6	68	6	65	109	.234

Overall Statistics

	G	AB	R	H	D	T	HR	RBI	SB	BB	SO	AVG
1989	61	87	10	16	4	2	0	6	3	4	13	.184
Career	107	160	16	36	7	2	0	11	8	5	19	.225

HITTING, FIELDING, BASERUNNING:

Domingo Ramos was the ultimate player off the bench last season. When called on to pinch hit he batted .429. He was able to give the regular infielders a day off because he played second, third and short-stop and played them very well. Finally, he did his best hitting late in the game and with runners in scoring position, which made him an excellent candidate for double switches. Ramos has always been an unpredictable hitter, with seasons .283 and .311 sand-wiched around years of .185, .196 and .182. He uses the heaviest bat on the team because he feels it keeps him from overswinging. He is a line drive hitter who hits the ball back up the middle, and will take a walk on occasion. He has no speed and does not get any leg hits. He is also not threat to run on a straight steal. Going from first to third can also be an experience for this stockily built infielder.

OVERALL:

Ramos is a good reserve because he can do a little of everything. He fields well, can hit a little and is happy with his role on the team. You never know what he'll hit, but Ramos's defense and versatility make him a valuable player.

HITTING, FIELDING, BASERUNNING:

The stock of Gary Varsho dropped dramatically last season. He began the year as one of the Cubs' backup outfielders but by year's end he barely had a spot on the 40-man roster. Offensively Varsho is a lefthanded hitter who likes to go to the opposite field. He has little home run power but is capable of hitting line drives into the gaps for doubles and triples. He can hit righties and likes the ball out over the plate. When he is jammed inside he often pops it up weakly to the middle infield. He can draw a walk, but lost his patience when he began to press last year. Defensively, Varsho is an adequate fielder. His arm is strong enough to allow him to play rightfield but his throws are not always accurate. On the basepaths Gary can be a threat. He can steal bases but needs work on reading a pitchers' move to first.

OVERALL:

Nearly 29, Varsho may be running out of chances with the Cubs. He has some skills but hasn't shown he can handle major league pitching. He might need to catch on with another organization.

CURTIS WILKERSON

Position: 3B/2B
Bats: B **Throws:** R
Ht: 5' 9" **Wt:** 160

Opening Day Age: 28
Born: 4/26/61 in Petersburg, VA
ML Seasons: 7

Overall Statistics

	G	AB	R	H	D	T	HR	RBI	SB	BB	SO	AVG
1989	77	160	18	39	4	2	1	10	4	8	33	.244
Career	687	1751	203	445	54	20	4	116	57	97	274	.254

HITTING, FIELDING, BASERUNNING:

Curtis Wilkerson is an excellent role player. He sprays the ball around and batted .370 as a pinch hitter last year. As an everyday player Curtis has been a .260 hitter who strikes out too often and has virtually no power. His only homer was a windblown Wrigley Field fly ball that went almost as high as it went far. Wilkerson can play second, third and shortstop and even the outfield in a pinch. He's best in the middle of the infield but his lack of range will preclude him receiving any fielding awards. His arm is good for an infielder and accurate if not quick. On the bases Curtis is an asset. He won't win any stolen base titles either but he is good going from first to third and can steal an occasional base if needed. He's still young and with a little more experience he can be an above average base stealer.

OVERALL:

Wilkerson is an excellent man off the bench. He can pinch hit, pinch run and play a variety of positions adequately enough to be trusted. He won't lead anybody to the World Series but he can play his role well for a team trying to get there.

STEVE WILSON

Position: RP/SP
Bats: L **Throws:** L
Ht: 6' 4" **Wt:** 195

Opening Day Age: 25
Born: 12/13/64 in Victoria, BC
ML Seasons: 2

Overall Statistics

	W	L	ERA	G	GS	Sv	IP	H	R	BB	SO	HR
1989	6	4	4.20	53	8	2	85.2	83	43	31	65	6
Career	6	4	4.34	56	8	2	93.1	90	48	35	66	7

PITCHING, FIELDING, HITTING:

Steve Wilson, a young lefthander, did not put up impressive numbers last season but nevertheless made an impression. He showed excellent composure for his age in the heat of a pennant race. His fastball has excellent movement and is complemented by a better than average changeup. Wilson will be given a chance to win a starting spot in the rotation but landing that spot is still likely to be a year or two away. Because he is used sparingly he has trouble with his stamina and averaged less than five innings per start in his eight starts last season. Wilson can field his position well. He knocks down most balls he can reach and he isn't afraid to go after the lead runner on comebackers. He is also decent at holding runners. Offensively Wilson is not going to help himself much. On the basepaths he seems to need a secondbase coach.

OVERALL:

Even with his limited experience, Wilson is excellent during his first 20 pitches. After that it is steadily downhill. At this time the Cubs organization has him ticketed as a starter in the future, but Wilson may be best used as a closer. He has the fastball and control to be a good one.

RICK
WRONA

Position: C
Bats: R **Throws:** R
Ht: 6' 0" **Wt:** 180

Opening Day Age: 26
Born: 12/10/63 in
Tulsa, OK
ML Seasons: 2

Overall Statistics

	G	AB	R	H	D	T	HR	RBI	SB	BB	SO	AVG
1989	38	92	11	26	2	1	2	14	0	2	21	.283
Career	42	98	11	26	2	1	2	14	0	2	22	.265

HITTING, FIELDING, BASERUNNING:

Due to injuries to Damon Berryhill, Rick Wrona was thrown into the majors at least a year or two before he was ready. But Wrona played excellently and surprised everyone except himself. Wrona is confident without being cocky. Offensively he is not intimidated at the plate but he is not patient either. In 95 plate appearances he drew only two walks. He was able to hit both the fastball and off-speed pitches. He is a pull hitter and goes to the opposite field only on rare occasions. Defensively, Wrona was good. He threw out 32% of the baserunners attempting to steal. He was also good at staying in front of pitches in the dirt and saving his pitchers from wild pitches. A slow man, he knows his abilities and takes no chances going for the extra bases on basehits.

OVERALL:

Wrona shows all the potential to be a regular major league catcher. If Damon Berryhill is healthy this year, Wrona can spend the season at Triple A rounding off his rough edges. Catchers are such a valuable commodity, Rick may prove to be a real golden nugget. With Berryhill, Girardi, and Wrona, the Cubs may have struck it rich at the catching position.

HITTING:

People who want to argue that Fenway is a great hitters' park will have some ammunition in the results from the Benzinger/Esasky switch. While Nick Esasky blossomed into an offensive force in Boston, Todd Benzinger withered on the vine in Cincinnati. Esasky hit 32 points over his lifetime average, while Benzinger dropped almost 20 points.

Benzinger is not really a great power hitter, but he swings hard, produces his share of homers, and strikes out a lot. The total performance amounts to a low on-base percentage, under .300 from both sides of the plate. His numbers would look good for a middle infielder; for a first baseman batting in the middle of the order, Benzinger is barely adequate as an offensive producer.

Benzinger likes to swing at the first pitch, and is generally not too selective. Pitchers accordingly give him many bad pitches. Benzinger is especially prone to chase anything down low, breaking balls or fastballs, inside or out. He frequently makes an awkward, lunging half-stroke that produces a miss, a foul, or a weak grounder.

BASERUNNING:

Anyone who gets caught stealing in seven of 10 attempts should consider loosening the shoe laces and giving the legs a rest. Benzinger was only 50% successful through 1988, and got worse in 1989. Lacking both instinct and raw speed, Todd should stay put more often, and rely entirely on coaches to make decisions for him.

FIELDING:

An outfielder by profession, Benzinger was pressed into first base service by the Red Sox in 1988, and he is still learning. Todd showed true progress in 1989, especially in the second half. In the early spring, he looked like a real butcher: unprepared, clumsy, and unsure where to throw the ball. Late in the season, he looked more sure of himself, had apparently developed a softer glove, and was making the 3-6 play with a hint of grace.

OVERALL:

Except for possibly lowering his strikeouts and raising his on-base average, Benzinger's performance is about all that can be expected. He will have increasing defensive value as he learns more about first base and/or returns to the outfield. Benzinger was the only Reds player who was in the opening day line-up and stayed off the disabled list all year. Cincinnati needs more durable performers like Benzinger if they are going to be contenders in 1990.

TODD BENZINGER

Position: 1B
Bats: B **Throws:** R
Ht: 6' 1" **Wt:** 185

Opening Day Age: 27
Born: 2/11/63 in Dayton, KY
ML Seasons: 3

Overall Statistics

	G	AB	R	H	D	T	HR	RBI	SB	BB	SO	AVG
1989	161	628	79	154	28	3	17	76	3	44	120	.245
Career	354	1256	162	319	67	5	38	189	10	88	241	.254

Where He Hits the Ball

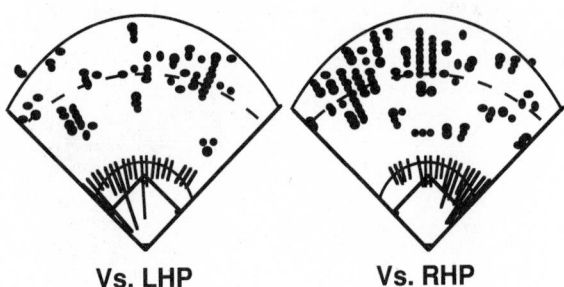

Vs. LHP　　　　　**Vs. RHP**

1989 Situational Stats

	AB	H	HR	RBI	AVG		AB	H	HR	RBI	AVG
Home	306	85	6	36	.278	LHP	231	56	7	23	.242
Road	322	69	11	40	.214	RHP	397	98	10	53	.247
Day	199	45	2	19	.226	Sc Pos	165	33	6	63	.200
Night	429	109	15	57	.254	Clutch	96	16	2	12	.167

1989 Rankings (National League)

➡ 1st in at bats (628)

➡ 3rd in sacrifice flies (8)

➡ 4th in plate appearances (686) and worst hitting with runners in scoring position (.200) - *players with 100 PA with runners in scoring position*

➡ 5th in games (161)

➡ Led the Reds in at bats, singles (106), intentional walks (13), times on base (200), runs (79), hits (154), doubles (28), strikeouts (120), plate appearance, games, and runs scored per time reached base (33.6%) - *team players with 502 PA*

➡ Led AL First Basemen in at bats, sacrifice bunts (4) and caught stealing (7)

WORKHORSE

TOM BROWNING

Position: SP
Bats: L **Throws:** L
Ht: 6' 1" **Wt:** 190

Opening Day Age: 29
Born: 4/28/60 in
Casper, WY
ML Seasons: 6

PITCHING:

Tom Browning is from the Robin Roberts/Catfish Hunter school of pitching. He gives up many fly balls, including some homers, but his total hit count is low, and he gives up very few walks. Browning is good for almost a dinger per game, but he will probably win anyway, if there are not two or three runners on base when the ball flies over the fence. He is the real workhorse of the Reds staff, and has thrown over 240 innings in three of the last four years.

Browning has more pitches than he has fingers on his throwing hand: a lukewarm fastball, two different screwballs (one hard and one a change), a curve, a slider, and a straight change-up. He uses the fastball only to hit locations and to set up the other pitches. The scroogie is his out pitch. When Browning has good control, spectators get to see a pitching clinic. He works very quickly and keeps the opposition off balance through entire games, many of which are finished in two and a half hours or less.

For a pitcher without overwhelming power, Browning produces a large number of low-hit games. His best, of course, was the 1988 perfect game against L.A. He just missed another perfect game in 1989, and had a number of one and two hitters. Browning's 15-12 record in 1989 could have been much better. The Reds were shut out in six of his starts.

FIELDING, HITTING, BASERUNNING:

Browning is a marvelous fielder. He was second only to Rick Mahler on the Reds in assists with 32, and participated in an impressive total of six double plays during 1989. Browning is superior at holding runners. Last year he allowed only 15 steals and a 63% success rate by the opposition. Tom hit only .090 in 1989, but he produced an amazing 14 sacrifice hits. He is much better than the average pitcher when it comes to offense. He can draw a walk, move a runner along, line an occasional hit, and swing-bunt at any time. He has appeared as a pinch runner on occasion and held his own on the basepaths.

OVERALL:

Ever since Browning won 20 games as a rookie in 1985, all his other accomplishments have been regarded as glittering indications of unfulfilled potential. At age 30, Browning has compiled a .600 lifetime winning percentage, with an ERA that looks like it belongs to a so-so pitcher. Conclusion: Browning may not be a superstar, but he is a winner, a money pitcher, and the one starter that Cincinnati can rely on for 1990.

Overall Statistics

	W	L	ERA	G	GS	Sv	IP	H	R	BB	SO	HR
1989	15	12	3.39	37	37	0	249.2	241	109	64	118	31
Career	78	52	3.72	185	184	0	1211.1	1141	552	337	675	149

Where They Hit the Ball

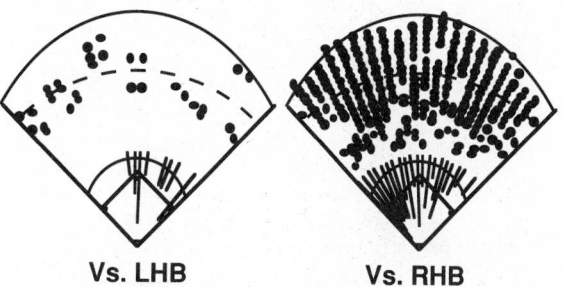

Vs. LHB　　　　**Vs. RHB**

1989 Situational Stats

	W	L	ERA	Sv	IP		AB	H	HR	RBI	AVG
Home	7	8	4.14	0	126.0	LHB	132	35	6	19	.265
Road	8	4	2.62	0	123.2	RHB	814	206	25	76	.253
Day	4	4	2.39	0	67.2	Sc Pos	171	44	2	54	.257
Night	11	8	3.76	0	182.0	Clutch	68	11	0	2	.162

1989 Rankings (National League)

➡ 1st in games started (37), least pitches thrown per batter (3.2), home runs allowed (31) and home runs allowed per 9 innings (1.11) - *pitchers with 162 IP*

➡ 2nd in hits allowed (241), batters faced (1,031), innings (249.2) and lowest grounder/flyball ratio (.68) - *pitchers with 162 IP*

➡ Led the Reds in wins (15), games started, innings, home runs allowed, walks allowed, pitches thrown (3,319), shutouts (2), complete games (9), batters faced, ERA (3.39), lowest batting average allowed (.255) and lowest on-base average allowed (.302) - *team pitchers with 162 IP*

PITCHING:

Norm Charlton finished strongly to become one of the Reds' few pleasant surprises of 1989, working in 69 games with good stats in almost every category. Charlton fulfilled the newly-defined specialist role of "pre-setup" man to fill in between the starter and the Dibble/Franco tag team.

Charlton relies primarily on his 90 MPH fastball and a complementary slider. He is especially tough on lefties (who hit .148 against him) but was no treat for righties to face either. He is capable of overpowering performances such as the 10 strikeouts he recorded against the Giants in just 4.1 innings. His control, while not a major problem, needs a little sharpening. Charlton allowed 40 walks in 95.1 innings last year, seven of those intentional.

Charlton seems to get tougher with each pitch he throws (.229 batting average on his first 15 pitches, .170 on 16 to 30, and .103 on pitches 31 and up), raising curiosity about what he might do in 1990 as a major league starter. In the minors Charlton was a successful starter, and he led the American Association in strikeouts in 1988. The Reds have a large number of starters already, but they also have a large number of problems. Charlton is a great asset, because he is one of the few Reds who offer the possibility of major improvement.

FIELDING, HITTING, BASERUNNING:

Charlton has good range and makes about as many plays as any Reds pitcher. He is somewhat error-prone, however, and will need to add a little poise and confidence to his long list of assets. He also needs to work on holding opposition baserunners. In 1989, nine of 12 steal attempts (75%) against Charlton were successful. He also committed four balks. At the plate, Charlton showed absolutely nothing in 1989. He came up only five times, and struck out four times. He showed some potential in the minors, however, and if he gets a role that requires more plate appearances, he will be able to do more than watch and wave.

OVERALL:

Charlton seems destined to make a big contribution in 1990, whatever his role. Whitey Herzog has been openly interested in Charlton, and the Reds may succumb to a tempting trade offer before opening day. The most interesting possibilities involve Charlton as a starter with Cincinnati. Lou Piniella has many unpleasant choices to make; how to use Charlton is one of his least painful decisions.

NORM CHARLTON

Position: RP
Bats: B **Throws:** L
Ht: 6' 3" **Wt:** 195

Opening Day Age: 27
Born: 1/6/63 in Fort Polk, LA
ML Seasons: 2

Overall Statistics

	W	L	ERA	G	GS	Sv	IP	H	R	BB	SO	HR
1989	8	3	2.93	69	0	0	95.1	67	38	40	98	5
Career	12	8	3.33	79	10	0	156.2	127	65	60	137	11

Where They Hit the Ball

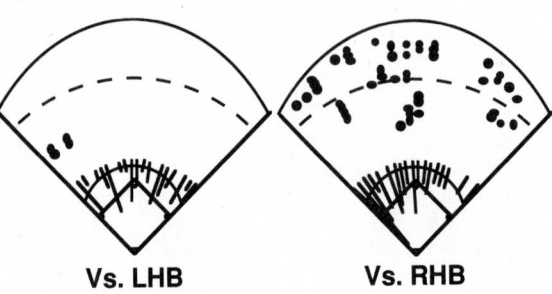

Vs. LHB   **Vs. RHB**

1989 Situational Stats

	W	L	ERA	Sv	IP		AB	H	HR	RBI	AVG
Home	2	1	2.93	0	46.0	LHB	81	12	0	5	.148
Road	6	2	2.92	0	49.1	RHB	259	55	5	26	.212
Day	0	2	2.93	0	30.2	Sc Pos	75	15	2	26	.200
Night	8	1	2.92	0	64.2	Clutch	143	26	1	8	.182

1989 Rankings (National League)

- ➡ 2nd in worst first batter efficiency (.300) - *pitchers in 40 relief games*
- ➡ 4th in fewest GDPs induced per GDP situation (3.1%) - *pitchers with 30 GDP situations*
- ➡ 8th in games (69)
- ➡ 9th in balks (4)
- ➡ Led the Reds in balks

ERIC DAVIS

Position: CF
Bats: R **Throws:** R
Ht: 6' 3" **Wt:** 185

Opening Day Age: 27
Born: 5/29/62 in Los Angeles, CA
ML Seasons: 6

IN HIS PRIME

HITTING:

Eric Davis has the most impressive bat speed in the game today. He hits pop-ups that go over the center field fence, and line drives that keep rising until they hit the upper seats.

Quietly, Davis had his second highest season batting average in 1989, and exceeded 30 home runs and 100 RBIs -- a bad year, according to his critics. Since Eric has improved his plate discipline, pitchers give him fewer high fastballs, more curves, and more fastballs way outside. The curve is the safest pitch, but if it doesn't break, look out. For the second consecutive year, Eric proved himself as a clutch hitter, producing significantly higher averages in late innings, with runners on, and with runners in scoring position.

Davis's only weakness is a tendency to strike out. But the super-fast swing is his biggest offensive weapon. Also, Eric has repeatedly shown the ability to miss a pitch wildly during one at bat, and park it in the seats the next time he sees it.

BASERUNNING:

Legend has it that Davis stole 80 bases in high school, and never had to slide even once. His blazing speed in the majors is a matter of record. Eric was slowed by hamstring problems in 1989, getting only four steals through June 30. In the second half, though, he stole 17. Davis says he gets more pleasure from a steal than from a homer (more opposing players take it personally). Eric's amazing running stat is his lifetime stolen base percentage of 87% (compared to Vince Coleman's 83% and Rickey Henderson's 81%). Davis obviously knows his pitchers and catchers.

FIELDING:

Davis has tremendous range and gets a good jump; if he can't catch a ball, no one can. His arm is more than adequate, and he rarely makes a mistake in judgment. Davis makes so many spectacular fielding plays that he sometimes calls attention to recently-missed playing time. The logic goes something like, "If he could make a play like that today, he must have been OK two days ago."

OVERALL:

Prophets and great athletes get no respect in their home towns. Cincinnati fans know that just as well as those in other cities, but they fall into the trap of looking only for peak performance from their best player. If he stole 80 bases in 1986, why not in 1989? Why doesn't he just play 160 games, so he can hit 50 homers? Such questions might help move Eric to another city, and leave Reds fans cheering for Herm Winningham.

Overall Statistics

	G	AB	R	H	D	T	HR	RBI	SB	BB	SO	AVG
1989	131	462	74	130	14	2	34	101	21	68	116	.281
Career	640	2119	431	582	83	16	142	413	212	316	561	.275

Where He Hits the Ball

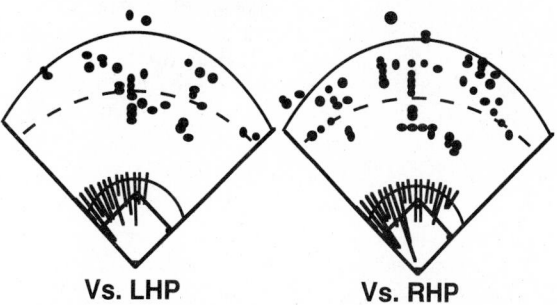

Vs. LHP **Vs. RHP**

1989 Situational Stats

	AB	H	HR	RBI	AVG		AB	H	HR	RBI	AVG
Home	204	59	15	51	.289	LHP	156	39	10	26	.250
Road	258	71	19	50	.275	RHP	306	91	24	75	.297
Day	149	36	8	24	.242	Sc Pos	110	35	11	66	.318
Night	313	94	26	77	.300	Clutch	80	26	8	26	.325

1989 Rankings (National League)

- ➡ 2nd in home run frequency (13.6 ABs per home run) and sacrifice flies (11) - *players with 502 PA*

- ➡ 3rd in home runs (34) and highest percentage of swings that missed (28.9%)

- ➡ 4th in slugging percentage (.541)

- ➡ Led the Reds in batting average (.281), total bases (250), home runs, RBIs (101), stolen bases (21), walks (68), GDPs (15), on-base average (.367), slugging percentage (.541), home run frequency, grounder/flyball ratio (1.18), pitches seen per plate appearance (3.6), steals of third (4) and hitting with runners in scoring position (.318) - *team players with 502 PA*

PITCHING:

After a promising trial in 1988, Rob Dibble was handed the Reds' set-up role last year when Rob Murphy went to Boston. Dibble responded with one of the finest seasons ever by a relief pitcher -- at least in terms of hits and strikeouts. Opposing hitters managed only a .176 batting average off Dibble, while they fanned at an amazing rate of almost 13 per nine innings. The phenomenal counterpart of the huge K ratio was Dibble's excellent control in 1989. He walked only 2.5 batter per nine innings. Dibble is effective when he pitches anywhere in the strike zone; there is no need for careful placement of the stuff he throws.

As the stats would indicate, Dibble is the owner of a fastball, arguably the best in the baseball. He was clocked at 100 MPH on several occasions in 1989. But the pitch that put his strikeout totals in the stratosphere was a slider that Dibble used like a change-up. Dibble would get to two strikes by throwing heat, then drop in an 88 MPH slider requiring an adjustment that few hitters could make. If and when Dibble needs another pitch, a true change-up would be a devastating weapon for him.

The big question about Dibble is his durability. His motion looks awkward and tiring: a very high leg kick, and a slingshot throwing motion. Dibble has already had knee surgery while in the minors, and was briefly disabled with a sore elbow in 1989. His future is more likely to be a short one; don't look for a Goose Gossage career.

FIELDING, HITTING, BASERUNNING:

Dibble has the worst range of any Reds pitcher, making only six assists last year. He is also the worst Cincinnati pitcher when it comes to baserunners. Rob allowed an unacceptable 91% (19 of 21) to steal from him in 1989. After the high kick, catchers have no chance, even when the ball arrives at 100 MPH. Since he bats lefty, you might think Dibble could hit, but he's 0 for 10 in his major league career.

OVERALL:

Dibble has the potential to be not just a great set-up man, but a great closer; the Reds have considered trading John Franco and handing Dibble the late-inning job. But Dibble is also a volatile personality, suspended three times in 1989 for acts like hitting batters deliberately, and throwing a bat onto the foul screen behind home plate. Intensity is great in a bullpen stopper, but one must wonder if Dibble himself knows what he is going to do next.

ROB DIBBLE

Position: RP
Bats: L **Throws:** R
Ht: 6' 4" **Wt:** 235

Opening Day Age: 26
Born: 1/24/64 in Bridgeport, CT
ML Seasons: 2

Overall Statistics

	W	L	ERA	G	GS	Sv	IP	H	R	BB	SO	HR
1989	10	5	2.09	74	0	2	99.0	62	23	39	141	4
Career	11	6	1.99	111	0	2	158.1	105	35	60	200	6

Where They Hit the Ball

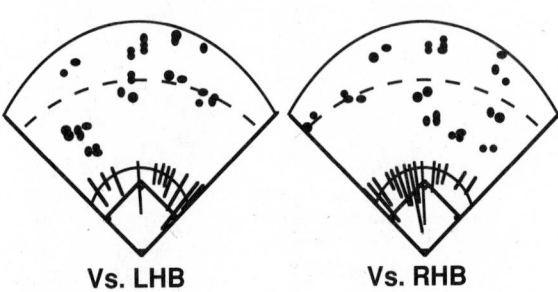

Vs. LHB   Vs. RHB

1989 Situational Stats

	W	L	ERA	Sv	IP		AB	H	HR	RBI	AVG
Home	4	2	1.00	0	45.0	LHB	172	32	1	15	.186
Road	6	3	3.00	2	54.0	RHB	180	30	3	17	.167
Day	4	0	1.80	0	30.0	Sc Pos	135	22	1	28	.163
Night	6	5	2.22	2	69.0	Clutch	220	44	4	22	.200

1989 Rankings (National League)

- ➡ 1st in holds (23)
- ➡ 2nd in games (74)
- ➡ 4th in strikeouts per 9 innings (12.8) - *all league players*
- ➡ 4th in lowest percentage of inherited runners scoring (19.7%) - *pitchers with 30 inherited runners*
- ➡ Led the Reds in games, holds, strikeouts (141), ERA (2.09), wild pitches (7), lowest batting average allowed (.176), lowest on-base average allowed (.261), lowest slugging percentage (.250), first batter efficiency (.209), lowest batting average with runners in scoring position (.163) and strikeous per 9 innings - *all team pitchers*

HITTING:

Mariano Duncan may have peaked in 1985 at the age of 22. Since then, he has failed to improve on his rookie performance in almost every offensive category. Duncan has simply failed to adjust and mature as most players do in their mid-twenties. Duncan took up switch hitting to be more effective against righties, but to no avail. While he hit .224 facing righthanders in 1985, he still only hit .226 against them in 1989. Mariano determined to lay off the high fastball and hit down on the ball to avoid strikeouts. In 1985, he had .20 strike outs per at bat. In 1989 he had .20 strike outs per at bat. And so on.

Duncan overswings from both sides of the plate, but more so from the left side. He is prone to chase high heat, especially when batting righthanded, and he will often swing at the first pitch. Lefties are well-advised not to serve up waist-high fastballs to Mariano, but opposing pitchers do not have any special approach to him. He is simply not a dangerous threat at the plate. Given a variety of pitches to hit, he will probably be overmatched by most of them. Just one rule: don't walk him.

BASERUNNING:

The man who once produced four bunt doubles in a single season can still run, even after various leg injuries. Duncan seemed to lose some traces of speed and judgment in 1989, however. His 64% stolen base percentage was the lowest of his career, and a serious drop from the 82% lifetime rate that he brought into the season.

FIELDING:

Like most shortstops from San Pedro de Macoris, Duncan has great range to both sides, acrobatic abilities to stand, turn, and throw in one fluid motion, and a strong if somewhat overenthusiastic throwing arm. Like the other aspects of his game, fielding is an area where Duncan could have improved, but didn't. In his rookie season he committed 30 errors playing full-time. In 1989, in about half of a season, he committed 14 errors.

OVERALL:

Since his rookie season raised high expectations, Duncan has repeatedly been relegated to the bench, the disabled list, and the minor leagues. His failure to improve, and the maddening immutability of unacceptable numbers from year to year, made the Dodgers give up. Now there is a slight possibility, with Larkin's injury and Oester's aging, that Duncan may have a second chance. But he will have to improve, and the odds are against it.

MARIANO DUNCAN

Position: SS
Bats: B **Throws:** R
Ht: 6' 0" **Wt:** 190

Opening Day Age: 27
Born: 3/13/63 in San Pedro de Macoris, Dominican Republic
ML Seasons: 4

Overall Statistics

	G	AB	R	H	D	T	HR	RBI	SB	BB	SO	AVG
1989	94	258	32	64	15	2	3	21	9	8	51	.248
Career	421	1488	184	350	54	9	23	108	106	93	304	.235

Where He Hits the Ball

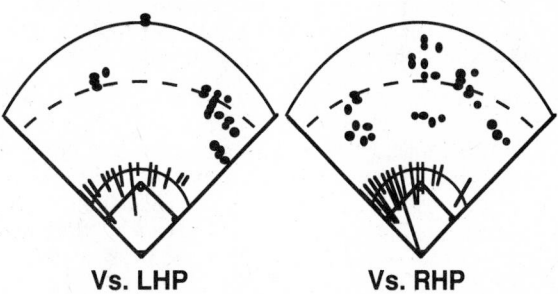

Vs. LHP   **Vs. RHP**

1989 Situational Stats

	AB	H	HR	RBI	AVG		AB	H	HR	RBI	AVG
Home	130	30	2	11	.231	LHP	99	28	2	14	.283
Road	128	34	1	10	.266	RHP	159	36	1	7	.226
Day	73	16	0	2	.219	Sc Pos	60	18	1	19	.300
Night	185	48	3	19	.259	Clutch	54	15	1	6	.278

1989 Rankings (National League)

- ➡ 8th in hit by pitch (5)
- ➡ Led the Reds in hit by pitch
- ➡ Led NL Shortstops in hit by pitch

PITCHING:

John Franco's reputation as the best closer in baseball took a beating in the second half of 1989. He blew half his save opportunities, including a four run lead over Montreal that fell to homers by Damaso Garcia and Rex Hudler. Thanks to a marvelous first half, however, John's full year numbers were good enough to be envied by almost every other pitcher.

Franco features a sinking fastball, a good slider, and a wicked screwball. John is not a strikeout pitcher; he mows down hitters by inducing them to hit grounders, not by blowing them away. He needs regular, short outings to maintain sharp control. Pete Rose apparently blundered by withholding Franco unless there was a save situation. He also put John in too early on other occasions, though that was due in good part to the fact that Rob Dibble was out with an injury. Franco normally looked great on his first 15 pitches: a .226 batting average and .243 slugging percentage. On pitches 16 and up, however, he gave up a .306 batting average and .414 slugging average.

It also appeared that hitters were learning to lay off the Franco screwball, which he usually throws out of the strike zone. He is not powerful enough to throw the fastball when hitters expect it; eventually they will catch up with him. Also, the media attention surrounding the Pete Rose Wagergate Scandal affected John Franco. John denied any concern, but such matters never help a pitcher.

FIELDING, HITTING, BASERUNNING:

Franco is an ace at holding runners and fielding his position. He has the best range of any Reds pitcher, and actually had more assists (19) than all but two of the starters. Three of five attempted base stealers were cut down. Like most closers, Franco rarely has to pick up a bat or stand on a base. When the occasion arises, however, John is ready. He had six hits in 1989, despite striking out in half of his at bats. On the bases, he is cautious but alert to opportunities.

OVERALL:

Though he wasn't as good in 1989, Franco has considerable value. If the Reds traded him, it would mainly be due to the fact that they have another potentially outstanding closer in Rob Dibble. Wherever Franco ends up, he'll probably get off to a hot start. He retired the first 32 batters he faced in 1987, had a 1.21 ERA until June of 1988, and was 1.35 with 22 saves before the All Star break of 1989. The question in 1990 is whether he can avoid an '89 style fadeout.

JOHN FRANCO

Position: RP
Bats: L **Throws:** L
Ht: 5'10" **Wt:** 185

Opening Day Age: 29
Born: 9/17/60 in Brooklyn, NY
ML Seasons: 6

Overall Statistics

	W	L	ERA	G	GS	Sv	IP	H	R	BB	SO	HR
1989	4	8	3.12	60	0	32	80.2	77	35	36	60	3
Career	42	30	2.49	393	0	148	528.0	460	174	210	367	27

Where They Hit the Ball

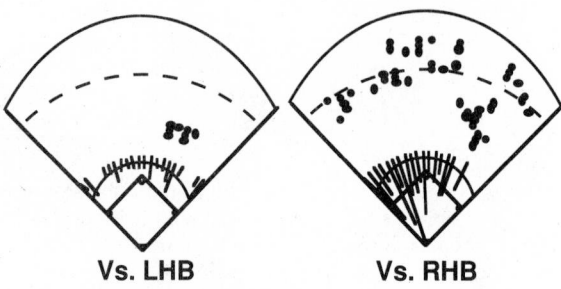

Vs. LHB   **Vs. RHB**

1989 Situational Stats

	W	L	ERA	Sv	IP		AB	H	HR	RBI	AVG
Home	4	4	3.92	17	41.1	LHB	50	10	0	4	.200
Road	0	4	2.29	15	39.1	RHB	249	67	3	30	.269
Day	2	3	4.02	9	31.1	Sc Pos	75	21	2	30	.280
Night	2	5	2.55	23	49.1	Clutch	243	60	3	29	.247

1989 Rankings (National League)

- ⇢ 3rd in saves (32) and save opportunities (39)
- ⇢ 5th in blown saves (7)
- ⇢ 7th in games finished (50)
- ⇢ Led the Reds in saves, blown saves, games finished, grounder/flyball ratio (2.46) and GDPs induced per 9 innings (.89) - *all team pitchers*

PITCHING:

Reds' pennant hopes in 1990 will depend on a return to form by Danny Jackson. Jackson never got into any kind of groove in 1989, and ruined his season by attempting to pitch while injured. Jackson changed his motion in an attempt to lessen pressure on his big toe, which had been diagnosed as having bone spurs. The new motion caused some injury to his wrist and shoulder. He had arthroscopic surgery on the shoulder last July, and got the toe fixed after the season ended. Medical reports are all favorable, but the proof is in the pitching.

Jackson is a two-pitch pitcher. He throws a fastball with fair velocity (mid to high 80's) and excellent movement. And he has a slider that can be devastating. These two pitches have as much movement as any fastball/slider combination in baseball. When he is pitching well, there will be several broken bats, and many ground balls. Jackson's fastball normally runs in on righthanders, away from lefties. He can also cut the fastball to give it extra sinking movement.

Jackson does not have great control, but he is so hard to hit that he can usually survive three or four walks per game without getting hurt. On occasion, Danny can have his good stuff and still get beat, through a combination of consecutive walks and broken-bat singles. Usually, though, when he's on, he wins.

FIELDING, HITTING, BASERUNNING:

Jackson sometimes looks awkward coming off the mound, but he has average range, is adequate at covering first, and is not prone to errors. He has improved his ability to hold runners, and gave up only six stolen bases last year, while five were caught trying. On offense, Jackson strikes out excessively (22 in 36 at bats last year), but he gets his share of hits for a pitcher (.222 batting average in '89).

OVERALL:

The biggest concern about Jackson is his health. Pete Rose worked him very hard in 1988, and Danny has not shown much since then. Although he never said anything, it was obvious from the start of the 1989 season that something was wrong. If he recovers and returns to his 1988 form, he will be the anchor of the Reds staff. If Jackson's physical problems recur, there will be real concern about his ability to work through them.

DANNY JACKSON

Position: SP
Bats: R **Throws:** L
Ht: 6' 0" **Wt:** 205

Opening Day Age: 28
Born: 1/5/62 in San Antonio, TX
ML Seasons: 7

Overall Statistics

	W	L	ERA	G	GS	Sv	IP	H	R	BB	SO	HR
1989	6	11	5.60	20	20	0	115.2	122	78	57	70	10
Career	66	68	3.66	174	162	1	1089.0	1043	509	433	661	59

Where They Hit the Ball

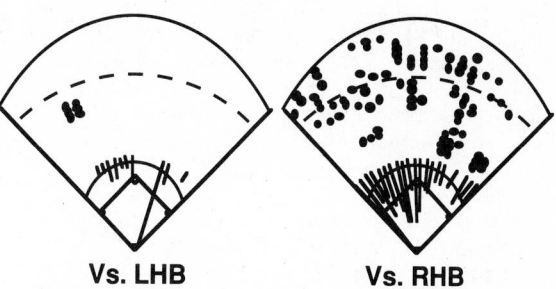

Vs. LHB   Vs. RHB

1989 Situational Stats

	W	L	ERA	Sv	IP		AB	H	HR	RBI	AVG
Home	3	5	5.10	0	60.0	LHB	66	18	1	11	.273
Road	3	6	6.14	0	55.2	RHB	385	104	9	56	.270
Day	3	6	6.54	0	53.2	Sc Pos	125	39	5	60	.312
Night	3	5	4.79	0	62.0	Clutch	21	4	1	2	.190

1989 Rankings (National League)

➡ Did not rank near the top or bottom in any category

BARRY LARKIN

FUTURE MVP?

Position: SS
Bats: R **Throws:** R
Ht: 6' 0" **Wt:** 185

Opening Day Age: 25
Born: 4/28/64 in Cincinnati, OH
ML Seasons: 4

HITTING:

When he went on the disabled list July 11, Barry Larkin was contending for the National League batting title. Larkin owns lefthanded pitchers, smacking them around for a .352 average in 1988 and .372 last year. When he started hitting righties with authority too, in 1989, he became one of the toughest outs in baseball.

Larkin has just about every skill you could want in a leadoff hitter, except that he does not take the base on balls very often. But an on-base percentage of .375 leaves little to be desired. Larkin simply likes to put the ball in play, and does it effectively. He strikes out so seldomly that he has a great lifetime strikeout to walk ratio (1.13) with only a couple dozen walks per year.

It is hard to find much weakness in a .342 hitter. If you had to get Larkin out, your best hope would be a righthanded junk-baller. Fastballs give him little difficulty regardless of location, and he adjusts well to changing speeds. Larkin is a line drive hitter with good power, but he does not try to pull the ball. Most teams give him the lines.

BASERUNNING:

One of the big factors in Larkin's ability to get on base is his great speed. He gets out of the box quickly, and has never grounded into more than eight double plays in a season. Barry's stolen base output has dropped sharply from his high mark of 40 in 1988, as opposing pitchers give him increased attention.

FIELDING:

Larkin has good range to both sides, and he can throw from an off-balance position, but he is still learning not to attempt the impossible. Larkin is prone to erratic throws in bunches, and he has produced some high error totals. But he looked more settled in 1989. At age 26, most shortstops are just trying to break into a line-up; Larkin has more than three full years under his belt, and is emerging as one of the steadiest and most effective shortstops in the National League.

OVERALL:

Larkin's elbow injury is a type that might ruin a pitcher's career, but it should detract little from his hitting prowess. There is still some concern about Larkin's ability to make good throws from deep short. The Reds have even discussed using him as a first baseman. More likely, however, he will shift to left field or second base if a change is needed. If he continues playing shortstop with unimpaired abilities, he could be Ozzie Smith's successor as the best in the league.

Overall Statistics

	G	AB	R	H	D	T	HR	RBI	SB	BB	SO	AVG
1989	97	325	47	111	14	4	4	36	10	20	23	.342
Career	414	1511	229	437	66	14	31	154	79	106	120	.289

Where He Hits the Ball

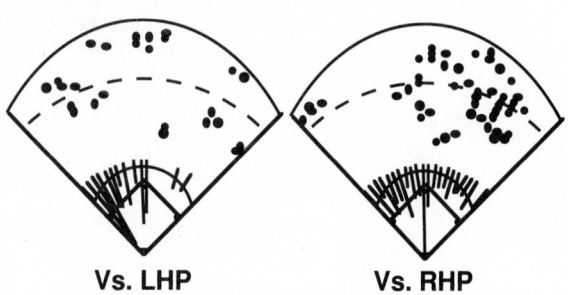

Vs. LHP   **Vs. RHP**

1989 Situational Stats

	AB	H	HR	RBI	AVG		AB	H	HR	RBI	AVG
Home	156	55	1	21	.353	LHP	121	45	2	16	.372
Road	169	56	3	15	.331	RHP	204	66	2	20	.324
Day	109	32	1	5	.294	Sc Pos	67	20	1	31	.299
Night	216	79	3	31	.366	Clutch	53	19	1	7	.358

1989 Rankings (National League)

➡ 1st in hitting on an 0-2 count (.379) - *players with 20 PA with an 0-2 count*

➡ 2nd in batting average with 2 strikes (.314) - *players with 162 PA with 2 strikes*

➡ 2nd in batting average vs. lefthanded pitchers (.372) - *players with 125 PA vs. LHP*

➡ Led the Reds in batting average with 2 strikes, hitting in the clutch, batting average vs. lefthanded pitchers and hitting on an 0-2 count

➡ Led NL Shortstops in sacrifice flies (8), batting average with 2 strikes, batting average vs. lefthanded pitchers and hitting on an 0-2 count

PITCHING:

Since a 12-12 season in 1986, Tim Leary's career has been up and down like a yo-yo. His last up year was 1988, when the introduction of the forkball (acquired in Mexico during the previous winter) transformed Leary into a dominating pitcher. Leary was overshadowed by Orel Hershiser, but he was just as vital to the Dodgers' pennant and World Championship. Last year, however, Leary became surplus to an overcrowded L.A. staff, and was the principal in the trade for Kal Daniels.

Leary was adequate on the mound in 1989, but he sometimes lacked the killer instinct that it takes to win, and suffered from the worst run support in the National League. In his last five starts for the Reds, his 2.18 ERA earned him an 0-2 record with three no-decisions. In his 13 losses as a starter, the Reds and Dodgers scored a grand total of 17 runs for him.

In addition to the forkball that propelled him in 1988, Leary has all the pitches that kept him in the majors for four years before that. His fastball is not the overpowering pitch that he had before hurting his arm in April 1981, but it is still above average. In addition, he has a decent curve, and a slider that can be his out-pitch when he throws it to the right spots. He usually has good control, averaging under three walks per nine innings and only 14.4 pitches per inning, a low average.

FIELDING, HITTING, BASERUNNING:

Leary is a good fielder, quick to cover first or provide backup wherever required. His pickoff move is only average, but he works hard to keep runners close. In 1989, the opposition got away with 19 of 27 stolen base attempts, just a little bit too much success. Tim's athletic ability makes him a fine hitter. He often helps himself, and has appeared as a pinch hitter with some success. His baserunning is more than acceptable for a pitcher.

OVERALL:

The Reds traded away a potential superstar slugger and reigning on-base average champ to get Leary. They need Leary to pitch as he is capable of doing if Cincinnati is to be a contender in 1990. Tim needs to use his fastball more extensively, and bear down on lefties. Cincinnati should note that Leary gets hit pretty hard after the 6th inning (.297 batting average, .494 slugging percentage). If he worked with a set pitch count, he might be able to exert himself with less concern in the early and middle innings, and maintain that extra intensity so critical to his success.

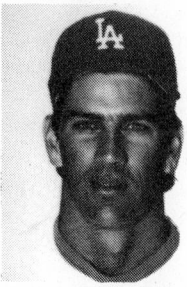

TIM LEARY

Position: SP
Bats: R **Throws:** R
Ht: 6' 3" **Wt:** 208

Opening Day Age: 31
Born: 12/23/58 in Santa Monica, CA
ML Seasons: 8

Overall Statistics

	W	L	ERA	G	GS	Sv	IP	H	R	BB	SO	HR
1989	8	14	3.52	33	31	0	207.0	205	84	68	123	17
Career	45	56	3.71	168	122	1	831.1	859	386	244	544	72

Where They Hit the Ball

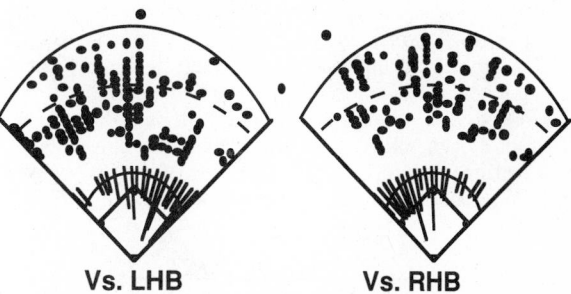

Vs. LHB   Vs. RHB

1989 Situational Stats

	W	L	ERA	Sv	IP		AB	H	HR	RBI	AVG
Home	4	8	3.43	0	118.0	LHB	404	122	12	47	.302
Road	4	6	3.64	0	89.0	RHB	382	83	5	30	.217
Day	4	3	2.13	0	67.2	Sc Pos	171	34	2	54	.199
Night	4	11	4.20	0	139.1	Clutch	84	23	1	9	.274

1989 Rankings (National League)

➡ 1st in worst run support per 9 innings (3.1) - *pitchers with 162 IP*

➡ 4th in losses (14), GDPs induced (20), lowest batting average allowed with runners in scoring position (.199) and most GDPs per 9 innings (.87) - *pitchers with 162 IP*

➡ 8th in least pitches thrown per batter (3.4) and lowest batting average allowed vs. right-handed batters (.217) - *pitchers facing 377 RHB*

➡ 9th in wild pitches (10)

PITCHING:

When Rick "Junk" Mahler pitched for the TBS-affiliated Atlanta Braves, he was on TV more than Phil Donahue. This guy gives you lots of innings, and lots of everything else: hits, runs, wins, losses. Everything.

Mahler throws the ball over the plate, and lets his fielders earn their salaries. He has led the National League in hits allowed four of the last five years. His walk ratios have been excellent (1.5 to 2.0 per 9 innings pitched) in the past two years, but his overall performance has been fairly mediocre. It is unclear exactly what the Reds wanted to get by signing Mahler as a free agent, but they didn't get much.

Rick has a full assortment of pitches and uses all of them (in approximate order of preference): curve, fastball, change-up, slider, forkball, screwball. The big, slow curve and slow slider are his main outpitches. The fastball rarely appears in the strike zone, but moves around outside of it, setting up the other pitches. Mahler depends on excellent location to be successful. When his control is off a little, hitters don't even bother to wait for walks; they simply take batting practice. Even on good days, Mahler is always on the edge of disaster, with runners dancing off the bases.

FIELDING, HITTING, BASERUNNING:

Mahler is probably the best overall fielder among Reds pitchers. He led the staff with 35 assists and 9 putouts in 1989. He gave up the most stolen bases, but also produced the most caught stealing. The stolen base success rate of 55% by opposing runners is low, reflecting his constant throwing to first and paying attention to holding runners close. Rick also helps himself with the bat. He banged out 11 hits, made three sacrifices, and drew four walks in 1989, while striking out only 8 times in 62 at bats.

OVERALL:

Mahler used to dominate the Reds when he pitched for Atlanta. If Cincinnati accomplished nothing else by signing Rick, they have at least taken him away from the opposition. But Mahler is another Reds pitcher whose role for 1990 is unsettled. He will turn 37 in August, and he was already out of the starting rotation last September to make room for younger arms. As a starter, he must be ranked number six or seven when everyone else is healthy, and as a reliever, his role is far from clear. It may not be too long before Mahler becomes the best pitcher in the Senior League.

RICK MAHLER

Position: SP/RP
Bats: R **Throws:** R
Ht: 6' 1" **Wt:** 202

Opening Day Age: 36
Born: 8/5/53 in Austin, TX
ML Seasons: 11

Overall Statistics

	W	L	ERA	G	GS	Sv	IP	H	R	BB	SO	HR
1989	9	13	3.83	40	31	0	220.2	242	113	51	102	15
Career	87	101	3.95	334	247	2	1750.2	1865	868	539	857	145

Where They Hit the Ball

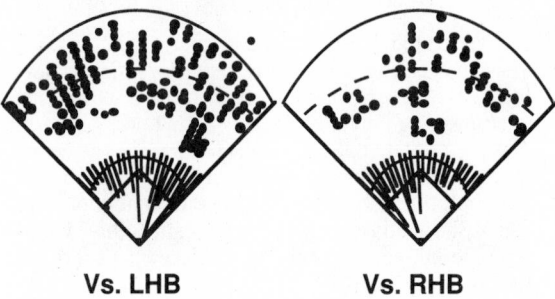

Vs. LHB   **Vs. RHB**

1989 Situational Stats

	W	L	ERA	Sv	IP		AB	H	HR	RBI	AVG
Home	6	6	4.43	0	120.0	LHB	488	149	8	54	.305
Road	3	7	3.13	0	100.2	RHB	371	93	7	49	.251
Day	2	3	3.97	0	47.2	Sc Pos	195	60	5	85	.308
Night	7	10	3.80	0	173.0	Clutch	45	12	1	7	.267

1989 Rankings (National League)

➡ 1st in hits allowed (242), runs allowed (113), caught stealing (17), hit batsmen (10) and worst batting average with runners in scoring position (.308) - *pitchers facing 150 batters with runners in scoring position*

➡ 2nd in worst ERA at home (4.43) - *pitchers with 81 IP at home*

➡ Led the Reds in caught stealing, lowest stolen base percentage allowed (55.3%), hits allowed, runs allowed, hit batsmen, worst batting average with runners in scoring position, stolen bases allowed (21), balks (4), pickoff throws (114) and least home runs allowed per 9 innings (.61) - *team pitchers with 162 IP*

PAUL O'NEILL

Position: RF
Bats: L **Throws:** L
Ht: 6' 4" **Wt:** 210

Opening Day Age: 27
Born: 2/25/63 in
Columbus, OH
ML Seasons: 5

OVERLOOKED

HITTING:

Except for a .305 season in 1985, Paul O'Neill's minor league career gave little indication that he would hit well in the majors. Nonetheless, Paul has now advanced from substitute, to platooner, to everyday player. If he shows the ability to hit lefthanded pitching with more authority, he could become a star.

Paul has trouble with most lefties, especially those who throw sharp breaking balls down and away. O'Neill has, however, showed significant progress against curveballs from righthanders. His plate discipline has also improved. O'Neill's 1.4 strikeout to walk ratio last year was his career best.

O'Neill is still young enough to improve against southpaws. In 1988 he showed that he can do much better than last year's pitiful .178 vs. LHP. The Reds want to see him play full time for a whole season, to show what he can do. Paul's 1989 season was injury-shortened after a great first half. Following the All Star break, he produced only three homers and 18 RBIs in 121 at bats. His mid-year numbers projected to 20+ home runs and 100+ RBI for a full year.

BASERUNNING:

The shortened second half took nothing away from O'Neill's running game, as he produced 11 of his 20 steals in limited use. Paul has good raw speed, but his biggest developments in 1989 were improved judgment and knowledge of National League pitchers. O'Neill improved his stolen base percentage from 57% in 1988 to 80% last year. In his last season the minors, Paul stole just one base, and in the majors, he had never swiped more than eight in a season. The improvement is noteworthy.

FIELDING:

O'Neill's speed gives him good range, and he pays attention on every pitch. His arm is not the high-powered gun that you often find in right field, but whatever he lacks in raw strength, he gets back in alertness and accuracy. Paul almost always hits the cutoff man and gets the ball to the right base quickly.

OVERALL:

The new-found baserunning speed that O'Neill unveiled in 1989 makes him a serious threat to become one of those 20 HR/20 SB men who give definition to the phrase, "all-around ball player." He is already a 15/15 man without yet playing a full season. The big issue with O'Neill is his ability to hit lefties. He seemed on the right track in 1988, but got derailed last year. Lifetime, he still has only five of 38 homeruns against southpaws. The ability to hit lefties will ultimately determine whether O'Neill will be an everyday star, or just a good platooner.

Overall Statistics

	G	AB	R	H	D	T	HR	RBI	SB	BB	SO	AVG
1989	117	428	49	118	24	2	15	74	20	46	64	.276
Career	354	1087	132	285	64	6	38	176	30	103	161	.262

Where He Hits the Ball

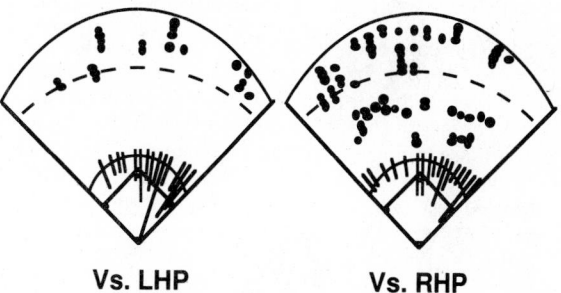

Vs. LHP   **Vs. RHP**

1989 Situational Stats

	AB	H	HR	RBI	AVG		AB	H	HR	RBI	AVG
Home	231	73	11	45	.316	LHP	152	27	4	25	.178
Road	197	45	4	29	.228	RHP	276	91	11	49	.330
Day	141	33	3	16	.234	Sc Pos	109	34	6	58	.312
Night	287	85	12	58	.296	Clutch	74	21	0	8	.284

1989 Rankings (National League)

➡ 2nd in hitting with the bases loaded (.556) - *players with 10 PA with the bases loaded*

➡ 4th in worst batting average vs. lefthanded pitchers (.178) and worst on-base percentage vs. lefthanded pitchers - *players with 125 PA LHP*

➡ 7th in hitting on a 3-1 count (.533) - *players with 10 PA on a 3-1 count*

➡ Led the Reds in stolen base percentage (80.0%), hitting with the bases loaded, hitting on a 3-1 count and batting average at home (.316)

➡ Led NL Right Fielders in hitting with the bases loaded, hitting on a 3-1 count and hitting at home

HITTING:

Like a returning war hero, Ron Oester took his old job back from Jeff Treadway in 1989, getting most of the playing time against righthanded pitchers. Oester is not really much of a hitter, and his age is beginning to show. Ron has little bat speed, little power, and a generally weak swing.

Oester is nominally a switch hitter, but against lefties he is ineffective and utterly devoid of power, so he does not face southpaws often. Ron likes pitches up in the strike zone, but has trouble with anything below the waist. He has also grown increasingly vulnerable to hard stuff in on the hands. Most pitchers now work him in and out with fastballs, inducing pop-ups, and give him low breaking balls that become fouls, weak grounders or clean misses. Oester strikes out more than he walks, and amasses strikeout totals that are really excessive for a hitter with no power.

The Reds have been using Oester as their #8 hitter -- something of a condemnation considering the other weak bats in their line-up. It would not be hard to find another player who could equal Oester's value, as far as offense is concerned. Oester has shown the ability to overcome slumps, however. Ron hit .186 through May 31 last year, and then returned to form. A weak start in 1990 does not necessarily mean curtains.

BASERUNNING:

Oester is a hard-nosed, hustling runner. He used to steal six to nine bases a year, but has given up such displays of speed. Ron would be well-advised to ease up on the rest of his running game, as well. Even at his advanced age, he still crosses the line from aggressiveness to over-optimism too frequently.

FIELDING:

The one strong aspect of Oester's play is his good defense. He has adequate range, sure hands, and a marvelous ability to turn the double play. If there were "special teams" in baseball, Ron would come onto the field every time his team needed to turn the double play.

OVERALL:

At age 33, Oester cannot be expected to improve, and he appears to be on a bubble regarding his role for 1990. Pete Rose's fondness for hustling, aggressive players was obviously a factor in keeping Oester active with the Reds, and there are many scenarios for 1990 in which Oester loses his job.

RON OESTER

Position: 2B
Bats: B **Throws:** R
Ht: 6' 2" **Wt:** 190

Opening Day Age: 33
Born: 5/5/56 in Cincinnati, OH
ML Seasons: 12

Overall Statistics

	G	AB	R	H	D	T	HR	RBI	SB	BB	SO	AVG
1989	109	305	23	75	15	0	1	14	1	32	47	.246
Career	1212	4060	448	1072	180	32	42	331	39	359	652	.264

Where He Hits the Ball

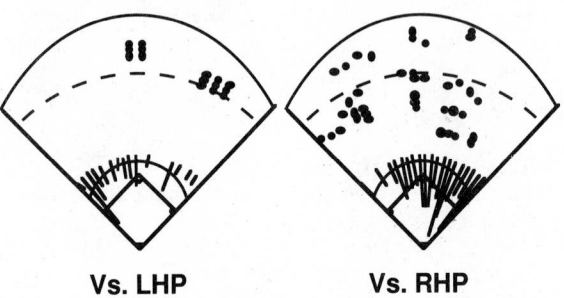

Vs. LHP	Vs. RHP

1989 Situational Stats

	AB	H	HR	RBI	AVG		AB	H	HR	RBI	AVG
Home	148	40	1	8	.270	LHP	63	11	0	1	.175
Road	157	35	0	6	.223	RHP	242	64	1	13	.264
Day	96	20	0	1	.208	Sc Pos	58	18	0	13	.310
Night	209	55	1	13	.263	Clutch	58	13	0	3	.224

1989 Rankings (National League)

➡ 4th in worst home run frequency (305 ABs per HR) and hitting on a 3-2 count (.400) - *players with 20 PA on a 3-2 count*

➡ 10th in most GDPs per GDP situation (16.9%) - *players with 50 PA in GDP situations*

➡ Led NL Second Basemen in intentional walks

HITTING:

On the strength of his hitting, Joe Oliver took the Cincinnati catching job away from Bo Diaz and Jeff Reed last summer. He then fractured a vertebra in a collision with Rick Dempsey, and missed the second half of September. Oliver looked great during his brief stint. In 151 at bats, Oliver produced 23 RBIs, while Reed and Diaz together produced only 31 ribbies in a combined 419 at bats.

There are still questions about Joe Oliver as a hitter. Can he hit righties? Last year's .192 BA would say no. Has he fully matured as a MINOR league hitter? He did just fine in 1989, and he hit over .300 in the Eastern League in 1987, but Joe Oliver's minor league stats do not suggest a star hitter at the major league level. As recently as 1988, he was unable to hold his own at the Triple A level. Does he know the strike zone? Probably not. Oliver's 4.7 strikeout to walk ratio is bad, even for a rookie. And he faced a full count in 10 at bats last year, without drawing a walk in any of them. It would be unfair to disqualify anyone on the basis of 150 at bats, but in the case of rookies, the burden of proof is always on them to show what they can do. At this point, Oliver must be regarded as an unproven hitter.

BASERUNNING:

A slow man, Oliver did not attempt to steal during 1989, and is not likely to be running much in 1990. He may, in fact, be a little over-conservative, and needs to extend himself a little in baserunning situations.

FIELDING:

Oliver is a good catcher who will just turn 25 this year. He has a good arm and has shown the ability to move around home plate pretty well. He needs to show more poise and confidence, however, and learn to play within his limits to avoid errors. Reds pitchers have grown accustomed to mature backstops. Oliver will need to establish himself as a game-caller and pitcher-handler in 1990.

OVERALL:

It appears likely that Joe Oliver will be given the Reds' starting catcher job in 1990, and will have the opportunity to play himself out of it. He seems to have all the tools, but many talented young catchers have failed in similar circumstances. Lou Piniella could do Joe a favor by batting him eighth, and taking some of the pressure off.

JOE OLIVER

Position: C
Bats: R **Throws:** R
Ht: 6' 3" **Wt:** 215

Opening Day Age: 24
Born: 7/24/65 in Memphis, TN
ML Seasons: 1

Overall Statistics

	G	AB	R	H	D	T	HR	RBI	SB	BB	SO	AVG
1989	49	151	13	41	8	0	3	23	0	6	28	.272
Career	49	151	13	41	8	0	3	23	0	6	28	.272

Where He Hits the Ball

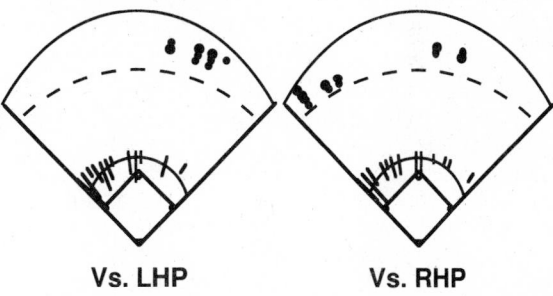

Vs. LHP   **Vs. RHP**

1989 Situational Stats

	AB	H	HR	RBI	AVG		AB	H	HR	RBI	AVG
Home	79	22	1	14	.278	LHP	78	27	1	13	.346
Road	72	19	2	9	.264	RHP	73	14	2	10	.192
Day	43	14	1	7	.326	Sc Pos	40	12	0	18	.300
Night	108	27	2	16	.250	Clutch	31	11	0	3	.355

1989 Rankings (National League)

➡ Did not rank near the top or bottom in any category

HITTING:

Luis Quinones is one of numerous 27 year old "prospects" trying to make the Reds this year. Luis has a better chance than most. The Reds are his fourth major league team, so he's been through the wars. Though his lifetime average is only .225, Quinones' talents always seem to be in demand. He's only been released once, and in his last two trades was dealt even up, first for Ron Cey and then for Bill Landrum.

Though a flawed hitter, Quinones has a little pop in his bat. He belted 12 homers last year in just 340 at bats, and while he was probably playing over his head, he was always a threat to hit 8-12 homers a year as a minor leaguer. Quinones hits the ball to all fields, and has both the speed and the strength to compile a decent number of triples -- he led the American Association with 12 in 1987, even though he batted only 287 times that year. Quinones' RBI totals have always been fine for a middle infielder, and his .301 average with men in scoring position last year shows he won't back down under pressure.

In the past, Quinones had always been helpless against lefthanded breaking ballers. Through '87, his lifetime average against lefties was only .119, with no extra base hits. But Quinones worked hard, and last year his performance against southpaws (nine homers in 142 at bats) was a revelation. He gave Cincinnati a fine half-season as a sub in 1989, and drew attention by hitting in 18 straight games.

BASERUNNING:

As a baserunner, Quinones is nothing special. His triples totals show he has good speed, but he's never been much of a threat to steal. Last year Quinones was thrown out in four of six stolen base attempts, a typical performance for him.

FIELDING:

Luis is a fine utility infielder. He can play second, short, and third, and his range and arm are adequate. His ability to turn the double play is a particular strength. Quinones can make all the routine plays, and occasionally show something extra. He needs to play within himself, however, being prone to errors when he tries to do too much.

OVERALL:

Quinones experimented with his batting in 1989, and made some progress working with Tony Perez. It is unlikely that Quinones is about to become a slugging second baseman, or even an everyday player, but he has shown that he can be very valuable as a utility man.

LUIS QUINONES

Position: 2B/3B
Bats: B **Throws:** R
Ht: 5'11" **Wt:** 175

Opening Day Age: 27
Born: 4/28/62 in Ponce, Puerto Rico
ML Seasons: 5

Overall Statistics

	G	AB	R	H	D	T	HR	RBI	SB	BB	SO	AVG
1989	97	340	43	83	13	4	12	34	2	25	46	.244
Career	259	641	77	144	25	8	13	68	7	41	94	.225

Where He Hits the Ball

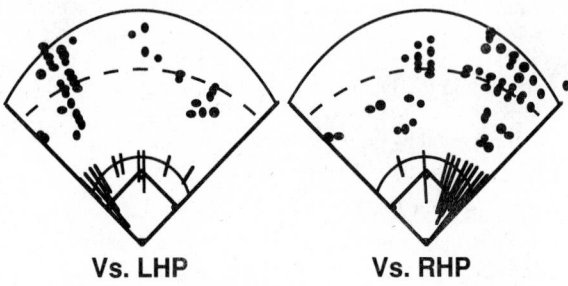

Vs. LHP   Vs. RHP

1989 Situational Stats

	AB	H	HR	RBI	AVG		AB	H	HR	RBI	AVG
Home	170	41	5	13	.241	LHP	142	34	9	20	.239
Road	170	42	7	21	.247	RHP	198	49	3	14	.247
Day	108	22	3	9	.204	Sc Pos	73	22	1	22	.301
Night	232	61	9	25	.263	Clutch	57	13	1	6	.228

1989 Rankings (National League)

→ Led the Reds in hit by pitch (3)

PITCHING:

Like many Reds in 1989, Jose Rijo was on his way to a great season when ill fate intervened. In Rijo's case, the problem was a lower back malady that sidelined him for rest of the season. Initially, he tried to pitch through the back problem, which was diagnosed as a fractured vertebra, but his effort to be heroic was short lived. His pitching deteriorated, and he finally went on the disabled list in July and was out for the season.

Rijo is a classic diamond-in-the-rough pitcher, just turning age 25 this year. On the mound, he looks like a righthanded version of a young Sid Fernandez: he gives up much less than a hit per inning, keeps the ball in the park, walks too many batters, and has trouble going the distance. Rijo has completed only six of 92 career starts. He is more effective in the early going, and loses his control when he runs out of gas.

Jose relies on a fastball, slider, and forkball. The forker is now his big out-pitch. Rijo is usually very good or very bad in each outing. On good days, he works ahead of the hitters, cruises through six or seven innings, and delivers a low score to the bullpen for safekeeping. On bad days, Rijo struggles mightily with his control, and is usually gone within three innings. Rarely does he perform at a happy medium between these two extremes. In 1989, his outings were mostly of the good type.

FIELDING, HITTING, BASERUNNING:

Rijo is a good fielder with average range. His follow-through leaves him in an awkward position, but he has worked on this problem and come a long way. He recovers quickly, gets to first base, and grabs an occasional blooper. Rijo is good at holding runners. Steal attempts were only 59% successful against him last year. Jose is also good with a bat. In 1989 he hit .211, put the ball in play over 70% of the time, and actually stole a base.

OVERALL:

The Reds went into spring training with an apparent surplus of starting pitchers for 1990. Last year, Pete Rose was toying with the idea that Rijo should return to the bullpen, and this idea might resurface under Lou Piniella. Rijo is probably better as a starter, but he did look especially effective against the first few hitters last year (.189 batting average on his first 15 pitches). Rijo has immense talent, and it is a pleasant problem to be worrying about where he fits.

JOSE RIJO

Position: SP
Bats: R **Throws:** R
Ht: 6' 2" **Wt:** 200

Opening Day Age: 24
Born: 5/13/65 in San Cristobal, Dominican Republic
ML Seasons: 6

Overall Statistics

	W	L	ERA	G	GS	Sv	IP	H	R	BB	SO	HR
1989	7	6	2.84	19	19	0	111.0	101	39	48	86	6
Career	39	44	3.87	164	92	3	675.0	630	335	321	601	58

Where They Hit the Ball

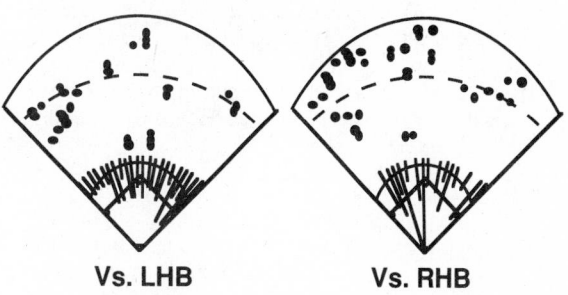

Vs. LHB   **Vs. RHB**

1989 Situational Stats

	W	L	ERA	Sv	IP		AB	H	HR	RBI	AVG
Home	2	2	3.16	0	42.2	LHB	242	66	5	20	.273
Road	5	4	2.63	0	68.1	RHB	163	35	1	15	.215
Day	0	2	2.84	0	31.2	Sc Pos	105	25	1	29	.238
Night	7	4	2.84	0	79.1	Clutch	25	9	0	3	.360

1989 Rankings (National League)

➡ Led the Reds in most GDPs induced per GDP situation (12.8%) - *pitchers with 30 GDP situations*

PITCHING:

In 1988, Ron Robinson suffered a severe elbow injury that kept him out of the line-up until July 1989. The Reds gave Robinson 15 starts in the second half. It was hoped that a regular work schedule would be most helpful to Ron's rehabilitation, so he went straight into the rotation without trial appearances as a reliever.

Robinson produced good numbers as a starter, especially in his first nine starts during July and August (3-1, 2.79 ERA). In September, he seemed to tire. Robinson was working only about five innings per start last year. His medical history includes other injuries besides the 1988 elbow problem; there is reason to be cautious.

Robinson was a power pitcher when he came up, but is making the transition to finesse and control. He walked 3.65 batters per nine innings pitched during his successful July/August appearances. He will have to reduce this total in 1990 (as he did in September), or the odds are going to catch up with him. Robinson throws a fastball, curve, slider and change. He now favors the curve as his main pitch. He needs to get the curve over to be effective.

FIELDING, HITTING, BASERUNNING:

Robinson is a superior all-around athlete -- he was a good quarterback in high school -- and fields his position well. His range is about as good as any of the Reds pitchers, and he can make correct decisions quickly. He was the Reds' ace at preventing stolen bases last year; five of seven attempts against him were cut down. Robinson struck out 14 times in 28 at bats last year, but still managed a .214 batting average. He is not adept at bunting, but when he gets on the bases, he has the smarts and athletic ability to stay out of trouble and occasionally help the offense.

OVERALL:

Not many teams can afford the luxury of a starter who throws only five innings a game, or a reliever who needs two or three days notice to get ready for an appearance. Robinson does not look good enough to push aside any of the younger Cincinnati relievers, but if he can improve his stamina and pitch effectively in the spring, and if some other starters have problems, Ron has a chance of getting a starter's role in 1990. Failing those possibilities, Robinson looks like the odd man out.

RON ROBINSON

Position: SP
Bats: R **Throws:** R
Ht: 6' 4" **Wt:** 230

Opening Day Age: 28
Born: 3/24/62 in Exeter, CA
ML Seasons: 6

Overall Statistics

	W	L	ERA	G	GS	Sv	IP	H	R	BB	SO	HR
1989	5	3	3.35	15	15	0	83.1	80	36	28	36	8
Career	33	27	3.60	195	66	19	580.2	568	269	185	390	51

Where They Hit the Ball

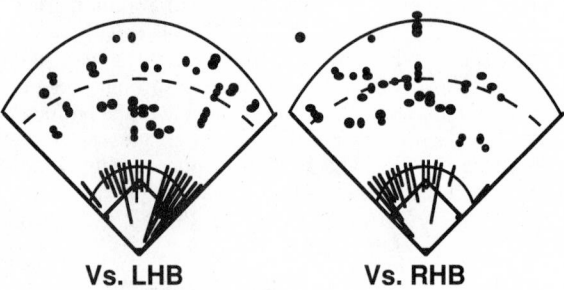

Vs. LHB   **Vs. RHB**

1989 Situational Stats

	W	L	ERA	Sv	IP		AB	H	HR	RBI	AVG
Home	2	1	3.04	0	26.2	LHB	172	47	3	16	.273
Road	3	2	3.49	0	56.2	RHB	145	33	5	15	.228
Day	1	0	3.71	0	17.0	Sc Pos	68	17	1	23	.250
Night	4	3	3.26	0	66.1	Clutch	5	2	0	0	.400

1989 Rankings (National League)

➡ Did not rank near the top or bottom in any category

HITTING:

Rolando Roomes is an exciting hitter. As a prospect with the Cubs, he attracted a loud following at spring training games. Rolando is a pure fastball hitter, with no ability (and apparently no inclination) to lay off the curve. He swings very hard, producing huge strikeout totals that would look more appropriate alongside a huge homer output. He has led three different minor leagues in strikeouts, and could lead the National League in whiffs if he played a full season.

Roomes burst upon the Cincinnati scene with a .362 average in May. But Roger Craig put an end to the fun with accurate scouting. In three games June 5-7, Giant pitchers grooved no fastballs to Rolando; he went 0-14 as his average plunged back to earth.

BASERUNNING:

Roomes has good raw speed and has amassed some impressive stolen base totals in the minors. With Cincinnati in 1989, he was cut down in six of his first 11 steal attempts. He became more careful, and after July 31, he got away with seven of nine attempts. Roomes is not overly aggressive to the point of always wanting to steal, but he is eager to go from first to third on almost any hit.

FIELDING:

Rolando played all three outfield positions in 1989, appearing mainly in right as a platoon partner or substitute for Paul O'Neill. He would probably be more adequate in left, and should get a long, hard look there in early 1990. Roomes' speed gives him decent range, and he has a good throwing arm, but just like his hitting, he is not as mature as most players his age. One full season in the major leagues should change that, however, because he has all the tools.

OVERALL:

Roomes is too old to be considered a prospect; he will probably show his full potential during 1990. Rolando will have to continue learning at the age of 28, if he hopes to be more than just a platooner against lefthanded pitching. Specifically, Roomes needs to improve his knowledge of the strike zone, make adjustments for the ball/strike count and baserunning situation, and (most importantly) learn to recognize what a curveball looks like between the mound and home plate, and act accordingly. He is not a big enough defensive asset to earn a position with his glove, and his high strikeout totals, without dominating power, make it unclear where he best fits in a batting order.

ROLANDO ROOMES

Position: RF/LF/CF
Bats: R **Throws:** R
Ht: 6' 3" **Wt:** 180

Opening Day Age: 28
Born: 2/15/62 in Kingston, Jamaica
ML Seasons: 2

Overall Statistics

	G	AB	R	H	D	T	HR	RBI	SB	BB	SO	AVG
1989	107	315	36	83	18	5	7	34	12	13	100	.263
Career	124	331	39	86	18	5	7	34	12	13	104	.260

Where He Hits the Ball

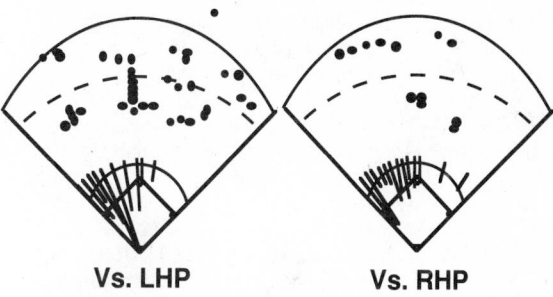

Vs. LHP   **Vs. RHP**

1989 Situational Stats

	AB	H	HR	RBI	AVG		AB	H	HR	RBI	AVG
Home	152	36	5	15	.237	LHP	160	47	2	16	.294
Road	163	47	2	19	.288	RHP	155	36	5	18	.232
Day	101	39	3	14	.386	Sc Pos	74	17	1	22	.230
Night	214	44	4	20	.206	Clutch	44	13	1	8	.295

1989 Rankings (National League)

- ⇒ 3rd in worst stolen base percentage (60.0%) - *players with 20 attempts*
- ⇒ 7th in least GDPs per GDP situation (3.4%) - *players with 50 PA in GDP situations*
- ⇒ Led the Reds in hit by pitch (3), triples (5) and least GDPs per GDP situation

HITTING:

Two years ago, Chris Sabo had a rookie honeymoon for half a year, hitting .315 with power as National League pitchers fed him weak cheese down the middle. The league wised up, however, and since July 1, 1988, Sabo is a .244 hitter with only 42 RBIs. He has shown a remarkable trait of hitting dozens of doubles without producing runs or ribbies.

Sabo likes to look at the first pitch, but pitchers are careful not to groove their first offering. Most organizations like to start him off with breaking balls and then switch to hard stuff. He can have trouble with any pitch if he is off balance and guessing, and he is still learning the strike zone. Sabo's .218 average after the sixth inning shows that starters can work him progressively through the course of a game, and it is also a negative reflection on Sabo's ability to adjust when facing relievers who look different from the starter. Sabo is obviously not the star hitter that some people thought he might become, and is among the weaker hitters who play third base.

BASERUNNING:

Sabo showed his excellent speed and aggressive style when he amassed 46 steals as a rookie. Unfortunately, his stolen base efficiency has dropped to 61% and makes his whole running game of questionable value. Sabo is *always* looking to steal a base. He frequently crosses the line from aggressive to foolish, and has been caught stealing third with two out in a close game more than once. If he would control his eagerness, and pay more attention to situations, Sabo's speed on the bases could be a greater asset.

FIELDING:

Chris is fully adequate at third. He has good range for a corner man, and his throwing arm is strong and quick, though occasionally wild. He stays alert, knows the hitters, and positions himself well. He plays with good intensity and concentration, but is more of a loner than a leader on the field. The Reds have discussed making a left fielder out of Sabo, to fill the gaping hole left by Kal Daniels. Chris could handle it.

OVERALL:

Sabo has quickly changed from a marvelous surprise to a huge question mark. The power that he showed earlier has fizzled, and the speed skills that made him a logical choice for leadoff or #2 are also becoming suspect. At age 28, he should be playing at the top of his ability. But there is a clear possibility that his "sophomore slump" is going to last longer than a year.

CHRIS SABO

Position: 3B
Bats: R **Throws:** R
Ht: 6' 0" **Wt:** 185

Opening Day Age: 28
Born: 1/19/62 in Detroit, MI
ML Seasons: 2

Overall Statistics

	G	AB	R	H	D	T	HR	RBI	SB	BB	SO	AVG
1989	82	304	40	79	21	1	6	29	14	25	33	.260
Career	219	842	114	225	61	3	17	73	60	54	85	.267

Where He Hits the Ball

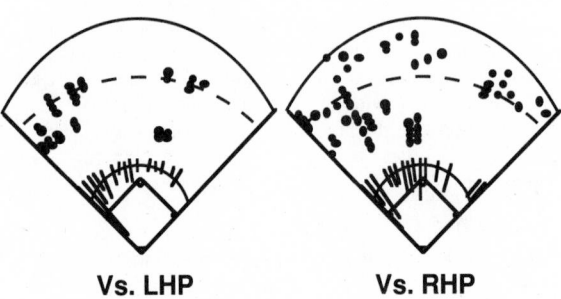

Vs. LHP   **Vs. RHP**

1989 Situational Stats

	AB	H	HR	RBI	AVG		AB	H	HR	RBI	AVG
Home	158	37	3	14	.234	LHP	100	29	0	6	.290
Road	146	42	3	15	.288	RHP	204	50	6	23	.245
Day	90	19	3	6	.211	Sc Pos	63	19	1	22	.302
Night	214	60	3	23	.280	Clutch	40	6	1	6	.150

1989 Rankings (National League)

➡ 5th in worst stolen base percentage (60.9%) - *players with 20 attempts*

➡ Led the Reds in caught stealing (9)

➡ Led NL Third Basemen in steals of third (3)

PITCHING:

Scott Scudder was probably the best pitching prospect in the Cincinnati organization and a big favorite of Pete Rose last year. And no wonder. The seventeenth player picked in the 1986 draft, Scudder has moved rapidly through the Reds' system. He started slowly, but turned a lot of heads when he went 14-3 for two clubs in 1988, with 178 strikeouts in 172 innings.

Though he'd barely pitched a half season in AA ball, Scudder was one of the last pitchers cut in spring training. He was sent to AAA Nashville, and continued to do well, and when the Reds experienced pitching problems, Scudder got a June call-up. Though the big club was in chaos with injuries and the Rose-gambling situation, Scudder responded with an early display of ability. After four starts, he was 2-1 with a 2.70 ERA, but then he blew up. From July 1 on, Scudder was only 2-8, and his ERA was a dismal 5.03. In September, out of the race, the Reds kept Scudder in the rotation. But he didn't respond.

Scudder's problem was control. He has a 90 MPH fastball, with a slider and change-up to mix in, as needed. The heater is difficult to hit, but if it's not over the plate, nobody cares how hard it is to hit. Scott's 5.5 walks per nine innings pitched will obviously have to come down, if he wants to make it in the majors. Scudder will also have to keep the ball in the ballpark. He got behind in the count a lot and was forced to take something off his pitches. He thus allowed 14 home runs in only 100.1 innings pitched.

FIELDING, HITTING, BASERUNNING:

Scudder looks adequate in the field. He has not yet turned 22, and is still learning. His range is just a little below average. He needs a lot of work in holding baserunners. With a high leg kick and trouble hitting the catcher's target, Scudder allowed 15 steals in 16 attempts during his 100 innings, one of the worst performances in the majors last year. Scott looks like he will be a good hitter, though. Last year he struck out 13 times in 32 plate appearances, but he also produced four hits, four sacrifices, and four walks.

OVERALL:

Going into spring training, Scudder was the youngest pitcher with a real shot at the Reds' 1990 roster. Scott will probably need a good spring to earn a trip north with the Reds in early 1990. But he should make it -- and make it big -- before long.

SCOTT SCUDDER

Position: SP/RP
Bats: R **Throws:** R
Ht: 6' 2" **Wt:** 180

Opening Day Age: 22
Born: 2/14/68 in Paris, TX
ML Seasons: 1

Overall Statistics

	W	L	ERA	G	GS	Sv	IP	H	R	BB	SO	HR
1989	4	9	4.49	23	17	0	100.1	91	54	61	66	14
Career	4	9	4.49	23	17	0	100.1	91	54	61	66	14

Where They Hit the Ball

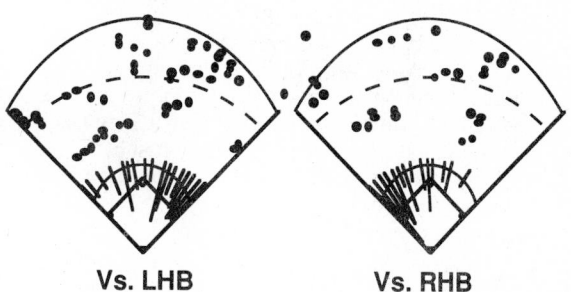

Vs. LHB   **Vs. RHB**

1989 Situational Stats

	W	L	ERA	Sv	IP		AB	H	HR	RBI	AVG
Home	2	4	4.95	0	43.2	LHB	194	42	4	15	.216
Road	2	5	4.13	0	56.2	RHB	186	49	10	34	.263
Day	1	6	7.00	0	36.0	Sc Pos	88	22	4	34	.250
Night	3	3	3.08	0	64.1	Clutch	27	6	1	1	.222

1989 Rankings (National League)

➡ 2nd in least GDPs induced per GDP situation (2.9%) - *pitchers with 30 GDP situations*

HITTING:

In 1989, Herm Winningham had his best offensive year, posting career highs in batting average and runs scored. But that's not saying much. Winningham gives definition to the term "thin hitter." He swings with an uppercut, but generates mainly pop-ups and fly balls. He hits a fair number of doubles, but uses speed, not power, to reach second base. In 1988, his .288 on-base percentage was actually higher than his slugging percentage. That's a serious lack of power.

Winningham has few positives in his offensive arsenal. His swing is inappropriate for someone with excellent footspeed and little arm strength. For someone with almost no power, he strikes out far too often. He is getting better at laying off the high, inside pitch, but he still has trouble with most pitchers who throw high hard stuff. His knowledge of the strike zone is only fair, so control pitchers can also give him fits.

With the Reds, Winningham has been used primarily in the leadoff spot, as a fill-in for the injured Barry Larkin. Winningham is not a good leadoff hitter: too many whiffs, not enough hits and walks. Few teams finish high in the standings when their first batter has an on-base average of only .316. As scouts have been saying for years, Winningham must try to be more of a slap hitter and let his legs do more of the work.

BASERUNNING:

If Winningham could get more playing time or get on base more effectively, he has the potential to steal 50 bases in a season. He has improved his knowledge of the pitchers and catchers, and had the second highest stolen base percentage of his career (.74%) in 1989.

FIELDING:

Speed is an asset in the outfield, but it is just about Herman's only asset. He has made some spectacularly bad plays and showed poor judgment. His arm is adequate, but is too often aimed in the wrong direction.

OVERALL:

It has been suggested that Winningham's greatest strength was the fact that Pete Rose liked him. Certainly, Herm got less playing time after Pete departed. Winningham is one of many Reds players in their late twenties, who should be having big, career years right now. If a .251 average and 40 runs scored is a career year for Winningham, he is in danger of joining that long list of high-potential players who proved "you can't steal first base."

HERM WINNINGHAM

Position: CF/LF/RF
Bats: L **Throws:** R
Ht: 5'11" **Wt:** 175

Opening Day Age: 28
Born: 12/1/61 in Orangeburg, SC
ML Seasons: 6

Overall Statistics

	G	AB	R	H	D	T	HR	RBI	SB	BB	SO	AVG
1989	115	251	40	63	11	3	3	13	14	24	50	.251
Career	581	1325	148	318	47	19	14	112	89	122	293	.240

Where He Hits the Ball

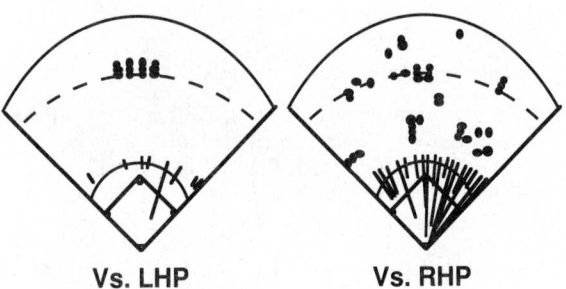

Vs. LHP   **Vs. RHP**

1989 Situational Stats

	AB	H	HR	RBI	AVG		AB	H	HR	RBI	AVG
Home	133	33	1	6	.248	LHP	37	8	1	1	.216
Road	118	30	2	7	.254	RHP	214	55	2	12	.257
Day	91	24	1	4	.264	Sc Pos	47	9	0	9	.191
Night	160	39	2	9	.244	Clutch	47	15	1	5	.319

1989 Rankings (National League)

→ Did not rank near the top or bottom in any category

JACK ARMSTRONG

Position: SP
Bats: R **Throws:** R
Ht: 6' 5" **Wt:** 220

Opening Day Age: 25
Born: 3/7/65 in Englewood, NJ
ML Seasons: 2

Overall Statistics

	W	L	ERA	G	GS	Sv	IP	H	R	BB	SO	HR
1989	2	3	4.64	9	8	0	42.2	40	24	21	23	5
Career	6	10	5.33	23	21	0	108.0	103	68	59	68	13

PITCHING, FIELDING, HITTING:

In addition to having a great name for a pitcher, Jack Armstrong has other assets. He possesses a good fastball, curve, and slider, and worked on an improved change-up last winter. The fourth pitch could make him a major league success. Armstrong has nothing further to prove at Triple A. In his spare time between stints on the Reds roster, Jack had time to be Nashville's most valuable player, going 13-9 with six shutouts, 12 complete games, and a 2.91 ERA. Armstrong showed outstanding fielding ability in his brief time with the Reds. He had the best range of any pitcher except John Franco, and made no errors. He was a bust at the plate, however, going hitless in eight at bats and usually fanning.

OVERALL:

The Reds have some tough choices to make in 1990. The decision to keep Jack Armstrong or Scott Scudder may be one of them. Both are #1 draft picks, one from 1986 and one from 1987. Last year, Scudder had the benefit of Pete Rose showing some interest in him. This year, it will probably come down to spring training to determine which one stays in the majors. Trades or injuries could make room for both of them, though perhaps not in Cincinnati.

TIM BIRTSAS

Position: RP
Bats: L **Throws:** L
Ht: 6' 7" **Wt:** 240

Opening Day Age: 29
Born: 9/5/60 in Clarkston, MI
ML Seasons: 4

Overall Statistics

	W	L	ERA	G	GS	Sv	IP	H	R	BB	SO	HR
1989	2	2	3.75	42	1	1	69.2	68	33	27	57	5
Career	13	11	4.12	109	30	1	277.1	255	144	146	190	30

PITCHING, FIELDING, HITTING:

Tim Birtsas has been the tenth man on the Cincinnati staff for two years now. Based on his appearance (6'7", 240 lbs.) you would expect him to be a hard thrower, but his stuff is more like Rick Mahler's than Rob Dibble's. Birtsas is very dependent on sharp control and ability to change speeds. He is capable of having some fine outings, but is also capable of getting shelled when he is unable to pitch to spots and does not have command of his full repertoire. Birtsas is not a good fielder. He has the worst range of any Reds pitcher except Rob Dibble, and did not cover first successfully even once in 1989, or catch a single pop-up. Birtsas does not come to bat often. He was one for four last year. That one hit was a homer, but Birtsas should not be regarded as an offensive factor.

OVERALL:

After two years on the bubble, Birtsas's number may finally be up in 1990. He looks like the most expendable member of an overcrowded pitching staff, with two or three younger players making serious bids for spots on the roster. If Birtsas remains in the majors, it will probably not be with Cincinnati.

BO
DIAZ

Position: C
Bats: R **Throws:** R
Ht: 5'11" **Wt:** 205

Opening Day Age: 37
Born: 3/23/53 in Cua,
Venezuela
ML Seasons: 13

Overall Statistics

	G	AB	R	H	D	T	HR	RBI	SB	BB	SO	AVG
1989	43	132	6	27	5	0	1	8	0	6	7	.205
Career	993	3274	327	834	162	5	87	452	9	198	429	.255

HITTING, FIELDING, BASERUNNING:

Bo Diaz's best days are obviously behind him. A .260 to .270 hitter through most of his career, he tailed of to .219 in 1988 and .205 last year. Diaz can no longer get around on the inside fastball, and his home run power has just about vanished. Long noted as a great clutch hitter, Diaz hit just .163 with men on base last year, and only .153 with runners in scoring position. Bo has no running game, but has managed to get caught stealing four times in the past two years, with no stolen bases. Bo has also lost what was once a very fine arm; he only threw out seven of 36 attempted base stealers in 1989. His fielding is much impaired by bad knees, but he surely knows his way around home plate.

OVERALL:

There's only one thing that may keep Bo Diaz off the scrap heap in 1990. That's his ability to handle a pitching staff. Reds pitchers posted their lowest ERA in 1989 with Bo behind the plate (3.57 with Bo, 3.63 with Jeff Reed, 4.15 with Joe Oliver). Even if the Reds are done with Diaz, he may find an organization that wants him.

KEN
GRIFFEY

Position: LF
Bats: L **Throws:** L
Ht: 6' 0" **Wt:** 210

Opening Day Age: 40
Born: 4/10/50 in
Donora, PA
ML Seasons: 17

Overall Statistics

	G	AB	R	H	D	T	HR	RBI	SB	BB	SO	AVG
1989	106	236	26	62	8	3	8	30	4	29	42	.263
Career	2000	7004	1100	2077	353	77	147	824	198	694	877	.297

HITTING, FIELDING, BASERUNNING:

As he approaches his fortieth birthday, Ken Griffey finds himself in a familiar position. Griffey has produced 2077 hits, sports a splendid .297 lifetime batting average, and was a star on the great Cincinnati teams of the seventies. Yet just as Griffey spent his prime in the shadow of Rose, Bench and Morgan, he now spends his declining years in the shadow of his son, Ken, Jr. No matter -- Griffey is still a useful player. His average last year was a sub-standard .263, but his home run percentage of 3.4 percent was the third highest of his career. Though his bat has slowed a little, he can still turn on a fastball. Griffey was best utilized as a spot player last year. He did not do well as a pinch hitter (8 for 42, .190) and was most effective when spotted as a platoon outfielder. He still has a little speed and stole four bases last year, but he is now a liability in the outfield, with reduced range and a weak arm.

OVERALL:

Griffey probably won't be back with the Reds, but he showed enough last year to be picked up by another team. He'd be useful as a substitute outfielder/first baseman/pinch-hitter/DH for an American League team. Like maybe his son's team?

SCOTTI MADISON

Position: 3B
Bats: B **Throws:** R
Ht: 5'11" **Wt:** 185

Opening Day Age: 30
Born: 9/12/59 in Pensacola, FL
ML Seasons: 5

Overall Statistics

	G	AB	R	H	D	T	HR	RBI	SB	BB	SO	AVG
1989	40	98	13	17	7	0	1	7	0	8	9	.173
Career	71	166	21	27	12	0	1	11	1	15	22	.163

HITTING, FIELDING, BASERUNNING:

The good news is that Scotti Madison raised his lifetime batting average in 1989. The bad news is that he raised it to .163 by hitting .173. Scotti has no illusions about his hitting ability or his utility role. He is a good Triple A hitter, overmatched and reduced to occasional line drives and warning track power in the bigs. After bouncing around with six organizations, Madison is happy to be getting major league meal money at age 30. Madison is capable of playing third base (as he did for the Reds), catcher, first, or the outfield. At his age and with his background, it is good to be flexible. Scotti was a backup quarterback at Vanderbilt, is a good all-around athlete, and can make his share of contributions in the field. Madison does not run well and has recorded only one stolen base as a major leaguer.

OVERALL:

Madison's career may have peaked in September 1989, when he went three for three with two walks and two runs scored in one game against the Padres. Of the many players who wore a Reds uniform last year, Scotti is one of the most questionable to return in 1990.

JEFF REED

Position: C
Bats: L **Throws:** R
Ht: 6'2" **Wt:** 190

Opening Day Age: 27
Born: 11/12/62 in Joliet, IL
ML Seasons: 6

Overall Statistics

	G	AB	R	H	D	T	HR	RBI	SB	BB	SO	AVG
1989	102	287	16	64	11	0	3	23	0	34	46	.223
Career	362	955	69	212	40	3	7	70	2	92	135	.222

HITTING, FIELDING, BASERUNNING:

Jeff Reed has been limited to journeyman's work, mainly because of his weak hitting. Reed seems to have settled in around the .220 level, with little hope of future improvement. Jeff swings hard, but he is not a pull hitter; he just doesn't get the bat around fast enough. Hard throwers, especially those who pitch inside, get him out rather easily. So do most lefties. Jeff likes to swing at the first pitch, but he has a good knowledge of the strike zone, and draws his share of walks. Reed has no speed. Infielders can take their time on his ground balls. Jeff has stolen only two bases over five major league seasons. He is no fool on the bases, however, paying attention and avoiding blunders. If Reed could hit, he would be playing a lot more. His defensive skills are definitely above average. He is a good handler of pitchers, and his ability to throw out runners is his greatest defensive asset.

OVERALL:

If Reed were ever going to rise above the multitude of good-field, no-hit catchers, he probably would have done it by age 27. He seems destined to play out his career as a backup catcher and defensive replacement, a role he handles fairly well.

JEFF RICHARDSON

Position: SS
Bats: R **Throws:** R
Ht: 6' 2" **Wt:** 175

Opening Day Age: 24
Born: 8/26/65 in Grand Island, NE
ML Seasons: 1

Overall Statistics

	G	AB	R	H	D	T	HR	RBI	SB	BB	SO	AVG
1989	53	125	10	21	4	0	2	11	1	10	23	.168
Career	53	125	10	21	4	0	2	11	1	10	23	.168

HITTING, FIELDING, BASERUNNING:

At age 24, Jeff Richardson is an excellent defensive shortstop, but he is at least a season away from being able to hit big league pitching. He came up in 1989 only because of the injury to Barry Larkin. Richardson looked completely overmatched in his early appearances. By September, he looked more confident, although his numbers failed to show improvement. Richardson ended up batting only .168 in 125 at bats, though he did belt two homers and showed a little patience at the plate. In the field, Jeff looked more at home. His slender, lanky build is ideally suited to the shortstop position, where Richardson has good range and a good arm. He really entertained the fans in 1989 with some sparkling play.

OVERALL:

It seems unlikely that Richardson will be able to win a regular job with the Reds until he can hit major league pitching. He is at the age when players show rapid improvement, however, and an outstanding spring training just might propel him to a good year. He has an added advantage in that many of the other "young" Reds are nearing age 30, while Richardson is a legitimate prospect at age 24.

MIKE ROESLER

Position: RP
Bats: R **Throws:** R
Ht: 6' 5" **Wt:** 195

Opening Day Age: 26
Born: 9/12/63 in Fort Wayne, IN
ML Seasons: 1

Overall Statistics

	W	L	ERA	G	GS	Sv	IP	H	R	BB	SO	HR
1989	0	1	3.96	17	0	0	25.0	22	11	9	14	4
Career	0	1	3.96	17	0	0	25.0	22	11	9	14	4

PITCHING, FIELDING, HITTING:

Mike Roesler is a wild card in the Reds' pitching outlook for 1990. He has been a relief specialist in the minors since 1987, and looks like he could be dominating. Roesler throws a fastball that has been clocked well into the 90s. He complements the heater with a slider and a forkball. The forker is inconsistent, or he would be a major league star already. Mike yielded a bit more than three walks per nine innings last year, but he is a direct worker. His 14.0 pitches per inning were the lowest of any Reds pitcher except Tom Browning. Roesler showed almost no fielding ability in his late season call-up, making just one play in 25 innings, and he never came to bat. He thus enters 1990 with a clean slate.

OVERALL:

One big improvement for Roesler in 1989 was the quality of hitter who smashed home runs off him. His first was yielded to pitcher Don Robinson, but then he became more selective, and gave up the next three to sluggers Andre Dawson, Terry Pendleton, and Glenn Davis. Roesler had a little discomfort working as a mop-up man. He seems to perform better when the pitcher and hitter are both worried about the situation.

PITCHING:

"To explain the success of Juan Agosto as a relief pitcher is to delve into the great unknown," insisted one baseball scout on a mid-season visit to Houston's Astrodome. The question put to him was, "What is it that makes Agosto so effective as a pitcher?" The scout looked mystified. "I don't know what he does," he answered. "I think he's got a mirror or something. He's a magician. He doesn't throw hard, but the ball tails and sinks a little bit."

Agosto is a situation pitcher, the guy who can come in and retire a tough lefthanded batter. He can give a club an inning or so before the closer enters the game. "What Agosto does have," says the scout, "is that big, running curveball that gives lefthanders fits when he's out there."

Agosto and veteran Dan Schatzeder provided lefty depth in a bullpen that carried a heavy load for the Astros in the month when Mike Scott and Jim Deshaies were the only dependable starters. Although Agosto failed to match his 10-2 record, 2.26 ERA, and four saves of the '88 season, his durability (83 innings in 71 games) was important to the team. He went 4-5 with a 2.93 ERA and nailed his one save in two opportunities. Those 71 appearances trailed only his club record total of 75 set the year before. Agosto is 15-8 in Houston after going 9-10 in the American League with Chicago and Minnesota. He was so ineffective in Chicago that he was practically booed out of town, and fans there are as amazed by his Houston success as the scouts are.

FIELDING, HITTING, BASERUNNING:

Agosto creates a lot of groundballs with his pitches and is adept at snagging balls hit back to the mound. He holds baserunners extremely well and has a slick move to first; he's capable of getting out of a jam with a pickoff. Agosto makes contact at the plate and had one single in five at-bats. He just doesn't swing a stick very often.

OVERALL:

Agosto is a good sinkerball pitcher who is spotted in certain situations to make him an effective reliever. The Astros tried a number of southpaws out of the bullpen without too much luck until they signed Agosto as a free agent. He's a finesse pitcher with a resilient arm, and there's no reason to think he won't continue his good work in 1990.

JUAN AGOSTO

Position: RP
Bats: L **Throws:** L
Ht: 6' 2" **Wt:** 190

Opening Day Age: 32
Born: 2/23/58 in Rio Piedras, Puerto Rico
ML Seasons: 9

Overall Statistics

	W	L	ERA	G	GS	Sv	IP	H	R	BB	SO	HR
1989	4	5	2.93	71	0	1	83.0	81	32	32	46	3
Career	24	18	3.46	344	1	23	392.1	382	175	158	195	19

Where They Hit the Ball

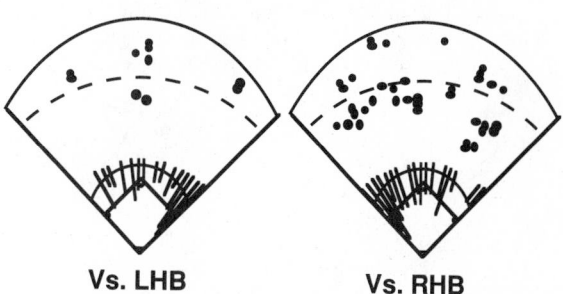

Vs. LHB   **Vs. RHB**

1989 Situational Stats

	W	L	ERA	Sv	IP		AB	H	HR	RBI	AVG
Home	3	2	2.66	0	44.0	LHB	109	24	0	14	.220
Road	1	3	3.23	1	39.0	RHB	207	57	3	23	.275
Day	2	0	1.88	1	28.2	Sc Pos	106	23	0	32	.217
Night	2	5	3.48	0	54.1	Clutch	80	24	1	12	.300

1989 Rankings (National League)

→ 1st in worst first batter efficiency (.333) - *pitchers in 40 games in relief*

→ 4th in games (71)

→ 6th in holds (14)

→ Led the Astros in games, blown saves (4) and lowest batting average vs. lefthanded batters (.220) - *team pitchers facing 125 LHB*

PITCHING:

The humor of Larry Andersen is unmatched in the Astros' clubhouse and now his pitching is equal to the fun times he shares with those within earshot of his locker. He is one of the National League's premier middle relief men, not just a clubhouse cut-up.

Andersen showed no signs of slowing down last year at age 36. His 4-4 record with three saves was topped off by a 1.54 ERA. For the better part of the season, his ERA was under 1.00, but a brief slump did not take the shine off his fourth campaign with the Astros.

Andersen was an impact pitcher while the Astros challenged for the National League West lead. He does the job with a sharp, biting slider. "Slider, slider, slider," says one league scout. "He's got a good one. I've seen him, at least twice, throw nothing but sliders in an inning and strike out the side. I tried to get our club to pick him up when the Phillies released him and I couldn't convince our people the guy could pitch. He's really done the job for Houston."

In 60 games, he retired the first batter he faced 44 times. He held opposing batters to a .198 average and notched saves three times in four opportunities. He struck out 85 batters in 87 2/3 innings. Playing for his fourth major league team, Andersen has the ideal disposition for a reliever. Every team has its resident flake, the player who is a true character. "On our club it happens to be me," he says. Flake or not, in one span in which this character made 33 appearances, covering 49 innings, he allowed only two earned runs.

FIELDING, HITTING, BASERUNNING:

Andersen has good reactions on balls hit back to the mound and he makes a strong, accurate throw to first base. He does not hold baserunners very well. He batted only three times, but cracked out a single for a .333 average.

OVERALL:

Strictly a power pitcher with his sharp slider and hard sinker, Andersen allows few home runs – only two in '89. He got his second wind, so to speak, when Houston signed him with the role of middle relief in mind. He is tough on righthanded hitters and could be a stopper for the Astros if they didn't have Dave Smith in that role.

LARRY ANDERSEN

Position: RP
Bats: R **Throws:** R
Ht: 6' 3" **Wt:** 205

Opening Day Age: 36
Born: 5/6/53 in Portland, OR
ML Seasons: 12

Overall Statistics

	W	L	ERA	G	GS	Sv	IP	H	R	BB	SO	HR
1989	4	4	1.54	60	0	3	87.2	63	19	24	85	2
Career	27	28	3.33	469	1	27	724.0	701	311	227	496	48

Where They Hit the Ball

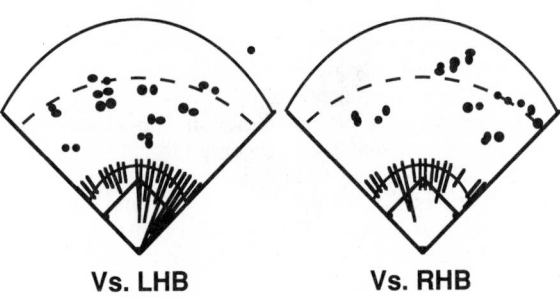

Vs. LHB   **Vs. RHB**

1989 Situational Stats

	W	L	ERA	Sv	IP		AB	H	HR	RBI	AVG
Home	2	3	1.22	2	51.2	LHB	164	41	2	17	.250
Road	2	1	2.00	1	36.0	RHB	154	22	0	12	.143
Day	0	1	1.33	2	27.0	Sc Pos	83	12	0	27	.145
Night	4	3	1.63	1	60.2	Clutch	133	29	1	14	.218

1989 Rankings (National League)

- ➡ 3rd in holds (16)
- ➡ 4th in least baserunners per 9 innings (8.9) - *all league pitchers*
- ➡ 9th in lowest batting average vs. righthanded batters (.143) - *all league pitchers*
- ➡ Led the Astros in ERA (1.54), holds, lowest opponent batting average (.198), first batter efficiency (.200), lowest batting average with runners in scoring position (.145), lowest on-base average allowed (.251) and lowest slugging percentage allowed (.245) - *all team pitchers*

HITTING:

Houston's search for additional home run thunder in the lineup may begin and end with young Eric Anthony. This California native who made his big league debut in late July, 1989, has flashed power signals everywhere he's played. He bashed 69 homers in three-plus minor league campaigns before his promotion from Class AA ball. He hit 4 homers in 61 official at bats with the Astros and knocked in 7 runs in 25 games. He batted only .180, but this wasn't a big issue with club officials. They wanted to give him some exposure at the top level and to get a gander at his power potential in a major league setting.

Anthony showed enough to project himself into the Astros outfield picture in 1990. The lefthanded swinger hit 35 homers in '89 -- 28 at Columbus, GA, and three at AAA Tucson, plus four with the Astros. He rips fastballs and has solid power to all fields. His bat speed is outstanding, and the adjustments he will need to make lie in how he handles breaking balls and off-speed pitches. With his rapid rise up the minor league ladder, Anthony appears to be a quick learner although he has much to discover in the ways of baseball. He has a powerful stroke that will not be limited by any park in which he plays. Anthony struck out 127 times at Columbus alone in 1989, and must make contact and cut down on his strikeouts to be effective.

BASERUNNING:

Anthony is a late-comer to baseball – he didn't play the game in high school – so he has much to learn about running the bases, getting a jump on pitchers and knowing when to take the extra base. He did steal 14 bases at Columbus, though none at the big league level. His talents are still raw, but very promising.

FIELDING:

Anthony is aggressive in the field, has excellent speed and can run down a ball. He still makes mistakes in judgment on occasion, but has a strong arm and skills to raise his game a notch or two with experience.

OVERALL:

Determined and a hard worker, Anthony has the ability to make his move in spring training and battle for a starting job. With the pop he has in his bat, he can be the answer to the needs of the power-starved Astros. He could well be the slugger who can take some of the pressure off Glenn Davis.

ERIC ANTHONY

Position: RF
Bats: L **Throws:** L
Ht: 6' 2" **Wt:** 195

Opening Day Age: 22
Born: 11/8/67 in San Diego, CA
ML Seasons: 1

Overall Statistics

	G	AB	R	H	D	T	HR	RBI	SB	BB	SO	AVG
1989	25	61	7	11	2	0	4	7	0	9	16	.180
Career	25	61	7	11	2	0	4	7	0	9	16	.180

Where He Hits the Ball

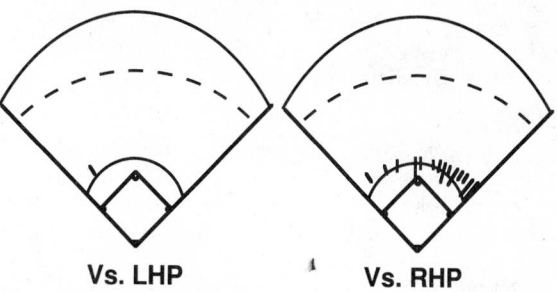

Vs. LHP   Vs. RHP

1989 Situational Stats

	AB	H	HR	RBI	AVG		AB	H	HR	RBI	AVG
Home	25	5	2	4	.200	LHP	5	0	0	0	.000
Road	36	6	2	3	.167	RHP	56	11	4	7	.196
Day	20	3	1	2	.150	Sc Pos	10	1	0	2	.100
Night	41	8	3	5	.195	Clutch	12	3	0	1	.250

1989 Rankings (National League)

➡ 6th in home run frequency (15.3 ABs per HR) - *all league players*

➡ Led the Astros in home run frequency - *all team players*

HITTING:

A healthy Kevin Bass is important to the Astros' pennant ambitions. He spent 76 days on the disabled list in '89 with a fractured bone in his right shin and his presence in the lineup was sorely missed. As it was, Bass batted .300, hit five homers and collected 44 RBIs in the 87 games he played. He also hit home runs from both sides of the plate in a game for the third time in his career. One was a grand-slam, hit righthanded, to beat Chicago's Mitch Williams.

A switch-hitter, Bass has had success from both sides of the plate. He hit better from the left side in '89 (.313 to .265), which is unusual for him; ordinarily he hits for a better average, and much more home run power, as a righthanded swinger. He likes the ball up as a righty hitter, down as a lefty. He'll chase bad pitches and is much more effective when he stays disciplined, as he did in '89. Bass has hit as many as 20 home runs in a season, but that total has declined in recent years. For the most part Bass is now a line drive hitter who hits the ball where it's pitched.

BASERUNNING:

Bass is aggressive on the basepaths, stealing 11 bags in 15 attempts despite his long layoff in '89. He takes the extra base when he sees the opportunity, and uses his speed to get into scoring position.

FIELDING:

When the Astros acquired Glenn Wilson from Pittsburgh, Bass moved to left field (from right). He gives them a strong arm in left, something they lacked in recent years; the arm is not always accurate, however. He is a sure fielder on ground balls to the outfield, and good at cutting off balls hit in the alleys.

OVERALL:

A subject of trade rumors during the early part of '89, Bass responded well to the low-key approach of Manager Art Howe and he is more comfortable in a relaxed atmosphere. This helped him, in part, to bounce back from an off-year in '88 (when he hit only .255). He is capable of hitting .300 and 20 home runs under Howe's gentle urging.

KEVIN BASS

Position: RF/LF
Bats: B **Throws:** R
Ht: 6' 0"   **Wt:** 180

Opening Day Age: 30
Born: 5/12/59 in Redwood City, CA
ML Seasons: 8

Overall Statistics

	G	AB	R	H	D	T	HR	RBI	SB	BB	SO	AVG
1989	87	313	42	94	19	4	5	44	11	29	44	.300
Career	947	3135	401	862	161	29	78	396	111	206	414	.275

Where He Hits the Ball

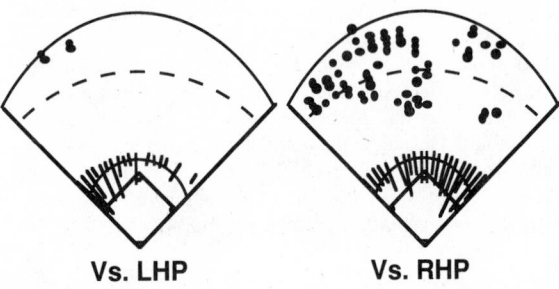

Vs. LHP   **Vs. RHP**

1989 Situational Stats

	AB	H	HR	RBI	AVG		AB	H	HR	RBI	AVG
Home	168	50	2	26	.298	LHP	83	22	2	14	.265
Road	145	44	3	18	.303	RHP	230	72	3	30	.313
Day	103	32	3	14	.311	Sc Pos	75	24	2	37	.320
Night	210	62	2	30	.295	Clutch	53	14	2	14	.264

1989 Rankings (National League)

➡ 5th in least GDPs per GDP situation (3.1%) - *players with 50 PA in GDP situations*

➡ Led the Astros in triples (4), least GDPs per GDP situation and batting average with 2 strikes (.260) - *team players with 162 PA with 2 strikes*

➡ Led NL Right Fielders in least GDPs per GDP situation

CRAIG BIGGIO

Position: C
Bats: R **Throws:** R
Ht: 5'11" **Wt:** 180

Opening Day Age: 24
Born: 12/14/65 in Smithtown, NY
ML Seasons: 2

FUTURE ALL-STAR

HITTING:

When was the last time you remember a catcher batting in the leadoff spot? Or playing centerfield? The Astros' Craig Biggio did this and more this past season. He also commandeered attention by becoming only the seventh catcher since 1900 to steal 20 bases in a season. He ended up with 21 steals in 24 attempts, which would be an outstanding success ratio for Rickey Henderson. Biggio also played left and centerfields in the final week of the season because manager Art Howe, noting the young man's versatility, wanted to see what other positions Biggio could play. There's even been talk of trying him at second base some day.

The Astros have been seeing Biggio's potential since they made him their first round selection in the 1987 draft. But they finally made a total commitment to him early in 1989, when -- though very much in the pennant race -- they released veteran receiver Alan Ashby and handed Biggio the number one job. His numbers were good, but equally important was the fire he lit under a team that had become set in its ways. His enthusiasm for the game proved contagious and the Astros contended for the National League West title until the final weeks.

Though a young hitter, Biggio has a surprising amount of discipline. He'll lay off bad offerings and pitchers find it increasingly difficult to throw a fastball by him. He is adjusting to the breaking ball and the mental aspects of the game.

BASERUNNING:

In his short career, Biggio has been thrown out only four times while stealing 27 bases. He's not only fast, he's a smart baserunner. He'll seldom make a foolish mistake on the bases.

FIELDING:

Biggio has a chance to be a good catcher. He calls a good game, handles pitches (and pitchers) well and shows great poise, considering his inexperience at the top level. His one problem is throwing out runners. The Astro pitchers don't help him much, but Biggio needs to improve in this area.

OVERALL:

It seems obvious that the former Seton Hall star is only going to improve with experience. Biggio is a leader on the field and in the dugout who throws off sparks with his all-out desire for the game.

Overall Statistics

	G	AB	R	H	D	T	HR	RBI	SB	BB	SO	AVG
1989	134	443	64	114	21	2	13	60	21	49	64	.257
Career	184	566	78	140	27	3	16	65	27	56	93	.247

Where He Hits the Ball

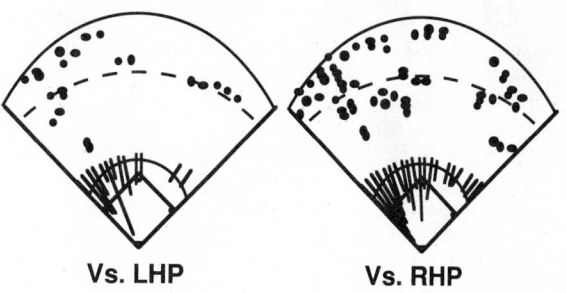

Vs. LHP   **Vs. RHP**

1989 Situational Stats

	AB	H	HR	RBI	AVG		AB	H	HR	RBI	AVG
Home	219	51	6	30	.233	LHP	122	33	1	15	.270
Road	224	63	7	30	.281	RHP	321	81	12	45	.252
Day	149	41	6	27	.275	Sc Pos	117	29	4	46	.248
Night	294	73	7	33	.248	Clutch	90	28	3	19	.311

1989 Rankings (National League)

➡ Worst catcher throwing out base stealers (17.2%) - *catchers with 75 attempts*

➡ 2nd in stolen base percentage (87.5%) - *players with 20 attempts*

➡ 7th in bunts in play (26)

➡ Led the Astros in bunts in play and hitting in the clutch (.311) - *team players with 50 PA in the clutch*

➡ Led NL Catchers in 22 categories including runs (64), hits (114), doubles (21), stolen bases (21), batting average (.257), stolen base percentage, plate appearances (509) and home run frequency (34.1 ABs per HR) - *catchers with 502 PA*

HITTING:

A year ago, the Astros came into spring training wondering who was going to play third base. Ken Caminiti produced a ringing answer to the question, constructing his best year in the major leagues. The same chance was given to Caminiti the previous year, but he failed to prosper under Hal Lanier and was returned to triple-A ball. In 1989, under new manager Art Howe, Caminiti found a gentler approach and an assurance that the job was his. The security Caminiti got from that assurance helped him put it all together. He responded with a .255 average and 10 home runs. His 72 RBIs were second only to Glenn Davis' club-leading total of 89.

The switch-hitting Caminiti batted .315 righthanded and .215 left-handed, repeating the extreme platoon differential he'd shown as a rookie in 1987. Thus far Caminiti's had a lot of problems from the left side -- he hit only .184 as a lefty swinger in '87 -- though he did hit six homers last year batting lefty. "He's showing flashes of what I saw the first year (1987) they brought him up," says one big league scout. "He's swinging the bat with a lot more authority." Caminiti and another Astro youngster, Craig Biggio, provided a spark to the team with their enthusiasm and combined for a total of 132 RBIs and 23 homers. He played in all but one game.

BASERUNNING:

Caminiti stole four bases in five attempts, but is an average runner at best. He runs hard and slides hard to break up the double play. He doesn't have the legs to take the extra base.

FIELDING:

Caminiti has it all in the field: a quick first step to either side, good hands, a gun for an arm and an ability to make spectacular plays at third base. Many of his 22 errors came on throws after making a standout stop. Says Howe: "There ought to be a new statistic for Ken -- runs saved on defense."

OVERALL:

Caminiti has the potential for a Gold Glove in his future after establishing his defensive credentials this past year. As a hitter he needs to make more contact at the plate and drive the ball a little harder to really come into his own. He also needs to improve a lot as a lefthanded hitter. Nonetheless he has the skills to become an Astro fixture for years to come.

KEN CAMINITI

Position: 3B
Bats: B **Throws:** R
Ht: 6' 0" **Wt:** 200

Opening Day Age: 26
Born: 4/21/63 in Hanford, CA
ML Seasons: 3

Overall Statistics

	G	AB	R	H	D	T	HR	RBI	SB	BB	SO	AVG
1989	161	585	71	149	31	3	10	72	4	51	93	.255
Career	254	871	86	214	40	4	14	102	4	68	155	.246

Where He Hits the Ball

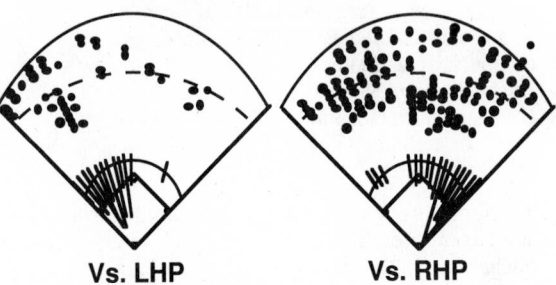

Vs. LHP   Vs. RHP

1989 Situational Stats

	AB	H	HR	RBI	AVG		AB	H	HR	RBI	AVG
Home	293	75	3	32	.256	LHP	165	52	4	22	.315
Road	292	74	7	40	.253	RHP	420	97	6	50	.231
Day	184	53	5	27	.288	Sc Pos	164	48	2	63	.293
Night	401	96	5	45	.239	Clutch	119	25	3	9	.210

1989 Rankings (National League)

- ➡ 5th in games (161)
- ➡ 6th in errors (22)
- ➡ 8th in hitting on a 3-1 count (.500) - *players with 10 PA on a 3-1 count*
- ➡ Led the Astros in at bats (585), singles (105), games, doubles (31), hitting on a 3-1 count and hitting with runners in scoring position (.293) - *team players with 100 PA with runners in scoring position*
- ➡ Led NL Third Basemen in hitting on a 3-1 count, lowest percentage of swings that missed (16.6%) and hit by pitch (3)

PITCHING:

Jim Clancy was a major disappointment for the Astros in 1989. When Nolan Ryan was lost to free agency, Clancy became the pitcher who was supposed to take up the slack after signing a lucrative free agent contract. But it didn't happen. His 7-14 record, 5.08 ERA and one complete game in 26 starts doesn't completely tell the torment he suffered this season. In his Toronto years, his hard slider and good arm earned 128 wins.

At age 34, Clancy has lost enough zip on his fastball to make one wonder if he can regain his winning form. His problem is that he's throwing all of his pitches at about the same speed, causing little confusion to the hitters. They enjoyed some big days at his expense with the hop missing from his fastball, and it became a struggle just to survive the early innings. He had four wins at San Diego's expense (the Padres finally beat him the last time around) and little success against the rest of the league. He used to challenge hitters with his fastball; he still managed to strike out 91 batters in 147 innings in 1989. But he yielded 155 hits and a whopping 100 runs in those innings. Clancy spent a brief spell in the bullpen to try to work out his problems, but nothing seemed to help. San Francisco beat him three times, including the game that officially eliminated the Astros from the pennant race. Montreal banged him around for two losses and 13 runs in 2.2 innings. He went 1-4 the first month of this season, then briefly found the winning touch and notched four straight victories. He went 2-10 the rest of the way.

FIELDING, HITTING, BASERUNNING:

When his pitching troubles began to mount, Clancy developed a problem throwing the ball to first base after fielding balls hit back to the mound. He was charged with seven errors in 33 games. He does only a fair job of holding baserunners. Clancy's not much of a runner, but he did stroke six singles and a double in 41 at-bats in his first experience as a major league hitter.

OVERALL:

At his age, Clancy needs to make some adjustments, if he can. He was working with a split-fingered fastball and this could provide a lift and give him more movement on his pitches. Certainly he'll have to improve on his '89 work if he wants to stick around as a regular starter.

JIM CLANCY

Position: SP/RP
Bats: R **Throws:** R
Ht: 6' 4" **Wt:** 220

Opening Day Age: 34
Born: 12/18/55 in Chicago, IL
ML Seasons: 13

Overall Statistics

	W	L	ERA	G	GS	Sv	IP	H	R	BB	SO	HR
1989	7	14	5.08	33	26	0	147.0	155	100	66	91	13
Career	135	154	4.16	385	371	1	2353.0	2340	1204	880	1328	232

Where They Hit the Ball

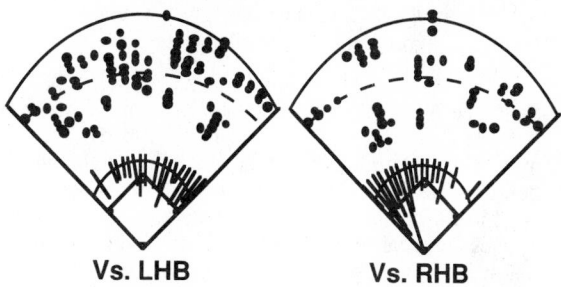

Vs. LHB   **Vs. RHB**

1989 Situational Stats

	W	L	ERA	Sv	IP		AB	H	HR	RBI	AVG
Home	4	5	5.66	0	62.0	LHB	316	91	10	49	.288
Road	3	9	4.66	0	85.0	RHB	260	64	3	29	.246
Day	0	6	5.18	0	40.0	Sc Pos	150	49	3	63	.327
Night	7	8	5.05	0	107.0	Clutch	47	9	2	2	.191

1989 Rankings (National League)

➡ 3rd in worst ERA on the road (4.66) - *pitchers with 81 IP on the road*

➡ 4th in losses (14)

➡ Led the Astros in losses, GDPs induced (14), runs allowed (100) and earned runs allowed (83)

➡ Led NL Pitchers in errors (7)

DANNY DARWIN

Position: RP
Bats: R **Throws:** R
Ht: 6' 3" **Wt:** 190

Opening Day Age: 34
Born: 10/25/55 in
Bonham, TX
ML Seasons: 12

PITCHING:

There's something of Nolan Ryan in Danny Darwin. Not the all-time strikeout and no-hit record. Not the many other career marks. But the style: tall, lanky, raw-boned and Texan. He traveled the opposite course of Ryan, going from the Texas Rangers to the Houston Astros (around a stopover in Milwaukee), and became a close friend of the future Hall of Famer before Ryan's exit to Texas.

At age 34, Darwin is working on the longevity end of it, too. He enjoyed one of his finest seasons in 1989 as a long reliever and occasional closer. And, like Ryan, he still depends on his ripping fastball. He won 11 games (losing four), tying a club record out of the bullpen. He saved seven other games in 68 outings. He pitched more innings (122) than any reliever in baseball. In addition, Darwin struck out 104 batters, the most ever by an Astro reliever. The bullpen, of which Darwin was a vital member, was what allowed the Astros to remain in the pennant chase for much of the season.

Says one National League scout, "Darwin throws a fastball in the 90s. It tails and really moves. Tails away from a lefthander and moves in on a righthander. Plus, he drops down and crossfires righthanders and hits the outside corner. He's good at it." Darwin's pitches are ideal for his craft: the good, hard fastball that runs in on a right-handed batter and a good, stiff slider that zips away at the outside of the plate. He remains versatile, too, being capable of starting (his first love), middle relieving or closing when needed.

FIELDING, HITTING, BASERUNNING:

Two hits in 17 at-bats shows Darwin's limits as a batter and two errors all season indicate his dependability in the field. He has not had much experience on basepaths. With his high leg kick and slow delivery, Darwin is an easy mark for base stealers.

OVERALL:

Everyone knows fastballs remain Darwin's best weapon. His power pitching style marks him as an asset to the Astros. He is sturdy and dependable and his career-high 68 appearances in '89 are the fourth-highest total in club history.

Overall Statistics

	W	L	ERA	G	GS	Sv	IP	H	R	BB	SO	HR
1989	11	4	2.36	68	0	7	122.0	92	34	33	104	8
Career	100	105	3.51	440	191	27	1750.2	1640	778	550	1156	150

Where They Hit the Ball

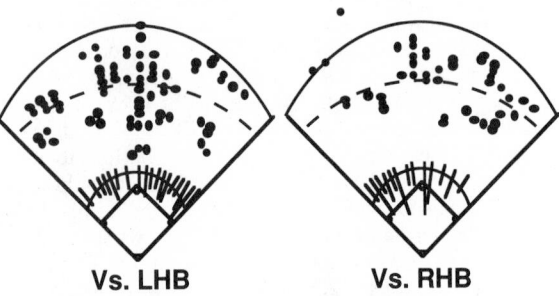

Vs. LHB   **Vs. RHB**

1989 Situational Stats

	W	L	ERA	Sv	IP		AB	H	HR	RBI	AVG
Home	7	0	1.98	4	72.2	LHB	241	59	3	26	.245
Road	4	4	2.92	3	49.1	RHB	193	33	5	22	.171
Day	2	2	2.81	2	25.2	Sc Pos	117	28	1	39	.239
Night	9	2	2.24	5	96.1	Clutch	242	48	5	22	.198

1989 Rankings (National League)

- ➡ 1st in most innings (122) - *all relievers*
- ➡ 3rd in won/loss percentage (.733) - *pitchers with 15 decisions*
- ➡ 4th in worst first batter efficiency (.283) - *pitchers with 40 games in relief*
- ➡ 10th in games (68)
- ➡ Led the Astros in won/loss percentage, blown saves (4) and lowest percentage of inherited runners (37.3%) - *team pitchers with 30 inherited runners*

IN HIS PRIME

GLENN DAVIS

Position: 1B
Bats: R **Throws:** R
Ht: 6' 3" **Wt:** 210

Opening Day Age: 29
Born: 3/28/61 in
Jacksonville, FL
ML Seasons: 6

HITTING:

Glenn Davis was the lone Houston hitter in double figures in home runs for much of the '89 season. Therein lies the problem for the slugging first baseman since his arrival in the major leagues. He has no partner in power, no one to back him up in the batting order so the opposition cannot pitch around him. Such an individual has yet to establish himself with the Astros, yet Davis continues about his duties with a mark of consistency. He became the first Astro to hit 30 or more homers in three seasons, reaching a career-high 34 this past year.

The book on Davis has always been to set him up with high and tight pitches, then try to get him to chase low and away breaking stuff. Since his power shots carry the club, Davis has a tendency to chase those bad pitches in an attempt to drive in runs. With a strong bat behind him, the Astros feel that the pressure would not be on Davis alone and pitchers would be forced to give him better offerings. The rap against Davis -- that he hits homers when they mean nothing -- has resulted in this search for a number five hitter. Why would anyone pitch to Davis in a tight situation if they can pitch around him?

BASERUNNING:

Davis stole four bases last year, matching his career high. He's not a stealing threat, but his overall speed is about average. He's a pretty conservative runner but doesn't always break quickly enough when a ball is hit.

FIELDING:

In his early years, Davis was still learning the position. Through a lot of hard work, he has become a good first baseman. His instincts and range are improved, but his throws to other bases leave something to be desired at times. He made 12 errors in 158 games.

OVERALL:

Davis has quietly grown into the team leader as he enters his peak years. The Astros traded for Glenn Wilson as a number five bat behind him late in '89, but this role may eventually fall to young Eric Anthony, the first power hitter produced by the organization since Davis. In four and a half years, Davis has struck 144 homers, marking him one of the game's premier power hitters.

Overall Statistics

	G	AB	R	H	D	T	HR	RBI	SB	BB	SO	AVG
1989	158	581	87	156	26	1	34	89	4	69	123	.269
Career	737	2705	383	713	135	6	144	454	15	264	436	.264

Where He Hits the Ball

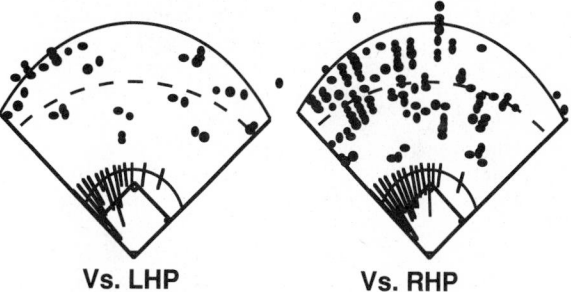

Vs. LHP   **Vs. RHP**

1989 Situational Stats

	AB	H	HR	RBI	AVG		AB	H	HR	RBI	AVG
Home	287	91	15	42	.317	LHP	146	42	14	26	.288
Road	294	65	19	47	.221	RHP	435	114	20	63	.262
Day	183	42	8	22	.230	Sc Pos	137	37	5	47	.270
Night	398	114	26	67	.286	Clutch	111	28	7	17	.252

1989 Rankings (National League)

➡ 3rd in home runs (34) and slugging percentage vs. lefthanded pitchers (.616) - *players with 125 PA vs. LHP*

➡ 5th in hit by pitch (7) and home run frequency (17.1 ABs per HR) - *players with 502 PA*

➡ 6th in strikeouts (123) and total bases (286)

➡ Led the Astros in batting average (.269), home runs, runs (87), hits (156), RBI (89), GDPs (9), on-base average (.350), slugging average (.492), strikeouts, home run frequency, total bases, sacrifice flies (6) and intentional walks (17) - *players with 502 PA*

➡ Led NL First Basemen in home runs and home run frequency

PITCHING:

The scout watched Jim Deshaies from the stands. "He's a mystery to me," he said. "How you can throw high fastballs and win, I don't know. But he does it." The scout tells hitters in his reports to lay off the high pitch "and we can beat this guy. And they go out there and keep swinging at the high pitch."

The lefthanded Deshaies keeps improving each year. He reached a career high of 15 wins in 1989 in establishing himself as the No. 2 man on the starting staff. He battled back from off-season arthroscopic surgery on his left shoulder in 1988 to win 11 games that year. This past season Deshaies recorded career highs in wins (15), innings (225.2), complete games (6) and strikeouts (153). His ERA was 2.91 as he still managed to prevail with that high fastball and crackling slider.

The rising fastball is the key to Deshaies' success. One league rival said, "Deshaies' fastball starts out about chest high and (Craig) Biggio ends up catching it standing up." When Deshaies has strong command of his slider, it sets up his fastball. He gets a lot of swinging strikes at the shoulders. He tries to keep things simple, trying not to overanalyze the situation. He has a good mix in his pitches and works the ball in and out, up and down. "He's become the kind of pitcher I wouldn't want to face," says teammate Billy Doran.

FIELDING, HITTING, BASERUNNING:

Deshaies does not have very quick reflexes on the mound and is not a good fielder. He does not hold runners well, either; base stealers were successful in 27 of 33 attempts with Deshaies on the mound last year, a very high rate of success against a southpaw. But it's not that he doesn't try; he made more throws to first (355) in 1989 than any other pitcher in the major leagues. As a hitter Deshaies strikes out a little over one-third of his at bats, but he stroked out nine hits, second only to Mike Scott's 10 among the Astros' pitchers. He's a very slow runner.

OVERALL:

Deshaies joins Mike Scott as a solid one-two starting team around which the Astros need to rebuild their staff. If he stays healthy, should he able to match or improve on his victory total this season.

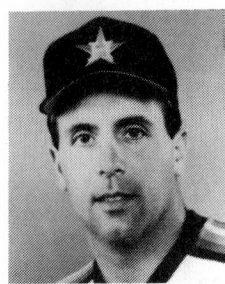

JIM DESHAIES

Position: SP
Bats: L **Throws:** L
Ht: 6' 4"   **Wt:** 222

Opening Day Age: 29
Born: 6/23/60 in Massena, NY
ML Seasons: 6

Overall Statistics

	W	L	ERA	G	GS	Sv	IP	H	R	BB	SO	HR
1989	15	10	2.91	34	34	0	225.2	180	80	79	153	15
Career	49	36	3.42	121	118	0	738.2	632	305	274	519	74

Where They Hit the Ball

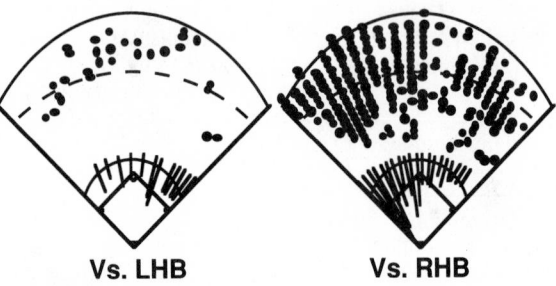

Vs. LHB   **Vs. RHB**

1989 Situational Stats

	W	L	ERA	Sv	IP		AB	H	HR	RBI	AVG
Home	8	4	3.13	0	118.0	LHB	120	31	0	6	.258
Road	7	6	2.67	0	107.2	RHB	709	149	15	57	.210
Day	5	2	2.37	0	68.1	Sc Pos	178	38	3	45	.213
Night	10	8	3.15	0	157.1	Clutch	75	15	2	5	.200

1989 Rankings (National League)

- ➡ 1st in pickoff throws (355)
- ➡ 3rd in worst stolen base percentage (81.8%) - *pitchers with 162 IP*
- ➡ 4th in games started (34) and lowest grounder/flyball ratio (.81)
- ➡ 5th in ERA on the road (2.68) and lowest batting average vs. righthanded batters (.210)
- ➡ Led the Astros in games started, ERA (2.91), hits allowed (180), walks allowed (79), pitches thrown (3,526), pickoff throws, shutouts (3), hit batsmen (4), wild pitches (8), lowest slugging percentage allowed (.331), strikeout/walk ratio (1.94) and ERA on the road - *team pitchers with 162 IP*

HITTING:

This is a subject Billy Doran would prefer to ignore after his decline in '89. In his own words: "I've given the word slump a whole new meaning. Instead of saying, 'I'm in a slump.' they say, 'I'm in a Billy Doran.'" How bad was it? On June 25, his average was at .280 with seven homers and 46 RBIs, after a season-high .304 average a month earlier. After the All-Star break, Doran hit .130 with no homers and only nine RBIs. This is from a veteran who came into the year with a .277 career batting mark. His final totals in '89: .219 (.229 righthanded, .215 left-handed), eight homers, 58 RBIs.

It was, by far, the worst slump of his career, though Doran has always had a tendency to go through long dry spells. In April of '87, for instance, he batted only .200; in August-September of '88 he hit just .197. But he'd never been through anything like this. Doran has always been considered a good fastball hitter but somewhat vulnerable to low breaking stuff. But during the drought he couldn't hit anything. Even being a switch-hitter failed to help. He had troubles from both sides of the place. Doran is such a strong competitor that his intensity worked against him as his numbers dwindled.

BASERUNNING:

Doran is an excellent base runner, even in a hitting slump. He was successful on 88 percent of his steal attempts -- 22 in 25 tries -- and he has natural instincts for the game. Doran has stolen as many as 42 bases in a season. His totals have gone down in recent years, but his success percentage has increased.

FIELDING:

Because he plays in the era of Ryne Sandberg, Doran has never won a Gold Glove, but he remains an excellent fielder. His competitiveness shows in the field, where he never gives up on a ball. He has good range to either side, can make the diving stop and come up throwing. Doran made 12 errors in 142 games, a low number but his highest total in three years.

OVERALL:

The third spot in the batting order is a vital one, and the Astros need Doran to regain his old touch in that position. With his speed and occasional pop in his bat, he has been one of the team's key clutch performers. No one can explain Doran's second-half slump, but he is expected to bounce back in 1990.

BILLY DORAN

Position: 2B
Bats: B **Throws:** R
Ht: 6' 0" **Wt:** 175

Opening Day Age: 31
Born: 5/28/58 in Cincinnati, OH
ML Seasons: 8

Overall Statistics

	G	AB	R	H	D	T	HR	RBI	SB	BB	SO	AVG
1989	142	507	65	111	25	2	8	58	22	59	63	.219
Career	1056	3920	562	1040	159	33	63	372	173	514	460	.265

Where He Hits the Ball

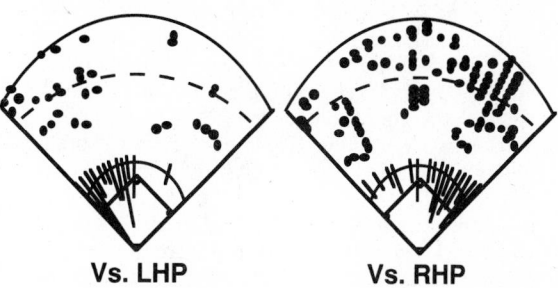

Vs. LHP   **Vs. RHP**

1989 Situational Stats

	AB	H	HR	RBI	AVG		AB	H	HR	RBI	AVG
Home	250	63	3	36	.252	LHP	140	32	4	17	.229
Road	257	48	5	22	.187	RHP	367	79	4	41	.215
Day	146	27	1	14	.185	Sc Pos	121	34	2	45	.281
Night	361	84	7	44	.233	Clutch	95	18	3	7	.189

1989 Rankings (National League)

➡ 1st in stolen base percentage (88.0%) - *players with 20 attempts*

➡ 2nd worst batting average (.219) - *players with 502 PA*

➡ Led the Astros in stolen base percentage

➡ Led NL Second Basemen in stolen base percentage and hitting with runners in scoring position (.281) - *second basemen with 100 PA with runners in scoring position*

PITCHING:

Bob Forsch is a pitcher for all occasions. In baseball circles, he is called a swingman, a pitcher who can start for a team or work out of the bullpen. In recent years, the 40-year old Forsch has played the dual roles with some success. He served as the Astros' No. 5 starter, filling in for Rick Rhoden when he was on the disabled list, and Forsch entered 22 other games in relief outings. Despite poor overall numbers, this marked him as a valuable asset. Such a pitcher helps hold a staff together in difficult times and this is what Forsch has done despite his advancing years. He throws all the pitches but has become more of finesse pitcher in recent seasons.

Just consider his performance chart in 1989: 3-4 as a starter, 1-1 as a reliever. He pitched five or more innings in 10 of 12 starts in one mid-season stretch and worked a season-high seven innings in long relief at Cincinnati. He blanked Los Angeles for seven innings in one start, too. It's just that at his age, a team cannot expect him to do this very often; his overall numbers (4-5, 5.32) were not good. But Forsch is a veteran who goes about his business and does his job to the best of his ability. He has been a good insurance policy against injuries to the Astros' pitching staff -- starters or relievers. He is one of the game's top competitors, too. His relief record in 1989 was only so-so. He allowed five of 17 inherited runners to score and he retired the first batter in 12 of the 22 games in which he worked out of the bullpen.

FIELDING, HITTING, BASERUNNING:

Forsch is one of the game's better hitting pitchers, a reputation he brought to the Astros from his days as a Cardinal. Although he hit only .167 this past year, he shows career totals of 12 homers and 84 RBIs. He is a sound fielder and runs the bases well for a pitcher.

OVERALL:

Forsch's value remains in that he will take the ball whenever you ask him to pitch, starting or relief. He may not give you seven innings as a starter, but he's good for five or six. He is also a good man in the clubhouse, a solid team player. But he'll need to lower that 5.32 ERA to keep his job.

BOB FORSCH

Position: RP/SP
Bats: R **Throws:** R
Ht: 6' 3" **Wt:** 215

Opening Day Age: 40
Born: 1/13/50 in Sacramento, CA
ML Seasons: 16

Overall Statistics

	W	L	ERA	G	GS	Sv	IP	H	R	BB	SO	HR
1989	4	5	5.32	37	15	0	108.1	133	68	46	40	10
Career	168	136	3.76	498	422	3	2795.0	2777	1319	832	1133	216

Where They Hit the Ball

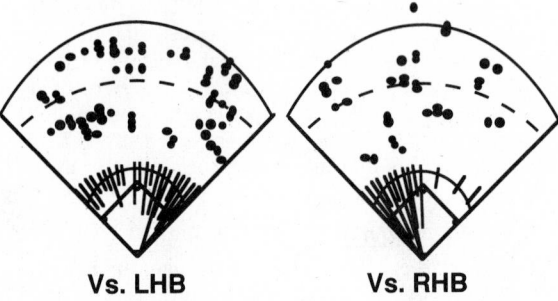

Vs. LHB   **Vs. RHB**

1989 Situational Stats

	W	L	ERA	Sv	IP		AB	H	HR	RBI	AVG
Home	2	1	4.92	0	56.2	LHB	259	79	6	39	.305
Road	2	4	5.75	0	51.2	RHB	180	54	4	22	.300
Day	3	0	3.81	0	26.0	Sc Pos	123	42	4	49	.341
Night	1	5	5.79	0	82.1	Clutch	36	8	0	2	.222

1989 Rankings (National League)

- ➡ 3rd in balks (5)
- ➡ 5th in worst batting average vs. lefthanded batters (.305) - *pitchers facing 125 LHB*
- ➡ Led the Astros in balks

PITCHING:

Mark down Mark Portugal as an overachiever. He made a long haul out of what was supposed to be a short run. Portugal was promoted to the big leagues because of a rash of injuries and a surplus of doubleheaders. The Astros needed a pinch starter so the call went out for help.

Portugal answered the summons in Tucson, Arizona and he drew his first start a day later in San Diego. The results were not encouraging: nine hits and six runs in a brief stint. After pitching twice more, he returned to Triple-A ball. On the recommendation of Tucson manager Bob Skinner, Mark was brought back up on July 15 and he went on a scintillating winning streak: seven straight decisions without a loss. He gained a foothold on the mound and never surrendered it, moving into the No. 3 starting role as others foundered.

After being 11-19 in parts of four seasons with the Minnesota Twins, Portugal has turned his career around. He now has control of his four pitches, the ability to change speeds, and uses a tantalizing change-up effectively. When he throws his fastball for strikes, or as an effective waste pitch inside, and gets over his curveball or slider, he is in full control. He becomes what some hitters label as "nasty." Portugal has confidence in his breaking ball when behind in the count. His performance over the final two months, as the Astros struggled to stay in the pennant race, won him ranking on the starting staff behind Mike Scott and Jim Deshaies, the only starters to post more wins.

FIELDING, HITTING, BASERUNNING:

Although a refugee from the American League, Portugal became one of four Astro pitchers with multi-hit games in 1989. He is aggressive in fielding his position, has good reactions and a strong throw to first base on ground balls hit back to him. Portugal also has an outstanding pickoff move for a righthander and holds baserunners very well.

OVERALL:

In his early starts as an Astro, Portugal was a five or six-inning pitcher as he battled to rebuild his stamina. He finished with a strong kick in some must-win games down the stretch. His timing was perfect for a starting staff desperate for help. At 27, Portugal is just entering his prime years.

MARK PORTUGAL

Position: SP/RP
Bats: R **Throws:** R
Ht: 6' 0" **Wt:** 200

Opening Day Age: 27
Born: 10/30/62 in Los Angeles, CA
ML Seasons: 5

Overall Statistics

	W	L	ERA	G	GS	Sv	IP	H	R	BB	SO	HR
1989	7	1	2.75	20	15	0	108.0	91	34	37	86	7
Career	18	20	4.39	92	41	4	346.2	345	176	142	224	44

Where They Hit the Ball

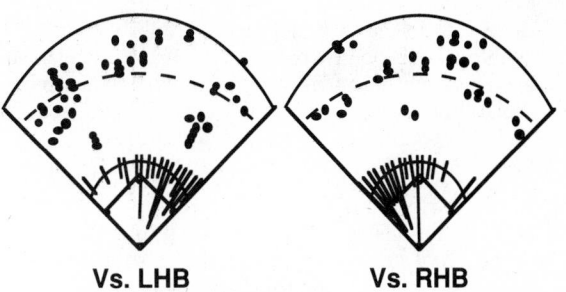

Vs. LHB   **Vs. RHB**

1989 Situational Stats

	W	L	ERA	Sv	IP		AB	H	HR	RBI	AVG
Home	4	1	3.12	0	52.0	LHB	214	48	3	15	.224
Road	3	0	2.41	0	56.0	RHB	178	43	4	15	.242
Day	2	0	2.34	0	34.2	Sc Pos	83	14	0	19	.169
Night	5	1	2.95	0	73.1	Clutch	39	9	0	2	.231

1989 Rankings (National League)

➡ Led the Astros in runners caught stealing (7)

HITTING:

Terry Puhl hasn't been a full time regular since 1984 when he put together a .301 batting average. Yet when they need his presence in the lineup, the lanky veteran responds with good numbers. This past season is representative of Puhl's value to the team. Pressed into regular duty when Kevin Bass went on the disabled list, Terry took Bass's place in right field and hit .293 with 10 RBIs during the month of June. Certainly Puhl contributed to the club's 18-10 mark that month. He is the Astros' security blanket: he fills in where he is needed, getting key hits and keeping a rally going.

That sort of performance has come to be expected of Puhl, who made his major league debut with the Astros in July, 1977, just three days after his 21st birthday. Among active players only Atlanta's Dale Murphy has logged more continuous time with the same club in the National League. Puhl has hit in double digits in homers only once (13 in 1980), but he makes a habit of finding the alleys with doubles and triples. His .271 season shows he can play a strong role as a fourth outfielder for the team in 1990.

A contact hitter, Puhl is very disciplined and seldom swings at a bad pitch. Pitchers try to get him out by working him inside and low, but he'll usually make them keep it in the strike zone. He's a stinging line drive hitter who belts the ball to all fields.

BASERUNNING:

Despite his years, Puhl continues to run well. He stole nine bases -- though he was caught eight times -- legged out 25 doubles and four triples in '89. Puhl is aggressive on the basepaths and will take the extra base. His legs remain an asset.

FIELDING:

Puhl has good range in the field, a good arm and he can play all three spots in the outfield. He cuts off the ball well on hits into the alleys and still gets a good jump on the ball.

OVERALL:

Puhl remains capable of filling more than a reserve role. He showed he can start over a period of time and not decline in performance. He's always been a good ballplayer and understands his role as the Astros enter the 1990s. Puhl has always put the team ahead of his personal goals.

TERRY PUHL

Position: RF/LF
Bats: L **Throws:** R
Ht: 6' 2" **Wt:** 197

Opening Day Age: 33
Born: 7/8/56 in Melville, Saskatchewan
ML Seasons: 13

Overall Statistics

	G	AB	R	H	D	T	HR	RBI	SB	BB	SO	AVG
1989	121	354	41	96	25	4	0	27	9	45	39	.271
Career	1479	4796	671	1345	225	56	62	424	216	497	498	.280

Where He Hits the Ball

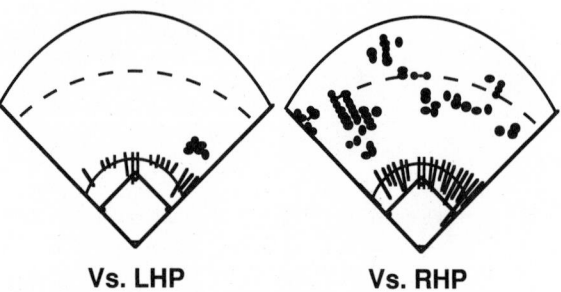

Vs. LHP   Vs. RHP

1989 Situational Stats

	AB	H	HR	RBI	AVG		AB	H	HR	RBI	AVG
Home	189	48	0	18	.254	LHP	57	14	0	5	.246
Road	165	48	0	9	.291	RHP	297	82	0	22	.276
Day	101	32	0	11	.317	Sc Pos	78	19	0	24	.244
Night	253	64	0	16	.253	Clutch	60	17	0	2	.283

1989 Rankings (National League)

➡ Led the Astros in triples (4)
➡ Led NL Right Fielders in sacrifice bunts (4) and bunts in play (11)

HITTING:

When Houston acquired Rafael Ramirez in a trade with Atlanta for two young prospects, he bore the label of a good-hitting shortstop who made too many errors in the field. That tag still holds after two seasons with the Astros. Although his batting average dipped to .246 (down from .276 the first year), Ramirez delivered a number of game-winning and clutch hits among his 54 RBIs (slightly off his career best of 59 in 1988). Included in his outbursts were a club-record seven RBIs in a game at Chicago's Wrigley Field. Five times in extra-inning games, he chased home the winning run with hits. "When you need a big base hit," says his double play partner, Billy Doran, "Raffy's been the guy that's been able to come up and get it for us." The other thing about Ramirez is that he's always smiling, whether he is going good or going bad.

Ramirez is a free swinger and drew only 29 walks in 537 at-bats. He has a quick bat and tries to hit the ball to the opposite field, especially in clutch situations. "I take what's given me," he says. He likes the ball low and outside, especially fastballs. But with his lack of discipline he chases numerous pitches, especially breaking pitches, that aren't strikes. For that reason his offensive value will always be limited.

BASERUNNING:

Ramirez is not much of a base stealing threat, although he did swipe three of four bases. He bats in the lower part of the order and scored just 46 runs as a lineup regular. Still, he goes first-to-third and second-to-home well, although his speed has diminished somewhat.

FIELDING:

Even playing on carpet, Ramirez makes too many errors. Many of them come on throws, when he unloads the ball off-balance or rushes his throws. At least he's consistent: 1989 was his sixth 30-error campaign and the sixth time he's led National League shortstops in that department. His range in the field is limited, too, although he's excellent on the double play.

OVERALL:

With Ramirez, what you see is what you get. He's 31 now and will always be an undisciplined hitter and a fielder who makes too many errors. Still, Ramirez works well with Doran and can be dangerous with the bat in the clutch, taking the pitch to the opposite field. He's one of the top RBI men among National League shortstops.

RAFAEL RAMIREZ

Position: SS
Bats: R **Throws:** R
Ht: 5'11" **Wt:** 190

Opening Day Age: 31
Born: 2/18/59 in San Pedro de Macoris, Dominican Republic
ML Seasons: 10

Overall Statistics

	G	AB	R	H	D	T	HR	RBI	SB	BB	SO	AVG
1989	151	537	46	132	20	2	6	54	3	29	64	.246
Career	1233	4640	484	1217	189	28	49	414	99	220	511	.262

Where He Hits the Ball

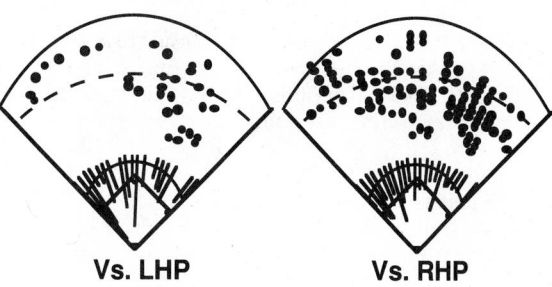

Vs. LHP   **Vs. RHP**

1989 Situational Stats

	AB	H	HR	RBI	AVG		AB	H	HR	RBI	AVG
Home	268	66	3	31	.246	LHP	156	42	2	18	.269
Road	269	66	3	23	.245	RHP	381	90	4	36	.236
Day	179	50	2	22	.279	Sc Pos	145	33	1	43	.228
Night	358	82	4	32	.229	Clutch	98	25	1	15	.255

1989 Rankings (National League)

- ➡ 2nd in errors (30)
- ➡ 4th in worst on-base average vs. righthanded pitchers (.269) - *players with 377 PA vs. RHP*
- ➡ 5th in worst slugging percentage vs. righthanded pitchers (.312)
- ➡ Led the Astros in errors
- ➡ Led NL Shortstops in errors

PITCHING:

Barely a month into his first season with Houston, Rick Rhoden went on the disabled list with an inflammation behind his right shoulder blade. After a lengthy absence, he could not locate a consistent winning touch. He was effective enough at times, but not enough to seize the win. That was a disappointment to the Astros, who surrendered three players to the New York Yankees to land Rhoden. They felt that Rick and Jim Clancy could put them into the thick of the National League West pennant race. Unfortunately, neither was a major contributor.

After his stint on the disabled list, Rhoden struggled to regain the velocity on his fastball in order to challenge the hitters. His control also deserted him. He wound up 2-6 with a 4.28 ERA and not a single complete game in 17 starts. He also yielded 108 hits in 96.2 innings to go with 41 walks. Rhoden's drop in velocity was a major problem after leaving the DL. He doesn't throw as hard as he used to so he has to master his control. He used to pitch inside to hitters as well as anyone in the game, but his time on the DL may have taken away this strength. He may have compensated for this since one manager, San Francisco's Roger Craig, complained that Rhoden scuffed the ball more than Mike Scott. Rhoden is a fierce competitor who knows how to pitch. He's lost a bit of speed, but uses a good slider, curveball, and change-up to advantage when he is on his game.

FIELDING, HITTING, BASERUNNING:

Rhoden is a good athlete and helps himself with the bat and the glove. He did not make an error in the field in his 20 outings. He also holds baserunners well and has an outstanding pickoff move. One of the best hitting pitchers of the modern era, he was a .239 career hitter coming into the '89 season and batted .222 as an Astro despite his lengthy inactivity.

OVERALL:

Rhoden has been a winner wherever he has pitched and that is what attracted the Astros to him. He averaged 13 wins and more than 200 innings a season for seven years prior to joining Houston. If he can regain some of the pop in his fastball, he can win again. But he'll be 37 early in the '90 season, and some early success is critical to him.

RICK RHODEN

Position: SP
Bats: R **Throws:** R
Ht: 6' 4" **Wt:** 203

Opening Day Age: 36
Born: 5/16/53 in Boynton Beach, FL
ML Seasons: 16

Overall Statistics

	W	L	ERA	G	GS	Sv	IP	H	R	BB	SO	HR
1989	2	6	4.28	20	17	0	96.2	108	49	41	41	7
Career	151	125	3.60	413	380	1	2593.1	2606	1143	801	1419	198

Where They Hit the Ball

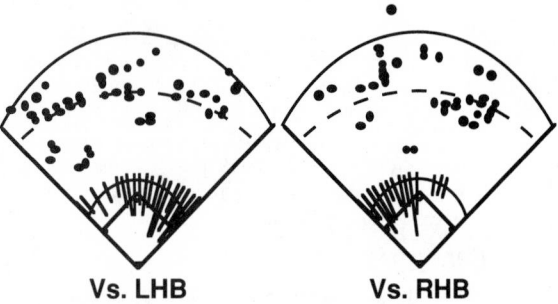

Vs. LHB   **Vs. RHB**

1989 Situational Stats

	W	L	ERA	Sv	IP		AB	H	HR	RBI	AVG
Home	1	6	4.42	0	57.0	LHB	227	61	4	27	.269
Road	1	0	4.08	0	39.2	RHB	147	47	3	18	.320
Day	0	1	4.50	0	20.0	Sc Pos	99	28	2	38	.283
Night	2	5	4.23	0	76.2	Clutch	9	2	0	0	.222

1989 Rankings (National League)

➡ Did not rank near the top or bottom in any category

PITCHING:

They say lefthanded relievers have nine lives, and Dan Schatzeder has certainly proven that. Schatzeder is 35, and has been around long enough to have once been traded for Ron LeFlore. He's pitching for his seventh major league club. But the southpaw is still hanging in there.

Schatzeder was invited to the Astros' spring camp after being granted free agency by the Minnesota Twins. His status depended on making a favorable impression to stay with the big club. But once Schatzeder got his bearings, he began to make strong contributions as a reliever. Before going on the disabled list with tendinitis in his left shoulder, he posted a 4-0 record with a 3.55 ERA. After a lengthy rehabilitation program, he struggled, and finished with a 4-1 mark, a 4.45 ERA and 56.2 innings of toil in 36 games.

"I had him at Detroit," says San Francisco Manager Roger Craig, "and he still throws good for Houston. He's got a young arm and he does a good job, the way they use him." One National League scout concurs, saying, "He's been around quite a bit. If he's used right, he can help a ball club. And Houston is using him right." That is, they pick the right spots for him out of the bullpen. He has a good breaking ball, throws the slider and spots his fastball well. "Usually he has good control," says the scout. "That's what he depends on. Use him an inning or two; don't let him go around the lineup twice. Use him against a couple of lefthanders. He can do the job for you when used this way. Dan's been around quite a bit and he knows how to pitch."

FIELDING, HITTING, BASERUNNING:

Although his opportunities are few now, Schatzeder is one of the best-hitting pitchers in the game. He has the natural stroke of a lefthanded swinger and makes good contact. Even so, he went zero for nine at the plate in 1989. He's a good baserunner. Schatzeder also fields his position well and has a fine move to first.

OVERALL:

Because of his stint on the DL, Schatzeder's final win in '89 came on June 25 at Atlanta. He wasn't effective late in the year, probably because he was still recovering. Still, he proved to the Astros he can contribute out of the bullpen when his health is good. If Houston doesn't want him, some other team will probably give him a chance.

DAN SCHATZEDER

Position: RP
Bats: L **Throws:** L
Ht: 6' 0" **Wt:** 195

Opening Day Age: 35
Born: 12/1/54 in Elmhurst, IL
ML Seasons: 13

Overall Statistics

	W	L	ERA	G	GS	Sv	IP	H	R	BB	SO	HR
1989	4	1	4.45	36	0	1	56.2	64	33	28	46	2
Career	68	65	3.80	445	119	10	1241.1	1180	585	445	705	126

Where They Hit the Ball

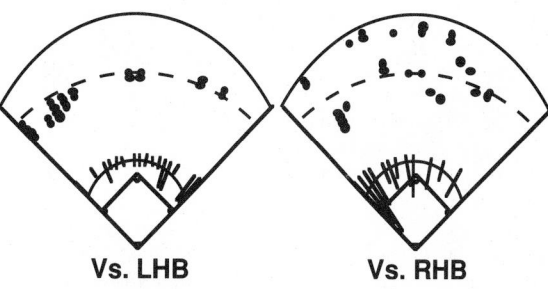

Vs. LHB   **Vs. RHB**

1989 Situational Stats

	W	L	ERA	Sv	IP		AB	H	HR	RBI	AVG
Home	1	1	3.73	0	31.1	LHB	80	23	0	11	.287
Road	3	0	5.33	1	25.1	RHB	143	41	2	23	.287
Day	2	0	5.33	0	25.1	Sc Pos	85	29	1	31	.341
Night	2	1	3.73	1	31.1	Clutch	65	10	0	3	.154

1989 Rankings (National League)

➡ Did not rank near the top or bottom in any category

PITCHING:

With his first 20-win season in '89, Mike Scott has become the consummate pitcher for the Astros. He's always had the arm, but now he is the leader of a starting staff much in need of direction without Nolan Ryan around. Consider his arsenal: a rising fastball in the 92-93 mph range and a sinker, plus one of the best split-finger pitches in the National League. He throws a slider, but doesn't depend on it. The split-finger fastball made Scott what he is today. When he gets ahead of the hitter, he can be overpowering. His strikeout total (172 in 229 innings) speaks for his ability to dominate a game. Scott's strikeouts have dwindled every year since his overpowering 1986 campaign, and he's battled a series of hamstring pulls the past two seasons. Even so, he became only the fourth Astros pitcher to win 20 games in a season. Five of Scott's 20 victories were at the expense of Los Angeles, tying a club record for most wins in a season against one team.

Scott didn't start out like Ryan, the legend he succeeded as the staff ace, with a 100-mph fastball. But he built his base with the split-finger and is now a better pitcher because he doesn't try to overpower every batter in a clutch spot. He always had the sinker and slider, but the rising fastball and split-finger made him one of the league's top three pitchers. Scott had a chance at even bigger numbers this past year. He recorded his 17th win on July 30 and didn't win again until Aug. 30. His season ended at 20-10 with a 3.10 ERA, two victories higher than his 18-win campaigns of 1985 and 1986.

FIELDING, HITTING, BASERUNNING:

Scott banged out the most hits (10) for the most total bases (13) among Astro pitchers. He's pretty slow and is a one-base-at-a-time runner. Scott committed four errors in the field, but is dependable in handling his position. He's never held baserunners well and is very easy to steal on.

OVERALL:

With his low-key approach to the game, Scott doesn't suffer the ups and downs of some pitchers. He has won 101 games since Houston acquired him from the New York Mets in a trade for Danny Heep after the 1982 season. Even at 35, he should make another run at 20 wins this year.

MIKE SCOTT

Position: SP
Bats: R **Throws:** R
Ht: 6' 3" **Wt:** 215

Opening Day Age: 34
Born: 4/26/55 in Santa Monica, CA
ML Seasons: 11

Overall Statistics

	W	L	ERA	G	GS	Sv	IP	H	R	BB	SO	HR
1989	20	10	3.10	33	32	0	229.0	180	87	62	172	23
Career	115	93	3.47	313	285	3	1855.1	1653	796	557	1345	144

Where They Hit the Ball

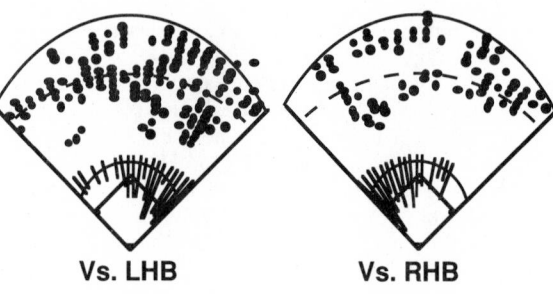

Vs. LHB   **Vs. RHB**

1989 Situational Stats

	W	L	ERA	Sv	IP		AB	H	HR	RBI	AVG
Home	12	6	3.03	0	133.2	LHB	482	119	14	43	.247
Road	8	4	3.21	0	95.1	RHB	366	61	9	36	.167
Day	8	5	3.59	0	85.1	Sc Pos	198	35	2	48	.177
Night	12	5	2.82	0	143.2	Clutch	78	14	1	2	.179

1989 Rankings (National League)

➡ 1st in wins (20), most stolen bases allowed (39) and worst stolen base percentage allowed (95.1%) - *pitchers with 162 IP*

➡ 2nd in lowest on-base average allowed (.267), lowest batting average allowed with runners in scoring position (.177), batting average vs. righthanded batters (.167) and home runs allowed (23)

➡ Led the Astros in wins, innings (229), home runs allowed, strikeouts (172), stolen bases allowed, lowest batting average allowed (.212), lowest on-base average allowed, complete games (9) and lowest opponent batting average with runners in scoring position - *team pitchers with 162 IP*

PITCHING:

If the 1980s mark the most successful years of the Astros franchise, they also celebrate the constancy of Dave Smith, their bullpen ace. He has been Mister Dependable. It's no coincidence the Astros won their first division title in 1980, the year Smith broke onto the scene. That rookie year, he was 7-5 with 10 saves. As he matured into a premier relief specialist, his numbers grew sharply after overcoming back problems. Smith has recorded 20 or more saves in each of the past five years. In 1989, he stashed away saves in 25 of 29 opportunities.

What Smith brings to the ballpark with him each night, usually, is a good curveball, a forkball that runs away from righthanders, and a fastball approaching 90 mph. He has a veteran's cunning and will fool a hitter. Manager Art Howe never wastes Smith's arm, reserving him for prime time when a game is on the line in the late innings. In this scenario, Smith made 52 appearances in 1989. He was the finishing pitcher in 44 of those games, an affirmation of the trust that is placed in him. Smith has yielded just two homers in his past 189.2 regular-season innings. One of those was Eddie Murray's three-run blast in the ninth that enabled Los Angeles to beat him 7-5. Normally, Smith doesn't get his sinker up, as he did in that game to Murray. He has converted 85.5 percent of the save opportunities (136 of 159) given him since 1985.

FIELDING, HITTING, BASERUNNING:

Despite always pitching in tight, game-on-the-line situations, Smith did not make an error all season. He is good at covering first base on balls hit in that direction. He is not very good at holding baserunners. Smith doesn't get to bat much, which is just as well. He struck out in his one official at-bat in 1989; he has only three hits in 10 major league seasons, covering 41 at bats, and only one since 1981.

OVERALL:

A good curveball and forkball make Smith's fastball more effective for the role he plays. He's been known to doctor the ball, if you believe some opponents. He's now 35 and one wonders how long he can hold up under the wear and tear of the many years, but he keeps doing the job.

DAVE SMITH

Position: RP
Bats: R **Throws:** R
Ht: 6' 1" **Wt:** 195

Opening Day Age: 35
Born: 1/21/55 in San Francisco, CA
ML Seasons: 10

Overall Statistics

	W	L	ERA	G	GS	Sv	IP	H	R	BB	SO	HR
1989	3	4	2.64	52	0	25	58.0	49	20	19	31	1
Career	47	41	2.54	514	1	176	702.0	601	236	240	479	24

Where They Hit the Ball

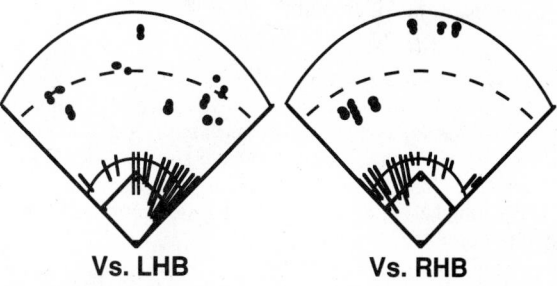

Vs. LHB   Vs. RHB

1989 Situational Stats

	W	L	ERA	Sv	IP		AB	H	HR	RBI	AVG
Home	3	1	3.81	12	28.1	LHB	118	29	1	16	.246
Road	0	3	1.52	13	29.2	RHB	92	20	0	4	.217
Day	1	2	4.86	6	16.2	Sc Pos	58	14	1	18	.241
Night	2	2	1.74	19	41.1	Clutch	157	33	1	15	.210

1989 Rankings (National League)

- ➡ 5th in save percentage (86.2%) - *pitchers with 20 save opportunites*
- ➡ 7th in saves (25)
- ➡ 8th in save opportunites (29)
- ➡ 9th in games finished (44)
- ➡ Led the Astros in saves, blown saves (4), games finished and save percentage

HITTING:

Not until mid-August did Houston complete a trade with Pittsburgh for outfielder Glenn Wilson, a player whom they had sought since the early months of '89. Wilson had little time to make much of an impact with his new team, but the reasons for his acquisition remain the same as the club goes into 1990. Namely, he is a proven RBI-man and a solid right fielder. Those are strong pluses in the Astros' book.

Wilson is not a great home run threat. He hit 15 homers with the '86 Phillies, and he clubbed 11 in '89 -- two with the Astros in 28 games. His forte is driving in runs. Wilson accumulated 15 RBIs with Houston to compile 64 for the year in 128 games. But he had 102 RBIs in 1985 batting behind Mike Schmidt, who drew 100 walks. The Astros hope the same formula works for the No. 5-hitting Wilson in taking some of the pressure off clean-up man Glenn Davis. If pitchers continue to work around Davis in the lineup, Wilson could make them pay a stiff penalty.

Wilson has always been a high fastball hitter who likes the ball away. He doesn't have a lot of discipline, so pitchers try to make him chase fastballs up and out of the strike zone. They also have success with low and away breaking balls; Wilson often tries to pull those pitches, and the result is that he grounds into a lot of double plays.

BASERUNNING:

Wilson has average or slightly below average speed. He stole only one base this past season and was thrown out 5 times, so he is no threat in that area. He is no plodder on the basepaths, however, in advancing as a runner.

FIELDING:

Wilson remains one of the best right fielders in the game. His arm is one of the strongest in the major leagues and he always hustles in the field, getting a good jump on the ball. Wilson doesn't have great range, but knows how to play hitters and he makes the plays.

OVERALL:

The Astros believe they might have caught San Francisco in '89 if they had landed Wilson early in the season. This year they can put that theory to the test. Wilson is not a high-average hitter, but his RBI total is what interests Houston.

GLENN WILSON

Position: RF
Bats: R **Throws:** R
Ht: 6' 1" **Wt:** 190

Opening Day Age: 31
Born: 12/22/58 in Baytown, TX
ML Seasons: 8

Overall Statistics

	G	AB	R	H	D	T	HR	RBI	SB	BB	SO	AVG
1989	128	432	50	115	26	4	11	64	1	37	53	.266
Career	1073	3769	409	1006	195	26	88	466	27	227	599	.267

Where He Hits the Ball

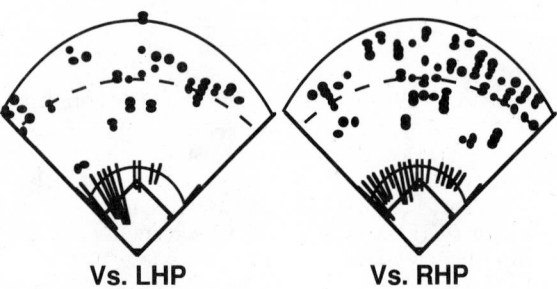

Vs. LHP   Vs. RHP

1989 Situational Stats

	AB	H	HR	RBI	AVG		AB	H	HR	RBI	AVG
Home	198	52	4	31	.263	LHP	143	46	4	25	.322
Road	234	63	7	33	.269	RHP	289	69	7	39	.239
Day	153	39	4	23	.255	Sc Pos	118	37	2	52	.314
Night	279	76	7	41	.272	Clutch	87	28	2	15	.322

1989 Rankings (National League)

➡ 5th in most GDPs per GDP situation (18.0%) - *players with 50 PA in GDP situations*

➡ 6th in batting average with 2 strikes (.270) - *players with 162 PA with 2 strikes*

➡ 7th in batting average vs. lefthanded pitchers (.322) - *players with 125 PA vs. LHP*

➡ 8th in slugging percentage vs. lefthanded pitchers (.517) and hitting in the clutch (.322) - *players with 50 PA in the clutch*

➡ Led NL Right Fielders in hitting in the clutch, hitting with runners in scoring position (.314), hitting vs. lefthanded pitchers, hitting with 2 strikes and percentage of extra bases taken as a runner (53.2%) - *right fielders with 40 opportunites to advance*

HITTING:

Some baseball people are still trying to make up their mind about Gerald Young. They love his speed, those flying feet zipping over the bases and flashing over ground in the outfield. Yet, after all the promise of his rookie year, Young suffered a serious decline at the plate in '89. From a .321 average in 71 games in '87, and 65 stolen bases in '88, he dropped to these numbers in '89: .233, 34 stolen bases, 25 times caught stealing.

"I don't know what to think about Gerald," admits one National League scout. "When I first saw him, I thought he was going to be one of the standout players in the league. He hit the ball good. Now, he's taking pitches like he's undecided whether to swing, take the pitch or what to do." Young needs to become more aggressive at the plate, even if it means striking out more. He also needs to stop uppercutting the ball so much, and instead hit down to get the ground ball and use his speed. Young has all a team looks for in a leadoff batter when he performs as he did the first year. But after the way he struggled in 1989, it's going to take some work for him to return to that form.

BASERUNNING:

Young's stolen base haul went down noticeably, partly because of leg and knee ailments. He had 33 stolen bases on July 17 and he managed just one more in 10 attempts thereafter. Although his stolen base total was half of the previous year, his runs (71) and walks (74) remained steady.

FIELDING:

Young turns the wrong way on line drives sometimes, and he occasionally gets a slow jump on the ball, but his speed compensates for these shortcomings. He runs in on the ball well and rates at the top of the class in running down drives into the gaps. He had a club-record for a centerfielder with 15 assists.

OVERALL:

When he puts the whole package together, Young is impressive. He was rushed to the big leagues and is still learning his profession as a centerfielder. Given time, Young can measure up to the high prospects baseball scouts envisioned for him after his rookie year.

GERALD YOUNG

Position: CF
Bats: B **Throws:** R
Ht: 6' 2" **Wt:** 185

Opening Day Age: 25
Born: 10/22/64 in Tele, Honduras
ML Seasons: 3

Overall Statistics

	G	AB	R	H	D	T	HR	RBI	SB	BB	SO	AVG
1989	146	533	71	124	17	3	0	38	34	74	60	.233
Career	366	1383	194	360	47	14	1	90	125	166	153	.260

Where He Hits the Ball

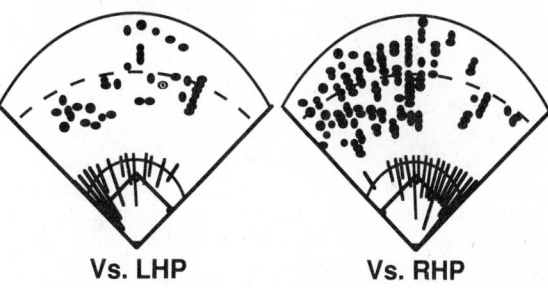

Vs. LHP   **Vs. RHP**

1989 Situational Stats

	AB	H	HR	RBI	AVG		AB	H	HR	RBI	AVG
Home	267	66	0	19	.247	LHP	147	35	0	11	.238
Road	266	58	0	19	.218	RHP	386	89	0	27	.231
Day	167	43	0	16	.257	Sc Pos	107	31	0	38	.290
Night	366	81	0	22	.221	Clutch	97	21	0	6	.216

1989 Rankings (National League)

→ 1st in caught stealing (25), worst slugging percentage (.276) and worst stolen base percentage (57.6%) - *players with 20 stolen base attempts*

→ 4th in highest percentage of pitches taken (62.9%) and lowest percentage of swings that missed (8.4%) - *players with 502 PA*

→ Led the Astros in caught stealing, stolen bases (34), walks (74), grounder/flyball ratio (1.45), lowest percentage of swings that missed, highest percentage of swings put into play (55.3%), pitches seen per plate appearance (3.5) and steals of third (7)

→ Led NL Center Fielders in caught stealing and walks

MARK DAVIDSON

Position: RF
Bats: R **Throws:** R
Ht: 6' 2" **Wt:** 190

Opening Day Age: 29
Born: 2/15/61 in Knoxville, TN
ML Seasons: 4

Overall Statistics

	G	AB	R	H	D	T	HR	RBI	SB	BB	SO	AVG
1989	33	65	7	13	2	1	1	5	1	7	14	.200
Career	271	389	66	84	16	2	3	31	15	36	82	.216

HITTING, FIELDING, BASERUNNING:

Mark Davidson's status is that of a role player -- a reserve outfielder and pinch hitter -- and there is no likelihood of change in 1990. With a surplus of outfielders, Davidson must create a spot for himself with his bat and his defensive play. He is an exceptional outfielder with a strong arm, and he has good range in the field. He played errorless ball in 33 games and had his moments with the bat. Davidson hit his first National League homer off Philadelphia's Dennis Cook. He unloaded two homers in 324 at-bats, during a three year reserve roll with the Twins. Davidson hammered 25 homers one year in the minors and hits the fastball well, but he has to cut down on his swing a bit to handle pinch hit duties.

OVERALL:

Davidson made a good impression on the Astros with his sharp glove work. But his hitting needs some polish. He whiffed 14 times in 65 at bats and needs to make better contact. Nonetheless Davidson has a good shot at being the righthanded hitter off the bench.

GREG GROSS

Position: RF
Bats: L **Throws:** L
Ht: 5'11" **Wt:** 180

Opening Day Age: 37
Born: 8/1/52 in York, PA
ML Seasons: 17

Overall Statistics

	G	AB	R	H	D	T	HR	RBI	SB	BB	SO	AVG
1989	60	75	2	15	0	0	0	4	0	11	6	.200
Career	1809	3745	449	1073	130	46	7	308	39	523	250	.287

HITTING, FIELDING, BASERUNNING:

Greg Gross would like to squeeze out one more year to make a final stab at Manny Mota's record for pinch hits. Mota finished his career with 150, Smokey Burgess is next with 145 and Gross is at 143 after a season in which he went seven for 38 as a pinch hitter. That was the most pinch hits for an Astro, yet his batting average leveled out at .200 for 60 games. Gross made a few starts at first base and played some in the outfield, but his value is almost entirely in his bat these days. Gross struck out only six times in 75 at bats so he remains a good contact hitter. He has always had a strong arm in the outfield, but his speed is gone and his playing time out there will be limited.

OVERALL:

Gross' niche now is strictly as a pinch hitter. He is getting near the end of the line and has no power at the plate. All of his 15 hits in '89 were singles. But he knows how to hit, to put the bat on the ball, and he found the holes often enough this past year to make one final run at Mota's mark in 1990.

LOUIE MEADOWS

Position: LF
Bats: L **Throws:** L
Ht: 5'11" **Wt:** 190

Opening Day Age: 28
Born: 4/29/61 in
Onslow County, NC
ML Seasons: 3

Overall Statistics

	G	AB	R	H	D	T	HR	RBI	SB	BB	SO	AVG
1989	31	51	5	9	0	0	3	10	1	1	14	.176
Career	72	99	11	19	0	1	5	13	6	7	22	.192

HITTING, FIELDING, BASERUNNING:

Louie Meadows has yo-yoed his way between the major leagues and Triple-A ball. He always seems to be on the bubble, so to speak, and becomes the odd man out. Meadows thought he had made the Houston club in spring training, but he found himself back at Tucson, Arizona. With the Astros, he has been a spot starter and pinch hitter. He has a bit of power, showing five big league homers. This past season, he hit only .176 with three homers and 10 RBI in 31 games. He has fared better as a starter, going two for 20 as a pinch hitter. Meadows has good speed and is strong, but he takes a long stroke at the plate and must make better contact. He has strength and speed, but needs to refine his batting stroke.

OVERALL:

Meadows' future with the Astros probably depends on his ability to shorten his swing. Since he is not projected as a starter, he needs to be able to make contact in a pinch-hit role. The big swing works against this need. He was not recalled in September and plans called for him to play winter ball, to work on a shorter cut at the plate.

ALEX TREVINO

Position: C
Bats: R **Throws:** R
Ht: 5'11" **Wt:** 179

Opening Day Age: 32
Born: 8/26/57 in
Monterrey, Mexico
ML Seasons: 12

Overall Statistics

	G	AB	R	H	D	T	HR	RBI	SB	BB	SO	AVG
1989	59	131	15	38	7	1	2	16	0	7	18	.290
Career	881	2344	242	585	112	10	22	231	19	198	306	.250

HITTING, FIELDING, BASERUNNING:

After two seasons as the backup catcher, Alex Trevino knows his role with Houston. He does a good job of supporting regular Craig Biggio and occasionally pinch-hitting. He batted .290 with two home runs and 16 RBI, but Trevino managed only a one for 21 as a pinch swinger. He played in 59 games this past season. He had his good streaks, going 12 for 16 with five RBI in one period of four starts. The last time he has appeared in over 100 games in a season was with Cincinnati in 1982. Trevino has played with every National League West team except San Diego in the years after his 1978 debut with the New York Mets. For a catcher, he runs pretty well. His catching skills are about average, but he doesn't have a particularly strong throwing arm.

OVERALL:

Trevino knows his job and doesn't complain, although he feels he needs more playing time to be effective. Hang a breaking ball in front of him and he has enough power to hit it out. Says one National League scout: "He can receive, he calls a good game, but his arm now, to me, is just adequate. He's got to have a break to throw somebody out."

ERIC YELDING

Position: SS
Bats: R **Throws:** R
Ht: 6' 1" **Wt:** 170

Opening Day Age: 25
Born: 2/22/65 in
Montrose, AL
ML Seasons: 1

Overall Statistics

	G	AB	R	H	D	T	HR	RBI	SB	BB	SO	AVG
1989	70	90	19	21	2	0	0	9	11	7	19	.233
Career	70	90	19	21	2	0	0	9	11	7	19	.233

HITTING, FIELDING, BASERUNNING:

After a year of exposure to the major leagues, short-stop Eric Yelding is in a position to make his bid for the lineup. Rafael Ramirez has put in two years as the Astros' regular, but his defensive play leaves something to be desired. So Yelding spent the off-season gaining playing experience in winter ball, preparing for the challenge. With his speed (4.3 in the 40-yard dash), the potential is there for Yelding to steal 60 to 70 bases a year. The only question is his hitting. He batted .233 gaining 90 at-bats in bits and pieces of 70 games. Yelding had two doubles among 21 hits, but the teasing statistic is this one: 11 steals in 16 attempts. In 1987, he pilfered 83 bases in the minors.

OVERALL:

With his quickness, shortstop is Yelding's best position and he prefers it over second base. Yelding can make the throw from the hole at short and is gaining confidence in his play around the bag. As a batter, he needs to make more contact and to hit breaking pitches better. All the other skills are there.

PITCHING:

Tim Belcher has always been somewhat temperamental and volatile. Last year he was more volatile than ever. He was also plenty good, winning 15 games, posting a 2.82 ERA, throwing a league-leading eight shutouts and striking out 200 batters -- missing the league title by one -- in 230 innings. The righthanded Belcher, at 28, has the potential to lead the league in virtually every category and win the Cy Young Award.

Belcher has only two pitches -- a 95 mph fastball and a hard slider -- and he gets in trouble at times with that limited repertoire. He's working on a change up and curve, and has used both pitches at one time or another. His fastball is outstanding because of the way it explodes. Batters cannot adjust to it for a few at bats. His smooth and fluid windup makes it appear that he's not throwing as hard as he really is. Because of that, he often blows hitters away. Belcher averaged 7.8 strikeouts per nine innings last year. Belcher's only problem last year was giving up homers; he permitted 20, after yielding only eight in 1988.

What's amazing is that before the Dodgers obtained him in a deal from the A's, Belcher was languishing in Oakland's farm system, walking batters left and right. A former No. 1 draft pick, Belcher led the Pacific Coast League with 133 walks in 163 innings in 1987. After coming over to the Dodgers in a trade that sent Rick Honeycutt to the A's, Belcher suddenly began fanning people, not walking them. The A's have been happy with Honeycutt, but they must be scratching their heads about Belcher, who taught Oakland some respect when he beat them in the World Series.

FIELDING, HITTING, BASERUNNING:

Belcher moves well for a big man and is a decent fielder. He has a slow delivery to the plate, but is improving at holding runners. He's not too bad of a hitter -- he had six RBIs on his seven hits last season.

OVERALL:

Belcher became extremely volatile this past season, especially when he was briefly moved to the bullpen in midseason. He sometimes exploded at his teammates. Once, after being lifted in the sixth inning of a game in Philadelphia, trailing 1-0, Belcher was heard yelling in the runway, "Don't be afraid to score some runs, guys." He'll need to harness that temper. But Belcher's a great talent, and should continue to be a steady winner.

TIM BELCHER

Position: SP/RP
Bats: R **Throws:** R
Ht: 6' 3" **Wt:** 210

Opening Day Age: 28
Born: 10/19/61 in Mount Gilead, OH
ML Seasons: 3

Overall Statistics

	W	L	ERA	G	GS	Sv	IP	H	R	BB	SO	HR
1989	15	12	2.82	39	30	1	230.0	182	81	80	200	20
Career	31	20	2.82	81	62	5	443.2	355	157	138	375	30

Where They Hit the Ball

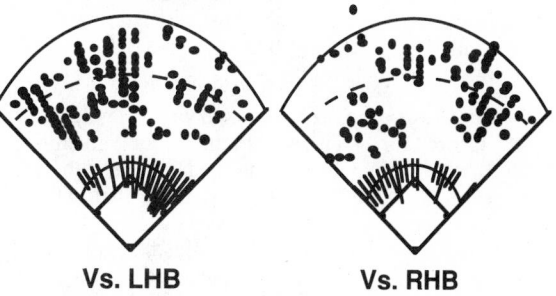

Vs. LHB   Vs. RHB

1989 Situational Stats

	W	L	ERA	Sv	IP		AB	H	HR	RBI	AVG
Home	10	4	2.10	0	124.1	LHB	475	105	7	36	.221
Road	5	8	3.66	1	105.2	RHB	363	77	13	34	.212
Day	3	5	3.68	1	73.1	Sc Pos	181	34	4	50	.188
Night	12	7	2.41	0	156.2	Clutch	128	25	2	9	.195

1989 Rankings (National League)

➡ 1st in shutouts (8) and complete games (10)

➡ 2nd in strikeouts (200) and pitches thrown (3,636)

➡ 3rd in strikeouts per 9 innings (7.8) and hit batsmen (7) - *pitchers with 162 IP*

➡ Led the Dodgers in shutouts, complete games, hit batsmen, wins (15), home runs allowed, strikeouts, pitches thrown, stolen bases allowed (22), win/loss percentage (.556), lowest batting average allowed (.217), lowest on-base average allowed (.289) and strikeouts per 9 innings - *team pitchers with 162 IP*

PITCHING:

After three seasons, Tim Crews has established himself as one of the best middle relievers in the big leagues. Like most middle relievers, he's underrated and anonymous. But if not for Crews, who is armed with a good fastball, curve, change-up and good control, the Dodgers might not have made it to the playoffs in 1988. Yet Crews was left off the playoff roster because management, feeling it needed another left-hander in the bullpen, chose to give a roster spot to Rick Horton.

Crews was infuriated, but he pushed past the emotional pain and had another good season in 1989. He posted a 3.21 ERA, struck out 56 batters in 61 2/3 innings and walked just 23, nine of those intentionally. He did this while continuing a curious inability to pitch well in his home park. In the last two years Crews has had road ERAs of 0.98 and 2.56; in Dodger Stadium, usually one of the best pitchers' parks in baseball, his figures have been 4.50 and 3.90.

Though he's entering only his third full major league season, Crews is no fuzzy-cheeked youngster. He's 29 and labored for seven years in the minors, mostly in the Brewer system; he came to the Dodgers with Tim Leary in the Greg Brock deal. With all that experience, it's no surprise that Crews is a smart pitcher equipped with a good arm, decent fastball and tough breaking pitch. He throws strikes and doesn't fall behind hitters often. If he does, he has the ability to get the hitter out using finesse and some power. He knows what he's doing on the mound.

FIELDING, HITTING, BASERUNNING:

Crews is a good fielder. He is quick off the mound and does not rush his throws. He has only a fair move to first and was one of the easier Dodger pitchers to steal on last year. Crews has been to bat only seven times in his major league career, with one hit.

OVERALL:

Crews started for his first six professional seasons, while in Milwaukee's chain. He has worked out of the bullpen since coming over to the Dodgers after the 1986 season. Crews doesn't throw hard enough to be a stopper and isn't durable enough to start. He's best suited for middle relief, and it's what he enjoys. He's a good man to have on your club.

TIM CREWS

Position: RP
Bats: R **Throws:** R
Ht: 6' 0" **Wt:** 190

Opening Day Age: 29
Born: 4/3/61 in Tampa, FL
ML Seasons: 3

Overall Statistics

	W	L	ERA	G	GS	Sv	IP	H	R	BB	SO	HR
1989	0	1	3.21	44	0	1	61.2	69	27	23	56	7
Career	5	2	3.05	106	0	4	162.1	176	65	47	121	12

Where They Hit the Ball

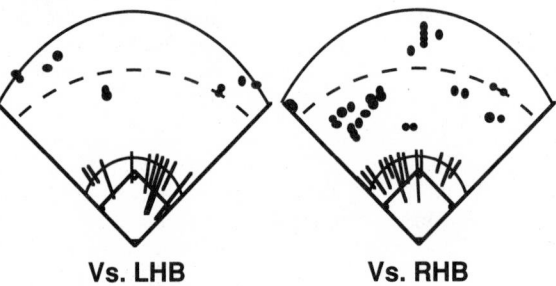

Vs. LHB   **Vs. RHB**

1989 Situational Stats

	W	L	ERA	Sv	IP		AB	H	HR	RBI	AVG
Home	0	0	3.90	0	30.0	LHB	110	27	2	17	.245
Road	0	1	2.56	1	31.2	RHB	133	42	5	23	.316
Day	0	1	0.86	1	21.0	Sc Pos	68	22	3	33	.324
Night	0	0	4.43	0	40.2	Clutch	45	14	0	5	.311

1989 Rankings (National League)

- ➡ 1st in highest percentage of inherited runners scoring (54.8%) - *pitchers with 30 inherited runners*
- ➡ 1st in least GDPs induced per GDP situation (2.6%) - *pitchers with 30 GDP situations*

HITTING:

Though he didn't show it in 1989, Kal Daniels is an exceptional batter who hits for average and power. He has the ability to spray hits to all fields. Within a span of two seasons (1986-87), he belted 44 homers in 248 games, basically a season and a half. His career average stood at .311 entering his fourth season, testament to how good this player is. He was the National League's on-base percentage leader in 1988.

The lefthanded hitting Daniels, traded from Cincinnati to Los Angeles midway through the season, is a low ball hitter who is patient and equipped with a sharp eye for the strike zone. Pitchers tend to throw him a lot of breaking pitches and move the ball around in an attempt to keep him off balance. But when they get into a hole, Daniels can hurt them. Daniels, a short-stroke line-drive hitter, suffered through an injury-plagued 1989 season, but he is so talented that even with bad knees, he was hitting .342 in 38 Dodger at bats when he underwent surgery. Overall, he batted .246 with four homers and 17 RBIs in 55 games. All those figures were career lows by a good margin.

Daniels has a problem hitting lefthanded pitching. That's one of the reasons the Reds dealt him away. Whether it's psychological or the fact he hasn't been given a chance to see enough lefties, it's hard to say. But Daniels hit .480 (12 for 25) against righties, .077 (one for 13) against lefties when he was with the Dodgers.

BASERUNNING:

Five knee operations during the last two seasons have taken their toll on Daniels. But Daniels has good speed, despite his leg problems, and has the ability to steal bases. He also has the smarts to take the extra base. He has swiped 26 bases before and there's been talk that he could be a 30-30 man.

FIELDING:

Daniels is a complete liability in the outfield because of his gimpy knees, a weak throwing arm and a reputation for not hustling. Playing next to Gibson for an extended period of time might convince Daniels to play more aggressively.

OVERALL:

If Daniels stays healthy (which he hasn't been able to do in his four big league seasons), sheds his moody attitude and plays with a little more intensity, he could become one of the best players in baseball. He's a potential batting champ.

KAL DANIELS

Position: LF
Bats: L **Throws:** R
Ht: 5'11" **Wt:** 195

Opening Day Age: 26
Born: 8/20/63 in Vienna, GA
ML Seasons: 4

Overall Statistics

	G	AB	R	H	D	T	HR	RBI	SB	BB	SO	AVG
1989	55	171	33	42	13	0	4	17	9	43	33	.246
Career	377	1215	235	367	76	6	54	168	77	212	219	.302

Where He Hits the Ball

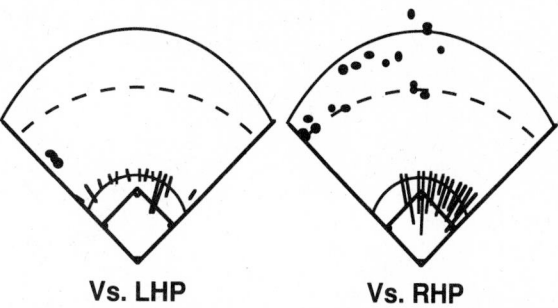

Vs. LHP   **Vs. RHP**

1989 Situational Stats

	AB	H	HR	RBI	AVG		AB	H	HR	RBI	AVG
Home	69	17	2	5	.246	LHP	57	11	1	5	.193
Road	102	25	2	12	.245	RHP	114	31	3	12	.272
Day	56	10	2	7	.179	Sc Pos	33	8	1	13	.242
Night	115	32	2	10	.278	Clutch	29	6	0	4	.207

1989 Rankings (National League)

➡ Did not rank near the top or bottom in any category

HITTING:

After winning the MVP award and starring in one of the most dramatic moments in World Series history in 1988, Kirk Gibson had a most frustrating season in 1989. Plagued by knee problems that eventually required surgery, Gibson could play in only 71 games, batting a career-low .213. Always the blood-and-guts type, Gibson attempted to play through the pain, but eventually had to go to the sidelines.

When healthy -- and sometimes when he can barely walk -- Gibson can hit for average and with power to all fields. He's particularly good at hitting low pitches, whether they're fastballs or breaking balls. Sliders down and in give him trouble, especially when he's down in the count. Fastballs up and in also give Gibson trouble. The game-winning homer he hit off Dennis Eckersley in Game One of the '88 World Series was off a 3-2 slider -- but that one was down and away, a pitch he can handle much more easily.

Gibson is a patient hitter, especially in situations when his club is trailing in crunch time. He's smart enough to know the importance of getting a good pitch to hit. But he can be overly aggressive at times, especially when he's going through a cold streak. One of the knocks against Gibson has always been that he couldn't hit lefthanders well. But he refuted the theory in 1988, hitting .294 with 11 homers off southpaws. He didn't have much of a chance to face righties, let alone lefties, in 1989.

BASERUNNING:

Aggressive is a mild description of Gibson's baserunning. He's like a runaway train. He's an exceptional base stealer with a terrific stolen base ratio and will take the extra base at every opportunity. He swiped 31 bases in 35 attempts during the '88 season and stole 12 in 15 attempts during his injury-riddled season last year.

FIELDING:

Though he can get to nearly every ball because of his speed, Gibson cannot throw well. His shoulder is weak because of football injuries. Everybody is given the green light to run on Gibson.

OVERALL:

Intense, fiery and temperamental, Gibson showed what an impact player he is when he transformed the Dodgers from fourth-place chumps to World Champs. He is a show stopper, a fan's delight. Players and managers say they'd pay to watch the electrifying Gibson play. His biggest problem is staying healthy. That's the reason Gibson is talking about retiring. The Kirk Gibson Show might be airing just one or two more seasons.

KIRK GIBSON

Position: LF/CF
Bats: L **Throws:** L
Ht: 6' 3" **Wt:** 215

Opening Day Age: 32
Born: 5/28/57 in Pontiac, MI
ML Seasons: 11

Overall Statistics

	G	AB	R	H	D	T	HR	RBI	SB	BB	SO	AVG
1989	71	253	35	54	8	2	9	28	12	35	55	.213
Career	1114	4005	669	1096	176	38	184	603	209	488	888	.274

Where He Hits the Ball

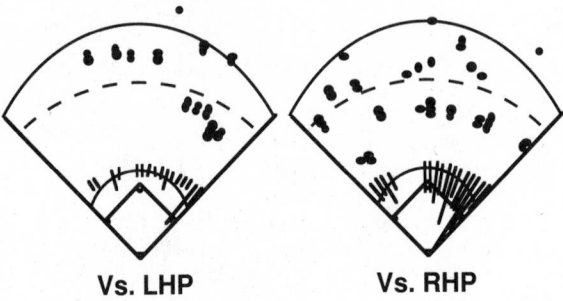

Vs. LHP   **Vs. RHP**

1989 Situational Stats

	AB	H	HR	RBI	AVG		AB	H	HR	RBI	AVG
Home	135	30	4	10	.222	LHP	95	12	4	10	.126
Road	118	24	5	18	.203	RHP	158	42	5	18	.266
Day	76	15	1	6	.197	Sc Pos	55	10	0	13	.182
Night	177	39	8	22	.220	Clutch	49	8	1	6	.163

1989 Rankings (National League)

➡ Led the Dodgers in stolen bases (12) and triples (2)

HITTING:

For four seasons, from 1985 through 1988, Jose Gonzalez had been shuffled back and forth from the minors to the majors. He had never really been given the chance to show what he could do on the big league level for an extended period of time -- until last season. When John Shelby played himself out of the lineup with his .156 average, the Dodgers finally turned to Gonzalez, who did well for awhile, hitting over .300. But it wasn't good enough for the Dodgers. They went out and acquired Kal Daniels to play left field and moved Kirk Gibson to centerfield. So much for Gonzalez's shot. He was a bit player after that and his average skidded to .268.

The righthanded hitting Gonzalez, who has been in the Dodgers' system nine years and is only 25, is a line-drive hitter who has occasional power (five homers in 405 career at-bats). He likes the fastball out over the plate and can hit it a long way on occasion. But breaking balls give him trouble and he struck out a lot. He is not too disciplined and uses only three-quarters of the field. He still has trouble taking the outside pitch to right field.

Given the chance to play full-time, Gonzalez might just surprise a few people in the Dodger organization. Jerked up and down the way he's been, it hasn't been easy for him to show what he can do. He's continually shuttled between Los Angeles and Albuquerque and was called up four different times in 1988. Last season was the first time he saw extended action.

BASERUNNING:

Forty-four stolen bases at AAA Albuquerque tells you all you need to know about Jose's baserunning. He is not as aggressive as he could be, but that stems from being afraid to make a mistake.

FIELDING:

A good defensive outfielder, Gonzalez can cover a lot of ground in centerfield. He has a good arm, and the Dodgers have used him a lot as a defensive replacement.

OVERALL:

Like Franklin Stubbs, probably the best thing for Gonzalez would be to get out of the Dodgers' organization. He would like a trade, but the Dodgers simply seem to want to hold onto him for insurance purposes. With an injury-prone outfield of Daniels, Gibson and Mike Marshall, it's not a bad idea. But, given an opportunity, Gonzalez would probably do a nice job for some other club.

JOSE GONZALEZ

Position: CF/RF
Bats: R **Throws:** R
Ht: 6' 2" **Wt:** 196

Opening Day Age: 25
Born: 11/23/64 in Puerto Plata, Dominican Republic
ML Seasons: 5

Overall Statistics

	G	AB	R	H	D	T	HR	RBI	SB	BB	SO	AVG
1989	95	261	31	70	11	2	3	18	9	23	53	.268
Career	230	405	61	98	21	3	5	25	22	34	97	.242

Where He Hits the Ball

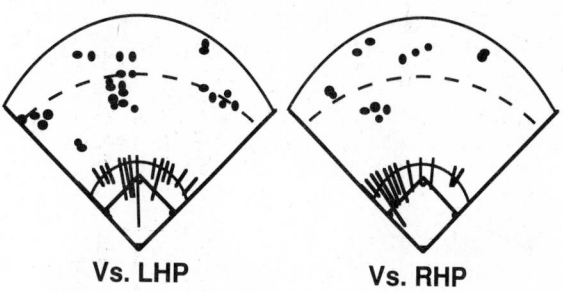

Vs. LHP　　　**Vs. RHP**

1989 Situational Stats

	AB	H	HR	RBI	AVG		AB	H	HR	RBI	AVG
Home	113	27	2	10	.239	LHP	134	41	2	10	.306
Road	148	43	1	8	.291	RHP	127	29	1	8	.228
Day	98	28	2	7	.286	Sc Pos	58	12	0	14	.207
Night	163	42	1	11	.258	Clutch	53	17	0	2	.321

1989 Rankings (National League)

→ 7th in percentage of extra bases taken as a runner (60.9%) - *players with 40 opportunities to advance*

→ 9th in hitting in the clutch (.321) - *players with 50 PA in the clutch*

→ Led the Dodgers in percentage of extra bases taken as a runner, hitting in the clutch and triples (2)

→ Led NL Center Fielders in hitting vs. left-handed pitchers - *center fielders with 125 PA vs. LHP*

HITTING:

Alfredo Griffin suffered through his worst offensive season (.199) during the Dodgers' World Championship season of 1988. But the switch-hitting shortstop rebounded in 1989 by hitting .247. Obviously, offense has never been Griffin's forte. The problem is that he's not a patient hitter. He's a bona fide bad-ball hitter without power or ability to hit for average. Griffin will swing at just about anything, whether the pitch is parallel with the tip of his helmet or brushing the dirt. The guy is a hacker, a slasher. He doesn't waste a pitcher's time. He's up there to swing, not to look. Griffin once went through an entire season walking only four times.

That tendency might be forgiven if Griffin was doing some sort of damage with his swings. But he's seldom hit for average and his power consists of occasional doubles. Griffin's had a couple of decent years with the bat, hitting in the .280s. But those moments have been rare -- the .280s are a better description of Griffin's career on-base percentage (.288).

At least Griffin makes contact, fanning an average of only 46 times a season during his 11-year career. He has no power, but has proven to be a tough out in clutch situations. He can also bunt for a hit on occasion.

BASERUNNING:

As a runner, Griffin is aggressive, but not too bright running the bases. There's nothing wrong with taking a risk, but don't forget the score or the inning. Sometimes Griffin does. Once a major base stealing threat, Griffin's only swiped 17 in two years for the Dodgers. But he can steal you a base when you need one.

FIELDING:

Superb ... steady ... reliable. Those are the terms baseball people use to describe Griffin's defense. Though he may make more errors than most shortstops, Griffin gets to more balls than most shortstops. Most of his errors are the result of throws. He has excellent range, both to his right and left.

OVERALL:

After Griffin batted .199 in 1988, he was one of the first players the Dodgers re-signed in the off-season. Griffin stabilized what was one of the league's worst infields, and management considered him as important to the title club as Kirk Gibson. Griffin is a student of the game and is considered future managerial material by some. He's a tremendous leader, albeit a quiet one. He has a strong influence on younger players.

ALFREDO GRIFFIN

Position: SS
Bats: B **Throws:** R
Ht: 5'11" **Wt:** 165

Opening Day Age: 33
Born: 3/6/57 in Santo Domingo, Dominican Republic
ML Seasons: 14

Overall Statistics

	G	AB	R	H	D	T	HR	RBI	SB	BB	SO	AVG
1989	136	506	49	125	27	2	0	29	10	29	57	.247
Career	1603	5724	658	1451	218	73	23	452	178	275	518	.253

Where He Hits the Ball

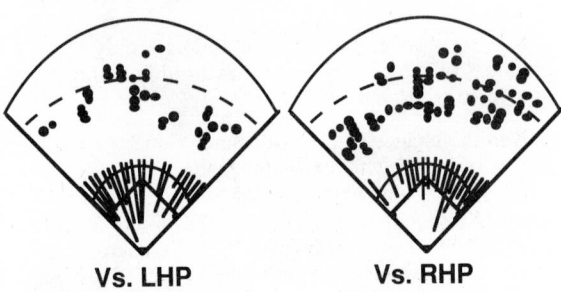

Vs. LHP   Vs. RHP

1989 Situational Stats

	AB	H	HR	RBI	AVG		AB	H	HR	RBI	AVG
Home	250	63	0	8	.252	LHP	177	50	0	10	.282
Road	256	62	0	21	.242	RHP	329	75	0	19	.228
Day	161	38	0	11	.236	Sc Pos	107	26	0	29	.243
Night	345	87	0	18	.252	Clutch	104	23	0	4	.221

1989 Rankings (National League)

→ 3rd in worst batting average with 2 strikes (.109) - *players with 162 PA with 2 strikes*

→ 4th in worst slugging percentage (.308) - *players with 502 PA*

→ 5th in bunts in play (29)

→ 6th in sacrifice bunts (11)

→ 8th in lowest percentage of pitches taken (48.5%)

→ Led the Dodgers in sacrifice bunts, grounder/flyball ratio (1.72), triples (2), caught stealing (7), bunts in play, runs scored per time reached base (27.7%) and steals of third (4) - *team players with 502 PA*

HITTING:

Jeff Hamilton drives the Dodgers' management and coaching staff batty with his inability to hit consistently. His lack of fire and intensity also drives them crazy. What's strange about Hamilton is that he was an exceptional hitter in the minors, compiling averages of .335, .332 and .360. But he simply has not been able to adjust to major-league pitching. He did have his best season, statistically, in 1989: .245, 12 homers, 56 RBIs, 35 doubles -- all career highs. But considering the buildup he's gotten, the Dodgers can't help being disappointed.

The shy and quiet Hamilton, still only 26, likes the ball down, which is rare for a righthanded hitter. So pitchers throw him inside fastballs and then breaking pitches down and away. Hamilton chases a lot of those bad pitches. But he's developed an ability to fight off inside pitches and go more to right field. That was one of the keys to his improvement in 1989.

Hamilton showed a little more patience at the plate this past season (20 walks) than in 1988, when he walked 10 times in 309 at bats. Still, 20 walks in 548 at-bats is too low for someone who doesn't hit for a high average or for power. Once very easy to fan, Hamilton doesn't really strike out that much any more (71 times). But he needs to be more selective.

BASERUNNING:

At 214 pounds, Hamilton has no speed whatsoever. After four seasons, he's yet to steal a base in the majors. He's a very conservative baserunner, but at least he knows his limitations.

FIELDING:

Defense is Hamilton's strength. Though unheralded, he is among the best in the league at third base. His range is only average, but he has excellent instincts, soft hands and a good arm.

OVERALL:

Don't look for Hamilton to be the Dodgers' third baseman for much longer -- unless he blossoms late and has a sterling 1990 season. He did do a decent job during the Dodgers' title season, but he simply has not been consistent enough to suit management. Defense has kept Hamilton in the major leagues. He might be given just one more chance to hit big league pitching. If he doesn't, he'll probably be relegated to the bench -- or packaged in a multi-player deal.

JEFF HAMILTON

Position: 3B
Bats: R **Throws:** R
Ht: 6' 3" **Wt:** 214

Opening Day Age: 26
Born: 3/19/64 in Flint, MI
ML Seasons: 4

Overall Statistics

	G	AB	R	H	D	T	HR	RBI	SB	BB	SO	AVG
1989	151	548	45	134	35	1	12	56	0	20	71	.245
Career	368	1087	106	258	57	3	23	109	0	39	187	.237

Where He Hits the Ball

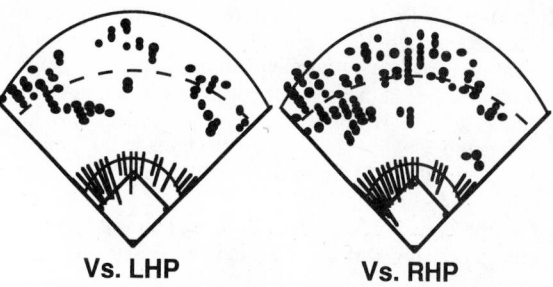

Vs. LHP   Vs. RHP

1989 Situational Stats

	AB	H	HR	RBI	AVG		AB	H	HR	RBI	AVG
Home	263	61	8	28	.232	LHP	210	44	2	16	.210
Road	285	73	4	28	.256	RHP	338	90	10	40	.266
Day	170	43	3	23	.253	Sc Pos	124	26	1	40	.210
Night	378	91	9	33	.241	Clutch	115	29	0	7	.252

1989 Rankings (National League)

➡ 2nd in lowest on-base percentage (.272), lowest percentage of pitches taken (44.4%) and least pitches seen per plate appearance (3.0) - *players with 502 PA*

➡ 5th in hitting with the bases loaded (.500) - *players with 10 PA with the bases loaded*

➡ 6th in doubles (35)

➡ Led the Dodgers in doubles, hitting with the bases loaded and errors (19)

➡ Led NL Third Basemen in hit by pitch (3), hitting with the bases loaded and highest percentage of swings put into play (47.7%)

HITTING:

There's something about Lenny Harris that's intriguing. He appears to have the ability, the talent, and the makeup to be a successful offensive player. Entering only his second full season, Harris, who bats lefthanded, is a line drive hitter with a little power (three homers). He has the potential to hit more, having belted as many as 10 during his minor league career. Mostly he's a gap hitter who legs out an occasional double or triple. From a compact swing, Harris sprays hits to all fields. He isn't terribly selective; he goes after too many bad pitches and doesn't draw a lot of walks. But he's a good contact man and doesn't strike out much. He had a lot of trouble with lefthanded pitching in his first major league shot last year.

Harris excelled as a pinch hitter last year. He was eight for 20 overall (.400) and six for 15 with three RBIs with the Dodgers. Harris, acquired with Kal Daniels for Tim Leary and Mariano Duncan, took the National League by storm when he was recalled at the end of the 1988 season. He hit .372 with eight RBIs in 16 games. He didn't follow that up the way he expected. He hit .252 with the Dodgers in 54 games, .236 overall. Judging from his minor league record, Harris appears unlikely to develop into a .300 hitter. But he has some offensive skills and showed decent run-producing ability for a middle infielder.

BASERUNNING:

If he ever plays regularly, Harris could steal 30-40 bases. He's already done it -- in the minors. Harris' problem right now is that he gets caught stealing a little too much (nine times in 23 attempts). With experience, Harris will become smarter and more aggressive. He'll also know the pitchers and catchers better.

FIELDING:

Disregard Harris' 15 errors last year. He is an exceptional defensive player who should get better with experience. He was twice voted best defensive player in the minors by managers. He has a good, accurate arm with good reactions and instincts. He can play second, short and third.

OVERALL:

Scouts claim Harris is a talent waiting to be tapped. They cite his hitting and defensive ability and his speed. The Dodgers might have found their third baseman of the future -- by accident. With Jeff Hamilton a disappointment so far and Willie Randolph getting up in years, Harris will probably get plenty of chances to show what he can do.

LENNY HARRIS

Position: 2B/3B/SS/LF
Bats: L **Throws:** R
Ht: 5'10" **Wt:** 195

Opening Day Age: 25
Born: 10/28/64 in Miami, FL
ML Seasons: 2

Overall Statistics

	G	AB	R	H	D	T	HR	RBI	SB	BB	SO	AVG
1989	115	335	36	79	10	1	3	26	14	20	33	.236
Career	131	378	43	95	11	1	3	34	18	25	37	.251

Where He Hits the Ball

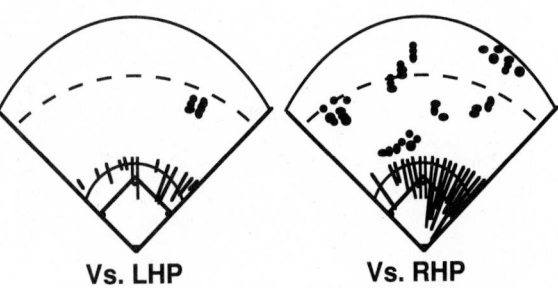

Vs. LHP   Vs. RHP

1989 Situational Stats

	AB	H	HR	RBI	AVG		AB	H	HR	RBI	AVG
Home	161	41	1	13	.255	LHP	68	13	0	3	.191
Road	174	38	2	13	.218	RHP	267	66	3	23	.247
Day	112	23	1	7	.205	Sc Pos	69	14	1	20	.203
Night	223	56	2	19	.251	Clutch	57	12	0	1	.211

1989 Rankings (National League)

→ 1st in most GDPs per GDP situation (21.9%)
- *players with 50 PA in GDP situations*

→ 4th in worst stolen base percentage (60.9%)
- *players with 20 attempts*

HITTING:

People simply do not realize how good a hitter Mickey Hatcher really is. All they seem to think about is his hustle, spirit, enthusiasm, his Little League approach. Yet this guy can hit. How many people realize Hatcher's career average is .283? For the last two seasons, he's been the Dodgers' leading hitter (.293 in 1988, .295 last season). He hit .282 the year before. He once hit .317 and .302 in back-to-back seasons (1983-84 with the Twins). If not for Orel Hershiser, Hatcher probably would have been the World Series MVP in 1988. He (uncharacteristically) bashed first-inning homers in Game 1 and Game 5. He hit .368 in the Series and drove in five runs. Not bad for a gray-haired 34-year old guy with gimpy knees.

Hatcher has an unorthodox stance and hitting mechanics, but he always seems to get the job done. He has a short stroke. He is a good contact, situation-type hitter who can spray to all fields. He seldom strikes out; he fanned just 16 times in 1989 and only seven times in '88. He doesn't walk much, either -- 13 times in '89, seven times in '88. He doesn't hit for power -- his World Series homers were a fluke -- but anytime he needs to move a runner over or get a runner in from third, Hatcher will do it.

Hatcher is a good high fastball hitter. He has trouble with breaking stuff and low pitches in general. He's best when he knows he can expect a fastball; that, along with his strong belief in himself, helps him in clutch situations.

BASERUNNING:

Hatcher runs -- and walks -- as if he just got off the operating table. Watching him walk is painful. He cannot run well, does not attempt to steal, does not take risks, but has good instincts. He has just one steal since 1987.

FIELDING:

Able to play left field, right field, first base and third base, Hatcher is not considered a fine fielder, but with his instincts, desire and hustle, he has a tendency to make the spectacular play. His throwing arm is below average.

OVERALL:

Hatcher is at his best when he is platooned and brought in off the bench. He is not nearly as effective when he plays regularly for an extended period of time. He's excellent to have on a club because of his personality and comic antics. The Dodgers probably wouldn't have won the World Series without him. But he only has a year or two left -- and he knows it.

MICKEY HATCHER

Position: LF/3B
Bats: R **Throws:** R
Ht: 6' 2" **Wt:** 202

Opening Day Age: 35
Born: 3/15/55 in Cleveland, OH
ML Seasons: 11

Overall Statistics

	G	AB	R	H	D	T	HR	RBI	SB	BB	SO	AVG
1989	94	224	18	66	9	2	2	25	1	13	16	.295
Career	1045	3245	336	918	169	19	38	362	11	158	224	.283

Where He Hits the Ball

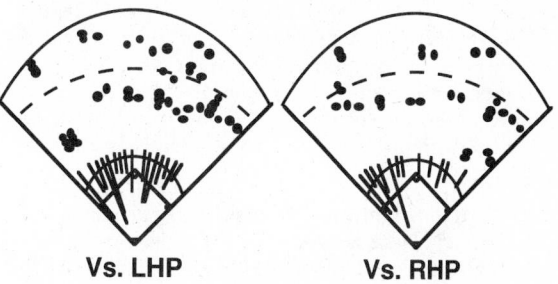

Vs. LHP   Vs. RHP

1989 Situational Stats

	AB	H	HR	RBI	AVG		AB	H	HR	RBI	AVG
Home	116	33	0	12	.284	LHP	131	42	2	17	.321
Road	108	33	2	13	.306	RHP	93	24	0	8	.258
Day	73	24	1	11	.329	Sc Pos	62	14	1	23	.226
Night	151	42	1	14	.278	Clutch	50	13	0	6	.260

1989 Rankings (National League)

➡ 10th in batting average vs. lefthanded pitchers (.321) - *players with 125 PA vs. LHP*

➡ Led the Dodgers in batting average vs. lefthanded pitchers and triples (2)

STAFF ACE

OREL HERSHISER

Position: SP
Bats: R **Throws:** R
Ht: 6' 3" **Wt:** 190

Opening Day Age: 31
Born: 9/16/58 in Buffalo, NY
ML Seasons: 7

PITCHING:

Orel Hershiser is a name that will live forever in baseball history. Hershiser's feats in 1988 -- a record scoreless inning streak, a postseason of total dominance, and finally a Cy Young Award -- are enough to make people remember him for years. But Hershiser seems intent on embellishing the legend.

What allows Hershiser to be so consistently good is an assortment of weapons: a tremendous sinking fastball, a hard-breaking curve, pin-point control, tremendous tenacity and great intelligence. He uses all his pitches effectively. The fastball and curve are his best offerings, but Hershiser mixes up his assortment and is a master at setting up hitters. There aren't many pitchers who are as smart, determined or better prepared than Hershiser. Even in bad Dodger seasons, like the last one, Hershiser still puts up outstanding numbers. He was only 15-15 due to lack of support, but his 2.31 ERA was second in the National League. He led the league with 256.2 innings pitched, yielded only nine homers, had eight complete games and four shutouts. If he had played for the Giants or Cubs, he'd have probably won 25 games. That's some kind of encore to his phenomenal 1988 Cy Young Award year.

Now 31, Hershiser must feel a little frustrated at times. It took him a little while to learn his trade, and he was 25 before he won a big league game. By then he was a polished hurler, and he's won 98 games in the last six seasons. But he should have won even more. Hershiser has finished in the top three in ERA in five of those years, but he's had to settle for a .500 record three times. It's not easy pitching for one of the weakest-hitting teams in baseball.

FIELDING, HITTING, BASERUNNING:

The agile Hershiser is an excellent fielder, a smart and aggressive baserunner, and one of the finest hitting pitchers around. Remember his three hits in Game 2 of the '88 World Series and how he shocked right fielder Jose Canseco by racing from first to third on a single? That's Hershiser, the complete player. He also has a fine pickoff move and allowed only 11 stolen bases last year.

OVERALL:

Hershiser's No. 1 on anyone's pitching chart. He's consistent, he's dedicated and he's a winner. Following the World Series, he was seen pitching every product imaginable on TV. During the season, baseball was his whole focus.

Overall Statistics

	W	L	ERA	G	GS	Sv	IP	H	R	BB	SO	HR
1989	15	15	2.31	35	33	0	256.2	226	75	77	178	9
Career	98	64	2.69	231	191	5	1457.0	1240	508	434	1011	75

Where They Hit the Ball

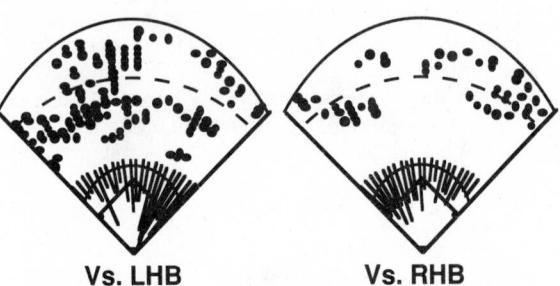

Vs. LHB **Vs. RHB**

1989 Situational Stats

	W	L	ERA	Sv	IP		AB	H	HR	RBI	AVG
Home	9	8	2.71	0	126.0	LHB	519	134	5	43	.258
Road	6	7	1.93	0	130.2	RHB	423	92	4	24	.217
Day	7	4	1.87	0	96.1	Sc Pos	221	37	3	57	.167
Night	8	11	2.58	0	160.1	Clutch	139	31	1	9	.223

1989 Rankings (National League)

➡ 1st in losses (15), innings (256.2), batters faced (1,047), GDPs induced (29), lowest batting average allowed with runners in scoring position (.167) and most GDPs induced per 9 innings (1.02) - *pitchers with 162 IP*

➡ 2nd in ERA (2.31) and least HRs per 9 innings (.316)

➡ Led the Dodgers in wins (15), losses, ERA, games started (33), innings, hits allowed (226), lowest slugging average allowed (.316), batters faced, balks (4), GDPS induced, grounder/flyball ratio (2.32), least HRs per 9 innings and most GDPs induced per 9 innings

STOPPER

JAY HOWELL

Position: RP
Bats: R **Throws:** R
Ht: 6' 3" **Wt:** 205

Opening Day Age: 34
Born: 11/26/55 in Miami, FL
ML Seasons: 10

PITCHING:

After emerging as one of the American League's top closers with 29 saves for Oakland in 1985, Jay Howell became a victim of severe arm problems. He posted 16 saves in 1986, most of them after the All-Star break, then 16 more in 1987, most of them before the All-Star break. Howell was inconsistent both years and had a terrible 5.89 ERA in '87.

Traded to the Dodgers before the 1988 season in the blockbuster Bobby Welch deal, Howell continued to have arm problems at the outset of the season. Then things clicked, and since then he has become one of the top closers in baseball. He finished '88 with 21 saves (most by a Dodger in 10 years). Last year he had 28 to establish an all-time Dodgers record. Howell is armed with a 90 mph fastball and excellent, sharpbreaking curve (despite Mets pitcher David Cone's comments to the contrary). Howell's curve can be as effective an out pitch as his exploding fastball. He has a slider but seldom uses it. His curve is hard to hit because of his big, overhand motion. Lefthanders have loads of trouble against him. They hit .169 against him in '88, .208 in '89. They've hit just one homer against him in each of the previous two seasons.

FIELDING, HITTING, BASERUNNING:

Howell gets to first base quickly. He reacts well and is a thinking man's pitcher. He is calm under pressure, enabling him to throw to bases well. For a right-handed power pitcher, Howell does a fine job of stopping the running game. As a closer, he hardly ever hits or runs the bases.

OVERALL:

Classy guy. Hard worker. Team player. As long as he stays healthy, Howell, though no kid at 34, should continue to be one of baseball's top closers. He relishes the role, too, no matter how much pressure he faces. Remember, after being ripped in the press by Cone, shamed and embarrassed by the infamous Pine Tar Scandal, criticized by the A's Don Baylor (who said Howell had no guts), then giving up a game-winning homer to Mark McGwire in Game 3 of the World Series, Howell rebounded to save Game 4 to give the Dodgers a three-games-to-one lead and put them on the threshold of an impossible dream.

Overall Statistics

	W	L	ERA	G	GS	Sv	IP	H	R	BB	SO	HR
1989	5	3	1.58	56	0	28	79.2	60	15	22	55	3
Career	39	36	3.58	344	21	117	579.0	551	245	210	472	34

Where They Hit the Ball

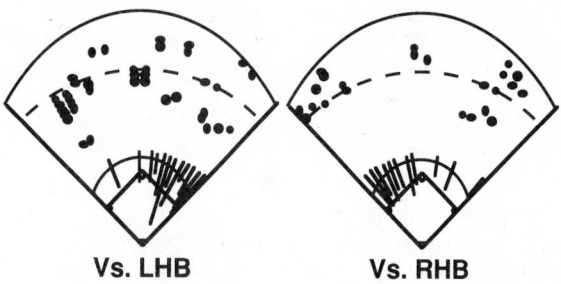

Vs. LHB   **Vs. RHB**

1989 Situational Stats

	W	L	ERA	Sv	IP		AB	H	HR	RBI	AVG
Home	4	3	1.16	16	46.2	LHB	159	33	1	12	.208
Road	1	0	2.18	12	33.0	RHB	125	27	2	7	.216
Day	2	0	1.11	11	32.1	Sc Pos	71	14	1	16	.197
Night	3	3	1.90	17	47.1	Clutch	239	50	2	15	.209

1989 Rankings (National League)

- ➡ 3rd in save percentage (87.5%) - *pitchers with 20 save opportunities*
- ➡ 4th in saves (28)
- ➡ 5th in save opportunities (32)
- ➡ 8th in most GDPs induced per GDP situation (17.3%) - *pitchers with 30 GDP situations*
- ➡ 9th in first batter efficiency (.173) - *pitchers with 40 games in relief*
- ➡ 10th in games finished (41)
- ➡ Led the Dodgers in games (56), games finished, saves, save percentage, first batter efficiency, blown saves (4) and lowest batting average allowed vs. lefthanded batters (.208) - *team pitchers with 125 PA vs. LHB*

HITTING:

Mike Marshall is now 30 and it looks like he's never going to achieve the stardom once predicted for him. Injuries have been a big factor, but even with all his assorted aches, Marshall has been a respectable run producer. From 1983 through 1988 Marshall averaged 20 homers and 72 RBIs, despite five stints on the disabled list. But in 1989 Marshall, bothered again by his chronic back problems, could manage only 11 homers and 42 RBIs. Those figures were by far the worst of any of his seven full seasons.

When healthy Marshall has outstanding power and the ability to carry a ballclub. A big man at 6'5", Marshall hits out of a crouch and uncoils with a powerful stroke. He loves high pitches and does his most damage on balls belt-high to the letters. He's mostly a pull hitter, but is capable of slamming opposite field homers because he drives the ball so well. Marshall has never been very patient -- he's struck out more than three times as much as he's walked in his career -- so the book on him is to feed him low and away breaking stuff and get him to go fishing. If the pitcher doesn't make a mistake, Marshall can be an easy out. But when they do make mistakes, he'll hurt them plenty.

BASERUNNING:

As would befit a 220-pounder with a bad back, Marshall is a slow and lumbering baserunner. Almost all his steals come on broken hit-and-run plays, and they don't come very often -- only 26 in 57 attempts during his career. Marshall had a fairly typical season on the bases last year, getting tossed out five times in seven attempts. As a baserunner he's as aggressive as his speed will permit.

FIELDING:

Marshall is best suited for first base, but the position is too aggravating to his back. So he plays the outfield, where he has little range but always hustles. Marshall's arm is both strong and accurate. He was a first baseman in the minors.

OVERALL:

Marshall wasn't expected to be around in 1989, but it was Pedro Guerrero, not Marshall, who was dealt. Then Marshall was signed to a three-year contract. All the Dodgers can hope for is that he stays healthy. If he does, he ranks among the top 15 outfielders in the league. But of course, he's never been able to stay healthy for very long.

MIKE MARSHALL

Position: RF
Bats: R **Throws:** R
Ht: 6' 5" **Wt:** 220

Opening Day Age: 30
Born: 1/12/60 in Libertyville, IL
ML Seasons: 9

Overall Statistics

	G	AB	R	H	D	T	HR	RBI	SB	BB	SO	AVG
1989	105	377	41	98	21	1	11	42	2	33	78	.260
Career	928	3249	395	882	155	6	137	484	26	236	724	.271

Where He Hits the Ball

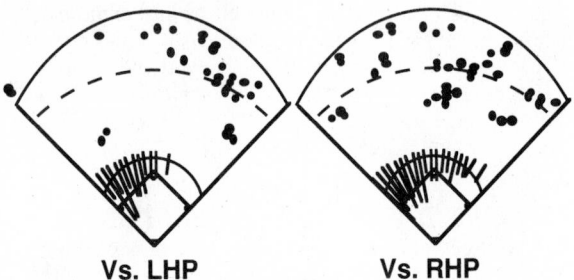

Vs. LHP   **Vs. RHP**

1989 Situational Stats

	AB	H	HR	RBI	AVG		AB	H	HR	RBI	AVG
Home	177	52	6	22	.294	LHP	130	32	7	17	.246
Road	200	46	5	20	.230	RHP	247	66	4	25	.267
Day	136	37	3	10	.272	Sc Pos	91	24	3	28	.264
Night	241	61	8	32	.253	Clutch	69	14	1	6	.203

1989 Rankings (National League)

➡ 8th in hit by pitch (5)

➡ Led the Dodgers in hit by pitch and hitting with runners in scoring position (.264) - *team players with 100 PA with runners in scoring position*

➡ Led NL Right Fielders in hit by pitch

TOP PROSPECT

PITCHING:

Ramon Martinez may be the next superstar right-hander in the National League. The Dodgers' top pitching prospect is equipped with a 92 mph fastball, a good curve and a change-up. Martinez, who is expected to be a fixture in the Dodgers' rotation for many years, is a stringbean at 6'4", 170 pounds. It looks as if like a strong breeze would blow him off the mound. But Martinez has an excellent arm, excellent pitching mechanics and strong work habits, all at the age of 22.

Martinez doesn't mess around on the mound. He throws strikes, doesn't fall behind hitters when he's in a groove, and displays a lot of poise for such a young man. He's a lot like Fernando Valenzuela in that he doesn't let a lot bother him -- not even getting demoted to the minors after pitching a major league shutout. He keeps his concentration, follows instructions and goes about his business.

Martinez gets in trouble when his curve isn't breaking. Hitters then sit on his fastball and have a tendency to shower him with line drives. He can fool them with his change of pace, but to be effective, he must have his curve. And while his control is outstanding when he's going good, Martinez is prone to streaks of wildness. He's walked nearly one batter for every two innings in his short major league career, a very high ratio.

After reaching the big leagues in 1988, Martinez opened the '89 season at Albuquerque. All he did was dominate the league. He was called up during a crunch of doubleheaders, shut out Atlanta, and was shipped right back to Albuquerque, which didn't do much for his confidence. But he came back once the Dodgers were out of it, and he continued to perform well.

FIELDING, HITTING, BASERUNNING:

Martinez is considered a good fielder because of his mobility and concentration. He has an excellent move to first, and he can hit. Martinez goes to the plate aggressively, not tentatively. He had three RBIs with his six hits.

OVERALL:

Martinez has great potential. Dodgers General Manager Fred Claire says he is untouchable as far as trades go, though clubs have nearly begged the Dodgers for him. Martinez needs to become more consistent, but he should be a part of the Dodger rotation for years to come.

RAMON MARTINEZ

Position: SP
Bats: R **Throws:** R
Ht: 6' 4" **Wt:** 172

Opening Day Age: 22
Born: 3/22/68 in Santo Domingo, Puerto Rico
ML Seasons: 2

Overall Statistics

	W	L	ERA	G	GS	Sv	IP	H	R	BB	SO	HR
1989	6	4	3.19	15	15	0	98.2	79	39	41	89	11
Career	7	7	3.35	24	21	0	134.1	106	56	63	112	11

Where They Hit the Ball

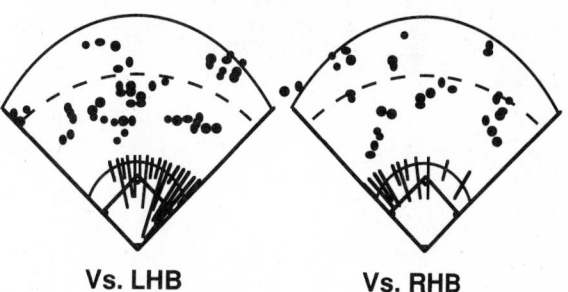

Vs. LHB   **Vs. RHB**

1989 Situational Stats

	W	L	ERA	Sv	IP		AB	H	HR	RBI	AVG
Home	3	3	2.17	0	49.2	LHB	199	50	6	18	.251
Road	3	1	4.22	0	49.0	RHB	161	29	5	14	.180
Day	1	0	6.14	0	14.2	Sc Pos	72	15	1	17	.208
Night	5	4	2.68	0	84.0	Clutch	27	8	0	1	.296

1989 Rankings (National League)

➥ Led the Dodgers in run support per 9 innings (5.5) - *all team pitchers*

PITCHING:

Mike Morgan is the major leagues' ultimate hard-luck pitcher; he opened the 1989 season with his sixth club in a career that started a couple months after he'd graduated from high school in 1978. Morgan, obtained from Baltimore for outfielder Mike Devereaux before last season, entered the year at 34-68 -- the worst won-lost ratio in the bigs. He had back-to-back 17-loss seasons in 1986-87 with Seattle and went 1-6 with Baltimore in 1988.

Then Morgan came over to the Dodgers and took the league by storm. He led the league in ERA through July, though his record certainly did not reflect it. What it reflected was that the Dodgers could not score any runs for him. At one point, he had 12 defeats and the Dodgers scored 10 runs in those games. After a couple of poor starts, he was moved to the bullpen. Given up on by some, Morgan did well there, also, with a 1.72 ERA as a reliever. He finished the year 8-11 but with an excellent 2.53 ERA, by far his career best.

Morgan has a sound arm and a good fastball, change-up and slider. Previously he had a tendency to hang his slider and seldom brushed guys off the plate. That led to problems. What he lacked was confidence and concentration. He acquired both qualities with the Dodgers, and became mentally tougher. He also began pitching inside more.

FIELDING, HITTING, BASERUNNING:

Last year Morgan was a terrible hitter and baserunner, mainly because he hadn't hit since high school. His fielding was also questionable because of his lack of concentration. But, with the Dodgers, he started jumping off the mound more quickly and reacting better. Morgan's pickoff move is decent, and since he has a very compact motion, he is tough to steal on.

OVERALL:

Morgan learned how to lose before he learned how to win. He was the number four player chosen in the 1978 draft, and Charley Finley, Oakland's eccentric owner, thrust him into the rotation one week after Morgan's high school prom. Morgan pitched well in his debut, but everything went downhill from there. Maybe Morgan's career will turn around with a winning organization which has a rich tradition of strong pitching. He has some wins left in that arm.

MIKE MORGAN

Position: RP/SP
Bats: R **Throws:** R
Ht: 6' 2" **Wt:** 215

Opening Day Age: 30
Born: 10/8/59 in Tulare, CA
ML Seasons: 9

Overall Statistics

	W	L	ERA	G	GS	Sv	IP	H	R	BB	SO	HR
1989	8	11	2.53	40	19	0	152.2	130	51	33	72	6
Career	42	79	4.51	197	138	2	938.0	1035	515	346	414	92

Where They Hit the Ball

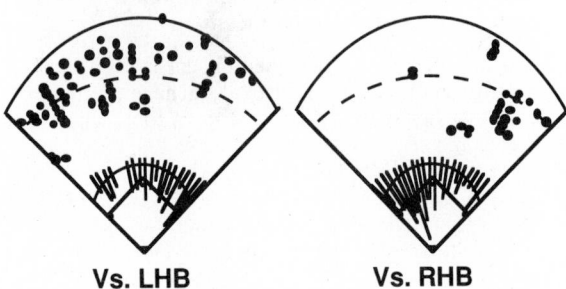

Vs. LHB   **Vs. RHB**

1989 Situational Stats

	W	L	ERA	Sv	IP		AB	H	HR	RBI	AVG
Home	4	6	2.27	0	87.1	LHB	300	77	5	34	.257
Road	4	5	2.89	0	65.1	RHB	255	53	1	16	.208
Day	4	3	2.32	0	42.2	Sc Pos	113	26	1	42	.230
Night	4	8	2.62	0	110.0	Clutch	83	16	1	6	.193

1989 Rankings (National League)

➡ 5th in most GDPs induced per GDP situation (18.1% - *pitchers with 30 GDP situations*) and ERA at home (2.27 - *pitchers with 18 IP at home*)

➡ 9th in most GDPs induced (17)

➡ Led the Dodgers in most GDPs induced per GDP situation

HITTING:

Not long ago, Eddie Murray was one of the most devastating and feared hitters in all of baseball. Murray is no longer in that category, but he's still a dangerous hitter. Though returning to his hometown didn't make Murray look any happier, his run production figures were fine, even though his home park hindered him a lot. And they were especially respectable considering that he didn't get much help from a weak Dodger lineup that suffered from injuries to Kirk Gibson and Mike Marshall. With no other viable threat in the batting order for most of the season, opposing managers gave Murray 24 intentional walks.

Murray's bat speed has slowed down, yet he is still able to hit -- and hit with power -- to all fields. Early in his career, Murray was considered an excellent fastball hitter, but he has hit breaking pitches just as well. He is also a good high ball hitter. The pitch that really gets on Murray's nerves is an inside fastball. Throw him that and you have a good chance of beating him. Lefthanders have had an easy time with the switch-hitting Murray in recent years. Last year, Murray hit .210 against southpaws, .268 against righties.

Murray's 20 homers were the second-lowest total of his career, but he hasn't lost his home run stroke. He was hampered by the big dimensions of Dodger Stadium, hitting only four there. Away from home Murray belted 16, one of the highest road-homer totals in the National League.

BASERUNNING:

Though not fast, Murray stole seven bases in nine attempts last year and is a career 72% stealer. He'll run if the defense is napping and usually make it. He does not take the extra base often on hits, however, and he seldom slides.

FIELDING:

A Gold Glove winner from 1982 to 84, Murray has also slumped in the field. His range is limited. He's moving a lot more slowly as the years pass. Murray is sure-handed, however, and committed only six errors.

OVERALL:

Though no longer a superstar, Murray is still productive. He batted a career low .247 last year, but drove in 88 runs, 32 more than any other Dodger. His attitude may not be great; his approach these days seems to be nonchalant, almost ho-hum, especially in the field. Perhaps that attitude hurts the Dodgers in the clubhouse. But Eddie Murray can still hit.

EDDIE MURRAY

Position: 1B
Bats: B **Throws:** R
Ht: 6' 2" **Wt:** 224

Opening Day Age: 34
Born: 2/24/56 in Los Angeles, CA
ML Seasons: 13

Overall Statistics

	G	AB	R	H	D	T	HR	RBI	SB	BB	SO	AVG
1989	160	594	66	147	29	1	20	88	7	87	85	.247
Career 1980	7439	1114	2168	380	26	353	1278	68	944	1012	.291

Where He Hits the Ball

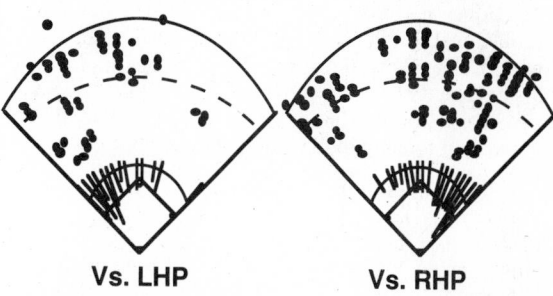

Vs. LHP   **Vs. RHP**

1989 Situational Stats

	AB	H	HR	RBI	AVG		AB	H	HR	RBI	AVG
Home	292	74	4	40	.253	LHP	210	44	4	21	.210
Road	302	73	16	48	.242	RHP	384	103	16	67	.268
Day	184	44	12	34	.239	Sc Pos	149	38	9	68	.255
Night	410	103	8	54	.251	Clutch	111	22	4	10	.198

1989 Rankings (National League)

- ➡ 3rd in plate appearances (690) and intentional walks (24)
- ➡ 5th in walks (87)
- ➡ 6th in pitches seen (2,391)
- ➡ 7th in at bats (594) and games (160)
- ➡ 8th in RBIs (88)
- ➡ Led the Dodgers in at bats, total bases (238), home runs (20), runs (66), RBIs, walks, intentional walks, GDPs (12), pitches seen, home run percentage (29.7 ABs per HR), slugging percentage (.401), sacrifice flies (7), plate appearances, games (160), and times on base (207)

PITCHING:

After back-to-back 12-win seasons and ERAs of 2.75 and 2.48 in 1983 and 1984, Alejandro Pena began having arm troubles. Bad arm troubles. He didn't get over them completely until 1988, when he was moved to the bullpen for good. Sound of arm again, Pena has developed into one of the best set-up men in baseball.

Though the 30-year old Pena has lost a little off his fastball because of surgery, he's excelled in the pen. He relishes being there and loves the life of a reliever. Pena had a terrific year in the Dodgers' World Championship season of 1988, with 12 saves, six wins, a 1.91 ERA, and 83 strikeouts in 94.1 innings. Last season, with the Dodgers having a down year, Pena saved just five games and won four. But he fanned 75 batters in 76 innings while walking just 18. His earned run average was outstanding again at 2.13.

Pena once had a 95 mph fastball, but with his arm problems, his velocity has dropped several miles an hour. But he can still reach the low nineties, and with his excellent curve, he can blow the ball past hitters. Pena has a forkball, but doesn't use it much. He likes the idea of it being in the hitters' minds, though.

About Pena's only problem is that he is a very slow worker. He frustrates his teammates by putting them to sleep. Two-inning stints turn into 45 minute affairs with Pena. He's also prone to giving up the long ball, but overall he's been an extremely effective reliever.

FIELDING, HITTING, BASERUNNING:

Pena is not a good fielder because he tends to go into a trance on some plays and freezes. When he should be backing up the catcher on a play to the plate, Pena can often be found at the mound, watching the action. He is below average at holding baserunners. Pena doesn't hit or run the bases often, but he swings the bat with enthusiasm.

OVERALL:

Now that he has found his niche in the bullpen, Pena is more valuable than ever. His role with the Dodgers is perfect for him because he can be utilized as a set-up man as well as the occasional closer. If he worked strictly as a closer, he probably wouldn't be able to handle the constant pressure. If he worked faster, he might be even more effective.

ALEJANDRO PENA

Position: RP
Bats: R **Throws:** R
Ht: 6' 1"   **Wt:** 205

Opening Day Age: 30
Born: 6/25/59 in Cambiaso, Dominican Republic
ML Seasons: 9

Overall Statistics

	W	L	ERA	G	GS	Sv	IP	H	R	BB	SO	HR
1989	4	3	2.13	53	0	5	76.0	62	20	18	75	6
Career	38	38	2.93	281	72	32	769.0	693	301	244	571	44

Where They Hit the Ball

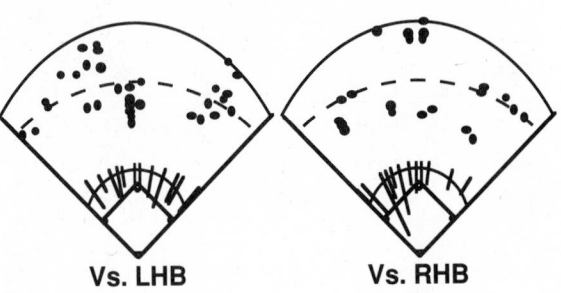

Vs. LHB   **Vs. RHB**

1989 Situational Stats

	W	L	ERA	Sv	IP		AB	H	HR	RBI	AVG
Home	1	0	2.80	2	35.1	LHB	151	35	4	7	.232
Road	3	3	1.55	3	40.2	RHB	131	27	2	12	.206
Day	3	1	1.59	2	28.1	Sc Pos	57	12	0	12	.211
Night	1	2	2.45	3	47.2	Clutch	163	41	5	16	.252

1989 Rankings (National League)

➠ Led the Dodgers in holds (5) and blown saves (4)

LOS ANGELES DODGERS

HITTING:

Willie Randolph is an excellent contact and situation hitter with tremendous leadership qualities. At the age of 35, he turned out to be one of the brightest spots in a dismal season for the Dodgers. Rebounding from his worst season in 1988 (career low .230 average), Randolph led the Dodgers with a .282 average in his first season in Los Angeles. It was his third highest average in his stellar 15-year career -- 13 of which were played with the Yankees.

A career .274 hitter, Randolph's major asset is that he's a patient batter who knows the strike zone. His career on-base average is a splendid .372, and he consistently draws 70 or more walks a season. Because he seldom swings at a bad pitch, pitchers like to work Randolph over with a variety of pitches, all at different speeds and locations. He gets a lot of fastballs because hurlers don't want to fall behind on the count against him; they know Randolph is doubly dangerous when he can expect one down the middle. He's a good high ball hitter, and pitchers tend to work him low and away or jam him with an inside fastball.

Randolph is a line drive hitter who averages three homers per season. But he has decent power to the gaps, often going to right-center on an outside pitch. He seldom strikes out and is an excellent number one or two hitter.

BASERUNNING:

At 35, Randolph has lost a step or two, but he is still a good baserunner because of his instincts, experience, and knowledge of opposing fielders. But his bad knees haven't allowed him to be much of a base stealer since swiping 30 in 1980. He stole seven bases last season, but was caught stealing six times - - certainly not a respectable ratio.

FIELDING:

Randolph's range, never great, has diminished with age, but he's very sure-handed and made only nine errors last year. He plays hitters well and is fearless, never backing down from hard-charging runners. He gets rid of the ball quickly and turns the double play as well as any second baseman in baseball.

OVERALL:

One of the nicest men in baseball, Randolph is considered future managerial material by many associates. He is a leader in the truest sense, the consummate professional ballplayer. He looked washed up after a .230 season in 1988, but made a strong comeback and should be good for at least a couple more years.

WILLIE RANDOLPH

Position: 2B
Bats: R **Throws:** R
Ht: 5'11" **Wt:** 163

Opening Day Age: 35
Born: 7/6/54 in Holly Hill, SC
ML Seasons: 15

Overall Statistics

	G	AB	R	H	D	T	HR	RBI	SB	BB	SO	AVG
1989	145	549	62	155	18	0	2	36	7	71	51	.282
Career	1869	6913	1098	1896	278	58	50	588	259	1083	569	.274

Where He Hits the Ball

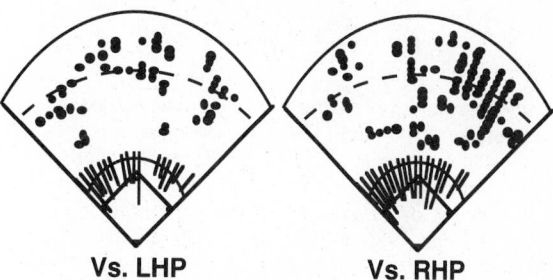

Vs. LHP   **Vs. RHP**

1989 Situational Stats

	AB	H	HR	RBI	AVG		AB	H	HR	RBI	AVG
Home	266	81	0	17	.305	LHP	191	57	1	13	.298
Road	283	74	2	19	.261	RHP	358	98	1	23	.274
Day	144	43	1	14	.299	Sc Pos	95	25	1	34	.263
Night	405	112	1	22	.277	Clutch	101	25	1	10	.248

1989 Rankings (National League)

➡ 1st in percentage of pitches taken (64.3%) - *players with 502 PA*

➡ 2nd in percentage of swings put into play (59.6%)

➡ 3rd in lowest slugging percentage vs. right-handed batters (.310) - *pitchers facing 377 RHB*

➡ Led the Dodgers in batting average (.282), singles (135), hits (155), on-base average (.366), percentage of pitches taken, percentage of swings put into play, lowest percentage of swings that missed (8.7%) and batting average with 2 strikes (.261) - *team players with 502 PA*

The Scouting Report:1990

HITTING:

Mike Scioscia may not hit many home runs, drive in many runs or hit for a high average often. But he is as solid as any catcher in the major leagues. Scioscia had one of his usual quiet, but effective, seasons last year. His .250 batting average was his lowest since 1982, and 11 points below his career mark. But Scioscia's 10 homers were a career high, and his 44 RBIs were the most he's recorded since 1985.

Now 31, the lefthanded hitting Scioscia has never been known for his hitting. But he has definite offensive virtues. He's a patient batter who can pull the inside pitch or take an outside offering to left field. One of the premier contact hitters in baseball, Scioscia has never struck out more than 31 times in a season. His career strikeout rate of one per 15.2 at bats is topped among active players only by Tony Gwynn (one per 17.5) and Don Mattingly (one per 16.9) -- not bad company. Scioscia can take a walk as well, and has walked more than twice as many times in his career than he's struck out.

Scioscia can hit breaking pitches as well as fastballs. He prefers high pitches, and has the ability to hit for a decent average; he hit .296 in 1985 and led National League hitters through April of 1988 with a .404 average. Scioscia, though, was the only player in the majors from 1986 to 1988 who hit below .200 with runners in scoring position and two outs (minimum of 50 at bats). He hit just .204 last year with runners in scoring position.

BASERUNNING:

Forget it. When Scioscia steals a base, it's a fluke. The Dodger dugout keels over in laughter when he runs. He looks like an overgrown turtle lumbering down the line. One of world's great mysteries is how Scioscia ever swiped seven bases in 1987. The only explanation is that opposing pitchers must have fallen asleep -- or the catchers attempting to throw Scioscia out were laughing too.

FIELDING:

Scioscia is a superb defensive catcher. No one blocks the plate better. He's a human highlight film when it comes to head-on collisions at home plate. For a guy who had arm surgery in 1983, Scioscia has recovered well. He's a very smart receiver and calls an excellent game.

OVERALL:

As tough as nails, the underrated Scioscia plays hurt and is the epitome of a gamer. How valuable is he? The Dodgers, who usually do not negotiate contracts during the season, re-signed Scioscia during the season.

MIKE SCIOSCIA

Position: C
Bats: L **Throws:** R
Ht: 6' 2" **Wt:** 219

Opening Day Age: 31
Born: 11/27/58 in Upper Darby, PA
ML Seasons: 10

Overall Statistics

	G	AB	R	H	D	T	HR	RBI	SB	BB	SO	AVG
1989	133	408	40	102	16	0	10	44	0	52	29	.250
Career	1070	3245	294	848	151	7	45	316	18	433	213	.261

Where He Hits the Ball

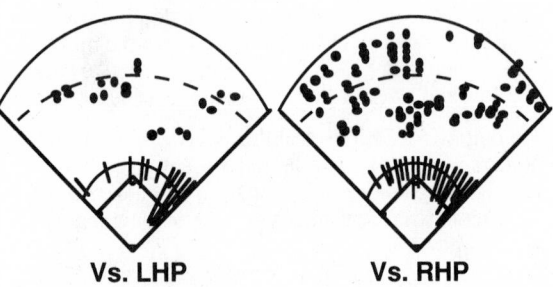

Vs. LHP   **Vs. RHP**

1989 Situational Stats

	AB	H	HR	RBI	AVG		AB	H	HR	RBI	AVG
Home	200	47	4	21	.235	LHP	100	23	3	8	.230
Road	208	55	6	23	.264	RHP	308	79	7	36	.256
Day	129	34	5	18	.264	Sc Pos	98	20	3	32	.204
Night	279	68	5	26	.244	Clutch	78	19	1	4	.244

1989 Rankings (National League)

➡ 2nd in throwing out base stealers (39.2%) - *catchers with 75 attempts*

➡ 10th in hitting on a 3-1 count (.480) - *players with 10 PA on a 3-1 count*

➡ Led the Dodgers in least GDPs per GDP situation (5.6%) - *team players with 50 PA in GDP situations*

➡ Led NL catchers in sacrifice bunts (7), batting average with 2 strikes (.238), walks (52), least GDPs per GDP situation and hitting on a 3-1 count - *catchers with 502 PA*

PITCHING:

Ray Searage is the ultimate journeyman; he has played in seven organizations in his 12 professional years. The only special characteristic Searage has is that he's lefthanded. Every club needs a lefthanded reliever, so Searage will probably continue to have a job.

At 34, Searage still has a good, live arm. He has a good fastball and an assortment of breaking pitches. He's generally tough on lefties, and that's what's kept him in the majors, but last year he was much tougher on righties. He changes speeds well. Control has always been a problem for Searage, who sometimes gets himself into trouble by walking people. He's not a power pitcher, but he can come in and get a needed strikeout on occasion.

After a poor season with the White Sox in '87, Searage was released by that pitching-poor club the next spring. He couldn't find a major league job, but Searage is a survivor and has always been willing to go back to the minors and prove himself again. He was signed by Albuquerque in the Dodger organization, and didn't dazzle anyone by turning in a 5.10 ERA. But that didn't matter. He was lefthanded, and he was available. When Rick Horton didn't impress the Dodgers last year, Searage got yet another major league chance. He didn't overwhelm anyone, going 3-4 with a 3.53 ERA and no saves. But he didn't embarrass himself, either. He was the ultimate specialist, working only 35.2 innings in his 41 games. He kept the ball in the park, yielding only one home run.

FIELDING, HITTING, RUNNING:

Searage is an average fielder. He doesn't get off the mound too well and his throws to first base aren't always on the mark. He's always had a good pickoff move and an ability to control the running game, skills which have helped him survive in the majors.

OVERALL:

As always, Searage has only marginal prospects for pitching in the majors next year. But he's lefthanded, and he's available -- like Paul Mirabella and Dan Schatzeder, he seems to have nine lives. If Searage doesn't land a major league job right away, he'll probably be willing to bide his time in the minors until someone just has to have a lefty reliever.

RAY SEARAGE

Position: RP
Bats: L **Throws:** L
Ht: 6' 1" **Wt:** 180

Opening Day Age: 34
Born: 5/1/55 in Freeport, NY
ML Seasons: 6

Overall Statistics

	W	L	ERA	G	GS	Sv	IP	H	R	BB	SO	HR
1989	3	4	3.53	41	0	0	35.2	29	15	18	24	1
Career	10	13	3.59	225	0	11	255.2	237	109	127	174	21

Where They Hit the Ball

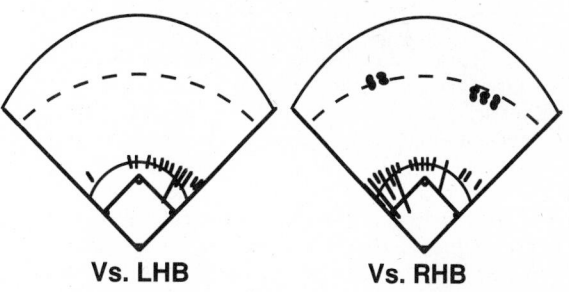

Vs. LHB   **Vs. RHB**

1989 Situational Stats

	W	L	ERA	Sv	IP		AB	H	HR	RBI	AVG
Home	2	1	0.87	0	10.1	LHB	45	13	0	7	.289
Road	1	3	4.62	0	25.1	RHB	84	16	1	15	.190
Day	1	2	5.79	0	9.1	Sc Pos	43	14	0	21	.326
Night	2	2	2.73	0	26.1	Clutch	45	12	1	12	.267

1989 Rankings (National League)

→ Led the Dodgers in lowest percentage of inherited runners scoring (39.5%) - *team players with 30 inherited runners*

HITTING:

Poor John Shelby. He was the starting centerfielder and No. 6 hitter for the 1988 World Series champions, but he found himself in the minor leagues in 1989. At the time of the demotion to AAA Albuquerque, Shelby was batting .159 with 66 strikeouts in 244 at bats. He came back to L.A., but wound up hitting just .183 in 108 games with 92 strikeouts in 345 at-bats, one homer and 12 RBIs.

Though the switch-hitting Shelby has nine years of big league experience, he still has a tendency to look like a rookie. His problem is that his swing is too big and he is too undisciplined. He is not patient and often chases ridiculously bad pitches. He cannot hit breaking balls well, either from lefthanders or righthanders. He has enough speed to bunt for hits, but he cannot bunt effectively because of his poor batting technique.

It upset Tom Lasorda to see Shelby exiled to the minors, since John is one of the manager's favorite individuals. But the move had to be made. Shelby was so confused and helpless at the plate, it was sad. He hardly seemed the same fellow who had breezed into Los Angeles in 1987 and proceeded to wallop 21 homers in only 120 games. The Dodgers didn't really expect Shelby to continue that kind of performance, but even a return to his '88 form (.263, 10 homers) would be a blessing.

BASERUNNING:

Shelby can run. He swiped 16 bases in 1987 and again in 1988. But his instincts aren't too sharp. He stole 10 bases in limited action last year, but was tossed out seven times. On the bases, he often makes foolish mistakes and runs himself into outs.

FIELDING:

This is what kept Shelby in the lineup the second half of the '88 season and the start of last season. He has the speed to catch up to balls. He has good instincts and reaction. His arm is average and he has a tendency to rush his throws in bigger parks, where players try to run on him.

OVERALL:

If Shelby can learn how to adjust, become more patient and learn how to hit the breaking ball, he might be able to win back his job. But a manager must have patience, too. Lasorda did, and last year it wasn't rewarded. At 32, Shelby isn't going to find it easy to win a regular position back.

JOHN SHELBY

Position: CF
Bats: B **Throws:** R
Ht: 6' 1" **Wt:** 175

Opening Day Age: 32
Born: 2/23/58 in Lexington, KY
ML Seasons: 9

Overall Statistics

	G	AB	R	H	D	T	HR	RBI	SB	BB	SO	AVG
1989	108	345	28	63	11	1	1	12	10	25	92	.183
Career	880	2701	346	656	110	20	63	283	94	164	590	.243

Where He Hits the Ball

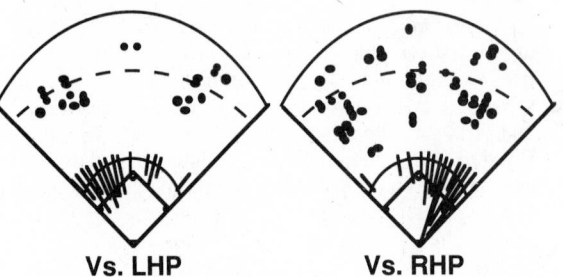

Vs. LHP   **Vs. RHP**

1989 Situational Stats

	AB	H	HR	RBI	AVG		AB	H	HR	RBI	AVG
Home	186	34	0	5	.183	LHP	125	21	0	4	.168
Road	159	29	1	7	.182	RHP	220	42	1	8	.191
Day	104	17	0	1	.163	Sc Pos	63	11	0	10	.175
Night	241	46	1	11	.191	Clutch	77	11	1	3	.143

1989 Rankings (National League)

➡ 1st in worst slugging percentage vs. left-handed pitchers (.208) - *players with 125 PA vs. LHP*

➡ 2nd in worst batting average vs. lefthanded pitchers (.168), worst on-base average vs. lefthanded pitchers (.206) and worst batting average with 2 strikes (.105) - *players with 162 PA with 2 strikes*

➡ 3rd in worst home run frequency (345 ABs per HR)

➡ 5th in worst batting average in the clutch (.143) - *players with 50 PA in the clutch*

➡ Led the Dodgers in strikeouts (92) and caught stealing (7)

PITCHING:

He's one of the most renowned lefthanders in history, and last year Fernando Valenzuela made an impressive and improbable recovery from his 1988 shoulder problems. After going only 5-8 with a 4.24 ERA in '88, he rebounded by winning 10 games, posting a 3.43 ERA and pitching 196.2 innings. Given up for dead, Fernando may be on the comeback trail.

All the innings Valenzuela logged over the years, all the screwballs he turned over, all the fastballs he flung, all the complete games, turned his shoulder into mush. He was a nonfactor during the World Championship season. Some people thought his career was finished. Most didn't think he'd figure in the 1989 season. Despite that, the Dodgers showed their appreciation to Fernando by signing him to a $1.8 million contract. And Fernando responded, moving from the No. 5 pitcher on the staff to No. 2 during one point late in the season. Valenzuela, who used to rely strictly on his screwball and fastball, was forced to think more and finesse hitters. By August, it was working. Though his fastball was clocked in the low 80's even in July, Valenzuela began to build some stamina and started to win. He started using his curve more, as well as a slider. Fernando has five pitches, two of which are screwballs. One tails away from lefthanders. The other is used as an off-speed pitch, a change-up. He never used his curveball much -- until last year. His curve needs work, however.

Only 29, Valenzuela is unflappable, a characteristic that has unquestionably been a factor in his success and his recovery. Nothing fazes him. He expects to walk a few batters, so getting behind in the count doesn't bother him. He's still able to come back and get hitters out.

FIELDING, HITTING, BASERUNNING:

Though he looks out of shape, Valenzuela is in good physical condition and moves extremely well. Few pitchers field their position better. He's a good hitter, as well, with seven career homers. He's a daring, aggressive baserunner, unusual for a pitcher. Valenzuela has been easy to steal on in the past, but in 1989 only half the 30 runners who tried to steal off him were successful.

OVERALL:

Valenzuela has never been the same since 1986, when Tommy Lasorda kept him on the mound for 20 complete games. At 29, he must now rely on finesse rather than power. But Valenzuela's always been one of the smartest pitchers in baseball, and in 1989 he showed that he might be able to make that very difficult transition.

FERNANDO VALENZUELA

Position: SP
Bats: L **Throws:** L
Ht: 5'11" **Wt:** 202

Opening Day Age: 29
Born: 11/1/60 in Navajoa, Mexico
ML Seasons: 10

Overall Statistics

	W	L	ERA	G	GS	Sv	IP	H	R	BB	SO	HR
1989	10	13	3.43	31	31	0	196.2	185	89	98	116	11
Career	128	103	3.19	298	287	2	2144.2	1876	869	838	1644	133

Where They Hit the Ball

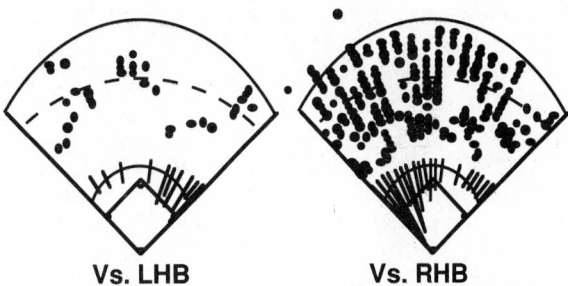

Vs. LHB   **Vs. RHB**

1989 Situational Stats

	W	L	ERA	Sv	IP		AB	H	HR	RBI	AVG
Home	4	6	3.26	0	99.1	LHB	125	32	1	7	.256
Road	6	7	3.61	0	97.1	RHB	613	153	10	65	.250
Day	4	2	2.90	0	62.0	Sc Pos	195	47	4	61	.241
Night	6	11	3.68	0	134.2	Clutch	46	17	1	6	.370

1989 Rankings (National League)

- ➡ 2nd in walks allowed (98)
- ➡ 3rd in highest on-base average allowed (.337) and lowest stolen base percentage allowed (50.0%) - *pitchers with 162 IP*
- ➡ 6th in least HRs allowed per 9 innings (.50)
- ➡ 8th in losses (13)
- ➡ Led the Dodgers in walks allowed, balks (4), pickoff throws (156), lowest stolen base percentage allowed, caught stealing (15) and run support per 9 innings (4.1) - *team pitchers with 162 IP*

PITCHING:

John Wetteland is yet another highly touted prospect to come off the Dodgers' pitching assembly line. The hard-throwing righthander has a great arm and tremendous potential. Opposing teams have already been on the telephone with the Dodgers to try to nab him in a trade. But GM Fred Claire considers Wetteland one of his "untouchables." The animated, quotable and comical Wetteland is a fastball/curveball pitcher who must learn control. He's too inconsistent at this point, but there's still a chance he might be in the Dodgers' starting rotation for the 1990 season. He might be better off with one more year at Triple A.

Wetteland, hard-nosed and competitive, uncorked an amazing 16 wild pitches in only 102.2 innings, illustrating his big problem. He has an excellent fastball that's been clocked at 93 mph. He's not afraid to come inside, either. The key for Wetteland is getting his curveball over. If he doesn't, hitters can sit on his fastball and clobber him. For Wetteland to be successful and consistent, he must develop another pitch and be able to use it 20 percent of the time.

With the Dodgers out of the race last season, Wetteland was able to get some valuable major league experience. He pitched in 31 games and started 12, most of them down the stretch. He was 5-8 with a 3.77 ERA, and was tough against both right- and left-handed hitters. He struck out 96 in 102 2/3 innings.

FIELDING, HITTING, BASERUNNING:

Wetteland is a good fielder who can become much better. He's agile. He has good mobility and quickness. But sometimes he rushes. Perhaps it can be attributed to last year being his first season in the bigs. He has the potential to be a productive hitting pitcher. He goes up there looking for hits. He doesn't consider himself an automatic out. One of his three hits (in 21 at bats) was a double. He also successfully sacrificed five times. With all of his problems controlling his pitches, Wetteland does not do a good job of holding runners.

OVERALL:

The Dodgers had enough confidence that Wetteland would be part of their rotation in 1990 or 1991 that they traded Tim Leary. Wetteland will satisfy the Dodgers' confidence in him only when he is able to get control of his pitches.

JOHN WETTELAND

Position: RP/SP
Bats: R **Throws:** R
Ht: 6' 2" **Wt:** 195

Opening Day Age: 23
Born: 8/22/66 in San Mateo, CA
ML Seasons: 1

Overall Statistics

	W	L	ERA	G	GS	Sv	IP	H	R	BB	SO	HR
1989	5	8	3.77	31	12	1	102.2	81	46	34	96	8
Career	5	8	3.77	31	12	1	102.2	81	46	34	96	8

Where They Hit the Ball

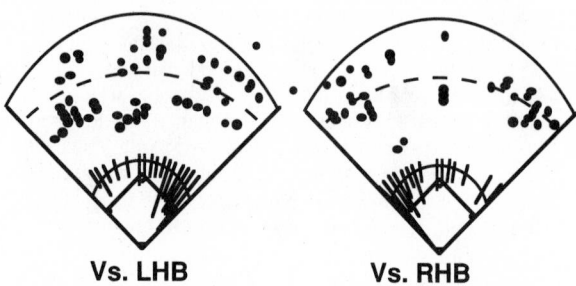

Vs. LHB   Vs. RHB

1989 Situational Stats

	W	L	ERA	Sv	IP		AB	H	HR	RBI	AVG
Home	4	3	3.45	1	47.0	LHB	193	41	3	16	.212
Road	1	5	4.04	0	55.2	RHB	178	40	5	25	.225
Day	1	3	6.66	0	25.2	Sc Pos	84	22	4	35	.262
Night	4	5	2.81	1	77.0	Clutch	64	15	0	3	.234

1989 Rankings (National League)

- ➡ 2nd in wild pitches (16)
- ➡ Led the Dodgers in wild pitches

DAVE ANDERSON

Position: SS/3B
Bats: R **Throws:** R
Ht: 6' 2" **Wt:** 191

Opening Day Age: 29
Born: 8/1/60 in
Louisville, KY
ML Seasons: 7

BILLY BEAN

Position: LF
Bats: L **Throws:** L
Ht: 6' 1" **Wt:** 185

Opening Day Age: 25
Born: 5/11/64 in Santa
Ana, CA
ML Seasons: 3

Overall Statistics

	G	AB	R	H	D	T	HR	RBI	SB	BB	SO	AVG
1989	87	140	15	32	2	0	1	14	2	17	26	.229
Career	662	1616	196	375	59	9	13	116	46	187	265	.232

Overall Statistics

	G	AB	R	H	D	T	HR	RBI	SB	BB	SO	AVG
1989	60	82	7	14	4	0	0	3	0	6	13	.171
Career	96	159	15	33	6	1	0	7	1	11	26	.208

HITTING, FIELDING, BASERUNNING:

The Dodgers thought Dave Anderson was their short-stop of the future after he won the job from long-time incumbent Bill Russell in 1984. But things haven't worked out for the Dodgers or Anderson as planned. Anderson, a righthanded hitter with a short, compact stroke, has been set back by injuries his whole career, preventing him from living up to his potential. He's a career .232 hitter with little power (13 homers in seven seasons). He strikes out too much and walks too little for a guy who's supposed to be a disciplined hitter. Anderson likes fastballs over the plate, especially when he's ahead in the count. But he doesn't go to the opposite field enough. Anderson has settled in as a good utility man who can play second, short and third, and he did a fabulous job filling in for the injured Alfredo Griffin during the 1988 World Championship season. He has good speed and is a smooth, surehanded fielder who makes all the routine plays.

OVERALL:

Anderson might have been something special if he hadn't developed chronic back problems. But he's turned into a solid utility man who can do a decent job in a pinch. He's a team player and a good leader.

HITTING, FIELDING, BASERUNNING:

Billy Bean is often confused with his former team-mate, Billy Beane, now with the A's. This Bean is a lefthanded contact hitter with good bat control. He goes with the pitch well and is a very patient, smart hitter. Some have thought him capable of hitting for a high average, though he did not show it when he played in 51 games for the Dodgers last year. He hit just .197. But the Tigers, Bean's former employer, were always high on him. Bean tied a record with four hits in his first major league game. He's a fiery, enthusiastic, versatile performer who can play all three outfield positions as well as first base. He commits too many errors in the outfield, but has good lateral movement and a fine throwing arm. Bean also has good speed and the potential to steal 15 to 20 bases.

OVERALL:

Bean is the type of player any organization would love. He's a fans' delight. He hustles. He works hard. He's enthusiastic. He's versatile. He makes things happen. Whether he can become an everyday major league outfielder is debatable. He can definitely be a fourth outfielder. He's as fundamentally sound as a player can be.

MIKE
DAVIS

Position: RF/LF
Bats: L **Throws:** L
Ht: 6' 3" **Wt:** 185

Opening Day Age: 30
Born: 6/11/59 in San Diego, CA
ML Seasons: 10

Overall Statistics

	G	AB	R	H	D	T	HR	RBI	SB	BB	SO	AVG
1989	67	173	21	43	7	1	5	19	6	16	28	.249
Career	963	2999	419	778	161	16	91	371	134	236	537	.259

HITTING, FIELDING, BASERUNNING:

Mike Davis' career as a Dodger has been a disaster. Signed to a three-year, three million dollar free-agent contract after the 1987 season, he was penciled in as the starting right fielder and No. 5 hitter. But Davis sprained his ankle in spring training 1988, came out of the gate slowly, and then lost his job when Mike Marshall's sore back necessitated a move back to the outfield. Davis hit only .196 in 1988, but improved that to .249, with five homers in 173 at bats, last year. Davis has a smooth stroke and has hit as many as 24 homers, but chases bad pitches when he gets behind in the count. He still has good speed, but base stealing is another thing he hasn't done in L.A. -- only 13 in two years after stealing as many as 32 for Oakland. He's a decent outfielder with an average arm.

OVERALL:

At 30, Davis is still young enough to do something with his career. But he's with a team that doesn't really believe in him. He has both speed and power, and might produce for another team if the Dodgers are willing to eat part of his salary.

RICK
DEMPSEY

Position: C
Bats: R **Throws:** R
Ht: 6' 0" **Wt:** 184

Opening Day Age: 40
Born: 9/13/49 in Fayetteville, TN
ML Seasons: 21

Overall Statistics

	G	AB	R	H	D	T	HR	RBI	SB	BB	SO	AVG
1989	79	151	16	27	7	0	4	16	1	30	37	.179
Career	1635	4408	495	1033	213	12	90	435	19	544	686	.234

HITTING, FIELDING, BASERUNNING:

The curtain is about to descend on Rick Dempsey's playing days. He wants to play next year to become a four-decade player -- a rarity in professional sports. Even though he's 40 and had one of his worst offensive seasons in 1989, hitting just .179 in 79 games, the righthanded hitting Dempsey is expected to be re-signed. He is still valuable as a backup receiver because of experience, knowledge, defense and handling a pitching staff. A career .234 hitter, Dempsey is a pull hitter who has a good eye, but his swing is a little wide and he is often fooled by breaking stuff, especially pitches down and in and down and away. Dempsey's always been a tough out and a clutch hitter. He's a smart baserunner, but one with no speed. Dempsey's defense is still excellent. His throwing arm is weaker, but he works well with pitchers and blocks low pitches in good fashion.

OVERALL:

Dempsey has had a fine career and was instrumental in the Dodgers' 1988 championship season, batting .400 in the playoffs against the Mets, and starring the last game of the Series when Mike Scioscia was injured. Dempsey is a leader on and off the field and a strong clubhouse influence.

CHRIS GWYNN

Position: LF
Bats: L **Throws:** L
Ht: 6' 0" **Wt:** 200

Opening Day Age: 25
Born: 10/13/64 in Los Angeles, CA
ML Seasons: 3

Overall Statistics

	G	AB	R	H	D	T	HR	RBI	SB	BB	SO	AVG
1989	32	68	8	16	4	1	0	7	1	2	9	.235
Career	61	111	11	25	5	1	0	9	1	4	18	.225

HITTING, FIELDING, BASERUNNING:

The Dodgers have always hoped that someday Chris Gwynn might wind up in the same hitting class as his big brother, Tony. Chris is very similar to Tony in that he has a smooth, compact, and level swing, good hand-eye coordination and the ability to hit line drives. But he's batted only .225 in 111 big league at bats and hasn't shown either much patience (four walks) or the ability to make contact (18 strikeouts). And unlike Tony, Chris appears to be injury prone. He has speed and is a good baserunner, but's not a stealer, with only one major league theft. He's a good outfielder -- but again, not as good as Tony -- with a fair arm.

OVERALL:

It can't be easy being the baby brother of a big star. Gwynn has some hitting talent, but the Dodgers have projected him as a .300 hitter, even though he's done that only once in the minors. Chris has some skills, but hasn't been healthy enough to show them at the big league level. The Dodgers haven't used him much even when he's been available, and will have to give Gwynn a longer look to really find out what he can do.

FRANKLIN STUBBS

Position: LF
Bats: L **Throws:** L
Ht: 6' 2" **Wt:** 218

Opening Day Age: 29
Born: 10/21/60 in Laurinburg, NC
ML Seasons: 6

Overall Statistics

	G	AB	R	H	D	T	HR	RBI	SB	BB	SO	AVG
1989	69	103	11	30	6	0	4	15	3	16	27	.291
Career	542	1377	166	313	48	7	59	178	31	131	346	.227

HITTING, FIELDING, BASERUNNING:

Just a few years ago, Franklin Stubbs looked like he'd be the Dodgers' regular first baseman for many years to come. But though he packs a lot of power, Stubbs strikes out far too much and is far too inconsistent to be an everyday player. That's why the Dodgers acquired Eddie Murray, leaving the lefthanded hitting Stubbs as a reserve and a pinch hitter -- a role he's handled well. He's turned out to be one of the National League's top pinch hitters, batting .308 with two homers in 1988 and belting six pinch hits, including a homer, last year. Stubbs has a big swing and a lot of holes for pitchers to exploit. He is easily fooled with breaking stuff, and is strictly a fastball hitter. Stubbs has very good speed for a big man and is a 77% career stealer. He is only so-so on defense, but much better at first base than the outfield.

OVERALL:

With Murray around, Stubbs isn't going to get much playing time. He's shown he can be a good bench player. He probably needs a different setting if he's going to get a chance to play every day again.

HITTING:

Mike Aldrete was a forgotten man on the Expos bench last season. After being acquired in a trade with the Giants for outfielder Tracy Jones, the lefthanded hitting Aldrete was told he could expect 400 at bats as a substitute for left fielder Hubie Brooks and first baseman Andres Galarraga, both righthanded hitters, and in spot duty throughout the outfield. But Aldrete got off to a slow start, hitting only .100 in 20 April at bats, and the expected playing time never appeared. When he did get his few playing chances, a rusty Aldrete wasn't able to produce, and found himself back on the bench for extended periods. Aldrete finished the season hitting .221 with one homer and 12 RBIs in 136 at bats.

Aldrete did have some pluses. He was an extremely effective pinch hitter, hitting .308 with four doubles and 10 RBIs in 26 at bats. Aldrete is a .302 hitter in pinch roles during his career. And he was reasonably patient, walking in about 12% of his plate appearances. On the other hand, he struck out once for every 4.5 at bats after having previously struck out about once every 6.5 at bats in his career. Obviously, Aldrete was lacking in confidence after getting off to a slow start. In his three previous seasons, Aldrete had shown himself to be a solid clutch hitter while hitting .325 in 357 at bats in 1987 and .267 in 389 at-bats in 1988. He'd had a career average of .321 with runners on base, .257 with the bases empty.

BASERUNNING:

Aldrete gets average marks as a baserunner -- not fleet of foot, not very aggressive and not excellent at rounding the bases. After stealing six bases in each of his two previous seasons, Aldrete stole only once last season and was caught three times.

FIELDING:

Aldrete is a capable defensive player and appeared at four positions for the Expos last season, splitting his time between first base and all three outfield positions. Most of his playing time came in right and left fields. An outfielder by trade, Aldrete has an average arm and is aggressive chasing down fly balls. He led National League left fielders with an average of 2.37 putouts per nine innings in 1988.

OVERALL:

With the Expos in desperate need of lefthanded hitters, Aldrete should get another chance at being the fourth outfielder and spare first baseman this season. But he will have to produce quickly for Montreal not to give up on him.

MIKE ALDRETE

Position: RF/LF
Bats: L **Throws:** L
Ht: 5'11" **Wt:** 185

Opening Day Age: 29
Born: 1/29/61 in Carmel, CA
ML Seasons: 4

Overall Statistics

	G	AB	R	H	D	T	HR	RBI	SB	BB	SO	AVG
1989	76	136	12	30	8	1	1	12	1	19	30	.221
Career	425	1098	133	304	59	6	15	138	14	151	179	.277

Where He Hits the Ball

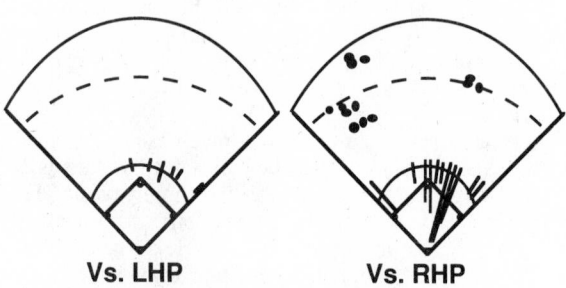

Vs. LHP   **Vs. RHP**

1989 Situational Stats

	AB	H	HR	RBI	AVG		AB	H	HR	RBI	AVG
Home	59	15	0	5	.254	LHP	17	4	0	3	.235
Road	77	15	1	7	.195	RHP	119	26	1	9	.218
Day	47	12	1	6	.255	Sc Pos	34	6	0	11	.176
Night	89	18	0	6	.202	Clutch	40	6	0	3	.150

1989 Rankings (National League)

→ 1st in worst hitting on a 3-2 count (.000) - *players with 20 PA on a 3-2 count*

HITTING:

Even a tremendous finish couldn't salvage Hubie Brooks' 1989 season. Despite hitting .384 with four home runs and 18 RBIs in September, Brooks suffered through his worst major league season since 1983. A prolonged slump through July (.178) and August (.202, one homer, five RBIs) led to his benching in late August and early September -- in favor of rookie Larry Walker -- as the Expos desperately tried to hang on in the National League East pennant race. For Brooks, an Expo mainstay since 1985, riding the bench while healthy was a new experience.

A fastball hitter who can be made to look bad on offspeed pitches (many a Brooks bat has ended up in the seats just behind the third-base dugout), Brooks hits to all fields, but his power is mainly to left. Brooks has tantalized Expos fans with displays of differing talents in his five years in Montreal, hitting .340 before being injured after 80 games in 1986, smacking 14 homers and driving in 72 runs while playing only 112 games in '87 and hitting 20 homers with 90 RBIs in a full 1988 season. Throughout, he has been known as Mr. Clutch, a devastating two-out hitter with runners on. But even that tailed off last season, as Brooks hit .265 with runners on and .279 with runners in scoring position.

BASERUNNING:

Brooks isn't catcher-slow, but he doesn't have much speed. He's decent at going from second to home or first to third, but Hubie has also been known to make the occasional baserunning blunder. Brooks stole only six bases while being caught 11 times last year, one of the worst success rates in the majors.

FIELDING:

Brooks plays right field like the converted third baseman and shortstop that he is. He turns every fly ball into an adventure, making routine plays heartstopping by overrunning balls and taking bad angles to the ball. In two years in the outfield, he has yet to learn to play balls off the wall or balls that bounce around in the corner. His one saving grace in the outfield is a strong arm that stops opposing baserunners in their tracks.

OVERALL:

Brooks is considered a steadying influence in the clubhouse, a player who does his work and stays out of trouble. He was extremely upset with his benching during a pennant race and has vowed to come back strong. For Brooks to bounce back, he will have to terrify lefthanders once again. Prior to last season, Brooks had four straight years of hitting .310 or better against lefties. Last year, that dropped to .284.

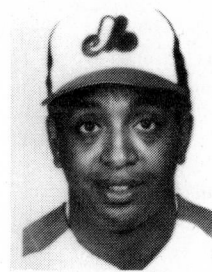

HUBIE BROOKS

Position: RF
Bats: R **Throws:** R
Ht: 6' 0" **Wt:** 200

Opening Day Age: 33
Born: 9/24/56 in Los Angeles, CA
ML Seasons: 10

Overall Statistics

	G	AB	R	H	D	T	HR	RBI	SB	BB	SO	AVG
1989	148	542	56	145	30	1	14	70	6	39	108	.268
Career	1198	4514	487	1244	224	29	103	609	55	285	752	.276

Where He Hits the Ball

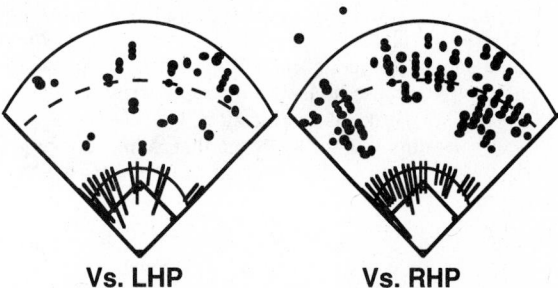

Vs. LHP   **Vs. RHP**

1989 Situational Stats

	AB	H	HR	RBI	AVG		AB	H	HR	RBI	AVG
Home	260	75	7	32	.288	LHP	162	46	6	23	.284
Road	282	70	7	38	.248	RHP	380	99	8	47	.261
Day	149	40	9	24	.268	Sc Pos	147	41	5	58	.279
Night	393	105	5	46	.267	Clutch	97	27	3	14	.278

1989 Rankings (National League)

➡ 3rd in sacrifice flies (8)
➡ 9th in caught stealing (11)
➡ 10th in GDPs (15)
➡ Led the Expos in sacrifice flies
➡ Led NL Right Fielders in batting average (.268), strikeouts (108), singles (100), sacrifice flies, caught stealing, hits (145), doubles (30), grounder/flyabll ratio (1.18) and errors (9) - *right fielders with 502 PA*

PITCHING:

Despite what will look in the yearbooks as a successful season, Tim Burke was a disappointment to the Expos in 1989. His numbers all look good -- 9-3 record, 28 saves, 2.55 earned run average -- but one number puts the season in perspective -- 11. That's how many save opportunities Burke frittered away. Those blown saves have Expos management wondering if Burke is suited to be the closer out of the bullpen.

Burke was the successful chairman of a bullpen-by-committee in 1987 and '88, but when Jeff Parrett was traded away before the start of the 1989 season, he found himself as the only closer. Tim had trouble handling the job on his own and will certainly find himself with more help in the bullpen this year.

Burke is primarily a two-pitch pitcher, with a sinking fastball and a slider. He relies on his infielders as the majority of his outs come on the ground, with the number of groundouts increasing when he is most effective. Because he isn't an overpowering pitcher, the key for Burke is his location. He allowed 2.33 walks per nine innings and even that is high for him -- in 1987 he allowed an average of only 1.67 walks per nine innings.

Tim sometimes gets into trouble by starting hitters off with a fat pitch. Batters hit .340 off him when putting the first pitch into play. While Burke was still effective against righthanders, he had his problems pitching to lefties, who hit .245 with five home runs in 159 at bats. By comparison, righthanders hit .203 with one homer in 149 at bats.

FIELDING, HITTING, BASERUNNING:

While Burke has an unconventional wind-up, keeping his hands apart until he plucks the ball from his glove, he is still an agile fielder who takes charge in the infield. Even when in the stretch, Burke is a little slow coming to the plate. Last year that resulted in eight stolen bases against him with only one caught stealing. Burke is a terrible hitter who, fortunately, doesn't have to swing the bat very often.

OVERALL:

Burke's career earned run average is the second best among National League pitchers with at least 450 innings pitched, behind only John Franco's. That proves he is more than capable as a reliever. Burke's inability to close out so many games, however, calls into question whether he is aptly suited to being a closer. He will certainly need more help against left-handed hitters.

TIM BURKE

Position: RP
Bats: R **Throws:** R
Ht: 6' 3" **Wt:** 200

Opening Day Age: 31
Born: 2/19/59 in Omaha, NE
ML Seasons: 5

Overall Statistics

	W	L	ERA	G	GS	Sv	IP	H	R	BB	SO	HR
1989	9	3	2.55	68	0	28	84.2	68	24	22	54	6
Career	37	19	2.48	330	2	76	479.1	405	147	154	323	32

Where They Hit the Ball

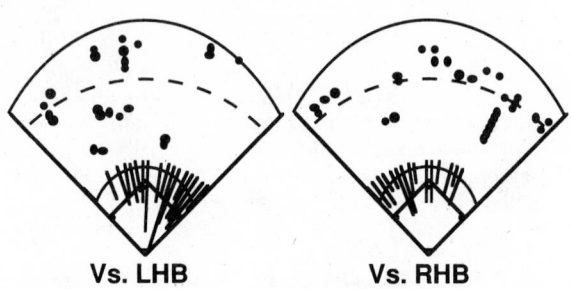

Vs. LHB   **Vs. RHB**

1989 Situational Stats

	W	L	ERA	Sv	IP		AB	H	HR	RBI	AVG
Home	7	0	2.35	13	46.0	LHB	159	39	5	16	.245
Road	2	3	2.79	15	38.2	RHB	143	29	1	21	.203
Day	2	0	1.00	10	27.0	Sc Pos	82	21	1	30	.256
Night	7	3	3.28	18	57.2	Clutch	222	51	4	31	.230

1989 Rankings (National League)

- ➡ 1st in blown saves (11)
- ➡ 2nd in worst save percentage (71.8%) - *pitchers with 20 save opportunities*
- ➡ 3rd in save opportunities
- ➡ 4th in saves (28)
- ➡ 6th in games finished (52)
- ➡ 10th in games (68)
- ➡ Led the Expos in games, games finished, saves, blown saves, lowest percentage of inherited runners scoring (37.8%) and first batter efficiency (.222) - *team pitchers with 40 relief games*

MIKE FITZGERALD

Position: C
Bats: R **Throws:** R
Ht: 5'11" **Wt:** 190

Opening Day Age: 29
Born: 7/13/60 in Long Beach, CA
ML Seasons: 7

HITTING:

Mike Fitzgerald appeared to have had a potentially brilliant catching career ended by a nasty finger injury in 1986. Subsequent surgery did little to help him regain any semblance of throwing effectiveness. The situation was so bad that Fitzgerald had to win a spot on the Expos roster for the 1989 season as a bench player. All but written off as a catcher, he was pencilled in as a pinch hitter and third man behind the plate. That was a role Mike refused to accept. Fitzgerald ended up playing in 100 games and logging 290 at bats, the third highest total of his career.

All of a sudden, three years after his career-threatening injury, Fitzgerald has improved his lot. "His value has gone up this year," manager Buck Rodgers said late last season. "He has proven to us that he can do more behind the plate than he could a year ago. And we already knew he is a good clutch hitter." Fitzgerald is basically a singles hitter with limited power. Not a patient hitter, he often swings at the first pitch. He is basically a fastball hitter, and good breaking ball pitchers can give this spray hitter trouble.

Rodgers often puts on the hit-and-run with Fitzgerald at the plate. Mike has become one of the team's most dependable hitters with the game on the line, especially against lefthanders. Fitzgerald managed 42 runs batted in with his 69 hits in 1989. In eight bases-loaded situations in 1988, Fitzgerald was three for six with a double, a home run and two sacrifice flies.

BASERUNNING:

Like most catchers, Fitzgerald is slow of foot. Consequently, he is a conservative baserunner who rarely gambles; he looks for his coaches and follows their signs.

FIELDING:

Fitzgerald has good range and his handling of pitchers is excellent. Since the finger injury, throwing has been his problem. The arm strength is there, but Mike needs consistency and confidence. There were signs he was regaining his touch last year. He has the confidence of the pitchers he works with. In his five seasons with the Expos, the team has had a winning record and a better ERA when Fitzgerald is behind the plate than they do with other catchers.

OVERALL:

A respectable season has changed Fitzgerald's status. He is now counted upon to share the catching with Nelson Santovenia and to step in as the starter if Santovenia should get injured. Mike's baseball instincts are sound and he is the type of player who may eventually become a coach.

Overall Statistics

	G	AB	R	H	D	T	HR	RBI	SB	BB	SO	AVG
1989	100	290	33	69	18	2	7	42	3	35	61	.238
Career	571	1616	148	389	70	6	29	207	17	188	303	.241

Where He Hits the Ball

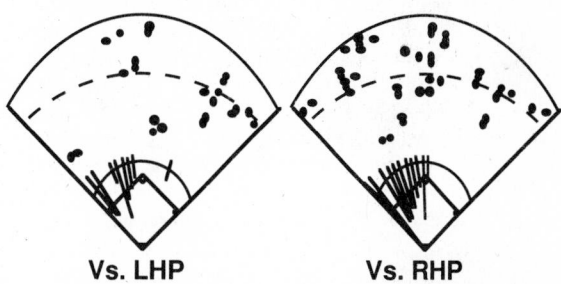

Vs. LHP   **Vs. RHP**

1989 Situational Stats

	AB	H	HR	RBI	AVG		AB	H	HR	RBI	AVG
Home	141	40	3	22	.284	LHP	101	27	2	12	.267
Road	149	29	4	20	.195	RHP	189	42	5	30	.222
Day	89	25	3	18	.281	Sc Pos	97	25	2	32	.258
Night	201	44	4	24	.219	Clutch	70	16	0	6	.229

1989 Rankings (National League)

➡ Did not rank near the top or bottom in any category

HITTING:

Tom Foley, who had taken two years to establish himself as a fine hitting second baseman, fell flat on his face last year. After quietly hitting .293 in 1987 and .260 in 1988, Foley had his 1989 season ruined by two prolonged mid-season slumps. He hit just .161 in June and .164 in August, finishing the season with a .229 batting average. That was well below Foley's career batting average of .254.

The platoon second baseman -- he plays almost exclusively against righthanded pitchers -- was in the No. 2 spot in the batting order for most of the season. He didn't seem comfortable in that spot. Foley found himself behind in the count often and wasn't able to dig himself out of those holes. Foley hit .199 after falling behind 0-1, .123 after 0-2 and .193 after 1-2.

A contact hitter with good bat control -- his 53 strikeouts last year were a career high -- Foley was able to sacrifice runners along and hit-and-run when called upon to do so by manager Buck Rodgers. He can hit the ball to all fields and can turn on mediocre inside pitches. Foley hit seven home runs in his 375 at-bats (winning a bet with teammate Spike Owen over who would hit the most homers) and laced 19 doubles. Foley showed more patience at the plate last year than ever before; his 45 walks were a career high by 15.

BASERUNNING:

For the third straight season, Foley was thrown out more often than he was successful in stolen base attempts. Foley was two for five last year after going two for nine in 1988 and six for 16 in 1987. Despite his penguin-like gait, however, Foley is an aggressive baserunner who often tries for the extra base.

FIELDING:

Unbeknownst to most fans, Foley is among the best fielding second basemen in the game and has manager Rodgers singing his praises. A converted shortstop, Foley shows great range to either side, though he seems to have more range to his right, and is equally adept at making diving plays to either side. Foley and Owen, acquired before the 1989 season, adapted to each other's play quickly and turned the double play well.

OVERALL:

Foley's fine defense means the Expos don't need a lot of hitting from him. But he'll have to hit more than .229. If Foley can revert back to form and hit .260, he'll be the lefthanded half of the platoon. If not, he may find himself on the bench.

TOM FOLEY

Position: 2B/3B
Bats: L **Throws:** R
Ht: 6' 1" **Wt:** 180

Opening Day Age: 30
Born: 9/9/59 in Columbus, GA
ML Seasons: 7

Overall Statistics

	G	AB	R	H	D	T	HR	RBI	SB	BB	SO	AVG
1989	122	375	34	86	19	2	7	39	2	45	53	.229
Career	721	1920	185	488	98	16	26	192	26	172	266	.254

Where He Hits the Ball

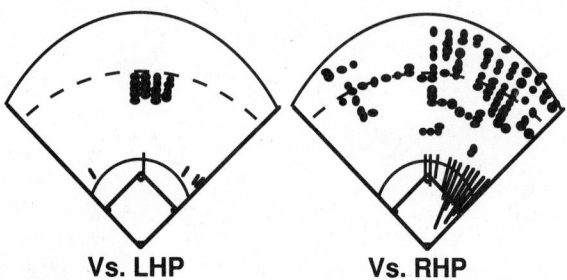

Vs. LHP   **Vs. RHP**

1989 Situational Stats

	AB	H	HR	RBI	AVG		AB	H	HR	RBI	AVG
Home	203	44	4	19	.217	LHP	23	6	0	2	.261
Road	172	42	3	20	.244	RHP	352	80	7	37	.227
Day	107	25	2	13	.234	Sc Pos	100	25	4	36	.250
Night	268	61	5	26	.228	Clutch	56	14	1	4	.250

1989 Rankings (National League)

➡ 3rd in least GDPs per GDP situation (2.8%) - *players with 50 PA in GDP situations*

➡ 5th in worst hitting on an 0-2 count (.043) - *players with 20 PA with an 0-2 count*

➡ Led NL Second Basemen in least GDPs per GDP situation

HITTING:

Andres Galarraga began last season in a battle with San Francisco's Will Clark to see which of the two would become the league's best first baseman. But while the Thrill lived up to his nickname, the Cat just chased his tail. For all intents and purposes, 1989 was a wasted season for the big Venezuelan. After hitting over .300 in each of his first two full seasons, and leading the league in hits and total bases in 1988, Galarraga slumped to .257 last year. His power was off, too, with his home run total dropping to 23 from 29 and his doubles to 30 from 42.

Worse still, Galarraga's problem with strikeouts -- he led the National League with 153 in 1988 -- didn't get better with experience. Galarraga struck out 158 times, his highest total yet. Although he didn't suffer through any prolonged slumps, Galarraga never found his stroke. His best month was June, when he hit .297 with five homers and 15 runs batted in.

When he's at the top of his game, Galarraga hits line drives into the gaps and monstrous home runs to all parts of the field, and generally eats lefthanders for lunch. But pitchers found his weakness and focused on it; Galarraga was unable to lay off low, outside breaking pitches.

BASERUNNING:

Galarraga has surprising speed and is an aggressive baserunner. While it takes him a few strides to get going, he can steal up to 15 bases and is one of the team's best in going from first to third or second to home.

FIELDING:

This is where Galarraga earned his nickname. The Cat is quickly gaining the reputation throughout the league as the successor to Keith Hernandez -- the finest fielder at first base. He is remarkably quick at going either to his left or right, has a strong, accurate arm, and is excellent at turning the 3-6-3 double play. His ability to dig balls out of the dirt saves the Expos infielders many errors.

OVERALL:

The Expos desperately need Galarraga's power and count on him to carry the team in stretches. A new batting coach last season, Joe Sparks, tried tinkering with Galarraga's mechanics but that only seemed to compound the problem. Galarraga was quoted several times during the season as saying he would go back to his old swing, but he could never seem to find it. The Expos hope that a new batting coach, Hal McRae, will put Galarraga back on the road to stardom.

ANDRES GALARRAGA

Position: 1B
Bats: R **Throws:** R
Ht: 6' 3" **Wt:** 235

Opening Day Age: 28
Born: 6/18/61 in Caracas, Venezuela
ML Seasons: 5

Overall Statistics

	G	AB	R	H	D	T	HR	RBI	SB	BB	SO	AVG
1989	152	572	76	147	30	1	23	85	12	48	158	.257
Career	585	2128	295	600	126	12	77	313	39	161	535	.282

Where He Hits the Ball

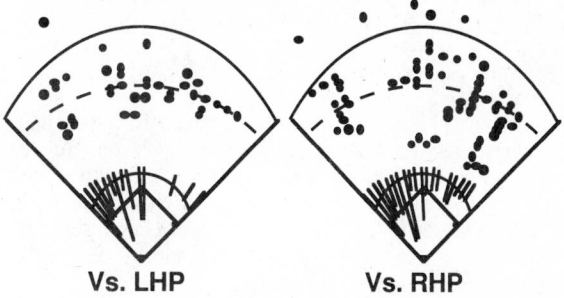

Vs. LHP **Vs. RHP**

1989 Situational Stats

	AB	H	HR	RBI	AVG		AB	H	HR	RBI	AVG
Home	286	69	13	50	.241	LHP	174	67	11	37	.385
Road	286	78	10	35	.273	RHP	398	80	12	48	.201
Day	147	34	3	15	.231	Sc Pos	144	32	5	54	.222
Night	425	113	20	70	.266	Clutch	118	28	6	17	.237

1989 Rankings (National League)

➡ 1st in strikeouts (158), hit by pitch (13), highest batting average vs. lefthanded pitchers (.385 - *players with 125 PA vs. LHP*) and lowest batting average vs. righthanded pitchers (.201 - *players with 377 PA vs. RHP*)

➡ 2nd in on-base average vs. lefthanded pitchers (.449), slugging percentage vs. left-handed pitchers (.672) and lowest percentage of swings put into play (35.1%) - *players with 502 PA*

➡ Led the Expos in strikeouts, home run frequency (24.9 ABs per HR), slugging percentage (.434), total bases (248), hit by pitch, home runs (23), runs (76), RBIs (85), pitches seen (2,339), grounder/flyball ratio (1.77)

HITTING:

Damaso Garcia fell just a few pages short of authoring the comeback story of the year. As it was, the 33-year old, nine-year major-league veteran made a stirring effort. Garcia was virtually out of baseball for two years, after suffering a knee injury which required surgery and a long period of recuperation. He was invited by the Expos to attend spring training with no promises attached. He impressed manager Buck Rodgers, and when camp broke, Damaso headed north with the team and contributed steadily, hampered at times by a heel injury rather than by the knee.

As the Expos stayed atop the National League East for 41 days, Garcia was an important cog in the offense, hitting .369 in 50 at bats in July and then .294 in August. Though not the hitter he was earlier in his career -- Garcia earned the Silver Slugger in 1982 as the best hitter at his position in the American League -- he was effective. Used in a platoon role at second base with lefthanded hitting Tom Foley, Garcia hit .298 for the season against lefthanded pitching.

One of the least patient hitters in baseball, Garcia has never drawn more than 24 walks in a season. He's a good high ball hitter who likes to go after the first pitch fastball; he has trouble with low-and-away breaking stuff. Though undisciplined, Garcia seldom strikes out. He's a good hit-and-run man and an excellent bunter.

BASERUNNING:

Garcia is an intelligent baserunner, but has lost his speed and aggressiveness. With the Toronto Blue Jays he stole 54, 31 and 46 bases during a three-year period in which he batted .300 overall. With the Expos he stole five bases but was caught four times.

FIELDING:

The knee injury has robbed Garcia of some of his range, but the veteran made up for that by positioning himself properly and adjusting depending on the pitch. His two-year absence from the game did nothing to dull his baseball instincts.

OVERALL:

Garcia was sent home a few weeks before the end of the season, but not in disgrace. The Expos had fallen out of the pennant race and the decision was made to give younger players a chance. Though the Expos aren't interested in re-signing him, Garcia could help another team as a backup and occasional starter.

DAMASO GARCIA

Position: 2B
Bats: R **Throws:** R
Ht: 6' 0" **Wt:** 185

Opening Day Age: 33
Born: 2/7/57 in Moca, Dominican Republic
ML Seasons: 11

Overall Statistics

	G	AB	R	H	D	T	HR	RBI	SB	BB	SO	AVG
1989	80	203	26	55	9	1	3	18	5	15	20	.271
Career	1032	3914	490	1108	183	27	36	323	203	130	322	.283

Where He Hits the Ball

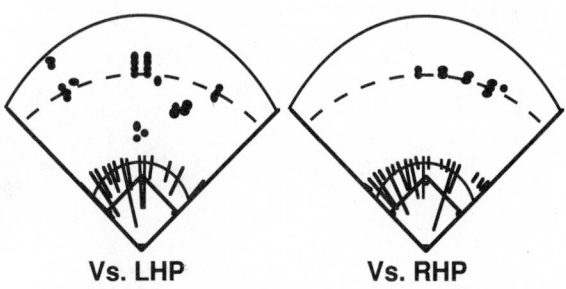

Vs. LHP   **Vs. RHP**

1989 Situational Stats

	AB	H	HR	RBI	AVG		AB	H	HR	RBI	AVG
Home	109	31	3	10	.284	LHP	131	39	3	10	.298
Road	94	24	0	8	.255	RHP	72	16	0	8	.222
Day	52	20	2	8	.385	Sc Pos	45	10	1	16	.222
Night	151	35	1	10	.232	Clutch	42	12	1	5	.286

1989 Rankings (National League)

➡ Did not rank near the top or bottom in any category

PITCHING:

Kevin Gross, a.k.a. Dr. Jekyll and Mr. Hyde, was like the little girl with the curl last season -- when he was good, he was very, very good; when he was bad, he was awful. Gross, acquired last off-season in a trade with the Phillies for Floyd Youmans and Jeff Parrett, had an exasperated Expos coaching staff working overtime trying to figure out what was wrong with him. Gross often followed complete games with one- or two-inning performances.

Gross, a power pitcher who struck out 158 batters in 201.1 innings, seemed to fall in love with a sidearm curveball last year. That was a pitch, coach Larry Bearnarth determined, that lefthanded hitters loved even more than Gross did. But even after eliminating the sidearm curve from his repertoire, which includes a fastball, a curve, and a slow curve, Gross seemed to have trouble with his release point and couldn't find any consistency.

Gross has had a problem throughout his career with the long ball and gave up 20 homers last year (his career high is 28 in 1986). Though his career record is below .500, Gross's value to a pitching staff comes in the fact that he is an inning-eater. He is one of only four National League pitchers to have gone over 200 innings pitched in each of the past five seasons. Gross likes to establish the inside corner of the plate and isn't afraid to brush back hitters (he led or tied for the National League lead in hit batsmen in 1986, '87 and '88 and hit six last year).

FIELDING:

A high leg kick and a move to first that is average at best make Gross susceptible to stolen bases. Last year, opposing baserunners stole 34 bases off Gross -- the third highest total in the major leagues -- and were caught only 13 times. His bulky throwing motion often puts Gross off-balance and in a poor position to field the ball. Gross is a capable hitter who hit a home run in each of the 1985, '86 and '87 seasons.

OVERALL:

The Expos counted heavily on Gross, a former All-Star, before the start of last season. But manager Buck Rodgers was beginning to lose his patience with Gross' up-and-down performances as the season wore on. Gross needs to find some consistency if he is ever to become a winner.

KEVIN GROSS

Position: SP
Bats: R **Throws:** R
Ht: 6' 5" **Wt:** 215

Opening Day Age: 28
Born: 6/8/61 in Downey, CA
ML Seasons: 7

Overall Statistics

	W	L	ERA	G	GS	Sv	IP	H	R	BB	SO	HR
1989	11	12	4.38	31	31	0	201.1	188	105	88	158	20
Career	71	78	3.95	234	195	1	1306.0	1276	626	518	885	124

Where They Hit the Ball

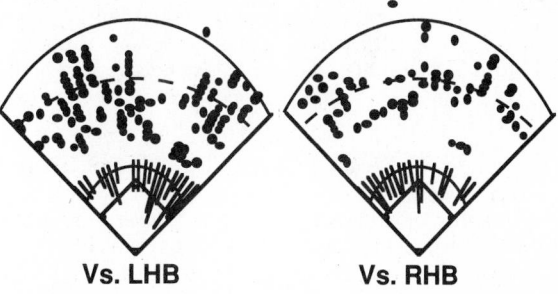

Vs. LHB   **Vs. RHB**

1989 Situational Stats

	W	L	ERA	Sv	IP		AB	H	HR	RBI	AVG
Home	6	4	4.29	0	94.1	LHB	418	101	10	44	.242
Road	5	8	4.46	0	107.0	RHB	342	87	10	42	.254
Day	2	0	1.46	0	37.0	Sc Pos	203	46	6	66	.227
Night	9	12	5.04	0	164.1	Clutch	50	12	1	4	.240

1989 Rankings (National League)

- 2nd in stolen bases allowed (34) and most pitches thrown per batter (3.9) - *pitchers with 502 IP*
- 3rd in worst ERA (4.38) and balks (5)
- 4th in walks allowed (88)
- 6th in shutouts (3)
- 8th in strikeouts per 9 innings (7.1) and hit batsmen (6)
- Led the Expos in caught stealing (13), balks, pitches thrown (3,370), stolen bases allowed, runs allowed (105) and earned runs allowed (98)

PITCHING:

Joe Hesketh appeared to have adjusted to the switch from starter to reliever admirably in 1988. However, after a horrible 1989 season, it appears that the lefthander's forte could be as a spot starter. A horrific May Day outing against the Reds seemed to destroy Hesketh's confidence, and he never recovered. That outing was the culmination of a slump in which Hesketh allowed runs in four consecutive appearances, and for all intents and purposes, it ended his season.

Hesketh finished with a 6-4 record and an awful 5.77 earned run average. But the season turned on that afternoon when the Reds nailed him for nine earned runs in one and a third innings on six hits, five walks, a wild pitch and a balk. The most disconcerting stat from the rout was that lefthanded batters were two for two with three walks. It was weeks before Hesketh could stop brooding about that outing and he had trouble with lefties for the rest of the season. Hesketh lost the bite on his slider for an extended period and was finally sent to the minors to regain his confidence.

The Expos have always liked Hesketh's arm. There was no loss in the velocity which had earned him the reputation of being a reliable power pitcher. Until last year, Hesketh had been tough on lefthanders. In 1988, he had limited lefties to a .205 batting average with 23 strikeouts in 78 at bats. Until 1989, he had allowed only two homers to lefties, one to Jose Cruz in 1985 and the other to John Kruk in 1987.

FIELDING, HITTING, BASERUNNING:

Probably the only highlight of Hesketh's 1989 season concerned his hitting. Or rather, his hit. When he singled against Dan Quisenberry on April 23, it ended a drought of 1,048 days. It would be his only hit of the season. Then again, he had only two at bats, so he hit .500. Hesketh was a fine baserunner early in his career, but understandably has never been the same since breaking his leg in a home-plate collision with the Dodgers' Mike Scioscia in August 1985.

OVERALL:

The Expos haven't given up on Hesketh and are counting on him to regain the bite on his slider. Though he's had some ups and downs, Hesketh has a 3.37 career ERA and has never had a losing season. Joe's inability to shake off a bad outing lends credence to the possibility that he will return to the starter's role he had when he first came up. There is too much talent there to waste.

JOE HESKETH

Position: RP
Bats: L **Throws:** L
Ht: 6' 2" **Wt:** 170

Opening Day Age: 31
Born: 2/15/59 in Lackawanna, NY
ML Seasons: 6

Overall Statistics

	W	L	ERA	G	GS	Sv	IP	H	R	BB	SO	HR
1989	6	4	5.77	43	0	3	48.1	54	34	26	44	5
Career	28	19	3.37	172	45	14	432.2	395	186	167	351	31

Where They Hit the Ball

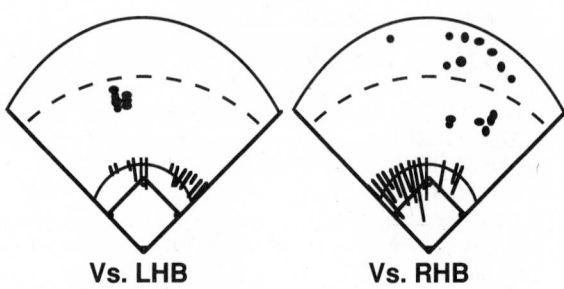

Vs. LHB   **Vs. RHB**

1989 Situational Stats

	W	L	ERA	Sv	IP		AB	H	HR	RBI	AVG
Home	1	3	8.00	1	27.0	LHB	57	17	2	15	.298
Road	5	1	2.95	2	21.1	RHB	128	37	3	17	.289
Day	3	1	4.26	1	19.0	Sc Pos	50	17	1	26	.340
Night	3	3	6.75	2	29.1	Clutch	73	20	2	12	.274

1989 Rankings (National League)

➡ Did not rank near the top or bottom in any category

HITTING:

Rex Hudler plays with an intensity more suited to football than baseball. After hitting a ninth-inning home run to tie a game, Expos teammates avoided a fired-up Hudler, fearing that his spirited high-fives might break a finger or two. His gung-ho approach to the game carries over to the batter's box, where he is a free-swinger who won't get cheated from taking his cuts.

Hudler, who languished in the minor leagues for nine years before being called up to the Expos midway through the 1988 season, showed flashes of power last season, hitting six home runs in 155 at bats. But Hudler's game is blinding speed, and his lack of discipline at the plate prevents him from taking full advantage of that talent. Hudler drew only six walks while striking out 23 times, resulting in a poor on-base average of .278.

Hudler appears to be made for platoon duty. Last year, he hit .254 with five home runs in 114 at bats against lefthanded pitchers while hitting only .220 with one homer in 41 at bats against righties. In 1988, Hudler hit .292 against lefties and .255 against righties. Though not very effective as a pinch hitter, hitting only .120, Hudler did have two home runs among his three pinch hits.

BASERUNNING:

Hudler is as aggressive as they come with his head-first slides on steal attempts and body blocks on fielders trying to turn double plays. Hudler stole 15 bases in 19 attempts last season. He was successful in his first 19 attempts after being called up in 1988, and finished that season with 29 steals in 36 attempts.

FIELDING:

Used mostly as a utility player, Hudler split his time between shortstop, second base and the outfield last season. A second baseman by trade, the Expos were so unimpressed with his defense that they signed Damaso Garcia to share time with Tom Foley at second base. When shortstop Spike Owen was injured in July, the Expos called up Jeff Huson from Triple A Indianapolis to play the position. The move to the outfield may have been an attempt to hide Hudler's glove.

OVERALL:

Hudler's speed makes him a valuable addition to a team, even if only as a pinch-runner in late innings. A streaky hitter (he hit .375 in April, .342 in June), Hudler can perform well in stretches and is capable enough to give position players an occasional rest. Learning patience at the plate could help him win a platoon role, but don't hold your breath.

REX HUDLER

Position: 2B/SS/LF
Bats: R **Throws:** R
Ht: 6' 2" **Wt:** 180

Opening Day Age: 29
Born: 9/2/60 in Tempe, AZ
ML Seasons: 5

Overall Statistics

	G	AB	R	H	D	T	HR	RBI	SB	BB	SO	AVG
1989	92	155	21	38	7	0	6	13	15	6	23	.245
Career	212	430	66	106	22	3	10	28	45	18	71	.247

Where He Hits the Ball

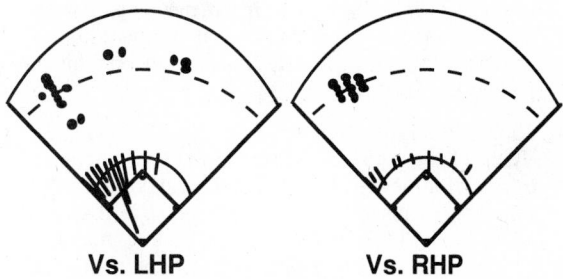

Vs. LHP   **Vs. RHP**

1989 Situational Stats

	AB	H	HR	RBI	AVG		AB	H	HR	RBI	AVG
Home	66	17	3	7	.258	LHP	114	29	5	12	.254
Road	89	21	3	6	.236	RHP	41	9	1	1	.220
Day	38	9	3	7	.237	Sc Pos	32	5	1	7	.156
Night	117	29	3	6	.248	Clutch	46	9	2	4	.196

1989 Rankings (National League)

➡ Did not rank near the top or bottom in any category

PITCHING:

Recognized as a power pitcher throughout his first five years in the major leagues, Mark Langston is working on finesse -- without losing the heat. While trying to add off-speed pitches to his repertoire and learning a new league (Langston was traded from the American League Mariners to the National League Expos on May 25), the lefthander equalled his strike-out total of 235 from the previous season. Langston has fanned 977 batters over the past four years.

Throwing the occasional junk ball -- and leaving the Kingdome -- had a profound effect on Langston's earned run average, which sunk to a career-low 2.74. Mark's ERA has sunk steadily since an injury-plagued 1985 season, when he posted a 5.47 ERA, dropping to 4.85, 3.84, 3.34 , and now to 2.74 in 1989. Langston's showcase pitch is a hard fastball, which on any given day will average around 92 miles per hour, and which he likes to ride in on the fists of right-handed hitters. However, Langston strikeout pitch is an excellent hard slider. He'll also fool some hitters with an occasional change-up.

Langston's unique delivery, with his high leg kick and flying elbows, adds to hitters' problems, making it difficult for them to pick up the release point. Under-standably, Langston is murder against lefthanders, who hit only .142 against him. Righthanders managed a weak .230. A durable pitcher, Langston completed eight games and, like many outstanding pitchers, often gets stronger as the game wears on. From the seventh inning on, Langston limited batters to a .202 batting average in 193 at bats. At 29, Langston appears to be entering his prime. Since making only 24 starts in 1985 because of a strained tendon in his left elbow, Langston has averaged 255 innings a year.

FIELDING, HITTING, BASERUNNING:

Langston didn't win a third straight Gold Glove last season, but he still proved himself to be a good athlete with his outstanding defensive work. His agility is such that few dare to bunt against him. He also has an excellent move to first. Langston also proved to be capable at the plate. Though he didn't have to hit in his five-plus seasons with the Mariners, Langston drove in three runs with 11 hits in 64 at bats (.172) after joining the Expos.

OVERALL:

Aside from the fact that he would be the ace of any rotation, Langston's superb work habits make him a tremendous asset for any team. He is capable of winning 20 games in a season, is ready to pitch every fifth day, and prepares meticulously both on game day and between starts.

MARK LANGSTON

Position: SP
Bats: R **Throws:** L
Ht: 6' 2" **Wt:** 183

Opening Day Age: 29
Born: 8/20/60 in San Diego, CA
ML Seasons: 6

Overall Statistics

	W	L	ERA	G	GS	Sv	IP	H	R	BB	SO	HR
1989	16	14	2.74	34	34	0	250.0	198	87	112	235	16
Career	86	76	3.80	200	197	0	1374.1	1206	653	668	1253	146

Where They Hit the Ball

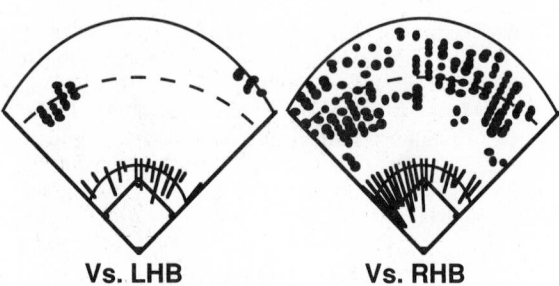

Vs. LHB   Vs. RHB

1989 Situational Stats

	W	L	ERA	Sv	IP		AB	H	HR	RBI	AVG
Home	8	5	3.58	0	113.0	LHB	113	16	1	4	.142
Road	8	9	2.04	0	137.0	RHB	792	182	15	75	.230
Day	4	7	3.91	0	71.1	Sc Pos	216	46	3	62	.213
Night	12	7	2.27	0	178.2	Clutch	127	26	2	9	.205

1989 Rankings (National League)

➡ 1st in strikeouts per 9 innings (8.9) and most pitches thrown per batter (4.0) - *pitchers with 162 IP*

➡ 2nd in ERA on the road (2.21) - *pitchers with 81 IP on the road*

➡ 3rd in ERA (2.39), walks allowed (93) and shutouts (4)

➡ Led the Expos in ERA, complete games (6), shutouts, walks allowed, strikeouts (175), lowest batting average allowed (.218), lowest slugging percentage allowed (.320), strikeouts per 9 innings and least HRs per 9 innings (.66) - *team pitchers with 162 IP*

HITTING:

Certain statistics support Dave Martinez' claim that he should be the Expos' everyday centerfielder. For instance, though May, June, July and August, when he played most of the time, Martinez's average was .293. On the other hand, to support the policy of platooning Martinez and Otis Nixon, manager Buck Rodgers can point to Martinez's .287 batting average against righthanders and .133 average versus lefties. In 30 at bats against southpaws, Martinez struck out 10 times.

Martinez has always been considered a platoon player. In 1987, he started 119 of the Cubs' 123 games against righthanders but none against lefties. In 1988, he started 105 games against righties but only six versus lefties. A singles hitter, Dave takes too many pitches and consistently falls behind in the count. Even though he is a fastball hitter, Martinez is often overmatched by pitchers who throw exceptional heat.

Martinez was a much better hitter on the road. In nearly equal at bats, he hit .339 on the road compared to .200 at home and had two home runs and 20 RBIs on the road compared to one and seven at home. Martinez did not thrive in clutch situations, hitting only .231 in the late innings of close games. However, with men in scoring position, he did hit .300. Martinez has thrived in pressure situations in other years. In 1988, he had seven hits, five for extra bases, in 13 at bats with the bases loaded. In 1987, he hit .371 in late-inning pressure situations.

BASERUNNING:

Martinez became more aggressive on the bases last year. Beside his 23 stolen bases in 27 attempts, he forced defenders into miscues on numerous occasions by making them rush their throws. Martinez often took big turns at first base and stretched singles into doubles.

FIELDING:

An excellent outfielder, Martinez is equally at home in left, center or right. He has great range, going to his left or his right with confidence. He goes back extremely well on fly balls, allowing him to play shallow. The Expos take advantage of his superior arm by playing him in center.

OVERALL:

A solid platoon player, Martinez has the chance to be more. He is assured of getting about 450 at bats as the starter against righties and may be given the chance to play full time if he can show more production against lefties. His happy disposition makes him a plus in the clubhouse.

DAVE MARTINEZ

Position: CF/RF
Bats: L **Throws:** L
Ht: 5'10" **Wt:** 150

Opening Day Age: 25
Born: 9/26/64 in New York, NY
ML Seasons: 4

Overall Statistics

	G	AB	R	H	D	T	HR	RBI	SB	BB	SO	AVG
1989	126	361	41	99	16	7	3	27	23	27	57	.274
Career	459	1375	175	362	48	22	18	116	66	128	269	.263

Where He Hits the Ball

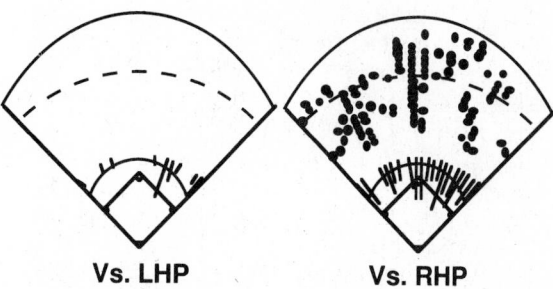

Vs. LHP   **Vs. RHP**

1989 Situational Stats

	AB	H	HR	RBI	AVG		AB	H	HR	RBI	AVG
Home	178	37	1	7	.208	LHP	30	4	0	1	.133
Road	183	62	2	20	.339	RHP	331	95	3	26	.287
Day	106	31	2	9	.292	Sc Pos	70	21	0	23	.300
Night	255	68	1	18	.267	Clutch	65	15	0	3	.231

1989 Rankings (National League)

➡ 2nd in least GDPs per GDP situation (2.0%) - *players with 50 PA in GDP situations*

➡ 4th in steals of third (7) and stolen base percentage (85.2%) - *players with 20 stolen base attempts*

➡ 9th in triples (7)

➡ Led the Expos in least GDPs per GDP situation, stolen base percentage and triples

➡ Led NL Center Fielders in least GDPs per GDP situation and stolen base percentage

DENNIS MARTINEZ

PINPOINT CONTROL

Position: SP
Bats: R **Throws:** R
Ht: 6' 1" **Wt:** 183

Opening Day Age: 34
Born: 5/14/55 in Granada, Nicaragua
ML Seasons: 14

PITCHING:

Over the years, Dennis Martinez has built the reputation of owning and controlling a wicked curveball. But that doesn't tell half the story. While his curve is among the five best in the game, Martinez also has a variety of pitches which he throws from any number of different angles. The Giants' Will Clark calls Martinez "the toughest righthander in the league" and he would have plenty of company in that assessment. In 1989, his 12th season, Martinez equalled his major league career high of 16 wins.

The 34-year old veteran depends on guile and craftiness and is what scouts call sneaky fast. He politely checks out scouting reports and listens to the words of the manager and coaches -- and then pitches the way he feels in that game. There have been few complaints. Martinez governs his vast repertoire (assorted fastballs, curves, and change-ups) for any particular game on how his pitches are working against each batter at that time. He often forces batters into a guessing game because he doesn't follow any set pattern. His next pitch is often determined by what the batter did on the previous pitch.

The Nicaraguan-born Martinez even confuses his own dugout with his pitch selection. Manager Buck Rodgers and his coaches have a game in the dugout trying to guess what pitch Martinez will throw next. "We aren't right that often," Rodgers says. "He has his own feel for the situation." Dennis also possesses excellent control. He only gave up 49 walks in 232 innings. Many of that already low total were intentional or semi-intentional; Martinez seldom issues a walk he hasn't thought about. A tough battler, Martinez refuses to give in to hitters. He is particularly tough in clutch situations and seldom loses leads.

FIELDING, HITTING, BASERUNNING:

Martinez works on all facets of his game. He holds runners fairly well, has a good move to first base, and is a decent fielder. Though he will never be mistaken for a hitter and bails out on almost every pitch, Martinez did manage nine singles and three runs batted in last year. He also helped himself with nine sacrifice bunts.

OVERALL:

A veteran of numerous pennant races, Martinez sets a fine example with his excellent work habits. He gets into trouble every now and then by spewing off to the media about team problems, but that's because he feels that, as a veteran, he has an obligation to stir things up when the team is playing poorly.

Overall Statistics

	W	L	ERA	G	GS	Sv	IP	H	R	BB	SO	HR
1989	16	7	3.18	34	33	0	232.0	227	88	49	142	21
Career	153	123	3.90	428	347	5	2485.1	2500	1192	755	1262	249

Where They Hit the Ball

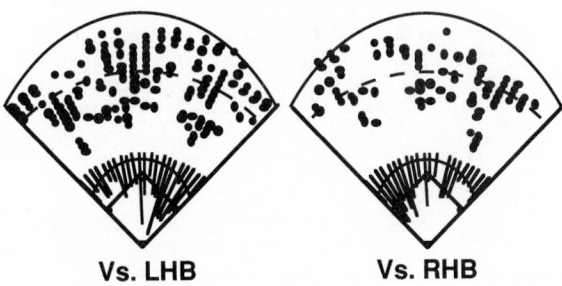

Vs. LHB **Vs. RHB**

1989 Situational Stats

	W	L	ERA	Sv	IP		AB	H	HR	RBI	AVG
Home	7	4	2.79	0	116.1	LHB	495	140	12	49	.283
Road	9	3	3.58	0	115.2	RHB	389	87	9	26	.224
Day	5	1	2.53	0	64.0	Sc Pos	189	39	4	49	.206
Night	11	6	3.43	0	168.0	Clutch	108	28	3	10	.259

1989 Rankings (National League)

→ 2nd in strikeout/walk ratio (2.9) - *pitchers with 162 IP*

→ 3rd in pickoff throws (251), hits allowed (227), hit batsmen (7) and GDPs induced (21)

→ 5th in win/loss percentage (.696) and lowest batting average allowed with runners in scoring position (.206) - *pitchers facing 150 batters with runners in scoring position*

→ Led the Expos in wins (16), games started (33), innings (232), home runs allowed (21), win/loss percentage, caught stealing (13), hits allowed, batters faced (950), hit batsmen, GDPs induced and run support per 9 innings (4.8) - *team pitchers with 162 IP*

PITCHING:

Andy McGaffigan, long a mainstay of the Expos bullpen, found himself shunted to a mop-up role more and more as last season progressed. Bullpen set-up men often go unrecognized, but McGaffigan had established himself as one of the National League's best. Until last year, that is, when Andy went 3-5 with a 4.68 earned-run average, stopping a streak of three straight seasons with ERAs of 2.76 or better.

For the first time in his career, McGaffigan gave up more hits than innings pitched (85 hits in 75 innings). Combined with the 30 walks he gave up, McGaffigan allowed almost 1.5 baserunners per inning, a disastrous amount for a pitcher who often comes into a game with runners already on base. Strangely enough, it was righthanded batters who did almost all of the damage against this righthanded pitcher, the second straight season McGaffigan has gone against the percentages. In 1987, McGaffigan was among the National Leagues toughest pitchers on righthanders, limiting them to a .193 batting average. But in 1988, that figure rose to .276 and last season it jumped even more, to an astounding .353, including three homers, in 150 at bats.

McGaffigan remains an effective pitcher against lefthanders, holding them to a .229 average, with no homers, in 140 at bats after limiting them to a .192 average in 1988. McGaffigan, a ground-ball type pitcher throughout his career, seemed to have lost some of his sinking action and gave up 14 doubles and three triples last year.

FIELDING, HITTING, BASERUNNING:

McGaffigan, though not blessed with cat-like quickness, is a capable fielder who can handle bunts to the mound. McGaffigan has only an average move to first base but has a stubborn streak that keeps baserunners close and sportswriters calling the office to check on deadlines. McGaffigan often throws to first seven or eight consecutive times to keep baserunners on their toes. The strategy had some success as he allowed eight stolen bases but gave his catchers the chance to throw out four potential thieves. Despite going one for one last year, McGaffigan is notorious for his bad hitting. His .048 lifetime average (six for 126) is one of the worst figures ever. He hasn't reached first enough to learn how to run the bases.

OVERALL:

The Expos showed little interest in re-signing McGaffigan after his disastrous season. The 33-year-old, nine-year veteran has had injury problems -- he has gone on the disabled list four times -- and may be reaching the end of his career.

ANDY MCGAFFIGAN

Position: RP
Bats: R **Throws:** R
Ht: 6' 3" **Wt:** 190

Opening Day Age: 33
Born: 10/25/56 in West Palm Beach, FL
ML Seasons: 9

Overall Statistics

	W	L	ERA	G	GS	Sv	IP	H	R	BB	SO	HR
1989	3	5	4.68	57	0	2	75.0	85	40	30	40	3
Career	34	30	3.31	331	51	23	742.0	674	297	260	554	47

Where They Hit the Ball

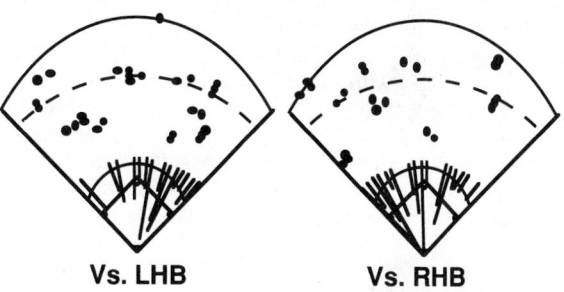

Vs. LHB   **Vs. RHB**

1989 Situational Stats

	W	L	ERA	Sv	IP		AB	H	HR	RBI	AVG
Home	3	2	4.66	0	36.2	LHB	140	32	0	16	.229
Road	0	3	4.70	2	38.1	RHB	150	53	3	32	.353
Day	2	2	4.76	1	22.2	Sc Pos	94	30	0	41	.319
Night	1	3	4.64	1	52.1	Clutch	106	28	0	12	.264

1989 Rankings (National League)

➡ Did not rank near the top or bottom in any category

HITTING:

Otis Nixon has the lightning but he doesn't have the lumber. Nixon, the brother of the Giants' Donnell Nixon, is an extremely fast, intelligent baserunner, but the problem has been finding a way to get him to first base. After a winter session with Harry "The Hat" Walker, Nixon was being counted on to hit more ground balls, allowing him to take advantage of his blazing speed. But the plan didn't work as Nixon's average dropped to .217 from .244. There is no question about Nixon's ability to wreak havoc once on base, as the Expos gained full value for Nixon's 56 hits in 258 at-bats. He stole 37 bases and scored 41 runs in his limited opportunities. Oddly, Nixon became most dependable when he was written off. Opposing managers often issued intentional walks with Nixon on-deck. Under those conditions, Nixon once cleared the bases with a double, and another time hit a two-run double. All told, Nixon picked up 10 of his 21 RBIs in bases-loaded situations. Ironically, Nixon, a player ideally suited to leadoff if he could get on base, hit .250 with runners in scoring position and .208 the rest of the time. A spray singles hitter, the switch-hitting Nixon hit .233 against lefthanders and only .194 against righthanders. Nixon has a tendency to wait for his pitch too often, falling behind in the count, and can be fooled by offspeed pitches.

BASERUNNING:

The backbone of Nixon's game. An aggressive baserunner, Nixon follows instructions well and makes things happen on the basepaths. He reads situations quickly on base hits. In 1988, he led the team in stolen bases with 46 despite playing in only 90 games.

FIELDING:

Nixon's speed helps compensate for his inferior throwing arm. He does hit the cutoff man and basically keeps runners honest. He plays a shallow centerfield and is excellent at going back on fly balls. The fleet Nixon gets to many balls other outfielders only dream of catching.

OVERALL:

Nixon didn't get his chances until late in his career and he is now a fading 31-year-old veteran. As long as he can keep his speed, he should find a job as a spare outfielder and pinch-runner. His numbers in 1989 were not as good as his 1988 totals, with a slight drop in stolen base percentage and a rise in grounding into double plays. Combined with his drop in batting average, even a slight drop in speed can be the difference for a one-dimensional player like Nixon.

OTIS NIXON

Position: CF
Bats: B **Throws:** R
Ht: 6' 2" **Wt:** 180

Opening Day Age: 31
Born: 1/9/59 in Evergreen, NC
ML Seasons: 7

Overall Statistics

	G	AB	R	H	D	T	HR	RBI	SB	BB	SO	AVG
1989	126	258	41	56	7	2	0	21	37	33	36	.217
Career	506	908	175	202	23	5	3	55	142	94	137	.222

Where He Hits the Ball

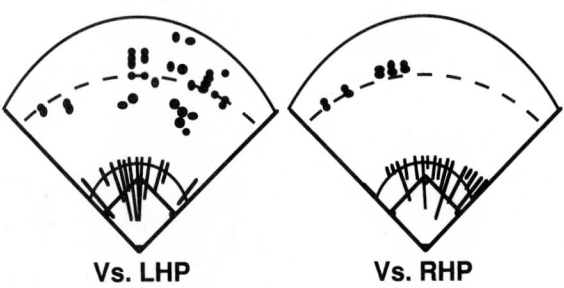

Vs. LHP   **Vs. RHP**

1989 Situational Stats

	AB	H	HR	RBI	AVG		AB	H	HR	RBI	AVG
Home	132	28	0	12	.212	LHP	150	35	0	12	.233
Road	126	28	0	9	.222	RHP	108	21	0	9	.194
Day	73	19	0	14	.260	Sc Pos	56	14	0	20	.250
Night	185	37	0	7	.200	Clutch	54	14	0	5	.259

1989 Rankings (National League)

- ➡ 2nd in steals of third (9)
- ➡ 5th in bunts in play (29) and caught stealing (12)
- ➡ 7th in stolen bases (37)
- ➡ 10th in hitting with the bases loaded (.400) - *players with 10 PA with the bases loaded*
- ➡ Led the Expos in caught stealing, bunts in play, steals of third and hitting on a 3-2 count (.296) - *team players with 20 PA on a 3-2 count*
- ➡ Led NL Center Fielders in steals of third and hitting with the bases loaded

HITTING:

For the first half of 1989, Spike Owen was the Expos' most valuable player. For the second half, he was just another Argenis Salazar. The combative shortstop did all the Expos could ask of him in the first four months of the season, getting timely hits and drawing important walks out of his No. 8 spot in the order. But Owen slumped badly in the second half and has Expos fans and management wondering just what they'll be paying more than $1 million for next season.

Owen is a slap hitter with good bat control (44 strikeouts), making him one of manager Buck Rodgers' favorite candidates for the hit-and-run. The diminutive shortstop has some power, having hit six home runs -- most of which hugged the left-field foul line and barely cleared the fence -- and 17 doubles, but the key to his success is patience at the plate. Owen drew 59 walks in his first 323 plate appearances, a valuable tool for an eighth place hitter. By getting on base with a walk, Owen, at worst, allowed the offense to bring the pitcher to the plate and start the next inning with the top of the order. During that successful span, Spike's on-base average was .384. But over his last 190 plate appearances, Owen walked only 17 times and had on on base average of .290.

BASERUNNING:

Like everything else about his game, Owen is aggressive on the bases. While his speed is limited (three stolen bases in five attempts), he rounds the bases well and goes for the extra base at every opportunity. He makes opposing second basemen and shortstops pay the price on double plays, sliding hard into second base.

FIELDING:

In the field Owen is smoother than peanut butter. Though he rarely makes flashy plays, Spike gobbles up everything he gets to, bobbling balls about as often as he hits homers. His heady play usually puts him in the right position to make up for his somewhat limited range. Owen's arm strength is only average, but he has an uncanny accuracy on throws to first base, even while on the run. He's a good pivot man on double plays.

OVERALL:

There's no doubt about Owen's will to win. His intensity and fiery play quickly made him one of the team leaders after he joined the Expos in a trade with Boston. However, Owen will have to regain the discipline he showed at the plate early in the season to be a valuable member of the team.

SPIKE OWEN

Position: SS
Bats: B **Throws:** R
Ht: 5'10" **Wt:** 165

Opening Day Age: 28
Born: 4/19/61 in Cleburne, TX
ML Seasons: 7

Overall Statistics

	G	AB	R	H	D	T	HR	RBI	SB	BB	SO	AVG
1989	142	437	52	102	17	4	6	41	3	76	44	.233
Career	867	2847	353	682	111	36	25	253	55	311	299	.240

Where He Hits the Ball

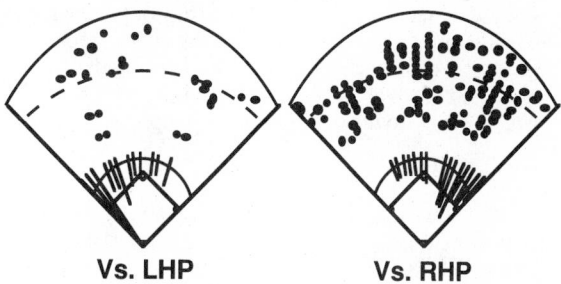

Vs. LHP   **Vs. RHP**

1989 Situational Stats

	AB	H	HR	RBI	AVG		AB	H	HR	RBI	AVG
Home	201	55	5	27	.274	LHP	131	36	2	14	.275
Road	236	47	1	14	.199	RHP	306	66	4	27	.216
Day	119	34	2	11	.286	Sc Pos	102	28	2	34	.275
Night	318	68	4	30	.214	Clutch	91	21	3	10	.231

1989 Rankings (National League)

➡ 1st in hitting on a 3-1 count (.636) - *players with 10 PA on a 3-1 count*

➡ 2nd in intentional walks (25) and hitting on a 0-2 count (.364) - *players with 20 PA on a 0-2 count*

➡ 3rd in highest percentage of pitches taken (63.2%) - *players with 502 PA*

➡ 7th in highest percentage of swings put into play (52.8%)

➡ 8th in pitches seen per plate appearance (3.7)

➡ Led the Expos in intentional walks, pitches seen per plate appearance, percentage of swings put into play, hitting on a 3-1 count and hitting on a 0-2 count

PITCHING:

Pascual Perez has been described as a marionette with one string missing -- he's all arms and legs as he high steps from the mound to first base, and from the mound to the dugout. Pascual's antics delight his fans and annoy opponents. He keeps runners close by peeking through his legs; he charges off the mound and is seated on the bench by the time a fly ball is caught for the third out. In short, he is the absolute hot dog.

But make no mistake about his ability. Perez can pitch. Pascual is a power pitcher with an absolutely devastating slider, a pitch which he throws as hard as many pitchers' fastballs, but with a tight, hard break. Even when opposing hitters expect the slider, they can't count on making contact. Perez's control is so good he sometimes thinks he's bulletproof. He has a tendency to challenge hitters too often instead of wasting a pitch. Perez's showmanship occasionally extends to his pitch selection. He throws an eephus pitch -- which resembles a softball lob and often comes down over the plate -- a couple of times a game, usually to the opposing team's top slugger.

Perez, who has a history of drug problems, spent spring training last year in a rehabilitation center and got off to a terrible start when he rejoined the Expos. At 0-6, he was sent to the bullpen on May 19 for a three week stay. When he returned to the starting rotation, Perez regained his mastery and was voted Expos' player of the month for August. After posting an earned run average of 6.83 in May, Perez was spectacular for the rest of the season, with ERAs of 2.03, 3.25, 2.27 and 2.60 in the ensuing months.

FIELDING, HITTING, BASERUNNING:

Despite the hijinx, Perez is an outstanding fielder. He holds runners well even if his methods are unorthodox. Pascual is a good enough baserunner that he was frequently used as a pinch-runner in 1988. That policy, however, was abandoned last season. Perez found a renewed vigor at the plate in '89. After breaking an 0-for-57 slump in September 1988, Perez, who uses heavily padded gloves when hitting, had 11 hits in 54 at-bats last season, driving in eight runs.

OVERALL:

Perez was signed by the Yankees to a big money contract – indeed, enormous money considering his past problems and won-loss record. Because of his nine-inning mentality, Perez can be a valuable man for his new club. However, he can quickly lose his confidence and needs constant positive reinforcement. Pitching in the Bronx Zoo isn't going to be easy for him, but he is perfectly capable of winning 15 games if handled right.

PASCUAL PEREZ

Position: SP/RP
Bats: R **Throws:** R
Ht: 6' 3" **Wt:** 180

Opening Day Age: 32
Born: 5/17/57 in San Cristobal, Dominican Republic
ML Seasons: 9

Overall Statistics

	W	L	ERA	G	GS	Sv	IP	H	R	BB	SO	HR
1989	9	13	3.31	33	28	0	198.1	178	85	45	152	15
Career	64	62	3.48	190	176	0	1156.1	1091	512	317	769	100

Where They Hit the Ball

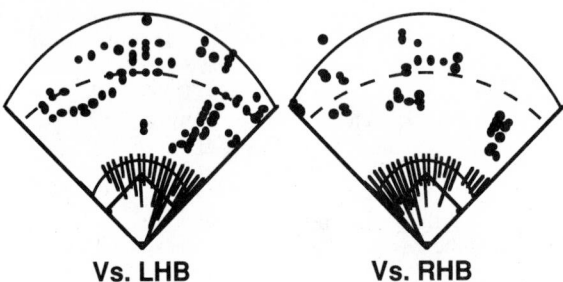

Vs. LHB   **Vs. RHB**

1989 Situational Stats

	W	L	ERA	Sv	IP		AB	H	HR	RBI	AVG
Home	6	9	2.80	0	125.1	LHB	417	100	9	38	.240
Road	3	4	4.19	0	73.0	RHB	334	78	6	35	.234
Day	1	3	3.92	0	43.2	Sc Pos	170	39	3	56	.229
Night	8	10	3.14	0	154.2	Clutch	67	27	0	11	.403

1989 Rankings (National League)

→ 1st in strikeout/walk ratio (3.4) - *pitchers with 162 IP*

→ 5th in least run support per 9 innings (3.5)

→ 8th in losses (13)

→ 9th in lowest on-base average allowed (.282) and highest strikeouts per 9 innings (6.9)

→ Led the Expos in losses, wild pitches (6) and grounder/flyball ratio (2.22)

CLUTCH HITTER

TIM RAINES

Position: LF
Bats: B **Throws:** R
Ht: 5' 8" **Wt:** 180

Opening Day Age: 30
Born: 9/16/59 in
Sanford, FL
ML Seasons: 11

HITTING:

Often called the National League's best leadoff hitter, Tim Raines found himself hitting cleanup for the first half of last season as the Expos tried to break up the righthanded threesome of Hubie Brooks, Andres Galarraga and Tim Wallach in the middle of their lineup. After driving in only 28 runs in 259 at-bats, Raines was switched back to leadoff as the Expos struggled for runs. Raines hit .286 with an on-base average of .395 and a slugging percentage of .418 for the season, very respectable numbers for most players but far below what is expected of Raines.

In '89, Tim's average was under .300 for the second straight year after he'd hit over .300 for four straight years. Raines is a first-ball hitter, putting the ball in play on the first pitch 90 times in 517 at-bats, but he also has a keen eye and won't swing unless he likes the pitch. He worked pitchers for 93 walks. He's a line-drive hitter with occasional power who hits to all parts of the field. Though he is among the fastest players in the league, he rarely tries to bunt and gets few infield hits because he hits the ball hard.

BASERUNNING:

Raines has lost much of the aggressiveness which once made him one of the most feared basestealers in the league. He stole 41 bases, but nine of those came in the final 10 games when the Expos had fallen out of the pennant race. He was thrown out only nine times, a success rate which should see him running much more often.

FIELDING:

Raines, who played second base until reaching the majors, has worked to make himself into a fine left fielder. His speed allows him to get to many balls and cut off hits into the gap, a necessity in spacious Olympic Stadium. He charges the ball well and gets into position to throw quickly. Although he has only an average arm, his throws are accurate and he rarely misses the cutoff man. Runners rarely try to take the extra base against him.

OVERALL:

Much is expected of this multi-talented player, but Raines's uninspired play over the past two seasons has made him the object of fans' wrath and numerous trade rumors. Raines needs to regain the aggressive attitude which once made him a dominant and intimidating player.

Overall Statistics

	G	AB	R	H	D	T	HR	RBI	SB	BB	SO	AVG
1989	145	517	76	148	29	6	9	60	41	93	48	.286
Career	1275	4848	869	1467	262	76	87	490	585	705	520	.303

Where He Hits the Ball

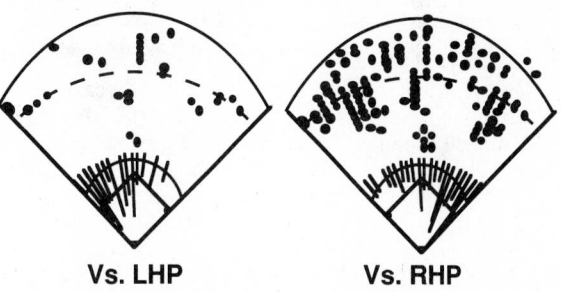

Vs. LHP **Vs. RHP**

1989 Situational Stats

	AB	H	HR	RBI	AVG		AB	H	HR	RBI	AVG
Home	258	70	6	30	.271	LHP	133	38	3	14	.286
Road	259	78	3	30	.301	RHP	384	110	6	46	.286
Day	154	45	4	18	.292	Sc Pos	105	35	1	48	.333
Night	363	103	5	42	.284	Clutch	97	33	1	15	.340

1989 Rankings (National League)

- ➡ 1st in on-base average batting leadoff (.399) - *players with 150 PA batting leadoff*
- ➡ 2nd in steals of third (9)
- ➡ 3rd in walks (93)
- ➡ 4th in stolen bases (41) and hitting with the bases loaded (.500) - *players with 10 PA with the bases loaded*
- ➡ 5th in on-base average (.395) and worst slugging percentage batting cleanup (.405) - *players with 150 PA batting clenup*
- ➡ Led the Expos in batting average (.286), singles (104), times on base (244), runs (76), stolen bases, walks, on-base average, steals of third, hitting with runners in scoring position and hitting in the clutch

HITTING:

Nelson Santovenia is proving to be a late bloomer. After breaking into the majors as a 27-year old in 1988, Santovenia has been a pleasant surprise for the Expos. Considering the dearth of offense from the catching position around the National League, Santovenia's .250 batting average, five home runs, 14 doubles and 31 RBIs in 304 at bats represents more than adequate production.

Santovenia was on his way to a fine season but he slumped in August (.222, no homers) and almost disappeared in September (.186, no homers). The Cuban-born, Miami-raised Santovenia, a member of the University of Miami Hurricanes National Champion baseball team in 1982, is generally a pull hitter with line-drive power whose doubles are usually off the wall in left field. He is a good fastball hitter who can be fooled by breaking pitches, especially from righthanders (30 strikeouts in 205 at bats against righthanders, seven in 99 at bats against lefthanders).

Santovenia cut his strikeouts drastically last year after striking out 77 times in 307 at bats in 1988. He also continued a pattern he began in 1988, when he hit .276 at home and only .198 on the road. In 1989, Santovenia hit .296 at home and .210 on the road.

BASERUNNING:

An agonizingly slow runner, Santovenia loses many hits because infielders can afford to play him deep, almost in the outfield on artificial surfaces. A full-fledged member in the Lumbering Catchers' Fraternity, his four career stolen bases have come when opposing catchers were laughing too hard to throw.

FIELDING:

Santovenia, who threw out Vince Coleman to stop Coleman's consecutive stolen base streak, has one of the strongest arms in the league. He can make all the plays on dribblers in front of the plate and is aggressive in pursuing pop-ups. However, Santovenia still needs to work on blocking pitches in the dirt and on blocking the plate. With manager Buck Rodgers, a former catcher, helping out, Santovenia has improved at calling the game.

OVERALL:

Santovenia has helped fill what had become a huge hole following the trade of Gary Carter. Although he's only been in the league two years, Santovenia is almost 29 years old, and his continued improvement as a player is unlikely unless he can avoid late-season collapses and can learn to hit on the road.

NELSON SANTOVENIA

Position: C
Bats: R **Throws:** R
Ht: 6' 3" **Wt:** 220

Opening Day Age: 28
Born: 7/27/61 in Pino del Rio, Cuba
ML Seasons: 3

Overall Statistics

	G	AB	R	H	D	T	HR	RBI	SB	BB	SO	AVG
1989	97	304	30	76	14	1	5	31	2	24	37	.250
Career	191	614	56	149	34	3	13	72	4	48	114	.243

Where He Hits the Ball

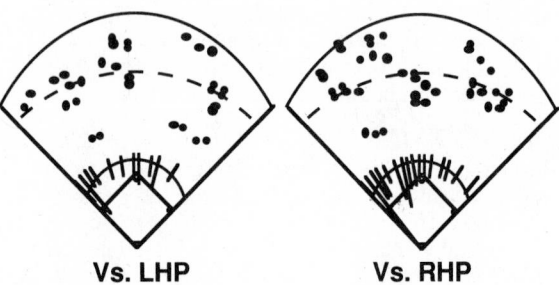

Vs. LHP   **Vs. RHP**

1989 Situational Stats

	AB	H	HR	RBI	AVG		AB	H	HR	RBI	AVG
Home	142	42	4	18	.296	LHP	99	28	2	9	.283
Road	162	34	1	13	.210	RHP	205	48	3	22	.234
Day	81	25	1	6	.309	Sc Pos	79	19	0	22	.241
Night	223	51	4	25	.229	Clutch	60	15	1	9	.250

1989 Rankings (National League)

➡ 4th in most GDPs per GDP situation (18.8%)
  - *players with 50 PA in GDP situations*

PITCHING:

Bryn Smith is the ultimate control pitcher. His ratio of walks per nine innings last year (2.26) was excellent, yet it was well off his 1988 performance. That season Smith walked 32 batters in 32 starts covering 198 innings, a league-leading average of 1.5 walks per nine innings. Despite the increase in walks, Smith probably became a better pitcher in 1989, developing a killer instinct. "This year he pitched better, finished hitters off better," pitching coach Larry Bearnarth said at the end of last season.

Smith also finished games off better, completing three games, more than in any season since 1985. It remains to be seen whether his stamina has improved or if the longer pitching stints were due to failures of the Expos' middle relievers. Following elbow surgery in 1986, Smith became a six- or seven-inning pitcher. However, when the Expos ran into bullpen problems this past season, all starters were forced to go longer. The longer outings may have contributed to Smith's second-half problems. The crafty righthander won nine of his first 21 starts but only once in his final 13.

A finesse pitcher, Smith moves the ball around the plate well. His velocity is only modest but he keeps hitters off-balance by changing speeds. His strikeout pitch is a palm ball, a tricky change-up which breaks down. His straight sinker is among the best. Smith doesn't waste pitches and likes to get ahead in the count quickly. Smith was extremely effective against lefthanded hitters, holding them to a .215 batting average and six home runs in 446 at bats. A dogged performer, Smith invariably is at his best in important games.

FIELDING, HITTING, BASERUNNING:

Smith is a good athlete and prides himself for trying to take care of all aspects of the game. He holds runners well and fields his position aggressively. He is a good bunter and led the Expos with 10 sacrifice bunts. Though nobody accuses him of being a sprint ace, Smith runs the bases intelligently.

OVERALL:

An excellent third or fourth starter on any staff -- 200 plus innings and 10-12 wins -- Smith's value to a team goes beyond numbers. His intelligent approach to pitching is an example for other pitchers, and his unselfish team-oriented attitude is an example to all his teammates.

Smith signed with the Cardinals in the off-season.

BRYN SMITH

Position: SP
Bats: R **Throws:** R
Ht: 6' 2" **Wt:** 205

Opening Day Age: 34
Born: 8/11/55 in Marietta, GA
ML Seasons: 9

Overall Statistics

	W	L	ERA	G	GS	Sv	IP	H	R	BB	SO	HR
1989	10	11	2.84	33	32	0	215.2	177	76	54	129	16
Career	81	71	3.28	284	193	6	1400.1	1310	592	341	838	108

Where They Hit the Ball

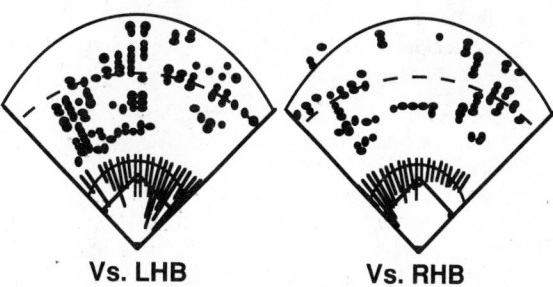

Vs. LHB   **Vs. RHB**

1989 Situational Stats

	W	L	ERA	Sv	IP		AB	H	HR	RBI	AVG
Home	5	5	2.73	0	125.1	LHB	446	96	6	34	.215
Road	5	6	2.99	0	90.1	RHB	348	81	10	29	.233
Day	4	5	3.00	0	84.0	Sc Pos	153	30	4	46	.196
Night	6	6	2.73	0	131.2	Clutch	58	16	2	2	.276

1989 Rankings (National League)

➡ 2nd in worst stolen base percentage (85.7%) - *pitchers with 162 IP*

➡ 4th in GDPs induced (20)

➡ 5th in GDPs per 9 innings (.84)

➡ 6th in lowest on-base average allowed (.274)

➡ 7th in grounder/flyball ratio (1.72)

➡ Led the Expos in lowest on-base average allowed, GDPs per 9 innings and least pitches thrown per batter (3.4)

TOUGH ON LEFTIES

ZANE SMITH

Position: RP/SP
Bats: L **Throws:** L
Ht: 6' 2" **Wt:** 195

Opening Day Age: 29
Born: 12/28/60 in
Madison, WI
ML Seasons: 6

PITCHING:

Zane Smith is Dave Dombrowski's insurance policy and it should pay in full in 1990. Dombrowski, the Expos' general manager, acquired Smith from the Atlanta Braves in the second half of 1989, in part to help out his struggling bullpen, but mostly in case the Expos couldn't sign Mark Langston after the season. Smith, a hard-throwing lefthander with enormous potential, had worn out his welcome in Atlanta, but his performance with the Expos almost certainly earned him a spot in the starting rotation in 1990.

Smith had been tantalizing the Braves since being picked in the third round of the 1982 June draft. After posting a 9-10 record with a 3.80 ERA as a rookie with the Braves in 1985, Smith was counted on to anchor their rotation for the next decade. He faltered in 1986 (8-16) but appeared to have come into his own in 1987 (15-10, league-leading 36 starts). But Smith fell apart in an injury-plagued 1988 season (5-10), and after starting 1989 at 1-12 was shipped to the Expos for three minor leaguers.

Converted to a reliever in Montreal, Smith was nothing short of sensational. He posted ERAs of 0.57 in July, 2.16 in August and 1.72 in September. With the Expos, Smith posted a 1.50 ERA over the final three months, allowing 39 hits in 48 innings. Quite a contrast to his first three months, when he had a 4.45 ERA and allowed 102 hits in 99 innings.

Smith has a good fastball and a hard slider, but still tries to finesse hitters by sometimes nibbling at the corners. He would be helped by a good offspeed pitch. He was murder on lefthanded batters, limiting them to a .143 batting average. Righthanders, however, hit him at a .289 clip.

FIELDING, HITTING, BASERUNNING:

At 6'3" and 195 pounds, Smith is a good athlete who fields his position well. Like many lefthanders, he has a good move to first base and can hold baserunners. Smith is a decent hitter who can help himself at the plate. Last year he had six hits in 32 at bats and laid down four sacrifice bunts. He led the National League with 14 sacrifice bunts in 1987.

OVERALL:

The Expos feel that Smith's poor first half last season was the result of the Braves rushing him back from elbow surgery late in the 1988 season. Now that he is fully recovered, the Expos are convinced he will be a consistent winner. Though Smith showed he can be an effective reliever last season, he will certainly be starting in 1990.

Overall Statistics

	W	L	ERA	G	GS	Sv	IP	H	R	BB	SO	HR
1989	1	13	3.49	48	17	2	147.0	141	76	52	93	7
Career	39	59	3.93	190	128	3	901.0	905	464	385	522	47

Where They Hit the Ball

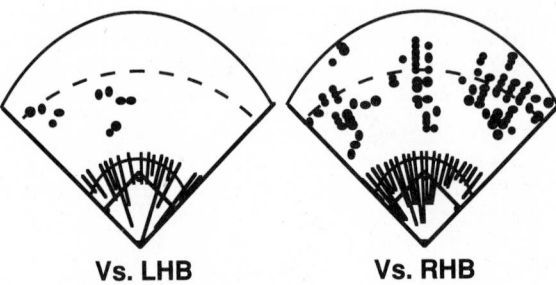

Vs. LHB   **Vs. RHB**

1989 Situational Stats

	W	L	ERA	Sv	IP		AB	H	HR	RBI	AVG
Home	1	5	2.81	1	77.0	LHB	140	20	1	11	.143
Road	0	8	4.24	1	70.0	RHB	419	121	6	56	.289
Day	0	1	3.30	0	30.0	Sc Pos	137	41	3	60	.299
Night	1	12	3.54	2	117.0	Clutch	139	36	2	12	.259

1989 Rankings (National League)

- 2nd in lowest batting average allowed vs. lefthanded hitters (.143) - *pitchers facing 125 LHB*
- 8th in losses (13)
- 9th in grounder/flyball ratio (2.90) - *all league pitchers*
- Led the Expos in ERA (1.50) and holds (6) - *all team pitchers*

HITTING:

Tim Wallach won the Expos' player-of-the-year award for the second time in three years in 1989, even though he didn't approach the numbers he put up the first time. It was the three-time Gold Glove third baseman's inability to emulate his career-year figures of 1987 (.298, 26 home runs, 123 runs batted in) which had some saying he had a bad year in 1989. But in fact his .277 average with 13 home runs and 77 RBIs placed him close to his career average in all three departments.

An out-and-out fastball hitter, Wallach has trouble with pitchers who can throw breaking balls at any stage in the count. Wallach is overly aggressive to a fault at the plate, often taking a full cut at the first pitch and showing little inclination to work the count in his favor. Although he came up as strictly a pull hitter, Wallach hits balls into the right-centerfield gap when he's in a groove. Tim is a doubles hitter; he tied for the league lead with Pedro Guerrero at 42 in 1989, hit 32 in 1988 and led the league with 42 in 1987.

When he's in a groove, Wallach comes through with the game on the line. But when he's in a slump, Tim chases breaking balls off the plate and tries to pull too many pitches. Manager Buck Rodgers tries to use the hit-and-run when Wallach is slumping to force him to go with the pitch.

BASERUNNING:

Wallach is a conservative baserunner for a very good reason. He has no speed. Don't let his three stolen bases fool you -- he was caught seven times.

FIELDING:

If a certain Hall of Famer named Mike Schmidt hadn't been so dominant in the eighties, Wallach would have gained recognition long before he did. Whether it's charging a bunt, diving to his left or right to stab a hot shot, or racing back to catch a ball over his shoulder, Wallach is at the front of his class of fellow third basemen. His arm is both strong and accurate.

OVERALL:

A solid veteran, Wallach is a team leader through action rather than words. Next to impossible to keep out of the lineup, he plays with injuries which would send others to the disabled list. Tim's laid-back approach and relaxed style make him appear indifferent, particularly when he is slumping, but he's actually a gamer.

TIM WALLACH

Position: 3B
Bats: R **Throws:** R
Ht: 6' 3" **Wt:** 200

Opening Day Age: 32
Born: 9/14/57 in Huntington Park, CA
ML Seasons: 10

Overall Statistics

	G	AB	R	H	D	T	HR	RBI	SB	BB	SO	AVG
1989	154	573	76	159	42	0	13	77	3	58	81	.277
Career	1305	4789	555	1259	272	24	161	675	40	372	739	.263

Where He Hits the Ball

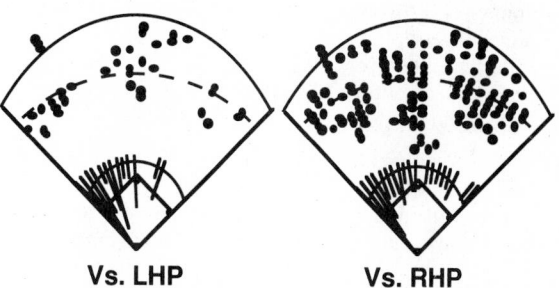

Vs. LHP   Vs. RHP

1989 Situational Stats

	AB	H	HR	RBI	AVG		AB	H	HR	RBI	AVG
Home	286	91	6	42	.318	LHP	160	46	8	25	.287
Road	287	68	7	35	.237	RHP	413	113	5	52	.274
Day	174	47	4	24	.270	Sc Pos	146	44	3	58	.301
Night	399	112	9	53	.281	Clutch	99	26	3	16	.263

1989 Rankings (National League)

➡ 1st in GDPs (21) and doubles (42)

➡ 6th in batting average at home (.318) - *players with 252 PA at home*

➡ Led the Expos in at bats (573), plate appearances (639), games (154), runs (76), hits (159), singles (104), doubles, GDPs, batting average at home and errors (18)

➡ Led NL Third Basemen in doubles, sacrifice flies (7), GDPs, and batting average at home

JOHN CANDELARIA

Position: RP/SP
Bats: B **Throws:** L
Ht: 6' 6" **Wt:** 225

Opening Day Age: 36
Born: 11/6/53 in Brooklyn, NY
ML Seasons: 15

JIM DWYER

Position: DH
Bats: L **Throws:** L
Ht: 5'10" **Wt:** 186

Opening Day Age: 40
Born: 1/3/50 in Evergreen, IL
ML Seasons: 17

Overall Statistics

	W	L	ERA	G	GS	Sv	IP	H	R	BB	SO	HR
1989	3	5	4.68	22	6	0	65.1	66	36	16	51	11
Career	167	107	3.27	420	353	16	2368.0	2236	958	539	1532	228

Overall Statistics

	G	AB	R	H	D	T	HR	RBI	SB	BB	SO	AVG
1989	101	235	35	74	12	0	3	25	2	29	24	.315
Career	1291	2698	402	707	115	17	76	344	26	390	395	.262

PITCHING, FIELDING, HITTING:

After knee problems ended the marvelous 1988 comeback season in which he led the Yankees in almost every pitching category, John Candelaria had little success in New York. The victim of overwhelmingly bad publicity, Candelaria became visibly unhappy, and his performance deteriorated.

Candelaria's great strengths are his excellent control and his ability to get out lefthanded hitters, both of which remained intact in 1989. John was able to contain lefty hitters to a .160 batting average, and he yielded only 2.2 walks per 9 innings. Unfortunately, the way the Yankees used Candelaria, righthanded hitters made up 80% of total opposition at bats. John also lost some of his long-standing ability to perform well in clutch situations. In 1989, he allowed opponents a .318 average with runners on base, though he held them to a .229 average in close game situations.

OVERALL:

Candelaria is obviously better than the numbers he produced in New York. After his August 30 trade to Montreal, he showed his old form with a 3.27 ERA and a strikeout per inning. Big, strong southpaws with good control and ability to retire lefties are eminently employable. There is plenty of baseball left in John Candelaria, even at age 36. John pitched exclusively in relief for Montreal in 1989. But with the loss of Bryn Smith and Pascual Perez, it's likely that John will enter the starting rotation for Montreal in 1990.

HITTING, FIELDING, BASERUNNING:

The aging process has taken its inevitable toll, but you'd never know it by looking at Jim Dwyer's batting average. Dwyer, who turned 40 in January, no longer gets around as quickly on inside fastballs as he once did. But the lefthanded batter has compensated by hitting more pitches to left field. The result: a .315 average last year, the highest of Dwyer's 17-year career. Dwyer is no longer much of a home run threat, but he still has enough line-drive power to reach the gaps by spraying the ball to left and center. He's a patient hitter who draws a good number of walks, but he doesn't strike out much. Not as slow as most 40-year olds, Dwyer is a smart baserunner who can be sent in hit-and-run situations. With poor range and a bad elbow, he's a definite liability when forced to play the outfield.

OVERALL:

A contending team will find Dwyer a valuable addition. He can still hit in the clutch and be a productive platoon designated hitter. On the other hand, Dwyer may be a luxury that a non-contending team can't afford, because he has no value defensively and is not an everyday designated-hitter type.

STEVE FREY

Position: RP
Bats: L **Throws:** L
Ht: 5' 9" **Wt:** 170

Opening Day Age: 26
Born: 7/29/63 in
Meadowbrook, PA
ML Seasons: 1

MARQUIS GRISSOM

Position: CF
Bats: R **Throws:** R
Ht: 5'11" **Wt:** 190

Opening Day Age: 22
Born: 4/17/67 in
Atlanta, GA
ML Seasons: 1

Overall Statistics

	W	L	ERA	G	GS	Sv	IP	H	R	BB	SO	HR
1989	3	2	5.48	20	0	0	21.1	29	15	11	15	4
Career	3	2	5.48	20	0	0	21.1	29	15	11	15	4

Overall Statistics

	G	AB	R	H	D	T	HR	RBI	SB	BB	SO	AVG
1989	26	74	16	19	2	0	1	2	1	12	21	.257
Career	26	74	16	19	2	0	1	2	1	12	21	.257

PITCHING, FIELDING, HITTING:

The Expos completed a Triple A transaction with the Mets last spring, and they feel the dividends from that move are yet to come. They sent infielder Tom O'Malley and catcher Mark Bailey to Tidewater in exchange for lefthanded pitcher Steve Frey. O'Malley went on to MVP honors at Tidewater, while Frey did not enjoy success with the Expos. But Steve was extremely effective in Indianapolis (1.78 earned run average with a 2-1 record and three saves in 21 outings). Montreal feels that's a better gauge of his ability. Frey was called up from Triple A in early May to help out a drifting bullpen. He did well at first, posting a 2-0 record in June. His fastball was alive but the curveball which served him well in the minors soon deserted him and Frey was hit hard. In Indianapolis, Frey walked six men in 25.1 innings, but in Montreal, his control left him. With hitters sitting on his fastball, Frey was hit hard. Righthanders tattooed him at a .339 clip.

OVERALL:

The Expos like what they have seen of Frey. They feel his minor league background with the pitching-rich Mets will serve him well. Frey is learning a new pitch in the winter leagues and is being counted on to handle lefthanded hitters out of the bullpen.

HITTING, FIELDING, BASERUNNING:

Marquis Grissom has been touted by members of the Expos' scouting and development departments as a potential star since his fourth-round selection out of Florida A&M in June 1988. A three-letter MVP in football, basketball and baseball at Lakeshore High School in College Park, Georgia, Grissom hit .448 and was 9-3 as a starting pitcher at Florida A&M. As a rookie pro in 1988, he led the New York-Penn league in several offensive categories. Quickly moving up the ladder in 1989, Grissom hit .299 at Double A Jacksonville, .278 at Triple A Indianapolis and .257 with the Expos. Grissom is a line-drive hitter and sprays his hits to the gaps. At the three levels, he totalled 27 doubles. Grissom feasts on fastballs but was overmatched by breaking ball pitchers after joining the Expos for the final five weeks of the season. An excellent outfielder with an accurate arm, Grissom is aggressive both at the plate and on the bases. He stole 41 sacks during the season, one with the major league Expos, in one attempt.

OVERALL:

Grissom could certainly develop into an outfield star. He will be given every opportunity to win a starting job in spring training. He adjusted well at every stop on the way up. The only question seems to be whether he would be better off with another year's experience in Triple A.

JEFF HUSON

Position: SS
Bats: L **Throws:** R
Ht: 6'3" **Wt:** 170

Opening Day Age: 25
Born: 8/15/64 in Scottsdale, AZ
ML Seasons: 2

Overall Statistics

	G	AB	R	H	D	T	HR	RBI	SB	BB	SO	AVG
1989	32	74	1	12	5	0	0	2	3	6	6	.162
Career	52	116	8	25	7	0	0	5	5	10	9	.216

HITTING, FIELDING, BASERUNNING:

Jeff Huson has proven to be an extremely handy young man. Brought along slowly after he was signed as a free agent in 1985, Huson has impressed with his hustle at every stop. Primarily a shortstop, Huson has also shown that he can play second base and the outfield. In 1989, Huson hit .304 at Triple A Indianapolis and stole 30 bases. Previously he stole 33 bases at Class A West Palm Beach (1987) and lead the league at AA Jacksonville with 56 in 1988. A singles hitter, Huson tries to take advantage of the whole field. He tends to swing at the first pitch too often and appeared to have trouble with breaking balls in his brief stint with the Expos. Huson's reputation is that of an excellent fielder. While with the Expos he showed excellent range at shortstop but an erratic throwing arm. However, that was attributed to a young man's nerves. While he had five doubles among his 12 hits with the Expos, he failed to produce with runners on base.

OVERALL:

Huson's future appears to be as a utility infielder. A hard worker and a good team player, his versatility puts him in good shape as he tries to win a job with the Expos.

WALLACE JOHNSON

Position: 1B
Bats: B **Throws:** R
Ht: 5'11" **Wt:** 185

Opening Day Age: 33
Born: 12/25/56 in Gary, IN
ML Seasons: 8

Overall Statistics

	G	AB	R	H	D	T	HR	RBI	SB	BB	SO	AVG
1989	85	114	9	31	3	1	2	17	1	7	12	.272
Career	381	520	46	137	16	6	4	54	18	45	52	.263

HITTING, FIELDING, BASERUNNING:

The odd thing about Wallace Johnson's 1989 season is that he didn't lead the league in pinch hits. His 14 pinch hits were second to Ken Oberkfell, who stroked 18 for the Braves and Giants. Johnson leads all major leaguers over the past four seasons with a total of 64 pinch hits. He led the National League once and was tied for the top spot twice before finishing second in 1989. Though he fell short of his 1988 mark (22 pinch hits in 64 at bats, .344 average), Johnson drove in 10 runs while performing the difficult role in 1989. Basically a singles hitter who is often used to start innings, the switch-hitting Johnson was much better against righthanders (.298 batting average) than against lefties (.150). An aggressive hitter, Johnson tends to swing at the first pitch. He prefers fastballs and can be counted on to produce in the clutch. An alert baserunner, Johnson is an ordinary fielder at first base, second base, and the outfield, with a below average arm.

OVERALL:

Johnson's work habits make him a role model for younger players. His preparation for his pinch hitting duties are exemplary and he always tries to be ready for an occasional start. Though he attributes his defensive shortcomings to rust from lack of use, Johnson's value is as a pinch hitter.

MARTY PEVEY

Position: C
Bats: L **Throws:** R
Ht: 6' 1" **Wt:** 185

Opening Day Age: 28
Born: 9/18/61 in Statesboro, GA
ML Seasons: 1

Overall Statistics

	G	AB	R	H	D	T	HR	RBI	SB	BB	SO	AVG
1989	13	41	2	9	1	1	0	3	0	0	8	.220
Career	13	41	2	9	1	1	0	3	0	0	8	.220

HITTING, FIELDING, BASERUNNING:

Marty Pevey is a genial 28-year old who has a couple of major shortcomings in his bid to become a major league catcher. The stocky Pevey has had trouble blocking pitches in the dirt. And he has yet to prove he can hit anything above Double A pitching. Despite the fact he had only a few opposite field bloopers during a 13-game (41 at bats) stay with the Expos in 1989, Pevey was a popular man with the team. Established members of the pitching staff appreciated his hustle and knowledgeable work behind the plate. But Pevey's biggest talent seemed to be off the field. He is a proficient barber and hair stylist, after being trained in his mother's hair salon. All spring, Pevey did clipping and coiffure work for both players and hangers-on. Marty was greeted with open arms when he was called up from Triple A Indianapolis May 14.

OVERALL:

Unfortunately for Pevey, his stay with the Expos was shortlived. When Nelson Santovenia came off the injury list, Pevey was sent back down. Worse still, he suffered a shoulder injury immediately upon returning to Triple A, was out for the season and was subsequently released. His future as a barber might be brighter than his future as a ballplayer.

RICH THOMPSON

Position: RP
Bats: B **Throws:** R
Ht: 5'11" **Wt:** 170

Opening Day Age: 31
Born: 11/1/58 in West Palm Beach, FL
ML Seasons: 2

Overall Statistics

	W	L	ERA	G	GS	Sv	IP	H	R	BB	SO	HR
1989	0	2	2.18	19	1	0	33.0	27	11	11	15	2
Career	3	10	5.10	76	1	5	113.0	122	74	59	45	10

PITCHING, FIELDING, HITTING:

Rich Thompson was not satisfied that he had been given a decent chance to make the grade in the major leagues. Released by three organizations, the righthander's only fling in the big leagues was in 1985 when he was 3-8 with a 6.30 earned run average with the Cleveland Indians. Thompson had been asked by the Indians to change from a sidearm to an overhand delivery. Obviously it didn't work. Thompson had bounced around the minor leagues for 10 years. He wanted one more opportunity, despite owning a law degree and being qualified to teach. When things seemed bleakest, in the spring of 1989, Thompson called Dan Duquette, a former teammate when they had attended Amherst College together in 1979. As director of the Expos minor league organizations, Duquette signed Thompson to a Triple A contract. Called up in August, Thompson came through for the Expos. Using a slider and fastball with his sidearm motion, Thompson had a stretch of 16 consecutive scoreless innings in relief.

OVERALL:

A Steve Rogers look-alike, Thompson impressed the Expos' brass with his ability to throw strikes. A starter for the past two years at the Triple A level, Thompson may have found his true calling in relief; he had an ERA of 1.27 over 28.1 innings out of the Expos bullpen. He's a solid candidate to begin the season with the Expos.

LARRY WALKER

Position: RF
Bats: L **Throws:** R
Ht: 6' 2" **Wt:** 185

Opening Day Age: 23
Born: 12/1/66 in Maple River, BC
ML Seasons: 1

Overall Statistics

	G	AB	R	H	D	T	HR	RBI	SB	BB	SO	AVG
1989	20	47	4	8	0	0	0	4	1	5	13	.170
Career	20	47	4	8	0	0	0	4	1	5	13	.170

HITTING, FIELDING, BASERUNNING:

The burden of becoming the Expos' first everyday Canadian player doesn't seem to be weighing down Larry Walker. The 23-year old appeared to be only a few months away from getting his first chance at the major leagues after hitting .287 with 26 home runs and 83 RBIs at Double A Jacksonville in 1987. However, a major knee injury while playing in the winter leagues, and subsequent surgery, wiped out the 1988 season. Walker bounced back last season and hit a solid .270 at Triple A Indianapolis with 12 home runs, 18 doubles and 58 RBIs in 395 at-bats before being called up. A line drive hitter with power, Walker feasts on offspeed pitches but can be handled by superior fastballs. Walker is patient, uses all of the field, and usually waits for his pitch. He's a good outfielder with a better than average arm. Walker is also an aggressive and intelligent baserunner. His 36 steals at Indianapolis demonstrate that knee surgery has not slowed him down, nor has it made him tentative on the base paths.

OVERALL:

Walker conjured up visions of a Canadian slugger when, as a 19-year-old, he belted 29 home runs at Class A Burlington in 1986. Realistically, he is an outfield candidate whose value depends on what off-season moves the Expos make.

PITCHING:

Don Aase's fastball has always been his main pitch. On his best days, the #1 is all he needs, but he also commands a good slider and can vary speeds to keep hitters off balance. Injuries have always plagued him, however. After accumulating 34 saves with Baltimore in 1986, Aase had developed shoulder problems, an ominous sign for a pitcher who had missed the entire 1983 season with arm miseries. When the last place Birds cut Aase loose after the '88 season, most organizations concluded that he was washed up. But the Mets took a chance on him, and Aase was a pleasant surprise from the beginning of spring training.

When Aase saved the Mets' opening day victory, it looked as if the Flushing Meadow front office had marshalled some marvelous insight in acquiring him. It was not to be. If the season had ended on June 30, Aase would have had a 2.48 ERA in 26 games. But whether it was the ill fate of the Mets, or New York pressures, or just plain fatigue and age, Aase was very hittable in the second half of '89 (5.74 ERA in 23 games). More hitters were looking for the fastball and getting it, and by late July, Don's heater had lost some zip and movement. Aase definitely tired easily in his 1989 appearances, holding opposition hitters to a .220 batting average through his first 30 pitches, but yielding a .500 average on pitches 31 and up. Unfortunately, the Mets often needed innings from their righty relievers, not just situational firefighting.

FIELDING, HITTING, BASERUNNING:

Aase is a fast worker who presents problems for base stealers. In 1989, only four steals against Don were successful, and three runners were caught trying. Aase's experience makes him adequate in the field, but he is no gazelle coming off the mound. His hitting is as weak as it looks, and since he was never on base, his running game in 1989 was nonexistent.

OVERALL:

Late in the season, Don was the victim of New York fans' wrath. Some accused him of being Doug Sisk with a moustache. It seems as if Aase's career is finally nearing an end. The Mets have apparently lost interest, and despite his proven ability to come back from injuries, other teams must realize that the odds are pretty long at age 35.

DON AASE

Position: RP
Bats: R **Throws:** R
Ht: 6' 3" **Wt:** 222

Opening Day Age: 35
Born: 9/8/54 in Orange, CA
ML Seasons: 12

Overall Statistics

	W	L	ERA	G	GS	Sv	IP	H	R	BB	SO	HR
1989	1	5	3.94	49	0	2	59.1	56	27	26	34	5
Career	63	59	3.76	416	91	79	1070.2	1052	479	438	617	84

Where They Hit the Ball

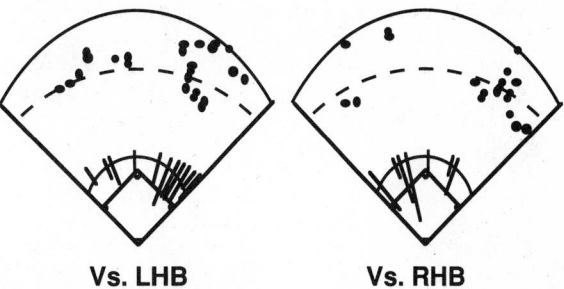

Vs. LHB   **Vs. RHB**

1989 Situational Stats

	W	L	ERA	Sv	IP		AB	H	HR	RBI	AVG
Home	1	2	4.06	2	31.0	LHB	114	31	1	14	.272
Road	0	3	3.81	0	28.1	RHB	115	25	4	14	.217
Day	1	3	4.18	1	28.0	Sc Pos	63	14	2	23	.222
Night	0	2	3.73	1	31.1	Clutch	91	22	3	13	.242

1989 Rankings (National League)

➡ 10th in lowest percentage of inherited runners scoring (29.0%) - *pitchers with 30 inherited runners*

➡ Led the Mets in holds (10)

HITTING:

There were few good moments for Carter in 1989, and few surprises. Gary's burning desire remained, but his bad right knee left him with a weak foundation. Continually unable to set up a strong stance at the plate, The Kid amassed only 10 hits before August.

In the final two months, Gary clicked with a .290 average, and had some exhilarating games (five hits in one, five RBIs in another). But his disastrous .183 full-year average is the number that everyone will remember. And even in his late season revival, Carter never regained much power. His two home runs are an accurate summary of the warning track power that he displayed all year.

Sliders and off-speed pitches have always been difficult for Carter, but in 1989 they really did him in. The only fastballs that he saw were in unhittable locations (inside or out) and his attempts to readjust were futile. Carter kept swinging like a strong, eager slugger, but in 1989 the equipment just wasn't working. He frequently put the first pitch in play, but rarely for a base hit. Both his home runs came on 2-1 counts.

BASERUNNING:

The Kid can't travel the bases like he used to, and he was never very fast. He used to steal a base or two per year, but the running days are behind him now. A sort of Ernie Lombardi of the 1980's, Gary's legs are 99% effort and 1% ability.

FIELDING:

There is no catcher in the National League with a better knowledge of hitters than Carter. Gary has been instrumental in the development of numerous young mound stars. Handling pitchers is the one great strength that Carter still brings onto the field. But in 1989, Carter made about as many errors per game as any catcher; he needs to adjust and play within his diminished abilities. His throwing arm seemed to improve slightly in 1989, but young pitchers learning better deliveries and pickoff moves helped the Mets as well. Carter is simply overmatched by the real burners in today's National League.

OVERALL:

Gary is hoping free agency will find him a team that wants to give him playing time. If the last two months of 1989 are a good indication, there should be a young franchise that can benefit from Carter's great experience and superior attitude. If Gary can put together a couple more solid years, he will greatly enhance his possibilities for entrance into Cooperstown.

GARY CARTER

Position: C
Bats: R **Throws:** R
Ht: 6' 2" **Wt:** 210

Opening Day Age: 36
Born: 4/8/54 in Culver City, CA
ML Seasons: 16

Overall Statistics

	G	AB	R	H	D	T	HR	RBI	SB	BB	SO	AVG
1989	50	153	14	28	8	0	2	15	0	12	15	.183
Career	2008	7194	955	1907	329	30	304	1143	36	768	903	.265

Where He Hits the Ball

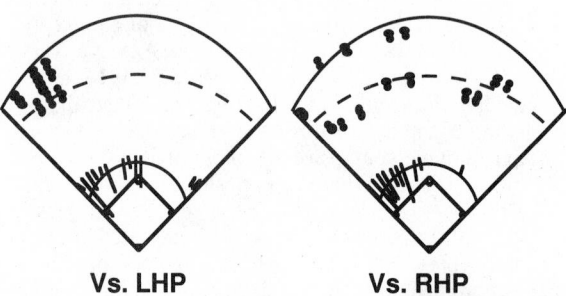

Vs. LHP   **Vs. RHP**

1989 Situational Stats

	AB	H	HR	RBI	AVG		AB	H	HR	RBI	AVG
Home	77	11	1	8	.143	LHP	66	11	2	7	.167
Road	76	17	1	7	.224	RHP	87	17	0	8	.195
Day	63	17	2	10	.270	Sc Pos	32	7	1	14	.219
Night	90	11	0	5	.122	Clutch	30	4	1	3	.133

1989 Rankings (National League)

➡ Did not rank near the top or bottom in any category

PITCHING:

The biggest difference between the David Cone of 1988 (20-3, third in Cy Young balloting) and the Cone of 1989 (14-8) was a jump in ERA of 1.3 runs per game, from 2.22 to 3.52. Cone suffered from an early slump and had two bad starts in September. But most of the season, he looked and pitched exactly like he had the year before, to the delight of the "Cone Heads" who appear at every one of his Shea Stadium outings.

Cone has all the pitches and uses them intelligently: popping fastball with good movement, nasty slider, sharp curve and an excellent change-up. He also features a sidearm delivery called "Laredo" because it comes from way down at the bottom of the map. The sidearm pitch is predictably tough on righthanders. Cone is very aggressive, a bit of a perfectionist, and he can get upset when umpires' calls go against him.

Cone is a flyball pitcher (20 home runs and only 5 double plays) who thrives in Shea Stadium. His two year home record is 18-3 with a 1.94 ERA in 30 starts, as good as any pitcher in any park. Last year, he continued to pitch well at Shea, going 8-2 with five no-decisions in 15 starts, with an ERA of 2.61. Although he got both of his shutouts on the road, he had many problems as a visitor, finishing at 6-6 with an ERA of 4.50.

FIELDING, HITTING, BASERUNNING:

Now that Roger McDowell is gone, Cone is the fielding star among Mets pitchers. He has a smooth follow-through and quick reflexes that give him good range, and often helps himself with a good play. Cone is not good at holding runners. The opposition swiped 27 bases from him in 1989. With 18 hits in '89, Cone led all National League pitchers and was never an easy out. A good bunter and baserunner, and a fine overall athlete, David usually finds a way to help the Mets line-up.

OVERALL:

Cone comes right at the hitter with justifiable confidence. There is no more combative pitcher in the league. His minor failures in 1989 simply prove that he is human; no one can have serious expectations of an .870 winning percentage. With the whole Mets team in a slump, Dave picked a good year to show that he can work through problems and regain his form. Considering his superior talent and youth (age 27), it looks like the Mets can rely on Cone to be effective for several more years.

DAVID CONE

Position: SP
Bats: L **Throws:** R
Ht: 6' 1" **Wt:** 185

Opening Day Age: 27
Born: 1/2/63 in Kansas City, MO
ML Seasons: 4

Overall Statistics

	W	L	ERA	G	GS	Sv	IP	H	R	BB	SO	HR
1989	14	8	3.52	34	33	0	219.2	183	92	74	190	20
Career	39	17	3.11	101	74	1	573.0	477	219	211	492	43

Where They Hit the Ball

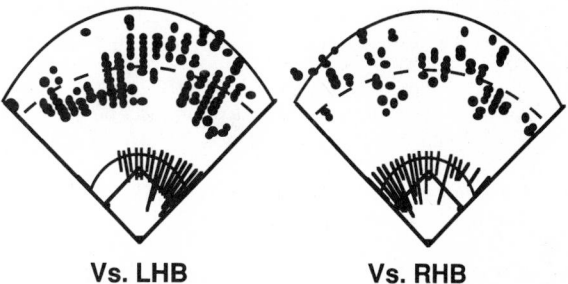

Vs. LHB   **Vs. RHB**

1989 Situational Stats

	W	L	ERA	Sv	IP		AB	H	HR	RBI	AVG
Home	8	2	2.61	0	113.2	LHB	449	105	9	46	.234
Road	6	6	4.50	0	106.0	RHB	373	78	11	38	.209
Day	4	4	3.81	0	85.0	Sc Pos	179	42	4	61	.235
Night	10	4	3.34	0	134.2	Clutch	91	26	1	7	.286

1989 Rankings (National League)

➡ 2nd in least GDPs per 9 innings (.25) - *pitchers with 162 IP*

➡ 3rd in highest run support per 9 innings (5.2), most pitches thrown per batter (3.9) and wild pitches (14)

➡ 4th in most strikeouts per 9 innings (7.8), strikeouts (190), pitches thrown (3,533) and lowest batting average allowed vs. right-handed batters (.209) - *pitchers facing 377 RHB*

➡ Led the Mets in complete games (7), wild pitches, wins (14), games started (33), shutouts (2), innings (219.2), pitches thrown and highest run support per 9 innings

PITCHING:

Although his fastball is not what it used to be, Ron Darling is still a power pitcher -- he averaged 6.3 strikeouts per nine innings last year. The difference is that he now relies more on his splitfinger fastball. Darling is a workhorse; he gives you 200-plus innings every year and does not complain about who's catching, where he's pitching, or how many runs he's getting. He has cut down on his walks in recent years, and in 1989 he threw the fewest pitches per inning (14.5) of any Mets starter.

Darling has difficulty getting out of trouble, and he gives up so many unearned runs (15 in 1989, by far the most of any Met) that there must be concern about his ability to remain composed after someone makes an error. Darling is also prone to lose some effectiveness after a walk. More than most pitchers, Darling really likes to be ahead in the count. On all two-strike counts, he held opposition hitters to a .152 average, but with less than two strikes, opposing batters hit .388 against him.

Darling has some of the most dramatic home/road differentials of any pitcher; since 1986 his ERA is 3.00 at Shea and 4.50 at other stadiums. Shea is a pitcher's park, but 50% more earned runs cannot be explained by fence locations. Considering all the other factors (loss of effectiveness after errors and walks, strong preference to pitch ahead in the count), one must conclude that Ron simply has trouble relaxing enough to throw his best pitches. Whether home or away, this factor deserves careful attention by his manager, coaches, catchers and infielders.

HITTING, FIELDING, BASERUNNING:

Darling is a good athlete. He is a workmanlike hitter who produces several extra base hits every year. Last year he clouted home runs in consecutive games. He is a good bunter and baserunner, and has been used as a pinch-runner on occasion. Darling is more than adequate as a fielder, normally alert and sure-handed. He used to have an excellent move to first, but opposition runners are apparently learning to read him better. They stole 26 bases (with a 70% success rate) against Ron in 1989.

OVERALL:

Darling's best years may be behind him, and the Mets have to consider him expendable for the right offer. His extreme home-road breakdown in an excellent pitcher's park could be troubling to other teams; but even if Ron is traded, he is intelligent enough to find winning methods wherever he lands.

RON DARLING

Position: SP
Bats: R **Throws:** R
Ht: 6' 3"   **Wt:** 195

Opening Day Age: 29
Born: 8/19/60 in Honolulu, HI
ML Seasons: 7

Overall Statistics

	W	L	ERA	G	GS	Sv	IP	H	R	BB	SO	HR
1989	14	14	3.52	33	33	0	217.1	214	100	70	153	19
Career	87	55	3.38	207	206	0	1391.2	1242	593	542	991	126

Where They Hit the Ball

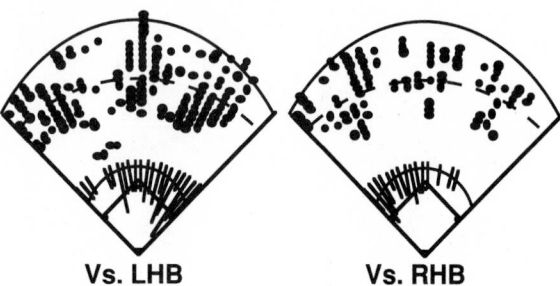

Vs. LHB   **Vs. RHB**

1989 Situational Stats

	W	L	ERA	Sv	IP		AB	H	HR	RBI	AVG
Home	8	6	3.04	0	121.1	LHB	482	136	9	49	.282
Road	6	8	4.13	0	96.0	RHB	347	78	10	39	.225
Day	0	3	3.72	0	29.0	Sc Pos	198	50	5	69	.253
Night	14	11	3.49	0	188.1	Clutch	57	15	1	5	.263

1989 Rankings (National League)

➡ 4th in losses (14) and lowest on-base average allowed to the leadoff batter (.254) - *pitchers facing 150 leadoff batters*

➡ 6th in wild pitches (12)

➡ 7th in games started (33)

➡ 8th in stolen bases allowed (26) and hits allowed (214)

➡ Led the Mets in wins (14), losses, games started, pickoff throws (161), least pitches thrown per batter (3.4), caught stealing (11), lowest stolen base percentage allowed (70.3%), hits allowed and batters faced (922)

HITTING:

Kevin Elster is an aggressive hitter, with an uppercut swing and a tendency to pull everything. Elster is no Cal Ripken, but he was the only National League shortstop to get 25 doubles and 10 homers last year. His favorite pitch is the hanging curve ball; make that mistake, and he can park it for you. While hitting all these long balls, and swinging at numerous others, Elster unfortunately strikes out too much. In 1989 his whiff count rose from 47 to 77, while his walks dropped slightly, not a good trend for a young player.

Until the All-Star break, all a pitcher had to do was throw a fastball near the outside part of the plate and Elster was done. Breaking balls worked too; he was helpless. Halfway through the season, his average was a paltry .208, his slugging percentage (despite all those big swings) was only .290, and his RBI count seemed stuck at 18. At the break, Davey Johnson announced he was benching Elster to keep both Hernandez and Magadan in the line-up. Kevin was upset. Three days later Hernandez was re-injured. Kevin returned and stayed at short for the rest of the season. In the second half, Elster hit .251, slugged .418, drove in 37 runs, and smashed eight of his 10 homers. Apparently the benching improved his concentration.

BASERUNNING:

Elster is not particularly fast, but he doesn't delude himself about it. He is a good, smart, safe baserunner. He doesn't steal many bases (six in two years), but he doesn't get thrown out much, either.

FIELDING:

Elster was a starter in the World Series at age 23. He is a poised and accomplished professional with good range, sure hands, a strong arm, and fine ability to turn the double play. Kevin's fielding totals (assists, double plays, etc.) do not reflect his true ability; Mets pitchers simply do not throw enough ground balls for him to get big numbers. In 1989, Elster set a record for the most consecutive games without an error (88). He is one defensive plus on a team of defensive minuses.

OVERALL:

Just 25, Elster is still improving. He may be ready to emerge as one of the best-hitting shortstops in the game today. Certainly his second half 1989 numbers show the potential. With Davey Johnson's fondness for offensive output from every position, Elster's career might depend on a little more development. Kevin could go either way in 1990: he might make the All-Star team, and he might land on the Mets' bench.

KEVIN ELSTER

Position: SS
Bats: R **Throws:** R
Ht: 6' 2" **Wt:** 195

Opening Day Age: 25
Born: 8/3/64 in San Pedro, CA
ML Seasons: 4

Overall Statistics

	G	AB	R	H	D	T	HR	RBI	SB	BB	SO	AVG
1989	151	458	52	106	25	2	10	55	4	34	77	.231
Career	324	904	97	202	39	3	19	93	6	72	133	.223

Where He Hits the Ball

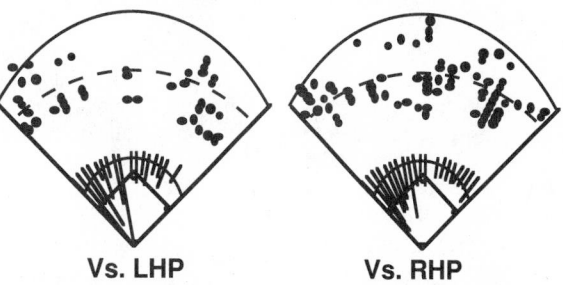

Vs. LHP   **Vs. RHP**

1989 Situational Stats

	AB	H	HR	RBI	AVG		AB	H	HR	RBI	AVG
Home	235	53	5	30	.226	LHP	159	41	2	13	.258
Road	223	53	5	25	.238	RHP	299	65	8	42	.217
Day	167	42	6	30	.251	Sc Pos	116	32	3	45	.276
Night	291	64	4	25	.220	Clutch	78	20	1	5	.256

1989 Rankings (National League)

- ➡ 3rd in sacrifice flies (8)
- ➡ 4th in lowest batting average at home (.226) - *players with 252 PA at home*
- ➡ 5th in worst hitting with the bases loaded (.100) - *players with 10 PA with the bases loaded*
- ➡ Led the Mets in sacrifice flies
- ➡ Led NL shortstops in sacrifice flies

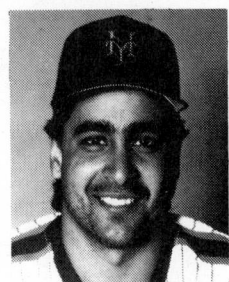

SID FERNANDEZ

Position: SP
Bats: L **Throws:** L
Ht: 6' 1" **Wt:** 230

Opening Day Age: 27
Born: 10/12/62 in Honolulu, HI
ML Seasons: 7

PITCHING:

Sid Fernandez has been perennial trade bait, and he became the odd man out in April 1989 when the Mets put him in the bullpen. When Sid later emerged as the N.Y. ace, people began questioning how the Mets could have undervalued him so. Sid improved in 1989, but he had long been the Mets leader in fewest hits and most strikeouts per inning.

Fernandez is a classic "sneaky fast" power pitcher who seems to hide the ball up his sleeve and deliver it with a motion that looks premature. He can make hitters climb the ladder reaching his rising fastball, and he can drop his slow curve on the outside corner like a dart-thrower tossing triple twenties. Sid's two main pitches are so distinctive, they can be readily identified from the upper deck.

Fernandez' big improvement in 1989 was due to mental adjustment, not a new pitch or delivery (he has always had a good change and a hard curve in his repertoire). Sid simply stopped worrying and went after hitters more directly. He gave up fewer walks, and got more people out with fewer pitches. The results included career highs for innings pitched and complete games, and a strikeout to walk ratio that jumped from a respectable 1.8 in the first half to a magnificent 3.6 after July 1.

Sid's games are characterized by many fly balls and strikeouts. He threw one game last year with no assists. The shortage of ground balls makes the infielders' jobs easy, and enables Davey Johnson to play Howard Johnson at shortstop whenever Fernandez pitches.

HITTING, FIELDING, BASERUNNING:

Despite his notorious girth, Fernandez is a true athlete and a good hitter. Against righthanded pitching he could actually pinch hit. He makes contact, and has sufficient warning track power for run-scoring fly balls. On the bases and in the field, Sid moves about as fast as Heinz ketchup. Sid's move to first is supposedly weak, but opposing runners know better. They stole only 11 bases off Fernandez in 1989.

OVERALL:

Fernandez' accomplishments in pennant races, All-Star games and postseason play are already impressive, and he currently ranks among the all-time leaders in lowest opponents' batting average and most strikeouts per innings pitched. Considering that left-handers normally mature later than righties, there may still be true greatness in this 27-year old southpaw.

Overall Statistics

	W	L	ERA	G	GS	Sv	IP	H	R	BB	SO	HR
1989	14	5	2.83	35	32	0	219.1	157	73	75	198	21
Career	69	45	3.22	169	163	1	1033.0	764	399	424	972	87

Where They Hit the Ball

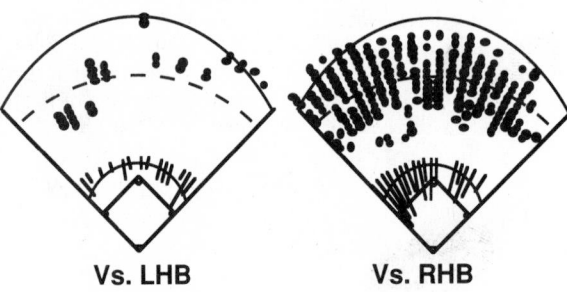

Vs. LHB   **Vs. RHB**

1989 Situational Stats

	W	L	ERA	Sv	IP		AB	H	HR	RBI	AVG
Home	7	2	2.78	0	129.2	LHB	117	23	2	8	.197
Road	7	3	2.91	0	89.2	RHB	677	134	19	58	.198
Day	4	1	2.77	0	65.0	Sc Pos	118	30	5	44	.254
Night	10	4	2.86	0	154.1	Clutch	71	19	3	4	.268

1989 Rankings (National League)

- ➡ 1st in win/loss percentage (.737) - *pitchers with 15 decisions*
- ➡ 2nd in lowest opponent batting average (.198) and strikeouts per 9 innings (8.1) - *pitchers with 162 IP*
- ➡ 3rd in strikeouts (198)
- ➡ 4th in lowest on-base average allowed (.271)
- ➡ Led the Mets in wins (14), shutouts (2), ERA (2.83), hit batsmen (6), home runs allowed (21), strikeouts, win/loss percentage, lowest opponent batting average, strikeouts per 9 innings, lowest on-base average allowed and lowest slugging percentage allowed (.334) - *team pitchers with 162 IP*

PITCHING:

Statistical analysis of Doc Gooden's 1989 season would be rather pointless. There is only one question about Doc: Is he healthy? If so, he is one of the three most dominant pitchers in the game today. Gooden wins over 70% of his decisions. He holds opponents to a meager .210 average, with an ERA under three, and a strikeout to walk ratio of nearly three to one.

From all medical reports, and judging from his two brief outings in September, Gooden returned from his injury with his heater working and "Lord Charles" intact. He even showcased his change. The fastball he threw in September had movement and velocity (93 mph). During July, the speed was there but the movement was not. He was throwing a straight fastball, and it got hit.

In September he also showed his great curve, the one which breaks from a batter's shoulder to his knee while going over the plate. Most encouraging is the fact that medical tests showed "no change" after his stint in Chicago. Love or hate the Mets, Gooden is a national phenomenon.

The real worry about Doc's injury is its peculiarity. Damage to muscles in front of and under the arm is mysterious, as is how to protect against a recurrence. A healthy Gooden will overpower batters with his fast ball, freeze them with his curve, and blow their minds with his 82 mph change-up. His best pitch depends on the day. Davey Johnson normally allows Doc 125 pitches, just enough to put him somewhere near the finish. Gooden has always shown the ability to turn it up a notch when the situation calls for it.

FIELDING, HITTING, BASERUNNING:

Gooden plays his position exceptionally well. His smooth delivery places him in good fielding position. He covers first well and quickly provides backup wherever needed. His one glaring deficiency is an inability to hold runners (30 stolen bases in a shortened season). Gooden loves to hit and does it quite well. He is a good bat-handler and can bunt when called upon. Doc also runs the bases well.

OVERALL:

If he is healthy, Gooden will anchor the best pitching staff in baseball. He is the stopper, the leader whose absence hurt so much. At age 25, his 100 wins and .719 percentage suggest wild possibilities for totals in a long career. But right now, everyone's concern is focused on 1990.

DWIGHT GOODEN

Position: SP
Bats: R **Throws:** R
Ht: 6' 3" **Wt:** 203

Opening Day Age: 25
Born: 11/16/64 in Tampa, FL
ML Seasons: 6

STAFF ACE

Overall Statistics

	W	L	ERA	G	GS	Sv	IP	H	R	BB	SO	HR
1989	9	4	2.89	19	17	1	118.1	93	42	47	101	9
Career	100	39	2.64	177	175	1	1291.0	1053	423	379	1168	65

Where They Hit the Ball

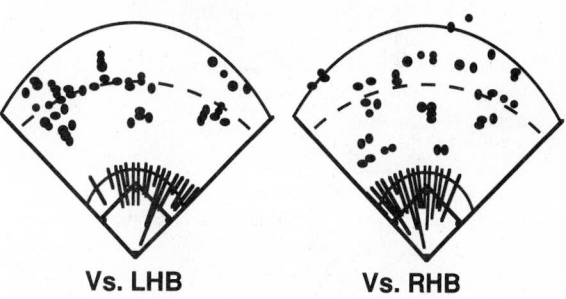

Vs. LHB   **Vs. RHB**

1989 Situational Stats

	W	L	ERA	Sv	IP		AB	H	HR	RBI	AVG
Home	6	1	2.33	0	65.2	LHB	230	42	3	17	.183
Road	3	3	3.59	1	52.2	RHB	211	51	6	21	.242
Day	3	2	4.03	1	44.2	Sc Pos	116	23	2	31	.198
Night	6	2	2.20	0	73.2	Clutch	62	14	1	6	.226

1989 Rankings (National League)

➡ 3rd in balks (5) and stolen bases allowed (30)

➡ 4th in lowest batting average allowed vs. lefthanded batters (.183) - *pitchers facing 125 LHB*

➡ Led the Mets in balks, stolen bases allowed and lowest batting average vs. lefthanded batters

HITTING:

At 35, Keith Hernandez knew that physical conditioning would be critical last year. He had suffered a loss of playing time, with lower production in 1988, mainly because of recurring hamstring injuries. So he followed a strenuous off-season training program. He was pleased with the improvement in his legs and looked forward to a comeback year in 1989.

Keith started slowly but got hot in May (.356), raising his season average to .282. Then he collided with Dodger shortstop Dave Anderson, cracking his knee. For Hernandez, this injury meant the end of his season's productivity. After returning in July, he hit .173 in part-time play and was not an offensive factor.

Hernandez has been one of the game's top hitters. He knows the strike zone as well as anyone, and umpires give him credit for this knowledge. He can handle pitches in all locations, eating up any fastball out over the plate. Well-placed, low inside breaking balls are about the only pitches that consistently give him trouble. Keith's biggest asset at the plate is an apparent ability to read pitchers' minds.

BASERUNNING:

If Hernandez were allowed one fantasy at this point in his career, it would probably be a designated runner to replace him when he gets on base. The basepaths have been at the center of his miseries these last two seasons. He was oh for three in steal attempts last year, and is likely to stop trying in 1990.

FIELDING:

Hernandez won nine consecutive Gold Gloves with his great knowledge and positioning, soft hands, and intense concentration on every pitch. At this stage, however, his range is limited by legs that won't do what they used to do. There will likely be no more Gold Gloves for Hernandez. However, he remains a defensive presence, a field leader with enough savvy to play an excellent first base despite his physical problems.

OVERALL:

Although the Mets have decided that they can live without Hernandez, it would be very surprising if some other team does not take advantage of his skill and experience. He has expressed an aversion to the American League, but he would make an excellent combination of DH, defensive replacement, and unofficial fielding coach and hitting instructor. Keith should be able to substantially bolster any contending team or lift an also-ran. Great players do these things and Hernandez has been one of the greats. The Mets will miss him.

KEITH HERNANDEZ

Position: 1B
Bats: L **Throws:** L
Ht: 6' 0" **Wt:** 205

Opening Day Age: 36
Born: 10/20/53 in San Francisco, CA
ML Seasons: 16

Overall Statistics

	G	AB	R	H	D	T	HR	RBI	SB	BB	SO	AVG
1989	75	215	18	50	8	0	4	19	0	27	39	.233
Career	2045	7240	1117	2156	424	60	161	1063	98	1056	995	.298

Where He Hits the Ball

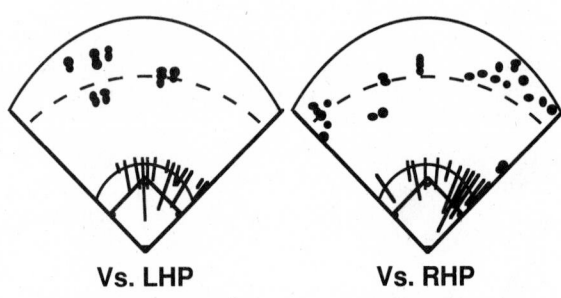

Vs. LHP   **Vs. RHP**

1989 Situational Stats

	AB	H	HR	RBI	AVG		AB	H	HR	RBI	AVG
Home	95	25	2	4	.263	LHP	79	23	1	8	.291
Road	120	25	2	15	.208	RHP	136	27	3	11	.199
Day	68	15	1	3	.221	Sc Pos	60	11	1	14	.183
Night	147	35	3	16	.238	Clutch	45	9	0	2	.200

1989 Rankings (National League)

➡ Did not rank near the top or bottom in any category

PITCHING:

One of the Mets' many disappointments of 1989 was the failure of Jeff Innis to emerge as a dominating sidearm set-up man to replace Terry Leach. In limited use in '87 and '88, Innis showed definite promise: an intimidating delivery with good downward movement on the sinkerball and a better tempo than Leach himself. But after Leach departed, Innis failed to impress Davey Johnson.

When he came up in late June, Innis had a good season going at Tidewater, and it continued for several weeks. But in August, Jeff gave up 12 hits and five earned runs in 8.2 innings. That could be a fair day's work for a journeyman starter, but it seemed to land Innis in the Johnson dog house. Timing is critical, and Innis seemed to become hittable just at those moments when emotions begged for an out. Jeff gave up only two homers all year, one to Bobby Bonilla and one to Candy Maldonado, but both of them were painful.

It is hard to judge a pitcher in less than 40 innings, but Innis' 1989 season looks pretty good on paper: less than a hit per inning, fewer than two walks per nine innings, only two home runs in 149 at bats, and a fine ERA. And Innis was outstanding against righthanded hitters, as a righty sidearmer should be. His left-right splits (.315 v. LHP, .221 v. RHP) were very similar to Terry Leach's; they suggest he probably can't be used as a closer, but that he can be very effective if spotted, just as Leach was. So what's the problem?

FIELDING, HITTING, BASERUNNING:

Innis fielded his position well in '89, and although he had few opportunities at the plate or on the bases, he always conveyed confidence, and handled himself adequately. Innis tries to hold runners close, and not too many runners tried to steal against him, but everyone who attempted in 1989 was successful.

OVERALL:

Davey Johnson likes having a sidearm relief specialist, but he does not exude much enthusiasm about having Jeff Innis. That could change in 1990 if Innis and the Mets get off to a good start. But it is also possible that Innis could find himself with a new team.

JEFF INNIS

Position: RP
Bats: R **Throws:** R
Ht: 6' 0" **Wt:** 170

Opening Day Age: 27
Born: 7/5/62 in Decatur, IL
ML Seasons: 3

Overall Statistics

	W	L	ERA	G	GS	Sv	IP	H	R	BB	SO	HR
1989	0	1	3.18	29	0	0	39.2	38	16	8	16	2
Career	1	3	2.88	58	1	0	84.1	86	31	14	58	7

Where They Hit the Ball

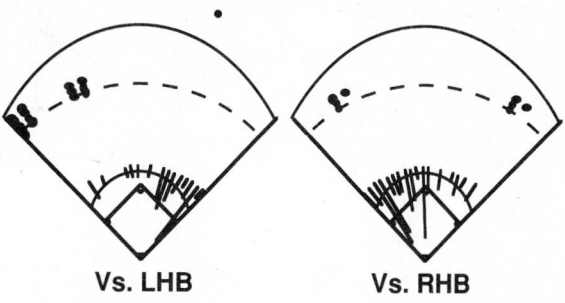

Vs. LHB   **Vs. RHB**

1989 Situational Stats

	W	L	ERA	Sv	IP		AB	H	HR	RBI	AVG
Home	0	1	2.01	0	22.1	LHB	54	17	1	7	.315
Road	0	0	4.67	0	17.1	RHB	95	21	1	9	.221
Day	0	1	4.00	0	18.0	Sc Pos	44	11	0	13	.250
Night	0	0	2.49	0	21.2	Clutch	21	8	1	4	.381

1989 Rankings (National League)

➡ 4th in most GDPs induced per GDP situation (19.4%) - *pitchers with 30 GDP situations*

➡ Led the Mets in most GDPs induced per GDP situation

HITTING:

Years from now, fans may make up trivia questions about Greg Jefferies' failure to win Rookie of the Year honors in 1989. Jefferies took himself out of the running by hitting .187 in his first 150 at bats. But Jefferies hit .288 after May 31, and .309 after July 31. He is one of those rare players who can hit major league pitching at an age when most future stars are still in college or AA. The pressure to get off to a good start got to Jefferies, and he was lunging at down and away pitches and chasing high heat in April and May. But, inevitably, his natural talent surfaced.

Discipline is important to Jefferies' success as a hitter. During his early slump, he drew only four walks in two months. That's real over-anxiety. He started to take off later in the year when Davey Johnson moved him into the leadoff spot. Batting first, Jefferies still didn't walk much, but he was much less apt to leave the dugout swinging. When Jefferies takes advantage of his small strike zone, he can hit a ball anywhere. Gregg is a line drive hitter who can smash any type of pitch. He uses all fields, and he should show good power some day. He should be hitting 20 to 30 homers eventually.

BASERUNNING:

Jefferies is still learning, but he has fine speed and uses it wisely. With 21 steals in 27 attempts last year, he looks like a cinch to steal 30 to 40 once he learns the pitchers better.

FIELDING:

The Mets trailed the National League in double plays last year, partly because Sid Fernandez can pitch without infielders, and partly because Gregg Jefferies is new at second base. Gregg needs practice and confidence to turn the double play; both will come with time. As a former shortstop and third baseman, Jefferies has proven that he has good range and a strong and accurate throwing arm. His tremendous athletic ability should blossom at second by mid-1990, if that is where the Mets want him.

OVERALL:

If you were starting a major league franchise today, Gregg Jefferies is one of two or three players you would most want. For two consecutive years, he has started slowly and then finished with a bang. The slow starts could be blamed on fans and media excess, but Jefferies must soon learn presence of mind at the plate. When he does this, he will be great.

GREGG JEFFERIES

Position: 2B/3B
Bats: B **Throws:** R
Ht: 5'10" **Wt:** 175

Opening Day Age: 22
Born: 8/1/67 in Burlingame, CA
ML Seasons: 3

Overall Statistics

	G	AB	R	H	D	T	HR	RBI	SB	BB	SO	AVG
1989	141	508	72	131	28	2	12	56	21	39	46	.258
Career	176	623	91	169	37	4	18	75	26	47	56	.271

Where He Hits the Ball

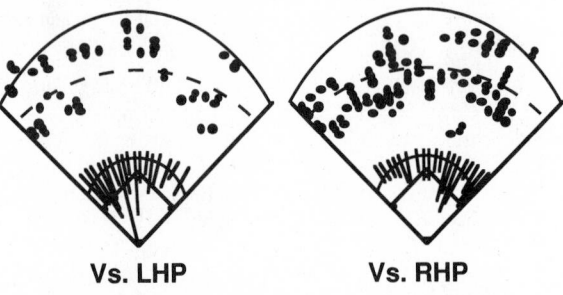

Vs. LHP   **Vs. RHP**

1989 Situational Stats

	AB	H	HR	RBI	AVG		AB	H	HR	RBI	AVG
Home	237	68	7	27	.287	LHP	174	44	5	24	.253
Road	271	63	5	29	.232	RHP	334	87	7	32	.260
Day	190	48	4	20	.253	Sc Pos	117	30	3	45	.256
Night	318	83	8	36	.261	Clutch	79	13	0	4	.165

1989 Rankings (National League)

➡ 7th in GDPs (16) and highest batting average with 2 strikes (.264) - *players with 162 PA with 2 strikes*

➡ 8th in hit by pitch (5) and runs scored per time reached base (36.5%) - *players with 502 PA*

➡ 9th in most GDPs per GDP situation (17.0%) - *players with 50 PA in GDP situations*

➡ Led the Mets in GDPs, grounder/flyball ratio (1.65), lowest percentage of swings that missed (10.9%), highest percentage of swings put into play (50.8%), batting average with 2 strikes,

➡ Led NL Second Basemen in GDPs and intentional walks (8)

FUTURE MVP?

HITTING:

Howard Johnson made a major change last year. Rather than look for fastballs and swinging way out in front of breaking balls, he concentrated on hitting the curve and adjusting to fastballs. The results were spectacular. Johnson produced a better average with more power, and instead of swatting curveballs for line drive fouls, he started hitting them for doubles down the line. His personal high in doubles jumped from 22 to 41, a Mets record.

HoJo is still a pull hitter from both sides. He loves to swing at the first pitch; in 1989 he put the initial offering in play 102 times and batted .382 on these swings. Pitchers can throw away their old books that recommend starting him off with a curve in the strike zone -- he'll punish it.

Although he is aggressive on the first pitch, Johnson can also show patience, and he draws a lot of walks. Last year on 3-0 and 3-1 counts, Howard walked 39 times while getting only four hits.

One offensive weakness is Johnson's tendency to wear out at year-end. Even last year, from September 1 on he hit just .252, and only .189 with runners in scoring position. Trying to steal 50 bases can be exhausting. Howard must try to pace himself for the good of the team.

BASERUNNING:

Johnson is extremely fast for a power-hitting third baseman. As a baserunner, he is aggressive and usually alert. He is a serious threat to steal at any time, and has a high success rate.

FIELDING:

At third, HoJo moves well to his right, but has little range to his left. He comes in on the ball well. His erratic throws and blundered pop-ups seem to be a mental problem, often occurring when he has plenty of time to get set. Howard's ability to play shortstop is a big plus for Davey Johnson, who loves double switches, position shifts, and line-ups overloaded with offense.

OVERALL:

Johnson's biggest weakness is that he overvalues his own abilities and openly puts his own accomplishments foremost. When he first won the Mets' third base job because of a teammate's disability, Johnson conveyed a lack of sympathy about the injury, and said he was glad to have the competition resolved. Such candor is admirable, but the attitude is not. Now that HoJo is an established star with a growing national reputation, he can afford to be more team-oriented.

HOWARD JOHNSON

Position: 3B/SS
Bats: B **Throws:** R
Ht: 5'10" **Wt:** 195

Opening Day Age: 29
Born: 11/29/60 in Clearwater, FL
ML Seasons: 8

Overall Statistics

	G	AB	R	H	D	T	HR	RBI	SB	BB	SO	AVG
1989	153	571	104	164	41	3	36	101	41	77	126	.287
Career	869	2805	427	724	135	10	136	422	127	374	592	.258

Where He Hits the Ball

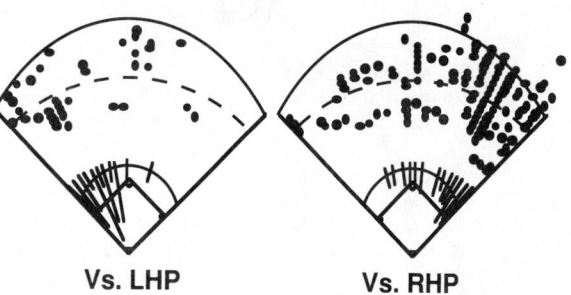

Vs. LHP   **Vs. RHP**

1989 Situational Stats

	AB	H	HR	RBI	AVG		AB	H	HR	RBI	AVG
Home	276	80	19	47	.290	LHP	194	54	7	25	.278
Road	295	84	17	54	.285	RHP	377	110	29	76	.292
Day	187	57	13	31	.305	Sc Pos	126	39	9	64	.310
Night	384	107	23	70	.279	Clutch	84	21	5	12	.250

1989 Rankings (National League)

➡ 1st in runs (104), slugging percentage vs. righthanded pitchers (.607) and lowest grounder/flyball ratio (.63) - *players with 502 PA*

➡ 2nd in slugging percentage (.559) and home runs (36)

➡ 3rd in home run frequency (15.9 ABs per HR), doubles (41), total bases (319) and runs scored per time reached base (40.6%)

➡ Led the Mets in 24 categories including home runs, runs, hits (164), doubles, triples (3), RBI (101), stolen bases (41), walks (77), batting average (.287), on-base average (.369), slugging percentage, strikeouts (126), total bases and at bats (571)

HITTING:

Barry Lyons has already proven himself a good enough hitter to play in the majors, but the world expects more from a regular starter than from a backup. Lyons has hit around .300 at every minor league level. It looks highly unlikely that he can hit .300 with the Mets, but .270 is not an outrageous goal, and would sure please the franchise.

Lyons has trouble with junkballing righthanders, but eats up hard throwers, especially lefties. Barry has decent power and can drive the ball anywhere from left field to right center. He is fairly disciplined, knows how to take a pitch and work the count, and he can usually hit behind the runner. While Lyons will never be a star, he is a workmanlike hitter already, and could still improve at age 29.

Lyons has a big hitch in his swing, which makes it difficult for him to wait on the slow curve. (If you hit .280 or smash 25 homers, it's called a trigger mechanism; if you hit like Barry Lyons, it's called a hitch.) Noting his ability to hit power pitchers, an adjustment should be possible if he gets enough playing time.

BASERUNNING:

"Barry Lyons baserunning" is an oxymoron. Lyons is oh for one lifetime in steal attempts, and these numbers are unlikely to change much during the 1990's. Barry has no speed. He does have sense enough to stay out of trouble. So he may hurt you with slowness, but he will rarely hurt you with foolishness.

FIELDING:

Lyons is still maturing as a catcher. He blocks the ball in the dirt well, a very important skill when catching the likes of Cone, Darling and Gooden, all of whom have thrown 55-foot breaking balls in game situations. Lyons calls a good game and sets a clear target. He has a quick arm and throws accurately. If the pitcher delivers the ball promptly enough to allow any play at all, Barry can throw out most of the base stealers in the National League.

OVERALL:

Lyons' major problem is that he is being compared to a potential Hall of Famer, Gary Carter. Once people get used to the idea that Barry cannot be a superstar, and evaluate him within the context of his own abilities, they will see that while he is not as good as wished, he is much better than feared.

BARRY LYONS

Position: C
Bats: R **Throws:** R
Ht: 6' 1" **Wt:** 205

Opening Day Age: 29
Born: 6/3/60 in Biloxi, MS
ML Seasons: 4

Overall Statistics

	G	AB	R	H	D	T	HR	RBI	SB	BB	SO	AVG
1989	79	235	15	58	13	0	3	27	0	11	28	.247
Career	188	465	36	112	24	2	7	64	0	23	66	.241

Where He Hits the Ball

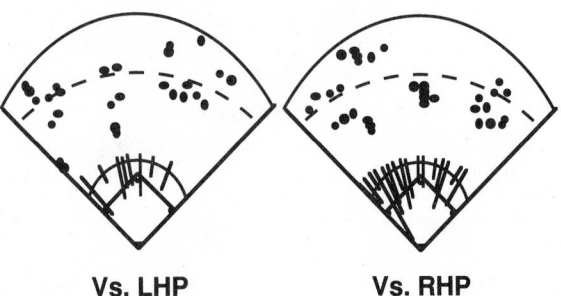

Vs. LHP   **Vs. RHP**

1989 Situational Stats

	AB	H	HR	RBI	AVG		AB	H	HR	RBI	AVG
Home	108	26	1	13	.241	LHP	84	25	3	10	.298
Road	127	32	2	14	.252	RHP	151	33	0	17	.219
Day	70	17	0	7	.243	Sc Pos	66	18	0	24	.273
Night	165	41	3	20	.248	Clutch	41	8	1	2	.195

1989 Rankings (National League)

➡ 5th in batting average on an 0-2 count (.300) - *players with 20 PA on an 0-2 count*

➡ Led the Mets in batting average on an 0-2 count

➡ Led NL Catchers in batting average on an 0-2 count

HITTING:

Dave Magadan will attempt to fill the shoes of Keith Hernandez in 1990. Offensively, he should come close to succeeding. Like Hernandez, Magadan is a patient, high average, line-drive hitter. Dave has an exceptional sense of his strike zone and is rarely fooled. His unorthodox stance makes him susceptible to the high inside pitch, but he can usually fight it off.

Magadan does not have much power and will amaze everyone if he ever hits 10 home runs in a season. He is a spray hitter with power in the alleys. He will hit around .300 with an on-base percentage closer to .400. Because of his bat control and patience, he is an ideal number two hitter, but could appear anywhere in the line-up except fourth. Most importantly, Magadan's offensive skill, cool, and discipline make him a money player.

BASERUNNING:

Magadan is flat out slow. But he is an intelligent, conservative base traveler who rarely blunders. Any pitcher who throws over to first to hold Magadan is either practicing or foolish. When Dave Magadan gets a steal, it means something has gone wrong. This man does not steal, but will take an extra base on rare occasions.

FIELDING:

Magadan is an adequate fielder. Unfortunately, he has a tough act to follow and will suffer from being compared to the great Keith Hernandez. In 1990, many observers will label Dave a lousy fielder, which he is not. Being righthanded, and lacking quickness, Magadan will have to work extra hard on his positioning, his knowledge of the hitters, and paying close attention on every pitch. He will also have to overcome a tendency to be tentative, and really take charge on plays involving the pitcher and second baseman. Dave has proven himself at third, so he brings a good package of skills to the game. The outlook is favorable for his rapid development as a fielder.

OVERALL:

Magadan should begin 1990 as the Mets' everyday first baseman, but if he has much trouble at bat or in the field, there are various candidates ready to platoon with him. Most likely, he will hit for high average, drive in his share of runs and do fine offensively. If his defense improves rapidly with regular work, he could become a star. But if he fails to show further development, he might find it difficult to keep his everyday status.

DAVE MAGADAN

Position: 1B/3B
Bats: L **Throws:** R
Ht: 6' 3" **Wt:** 195

Opening Day Age: 27
Born: 9/30/62 in Tampa, FL
ML Seasons: 4

Overall Statistics

	G	AB	R	H	D	T	HR	RBI	SB	BB	SO	AVG
1989	127	374	47	107	22	3	4	41	1	49	37	.286
Career	334	898	110	263	50	4	8	103	1	134	99	.293

Where He Hits the Ball

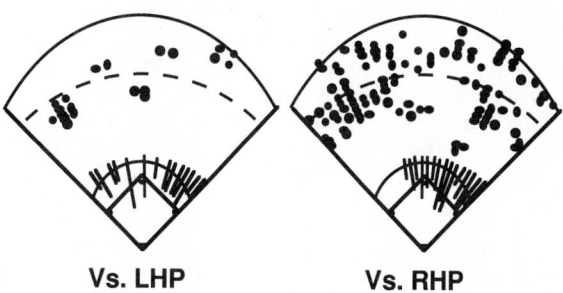

Vs. LHP   **Vs. RHP**

1989 Situational Stats

	AB	H	HR	RBI	AVG		AB	H	HR	RBI	AVG
Home	183	56	3	22	.306	LHP	92	24	0	8	.261
Road	191	51	1	19	.267	RHP	282	83	4	33	.294
Day	135	40	1	12	.296	Sc Pos	94	28	1	35	.298
Night	239	67	3	29	.280	Clutch	68	17	2	9	.250

1989 Rankings (National League)

➡ 4th in least GDPs per GDP situation (2.9%) - *players with 50 PA in GDP situations*

➡ Led the Mets in triples (3) and least GDPs per GDP situation

➡ Led NL First Basemen in hitting on a 3-2 count (.342) - first basemen with 20 PA on a 3-2 count

HITTING:

In early 1986, when he started to hit righthanders consistently, Kevin McReynolds emerged as one of the National League premier sluggers. For three years he performed at a high and ultra-consistent level: 26-29 home runs, 95-99 RBIs, 82-89 runs scored, and .276 -.288 batting average. Perhaps it was inevitable that these numbers should decline somewhat in 1989. But Kevin's "off year" was not all that bad.

McReynolds is an aggressive pull hitter. In 1989 he hit six homers on first-pitch swings, and five more on 1-0 counts. His basic approach at the plate is to look for anything inside that he can jerk toward left field. Most pitchers work him with breaking balls on the outside corner, fastballs well off the plate, and occasional (careful) inside stuff that will be fouled into the seats.

Not only is McReynolds aggressive, but he becomes increasingly aggressive in the second half of each season. During each of his three years with the Mets, Kevin's strikeout/walk ratio has risen from about 1.3 in the first half to about 2.0 in the second half, and his home runs have come every 25 at bats in the first half, but every 19 at bats in the second half.

BASERUNNING:

A loss of speed was a definite factor dragging down McReynolds' batting stats, and the impact on baserunning was even more visible. McReynolds dropped off his record-setting stolen base performance of 21 for 21 attempts in 1988, and settled down to 15 for 22 in 1989. Kevin is not a true burner, but he is extremely wise in his selection of opportunities.

FIELDING:

McReynolds did not repeat his Gold Glove level performance of 1988, but he remained a solid outfielder last year. His combined abilities to move toward a ball quickly and throw with power and accuracy to any spot on the field make him one of the most dangerous outfielders to run on. His assists dropped off his league-leading pace of 18 in 1988, partly because of runners' respect and partly because of minor physical problems.

OVERALL:

McReynolds' amazing consistency in 1986-1988 raised unreasonable expectations and caused disproportionate disappointment in his 1989 performance. True, the numbers were down a bit, the weight was up a bit, and he left a few games with unprofessional haste. But two bad months in four years do not make a player a bum. Kevin's bad season wasn't that bad, and a return to physical health, and better conditioning, should restore him to a level near superstar.

KEVIN MCREYNOLDS

Position: LF
Bats: R **Throws:** R
Ht: 6' 1" **Wt:** 215

Opening Day Age: 30
Born: 10/16/59 in Little Rock, AR
ML Seasons: 7

Overall Statistics

	G	AB	R	H	D	T	HR	RBI	SB	BB	SO	AVG
1989	148	545	74	148	25	3	22	85	15	46	74	.272
Career	942	3476	475	940	171	27	143	539	67	278	462	.270

Where He Hits the Ball

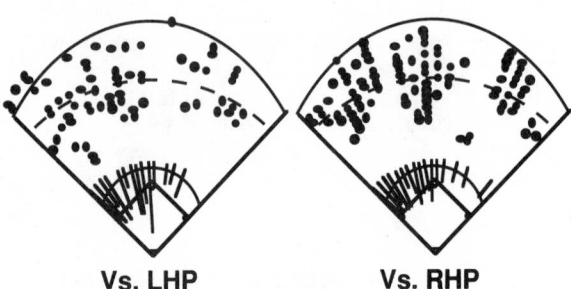

Vs. LHP   **Vs. RHP**

1989 Situational Stats

	AB	H	HR	RBI	AVG		AB	H	HR	RBI	AVG
Home	274	73	12	40	.266	LHP	189	56	10	32	.296
Road	271	75	10	45	.277	RHP	356	92	12	53	.258
Day	188	48	5	21	.255	Sc Pos	139	38	5	62	.273
Night	357	100	17	64	.280	Clutch	99	31	5	9	.313

1989 Rankings (National League)

→ 4th in lowest grounder/flyball ratio (.80) - *players with 502 PA*

→ 6th in percentage of extra bases taken as a runner (60.9%) - *players with 40 opportunities to advance*

→ 7th in hitting with the bases loaded (.471) - *players with 10 PA with the bases loaded*

→ 10th in home run frequency (24.8 ABs per HR) and RBI (85)

→ Led the Mets in singles (98), triples (3), percentage of extra bases taken as a runner and hitting in the clutch (.313)

→ Led NL Left Fielders in sacrifice flies (7) and errors (10)

PITCHING:

Randy Myers is a typical short relief specialist: he comes in and overpowers you. He throws a fastball well over 90 mph, and an occasional wicked slider. He had marvelous control in 1988 (2.25 walks per nine innings pitched), but became shaky in 1989 (4.26 walks per nine innings) immediately after adopting Mitch Williams' theme song, "Wild Thing."

In 1988 Myers was devastating with the game on the line. In 1989 he was tough at home, but the road was another story. He allowed four game-winning homers, two to lefties. Those two homers notwithstanding, lefties had little success against Myers, only a .164 average. For that matter, righties hit only .219.

Myers had an ERA of 1.45 for the first half and 3.63 for the second. He was virtually unhittable in April and May, then around the third week in June he seemed to lose his rhythm. He carried a heavy workload the first three months, appearing in 36 games. Some observers thought he was tired. Myers claimed the opposite, that he wasn't being used enough. The ERA remained low through July and August, as he tended to give up other pitchers' runs, but in September, his ERA jumped, giving support to the "tired" theory. Davey Johnson has always used a two-man bullpen (Orosco/McDowell, Myers/McDowell, Myers/Aguilera). The delineation between set-up man and closer changes day to day. But when Aguilera left, the Mets used Myers as their only closer, without great success. A righty to complement Myers looks like a necessity for 1990.

HITTING, FIELDING, BASERUNNING:

Myers seldom participates in the Mets' offense. He seems to enjoy his rare appearances at bat or on the bases, but has not batted often enough to give any real indication of his offensive abilities. Like many hard throwers, Randy's follow-through leaves him poorly set for fielding activity. He does not help himself much. Myers does, however, hold runners very effectively (just six steals allowed in 1989) and shows a great pickoff move on occasion.

OVERALL:

A key player for the Mets in 1990, Myers will be their only legitimate stopper unless trades produce a righty counterpart. Myers does not have the long credentials of some National League closers, but he has accomplished a great deal in his short time with the Mets. Despite the weak finish in 1989, he must be considered a top-flight closer until he proves he cannot do the job.

RANDY MYERS

Position: RP
Bats: L **Throws:** L
Ht: 6' 1" **Wt:** 208

Opening Day Age: 27
Born: 9/19/62 in Vancouver, WA
ML Seasons: 5

Overall Statistics

	W	L	ERA	G	GS	Sv	IP	H	R	BB	SO	HR
1989	7	4	2.35	65	0	24	84.1	62	23	40	88	4
Career	17	13	2.74	185	0	56	240.0	179	79	97	264	16

Where They Hit the Ball

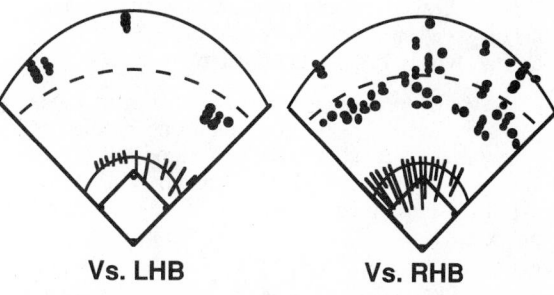

Vs. LHB   **Vs. RHB**

1989 Situational Stats

	W	L	ERA	Sv	IP		AB	H	HR	RBI	AVG
Home	4	0	2.02	17	49.0	LHB	73	12	2	8	.164
Road	3	4	2.80	7	35.1	RHB	228	50	2	20	.219
Day	1	1	3.04	5	26.2	Sc Pos	102	17	2	23	.167
Night	6	3	2.03	19	57.2	Clutch	250	50	4	24	.200

1989 Rankings (National League)

➡ 3rd in lowest GDPs induced per GDP situation (3.0%) and lowest percentage of inherited runners scoring (18.5%) - *pitchers with 30 inherited runners*

➡ 6th in first batter efficiency (.155) - *pitchers with 40 relief games*

➡ 7th in save percentage (82.8%) - *pitchers with 20 save opportunities*

➡ 8th in saves (24), games finished (47), save opportunities (29) and blown saves (5)

➡ Led the Mets in games (65), games finished, saves, save percentage, lowest percentage of inherited runners scoring, first batter efficiency and blown saves

PITCHING:

The freak accident that practically severed Bobby Ojeda's fingertip in 1988, and the successful healing that followed, raised some unusual questions. Would Ojeda still be able to squeeze the ball far enough back into his palm to make the change work? With the re-grown finger, Bob was actually able to throw a quicker fastball, but he lost some of the downward movement that had enhanced his tepid heater. Would the new fastball be effective?

Ojeda was concerned about such questions and was tentative in the first half of '89. Before the All-Star break, he was 5-8 with a 3.96 ERA. After the break, while the Mets were playing "only" .541 baseball, Ojeda improved to 8-3 with a 3.10 ERA.

Ultimately, Ojeda's increased speed allowed him to work inside against righthanded hitters more than before. The new velocity gave him a better set-up for his off-speed stuff, especially the famous "dead-fish" change, which was clearly effective in late 1989.

Ojeda works very carefully and will often issue walks because he refuses to give in to hitters, not because he is unable to throw strikes. The opposition batted only .059 against him after 3-0 counts, and only .179 after 3-1. Like most groundball pitchers, Ojeda prefers grass, and he loves Shea Stadium. Bob is susceptible to first inning snake-bit pitching, sometimes suffering bizarre episodes of walks, balks, bunts, stolen bases, sac flies, errors and/or pitches evading the catcher. Ojeda gave up 30% of all his runs on the first 15 pitches of each game, allowing a .305 batting average, and five stolen bases without a caught stealing to those who faced him early.

FIELDING, HITTING, BASERUNNING:

Ojeda is not good at holding runners. Opponents stole 28 bases in 1989, but were cut down 10 times. He is vulnerable only because he uses slowballs extensively, not because of any weakness in his hold or delivery. Ojeda showed his athletic ability with a few key hits in 1989. He is usually alert and disciplined at bat and on the base paths, but occasionally looks like an alumnus of the American League. Bob is a good fielder with decent range and superior presence of mind.

OVERALL:

It would appear that any doubts about Ojeda's ability (including his own) have been dispelled by the second half success and, barring a trade, the Mets should benefit greatly from Ojeda's presence in 1990.

BOBBY OJEDA

Position: SP
Bats: L **Throws:** L
Ht: 6' 1"   **Wt:** 195

Opening Day Age: 32
Born: 12/17/57 in Los Angeles, CA
ML Seasons: 10

Overall Statistics

	W	L	ERA	G	GS	Sv	IP	H	R	BB	SO	HR
1989	13	11	3.47	31	31	0	192.0	179	83	78	95	16
Career	88	73	3.65	242	210	1	1364.1	1301	615	458	822	106

Where They Hit the Ball

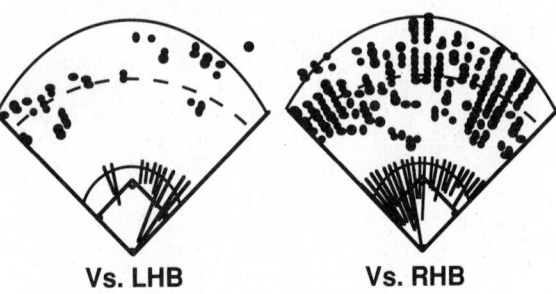

Vs. LHB   **Vs. RHB**

1989 Situational Stats

	W	L	ERA	Sv	IP		AB	H	HR	RBI	AVG
Home	6	4	2.95	0	85.1	LHB	161	38	5	12	.236
Road	7	7	3.88	0	106.2	RHB	570	141	11	62	.247
Day	5	7	4.36	0	88.2	Sc Pos	164	42	2	53	.256
Night	8	4	2.70	0	103.1	Clutch	43	9	1	4	.209

1989 Rankings (National League)

➡ 5th in stolen bases allowed (28) and lowest strikeout/walk ratio (1.22) - *pitchers with 162 IP*

➡ 9th in grounder/flyball ratio (1.62)

➡ Led the Mets in shutouts (2), GDPs induced (13), walks (78), grounder/flyball ratio, least HRs per 9 innings (.75) and most GDPs induced per 9 innings (.609) - *team pitchers with 162 IP*

HITTING:

Apparently someone told Juan Samuel that a good hitter must reach the outside pitch. Unfortunately, this advice ignored the issue of strike zone. If a pitch isn't over Juan's shoulders, and if he doesn't have to duck it, Samuel will swing. One look at his strikeout totals will tell you this is not a secret to National League pitchers.

One positive result from leaning across the plate is a tendency to get hit by pitches; once Juan gets on base, he's wonderful. He just doesn't get to first often enough. Juan hits to all fields, and has traditionally hit with men in scoring position; but he was awful last year (.212 batting average in 132 at bats).

Samuel's biggest problem as a Met is Shea Stadium. His game is speed, manifested in doubles and triples. His style cries out for a turf field (like Veterans Stadium). Samuel's numbers with Philadelphia showed big home park advantages, but this year he was actually worse at home. His career may not survive Shea Stadium.

BASERUNNING:

Samuel is an excellent runner, fast and aggressive. He just has to get on base to show his abilities. He also hustles out of the box on ground balls, which last year enabled him to beat out an inordinate number of would-be double plays.

FIELDING:

Samuel's conversion to centerfield has not been a complete success. He has great lateral range and an adequate arm. But he isn't really sound on balls hit in front of him, and he hasn't a clue on balls hit over his head. Still, he has the skills to become a good outfielder. But what for? As Casey Stengel once said, "his potential is behind him now." Someone should just move him back to second, not because he can field so well there, but because at least his bat would be a great asset instead of a possible liability.

OVERALL:

As a second baseman, Samuel was an offensive gem. As an outfielder, his offensive value is questionable. Where in the Mets line-up do you put a centerfielder who has speed and power, but hits for a low average and strikes out excessively? Stated differently, why did the Mets want this particular individual in exchange for two highly marketable players like Dykstra and McDowell? Samuel just doesn't seem to fit the Mets equation. Something will have to give soon, to address these unanswered questions.

JUAN SAMUEL

Position: CF
Bats: R **Throws:** R
Ht: 5'11" **Wt:** 170

Opening Day Age: 29
Born: 12/9/60 in San Pedro de Macoris, Dominican Republic
ML Seasons: 7

Overall Statistics

	G	AB	R	H	D	T	HR	RBI	SB	BB	SO	AVG
1989	137	532	69	125	16	2	11	48	42	42	120	.235
Career	938	3836	560	997	189	72	103	441	280	232	900	.260

Where He Hits the Ball

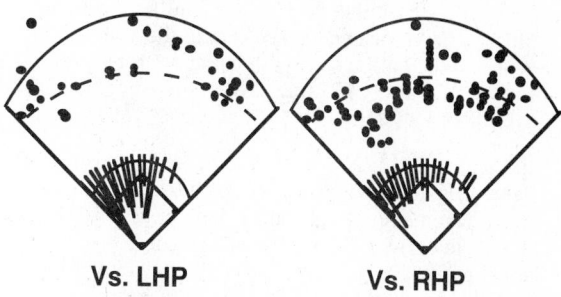

Vs. LHP   **Vs. RHP**

1989 Situational Stats

	AB	H	HR	RBI	AVG		AB	H	HR	RBI	AVG
Home	269	62	5	25	.230	LHP	190	49	6	22	.258
Road	263	63	6	23	.240	RHP	342	76	5	26	.222
Day	149	30	4	10	.201	Sc Pos	132	28	0	33	.212
Night	383	95	7	38	.248	Clutch	73	18	1	8	.247

1989 Rankings (National League)

➤ 2nd in stolen bases (42)

➤ 3rd in hit by pitch (11) and most pitches seen per plate appearance (3.8) - *players with 502 PA*

➤ 4th in highest percentage of swings that missed (28.2%) and lowest percentage of swings put into play (36.6%)

➤ 5th in caught stealing (12)

➤ Led the Mets in caught stealing (9) and hit by pitch (10)

➤ Led NL Center Fielders in hit by pitch, stolen bases and most pitches seen per plate appearance

HITTING:

The Mets obtained Mackey Sasser to provide backup catching and lefthanded hitting. He has done both well. Sasser is a free swinger who consistently puts the ball in play. He walked only seven times in 1989, and rarely worked the count as far as ball three. Considering his lack of discipline, he makes remarkably good contact. He swings at almost anything near the strike zone, but he has quick hands, and does not swing excessively hard.

Sasser likes the ball low and out over the plate. He can handle fastballs better than breaking stuff. Slow curves inside bother him the most, because he normally looks for a fastball and tries to adjust after committing himself. He is not a power hitter, but hits plenty of hard grounders and line drives.

Sasser plays against righthanded pitching exclusively. He is unlikely to see a southpaw except for occasions when he is the last available catcher. Mackey has appeared everywhere in the bottom half of the Mets' batting order, showing a strong preference for the #6 or #7 spot (.310 composite average) over #8 or #9 (.250).

BASERUNNING:

Sasser has "average speed for a catcher," meaning that if he played any other position, he would have to be called slow. He is definitely not a threat to steal, and rarely grabs an extra base. Mackey is quick out of the batter's box, however, making good use of the lefthanded hitter's head start toward first base. For a slow runner who hits a lot of grounders, he is very good at staying out of the double play.

FIELDING:

Sasser has come a long way since first converting from the outfield to catcher in 1986. His growth with New York has been visible and rewarding to fans and management. Sasser is not one of the top-gun throwers in the league, but he has a quick release and fair accuracy. One annoying problem is that Mackey tends to double-pump when throwing back to the pitcher. A few teams have stolen bases on this move, and he will have to correct it.

OVERALL:

Sasser should provide more than adequate backup for Barry Lyons in 1990. He is strong enough to catch 100 or more games, and will often appear for offensive purposes, in addition to giving Lyons some days off. An excellent pinch hitter and team player, he has the added abilities to play first base, third base and the outfield, valuable attractions to a manager who must balance a 24-man roster.

MACKEY SASSER

Position: C
Bats: L **Throws:** R
Ht: 6' 1" **Wt:** 210

Opening Day Age: 27
Born: 8/3/62 in Fort Gaines, GA
ML Seasons: 3

Overall Statistics

	G	AB	R	H	D	T	HR	RBI	SB	BB	SO	AVG
1989	72	182	17	53	14	2	1	22	0	7	15	.291
Career	146	332	28	93	24	3	2	41	0	13	26	.280

Where He Hits the Ball

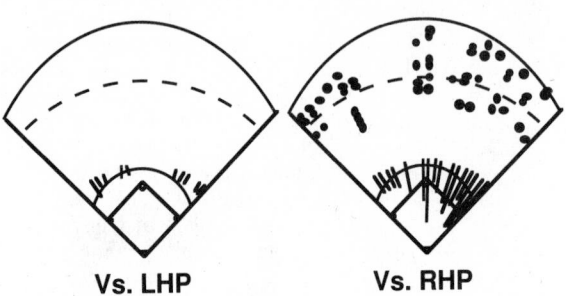

Vs. LHP   **Vs. RHP**

1989 Situational Stats

	AB	H	HR	RBI	AVG		AB	H	HR	RBI	AVG
Home	92	27	1	14	.293	LHP	24	5	0	1	.208
Road	90	26	0	8	.289	RHP	158	48	1	21	.304
Day	64	20	1	12	.313	Sc Pos	47	13	0	20	.277
Night	118	33	0	10	.280	Clutch	34	9	0	3	.265

1989 Rankings (National League)

➡ Did not rank near the top or bottom in any category

HITTING:

Taunted on the road, and booed at home, Darryl Strawberry is surrounded by so much emotion that an objective assessment of his skills becomes difficult. Blessed with awesome talent, he has a maddening tendency to look awkward, and worse, like he just doesn't care. Reading Darryl's mind is a cottage industry among New York fans and media; they would all be better off just reading his stats.

Another problem in analyzing Darryl's hitting is that he is so inconsistent. One day he can look like superman, with stats to match; the next day he can look like a clumsy giant swinging a bat for the first time. Tendencies do emerge, however. Darryl hits better at home than on the road. His batting average, on-base percentage and slugging percentage are all higher against righties, but he still hits a lot of homers off southpaws (16 in '87, 20 in '88).

Strawberry likes to extend his arms, but if pitchers come inside and miss by a little, he'll probably bounce one off the scoreboard. The big homer output against lefties is largely attributable to optimists trying to pitch him inside. Darryl has been proficient at drawing the base on balls, but his annual walk totals have been declining: from 97 to 85 to 61 over the last three years. Strawberry may have to earn back the respect that makes pitchers extra careful.

BASERUNNING:

Despite his speed (and he has plenty of it) Strawberry is not a good baserunner. He gets picked off, he runs through stop signs, he just gets lost. He is a good but not great base stealer, using raw speed. His success percentage was higher when he was starting out.

FIELDING:

Strawberry has marvelous skills but doesn't use them. He wastes his great arm by overthrowing cut-off men and throwing to the wrong base. He gets a bad jump on the ball. And like all Met outfielders, he plays too deep. This is a special harm to Darryl, because he cannot use his speed to race back to the wall, and he does not have much ability to come in on a ball.

OVERALL:

After a miserable 1989, people are already forgetting that Strawberry was arguably the best hitter in the National League in '87 and '88. It is fashionable to give up on Darryl. But other great hitters have come back from bad years. So could Darryl. He's only 28, and there could be 400 home runs left in that bat. He is still a potential Hall of Famer.

DARRYL STRAWBERRY

Position: RF
Bats: L **Throws:** L
Ht: 6' 6" **Wt:** 195

Opening Day Age: 28
Born: 3/12/62 in Los Angeles, CA
ML Seasons: 7

Overall Statistics

	G	AB	R	H	D	T	HR	RBI	SB	BB	SO	AVG
1989	134	476	69	107	26	1	29	77	11	61	105	.225
Career	957	3361	570	875	169	29	215	625	176	510	850	.260

Where He Hits the Ball

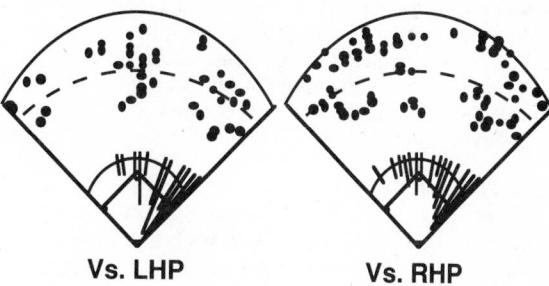

Vs. LHP   **Vs. RHP**

1989 Situational Stats

	AB	H	HR	RBI	AVG		AB	H	HR	RBI	AVG
Home	224	61	15	41	.272	LHP	178	39	9	33	.219
Road	252	46	14	36	.183	RHP	298	68	20	44	.228
Day	163	42	10	28	.258	Sc Pos	147	33	6	45	.224
Night	313	65	19	49	.208	Clutch	82	11	3	8	.134

1989 Rankings (National League)

➡ 1st in lowest batting average on the road (.183) and lowest batting average on a 0-2 count (.000) -*players with 20 PA on a 0-2 count*

➡ 3rd in lowest batting average (.225) and worst hitting in the clutch (.134) - *players with 502 PA*

➡ 4th in home run frequency (16.4 ABs per HR) and lowest batting average with the bases loaded (.091)

➡ 6th in home runs (29)

➡ 7th in runs scored per time reached base (37.7%)

➡ Led the Mets in pitches seen per plate appearance (3.7) and intentional walks (13)

HITTING:

A former number one draft choice who has made the transition from regular to utility man, Tim Teufel is a line drive, doubles hitter with occasional power. He has suffered from hand injuries the last two years, but when he is well, he flashes a quick swing that can catch up with almost any fastball or adjust to unexpected curves.

Tim has much better success against lefthanded pitchers than righties, making him a natural as a platooner or pinch hitter. He hits to all fields, but his power is to the left side. His most natural swing is somewhat low and toward the outer part of the plate, so he is vulnerable to inside pitches.

Teufel is a patient batsman, a good quality for someone who is getting increased usage as a pinch hitter. On 3-0 and 3-1 counts in 1989, Teufel drew 18 walks while putting the ball in play only six times. Tim has versatile hitting skills that can be useful in any situation. He appeared in every batting order spot except cleanup in 1990, showing a definite preference for the upper half. In positions one to five, he hit .296, but in the lower spots, just .212.

BASERUNNING:

Teufel does not have much speed; he was caught stealing in three of his four attempts last year. Generally, he is an intelligent runner who does not make baserunning mistakes, but he is not the person to ignite a rally with exciting footwork.

FIELDING:

Teufel has spent most of his career at second base. His hands are a little hard, and his range is limited, but he excels at the important skill of turning the double play. Recently he has put in time at both third and first, and looks thoroughly competent at these positions, where the range factor is less critical. With the departure of Hernandez and Mazzilli, Teufel is likely to get more playing time at first in 1990. He is still improving on fine points like picking low throws out of the dirt, but his progress is encouraging.

OVERALL:

Teufel is the kind of hustling veteran player who is a major asset to a contending team. He can contribute to any franchise, and he has matured into a fine infield utility man. While Tim will never be the superstar the Twins hoped he would be, the Mets are pleased to have him. He should continue to play productive, multifaceted roles on offense and defense for the Mets in 1990.

TIM
TEUFEL

Position: 2B/1B
Bats: R **Throws:** R
Ht: 6' 0" **Wt:** 175

Opening Day Age: 31
Born: 7/7/58 in Greenwich, CT
ML Seasons: 7

Overall Statistics

	G	AB	R	H	D	T	HR	RBI	SB	BB	SO	AVG
1989	83	219	27	56	7	2	2	15	1	32	50	.256
Career	679	2150	297	567	137	10	51	255	10	263	337	.264

Where He Hits the Ball

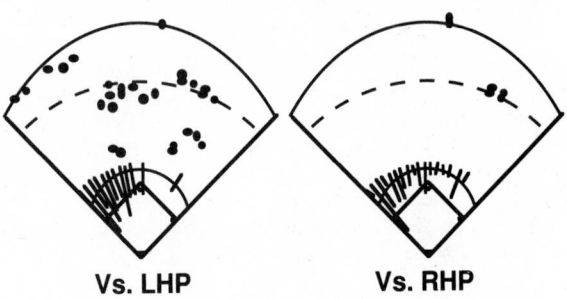

Vs. LHP   **Vs. RHP**

1989 Situational Stats

	AB	H	HR	RBI	AVG		AB	H	HR	RBI	AVG
Home	107	23	1	7	.215	LHP	132	36	1	9	.273
Road	112	33	1	8	.295	RHP	87	20	1	6	.230
Day	75	18	1	5	.240	Sc Pos	53	12	0	11	.226
Night	144	38	1	10	.264	Clutch	33	8	1	2	.242

1989 Rankings (National League)

➡ Did not rank near the top or bottom in any category

PITCHING:

Frank Viola came home to New York in 1989 after seven years in the Midwest. He won 115 games for the Twins, including 3 in postseason play in 1987. But life was not sweet enough, even with a Cy Young award in 1988. After a contract dispute and a lackluster first half in '89, Frank OK'd a trade to the Mets. Ironically, the Mets' immediate need was to replace the injured Doc Gooden, another Cy Young winner, in their rotation.

Viola joined the richest (in salary and talent) pitching staff in baseball. A former star pitcher for St. John's University, he seemed to settle in comfortably with a four-hitter against the Cardinals on August 2 and allowed only five hits in seven innings against the Phillies on August 7. After some mediocre performances, he tossed a three-hit, 1-0 shutout against Orel Hershiser in the world's first match-up of reigning Cy Young winners. September brought more of the same: alternating excellence and so-so performances.

Statistically, Viola's last months with Minnesota were unimpressive. He was 8-12 with a 3.81 ERA and disappointed many people, especially those who ogled his big new contract. But with the Mets, Viola performed admirably, better than his 5-5 record and 3.38 ERA would indicate. He held the opposition to two runs or less in seven of 12 starts, while the Mets offense exceeded two runs only four times for Frank.

Viola's fastball reached a plateau of velocity, control and movement in the spring of 1987, and the heater remains his best pitch. He also has an outstanding change-up and a sharp curve, both of which Mel Stottlemyre would like to see Viola use more extensively. Mel has also advised Frank concerning a tendency to tip his fastball during delivery.

FIELDING, HITTING, BASERUNNING:

Viola's lack of quickness makes him an adequate fielder at best. He is, however, excellent at holding runners. Historically the opposition is barely 50% successful in stolen base attempts; in 1989 they got away with 59%, still quite low. At bat and on the bases, Frank looks like a refugee from the junior circuit.

OVERALL:

The Sweet Music emanating from Shea Stadium in 1990 could just be the beginning of a long and pleasant refrain. If the Mets recapture some of their run-scoring effectiveness in the 90's, Viola's contributions could result in just what all Met fans clamor for: World Championships.

FRANK VIOLA

Position: SP
Bats: L **Throws:** L
Ht: 6' 4" **Wt:** 209

Opening Day Age: 29
Born: 4/19/60 in Hempstead, NY
ML Seasons: 8

Overall Statistics

	W	L	ERA	G	GS	Sv	IP	H	R	BB	SO	HR
1989	13	17	3.66	36	36	0	261.0	246	115	74	211	22
Career	117	98	3.84	272	271	0	1858.0	1850	877	548	1287	218

Where They Hit the Ball

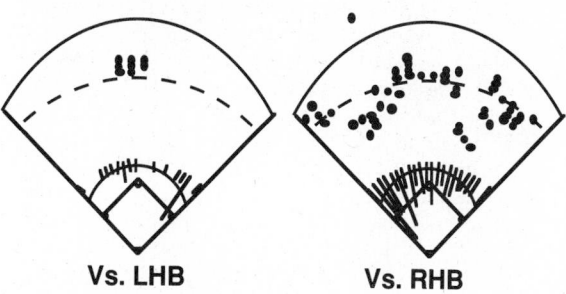

Vs. LHB   **Vs. RHB**

1989 Situational Stats

	W	L	ERA	Sv	IP		AB	H	HR	RBI	AVG
Home	6	9	3.52	0	128.0	LHB	172	46	3	15	.267
Road	7	8	3.79	0	133.0	RHB	814	200	19	90	.246
Day	5	5	4.14	0	76.0	Sc Pos	226	58	5	77	.257
Night	8	12	3.45	0	185.0	Clutch	99	17	1	3	.172

1989 Rankings (National League)

➡ Did not rank near the top or bottom in any category

MARK CARREON

Position: RF/LF
Bats: R **Throws:** L
Ht: 6' 0" **Wt:** 194

Opening Day Age: 26
Born: 7/19/63 in Chicago, IL
ML Seasons: 3

Overall Statistics

	G	AB	R	H	D	T	HR	RBI	SB	BB	SO	AVG
1989	68	133	20	41	6	0	6	16	2	12	17	.308
Career	84	154	25	49	8	0	7	18	2	15	19	.318

HITTING, FIELDING, BASERUNNING:

Mark Carreon is emerging as a fine major league hitter. He has excellent power, and he is disciplined enough to wait for a pitcher's mistake. For a young hitter, he can adapt well, just making contact or trying to jerk one into the bleachers, as the situation may require. Carreon has good speed, but not great. He got thrown out on three of five stolen base attempts in 1989, and they weren't really close. Mark did steal 31 bases at Tidewater in 1987, but he needs to study the pitchers more, and show greater respect for major league throwing arms. Twice last season Mark made the weird play of blocking a home run with his glove and catching it barehanded. Despite such heroics, or perhaps because of them, Carreon's fielding remains suspect. He can botch easy plays, and has a lot to learn.

OVERALL:

The son of former White Sox catcher Camilo Carreon, Mark shows a lot of poise for a young player. Carreon offers the Mets youthful enthusiasm and fine potential. He has a solid minor league record, and did well as a spare player in his first real chance last year. He may not play a lot for the Mets in 1990, but he figures to contribute.

PHIL LOMBARDI

Position: C
Bats: R **Throws:** R
Ht: 6' 2" **Wt:** 205

Opening Day Age: 27
Born: 2/20/63 in Abilene, TX
ML Seasons: 3

Overall Statistics

	G	AB	R	H	D	T	HR	RBI	SB	BB	SO	AVG
1989	18	48	4	11	1	0	1	3	0	5	8	.229
Career	43	92	10	22	4	0	3	9	0	9	17	.239

HITTING, FIELDING, BASERUNNING:

With four years of AAA experience, Lombardi has proven himself as a power hitter (home run ratio 3.0%) and a good judge of the strike zone (more walks than strikeouts). Offensively, he has been ready for the major leagues for a couple of years or longer. Lombardi has never stolen a base in his three major league stints; he is not likely to begin running at age 27. His baserunning is about what you expect from a veteran catcher. Why has this man spent four years at the AAA level? Simple: he can't field. He's willing to try. He has caught, played first, the outfield, third, even shortstop. He can play many positions, but none of them well. He now spends more time at first then behind the plate. Still, he has to be given points for versatility, a big asset in the era of the 24 man roster.

OVERALL:

Lombardi is too old to be called a prospect, but if the Mets simply keep the catchers they had in '89, Phil should be one of them. He's a perfect third-stringer: he can hit a homer, draw a walk, make contact, and play several positions.

JULIO MACHADO

Position: RP
Bats: R **Throws:** R
Ht: 5' 9" **Wt:** 160

Opening Day Age: 24
Born: 12/1/65 in
Zulia, Venezuela
ML Seasons: 1

Overall Statistics

	W	L	ERA	G	GS	Sv	IP	H	R	BB	SO	HR
1989	0	1	3.27	10	0	0	11.0	9	4	3	14	0
Career	0	1	3.27	10	0	0	11.0	9	4	3	14	0

PITCHING, FIELDING, HITTING:

After four seasons in the minors, Julio Machado was released by the Phillies after spring training '89. This move may be a comment on the state of Phillies pitching, because young Julio has a live arm. The Mets promptly signed him and gave him a tour of North America. Machado played in five (!) leagues last year, finishing with the National League Mets. His most impressive work was at Tidewater, where his 0.62 ERA and 37 strike outs in 29 innings pitched earned him a trip to the majors. Machado is a classic power pitcher with a live, rising fastball. He likes to pitch inside. Like many hard throwers, he has struggled with control early in his career. At Tidewater, he averaged 5.3 walks (but only five hits) per nine innings. With New York, his control looked much better: just three walks in 11 innings pitched, and he rarely let the count go as far as ball three. Machado fields and holds runners like a typical youngster: not too effectively. The opposition stole three bases from him (one caught stealing) in just 42 at bats.

OVERALL:

Randy Myers needs help, and Machado may be able to provide it. If he has good control in 1990, he could be highly effective.

KEITH MILLER

Position: 2B
Bats: R **Throws:** R
Ht: 5'11" **Wt:** 180

Opening Day Age: 26
Born: 6/12/63 in
Midland, MI
ML Seasons: 3

Overall Statistics

	G	AB	R	H	D	T	HR	RBI	SB	BB	SO	AVG
1989	57	143	15	33	7	0	1	7	6	5	27	.231
Career	122	264	38	67	10	3	2	13	14	13	43	.254

HITTING, FIELDING, BASERUNNING:

Keith Miller is a question mark. His aggressiveness and hustle are impressive. He is "in the game." However, he has yet to be given the playing time to prove his offensive skills at the major league level. Miller uses a closed stance. He is a spray, line-drive hitter. Keith likes low balls and pitches on the outside of the plate. He has problems hitting the curve, especially inside, and is susceptible to a high inside heater. Miller has good bat control. He can bunt for a sacrifice, or for a hit. Keith is a speedy, aggressive, and smart baserunner. He can steal (six for six in '89) and can go from first to third on most hits. As a fielder, Miller has good range and a strong arm. He can play second, short and centerfield. His speed, range, and versatility make him a big defensive asset.

OVERALL:

In early 1989, the Mets' long range plan had Magadan at first base, Miller at second base, Jefferies at third base, and Elster at shortstop: "the infield that would last a decade." Howard Johnson's new-found ability to hit the curveball has changed all this. Miller is the odd man out, at least for 1990.

JEFF MUSSELMAN

Position: RP/SP
Bats: L **Throws:** L
Ht: 6' 0" **Wt:** 185

Opening Day Age: 26
Born: 6/21/63 in
Doylestown, PA
ML Seasons: 4

Overall Statistics

	W	L	ERA	G	GS	Sv	IP	H	R	BB	SO	HR
1989	3	3	5.30	25	3	0	37.1	46	26	23	14	3
Career	23	13	4.11	114	19	3	216.2	209	110	112	111	15

PITCHING, FIELDING, HITTING:

Jeff Musselman's 1989 season took a wrong turn in spring training. While with Toronto he plunked Darryl Strawberry and then made a celebrated retreat toward third base when Straw Man charged the mound. No one will ever accuse Musselman of stupidity. But he never got back on track after this incident. He pitched horribly for Toronto (10.64 ERA), and when the Mets offered Mookie Wilson, the Jays jumped at the trade. Often compared to Jimmy Key while he worked in Toronto, Musselman has a good fastball but relies extensively on breaking pitches. He has a big-breaking curveball that may appear on any count, and a sharp slider. He can run the fastball in to righthanders, or make it sink. During the past two years, he has had more trouble with lefties than righties. Musselman made 15 starts without a complete game in 1988; he is clearly better suited for relief work.

OVERALL:

A Harvard grad, Musselman is an intelligent worker who is still just 26, and appears capable of a comeback. His 23-13 lifetime win/loss mark is not too shabby. The New York scenery appeared to help him, as he went 3-2 with a 3.08 ERA for the Mets.

PITCHING:

In 1989 Don Carman allowed more hits and walks per inning than he ever had before. His ERA, steadily climbing since 1984, shot up to a career-threatening 5.24 because he could not throw his curve ball consistently for strikes.

When Carman's curve drops, he is able to throw it up in the strike zone so that it flops downward for a called strike. For most of 1989, curve balls thrown up became curve balls hit out. This forced Carman to throw it down, where it was less apt to cause him trouble. But then the pitch often broke into the dirt, making it unusable with runners on base, or when he was behind in the count.

The failure of his curve allowed hitters to sit on Carman's best pitch, a hard fastball which tails slightly. He throws fastballs two-thirds of the time, but when he couldn't get his curve over, he would need five and six pitches for each hitter, tiring his arm, and losing his motion on his fastball.

Carman gets less power from his body and legs than any other fastball pitcher in the league. His legs remain almost straight as he bends at the waist powering each pitch with his arms and back. This can be an advantage for him. If he releases the fastball low, a hitter expecting Carman's change-up or curveball, will watch the fastball sail in for a strike. The disadvantage is that Carman tires from throwing so many hard pitches using so small a portion of his body's muscles. Fatigue straightens his fastball, and sends him to the showers by the middle of most starts. This doesn't affect him as much in relief; hitters facing Carman in the first inning of each outing were unable to do anything but draw walks.

FIELDING, HITTING, BASERUNNING:

Carman has only an average move to first base, but a quick delivery home, which helped his catchers catch half the attempted base-stealers. His delivery leaves him in good shape to field grounders and cover first. He is unable to hit or bunt successfully, and has endured multi-game streaks where he failed to even foul a pitch.

OVERALL:

After seven years in the majors, Don Carman is still a one-pitch pitcher. This spring he'll battle for a bullpen spot, but without a curveball, he's a one inning pitcher. One pitch and one inning is not the recipe for a long career.

DON CARMAN

Position: RP/SP
Bats: L **Throws:** L
Ht: 6' 3" **Wt:** 195

Opening Day Age: 30
Born: 8/14/59 in
Oklahoma City, OK
ML Seasons: 7

Overall Statistics

	W	L	ERA	G	GS	Sv	IP	H	R	BB	SO	HR
1989	5	15	5.24	49	20	0	149.1	152	98	86	81	21
Career	47	50	4.04	253	101	9	796.2	736	393	321	523	94

Where They Hit the Ball

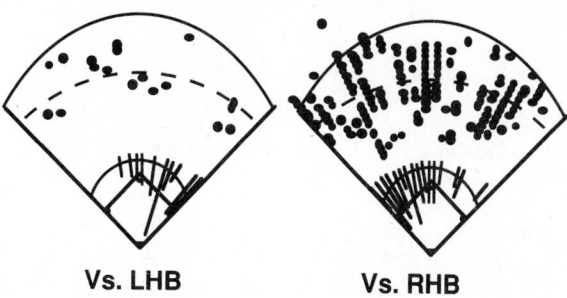

Vs. LHB   Vs. RHB

1989 Situational Stats

	W	L	ERA	Sv	IP		AB	H	HR	RBI	AVG
Home	4	5	4.26	0	76.0	LHB	108	24	6	16	.222
Road	1	10	6.26	0	73.1	RHB	476	128	15	59	.269
Day	1	5	4.85	0	55.2	Sc Pos	140	37	2	52	.264
Night	4	10	5.48	0	93.2	Clutch	61	13	1	4	.213

1989 Rankings (National League)

- ➡ 1st in losses (15) and lowest win/loss percentage (.250) - *pitchers with 15 decisions*
- ➡ 5th in walks allowed (86)
- ➡ 6th in home runs allowed (21)
- ➡ Led the Phillies in losses, walks allowed, home runs allowed, balks (3), runs allowed (98) and earned runs allowed (87)

PITCHING:

Dennis Cook was an All-Southwest Conference out-fielder on the same Texas teams as Bruce Ruffin and Greg Swindell. Now at age 26, after one successful trip around the National League, Cook faces the test which Ruffin failed and Swindell passed: to develop faster than the hitters adapt, and to throw strikes they can't hit.

Cook challenges hitters with variations on three pitches; a high 80's fastball, a split-finger sinker, and a slider. He changes speeds on all three pitches, but can throw his slider nearly as hard as his fastball. Hitters usually can't do anything their first time against him, and with his strength, Cook doesn't tire late. If the hitters don't get to Cook during the fifth or sixth innings, he will usually turn in a gem. The problem is when they do get to him. Cook gave up 18 home runs last year in only 121 innings pitched.

Cook throws his fastball just under half the time, and will hardly ever throw two in a row, preferring to set it up with the hard slider or split-finger pitch. He needs to keep the ball down, and have good rotation on his fastball to keep opposing hitters from driving it. Opposing hitters read Cook's inconsistent leg kick in '89. The higher he kicked, the higher the ball would be thrown in the strike zone. Lonnie Smith apparently used this to hit home runs against Cook in consecutive starts. After late August, Cook appeared to standard-ize his kick, and he pitched better.

FIELDING, HITTING, BASERUNNING:

An aggressive fielder, Cook covers a lot of ground between the mound and home. He has an outstanding move to first, but couples it with a penchant for throwing pickoff darts into the dirt. Cook is a genuine threat at bat, able to pull high strikes sharply, to bunt, and to direct ground balls.

OVERALL:

Though he was mostly a starter last year, the Phillies would like Cook to be their set-up man if they can find five solid starters. His strong first inning and aggres-sive demeanor suit him for relief. On the other hand, his hitting, his sheer ability level, and the Phils' weak rotation may keep him a starter. Developing consis-tent mechanics will put Cook on the road to success, whatever his role. But he'll also have to learn to keep the ball in the park.

DENNIS COOK

Position: SP/RP
Bats: L **Throws:** L
Ht: 6' 3" **Wt:** 185

Opening Day Age: 27
Born: 10/4/62 in Lamarque, TX
ML Seasons: 2

Overall Statistics

	W	L	ERA	G	GS	Sv	IP	H	R	BB	SO	HR
1989	7	8	3.72	23	18	0	121.0	110	59	38	67	18
Career	9	9	3.59	27	22	0	143.0	119	67	49	80	19

Where They Hit the Ball

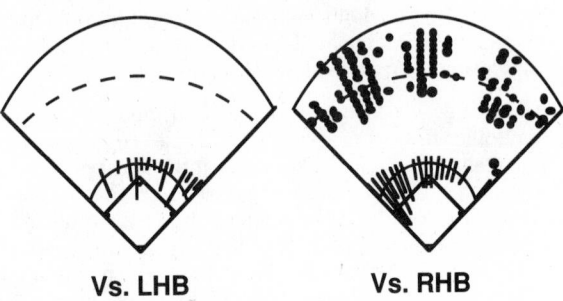

Vs. LHB   **Vs. RHB**

1989 Situational Stats

	W	L	ERA	Sv	IP		AB	H	HR	RBI	AVG
Home	5	3	2.54	0	71.0	LHB	63	13	4	10	.206
Road	2	5	5.40	0	50.0	RHB	389	97	14	42	.249
Day	4	5	3.64	0	64.1	Sc Pos	91	27	4	33	.297
Night	3	3	3.81	0	56.2	Clutch	33	6	1	2	.182

1989 Rankings (National League)

➟ Led the Phillies in shutouts (1)

HITTING:

Until the collision which damaged his left knee in 1986, Darren Daulton was essentially a Darrell Porter clone as a hitter. He made up for low batting averages with excellent walk totals and good power.

That solid platoon contributor is gone. In 234 games since the injury, Daulton's batting average has dropped from the .230's to the .200's. His best asset, his judgement of the strike zone and willingness to wait for his pitch, simply isn't enough. Last season showed how easy it is for pitchers to shut down Darren Daulton. Through April, Daulton looked like the 1986 version again. He waited for pitchers to throw hard and inside and pulled them sharply for hits and homers when they challenged him.

Daulton didn't change after April, but the league did. He kept waiting for knee-high inside fastballs, but opposing pitchers refused to throw them. Instead they kept throwing curves, sliders, and fastballs low and away, capitalizing on his left knee's diminished ability to pivot. When Daulton's fine strike zone judgement told him he had to swing, he mostly lofted curves to centerfield, or topped fastballs to second base.

BASERUNNING:

This is the one area where Daulton's injury should show up most, but doesn't. His frequent walks usually put him on first ahead of the pitcher, and he gamely tries to take out the relay man on double plays. He takes extra bases when he can, and slides vigorously and well. No speed, but plenty of smarts and hustle.

FIELDING:

The Phillies tied the National League record of 91 wild pitches in 1989, and balls in the dirt continually overtaxed Daulton's reactions. He tends to drop his target early in a pitcher's delivery, and hold it pointing down as the pitcher delivers. This contributes to the control problems which plague the Phillies, and delays his wrist flip to catch balls in the dirt. Despite these flaws, Daulton seemed to keep the confidence of his pitchers. His arm is strong, but not pinpoint accurate; Daulton was one of the Phillies who benefited most from the smooth tags of Tom Herr and Dickie Thon, who helped him cut down stealers.

OVERALL:

After an excruciating injury, and a year caddying for Lance Parrish, the Phillies handed Daulton 131 games behind the plate. After that long look, the Phillies decided to acquire another catcher. Barring injuries to the other catchers, and assuming he recovers defensively, Daulton will have to fight for a job as a back-up.

DARREN DAULTON

Position: C
Bats: L **Throws:** R
Ht: 6' 2" **Wt:** 190

Opening Day Age: 28
Born: 1/3/62 in
Arkansas City, KS
ML Seasons: 6

Overall Statistics

	G	AB	R	H	D	T	HR	RBI	SB	BB	SO	AVG
1989	131	368	29	74	12	2	8	44	2	52	58	.201
Career	329	885	85	182	31	3	24	101	9	140	200	.206

Where He Hits the Ball

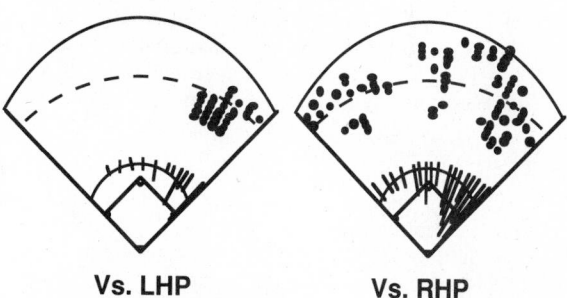

Vs. LHP   **Vs. RHP**

1989 Situational Stats

	AB	H	HR	RBI	AVG		AB	H	HR	RBI	AVG
Home	172	28	2	20	.163	LHP	58	14	1	9	.241
Road	196	46	6	24	.235	RHP	310	60	7	35	.194
Day	109	20	2	9	.183	Sc Pos	91	22	3	35	.242
Night	259	54	6	35	.208	Clutch	69	14	0	6	.203

1989 Rankings (National League)

➡ Led the Phillies in hitting with the bases loaded (.273) - *team players with 10 PA with the bases loaded*

➡ Led NL Catchers in walks (52)

HITTING:

Bob Dernier began the season as the Phillies starting center fielder when Juan Samuel was injured, and he played well for the season's first two weeks, slapping base hits and drawing walks. After his return to the bench, however, he completely lost his stroke, and endured his most futile year as a professional.

After April, Dernier could no longer get around on a good fastball from either a righty or a lefty, and lost the confidence which used to help him lay off balls, draw walks, and slap hits up the middle. He could still slap the ball, but was unable to drive it through the middle infielders and pitcher. Pitches up and over the plate, which he used to blast into gaps, turned into indifferent liners which held up in the air to be caught.

The National League refused to throw Dernier a curveball, crowding him down, or keeping the ball low and away. Even lefthanders, whom he had crushed at a .300 pace for years, mastered Bob Dernier in 1989. Dernier could not even pinch-hit above .100 last year.

BASERUNNING:

Dernier is still an outstanding baserunner. He has a terrific first step and outstanding acceleration. He does not see the ball well when running from first base, but he usually wins the challenges he puts to outfield arms. In fact, without his speed, which gave him several infield singles, Dernier might no longer be in the major leagues. Bob grounded into only one double play in over 200 plate appearances, a testament to his hustle.

FIELDING:

In a season where his bat ran away and hid, Dernier's arm returned with a vengeance. Dernier had always been able to run down balls, but his throws from centerfield were frequently challenged by opposing baserunners. Throughout April, they lost several of those challenges, and stopped taking liberties. Dernier's arm is still below average for right field, but his speed, experience, and knowledge of opposing hitters makes him competent in all three outfield positions.

OVERALL:

Dernier must recapture his command of the strike zone if he wants to stay in the majors. His fielding and baserunning will keep him there as long as he can hit lefties, particularly coming off the bench. Laying off bad pitches and restoring his bat speed are the keys to rejuvenating his offensive contributions and saving his career.

BOB DERNIER

Position: CF/LF/RF
Bats: R **Throws:** R
Ht: 6' 0" **Wt:** 165

Opening Day Age: 33
Born: 1/5/57 in Kansas City, MO
ML Seasons: 10

Overall Statistics

	G	AB	R	H	D	T	HR	RBI	SB	BB	SO	AVG
1989	107	187	26	32	5	0	1	13	4	14	28	.171
Career	904	2483	374	634	92	16	23	152	218	222	301	.255

Where He Hits the Ball

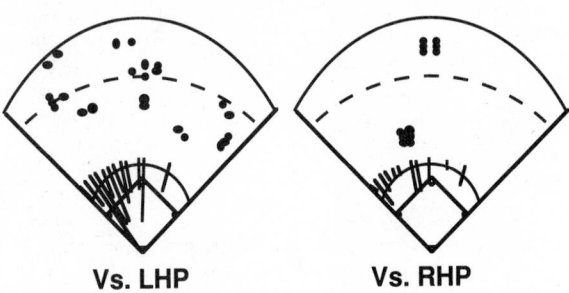

Vs. LHP   **Vs. RHP**

1989 Situational Stats

	AB	H	HR	RBI	AVG		AB	H	HR	RBI	AVG
Home	97	16	1	6	.165	LHP	132	26	1	10	.197
Road	90	16	0	7	.178	RHP	55	6	0	3	.109
Day	57	11	1	4	.193	Sc Pos	40	7	1	12	.175
Night	130	21	0	9	.162	Clutch	47	11	1	5	.234

1989 Rankings (National League)

➡ 5th in worst slugging percentage vs. left-handed pitchers (.250) - *players with 125 PA vs. LHP*

HITTING:

Adrenaline-charged and fiery Lenny Dykstra doesn't see any reason why he can't play every day, against every pitcher. Unfortunately, that argument doesn't make his record against lefties go away.

For a small man with a Pete Rose stance, Dykstra has surprising power, and an inclination to hit line drives and fly balls rather than ground balls. His power zone extends from the middle of the plate in, halfway up his thigh to his waist. Two weeks of clutch RBI doubles for the Phillies in June made him fall in love with his power stroke, rather than working to reach base.

Lefthanders are consistently able to fool Dykstra with breaking pitches. He commits early and swings, but instead of driving these pitches to the right-center gap, he lofts them up to center or right-center. He is able to take outside pitches, but unable to hit outside strikes anywhere useful. Against righthanders Dykstra is able to pick up pitches earlier, which helps him stay with the breaking pitches that victimize him from the left side. The majority of his hits come against fastballs; he can put any righty's heater into play.

BASERUNNING:

Dykstra continually matched his aggressiveness and speed against opponents last year with positive results. He took extra bases more often than any other Phillie, and reached the 30 stolen base level for the third time. He's an asset on the bases; he just needs to reach them more often.

FIELDING:

While Dykstra drew criticism last year for unnecessary diving, his defense continues to be well above average. He runs down many more short liners and fly balls each season than his peers do, and cuts off balls well to both sides. He is more comfortable coming forward than going back for balls, but now that he is used to playing in the Vet, he should improve dramatically on deep flies. His arm is adequate, accurate, and he has a good release.

OVERALL:

Dykstra had a chance to prove himself as a regular, but lefthanded pitching and his pursuit of power hitting undid him. He must restore his stroke against righties, and hit the ball on the ground more to maintain his value as a platoon player. In '89, he failed even in that role.

LENNY DYKSTRA

Position: CF
Bats: L **Throws:** L
Ht: 5'10" **Wt:** 170

Opening Day Age: 27
Born: 2/10/63 in Santa Ana, CA
ML Seasons: 5

Overall Statistics

	G	AB	R	H	D	T	HR	RBI	SB	BB	SO	AVG
1989	146	511	66	121	32	4	7	32	30	60	53	.237
Career	634	2038	326	547	124	20	34	172	133	218	242	.268

Where He Hits the Ball

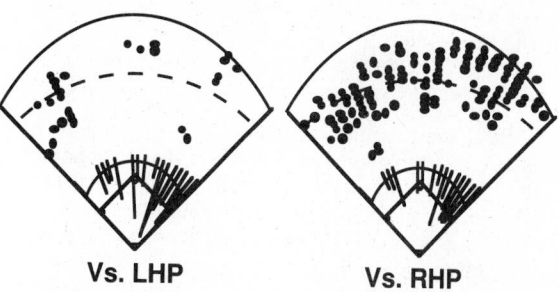

Vs. LHP   **Vs. RHP**

1989 Situational Stats

	AB	H	HR	RBI	AVG		AB	H	HR	RBI	AVG
Home	234	59	5	13	.252	LHP	153	34	0	7	.222
Road	277	62	2	19	.224	RHP	358	87	7	25	.243
Day	156	35	3	13	.224	Sc Pos	80	16	0	21	.200
Night	355	86	4	19	.242	Clutch	87	22	0	5	.253

1989 Rankings (National League)

→ 3rd in worst hitting with the bases loaded (.091) - *players with 10 PA with the bases loaded*

→ 5th in caught stealing (12)

→ 7th in lowest percentage of swings that missed (9.1%) - *players with 502 PA*

→ 10th in doubles (32), steals of third (5) and highest percentage of swings put into play (51.7%)

→ Led the Phillies in caught stealing (11) and steals of third (4)

→ Led NL Center Fielders in doubles

HITTING:

Curt Ford played his best baseball in May and June when he filled a regular platoon role for the Phillies. That was the same role he handled as a playoff and World Series offensive hero for the 1987 Cardinals. Lee Thomas and Nick Leyva acquired Ford to play that kind of baseball for the Phillies, and -- except for the brief early spurt -- they're still waiting.

Ford is a short, slender man whose compact swing can generate surprising power. His wrists and elbows hover almost on the inside edge of the plate, so that he can easily get around to pull any pitch from the outside corner in.

Pitchers were successful in 1989 throwing him breaking balls low and inside, and fastballs high and inside. His stance was so over-adjusted to pull every pitch that these normally pullable pitches ended up in on his hands. In past years, he kept pitchers honest by driving inside pitches for extra bases every 10-12 at bats. But in '89, he wasn't able to turn on inside pitches, so that was all he saw.

Ford doesn't swing at many bad pitches and drew an above average number of walks last year. This helped him in pinch-hitting roles, often adding a valuable baserunner in the late innings. But Ford's habit of pulling everything ironically tended to deprive him of his power.

BASERUNNING:

Ford's excellent speed and hustle make every ground ball a close play, and keep him from hitting into more double play ground balls than a hitter of his style ordinarily would. He is adept at picking up extra bases on opposing outfielders, and slides not only hard, but skillfully. He had a poor year stealing bases in 1989, and by the end of the summer, Leyva stopped sending him.

FIELDING:

Ford is most comfortable in left or right field. He does an adequate job, but does not pick the ball up off the bat well or throw impressively. He uses his speed to outrun most fly balls, and always hits the cut-off man or gets the ball to the right base. He has also played first, second and third sparingly in the majors.

OVERALL:

Ford's only solid offensive months last year came as a platoon starter. While he may get another chance in that role, he must also get some hits as a pinch-hitter, not just walks. Ford has to prove to Thomas and Leyva that he is still as "clutch" as they remember.

CURT FORD

Position: LF/RF
Bats: L **Throws:** R
Ht: 5'10" **Wt:** 150

Opening Day Age: 29
Born: 10/11/60 in Jackson, MS
ML Seasons: 5

Overall Statistics

	G	AB	R	H	D	T	HR	RBI	SB	BB	SO	AVG
1989	108	142	13	31	5	1	1	13	5	16	33	.218
Career	384	724	88	180	37	8	7	89	36	65	121	.249

Where He Hits the Ball

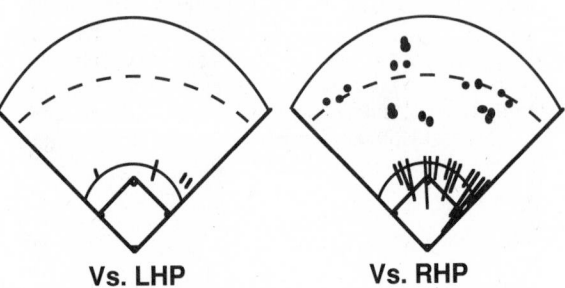

Vs. LHP   **Vs. RHP**

1989 Situational Stats

	AB	H	HR	RBI	AVG		AB	H	HR	RBI	AVG
Home	58	15	0	10	.259	LHP	15	4	0	3	.267
Road	84	16	1	3	.190	RHP	127	27	1	10	.213
Day	48	12	0	5	.250	Sc Pos	31	8	0	12	.258
Night	94	19	1	8	.202	Clutch	42	9	0	2	.214

1989 Rankings (National League)

➤ Did not rank near the top or bottom in any category

PITCHING:

Todd Frohwirth is a side-arming sinker-ball pitcher who earned a season long spot in the Phillies bullpen by reducing righthanded batters to a .159 batting average. However, Frohwirth's control problems and his inability to retire lefties severely limited his role in 1989.

Frohwirth fell in love with strikeouts early last season, and it led him to overpitch, rather than obey the Tekulve-Quisenberry cardinal rule of sinkerballers: "I just make them hit it on the ground; the other guys get them out." In the 32 innings where he had one or more strikeouts, Frohwirth's ERA for was 6.18; in the 25 innings where he struck out no one, his ERA was under 1.00. Fifteen of Frohwirth's 18 walks came in outings where he recorded a strikeout.

Frohwirth lost confidence when lefthanders lit him up. He tried to hit the corners and to throw the ball past hitters. Like the knuckle ball, a side-arm sinker is a touch pitch, and Frohwirth's tends to flatten out, or even rise slightly when he overthrows, exacerbating his problems. The key to throwing his sinker-ball is getting it over the "hump," making it break a few yards before the plate, so that the hitter swings over the ball. This requires consistency of grip, velocity and delivery, the three things that vary most when a pitcher has confidence problems.

One sign that Frohwirth's problem is mainly confidence is that before 1989, he had only faced Eastern Division clubs. He continued to pitch well against the East last year. Western Division teams were the main source of his troubles, and he improved markedly the second time he faced them.

FIELDING, HITTING, BASERUNNING:

Frohwirth's delivery and motion make him vulnerable to the stolen base. He has a good move to first, but his pitches dip down so that the catcher usually can't get the ball quickly into throwing position and fire to second base. A sinker-ball pitcher has to wield a nimble glove to survive, and Frohwirth does. He rarely bats and never hits the ball squarely.

OVERALL:

Frohwirth's confidence problem should be solved as he starts his third trip around the League. But to become more than a one inning pitcher, he must challenge lefties as he does righties: throw strikes with a consistent motion, down in the strike zone, and make the batter hit it past the infield to get on base.

TODD FROHWIRTH

Position: RP
Bats: R **Throws:** R
Ht: 6' 4" **Wt:** 195

Opening Day Age: 27
Born: 9/28/62 in Milwaukee, WI
ML Seasons: 3

Overall Statistics

	W	L	ERA	G	GS	Sv	IP	H	R	BB	SO	HR
1989	1	0	3.59	45	0	0	62.2	56	26	18	39	4
Career	3	2	3.78	67	0	0	85.2	84	37	31	59	6

Where They Hit the Ball

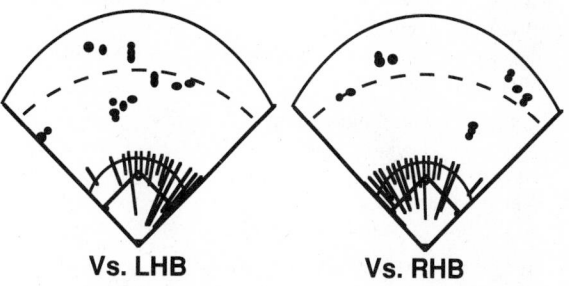

Vs. LHB   Vs. RHB

1989 Situational Stats

	W	L	ERA	Sv	IP		AB	H	HR	RBI	AVG
Home	0	0	3.96	0	36.1	LHB	100	35	3	21	.350
Road	1	0	3.08	0	26.1	RHB	132	21	1	11	.159
Day	0	0	6.11	0	17.2	Sc Pos	66	20	2	29	.303
Night	1	0	2.60	0	45.0	Clutch	45	11	0	2	.244

1989 Rankings (National League)

→ Led the Phillies in holds (6) and lowest percentage of inherited runners scoring (35.3%)
- team players with 30 inherited runners

HITTING:

He arrived a year later, but Charlie Hayes showed most of the same virtues and flaws as 1988 phenom Ricky Jordan. He hit for unexpected power, and goes into '90 as the Phils' regular third baseman.

Hayes's eight home runs in a half season were his second-highest total in six pro seasons. In RBI situations, Hayes made consistent contact even against good fastballs, and showed excellent power. He particularly excelled at hitting with runners on first base, and in driving runners home from third with less than two out. However, his good contact vanished without runners on, and his desire to go after every fastball in the strike zone prevented him from reaching base on walks.

Hayes takes a very small step on inside pitches above the belt, and a big stride on outside pitches. This means he has to make an early decision about each pitch. As a result, Hayes is often the victim of breaking balls and cut fastballs, and the veterans who throw them.

The righthanded hitting Hayes had a respectable batting average against lefties last year (.267), but he hit only one homer against southpaws in 105 at bats. Since he plays a power position, Hayes will have to improve in this area if he wants to keep his job.

BASERUNNING:

Hayes gets out of the box swiftly and shows good speed between bases on extra-base hits. He is not an aggressive baserunner, and does not attempt to steal often.

FIELDING:

Hayes has terrific range toward the third base bag, an extremely strong arm, and good range on foul flies. But spending the season's early months in the outfield dulled his reactions at the hot corner, so that he topped 20 errors in a half season. These errors fell mostly into two categories: one hop throws dropped by Jordan, and balls Hayes couldn't get out of his glove. After Hayes came up with the ball, his motion kept coming unglued between his glove and his release point. Winter ball should correct this mechanical flaw, but only Jordan or manager Nick Leyva can correct the other problem.

OVERALL:

Like Ricky Jordan, Hayes must stop swinging at junk, reach base more often, drive the ball consistently, and correct mechanical flaws in his defense. That's a tall order, and Hayes may end up losing his fulltime job.

CHARLIE HAYES

Position: 3B
Bats: R **Throws:** R
Ht: 6' 0" **Wt:** 190

Opening Day Age: 24
Born: 5/29/65 in Hattiesburg, MS
ML Seasons: 2

Overall Statistics

	G	AB	R	H	D	T	HR	RBI	SB	BB	SO	AVG
1989	87	304	26	78	15	1	8	43	3	11	50	.257
Career	94	315	26	79	15	1	8	43	3	11	53	.251

Where He Hits the Ball

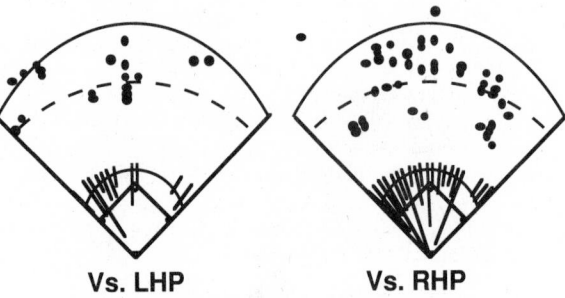

Vs. LHP   Vs. RHP

1989 Situational Stats

	AB	H	HR	RBI	AVG		AB	H	HR	RBI	AVG
Home	156	36	3	24	.231	LHP	105	28	1	14	.267
Road	148	42	5	19	.284	RHP	199	50	7	29	.251
Day	84	26	4	16	.310	Sc Pos	83	21	2	36	.253
Night	220	52	4	27	.236	Clutch	52	10	2	7	.192

1989 Rankings (National League)

➡ 6th in errors (22)
➡ Led the Phillies in errors (22)

HITTING:

Von Hayes rebounded from a disappointing, injury-curtailed season with a solid 1989 season. He set a career high in home runs with 26, scored 93 runs, drew 101 walks, and rejuvenated his bat against left-handers.

After hitting .129 against lefties in 1988, Hayes entered last season with an entirely new stance. Gone was the widest front-to-back stance in the major leagues, replaced by a closed stance with Hayes' feet no farther apart than his shoulder-blades. Hayes shortened his stroke, improving his ability to adjust to breaking balls headed for the dirt, the main factor in his futile efforts against lefties in 1988. Able to wait longer and strike more quickly, Hayes not only was able to hit lefties for average and draw walks, he recovered his line drive power against them.

Even more noticeable was the effect of Hayes' new stance on righthanded pitching. Rather than driving weak pitches into the gaps as he had in '88, Hayes drove mistakes into the seats last season, winning several games on the last pitch. Unfortunately, no batting stance can make opponents throw strikes. After April, as the Phillies' only remaining dangerous hitter, Hayes saw few strikes and fewer fastballs, while his manager continued to pressure him to be more aggressive. More swings at fewer strikes dropped his batting average to its lowest since coming over from Cleveland, seven years ago.

BASERUNNING:

Hayes demonstrated last season that his reputation for running into outs on the basepaths was undeserved. He advanced on opponents all year without ever being thrown out. He gets a good lead, and stole 28 bases with an 80% success rate.

FIELDING:

Hayes is the best defensive first baseman on the Phillies, fielding and scooping balls adeptly, and making all the throws. Two brief experiments returning him to third base have shown that he lacks the quick range needed for the hot corner. But Hayes will play regularly in either right or centerfield in 1990. His best defensive attributes are his speed, his ability to charge balls aggressively, cut off hits in the alleys, and relay the ball to the infield swiftly. He rarely throws anyone out at home or third.

OVERALL:

Nick Leyva would like to bat Hayes leadoff next season, adapting Hayes' offensive role to his skills. If he leads off all season, look for Hayes to bust out with a .300 average, 120 runs, and deserved recognition as a preeminent player.

VON HAYES

Position: RF/1B/CF
Bats: L **Throws:** R
Ht: 6' 5" **Wt:** 180

Opening Day Age: 31
Born: 8/31/58 in Stockton , CA
ML Seasons: 9

Overall Statistics

	G	AB	R	H	D	T	HR	RBI	SB	BB	SO	AVG
1989	154	540	93	140	27	2	26	78	28	101	103	.259
Career	1195	4191	619	1147	236	31	122	573	217	557	627	.274

Where He Hits the Ball

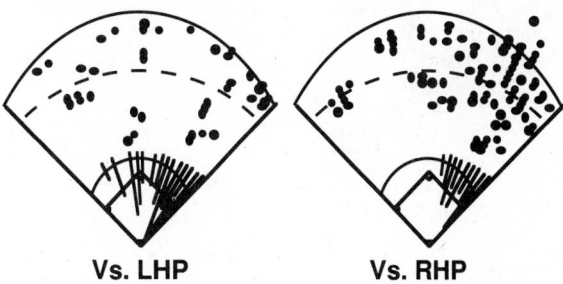

Vs. LHP   **Vs. RHP**

1989 Situational Stats

	AB	H	HR	RBI	AVG		AB	H	HR	RBI	AVG
Home	257	64	15	40	.249	LHP	208	51	8	29	.245
Road	283	76	11	38	.269	RHP	332	89	18	49	.268
Day	147	43	7	25	.293	Sc Pos	132	34	8	55	.258
Night	393	97	19	53	.247	Clutch	89	20	4	9	.225

1989 Rankings (National League)

➡ 1st in pitches seen (2,533)

➡ 2nd in walks (101) and pitchers seen per plate appearance (3.9) - *players with 502 PA*

➡ 5th in highest percentage of pitches taken (62.9%)

➡ Led the Phillies in home runs, runs (93), doubles (27), RBIs (78), stolen bases (28), walks, pitches seen, pitches seen per plate appearance, on-base average (.376), slugging percentage (.461), stolen base percentage (.800), strikeouts (103), total bases (249), home run frequency (20.8 ABs per HR), intentional walks (14), times on base (245), plate appearances (652) and games (154) - *team players with 502 PA*

HITTING:

Tom Herr is a patient slap hitter, one who uses outstanding judgement and bat control to slap the ball where they ain't. He'll let pitchers put him on base if they won't throw strikes. Herr has mastered the old Pete Rose tactic of reading each pitch three ways when he has two strikes. First he reads strike or ball. If it's a strike, he decides whether he can make solid contact. If he can't, his bat whips out like a lizard's tongue to flick the ball foul, earning him another pitch.

Herr owes his continued success to artificial turf. On natural sod, his sharp singles turn into groundouts, and his doubles into singles, because dirt doesn't add torque and momentum to a batted ball.

Pitchers have their greatest success against him when they jam him low and inside, particularly with breaking balls. Herr tends to top pitches slightly, and topping and pulling a ball usually means a grounder to the right side. When those curves stay up however, it's extra-base time.

While Nick Leyva was disappointed with Herr's RBI totals, no one can drive in 60-100 runs unless the table is set. Herr hit about the same with men on base as he did in the mid-1980s; there were just a lot fewer runners to drive home in '89.

BASERUNNING:

Herr's baserunning was the only aspect of his play which legitimately disappointed the Phillies. Due to a long-time back condition, Herr stole just 10 bases, and was caught over 40 percent of the time. He still runs intelligently, but with only average speed to fuel his aggressiveness.

FIELDING:

Herr takes away almost one hit per week from opposing teams purely by positioning himself according to hitter and pitch. While he has lost a step toward second base on hits up the middle, his range towards first has allowed the Phillies to keep Ricky Jordan there, even though Jordan has limited range to his right. Herr is a half second faster in gloving the ball and then releasing it than most major league second baseman. This led to a major increase in double plays for the Phillies in '89.

OVERALL:

Now 34, Herr had his best season last year since 1985. He was clearly back at home in the National League, playing for a disciple of Whitey Herzog. Herr plays baseball with canny professionalism and smooth competence. His best days are behind him, but he appears to have some good ones left.

TOMMY HERR

Position: 2B
Bats: B **Throws:** R
Ht: 6' 0" **Wt:** 185

Opening Day Age: 34
Born: 4/4/56 in Lancaster, PA
ML Seasons: 11

Overall Statistics

	G	AB	R	H	D	T	HR	RBI	SB	BB	SO	AVG
1989	151	561	65	161	25	6	2	37	10	54	63	.287
Career	1266	4587	605	1262	220	37	22	493	172	532	498	.275

Where He Hits the Ball

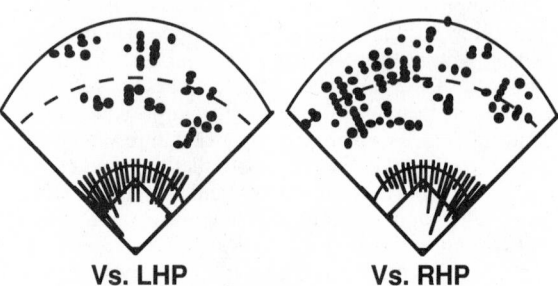

Vs. LHP   **Vs. RHP**

1989 Situational Stats

	AB	H	HR	RBI	AVG		AB	H	HR	RBI	AVG
Home	270	77	0	16	.285	LHP	229	66	1	14	.288
Road	291	84	2	21	.289	RHP	332	95	1	23	.286
Day	149	45	0	10	.302	Sc Pos	112	29	0	33	.259
Night	412	116	2	27	.282	Clutch	100	26	1	12	.260

1989 Rankings (National League)

➡ 2nd in hitting on a 3-2 count (.419) - *players with 20 PA on a 3-2 count*

➡ 5th in singles (128) and worst home run frequency (280.5 ABs per HR)

➡ 6th in hitting on an 0-2 count (.286) - *players with 20 PA on a 0-2 count*

➡ 7th in grounder/flyball ratio (1.74) - *players with 502 PA*

➡ Led the Phillies in batting average (.287), at bats (561), singles (128), hits (161), triples (6), grounder/flyball ratio, lowest percentage of swings that missed (11.8%), highest percentage of swings put into play (49.4%) and hitting on a 3-2 count - *team players with 502 PA*

PITCHING:

After 190 games in the Dodger's bullpen, Ken Howell proved that he was a bona fide major league starter last season. Leading the Phillies in starts, innings and wins, Howell was the only year-long member of the Phillies starting rotation, and is the fixed point on which the Phillies will build their 1990 staff.

Howell's strength is that he throws hard, and his pitches veer and slide on the hitter, overpowering them with speed and placement. His fastball runs in on righties and away from lefties, zooming in at 90+ mph, while his slider, clocked in the high 80's, moves the opposite direction. His change of pace, a forkball, breaks downward sharply, either drawing a futile swing or being registered as a ball. Howell's Three Rules of Pitching are simple and effective: throw the ball hard, let the ball move, keep the ball down.

This combination of movement and power can make Howell as difficult to catch as he is to hit. Last season he threw 21 wild pitches and made several contributions to the passed ball totals of Darren Daulton. Nearly every problem inning for Howell can be traced to one of two sources: walks or wild pitches. When Howell lost his control, he lost it early -- in six starts he didn't retire anyone after the 4th, and in those games he walked 22 men in 17 innings.

After a few trips around the league, Howell made real progress with his control, gaining the confidence to throw fewer pitches and more strikes. Don't be fooled by his win/loss: Howell was a decent pitcher up til the All-Star break, and a terrific one after it. With the status of a number one starter, and the certainty of a start every fifth day, Howell's development should continue.

FIELDING, HITTING, BASERUNNING:

Howell's relief experience left him with a good move to first base and quick delivery of fast pitches, which helps his catchers control baserunners. His fielding's okay, although he tends to wind-up on throws to first. He sometimes gets his bat on the ball, but can't drive it, or control his bunts. He is a station-to-station baserunner.

OVERALL:

Though he came to the Phillies as a project, recovering from shoulder surgery, Howell did not miss a turn all year, amply justifying the investment of Phil Bradley to acquire him. By continuing to challenge hitters and adapt, Ken Howell has developed to the point where good offensive support would make him a big winner.

KEN HOWELL

Position: SP
Bats: R **Throws:** R
Ht: 6' 3" **Wt:** 228

Opening Day Age: 29
Born: 11/28/60 in Detroit, MI
ML Seasons: 6

Overall Statistics

	W	L	ERA	G	GS	Sv	IP	H	R	BB	SO	HR
1989	12	12	3.44	33	32	0	204.0	155	84	86	164	11
Career	30	41	3.80	227	36	31	506.2	428	236	226	479	34

Where They Hit the Ball

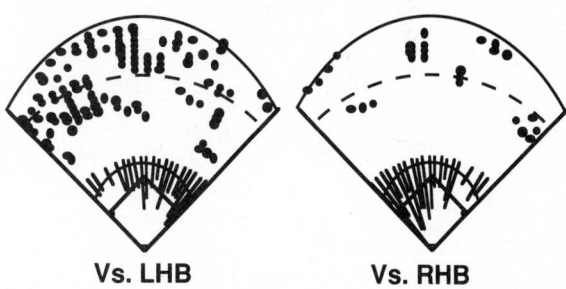

Vs. LHB   **Vs. RHB**

1989 Situational Stats

	W	L	ERA	Sv	IP		AB	H	HR	RBI	AVG
Home	4	5	3.19	0	101.2	LHB	413	97	6	32	.235
Road	8	7	3.69	0	102.1	RHB	309	58	5	36	.188
Day	0	3	7.57	0	27.1	Sc Pos	147	36	3	54	.245
Night	12	9	2.80	0	176.2	Clutch	55	14	0	4	.255

1989 Rankings (National League)

➡ 1st in wild pitches (21)

➡ 2nd in caught stealing (15)

➡ 3rd in lowest slugging percentage allowed (.313) - *pitchers with 162 IP*

➡ Led the Phillies in ERA (3.44), wins (12), games started (32), shutouts (1), walks allowed (86), strikeouts (164), pitches thrown (3,086), stolen bases allowed (26), caught stealing, lowest slugging percentage allowed, lowest on-base average allowed (.297), lowest stolen base percentage allowed (63.4%), lowest batting average allowed (.215), strikeout/walk ratio (1.9) and least HRs per 9 innings (.49) - *team pitchers with 502 PA*

HITTING:

Richie Ashburn and Mike Schmidt have said for years that Steve Jeltz has the athletic ability and strike zone judgement to be a more productive hitter than he has been. Either their hints or their confidence spurred Jeltz's first decent offensive season. Steve even hit home runs from each side of the plate against the Pirates, who have been the victims of three of his five lifetime home runs.

Ashburn advised Steve to concentrate on using a version of Schmidt's stroke, slightly topping the ball to produce low line drives and ground balls. Jeltz responded by torching lefthanded pitching. A right-handed batter until 1986, Jeltz switch-hit .197 against lefties and .200 against righties from 1986 to 1988, until Ashburn's advice rejuvenated at least his righty bat.

Batting righthanded, Jeltz learned to rifle fastballs past the shortstop and third baseman. Against break-ing pitches, he tries to spray soft liners for extra bases down the lines, or for base hits just onto the outfield grass. Batting lefthanded, Jeltz is a pure pull hitter who is overmatched by a good fastball, usually top-ping them to either side of the second baseman. About fifteen times a year he will get a high hanging curve-ball, and either pull it over the wall, past the first baseman, or dump it into left field.

From each side, Jeltz may be the most patient hitter in the National League. He is extremely deft at working walks, and turned out to be a fine righthanded pinch hitter for the Phils in '89. He is a precise and accurate bunter.

BASERUNNING:

Jeltz runs well with a smooth first step and good speed, but he is not a chance-taker or particularly good at breaking up double plays. He rarely attempts to steal.

FIELDING:

Jeltz is an outstanding fielder. He has exceptional range to his right and left, and saves the Phillies 10-15 bases per year with diving stops which keep ground-ers in the infield and limit the advance of baserunners. His arm is strong and accurate. Jeltz's positioning has sometimes been questioned, but he can usually out-glove his mistakes. He is an adept fill-in at second, third, and the outfield.

OVERALL:

Steve Jeltz played well last year, giving the Phils an outstanding defensive back-up at each infield posi-tion, and contributing with Greg Gross-style offense. If he can retain his new-found righty bat, he could play five more seasons at least.

STEVE JELTZ

Position: SS/2B/3B
Bats: B **Throws:** R
Ht: 5'11" **Wt:** 180

Opening Day Age: 30
Born: 5/28/59 in Paris, FR
ML Seasons: 7

Overall Statistics

	G	AB	R	H	D	T	HR	RBI	SB	BB	SO	AVG
1989	116	263	28	64	7	3	4	25	4	45	44	.243
Career	653	1646	172	351	42	20	5	120	17	242	321	.213

Where He Hits the Ball

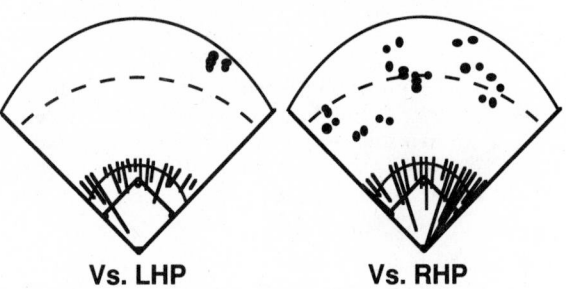

Vs. LHP   **Vs. RHP**

1989 Situational Stats

	AB	H	HR	RBI	AVG		AB	H	HR	RBI	AVG
Home	130	36	3	17	.277	LHP	71	19	1	9	.268
Road	133	28	1	8	.211	RHP	192	45	3	16	.234
Day	83	22	2	10	.265	Sc Pos	65	17	1	20	.262
Night	180	42	2	15	.233	Clutch	62	12	1	3	.194

1989 Rankings (National League)

➡ Led NL Shortstops in hitting on a 3-2 count (.265) - *shortstops with 20 PA on a 3-2 count*

HITTING:

Ricky Jordan is a line-drive spray hitter – Mickey Rivers trapped in the body of a first baseman. If they ever create a category for percentage of pitches swung at, Ricky's place in the record books is ensured.

Jordan's eagerness shows on every pitch. Keeping his weight back early in the pitcher's wind-up, he throws it forward earlier than any other Phillie. Once it's clear that the ball will be within a few inches of the strike zone, Jordan commits. His swing can produce a long ball on occasion, but when he isn't exactly right, Jordan is a slice and slap hitter. His quick wrists usually can make contact with two strikes or in the clutch, but cannot drive the ball consistently as most clubs want a first baseman to do. It also means that he rarely walks, since his habits enlarge an already generous strike zone.

Jordan's eagerness works better against lefthanders, whom he gets an earlier look at. Unlike in '88, Ricky was unable to hit righthanded pitching for power or average last year. Righthanders who changed speeds and employed deceptive motions rang up many strikeouts against Jordon by keeping him off-balance.

BASERUNNING:

Jordan possesses average major league speed, which means that he is faster than opposing outfielders expect a first baseman to be. His aggressiveness results in about two bases a month he shouldn't get. A base-stealer in the minors, Jordan's poor first step has kept him from pilfering in the majors.

FIELDING:

Unable to make basic plays consistently, Jordan thrives on the difficult ones. He muffs one-hop throws from short or third, but he fields ground balls in front of him or towards the line smoothly. Jordan excels at catching wild throws that are high and is good at making a sweep tag when pulled off the base. He is fine on pop-ups. He has difficulty making throws, however, and can't make the throw to second for a force or 3-6-3 double play to save his life.

OVERALL:

Unlike last season, when he was fighting a wrist injury for the first third of the season, Jordan should be healthy in 1990. But Ricky must either hit righties harder or draw more walks, and must improve on basic plays at first base. Without real progress in these areas, he faces a platoon role.

RICKY JORDAN

Position: 1B
Bats: R **Throws:** R
Ht: 6' 3" **Wt:** 210

Opening Day Age: 24
Born: 5/26/65 in Richmond, CA
ML Seasons: 2

Overall Statistics

	G	AB	R	H	D	T	HR	RBI	SB	BB	SO	AVG
1989	144	523	63	149	22	3	12	75	4	23	62	.285
Career	213	796	104	233	37	4	23	118	5	30	101	.293

Where He Hits the Ball

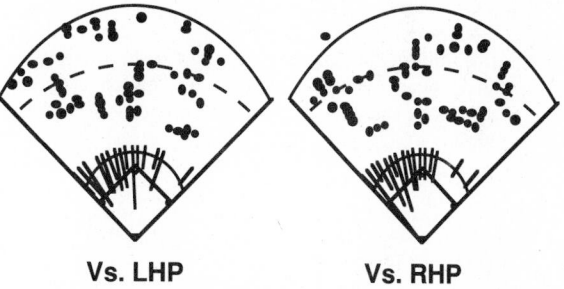

Vs. LHP   **Vs. RHP**

1989 Situational Stats

	AB	H	HR	RBI	AVG		AB	H	HR	RBI	AVG
Home	266	73	7	37	.274	LHP	201	67	4	29	.333
Road	257	76	5	38	.296	RHP	322	82	8	46	.255
Day	154	42	3	30	.273	Sc Pos	137	37	1	53	.270
Night	369	107	9	45	.290	Clutch	87	27	2	19	.310

1989 Rankings (National League)

- ➡ 3rd in sacrifice flies (8) and GDPs (19)
- ➡ 4th in hitting on an 0-2 count (.315) and least pitches seen per plate appearance (3.1) - *players with 502 PA*
- ➡ 5th in batting average vs. lefthanded pitchers (.333) - *players with 125 PA vs. LHP*
- ➡ 6th in lowest percentage of pitches taken (45.7%)
- ➡ Led the Phillies in sacrifice flies, hit by pitch (5), GDPs, hitting vs. lefthanded pitchers, hitting on an 0-2 count and hitting in the clutch (.310) - *team players with 50 PA in the clutch*
- ➡ Led NL First Basemen in GDPs and hitting on an 0-2 count

HITTING:

"Krucker," as Phillie announcer Harry Kalas calls him, was an outstanding addition to the Phillies last year. John Kruk loves to play as much as fans love to watch him. And what is even more useful to Lee Thomas and Nick Leyva, he can hit.

Kruk is a classic opposite-field hitter who holds his body back so that he can extend his arms on every pitch. What makes Kruk unique is that most opposite-field hitters are content to drive the ball over the infield on arms and wrists alone. Kruk's short arms, swinging a brief stroke, can drive the ball into the left field seats. Keeping back until the last second also ensures that Kruk only swings at strikes, and reaches base often. He strokes inside pitches into right and right center for gap doubles, and waits for letter-high fastballs away to drive into the seats.

Most clubs try to crowd Kruk with low breaking balls. Lefthanders keep the ball down and in on him, trading a fair number of walks in exchange for short-circuiting his power. Opposing righties still haven't found anything but the law of averages to help them get Kruk out.

BASERUNNING:

Kruk's baserunning style led him to be nicknamed "The Human Weebil" -- John Kruk wobbles but won't fall down. Kruk has more moving parts and pistons than any average-speed runner in the majors. He is not particularly adventurous, but reads hits extremely well and slides hard on close plays. Kruk stole 18 bases for the '87 Padres, but has only eight in two seasons since then.

FIELDING:

Kruk is versatile and able to contribute defensively. He wields an above average glove in left field and at first base, and is passable in right. At first base, he picks low throws and ground balls cleanly and expertly, and can make all the throws. His lack of size means that high throws are a problem. In the outfield, Kruk's greatest strength is his anticipation and field sense. He takes away extra bases by aggressively cutting balls hit in front of him, but has trouble going back on balls over his head.

OVERALL:

John Kruk was acquired for his hitting, and to show the next generation of Phillies how to fully engage their talents. If Ricky Jordan doesn't show progress, or Ron Jones fails to recover from injuries, Kruk could move out of his platoon role and into the every-day line-up.

JOHN KRUK

OVERLOOKED

Position: LF/RF
Bats: L **Throws:** L
Ht: 5'10" **Wt:** 195

Opening Day Age: 29
Born: 2/9/61 in Charleston, WV
ML Seasons: 4

Overall Statistics

	G	AB	R	H	D	T	HR	RBI	SB	BB	SO	AVG
1989	112	357	53	107	13	6	8	44	3	44	53	.300
Career	492	1460	212	424	60	11	41	217	28	242	272	.290

Where He Hits the Ball

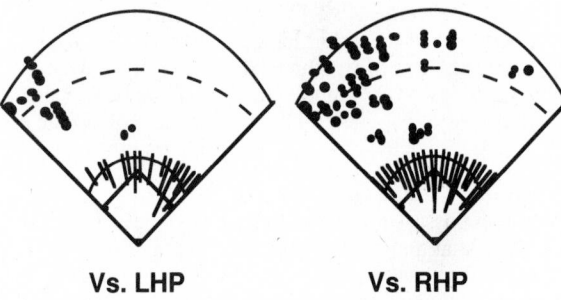

Vs. LHP   **Vs. RHP**

1989 Situational Stats

	AB	H	HR	RBI	AVG		AB	H	HR	RBI	AVG
Home	192	60	6	30	.313	LHP	101	27	0	7	.267
Road	165	47	2	14	.285	RHP	256	80	8	37	.313
Day	101	29	2	16	.287	Sc Pos	99	22	1	30	.222
Night	256	78	6	28	.305	Clutch	44	14	3	11	.318

1989 Rankings (National League)

➡ Led the Phillies in triples (6), batting average with 2 strikes (.259) and hitting on a 3-1 count (.462) - *team players with 10 PA on a 3-1 count*

HITTING:

Steve Lake knows that if he can spray enough singles over the infield to hit around .250, he'll get to play. He achieved that goal as a hitter in 1989, but that's about all.

Lake has problems with good fastballs. Hard fastballs simply whiz by him. He can hit sinkers, splitters, and under 90-mph fastballs that have good movement. But usually he hits them on the ground, where his lack of speed turns them into outs. He has excellent bat control and is a good hit-and-run man and pinch-hitter. Lake's problem is that most National League pitchers have a good fastball, and Lake can't hit one. His power, however, comes once or twice every year against someone who tries to throw him six or seven really nasty fastballs in a row. One of them turns ordinary on the way to the plate, and ends up as a souvenir for the fans.

Steve has much better luck against breaking pitches. He is a disciplined punch-and-judy hitter who stays back even on good curveballs, lofting them into the outfield for singles.

BASERUNNING:

Lake is a student of the game who knows the capabilities of every outfield throwing arm in the National League; he knows they can all throw him out.

FIELDING:

Steve Lake has caught four no-hitters in professional baseball, including a perfect game, which demonstrates his abilities to set up hitters with canny pitch calling. He is a student of his staff and his opponents, and will often adjust pitch strategies in a game if he notices that the batter has changed his stance or swing. He keeps his glove up until the pitcher commits, giving a Phillies staff prone to wildness a clear target. On a team which tied a National League record for wild pitches, he was not charged with a passed ball all season. He threw out nearly half the runners who attempted to steal on him last year, and has thrown out over 45 percent for his career. Quite simply, Steve Lake was one of the best defensive catchers in the National League last year.

OVERALL:

Steve Lake's offense may suffer if the Phillies' new starting catcher is righthanded, forcing him to make some starts against righties. But his roster spot is assured if his knee makes a complete recovery. In the next two seasons the Phillies will bring up a half-dozen young pitchers, and Lake's job will be to teach them how to get major league hitters out.

STOPPER

STEVE LAKE

Position: C
Bats: R **Throws:** R
Ht: 6' 1" **Wt:** 190
Opening Day Age: 33
Born: 3/14/57 in Inglewood, CA
ML Seasons: 7

Overall Statistics

	G	AB	R	H	D	T	HR	RBI	SB	BB	SO	AVG
1989	58	155	9	39	5	1	2	14	0	12	20	.252
Career	325	714	59	171	27	4	11	76	1	33	94	.239

Where He Hits the Ball

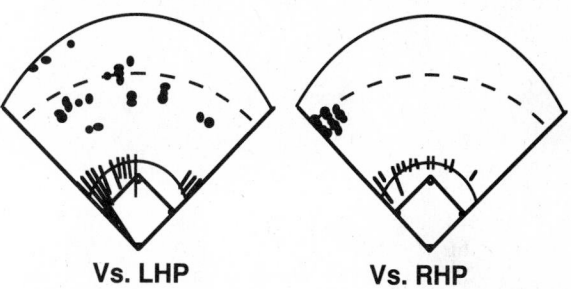

Vs. LHP   Vs. RHP

1989 Situational Stats

	AB	H	HR	RBI	AVG		AB	H	HR	RBI	AVG
Home	78	21	1	7	.269	LHP	121	29	1	10	.240
Road	77	18	1	7	.234	RHP	34	10	1	4	.294
Day	44	11	1	3	.250	Sc Pos	37	8	0	11	.216
Night	111	28	1	11	.252	Clutch	25	8	0	1	.320

1989 Rankings (National League)

➡ Did not rank near the top or bottom in any category

PITCHING:

The Phillies have a stable of guys who let the other team hit the ball. Roger McDowell is the only one who lets them hit the ball where the Phillies can generally catch it. A sinker-baller with a resilient arm, McDowell not only replaced Steve Bedrosian, but last year he surpassed Bedrosian's post-Cy Young Award efforts.

McDowell's hard sinker is very difficult for batters to meet or lift. This produces many ground balls, but it also perpetuates a major misconception about him. From 1985-1988, McDowell's ERA was over 4.00 on turf and under 2.50 on grass. But when he was traded to the Phillies, his ERAs on turf and grass both stayed around 2.00. It wasn't McDowell who had the problem on turf. It was simply that his Met infielders were below average at turning grounders into outs and double plays. Their deficiencies were particularly exposed on turf's faster surface, but McDowell got the blame. The Phillies infield was above average, so Phillies GM Lee Thomas rightly saw that McDowell's "turf weakness" was unlikely to recur in Philadelphia.

McDowell has fine control, throwing 56.2 innings of sinkerballs for the Phils last year with no wild pitches. One unfortunate consequence of that control is that during the few games a year the sinker doesn't sink, it flies hard and far into Bleacherland. But in the other games, McDowell can't be hit for distance. When he's on the beam, it takes three groundball singles to produce a run. That's why Roger McDowell is a successful pitcher.

FIELDING, HITTING, BASERUNNING:

McDowell is a fine athlete with quick reactions off the mound, and he devours bunts and come-back grounders up the middle. He has a quick delivery homeward, but his sinkerball and only average move allowed seven of nine base stealers to succeed against him. While he did not get a hit last year, he was three for nine in '88, and loves to hit. He can run the bases well when he gets the chance.

OVERALL:

McDowell was acquired as much to change the spirit of the Phillies as to throw the sinkerball. Giving hot-feet to coaches, pratfalling in the dugout, and making baseball fun again were Roger's way of renewing the Phillies. With a strong defense behind him, he is a tremendous asset in the bullpen.

ROGER MCDOWELL

Position: RP
Bats: R **Throws:** R
Ht: 6' 1" **Wt:** 185

Opening Day Age: 29
Born: 12/21/60 in Cincinnati, OH
ML Seasons: 5

Overall Statistics

	W	L	ERA	G	GS	Sv	IP	H	R	BB	SO	HR
1989	4	8	1.96	69	0	23	92.0	79	36	38	47	3
Career	36	32	2.91	324	2	103	525.0	469	199	176	260	24

Where They Hit the Ball

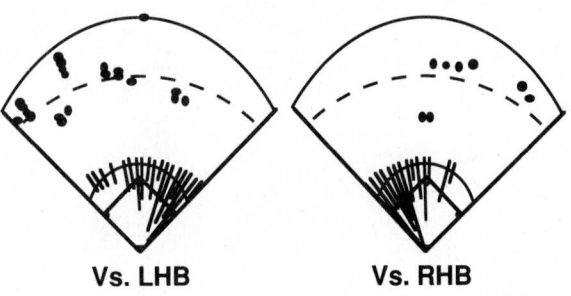

Vs. LHB   **Vs. RHB**

1989 Situational Stats

	W	L	ERA	Sv	IP		AB	H	HR	RBI	AVG
Home	4	5	1.38	10	39.0	LHB	185	49	3	24	.265
Road	0	3	2.38	13	53.0	RHB	154	30	0	18	.195
Day	1	3	2.54	5	28.1	Sc Pos	116	23	2	40	.198
Night	3	5	1.70	18	63.2	Clutch	190	44	2	20	.232

1989 Rankings (National League)

- ➟ 2nd in grounder/flyball ratio (3.89) - *all league players*
- ➟ 4th in games finished (56)
- ➟ 8th in games (69), blown saves (5) and save percentage (82.1%) - *pitchers with 20 save opportunities*
- ➟ 9th in saves (23)
- ➟ Led the Phillies in games finished (41), ERA (1.11), saves (19) and GDPs induced per GDP situation (16.3%) - *team pitchers with 30 GDP situations*

PITCHING:

Terry Mulholland is a slender lefthanded sinker-baller with an economical motion. He will remind you of a young Tommy John. Except for the results, which remind you of the very old Tommy John. Mulholland throws four pitches, all down in the strike zone. He relies on a compact, uniform delivery to deceive hitters. He throws a fastball about once every five pitches, his slider about as often, and a change-up two or three times each inning. Their main job is to set up his money pitch, the split-fingered fastball.

If Mulholland is able to throw the splitter and slider for strikes, opposing hitters put an early pitch into play, and he is generally successful. If Mulholland's low stuff comes in below the knee, hitters take it and slam the rest of his repertoire. Mulholland has an advantage against lefthanders, who have more trouble picking up his pitches. From the stretch, he shortens his delivery and seems to lose control of his sinker, leading to wild pitches and walks.

The key to any Mulholland start is the pitch count. If he throws more than 16 to 18 pitches an inning, he isn't throwing his splitter for strikes. It also appears that in September, opposing righthanded batters noticed a delivery difference between the splitter and the fastball, and were able to wait for the ordinary heater or the change-up. For a ground ball pitcher, Mulholland does not have much stamina. In an average start, his pitch velocity will be down in the 80's, and he'll be almost out of gas by the fifth or sixth inning.

Good, long term sinker-ball starting pitchers like Tommy John always have one statistic in common: seven to nine hits for every nine innings pitched. Mulholland's lifetime major league number is closer to 11. Looking alike isn't pitching alike.

FIELDING, HITTING, BASERUNNING:

Mulholland is a smooth fielding pitcher, partly because his delivery leaves him balanced as the pitch is released. He has an astoundingly quick flip-move to first base which caught several base-runners unawares, and twice embarrassed first baseman Ricky Jordan. Mulholland can bunt reliably, but his statistics say it all about his hitting ability; three for 67 (.045) lifetime.

OVERALL:

As long as Mulholland can get lefthanders out, he will be able to pitch in at least a limited relief role. He must improve his splitter's reliability and his stretch delivery to deserve anything more.

TERRY MULHOLLAND

Position: SP/RP
Bats: R **Throws:** L
Ht: 6' 3" **Wt:** 200

Opening Day Age: 27
Born: 3/9/63 in Uniontown, PA
ML Seasons: 3

Overall Statistics

	W	L	ERA	G	GS	Sv	IP	H	R	BB	SO	HR
1989	4	7	4.92	25	18	0	115.1	137	66	36	66	8
Career	7	15	4.67	49	34	0	216.0	238	119	78	111	14

Where They Hit the Ball

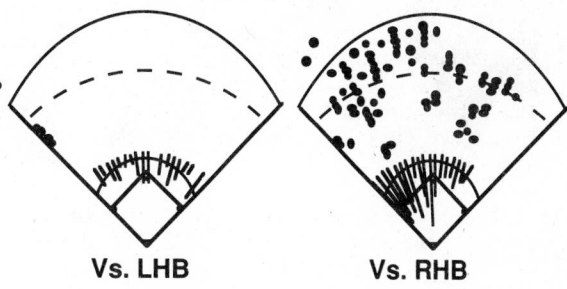

Vs. LHB   Vs. RHB

1989 Situational Stats

	W	L	ERA	Sv	IP		AB	H	HR	RBI	AVG
Home	2	3	3.94	0	59.1	LHB	85	18	0	9	.212
Road	2	4	5.95	0	56.0	RHB	380	119	8	51	.313
Day	0	3	7.18	0	26.1	Sc Pos	109	34	1	46	.312
Night	4	4	4.25	0	89.0	Clutch	26	9	0	3	.346

1989 Rankings (National League)

➡ 1st in worst batting average vs. righthanded batters (.313) - *pitchers facing 377 RHB*

➡ Led the Phillies in complete games (2), shutouts (1) and hit batsmen (4)

PITCHING:

Jeff Parrett oddly resembles Kevin Gross, the man the Phillies traded to acquire him. Both are durable and reliable. Both throw one of the best-regarded breaking balls in the league, and add to it a fine fastball with good movement. Both have yet to turn "great stuff" into a great season. While Parrett's win-loss and ERA numbers last year look impressive, he earned his six saves in 12 save opportunities, a poor record. Further, his 18 decisions as a reliever show that he has trouble holding leads. He also allowed over 46% of the runners he inherited from other pitchers to score.

Parrett's performance depended upon the amount of rest he had between appearances. When he worked on two or more days of rest, his ERA was 2.30, and he walked a batter slightly less than once every three innings. With zero or one day's rest, Parrett's ERA rose almost a full run to 3.22, and he walked a batter every 2.1 innings.

Despite his somewhat spotty record, Parrett's repertoire is genuinely impressive. His fastball, which he throws two-thirds of the time, has been clocked at 93 mph. It sets up a slider which usually yields one of three outcomes: a called ball, a grounder, or a strikeout. Both pitches move sharply, the fastball sailing up and in on righthanded hitters, the slider dive-bombing down and swerving from left to right. His change is a splitter which looks like a lifeless straight heater in the mid-80's, then dives for the dirt. Parrett loses neither velocity nor movement from the stretch.

Parrett's biggest concern is his control. When his slider draws swings and can notch up called strikes, he is virtually unhittable. He must work to keep the ball out of the dirt, as he finished second on the Phils in wild pitches per inning.

FIELDING, BASERUNNING, HITTING:

Parrett's quick, balanced delivery leaves him in position to smoothly field bunts and grounders. He alternates a labored, by-the-numbers move with a lightning-fast hop-swivel-throw move to keep runners close to first base. He has neither hit nor run the bases enough to make either look like professionals' work.

OVERALL:

The Phillies think they can tap Parrett's potential by making him a starter in '90. He will have to throw his slider consistently for strikes and keep it and his splitter out of the dirt. This year could well be the last year Parrett is considered a "could be" pitcher.

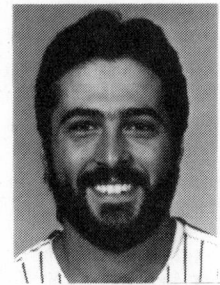

JEFF PARRETT

Position: RP
Bats: R **Throws:** R
Ht: 6' 3"   **Wt:** 200

Opening Day Age: 28
Born: 8/26/61 in Indianapolis, IN
ML Seasons: 4

Overall Statistics

	W	L	ERA	G	GS	Sv	IP	H	R	BB	SO	HR
1989	12	6	2.98	72	0	6	105.2	90	43	44	98	6
Career	31	17	3.28	190	0	18	279.2	228	116	132	237	25

Where They Hit the Ball

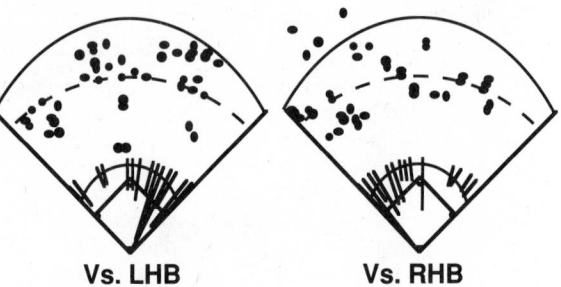

Vs. LHB   **Vs. RHB**

1989 Situational Stats

	W	L	ERA	Sv	IP		AB	H	HR	RBI	AVG
Home	7	0	2.22	3	48.2	LHB	204	44	0	23	.216
Road	5	6	3.63	3	57.0	RHB	184	46	6	30	.250
Day	4	2	3.24	0	25.0	Sc Pos	112	31	1	44	.277
Night	8	4	2.90	6	80.2	Clutch	189	43	4	27	.228

1989 Rankings (National League)

- → 3rd in games (72) and highest percentage of inherited runners scoring (46.3%) - *pitchers with 30 inherited runners*
- → 5th in worst first batter efficiency (.281) - *pitcher in 40 relief games*
- → 6th in blown saves (6)
- → 9th in win/loss percentage (.667) - *pitchers with 15 decisions*
- → Led the Phillies in games, balks (3), wins (12), pickoff throws (125), holds (6), win/loss percentage and blown saves

HITTING:

For a decent hitter, Randy Ready has the most walk-oriented batting stance in the majors. He is a genuine guess hitter who sets his stance in the early stages of the pitcher's delivery, depending on whether or not he plans to swing.

As the pitcher comes set, Ready picks up his front (left) foot, and sets it down in a closed stance, with his left knee sharply bent up and in, and his right knee pointed down and toward first. It's an imbalanced stance, placing his weight forward, and creating as small a strike zone as possible. He assumes this stance on every pitch, and then as the pitcher delivers, he either stays in it to take, or uses it as a timing mechanism, straightening his front foot as he throws his weight into the pitch.

Despite this complicated ritual, Ready has good bat control, an excellent strike out to walk ratio, and has excelled in sacrifice fly opportunities and hit-and-run plays. More noticeable last year was his power. Ready outslugged all Phillies' righthanded batters, but struggled against righty pitching for the first time in his career, which limited his playing time.

BASERUNNING:

Ready is a cautious base runner who rarely attempts to stretch a hit or move up on what would be a close call. He runs vigorously, however, and is more than willing to slide hard or collide forcefully with fielders on close tag plays. He is too slow to be a threat to steal bases.

FIELDING:

Moved between second, third, and the outfield for three seasons, Ready generally stays at a position long enough to show his slow first-step reactions, but not long enough to develop good habits. In left field, he doesn't track down fly balls confidently, and can't seem to turn a quick release and a good arm into outfield assists.

OVERALL:

Ready's righthanded bat, excellent attitude and versatility make him a strong contributor to any club. Look for him to take up the slack if Jones, Jordan or Charlie Hayes can't hold their jobs. On a team which could start five lefthanded batters, he should see plenty of platoon and spot action.

RANDY READY

Position: LF/3B
Bats: R **Throws:** R
Ht: 5'11" **Wt:** 180

Opening Day Age: 30
Born: 1/8/60 in San Mateo, CA
ML Seasons: 7

Overall Statistics

	G	AB	R	H	D	T	HR	RBI	SB	BB	SO	AVG
1989	100	254	37	67	13	2	8	26	4	42	37	.264
Career	459	1358	207	364	77	18	33	163	19	191	173	.268

Where He Hits the Ball

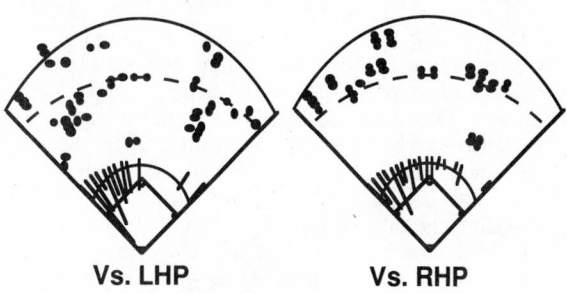

Vs. LHP   Vs. RHP

1989 Situational Stats

	AB	H	HR	RBI	AVG		AB	H	HR	RBI	AVG
Home	114	30	3	9	.263	LHP	150	42	5	14	.280
Road	140	37	5	17	.264	RHP	104	25	3	12	.240
Day	55	17	2	6	.309	Sc Pos	68	12	1	18	.176
Night	199	50	6	20	.251	Clutch	35	9	1	6	.257

1989 Rankings (National League)

➡ Did not rank near the top or bottom in any category

PITCHING:

Every year, the Phillies pinpoint exactly why Bruce Ruffin has not become a consistent ground-ball throwing starter, a la Tommy John. Every year in spring training, Ruffin cuts down his walks and hits allowed and reels off some good starts. Every year, starting in April, he starts walking people and giving up line drives all over again.

Ruffin's problem last April was simple. He relied on a sinking fastball and a slider. His sinker either stayed up or sunk out of the strike zone for wild pitches. His slider either hung or corkscrewed wide of the plate. Hitters were waiting for a cripple, and getting one often enough to chase Ruffin before the fifth inning in four of his first six starts.

After he'd spent a month in AAA Scranton, the Phillies decided that Ruffin, who throws a sinking fastball most of the time, was straightening his arm at the elbow, dropping from a three-quarters delivery to almost side-arm the ball. This stripped the movement from his ball and let the opponents pick it up earlier. Restoring his motion to three-quarters was credited as the difference between the Bruce Ruffin whose April-June featured rocketing line drives and an ERA of 8.67, and the pitcher whose July-October featured ground balls and an ERA of 3.28. But Ruffin's second half ERA's have all been better than his first halves except for 1988, when both halves were terrible.

Stamina remains a major problem for Ruffin. He has a history of being lit up after the sixth inning. Even during his successful string after the All-Star break, he averaged only five and one-third innings per start, largely because he was pulled regularly in the sixth and seventh innings at the first sign of trouble.

FIELDING, BATTING, BASERUNNING:

Ruffin's economical motion allows him to anticipate batted balls and cover ground. He has a good move and a quick delivery to home, which helps the catcher against baserunners who like to steal on sinkerballers. He is a nimble, heads-up fielder. Ruffin has made real progress as a hitter, hitting .176 last year, second best among Phillies pitchers, and bunting reliably. His first step is quick, but he rarely runs.

OVERALL:

Bruce Ruffin may have found the physical key to keeping his sinker down, but without more stamina, he won't keep a rotation spot on any club above the cellar.

BRUCE RUFFIN

Position: SP
Bats: L **Throws:** L
Ht: 6' 2" **Wt:** 205

Opening Day Age: 26
Born: 10/4/63 in Lubbock, TX
ML Seasons: 4

Overall Statistics

	W	L	ERA	G	GS	Sv	IP	H	R	BB	SO	HR
1989	6	10	4.44	24	23	0	125.2	152	69	62	70	10
Career	32	38	3.94	135	94	3	621.0	677	326	259	315	40

Where They Hit the Ball

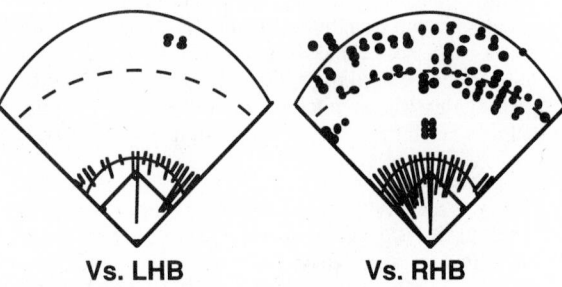

Vs. LHB   **Vs. RHB**

1989 Situational Stats

	W	L	ERA	Sv	IP		AB	H	HR	RBI	AVG
Home	4	7	4.90	0	75.1	LHB	64	18	1	7	.281
Road	2	3	3.75	0	50.1	RHB	441	134	9	56	.304
Day	1	3	5.40	0	31.2	Sc Pos	143	43	2	51	.301
Night	5	7	4.12	0	94.0	Clutch	18	4	0	1	.222

1989 Rankings (National League)

➡ 3rd in worst batting average vs. righthanded batters (.304) - *pitchers facing 377 RHB*

HITTING:

Dickie Thon was reborn as a major league starter in 1989. More than compiling good numbers, Thon did what he had been unable to do since Mike Torrez's beanball diminished his horizons and blurred his vision in 1984: hit righthanded pitching.

An aggressive hitter, Thon has always started with an extremely closed stance against lefties. That allowed him to open up on balls over the plate and inside, or stride in on balls pitched outside. Against righthanders, Thon had developed a habit of sliding his front foot away from the plate as the pitcher delivered; this left him standing almost upright and reaching for the ball. It kept his shoulders and head out of danger, but also took away his power most of the time.

Batting second early last season also contributed to the continuation of Thon's slump. He is an aggressive hitter, and having to lead off and hit behind runners exposed his weaknesses rather than build on his strengths. But in midseason Thon was moved to seventh in the order, where his job was to drive in John Kruk and Von Hayes, who were frequently on base. This increased not only his comfort level, but his RBI opportunities, and Thon lost his bad, five-year-old batting habits. He stopped pulling his foot and started pulling the ball sharply, becoming the Phillies' best RBI man for the last half of the season. With men on base, and with men in scoring position, Thon was as clutch as they come.

BASERUNNING:

Thon reads batted balls and fielders extremely well, and advances aggressively. His speed no longer makes him an 20 stolen base threat, but he is a good percentage stealer, who could easily steal 10-12 next season.

FIELDING:

Thon's anticipation of batted balls and knowledge of opposing hitter's tendencies are his strengths. He has excellent range to his left, but is less sure on balls to his right. He tends to retreat on balls towards third, to charge balls hit towards second.

OVERALL:

Thon not only displayed his talents last season, he showed genuine courage. He resumed a batting stance which almost cost him his vision the last time he employed it. With all respect to Lonnie Smith, no one came back further in 1989 than Dickie Thon.

DICKIE THON

Position: SS
Bats: R **Throws:** R
Ht: 5'11" **Wt:** 175

Opening Day Age: 31
Born: 6/20/58 in South Bend, IN
ML Seasons: 11

Overall Statistics

	G	AB	R	H	D	T	HR	RBI	SB	BB	SO	AVG
1989	136	435	45	118	18	4	15	60	6	33	81	.271
Career	912	2838	345	765	130	30	49	273	126	244	418	.270

Where He Hits the Ball

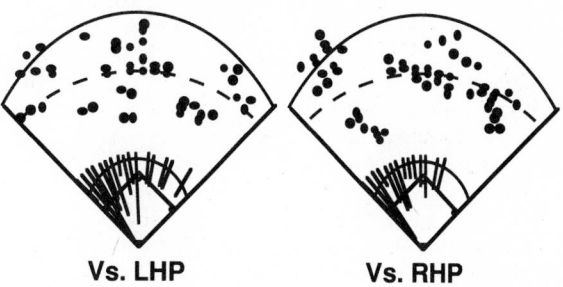

Vs. LHP   Vs. RHP

1989 Situational Stats

	AB	H	HR	RBI	AVG		AB	H	HR	RBI	AVG
Home	208	55	8	29	.264	LHP	176	48	6	22	.273
Road	227	63	7	31	.278	RHP	259	70	9	38	.270
Day	118	34	2	13	.288	Sc Pos	102	37	6	47	.363
Night	317	84	13	47	.265	Clutch	67	18	2	10	.269

1989 Rankings (National League)

➡ 4th in hitting with runners in scoring position (.363) - *players withh 100 PA with runners in scoring position*

➡ 10th in hitting on an 0-2 count (.250) - *players with 20 PA on an 0-2 count*

➡ Led the Phillies in hitting with runners in scoring position and percentage of extra bases taken as a runner (50.7%) - *team player with 40 opportunities to advance*

➡ Led NL Shortstops in home runs (15), RBIs (60), hitting with runners in scoring posision and home run frequency (29 ABs per HR)

PAT
COMBS

Position: SP
Bats: L **Throws:** L
Ht: 6' 4" **Wt:** 205

Opening Day Age: 23
Born: 10/29/66 in
Newport, RI
ML Seasons: 1

Overall Statistics

	W	L	ERA	G	GS	Sv	IP	H	R	BB	SO	HR
1989	4	0	2.09	6	6	0	38.2	36	10	6	30	2
Career	4	0	2.09	6	6	0	38.2	36	10	6	30	2

PITCHING, FIELDING, HITTING:

Pat Combs rose from A, AA, AAA and finally to the majors in one season. Except for a brief spell at AA Reading, nobody hit him hard all year. Combs throws an 87-88 mph fastball, a splitter and a slider, both hurled with good velocity. His success springs from his uniform delivery, which is smooth and unvaried, from the windup or stretch, no matter which pitch is coming. Last year opposing hitters were unable to tell his splitter from his fastball, and had trouble reading the change-up as well. Combs also showed great control all year, walking only six batters in 38.2 innings during his big league stint. Combs, who runs very aggressively, knows the strike zone as a batter, but needs to bunt with more touch and less force. He has a terrific move to first, and fields capably.

OVERALL:

The Phillies keep having a Pat Combs nightmare. In it, they see Don Carman and Bruce Ruffin all over again; initial success, then hitters deciphering his delivery, taking his breaking pitches, walking, then lighting up his fastball. On the other hand, if Combs gets his splitter and slider over when hitters try that this year, he could become the Phillies' anchor for the 90s.

RON
JONES

Position: RF
Bats: L **Throws:** R
Ht: 5'10" **Wt:** 200

Opening Day Age: 25
Born: 6/11/64 in
Seguin, TX
ML Seasons: 2

Overall Statistics

	G	AB	R	H	D	T	HR	RBI	SB	BB	SO	AVG
1989	12	31	7	9	0	0	2	4	1	9	1	.290
Career	45	155	22	45	6	1	10	30	1	11	15	.290

HITTING, FIELDING, BASERUNNING:

The Phils' best pure hitting prospect was Ron Jones who crushed the ball for the season's first week until he was crushed by the outfield wall, seriously injuring his already sore knees. Jones underwent surgery, ending his season and potentially threatening his career. If he recovers, the lefthanded hitting Jones can rejuvenate the Phillies. Throughout his professional career, he has forced pitchers to throw strikes, walked more than he has struck out, and has shown the ability to drive the ball to all three fields. A barrel-chested Tony Gwynn-style line drive hitter, Jones has hit lefthanders better than righties in his 166 major league plate appearances, a talent the Phillies' offense can use. For a young player, he hits breaking balls with confidence. Fast and very aggressive both in the outfield and on the bases before his injury, Jones's aggressiveness will very likely return, and he may recover most of his speed as well.

OVERALL:

Throughout his short professional career, only injuries and sore knees have stopped Ron Jones. If he can recover enough to hit, but not enough to play left, the Phillies may have to make room for him at first base. He's that promising a hitter.

MIKE MADDUX

Position: RP/SP
Bats: R **Throws:** R
Ht: 6' 2" **Wt:** 180

Opening Day Age: 28
Born: 8/27/61 in Dayton, OH
ML Seasons: 4

Overall Statistics

	W	L	ERA	G	GS	Sv	IP	H	R	BB	SO	HR
1989	1	3	5.15	16	4	1	43.2	52	29	14	26	3
Career	10	13	4.51	64	33	1	227.1	248	131	87	144	15

PITCHING, FIELDING, HITTING:

Mike Maddux and his brother Greg were the first siblings ever to duel each other as National League rookies. Their rivalry stands at 1-1, and if they never face each other again, it won't be Greg's fault. While Greg has gone on to stardom, Mike has never won more than four games in a season. Mike has to keep his fastball down to be successful. When he releases it a fraction too early, the ball stays up, where hitters can turn on it for extra bases. Maddux throws two curveballs, one that sails away from righties, and one that drops. He could not make either break sharply often enough last year, and hitters could extend their arms and tee off on him. Maddux is a decent athlete, and it shows in his able baserunning and fielding. He makes contact at the plate, but is not a sure bet to bunt successfully.

OVERALL:

Given every chance to earn a spot on a chaotic Phils pitching staff, Mike's mechanics failed him. With young arms now bubbling up from the Phillies farm system, Maddux must find his stuff by spring to stay in the majors.

DWAYNE MURPHY

Position: LF/RF
Bats: L **Throws:** R
Ht: 6' 1" **Wt:** 185

Opening Day Age: 35
Born: 3/18/55 in Merced, CA
ML Seasons: 12

Overall Statistics

	G	AB	R	H	D	T	HR	RBI	SB	BB	SO	AVG
1989	98	156	20	34	5	0	9	27	0	29	44	.218
Career	1360	4347	648	1069	139	20	166	609	100	747	953	.246

HITTING, FIELDING, BASERUNNING:

From 1980 to 1985, with the Oakland A's, Dwayne Murphy won six consecutive American League Gold Gloves, hit 125 home runs, stole 77 bases, and averaged 80 walks per year as part of one of the best outfields of the decade. He retains his power and his batting eye, but the physical tools which once ranked him with the likes of Gary Pettis are gone. Injuries to Murphy's feet and knees have taken away his base stealing ability and outfield range. His quick release and accuracy cannot make up for his weak arm in right field. A canny competitor, Murphy suffered in every aspect from not being able to use the data on opponents and ballparks he had stored up in 11 seasons in the American League. Murphy is a patient hitter who attempts to manipulate every count into either a walk or a chance to drive the ball. He tends to overswing, and strikes out nearly one out of every four plate appearances. His power comes from pulling low and inside pitches to right field. Pitchers have success climbing his ladder with outside pitches.

OVERALL:

Murphy can still play left or right and hit for power. He will compete in the spring for a platoon role against righthanders. In his new role as a part-timer, pinch-hitting and RBI efficiency are vital.

RANDY O'NEAL

Position: RP
Bats: R **Throws:** R
Ht: 6' 2" **Wt:** 195

Opening Day Age: 29
Born: 8/30/60 in Ashland, KY
ML Seasons: 6

Overall Statistics

	W	L	ERA	G	GS	Sv	IP	H	R	BB	SO	HR
1989	0	1	6.23	20	1	0	39.0	46	28	9	29	5
Career	16	19	4.41	116	46	3	393.2	403	217	131	218	45

PITCHING, FIELDING, HITTING:

Randy O'Neal believes in challenging hitters, and making them beat you with their bats. Last year the hitters won. O'Neal's low 80's fastball, thrown high, is a good set-up for his split-fingered sinker because he releases both high. However, he can't throw his slider for consistent strikes, and uses the sinker sparingly as his out pitch. This leaves an enormous burden on an unexceptional fastball. To throw a fastball two-thirds of the time, it has to be fast or have a lot of movement. O'Neal's doesn't, so while he usually manages to put it somewhere where it can't be hit out of the park, it is often ripped hard up the middle. O'Neal's slow delivery is easy to steal on. Though he disguises it well, his sinker is the pitch of choice when he's ahead in the count, and base-stealers know that. He is slow off the mound and on the bases, and no help at the plate.

OVERALL:

The Phillies need a solid righthanded middle reliever. If O'Neal can get his slider over, he could fill that slot. If he can't make the Phillies, he probably can't pitch in the majors.

FLOYD YOUMANS

Position: SP
Bats: R **Throws:** R
Ht: 6' 1" **Wt:** 200

Opening Day Age: 25
Born: 5/11/64 in Tampa, FL
ML Seasons: 5

Overall Statistics

	W	L	ERA	G	GS	Sv	IP	H	R	BB	SO	HR
1989	1	5	5.70	10	10	0	42.2	50	31	25	20	7
Career	30	34	3.74	94	90	0	539.0	428	249	280	424	45

PITCHING, FIELDING, HITTING:

When Floyd Youmans could throw his 93 mph fastball 70 times per game, it made his change-up a weapon and his slider downright unfair. But except for '86 and a few weeks in '88, persistent tendinitis in Floyd's right shoulder has made his fastball drop alarmingly in velocity. Youmans finally needed surgery on the shoulder. When he's healthy and his fastball is cooking, Youmans can be extremely tough. In 1986 he allowed just under six hits per nine innings, and a home run every 16 innings. In 1989, opponents blasted 11 hits per nine innings and reaching the bleachers once every six innings. Youmans has a poor move and a slow wind-up, which allow opponents to steal freely. He has gained weight over the last year or two and, despite good athletic ability, his fielding is neither practiced nor confident. At the plate, he likes to swing, but is only valuable because he can lay down a good bunt.

OVERALL:

If Youmans's shoulder recovers and fastball returns, he will start for the Phillies. But how will they know? Youmans insisted he was able to pitch right up until he was threatened with his release. He has to be mature enough to let himself recover before trying to pitch again.

PITCHING:

Doug Bair's up-and-down fortunes took a sharp turn for the better last season. When spring training started, Bair was in the Toronto Blue Jays' minor-league camp working out with players young enough to be his sons. By the end of summer, Bair was a key figure in the Pittsburgh Pirates' bullpen. There were snickers when the Pirates, desperate for pitching help, purchased Bair from Toronto's Syracuse farm club. But Bair, who turned 40 last August, provided a steadying influence in the bullpen. He also provided versatility, performing well as a long man, middle reliever and set-up man. By season's end, he had made 44 appearances and compiled an outstanding 2.27 ERA with a 2-3 record and one save. The wins were his first in the majors in two seasons and the save his first in three years.

Bair is a hard worker. He gets to the ballpark early and is working out long before a lot of other players arrive. He realizes the importance of conditioning at his age. Despite his years, Bair can run the fastball up in a hurry and it is still his best pitch. He has also has a sharp-breaking curveball. And he throws strikes, issuing just 18 unintentional walks in 67.1 innings. More than anything, Bair provides experience. He has been in the major leagues since 1976, hitting the circuit with stops in Pittsburgh (twice), Oakland (twice), Cincinnati, St. Louis (twice), Detroit, Philadelphia and Toronto. After that many years and that many stops, the man has some pretty solid clues about how to pitch.

FIELDING, HITTING, BASERUNNING:

Bair knows how to do the little things to help himself. He fields his position well, is quick off the mound on bunts and holds runners. Bair rarely gets to the plate to bat and gets on base even more infrequently. However, he did smack a double in his first plate appearance in two seasons. He does not have to worry much about honing his baserunning skills.

OVERALL:

Bair has been traded, released and signed as a free agent over and over. Yet he continues to hang on. He proved in 1989 that, even though he is 40, he can still get major-league hitters out with his live arm. He does not figure in Pittsburgh's five-year plan, but he can be an effective role reliever for a club shy on bullpen depth.

DOUG BAIR

Position: RP
Bats: R **Throws:** R
Ht: 6' 0" **Wt:** 180

Opening Day Age: 40
Born: 8/22/49 in Defiance, OH
ML Seasons: 14

Overall Statistics

	W	L	ERA	G	GS	Sv	IP	H	R	BB	SO	HR
1989	2	3	2.27	44	0	1	67.1	52	19	28	56	4
Career	55	43	3.61	562	5	81	883.2	809	383	394	670	83

Where They Hit the Ball

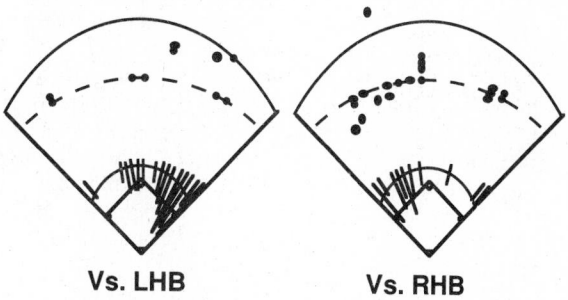

Vs. LHB   Vs. RHB

1989 Situational Stats

	W	L	ERA	Sv	IP		AB	H	HR	RBI	AVG
Home	2	2	1.59	0	39.2	LHB	120	23	1	10	.192
Road	0	1	3.25	1	27.2	RHB	126	29	3	14	.230
Day	0	1	0.00	0	17.2	Sc Pos	77	14	1	20	.182
Night	2	2	3.08	1	49.2	Clutch	112	24	3	13	.214

1989 Rankings (National League)

➡ 5th in highest percentage of inherited runners scoring (43.3%) - *pitchers with 30 inherited runners*

➡ 7th in holds (13) and lowest batting average vs. lefthanded hitters (.192) - *pitchers facing 125 LHB*

➡ Led the Pirates in holds

JAY BELL

Position: SS
Bats: R **Throws:** R
Ht: 6' 1" **Wt:** 180

Opening Day Age: 24
Born: 12/11/65 in Pensacola, FL
ML Seasons: 4

HITTING:

After disappointing in Cleveland, young Jay Bell emerged as a solid hitter in Pittsburgh during the second half of the 1989 season. Bell came over to Pittsburgh in a spring training deal and began the season as the Pirates' starting shortstop, but went one for 20 and was sent to the minors. He came back in mid-July to stay, thanks to an adjustment in his swing. Bell began his swing by resting the bat on his right shoulder, eliminating a severe hitch and enabling him to get full extension.

Bell's hitting also picked up when he was moved up in the batting order from eighth to second. He began to see more fastballs and also proved to be an adept hit-and-run man and bunter. He batted second in the final 48 games and had a .309 average with 29 runs and 18 multiple-hit games. Curveballs can give Bell problems, particularly ones low and away. Good fastballs up and away can also cause him to swing weakly. However, his knowledge of the strike zone keeps improving and he is becoming a much better hitter against righthanders. Bell also showed signs of becoming a dangerous clutch hitter in the season's final weeks. He had 14 hits in his last 21 at-bats with runners in scoring position, driving in 14 runs. Bell has a live bat and can hit the ball far the other way. He can be expected to reach double figures in homers at some point in his career.

BASERUNNING:

Bell is not blessed with blazing speed, but moves quite well. He can steal an occasional base and he hit the Pirates' first inside-the-park home run in two seasons last September. He is an intelligent baserunner, who will take a risk when he feels the odds are in his favor.

FIELDING:

Bell came to the Pittsburgh with the rap of being a good-hit, no-field shortstop. He disproved the no-field tag, though, finishing with 10 errors, many on difficult plays. He made all of the routine plays and showed a very strong arm. He is not blessed with outstanding range. However, Bell compensates by studying hitters and should improve with more experience.

OVERALL:

Shortstop has been a problem spot with the Pirates since Gene Alley's heyday in the late '60s. However, they feel they have finally found their man. The Pirates took heat early for the trade that sent Felix Fermin to Cleveland for Bell. By the end of the season, they were more than pleased with their end of the bargain.

Overall Statistics

	G	AB	R	H	D	T	HR	RBI	SB	BB	SO	AVG
1989	78	271	33	70	13	3	2	27	5	19	47	.258
Career	194	621	73	148	29	5	7	65	11	50	134	.238

Where He Hits the Ball

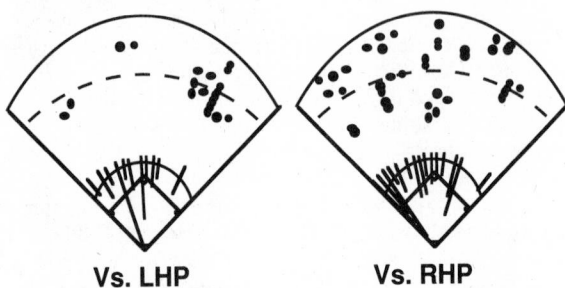

Vs. LHP   **Vs. RHP**

1989 Situational Stats

	AB	H	HR	RBI	AVG		AB	H	HR	RBI	AVG
Home	141	36	1	11	.255	LHP	107	29	1	10	.271
Road	130	34	1	16	.262	RHP	164	41	1	17	.250
Day	78	21	1	9	.269	Sc Pos	53	19	0	23	.358
Night	193	49	1	18	.254	Clutch	48	9	0	7	.188

1989 Rankings (National League)

→ 4th in hitting on a 3-1 count (.545) - *players with 10 PA on a 3-1 count*

→ 9th in sacrifice bunts (10)

→ Led the Pirates in hitting with runners in scoring position (.358) - *all team players*

HITTING:

Barry Bonds does not like to be compared to his father, former major league star Bobby Bonds. Yet, it seems that people never know quite what to do with Barry, just as was the case with his oft-traded father. For openers, Pittsburgh still is unsure exactly where Bonds should fit into the batting order. Bonds has been mainly a leadoff man with Pittsburgh and has done well in that role, getting on base and averaging 97 runs scored over the last three years. But Bonds also has home run power, making people think he could hit lower in the order. Remind you of anyone?

What makes the idea of batting Bonds in the middle of the order an iffy proposition is his lack of clutch hitting. Barry has generally hit poorly with runners in scoring position, batting just .227 last year. He goes after too many bad pitches with men on base, and particularly when the game is on the line.

Bonds is a rare lefthanded hitter in that he fares better against lefthanded pitchers. He particularly hits breaking balls well from lefties. Bonds, who can hit with power to all fields, often falls into the rut of holding his hands too close to his body. Thus, he is very vulnerable to hard stuff inside from righthanders. They will then work him away and force him to chase off-speed pitches. Often, he will refuse to swing at any inside pitch and is frequently called out on strikes.

BASERUNNING:

Bonds has outstanding speed and led the Pirates with 32 stolen bases last year. It was the third time in four seasons he has stolen 30 or more bases. An aggressive baserunner, Bonds sometimes runs into outs on the basepaths, gambling for the extra base when the odds are slim.

FIELDING:

Bonds is perfectly suited to left field and has become one of the top defensive players in the league at that position. He has a smooth gait and gets under even what appear to be the most difficult of fly balls. He can come in on balls and go to the wall with equal effectiveness. His throwing arm is considered below average, but he was second in the league with 14 outfield assists in '89.

OVERALL:

Bonds has performed well for Pittsburgh, providing speed, power, defense and run-scoring ability. Yet the Pirates seem ready to give up on him at the age of 25. Will Barry spend his career modeling uniforms ... just like his daddy?

BARRY BONDS

Position: LF
Bats: L **Throws:** L
Ht: 6' 1" **Wt:** 185

Opening Day Age: 25
Born: 7/24/64 in Riverside, CA
ML Seasons: 4

Overall Statistics

	G	AB	R	H	D	T	HR	RBI	SB	BB	SO	AVG
1989	159	580	96	144	34	6	19	58	32	93	93	.248
Career	566	2082	364	532	124	23	84	223	117	284	365	.256

Where He Hits the Ball

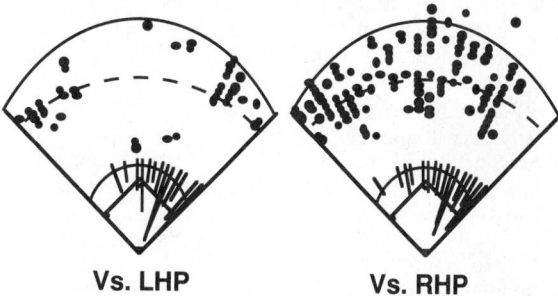

Vs. LHP   **Vs. RHP**

1989 Situational Stats

	AB	H	HR	RBI	AVG		AB	H	HR	RBI	AVG
Home	280	57	7	28	.204	LHP	178	47	4	24	.264
Road	300	87	12	30	.290	RHP	402	97	15	34	.241
Day	200	52	5	19	.260	Sc Pos	97	22	3	36	.227
Night	380	92	14	39	.242	Clutch	98	21	1	8	.214

1989 Rankings (National League)

➡ 2nd in pitches seen (2,528) and lowest batting average at home (.204) - *players with 252 PA at home*

➡ 3rd in walks (93)

➡ 4th in steals of third (7) and intentional walks (22)

➡ Led the Pirates in runs (96), stolen bases (32), walks, pitches seen, runs scored per time reached base (37.9%), steals of third, batting average on the road (.290), caught stealing and intentional walks (22) - *team players with 502 PA*

➡ Led NL Left Fielders in at bats (580), plate appearances (679), games (159), doubles (34), walks and pitches seen

HITTING:

Big, switch-hitting Bobby Bonilla continues to emerge as one of the game's premier hitters. After hitting .274 with 24 home runs and 100 RBIs in 1988, his breakthrough season into stardom, Bonilla posted numbers of .281, 24, 86 last season. He compiled those statistics despite the fact that Jose Lind and Andy Van Slyke, the players who most often bat in front of Bonilla, had poor seasons. Bonilla goes to the plate with one thing in mind: get his pitch and hit it hard.

Bonilla shows good patience at the plate for a young player. He has a keen eye for the strike zone and will wait for his pitch. After a consistent season from both sides of the plate in '88, Bonilla struggled from the right side in '89. He developed a long, looping swing when batting righthanded and lefthanders were able to tie him up with hard stuff inside and low. He does have success against breaking pitches when batting from the right side. When Bonilla bats lefty, pitchers can have a moderate amount of success by throwing off-speed pitches away. He will kill fastballs, particularly over the middle of the plate and in. A two-time All-Star, Bonilla has proven he can knock home 100 runs in a season. It is just a matter of having someone on base to bring in.

BASERUNNING:

Bonilla has deceptive speed. He can get his big body moving in a hurry when going from first to third and second to home. Though pitchers and catchers do not fear Bonilla, he can steal a base if the battery does not pay attention. He finished with eight last season. He will also go in hard to break up double plays.

FIELDING:

Bonilla's problems at third base have been well documented. He's committed 67 errors over the last two season, both on throws and on bullets hit right at him. Bonilla makes difficult plays at times, but, considering his awesome hitting potential, he would undoubtedly be better off at a position he can handle more easily. A move to first base or right field might be in order.

OVERALL:

Over the last two years, Bonilla has earned a reputation as one of the best hitters in the National League. He might be able to do even better if he wasn't being forced to play such a demanding position.

BOBBY BONILLA

Position: 3B
Bats: B **Throws:** R
Ht: 6' 3" **Wt:** 230

Opening Day Age: 27
Born: 2/23/63 in New York, NY
ML Seasons: 4

Overall Statistics

	G	AB	R	H	D	T	HR	RBI	SB	BB	SO	AVG
1989	163	616	96	173	37	10	24	86	8	76	93	.281
Career	601	2092	296	582	118	24	66	306	22	262	327	.278

Where He Hits the Ball

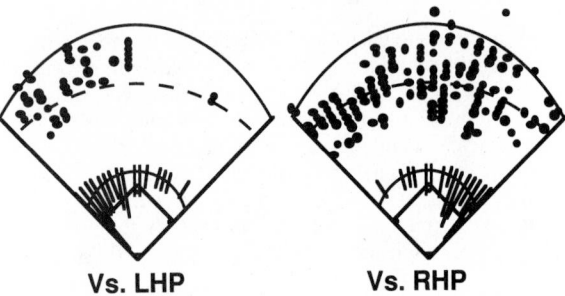

Vs. LHP   **Vs. RHP**

1989 Situational Stats

	AB	H	HR	RBI	AVG		AB	H	HR	RBI	AVG
Home	296	92	13	42	.311	LHP	221	50	8	30	.226
Road	320	81	11	44	.253	RHP	395	123	16	56	.311
Day	214	60	10	31	.280	Sc Pos	143	41	3	57	.287
Night	402	113	14	55	.281	Clutch	123	27	5	15	.220

1989 Rankings (National League)

➡ 1st in games (163) and errors (35)

➡ 2nd in triples (10) and plate appearances (698)

➡ 3rd in at bats (616)

➡ 4th in totals bases (302), times on base (250) and slugging percentage vs. righthanded pitchers (.547) - *players with 377 PA vs. RHP*

➡ Led the Pirates in at bats, total bases, home runs (24), runs (96), hits (173), doubles (37), triples, RBIs (86), batting average (.281), on-base average (.358), slugging percentage (.490), home run frequency (25.7 ABs per HR), times on base, plate appearances and games

HITTING:

John Cangelosi is like a young Eddie Gaedel: his main weapon -- lately, almost his only weapon -- is his ability to draw a walk. The 5'8" Cangelosi, a switch hitter, bats out of a severely-crouched stance and dares the pitcher to try and throw a strike. Pitchers have trouble doing that, so Cangelosi often walks to first base, where he can use his speed. That's why Cangelosi, who hit only .219 last year, is still in the majors.

Cangelosi will usually wait until he gets a called strike before swinging. Often he will wait until he gets to two strikes. It's a very passive style, but one Cangelosi needs to use because he doesn't do much damage when he swings the bat. Cangelosi has not hit a home run during the past two seasons, and only 11 of his 65 hits during that time have gone for extra bases. A switch hitter, he has a little more extra-base power from the right side. Like many switchers, he likes the ball low from righthanders and high from lefthanders. He hits fastballs better than breaking balls.

Though his on-base percentage continues to be respectable (.365 last year) due to all the walks, Cangelosi hasn't helped the Pirates as much as they'd like. His batting average has declined from .275 to .254 to .219 in three seasons. He's also struggled as a pinch hitter, a role in which he's been used extensively. Cangelosi batted only .176 (12 for 68) last year, though he did draw 12 pinch walks.

BASERUNNING:

Along with his ability to draw walks, Cangelosi's speed has kept him in the major leagues. But last year he was only 11 of 19 in steal attempts, an unacceptably low percentage. Cangelosi, a real hustler, is aggressive on the basepaths and is always looking to take the extra base. He slides head first and is not afraid to give his compact body a pounding.

FIELDING:

With his outstanding natural speed, Cangelosi can get to almost any fly ball hit into the alley. He comes in and goes back on balls well and is not afraid of running into fences. His arm is weak, so he's best suited to left field.

OVERALL:

Cangelosi has been a role player for the last three years, and has generally served the Pirates well. He'll always be able to get on base via the walk. But he needs to run better and hit better, especially in a pinch role, in order to survive.

JOHN CANGELOSI

Position: CF/LF
Bats: B **Throws:** L
Ht: 5' 8" **Wt:** 150

Opening Day Age: 27
Born: 3/10/63 in Brooklyn, NY
ML Seasons: 5

Overall Statistics

	G	AB	R	H	D	T	HR	RBI	SB	BB	SO	AVG
1989	112	160	18	35	4	2	0	9	11	35	20	.219
Career	433	900	147	218	32	9	6	67	91	169	131	.242

Where He Hits the Ball

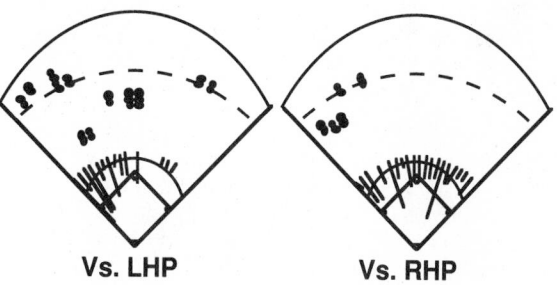

Vs. LHP　　　　Vs. RHP

1989 Situational Stats

	AB	H	HR	RBI	AVG		AB	H	HR	RBI	AVG
Home	78	21	0	3	.269	LHP	82	17	0	6	.207
Road	82	14	0	6	.171	RHP	78	18	0	3	.231
Day	56	13	0	2	.232	Sc Pos	28	5	0	9	.179
Night	104	22	0	7	.212	Clutch	67	13	0	2	.194

1989 Rankings (National League)

→ Did not rank near the top or bottom in any category

OVERLOOKED

DOUG DRABEK

Position: SP
Bats: R **Throws:** R
Ht: 6' 1" **Wt:** 185

Opening Day Age: 27
Born: 7/25/62 in
Victoria, TX
ML Seasons: 4

PITCHING:

Doug Drabek finally found consistency over a full season in 1989. In the past, Drabek started slowly and finished strongly. During his first three major league seasons, Doug was 8-15 before the All-Star break and 25-12 after. His career ERA was also a full run lower in the second half. Drabek put it together over a full season last year, though his 14-12 record is not a fair indicator of how well he pitched. He was just 6-6 at the break despite a 2.19 earned run average. Drabek had a poor month of July, but he was outstanding in August and September (2.56 ERA) as he went 8-6 during the second half.

Drabek is at his best when he mixes all of his pitches. He has an above-average fastball with good movement, but his best pitches are his breaking balls. He throws a sharp-breaking curveball from straight over the top and has a slider with bite. He also mixes in a decent changeup and is not scared to throw inside. Drabek can be close to untouchable when all of his pitches are working. He threw five shutouts last season, including three in his final four starts.

Drabek, a low-key guy off the field but a tenacious competitor on the mound, continued to improve mentally in '89. In the past, he would tend to rely on one pitch too much if the others were not up to his standards. But he learned to relax and not let mistakes bother him as much. He was the workhorse of the Pirates' staff last season, racking up 244.1 innings and eight complete games. He went at least seven innings in 23 of his 34 starts. Drabek tied for the club lead with 123 strikeouts, but he does not try to blow the ball by hitters. He also has good control and rarely beats himself with walks.

FIELDING, HITTING, BASERUNNING:

Drabek is top-notch fielder. He handles bunts well, covers first base well on grounders to the right side and stabs balls hit back up the middle. He also has a very good pickoff move, particularly for a righthander (eight pickoffs in 1989). Drabek is a poor hitter, going eight for 77 (.104) with three RBIs last year, but he runs the bases well and is sometimes used as a pinch runner.

OVERALL:

Drabek has won 40 games over the last three years, while lowering his ERA each year. At the age of 27, he seems on the brink of stardom. Drabek is good enough to be a 20-game winner in 1990.

Overall Statistics

	W	L	ERA	G	GS	Sv	IP	H	R	BB	SO	HR
1989	14	12	2.80	35	34	0	244.1	215	83	69	123	21
Career	47	39	3.35	124	115	0	771.2	700	316	215	446	77

Where They Hit the Ball

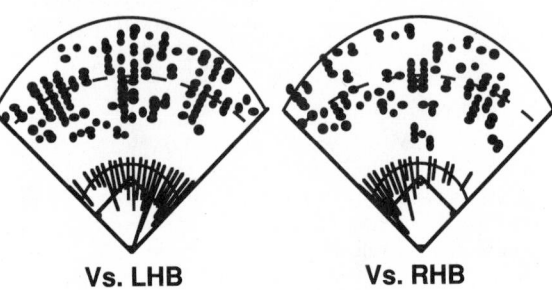

Vs. LHB   **Vs. RHB**

1989 Situational Stats

	W	L	ERA	Sv	IP		AB	H	HR	RBI	AVG
Home	8	5	1.85	0	136.0	LHB	495	123	7	29	.248
Road	6	7	3.99	0	108.1	RHB	407	92	14	47	.226
Day	3	3	3.27	0	55.0	Sc Pos	202	46	5	57	.228
Night	11	9	2.66	0	189.1	Clutch	146	31	2	7	.212

1989 Rankings (National League)

➡ 2nd in ERA at home (1.85), shutouts (5) and least run support per 9 innings (3.2) - *pitchers with 162 IP*

➡ 4th in games started (34) and batters faced (994)

➡ 5th in innings (244.1) and pitches thrown (3,532)

➡ 6th in ERA (2.80), home runs allowed (21) and complete games (8)

➡ Led the Pirates in ERA, wins (14), games started, innings, walks allowed (69), strikeouts (123), pitches thrown, complete games, shutouts, hits allowed (215) and lowest batting average allowed with runners in scoring position (.228) - *team pitchers with 162 IP*

HITTING:

Slapping the ball around and making things happen on the basepaths is what Billy Hatcher likes to do. And that is what the Pirates wanted to see Hatcher do when they acquired him in a trade from the Houston Astros in exchange for Glenn Wilson on Aug. 18. However, the Pirates never really got a good look at Hatcher because he sprained a knee ligament and missed most of the season's final three weeks.

The Pirates envision Hatcher as a possible leadoff hitter, which would allow them to drop Barry Bonds into an RBI slot. Hatcher was Houston's leadoff hitter until the emergence of Gerald Young. However, he does not seem to have the patience necessary to be a premier No. 1 hitter. Billy is a free swinger and has a tendency to chase pitches out of the strike zone. He's never walked more than 42 times in a season.

Hatcher is a notorious streak hitter. He will go through some stretches where he is impossible to get out. At other times, he will struggle terribly. Hatcher has problems against righthanders, particularly with breaking balls outside. He will lunge at those pitches. However, he kills fastballs on the inside part of the plate and will make pitchers pay for mistakes. Though not an RBI man, Hatcher has usually hit well in pressure situations during his career.

BASERUNNING:

Hatcher is a strong base stealer who's swiped as many as 53 in a season, though he slumped to 24 steals last season. He has outstanding speed but can get caught running in the wrong situations and is susceptible to pitchouts. Hatcher is aggressive on the bases and always looks to turn a single into a double and a double into a triple.

FIELDING:

Hatcher has started at all three outfield positions and has no preference. He has a strong enough arm to play right and enough range to play center. Hatcher does have some problems on balls hit over his head and is better at coming in on flies than going back. He can also fall into ruts where he misses cut-off men and throws to wrong bases. However, his speed allows him to cover a lot of his mistakes.

OVERALL:

Hatcher's only had one good hitting season -- 1987, the year he was caught using a corked bat late in the campaign. He'll give the Pirates speed and aggressiveness. But unless he can hit a lot better than he did in 1989, he won't be the answer to Pittsburgh's leadoff problems.

BILLY HATCHER

Position: LF/CF
Bats: R **Throws:** R
Ht: 5' 9" **Wt:** 175

Opening Day Age: 29
Born: 10/4/60 in Williams, AZ
ML Seasons: 6

Overall Statistics

	G	AB	R	H	D	T	HR	RBI	SB	BB	SO	AVG
1989	135	481	59	111	19	3	4	51	24	30	62	.231
Career	609	2166	314	569	99	15	30	212	151	140	252	.263

Where He Hits the Ball

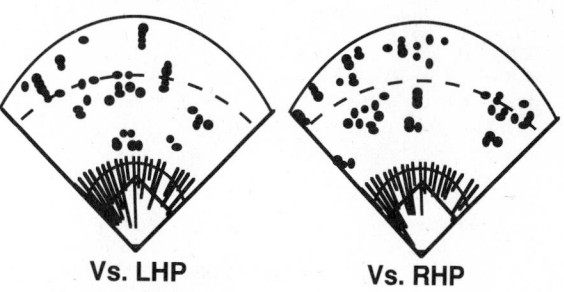

Vs. LHP   **Vs. RHP**

1989 Situational Stats

	AB	H	HR	RBI	AVG		AB	H	HR	RBI	AVG
Home	231	54	0	23	.234	LHP	193	52	2	20	.269
Road	250	57	4	28	.228	RHP	288	59	2	31	.205
Day	134	35	1	20	.261	Sc Pos	129	32	1	47	.248
Night	347	76	3	31	.219	Clutch	81	16	1	6	.198

1989 Rankings (National League)

→ 2nd in percentage of extra bases taken as a runner (61.4%) - *players with 40 opportunities to advance*

→ 3rd in worst on-base average (.277) and worst slugging percentage (.308) - *players with 502 PA*

→ 5th in worst batting average (.231)

→ Led NL Left Fielders in percentage of extra bases taken as a runner

PITCHING:

Neal Heaton is versatile pitcher, a lefthander who can both start and relieve. Heaton performed in both roles during a roller-coaster 1989 with the Pirates. He began the year in rotation and pitched well, then was exiled to the bullpen after some rocky outings during May. Heaton continued to struggle as a reliever and at the end of June sported a 4.56 ERA. But then he turned things around completely. Heaton pitched well in July and really caught fire in August, allowing only one run in 19.1 innings over a stretch of 12 appearances. In September he went back into the rotation and continued to pitch well, going 3-0, 1.59 in six starts. From July 1, Heaton was 5-1 with a 1.62 ERA.

Heaton relies primarily on an effective fastball with good movement. He gets into trouble with it at times, though, because it moves too well and slides out of the strike zone. He also throws a slider and curve. The fastball was the only pitch working for Heaton early in the season, and it wasn't enough. Once he regained command of his breaking pitches and mixed in a changeup, he started to click. He was devastating against lefthanded hitters, holding them to a .137 average for the season.

Heaton has had shoulder problems in the past, and while exercise has strengthened the area, he needs to be used carefully. He had only one complete game last year and often tired in the late innings. For the first 75 pitches of his appearances, he help opponents to a .222 average; from pitch 76 on, they batted .333.

FIELDING, HITTING, BASERUNNING:

Heaton is an average fielder, though his motion causes him to fall away from the plate. He has a decent move to first, but his motion to home is on the slow side, making him vulnerable to base stealers. Heaton takes pride in his hitting. He hit .214 last year (nine for 42) and has a respectable .200 lifetime average. He makes contact, and the Pirates will even hit-and-run with Heaton at the plate. He handles himself well on the bases.

OVERALL:

After an All-American career at the University of Miami, Heaton has struggled to a 61-83 record in the major leagues. His '89 second half was his best stretch of pitching ever, and it's not easy to assume he can sustain it. Heaton is eligible for free agency and could generate some interest, especially since he can both start and relieve. The Pirates wouldn't mind having him back.

NEAL HEATON

Position: RP/SP
Bats: L **Throws:** L
Ht: 6' 1" **Wt:** 195

Opening Day Age: 30
Born: 3/3/60 in Jamaica, NY
ML Seasons: 8

Overall Statistics

	W	L	ERA	G	GS	Sv	IP	H	R	BB	SO	HR
1989	6	7	3.05	42	18	0	147.1	127	55	55	67	12
Career	61	83	4.46	260	177	10	1223.1	1297	661	431	551	129

Where They Hit the Ball

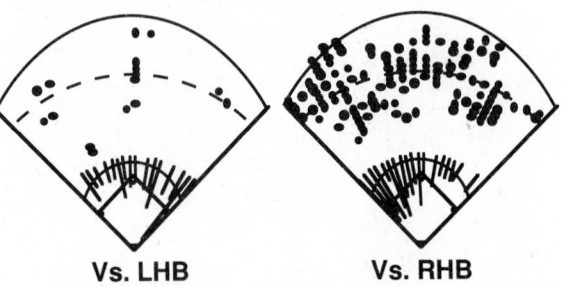

Vs. LHB   **Vs. RHB**

1989 Situational Stats

	W	L	ERA	Sv	IP		AB	H	HR	RBI	AVG
Home	2	4	2.52	0	75.0	LHB	117	16	0	4	.137
Road	4	3	3.61	0	72.1	RHB	427	111	12	47	.260
Day	1	2	3.76	0	40.2	Sc Pos	154	33	2	37	.214
Night	5	5	2.78	0	106.2	Clutch	49	12	1	5	.245

1989 Rankings (National League)

➤ 1st in lowest batting average allowed vs. lefthanded batters (.137) - *pitchers facing 125 LHB*

➤ 8th in hit batsmen (6)

➤ Led the Pirates in balks (5) and lowest batting average allowed vs. lefthanded batters

HITTING:

Great expectations have been placed on Jeff King since the day he left the University of Arkansas. The Pirates made King the first pick in the June 1986 amateur draft and expected him to eventually become one of the premier players in the game. King did not even get to Class AAA until 1989. However, he didn't stay there long as the Pirates called him up in June. Still, his development has taken longer than the Pirates had hoped.

Once he got to the majors, King began to show flashes of being the bomber the Pirates were looking for. King hit just .195 in 75 games. However, 21 of his 42 hits were for extra bases, including five home runs. Though the righthanded hitter saw a majority of his action against lefties, all five of his homers came off righthanders. A blast off Montreal's Kevin Gross to dead centerfield at Three Rivers Stadium in August was estimated to have traveled 429 feet. King does not get cheated when he is at the plate. He swings hard and hits rockets. Like many young hitters, good breaking pitches can fool him but he has a pretty good idea of what to do at the plate. He makes contact well for a young power hitter.

BASERUNNING:

King has average speed, good enough that he can be used on hit-and-run plays. He can get from first to third on singles to the right. King stole only 19 bases in the minors but did manage four in limited duty with the Pirates last season.

FIELDING:

King was drafted as a third baseman but his future there is cloudy. He underwent shoulder surgery following the '88 season and his arm may not recover enough to be able to take the daily grind of making long throws across the infield. King has seen most of his major league action at first, a position he's still learning. He also played both second base and shortstop and performed adequately, though he probably couldn't handle those positions on a regular basis.

OVERALL:

Quietly, some members of the Pirates' organization thought they had made a mistake in choosing King with the first pick in the '86 draft. He's taken longer to develop than expected but, has shown signs of improvement as he got closer to the big leagues. He may not reach the superstar level, but he should become a quality regular player in the major leagues.

JEFF KING

Position: 1B/3B
Bats: R **Throws:** R
Ht: 6' 1" **Wt:** 175

Opening Day Age: 25
Born: 12/26/64 in Marion, IN
ML Seasons: 1

Overall Statistics

	G	AB	R	H	D	T	HR	RBI	SB	BB	SO	AVG
1989	75	215	31	42	13	3	5	19	4	20	34	.195
Career	75	215	31	42	13	3	5	19	4	20	34	.195

Where He Hits the Ball

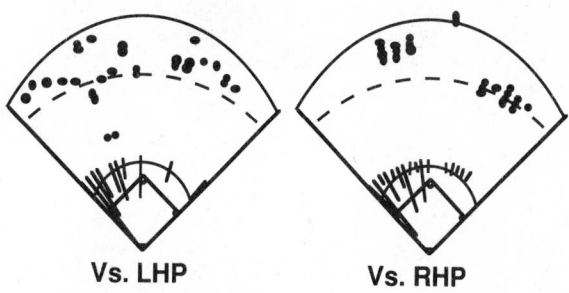

Vs. LHP   Vs. RHP

1989 Situational Stats

	AB	H	HR	RBI	AVG		AB	H	HR	RBI	AVG
Home	119	22	3	10	.185	LHP	112	22	0	8	.196
Road	96	20	2	9	.208	RHP	103	20	5	11	.194
Day	58	11	2	5	.190	Sc Pos	50	9	0	12	.180
Night	157	31	3	14	.197	Clutch	42	11	2	5	.262

1989 Rankings (National League)

➡ 3rd in percentage of extra bases taken as a runner (61.4%) - *players with 40 opportunities to advance*

➡ 5th in worst batting average vs. lefthanded pitchers (.196) - *batters with 125 PA vs. LHP*

➡ Led the Pirates in percentage of extra bases taken as a runner

PITCHING:

Bob Kipper has gone from being a promising rookie lefthanded starter to being sent to the minors to being a reliever. And he still won't turn 26 until July. After he'd struggled for two years in a starting role, the Pirates moved him to the pen in 1988, and Kipper has turned his career in the right direction.

Kipper has become the Pirates' main lefthanded reliever the past two seasons, making 102 appearances, and he has grown into the role. In '88, he was used mainly to get lefthanders out. Last year, he was left in the game to face righthanders, too. By the end of the season, he was closing out games. As a starter, Kipper was always haunted by home run balls, yielding 25 in only 110.2 innings in 1987. However, he cut back on the gopher balls last season, allowing only five in 83 innings.

The main reason for Kipper's success is that, like so many of the Pirates, he has learned to master the change-up. That change of pace dissuades hitters from sitting on his hard stuff. It complements Kipper's fastball, which he cuts, and his slider. Kipper has also helped himself by keeping the ball down in the strike zone. When he was younger, he had the tendency to get pitches up and they often wound up in the bleachers. Kipper's confidence was somewhat shaken by his early struggles as a starter. However, he has flourished as a reliever and rarely lets the pressure of pitching in a tight game bother him.

FIELDING, HITTING, BASERUNNING:

Kipper is an average fielder. He has improved at holding runners, mainly because he pitches almost exclusively from the stretch position now that he is a reliever. He can occasionally pick a napping runner off. Kipper swings and hopes the ball hits his bat. He is a career .138 hitter. He drove in one run last season to double his career total. Kipper shows pretty good speed when he gets on base, but the opportunities are rare.

OVERALL:

Bob Kipper was rushed to the major leagues by the California Angels before he was even old enough to go into a bar and order a drink. He went through some very rough stretches early in his career, but never gave in. Since being moved to relief duty, he has shown great improvement. Down the road, he will likely become a starter again.

BOB KIPPER

Position: RP
Bats: R **Throws:** L
Ht: 6' 2" **Wt:** 175

Opening Day Age: 25
Born: 7/8/64 in Aurora, IL
ML Seasons: 5

Overall Statistics

	W	L	ERA	G	GS	Sv	IP	H	R	BB	SO	HR
1989	3	4	2.93	52	0	4	83.0	55	29	33	58	5
Career	17	30	4.49	153	44	4	400.2	377	220	155	274	59

Where They Hit the Ball

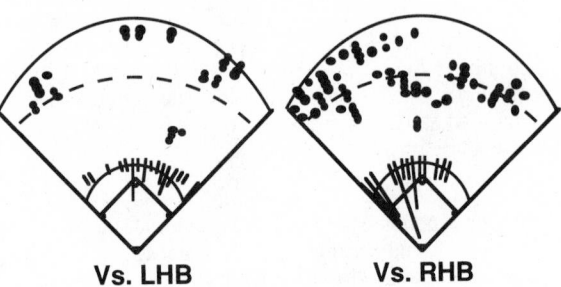

Vs. LHB   **Vs. RHB**

1989 Situational Stats

	W	L	ERA	Sv	IP		AB	H	HR	RBI	AVG
Home	2	0	1.85	1	39.0	LHB	94	16	0	8	.170
Road	1	4	3.89	3	44.0	RHB	199	39	5	20	.196
Day	2	3	3.14	4	43.0	Sc Pos	69	15	1	22	.217
Night	1	1	2.70	0	40.0	Clutch	121	19	2	9	.157

1989 Rankings (National League)

➡ 3rd in first batter efficiency (.125) - *pitchers with 40 relief games*

➡ 8th in lowest percentage of inherited runners scoring (27.3%) - *pitchers with 30 inheritied runners*

➡ 9th in holds (12)

➡ Led the Pirates in first batter efficiency, lowest percentage of inherited runners scoring and blown saves (4)

PITCHING:

Randy Kramer was very good at times during his 1989 rookie year. He was also very bad at times. In his third start, Kramer took a no-hitter into the eighth inning in Cincinnati before Ron Oester's two-out double broke it up. He settled for a one-hit shutout. Things were never quite the same after that, though. Following the one-hitter, Pirates manager Jim Leyland decided to make Kramer the closer in an effort to plug a gaping hole in his injured and ineffective bullpen. Kramer failed in that role and finished out the year by splitting time between starting, long relief and middle relief.

Kramer has a live arm and can crank his fastball up into the mid-90s. That is his bread-and-butter pitch, though he also throws a slider, a curve and a change. What holds Kramer back from being a good pitcher is his inability to throw strikes. He continually killed himself with walks, particularly to the leadoff batters of innings. Kramer also struggles to establish his first pitch for a strike. He falls behind in the count and is forced to lay the fastball down the middle. Those problems caused him to get to the seventh inning in just three of his 15 starts. The control problems unnerve Kramer at times. He tries to muscle up on the fastball and it winds up sailing even farther out of the strike zone. Thus, he often becomes his own worst enemy.

FIELDING, HITTING, BASERUNNING:

Kramer is an adequate fielder who did not commit an error last season. He needs more work at holding runners on. At the plate, Randy kind of flails away, but will occasionally slap a hit the other way. He was five for 33 last season. He has problems getting the bunt down, though. Kramer, a good athlete, is quick and runs the bases well. He was the only Pirate pitcher to steal a base last season and was called on as a pinch runner.

OVERALL:

Randy Kramer can blow people away with his fastball. However, controlling that heat is a different matter. Kramer never had a professional earned run average below 4.38 until 1988, yet his great arm always kept getting him chances. In his first full shot at the majors in '89, Kramer had mixed success. He is 29 years old, though, and has to produce now if he's going to stick around much longer.

RANDY KRAMER

Position: RP/SP
Bats: R **Throws:** R
Ht: 6' 2" **Wt:** 180

Opening Day Age: 29
Born: 9/20/60 in Palo Alto, CA
ML Seasons: 2

Overall Statistics

	W	L	ERA	G	GS	Sv	IP	H	R	BB	SO	HR
1989	5	9	3.96	35	15	2	111.1	90	53	61	52	10
Career	6	11	4.08	40	16	2	121.1	102	59	62	59	11

Where They Hit the Ball

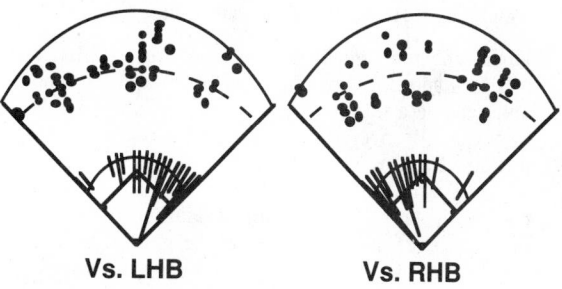

Vs. LHB   Vs. RHB

1989 Situational Stats

	W	L	ERA	Sv	IP		AB	H	HR	RBI	AVG
Home	2	4	4.66	2	48.1	LHB	220	50	6	30	.227
Road	3	5	3.43	0	63.0	RHB	181	40	4	17	.221
Day	1	4	3.33	0	46.0	Sc Pos	112	26	3	37	.232
Night	4	5	4.41	2	65.1	Clutch	81	24	2	11	.296

1989 Rankings (National League)

- ➡ 3rd in hit batsmen (7)
- ➡ Led the Pirates in hit batsmen, blown saves (4) and most GDPs induced per GDP situation (11.6%) - *team pitchers with 30 GDP situations*

PITCHING:

Bill Landrum came out of obscurity to become perhaps the Pirates' most valuable player in 1989. Landrum was signed as a six-year, minor-league free agent prior to spring training and surprisingly made the club. However, he was sent to the minors two weeks later. Three weeks after that, Landrum was back in the big leagues and never went back down.

Of course, it's hard to send down a guy who leads your club in saves and gives up just over two earned runs a month. With Jim Gott injured and Jeff Robinson ineffective, the Pirates' bullpen cried for a hammer and Landrum stepped into the breach. At one point, he converted 15 save opportunities in a row. He failed to allow an earned run in 22 straight appearances that covered 37 innings. All this from a fellow who had compiled a less than impressive 5.16 career ERA while spending parts of the previous three seasons with the Cincinnati Reds and Chicago Cubs.

Under the tutelage of Pirates' pitching coach Ray Miller, Landrum learned a change-up and curveball and became a totally different pitcher. That enabled him to finally overcome the rap of having good stuff but no idea how to use it. Prior to coming to Pittsburgh, Landrum relied strictly on his fastball, which can reach the mid-90s. Once he learned to mix the breaking stuff in with his heater, he got hitters completely off balance and became a dominant closer.

FIELDING, HITTING, BASERUNNING:

Landrum fields his position adequately and handles bunts well. He also showed the ability to hold runners on, though few got on base against him last season. As a short reliever, Landrum rarely bats. He never had to worry about testing his bad knee on the basepaths as he did not get on all season.

OVERALL:

It seems like someone comes out of the woodwork every season to become a major surprise. Last year, it was Landrum. As bad as the Pirates finished, going 74-88, pity the thought of where they may have ended if not for Landrum's emergence. He established himself as a top-flight closer and could provide the Pirates with a pleasant problem in 1990. Should Gott return from his elbow surgery, the Pirates will have two hammers in the bullpen.

BILL LANDRUM

Position: RP
Bats: R **Throws:** R
Ht: 6' 2" **Wt:** 185

Opening Day Age: 32
Born: 8/17/57 in Columbia, SC
ML Seasons: 4

Overall Statistics

	W	L	ERA	G	GS	Sv	IP	H	R	BB	SO	HR
1989	2	3	1.67	56	0	26	81.0	60	18	28	51	2
Career	6	5	3.51	117	2	28	171.2	170	72	69	113	6

Where They Hit the Ball

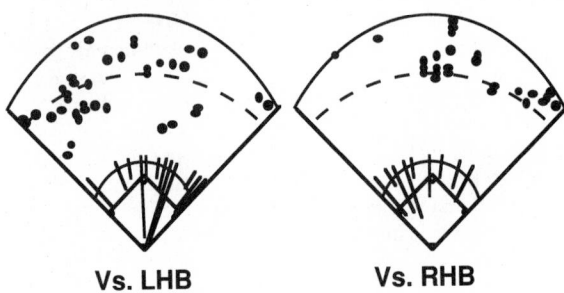

Vs. LHB   **Vs. RHB**

1989 Situational Stats

	W	L	ERA	Sv	IP		AB	H	HR	RBI	AVG
Home	1	2	2.75	11	36.0	LHB	159	28	0	8	.176
Road	1	1	0.80	15	45.0	RHB	133	32	2	17	.241
Day	0	2	2.30	9	31.1	Sc Pos	79	19	0	21	.241
Night	2	1	1.27	17	49.2	Clutch	199	38	1	18	.191

1989 Rankings (National League)

- ⇒ 2nd in save percentage (89.7%) - *pitchers with 20 save opportunities*
- ⇒ 3rd in lowest batting average allowed vs. lefthanded pitchers (.176) - *pitchers facing 125 LHB*
- ⇒ 6th in saves (26)
- ⇒ 8th in save opportunities (29)
- ⇒ Led the Pirates in games (56), games finished (40), saves, save opportunities and save percentage

HITTING:

Mike LaValliere has limitations as a hitter, but he lives within them quite well. The stocky catcher has little power and is no threat to beat out an infield hit. However, he has a good eye and makes contact. LaValliere had the reputation of being a pull hitter in his first few seasons, but he's becoming adept at taking the pitch the other way. He is becoming a master at dumping singles the opposite way into short left field.

LaValliere hit a career-high .316 in 1989, including a .325 mark after missing more than two months following knee surgery. The only drawback is that just 12 of his 60 hits were for extra bases. LaValliere is a good fastball hitter. Though he has increasingly begun to go the other way, he can still pull low fastballs. On rare occasions, he will take one out of the park. Breaking balls give him some trouble, but he can usually fight them off until he gets a pitch to his liking.

A lefthanded hitter, LaValliere almost never plays when a fellow lefty pitches. LaValliere would be the ideal Number 2 hitter in a batting order because of his ability to make contact and his knowledge of situational hitting. However, his lack of speed forces him to hit lower in the order where he can still do damage because of good clutch-hitting abilities.

BASERUNNING:

In 1988, LaValliere bragged about joining the 2-2 club -- two home runs and two stolen bases in the same year. Mike is among the slowest runners in the game and his latest knee surgery, the third, has slowed him even more. LaValliere clearly understands his limitations on the bases and rarely runs himself into an out.

FIELDING:

Pirate pitchers love to pitch to LaValliere. He presents a low, steady target and has an uncanny sense of knowing the right pitch to call in every situation. Mike has a good arm and emerges from the crouch in a hurry, with a quick release. However, he had a poor year throwing out baserunners in 1989, catching only 17.7% of them. He is fearless blocking the plate. A Gold Glove winner in 1987, he's clearly one of baseball's best defensive catchers.

OVERALL:

It has been suggested that LaValliere would make a good manager when his playing days are over. That is a testament to his knowledge of and feel for the game. He is a solid, if unspectacular, hitter, and outstanding defensively. It is no coincidence that the Pirates' pitching staff seemed to come together last year once LaValliere returned from the disabled list.

MIKE LAVALLIERE

Position: C
Bats: L **Throws:** R
Ht: 5' 9" **Wt:** 190

Opening Day Age: 29
Born: 8/18/60 in Charlotte, NC
ML Seasons: 6

Overall Statistics

	G	AB	R	H	D	T	HR	RBI	SB	BB	SO	AVG
1989	68	190	15	60	10	0	2	23	0	29	24	.316
Career	437	1226	92	330	58	2	8	142	3	167	132	.269

Where He Hits the Ball

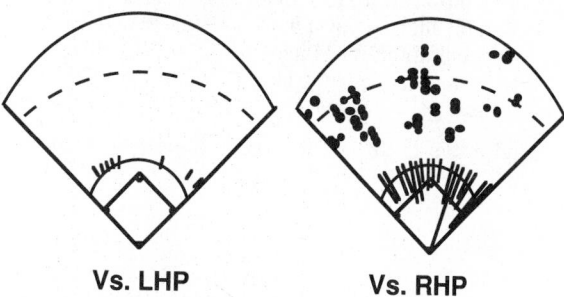

Vs. LHP   **Vs. RHP**

1989 Situational Stats

	AB	H	HR	RBI	AVG		AB	H	HR	RBI	AVG
Home	98	37	2	16	.378	LHP	25	7	0	2	.280
Road	92	23	0	7	.250	RHP	165	53	2	21	.321
Day	67	17	0	7	.254	Sc Pos	61	16	1	22	.262
Night	123	43	2	16	.350	Clutch	26	8	1	5	.308

1989 Rankings (National League)

- ➡ 1st in lowest percentage of extra bases taken as a runner (20.0%) - *players with 40 opportunities to advance*
- ➡ 2nd worst catcher throwing out base stealers (17.7%) - *catchers with 75 attempts*
- ➡ 3rd in hitting on a 3-2 count (.409) - *players with 20 PA on a 3-2 count*
- ➡ Led the Pirates in hitting on a 3-2 count
- ➡ Led NL Catchers in hitting on a 3-2 count

HITTING:

Like the team he plays for, Jose Lind's performance dropped from 1988 to 1989. Lind hit .322 in a late-season trial with the Pirates in 1987 and followed that with a solid .262 mark in 1988, his first full major league season. However, Lind battled a season-long slump in 1989 and finished with a .232 average. It got so bad that he was removed from his familiar second slot in the batting order in August and dropped to the bottom of the order.

Lind is an effective second-place hitter when things are going well. He takes the ball the other way and is outstanding at making contact on the hit-and-run. If he would improve his bunting skills, Lind could be even more help hitting behind the leadoff man. Lind's primary problem comes from being overly concerned with going to the opposite field. Though he is capable, Lind almost refuses to turn on a ball. When he does, he can hit doubles down the left-field line and add an occasional home run. Pitchers will jam Lind inside with hard stuff, knowing he will not try to pull. That often results in lazy pop flies for easy outs.

Lind drove in 48 runs last year despite his batting problems. He has the potential to drive in 65 or more if he can get his average up.

BASERUNNING:

Lind is aggressive on the bases and will take the extra base when it is there. He is also an intelligent base stealer and picks his spots well. He was successful on his first 15 attempts last season before Chicago's Joe Girardi caught him in his final try. If he increases his batting average, his stolen base total should rise proportionately.

FIELDING:

Lind seemed primed to be a Gold Glove winner after a sparkling first full year. However, this part of his game also slipped last season. Lind came to spring training overweight and then underwent arthroscopic surgery to remove bone chips in his elbow after one exhibition game. Whether it was the weight or the injuries Lind seemed tentative in all stages of defense. In all, Lind committed 18 errors and did not approach his acrobatics of 1988.

OVERALL:

Lind slipped badly in 1989 after looking like a future star in '88. He seemed to rest on his laurels and showed up for spring training out of shape. Lind is only 25, though, and should be able to bounce back if he makes the mental and physical adjustments.

JOSE LIND

Position: 2B
Bats: R **Throws:** R
Ht: 5'11" **Wt:** 170

Opening Day Age: 25
Born: 5/1/64 in Toabaja, Puerto Rico
ML Seasons: 3

Overall Statistics

	G	AB	R	H	D	T	HR	RBI	SB	BB	SO	AVG
1989	153	578	52	134	21	3	2	48	15	39	64	.232
Career	342	1332	155	340	53	11	4	108	32	89	151	.255

Where He Hits the Ball

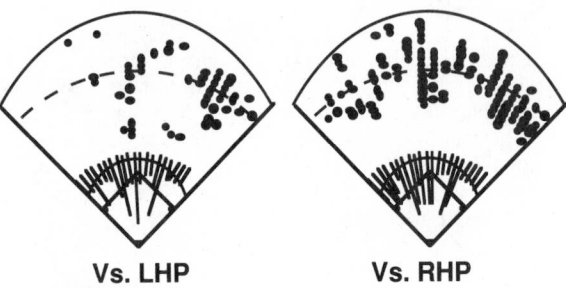

Vs. LHP   **Vs. RHP**

1989 Situational Stats

	AB	H	HR	RBI	AVG		AB	H	HR	RBI	AVG
Home	296	65	2	24	.220	LHP	195	50	1	21	.256
Road	282	69	0	24	.245	RHP	383	84	1	27	.219
Day	192	39	1	22	.203	Sc Pos	150	39	0	45	.260
Night	386	95	1	26	.246	Clutch	107	23	0	5	.215

1989 Rankings (National League)

→ 1st in worst hitting on a 3-1 count (.148 - *players with 10 PA*), worst hitting with the bases loaded (.000 - *players with 10 PA*) and worst slugging percentage vs. righthanded pitchers (.272) - *players with 377 PA vs. RHP*

→ 2nd in worst slugging percentage (.289)

→ 3rd in worst on on-base average vs. right-handed pitchers (.262) and worst home run frequency (289 ABs per HR) - *players with 502 PA*

→ Led the Pirates in singles (108), sacrifice bunts (13), GDPs (13), grounder/flyball ratio (1.66), bunts in play (18), lowest percentage of swings that missed (10.5%) and hitting on an 0-2 count (.227)

HITTING:

For a couple of years, the Pittsburgh Pirates had a good situation at catcher. Gold Glover Mike LaValliere would play against righthanders and right-handed hitting Junior Ortiz would start against lefties. The platoon role kept both players fresh, and each performed well on both offense and defense.

The Pirates felt Ortiz was such an important part of their club that they signed him to a two-year contract after the 1988 season, ensuring that he would not file for free agency. But things changed suddenly in the opening weeks of the season. LaValliere underwent knee surgery and was forced to the sidelines for over two months. Thrust into a more regular role, Ortiz struggled and wound up with a .217 average in a career-high 91 games. Though he was always a useful sub, Junior couldn't handle playing five times a week.

Until 1989, Ortiz had always been a fine hitter for the Bucs, though one with little power. From 1985 to 1988, Junior hit at least .271 every year, with a .336 mark in 110 at bats in '86. He was able to take the ball the other way, was good on the hit-and-run, and could come up with the clutch hit off a tough lefthander. However, Ortiz stopped hitting in '89, ending the year by going zero for 23. The Pirates became so disenchanted that they never put Ortiz in the starting lineup after Aug. 30. For the final month they went with journeyman Dann Bilardello, a September callup, as LaValliere's righthanded hitting complement.

BASERUNNING:

For a catcher, Ortiz runs decently but he is not a serious threat on the bases. He will usually go station-to-station on the bases and rarely will try to steal a base. Uncharacteristically, he made several mistakes while running the bases last season, costing the Pirates runs.

FIELDING:

Like his offense, Ortiz' defense declined in '89. He had trouble throwing out runners, got lackadaisical in blocking balls, and some pitchers privately complained about his handling of the staff. In previous seasons, Ortiz had rated high marks for his arm and calling of a game. The sudden dropoff of his skills was baffling.

OVERALL:

Seemingly overnight, Ortiz went from being a catcher coveted by catching-thin teams to a guy whose career may be in jeopardy. Ortiz, a big favorite in the clubhouse because of his willingness to be the butt of jokes and pranks, has one year remaining on a two-year contract. He will almost certainly be finishing the contract somewhere other than Pittsburgh.

JUNIOR ORTIZ

Position: C
Bats: R **Throws:** R
Ht: 5'11" **Wt:** 176

Opening Day Age: 30
Born: 10/24/59 in Humacao, Puerto Rico
ML Seasons: 8

Overall Statistics

	G	AB	R	H	D	T	HR	RBI	SB	BB	SO	AVG
1989	91	230	16	50	6	1	1	22	2	20	20	.217
Career	407	1021	73	262	37	2	5	104	6	66	134	.257

Where He Hits the Ball

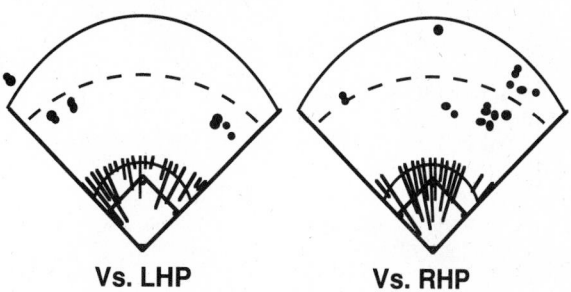

Vs. LHP   **Vs. RHP**

1989 Situational Stats

	AB	H	HR	RBI	AVG		AB	H	HR	RBI	AVG
Home	117	29	0	16	.248	LHP	97	21	1	8	.216
Road	113	21	1	6	.186	RHP	133	29	0	14	.218
Day	65	15	1	8	.231	Sc Pos	63	14	1	20	.222
Night	165	35	0	14	.212	Clutch	53	11	0	5	.208

1989 Rankings (National League)

➡ 3rd worst catcher throwing out base-stealers (23.7%) - *catchers with 75 attempts*

HITTING:

Gary Redus has the potential to make something happen every time he steps to the plate. He is a line-drive hitter who has the ability to hit for extra bases because of his outstanding speed. At the same time, he has enough pop in his bat to hit an occasional homer. Redus filled in ably for the Pirates in the outfield and at first base last year, producing career highs in batting average (.283), on-base average (.372) and slugging percentage (.462).

Used primarily as a leadoff man through most of his career, Redus may have benefitted from the fact that the Pirates usually batted him lower in the order. Gary had always produced in the number one spot, stealing bases and scoring runs, but people constantly pressured him to change his hitting style. They wanted him to slap groundballs and bunt for base hits, using his speed. But Redus is a notorious flyball hitter, and has found it difficult, if not impossible, to change his hitting style.

Last year the Pirates batted Redus primarily in the fifth and sixth spots. Free to hit his own way, Redus batted .310 in those two slots, with good power. Batting first or second, he hit only .189. Pitchers can get Redus out by keeping the ball low and away, and he has trouble with lefty breaking ballers. But Redus is a patient hitter who will make the pitcher throw strikes.

BASERUNNING:

Despite his age (33), Redus still has great speed and remains one of the best percentage stealers in the majors (81% for his career). He is one of the game's top baserunners as well. Redus accelerates quickly, goes from first to third on any single hit to center or right and scores from first on just about any double.

FIELDING:

Primarily an outfielder, Redus saw the majority of his action at first base last year when Sid Bream reinjured his knee. Redus adjusted to the position adequately, making the routine plays. He's a little shaky on bunts. He is better in the outfield, where he can use his great speed. Runners can take liberties on his throwing arm, however.

OVERALL:

Redus was one of the Pirates' most valuable players in 1989, hitting well and filling in ably at a foreign position. A consummate professional, he never complains and provides a steadying veteran influence in the clubhouse. Used properly and freed to hit his own way, Redus is a player of considerable value.

GARY REDUS

Position: 1B
Bats: R **Throws:** R
Ht: 6' 1" **Wt:** 185

Opening Day Age: 33
Born: 11/1/56 in Athens, AL
ML Seasons: 8

Overall Statistics

	G	AB	R	H	D	T	HR	RBI	SB	BB	SO	AVG
1989	98	279	42	79	18	7	6	33	25	40	51	.283
Career	794	2603	458	650	136	39	68	260	279	376	545	.250

Where He Hits the Ball

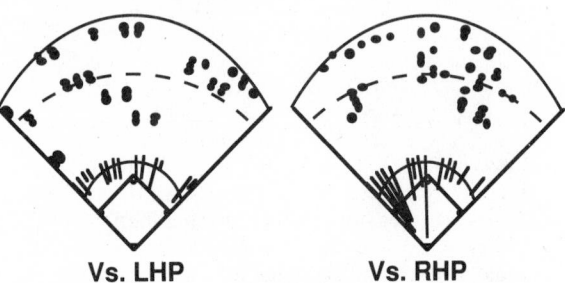

Vs. LHP   **Vs. RHP**

1989 Situational Stats

	AB	H	HR	RBI	AVG		AB	H	HR	RBI	AVG
Home	137	38	3	16	.277	LHP	113	33	3	15	.292
Road	142	41	3	17	.289	RHP	166	46	3	18	.277
Day	93	26	3	16	.280	Sc Pos	69	19	3	27	.275
Night	186	53	3	17	.285	Clutch	61	19	3	6	.311

1989 Rankings (National League)

- ➡ 2nd in hitting on a 3-1 count (.615) - *players with 10 PA on a 3-1 count*
- ➡ 6th in slugging percentage vs. lefthanded pitchers (.558) - *players 125 PA vs. LHP*
- ➡ 8th in stolen base percentage (80.6%) - *players with 20 stolen base attempts*
- ➡ 9th in triples (7)
- ➡ Led the Pirates in hitting on a 3-1 count
- ➡ Led NL First Basemen in stolen bases (25), stolen base percentage, steals of third (2) and hitting on a 3-1 count

HITTING:

R.J. Reynolds admits to being a hacker. The switch-hitter goes to the plate looking to swing the bat and loves to jump on the first offering. The book on Reynolds for a long time was that he was a much better hitter from the left side. That changed a bit last season as Reynolds batted .284 from the right side, compared to .263 while hitting lefthanded. However, five of Reynolds' six home runs came while batting lefty.

Reynolds is a contact hitter, though he will occasionally hit the long ball. He is most effective when he tries to hit the ball into the gap and use his speed. He feasts on balls up in the strike zone, particularly fastballs. However, pitchers can sometimes work Reynolds up the ladder with fastballs, getting him to swing at helmet-high pitches. Reynolds is a decent breaking ball hitter lefthanded, but struggles with the off-speed when batting righty. Though not a big RBI guy, Reynolds seems to have a knack for coming up with the big hit in the right situation. He likes pressure situations and can produce as a pinch hitter. R.J. has 16 pinch-hit RBIs over the past two seasons.

BASERUNNING:

Reynolds has above average speed and knows how to use it as a weapon. He reads pitchers well and senses when the time is most opportune to steal. Reynolds is an aggressive man on the bases and accelerates well from first to third and second to home. He will go in hard at second base and has no qualms about a collision at the plate on close plays.

FIELDING:

Reynolds plays all three outfield spots in his role as the fourth outfielder. He is steady at all three. His good speed enables him to get to fly balls in the gaps, and he will not shy away from fences. R.J. has a strong, but erratic, arm. His throwing problems stem from inconsistent release points that can cause the ball to sink or sail on him.

OVERALL:

Though he has never reached the stardom once predicted for him, Reynolds has become a very competent major league role player. He is reliable in all phases of the game. Reynolds yearns to be an everyday player, but his upbeat attitude helps him accept his situation.

R.J. REYNOLDS

Position: RF/CF
Bats: B **Throws:** R
Ht: 6' 0" **Wt:** 180

Opening Day Age: 29
Born: 4/19/60 in Sacramento, CA
ML Seasons: 7

Overall Statistics

	G	AB	R	H	D	T	HR	RBI	SB	BB	SO	AVG
1989	125	363	45	98	16	2	6	48	22	34	66	.270
Career	691	2055	263	543	111	16	35	275	97	167	384	.264

Where He Hits the Ball

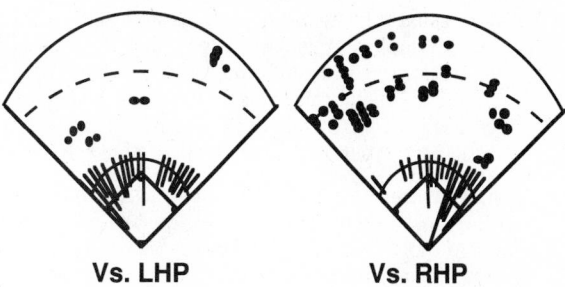

Vs. LHP   **Vs. RHP**

1989 Situational Stats

	AB	H	HR	RBI	AVG		AB	H	HR	RBI	AVG
Home	204	61	3	27	.299	LHP	116	33	1	11	.284
Road	159	37	3	21	.233	RHP	247	65	5	37	.263
Day	132	43	4	19	.326	Sc Pos	106	28	1	38	.264
Night	231	55	2	29	.238	Clutch	86	25	0	7	.291

1989 Rankings (National League)

➡ 7th in stolen base percentage (81.5%) - *players with 20 stolen base attempts*

➡ 10th in steals of third (5)

➡ Led the Pirates in GDPs (13) and stolen base percentage

➡ Led NL Right Fielders in stolen base percentage and steals of third

PITCHING:

Long an outstanding middle reliever, Jeff Robinson had always been considered a potentially outstanding closer who'd never been given a chance. Robinson got that chance last year when Jim Gott went out for the season, but he did not seize the opportunity. Jeff was hit hard in late relief and lost the job by late May. Eventually put in the starting rotation, Robinson did reasonably well. As a starter last year, Robinson was 5-7 with a respectable 3.53 ERA. In relief, his ERA was a hideous 7.32.

Robinson's failure as a closer was mystifying, because he'd been one of the game's top set-up men in both San Francisco and Pittsburgh. He certainly has the stuff to succeed. Robinson's best pitch is a nasty split-finger fastball that can drop nearly a foot when it enters the strike zone. To be effective with it, Robinson must throw it just slightly slower than his straight fastball. Last year he pressed and threw the splitter too hard in crucial situations, and the result was a total loss of effectiveness. Moved into the starting rotation, he relaxed and his pitches began working again. Robinson even dusted off an old curveball he had put on the shelf back in high school.

Though he didn't do badly as a starter, Robinson's future almost certainly is back in the bullpen. He didn't go more than seven innings in any of his 19 starts and was markedly less effective after he'd thrown only 45 pitches, about three innings worth. That sort of durability always served Robinson perfectly as a set-up man. Jeff led National League firemen in relief innings in both '87 and '88 while working a whopping 156 games. A real bullpen workhorse, Robinson has said he would relish the opportunity to pitch one inning in all 162 games some season.

FIELDING, HITTING, BASERUNNING:

Robinson has some problems as a fielder, particularly on wild pickoff throws. He did not hold baserunners well last year, either, perhaps because of his pitching problems; Robinson has been very effective at stopping the running game in the past. He was surprising as a hitter, leading all Pirates' pitchers with a .229 average and homering off David Cone. Robinson knows what he's doing on the basepaths.

OVERALL:

Robinson became a starter last year out of necessity, but he should be back in the bullpen in 1990. More than likely, Jeff will return to his familiar set-up role. And also more than likely, Robinson will handle that role effectively once again.

JEFF ROBINSON

Position: RP/SP
Bats: R **Throws:** R
Ht: 6' 4" **Wt:** 200

Opening Day Age: 29
Born: 12/13/60 in Santa Ana, CA
ML Seasons: 6

Overall Statistics

	W	L	ERA	G	GS	Sv	IP	H	R	BB	SO	HR
1989	7	13	4.58	50	19	4	141.1	161	92	59	95	14
Career	39	45	3.80	312	53	35	677.2	666	335	246	483	53

Where They Hit the Ball

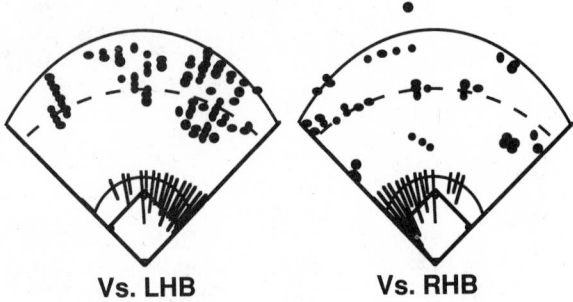

Vs. LHB   **Vs. RHB**

1989 Situational Stats

	W	L	ERA	Sv	IP		AB	H	HR	RBI	AVG
Home	3	6	4.16	2	62.2	LHB	307	81	5	39	.264
Road	4	7	4.92	2	78.2	RHB	262	80	9	46	.305
Day	4	5	3.12	3	60.2	Sc Pos	182	47	4	72	.258
Night	3	8	5.69	1	80.2	Clutch	119	37	3	24	.311

1989 Rankings (National League)

➡ 3rd in wild pitches (14)
➡ 8th in losses (13)
➡ 10th in stolen bases allowed (25)
➡ Led the Pirates in wild pitches, losses and blown saves (4)

JOHN SMILEY

Position: SP
Bats: L **Throws:** L
Ht: 6' 4" **Wt:** 195

Opening Day Age: 25
Born: 3/17/65 in Phoenixville, PA
ML Seasons: 4

PITCHING:

In just his third major league season, John Smiley continued to establish himself as one of the game's up-and-coming lefthanded starting pitchers. Smiley has risen rapidly since struggling to a 5-5 record with a 5.76 ERA as a reliever in 1987, his first full season. Since moving into the rotation at the start of 1988, he is 25-19 with a 3.20 ERA.

Smiley has all of the ingredients necessary to be a big winner. For openers, he has a live fastball that easily reaches the 90s. He then has a big breaking pitch, a hard slider that moves. He complements those pitches with a change-up that has improved dramatically. Smiley will now throw the change to anyone on any count, keeping hitters off guard.

Smiley, who will also throw an occasional curve just to make hitters think, delivers his pitches from a rather awkward motion. That makes his pitches harder to pick up. Smiley also exhibits outstanding control for such a young pitcher. He has allowed just over two walks per nine innings in his two seasons as a starter. Smiley can also get the strikeout when necessary, though he will just as gladly take a fly out or ground out.

There may be a slight question about Smiley's durability. The eight complete games may have taken a toll on his left elbow last season. He missed three starts in early September then called it a year with 10 days remaining in the season. One day after the season concluded, he underwent arthroscopic surgery to remove bone chips from the elbow.

FIELDING, HITTING AND BASERUNNING:

The gangly Smiley is anything but smooth defensively, but he makes the plays. His somewhat slow delivery allows runners to get a decent jump. However, he is improving his pickoff move and had more success keeping runners close last season. Smiley hits some shots in batting practice but it rarely translates in game situations; his lifetime batting average is .111. He takes it one base at a time when he gets on.

OVERALL:

Smiley will be only 25 years old when the 1990 season opens so he should get even better. He has great stuff, outstanding control and a tenacious attitude. The elbow surgery raises a small caution flag but the Pirates are confident Smiley will have a quick and full recovery. If he does, he has the potential to be a big winner for a long time.

Overall Statistics

	W	L	ERA	G	GS	Sv	IP	H	R	BB	SO	HR
1989	12	8	2.81	28	28	0	205.1	174	78	49	123	22
Career	31	24	3.46	137	60	4	497.0	432	214	149	319	46

Where They Hit the Ball

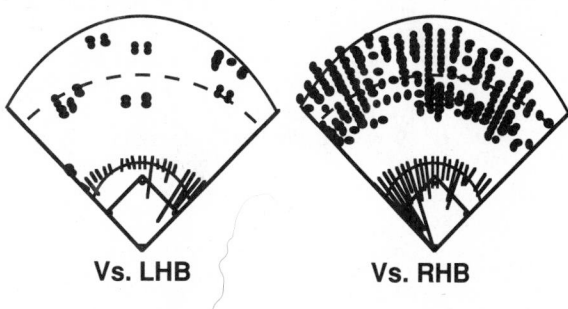

Vs. LHB   **Vs. RHB**

1989 Situational Stats

	W	L	ERA	Sv	IP		AB	H	HR	RBI	AVG
Home	8	4	2.64	0	109.0	LHB	103	25	1	7	.243
Road	4	4	2.99	0	96.1	RHB	667	149	21	64	.223
Day	5	4	2.94	0	82.2	Sc Pos	148	34	5	50	.230
Night	7	4	2.71	0	122.2	Clutch	103	24	5	12	.233

1989 Rankings (National League)

➡ 3rd in home runs allowed (22) and lowest grounder/flyball ratio (.77) - *pitchers with 162 IP*

➡ 4th in stolen bases allowed (29) and most HRs allowed per 9 innings (.96)

➡ 5th in lowest on-base average allowed (.273) and highest stolen base percentage allowed (76.3%)

➡ Led the Pirates in complete games (8), home runs allowed, strikeouts (123), stolen bases allowed, win/loss percentage (.600), lowest batting average allowed (.226), lowest on-base average allowed, lowest slugging percentage allowed (.349) and stikeouts per 9 innings (5.4) - *team pitchers with 162 IP*

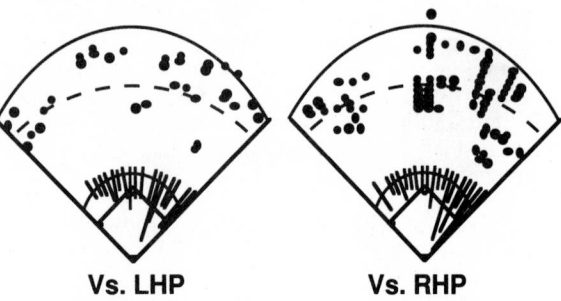

STRONG ARM

HITTING:

Few players saw their offensive statistics fall off more dramatically in 1989 than Andy Van Slyke. He went from a .288 average with 25 home runs and 100 RBIs in 1988 to .237, nine and 53 in '89. Injuries played a key role in the dropoff. A strained rib cage muscle in mid-April forced Van Slyke out of action for a month, and he also suffered shoulder and knee problems.

When he is right, Van Slyke is one of the top offensive threats in the league. He's an aggressive hitter who will strike out a lot, but he's made up for that with his powerful production. Van Slyke's biggest drawback has been his inability to hit lefthanders (.208 lifetime through 1988). Van Slyke did better against southpaws in 1989 (.247), but he's still often overpowered by lefties' hard stuff, and will take weak, one-handed swings on off-speed pitches outside.

Van Slyke makes up for that -- or did until 1989 -- with his success against righties. Prior to last year, about the only success a righty had against Van Slyke was by painting the outside corner with fastballs. He murdered anything else. Andy's problems against righties in '89 were undoubtedly injury-related; he simply couldn't turn and pull a good fastball. Van Slyke is an adept drag bunter and can leg bunt singles on occasion.

BASERUNNING:

From the moment his bat meets the ball, Van Slyke is thinking extra bases. He charges out of the batter's box and looks for a triple on any ball hit into the gap. Van Slyke is also a prime base-stealing threat when healthy. He reads pitchers well and uses his outstanding speed to full advantage.

FIELDING:

Injuries hampered Van Slyke in the field during 1989, but there is no better defensive centerfielder in the game. Van Slyke can track down any ball hit into the gap. He comes in and goes back on balls equally well. And his arm is a howitzer, both strong and accurate. Van Slyke has a sixth sense about playing centerfield and always seems to make the right play at the right time.

OVERALL:

After establishing himself as a superstar in 1988, Van Slyke suffered through a terribly frustrating year in 1989. As he put it, he could never get into the "Andy Van Slyke mode" because of his injuries. With a winter of rest and recovery, there is no reason to believe Van Slyke will not return to his old form again.

ANDY
VAN SLYKE

Position: CF
Bats: L **Throws:** R
Ht: 6' 2" **Wt:** 190

Opening Day Age: 29
Born: 12/21/60 in Utica, NY
ML Seasons: 7

Overall Statistics

	G	AB	R	H	D	T	HR	RBI	SB	BB	SO	AVG
1989	130	476	64	113	18	9	9	53	16	47	100	.237
Career	962	3139	463	839	156	57	96	439	184	363	622	.267

Where He Hits the Ball

Vs. LHP   Vs. RHP

1989 Situational Stats

	AB	H	HR	RBI	AVG		AB	H	HR	RBI	AVG
Home	216	46	4	22	.213	LHP	162	40	1	19	.247
Road	260	67	5	31	.258	RHP	314	73	8	34	.232
Day	154	41	4	21	.266	Sc Pos	113	31	1	40	.274
Night	322	72	5	32	.224	Clutch	96	19	1	10	.198

1989 Rankings (National League)

- ➤ 3rd in triples (9)
- ➤ 5th in percentage of extra bases taken as a runner (61.0%) - *players with 40 opportunities to advance*
- ➤ 6th in pitches seen per plate appearance (3.8)
- ➤ Led the Pirates in strikeouts (100), hit by pitch (3), GDPs (13) and pitches seen per plate appearance
- ➤ Led NL Center Fielders in triples

PITCHING:

Bob Walk does nothing fancy. He does not have a blazing fastball or a trick pitch like a knuckler. All he does is force hitter after hitter to hit ground balls or lift lazy flies. Walk has never reached the stardom expected when he was Philadelphia's starting pitcher in the first game of the 1980 World Series. But after a few years of bouncing back and forth from the minors to the majors, he has established himself a solid veteran starting pitcher.

Walk won 13 games for the Pirates last season, his career best. Over the last three years, he's gone 33-22 while increasing his victory total each year. Walk has a smooth delivery and is sneaky fast. He seems to be throwing soft but the fastball, which sinks, can get to the plate in a hurry. His best pitch, though, is a sharp-breaking curveball. He also throws an effective slider and will mix in a change-up. Walk's strong suit is his ability to throw to spots and his knowledge of opposing hitters. Since he tends to give up a lot of hits, control is crucial to his success. Though not terrible, Walk's control was off at times last year, probably due to a groin injury that forced him to change his motion at times. The injury made him less effective, and that's one reason he had a high ERA (4.41).

FIELDING, HITTING, BASERUNNING:

Walk enjoys all aspects of the game. Many times, his uniform will be as dirty as any position player's by game's end. He is an aggressive fielder who will try to nail the lead runner on bunts, and covers first base well. He holds runners close and has a good "balk" move to first. Walk can handle the bat and is particularly adept at the "slug" bunt in which he fakes a bunt then swings away. He went 13 for 70 (.186) last year with two doubles and two triples, and his nine RBIs led the Pirates' staff. Walk is an aggressive baserunner who will take the extra base and is not afraid to slide.

OVERALL:

Bob Walk is a good guy to have on a pitching staff. He is a veteran who knows how to pitch. He won't be a big winner but he can be relied on to win 12 to 15 games, perhaps one or two more if everything breaks right. He is the kind of reliable third or fourth starter coveted by many teams.

BOB WALK

Position: SP
Bats: R **Throws:** R
Ht: 6' 4" **Wt:** 217

Opening Day Age: 33
Born: 11/26/56 in Van Nuys, CA
ML Seasons: 10

Overall Statistics

	W	L	ERA	G	GS	Sv	IP	H	R	BB	SO	HR
1989	13	10	4.41	33	31	0	196.0	208	106	65	83	15
Career	66	54	3.93	231	164	2	1099.1	1085	542	422	568	83

Where They Hit the Ball

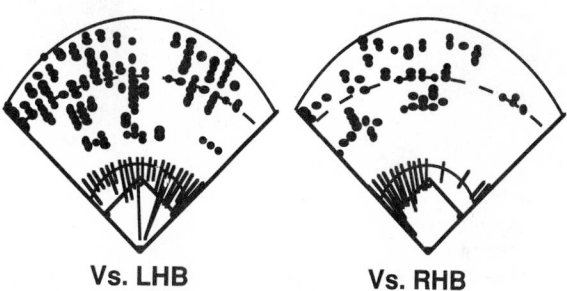

Vs. LHB   Vs. RHB

1989 Situational Stats

	W	L	ERA	Sv	IP		AB	H	HR	RBI	AVG
Home	7	4	3.28	0	90.2	LHB	435	124	9	49	.285
Road	6	6	5.38	0	105.1	RHB	333	84	6	38	.252
Day	4	1	4.01	0	49.1	Sc Pos	180	57	5	71	.317
Night	9	9	4.54	0	146.2	Clutch	49	14	2	5	.286

1989 Rankings (National League)

➡ 1st in run support per 9 innings (5.4) and worst ERA on the road (5.38) - *pitchers with 162 IP*

➡ 2nd in worst ERA (4.41) and least strikeouts per 9 innings (3.8)

➡ 4th in worst opponent batting average (.271)

➡ 9th in balks (4)

➡ 10th in pickoff throws (172) and hits allowed (208)

➡ Led the Pirates in caught stealing (11), lowest stolen base percentage allowed (68.6%), pickoff throws (172), grounder/flyball ratio (1.55), run support per 9 innings, HRs allowed per 9 innings (.69) and GDPs per 9 innings (.55) - *team pitchers with 162 IP*

RAFAEL BELLIARD

Position: SS/2B
Bats: R **Throws:** R
Ht: 5' 6" **Wt:** 150

Opening Day Age: 28
Born: 10/24/61 in Pueblo Nuevo, Dominican Republic
ML Seasons: 8

Overall Statistics

	G	AB	R	H	D	T	HR	RBI	SB	BB	SO	AVG
1989	67	154	10	33	4	0	0	8	5	8	22	.214
Career	437	997	105	218	13	9	1	66	34	80	155	.219

HITTING, FIELDING, BASERUNNING:

Rafael Belliard is the epitome of the good-field/no-hit shortstop. He is simply overmatched by major league pitching. Fastballs overpower him and can knock the bat right out of his hands. Breaking balls baffle him and he flails at them. Belliard has tried light bats and heavy bats, but nothing works. He has no power, as evidenced by his one home run in 997 major league at bats. He also shows little patience at the plate, rarely drawing a walk. He is an adept bunter, but that is about the only way he can get on base. Belliard is speedy, runs the bases well and can steal a base. It's a shame he can't hit, because outside of Ozzie Smith, there is no better defensive shortstop in the National League. Belliard has great range, a strong arm and rarely botches the routine play. He is also a superb second baseman and adequate at third base. Belliard led National League shortstops in fielding percentage in 1988, breaking Smith's four-year hold on the title.

OVERALL:

Not many teams can afford to keep a .219 career hitter in their lineup, no matter how good his glove. With young Jay Bell entrenched as the Pirates' shortstop, Belliard will be lucky to stick with the club even as a utilityman.

SID BREAM

Position: 1B
Bats: L **Throws:** L
Ht: 6' 4" **Wt:** 220

Opening Day Age: 29
Born: 8/3/60 in Carlisle, PA
ML Seasons: 7

Overall Statistics

	G	AB	R	H	D	T	HR	RBI	SB	BB	SO	AVG
1989	19	36	3	8	3	0	0	4	0	12	10	.222
Career	562	1744	210	457	112	8	45	240	32	194	251	.262

HITTING, FIELDING, BASERUNNING:

Sid Bream had a nightmarish 1989. He appeared in only 19 games as a result of three operations on his right knee. He did not play after May 28. Bream had been a steady, if unspectacular, player with the Pirates from 1986-88. He is not a major home run threat for a first baseman, but he has power to the alleys, with a knack for hitting doubles. He is effective against any high pitch, particularly fastballs, but struggles with low balls. Bream is a streak hitter who likes to pull the ball, even inside fastballs. Before his knee injuries, Bream was capable of stealing a base, but that appears to be a thing of the past: he was zero for four in '89. The Pirates missed Bream's defense. He doesn't always get hard-hit balls down the line, but he is excellent at charging bunts and will often nab the lead runner. He is also good at scooping low throws. The Pirates feel he is a Gold Glove candidate.

OVERALL:

Bream has a good work ethic and is expected to be ready by spring training. Though he lacks good run production for a first baseman, the Pirates are hopeful he can return and be an everyday player again. He is a steadying influence in the lineup.

BENNY DISTEFANO

Position: 1B
Bats: L **Throws:** L
Ht: 6' 1" **Wt:** 200

Opening Day Age: 28
Born: 1/23/62 in
Brooklyn, NY
ML Seasons: 4

Overall Statistics

	G	AB	R	H	D	T	HR	RBI	SB	BB	SO	AVG
1989	96	154	12	38	8	0	2	15	1	17	30	.247
Career	188	300	31	68	13	3	7	35	1	26	52	.227

HITTING, FIELDING, BASERUNNING:

Benny Distefano waited a long time for his chance to be an everyday major league player. It came in 1989 when first baseman Sid Bream injured his knee early in the season, but Distefano failed to capitalize. Benny has shown power in the minor leagues, but he managed just two home runs in 154 at bats last year. Distefano looks to pull the ball at all times and can be overaggressive. Pitchers will feed him a diet of breaking balls and low-and-away fastballs. He can crush a mistake pitch, particularly inside fastballs. Distefano fared well as a pinch hitter, hitting .271 (13 for 48) with a club-high seven RBIs. Not a fast runner or a base stealer, Distefano will nonetheless go all out on the bases. He's an adequate first baseman and somewhat of a liability in the outfield. However, he made his mark in 1989 on defense -- as the majors' first lefthanded catcher since 1980.

OVERALL:

Though he failed as regular last year, Distefano proved useful as a substitute. He can hit coming off the bench, and his ability to fill in behind the plate is an added bonus. He may be able to stick in the majors as a 24th man.

BRIAN FISHER

Position: RP/SP
Bats: R **Throws:** R
Ht: 6' 4" **Wt:** 210

Opening Day Age: 28
Born: 3/18/62 in
Honolulu, HI
ML Seasons: 5

Overall Statistics

	W	L	ERA	G	GS	Sv	IP	H	R	BB	SO	HR
1989	0	3	7.94	9	3	1	17.0	25	17	10	8	2
Career	32	31	4.34	196	51	22	543.2	549	287	205	343	60

PITCHING, FIELDING, HITTING:

Brian Fisher would like to strike the entire year of 1989 from the record. Fisher's woes began immediately after the 1988 season when he underwent surgery on his right shoulder and left knee. He began last season in extended spring training before being activated in mid-April. He was never completely healthy, though, and pitched just 17 ineffective innings. Fisher was sent to the minors twice on rehabilitation assignments and further hampered his comeback when he injured his right knee while pitching for Class AAA Buffalo. That prompted yet another operation. When healthy, Fisher can throw four pitches with relative success. He has a fastball that reaches 90, a sharp-breaking curve, a slider with good movement and a decent change-up. However, he tries to be too fine with his pitches and hurts himself getting behind in the count. Fisher hurts himself in other phases of the game, too. He is a poor fielder and does not hold runners well. His hitting borders on the pathetic, and he lumbers on the bases.

OVERALL:

The career of the star-crossed Fisher is in jeopardy. He now has two bad legs and a bad arm which doesn't leave that many good body parts left. Fisher is a conditioning buff and has worked hard to rehabilitate. Still, it's going to be an uphill climb.

JIM GOTT

Position: RP
Bats: R **Throws:** R
Ht: 6' 4" **Wt:** 220

Opening Day Age: 30
Born: 8/3/59 in Hollywood, CA
ML Seasons: 8

Overall Statistics

	W	L	ERA	G	GS	Sv	IP	H	R	BB	SO	HR
1989	0	0	0.00	1	0	0	0.2	1	0	1	1	0
Career	35	48	4.17	257	96	50	748.2	732	391	310	530	60

PITCHING, FIELDING, HITTING:

Jim Gott's 1989 season lasted all of two-thirds of an inning. He suffered an elbow injury in the Pirates' third game, his first appearance of the season, and underwent season-ending surgery in May. It was frustrating for Gott, who had finally lived up to his great potential by recording a Pittsburgh record 34 saves in 1988. When healthy, Gott throws strictly heat, relying on a fastball that can reach the high 90s and a hard slider that breaks sharp and late. He will toss in an occasional curveball, but does not need to throw it often because his hard stuff is so effective. Gott is quick off the mound and a good fielder, but he doesn't hold baserunners very well. A good hitter, he's belted four major league homers.

OVERALL:

The effects of the elbow injury on Gott's velocity remain to be seen. He did bounce back from rotator cuff surgery in 1986, though. Gott, an eternal optimist, was able to long toss by September and is confident he will be 100 percent by spring training. Despite the emergence of Bill Landrum last year, the Pirates would love to have Gott back.

TOM PRINCE

Position: C
Bats: R **Throws:** R
Ht: 5'11" **Wt:** 185

Opening Day Age: 25
Born: 8/13/64 in Kankakee, IL
ML Seasons: 3

Overall Statistics

	G	AB	R	H	D	T	HR	RBI	SB	BB	SO	AVG
1989	21	52	1	7	4	0	0	5	1	6	12	.135
Career	54	135	5	22	7	0	1	13	1	10	29	.163

HITTING, FIELDING, BASERUNNING:

Once considered one of the crown jewels of the Pirates' farm system, Tom Prince failed miserably when he got the chance to catch on at the major league level. Prince has seen action for the Pirates in the last three seasons and batted .222, .176 and .135. A homer off the Mets' Bob Ojeda in his '87 callup has been Prince's only major league highlight. Prince, never more than an adequate hitter in the minors, has struggled against all types of major league pitching. He has been overmatched and shows a decided lack of confidence. Defense is Prince's calling card but that ability, too, has yet to surface in his major league stints. He has had problems throwing out baserunners and does not have a feel for handling pitchers at the major league level. He shows toughness behind the plate and is not afraid to block balls or get involved in collisions.

OVERALL:

Tom Prince has been a major disappointment for Pittsburgh. The Pirates have looked to him for help in each of the last two years and he has failed them each time. His star has definitely faded in the Pirates' organization.

REY QUINONES

Position: SS
Bats: R **Throws:** R
Ht: 5'11" **Wt:** 185

Opening Day Age: 26
Born: 11/11/63 in Rio Piedras, Puerto Rico
ML Seasons: 4

Overall Statistics

	G	AB	R	H	D	T	HR	RBI	SB	BB	SO	AVG
1989	78	244	23	49	11	0	3	29	0	16	41	.201
Career	451	1533	173	373	75	6	29	159	5	89	240	.243

HITTING, FIELDING, BASERUNNING:

At 26, Rey Quinones ended 1989 as a man without a team ... and maybe a man without a future. It's not that he lacks talent. Three years ago, Quinones hit .276 with 12 homers for the Mariners; many felt he could be the best young shortstop in baseball. But it's been all downhill since then. In 1988 Quinones missed time with various problems, saw his average dip to .248, and showed no progress afield with 23 errors. When 1989 started the same way, Seattle shipped Quinones to the Pirates, who saw Rey as the answer to their longstanding shortstop problem. But this stop was worse than ever. Quinones committed 19 errors in 71 games, batted only .209, and did nothing to enhance the idea that he was a team player. The Pirates finally shipped Quinones to the minors, where he's basically available to anyone who wants him. Thus far teams haven't exactly been lining up.

OVERALL:

Quinones has fallen so far in three years that maybe he's finally hit bottom. Rey can field brilliantly and has the potential to be one of the best hitting shortstops in the majors. He still has a chance, but he'd better get his head together in a hurry.

RICK REED

Position: RP/SP
Bats: R **Throws:** R
Ht: 6'0" **Wt:** 195

Opening Day Age: 25
Born: 8/16/64 in Huntington, WV
ML Seasons: 2

Overall Statistics

	W	L	ERA	G	GS	Sv	IP	H	R	BB	SO	HR
1989	1	4	5.60	15	7	0	54.2	62	35	11	34	5
Career	2	4	5.13	17	9	0	66.2	72	39	13	40	6

PITCHING, FIELDING, HITTING:

Rick Reed has yet to top his hard-to-be-believed major league debut. After moving rapidly through the Pirate system after a season which began in Class A, Reed was recalled by Pittsburgh late in 1988. Rick pitched eight shutout innings against the eventual National League East champion New York Mets in his debut. Reed returned to the majors last season, but failed to impress either as a starter or a reliever. Reed's main problem is that only one pitch has worked for him in the majors, his fastball. His curveball and change-up have been ineffective, leaving him with just the one pitch, which is not good enough to overpower major league hitters. Reed does show excellent control for a young pitcher and also exhibits great poise. He's a decent fielder, but he needs to learn how to hold runners better. Reed has only one hit in 17 at-bats for a lifetime average of .059. He is not a good bunter, either.

OVERALL:

Reed went from being a nonprospect to a pitcher of great promise in only four months of the 1988 season. He struggled last season, though. He has the poise to pitch in the major leagues but needs more time in the minors to work on his pitches.

MIKE
SMITH

Position: RP
Bats: B **Throws:** R
Ht: 6' 1" **Wt:** 195

Opening Day Age: 29
Born: 2/23/61 in
Jackson, MS
ML Seasons: 5

Overall Statistics

	W	L	ERA	G	GS	Sv	IP	H	R	BB	SO	HR
1989	0	1	3.75	16	0	0	24.0	28	12	10	12	1
Career	1	1	4.71	33	1	1	49.2	55	28	22	26	4

PITCHING, FIELDING, HITTING:

"Mississippi" Mike Smith can henceforth be known as just Mike Smith again after a 1989 minor league trade brought him to the Pittsburgh Pirates. Smith picked up the Mississippi tag last year in spring training when he was one of two pitchers named Michael Anthony Smith -- the other was known as "Texas" -- in the Baltimore Orioles' camp. Smith did little to make a name for himself in a two-month stint with the Pirates at the end of the '89 season. He has a live fastball but no outstanding off-speed pitch to complement it. He throws two curves, one a slow roundhouse type and the other thrown at regular speed. He has a change-up but does not have control of it. He's always had problems getting the ball over the plate. Smith is an average fielder, but has trouble holding runners. He enjoys hitting but is not very good at it. His baserunning abilities are unknown as he never gets on base.

OVERALL:

Smith has gotten cups of coffee with Cincinnati, Montreal, Baltimore and Pittsburgh in the past six seasons. He has never warranted a second cup. He keeps getting opportunities because of his live arm but seems about out of chances at 29.

HITTING:

Tom Brunansky is a consistent power hitter who has averaged 26 home runs over the last eight seasons, and 84 RBIs over the last seven. Bruno's RBI production has been eerily consistent since 1983: he's had fewer than 82 only once (when he drove home 75), and more than 85 only once (when he had 90). Tom has driven home exactly 85 runs four times, including the last three years in succession.

What's remarkable is that Brunansky has maintained that consistency while switching from the Metrodome, a park which helped him, to Busch Stadium, a yard which is absolutely killing him. Busch is a park where uppercutting the ball results in a lot of flyouts and few homers. And Brunansky is an uppercutter. He continues to be a big home run hitter on the road, with 31 homers in less than two seasons as a National Leaguer. But Tom has belted only 11 home runs at Busch over the same span, including just four last year. Since the trade, Bruno's batted .254 on the road; at Busch, he's hit only .229. In St. Louis, pitchers are able to challenge Brunansky, knowing his long shots are apt to be caught. As a consequence, his walk total, once one of his strengths, dropped by 27 last year.

Traditionally, Bruno could be counted on for one tremendous hot streak during the year. His first half/second half batting splits have always been extreme. Last year, however, the hot streak did not come, and it may have cost the Cardinals the division.

BASERUNNING:

Tom can run, and seemed to be developing into a base stealing threat when he stole 16 in 22 attempts in his Cardinal debut in '88. But last year he was a woeful five for 14. He is, however, an excellent first-to-third runner.

FIELDING:

Bruno is an excellent outfielder. He has both good range and a very good arm. He makes few mental mistakes, despite the weeping and wailing in St. Louis over one that cost the Cards a September game in Chicago.

OVERALL:

If Bruno ever learned to hit the line drives that succeed in Busch Stadium, he'd be one of the most dangerous hitters in the National League. But at 29, it's unrealistic to think he'll change. As long as he's a Cardinal, Brunansky seems destined to be a .240 hitter, though one with 85 RBIs and great power on the road.

TOM BRUNANSKY

Position: RF
Bats: R **Throws:** R
Ht: 6' 4" **Wt:** 216

Opening Day Age: 29
Born: 8/20/60 in Covina, CA
ML Seasons: 9

Overall Statistics

	G	AB	R	H	D	T	HR	RBI	SB	BB	SO	AVG
1989	158	556	67	133	29	3	20	85	5	59	107	.239
Career	1228	4425	593	1095	205	20	208	639	58	540	788	.247

Where He Hits the Ball

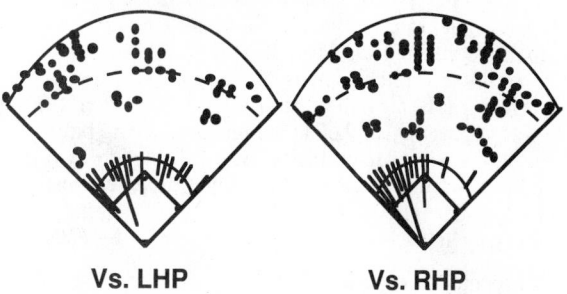

Vs. LHP   **Vs. RHP**

1989 Situational Stats

	AB	H	HR	RBI	AVG		AB	H	HR	RBI	AVG
Home	263	61	4	34	.232	LHP	220	52	11	31	.236
Road	293	72	16	51	.246	RHP	336	81	9	54	.241
Day	183	42	5	26	.230	Sc Pos	166	43	7	64	.259
Night	373	91	15	59	.244	Clutch	86	18	3	14	.209

1989 Rankings (National League)

➡ 2nd in lowest grounder/flyball ratio (.69) and worst hitting with the bases loaded (.071) - *players with 10 PA with the bases loaded*

➡ 5th in most pitches seen per plate appearance (3.8) - *players with 502 PA*

➡ 10th in games (158), RBI (85) and pitches seen (2,349)

➡ Led the Cardinals in strikeouts (107), home run frequency (27.8 ABs per HR), home runs (20) and pitches seen per plate appearance

➡ Led NL Right Fielders in at bats (556), games and RBI

PITCHING:

Cris Carpenter is a number one draft choice of enormous potential – he reached the major leagues in 1988 after only 13 games in professional baseball. That he struggled as a rookie (2-3, 4.72) was understandable; Cris had never played a full season in organized baseball, and he developed some shoulder tightness late in the year. Carpenter was expected to do better in 1989, and he did, reducing his ERA to a respectable 3.18. But Cris had a midseason slump and needed to be sent back to the minors. He did better when he returned in September, but still hasn't overpowered anyone, and now some people are doubting his chances.

Part of the problem is that, after two years, the Cardinals have not yet found a niche for Carpenter. Cris was an outstanding reliever at the University of Georgia, and starred as a closer for the U.S. in the 1987 Pan American Games. But the Cardinals already had a bullpen ace in Todd Worrell, and since they wanted Carpenter to pitch as many innings as possible, they let him make his minor league debut as a starter. Cris was successful, so they kept him as a starting pitcher when he arrived in the majors in '88. That didn't work very well, so last year St. Louis used Carpenter mostly as a middle reliever, letting him start five games along the way. In each role Cris was good, but not great.

Carpenter throws several pitches, but the best is a fastball that approaches 90 miles per hour. In college, Cris's fastball simply overpowered hitters, but in the majors he's barely averaged a strikeout for every two innings. Carpenter has worked hard to develop a slider and an offspeed pitch, but he's still learning.

FIELDING, HITTING, BASERUNNING:

An outstanding all-around athlete, Carpenter was also the punter for the Georgia football team. His athletic ability shows in his fielding, where he's very quick off the mound, and in his alert baserunning. Cris is also a decent hitter and a fine bunter. Carpenter needs work on holding baserunners, however, though he figures to improve with experience.

OVERALL:

Carpenter will be 25 at the start of the '90 season, but he's still only had two years in organized ball. He showed improvement in his second season, and had a 1.93 ERA in September. Cris had 11 saves in only 27 appearances at Louisville last year; with Worrell out for at least a while, Carpenter may finally get a chance to show whether or not he can save games on the major league level.

CRIS CARPENTER

Position: RP/SP
Bats: R **Throws:** R
Ht: 6' 1" **Wt:** 185

Opening Day Age: 25
Born: 4/5/65 in St. Augustine, FL
ML Seasons: 2

Overall Statistics

	W	L	ERA	G	GS	Sv	IP	H	R	BB	SO	HR
1989	4	4	3.18	36	5	0	68.0	70	30	26	35	4
Career	6	7	3.81	44	13	0	115.2	126	57	35	59	7

Where They Hit the Ball

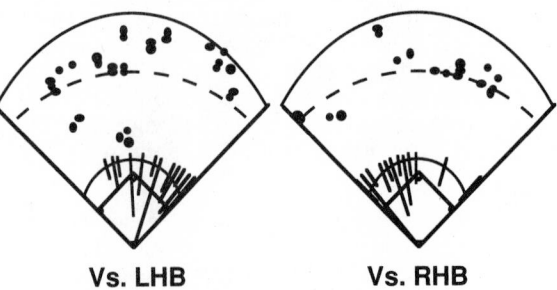

Vs. LHB   **Vs. RHB**

1989 Situational Stats

	W	L	ERA	Sv	IP		AB	H	HR	RBI	AVG
Home	1	3	4.42	0	36.2	LHB	138	39	1	13	.283
Road	3	1	1.72	0	31.1	RHB	129	31	3	22	.240
Day	4	2	3.75	0	36.0	Sc Pos	76	19	1	30	.250
Night	0	2	2.53	0	32.0	Clutch	46	11	0	7	.239

1989 Rankings (National League)

➡ Did not rank near the top or bottom in any category

HITTING:

Vince Coleman's ability to stay in the major leagues is completely dependant on his on-base average. He has no power at all, and his speed is useless if he can't get on base to start with. Consequently, his career has been an ongoing struggle to get himself to first. By 1987, Vince looked like he was winning the war. He hit .289, drew 70 walks, had an on-base average of .363 and scored 121 runs. He seemed to have learned to slap down on low pitches, creating infield choppers that he could use his speed to beat out, thereby effectively stealing first base. He also learned to bunt, and had become a true force as a leadoff man.

But for the last two years, Vince's numbers have declined to his rookie level ... a little below it, in fact. He now looks like he'll go through his career with a .315 on-base average, which is low for a leadoff man no matter how many bases he steals. It may be that Coleman created unrealistic expectations in 1987, an extreme hitters' year. Vince is only one of many players who have been unable to duplicate their '87 figures.

BASERUNNING:

After stealing over 100 bases each season from 1985 through 1987, Coleman's totals have declined to 81 and 65 the last two years. Vince's success percentage remained high at 87% in 1989, but he seemed obsessed with not getting caught. Vince set a record for consecutive steals, but did that in good part by not running on the tough throwing arms. Considering that his percentage was never less than 81% in the years that he was stealing 107 to 110 bases, Vince's caution may not have helped his ball club.

FIELDING:

Vince is an underrated outfielder, though his range is not as good as his speed might indicate. He throws out a very large number of baserunners, not because his arm is strong, but because his arm's weakness is legendary and everyone runs on him. Still, since the runners thrown out by a left fielder are usually past second base to start with, those are extremely valuable outs. Vince could probably play center in a ballpark that wasn't as large as Busch Stadium.

OVERALL:

The Cardinals have grown weary of Coleman's failure to improve, and last year gave Milt Thompson a long look while Vince was injured. Thompson did a good job, and it is possible that Vince will be traded. He might be more valuable to a team that needed a center fielder and played in a hitters' park with a small outfield, like Wrigley Field or Fenway Park.

VINCE COLEMAN

Position: LF
Bats: B **Throws:** R
Ht: 6' 0" **Wt:** 170

Opening Day Age: 28
Born: 9/22/61 in Jacksonville, FL
ML Seasons: 5

Overall Statistics

	G	AB	R	H	D	T	HR	RBI	SB	BB	SO	AVG
1989	145	563	94	143	21	9	2	28	65	50	90	.254
Career	754	3038	493	792	88	47	9	178	472	279	540	.261

Where He Hits the Ball

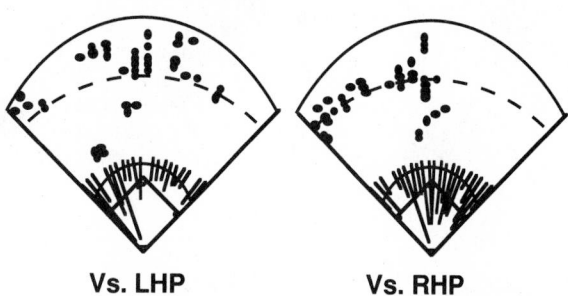

Vs. LHP   **Vs. RHP**

1989 Situational Stats

	AB	H	HR	RBI	AVG		AB	H	HR	RBI	AVG
Home	277	72	1	20	.260	LHP	264	62	2	17	.235
Road	286	71	1	8	.248	RHP	299	81	0	11	.271
Day	185	50	1	9	.270	Sc Pos	115	23	0	26	.200
Night	378	93	1	19	.246	Clutch	91	19	0	5	.209

1989 Rankings (National League)

➡ 1st in stolen bases (65), steals of third (17), pickoffs (4) and runs scored per time reached base (41.6%) - *players with 502 PA*

➡ 2nd in bunts in play (40)

➡ 3rd in triples (9) and stolen base percentage (86.7%) - *players with 20 stolen base attempts*

➡ 4th in grounder/flyball ratio (1.93) and worst home run frequency (281.5 ABs per HR)

➡ Led the Cardinals in stolen bases, steals of third, pickoffs, runs scored per time reached base, bunts in play, triples, stolen base percentage, caught stealing (10), runs (94), least GDPs per GDP situation (5.6%) and batting average on a 3-2 count (.348)

PITCHING:

John Costello is your basic developing fastball pitcher. His breaking pitch and change-up aren't much yet, but his heat gets him a good number of strikeouts. Costello gets the ball up in the strike zone, and is prone to the home run pitch. Like most such hurlers, he benefits from pitching in Busch Stadium, where the outfield contains the flyballs that are hit off the high hard one. In fact, he had the best ERA of any Cardinal pitcher in Busch. On the other hand, he had the highest road ERA of any Cardinal pitcher who had more than 10 innings.

Normally, that sort of split would lead to the pitcher getting much more work at home than on the road, especially with Whitey Herzog as manager. However, John was the unfortunate victim of Whitey's late-season experiment with Ricky Horton. Horton came back to the Cardinals with a questionable arm, and Whitey decided that, while he needed Ricky in the rotation, he couldn't give him much more than five innings at a time. So, John was assigned to relieve Ricky in the sixth, whatever the score or situation. Unfortunately for John, most of Ricky's starts turned out to be road games, and John ended up blowing a couple of performances in August, wrecking his ERA in the process. He came back to pitch effectively in September, however.

FIELDING, HITTING, BASERUNNING:

Costello hasn't really had enough opportunity to show his stuff at the plate or on the bases. He is just an adequate fielder. He had some trouble holding baserunners, allowing nine steals in only 62.1 innings.

OVERALL:

Though he's no kid at 29, Costello is an intriguing prospect. His wonderful home stats are hard to ignore when pencilling in possible futures. He was effective against both right and lefthanded hitters last year, and particularly good in the first innings of his appearances. With Todd Worrell out for a while and the Cards probably going back to the bullpen-by-committee they used so effectively before Worrell came up in 1985, Costello figures to get plenty of work this year.

JOHN COSTELLO

Position: RP
Bats: R **Throws:** R
Ht: 6' 1" **Wt:** 180

Opening Day Age: 29
Born: 12/24/60 in New York, NY
ML Seasons: 2

Overall Statistics

	W	L	ERA	G	GS	Sv	IP	H	R	BB	SO	HR
1989	5	4	3.32	48	0	3	62.1	48	24	20	40	5
Career	10	6	2.65	84	0	4	112.0	92	39	45	78	8

Where They Hit the Ball

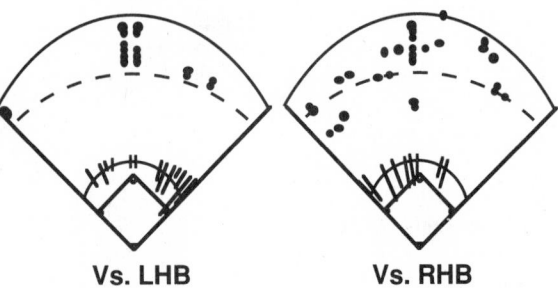

Vs. LHB   Vs. RHB

1989 Situational Stats

	W	L	ERA	Sv	IP		AB	H	HR	RBI	AVG
Home	4	2	1.44	1	31.1	LHB	88	20	1	4	.227
Road	1	2	5.23	2	31.0	RHB	137	28	4	26	.204
Day	0	1	3.49	2	28.1	Sc Pos	54	14	1	24	.259
Night	5	3	3.18	1	34.0	Clutch	101	25	1	13	.248

1989 Rankings (National League)

➡ 9th in holds (12)

PITCHING:

If there were more lefthanded people in the world than righthanded, Ken Dayley might have been the Cardinal closer the last few years, rather than Todd Worrell. They are reasonably similar pitchers, but Ken pitches better against southpaw batters, while Todd gains the platoon differential against the more common sort. Between the two of them, of course, the Cardinals have had an excellent closing combination.

Like Worrell, Dayley has the basic three pitches: fastball, breaking pitch and change-up. Again like Todd, the change isn't really that great of an option, and he doesn't throw it much. However, unlike Worrell, who throws a slider on occasion, Dayley throws a curveball, and it's considerably better than his fastball. In fact, it is one of the very best, hardest and sharpest curves in baseball. Ken also can consistently keep it down in the strike zone, and can even move it around inside and out while it still stays down. The result is an awful lot of double plays for such a hard thrower. All in all, it's one of the prettiest pitches around to watch -- from the stands.

Again like Worrell, Dayley became a short reliever after being tried for several years as a starter. The reason for the conversion was the same as well: he loses several miles per hour off his hard stuff after just a couple of innings. In fact, there is a rumor that what happened to Dayley was the reason for using the radar gun on Worrell in the first place.

FIELDING, HITTING, BASERUNNING:

Dayley is a decent, veteran fielder, though he doesn't have any great specialty or flashy skill. He just consistently gets to the bunts, stops his share of what's hit up the middle, and reliably backs up his bases. His move to first is only so-so. Dayley isn't much of a batter, though he can bunt a little. He is not a good baserunner.

OVERALL:

Though he's shared the closer's role with Worrell in good part, Dayley has always played second fiddle and has never had more than 12 saves in a season. There's always been a question of whether he could handle the top job on his own. Worrell, and Dayley's history of arm trouble, always stood in the way. Now Dayley's arm is sound, and Worrell's the one with the injured wing. Dayley may finally get his chance in 1990.

KEN DAYLEY

Position: RP
Bats: L **Throws:** L
Ht: 6' 0" **Wt:** 180

Opening Day Age: 31
Born: 2/25/59 in Jerome, ID
ML Seasons: 8

Overall Statistics

	W	L	ERA	G	GS	Sv	IP	H	R	BB	SO	HR
1989	4	3	2.87	71	0	12	75.1	63	26	30	40	3
Career	29	41	3.63	317	33	37	495.1	493	236	186	350	37

Where They Hit the Ball

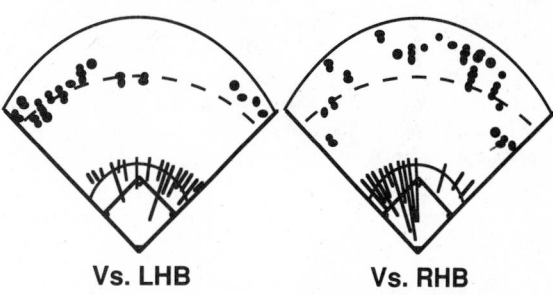

Vs. LHB   Vs. RHB

1989 Situational Stats

	W	L	ERA	Sv	IP		AB	H	HR	RBI	AVG
Home	2	1	3.65	8	37.0	LHB	101	19	1	8	.188
Road	2	2	2.11	4	38.1	RHB	175	44	2	16	.251
Day	0	2	3.27	3	22.0	Sc Pos	74	17	1	19	.230
Night	4	1	2.70	9	53.1	Clutch	187	45	3	19	.241

1989 Rankings (National League)

➡ 2nd in holds (22) and lowest percentage of inherited runners scoring (16.7%) - *pitchers with 30 inherited runners*

➡ 4th in games (71) and first batter efficiency (.131) - *pitchers with 40 relief games*

➡ 8th in blown saves (5)

➡ Led the Cardinals in games, holds, lowest percentage of inherited runners scoring, first batter efficiency and blown saves

PITCHING:

The key to understanding Jose DeLeon's career is to realize that it is much harder to master four pitches than it is three. Jose had all the basic stuff you'd want in a hard-throwing starter: the fastball, the breaking pitch and the change-up. The breaking pitch is the weak one, and the fastball rises in the strike zone, so the big power hitters can sit on the heat and then punish it. To counter this, Jose long ago developed a forkball (that is, a slow split-finger pitch) which drops down in contrast to the high hard one. The many strikeouts he gets are due to the contrast in pitch direction, and the many walks he issues are due to the fact that he doesn't always have all four pitches in command.

With the four pitches, Jose's potential is almost unlimited, which is why teams keep putting him out there even when he is not on his game. If he should ever master all four pitches consistently, there's a real possibility for 20 wins or more. His perfectly good 16-12 year in 1989 was not the result of a final maturing. It was the result of, first, a ballpark in which he could rely on the fastball even if the forkball wasn't working, and second, Whitey Herzog's realization that when Jose starts to weaken, he collapses quickly, and therefore requires a quick hook.

FIELDING, HITTING, BASERUNNING:

Jose shows a few signs of Joaquin Andujar's disease -- overswinging in the belief that he is really a good hitter. He lacks, however, the occasional power that let Joaquin get away with it. He bunts badly and doesn't run the bases very well, though he has some raw speed. With time, he might become a better fielder, too, though he isn't all that awful now, with decent reflexes and pretty good attention to the batter on the swing. DeLeon has worked on holding baserunners, but still isn't very good at it.

OVERALL:

DeLeon has come a long way since the days when he was known, derisively, as "the best 2-and-19 pitcher in baseball." The knock on Jose was that he had a great arm, but always pitched just well enough to lose. You don't hear that kind of talk any more about DeLeon; you hear about how many more games he's going to win.

JOSE DeLEON

Position: SP
Bats: R **Throws:** R
Ht: 6' 3" **Wt:** 211

Opening Day Age: 29
Born: 12/20/60 in
Rancho Viejo,
Dominican Republic
ML Seasons: 7

Overall Statistics

	W	L	ERA	G	GS	Sv	IP	H	R	BB	SO	HR
1989	16	12	3.05	36	36	0	244.2	173	96	80	201	16
Career	61	77	3.70	201	183	4	1234.1	974	558	550	1061	92

Where They Hit the Ball

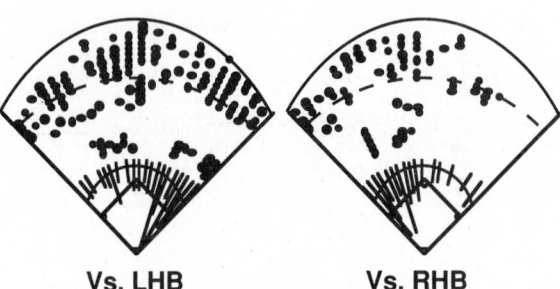

Vs. LHB **Vs. RHB**

1989 Situational Stats

	W	L	ERA	Sv	IP		AB	H	HR	RBI	AVG
Home	8	6	2.55	0	134.1	LHB	512	119	10	53	.232
Road	8	6	3.67	0	110.1	RHB	366	54	6	25	.148
Day	5	6	3.63	0	94.1	Sc Pos	173	42	2	55	.243
Night	11	6	2.69	0	150.1	Clutch	99	13	1	5	.131

1989 Rankings (National League)

➡ 1st in lowest batting average allowed (.197), lowest slugging percentage allowed (.309), strikeouts (201), pitches thrown (3,671) and lowest batting average vs. righthanded batters (.148) - *pitchers facing 377 RHB*

➡ 2nd in games started (36) and least baserunners allowed per 9 innings (9.5) - *pitchers with 162 IP*

➡ Led the Cardinals in games started, shutouts (3), innings (244.2), home runs allowed (16), hit batsmen (6), strikeouts, lowest batting average allowed, lowest on-base average allowed (.268), lowest slugging percentage allowed, caught stealing (12) and most strikeouts per 9 innings (7.4)

PITCHING:

Frank DiPino's outstanding success in 1989 had to be one of the more unlikely occurrences of the year. At 32, DiPino had pretty well established his niche as a lefty specialist of limited skill, surviving mainly on his ability to retire lefthanded hitters. Di-Pino had some success in his eight-year career, including a 20-save season in 1983. But he'd gotten his earned run average under three only once, and his career won-lost record was a terrible 20-35, with no winning seasons. So could this really be Frank DiPino --with a 9-0 record and a 2.45 ERA?

Indeed it was. Though he'd been mostly a fastball pitcher throughout his career, the key pitch in Frank's 1989 repertoire was a slider which broke strongly, and over which he had unusual control. DiPino's fastball is no longer overpowering; in fact, his strikeout rate declined in '89 from 6.9 strike outs per nine innings to 4.5. But the slider was effective against both righties and lefties, and DiPino was able to mix in a changeup as well. With a more complete repertoire, he had the greatest success of his career.

Along with a better selection of pitches, there were a couple of other important factors in DiPino's '89 success. He continued to be as effective against left-handed hitters as ever, holding them to a .209 average with only five extra base hits, all doubles. But Frank improved markedly against righties, reducing his righthanded opponents' batting average from .335 in '88 to .240 in 1989. DiPino also pitched very well in Busch Stadium, with a 1.58 ERA. A high-baller who'd always be susceptible to the home run ball, DiPino found Busch's deep power alleys made to order for him.

FIELDING, HITTING, BASERUNNING:

Frank doesn't hit well, though he can bunt just a little if he gets a good pitch. He runs the bases poorly. His fielding isn't anything special, either, though he can track down a bunt better than the average pitcher. He does back up the right base. DiPino's move to first has always been good, and he holds runners well.

OVERALL:

DiPino's role on Herzog's staff was inherited from Ricky Horton, and the Cardinals have Horton back. If Whitey returns Horton to the lefty setup man role, Frank's job is going to be redefined. DiPino will have to prove in 1990 that he can maintain his newfound success.

FRANK DiPINO

Position: RP
Bats: L **Throws:** L
Ht: 6' 0" **Wt:** 180

Opening Day Age: 33
Born: 10/22/56 in Syracuse, NY
ML Seasons: 9

Overall Statistics

	W	L	ERA	G	GS	Sv	IP	H	R	BB	SO	HR
1989	9	0	2.45	67	0	0	88.1	73	26	20	44	6
Career	29	35	3.69	432	6	53	592.0	551	273	229	453	43

Where They Hit the Ball

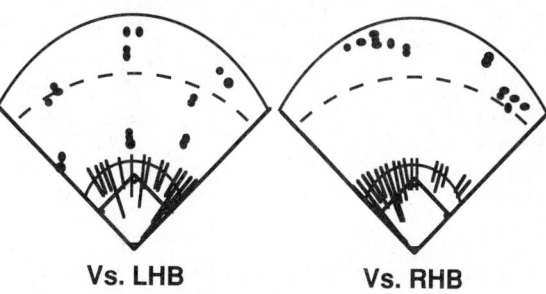

Vs. LHB   **Vs. RHB**

1989 Situational Stats

	W	L	ERA	Sv	IP		AB	H	HR	RBI	AVG
Home	4	0	1.58	0	45.2	LHB	129	27	0	12	.209
Road	5	0	3.38	0	42.2	RHB	192	46	6	24	.240
Day	2	0	3.23	0	30.2	Sc Pos	89	20	2	29	.225
Night	7	0	2.03	0	57.2	Clutch	57	13	2	6	.228

1989 Rankings (National League)

➡ 6th in lowest percentage of inherited runners scoring (24.4%) - *pitchers with 30 inherited runners*

➡ 8th in first batter efficiency (17.2%) - *pitchers in 40 relief games*

➡ 9th in most GDPs induced per GDP situation - *pitchers with 30 GDP situations*

➡ Led the Cardinals in ERA (2.45), lowest batting average allowed vs. lefthanded batters (.209) and least baserunners allowed per 9 innings (9.5) - *all team pitchers*

HITTING:

Watching Pedro Guerrero adjust to hitting for the Cardinals was a true education in the abilities of a great hitter. Previously an uppercutting home run hitter, Pedro now plays half his games in Busch Stadium, where flyballs die in the cavernous confines, but line drives go to the walls and the Astroturf skips grounders right along. Pedro switched parks and went from a 30-homer man to fewer than 20, but led the league in doubles and was fifth in batting average. He also was second in the league in RBIs to Kevin Mitchell, who out-homered him by 30.

Pedro alternated styles during the year. Out of Busch, he reverted to the uppercut, and all but three of his homers were hit in away games. At Busch, he became a line drive hitter. Guerrero has what could be called "bat accuracy." Though he takes a big swing, he seldom misses the ball. Guerrero hit almost as well against righties as against lefties, as he predicted would happen in April.

Pedro was an awesome performer for the Cards in key situations. He hit .400 with runners in scoring position. With the lack of punch behind him in the lineup, it's a wonder that he wan't intentionally walked more often (13 times in 1989).

BASERUNNING:

Guerrero has no running speed left, though he was successful in both his stolen base attempts last year. He is a good baserunner and a master at milking a rundown long enough for succeeding runners to move up.

FIELDING:

With bad knees, Guerrero cannot make any play that requires twisting his body, and so has no range at all. Installing him at first base was a move that was long overdue even when he was with Los Angeles. In fact, it is very likely the reason for Pedro's 162-game durability.

OVERALL:

Guerrero was calm and non-controversial last year for the first time in his career. With the injury-free year and the complete reestablishment of his offensive ability, Pedro's future looks brighter than it has in years. Pedro may have several years left as a dominant offensive force. After all, he has already lost his speed, so there is no reason to expect him to fall apart until age takes either his strength or his eyes. He could very well just plod along into his forties as an All-Star first baseman.

PEDRO GUERRERO

Position: 1B
Bats: R **Throws:** R
Ht: 6' 0" **Wt:** 195

Opening Day Age: 33
Born: 6/29/56 in San Pedro de Macoris, Dominican Republic
ML Seasons: 12

Overall Statistics

	G	AB	R	H	D	T	HR	RBI	SB	BB	SO	AVG
1989	162	570	60	177	42	1	17	117	2	79	84	.311
Career	1242	4321	637	1330	218	26	193	732	90	517	721	.308

Where He Hits the Ball

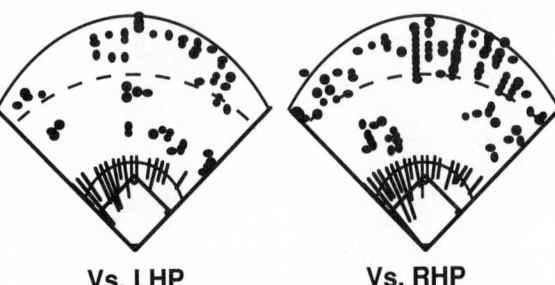

Vs. LHP   **Vs. RHP**

1989 Situational Stats

	AB	H	HR	RBI	AVG		AB	H	HR	RBI	AVG
Home	281	81	3	49	.288	LHP	218	69	8	41	.317
Road	289	96	14	68	.332	RHP	352	108	9	76	.307
Day	183	61	7	43	.333	Sc Pos	170	68	6	100	.400
Night	387	116	10	74	.300	Clutch	85	24	2	23	.282

1989 Rankings (National League)

- → 1st in doubles (42), sacrifice flies (12) and least runs scored per time reached base (21.3%) - *players with 502 PA*

- → 2nd in RBI (117), times on base (260) and hitting with runners in scoring position (.400) - *players with 100 PA with runners in scoring position*

- → Led the Cardinals in doubles, sacrifice flies, RBI, times on base, hitting with runners in scoring position, hitting on a 3-1 count (.571), hitting on the road (.332), batting average (.311), on-base average (.391), slugging percentage (.477), total bases (272), hits (177), walks (79) and pitches seen (2,358)

PITCHING:

Considering his tremendous athletic ability, it is not easy to see why Ken Hill was never drafted by a major league team. The big righthander was signed as a free agent by the Tigers, and after a couple of years in the low minors, came to St. Louis in the deal in which the Cards surrendered Mike Heath. Since then, Hill has progressed rapidly, and has often displayed outstanding pitching stuff. Everything Hill throws breaks, and breaks hard. However, like many breaking ball pitchers, he has had trouble getting his mechanics down so that the ball breaks in the strike zone. When it does, he is almost unhittable. When the control is not there, Hill gets bombed so thoroughly and so quickly that the game is usually out of reach before the relief can arrive.

Thus the 7-15 won/lost record in spite of a decent ERA. Hill walked 4.5 batters per nine innings last year, a high ratio, and he was usually gone early when his control was off. He also threw 11 wild pitches, the second highest total on the Cardinal staff. You can see Ken's difficulty if you watch his motion. When his motion is rough he is wild, and when his motion is smooth he gets the ball over. Hill had a good first half, then struggled, going 1-8 after August 1.

FIELDING, HITTING, BASERUNNING:

Hill fields well when he is in position, but can be occasionally found completely out of place. He does a respectable job of controlling the running game, especially in view of the fact that many of his pitches end up in the dirt. Ken is a wonderful hitter for a pitcher, with the potential to become the best hitting pitcher in the game. He has a smooth sweet swing that would do any position player proud. He is a very fast runner.

OVERALL:

It is worth noting that Whitey Herzog didn't want to promote Hill to the majors at all. In fact, he was slated to start the season in AA Arkansas, rather than AAA Louisville, so he could work on his mechanics without worrying about getting bombed by better hitters. Moved up because of injuries to other hurlers, Hill did get cuffed around a bit. But he showed enough potential to indicate he'll be a good one when his mechanics improve.

KEN HILL

Position: SP
Bats: R **Throws:** R
Ht: 6' 2" **Wt:** 175

Opening Day Age: 24
Born: 12/14/65 in Lynn, MA
ML Seasons: 2

Overall Statistics

	W	L	ERA	G	GS	Sv	IP	H	R	BB	SO	HR
1989	7	15	3.80	33	33	0	196.2	186	92	99	112	9
Career	7	16	3.89	37	34	0	210.2	202	101	105	118	9

Where They Hit the Ball

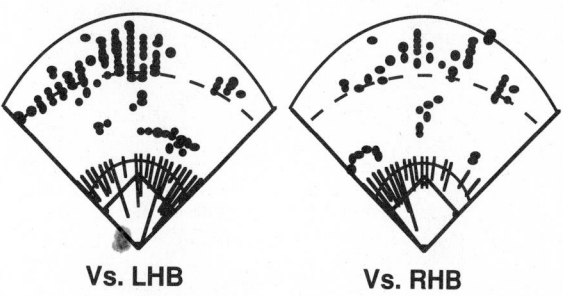

Vs. LHB   **Vs. RHB**

1989 Situational Stats

	W	L	ERA	Sv	IP		AB	H	HR	RBI	AVG
Home	2	5	3.80	0	97.0	LHB	399	107	3	40	.268
Road	5	10	3.79	0	99.2	RHB	340	79	6	37	.232
Day	1	4	3.54	0	56.0	Sc Pos	187	47	3	66	.251
Night	6	11	3.90	0	140.2	Clutch	31	16	1	8	.516

1989 Rankings (National League)

- ➡ 1st in losses (15) and walks allowed (99)
- ➡ 2nd in highest on-base average allowed (.342) and lowest strikeout/walk ratio (1.1) - *pitchers with 162 IP*
- ➡ 3rd in least HRs per 9 innings (.41)
- ➡ 4th in grounder/flyball ratio (2.02)
- ➡ 5th in worst win/loss percentage (.318) - *pitchers with 15 decisions*
- ➡ 7th in games started (33)
- ➡ Led the Cardinals in losses, walks allowed, pickoff throws (106) and grounder/flyball ratio

PITCHING:

Ricky Horton is capable of outstanding pitching when managed properly, but there is so little margin for error that even minor mismanagement can cause his arm to just collapse. He has trouble going more than five or six innings in a start, but he needs regular work to be effective. Jim Fregosi installed Ricky as his staff ace, then asked Horton to start pitching complete games, and Ricky's arm can't stand that. Tommy Lasorda then acquired him, but never did give him any regular role, and Horton couldn't get untracked. Last September Whitey Herzog tried to give Ricky five or six innings of work, then let John Costello take over. It didn't work because Costello has serious troubles away from Busch Stadium. If Horton is used in relief, one should avoid pitching him against tough righthanded hitters (like Kevin McReynolds). Horton is not going to get you the clutch strikeout, but he can induce the double play, so you should try to get him in the game before opposition runners get past first base.

Horton has the basic John Tudor collection: a mediocre fastball, a decent curve, an outstanding change-up, and great control. His arm isn't very strong, and he needs it full strength to keep his fastball up to the major league minimum. If what little heat he has goes, batters just wait on the change-up and kill it.

FIELDING, HITTING, BASERUNNING:

Ricky is a good fielder, though unspectacular. He has possibly the best pickoff move in the game now that Steve Carlton is retired, and used to get some outs that way. Now, no one tries to take a decent lead. He is starting to develop into a decent hitter for a pitcher, and can bunt some. He is slow on the basepaths and plays it safe.

OVERALL:

Between Horton's flexibility and Whitey's inventiveness, it is impossible to divine what Ricky's role will be this year. A couple of years ago, Whitey evolved a system wherein Horton was actually the closer early in the year, before the weather got hot enough for Todd Worrell to cut loose. However, Ricky will probably end up in the rotation from simple lack of any other lefty starter behind Joe Magrane. There is some question about Horton's arm and he hasn't pitched well since '87. But if the arm is sound, Ricky could prove to be an effective starter, though one with limited stamina.

RICKY HORTON

Position: RP/SP
Bats: L **Throws:** L
Ht: 6' 2" **Wt:** 197

Opening Day Age: 30
Born: 7/30/59 in Poughkeepsie, NY
ML Seasons: 6

Overall Statistics

	W	L	ERA	G	GS	Sv	IP	H	R	BB	SO	HR
1989	0	3	4.85	34	8	0	72.1	85	39	21	26	3
Career	31	26	3.68	293	53	14	631.1	644	276	200	301	52

Where They Hit the Ball

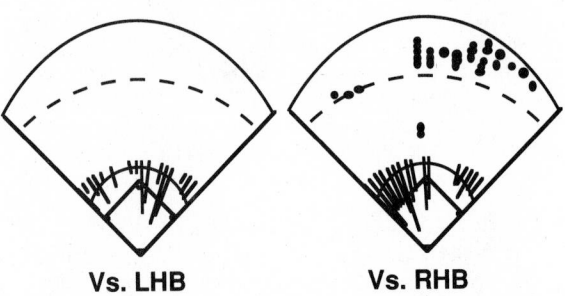

Vs. LHB   **Vs. RHB**

1989 Situational Stats

	W	L	ERA	Sv	IP		AB	H	HR	RBI	AVG
Home	0	2	4.62	0	37.0	LHB	70	24	0	13	.343
Road	0	1	5.09	0	35.1	RHB	209	61	3	26	.292
Day	0	0	2.00	0	9.0	Sc Pos	83	26	0	33	.313
Night	0	3	5.26	0	63.1	Clutch	18	8	0	6	.444

1989 Rankings (National League)

➡ 10th in most GDPs induced per GDP situation (16.4%) - *pitchers with 30 GDP situations*

PITCHING:

Joe Magrane augments his 6'6" height with a brutal overhand motion as he hurls his wide assortment of sinking stuff. The fastball stays low. The curve sinks. So does the slider and the change. When Joe has his good control, they all slip right past the front edge of the plate just at knee height for unhittable strikes, and then dive for the back corner of the plate.

Typed as a curveball pitcher when he came out of college, Joe actually had to be sent to what amounted to "fastball school" to learn to throw as hard as he could. This means Joe's pitch selection is different from other pitchers with the same stuff, as he regards the curve as his number one pitch. Batters often swing helplessly at one of Magrane's pitches and then look completely befuddled that Joe would throw that pitch on that count.

Magrane was injured during the 1989 season, and when he came back he had a few weak outings. He looked, frankly, like a just-better-than-average National League pitcher for a while. Later Joe revealed that when he first came back from the injury, his arm was not completely healed and he couldn't throw his curve at all. That is, he was working without his best pitch -- and was "only" performing at about the average. That's what kind of ability wins ERA titles.

FIELDING, HITTING, BASERUNNING:

Magrane is a decent fielder, though he looks gangly. He has quick reflexes and gets to his share of the balls hit in his area. He also has a good move to first, though it could still use some improvement. Magrane and Whitey Herzog both think he could be a good hitter. He has enough strength to hit with power if he were batting on a regular basis. Joe looks lost out there on the bases, though he is fast enough to be used as a pinch runner.

OVERALL:

The Cardinals had the foresight to draft Magrane, who didn't have a fastball in college, because they saw that he was strong enough to develop a big league heater. The Cardinal minor league organization was up to the task of developing that potential, and Magrane has become a first-class pitcher. Joe has the reputation of being a flake, partly because he is left-handed, and partly because he amuses himself by giving odd responses to sportswriters. His oddities do not extend to his work habits, which are good, dedicated, and sober.

JOE MAGRANE

Position: SP
Bats: R **Throws:** L
Ht: 6'6" **Wt:** 230

Opening Day Age: 25
Born: 7/2/64 in Des Moines, IA
ML Seasons: 3

Overall Statistics

	W	L	ERA	G	GS	Sv	IP	H	R	BB	SO	HR
1989	18	9	2.91	34	33	0	234.2	219	81	72	127	5
Career	32	25	2.89	85	83	0	570.1	509	213	183	328	20

Where They Hit the Ball

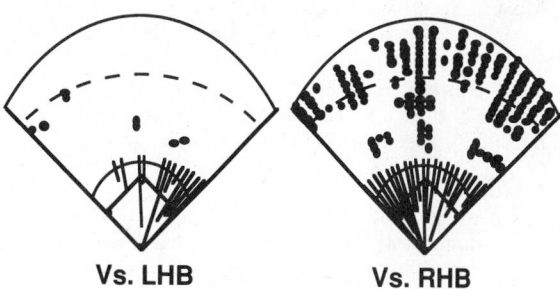

Vs. LHB   Vs. RHB

1989 Situational Stats

	W	L	ERA	Sv	IP		AB	H	HR	RBI	AVG
Home	9	5	3.09	0	119.1	LHB	127	30	0	13	.236
Road	9	4	2.73	0	115.1	RHB	744	189	5	53	.254
Day	6	2	4.58	0	72.2	Sc Pos	203	54	0	56	.266
Night	12	7	2.17	0	162.0	Clutch	88	17	0	4	.193

1989 Rankings (National League)

- ➡ 1st in least HRs per 9 innings (.19) - *pitchers with 162 IP*
- ➡ 2nd in GDPs induced (24) and worst batting average allowed with runners in scoring position (.266) - *pitchers facing 150 batters with runners in scoring position*
- ➡ 3rd in most GDPs induced per 9 innings (.92), wins (18), complete games (9), wild pitches (14) and balks (5)
- ➡ Led the Cardinals in ERA (2.92), wins, win/loss percentage (.667), complete games, shutouts (3), hits allowed (219), wild pitches, balks, GDPs induced, stolen bases allowed (24), run support per 9 innings (4.6) and most GDPs induced per 9 innings

HITTING:

If Willie McGee had even the faintest idea of where the strike zone is, he would be a wonderful hitter. As it is, he has been able to hit over .290 by swinging at anything, and particularly torments such hurlers as Dwight Gooden, who can't find anyplace to throw the ball where it is out of Willie's reach.

Willie has convinced himself that he is a leadoff man, without, unfortunately, learning to take enough walks to support the decision. He has developed a phobia about batting fifth, and goes into a monumental slump immediately upon being placed there. This is part of what has led to the friction between McGee and Whitey Herzog that is reported occasionally in the newspapers.

One way to pitch to McGee is to throw rising fastballs and let them slip out of his reach as he chases them. Most of his strikeouts come from failures there. Another approach is to throw breaking balls in the dirt. Willie can actually hit those low pitches a little, which is the reason he is a starter in the major leagues. Of course, he does hit them on the ground, which is why, despite his speed, he hits into so many double plays.

BASERUNNING:

Willie's injury and lack of playing time cut into his baserunning last year, but he has only had one other poor year, 1986, and that was also in somewhat limited playing time. When healthy Willie steals at about an 80% success rate, and will nab around 40 bases. Those who remember the '82 playoffs know that McGee is prone to mental lapses on the bases.

FIELDING:

McGee was a Gold Glove candidate before he hurt his ankles and lost some speed. His unique skill is the ability to pick balls right off his shoetops while running full out. He has a strong throwing arm, but the throws have "hang time," which is only useful in football. The better baserunners take advantage of Willie's arm.

OVERALL:

With the ankle injuries reducing his speed, Willie is not the player he used to be. He works hard and has great desire to win, but he doesn't appear to have learned much since he was a rookie. He is, though, an asset in the clubhouse. Willie picked up the skill of helping rookies get their feet on the ground from Ozzie Smith. He was widely credited with smoothing both Vince Coleman's and Terry Pendleton's transitions to the majors. When healthy, he's a good, valuable player.

WILLIE McGEE

Position: CF
Bats: B **Throws:** R
Ht: 6' 1" **Wt:** 176

Opening Day Age: 31
Born: 11/2/58 in San Francisco, CA
ML Seasons: 8

Overall Statistics

	G	AB	R	H	D	T	HR	RBI	SB	BB	SO	AVG
1989	58	199	23	47	10	2	3	17	8	10	34	.236
Career	1039	4084	551	1194	172	71	49	483	246	204	612	.292

Where He Hits the Ball

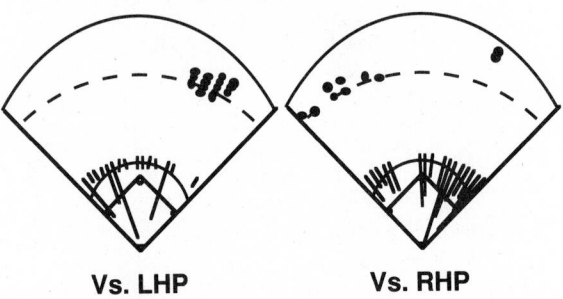

Vs. LHP   Vs. RHP

1989 Situational Stats

	AB	H	HR	RBI	AVG		AB	H	HR	RBI	AVG
Home	106	27	1	6	.255	LHP	77	12	2	10	.156
Road	93	20	2	11	.215	RHP	122	35	1	7	.287
Day	63	16	2	10	.254	Sc Pos	41	11	0	13	.268
Night	136	31	1	7	.228	Clutch	40	11	0	3	.275

1989 Rankings (National League)

➡ Did not rank near the top or bottom in any category

HITTING:

At the age of 19, Jose Oquendo was tossed into a terrible sinkhole in the middle of the New York Met infield. Horribly outmatched physically by major league personnel, he failed, and he failed spectacularly. The Mets cast him into the scrap heap of released ballplayers, where something about him caught the eye of someone in the Cardinal organization. Maybe it was work ethic. It sure *looks* like work ethic.

Jose learned how to switch hit. He learned how to bunt. He learned how to take pitches. He stole one of Rod Carew's lefthanded batting stances, the one with the exaggerated crouch that left him with no strike zone, and he learned how to slap the ball to left field from that stance. He stayed at the AAA level until the Cardinals decided he was ready, first serving as Ozzie Smith's caddy, and only getting his chance to play regularly after Tommy Herr was traded and Luis Alicea washed out. Oquendo proceeded to hit .291, take 79 walks and sneak in a little doubles power. His manager has even started to move him up in the batting order occasionally from his accustomed seventh spot. Señor Horatio Algerio would have been proud.

BASERUNNING:

Jose's greatest weakness is lack of running speed. If he could run, he'd be a tremendous leadoff man. As it is, he steals no bases, hits into more double plays than he should and isn't particularly good at taking the extra base when someone gets a hit behind him, either.

FIELDING:

Oquendo is on his way to the Gold Glove. What we have here is a first-rate major league shortstop playing a lesser position than he could handle because Ozzie Smith happens to be on the same team. A description of Oquendo as a second baseman reflects this: great range and a ridiculously strong arm. He had to work a little to get the double-play pivot down. Jose quit making errors totally in the second half of last season.

OVERALL:

It is quite possible that Jose Oquendo is the best second baseman in the National League whose name is not Ryne. He has at least a decade left of All-Star play, at whatever position his team should require. This player, who was considered washed up at age 20, has a golden future at age 26. There's a lot to be said for work ethic.

JOSE OQUENDO

Position: 2B
Bats: B **Throws:** R
Ht: 5'10" **Wt:** 156

Opening Day Age: 26
Born: 7/4/63 in Rio Piedras, Puerto Rico
ML Seasons: 6

Overall Statistics

	G	AB	R	H	D	T	HR	RBI	SB	BB	SO	AVG
1989	163	556	59	162	28	7	1	48	3	79	59	.291
Career	704	1910	210	511	63	9	10	158	31	234	234	.268

Where He Hits the Ball

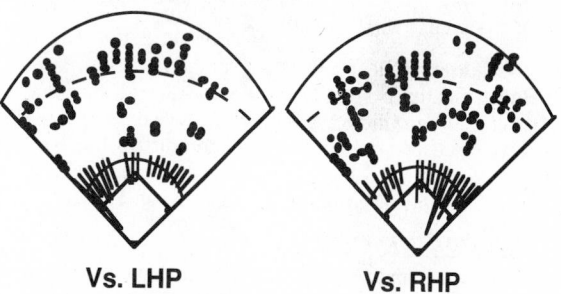

Vs. LHP   **Vs. RHP**

1989 Situational Stats

	AB	H	HR	RBI	AVG		AB	H	HR	RBI	AVG
Home	269	81	0	26	.301	LHP	229	61	0	14	.266
Road	287	81	1	22	.282	RHP	327	101	1	34	.309
Day	179	44	0	18	.246	Sc Pos	141	36	0	47	.255
Night	377	118	1	30	.313	Clutch	91	28	0	4	.308

1989 Rankings (National League)

- ➡ 1st in games (163) and worst home run frequency (556 ABs per home run)
- ➡ 2nd in least runs scored per time reached base (22.8%) - *players with 502 PA*
- ➡ 3rd in sacrifice flies (8)
- ➡ 4th in batting average with 2 strikes (.288) - *players with 162 PA with 2 strikes*
- ➡ 5th in on-base average vs. righthanded pitchers (.309) - *players with 277 PA vs. RHP*
- ➡ Led the Cardinals in games, singles (126), walks (79), batting average with 2 strikes, batting average vs. righthanded pitchers (.309) and hitting on an 0-2 count (.276) - *team players with 20 PA on an 0-2 count*

HITTING:

Tony Pena is no longer the .290 hitter of his prime, but he has recovered nicely from his horrible 1987. Eye problems have cost Pena his ability to hit inside pitching, or at least that's what they say in St. Louis. In response, Tony has learned to slap high, outside pitches into right field, which has made him into a tremendous hit-and-run man. In fact, it is quite possible that Pena would be better off trying to hit to right even more often. It would cost him his power, but he's no 20-homer man anyway.

Pitchers try to pitch Tony low and outside or high and inside. If they try inside and get the pitch a bit out over the plate, Tony can occasionally take it over the fence, but it is still the best place to pitch him. If you get the outside pitch even a little up, he'll hit a line drive between first and second. Tony has neither good strike zone judgement nor much patience at the plate, as reflected in his low walk totals.

It is curious that Tony didn't hit better at home in Busch Stadium. He has a little speed, and hits line drives and grounders, but he hit much better on the road. He also has an extreme platoon differential, and is a very good hitter against lefthanded pitching. Against righties, however, he was poor in 1989.

BASERUNNING:

Tony is fast and Whitey Herzog will have him steal on occasion. He is a very good first-to-third runner, but not so good at second-to-home. His legs have held up well, particularly for a catcher, and that indicates that Tony has been blessed with great lower body strength.

FIELDING:

Tony's trademark is the almost-sitting position with one leg thrust out, which allows his body to block even the lowest of sinkers. He is so agile that he can spring up from this position and still throw out more than his share of runners. The Cardinals asked Tony to use only the most productive of his odd squats, but he is still a completely unique catcher to watch, and still effective.

OVERALL:

All of the statistical systems for rating catchers still put Pena near the top of the National League. Now with Boston, he'll start the 1990 season as one of the favorites for the All-Star team in the American League. It is true that this is partially a tribute to the lack of Johnny Benches and Thurman Munsons among catchers, but Pena's skills remain strong enough to make him a very valuable receiver.

TONY PENA

Position: C
Bats: R **Throws:** R
Ht: 6' 0" **Wt:** 184

Opening Day Age: 32
Born: 6/4/57 in Monte Cristi, Dominican Republic
ML Seasons: 10

Overall Statistics

	G	AB	R	H	D	T	HR	RBI	SB	BB	SO	AVG
1989	141	424	36	110	17	2	4	37	5	35	33	.259
Career	1207	4185	438	1146	193	22	82	472	59	278	519	.274

Where He Hits the Ball

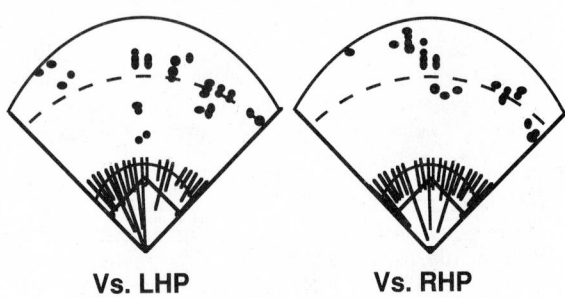

Vs. LHP   **Vs. RHP**

1989 Situational Stats

	AB	H	HR	RBI	AVG		AB	H	HR	RBI	AVG
Home	201	46	3	15	.229	LHP	170	50	2	17	.294
Road	223	64	1	22	.287	RHP	254	60	2	20	.236
Day	125	34	0	13	.272	Sc Pos	118	27	0	30	.229
Night	299	76	4	24	.254	Clutch	76	15	1	4	.197

1989 Rankings (National League)

- ➡ 2nd in most GDPs per GDP situation (20.2%) - *players with 50 PA in GDP situations*
- ➡ 3rd in GDPs (19)
- ➡ 6th in intentional walks (19)
- ➡ Led the Cardinals in GDPs and intentional walks
- ➡ Led NL Catchers in games (141), singles (87), intentional walks (19) and batting average vs. lefthanded pitchers (.294) - *catchers with 125 PA vs. LHP*

HITTING:

What an unpredictable hitter Terry Pendleton is! When he first came to St. Louis in midseason 1984, Pendleton hit .324, but with absolutely no plate discipline. By the beginning of 1985, National League pitchers had figured out that he would swing at anything, and stopped throwing him strikes. Terry's offense collapsed. For two years, he was about as bad a hitter as any major league starter, hitting .240 and .239 with no power. Then, just when people were about to give up on him, Pendleton turned in an outstanding season in 1987, hitting .286 with 96 RBIs and 70 walks. He was injured in '88 and his numbers declined, but Pendleton came back last year to have another good year with the bat. He drew only 44 walks, but that was double his '88 total, and his average improved by 11 points to .264. More than anything, the Cardinals were pleased with his run production. Playing in 162 games, Pendleton hit 13 homers and scored 83 runs last year, both career highs. He drove home 74, his second best total.

The pitching book on Pendleton is that you can make him "climb the ladder." The only problem is keeping him from hitting that first high strike. Terry hit more homers in Busch Stadium than anyone else on the 1989 Cardinals, many on high pitches. If you have to pitch him low, he'll play the same slap-and-go game as Ozzie Smith and Vince Coleman, though he's not as fast as those two.

BASERUNNING:

Although he stole 24 bases in 1986, Pendleton has not been a good base stealer in recent years. He hasn't stolen in double figures in three years, and his success percentages have not been good. Terry is a little better at running the bases on hits, but even there, he's nothing special.

FIELDING:

There is no doubt that Pendleton has deserved the Gold Glove at third for some time now. His range, in particular, is incredible. His specialty is the chase back on the foul pop-up, with the resulting catch over the shoulder. It is quite possible that no third baseman has ever been better on that play. It can safely be said that there is no skill nor tool that Pendleton is lacking.

OVERALL:

Pendleton's career has been so up and down that it's almost impossible to predict how he'll do in 1990. If he stays at his '89 level, he'll be a good run producer with an outstanding glove at third. The Cards would gladly settle for that, but they know they can't depend on it.

TERRY PENDLETON

Position: 3B
Bats: B **Throws:** R
Ht: 5' 9" **Wt:** 178

Opening Day Age: 29
Born: 7/16/60 in Los Angeles, CA
ML Seasons: 6

Overall Statistics

	G	AB	R	H	D	T	HR	RBI	SB	BB	SO	AVG
1989	162	613	83	162	28	5	13	74	9	44	81	.264
Career	806	2986	358	785	135	22	38	384	92	222	372	.263

Where He Hits the Ball

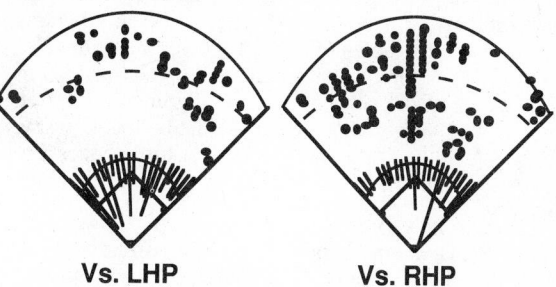

Vs. LHP	Vs. RHP

1989 Situational Stats

	AB	H	HR	RBI	AVG		AB	H	HR	RBI	AVG
Home	295	80	8	42	.271	LHP	247	69	2	20	.279
Road	318	82	5	32	.258	RHP	366	93	11	54	.254
Day	190	58	6	23	.305	Sc Pos	154	41	3	60	.266
Night	423	104	7	51	.246	Clutch	97	22	2	9	.227

1989 Rankings (National League)

- ➡ 3rd in games (162)
- ➡ 4th in at bats (613)
- ➡ 5th in lowest percentage of pitches taken (46.1%) - *players with 502 PA*
- ➡ 7th in GDPs (16)
- ➡ 9th in hits (162)
- ➡ 10th in runs scored per time reached base (36.2%)
- ➡ Led the Cardinals in at bats
- ➡ Led NL Third Basemen in singles (116) and grounder/flyball ratio (1.40)

PITCHING:

Back in 1981, Ted Power, with a 18-3 record, was the unquestioned pitching star of an Albuquerque Duke team that won 94 games while losing only 38. The Duke roster included such future major leaguers as Mike Marshall, Candy Maldonado, Rudy Law, Jack Perconte, Ron Roenicke, Dave Anderson, Brian Holton, Ricky Wright and Alejandro Pena. Like most of the bigger names on that Dodger farm club, Power has had a somewhat disappointing major league career, considering the buildup. He's had one 27-save season in relief, but mostly he's been a mediocre starter who's never won more than 10 games. But at 35, Power continues to survive on the major league level.

A year ago, it looked like it might be all over for Power. Cut loose by the lowly Tigers, Ted couldn't find a major league opening and had to sign with the Cardinals' Louisville farm team. Eventually he was recalled, and down the stretch Power was a regular member of the St. Louis rotation. He pitched well in the heat of the pennant race while going 7-7. A free agent at year's end, Power suddenly found teams engaged in a minor bidding war for his services. He finally signed with the Pirates.

Though he's getting up there in years, Power still relies mainly on his fastball. He's not afraid to work high and inside, and for that reason, he's prone to give up the home run ball. Power also throws a slider and a sinker; he'll usually set up hitters with a high and tight fastball, then go low and away with the breaking stuff. Power has always been markedly more effective against lefthanded hitters than versus righties.

HITTING, BASERUNNING, FIELDING:

Power is a good athlete and handles himself well with the glove. A high leg-kicker, he does not hold baserunners very well. Ted is a Power hitter in name only; he has only one major league homer in nine years, and generally swings a weak stick. As befits a man who is 6'4", 220, and 35 years old, he does not run the bases very well.

OVERALL:

Power's services were still in demand in the off-season because he can both start and relieve. He's a veteran who usually won't beat himself, and he seems able to handle whatever role his club gives him. He's a thorough professional and a good influence on young pitchers.

TED POWER

Position: SP/RP
Bats: R **Throws:** R
Ht: 6' 4" **Wt:** 220

Opening Day Age: 35
Born: 1/31/55 in Guthrie, OK
ML Seasons: 9

Overall Statistics

	W	L	ERA	G	GS	Sv	IP	H	R	BB	SO	HR
1989	7	7	3.71	23	15	0	97.0	96	47	21	43	7
Career	57	56	4.15	347	85	41	876.1	877	447	352	530	76

Where They Hit the Ball

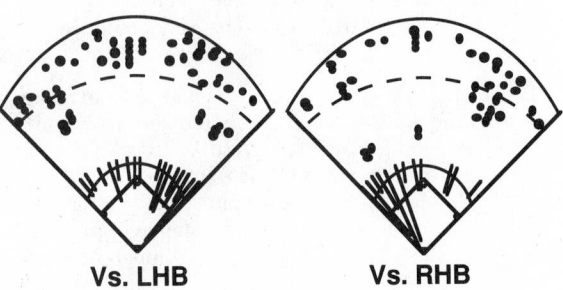

Vs. LHB   **Vs. RHB**

1989 Situational Stats

	W	L	ERA	Sv	IP		AB	H	HR	RBI	AVG
Home	3	2	2.95	0	39.2	LHB	207	58	3	20	.280
Road	4	5	4.24	0	57.1	RHB	170	38	4	22	.224
Day	1	3	5.40	0	18.1	Sc Pos	96	28	3	36	.292
Night	6	4	3.32	0	78.2	Clutch	12	4	0	1	.333

1989 Rankings (National League)

➡ Did not rank near the top or bottom in any category

PITCHING:

Once one of baseball's premier late-inning relievers, Dan Quisenberry lost that role, and almost his career, because of an inability to retire lefthanded hitters and a slight weakening of his pinpoint control. Signed by Whitey Herzog's Cardinals and placed in middle relief, where he could face a more even mix of hitters, Quisenberry has revived his career. Quisenberry's shaken confidence is now restored and his control, always a key to his success, is sharper than ever.

Quisenberry has an ordinary fastball, just quick enough to get a batter out if he is expecting something slower; a decent breaking ball; and a tremendous change-up. Because of his submarine delivery, the stuff looks like it is rising into the strike zone, and then it drops back down at the last minute. In order to get batters out, he absolutely must keep that stuff at the knees or even lower. When he was having his troubles the last few years, it was the fastball that wouldn't stay down at the knees, and hitters, especially lefties, sat on the change-up.

At his best, Quisenberry keeps the ball away from the batter, as well as down by the knees. This results in a lot of grounders to the opposite field, and Dan was definitely helped by the Cardinal defense when he was pitching against lefthanded batters. Against righties, Dan pitched inside, to get the batters to hit the ball towards Smith and Pendleton, and away from Pedro Guerrero.

FIELDING, HITTING, BASERUNNING:

Dan is a good, unspectacular fielder. He is especially good on bunts down the third base line. He throws underhand to first, just like he pitches, which can cause the first baseman some trouble gauging the throw. He holds baserunners well. Dan spent most of his career in the American League; he cannot hit at all.

OVERALL:

Submarine pitching places tremendous stress on the wrist, and Quisenberry must be absolutely precise with his motion and release to maintain the pinpoint control he must have to be effective. Dan pitched a light load of innings in 1989, and the question remains as to whether his body could stand the strain of a serious closer role. With Todd Worrell out until at least mid-1990, Quisenberry may get his chance. He'll have to deal with opponents who save their lefty swingers for him, the weakness that got him into trouble with the Royals.

DAN QUISENBERRY

Position: RP
Bats: R **Throws:** R
Ht: 6' 2" **Wt:** 185

Opening Day Age: 37
Born: 2/7/53 in Santa Monica, CA
ML Seasons: 11

Overall Statistics

	W	L	ERA	G	GS	Sv	IP	H	R	BB	SO	HR
1989	3	1	2.64	63	0	6	78.1	78	25	14	37	2
Career	56	45	2.69	669	0	244	1036.0	1051	344	159	377	58

Where They Hit the Ball

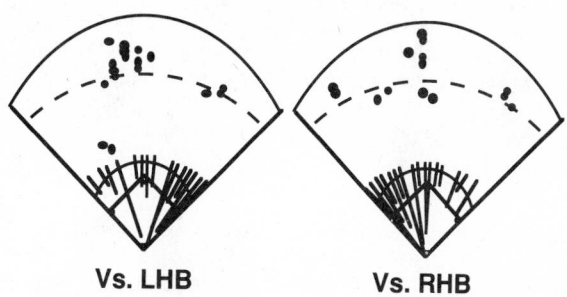

Vs. LHB   **Vs. RHB**

1989 Situational Stats

	W	L	ERA	Sv	IP		AB	H	HR	RBI	AVG
Home	3	0	4.30	4	37.2	LHB	143	34	2	8	.238
Road	0	1	1.11	2	40.2	RHB	156	44	0	19	.282
Day	3	0	3.07	2	29.1	Sc Pos	81	25	1	25	.309
Night	0	1	2.39	4	49.0	Clutch	72	19	0	6	.264

1989 Rankings (National League)

➡ 3rd in most GDPs induced per GDP situation (20.0%) - *pitchers with 30 GDP situations*

➡ Led the Cardinals in most GDPs induced per GDP situation

HITTING:

While with the Padres, Ozzie Smith learned exceptional plate discipline and strike zone judgement. His walk/strikeout ratios have been consistently among the highest in the league, and his on-base percentages are excellent. After being traded to the Cardinals, Ozzie went on Mackie Shilstone's strength program and developed enough power to cause outfielders to play him at normal depths. While he still doesn't hit many homers, he now manages good doubles totals, and his batting average is way up from his early years, as his soft liners now fall in front of the backed-up fielders.

Smith's strength as a hitter is placement. Ozzie is a great hit-and-run man, because he can hit almost any pitch to right field. He is also a fine bunter. He is particularly good at bunting the high pitch, one of the most difficult skills in baseball. Ozzie's basic approach is to slap grounders through the infield, going with the pitch. The best place to pitch Ozzie is up in the strike zone. While he can hit the high pitch, he won't take your high mistakes out of the park. There is no type of pitcher that gives Ozzie real trouble.

BASERUNNING:

Ozzie doesn't steal for great volume, but he seldom gets caught. At his level of attempts (he consistently steals about 30 bases a year), he is the among the very best. He is seldom thrown out running on hits. In fact, Ozzie is as intelligent, fast and skilled a baserunner as you'll find.

FIELDING:

Smith's unique acrobatic ability helps him continue to be a tremendous fielder. Now past 30, his range is down, reflecting a little lost speed. Smith has had shoulder problems for a few years, and his throws from the hole don't always beat the faster runners any more. He's not quite what he once was, but then no one else is what Ozzie once was, either.

OVERALL:

For a few years, say 1985 to 1987, Smith was a serious MVP candidate. At 35, his skills are declining, but Ozzie still has great value. Even late in his career, he does everything very well: fields, steals, hits a fine number two, and is a leader in the clubhouse. Ozzie has worked very hard to make new players on the Cardinals feel welcome and to help them settle into the area. You have to have some sort of player leadership on a team, and this is the sort you want.

OZZIE SMITH

Position: SS
Bats: B **Throws:** R
Ht: 5'10" **Wt:** 155

Opening Day Age: 35
Born: 12/26/54 in Mobile, AL
ML Seasons: 12

Overall Statistics

	G	AB	R	H	D	T	HR	RBI	SB	BB	SO	AVG
1989	155	593	82	162	30	8	2	50	29	55	37	.273
Career	1783	6507	849	1668	276	51	18	550	432	746	421	.256

Where He Hits the Ball

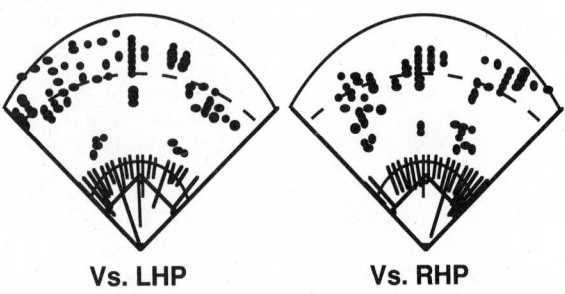

Vs. LHP   **Vs. RHP**

1989 Situational Stats

	AB	H	HR	RBI	AVG		AB	H	HR	RBI	AVG
Home	297	75	1	29	.253	LHP	248	71	1	16	.286
Road	296	87	1	21	.294	RHP	345	91	1	34	.264
Day	180	59	1	18	.328	Sc Pos	144	42	0	43	.292
Night	413	103	1	32	.249	Clutch	83	30	0	8	.361

1989 Rankings (National League)

→ 1st in hitting in the clutch (.361 - *players with 50 PA in the clutch*) and lowest percentage of swings that missed (6.2%) - *players with 502 PA*

→ 2nd in worst home run frequency (296.5 ABs per HR)

→ 6th in triples (8) and hitting on the road (.294) - *players with 252 PA on the road*

→ Led the Cardinals in lowest percentage of swings that missed, hitting in the clutch, sacrifice bunts (11) and errors (17)

→ Led NL Shortstops in games (155), runs (82), hits (162), doubles (30), triples, sacrifice bunts, stolen bases (29), at bats (593), singles (122) and total bases (214)

PITCHING:

Scott Terry is a converted third baseman/outfielder. He throws hard, with a very precise motion that does not look completely natural. His footwork looks delicate, but he throws very hard and finishes with a strong spring off the mound. The stuff is basic: fastball, slider and change-up. Terry's breaking pitch isn't all that hot, and he depends on his heat and his control. When his fastball rides up in the strike zone, he has trouble, though he throws hard enough to overpower weaker hitters. He gives up a lot of home runs on those high fastballs; in fact, it's his major weakness. When Terry keeps the ball down, he gets a lot of ground ball outs. He's not much of a strikeout pitcher.

A main strength of Terry's precise motion is that hitters do not seem to be able to guess the pitches at all; hence his change-up is an above-average weapon. He pitches with deliberation, taking his time, keeping his mechanics correct.

Whitey Herzog is talking about making a reliever out of Terry, mostly because he has not shown a lot of stamina in late innings. That's also supported by the high homer totals, which indicate a fastball that gets slow enough for major league hitters to time it.

FIELDING, HITTING, BASERUNNING:

The converted position player shows through in Scott's supplemental skills. He is an outstanding hitter for a pitcher, with power and placement. He is also excellent in the field. His motion leaves him in perfect position, and he is third baseman quick, a great asset in fielding a position only 60 feet away from the plate. In particular, he is great at snaring the hot shot through the box, and can truly pounce on bunts. Terry also does a decent job of holding baserunners. He is used as a pinch runner, and is particularly aggressive going from first to third.

OVERALL:

Terry has developed into an above-average pitcher, which seems to surprise everyone who saw him making the conversion in the first place. The center of his ability is a good combination of strength and quickness; it is hard to imagine why that combination wasn't enough to make a major league position player out of him. Though he's 30, Terry has only been pitching full-time since 1984. He still has time to develop his pitching skills even more.

SCOTT TERRY

Position: SP/RP
Bats: R **Throws:** R
Ht: 5'11" **Wt:** 195

Opening Day Age: 30
Born: 11/21/59 in Hobbs, NY
ML Seasons: 4

Overall Statistics

	W	L	ERA	G	GS	Sv	IP	H	R	BB	SO	HR
1989	8	10	3.57	31	24	2	148.2	142	65	43	69	14
Career	18	18	3.73	121	38	5	347.0	340	158	117	175	27

Where They Hit the Ball

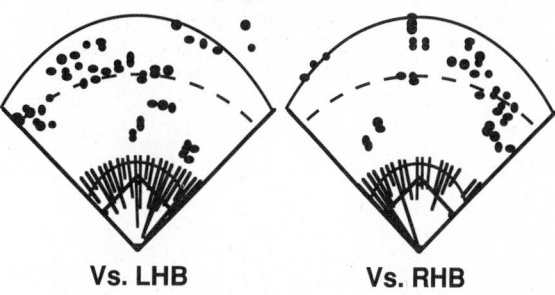

Vs. LHB   **Vs. RHB**

1989 Situational Stats

	W	L	ERA	Sv	IP		AB	H	HR	RBI	AVG
Home	6	4	3.08	1	87.2	LHB	280	73	6	25	.261
Road	2	6	4.28	1	61.0	RHB	281	69	8	34	.246
Day	1	4	6.03	0	31.1	Sc Pos	134	32	4	42	.239
Night	7	6	2.91	2	117.1	Clutch	54	13	1	6	.241

1989 Rankings (National League)

➡ Did not rank near the top or bottom in any category

HITTING:

Milt Thompson suffers in reputation because he is not flashy or spectacular. As a hitter, he has a good batting average, which floats just around .300, decent but not great plate discipline, and marginal power. He doesn't bunt well or often, nor does he have good bat control. He is a decent hit-and-run man only because he is lefthanded. The end result is that he is hard to describe and easy to overlook. The combination, however, has few serious weaknesses to go with the few obvious strengths, and Milt remains a fine major league hitter. He's very consistent, having hit between .288 and .303 in all but one of his six major league seasons. Thompson also gave the Cardinals excellent RBI production last year; his 68 ribbies were a career high by 25.

Most pitchers just use their best stuff in their best location against Milt, rather than trying to exploit any real weakness or oddity. Milt used to have the rap that he didn't hit lefthanded pitching, but he did reasonably well versus southpaws last year. Again, he lacks any idiosyncrasy that would cause people to notice him.

BASERUNNING:

Thompson is very fast and a fine base stealer, having swiped as many as 46 in a season. He's a good percentage stealer, 78% for his career. Now that he's had a year in St. Louis, the Cardinals would like him to run even more than he did a year ago, when he was 27 for 35. He was the best runner on the team at taking an extra base.

FIELDING:

Milt played a lot of centerfield for the Cardinals last year, but that was mainly out of necessity with Willie McGee hurt. Thompson has good range but doesn't possess a very strong arm. He's best suited for left field, and will be the regular there if the Cardinals unload Vince Coleman.

OVERALL:

The Cardinals knew pretty much what to expect when they obtained Thompson for Curt Ford and Steve Lake a year ago: a .290 bat with power in the gaps, excellent speed, and good outfield range. But Milt's RBI production and his ability to hit lefties were welcome bonuses. Thompson's stock has risen in St. Louis. The Cards now know he can play every day, which allows them to consider trading Coleman or McGee. If they don't make a deal, Thompson's presence gives the Redbirds an excellent alternative if the others are injured or unproductive.

MILT THOMPSON

Position: CF/LF
Bats: L **Throws:** R
Ht: 5'11" **Wt:** 170

Opening Day Age: 31
Born: 1/5/59 in Washington, DC
ML Seasons: 6

Overall Statistics

	G	AB	R	H	D	T	HR	RBI	SB	BB	SO	AVG
1989	155	545	60	158	28	8	4	68	27	39	91	.290
Career	621	2030	270	586	85	22	21	177	132	164	346	.289

Where He Hits the Ball

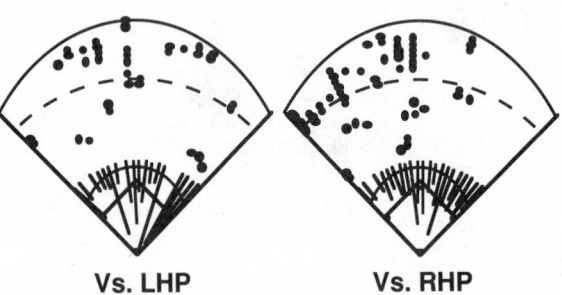

Vs. LHP   **Vs. RHP**

1989 Situational Stats

	AB	H	HR	RBI	AVG		AB	H	HR	RBI	AVG
Home	271	82	2	39	.303	LHP	210	56	1	28	.267
Road	274	76	2	29	.277	RHP	335	102	3	40	.304
Day	183	46	1	24	.251	Sc Pos	151	48	3	64	.318
Night	362	112	3	44	.309	Clutch	85	25	0	8	.294

1989 Rankings (National League)

- ➡ 1st in grounder/flyball ratio (2.43) - *players with 502 PA*
- ➡ 2nd in worst batting average on an 0-2 count (..029) - *players with 20 PA on an 0-2 count*
- ➡ 6th in triples (8) and highest batting average on a 3-1 count (.542) - *players with 10 PA on a 3-1 count*
- ➡ 9th in singles (118)
- ➡ 10th in hitting with runners in scoring position (.318) - *players with 100 PA with runners in scoring position*
- ➡ Led the Cardinals in hit by pitch (4), grounder/flyball ratio, hitting with the bases loaded (.385) and percentage of extra bases taken as a runner (55.4%)

PITCHING:

Todd Worrell, one of the finest relievers of the last five years, faces a clouded future. Worrell began suffering elbow problems last year, and missed most of the last month of the season. Rest didn't cure the problem, and Worrell ended up needing complicated reconstructive surgery. Recovery will be slow and, at best, Worrell will miss the early part of the 1990 season. He could be gone even longer.

When he's healthy, there's nothing complicated about Todd Worrell's pitching. He throws the fastball as hard as he can for as long as his arm holds out, and hopes the game ends before he gets pounded. While he is on, the hard one hops as it reaches the plate. When he runs out of gas, it is flat and loses about three miles per hour. When that happens, his slider and his ordinary change-up will not save him. Because he tries to throw as hard as he can, his control is not going to save him, either. When Worrell tires he cannot keep the ball down, and it loses its hop and rises into the strike zone at the same time. He is, therefore, not a pitcher who can get by for a couple of batters when he loses his stuff, and consequently, Whitey uses a quick hook on him.

The best strategy for a team facing Todd is to take a lot of pitches, hoping to exhaust his supply of the good, hopping fastball. It was to counter this tactic that Whitey made it a rule not to bring Todd in before the eighth inning.

FIELDING, HITTING, BASERUNNING:

Worrell is lacking in all these departments. Todd is not the best fielder among pitchers, and is also none too disciplined at backing up the right base. Worrell does not have a good move to first, either. He is also a lousy hitter, awkward and with a slow bat. As should be expected, he is a plodding, inexperienced baserunner on the rare occasion that he is actually on base.

OVERALL:

For a pitcher who depends on blowing the ball past hitters with his strong right arm, Worrell's injury has to be more than a little frightening. At this point, any contribution the Cards receive from Worrell in 1990 will be considered a bonus.

TODD WORRELL

Position: RP
Bats: R **Throws:** R
Ht: 6' 5" **Wt:** 210

Opening Day Age: 30
Born: 9/28/59 in Arcadia, CA
ML Seasons: 5

Overall Statistics

	W	L	ERA	G	GS	Sv	IP	H	R	BB	SO	HR
1989	3	5	2.96	47	0	20	51.2	42	21	26	41	4
Career	28	30	2.64	281	0	126	361.2	300	118	142	301	30

Where They Hit the Ball

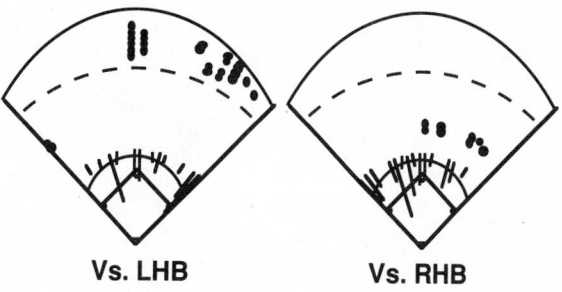

Vs. LHB   **Vs. RHB**

1989 Situational Stats

	W	L	ERA	Sv	IP		AB	H	HR	RBI	AVG
Home	3	4	3.08	12	26.1	LHB	90	22	3	14	.244
Road	0	1	2.84	8	25.1	RHB	99	20	1	11	.202
Day	2	0	3.45	3	15.2	Sc Pos	70	14	1	20	.200
Night	1	5	2.75	17	36.0	Clutch	140	30	2	19	.214

1989 Rankings (National League)

➡ 4th in save percentage (87.0%) - *pitchers with 20 save opportunities*

➡ 7th in lowest percentage of inherited runners scoring (26.7%) - *pitchers with 30 inherited runners*

➡ Led the Cardinals in saves (20), save opportunities (23), save percentage and games finished (39)

HITTING:

Todd Zeile's 1989 statistics are similar to Tony Pena's. Tony doesn't hit righthanded pitching at all, and neither did Todd, but both did very well against lefties. Each hit considerably better on the road than at home. The biggest difference between them was that, on average, Todd struck out a lot more than Tony, and also walked more.

Zeile, however, was just up for his first cup of coffee, while Tony is presumably not going to get any better. Also, Todd was obviously trying to decide how much of his minor league power he could count on in the caverns of Busch Stadium. From the first quick look, it seems like he won't retain much of it. By the end of the season he was trying to hit hard line drives, as if he were Ted Simmons, rather than swing for home runs. He was pulling everything, but not hitting the ball in the air as much as expected.

Pitchers first tried getting him out with stuff on the outside corner, but his bat is quick enough to not only hit such fare, but pull it. Then they tried jamming him, and he did have a little slump before he started to wait and let the close ones go by.

BASERUNNING:

Whitey Herzog had Todd batting third for a while, in front of Pedro Guerrero. That means that Todd is not nearly as slow as the archetypal catcher, though it may also have been an attempt to get Todd some good pitches to hit to bolster his confidence. Todd is not a threat to steal, and does not have the good speed for a catcher that Pena has.

FIELDING:

Zeile comes up with a rap against his arm, but that may not be true. Todd probably won't turn into Benito Santiago, but he seems likely to throw out his share of runners. His pitch-calling seemed very standard and conservative, but he was, after all, a rookie. He moves well fielding balls in play.

OVERALL:

The Cardinals are committed to Zeile for the next year, and probably for a couple, even if he does poorly. They have prepared him well, keeping him in Triple A longer than he probably needed. With Whitey's help on defense and pitch-calling, and his apparent decision not to try to hit 20 home runs in Busch, he is a very good bet to succeed.

TODD ZEILE

Position: C
Bats: R **Throws:** R
Ht: 6' 1" **Wt:** 190

Opening Day Age: 24
Born: 9/9/65 in Van Nuys, CA
ML Seasons: 1

Overall Statistics

	G	AB	R	H	D	T	HR	RBI	SB	BB	SO	AVG
1989	28	82	7	21	3	1	1	8	0	9	14	.256
Career	28	82	7	21	3	1	1	8	0	9	14	.256

Where He Hits the Ball

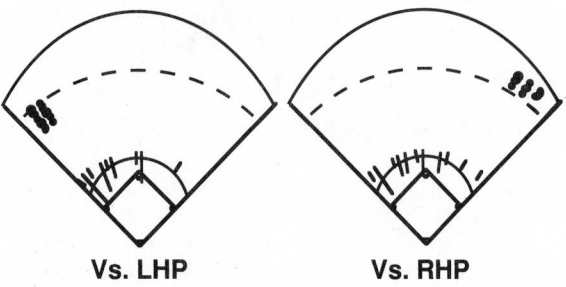

Vs. LHP   **Vs. RHP**

1989 Situational Stats

	AB	H	HR	RBI	AVG		AB	H	HR	RBI	AVG
Home	39	9	0	6	.231	LHP	39	11	0	5	.282
Road	43	12	1	2	.279	RHP	43	10	1	3	.233
Day	29	10	1	4	.345	Sc Pos	22	6	0	7	.273
Night	53	11	0	4	.208	Clutch	17	3	0	0	.176

1989 Rankings (National League)

➡ Did not rank near the top or bottom in any category

TIM JONES

Position: SS
Bats: L **Throws:** R
Ht: 5'10" **Wt:** 172

Opening Day Age: 27
Born: 12/1/62 in Sumter, SC
ML Seasons: 2

Overall Statistics

	G	AB	R	H	D	T	HR	RBI	SB	BB	SO	AVG
1989	42	75	11	22	6	0	0	7	1	7	8	.293
Career	73	127	13	36	6	0	0	10	5	11	18	.283

HITTING, FIELDING, BASERUNNING:

In the minors, Tim Jones displayed a little power, and you'd think he would retain at least some pop in the majors. However, he has hit mostly singles in his two partial seasons with St. Louis. Even as a singles hitter, Tim hits high pitching well, though usually to the opposite field. A good base stealer, he has enough speed to beat out some grounders. Jones is also used as a pinch runner on occasion. He has good plate discipline, and takes his walks. Tim is a good infielder and has become extremely versatile, even learning how to catch. If Ozzie Smith and Jose Oquendo hadn't been healthy all year, he would have been quite able to fill Jose's old "secret weapon" role.

OVERALL:

Whitey Herzog prefers to keep potential regulars in the minors, where they can get some experience, until he is willing to start them on the Cardinals. Since Jones is a young reserve, Whitey probably thinks Tim is going to be a career benchwarmer. It is worth noting that Whitey has made only one mistake in this regard, Jose Oquendo. However, Tim Jones resembles Jose Oquendo more than any other player in Whitey's organization.

JIM LINDEMAN

Position: 1B
Bats: R **Throws:** R
Ht: 6' 1" **Wt:** 200

Opening Day Age: 28
Born: 1/10/62 in Evanston, IL
ML Seasons: 4

Overall Statistics

	G	AB	R	H	D	T	HR	RBI	SB	BB	SO	AVG
1989	73	45	8	5	1	0	0	2	0	3	18	.111
Career	184	350	38	71	16	0	11	43	4	18	93	.203

HITTING, FIELDING, BASERUNNING:

Although it may seem that Jim Lindeman's career has been dominated by injuries, it is equally a story of the importance of plate discipline. Lindeman swings at absolutely everything, and all the pitchers know it. Three years ago, he might have been able to learn to take pitches, but he has lost those years to injury, and is now only the most marginal of prospects. Low pitches are best against him, as Jim will occasionally punish the high ones for homers if they get too close, which the Giants learned to their dismay in 1987. Lindeman has hardly had any time to work on his baserunning. He has a little speed, but remains well below major league levels as a runner, and can't steal at all. Jim is also a poor fielder, having failed in chances at third base and right field.

OVERALL:

To be blunt, Jim Lindeman is now a major league player in name only. If he had not been injured so much, he would have washed out completely as a prospect. Only the chance that he still can fulfill the potential of three years ago keeps him in the majors, and now he also has to fight a reputation as injury-prone. He's about on his last chance.

JOHN MORRIS

Position: RF
Bats: L **Throws:** L
Ht: 6' 1" **Wt:** 185

Opening Day Age: 29
Born: 2/23/61 in
Freeport, NY
ML Seasons: 4

Overall Statistics

	G	AB	R	H	D	T	HR	RBI	SB	BB	SO	AVG
1989	96	117	8	28	4	1	2	14	1	4	22	.239
Career	256	412	41	104	12	7	6	54	12	23	66	.252

HITTING, FIELDING, BASERUNNING:

John Morris has tremendous athletic ability, and shows signs of developing into a quality hitter when he isn't suffering from one of his frequent injuries. He has hit for average and a little power at times, and has developed into a fine pinch hitter. Though fast, Morris shows no sign of utilizing the slap-and-go game that so many of the Cardinals have found useful. It might help him, because he's not much of a home run threat. Morris has little bat control, though as a lefthanded pull hitter, he can regularly hit the ball to the right side, a thing that Whitey Herzog harps on. He has a excellent glove, with centerfield speed and plenty of arm for right. Morris shows a good jump and seems to be well drilled in throwing to the right base or cutoff man.

OVERALL:

A lesser athletic talent might be in trouble if he had Morris's injury history, but, as long as he still has the arm and the speed, John will be able to find someone to give him a tryout. In the meantime, he is a good enough fielder to make a decent living in the majors as a backup and pinch hitter.

TOM PAGNOZZI

Position: C
Bats: R **Throws:** R
Ht: 6' 1" **Wt:** 190

Opening Day Age: 27
Born: 7/30/62 in
Tucson, AZ
ML Seasons: 3

Overall Statistics

	G	AB	R	H	D	T	HR	RBI	SB	BB	SO	AVG
1989	52	80	3	12	2	0	0	3	0	6	19	.150
Career	160	323	28	76	12	0	2	27	1	21	64	.235

HITTING, FIELDING, BASERUNNING:

A righthanded hitter with some power, Tom Pagnozzi has never had enough playing time to get into a groove and display a consistent stroke. He pulls the ball too often, and is vulnerable to the curve and the sinker. Tom hits much better when in the starting lineup than when pinch hitting, and might well be capable of handling a full-time job on a team that doesn't have Tony Pena or Todd Zeile. A decent runner for a catcher, Tom still isn't going to steal any bases or make many mad dashes from first to third. He's a good, solid fielder with an above average arm. He needs work at calling games, but part of his problem there is due to lack of major league experience.

OVERALL:

Tom is a classic Whitey Herzog reserve. There are certainly teams he could start for, but Whitey keeps him around, secure in the knowledge that he is the best available protection against an injury to his starter. It is Herzog's ability to find and keep people like Pagnozzi that allows him to choose between Tony Pena and Todd Zeile, rather than trying to find some mad plan to keep both of them happy.

DENNY WALLING

Position: 1B
Bats: L **Throws:** R
Ht: 6' 1" **Wt:** 185

Opening Day Age: 35
Born: 4/17/54 in
Neptune, NJ
ML Seasons: 15

Overall Statistics

	G	AB	R	H	D	T	HR	RBI	SB	BB	SO	AVG
1989	69	79	9	24	7	0	1	11	0	14	12	.304
Career	1166	2771	363	766	136	30	48	359	44	297	293	.276

HITTING, FIELDING, BASERUNNING:

Denny Walling managed to hit over .300 last year under the worst possible circumstances. He was 35 years old, he was used sporadically, and his appearances varied between pinch-hitting and spot starting. Used to the Astrodome, where he played for 12 years, Walling has more than enough experience not to frustrate himself trying to hit homers out of Busch Stadium. Instead, he hits hard liners up the right-center alley. Pitching Walling away didn't bother him. He has very good bat control, again, presumably, from all those years in the Dome. Walling has lost his speed, and has learned to play safe, station-to-station baseball. Denny's jobs on the Cardinals were to play backup for Terry Pendleton at third and for Pedro Guerrero at first. The same reflexes that still let him get around on the outside fastball also make him quick enough to play third.

OVERALL:

After Walling hit only .239 in 1988, not many people thought he had anything left. But he showed he still can play third and still can hit righties. On a team with two brittle men at the corners of the infield, that's a valuable player in a necessary role. That Walling turned in an exceptional season as a pinch hitter was a bonus.

HITTING:

Roberto Alomar is on the brink of becoming an accomplished big league switch-hitter. But in his first two major league seasons, Alomar has continued to have problems hitting from the right side of the plate. Though he hit .295 overall last season, Alomar hit .256 swinging against lefthanders -- two points less than his rookie season (1988).

Just 22, Alomar has spent many batting practice hours trying to improve in this area, but the only real elixir may be experience. Alomar certainly has the talent to eliminate any of his hitting weaknesses. He has a quick bat and can belt the ball to all fields. Alomar is not a power hitter, but he can drive the ball at times, with seven homers and a club-leading (with Tony Gwynn) 27 doubles a year ago. He's also an outstanding bunter.

Along with a few problems batting righty, Alomar needs to acquire more patience. He only walked 53 times in 702 plate appearances a year ago. But that was an improvement by six over his rookie total, and not a bad figure for such a young player. While walking more, Alomar also reduced his strikeouts last year from 83 to 76.

BASERUNNING:

A good, swift baserunner, Alomar stole 42 bases last year, an improvement of 18 over his rookie season. He's a great player to keep in perpetual motion on the bases, particularly when batting in the number two hole ahead of Tony Gwynn.

FIELDING:

Despite 28 errors last season (up from 16 in 1988), Alomar could easily become an annual All-Star selection at second base. He has tremendous range to both sides and a very strong arm. Roberto makes the same type of acrobatic plays at his position as Ozzie Smith does at shortstop, and moving him to shortstop eventually is a viable option for the Padres. Roberto is often nailed for errors when he boots balls that many second basemen cannot reach. He also has a penchant for making wild throws across his body when he snares balls to his right and is fading away from first base. Alomar must learn to hold the ball more often in those circumstances, but that is a matter of experience.

OVERALL:

The sky is the limit for Roberto Alomar. In two seasons, he has only touched the surface of his vast potential. Alomar is a hard worker who toils even harder to overcome the problems in his game. But there aren't many problems, and Roberto would be a fine player with the skills he has already mastered.

ROBERTO ALOMAR

Position: 2B
Bats: B **Throws:** R
Ht: 6' 0" **Wt:** 155

Opening Day Age: 22
Born: 2/5/68 in St. Augustine, Puerto Rico
ML Seasons: 2

Overall Statistics

	G	AB	R	H	D	T	HR	RBI	SB	BB	SO	AVG
1989	158	623	82	184	27	1	7	56	42	53	76	.295
Career	301	1168	166	329	51	7	16	97	66	100	159	.282

Where He Hits the Ball

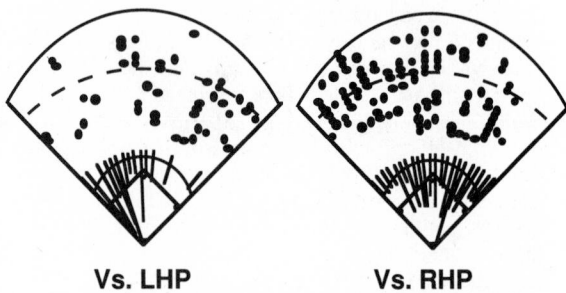

Vs. LHP   **Vs. RHP**

1989 Situational Stats

	AB	H	HR	RBI	AVG		AB	H	HR	RBI	AVG
Home	286	94	3	34	.329	LHP	195	50	4	20	.256
Road	337	90	4	22	.267	RHP	428	134	3	36	.313
Day	173	51	3	18	.295	Sc Pos	128	32	0	44	.250
Night	450	133	4	38	.296	Clutch	94	30	1	7	.319

1989 Rankings (National League)

- ➡ 1st in sacrifice bunts (17)
- ➡ 2nd in stolen bases (42), singles (149) and caught stealing (17)
- ➡ 3rd in hits (184), pitches seen (2,520), bunts in play (37) and sacrifice flies (8)
- ➡ Led the Padres in at bats (623), games (158), runs (82), doubles (27), stolen bases, sacrifice bunts, caught stealing, pitches seen, sacrifice flies, bunts in play, steals of third (7) and errors (28)
- ➡ Led NL Second Basemen in batting average (.295), at bats, singles, sacrifice bunts, sacrifice flies, stolen bases, caught stealing, hits, bunts in play, steals of third, percentage of extra bases taken (58.2%) and errors

HITTING:

Sandy Alomar, Jr., Baseball America's 1989 Minor League Player of the Year, has done it all at the Triple A level. During the 1988 and 1989 seasons at Las Vegas, Alomar won the Pacific Coast League MVP both years. Obviously, Sandy has proven he's ready for the big leagues. He would have made it a year ago, if the Padres had been able to trade Benito Santiago.

After an outstanding AAA season in 1988, Alomar was even better a year ago. He batted .306, nine points higher than 1988, and drove in 101 runs, 30 more than the previous season. He did it all despite a slump during which he bottomed out at .232 on June 5. Riding the crest of a 19-game hitting streak, Alomar hit .351 for the rest of the season.

Alomar will probably not be a big home run hitter at the major league level, but he has decent power and the capability of homering in double figures. Sandy opened some eyes with a 450-foot homer in the AAA All-Star game last year. He has shown all the traits of a successful hitter: the ability to hit to all fields, good numbers of both doubles (33 a year ago) and triples (8), decent plate discipline for a young hitter (his walks have increased the last four years, to 42 a year ago), and the ability to make contact (only 58 strike-outs).

BASERUNNING:

Though a catcher and a big man at 6'5", 200 lbs, Alomar has good speed. He stole 30 bases at Charleston in 1985, though he hasn't more than three in a season since then. He probably won't steal a lot of bases in the majors, but he runs the bases well.

FIELDING:

As a young catcher, Alomar suffers only in comparison to the man whose job he's after, Benito Santiago. He can't throw with Benito, but no one can; Sandy threw out 34 percent of attempted base stealers last year, which is acceptable. He may be even better than Santiago at calling a game, and is certainly better at blocking pitches, with only three passed balls last year.

OVERALL:

Alomar is a class player and a class kid from a long-time baseball family, on a Padres team where his father is a coach and his brother is the second baseman. Alomar was justifiably upset when he was sent back to the minors last year, but he recovered and had an even better year than in '88. Alomar has everything it takes to be an outstanding major league player.

SANDY ALOMAR JR.

Position: C
Bats: R **Throws:** R
Ht: 6' 5" **Wt:** 200

Opening Day Age: 23
Born: 6/18/66 in Salinas, Puerto Rico
ML Seasons: 2

Overall Statistics

	G	AB	R	H	D	T	HR	RBI	SB	BB	SO	AVG
1989	7	19	1	4	1	0	1	6	0	3	3	.211
Career	8	20	1	4	1	0	1	6	0	3	3	.200

Where He Hits the Ball

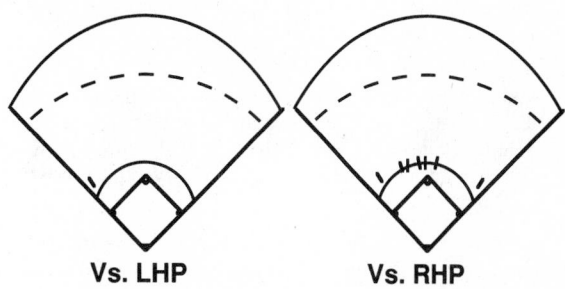

Vs. LHP　　　　**Vs. RHP**

1989 Situational Stats

	AB	H	HR	RBI	AVG		AB	H	HR	RBI	AVG
Home	18	4	1	6	.222	LHP	5	0	0	0	.000
Road	1	0	0	0	.000	RHP	14	4	1	6	.286
Day	7	1	0	2	.143	Sc Pos	7	3	1	6	.429
Night	12	3	1	4	.250	Clutch	1	0	0	0	.000

1989 Rankings (National League)

➡ Did not rank near the top or bottom in any category

PITCHING:

Andy Benes, the top pick in the 1988 amateur draft, was brought to the big leagues last Aug. 10 with a reputation for a live arm and not much else. An outstanding pitcher at the University of Evansville, Benes had been a member of the Olympic baseball team that won a gold medal in the 1988 Summer Olympics. After an outstanding debut at Class AA Wichita, Benes was quickly moved up to AAA Las Vegas last summer. There he appeared completely overmatched, with an 8.10 ERA in his five starts. But with Eric Show on the disabled list and the Padres badly in need of another starter, the decision was made to use the final six weeks of San Diego's season as Benes's training ground. Frankly, not much was expected of him.

When Benes arrived on the scene, pitching coach Pat Dobson was disheartened by his mechanics and approach. Dobson believed Benes actually slid backward in the club's minor-league system. After one very shaky start, Dobson trashed Benes' breaking ball and equipped him with a slider and change-up to go along with his 92-mph heater. At that point in his career, Benes had never thrown a slider in game action, and had used a change-up only on a limited basis.

Benes, a quick study, adapted well in the big leagues to his new repertoire. After two losses, he ran off a string of six victories in a row, convincing Padres management that, at 22, he is ready to become a capable big-league pitcher for the long term.

FIELDING, HITTING, BASERUNNING:

Benes is a fine athlete who seems to excel in every phase of the game. He can handle the bat, hitting his first major-league homer, a two-run shot, last Sept. 3 in a victory over Philadelphia. He's also a fine bunter and a good baserunner with decent speed. Benes, at 6-6, 235 pounds, probably could have been a pretty good position player had he decided to head in that direction. He is already competent at both fielding and holding baserunners.

OVERALL:

Upon his arrival in the major leagues, Benes did not appear even remotely ready. But Andy's quick grasp of Dobson's principals erased the doubts almost overnight. The Padres are now counting on Benes to be a key part of their starting rotation for many seasons to come. With his body, arm and sharp mind, there's no reason to believe that Benes will fail as long as he stays healthy.

ANDY BENES

Position: SP
Bats: R **Throws:** R
Ht: 6' 6" **Wt:** 235

Opening Day Age: 22
Born: 8/20/67 in Evansville, IN
ML Seasons: 1

Overall Statistics

	W	L	ERA	G	GS	Sv	IP	H	R	BB	SO	HR
1989	6	3	3.51	10	10	0	66.2	51	28	31	66	7
Career	6	3	3.51	10	10	0	66.2	51	28	31	66	7

Where They Hit the Ball

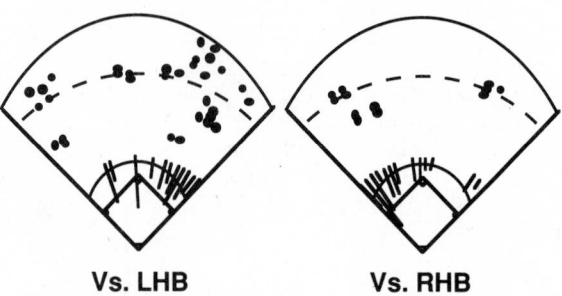

Vs. LHB　　　　**Vs. RHB**

1989 Situational Stats

	W	L	ERA	Sv	IP		AB	H	HR	RBI	AVG
Home	3	2	4.38	0	39.0	LHB	134	30	4	13	.224
Road	3	1	2.28	0	27.2	RHB	106	21	3	13	.198
Day	2	0	2.03	0	13.1	Sc Pos	48	14	1	18	.292
Night	4	3	3.88	0	53.1	Clutch	23	7	0	3	.304

1989 Rankings (National League)

➠ Led the Padres in balks (3)

HITTING:

Jack Clark is a streaky power hitter whose streaks invariably correspond to his moods. When Jack is hot, he can carry a club for months as he did for the St. Louis Cardinals during July and August of 1987. When he is not, he tends to become morose, questioning his own ability and fortitude.

Clark is a dead fastball hitter who can be thwarted by a steady diet of slow breaking pitches off the outside corner of the plate. During the opening months of the 1989 season, National League pitchers taunted Clark, giving him nothing of substance to hit. Consequently, Clark engaged in a battle of attrition. With no protection behind him in the batting order, Clark chose either to swing wildly in frustration or not to swing at all. Thus, at the All-Star break, Clark already had walked 70 times and struck out 91 times. He concluded the season with a strong second half, having finally come out of a malaise that at one point had him considering an early retirement.

BASERUNNING:

Clark is not very fast, but he's a smart baserunner. When his head is in the game, he is capable of taking the extra base. Recently, Jack seems to have been able to stay away from his tendency to sustain disabling leg or foot injuries. As a runner, Clark is a good man to hit-and-run with to avoid the double-play.

FIELDING:

Clark has been a regular at first base just four full seasons in his career and is obviously still learning the nuances of the position. His throwing arm is erratic and he is not particularly adept at digging infielder's throws out of the dirt. He has decent range, but will never be confused with Keith Hernandez. Clark still can play the outfield on occasion, but because of his fragile legs, he is no more than a spot player at his former position of right field.

OVERALL:

A limited player, Jack Clark came to the majors with a talent for crushing a fastball into the far reaches of the ionosphere. In his major league career, he has developed the taking of a walk to a high art. But Clark has also cultivated leadership ability as he has matured during an often controversial career. Clark has become a student of the game, and a man who does not mind sharing his wisdom with teammates during clubhouse bull sessions. What he lacks on the field in dimension he gets back with sheer determination. At 34, he is still a formidable player.

JACK CLARK

Position: 1B/RF
Bats: R **Throws:** R
Ht: 6' 3" **Wt:** 205

Opening Day Age: 34
Born: 11/10/55 in New Brighton, PA
ML Seasons: 15

Overall Statistics

	G	AB	R	H	D	T	HR	RBI	SB	BB	SO	AVG
1989	142	455	76	110	19	1	26	94	6	132	145	.242
Career	1658	5775	952	1563	291	37	282	998	72	1006	1130	.271

Where He Hits the Ball

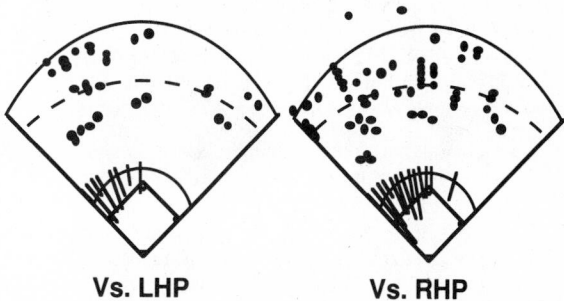

Vs. LHP   **Vs. RHP**

1989 Situational Stats

	AB	H	HR	RBI	AVG		AB	H	HR	RBI	AVG
Home	211	49	11	48	.232	LHP	125	34	4	16	.272
Road	244	61	15	46	.250	RHP	330	76	22	78	.230
Day	108	26	5	21	.241	Sc Pos	145	39	12	72	.269
Night	347	84	21	73	.242	Clutch	77	17	6	24	.221

1989 Rankings (National League)

➡ 1st in walks (132), highest percentage of swings that missed (32.1%), pitches seen per plate appearance (3.9) and on-base average vs. lefthanded pitchers (.474)

➡ 2nd in strikeouts (145), percentage of pitches taken (63.6%) and on-base average (.410) - *players with 502 PA*

➡ 6th in home run frequency (17.5 ABs per HR) and hitting with the bases loaded (.500) - *players with 10 PA with the bases loaded*

➡ Led the Padres in strikeouts, home run frequency, slugging percentage (.459), intentional walks (18), home runs (26), RBIs (94), walks, on-base average and hitting with the bases loaded

PITCHING:

Pat Clements is a journeyman lefthanded reliever who has pitched for four teams in only five major league seasons. Until 1989, Pat had worked in middle relief with little distinction. But last year Clements enjoyed his most successful season since 1986. The fact that he was used sparingly did not impede his ability to be ready when called.

In spring training last year, Padre pitching coach Pat Dobson found Clements to be a pitcher in complete disarray. Dobson was forced to rebuild Clements' mechanics, beginning with his position on the mound and the direction his arm traveled as he launched the ball toward the plate. When a decision had to be made near the end of the spring, the Padres elected to send Clements to Class AAA Las Vegas and keep Dave Leiper, another journeyman lefthander. Leiper eventually blew out his elbow and Clements was recalled on June 16. Except for a few bad outings in August and one disastrous start (only the second of his career), Clements pitched well. He recorded a 3.00 ERA as a reliever and held lefties to a .178 batting average.

A basic junkball pitcher who relies mostly on his curveball, Clements is a quiet man who goes about doing his job without fanfare. He is so modest that reporters can literally go a season without asking for his insight. That may be the result of his shy personality and the fact that Clements does not seek attention. He seems comfortable enough simply going about his job.

FIELDING, HITTING, BASERUNNING:

Clements, as a middle-inning reliever, was rarely in a position to exhibit his talents as a hitter or baserunner. After spending the better part of two seasons in the American League, it is safe to say that Clements has not had much recent experience with the stick, anyway. He has a decent lefthander's move to first base and appears more than adequate at fielding his position. He has accommodated such strategies as the slide step without problems.

OVERALL:

A quick learner, Clements proved last year that he was adaptable to all suggestions made by Pat Dobson. The fact that he worked so diligently to implement the suggestions endeared him to both Dobson and manager Jack McKeon. The bottom line is that Clements has an edge simply because he is that rare commodity -- a lefthanded reliever. He seems to have a better than even chance of sticking around as a middle man in 1990.

PAT CLEMENTS

Position: RP
Bats: R **Throws:** L
Ht: 6' 0" **Wt:** 180

Opening Day Age: 28
Born: 2/2/62 in McCloud, CA
ML Seasons: 5

Overall Statistics

	W	L	ERA	G	GS	Sv	IP	H	R	BB	SO	HR
1989	4	1	3.92	23	1	0	39.0	39	17	15	18	4
Career	12	10	3.89	217	2	12	284.2	281	127	121	124	16

Where They Hit the Ball

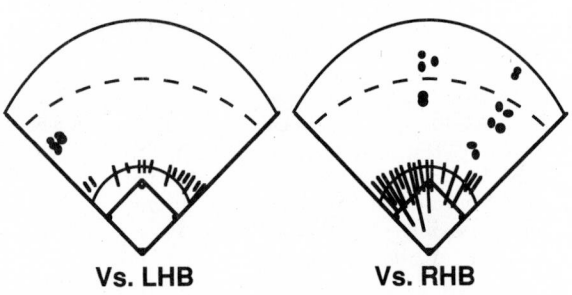

Vs. LHB   **Vs. RHB**

1989 Situational Stats

	W	L	ERA	Sv	IP		AB	H	HR	RBI	AVG
Home	1	0	3.80	0	21.1	LHB	45	8	0	4	.178
Road	3	1	4.08	0	17.2	RHB	101	31	4	14	.307
Day	2	0	3.21	0	14.0	Sc Pos	31	9	0	13	.290
Night	2	1	4.32	0	25.0	Clutch	35	10	2	5	.286

1989 Rankings (National League)

➡ Did not rank near the top or bottom in any category

PITCHING:

As his 44 saves and 1989 Cy Young Award attest, Mark Davis has developed into baseball's premier lefthanded relief pitcher. Certainly, it didn't happen overnight. When Davis was traded by the San Francisco Giants to the Padres in 1987, he was a marginal pitcher who had been bumped back and forth from the bullpen to the starting rotation with less than satisfactory results. Davis adjusted his motion to come over the top with his big curveball. As soon as he gained the confidence to throw that particular pitch consistently for strikes, his star began to shine.

The curve is now Davis' out pitch in any situation. Mixing it with a sneaky fastball, Davis has become a terror in critical situations. Last year, his 44 saves came in 48 opportunities. Three of the blown saves occurred during the same week in June during a 1-9 road trip. His only slump of the year was indicative of the way Davis used to pitch. He became anxious, overthrew, and was unable to put the ball in the strike zone.

FIELDING, HITTING, BASERUNNING:

Considering he almost never gets to hit, Davis can be potent at times with the bat. He hit his first and only major league homer in 1987 to help beat the Giants. Davis is rarely on the base paths, so an assessment of his base running is academic. As a fielder, Davis jumps off the mound with aplomb. His quick reflexes have helped him save more than one game by knocking down ground balls with his bare hand. He has the usual good move to first of a lefthanded pitcher.

OVERALL:

Without Davis and his 22 saves during the first half of last season, the Padres would have been in no position to make a late run at the division title -- in fact, they would have been a fifth place team. Part of Davis' sudden success can be attributed to his ability to block out almost all distractions except the job at hand. He says that dwelling on statistics only overloads his system. On a given day during the season, Davis may not know how many wins, saves or strikeouts he currently has. "I only have one (brain) cell up there," he said, only half in jest. "If I overload it, it explodes." Whatever mental gyrations he has undergone obviously have worked in spades.

MARK DAVIS

Position: RP
Bats: L **Throws:** L
Ht: 6' 4" **Wt:** 200

Opening Day Age: 29
Born: 10/19/60 in Livermore, CA
ML Seasons: 9

Overall Statistics

	W	L	ERA	G	GS	Sv	IP	H	R	BB	SO	HR
1989	4	3	1.85	70	0	44	92.2	66	21	31	92	6
Career	40	65	3.76	416	71	85	858.1	758	394	340	754	87

Where They Hit the Ball

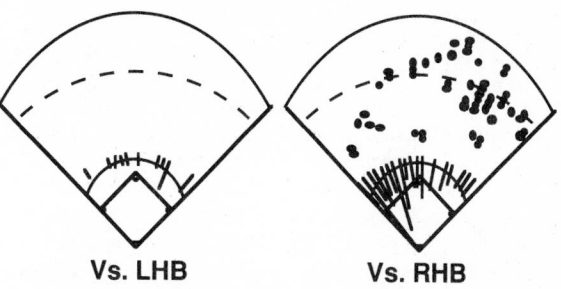

Vs. LHB   Vs. RHB

1989 Situational Stats

	W	L	ERA	Sv	IP		AB	H	HR	RBI	AVG
Home	2	0	1.17	21	46.0	LHB	46	11	2	9	.239
Road	2	3	2.51	23	46.2	RHB	284	55	4	25	.194
Day	0	1	2.30	13	27.1	Sc Pos	106	13	1	24	.123
Night	4	2	1.65	31	65.1	Clutch	258	50	5	30	.194

1989 Rankings (National League)

→ 1st in saves (44), save opportunities (48), games finished (65) and save percentage (91.7%) - *pitchers with 20 save opportunities*

→ 5th in lowest percentage of inherited runners scoring (21.3%) - *pitchers with 30 runners inherited*

→ 6th in games (70)

→ 10th in first batter efficiency (.194) - *pitchers in 40 relief games*

→ Led the Padres in saves, games, games finished, ERA (1.85), wild pitches (8), save percentage, lowest percentage of inherited runners scoring and blown saves (4) - *all team players*

PITCHING:

Since Mark Grant was a youngster with the Giants, the big rap on him has been his lack of maturity. During the early stages of his career, Grant gave management the perception that he was more interested in having a good time than doing his job. In the year after the July 4, 1987 trade that sent Grant to San Diego, little of that changed. Grant was known more as a cut-up than for a cut fastball -- a perception that was highlighted when he was caught on camera administering a hot foot to a teammate one night, early in McKeon's managerial tenure.

But in 1989, Grant may have finally found his niche -- as a middle-inning reliever. Grant has bounced back and forth from the bullpen to the starting rotation since the Giants first brought him up in 1984. Until 1989, Grant had showed signs of developing, but each step forward would usually be followed by two steps backward.

Under the watchful eye of Padre pitching coach Pat Dobson, Grant has made significant progress. A two-pitch pitcher basically relying on an average fastball and slider, Mark has been working on adding a change up to his repertoire. More importantly, Dobson seems to have been able to teach Grant how to pitch with his head: when to throw certain pitches in certain situations, how to approach particular hitters and pitch away from their strengths.

Grant, responding well, recorded career bests with an 8-2 mark, a 3.33 ERA, and a pair of saves in 1989. Better yet, he walked just 32 batters and allowed 105 hits in his 116.1 innings of work. At 26, Grant may have finally turned the corner, giving Padre management the clear impression that his best is ahead of him.

FIELDING, HITTING, BASERUNNING:

Grant is an average athlete who does not seem to excel in areas other than pitching. He's still learning the game and at times is prone to the mistakes that occur during the split-second when a decision must be made. He does have the capability of playing his position well. Grant has an average move to first base.

OVERALL:

Last season, Mark Grant began to put everything into place. Though he will always love having a good time, Mark has shown he can get down to business when it comes to doing his job. Perhaps that maturing process was just as big a reason for Grant's emergence last season as was his developing physical ability.

MARK GRANT

Position: RP
Bats: R **Throws:** R
Ht: 6' 2" **Wt:** 205

Opening Day Age: 26
Born: 10/24/63 in Aurora, IL
ML Seasons: 5

Overall Statistics

	W	L	ERA	G	GS	Sv	IP	H	R	BB	SO	HR
1989	8	2	3.33	50	0	2	116.1	105	45	32	69	11
Career	18	24	4.12	131	47	4	441.0	434	218	165	257	53

Where They Hit the Ball

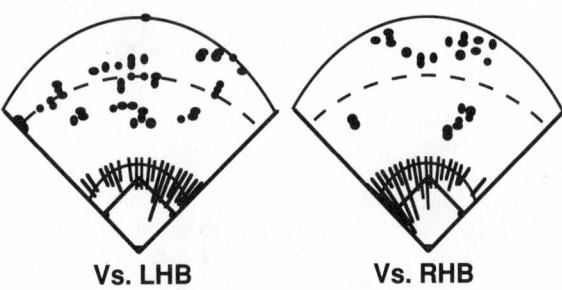

Vs. LHB   **Vs. RHB**

1989 Situational Stats

	W	L	ERA	Sv	IP		AB	H	HR	RBI	AVG
Home	3	1	4.33	2	54.0	LHB	200	49	4	24	.245
Road	5	1	2.45	0	62.1	RHB	224	56	7	24	.250
Day	2	0	2.93	2	43.0	Sc Pos	97	20	4	37	.206
Night	6	2	3.56	0	73.1	Clutch	96	22	2	8	.229

1989 Rankings (National League)

➡ 6th in most GDPs induced per GDP situation - *pitchers with 30 GDP situations*

➡ Led the Padres in most GDPs induced per GDP situation

HITTING:

Tony Gwynn has won three consecutive National League batting titles simply by executing his own personal theory of hitting: seeing the ball and putting it in play. Gwynn knows the strike zone like a pitcher, and has the knack of hitting the ball exactly where it is pitched.

Gwynn is a monster at going to the opposite field with a pitch on the outside corner of the plate. He is that rare player who is virtually impossible to stop. A manager must play his fielders straight away and a pitcher must hope Gwynn does not swing at his weakest offerings.

Tony has proven in the past that he is capable of turning on the ball and pulling it to right field. But he has shunned that approach, feeling it might cost him 10 to 20 points on his batting average. Thus, his run production remains low. Gwynn's best home run year (14) was 1986 -- the last year he did not win the batting title. He has never driven in more than 71 runs in a single season. Certainly, Tony has been miscast as a No. 3 hitter the last few years. He is most comfortable hitting in the second spot in the batting order.

BASERUNNING:

Gwynn has improved tremendously in this department, developing into a viable 40-steal a year player. He has overcome the tendency to make bad baserunning decisions, a syndrome that plagued him during the early years of his career. Gwynn is now given a green light to steal regardless of the situation.

FIELDING:

A mediocre left fielder when he came up, Gwynn developed into a two-time Gold Glove winner for his play in right (1986-87). Since the latter part of the 1988 season, though, Gwynn has been asked to shuttle between right and center -- a situation which has made him quite anxious. Gwynn is not comfortable in centerfield, feeling that covering all the ground wears down his legs. He's barely passable there, but still one of the league's best in right. His arm is average in stregth but excellent in accuracy..

OVERALL:

What Tony Gwynn offers on the field is personified by what he offers off the field. Gwynn is one of those who lead by example. His work habits are second to none. No matter how well he is hitting, he can be found in the batting cage or studying videos. He also has no qualms about playing hurt, and won his last two batting titles while playing with injuries.

TONY GWYNN

Position: CF/RF
Bats: L **Throws:** L
Ht: 5'11" **Wt:** 199

Opening Day Age: 29
Born: 5/9/60 in Los Angeles, CA
ML Seasons: 8

Overall Statistics

	G	AB	R	H	D	T	HR	RBI	SB	BB	SO	AVG
1989	158	604	82	203	27	7	4	62	40	56	30	.336
Career	1060	4078	617	1354	192	51	45	416	221	382	233	.332

Where He Hits the Ball

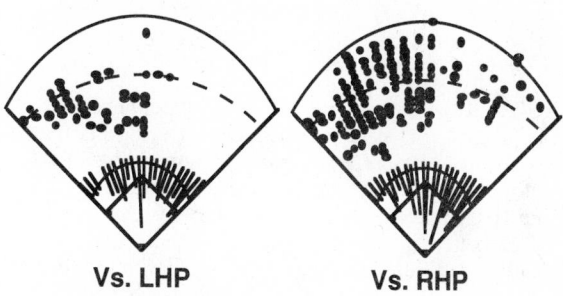

Vs. LHP   **Vs. RHP**

1989 Situational Stats

	AB	H	HR	RBI	AVG		AB	H	HR	RBI	AVG
Home	288	94	3	29	.326	LHP	200	61	0	23	.305
Road	316	109	1	33	.345	RHP	404	142	4	39	.351
Day	170	62	1	21	.365	Sc Pos	130	42	1	55	.323
Night	434	141	3	41	.325	Clutch	94	33	0	13	.351

1989 Rankings (National League)

→ 1st in batting average (.336), hits (203), percentage of swings put into play (61.0%), singles (165), batting average with 2 strikes (.315) and batting average vs. righthanded pitchers (.351) - *players with 377 vs. RHP*

→ 2nd in times on base (260) and grounder/flyball ratio (2.10) - *players with 502 PA*

→ Led the Padres in batting average, singles, total bases (256), times on base, runs (82), hits, doubles (27), games (158), grounder/flyball ratio, stolen base percentage (71.4%), percentage of swings put into play, steals of third (7), batting average with 2 strikes, hitting with runners in scoring position (.323) and hitting in the clutch (.351)

PITCHING:

In his rookie season, Greg Harris filled the Padres' desperate need for a righthanded short man. Groomed as a starter from the start of his career, Harris was chosen last spring to succeed Lance McCullers as the righty set-up man and alternate closer for Mark Davis. Though new to a relief role, Harris handled it in outstanding fashion.

Harris, 26, came through the organization as a basic fastball pitcher. The challenge for Greg was to learn to throw his more-than-acceptable breaking pitches in crucial situations. By midseason, the breaking ball, not the fastball, had become his out pitch.

After an early rib cage injury, Harris worked in relief for nearly half a season before making eight emergency starts because of various injuries to members of the rotation. In the final six weeks, with the Padres pressing San Francisco in the National League West, Harris moved back to the pen, where he helped the club in its aborted stretch run.

Given a choice, Harris would undoubtedly choose to be a starter. That is his orientation. During his four years in the minors, Harris made 93 appearances -- 92 of them starts. In his eight starts last year, Harris did fairly well, going 3-4 with a 3.51 ERA. But he was even better as a reliever, with a 5-5 mark, six saves and a sparkling 2.04 ERA. Overall, Greg grew progressively less effective the longer he stayed in a game. On pitches one to 30 of his appearances last year, opponents hit only .178 against Harris. On pitches 31 to 60, they batted .256. And on pitches 61 to 90, they walloped Greg for a .327 mark. That doesn't mean that Harris doesn't have a future as a starter. But it might make the Padres reluctant to shift him just yet.

FIELDING, HITTING, BASERUNNING:

A better than average athlete, Harris fields his position well. He has a fairly snappy move to first base for a righthanded pitcher. It's hard to discern what kind of hitter or baserunner Greg is, since he had so few chances to hit in 1989.

OVERALL:

Harris has been much coveted by other clubs in the league. Last spring the Padres seemed willing to part with Greg in a multi-player deal for Dale Murphy. When that trade never came off, Harris was taken off the market, and his future, whether as a starter or in relief, now appears to be in San Diego. That future looks pretty bright.

GREG W. HARRIS

Position: RP/SP
Bats: R **Throws:** R
Ht: 6' 2" **Wt:** 190

Opening Day Age: 26
Born: 12/1/63 in Greensboro, NC
ML Seasons: 2

Overall Statistics

	W	L	ERA	G	GS	Sv	IP	H	R	BB	SO	HR
1989	8	9	2.60	56	8	6	135.0	106	43	52	106	8
Career	10	9	2.47	59	9	6	153.0	119	46	55	121	8

Where They Hit the Ball

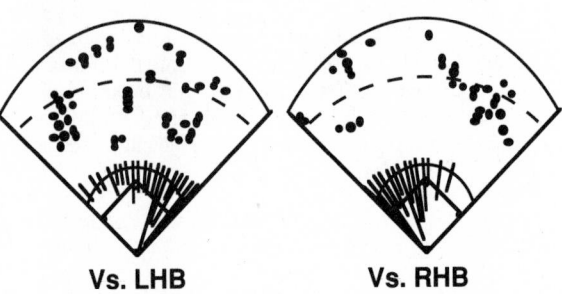

Vs. LHB   **Vs. RHB**

1989 Situational Stats

	W	L	ERA	Sv	IP		AB	H	HR	RBI	AVG
Home	6	4	2.36	1	61.0	LHB	284	56	2	17	.197
Road	2	5	2.80	5	74.0	RHB	209	50	6	19	.239
Day	3	3	1.59	1	45.1	Sc Pos	98	22	1	26	.224
Night	5	6	3.11	5	89.2	Clutch	176	37	1	13	.210

1989 Rankings (National League)

➡ 1st in first batter efficiency (.113) - *players with 40 relief games*

➡ 9th in lowest batting average allowed vs. lefthanded batters (.197) - *pitchers facing 125 LHB*

➡ Led the Padres in balks (3), holds (6), first batter efficiency and lowest batting average allowed vs. lefthanded batters

PITCHING:

After a slow start, Bruce Hurst proved to be the gutty, gritty lefthanded pitcher everyone in San Diego hoped he would be when the Padres signed him to a three-year, $5.25 million contract. Because of a season-ending back injury to Eric Show and the first-half blowout by Walt Terrell, Hurst was forced to be the bulwark of a starting rotation for the first time in his career. Last season, there was no Roger Clemens to shield him. Hurst was the guy, and after a period of adjustment to a new league and a new environment, he responded.

Hurst mixes several breaking pitches -- including a fork ball, slider and slow curve -- with a decent fastball. When he is on, his ability to paint corners and place the ball exactly where he wants is a thing of beauty. He walked just 2.42 batters per nine innings last season. When he has problems, he seems to drop his shoulder, thus elevating the ball in the strike zone, where his pitches are easier to hit.

Hurst came to the Padres after getting over soreness in his left shoulder that had bothered him late in 1988. During spring training last year, Hurst suffered from tendinitis in the same shoulder. Pitching coach Pat Dobson made several mechanical adjustments in Hurst's delivery, relieving the pressure that evidently had caused the problems.

FIELDING, HITTING, BASERUNNING:

Hurst is not one of your magnificent athletes. Coming up in the American League, he had never had to hit regularly until this past season. He proved to be abominable at the plate. He is clearly the type of player who, when he is on base, must avoid being maimed at all costs. Hurst does field his position well. His move to first base is excellent. Hurst picked off four runners last season, tops among Padre pitchers.

OVERALL:

Hurst, a fierce competitor who hates to lose, is a practicing Mormon who does not partake in the usual clubhouse high jinx. He is a constant butt of clubhouse jokes about his lifestyle, which includes no liquor and no caffeine. On almost all occasions, he takes the ribbing with a good sense of humor. Hurst, who has pitched in two playoff series and won a pair of 1986 World Series games, has developed into a quiet leader. He's the type of guy you'd feel good about sitting at your dinner table, or pitching the final game of the World Series.

BRUCE HURST

Position: SP
Bats: L **Throws:** L
Ht: 6' 3" **Wt:** 215

Opening Day Age: 32
Born: 3/24/58 in St. George, UT
ML Seasons: 10

Overall Statistics

	W	L	ERA	G	GS	Sv	IP	H	R	BB	SO	HR
1989	15	11	2.69	33	33	0	244.2	214	84	66	179	16
Career	103	84	4.01	270	250	0	1704.0	1783	831	545	1222	189

Where They Hit the Ball

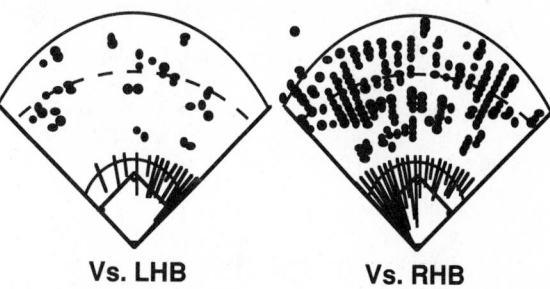

Vs. LHB   Vs. RHB

1989 Situational Stats

	W	L	ERA	Sv	IP		AB	H	HR	RBI	AVG
Home	9	6	2.58	0	139.2	LHB	144	43	2	16	.299
Road	6	5	2.83	0	105.0	RHB	759	171	14	58	.225
Day	3	3	2.13	0	55.0	Sc Pos	187	47	1	53	.251
Night	12	8	2.85	0	189.2	Clutch	114	23	3	4	.202

1989 Rankings (National League)

- ➡ 3rd in innings (244.2)
- ➡ 4th in caught stealing (14) and strikeout/walk ratio (2.7) - *pitchers with 162 IP*
- ➡ 5th in ERA (2.69) and lowest stolen base percentage allowed (51.7%)
- ➡ Led the Padres in innings, caught stealing, lowest stolen base percentage allowed, lowest slugging percentage allowed (.339), games started (33), complete games (10), shutouts (2), hits allowed (214), wild pitches (8), strikeouts (179), pitches thrown (3,479), pickoff throws (253), stolen bases allowed (15), grounder/flyball ratio (1.38), least HRS per 9 innings (.59) and most strikeouts per 9 innings (6.6) - *team pitchers with 162 IP*

HITTING:

At 27, Chris James has yet to really find his niche. He has some power, with 49 homers over the last three years. But James is so streaky that he may never hit for average. His monthly averages last year were almost schizophrenic: .302, .103, .167, .321, .333, .182. At the All-Star break last year, James went home and jokingly said he thought about killing himself. The constant ebb and flow of his offensive performance turns Chris into a mental dish rag. Without crawling inside his head, it's impossible to discern what feeds what -- his own instability, or his problems at the plate.

A fastball hitter, James can be driven batty by breaking pitches off the outside corner of the plate. When Chris is hot, the breaking pitch ceases to be a problem. But when he is in a prolonged slump, he'd have trouble competing at slow-pitch softball.

James compensates for his shortcomings with his desire and work habits. He comes to the park early and is usually available for extra work. He always seems to be playing through some sort of nagging injury. James usually gets those injuries when he's giving a little bit of extra effort.

BASERUNNING:

Below average on the base paths, James must overcome his problem of pulling muscles in his legs when he tries to turn it up a notch going for an extra base. He's fairly intelligent, though, and does not seem to make critical baserunning mistakes. James is capable of stealing five to 10 bases per year.

FIELDING:

James is a third baseman who hates to play third base, and an outfielder who has a lot of problems covering ground. After obtaining James from the Phillies, manager Jack McKeon hoped that Chris would solve San Diego's third base problem. But McKeon soon moved James to the outfield and dealt for third baseman Mike Pagliarulo. As an outfielder, James misjudges balls hit toward the fence and seems in constant jeopardy of hurting himself. He has a better than average arm.

OVERALL:

With his wild fluctuations, it's hard to tell exactly what to expect from Chris James. James hit .264 with 11 homers in 303 at bats after the trade to San Diego last year, and the Padres would probably settle for that kind of production. They'd just like to see him avoid those .103 months.

CHRIS JAMES

Position: LF/3B/RF
Bats: R **Throws:** R
Ht: 6' 1" **Wt:** 190

Opening Day Age: 27
Born: 10/4/62 in Rusk, TX
ML Seasons: 4

Overall Statistics

	G	AB	R	H	D	T	HR	RBI	SB	BB	SO	AVG
1989	132	482	55	117	17	2	13	65	5	26	68	.243
Career	413	1452	165	372	64	9	50	190	15	85	221	.256

Where He Hits the Ball

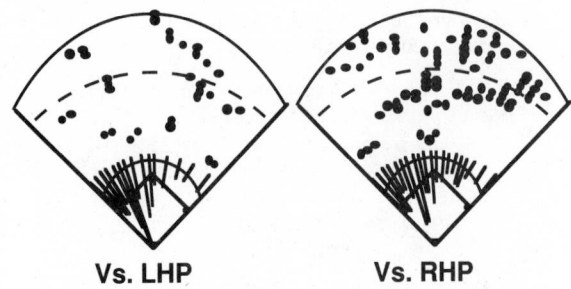

Vs. LHP   Vs. RHP

1989 Situational Stats

	AB	H	HR	RBI	AVG		AB	H	HR	RBI	AVG
Home	210	56	7	36	.267	LHP	168	49	7	33	.292
Road	272	61	6	29	.224	RHP	314	68	6	32	.217
Day	130	31	5	17	.238	Sc Pos	149	38	4	53	.255
Night	352	86	8	48	.244	Clutch	79	17	2	11	.215

1989 Rankings (National League)

- ➡ 2nd in GDPs (20)
- ➡ 5th in lowest on-base average (.281) - *players with 502 PA*
- ➡ 8th in most GDPs per GDP situation (17.5%) - *players with 50 PA in GDP situations*
- ➡ Led NL Left Fielders in GDPs

HITTING:

The 1989 season was an ugly one for Carmelo Martinez. After a wonderful spring in which Martinez plowed his way through the Cactus League with six homers and 17 RBIs, Carmelo opened the season as the starting left fielder. But by early June, after the Padres obtained Chris James from Philadelphia, a horrid slump (.200, three homers, 19 RBIs) found Martinez relegated to the bench for good.

During Martinez's six-year Padre tenure, his pattern almost always followed the same blue print. Good springs seemed to be followed by a first-half slump, and a mighty late-season comeback. Last year, no comeback ever materialized. Martinez seemed to be baffled by all kinds of pitching.

After leading the team with 18 homers in 1988, Martinez felt it imperative last year to supply much needed power to the listless middle of the Padre lineup. As he put himself under more pressure, he became more ineffective, literally jumping at the ball with his lead foot. Consequently, his strikeouts went up while his power numbers stagnated.

BASERUNNING:

Martinez, an average base runner at best, hurts himself with silly mental mistakes on the base paths. On April 28 at Chicago, Martinez was picked off second base by Mitch Williams to end the game with the tying runs on base. After that, he became extra cautious, further diminishing his viability as a baserunner. His speed is typical of the plodding power hitter, forcing his manager to play station-to-station baseball when he is on base.

FIELDING:

Martinez is a fine fielder at his natural position -- first base -- but has never had the opportunity to play there regularly with the Padres. He's found Steve Garvey, John Kruk and now Jack Clark holding the position. Out of necessity, Martinez has gone to the outfield. He's worked hard to become a decent outfielder, but it's a little like asking a long distance runner to win one sprint for the Gipper. The move hasn't really been fair to either Martinez or the ball club.

OVERALL:

When things are not going well for Martinez, he has a tendency to be a brooder. Unwittingly, his attitude becomes a corrosive element in the clubhouse. Last season even Jack McKeon, long a Martinez supporter, finally discovered that Carmelo's assets don't outweigh his limitations. Suddenly, after six big-league seasons, Martinez may find himself on the outside looking in.

CARMELO MARTINEZ

Position: LF/1B
Bats: R **Throws:** R
Ht: 6' 2" **Wt:** 220

Opening Day Age: 29
Born: 7/28/60 in Dorado, Puerto Rico
ML Seasons: 7

Overall Statistics

	G	AB	R	H	D	T	HR	RBI	SB	BB	SO	AVG
1989	111	267	23	59	12	2	6	39	0	32	54	.221
Career	812	2414	294	600	114	7	88	353	8	331	422	.249

Where He Hits the Ball

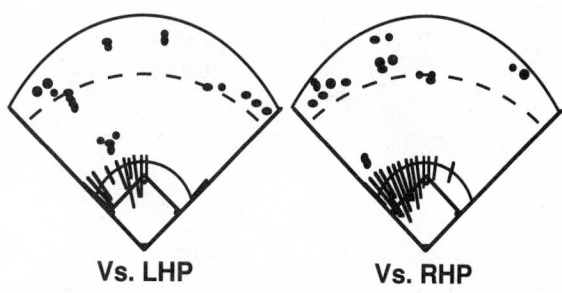

Vs. LHP   **Vs. RHP**

1989 Situational Stats

	AB	H	HR	RBI	AVG		AB	H	HR	RBI	AVG
Home	121	20	2	12	.165	LHP	118	32	2	21	.271
Road	146	39	4	27	.267	RHP	149	27	4	18	.181
Day	82	19	0	9	.232	Sc Pos	91	17	3	35	.187
Night	185	40	6	30	.216	Clutch	60	12	2	12	.200

1989 Rankings (National League)

➡ 2nd in worst hitting with runners in scoring position (.187) - *players with 100 PA with runners in scoring position*

➡ Led NL Left Fielders in hitting on an 0-2 count (.238) - *left fielders with 20 PA with an 0-2 count*

HITTING:

Somewhere, somehow, Mike Pagliarulo has lost the lefthanded swing that made him such a power threat as a member of the New York Yankees. Pags hit just .196 with three homers and 14 RBIs after the July 22 trade that brought him over from New York. Manager Jack McKeon, trying to fill a gaping hole at third base, installed Pagliarulo in the lineup everyday in the early going. But by the end of the season, when the Padres were making a run at the division title, Pagliarulo found himself displaced by Bip Roberts.

Pags will be the first to tell you he has been uncomfortable at the plate and therefore appears clueless. A fastball hitter, he is now seeing a relentless diet of breaking pitches, particularly from lefthanders, who obviously have his number. Is it his eyesight, or is he simply unable to make the necessary adjustments? Watch closely and you will notice that Pags swings in almost the same spot no matter where the ball is pitched. Surgery to repair a damaged ulna nerve in his right elbow after the 1988 season may be a contributing factor to his problems.

BASERUNNING:

Pagliarulo isn't much of a base stealer; he's stolen only nine bases in his career, but was two for two with the Padres. He's a smart baserunner, able to read situations well and won't make silly mistakes. He should probably be rated average in this department at best.

FIELDING:

People who watched Pagliarulo play in New York say his defensive skills have deteriorated, but he's the best fielding third sacker the Padres have had for quite some time. He can still go to both sides well for the ball and, with his quick reactions, is capable of turning in the big play. After elbow surgery, his arm is probably a tad below average, but he has enough juice in it to make the long throw from behind the bag. Again, he is the type of player who won't make many careless mistakes.

OVERALL:

Pagliarulo is the type of guy you hate to give up on because he has a tireless work ethic. He works endlessly in the batting cage trying to eliminate his problems, but it's possible he dwells on them too much. Mike must be content to work on his own skills and be himself, rather than trying to emulate his idol, Don Mattingly, as he's prone to do. Even so, it's highly likely those 32-homer, 87-RBI seasons (1987) are behind him.

MIKE PAGLIARULO

Position: 3B
Bats: L **Throws:** R
Ht: 6' 2" **Wt:** 195

Opening Day Age: 30
Born: 3/15/60 in Medford, MA
ML Seasons: 6

Overall Statistics

	G	AB	R	H	D	T	HR	RBI	SB	BB	SO	AVG
1989	124	371	31	73	17	0	7	30	3	37	82	.197
Career	753	2422	303	550	118	12	108	351	9	241	549	.227

Where He Hits the Ball

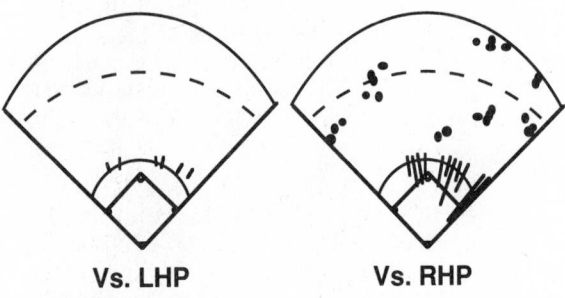

Vs. LHP   Vs. RHP

1989 Situational Stats

	AB	H	HR	RBI	AVG		AB	H	HR	RBI	AVG
Home	182	36	5	18	.198	LHP	59	12	0	5	.203
Road	189	37	2	12	.196	RHP	312	61	7	25	.196
Day	118	20	2	8	.169	Sc Pos	87	20	1	21	.230
Night	253	53	5	22	.209	Clutch	63	18	0	3	.286

1989 Rankings (National League)

➡ Did not rank near the top or bottom in any category

HITTING:

It's hard to tell just what Mark Parent is capable of as a hitter because he starts so few games. In his two full big league seasons, the big righthanded hitter has played in only 41 games and 52 games, respectively. Mark has strictly been a backup to Benito Santiago, who bristles when given a day off for any reason less serious than a gunshot wound.

Without the benefit of continuity, Parent has responded by hitting .195 in 1988 and .191 in 1989. But his power numbers are what is interesting. Two years ago, Parent hit six homers in 118 at bats. Last season, he hit seven homers in 141 at bats. Compare that to Santiago, who hit 26 homers in 954 at bats over the course of the same two seasons. It's easy to theorize that if Parent played more, his average would go up at least marginally. And he'd be a power threat, capable of 15 homers or more.

Realistically, Parent can't hope to develop as a consistent big-league hitter if he continues to play under the same circumstances. Mark usually takes his role in stride, but he wasn't pleased when he was benched for both Santiago and Sandy Alomar during the last 32 games. Santiago started 28 of those games, playing virtually every day while the Padres made their aborted stretch run. Parent, meanwhile, didn't start after August 27.

BASERUNNING:

At 6'5", 225 pounds, Parent is about as quick on the base paths as a water buffalo. But his nine seasons in the Padre farm system have helped him build strong fundamental instincts. Parent has a fine grasp of the game, and will rarely hurt his team by making a bad judgment.

FIELDING:

Parent has developed into a fine defensive catcher and is even compared at times to Santiago. Mark has a better than average arm, but does not possess Benito's amazing quickness. He blocks the plate well and does not make many mistakes. Parent has been lauded by pitchers for his ability to call a game, and has often been paired with Eric Show and Bruce Hurst. Mark is probably better than Santiago in this department.

OVERALL:

Parent has some skills, but they probably won't develop with San Diego. With the Padres, he seems doomed to a career backup role behind either Santiago or Sandy Alomar, Jr. At times Parent has asked to be traded, but the club has resisted. At 28, they figure that Mark is the perfect number two man to sit behind their top stud catcher, whoever that turns out to be.

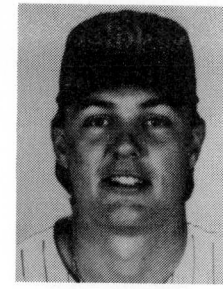

MARK PARENT

Position: C
Bats: R **Throws:** R
Ht: 6'5" **Wt:** 224

Opening Day Age: 28
Born: 9/16/61 in Ashland, OR
ML Seasons: 4

Overall Statistics

	G	AB	R	H	D	T	HR	RBI	SB	BB	SO	AVG
1989	52	141	12	27	4	0	7	21	1	8	34	.191
Career	113	298	22	54	7	0	13	38	1	15	69	.181

Where He Hits the Ball

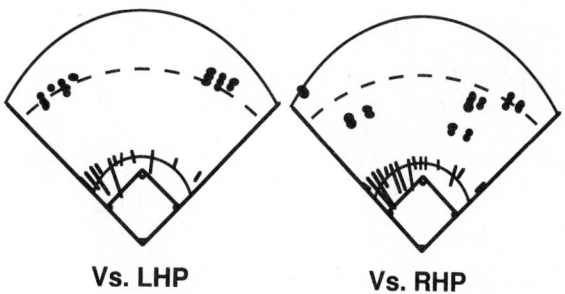

Vs. LHP   **Vs. RHP**

1989 Situational Stats

	AB	H	HR	RBI	AVG		AB	H	HR	RBI	AVG
Home	69	17	6	17	.246	LHP	51	10	2	4	.196
Road	72	10	1	4	.139	RHP	90	17	5	17	.189
Day	85	14	2	8	.165	Sc Pos	29	5	1	14	.172
Night	56	13	5	13	.232	Clutch	27	3	0	0	.111

1989 Rankings (National League)

➡ Did not rank near the top or bottom in any category

PITCHING:

When Dennis Rasmussen was traded from the Reds to the Padres in June of '88, it was mainly because he had infuriated Reds manager Pete Rose with his seeming unwillingness to attack hitters. After tinkering with Rasmussen's mechanics for 15 minutes, Padre pitching coach Pat Dobson seemed to have solved the problem. Rasmussen was dropping his shoulder, thus allowing his arm to swing across his body and the ball to ride out of the strike zone. With Rasmussen coming over the top with his array of breaking pitches mixed with a modest fastball, he again began to win. The results were stunning. During his Padre stay in 1988 Rasmussen won 14 games in 18 decisions, including a pair of five-game winning streaks.

Then came 1989. Suddenly, the old Rasmussen returned. He was 10-10, winning only three games from April 7 through August 6. Rasmussen was so ineffective that, in his first 13 starts, he allowed 18 runs and 31 hits during the first inning alone. Dennis so angered manager Jack McKeon with his penchant to pick at the corners that McKeon finally lifted him during the third inning of a Sept. 10 loss to the Los Angeles Dodgers. The incident incensed Rasmussen and only further inflamed already strained relations between the pitcher and manager.

All season Rasmussen seemed to toe a very thin line. As player rep, he was perceived by the manager and coaches as a disruptive element. A general feeling began to emerge that Rasmussen was more interested in off-field matters than he was about doing his job on the mound. That analysis may be a bit off base, but Rasmussen's poor pitching didn't help his cause.

FIELDING, HITTING, BASERUNNING:

Rasmussen is impotent at the plate and a plodder on the base paths. He's slow getting off the mound to field his position, but is capable of doing an adequate job. His move to first base is mediocre, at best, for a lefthanded pitcher.

OVERALL:

Will the real Dennis Rasmussen please stand up? After outstanding pitching in 1988, Dennis just couldn't seem to get it together last season. At 6'7" and 233 pounds, the perception is that Rasmussen should be more of a take-charge pitcher. But unless something stirs him, he isn't. In 1988, Rasmussen was stirred by the fifth trade in a career that began in 1980. He worked in 1989 seemingly without much motivation, and will definitely need to do better in 1990.

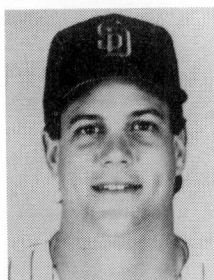

DENNIS RASMUSSEN

Position: SP
Bats: L **Throws:** L
Ht: 6' 7" **Wt:** 225

Opening Day Age: 30
Born: 4/18/59 in Los Angeles, CA
ML Seasons: 7

Overall Statistics

	W	L	ERA	G	GS	Sv	IP	H	R	BB	SO	HR
1989	10	10	4.26	33	33	0	183.2	190	100	72	87	18
Career	69	45	4.07	178	168	0	1044.2	967	515	381	644	126

Where They Hit the Ball

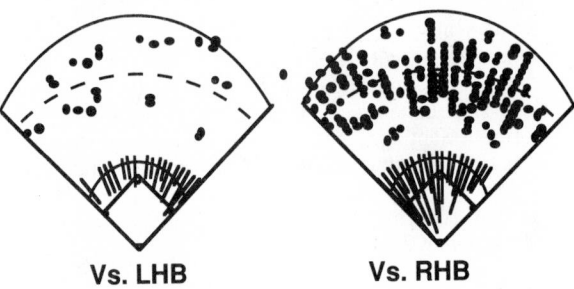

Vs. LHB **Vs. RHB**

1989 Situational Stats

	W	L	ERA	Sv	IP		AB	H	HR	RBI	AVG
Home	5	4	3.42	0	76.1	LHB	133	33	4	24	.248
Road	5	6	4.86	0	107.1	RHB	571	157	14	62	.275
Day	2	4	5.28	0	46.0	Sc Pos	149	42	3	59	.282
Night	8	6	3.92	0	137.2	Clutch	41	11	1	3	.268

1989 Rankings (National League)

- ➡ 2nd in GDPs per 9 innings (.93) - *pitchers with 162 IP*
- ➡ 4th in worst ERA (4.26), worst on-base average allowed (.335) and worst strikeout/walk ratio (1.2)
- ➡ 5th in worst batting average allowed (.270), worst slugging percentage allowed (.403) and lowest strikeouts per 9 innings (4.3)
- ➡ 6th in most GDPS induced (19)
- ➡ 7th in games started (33)
- ➡ Led the Padres in games started, GDPs induced, walks allowed (72), GDPs per 9 innings and run support per 9 innings (4.3) - *team pitchers with 162 IP*

HITTING:

Bip Roberts may have flopped in 1986 as a rookie, but he was perhaps the biggest surprise on the Padre ballclub last season. After two seasons at Class AAA Las Vegas, Roberts emerged last year as a bonafide big league switch-hitter. A .301 hitter in 117 games, Bip hit .288 from the left side and .325 from the right side.

What changed? In his two Triple A seasons, Roberts learned how to cut down on his swing and put the ball in play. In '86, Bip had a penchant for taking too big a swing and undercutting the ball. The result was a bevy of short flies and pop-ups that drove Padre management crazy. Last season, Roberts was a tough out because he laid off pitches out of the strike zone. He also became adept at hanging in against breaking balls.

With 49 walks and a .391 on base percentage, Roberts filled a hole in the leadoff spot that has plagued the Padres since Alan Wiggins was banished in 1985 due to drug problems. When Roberts was finally placed in the starting lineup for good during the second half of the season, he was a catalyst in the club's late run at the National League West title.

BASERUNNING:

Roberts has become a smarter baserunner, as well. In 1986, when he stole just 14 bases in 26 attempts, Bip was easy prey because he often ran in the wrong situations. Last year Roberts was 21 for 32, the third best theft mark on a club that swiped 136 bases. Often used on the hit-and-run, Bip scored 81 runs in 117 games, just one behind both Roberto Alomar and Tony Gwynn, who each played in 158 games.

FIELDING:

This is a real flaw in Bip's game. A natural second baseman, Roberts has been aced out of that spot by Roberto Alomar, who has much more range and a much better arm. The versatile Roberts can also play short, third, left and right, but none of them particularly well. Bip settled in mostly at third base and left field last year. But he is too small for the hot corner and his limited throwing arm makes him a liability anywhere in the outfield. Still, Roberts' offensive contributions make it imperative that he be used someplace.

OVERALL:

Roberts' attitude change was perhaps the biggest reason for his resurgence. Once brash and cocky, Bip has become a consummate team player. Roberts is one of those players so integral to any club with championship ambitions, and he figures to be San Diego's leadoff man again in 1990.

BIP ROBERTS

Position: 3B/SS/LF/RF
Bats: B **Throws:** R
Ht: 5' 7" **Wt:** 160

Opening Day Age: 26
Born: 10/27/63 in Berkeley, CA
ML Seasons: 3

Overall Statistics

	G	AB	R	H	D	T	HR	RBI	SB	BB	SO	AVG
1989	117	329	81	99	15	8	3	25	21	49	45	.301
Career	223	579	116	163	20	10	4	37	35	64	76	.282

Where He Hits the Ball

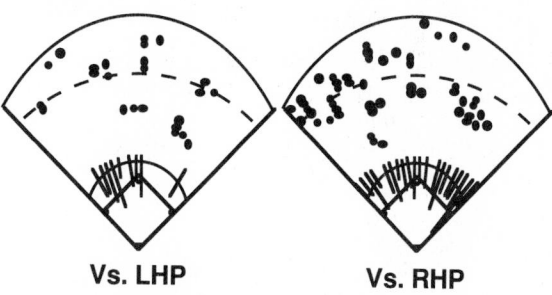

Vs. LHP   **Vs. RHP**

1989 Situational Stats

	AB	H	HR	RBI	AVG		AB	H	HR	RBI	AVG
Home	159	48	2	15	.302	LHP	117	38	3	13	.325
Road	170	51	1	10	.300	RHP	212	61	0	12	.288
Day	98	34	0	3	.347	Sc Pos	57	16	2	22	.281
Night	231	65	3	22	.281	Clutch	48	15	0	4	.313

1989 Rankings (National League)

➡ 3rd in batting average with 2 strikes (.302) - *players with 162 PA with 2 strikes*

➡ 4th in percentage of extra bases taken as a runner (61.3%) - *players with 40 opportunities to advance*

➡ 6th in triples (8) and batting average vs. lefthanded pitchers (.325) - *players with 125 PA vs. LHP*

➡ Led the Padres in triples, percentage of extra bases taken as a runner, hitting on an 0-2 count (.346) and batting average vs. lefthanded pitchers

HITTING:

Benito Santiago has been the source of trade talk for two seasons, as young Sandy Alomar, Jr. waits in the wings. But Benito has such potential that the deal could prove a nightmare. In three seasons Santiago has won the Rookie of the Year, set a rookie record by hitting in 34 straight games, won a Gold Glove and been elected the starting catcher for the All-Star team.

Only 25, Santiago can hit with power (16 homers last year) and batted .300 as a rookie in '87. But Santiago slumped to a career-low .236 last year. The '89 season became a long struggle between Benito and manager Jack McKeon. Santiago, a free swinger, felt the manager was impinging on his style by asking him to be more selective at the plate, particularly with runners in scoring position. Indeed, the righthanded swinging Santiago has become an easy fish for pitchers who simply throw him a high fastball or one off the outside corner with two strikes.

It wasn't until the final six weeks of the season that the logjam between player and manager ended. Santiago failed to improve his hitting, but he was much more relaxed. Perhaps not coincidentally, the Padres went on their only tear of the season and played .744 ball the rest of the way.

BASERUNNING:

Lithe and quick, Santiago can steal bases. He was fourth on the club in 1989 with 11 steals, and has swiped as many as 21. With his speed, Benito is a perfect candidate for the hit-and-run. If Santiago ever learns to take more walks, he will be able to do more damage on the bases.

FIELDING:

Santiago has the ability to be one of the greatest defensive catchers of all-time. With his slingshot arm, opponents have simply been taken out of their running game the last three years. His 14 pickoffs last year accounted for 30% of the major league total for all catchers in 1989. Calling games has been a weakness for him, but the Padres are now less inclined to call pitches from the bench with Santiago behind the plate. Benito still makes way too many errors (20 in 1989), mostly because of his penchant to try and pick off runners.

OVERALL:

Santiago has a tendency to be moody and temperamental. When he begins making mental mistakes, both McKeon and former Padre manager Larry Bowa found it advantageous to take him out of the lineup for a couple of days. But Benito is a competitor who plays even when injured. Wherever he ends up, he can only get better as he continues to grow.

BENITO SANTIAGO

Position: C
Bats: R **Throws:** R
Ht: 6' 1" **Wt:** 185

Opening Day Age: 25
Born: 3/9/65 in Ponce, Puerto Rico
ML Seasons: 4

Overall Statistics

	G	AB	R	H	D	T	HR	RBI	SB	BB	SO	AVG
1989	129	462	50	109	16	3	16	62	11	26	89	.236
Career	431	1562	173	413	73	7	47	193	47	68	295	.264

Where He Hits the Ball

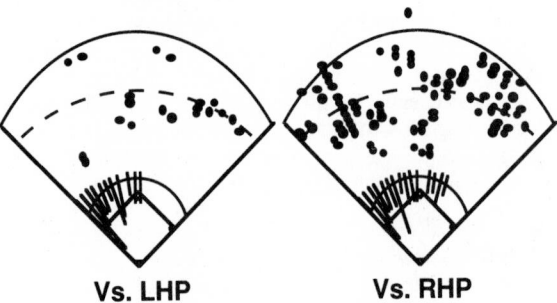

Vs. LHP   Vs. RHP

1989 Situational Stats

	AB	H	HR	RBI	AVG		AB	H	HR	RBI	AVG
Home	212	56	8	30	.264	LHP	117	26	2	12	.222
Road	250	53	8	32	.212	RHP	345	83	14	50	.241
Day	77	17	4	15	.221	Sc Pos	142	34	5	47	.239
Night	385	92	12	47	.239	Clutch	84	19	1	10	.226

1989 Rankings (National League)

➡ 1st in catcher pickoffs (14) and throwing out base stealers (41.0%) - *catchers with 75 attempts*

➡ 9th in errors (20)

➡ Led NL Catchers in strikeouts (89), at bats (462), total bases (179), caught stealing (6), home runs (16), triples (3), RBIs (62) and errors

PITCHING:

Calvin Schiraldi's career has been one of a man with neither a team nor a defined role on a pitching staff. The Padres are the fourth team he has pitched for in his six year career. During those six years he has gone from middle reliever to starting pitcher to closer and back again to starter.

No matter what Calvin's role has been, his style has been the same. He is a fastball pitcher who throws as hard as he can. His fastball has some movement and, because of it, he has averaged over eight strikeouts per nine innings pitched during his career. His uses both a curveball and a slider as off speed pitches, but both are average at best. Because Schiraldi is not a control pitcher, he only goes to the off-speed stuff when he is ahead in the count.

The Padres used Calvin as a starting pitcher after they acquired him from the Cubs last season. Because Mark Davis is the closer, Schiraldi will have to be a starter or middle man. The Cubs attempted to make him a starter in 1988, but he had little success and had to be moved back to the bullpen.

Schiraldi's four starts in September yielded good results, but there were telltale signs that a full season in the rotation could be hazardous. During those starts he averaged 5.5 walks per nine innings. He also averaged less than five innings per start, which makes endurance another problem. These difficulties are not new to Calvin and will probably reappear if he remains in the rotation for San Diego.

FIELDING, HITTING, BASERUNNING:

Schiraldi is average at fielding balls hit back at him, but slow at covering first. Bunts also give him more than his share of problems. For a power pitcher, Calvin does a good job of controlling the running game. At the plate, Schiraldi is a classic no-hit pitcher. His base hit last season was a windblown fly ball that cleared the fence for a homer. It will probably be the last of his career. He's a slow baserunner.

OVERALL:

Once considered a glittering prospect, Schiraldi has never seemed to recover from his unfortunate postseason experiences in 1986 when he got rocked as Boston lost the Series. That said, he can still be a useful member of a pitching staff. His fastball is still major league quality and he is successful against both lefties and righties. Since he doesn't seem to have the stamina to start, his best role may be that of a set-up man.

CALVIN SCHIRALDI

Position: RP/SP
Bats: R **Throws:** R
Ht: 6' 5" **Wt:** 215

Opening Day Age: 27
Born: 6/16/62 in Houston, TX
ML Seasons: 6

Overall Statistics

	W	L	ERA	G	GS	Sv	IP	H	R	BB	SO	HR
1989	6	7	3.51	59	4	4	100.0	72	40	63	71	8
Career	29	30	4.17	190	39	20	444.2	412	220	202	396	48

Where They Hit the Ball

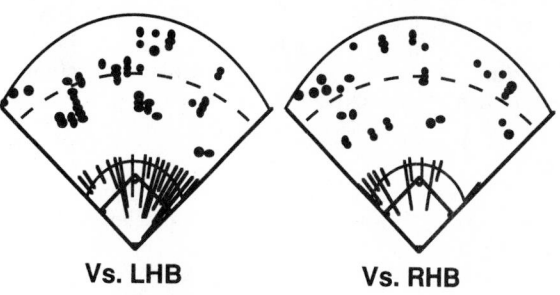

Vs. LHB   **Vs. RHB**

1989 Situational Stats

	W	L	ERA	Sv	IP		AB	H	HR	RBI	AVG
Home	3	4	3.91	1	53.0	LHB	201	41	3	19	.204
Road	3	3	3.06	3	47.0	RHB	160	31	5	19	.194
Day	3	4	3.50	1	54.0	Sc Pos	89	15	1	25	.169
Night	3	3	3.52	3	46.0	Clutch	140	31	5	17	.221

1989 Rankings (National League)

➡ 2nd in first batter efficiency (.130) - *pitchers with 40 games in relief*
➡ 3rd in holds (16)

PITCHING:

Eric Show has been a central figure in the Padres starting rotation since 1983, but neither he, nor many people in the Padres front office, believe he has ever reached his potential despite three seasons of 15 or more wins. An intelligent and religious man with many interests outside baseball, Show is an accomplished jazz guitarist who has recorded and produced several albums. His political interests and affiliation with the John Birch Society have garnered him much unwanted publicity and plenty of awkward stares and comments from teammates.

Last May, Show became the winningest pitcher in Padres history when he recorded his 92nd career victory with a 3-2 win over the New York Mets. But he went down a month later with back spasms. At first some people, including several teammates, doubted the authenticity of the injury. But Show needed mid-summer surgery to remove the L5 disc in his lumbar region, plus several bone fragments, from the injured area. Though he claims to have recovered nicely in post-surgery rehabilitation, only the test of pitching again this spring can determine how effective he will ever be again.

Prior to the injury, Show had been making a nice evolution from a strict fastball pitcher to one equipped to throw a sinker and change up for strikes. Show had finally begun to throw the ball down in the strike zone rather than challenge hitters with fastballs. The result has been more ground outs, fewer strikeouts and less homers allowed. Show says he would like to add a Bruce Hurst-type slow curve to his repertoire when he returns to action this season.

FIELDING, HITTING, BASERUNNING:

Show views himself as an athlete capable of doing more than just pitch. He is constantly taking extra batting practice and is very serious about his hitting. Consequently, he is able to help himself with the bat on occasion. He is an adequate base runner and fields his position well. With the incorporation of the slide step, he is fairly adept at holding a runner on base.

OVERALL:

Show is the proverbial round peg trying to fit into a square hole in the setting of the baseball clubhouse. No matter how hard he tries to fit in -- and in recent years he has made quite an effort to do so -- he still has a hard time winning acceptance. A strong return from back surgery might help him gain that acceptance.

ERIC SHOW

Position: SP
Bats: R **Throws:** R
Ht: 6' 1" **Wt:** 190

Opening Day Age: 33
Born: 5/19/56 in Riverside, CA
ML Seasons: 9

Overall Statistics

	W	L	ERA	G	GS	Sv	IP	H	R	BB	SO	HR
1989	8	6	4.23	16	16	0	106.1	113	59	39	66	9
Career	94	79	3.43	270	218	6	1497.0	1333	629	552	896	150

Where They Hit the Ball

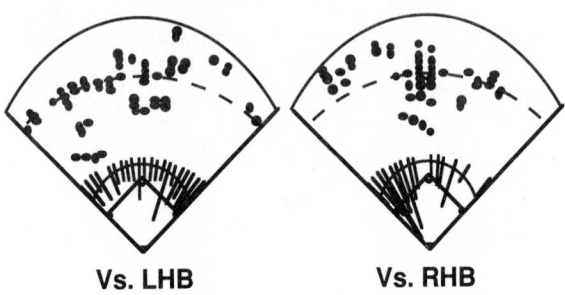

Vs. LHB   **Vs. RHB**

1989 Situational Stats

	W	L	ERA	Sv	IP		AB	H	HR	RBI	AVG
Home	4	3	4.37	0	55.2	LHB	234	63	4	19	.269
Road	4	3	4.09	0	50.2	RHB	178	50	5	32	.281
Day	2	3	6.98	0	29.2	Sc Pos	95	29	6	44	.305
Night	6	3	3.17	0	76.2	Clutch	54	13	0	4	.241

1989 Rankings (National League)

➥ Did not rank near the top or bottom in any category

HITTING:

The switch-hitting Garry Templeton may be in the twilight of his career, but he was able to rebound in 1989 after a pair of disastrous offensive seasons. Plagued by a chronically arthritic left knee that required arthroscopic surgery last winter, Templeton has become a shell of his former self from the left side of the plate. Breaking down his .255 batting average -- his highest single-season mark since 1985 -- Templeton hit .317 from the right side (46 for 145) and .230 (83 for 361) from the left. Templeton has toyed with the idea of batting righthanded only to take the strain off of his left knee, but has not made that commitment.

Complicating matters has been Templeton's resistance to becoming more selective. Always a free swinger, Templeton insists on swinging at the first few pitches in the count whether those pitches are in the strike zone or not.

Though his offensive numbers are not what they were in his youth, Templeton has helped the Padres in other ways. Garry was made the Padres' team captain in 1987 and began to take the role very seriously last season. He deserves much of the credit for the emergence of Bip Roberts, whom Templeton worked with for much of the year.

BASERUNNING:

Because of his gimpy knee, Templeton is no longer a base-stealing threat as his statistics for the past two seasons attest. He stole just eight sacks in 1988 and one in 1989. Templeton has admitted losing two or three steps from the days when one of his infield choppers was an automatic hit.

FIELDING:

Though he still possesses a strong arm, Templeton's range has diminished because of his aching legs. Balls that were once a sure out up the middle are now base hits. Plus, going into the hole to his left has become a problem because he no longer can make the same quick stop and throw like he could in the old days. Yet, Templeton's experience and savvy make him an aging, but elegant shortstop. He is brilliant at the double play pivot, and with that arm is still an effective cutoff man for plays at the plate.

OVERALL:

The responsibility of being team captain seems to have made Templeton more mature. Signed to a new two-year deal last winter, management recognizes the fact that at 34, Templeton can still be a major contributor in a more minor role. Expect Templeton to play in 110 to 120 games this season in an attempt to keep his legs fresh.

GARRY TEMPLETON

Position: SS
Bats: B **Throws:** R
Ht: 5'11" **Wt:** 190

Opening Day Age: 34
Born: 3/24/56 in Lockney, TX
ML Seasons: 14

Overall Statistics

	G	AB	R	H	D	T	HR	RBI	SB	BB	SO	AVG
1989	142	506	43	129	26	3	6	40	1	23	80	.255
Career	1823	6940	823	1910	294	101	58	643	238	341	995	.275

Where He Hits the Ball

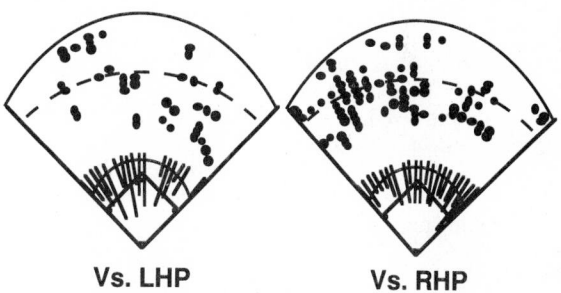

Vs. LHP   **Vs. RHP**

1989 Situational Stats

	AB	H	HR	RBI	AVG		AB	H	HR	RBI	AVG
Home	255	66	5	20	.259	LHP	145	46	1	18	.317
Road	251	63	1	20	.251	RHP	361	83	5	22	.230
Day	141	32	0	8	.227	Sc Pos	106	23	1	32	.217
Night	365	97	6	32	.266	Clutch	90	18	0	4	.200

1989 Rankings (National League)

➡ 1st in lowest percentage of pitches taken (41.9%) - *players with 502 PA*

➡ 2nd in worst on-base average vs. right-handed pitchers (.261) - *players with 377 PA vs. RHP*

➡ 3rd in lowest percentage of extra bases taken as a runner (26.0%) and least runs scored per time reached base (24.3%)

➡ 5th in least pitches seen per plate appearance (3.1)

➡ 8th in grounder/flyball ratio (1.73)

➡ 9th in errors (20)

➡ Led the Padres in GDPs (15)

➡ Led NL Shortstops in gounder/flyball ratio

PITCHING:

Now that he's approaching his 35th birthday, Ed Whitson has finally come into his own as a dominant big-league pitcher. He has won 29 games in two years, including last season's 16-11 record that earned him a new three-year contract. For much of the first half of the season, with Bruce Hurst adapting to his new environment and Eric Show struggling to overcome back problems, Whitson was the staff's stopper. Whitson was 9-2 through June 5, when the Padres were near .500 and struggling to stay alive in the National League West.

Whitson, long a journeyman righthander, credits his emergence to adding a change up he can throw for strikes to his varied repertoire. The change-up has added dimension to a good slider and curve. Whitson has also learned how to change speeds on his fastball, giving him as many as four pitches to work with in any given game.

Whitson's nemesis has long been the home run ball. Last year he led the Padre pitching staff with 22 homers allowed. Like most pitchers who rely on control to circumvent the lack of overpowering stuff, Whitson must keep the ball down in the strike zone. When his fastball is up or when he misses high with a breaking pitch, he gets into big trouble.

Whitson has always possessed a live arm, but much of the reason he developed so late was mental. Part of the problem was continuity. From 1979 to 1985, Whitson played for five organizations. Then, just when he achieved major league success in 1984, Whitson signed a big free agent contract with the Yankees. That decision proved a disaster, and even after he'd come back to San Diego, it took Whitson a good two years to get his head back on straight.

FIELDING, HITTING, BASERUNNING:

Whitson will help himself on occasion at the plate, but is really not a significant factor with the bat. On the bases he usually won't hurt you with silly mistakes. In the field he's been known to take shots off his body. Whitson has had hand and ankle injuries from drives hit back through the box. His move to first base has been aided greatly by the Padres' move to the slide step during the last two seasons.

OVERALL:

The coming season will be the first time in Whitson's 11-year career that he will be starting three seasons with the same organization. Finally, Whitson seems comfortable in his ability to perform, and about the place he is performing.

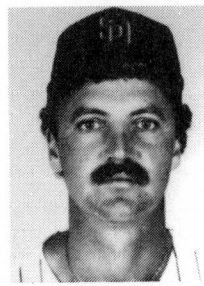

ED WHITSON

Position: SP
Bats: R **Throws:** R
Ht: 6' 3" **Wt:** 195

Opening Day Age: 34
Born: 5/19/55 in Johnson City, TN
ML Seasons: 13

Overall Statistics

	W	L	ERA	G	GS	Sv	IP	H	R	BB	SO	HR
1989	16	11	2.66	33	33	0	227.0	198	77	48	117	22
Career	108	108	3.88	407	289	8	1933.1	1932	925	634	1099	185

Where They Hit the Ball

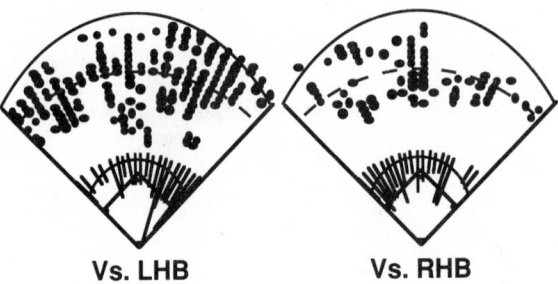

Vs. LHB   **Vs. RHB**

1989 Situational Stats

	W	L	ERA	Sv	IP		AB	H	HR	RBI	AVG
Home	9	6	2.98	0	124.0	LHB	501	132	16	49	.263
Road	7	5	2.27	0	103.0	RHB	340	66	6	21	.194
Day	4	4	3.81	0	54.1	Sc Pos	145	34	2	44	.234
Night	12	7	2.29	0	172.2	Clutch	88	19	2	5	.216

1989 Rankings (National League)

- ➡ 3rd in home runs allowed (22)
- ➡ 4th in ERA (2.66) and least pitches thrown per batter (3.3) - *pitchers with 162 IP*
- ➡ 6th in wins (16)
- ➡ 7th in lowest on-base average allowed (.278) and games started (33)
- ➡ Led the Padres in ERA, wins, games started, home runs allowed, balks (3), win/loss percentage (.593), lowest batting average allowed (.235), lowest on-base average allowed, hit batsmen (5) and least pitches thrown per batter - *team pitchers with 162 IP*

SHAWN ABNER

Position: CF
Bats: R **Throws:** R
Ht: 6' 1" **Wt:** 190

Opening Day Age: 23
Born: 6/17/66 in Hamilton, OH
ML Seasons: 3

Overall Statistics

	G	AB	R	H	D	T	HR	RBI	SB	BB	SO	AVG
1989	57	102	13	18	4	0	2	14	1	5	20	.176
Career	110	232	24	46	10	1	6	26	2	11	47	.198

HITTING, FIELDING, BASERUNNING:

Shawn Aber was the first player selected in the 1984 draft, but he has failed to develop into a major league player. A decent outfielder with good speed, Abner hasn't been able to put it together at the plate for three seasons now. His numbers in both the majors and minors have been absolutely consistent for the last two years. In 1988, after making the Padres out of spring training, Abner hit .181 before he was sent back to AAA Las Vegas, where he batted .254. Last season, Abner started with Vegas, and was recalled after a .269 beginning. Used by the Padres as a spot starter and late-inning defensive replacement, Shawn hit only .176. Abner does not appear capable of hitting a good fastball or any type of breaking pitch. He's got a little power and has homered off both Doc Gooden and Orel Hershiser in his career, but those moments have been rare. He's not a base stealing threat.

OVERALL:

Abner is still only 23, and the Padres have patiently waited for three years hoping he would develop. He's had some good minor league numbers, batting .300 with 85 RBIs at Vegas in '87, but his failure to hit over the last two years is disturbing. By now, San Diego may be on the verge of giving up on him.

DARRIN JACKSON

Position: CF/RF
Bats: R **Throws:** R
Ht: 6' 0" **Wt:** 185

Opening Day Age: 26
Born: 8/22/63 in Los Angeles, CA
ML Seasons: 4

Overall Statistics

	G	AB	R	H	D	T	HR	RBI	SB	BB	SO	AVG
1989	70	170	17	37	7	0	4	20	1	13	34	.218
Career	182	374	48	92	19	3	10	40	5	18	65	.246

HITTING, FIELDING, BASERUNNING:

Darrin Jackson was obtained from the Chicago Cubs on Aug. 30 and was instantly recognized as the best defensive centerfielder the Padres have had in recent years. Jackson's range and arm were a great aid to the Padres as they made a late run at San Francisco in the National League West. And with Jackson in center, Tony Gwynn could move back to right, where he is much more comfortable. But though he helped the Padres, it is obvious that Jackson needs to develop as a hitter. The Cubs used Darrin, a righthanded hitter, primarily against lefthanded pitching. In San Diego, Jack McKeon used Jackson against all types of pitching and, ironically, Jackson hit better against righthanders. But with a .218 overall average, Jackson obviously had trouble against all kinds of pitching.

OVERALL:

Since trading Kevin McReynolds to the Mets in 1986, the Padres have used the likes of Stan Jefferson, Shawn Abner, Shane Mack, Marvell Wynne, Gwynn and Jackson in centerfield, with no one really taking charge. Gwynn was the best, but playing center is tough on Tony's body. The Padres would love for Jackson to win the job permanently, but Darrin is probably ticketed as a spot starter and defensive replacement unless he hits a lot better.

ROB
NELSON

Position: 1B
Bats: L **Throws:** L
Ht: 6' 4" **Wt:** 215

Opening Day Age: 25
Born: 5/17/64 in
Pasadena, CA
ML Seasons: 4

DON
SCHULZE

Position: SP
Bats: R **Throws:** R
Ht: 6' 3" **Wt:** 230

Opening Day Age: 27
Born: 9/27/62 in
Roselle, IL
ML Seasons: 6

Overall Statistics

	G	AB	R	H	D	T	HR	RBI	SB	BB	SO	AVG
1989	42	82	6	16	0	1	3	7	1	20	29	.195
Career	71	147	12	27	2	1	4	11	1	24	62	.184

Overall Statistics

	W	L	ERA	G	GS	Sv	IP	H	R	BB	SO	HR
1989	3	2	5.09	9	6	0	35.1	50	25	11	20	7
Career	15	25	5.47	76	59	0	338.2	422	231	105	144	40

HITTING, FIELDING, BASERUNNING:

In the spring of 1987, the Oakland A's had two young sluggers competing for their first base job. Mark McGwire had the bigger reputation, but many thought that Rob Nelson was a better prospect. When the '87 season opened, Mark and Rob formed a first base platoon, but the lefty-swinging Nelson was slated to get most of the action. That didn't last long; McGwire started hitting homers right away, while Nelson struck out 20 times in his first 35 at bats to win a ticket back to the minors. Before the year was out Nelson went to the Padres in the Storm Davis deal, and he's shown nothing in three brief shots with San Diego. In four major league seasons Nelson has struck out 62 times in only 147 at bats, while hitting just four homers. He batted .195 in last season's 82 at bat trial, and the Padres lost interest. Nelson, a lumbering runner, has a decent glove at first. His problem is hitting the ball.

OVERALL:

Not yet 26, Nelson has belted 133 minor league homers. His stats suggest a young Rob Deer: low average, some walks, great power, a million strikeouts. Nelson hasn't shown power at the major league level yet, but some curious club may give him a longer look. It probably won't be the Padres.

PITCHING, FIELDING, HITTING:

Now 27, Don Schulze is a big lefthander who throws a high-eighties fastball and a good hard sinker. Stuff like his intrigues major league scouts, and Schulze has had trials with the Cubs, Indians, Mets, Yankees and now the Padres. But after six years, he's still best known for suffering a separated left shoulder during some on-field hijinx by the Chicken. Schulze sued the Chicken over that incident, and lost, which about sums up his career. He doesn't really throw hard enough to overpower hitters, and his sinker tends to be erratic. Don also gives up a lot of homers. His San Diego trial was typical: Schulze allowed 38 hits in 24.1 innings, with a 5.55 ERA. He was even worse against lefties (.370) than versus righties (.307), which is not what you like to see in a young southpaw. Don's an average fielder with a fair move to first, and not much of a hitter.

OVERALL:

Schulze's career totals are a horror story: a 15-25 record, 422 hits and 40 home runs allowed in 338.2 innings, a 5.47 ERA. Schulze keeps getting chances, but he has to be running out of them by now.

PITCHING:

Steve Bedrosian was acquired from Philadelphia in mid-June last year to supply the major element the Giants were lacking -- a first-class closer. Bedrock had been unable to get in a groove with the Phillies, since save opportunities were few and far between. But Steve gave the Giants an immediate boost at a time when they were struggling, picking up six saves in his first two weeks with the club.

After that burst, Bedrock enjoyed a Jekyll and Hyde season with San Francisco. At Candlestick Bedrosian was virtually untouchable. Away from the "friendly confines" of the Stick, opposing hitters found Bedrock's offerings much more hittable. Bedrosian ending up blowing eight saves over the course of the season, and was definitely not the pitcher he'd been in 1987, when he saved 40 games and captured the Cy Young Award. Nonetheless, he did the job, and having an established stopper did wonders for the Giants' psyche.

Bedrosian is predominantly a fastball pitcher, capable of reaching the low nineties. When he is on, Bedrock mixes in a hard slider, especially against righthanded batters. Steve is increasingly vulnerable to the home run -- his '89 homer rate of 1.28 per nine innings was by far the highest of his career. Bedrosian has lost a bit of velocity off his fastball, and, perhaps more damaging, his slider hangs up in the hitting zone too frequently.

Steve is now 32 years old. The Giants hope that Bedrosian has a few more seasons of effectiveness before he succumbs to the ravages of age. Although "experience" can be an asset for a starting pitcher, once a reliever loses his blazing fastball, there is little chance that he will be effective over the long haul.

FIELDING, HITTING, BASERUNNING:

As a closer, Bedrosian gets up to bat infrequently. Understandably, he is a poor hitter. Even bunting a runner along seems beyond his capabilities. On the plus side of the ledger, Bedrosian is a decent fielder. Bedrock has only a fair move to first and has always been easy to steal on.

OVERALL:

The acquisition of Bedrosian may have been more important for what it symbolized than for his actual on-field performance. By trading youngsters for an established star reliever, management sent a clear signal to the Giants and the rest of the league that they were going all out to win the pennant now, and let the future bring what it may. The Giants are counting heavily on Bedrosian for 1990.

STEVE BEDROSIAN

Position: RP
Bats: R **Throws:** R
Ht: 6' 3" **Wt:** 205

Opening Day Age: 32
Born: 12/6/57 in Methuen, MA
ML Seasons: 9

Overall Statistics

	W	L	ERA	G	GS	Sv	IP	H	R	BB	SO	HR
1989	3	7	2.87	68	0	23	84.2	56	31	39	58	12
Career	56	61	3.23	484	46	161	910.1	769	362	395	736	83

Where They Hit the Ball

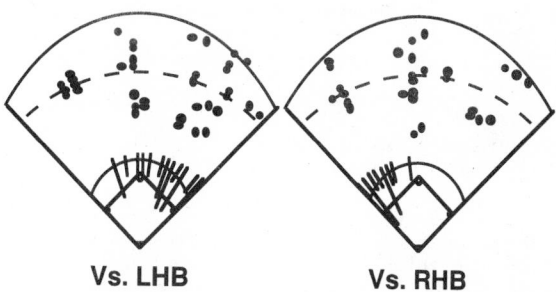

Vs. LHB   **Vs. RHB**

1989 Situational Stats

	W	L	ERA	Sv	IP		AB	H	HR	RBI	AVG
Home	2	2	1.96	14	46.0	LHB	166	33	8	26	.199
Road	1	5	3.96	9	38.2	RHB	131	23	4	12	.176
Day	1	1	1.59	7	28.1	Sc Pos	77	18	7	33	.234
Night	2	6	3.51	16	56.1	Clutch	178	37	8	27	.208

1989 Rankings (National League)

- ➡ 3rd in games finished (60) and worst save percentage (74.2%) - *pitchers with 20 save opportunities*
- ➡ 4th in blown saves (8)
- ➡ 5th in first batter efficiency (.140) - *pitchers in 40 relief games*
- ➡ 6th in save opportunities (31)
- ➡ 9th in saves (23)
- ➡ Led the Giants in games finished (33) and blown saves (5)

PITCHING:

Jeff Brantley, a 25-year old rookie, was able to help the Giants immediately last year in middle relief. Brantley does not have the greatest raw ability. What he does have is the attitude that he can get any hitter out.

The story behind Brantley's rise to the majors is worthy of note. Jeff, a college teammate of Will Clark at Mississippi State, was not even on the Giants' 40-man off-season roster. San Francisco left him unprotected last winter, and in a clear demonstration of Brantley's perceived worth, no other team claimed him. This affront prodded Jeff to pitch in the Puerto Rican winter league in a last-ditch attempt to improve his split-finger fastball. Brantley showed off his new-found abilities in Phoenix before the Giants brought him up.

Pitching in middle relief and often entering the game with the Giants behind, Brantley won his first six decisions despite an ERA of over 4.00. Jeff lost for the first time last season when he was pressed into an emergency starting role. Except for that one disastrous outing, Brantley pitched reasonably well, recording a 3.77 ERA as a reliever.

Brantley is a control pitcher who gets by mostly on his split-finger fastball. Jeff has only a fair-to-middling fastball. He throws a little curveball and spots his fastball, but when in a jam relies on the splitter. For variety, Brantley drops down to a three-quarters delivery occasionally to righthanded batters. When major league hitters got to see him the second time around the league, they often teed off on his offerings, which may not augur well for Brantley's future.

FIELDING, HITTING, BASERUNNING:

Brantley's follow-through leaves him in good fielding position, which allows him to wear the fifth infielder tag. Jeff is quick on his feet handling bunts and covering first base. To the uninitiated, Brantley unleashes a good pick-off move, but he permitted 12 steals in 14 attempts in his limited action.

OVERALL:

Roger Craig loves Brantley, since he comes right after the hitters. Jeff is not afraid to throw strikes. While his work in 1989 casts some doubts on his ability to be effective in the long term, Brantley will start 1990 with a job reserved for him.

JEFF BRANTLEY

Position: RP
Bats: R **Throws:** R
Ht: 5'11" **Wt:** 180

Opening Day Age: 26
Born: 9/5/63 in Florence, AL
ML Seasons: 2

Overall Statistics

	W	L	ERA	G	GS	Sv	IP	H	R	BB	SO	HR
1989	7	1	4.07	59	1	0	97.1	101	50	37	69	10
Career	7	2	4.35	68	2	1	118.0	123	63	43	80	12

Where They Hit the Ball

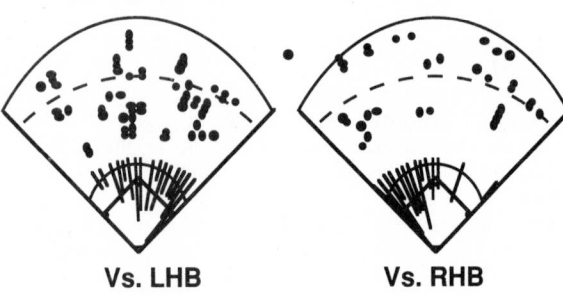

Vs. LHB   **Vs. RHB**

1989 Situational Stats

	W	L	ERA	Sv	IP		AB	H	HR	RBI	AVG
Home	4	1	3.60	0	45.0	LHB	198	59	4	19	.298
Road	3	0	4.47	0	52.1	RHB	175	42	6	27	.240
Day	3	0	3.57	0	35.1	Sc Pos	97	29	3	36	.299
Night	4	1	4.35	0	62.0	Clutch	85	18	0	4	.212

1989 Rankings (National League)

➡ 9th in lowest percentage of inherited runners scoring (28.6%) - *pitchers with 30 inherited runners*

➡ Led the Giants in lowest percentage of inherited runners scoring and first batter efficiency (.196) - *team pitchers in 40 relief games*

HITTING:

Brett Butler had another fine season in 1989, batting .283 and scoring 100 runs. Brett has always been the prototypical leadoff hitter. He draws a lot of walks, and with his speed beats out many bunts (23 bunt singles last season) and other infield hits. But Butler's 59 walks last year were 38 fewer than his 1988 total, and his production declined in almost every offensive category from '88 to '89. At 32, age may be starting to catch up to Butler a little.

Brett is an opposite-field line drive hitter with virtually no power. When he is going well, Butler chops down on pitches high in the strike zone. Brett has one of the best eyes in baseball, with his strikeout to walk ratio consistently among the league leaders. Since he has little power and is a good curveball hitter, Brett sees a lot of fastballs. His inside-out stroke results in many flares down the left field line.

Butler is one of the few lefthanded batters to have a higher career batting average off lefties (.288) than off of righties (.279). Unlike most lefthanded hitters, Butler is a good high ball hitter. If the pitcher comes down and in, Brett is able to lace the ball down the right field line, so he is difficult to defense.

BASERUNNING:

Butler has always stolen a lot of bases, but his 31 steals last year were his lowest total since 1982. The down side of his game is that he's always been thrown out a lot, including 16 times in 1989. Overall, his stealing is only marginally productive, if that. Brett likes to take the extra base whenever possible. He runs hard from home to first, which allows him to get several "leg doubles" during the season.

FIELDING:

For many years, Brett has been among the best defensive centerfielders in baseball. His range afield is his main attribute. Playing a rather deep center, Butler is adept at dashing in to catch looping liners. Butler's arm is underrated. Although it is slightly below average in strength, he is able to throw out many aggressive baserunners with accuracy.

OVERALL:

Though his skills may be declining a little, Butler is still one of the premier leadoff men in the National League. He has scored over 90 runs for six straight seasons, and reached the century mark in both his seasons with the Giants. Butler is the catalyst of the Giants' offense and a very good centerfielder as well.

BRETT BUTLER

Position: CF
Bats: L **Throws:** L
Ht: 5'10" **Wt:** 170

Opening Day Age: 32
Born: 6/15/57 in Los Angeles, CA
ML Seasons: 9

Overall Statistics

	G	AB	R	H	D	T	HR	RBI	SB	BB	SO	AVG
1989	154	594	100	168	22	4	4	36	31	59	69	.283
Career	1200	4379	742	1232	169	74	36	318	307	564	465	.281

Where He Hits the Ball

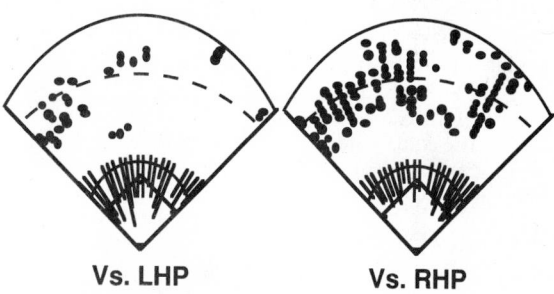

Vs. LHP   **Vs. RHP**

1989 Situational Stats

	AB	H	HR	RBI	AVG		AB	H	HR	RBI	AVG
Home	296	90	2	21	.304	LHP	200	56	1	15	.280
Road	298	78	2	15	.262	RHP	394	112	3	21	.284
Day	231	59	2	18	.255	Sc Pos	99	25	0	32	.253
Night	363	109	2	18	.300	Clutch	92	27	1	9	.293

1989 Rankings (National League)

➡ 1st in bunts in play (49) and percentage of extra bases taken as a runner (63.0%) - *players with 40 opportunities to advance*

➡ 3rd in caught stealing (16)

➡ 4th in runs (100), pitches seen (2,496), sacrifice bunts (13) and runs scored per time reached base (39.4%) - *players with 502 PA*

➡ Led the Giants in at bats (594), singles (138), caught stealing, stolen bases (31), pitches seen, grounder/flyball ratio (1.61), bunts in play, lowest percentage of swings that missed (8.0%) and percentage of extra bases taken as a runner

HITTING:

Will Clark is probably the best hitter in the National League, with his potent combination of high batting average and home run power. Whereas in the past he was pull-conscious, Clark used the whole field last year. He made his greatest improvement against left-handed pitchers, raising his average vs. southpaws from .262 in '88 to .321 last year.

Will is an intelligent hitter and keeps a comprehensive book on every pitch he is thrown, in order to recognize the pitcher's pattern. He has the ability to wait until the last possible instant before whipping his bat through the hitting zone. Clark excels against the flame-throwers of the league. He is especially tough in "game" situations (.389 with runners in scoring position). About the only way to get him out on anything resembling a consistent basis is with high and tight heat.

Anyone playing at Candlestick is fighting the odds in trying to win a batting title. Before Clark's 1989 season, Willie McCovey's .320 average in 1969 was the best for a Giant player since the team moved to the Stick. The cold, wind, tall infield grass, and large foul territories of Candlestick Park have a stultifying effect on many players' batting averages.

BASERUNNING:

Clark has little footspeed. He was once a terrible base stealer, going 9 for 33 in steal attempts during his first two years. But Clark has worked hard and completely overcome this former weakness. Over the last two years, he's 17 for 21. Will is a hard-nosed ballplayer in all aspects of the game, including sliding hard into second attempting to break up double plays.

FIELDING:

Like Don Mattingly, Clark's offense is so noteworthy that his defense gets little attention. Nonetheless, Clark is among the best in the league at his position. He is particularly adept at fielding bunts and throwing out the lead runner. Will scoops the low throw to first out of the dirt very well, and is one of the best in the league at catching foul pops down the right field line. The only area in which he may be deficient is his range afield.

OVERALL:

At 26, Clark may be the best player in the National League for several seasons to come. Though not possessing awesome power, Will has belted 87 home runs in the past three years. Emblematic of his maturation, Clark has elevated his batting average to the top of the league as well.

WILL CLARK

Position: 1B
Bats: L **Throws:** L
Ht: 6' 1" **Wt:** 190

Opening Day Age: 26
Born: 3/13/64 in New Orleans, LA
ML Seasons: 4

Overall Statistics

	G	AB	R	H	D	T	HR	RBI	SB	BB	SO	AVG
1989	159	588	104	196	38	9	23	111	8	74	103	.333
Career	582	2100	361	638	125	22	98	352	26	257	406	.304

Where He Hits the Ball

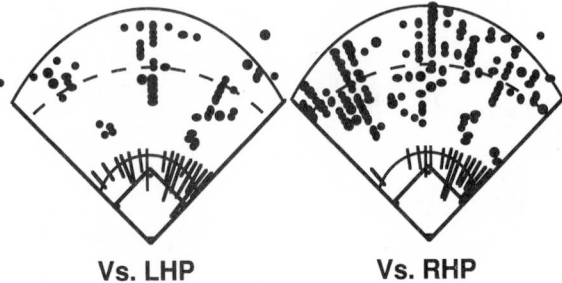

Vs. LHP	Vs. RHP

1989 Situational Stats

	AB	H	HR	RBI	AVG		AB	H	HR	RBI	AVG
Home	277	90	9	57	.325	LHP	215	69	8	54	.321
Road	311	106	14	54	.341	RHP	373	127	15	57	.340
Day	233	83	9	48	.356	Sc Pos	144	56	9	86	.389
Night	355	113	14	63	.318	Clutch	90	27	5	20	.300

1989 Rankings (National League)

- ➡ 1st in runs (104) and times on base (275)

- ➡ 2nd in batting average (.333), hits (196) and total bases (321) - *players with 502 PA*

- ➡ 3rd in RBIs (111), sacrifice flies (8), triples (9), on-base average (.407), slugging percentage (.546) and hitting with runners in scoring position (.389)

- ➡ Led the Giants in batting average, sacrifice flies, times on base, plate appearances (675), runs, hits, doubles (38), on-base average and hitting with runners in scoring position

- ➡ Led NL First Basemen in batting average, slugging percentage, singles, total bases, times on base, runs scored per time reached base (35.3%), runs, hits and triples

PITCHING:

Picked by a prominent national magazine as the pre-season favorite to win the Cy Young award, Kelly Downs had a miserable and injury-filled 1989. Kelly pitched poorly in April and early May before a serious injury was discovered in his pitching shoulder. There was some speculation that Downs was already injured at the time he was struggling.

Downs was forced to spend six weeks of inactivity to rest his inflamed shoulder. Thereafter he worked for the better part of three months on learning a new pitching motion to take the pressure off his shoulder. It was obvious to many observers that Downs' unorthodox delivery placed a lot of strain on his arm and shoulder. These same people, not in the organization, have questioned the Giants on their failure to take measures which may have prevented a career-influencing injury.

Downs's fastball had been clocked around 93 mph when he was completely healthy, but Kelly has not yet regained his former velocity. His best pitch, of course, is the famed split-finger fastball. Downs has the ability to throw the splitter very hard, somewhat like Mike Scott. Kelly has enjoyed his finest success when he changed speeds on his split-finger, something he did only rarely last season.

When he returned to the Giants in mid-August, Downs was restored to the starting rotation. His lack of stamina restricted his effectiveness and overall chances of success, and ultimately earned Kelly a trip to the bullpen in September. The few good outings Downs enjoyed late in the year should eliminate the self-doubt that can haunt an injured pitcher's off-season.

FIELDING, HITTING, BASERUNNING:

Downs is one of the more athletic pitchers on the Giants staff. He is able to do many of the little things which help to win ball games. Downs is a capable fielder, and though he is not a good hitter, he is an adequate bunter. He also has an outstanding move to first, allowing only one successful steal last year.

OVERALL:

A serious shoulder injury is nothing to be taken lightly. The Giants are not counting on Kelly to be the ace of the staff for their upcoming season. The inflated expectations coming into last season surely worked against him. If Kelly bounces back from his injury, he should once more be the steady pitcher who went 12-9, then 13-9 in 1987 and '88.

KELLY DOWNS

Position: SP
Bats: R **Throws:** R
Ht: 6' 4" **Wt:** 200

Opening Day Age: 29
Born: 10/25/60 in Ogden, UT
ML Seasons: 4

Overall Statistics

	W	L	ERA	G	GS	Sv	IP	H	R	BB	SO	HR
1989	4	8	4.79	18	15	0	82.2	82	47	26	49	7
Career	33	30	3.57	100	83	1	525.0	485	226	170	368	37

Where They Hit the Ball

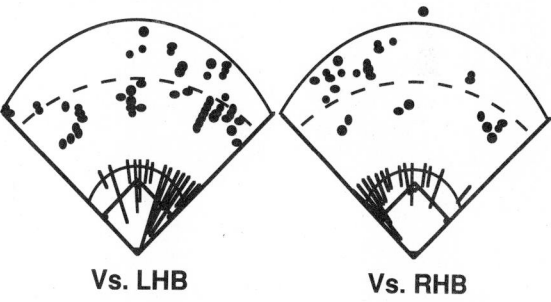

Vs. LHB   **Vs. RHB**

1989 Situational Stats

	W	L	ERA	Sv	IP		AB	H	HR	RBI	AVG
Home	3	2	5.09	0	40.2	LHB	181	55	4	26	.304
Road	1	6	4.50	0	42.0	RHB	133	27	3	14	.203
Day	1	2	4.21	0	25.2	Sc Pos	64	22	1	27	.344
Night	3	6	5.05	0	57.0	Clutch	31	7	1	3	.226

1989 Rankings (National League)

➥ Did not rank near the top or bottom in any category

PITCHING:

Last year, Scott Garrelts led the National League with a scintillating 2.28 ERA. Although he spent two separate stints on the disabled list, Garrelts would have been a serious Cy Young candidate had the Giants scored some more runs for him. In a stretch of seven starts in the middle of the season, Garrelts pitched very well, yet had only one win and six no-decisions to show for it.

In what the Giants hope was a breakthrough season, Scottie seemed to mature overnight. His road to success was nothing novel; Garrelts cut his walks allowed in half, while not trying to strike out every hitter. Scottie seemed to demonstrate that he belongs in the starting rotation, after pitching mostly from the bullpen in previous years. At Candlestick, the scene of past trials and tribulations, including unmerciful booing in the second half of the 1988 season, Garrelts pitched very well last season.

A 93 mph fastball, two different types of sliders (one predominantly to lefties, and one to righties), and a hard split-fingered fastball make up Garrelts' repertoire. As has been known for years, Garrelts has the best pure "stuff" on the Giants staff. Norm Sherry and Roger Craig have spent a long time trying to get Scottie's ability to be reflected in the win/loss column.

Garrelts is now pitching with an idea about how to go about setting up and getting out hitters, rather than rearing back and seeing how hard he could throw. As a result, Scottie works more deliberately and in more control than in past seasons. He used to pitch very rapidly, almost as if he were afraid to give himself time to think. Still relatively young, the Giants hope that Garrelts has just entered his pitching prime.

FIELDING, HITTING, BASERUNNING:

Having decent baserunning speed can be a curse for a pitcher. Garrelts is not a good baserunner, although he was used as a pinch runner on several occasions. Indeed, Garrelts went on the DL last season for an injury sustained while running out a triple. Garrelts is a decent fielder, but his move to first is below average.

OVERALL:

Garrelts has made a spectacular and successful transition from a thrower to a pitcher. While careful not to put undue pressure on him, the Giants expect the 28-year old Garrelts to be the ace of the Giants for several seasons to come. Despite his troubles in post-season play, Garrelts now has the maturity and confidence the Giants have been looking for.

SCOTT GARRELTS

Position: SP
Bats: R **Throws:** R
Ht: 6' 4" **Wt:** 205

Opening Day Age: 28
Born: 10/30/61 in Urbana, IL
ML Seasons: 8

Overall Statistics

	W	L	ERA	G	GS	Sv	IP	H	R	BB	SO	HR
1989	14	5	2.28	30	29	0	193.1	149	58	46	119	11
Career	56	41	3.01	313	55	48	757.2	600	290	334	615	53

Where They Hit the Ball

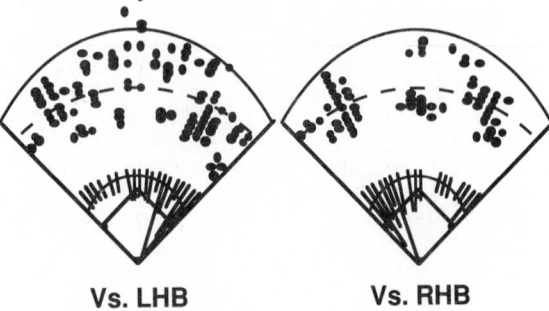

Vs. LHB   **Vs. RHB**

1989 Situational Stats

	W	L	ERA	Sv	IP		AB	H	HR	RBI	AVG
Home	10	2	1.57	0	108.2	LHB	378	89	6	38	.235
Road	4	3	3.19	0	84.2	RHB	326	60	5	17	.184
Day	5	3	3.25	0	63.2	Sc Pos	142	27	3	42	.190
Night	9	2	1.80	0	129.2	Clutch	53	13	1	3	.245

1989 Rankings (National League)

➡ 1st in ERA (2.28), lowest on-base average allowed (.258), and ERA at home (1.57) - *pitchers with 162 IP*

➡ 2nd in lowest slugging percentage allowed (.313)

➡ 4th in lowest batting average allowed (.212)

➡ 7th in least HRs allowed per 9 innings (.51)

➡ Led the Giants in ERA, lowest batting average allowed, lowest on-base average allowed, lowest slugging percentage allowed, wild pitches (7), strikeouts (119), win/loss percentage (.737), ERA at home, least HRs allowed per 9 innings and most strikeouts per 9 innings (5.5) - *team pitchers with 162 IP*

PITCHING:

In terms of continuous service, Atlee Hammaker has been with the Giants longer than anyone on the current roster. Hammaker has worked long and hard to recover from serious shoulder surgery. But in the "what have you done for me lately" world of professional athletics, that only carries a player so far. Atlee's once-biting slider now all too often invitingly hangs in the hitting zone. Along those same lines, Hammaker needs to have his pin-point control, since he no longer has the same "stuff" he had in 1983. After 1984 rotator-cuff surgery, very little remains of what was once a good fastball.

Hammaker began last season in the starting rotation, but by late April had been moved to the bullpen. Atlee had lost his confidence, perhaps due to not being comfortable with his ever-changing role on the staff. Hammaker wants to be a starter, but his ineffectiveness makes that strategy a risk. He is caught in the familiar Catch-22 situation: Hammaker needs to pitch regularly to be effective, but Roger Craig will not pitch him regularly until he is effective.

For a variety of unkind, although not necessarily invalid, reasons, Atlee is not particularly well liked by Giants fans and players. After his serious knee injury in early August, one of Hammaker's teammates said he regretted that the injury was not a career-ending injury. Atlee was able to come back in late September and pitch a few innings to successfully test his knee.

FIELDING, HITTING, BASERUNNING:

The Hammer is a terrible hitter. Hitting .368 (seven for 19) in 1989 was a fluke, and brought his career batting average up to only .119. However, if he ever finds himself on base, Atlee is a most "entertaining" baserunner. His follow-through leaves Hammaker in good fielding position, but he is not a good fielder. Only while delivering the ball to the plate does Hammaker have a baseball player's instincts. Atlee is not known for having a good move to first, but he allowed only three stolen bases last year, with two caught stealing.

OVERALL:

Hammaker is a tough case to evaluate. He once had the promise to become one of the best pitchers in the league, but arm and shoulder injuries have robbed Atlee of his best stuff. The Giants are hoping that he can come all the way back, but the fact is that Hammaker has struggled the past two seasons, and can't be counted on much in the future.

ATLEE HAMMAKER

Position: RP/SP
Bats: L **Throws:** L
Ht: 6' 2" **Wt:** 200

Opening Day Age: 32
Born: 1/24/58 in Carmel, CA
ML Seasons: 8

Overall Statistics

	W	L	ERA	G	GS	Sv	IP	H	R	BB	SO	HR
1989	6	6	3.76	28	9	0	76.2	78	34	23	30	5
Career	55	57	3.54	199	144	5	979.2	946	433	249	566	84

Where They Hit the Ball

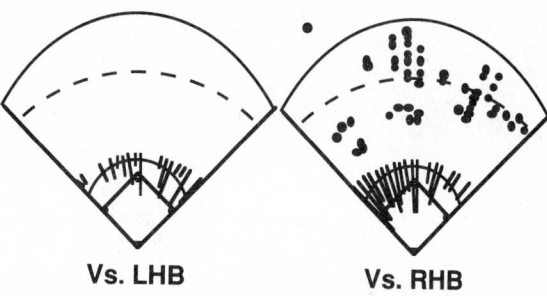

Vs. LHB   Vs. RHB

1989 Situational Stats

	W	L	ERA	Sv	IP		AB	H	HR	RBI	AVG
Home	3	1	2.55	0	35.1	LHB	64	18	0	4	.281
Road	3	5	4.79	0	41.1	RHB	224	60	5	24	.268
Day	4	4	2.70	0	36.2	Sc Pos	55	16	1	22	.291
Night	2	2	4.72	0	40.0	Clutch	68	19	0	4	.279

1989 Rankings (National League)

→ 2nd in most GDPs induced per GDP situation (20.0%) - *pitchers with 30 GDP situations*

HITTING:

Terry Kennedy began last season well, but finished the year batting only .239. Terry is now very weak against lefthanded pitching (a paltry .154 average last year), and will surely continue to be platooned for the remainder of his career.

Age has slowed Kennedy's bat, making him vulnerable to high and tight fastballs. Since joining the Giants, Kennedy has become more of a pull hitter, though no longer one with much power. Terry hit very well with runners in scoring position (.282) last season. Like most lefties, Kennedy prefers the ball down in the strike zone and handles the low fastball well. Terry has a good eye and has become a more patient hitter.

Once a decent power hitter who homered in double figures every year from 1982 through 1987, Kennedy appears to have lost his home run stroke. He had only three a year ago, his lowest total since 1981. The many years of wear and tear, catching over 100 games a season, have made Kennedy one of the slowest runners in the majors; he's not going to leg out any hits.

BASERUNNING:

Terry is one the most plodding baserunners in the majors. It is no cliche to report that it takes a double to get Terry home from second base. He did steal a base in 1989, matching his career high, but it took him four attempts. Kennedy's footspeed brings back memories of Milt May, the Giants' ponderous catcher of the early 1980s.

FIELDING:

Kennedy has never been known for his defense, with good reason. He was able to throw out a better percentage of baserunners this season only because the Giants' pitching staff is so good at holding runners. Terry's slowness makes him susceptible to wild pitches that a more agile catcher would block. The veteran Kennedy is capable of handling a pitching staff, but since Roger Craig takes almost total control of the Giants' staff (including calling the pitches), that skill is negated in this case.

OVERALL:

Kennedy has always been a good hitting/poor fielding catcher. The strain of catching has now caused his offense to slip below the level a major league team can afford from their regular catcher. Kennedy has aged rapidly the past few seasons, and his future in the majors is not likely to last much longer.

TERRY KENNEDY

Position: C
Bats: L **Throws:** R
Ht: 6' 4" **Wt:** 224

Opening Day Age: 33
Born: 6/4/56 in Euclid, OH
ML Seasons: 12

Overall Statistics

	G	AB	R	H	D	T	HR	RBI	SB	BB	SO	AVG
1989	125	355	19	85	15	0	5	34	1	35	56	.239
Career	1315	4505	437	1189	215	11	108	589	5	323	786	.264

Where He Hits the Ball

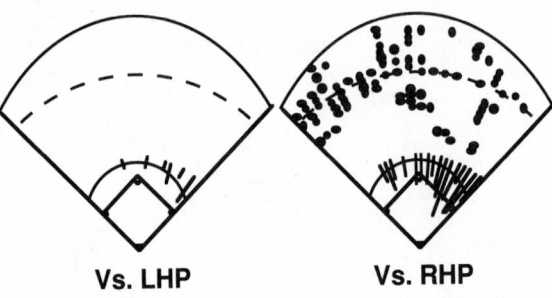

Vs. LHP   **Vs. RHP**

1989 Situational Stats

	AB	H	HR	RBI	AVG		AB	H	HR	RBI	AVG
Home	172	46	1	16	.267	LHP	39	6	0	3	.154
Road	183	39	4	18	.213	RHP	316	79	5	31	.250
Day	140	28	2	16	.200	Sc Pos	78	22	0	27	.282
Night	215	57	3	18	.265	Clutch	51	12	1	7	.235

1989 Rankings (National League)

➡ 3rd in throwing out base stealers (37.1%) - *catchers with 75 attempts*

➡ 4th in lowest percentage of extra bases taken as a runner (26.9%) - *players with 40 opportunities to advance*

PITCHING:

A 33-year old veteran now pitching for his fourth major league team, Mike LaCoss has served the Giants well in his four San Francisco seasons. LaCoss's main asset is the ability to switch between starting and relieving, depending on how his club needs him. He handled that role in fine fashion last year, winning 10 games, saving six, and turning in his lowest ERA since 1982. When Scott Garrelts was moved into the Giants' rotation last spring, LaCoss began the year as a late-inning reliever. He didn't do all that badly, recording six saves and a 2.06 ERA during the first two months. But Mike got into hot water with frequent bouts of wildness, including walking in the winning run on several occasions. Eventually the Giants obtained Steve Bedrosian, and LaCoss was moved back into the starting rotation. He went 7-4 after the All-Star break and was a big help in the Giants' drive to the National League pennant.

LaCoss possesses two different fastballs, a curveball and a split-finger. His "out" pitch is the splitter, which breaks down and away from lefthanded batters. Mike is a noted groundball pitcher with a career ratio of groundball outs to flyball outs of nearly two to one. The Giants' smooth fielding keystone combination of Uribe and Thompson bails him out of many jams by turning the double play. Mike was bothered by a tender elbow (allegedly caused by throwing too many split-finger fastballs) early last year, and was unable to use his curveball much during the season's first few months. LaCoss got by, but he was obviously more effective when able to use his complete arsenal.

FIELDING, HITTING, BASERUNNING:

LaCoss' defense is paradoxical. Mike seems to follow through in good position, but many grounders trickle through his legs, or some other unusual event jumps up and bites him. His move to first is not outstanding, but he did a fine job of controlling the running game last year. Whereas LaCoss is a fair bunter, he is a woeful hitter. Like many pitchers, LaCoss on the bases is like a fish out of water.

OVERALL:

Not blessed with great raw ability, LaCoss relies on bulldog determination. He has the sort of versatility that is always welcome on a pitching staff. It is unclear whether Mike will be able to break into the Giants' rotation this season, since he'll have lots of competition. But LaCoss will probably find some sort of useful role.

MIKE LACOSS

Position: RP/SP
Bats: R **Throws:** R
Ht: 6' 4" **Wt:** 200

Opening Day Age: 33
Born: 5/30/56 in Glendale, CA
ML Seasons: 12

Overall Statistics

	W	L	ERA	G	GS	Sv	IP	H	R	BB	SO	HR
1989	10	10	3.17	45	18	6	150.1	143	62	65	78	3
Career	91	94	3.93	384	226	12	1614.2	1650	809	662	714	90

Where They Hit the Ball

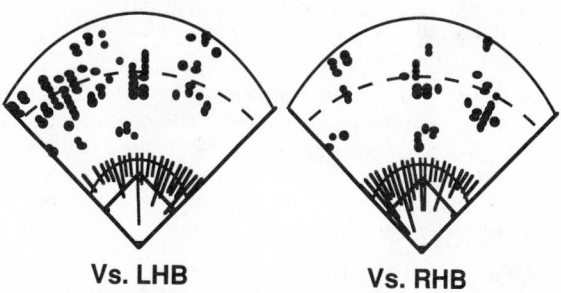

Vs. LHB   Vs. RHB

1989 Situational Stats

	W	L	ERA	Sv	IP		AB	H	HR	RBI	AVG
Home	6	4	2.90	4	68.1	LHB	311	83	3	33	.267
Road	4	6	3.40	2	82.0	RHB	249	60	0	24	.241
Day	5	3	3.05	3	65.0	Sc Pos	143	33	2	53	.231
Night	5	7	3.27	3	85.1	Clutch	103	26	2	16	.252

1989 Rankings (National League)

➡ 3rd in balks (5) and hit batsmen (7)

➡ Led the Giants in balks, hit batsmen, GDPs induced (14) and walks allowed (65)

PITCHING:

Without a doubt, Craig Lefferts' 1989 season was his career best. He began the year in middle relief while the Giants experimented with several ineffective stoppers. For the first six weeks Lefty was untouchable, compiling an ERA under 1.00, and allowing only one inherited baserunner to score. As belated reward, Lefferts was eventually promoted from his role as lefthanded relief specialist to full-time closer in late May. When Steve Bedrosian was acquired in mid-June, Lefferts reluctantly resumed his earlier status.

Lefferts has a fastball, a slider, a screwball, and a newly developed cut fastball (which runs away from lefthanded batters). Lefferts showcases his fastball. Against righthanded batters, he uses a good screwball. Facing lefthanded hitters, Craig uses his nasty slider almost exclusively. Occasionally Lefferts drops down sidearm to make it even tougher to stand in against him.

Lefferts' signature, when he enters the game, is his sprint in from the bullpen, a habit retained from his collegiate days. Most late-inning specialists rely on getting ground balls and/or strikeouts. Lefferts is an exception in that he is a flyball pitcher who does not strike out a preponderance of hitters.

Although Lefferts has the reputation of a "rubber armed" reliever, last year he was noticeably less effective in the second of consecutive appearances. In addition, Lefty seemed to tire in the second half of the season and was on the shelf in the latter part of September with a sore shoulder. That was probably due to Roger Craig's habit of going to the same man until he drops dead from fatigue.

FIELDING, HITTING, BASERUNNING:

Lefferts is a decent fielder, but has the tendency to throw the ball away on bunt plays. With his good pickoff move and quick delivery to the plate, he shuts down the opposition running game. As a short reliever, Craig rarely has batted in his career. In his small number of at bats, Lefferts has not demonstrated any ability to hit, and is also a poor bunter.

OVERALL:

Lefferts had 20 saves last year, and has aspirations to be a full-time closer. The Giants, however, have found that Craig is most effective as the lefthanded specialist. In the second half of last season, Lefferts was used with great success as Bedrosian's set-up man. The same potent combination will be employed this season as well.

CRAIG LEFFERTS

Position: RP
Bats: L **Throws:** L
Ht: 6' 1" **Wt:** 210

Opening Day Age: 32
Born: 9/29/57 in Munich, West Germany
ML Seasons: 7

Overall Statistics

	W	L	ERA	G	GS	Sv	IP	H	R	BB	SO	HR
1989	2	4	2.69	70	0	20	107.0	93	38	22	71	11
Career	32	39	3.00	472	5	54	683.2	600	257	205	422	59

Where They Hit the Ball

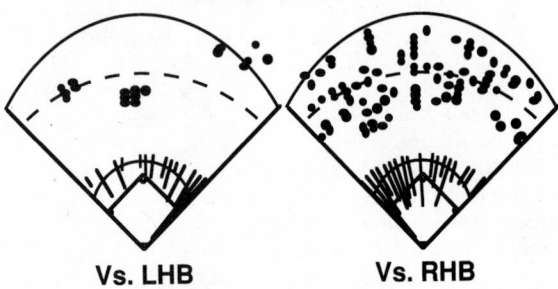

Vs. LHB   Vs. RHB

1989 Situational Stats

	W	L	ERA	Sv	IP		AB	H	HR	RBI	AVG
Home	0	2	2.28	10	55.1	LHB	85	17	2	5	.200
Road	2	2	3.14	10	51.2	RHB	314	76	9	42	.242
Day	0	2	2.49	10	47.0	Sc Pos	118	19	5	36	.161
Night	2	2	2.85	10	60.0	Clutch	229	50	5	22	.218

1989 Rankings (National League)

➡ 6th in games (70) and save percentage (83.3%) - *players with 20 save opportunities*

➡ 9th in holds (12)

➡ Led the Giants in games, save percentage, saves (20), holds and save opportunities (24)

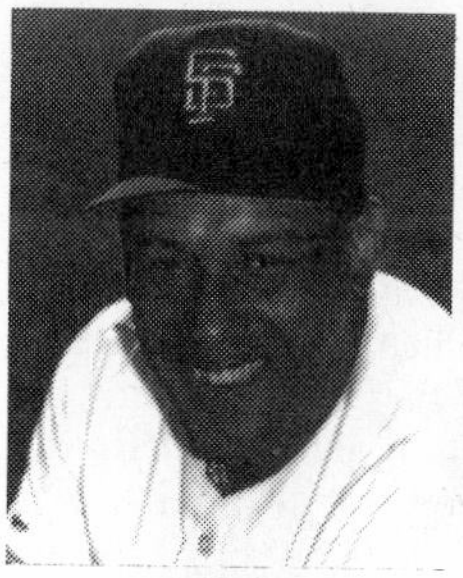

CANDY MALDONADO

Position: RF
Bats: R **Throws:** R
Ht: 6' 0" **Wt:** 195

Opening Day Age: 29
Born: 9/5/60 in Humacao, Puerto Rico
ML Seasons: 9

Overall Statistics

	G	AB	R	H	D	T	HR	RBI	SB	BB	SO	AVG
1989	129	345	39	75	23	0	9	41	4	37	69	.217
Career	818	2236	260	562	127	10	70	332	23	172	403	.251

Where He Hits the Ball

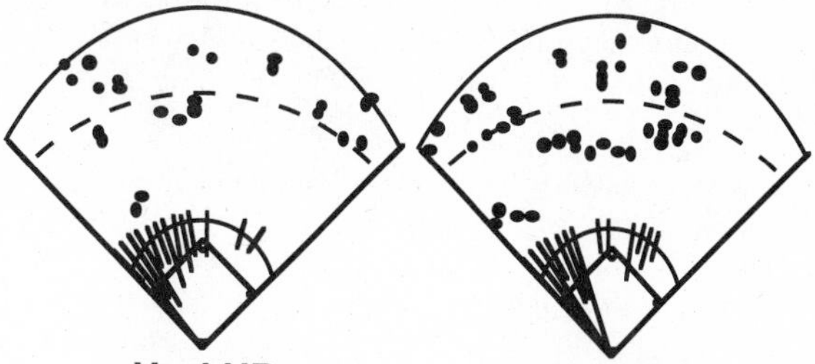

Vs. LHP   Vs. RHP

1989 Situational Stats

	AB	H	HR	RBI	AVG		AB	H	HR	RBI	AVG
Home	156	31	1	14	.199	LHP	147	31	2	9	.211
Road	189	44	8	27	.233	RHP	198	44	7	32	.222
Day	130	23	6	16	.177	Sc Pos	100	21	1	29	.210
Night	215	52	3	25	.242	Clutch	65	15	1	5	.231

1989 Rankings (National League)

➟ Led the Giants in GDPs (8)

HITTING:

Going into 1989, the Giants figured their pennant chances depended in good measure on a strong performance by Candy Maldonado. They were wrong. Maldonado had a miserable year, the worst of his career in fact. But carried by other players, the Giants won anyway.

Currently the Bay Area's favorite whipping boy (a la Bobby Murcer of the mid-1970s), Maldonado is someone Giants' fans love to hate. Candy gave them more than enough ammunition, hitting in the low .200's, and belting only one of his nine home runs at Candlestick. He also hit only .201 in 174 at bats as the number five hitter, a key reason Kevin Mitchell was given a whopping 32 intentional walks. Maldonado got off to a slow start last season when he tried to pull every ball. He then spent the rest of the year trying to right himself. Hitting coach Dusty Baker worked tirelessly with Candy to get him to cut down his swing and go with the pitch more. Maldonado did improve in midseason, batting .282 with five homers in June and July. But then he fell apart, batting only .164 from August 1 on.

Candy is a good low ball fastball hitter, but has noted trouble with off-speed pitches. He has good power and, when he is going well, is a good RBI man for the middle of the Giants' lineup. Maldonado has never been a patient hitter. His 37 walks last year tied his career high.

BASERUNNING:

Maldonado has decent speed but is known for baserunning blunders. He is not a good base stealer, and is frequently thrown out on the bases trying to take an extra base at inopportune times. To Candy's credit, he takes pleasure in sliding hard into second and breaking up double plays.

FIELDING:

On one occasion last year, Candy tried to throw out a runner at the plate in the bottom of the ninth with the Giants ahead by three runs. That allowed the tying run to get into scoring position, and the Giants lost the game. Another time, Candy dropped a flyball with the bases loaded while trying to make a gratuitous sliding catch, costing the Giants another game. Maldonado made a similar play in the nightmarish 1987 playoffs. He does possess a strong throwing arm.

OVERALL:

Although Maldonado is a talented individual, the Giants have given up on him as their regular right fielder, opting to sign Kevin Bass as a free agent. Unfortunately, Candy's trade value is none too high.

HITTING:

As a rookie, Kirt Manwaring was platooned for much of the season with Kennedy. Kirt's season effectively ended on August 31 when he was hit by a Terry Mulholland pitch, suffering a hairline fracture on his left foot. A rookie catcher is often overwhelmed at the major league level, since he has so much to learn about his team's pitchers and the opposition hitters. Manwaring proved no exception. The Giants are a trifle miffed that Kirt did not improve his offense over the course of the season.

Judging from his past performance, Manwaring does not figure to hit for much average. He does not have any power either, as evidenced by his absence of home runs. Kirt is basically a banjo hitter who strikes out too often. Manwaring is something like the Astros' Craig Biggio, not a great defensive catcher, but possessing some footspeed. Although Biggio could conceivably be moved to another defensive position to keep his bat in the lineup, Manwaring's impotent bat precludes this option.

BASERUNNING:

Since he is still rather young and unbattered as a catcher, Kirt has some of his innate quickness left in him. Although he was not asked to steal much, Manwaring was aggressive on the bases. He runs with a vigorous, choppy style that is unfortunately not rewarded with an increase in velocity.

FIELDING:

Manwaring has an average arm, but his quick release allowed him to throw out an excellent 37% of potential base stealers. A rather small man, Kirt is agile behind the plate, and is especially good at blocking the ball in the dirt. Since Roger Craig calls virtually every pitch, Manwaring's ability to "call a good game" is unknown at this stage. Craig's strategy has a side-effect in that Giants' catchers are not able to take charge of their pitching staff. For this reason, Manwaring may not be able to fulfill his potential as a major league receiver.

OVERALL:

Manwaring was expected to fill the role of right-handed platoon catcher with Terry Kennedy. It is often not fair to evaluate a catcher based solely on his first year, but it appears that Manwaring is not destined to be a star. Indeed he will need to improve in virtually all areas to become a regular in the major leagues.

KIRT MANWARING

Position: C
Bats: R **Throws:** R
Ht: 5'11" **Wt:** 185

Opening Day Age: 24
Born: 7/15/65 in Elmira, NY
ML Seasons: 3

Overall Statistics

	G	AB	R	H	D	T	HR	RBI	SB	BB	SO	AVG
1989	85	200	14	42	4	2	0	18	2	11	28	.210
Career	131	323	26	72	11	2	1	33	2	13	50	.223

Where He Hits the Ball

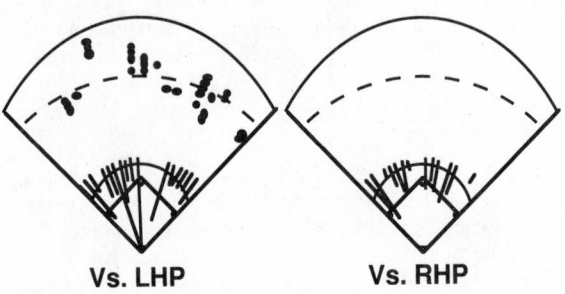

Vs. LHP   Vs. RHP

1989 Situational Stats

	AB	H	HR	RBI	AVG		AB	H	HR	RBI	AVG
Home	96	21	0	13	.219	LHP	132	27	0	8	.205
Road	104	21	0	5	.202	RHP	68	15	0	10	.221
Day	75	19	0	7	.253	Sc Pos	48	13	0	18	.271
Night	125	23	0	11	.184	Clutch	29	4	0	2	.138

1989 Rankings (National League)

➡ 3rd in worst slugging percentage vs. left-handed pitchers (.235) - *players with 125 PA vs. LHP*

➡ Led NL Catchers in sacrifice bunts (7)

HITTING:

In 1989, Kevin Mitchell had a career year in which he hit 47 homers, had 87 extra base hits and was the overwhelming choice as the National League's Most Valuable Player. Kevin's 125 runs batted in were the most by a Giant since Willie McCovey's 126 RBIs in 1970. He did all this while raising his batting average 40 points to a career high .291.

One of the strongest players in the league, Mitchell has awesome power when he is able to extend his arms -- especially against lefties, versus whom he had a Ruthian .725 slugging average. Pitchers try to keep the ball up in Kevin's eyes, thereby tying him up. Some of Mitchell's longest home runs were hit off down and in curveballs. Kevin is difficult to pitch around since he crowds the plate and is such a good bad-ball hitter. Mitchell is strong enough to muscle balls that jam ordinary hitters, and can hit opposite field home runs off pitches on the outer half of the plate.

Mitchell cites several factors as contributing to his spectacular season. They include being moved to the outfield from third base, having taken tons of off-season batting practice with a whiffle ball, wearing contact lenses for the first time, and no longer being troubled with headaches following a 1986 beanball.

BASERUNNING:

Not blessed with good speed, Kevin stole only three bases last year, but he makes his presence known. Mitchell's bad knees would prefer that he take it easier on the bases, but he plays the game at only one speed -- full-throttle. While Kevin goes into each base hard, he does not take many chances for extra bases on hits or outs.

FIELDING:

After learning the finer points of outfield defense from Willie Mays, Mitchell proved that he can catch with either hand. Kevin made the highlight-film catch of the year when he misjudged a foul fly down the line, and caught it bare-handed. Kevin has a decent arm for a left fielder, which is faint praise indeed. Mitchell's defense did show signs of improvement over the course of the season, so it should not be a major concern for next year.

OVERALL:

Having led the league in RBIs and home runs, several of them of the 475 foot variety, there is little doubt that Mitchell is the league's toughest new power hitter. It is crucial to the Giants' success that Mitchell have a great season, since he follows Will Clark in the batting order.

KEVIN MITCHELL

Position: LF
Bats: R **Throws:** R
Ht: 5'11" **Wt:** 210

Opening Day Age: 28
Born: 1/13/62 in San Diego, CA
ML Seasons: 5

Overall Statistics

	G	AB	R	H	D	T	HR	RBI	SB	BB	SO	AVG
1989	154	543	100	158	34	6	47	125	3	87	115	.291
Career	548	1854	279	509	101	17	100	319	20	216	352	.275

Where He Hits the Ball

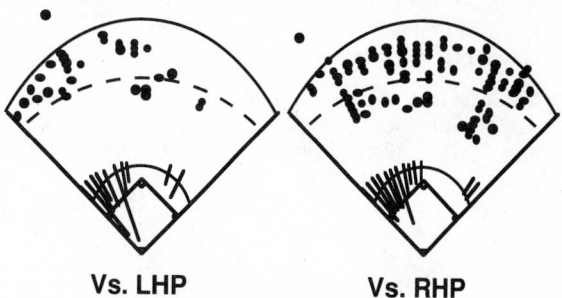

Vs. LHP   Vs. RHP

1989 Situational Stats

	AB	H	HR	RBI	AVG		AB	H	HR	RBI	AVG
Home	255	76	22	66	.298	LHP	171	52	19	40	.304
Road	288	82	25	59	.285	RHP	372	106	28	85	.285
Day	212	60	17	38	.283	Sc Pos	140	40	12	74	.286
Night	331	98	30	87	.296	Clutch	76	23	6	15	.303

1989 Rankings (National League)

➡ 1st in home runs (47), home run frequency (11.6 ABs per HR), slugging percentage (.635), RBI (125), total bases (345) and intentional walks (32) - *players with 502 PA*

➡ 3rd in lowest grounder/flyball ratio (.71)

➡ 4th in runs (100)

➡ 5th in walks (87) and times on base (248)

➡ Led the Giants in home runs, home run frequency, slugging percentage, RBIs, total bases, intentional walks, walks, least GDPs per GDP situation (4.2%), hitting in the clutch (.303) and hitting with the bases loaded (.444)

HITTING:

In the Giants' season-long search for an everyday right fielder, Donell Nixon played regularly for two stints, once in May and again in August. Donell hit .302 in 63 at bats as a right fielder, but since he has no power (only three extra-base hits last year), doesn't draw many walks, and has a weak throwing arm, the experiments ended rather quickly.

Often compared to his older brother Otis, Donell is in fact a much better hitter -- .277 lifetime, vs. Otis's .222. In the minors, he batted over .320 in three separate leagues. Though used sporadically in three major league seasons, Donell has never hit less than .250 and even batted an improbable .346 for 78 at bats in 1988. At his '89 level (.265 BA, 11 walks), Donell lacks the overall offensive skills to play every day. But Nixon is more than adequate as a fill-in, and would be even more valuable if he could learn to pinch hit. Donell batted only .200 (five for 25) in pinch roles last year.

While he is the first to recognize Nixon's limitations, Roger Craig likes Donell, since he never complains about lack of playing time. Craig loves to work for every advantage he can, so he finds opportunities to employ Nixon's limited, but nonetheless useful, skills.

BASERUNNING:

Nixon is very fast and stole 10 bases in 13 attempts last year. He has the potential to steal many more -- Donell swiped an amazing 144 bases at Bakersfield in 1983, and led three other minor leagues with 46, 85, and 102 steals. Often used as a pinch runner, Nixon is very useful in that role, but often guilty of over-aggressiveness. Several times a year Donell goes into a "keep running until tagged out" mode.

FIELDING:

Donell is a capable outfielder, with pretty good range. He is not a very good judge of flyballs, but his speed allows him to outrun most of his mistakes. He has played all three outfield positions, but with his weak arm, he is best suited for left field. Unfortunately for Nixon, Kevin Mitchell has that spot staked out on the Giants.

OVERALL:

At 28, Nixon has made a place for himself as a major league bench player. He can hit a little, run a lot, and he's a capable outfielder. If he can learn a little more patience at the plate, Donell might interest some club looking for a left fielder and leadoff man.

DONELL NIXON

Position: RF/CF
Bats: R **Throws:** R
Ht: 6' 1" **Wt:** 185

Opening Day Age: 28
Born: 12/31/61 in Evergreen, NC
ML Seasons: 3

Overall Statistics

	G	AB	R	H	D	T	HR	RBI	SB	BB	SO	AVG
1989	95	166	23	44	2	0	1	15	10	11	30	.265
Career	200	376	55	104	9	0	4	33	42	34	70	.277

Where He Hits the Ball

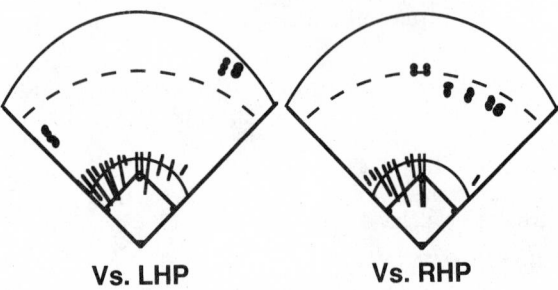

Vs. LHP	Vs. RHP

1989 Situational Stats

	AB	H	HR	RBI	AVG		AB	H	HR	RBI	AVG
Home	78	23	0	8	.295	LHP	83	20	0	6	.241
Road	88	21	1	7	.239	RHP	83	24	1	9	.289
Day	69	16	0	6	.232	Sc Pos	38	10	0	14	.263
Night	97	28	1	9	.289	Clutch	26	4	0	3	.154

1989 Rankings (National League)

➡ Did not rank near the top or bottom in any category

HITTING:

The Giants acquired Ken Oberkfell from the Pirates in early May, right after Matt Williams was sent down to the minors. Since manager Roger Craig is a master of the double switch, an extra infielder was particularly valuable at the time. Besides being able to fill in at all four infield positions -- and hitting .319 in a San Francisco uniform -- Oberkfell turned into the league's best pinch hitter, setting a Giants record with 18 pinch hits. It seemed that whenever the Giants needed to start a rally, or keep one alive, Oberkfell was able to produce off the bench. Because of this sort of professionalism, Obie is one of the most popular Giants in the clubhouse.

Oberkfell is the prototypical line drive hitter. He always hits for a good batting average, but has virtually no power. Lefties give him fits (an .095 average last year). Oberkfell is a patient hitter, unwilling to give in to the pitcher. He's a good high ball hitter, and loves the inside pitch. So hurlers tend to work him low and away continually.

BASERUNNING:

Oberkfell is an intelligent baserunner. The rare times he takes chances on the bases are calculated to be the times when there is the greatest reward. For the most part, Obie has become a station to station denizen of the basepaths. He's not a base stealing threat.

FIELDING:

At this stage of his career, Oberkfell is not expected to play regularly in the field. He can capably fill in for an injured starter at second or third base, or go in as a late inning replacement. Oberkfell's range is restricted by his advancing years and his many seasons of playing on artificial turf. Combined with a weak arm, Obie is currently a rather poor defensive player. One saving grace is that he is sure-handed, and has not lost his quick hands at third base. Thus Oberkfell is able to make the routine play on any ball he gets to.

OVERALL:

The contribution that Oberkfell made to the Giants' pennant drive does not adequately show up in the statistics. While he is not the player he once was, Obie will likely remain a valuable role-player and spot starter for the Giants for a couple more seasons. He has taken over the mantle of best pinch hitter in the National League.

KEN OBERKFELL

Position: 3B/1B
Bats: L **Throws:** R
Ht: 6' 1" **Wt:** 210

Opening Day Age: 33
Born: 5/4/56 in Maryville, IL
ML Seasons: 13

Overall Statistics

	G	AB	R	H	D	T	HR	RBI	SB	BB	SO	AVG
1989	97	156	19	42	6	1	2	17	0	10	10	.269
Career	1431	4563	535	1283	226	43	28	410	61	509	326	.281

Where He Hits the Ball

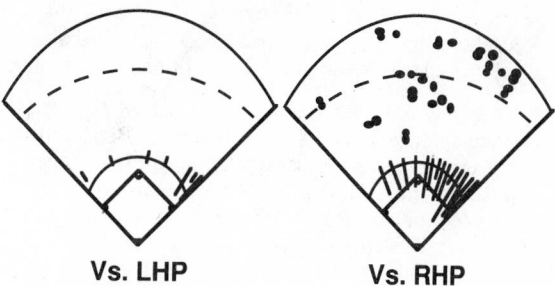

Vs. LHP   **Vs. RHP**

1989 Situational Stats

	AB	H	HR	RBI	AVG		AB	H	HR	RBI	AVG
Home	67	19	1	12	.284	LHP	21	2	0	1	.095
Road	89	23	1	5	.258	RHP	135	40	2	16	.296
Day	68	18	1	5	.265	Sc Pos	37	7	1	16	.189
Night	88	24	1	12	.273	Clutch	43	15	0	4	.349

1989 Rankings (National League)

➡ 1st in pinch hits (18)

PITCHING:

Rick Reuschel had a great first half in 1989, including the month of May when he was 6-0 with an 0.84 ERA. Riding a nine-game winning streak, Big Daddy was perched at 12-3 at the All-Star break. Named the National League's starting pitcher for the mid-summer classic, Rick will forever be remembered for serving up the awesome leadoff home run to Bo Jackson. Bothered with a nagging groin pull for much of the second half of the season, Reuschel was unable to match his first half numbers. Nevertheless the Giants were quite happy with his overall 17-8 record, and fine 2.94 ERA.

Rick is one of the few pitchers who can get by essentially on one pitch, a sinking fastball on which he changes speeds. For variety, Reuschel throws an occasional curveball, mostly for show and rarely in the strike zone. Admitting that he might be too old to learn new tricks, and is sufficiently effective anyway, Reuschel is the only pitcher on the Giants roster that Roger Craig has not taught the split-fingered fastball.

Reuschel is now the leader among active National League pitchers with 211 career victories. Big Daddy is the consummate professional, and rarely changes expression or mood. This sets a good example for the youngsters on the roster. Working quickly and not attempting to strike out hitters, Reuschel strives to keep hitters off balance. The result is a steady stream of routine grounders taking full advantage of Candlestick's thick infield grass and sparkling defensive keystone combination of Uribe and Thompson.

FIELDING, HITTING, BASERUNNING:

One of the best fielders in the league, Reuschel is surprisingly agile. Reuschel has learned to shut down the opposition running game. He uses the newfangled "slide step" to get the ball to home plate quickly. Occasionally when batting, Rick stands motionless, as far from home plate as possible, with the bat on his shoulder. If the opposing pitcher is able to throw three strikes before four balls, Reuschel is satisfied to accept a strikeout. But he's not really a bad hitter, and he's a surprisingly good baserunner for such a big man.

OVERALL:

Reuschel gives the impression that he could pitch at his present All-Star level indefinitely. Big Daddy will be "only" 41 this season, and is pitching better, and for a much better team, than he did 10 years ago. Roger Craig loves to have a veteran pitching staff. Of course, Father Time catches up with all men -- eventually.

RICK REUSCHEL

Position: SP
Bats: R **Throws:** R
Ht: 6' 3"   **Wt:** 240

Opening Day Age: 40
Born: 5/16/49 in Quincy, IL
ML Seasons: 17

Overall Statistics

	W	L	ERA	G	GS	Sv	IP	H	R	BB	SO	HR
1989	17	8	2.94	32	32	0	208.1	195	75	54	111	18
Career	211	183	3.36	538	515	4	3452.0	3469	1449	897	1962	213

Where They Hit the Ball

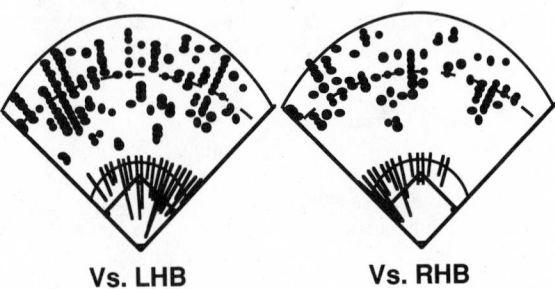

Vs. LHB   **Vs. RHB**

1989 Situational Stats

	W	L	ERA	Sv	IP		AB	H	HR	RBI	AVG
Home	8	5	2.79	0	109.2	LHB	445	116	5	33	.261
Road	9	3	3.10	0	98.2	RHB	345	79	13	36	.229
Day	7	3	1.98	0	81.2	Sc Pos	161	37	3	49	.230
Night	10	5	3.55	0	126.2	Clutch	85	21	0	5	.247

1989 Rankings (National League)

➡ 2nd in sacrifice bunts as a hitter (16)

➡ 3rd in least pitches thrown per batter (3.3) - *pitchers with 162 IP*

➡ 5th in wins (17) and run support per 9 innings (5.0)

➡ 6th in win/loss percentage (.680) - *pitchers with 15 decisions*

➡ Led the Giants in sacrifice bunts as a hitter, wins, games started (32), innings (208.1), pitches thrown (2,823), strikeout/walk ratio (2.1), grounder/flyball ratio (1.24), least pitches thrown per batter, run support per 9 innings, lowest stolen base percentage allowed (56.3%), hits allowed (195) and batters faced (860) - *team players with 162 IP*

HITTING:

Ernest Riles was acquired from Milwaukee during the 1988 season and proved to be a good man to have in the midst of a pennant race. His versatility is extremely valuable, especially given the way Roger Craig uses the entire 24-man roster.

A solid major league batsman, Riles is a line-drive hitter with occasional power. Ernest, a lefthanded hitter, likes the fastball up and out over the plate, driving this offering to left-centerfield. His other favorite strategy is to golf low fastballs to all points. Just to show that he can rise to any occasion, Riles hit one of the Giants' most dramatic home runs of the season, a two-out, game-winning grand slam off of the Phillies' Roger McDowell in late August.

Nicknamed "Easy" by his teammates for the manner in which he goes about his business, Riles is a stabilizing influence on the often overemotional Giants. Never one to rush things, Ernest is a patient hitter, although he is not a great proponent of the bases on balls. He is a very weak hitter against lefties, with only a .219 career average.

BASERUNNING:

For a player with fair speed, Riles is not a good base stealer. Roger Craig likes to start Ernest on the front end of a hit-and-run, but he was zero for six in steal attempts last year and is a terrible 15 for 38 (39 percent) in his career. Ernest is an aggressive baserunner, willing to try for the extra base at every opportunity.

FIELDING:

Riles, formerly an everyday shortstop with the Brewers, filled in capably at third base when Matt Williams was dispatched to the minors. Riles' arm is only average for a third baseman, and below average if asked to play shortstop. He does have quick reflexes, though, which help make up for his lack of range and sub-par arm. When nobody else was doing the job, Riles was asked to play right field late in the season. Ernest looked understandably shaky shagging flyballs. All in all, Riles is an adequate back-up at second, third, or shortstop.

OVERALL:

Riles will never again be more than a role player. His defense is not good enough to play regularly at second base or shortstop, nor is his power sufficient to allow a team to play him regularly at third base. His unsuccessful experiment in right field convinced all that Riles' future remains as a utility infielder. In that role, he is more than adequate.

ERNEST RILES

Position: 3B/2B
Bats: L **Throws:** R
Ht: 6' 1" **Wt:** 180

Opening Day Age: 29
Born: 10/2/60 in Bainbridge, GA
ML Seasons: 5

Overall Statistics

	G	AB	R	H	D	T	HR	RBI	SB	BB	SO	AVG
1989	122	302	43	84	13	2	7	40	0	28	50	.278
Career	586	1864	237	503	73	15	29	207	15	165	290	.270

Where He Hits the Ball

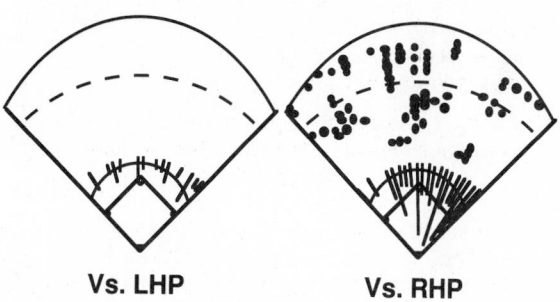

Vs. LHP   Vs. RHP

1989 Situational Stats

	AB	H	HR	RBI	AVG		AB	H	HR	RBI	AVG
Home	130	32	5	17	.246	LHP	39	7	0	2	.179
Road	172	52	2	23	.302	RHP	263	77	7	38	.293
Day	113	26	2	10	.230	Sc Pos	75	20	4	36	.267
Night	189	58	5	30	.307	Clutch	46	13	1	7	.283

1989 Rankings (National League)

➡ Led the Giants in batting average with 2 strikes (.242) - *team players with 162 PA with 2 strikes*

PITCHING:

The Giants' recent success can be traced to their mid-season 1987 acquisitions of Don Robinson and Rick Reuschel in separate deals with the Pirates, and the trade for Kevin Mitchell, Dave Dravecky and Craig Lefferts with the Padres. While the others may get more recognition, Robinson deserves his fair share of the credit.

Robinson pitched in the starting rotation for virtually the entire '89 season. For Don, that was a welcome change from seasons past when he was switched back and forth from the rotation to the bullpen. Until sidelined with his chronic knee trouble in mid-September, Don was one of the few Giants' hurlers to remain relatively healthy over the past two seasons. Several times "Caveman" was able to go the distance when the Giants' bullpen was unavailable from overuse. Roger Craig claimed that Robinson pitched the "biggest game of the year" three separate times during the Giants' pennant drive, and he may not have been exaggerating.

At 32, Robinson is still a power pitcher with a good live fastball. Don had his greatest success last season when he went back to his earlier power style -- shelving his newly developed split-finger fastball. When his curveball is right, Robinson is particularly tough. Like most strikeout pitchers, Robinson pitches up in the strike zone. Thus he is a flyball pitcher, and is subject to the longball. A few times last season, Giants' fielders flirted with not having a single assist behind Robinson. As he has done the past several seasons, Robinson's walks to innings pitched ratio is among the best in the league, a feature not provided by most power pitchers.

FIELDING, HITTING, BASERUNNING:

Robinson is an excellent hitter, better than many non-pitchers in the majors. He even has sporadic power, and is used several times a season as a pinch hitter. However, Don has terrible knees, and often is forced to wear a cumbersome knee brace. Thus he cannot run or field well any more. Robinson has a good move to first, but has a high leg kick and is somewhat vulnerable to the stolen base.

OVERALL:

Robinson has been a pleasant surprise for the Giants. Although his knees are permanently damaged, Robinson's arm and head are quite healthy. Caveman has been one of the stalwarts of the Giants pitching staff since his arrival. While he is not the ace of the staff, Robinson may very well be the Giants' most dependable starter.

DON ROBINSON

Position: SP
Bats: R **Throws:** R
Ht: 6' 4" **Wt:** 231

Opening Day Age: 32
Born: 6/8/57 in Ashland, KY
ML Seasons: 12

Overall Statistics

	W	L	ERA	G	GS	Sv	IP	H	R	BB	SO	HR
1989	12	11	3.43	34	32	0	197.0	184	80	37	96	22
Career	92	86	3.62	453	177	56	1618.2	1530	723	545	1069	138

Where They Hit the Ball

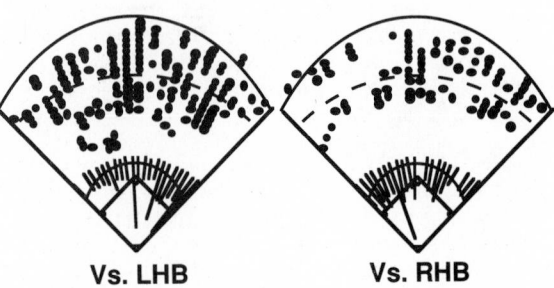

Vs. LHB   Vs. RHB

1989 Situational Stats

	W	L	ERA	Sv	IP		AB	H	HR	RBI	AVG
Home	9	4	2.10	0	120.0	LHB	438	114	13	43	.260
Road	3	7	5.49	0	77.0	RHB	305	70	9	27	.230
Day	5	5	3.46	0	78.0	Sc Pos	147	32	2	43	.218
Night	7	6	3.40	0	119.0	Clutch	69	14	1	4	.203

1989 Rankings (National League)

➡ 2nd in most HRs allowed per 9 innings (1.01) - *pitchers with 162 IP*

➡ 3rd in home runs allowed (22)

➡ 8th in pickoff throws (176)

➡ 9th in balks (4) and least baserunners allowed per 9 innings (10.2)

➡ Led the Giants in games started (32), losses (11), complete games (5), pickoff throws, stolen bases allowed (18), caught stealing (10) and most GDPs per 9 innings (.50) - *team pitchers with 162 IP*

HITTING:

A late season batting slump was the only thing that prevented 1989 from being Robby Thompson's career year. He was the first Giant since Gary Matthews and Garry Maddox in 1973 to rack up double figures in doubles, triples, home runs, and steals.

Many complain that Robby's strikeouts (133) are not tolerable for a number two hitter in the line-up, but they do not seem to bother either Thompson or his manager. Contrary to popular belief, Robby has fair bat control and is a good bunter, a strange combination with his strikeout proclivity. Since Thompson crowds the plate, and is such an aggressive hitter, he is hit by many pitches.

Thompson is a spray hitter with more power than he is given credit for. The trouble is that Robby becomes overanxious with runners in scoring position, as evidenced by his .175 average and strikeouts in nearly 30% of these plate appearances. Pitchers try to jam Robby with inside fastballs. However, Thompson can handle the high fastball over the plate and gets many of his extra-base hits down the left field line. Robby hits lefthanded pitchers especially well, with a career average over .300 vs. portsiders. However, he's had problems against righties throughout his career.

BASERUNNING:

Thompson has good footspeed and was 12 for 14 in stolen base attempts last year. Robby does not always get a good jump on stolen base attempts, so Roger Craig frequently uses him as the front man in a hit-and-run. Thompson is an aggressive and often reckless baserunner.

FIELDING:

Robby is among the best defensive second basemen in the league due to his quick double play pivot. His arm is good, especially demonstrated by relay throws from the outfield. Candlestick's thick infield grass, Roger Craig's love of the intentional walk, and the Giants' pitchers' reliance on the split-fingered fastball are among the factors which add to Thompson's double play totals. Robby's main deficiency is his lack of durability. Due to his chronic back trouble, and penchant for diving after nearly every ball, Thompson is forced to sit out several games a year.

OVERALL:

Thompson is a hard-nosed throwback to baseball's olden days: someone who plays all out and loves to get his uniform dirty. If Thompson can maintain his power while raising his batting average in seasons to come, Robby will have to be considered among the league's top second basemen.

ROBBIE THOMPSON

Position: 2B
Bats: R **Throws:** R
Ht: 5'11" **Wt:** 170

Opening Day Age: 27
Born: 5/10/62 in West Palm Beach, FL
ML Seasons: 4

Overall Statistics

	G	AB	R	H	D	T	HR	RBI	SB	BB	SO	AVG
1989	148	547	91	132	26	11	13	50	12	51	133	.241
Career	567	1993	292	517	103	25	37	189	54	173	447	.259

Where He Hits the Ball

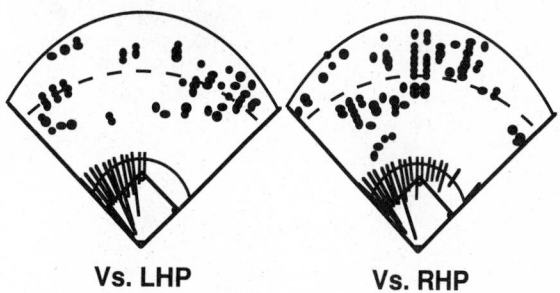

Vs. LHP   **Vs. RHP**

1989 Situational Stats

	AB	H	HR	RBI	AVG		AB	H	HR	RBI	AVG
Home	286	76	7	29	.266	LHP	194	59	5	17	.304
Road	261	56	6	21	.215	RHP	353	73	8	33	.207
Day	232	51	6	22	.220	Sc Pos	126	22	4	31	.175
Night	315	81	7	28	.257	Clutch	86	20	3	10	.233

1989 Rankings (National League)

➡ 1st in triples (11), hit by pitch (13) and worst batting average with runners in scoring position (.175) - *players with 100 PA with runners in scoring position*

➡ 2nd in most runs scored per time reached base (41.4%) and worst batting average vs. righthanded pitchers (.207) - *players with 377 PA vs. RHP*

➡ 4th in strikeouts (133) and worst hitting on an 0-2 count (.043) - *players with 20 PA on an 0-2 count*

➡ Led the Giants in strikeouts, hit by pitch, triples, runs scored per time reached base and hitting on a 3-1 count (.467) - *players with 10 PA on a 3-1 count*

HITTING:

A switch-hitter, Jose Uribe was so messed up last year that he experimented for a while with batting right-handed exclusively. When his knees buckled on every curveball and he batted a woeful .136 as a righty vs. righthanded pitching, Uribe quickly went back to switch hitting. By then he was messed up from both sides of the plate. All in all, Jose's 1989 offensive season, with its .221 batting average and .280 slugging percentage, will be one he will try to forget.

Uribe is a good low ball hitter who can be overpowered by high fastballs, especially as a righthanded batter. Since he gets down the baseline so rapidly, Jose grounds into few double plays. But he has almost no power, with only 19 extra base hits last year.

Uribe wielded a slow bat late last season partly due to his rarely taking a day off. He was pinch hit for quite frequently, much to his displeasure. To become a more effective hitter, Jose must work for more walks. He drew only 34 bases on balls in nearly 500 plate appearances last season, which contributed to an anemic .273 on-base percentage.

BASERUNNING:

While he has good speed, as an eighth place hitter Jose is not asked to steal many bases. That may be just as well, since he was only six for 12 last year. In other aspects of baserunning, Uribe is productive. He is able to go from first to third, or score from second, on a single.

FIELDING:

Last season Uribe's defense slipped a notch, and Giants fans are no longer apt to compare him to Ozzie Smith. A flamboyant fielder, he employs the "matador" defense, taking grounders off to one side, a style developed on the poorly conditioned Dominican infields of his youth. Uribe's arm is slightly below average in strength, but his quick release more than makes up for it. His best play is fielding the grounder up the middle. Along with Robby Thompson, Jose makes up part of one of the league's best double play combinations.

OVERALL:

Although he has always been introspective and moody, last season Jose seemed to lose his joie de vivre which had previously made him a good major league player. A .291 batter in 1987, he has slipped to the point where he is one of the weakest hitters in the majors. Replacing Uribe at shortstop, something that was unthinkable two seasons ago, is currently being contemplated by the Giants organization.

JOSE URIBE

Position: SS
Bats: B **Throws:** R
Ht: 5'10" **Wt:** 165

Opening Day Age: 30
Born: 1/21/60 in San Cristobal, Dominican Republic
ML Seasons: 6

Overall Statistics

	G	AB	R	H	D	T	HR	RBI	SB	BB	SO	AVG
1989	151	453	34	100	12	6	1	30	6	34	74	.221
Career	699	2203	221	532	73	23	15	167	63	185	313	.241

Where He Hits the Ball

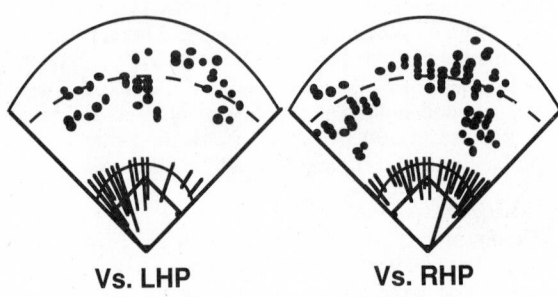

Vs. LHP   Vs. RHP

1989 Situational Stats

	AB	H	HR	RBI	AVG		AB	H	HR	RBI	AVG
Home	214	48	0	13	.224	LHP	150	32	0	13	.213
Road	239	52	1	17	.218	RHP	303	68	1	17	.224
Day	184	37	0	7	.201	Sc Pos	99	25	1	30	.253
Night	269	63	1	23	.234	Clutch	56	12	0	1	.214

1989 Rankings (National League)

➡ 2nd in worst home run frequency (453 ABs per HR)
➡ Led the Giants in errors (18)

HITTING:

The Giants pinned much of their pennant hopes on Matt Williams in pre-season, then were forced to send Matt down to Phoenix in May when he was hitting .130. After blasting 26 home runs in 10 weeks of Triple A pitching, Williams regained his confidence. Following his late-July recall, Williams was a new man, belting prodigious home runs at a healthy clip. Matt will likely never hit for a high batting average, but the Giants feel they now have a feared number five hitter to follow Clark and Mitchell in the batting order.

Williams was shuttled back and forth between Phoenix and the big club several times in the last two years. He had previously struggled with San Francisco, and whenever Williams was sent down he set the Pacific Coast League on fire. It now appears as if Matt is in the majors to stay.

It has long been obvious that Williams has major league power. However, Matt has had problems chasing curveballs out of the strike zone. For the most part, he is able to handle curveballs in the strike zone. While Matt feasts on low fastballs, he must work on learning to lay off the low and away curveball.

BASERUNNING:

As befits a slugger with more home runs than doubles, Williams is fairly slow. His lack of speed makes a stolen base attempt a rarity. Nevertheless, whenever he gets the chance to take an extra base, Matt is an aggressive baserunner.

FIELDING:

Williams has soft hands and one of the strongest arms in the league. As proof that he is a good glove man at third base, Matt is often asked to play shortstop when they pinch hit for Jose Uribe. Still rough around the edges, Williams will occasionally butcher a routine grounder, and then turn around and make a fabulous stop on a blue-darter. Since Candlestick has such large foul territories, Matt's good range on foul pop-ups is often of crucial value. Williams is among the best in the league at fielding grounders in the hole to his left.

OVERALL:

Williams has been compared to Mike Schmidt and Dale Murphy at comparable stages of their careers; each needed a few seasons before becoming super-stars. Williams' defense at third base has never been questioned. When Matt learns to hit home runs to the opposite field, he may well blossom into a very good major leaguer for years to come.

MATT D. WILLIAMS

Position: 3B/SS
Bats: R **Throws:** R
Ht: 6' 2" **Wt:** 205

Opening Day Age: 24
Born: 11/28/65 in Bishop, CA
ML Seasons: 3

Overall Statistics

	G	AB	R	H	D	T	HR	RBI	SB	BB	SO	AVG
1989	84	292	31	59	18	1	18	50	1	14	72	.202
Career	220	693	76	137	33	4	34	90	5	38	181	.198

Where He Hits the Ball

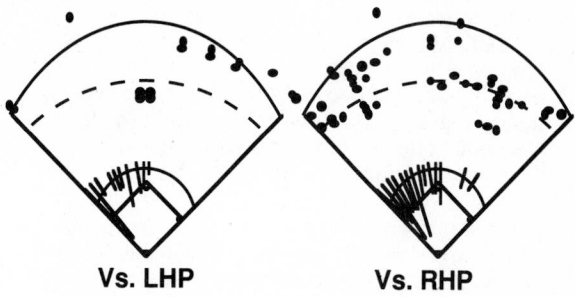

Vs. LHP   **Vs. RHP**

1989 Situational Stats

	AB	H	HR	RBI	AVG		AB	H	HR	RBI	AVG
Home	144	31	10	33	.215	LHP	87	23	9	21	.264
Road	148	28	8	17	.189	RHP	205	36	9	29	.176
Day	98	24	8	25	.245	Sc Pos	80	12	5	29	.150
Night	194	35	10	25	.180	Clutch	36	7	0	2	.194

1989 Rankings (National League)

➡ Did not rank near the top or bottom in any category

ERNIE CAMACHO

Position: RP
Bats: R **Throws:** R
Ht: 6' 1" **Wt:** 180

Opening Day Age: 34
Born: 2/1/56 in Salinas, CA
ML Seasons: 9

Overall Statistics

	W	L	ERA	G	GS	Sv	IP	H	R	BB	SO	HR
1989	3	0	2.76	13	0	0	16.1	10	5	11	14	1
Career	10	20	4.14	179	3	45	247.2	251	119	119	144	13

PITCHING, FIELDING, HITTING:

The Giants signed Ernie Camacho as a free agent last June. Ernie had been Cleveland's closer in the mid-1980s, racking up more than 20 saves in two separate seasons. Although he used to rely exclusively on his fastball, as he has aged Camacho developed a split-fingered fastball and a decent curveball. The Giants were quite impressed with his remaining velocity -- Camacho can still register 90+ on the radar gun. After a short stint at Phoenix, the Giants brought him up to serve as the "closer of the week" (following in the footsteps of LaCoss, Lefferts, and Gossage). Soon thereafter, Al Rosen swung the Bedrosian trade, and Ernie was sent to the minors for a while. Recalled in August, he had a 1.98 ERA over the last two months, including a 1.08 mark in seven September appearances. Like many of his teammates, Ernie is known to suffer from bouts of periodic wildness. He's a decent fielder and holds baserunners well. His hitting is an unknown quantity, since he hardly ever bats.

OVERALL:

At 34, Camacho's role with the Giants is uncertain. While Roger Craig speaks highly of him, even talking about putting Camacho into the rotation, there is little reason to believe that Ernie will play anything but a minor role in the upcoming season.

BOB KNEPPER

Position: SP/RP
Bats: L **Throws:** L
Ht: 6' 2" **Wt:** 210

Opening Day Age: 35
Born: 5/25/54 in Akron, OH
ML Seasons: 14

Overall Statistics

	W	L	ERA	G	GS	Sv	IP	H	R	BB	SO	HR
1989	7	12	5.13	35	26	0	165.0	190	98	75	64	16
Career	143	152	3.64	433	406	1	2663.1	2681	1230	838	1449	221

PITCHING, FIELDING, HITTING:

Bob Knepper began 1989 in the Astros starting rotation, but was banished to the bullpen in late July. Knepper's second win of the season set the Houston career record with 91 victories (eclipsed soon thereafter by Mike Scott). At age 35, Bob has become a disciple of the slow, slower, slowest school of pitching. Knepper won a game for the first time in six weeks when he was ordered by his manager never to shake off a sign from the catcher. The idea was that Bob was out-thinking himself, worrying too much about his mechanics. Knepper was ultimately released by Houston in late July with a poor 4-10 record and frightening 5.89 ERA. However, Bob was signed by the Giants in early August, the exact situation that the Astros had feared. Since Knepper beat the Astros twice down the stretch, Houston essentially was paying him to knock them out of the pennant race.

OVERALL:

Knepper helped the Giants win the division, with a smattering of solid starts when San Francisco most needed them. Truth be told though, Knepper is no longer an effective major league pitcher (opponents hit .294 off him). The Giants will likely give Knepper another shot only as insurance for their other ailing starters.

MIKE KRUKOW

Position: SP
Bats: R **Throws:** R
Ht: 6' 4" **Wt:** 205

Opening Day Age: 38
Born: 1/21/52 in Long Beach, CA
ML Seasons: 14

GREG LITTON

Position: 3B
Bats: R **Throws:** R
Ht: 6' 0" **Wt:** 175

Opening Day Age: 25
Born: 7/13/64 in New Orleans, LA
ML Seasons: 1

Overall Statistics

	W	L	ERA	G	GS	Sv	IP	H	R	BB	SO	HR
1989	4	3	3.98	8	8	0	43.0	37	20	18	18	5
Career	124	117	3.90	369	355	1	2190.0	2188	1069	767	1478	196

Overall Statistics

	G	AB	R	H	D	T	HR	RBI	SB	BB	SO	AVG
1989	71	143	12	36	5	3	4	17	0	7	29	.252
Career	71	143	12	36	5	3	4	17	0	7	29	.252

PITCHING, FIELDING, HITTING:

Mike Krukow began last season on the disabled list with a rotator cuff injury suffered in the second half of the 1988 season. Reactivated in late April, Mike pitched with middling success until early June, when severe bursitis was discovered in his right shoulder. Arthroscopic surgery in late June ended his season. Since he will be 38 next season, there is more than an outside chance that the surgery ended Krukow's career as well. Essentially a curveball pitcher of the old-fashioned round-house variety, age has left Krukow with only a mediocre fastball. However, Mike is not afraid to pitch high and tight to drive hitters off the plate. Like most curveball artists, Krukow is a control pitcher, with few walks or strikeouts. While he is a proponent of the split-fingered fastball, Krukow is a flyball pitcher. As one of the best competitors in the game, Krukow remained a team leader even after he couldn't pitch any more.

OVERALL:

The pitching career of Mike Krukow may be all but over, but he will be around for at least one more season. Krukow is a club leader in many respects. Roger Craig especially likes Krukow's professionalism and his ability to take young pitchers under his wing.

HITTING, FIELDING, BASERUNNING:

Any team which has a great season will have received significant contributions from unexpected sources. Greg Litton is the 1989 Giants' prime example. He rode the Phoenix-San Francisco shuttle a couple of times during the season before finally sticking. The Giants, needing Litton's steady glove and versatility in the infield, called him up in June despite a sub-.200 Triple A batting average. Litton gave them defense and much more. He is a wiry guy who has deceiving power, but is usually content to put the ball in play. Pitchers try to get Greg out by jamming him with inside fastballs. Even though he is a more than adequate defensive third baseman, the Giants have debated about moving Litton to right field, where he played a bit in the minors. Third base is his best defensive position, but Matt Williams should be the Giants' regular third sacker for years to come.

OVERALL:

Although Litton will likely never be a regular in the majors, the 24-man roster makes his versatility a worthy asset. Litton can play the infield or outfield, and can serve as the Giants' third catcher, which is even more valuable under Roger Craig's managerial style.

RANDY McCAMENT

Position: RP
Bats: R **Throws:** R
Ht: 6' 3" **Wt:** 180

Opening Day Age: 27
Born: 7/29/62 in Albequerque, NM
ML Seasons: 1

Overall Statistics

	W	L	ERA	G	GS	Sv	IP	H	R	BB	SO	HR
1989	1	1	3.93	25	0	0	36.2	32	22	23	12	4
Career	1	1	3.93	25	0	0	36.2	32	22	23	12	4

PITCHING, FIELDING, HITTING:

Randy McCament was recalled last season when the Giants were in critical need of pitchers. McCament was used primarily in middle relief with the Giants, a role he worked in the minors as well. Since the requirement for promotion to the majors was little more than being a warm body who could pitch some innings, the Giants were satisfied with McCament's performance. The possessor of a pretty good fastball, McCament has little else. His off-speed pitches tend to be a bit too slow, giving major league hitters sufficient time to recognize what is coming, and then tear into it. Randy has never been one to strike out a lot of hitters, but has relied instead upon his control. Nevertheless, McCament walked far too many hitters in his short stint with the Giants, perhaps out of too much respect for major league hitters. His move to first did not appear to be good.

OVERALL:

McCament made his major league debut at age 27; his stuff does not appear to be of major league caliber. Randy filled in capably when the Giants ran out of pitchers, but San Francisco is hoping that they will not have reason to call on McCament next season.

PAT SHERIDAN

Position: RF/LF
Bats: L **Throws:** R
Ht: 6' 3" **Wt:** 175

Opening Day Age: 32
Born: 12/4/57 in Ann Arbor, MI
ML Seasons: 8

Overall Statistics

	G	AB	R	H	D	T	HR	RBI	SB	BB	SO	AVG
1989	120	281	36	62	6	4	6	29	8	30	66	.221
Career	814	2306	306	588	88	21	47	250	85	223	471	.255

HITTING, FIELDING, BASERUNNING:

Ex-Tiger Pat Sheridan came to the Giants last June in exchange for the disgruntled Tracy Jones. Pat felt his way around the National League, facing most pitchers for the first time. When Sheridan's bat did not improve, he was benched in favor of September call-ups. As a hitter, Sheridan takes a lot of pitches, including too many called third strikes. While he is a spray hitter, the majority of Sheridan's safeties are balls hit up the middle. Making use of his good speed, Sheridan is an aggressive baserunner. Pat is an above average defensive right fielder, with good range and a decent arm. While Sheridan has a bit of trouble going back on flyballs, he is good at cutting off line drives in the gaps. Last year the Giants used Sheridan in an unproductive right field platoon with Candy Maldonado, but the acquisition of Kevin Bass will put an end to that.

OVERALL:

Sheridan is a player without any noticeable strengths or weaknesses. Pat has been used as a defensive replacement, as a pinch hitter, and as a pinch runner. Nevertheless, Roger Craig is not overly impressed with Sheridan and Pat is not likely to figure significantly in the Giants' plans for 1990.

TREVOR WILSON

Position: RP/SP
Bats: L **Throws:** L
Ht: 6' 0" **Wt:** 175

Opening Day Age: 23
Born: 6/7/66 in
Torrance, CA
ML Seasons: 2

Overall Statistics

	W	L	ERA	G	GS	Sv	IP	H	R	BB	SO	HR
1989	2	3	4.35	14	4	0	39.1	28	20	24	22	2
Career	2	5	4.26	18	8	0	61.1	53	34	32	37	3

PITCHING, FIELDING, HITTING:

Trevor Wilson began last season in Phoenix and was called up to the Giants in early July. In his first start, Trevor walked the bases loaded in the first inning with nobody out. Seemingly Trevor's moment of truth had arrived. He then showed his "intestinal fortitude" by getting out of the inning with only one run scoring. But in early August, after showing signs of becoming comfortable in the majors, Wilson walked the opposing pitcher to force in the winning run. He thereby earned a dispatch to the minors the very next day. After his September recall to San Francisco, Trevor pitched quite capably. Wilson has an above average fastball which he is not afraid to throw inside. However, to complement his hard slider and good fastball he must work on an off-speed pitch. His move to first appears to be good.

OVERALL:

There are few players in baseball that are more coveted than a young pitcher with unlimited potential, especially a lefthander. Although Wilson was previously thought to fall into this category, it now appears that Trevor will eventually be a fourth or fifth starter, and not the star that many had hoped.

About STATS Inc.

It all starts with the system. The STATS scoring method, which includes pitch-by-pitch and the direction, distance, and velocity of each ball hit into play, yields an immense amount of information. Sure, we have all the statistics you're used to seeing, but where other statistics sources quit, STATS is just getting started.

Then, there is the network. We get our game reports via computer so that they are timely. Statistics are checked, rechecked, and are updated and available daily.

Analysis comes next. STATS constantly searches for new ways to use this wealth of information to open windows into the workings of Baseball. Accurate numbers, intelligent computer programming, and a large dose of imagination all help coax the most valuable information from its elusive cover.

Finally, distribution!

STATS has served Major League teams for 10 years now including the World Champion Oakland A's, the New York Yankees and the Chicago White Sox. *Sports Illustrated* and *The Sporting News* regularly feature STATS, Inc., as do *The New York Post, The St. Petersburg Times,* and many other national and regional publications. We provide statistics for *Earl Weaver Baseball, Rotisserie Baseball, The Los Angeles Times'* Dugout Derby, and other baseball games and fantasy leagues all over the country.

For the baseball fan, STATS publishes monthly and year-end reports on each Major League team. We offer a host of year-end statistical breakdowns on paper or disk that cover hitting, pitching, catching, baserunning, throwing, and more. STATS also produces custom reports on request.

Computer users with modems can access the STATS computer for information with *STATS Online.* If you own a computer with a modem, there is no other source with the scope of baseball information that STATS can offer.

STATS and Bill James enjoy an on-going affiliation that has produced several baseball products including *STATS 1990 Major League Handbook* and *Bill James Fantasy Baseball*, a game designed by Bill which allows you to own and manage your own team and compete with other team owners around the country.

Keep an eye out for other exciting future projects.

It is STATS, Inc.'s purpose to make the best possible Baseball information available to all Baseball interests: fans, players, teams, or media. Write to:

STATS, Inc.
7250 North Cicero
Lincolnwood, IL 60646

...or call us at **1-708-676-3322**. We can send you a STATS brochure, a free *Bill James Fantasy Baseball* information kit, and/or information on *STATS Online*.

To maintain its information, STATS hires scorers around the country to cover games. If you are interested in applying for a scorer's position, please write or call STATS.

Finally, look for *The STATS Baseball Scoreboard* in your bookstores this year. If you like *The Scouting Report: 1990* and our features in *Sports Illustrated*, you'll enjoy the *Scoreboard* with its great writing, great graphics and stats you won't find anywhere else.

Downs, Kelly	649
Drabek, Doug	576
Ducey, Rob	366
Duncan, Mariano	427
Dunne, Mike	300
Dunston, Shawon	401
Dwyer, Jim	518
Dyer, Mike	240
Dykstra, Lenny	551

E

Eckersley, Dennis	271
Eichhorn, Mark	377
Eisenreich, Jim	171
Elster, Kevin	527
Esasky, Nick	47
Espinoza, Alvaro	246
Espy, Cecil	322
Evans, Darrell	378
Evans, Dwight	48

F

Farr, Steve	172
Farrell, John	122
Felder, Mike	198
Felix, Junior	349
Fermin, Felix	123
Fernandez, Sid	528
Fernandez, Tony	350
Filer, Tom	215
Finley, Chuck	70
Finley, Steve	19
Fisher, Brian	593
Fisk, Carlton	91
Fitzgerald, Mike	499
Flanagan, Mike	351
Fletcher, Scott	92
Foley, Tom	500
Ford, Curt	552
Forsch, Bob	458
Fossas, Tony	199
Franco, John	428
Franco, Julio	323
Francona, Terry	200
Fraser, Willie	71

Frey, Steve	519
Frohwirth, Todd	553

G

Gaetti, Gary	224
Gagne, Greg	225
Galarraga, Andres	501
Gallagher, Dave	93
Gallego, Mike	272
Gant, Ron	379
Gantner, Jim	201
Garcia, Damaso	502
Gardner, Wes	49
Garrelts, Scott	650
Gedman, Rich	50
Geren, Bob	247
Gibson, Kirk	474
Gibson, Paul	143
Girardi, Joe	402
Gladden, Dan	226
Glavine, Tom	380
Gonzales, Rene	36
Gonzalez, German	227
Gonzalez, Jose	475
Gooden, Dwight	529
Gordon, Tom	173
Gossage, Goose	264
Gott, Jim	594
Gozzo, Mauro	366
Grace, Mark	403
Grant, Mark	628
Greenwell, Mike	51
Gregg, Tommy	381
Griffey, Ken	444
Griffey Jr., Ken	301
Griffin, Alfredo	476
Grissom, Marquis	519
Gross, Greg	468
Gross, Kevin	503
Gruber, Kelly	352
Guante, Cecilio	324
Gubicza, Mark	174
Guerrero, Pedro	604
Guetterman, Lee	248
Guillen, Ozzie	94
Guthrie, Mark	241

Gwynn, Chris	495		Horton, Ricky	606
Gwynn, Tony	629		Hough, Charlie	326
			Howell, Jack	73
			Howell, Jay	481
			Howell, Ken	557
			Hrbek, Kent	229

H

			Hudler, Rex	505
Hale, Chip	241		Hulett, Tim	37
Hall, Drew	325		Hurst, Bruce	631
Hall, Mel	249		Huson, Jeff	520
Hamilton, Jeff	477			
Hammaker, Atlee	651			
Hanson, Erik	302			
Harnisch, Pete	20			

I

Harper, Brian	228			
Harris, Gene	315		Incaviglia, Pete	327
Harris, Greg	61		Innis, Jeff	531
Harris, Greg W.	630			
Harris, Lenny	478			
Harvey, Bryan	72			
Hassey, Ron	273			

J

Hatcher, Billy	577			
Hatcher, Mickey	479		Jackson, Bo	175
Hawkins, Andy	250		Jackson, Danny	429
Hayes, Charlie	554		Jackson, Darrin	643
Hayes, Von	555		Jackson, Michael	304
Heath, Mike	144		Jacoby, Brook	124
Heaton, Neal	578		James, Chris	632
Heep, Danny	52		James, Dion	125
Henderson, Dave	274		Javier, Stan	277
Henderson, Rickey	275		Jeffcoat, Mike	328
Henke, Tom	353		Jefferies, Gregg	532
Henneman, Mike	145		Jefferson, Stan	37
Hernandez, Keith	530		Jeltz, Steve	558
Hernandez, Willie	146		Johnson, Dave	38
Herr, Tommy	556		Johnson, Howard	533
Hershiser, Orel	480		Johnson, Lance	97
Hesketh, Joe	504		Johnson, Randy	305
Hetzel, Eric	61		Johnson, Wallace	520
Hibbard, Greg	95		Jones, Barry	111
Hickey, Kevin	21		Jones, Doug	126
Higuera, Ted	202		Jones, Jimmy	264
Hill, Glenallen	367		Jones, Ron	568
Hill, Ken	605		Jones, Tim	619
Hillegas, Shawn	96		Jones, Tracy	147
Hoffman, Glenn	86		Jordan, Ricky	559
Holman, Brian	303		Jose, Felix	291
Holton, Brian	22		Joyner, Wally	74
Honeycutt, Rick	276			
Horn, Sam	62			

K

Karkovice, Ron	98
Kelly, Roberto	251
Kennedy, Terry	652
Key, Jimmy	354
Kilgus, Paul	404
King, Eric	99
King, Jeff	579
Kingery, Mike	316
Kipper, Bob	580
Kittle, Ron	100
Knepper, Bob	666
Knudson, Mark	203
Komminsk, Brad	127
Kramer, Randy	581
Kreuter, Chad	329
Krueger, Bill	204
Kruk, John	560
Krukow, Mike	667
Kunkel, Jeff	330
Kutcher, Randy	62

L

LaCoss, Mike	653
Lake, Steve	561
Lamp, Dennis	53
Lancaster, Les	405
Landrum, Bill	582
Langston, Mark	506
Lansford, Carney	278
LaPoint, Dave	252
Larkin, Barry	430
Larkin, Gene	230
Laudner, Tim	231
LaValliere, Mike	583
Law, Vance	406
Lawless, Tom	367
Leach, Rick	331
Leach, Terry	176
Leary, Tim	431
Lee, Manny	355
Lefferts, Craig	654
Leibrandt, Charlie	177
Leiter, Al	368
Lemon, Chet	148
Leonard, Jeff	306

Lilliquist, Derek	382
Lind, Jose	584
Lindeman, Jim	619
Liriano, Nelson	356
Litton, Greg	667
Lombardi, Phil	544
Long, Bill	112
Luecken, Rick	189
Lusader, Scott	162
Lynn, Fred	149
Lyons, Barry	534
Lyons, Steve	101

M

Macfarlane, Mike	178
Machado, Julio	545
Maddux, Greg	407
Maddux, Mike	569
Madison, Scotti	445
Magadan, Dave	535
Magrane, Joe	607
Mahler, Rick	432
Maldonado, Candy	655
Manrique, Fred	332
Manwaring, Kirt	656
Marshall, Mike	482
Martinez, Carlos	102
Martinez, Carmelo	633
Martinez, Dave	507
Martinez, Dennis	508
Martinez, Edgar	316
Martinez, Ramon	483
Mattingly, Don	253
Mazzilli, Lee	368
McCament	668
McCarthy, Tom	103
McCaskill, Kirk	75
McClendon, Lloyd	408
McClure, Bob	76
McCullers, Lance	254
McDowell, Oddibe	383
McDowell, Roger	562
McGaffigan, Andy	509
McGee, Willie	608
McGriff, Fred	357
McGwire, Mark	279
McLemore, Mark	87

McMurtry, Craig	343	
McReynolds, Kevin	536	
McWilliams, Larry	189	
Meadows, Louie	469	
Medina, Luis	137	
Melvin, Bob	23	
Meulens, Hensley	265	
Mielke, Gary	333	
Milacki, Bob	24	
Miller, Keith	545	
Milligan, Randy	25	
Minton, Greg	77	
Mitchell, Kevin	657	
Mohorcic, Dale	255	
Molitor, Paul	205	
Monteleone, Rich	78	
Montgomery, Jeff	179	
Moore, Mike	280	
Morgan, Mike	484	
Morris, Jack	150	
Morris, John	620	
Moseby, Lloyd	358	
Moses, John	232	
Moyer, Jamie	334	
Mulholland, Terry	563	
Mulliniks, Rance	359	
Murphy, Dale	384	
Murphy, Dwayne	569	
Murphy, Rob	54	
Murray, Eddie	485	
Musselman, Jeff	546	
Myers, Randy	537	

N

Navarro, Jaime	206
Nelson, Gene	281
Nelson, Rob	644
Newman, Al	233
Nichols, Rod	128
Niedenfuer, Tom	317
Nixon, Donell	658
Nixon, Otis	510
Nokes, Matt	151
Nolan, Ryan	339
Nunez, Ed	162

O

O'Brien, Charlie	207
O'Brien, Pete	129
O'Neal, Randy	570
O'Neill, Paul	433
Oberkfell, Ken	659
Oester, Ron	434
Ojeda, Bobby	538
Olin, Steve	130
Oliver, Joe	435
Olson, Gregg	26
Oquendo, Jose	609
Orosco, Jesse	131
Orsulak, Joe	27
Ortiz, Junior	585
Orton, John	87
Owen, Spike	511

P

Pagliarulo, Mike	634
Pagnozzi, Tom	620
Palacios, Rey	190
Pall, Donn	104
Palmeiro, Rafael	335
Parent, Mark	635
Parker, Clay	256
Parker, Dave	282
Parrett, Jeff	564
Parrish, Lance	79
Pasqua, Dan	105
Patterson, Ken	112
Pecota, Bill	190
Pedrique, Al	163
Pena, Alejandro	486
Pena, Tony	610
Pendleton, Terry	611
Perez, Melido	106
Perez, Pascual	512
Perry, Gerald	385
Petralli, Geno	336
Petry, Dan	88
Pettis, Gary	152
Pevey, Marty	521
Phelps, Ken	283
Phillips, Tony	284
Pico, Jeff	418

Plesac, Dan	208
Plunk, Eric	257
Polidor, Gus	209
Polonia, Luis	258
Portugal, Mark	459
Powell, Dennis	317
Power, Ted	612
Presley, Jim	307
Price, Joe	63
Prince, Tom	594
Puckett, Kirby	234
Puhl, Terry	460
Puleo, Charlie	395

Q

Quinones, Luis	436
Quinones, Rey	595
Quintana, Carlos	63
Quirk, Jamie	38
Quisenberry, Dan	613

R

Raines, Tim	513
Ramirez, Rafael	461
Ramos, Domingo	419
Randolph, Willie	487
Rasmussen, Dennis	636
Rawley, Shane	235
Ray, Johnny	80
Ready, Randy	565
Reardon, Jeff	236
Redus, Gary	586
Reed, Jeff	445
Reed, Jerry	308
Reed, Jody	55
Reed, Rick	595
Reuschel, Rick	660
Reuss, Jerry	215
Reynolds, Harold	309
Reynolds, R.J.	587
Rhoden, Rick	462
Rice, Jim	56
Richardson, Jeff	446
Righetti, Dave	259
Rijo, Jose	437

Riles, Ernest	661
Ripken, Billy	28
Ripken, Cal	29
Ritz, Kevin	163
Rivera, Luis	57
Roberts, Bip	637
Robinson, Don	662
Robinson, Jeff	588
Robinson, Jeff M.	153
Robinson, Ron	438
Roesler, Mike	446
Rogers, Ken	337
Romero, Ed	216
Romine, Kevin	58
Roomes, Rolando	439
Rosenberg, Steve	107
Ruffin, Bruce	566
Russell, Jeff	338
Russell, John	386

S

Saberhagen, Bret	180
Sabo, Chris	440
Salas, Mark	138
Salazar, Luis	409
Samuel, Juan	539
Sandberg, Ryne	410
Sanders, Deion	265
Sanderson, Scott	411
Santiago, Benito	638
Santovenia, Nelson	514
Sasser, Mackey	540
Sax, Steve	260
Schatzeder, Dan	463
Schiraldi, Calvin	639
Schmidt, Dave	30
Schofield, Dick	81
Schooler, Mike	310
Schroeder, Bill	82
Schu, Rick	154
Schulze, Don	644
Schwabe, Mike	164
Scioscia, Mike	488
Scott, Mike	464
Scudder, Scott	441
Searage, Ray	489
Seitzer, Kevin	181

Sheets, Larry	31		Teufel, Tim	542
Sheffield, Gary	210		Thigpen, Bobby	109
Shelby, John	490		Thomas, Andres	391
Sheridan, Pat	668		Thompson, Milt	616
Show, Eric	640		Thompson, Rich	521
Sierra, Ruben	340		Thompson, Robbie	663
Skinner, Joel	132		Thon, Dickie	567
Slaught, Don	261		Thurman, Gary	191
Smiley, John	589		Thurmond, Mark	33
Smith, Bryn	515		Tibbs, Jay	39
Smith, Dave	465		Traber, Jim	39
Smith, Dwight	412		Trammell, Alan	157
Smith, Lee	59		Treadway, Jeff	392
Smith, Lonnie	387		Trevino, Alex	469
Smith, Mike	596			
Smith, Ozzie	614			
Smith, Pete	388		**U**	
Smith, Roy	237			
Smith, Zane	516		Uribe, Jose	664
Smithson, Mike	60			
Smoltz, John	389			
Snyder, Cory	133		**V**	
Sosa, Sammy	108			
Spiers, Bill	211		Valdez, Sergio	395
Stanley, Mike	344		Valenzuela, Fernando	491
Stanton, Mike	390		Valle, Dave	312
Steinbach, Terry	285		Van Slyke, Andy	590
Stewart, Dave	286		Varsho, Gary	419
Stieb, Dave	360		Vaughn, Greg	216
Stillwell, Kurt	182		Velarde, Randy	266
Stottlemyre, Todd	361		Venable, Max	88
Strange, Doug	155		Ventura, Robin	113
Strawberry, Darryl	541		Viola, Frank	543
Stubbs, Franklin	495		Vizquel, Omar	313
Surhoff, B.J.	212			
Sutcliffe, Rick	413			
Swift, Billy	311		**W**	
Swindell, Greg	134			
			Walk, Bob	591
			Walker, Greg	110
T			Walker, Larry	522
			Wallach, Tim	517
Tabler, Pat	183		Walling, Denny	621
Tanana, Frank	156		Walton, Jerome	414
Tartabull, Danny	184		Ward, Duane	362
Templeton, Garry	641		Ward, Gary	158
Terrell, Walt	262		Washington, Claudell	83
Terry, Scott	615		Wayne, Gary	238
Tettleton, Mickey	32			

Webster, Mitch	415
Wegman, Bill	217
Weiss, Walt	287
Welch, Bob	288
Wellman, Brad	185
Wells, David	363
West, David	239
Wetherby, Jeff	396
Wetteland, John	492
Whitaker, Lou	159
White, Devon	84
White, Frank	186
Whited, Ed	396
Whitson, Ed	642
Whitt, Ernie	364
Wilkerson, Curtis	420
Williams, Eddie	113
Williams, Frank	160
Williams, Ken	161
Williams, Matt	665
Williams, Mitch	416
Williamson, Mark	34
Wills, Frank	369
Wilson, Glenn	466
Wilson, Mookie	365
Wilson, Steve	420
Wilson, Trevor	669
Wilson, Willie	187
Winningham, Herm	442
Winters, Matt	191
Witt, Bobby	341
Witt, Mike	85
Worrell, Todd	617
Worthington, Craig	35
Wrona, Rick	421
Wynne, Marvell	417

Y

Yelding, Eric	470
Yett, Richard	135
Youmans, Floyd	570
Young, Curt	289
Young, Gerald	467
Young, Matt	291
Young, Mike	138
Yount, Robin	213

Z

Zavaras, Clint	318
Zeile, Todd	618
Zuvella, Paul	139